P9-DEY-505

macroeconomics

Paul Krugman

Princeton University

Robin Wells

Princeton University

WORTH PUBLISHERS

To beginning students everywhere, which we all were at one time.

Photo Credits

Grateful acknowledgment is given for permission to reprint the following cover photos:

Publishers: Catherine Woods and Craig Bleyer
Senior Acquisitions Editor: Charlie Van Wagner
Executive Development Editor: Sharon Balbos
Development Editor: Marilyn Freedman
Associate Editor: Marie McHale
Consultant: Andreas Bentz
Director of Market Development: Steven Rigolosi
Marketing Manager: Scott Guile
Associate Managing Editor: Tracey Kuehn
Project Editor: Anthony Calcara
Art Director, Cover Designer: Babs Reingold
Interior Designer: Babs Reingold
Layout Designer: Lee Ann Mahler
Illustrations: TSI Graphics and Lyndall Culbertson
Photo Research Manager: Patricia Marx
Photo Researcher: Elyse Rieder
Production Manager: Barbara Anne Seixas
Composition: TSI Graphics
Printing and Binding: R. R. Donnelley and Sons

ISBN: 0-7167-5228-X (EAN: 9780716752288)

Library of Congress Control Number: 2005936306

Worth Publishers
41 Madison Avenue
New York, NY 10010
www.worthpublishers.com

About the Authors

Paul Krugman is Professor of Economics at Princeton University, where he regularly teaches the principles course. He received his BA from Yale and his PhD from MIT. Prior to his current position, he taught at Yale, Stanford, and MIT. He also spent a year on the staff of the Council of Economic Advisers in 1982–1983. His research is mainly in the area of international trade, where he is one of the founders of the "new trade theory," which focuses on increasing returns and imperfect competition. He also works in international finance, with a concentration in currency crises. In 1991, Krugman received the American Economic Association's John Bates Clark medal. In addition to his teaching and academic research, Krugman writes extensively for nontechnical audiences. Krugman is a regular op-ed columnist for the *New York Times*. His latest trade book is a best-selling collection of his *Times* articles entitled *The Great Unraveling: Losing Our Way in the New Century*. His earlier books, *Peddling Prosperity* and *The Age of Diminished Expectations*, have become modern classics.

Robin Wells is Researcher in Economics at Princeton University, where she regularly teaches undergraduate courses. She received her BA from the University of Chicago and her PhD from the University of California at Berkeley; she then did postdoctoral work at MIT. She has taught at the University of Michigan, the University of Southampton (United Kingdom), Stanford, and MIT. Her teaching and research focus on the theory of organizations and incentives. She writes regularly for academic journals.

Preface

FROM PAUL

Robin and I like to think that we wrote this book with Orwell's injunction in mind. We wanted to write a different sort of book, one that gives as much attention to the task of making sure the student understands how economic models apply to the real world as it gives to the models themselves. We wanted to adapt Orwell's principle to the writing of an economics textbook: to let the purpose of economics—to achieve a deeper understanding of the world—rather than the mechanics of economics dictate the writing.

We believe that writing in this style reflects a commitment to the reader—a commitment to approach the material from a beginner's point of view, to make the material entertaining and accessible, to make discovery a joy. That's the fun part. But we also believe that there is another, equally compelling obligation on the part of an author of a principles of economics text. Economics is an extremely powerful tool. Many of us who are economists originally started in other disciplines (I started in history, Robin in chemistry). And we fell in love with economics because we believed it offers a coherent worldview that offers real guidelines to making the world a better place. (Yes, most economists are idealists at heart.) But like any powerful tool, economics should be treated with great care. For us, this obligation became a commitment that students would learn the appropriate use of the models—understand their assumptions and know their limitations as well as their positive uses. Why do we care about this? Because we don't live in a "one model of the economy fits all" world. To achieve deeper levels of understanding of the real world through economics, students must learn to appreciate the kinds of trade-offs and ambiguities that economists and policy makers face when applying their models to real-world problems. We hope this approach will make students more insightful and more effective participants in our common economic, social, and political lives.

To those familiar with my academic work, this perspective will probably look familiar. There I tried to make the problem to be solved the focus and to avoid unnecessary technique. I tried to simplify. And I tried to choose topics that had important real-world implications. Writing for a large, nontechnical audience has only reinforced and expanded these tendencies. I had to begin with the working assumption that readers initially have no reason to care about what I am writing about—that it is my responsibility to show them why they should care. So the beginning of each chapter of this book is written according to the dictum: "If you haven't hooked them by the third sentence, then you've lost them." I've also learned that about all you can take for granted in writing for a lay audience is basic numeracy—addition and subtraction, but no more than that. Concepts must be fully explained; likely confusions must be anticipated and headed off. And most of all, you must be judicious in choosing the content and pacing of the writing—don't overwhelm your reader.

FROM ROBIN

Like Paul, I wanted to write a book that appeals to students without unduly sacrificing an instructor's obligation to teach economics well. I arrived at a similar perspective on how this book should be written, but by a different path. It came from my experiences teaching economics in a business school for a few years. Facing students who were typically impatient with abstraction and often altogether unhappy to be taking economics (and who would often exact bloody revenge in teaching evaluations), I learned how important it is to hook the students into the subject matter. Teaching with case studies, I found that concepts had been truly learned only when students could successfully apply them. And one of the most important lessons I learned was not to patronize. We—economists, that is—often assume that people who aren't familiar with conceptual thinking aren't smart and capable. Teaching in a business school showed me otherwise. The majority of my students were smart and capable, and many had shouldered a lot of responsibility in their working lives. Although adept at solving practical problems, they weren't trained to think conceptually. I had to learn to acknowledge the practical skills that they did have, but also show them the importance of the conceptual skills they didn't have. Although I eventually returned to an economics department, the lessons I learned about teaching economics in a business school stayed with me and, I believe, have been crucial ingredients in writing this textbook.

Advantages of This Book

Despite our fine words, why should any instructor use our text? We believe our book distinguishes itself in several ways that will make your introductory macroeconomics course an easier and more successful undertaking for the following reasons:

- **Chapters build intuition through real examples.** In every chapter, we use real-world examples, stories, applications, and case studies to teach concepts and motivate student learning. We believe that the best way to introduce concepts and reinforce them is through real-world examples; students simply relate more easily to them. In addition, we stress throughout the book that economic models aren't just intellectual games; they are ways to understand the real world and the dilemmas faced by policy makers. The real-world examples, stories, applications, and case studies are drawn from a wide variety of sources—individual stories, economic history, and recent experience, with a strong emphasis on international cases.

- **Real-world data illustrate concepts.** Examples are often accompanied by real-world data so that students can see what real macroeconomic numbers look like and how they relate to the models.

- **Pedagogical features reinforce learning.** We've worked hard to craft a set of features that will be genuinely helpful to students. We describe these features in the next section, "Tools for Learning."

- **Chapters have been written to be accessible and entertaining.** We have used a fluid and friendly writing style that makes the concepts accessible. And we have tried whenever possible to use examples that matter directly to students; for example, considering why decisions made by economic policy makers have important implications for what the job market will look like when they graduate.

- **Although easy to understand, the book also prepares students for further coursework.** Too often, instructors find that selecting a textbook means choosing between two unappealing alternatives: a textbook that is "easy to teach" but leaves major gaps in students' understanding, or a textbook that is "hard to teach" but adequately prepares students for future coursework. We have worked very hard to create an easy-to-understand textbook that offers the best of both worlds.

- **The book permits flexible yet conceptually structured use of chapters.** We recognize that instructors will have different preferences about which topics to emphasize and how much detail to give tools of analysis. Chapters were written with this in mind, allowing instructors to craft a course that fits their needs. For a detailed look at the organization of chapters and ways to use them, see pages ix through xv of this preface.

Tools for Learning

We have structured each of the chapters around a common set of features. The following features are intended to help students learn better while also keeping them engaged.

"What You Will Learn in This Chapter"

To help readers get oriented, the first page of each chapter contains a preview of the chapter's contents, in an easy-to-review bulleted list format, that alerts students to the critical concepts and details the objectives of the chapter.

Opening Story

In contrast to other books in which each chapter begins with a recitation of some aspect of economics, we've adopted a unique approach: we open each chapter with a compelling story that often extends through the entire chapter. Stories were chosen to accomplish two things: to illustrate important concepts in the chapter and then to encourage students to want to read on to learn more.

As we've mentioned, one of our main goals is to build intuition with realistic examples. Because each chapter is introduced with a real-world story, students will relate more easily to the material. For example, we introduce Chapter 7, on macroeconomic data—usually one of the driest subjects in macroeconomics—with the story of how an accurate estimate of real GDP growth steadied nervous Portuguese officials and helped the country make the transition from dictatorship to democracy (see "After the Revolution" on page 159). We introduce Chapter 15, on unemployment, with a story of two lives changed by job loss (see "Two Paths to Unemployment" on page 368). For a list of our opening stories, see the inside front cover.

"Economics in Action" Case Studies

In addition to introducing chapters with vivid stories, we conclude virtually every major text section with still more examples: a real-world case study called "Economics in Action." This feature provides a short but compelling application of the major concept just covered in that section. Students will experience an immediate payoff from being able to apply the concepts they've just read about. For example, our discussion of long-run fiscal issues (in Chapter 12, "Fiscal Policy"), which includes the question of solvency, is followed by an account of Argentina's debt default (see "Argentina's Creditors Take a Haircut," on page 313). In Chapter 19, "Open-Economy Macro-economics," we follow the discussion of exchange rate policy with an account of China's massive intervention to keep the yuan from rising (see "China Pegs the Yuan" on page 482). For a complete list of all the "Economics in Action" cases in the text, see the inside front cover and our table of contents.

Unique End-of-Section Review: "Quick Review" and "Check Your Understanding" Questions

In contrast to most other textbooks, which offer a review of concepts only at the end of each chapter, we include review material at the end of each major section within a chapter.

Economics contains a lot of jargon and abstract concepts that can quickly overwhelm the principles student. So we provide **"Quick Reviews,"** short bulleted summaries of concepts at the end of each major section. This review helps ensure that students understand what they have just read.

The **"Check Your Understanding"** feature, which appears along with every "Quick Review," consists of a short set of review questions; solutions to these questions appear at the back of the book in the section set off with a burgundy tab at the edge of each page. These questions and solutions allow students to immediately test their understanding of the section just read. If they're not getting the questions right, it's a clear signal for them to go back and reread before moving on.

The "Economics in Action" cases, followed by the "Quick Reviews" and "Check Your Understanding" questions comprise our unique end-of-section pedagogical set that encourages students to apply what they've learned (via the "Economics in Action") and then review it (with the "Quick Reviews" and "Check Your Understanding" questions). Our hope is that students will be more successful in the course if they use this carefully constructed set of study aids.

"For Inquiring Minds" Boxes

To further our goal of helping students build intuition with real-world examples, almost every chapter contains one or more "For Inquiring Minds" boxes, in which concepts are applied to real-world events in unexpected and sometimes surprising ways, generating a sense of the power and breadth of economics. These boxes help impress on students that economics can be fun despite being labeled "the dismal science."

In a Chapter 8 box, for example, students learn how a substantial portion of recent productivity gains in the United States can be attributed to a rather unglamorous industry, one that most of us take for granted—retailing

(see "The Wal-Mart Effect" on page 193). In Chapter 13, "Money, Banking, and the Federal Reserve System," we point out the puzzling fact that there's $2,500 worth of currency in circulation for every man, woman, and child in the United States (how many people do you know who keep $2,500 in their wallets?). We then explain how currency in domestic cash registers and in the hands of foreigners resolves the puzzle (see "What's with All The Currency?" on page 325.) For a list of "For Inquiring Minds" boxes, see the inside front cover and our table of contents.

"Pitfalls" Boxes

Certain concepts are prone to be misunderstood when students begin their study of economics. We try to alert students to these mistakes in "Pitfalls" boxes, where common misunderstandings are spelled out and corrected. For example, in Chapter 19 on open-economy macroeconomics, we address the tricky business of how to read an exchange rate (see "Which Way Is Up?" on page 470). For a list of all "Pitfalls" boxes see the table of contents.

Student-Friendly Graphs

Comprehending graphs is often one of the biggest hurdles for principles students. To help alleviate that problem, this book has been designed so that figures are large, clear, and easy for students to follow. Many contain helpful annotations—in an easy-to-see balloon label format—that link to concepts within the text. Figure captions have been written to complement the text discussion of figures and to help students more readily grasp what they're seeing.

We've worked hard to make these graphs student-friendly. For example, to help students navigate one of the stickier thickets—the distinction between a shifting curve and movement along a curve—we encourage students to see this difference by using two types of arrows: a shift arrow (⟶) and what we call a "movement-along" arrow (⟶). You can see these arrows in Figures 3-12 and 3-13 on pages 73 and 74.

In addition, several graphs in each chapter are accompanied by the icon >web…, which indicates that these graphs are available online as simulations (the graphs are animated in a Flash format and can be manipulated). Every interactive graph is accompanied by a quiz on key concepts to further help students in their work with graphs.

Instructing students in the use of graphs is also enhanced by our use of real-world data, often presented in charts that can be compared directly to the analytical figures. For example, the aggregate supply curve can seem like a highly abstract concept, but in Chapter 10, "Aggregate Supply and Aggregate Demand," we make it less abstract by illustrating the concept with the actual behavior of aggregate output and the aggregate price level during the 1930s (see Figure 10-6 on p. 245).

Helpful Graphing Appendix For students who would benefit from an explanation of how graphs are constructed, interpreted, and used in economics, we've included a detailed graphing appendix after Chapter 2 on page 41. This appendix is more comprehensive than most because we know that some students need this helpful background, and we didn't want to breeze through the material. Our hope is that this comprehensive graphing appendix will better prepare students to use and interpret the graphs in this textbook and then out in the real world (in newspapers, magazines, and elsewhere).

Definitions of Key Terms

Every key term, in addition to being defined in the text, is also placed and defined in the margin to make it easier for students to study and review.

"A Look Ahead"

The text of each chapter ends with "A Look Ahead," a short overview of what lies ahead in upcoming chapters. This concluding section provides students with a sense of continuity among chapters.

End-of-Chapter Review

In addition to the "Quick Review" at the end of each major section, each chapter ends with a complete but brief **Summary** of the key terms and concepts. In addition, a list of the **Key Terms** is placed at the end of each chapter along with page references.

For each chapter we have a comprehensive set of **End-of-Chapter Problems** that test intuition and the ability to calculate important variables. Much care has been devoted to the creation of these problems. Instructors can be assured that they provide a true test of students' learning.

Macroeconomic Data

To supplement our in-chapter use of real-world data to illustrate macroeconomic concepts, we've included a broad selection of macroeconomic data at the back of the book in a section set off with blue tabs at the edge of each page. These data series include most of the important macroeconomic variables for the United States. Selected early years illustrate the behavior of the economy during the Great Depression and the post–World War II boom. The series also include data for each year from 1970 to 2004 for full coverage of recent years.

The Organization of This Book and How to Use It

This book is organized as a series of building blocks in which conceptual material learned at one stage is clearly built upon and then integrated into the conceptual material covered in the next stage. These building blocks correspond to the eight parts into which the chapters are divided. We'll walk through those building blocks shortly. First, however, let's talk about the general question of the order in which macroeconomic topics are best covered.

Teaching Macroeconomics: Short Run or Long Run First? The history of macroeconomic theory is one in which short-run and long-run issues vie for priority. The long-run focus of classical economists gave way to the short-run focus of Keynesian economics; then the pendulum swung back to the long run, and lately it seems to be swinging back to the short run. This struggle over priority is reproduced every time an instructor must decide how to teach the subject. Two issues are particularly tricky. First, should long-run economic growth be covered early or later, after the business cycle has been discussed? Second, should classical, full-employment analysis of the price level come before or after business-cycle analysis?

We have chosen to cover long-run growth early (Part 4, Chapters 8 and 9) because we feel that an early discussion of the long-run growth of real GDP helps students understand why the business cycle involves fluctuations around an upward trend. We have, however, structured the subsequent short-run analysis (Part 5, Chapters 10–14) in a way that allows instructors to reverse this order, deferring our chapter on long-run growth (Chapter 8) until later in the course. However, we've taken a firmer stand when it comes to the second question. We believe that the fundamental approach of this book—to tie macroeconomics to real-world concerns—requires that a discussion of the short-run effects of demand and supply shocks come before a discussion of the classical model.

Although some macroeconomics textbooks treat the classical model first, and some even devote more space to long-run analysis than to the short run, we believe—based on our own teaching experience—that this is a formula for losing the interest of beginning students. We are, after all, living in a time of activist monetary and fiscal policy. Students are likely to read newspaper accounts of the Federal Reserve's attempts to stabilize the economy or of debates over the impact of tax cuts on job creation. If students begin their study of macroeconomics with models in which monetary policy has no effect on aggregate output, they will get the impression that what they are learning in the classroom is irrelevant to the real world. In this book we explain early why demand shocks have no effect on output in the long run, but we don't emphasize the long-run neutrality of money before describing how monetary and fiscal policy work in the short run.

We also believe that students could lose their sense that macroeconomics is relevant if the book starts with a model best used to explain inflation. We're living in a time when sustained high inflation is a distant memory in wealthy nations—and even in many developing countries. The great majority of students likely to use this book hadn't been born the last time the U.S. core inflation rate was above 6%. In contrast, the effects of short-run demand and supply shocks—such as the 2001 recession and the subsequent jobless recovery, or the surge in energy prices from 2003 to 2005—are fresh in our memories. We believe that a book aimed at showing students how economics applies to the real world must emphasize early on, rather than later, how macroeconomic models help us understand such events.

We believe that the diffidence with which some textbooks approach the short run is partly driven by reluctance to enter an area that was marked by fierce debates in the 1970s and 1980s. But the ferocity of those debates, like double-digit inflation, has receded into the past. Yes, there are still serious disputes about macroeconomic theory and policy. But as we explain in Chapter 17, "The Making of Modern Macroeconomics," there is also far more consensus than in the past. Students are best served by a book that emphasizes the macroeconomic issues that matter most to public debate rather than downplays these issues out of fear of stepping into contentious areas. That's why we have chosen to provide an extended early discussion of the short-run effects of demand and supply shocks and the role of fiscal and monetary policy in responding to these shocks.

Finally, one last issue involves the order in which the short run should be taught. Some instructors prefer to begin their coverage with a traditional Keynesian discussion of the determinants of aggregate expenditure. Some prefer to place that discussion after a basic introduction to aggregate supply and aggregate demand. And a third group prefers to skip that analysis altogether. We've used a structural innovation to make all three approaches work, by including an intuitive discussion of the multiplier in Chapter 10, "Aggregate supply and Aggregate Demand," followed by a more detailed, algebraic discussion in Chapter 11, "Income and Expenditure." Instructors who follow the table of contents, teaching Chapter 11 after Chapter 10, can treat the famous 45-degree diagram and its associated algebra as a more in-depth discussion of the multiplier principle students have already learned. Instructors who choose to teach Chapter 11 first can treat Chapter 10's discussion as a reinforcement of the graphical and algebraic analysis. And instructors who skip Chapter 11 will find that the intuitive discussion of the multiplier in Chapter 10 is sufficient for the analysis of fiscal and monetary policy.

With that, let's walk through the book's organization.

Part 1: What Is Economics?

In the **Introduction, "The Ordinary Business of Life,"** students are initiated into the study of economics in the context of a shopping trip on any given Sunday in everyday America. It provides students with basic definitions of terms such as *economics,* the *invisible hand,* and *market structure.* In addition, it serves as a "tour d'horizon" of economics, explaining the difference between microeconomics and macroeconomics.

In **Chapter 1, "First Principles,"** nine principles are presented and explained: four principles of individual choice, covering concepts such as opportunity cost, marginal analysis, and incentives; and five principles of interaction between individuals, covering concepts such as gains from trade, market efficiency, and market failure. In later chapters, we build intuition by frequently referring to these principles in the explanation of specific models. Students learn that these nine principles form a cohesive conceptual foundation for all of economics.

Chapter 2, "Economic Models: Trade-offs and Trade," shows students how to think like economists by using three models—the production possibility frontier, comparative advantage and trade, and the circular-flow diagram—to analyze the world around them. It gives students an early introduction to gains from trade and to international comparisons. The **Chapter 2 appendix** contains a comprehensive math and graphing review.

Part 2: Supply and Demand

In this part we provide students with the basic analytical tools they need to understand how markets work, tools that are common to microeconomics and macroeconomics.

Chapter 3, "Supply and Demand," covers the standard material in a fresh and compelling way: supply and demand, market equilibrium, and surplus and shortage are all illustrated using an example of the market for scalped tickets to a sports event. Students learn how the demand and supply curves of scalped tickets shift in response to the announcement of a star player's impending retirement.

Chapter 4, "The Market Strikes Back," covers various types of market interventions and their consequences: price and quantity controls, inefficiency and deadweight loss, and excise taxes. Through tangible examples such as New York City rent control regulations and New York City taxi licenses, the costs generated by attempts to control markets are made real to students.

Chapter 5, "Consumer and Producer Surplus," is designed to be optional. In the chapter, students learn how markets increase welfare through examples such as a market for used textbooks and eBay. Although the concepts of market efficiency and deadweight loss are strongly emphasized, we also describe the ways in which a market can fail. This chapter will be particularly helpful for instructors who teach Chapter 18 on international trade.

Part 3: Introduction to Macroeconomics

Chapter 6, "Macroeconomics: The Big Picture," introduces the big ideas in macroeconomics. Starting with an example close to students' hearts—how the business cycle affects the job prospects of graduates—this chapter provides a quick overview of recessions and expansions, employment and unemployment, long-run growth, inflation versus deflation, and the open economy.

Chapter 7, "Tracking the Macroeconomy," explains how the numbers macroeconomists use are calculated, and why. We start with a real-world example of how an estimate of real GDP helped save a country from policy mistakes, then turn to the basics of national income accounting, unemployment statistics, and price indexes.

Long-Run Growth We begin our discussion of macroeconomic models with long-run economic growth. We believe that students are best prepared to understand the significance of fluctuations around long-run trends if they first acquire an understanding of where long-run trends come from. Instructors can, however, defer Chapter 8 until later in the course if they choose.

Part 4: The Economy in the Long Run

Chapter 8, "Long-Run Economic Growth," starts with a reality TV show—a BBC series about a family that spent three months living life as it was in 1900—to illustrate the human significance of economic growth. When we turn to economic data, we emphasize an international perspective—economic growth is a story about the world as a whole, not just the United States. The chapter uses a streamlined approach to the aggregate production function to present an analysis of the sources of economic growth and the reasons some countries have been more successful than others.

Chapter 9, "Savings, Investment Spending, and the Financial System," introduces students to financial markets and institutions. We group it with Chapter 8 in this part because it highlights the role of these markets and institutions in economic growth. Chapter 9 is also, however, integral to short-run analysis, for two reasons. First, its analysis of the market for loanable funds and the determination of interest rates provides an analytical tool that will be helpful for understanding monetary policy, international capital flows, and other topics covered later in the book. Second, its discussion of financial institutions provides background when we turn to the role of banks in creating money.

The Short Run Macroeconomics as we know it emerged during the Great Depression, and the effort to understand short-run fluctuations and the effects of monetary and fiscal policy remains as important as ever. So we devote a large block of chapters (Chapters 10–14) to short-run fluctuations. These chapters are, however, structured to allow instructors to choose their preferred level of detail. In particular, we know that some instructors want to place more emphasis than others on the consumption function and the multiplier. So we provide a basic, intuitive explanation of the multiplier in Chapter 10 but reserve a detailed discussion of consumer behavior and how it relates to the 45-degree diagram for Chapter 11, which is designed to be optional (but can be taught before Chapter 10, if instructors choose to do so).

There is also an ongoing debate among economics instructors about whether the traditional presentation of aggregate supply and aggregate demand, which treats the aggregate quantities of goods and services demanded and supplied as functions of the price *level*, should be replaced with a framework that treats them as functions of the *inflation rate*. In this alternative framework, the "aggregate supply curve" is really the short-run Phillips curve, and the "aggregate demand curve" is really a representation of the effects of monetary policy that leans against inflation. We understand the appeal of such a presentation, which makes for an easier transition to the discussion of inflation. But we believe that this approach blurs the important distinction between the private sector's behavior and the effects of policy responses on that behavior. Furthermore, a crucial insight from the traditional aggregate supply–aggregate demand approach is the economy's ability to correct itself in the long run. This insight is lost in the alternative approach. So we introduce short-run macroeconomics with a traditional focus on the aggregate price level, and we treat ongoing inflation as a "medium-run" issue, reserved for Part 6.

Part 5: Short-Run Economic Fluctuations

Part 5 begins with **Chapter 10, "Aggregate Supply and Aggregate Demand."** This chapter's opening story covers the economic slump of 1979–1982, which startled Americans with its combination of recession and inflation. This leads into an analysis of how both demand shocks and supply shocks affect the economy. In analyzing demand shocks, we offer a simple, intuitive explanation of the concept of the multiplier, using the idea of successive increases in spending after an initial shock to explain how the aggregate demand curve shifts. In analyzing supply shocks, we emphasize positive shocks, such as the productivity surge of the late 1990s, as well as negative shocks. The chapter concludes with the key insight that demand shocks affect only output in the short run.

Chapter 11, "Income and Expenditure," is an optional chapter for instructors who want to go into some detail about the sources of changes in aggregate demand. We use real-world data to delve more deeply into the determinants of consumer and investment spending, introduce the famous 45-degree diagram, and present a fully fleshed-out explanation of the logic of the multiplier. For instructors who would like more algebraic detail, the **Chapter 11 appendix** shows how to derive the multiplier algebraically.

Chapter 12, "Fiscal Policy," starts in Japan, where discretionary fiscal policy has taken the form of huge public works projects, often of doubtful value. This leads into an analysis of the role of discretionary fiscal policy in shifting the aggregate demand curve, which makes use of the intuitive explanation of the multiplier from Chapter 10. We also cover automatic stabilizers—using the woes of Europe's "stability pact" to illustrate their importance—and long-run issues of debt and solvency. The **Chapter 12 appendix** shows how to introduce taxes into the analysis. It shows more specifically than the main text how the size of the multiplier depends on the tax rate, and it provides an intuitive explanation, in terms of successive rounds of spending, of how taxes reduce the multiplier.

Part 5 concludes with two monetary chapters. **Chapter 13, "Money, Banking, and the Federal Reserve System,"** covers the roles of money, the ways in which banks create money, and the structure and role of the Federal Reserve and other central banks. We use episodes from U.S. history together with the story of the creation of the euro to illustrate how money and monetary institutions have evolved.

Chapter 14, "Monetary Policy," covers the role of Federal Reserve policy in driving interest rates and aggregate demand. In the real-world examples, we took full advantage of the dramatic developments in monetary policy since 2000, which make it easier than ever before to illustrate what the Federal Reserve does. We also made a special effort to build a bridge between the short run and the long run. For example, we carefully explain how the Federal Reserve can set the interest rate in the short run, even though that rate reflects the supply and demand for savings in the long run.

The Medium Run An important set of questions in macroeconomics revolves around unemployment and inflation: can monetary and fiscal policy be used to reduce unemployment, does the attempt to reduce unemployment cause inflation, is there a trade-off between inflation and unemployment? These questions fall into the category of "medium-run" issues, which apply to periods long enough that wages and prices can't be taken as given, but short enough that productivity and population growth don't dominate the story.

Part 6: The Supply Side and the Medium Run

Chapter 15, "Labor Markets, Unemployment, and Inflation," begins with stories of how real people move into and out of unemployment. It explains why there is always some frictional and structural unemployment, illustrated by the problem of "Eurosclerosis." It then turns to the relationship between unemployment and the output gap. It concludes with the Phillips curve, the role of inflation expectations, and how this relates to the natural rate hypothesis.

Chapter 16, "Inflation, Disinflation, and Deflation," covers the causes and consequences of inflation, as well as the reasons disinflation imposes large costs in lost output and employment. A unique final section analyzes the effects of deflation and the problems that a "zero bound" poses for monetary policy. As we explain, these issues, dormant for more than half a century after the Great Depression, surfaced in Japan in the 1990s and have had a major impact on policy thinking.

If There's Time We recognize that many instructors will find that there's only enough time to cover the core chapters up through Chapter 16 on inflation. For those with enough time, however, Parts 7 and 8 (and Chapter 8, on long-run growth, for instructors who choose to cover it later) broaden the analysis. Part 7 offers a brief history of macroeconomic thought. Part 8 takes the analysis into international economics.

Part 7: Events and Ideas

Macroeconomics has always been a field in flux, with new policy issues constantly arising and traditional views often challenged. **Chapter 17, "The Making of Modern Macroeconomics,"** provides a unique overview of the history of macroeconomic thought, set in the context of changing policy concerns, then turns to a description of the current state of macroeconomic debates (there's more agreement than people think.)

Part 8: The Open Economy

Chapter 18, "International Trade," contains a recap of comparative advantage, traces the sources of comparative advantage, considers tariffs and quotas, and explores the politics of trade protection. In response to current events, we give in-depth coverage to the controversy over imports from low-wage countries.

Chapter 19, "Open-Economy Macroeconomics," analyzes the special issues raised for macroeconomics by the open economy. We frame the discussion with real-world concerns: Britain's debate over whether to adopt the euro, America's current account deficit, China's accumulation of dollar reserves.

For instructors and students who want to delve more deeply into international macroeconomics, we provide a supplemental chapter—available on the Web, at www.worthpublishers.com/krugmanwells, and in booklet form. **This chapter, "Currencies and Crises,"** takes students into the world of currency speculation and international financial crises, with an emphasis on the dramatic events that have unfolded in developing countries over the past decade.

Core and Optional Chapters Plus Possible Outlines

For an overview of what chapters are considered core and optional, see page xiv of this preface. For ideas on using this book to meet specific course goals, see the outlines on page xv.

Supplements and Media

Worth Publishers is pleased to offer an exciting and useful supplements and media package to accompany this textbook. The package has been crafted to help instructors teach their principles course and to help students grasp concepts more readily.

The entire package has been coordinated by Martha Olney, University of California-Berkeley, to provide consistency in level and quality. Rosemary Cunningham, Agnes Scott College, has coordinated all of the quizzing materials in the Study Guide, Test Bank, and all the online materials to guarantee uniformity.

Since accuracy is so critically important, all the supplements have been scrutinized and double-checked by members of the supplements team, reviewers, and a team of additional accuracy checkers. The time and care that have been put into the supplements and media ensure a seamless package.

Companion Website for Students and Instructors

econ X change

(www.worthpublishers.com/krugmanwells)
The companion website for the Krugman/Wells text offers valuable tools for both the instructor and students.

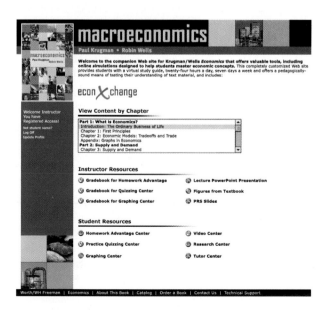

For instructors, this completely customized website offers many opportunities for quizzing and, most important, powerful grading tools. The site gives you the ability to track students' interaction with the Practice Quizzing Center and the Graphing Center by accessing an online gradebook. Instructors have the option to have student results e-mailed directly to them.

For students, the site offers many opportunities to practice, practice, practice. On the site, students can find animated graphs, practice quizzes, videos, graphing tutorials, and links to many other resources designed to help them master economic concepts. In essence, this site provides students with a virtual study guide, twenty-four hours a day, seven days a week by offering a pedagogically sound means of testing their understanding of text material.

This helpful, powerful site contains the following:

Homework Advantage Center Worth's secure, interactive, online homework system is accessible through the Krugman/Wells website. Using the Homework Advantage Center, instructors can easily create automatically graded homework assignments, quizzes, and tests. This online quizzing engine, which includes algorithmically generated questions, allows for repeatable, varied assignments for students. Students get immediate, individualized results after submitting their work. All student responses are stored in an electronic gradebook so that instructors can easily grade exams and generate reports. The gradebook has the following features that allow for flexibility in assessing students' abilities.

➤ Grades can be organized into as many as 25 related categories (tests, papers, homework, etc.).

➤ Assignments can be independently weighted.

➤ Letter grade cutoffs can be adjusted, and custom grading created ("Fair," "Good," "Excellent," and so on).

➤ Assignment scores and category averages can be entered or displayed as percentages, points, letter grades, or according to your own customized grading scheme.

➤ Gradebooks can be set up to report final averages as points earned across all categories.

➤ Student properties can include ID number, password (for online testing), e-mail address, and status (active, withdraw, incomplete).

➤ Grades can be dropped manually or automatically.

➤ Assignment, category, and final scores can be curved.

➤ Numerous reports can be customized and printed with an interactive print preview.

➤ Results can be merged from TheTestingCenter.Com.

➤ Student rosters can be imported and exported.

WHAT'S CORE, WHAT'S OPTIONAL: AN OVERVIEW

As noted earlier, we realize that some of our chapters will be considered optional. Below is a list of what we view as core chapters and those that could be considered optional. We've annotated the list of optional chapters to indicate what they cover should you wish to consider incorporating them into your course.

Core

1. First Principles
2. Economic Models: Trade-offs and Trade

3. Supply and Demand
4. The Market Strikes Back

6. Macroeconomics: The Big Picture
7. Tracking the Macroeconomy
8. Long-Run Economic Growth
9. Savings, Investment Spending, and the Financial System
10. Aggregate Supply and Aggregate Demand

12. Fiscal Policy
13. Money, Banking, and the Federal Reserve System
14. Monetary Policy
15. Labor Markets, Unemployment, and Inflation
16. Inflation, Disinflation, and Deflation

Optional

Introduction: The Ordinary Business of Life

Appendix: Graphs in Economics
> A comprehensive review of graphing and math for students who would find such a refresher helpful.

5. Consumer and Producer Surplus
> A brief introduction to welfare economics, which helps drive home the reasons markets are usually efficient. This chapter will be particularly helpful for instructors who teach international trade (Chapter 18).

11. Income and Expenditure plus Appendix: Deriving the Multiplier Algebraically
> A chapter for instructors who want to provide full details on the determinants of aggregate demand: the consumption function, the determinants of investment spending, and the determination of equilibrium by the requirement that planned spending equal GDP. The appendix offers an algebraic treatment of the multiplier for instructors who want to supplement the graphical analysis

Appendix: Taxes and the Multiplier
> A more rigorous derivation of the role of taxes in reducing the multiplier and acting as an automatic stabilizer

17. The Making of Modern Macroeconomics
> A chapter for instructors who like to cover the history of economic ideas and the current state of policy debate. It offers a unique survey of changing macroeconomic thought, leading up to current debates about monetary policy.

18. International Trade
> This chapter recaps comparative advantage, considers tariffs and quotas, and explores the politics of trade protection. Coverage here links back to the international coverage in Chapter 2 and makes use of the welfare economics introduced in Chapter 5.

19. Open-Economy Macroeconomics
> A chapter for instructors who take a more international approach. It covers the ways in which capital flows affect financial markets, the importance of exchange rates and exchange rate regimes, and the effects of monetary policy changes under fixed and floating rates.

Supplemental chapter: Currencies and Crises
> Available on the Web, at www.worthpublishers.com/krugmanwells, and in booklet form for instructors and students who want to cover currency speculation and international financial problems.

THREE POSSIBLE OUTLINES

To illustrate how instructors can use this book to meet their specific goals, we offer a selection of possible outlines that are alternatives to simply covering the chapters in order. By no means exclusive, these outlines reflect a likely range of different ways in which this book could be used.

Basic macroeconomics

Part 1
1. First Principles
2. Economic Models: Trade-offs and Trade

   Appendix: Graphs in Economics

Part 2
3. Supply and Demand
4. The Market Strikes Back

Part 3
6. Macroeconomics: The Big Picture
7. Tracking the Macroeconomy

Part 4
8. Long-Run Economic Growth
9. Savings, Investment Spending, and the Financial System

Part 5
10. Aggregate Supply and Aggregate Demand
12. Fiscal Policy
13. Money, Banking, and the Federal Reserve System
14. Monetary Policy

Part 6
15. Labor Markets, Unemployment, and Inflation
16. Inflation, Disinflation, and Deflation

And, if there is time: **Part 8**
18. International Trade
19. Open-Economy Macroeconomics

Expenditure first

Part 1
1. First Principles
2. Economic Models: Trade-offs and Trade

   Appendix: Graphs in Economics

Part 2
3. Supply and Demand
4. The Market Strikes Back

Part 3
6. Macroeconomics: The Big Picture
7. Tracking the Macroeconomy

Part 4
8. Long-Run Economic Growth
9. Savings, Investment Spending, and the Financial System

Part 5
11. Income and Expenditure
10. Aggregate Supply and Aggregate Demand
12. Fiscal Policy
13. Money, Banking, and the Federal Reserve System
14. Monetary Policy

Part 6
15. Labor Markets, Unemployment, and Inflation
16. Inflation, Disinflation, and Deflation

And, if there is time: **Part 8**
18. International Trade
19. Open-Economy Macroeconomics

Long run later

Part 1
1. First Principles
2. Economic Models: Trade-offs and Trade

   Appendix: Graphs in Economics

Part 2
3. Supply and Demand
4. The Market Strikes Back

Part 3
6. Macroeconomics: The Big Picture
7. Tracking the Macroeconomy

Part 4
9. Savings, Investment Spending, and the Financial System

Part 5
10. Aggregate Supply and Aggregate Demand
12. Fiscal Policy
13. Money, Banking, and the Federal Reserve System
14. Monetary Policy

Part 6
15. Labor Markets, Unemployment, and Inflation
16. Inflation, Disinflation, and Deflation
8. Long-Run Economic Growth

And, if there is time: **Part 8**
18. International Trade
19. Open-Economy Macroeconomics

Practice Quizzing Center   Developed by Debbie Mullin, University of Colorado-Colorado Springs, this quizzing engine provides 20 multiple-choice questions per chapter with appropriate feedback and page references to the textbook. The questions as well as the answer choices are randomized to give students a different quiz with every refresh of the screen. All student answers are saved in an online database that can be accessed by instructors.

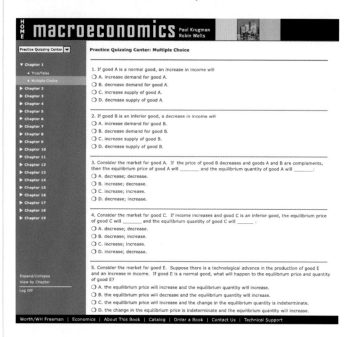

Graphing Center   Developed by Cadre LLC in conjunction with Debbie Mullin, University of Colorado-Colorado Springs, the Graphing Center includes selected graphs from the textbook that have been animated in a Flash format. Approximately five graphs from each chapter have been animated and are identified in the textbook by a web icon **>web...** within the appropriate figure. Working with these animated figures enhances student understanding of the effects of the shifts and movements

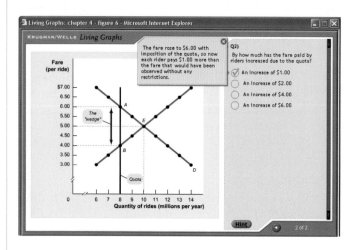

of the curves. Every interactive graph is accompanied by questions that quiz students on key concepts from the textbook and provide instructors with feedback on student progress. Student responses and interactions are tracked and stored in an online database that can be accessed by the instructor.

Research Center   Created and continually updated by Jules Kaplan, University of Colorado-Boulder, the Research Center allows students to easily and effectively locate outside resources and readings that relate to topics covered in the textbook. It lists web addresses that hotlink to relevant websites; each URL is accompanied by a detailed description of the site and its relevance to each chapter, allowing students to conduct research and explore related readings on specific topics with ease. Also hotlinked are relevant articles by Paul Krugman and other leading economists.

Video Center   In video interviews, the text's authors, Paul Krugman and Robin Wells, comment on specific aspects of each chapter and their relevance to students' lives. Each video is embedded in a Flash format with other pedagogical features and a running transcript of the authors' remarks. Videos can be presented in class to generate discussion or assigned as homework to give students a deeper understanding of key topics in the textbook.

Student Powerpoint   Created by Can Erbil, Brandeis University, this PowerPoint presentation is ideal for students who need extra help in understanding the concepts in each chapter. The PowerPoint presentations for each chapter come complete with animations, notes, summaries, and graphics. This tool enables students to review and practice and helps them to more readily grasp economic concepts.

➤ **Aplia**

 Aplia, founded by Paul Romer, Stanford University, is the first web-based company to integrate pedagogical features from a textbook with interactive media. Specifically designed for use with the Krugman/Wells text, the figures, end-of-chapter problems, boxes, text, and other pedagogical resources have been combined with Aplia's interactive media to save time for professors and encourage students to exert more effort in their learning.

The integrated online version of the Aplia media and the Krugman/Wells text includes:

➤ Extra problem sets suitable for homework and keyed to specific topics from each chapter

➤ Regularly updated news analyses

➤ Real-time online simulations of market interactions

➤ Interactive tutorials to assist with math

➤ Graphs and statistics

➤ Instant online reports that allow instructors to target student trouble areas more efficiently

With Aplia, you retain complete control and flexibility for your course. You choose the topics you want students to cover, and you decide how to organize it. You decide whether online activities are practice (ungraded or graded). You can even edit the Aplia content—making cuts or addtions as you see fit for your course.

For a preview of Aplia materials and to learn more, visit http://www.aplia.com.

Additional Student Supplements

Student CD-ROM This CD-ROM contains all of the multimedia content found on the Krugman/Wells Companion website, including the practice quizzes, interactive graphs, Krugman/Wells videos, and the student PowerPoint slides. This CD-ROM is ideal for students with limited web access or for use in a lab setting. Available upon request, this CD can be packaged with the textbook at no additional cost to the student.

Study Guide Prepared by Rosemary Cunningham, Agnes Scott College, and Elizabeth Sawyer-Kelly, University of Wisconsin-Madison, the Study Guide reinforces the topics and key concepts covered in the text. For each chapter, the Study Guide provides:

➤ An introduction

➤ A fill-in-the-blank chapter review

➤ Learning tips with graphical analysis

➤ Four or five comprehensive problems and exercises

➤ Twenty multiple-choice questions

➤ Solutions to all fill-in-the-blank reviews, problems, exercises, and quizzes found in the Study Guide.

Additional Instructor Supplements

Instructor's Resource Manual The Instructor's Resource Manual written by David Findlay, Colby College, and Diane Keenan, Cerritos Community College, is an ideal resource for instructors teaching principles of economics. The manual includes:

➤ Chapter-by-chapter learning objectives

➤ Chapter outlines

➤ Teaching tips and ideas

➤ Hints on how to create student interest

➤ Common misunderstandings that are typical among students

➤ Activities that can be conducted in or out of the classroom

➤ Detailed solutions to every end-of-chapter problem from the textbook

Printed Test Bank The Test Bank, coordinated by Rosemary Cunningham, Agnes Scott College, with contributing authors Doris Bennett, Jacksonville State University; Diego Mendez-Carbajo, Illinois Wesleyan University; Richard Gosselin, Houston Community College; Gus W. Herring, Brookhaven College; James Swofford, University of South Alabama; and James Wetzel, Virginia Commonwealth University, provides a wide range of creative and versatile questions ranging in levels of difficulty. Selected questions are paired with original graphs and graphs from the textbook to reinforce comprehension. Totaling over 2,800 questions, the Test Bank offers 150 multiple-choice questions and 20 true/false questions per chapter assessing comprehension, interpretation, analysis, and synthesis. Each question is conveniently cross-referenced to the page number in the text where the appropriate topic is discussed. Questions have been checked for continuity with the text content, reviewed extensively, and checked again for accuracy.

Diploma 6 Computerized Test Bank The Krugman/ Wells printed Test Bank is also available in CD-ROM format, powered by Brownstone, for both Windows and Macintosh users.  With Diploma, you can easily create tests, write and edit questions, and create study sessions for students. You can add an unlimited number of questions; scramble questions; and include pictures, equations, and multimedia links. Tests can be printed in a wide range of formats or administered to students with Brownstone's network or Internet testing software. The software's unique synthesis of flexible word-processing and database features creates a program that is extremely intuitive and capable. With Diploma, you can:

➤ Work with complete word-processing functions (including creating tables).

➤ Work with myriad question formats, including multiple choice, true/false, short answer, matching, fill in the blank, and essay.

➤ Attach feedback (rationales) to questions (or answers).

➤ Create, install, and use an unlimited number of question banks.

➤ Incorporate references (including tables, figures, and case studies).

➤ Attach customized instructions.

> Use multiple graphic formats (BMP, DIB, RLE, DXF, EPS, FPX, GIF, IMG, JPG, PCD, PCX, DCX, PNG, TGA, TIF, WMF, and WPG).

> Take advantage of a powerful algorithm engine for complex, dynamic question types and dynamic equations.

> Export self-grading tests (in HTML formats) for use with web browsers.

> Export test files in Rich Text File format for use with any word-processing program.

> Export test files to EDU, WebCT, and Blackboard course management systems.

> Preview and re-format tests before printing them.

> Include custom splash screens that feature graphics or images.

> Post tests to Diploma's online testing site, TheTestingCenter.com.

This computerized Test Bank is accompanied by a grade-book that enables you to record students' grades throughout a course; it also includes the capacity to track student records and view detailed analyses of test items, curve tests, generate reports, add weights to grades, and allows you to:

> Organize grades into as many as 25 related categories.

> Adjust letter grade cutoffs and create customized grading.

> Enter/display assignment scores and category averages as percentages, points, letter grades, or according to your own customized grading scheme.

> Report final averages as points earned across all categories.

> Customize student properties (including ID number, password, e-mail address, and status).

> Drop grades either manually or automatically.

> Import and export student rosters.

Diploma Online Testing at www.brownstone.net is another useful tool within the Brownstone software that allows instructors to provide online exams for students using Test Bank questions. With Diploma, you can easily create and administer secure exams over a network and over the Internet, with questions that incorporate multimedia and interactive exercises. The program allows you to restrict tests to specific computers or time blocks, and it includes an impressive suite of gradebook and result-analysis features.

Lecture PowerPoint Presentation Created by Can Erbil, Brandeis University, the enhanced PowerPoint presentation slides are designed to assist you with lecture preparation and presentation by providing original animations, graphs from the textbook, data tables, and bulleted lists of key concepts suitable for large lecture presentation. Although the slides are organized by topic from the text's table of contents, you can customize these slides to suit your individual needs by adding your own data, questions, and lecture notes. You can access these files on the instructor's side of the website or on the Instructor's Resource CD-ROM.

Instructor's Resource CD-ROM Using the Instructor's Resource CD-ROM, you can easily build classroom presentations or enhance your online courses. This CD-ROM contains all text figures (in JPEG and GIF formats), video clips of interviews with Paul Krugman and Robin Wells, animated graphs, and enhanced PowerPoint slides. You can choose from the various resources, edit, and save for use in your classroom.

Overhead Transparencies Worth is also happy to provide you with more than 100 vivid color acetates of text figures designed for superior projection quality.

Web-CT E-pack The Krugman/Wells WebCT E-Packs enable you to create a thorough, interactive, and pedagogically sound online course or course website. The Krugman/Wells E-Pack provides you with cutting-edge online  materials that facilitate critical thinking and learning, including course outlines, preprogrammed quizzes, links, activities, threaded discussion topics, animated graphs, and a whole array of other materials. Best of all, this material is pre-programmed and fully functional in the WebCT environment. Prebuilt materials eliminate hours of course-preparation work and offer significant support as you develop your online course. You can also obtain a WebCT-formatted version of the text's test bank.

Blackboard The Krugman/Wells Blackboard Course Cartridge allows you to combine Blackboard's popular tools and easy-to-use interface with the Krugman/Wells' text-specific, rich web content, including course outlines, preprogrammed quizzes, links, activities, interactive graphs, and a whole array of other materials. The result: an interactive, comprehensive online course that allow for effortless implementation, management, and use. The Worth electronic files are organized and prebuilt to work within the Blackboard software and can be easily downloaded from the Blackboard content showcases directly onto your department server. You can also obtain a Blackboard-formatted version of the book's test bank.

Dallas TeleLearning videos The Krugman/Wells text was chosen to accompany the economics telecourse developed by the Dallas Community College District (DCCCD). For use in class, instructors have access to videos produced by the DCCCD, the nation's leading developer of distance-learning materials. These videos dramatize key economic concepts and can be used in a classroom setting.

EduCue Personal Response System (PRS)— "Clickers"

Instructors can create a dynamic, interactive classroom environment with a personal response system, powered by EduCue. This wireless remote system allows you to ask your students questions, record their responses, and calculate grades instantly during lectures. Students use a hand-held wireless device (about the size of a television remote control) to transmit immediate feedback to a lecture hall receiver.

Wall Street Journal Edition

For adopters of the Krugman/Wells text, Worth Publishers and the *Wall Street Journal* are offering a 10-week subscription to students at a tremendous savings. Professors also receive their own free *Wall Street Journal* subscription plus additional instructor supplements created exclusively by the *Wall Street Journal*. Please contact your local sales rep for more information or go to the *Wall Street Journal* online at www.wsj.com.

Financial Times Edition

For adopters of the Krugman/Wells text, Worth Publishers and the *Financial Times* are offering a 15-week subscription to students at a tremendous savings. Professors also receive their own free *Financial Times* subscription for one year. Students and professors may access research and archived information at www.ft.com.

Acknowledgments

Writing a textbook is a team effort and we could never have reached this point without all of the talented and thoughtful consultants, reviewers, focus-group participants, class testers, and others who have been so generous with their insights on our work.

We are indebted to the following reviewers and other consultants for their suggestions and advice on our chapters:

Ashley Abramson, *Barstow College*

Ljubisa Adamovich, *Florida State University*

Lee Adkins, *Oklahoma State University*

Elena Alvarez, *State University of New York, Albany*

David A. Anderson, *Centre College*

Fahima Aziz, *Hamline University*

Sheryl Ball, *Virginia Polytechnic Institute and State University*

Charles L. Ballard, *Michigan State University*

Cynthia Bansak, *San Diego State University*

Richard Barrett, *University of Montana*

Daniel Barszcz, *College of DuPage*

Charles A. Bennett, *Gannon University*

Andreas Bentz, *Dartmouth College*

Ruben Berrios, *Clarion University*

Joydeep Bhattacharya, *Iowa State University*

Harmanna Bloemen, *Houston Community College*

Michael Bordo, *Rutgers University, NBER*

James Bradley, Jr., *University of South Carolina*

William Branch, *University of Oregon*

Michael Brandl, *University of Texas, Austin*

Greg Brock, *Georgia Southern University*

Raymonda L. Burgman, *DePauw University*

Charles Callahan III, *State University of New York, Brockport*

James Carden, *University of Mississippi*

Bill Carlisle, *University of Utah*

Leonard A. Carlson, *Emory University*

Andrew Cassey, *University of Minnesota*

Shirley Cassing, *University of Pittsburgh*

Yuna Chen, *South Georgia College*

Jim Cobbe, *Florida State University*

Eleanor D. Craig, *University of Delaware*

Rosemary Thomas Cunningham, *Agnes Scott College*

James Cypher, *California State University, Fresno*

Susan Dadres, *Southern Methodist University*

Ardeshir Dalal, *Northern Illinois University*

A. Edward Day, *University of Texas, Dallas*

Dennis Debrecht, *Carroll College*

Stephen J. DeCanio, *University of California, Santa Barbara*

J. Bradford DeLong, *University of California, Berkeley*

Julie Derrick, *Brevard Community College*

Carolyn Dimitri, *Montgomery College, Rockville*

Patrick Dolenc, *Keene State College*

Amitava Dutt, *University of Notre Dame*

Jim Eaton, *Bridgewater College*

Jim Eden, *Portland Community College*

Rex Edwards, *Moorpark College*

Can Erbil, *Brandeis University*

Sharon J. Erenburg, *Eastern Michigan University*

Joe Essuman, *University of Wisconsin, Waukesha*

David N. Figlio, *University of Florida*

David W. Findlay, *Colby College*

Eric Fisher, *Ohio State University/University of California, Santa Barbara*

Oliver Franke, *Athabasca University*

Rhona Free, *Eastern Connecticut State University*

K. C. Fung, *University of California, Santa Cruz*

Susan Gale, *New York University*

Neil Garston, *California State University, Los Angeles*

E. B. Gendel, *Woodbury University*

J. Robert Gillette, *University of Kentucky*

Lynn G. Gillette, *University of Kentucky*

James N. Giordano, *Villanova University*

Robert Godby, *University of Wyoming*

David Goodwin, *University of New Brunswick*

Lisa Grobar, *California State University, Long Beach*

Philip Grossman, *St. Cloud State University*

Wayne Grove, *Syracuse University*

Alan Gummerson, *Florida International University*

Jang-Ting Guo, *University of California, Riverside*

Jonathan Hamilton, *University of Florida*

Mehdi Haririan, *Bloomsburg University of Pennsylvania*

Hadley Hartman, *Santa Fe Community College*

Julie Heath, *University of Memphis*

John Heim, *Rensselaer Polytechnic Institute*

Jill M. Hendrickson, *University of the South*

Rob Holm, *Franklin University*

David Horlacher, *Middlebury College*

Robert Horn, *James Madison University*

Scott Houser, *California State University, Fresno*

Patrik T. Hultberg, *University of Wyoming*

Aaron Jackson, *Bentley College*

Nancy Jianakoplos, *Colorado State University*

Donn Johnson, *Quinnipiac University*

Bruce Johnson, *Centre College*

Philipp Jonas, *Western Michigan University*

Michael Jones, *Bridgewater State College*

James Jozefowicz, *Indiana University of Pennsylvania*

Kamran M. Kadkhah, *Northeastern University*

Matthew Kahn, *Columbia University*

Barry Keating, *University of Notre Dame*

Diane Keenan, *Cerritos College*

Bill Kerby, *California State University, Sacramento*

Kyoo Kim, *Bowling Green University*

Philip King, *San Francisco State University*

Sharmila King, *University of the Pacific*

Kala Krishna, *Penn State University, NBER*

Jean Kujawa, *Lourdes College*

Maria Kula, *Roger Williams University*

Michael Kuryla, *Broome Community College*

Tom Larson, *California State University, Los Angeles*

Susan K. Laury, *Georgia State University*

Jim Lee, *Texas A&M University, Corpus Christi*

Tony Lima, *California State University, Hayward*

Solina Lindahl, *California State Polytechnic University, Pomona*

Malte Loos, *Christian-Albrechts Universität Kiel*

Marty Ludlum, *Oklahoma City Community College*

Mark Maier, *Glendale Community College*

Rachel McCulloch, *Brandeis University*

Doug Meador, *William Jewell College*

Diego Mendez-Carbajo, *Illinois Wesleyan University*

Juan Mendoza, *State University of New York at Buffalo*

Jeffrey Michael, *Towson University*

Jenny Minier, *University of Miami*

Ida A. Mirzaie, *John Carroll University*

Kristen Monaco, *California State University, Long Beach*

Marie Mora, *University of Texas, Pan American*

W. Douglas Morgan, *University of California, Santa Barbara*

Peter B. Morgan, *University of Michigan*

Tony Myatt, *University of New Brunswick, Fredericton*

Kathryn Nantz, *Fairfield University*

John A. Neri, *University of Maryland*

Charles Newton, *Houston Community College*

Joe Nowakowski, *Muskingum College*

Seamus O'Cleireacain, *Columbia University/State University of New York, Purchase*

Martha Olney, *University of California, Berkeley*

Kerry Pannell, *DePauw University*

Chris Papageorgiou, *Louisiana State University*

Brian Peterson, *Central College*

John Pharr, *Dallas County Community College*

Clifford Poirot, *Shawnee State University*

Raymond E. Polchow, *Zane State College*

Adnan Qamar, *University of Texas, Dallas*

Jeffrey Racine, *University of South Florida*

Matthew Rafferty, *Quinnipiac University*

Dixie Watts Reaves, *Virginia Polytechnic Institute and State University*

Siobhán Reilly, *Mills College*

Thomas Rhoads, *Towson University*

Libby Rittenberg, *Colorado College*

Malcom Robinson, *Thomas More College*

Michael Rolleigh, *Williams College*

Christina Romer, *University of California, Berkeley*

Brian P. Rosario, *University of California, Davis*

Bernard Rose, *Rocky Mountain College*

Patricia Rottschaefer, *California State University, Fullerton*

Jeff Rubin, *Rutgers University*

Henry D. Ryder, *Gloucester Community College*

Allen Sanderson, *University of Chicago*

Rolando Santos, *Lakeland Community College*

Christine Sauer, *University of New Mexico*

Elizabeth Sawyer-Kelly, *University of Wisconsin, Madison*

Edward Sayre, *Agnes Scott College*

Robert Schwab, *University of Maryland*

Adina Schwartz, *Lakeland College*

Gerald Scott, *Florida Atlantic University*

Stanley Sedo, *University of Maryland*

William Shambora, *Ohio University*

Gail Shields, *Central Michigan University*

Amy Shrout, *West High School*

Eugene Silberberg, *University of Washington*

Bill Smith, *University of Memphis*

Ray Smith, *College of St. Scholastica*

Judy Smrha, *Baker University*

Marcia S. Snyder, *College of Charleston*

John Solow, *University of Iowa*

David E. Spencer, *Brigham Young University*

Denise Stanley, *California State University, Fullerton*

Martha A. Starr, *American University*

Richard Startz, *University of Washington*

Carol Ogden Stivender, *University of North Carolina, Charlotte*

Jill Stowe, *Texas A&M University, Austin*
William Stronge, *Florida Atlantic University*
Rodney Swanson, *University of California, Los Angeles*
Sarinda Taengnoi, *Western New England College*
Lazina Tarin, *Central Michigan University*
Jason Taylor, *University of Virginia*
Mark Thoma, *University of California, San Diego*
Mehmet Tosun, *West Virginia University*
Karen Travis, *Pacific Lutheran University*
Sandra Trejos, *Clarion University*
Arienne Turner, *Fullerton College*
Neven Valev, *Georgia State University*
Kristin Van Gaasbeck, *California State University*
Abu Wahid, *Tennessee State University*
Stephan Weiler, *Colorado State University*
James N. Wetzel, *Virginia Commonwealth University*
Robert Whaples, *Wake Forest University*
Roger White, *University of Georgia*
Jonathan B. Wight, *University of Richmond*
Mark Wohar, *University of Nebraska, Omaha*
William C. Wood, *James Madison University*
Ken Woodward, *Saddleback College*
Bill Yang, *Georgia Southern University*
Cemile Yavas, *Pennsylvania State University*
Andrea Zanter, *Hillsborough Community College*

We must also thank the following graduate student reviewers for their assistance: Kristy Piccinini, University of California, Berkeley; Lanwei Yang, University of California, Berkeley; Casey Rothschild, Massachusetts Institute of Technology; and Naomi E. Feldman, University of Michigan, Ann Arbor.

During the course of drafting our manuscript, we met with instructors of principles courses for face-to-face focus-group sessions that afforded us invaluable input. We appreciate the forthright advice and suggestions from these colleagues:

Michael Bordo, *Rutgers University*
Jim Cobbe, *Florida State University*
Tom Creahan, *Morehead State University*
Stephen DeCanio, *University of California, Santa Barbara*
Jim Eden, *Portland Community College, Sylvania*
David Flath, *North Carolina State University*
Rhona Free, *Eastern Connecticut State University*
Rick Godby, *University of Wyoming*
Wayne Grove, *Syracuse University*
Jonathan Hamilton, *University of Florida*
Robert Horn, *James Madison University*
Patrik Hultberg, *University of Wyoming*
Bruce Johnson, *Centre College*
Jim Jozefowicz, *Indiana University of Pennsylvania*

Jim Lee, *Texas A&M University, Corpus Christi*
Rachel McCulloch, *Brandeis University*
Ida Mirzaie, *John Carroll University*
Henry D. Ryder, *Gloucester Community College*
Marcia Snyder, *College of Charleston*
Brian Trinque, *University of Texas, Austin*
William C. Wood, *James Madison University*

Many thanks to the class testers who took the time to use early drafts of our chapters in their classrooms. The following instructors should know that we made use of their helpful suggestions. We also extend special thanks to so many of your students who filled out user surveys about our chapters. This student input inspired us.

Ashley Abramson, *Barstow College*
Terry Alexander, *Iowa State University*
Fahima Aziz, *Hamline University*
Benjamin Balak, *Rollins College*
Leon Battista, *Bronx Community College*
Richard Beil, *Auburn University*
Charles Bennett, *Gannon University*
Scott Benson, *Idaho State University*
Andreas Bentz, *Dartmouth College*
John Bockino, *Suffolk County Community College*
Ellen Bowen, *Fisher College, New Bedford*
Anne Bresnock, *University of California, Los Angeles*
Bruce Brown, *California State Polytechnic University, Pomona*
John Buck, *Jacksonville University*
Raymonda Burgman, *University of Southern Florida*
William Carlisle, *University of Utah*
Kevin Carlson, *University of Massachusetts, Boston*
Fred Carstensen, *University of Connecticut*
Shirley Cassing, *University of Pittsburgh*
Ramon Castillo-Ponce, *California State University, Los Angeles*
Emily Chamlee-Wright, *Beloit College*
Anthony Chan, *Santa Monica College*
Mitch Charkiewiecz, *Central Connecticut State University*
Yuna Chen, *South Georgia College*
Maryanne Clifford, *Eastern Connecticut State University*
Julia Chismar, *St. Joseph's High School*
Gregory Colman, *Pace University*
Sarah Culver, *University of Alabama*
Rosa Lea Danielson, *College of DuPage*
Lew Dars, *University of Massachusetts/Dartmouth*
Stephen Davis, *Southwest Minnesota State University*
Tom DelGiudice, *Hofstra University*
Arna Desser, *United States Naval Academy*
Nikolay Dobrinov, *University of Colorado*
Patrick Dolenc, *Keene State College*
Stratford Douglas, *West Virginia University*
Julie Dvorak, *Warren Township High School*

Dorsey Dyer, *Davidson County Community College*

Mary Edwards, *St. Cloud State University*

Fritz Efaw, *University of Tennessee, Chattanooga*

Herb Elliot, *Alan Hancock College*

Can Erbil, *Brandeis University*

Yee Tien Fu, *Stanford University*

Yoram Gelman, *Lehman College, The City University of New York*

E.B. Gendel, *Woodbury College*

Doug Gentry, *St. Mary's College*

Tommy Georgiades, *DeVry University*

Satyajit Ghosh, *University of Scranton*

Richard Glendening, *Central College*

Patrick Gormely, *Kansas State University*

Richard Gosselin, *Houston Community College, Central*

Patricia Graham, *University of Northern Colorado*

Kathleen Greer Rossman, *Birmingham Southern College*

Wayne Grove, *Syracuse University*

Eleanor Gubins, *Rosemont College*

Alan Haight, *State University of New York, Cortland*

Gautam Hazarika, *University of Texas, Brownsville*

Tom Head, *George Fox University*

Susan Helper, *Case Western Reserve University*

Paul Hettler, *Duquesne University*

Roger Hewett, *Drake University*

Michael Hilmer, *San Diego State University*

Jill Holman, *University of Wisconsin, Milwaukee*

Scott Houser, *California State University, Fresno*

Ray Hubbard, *Central Georgia Technical College*

Murat Iyigun, *University of Colorado*

Habib Jam, *Rowan University*

Louis Johnston, *College of St. Benedict/St. John's University*

Jack Julian, *Indiana University of Pennsylvania*

Soheila Kahkashan, *Towson University*

Charles Kaplan, *St. Joseph's College*

Jay Kaplan, *University of Colorado, Boulder*

Bentzil Kasper, *Broome Community College*

Kurt Keiser, *Adams State College*

Ara Khanjian, *Ventura College*

Sinan Koont, *Dickinson College*

Emil Kreider, *Beloit College*

Kenneth Kriz, *University of Nebraska, Omaha*

Tom Larson, *California State University, Los Angeles*

Delores Linton, *Tarrant County College, Northwest*

Rolf Lokke, *Albuquerque Academy*

Ellen Magenheim, *Swarthmore College*

Diana McCoy, *Truckee Meadows Community College*

Garrett Milam, *Ryerson University*

Robert Miller, *Fisher College, New Bedford Campus*

Michael Milligan, *Front Range Community College*

Cathy Miners, *Fairfield University*

Larry Miners, *Fairfield University*

Kristen Monaco, *California State University, Long Beach*

Marie Mora, *University of Texas, Pan American*

James Mueller, *Alma College*

Ranganath Murthy, *Bucknell University*

Sylvia Nasar, *Columbia University*

Gerardo Nebbia, *Glendale Community College*

Anthony Negbenebor, *Gardner-Webb University*

Joseph Nowakowski, *Muskingum College*

Charles Okeke, *Community College of Southern Nevada*

Kimberley Ott, *Kent State University, Salem Campus*

Philip Packard, *St. Mary's College*

Jamie Pelley, *Mary Baldwin College*

Michael Perelman, *California State University*

Mary K. Perkins, *Howard University*

John Pharr, *Dallas Community College, Cedar Valley*

Jerome Picard, *Mount Saint Mary College*

Ray Polchow, *Muskingum Area Technical College*

Ernest Poole, *Fashion Institute of Technology*

Reza Ramazani, *St. Michael's College*

Charles Reichheld, *Cuyahoga Community College*

Siobhan Reilly, *Mills College*

Michael Righi, *Bellevue Community College*

Carl Riskin, *Queens College, The City University of New York*

Malcolm Robinson, *Thomas More College*

Charles Rock, *Rollins College*

Richard Romano, *Broome Community College*

Jeff Romine, *University of Colorado, Denver*

Bernie Rose, *Rocky Mountain College*

Dan Rubenson, *Southern Oregon University*

Jeff Rubin, *Rutgers University*

Lynda Rush, *California State Polytechnic University, Pomona*

Martin Sabo, *Community College of Denver*

Sara Saderion, *Houston Community College, Southwest*

George Sawdy, *Providence College*

Ted Scheinman, *Mt. Hood Community College*

Russell Settle, *University of Delaware*

Anna Shostya, *Pace University*

Amy Shrout, *West High School*

Millicent Sites, *Carson-Newman College*

Judy Smrha, *Baker University*

John Somers, *Portland Community College*

Jim Spellicy, *Lowell High School*

Tesa Stegner, *Idaho State University*

Kurt Stephenson, *Virginia Tech*

Charles Stull, *Kalamazoo College*

Laddie Sula, *Loras College*

David Switzer, *University of Northern Michigan*

Deborah Thorsen, *Palm Beach Community College*

Andrew Toole, *Cook College/Rutgers University*

Arienne Turner, *Fullerton College*

Anthony Uremovic, *Joliet Junior College*

Jane Wallace, *University of Pittsburgh*

Tom Watkins, *Eastern Kentucky University*

James Wetzel, *Virginia Commonwealth University*

Mark Witte, *Northwestern University*

Larry Wolfenbarger, *Macon State College*

James Woods, *Portland State University*

Mickey Wu, *Coe College*

David Yerger, *Indiana University of Pennsylvania*

Eric Young, *Bishop Amat Memorial High School*

Lou Zaera, *Fashion Institute of Technology*

Andrea Zanter, *Hillsborough Community College, Dale Mabry Campus*

Stephen Zill, *De Anza College*

We also appreciate the contributions of our Two-Year/Community College Advisory Panel:

Kathleen Bromley, *Monroe Community College*

Barbara Connolly, *Westchester Community College*

Will Cummings, *Grossmont College*

Richard Gosselin, *Houston Community College, Central*

Gus Herring, *Brookhaven College*

Charles Okeke, *Community College of Southern Nevada*

Charles Reichheld, *Cuyahoga Community College*

Sara Saderion, *Houston Community College, Southwest*

Ted Scheinman, *Mt. Hood Community College*

J. Ross Thomas, *Albuquerque Technical Vocational Institute*

Deborah Thorsen, *Palm Beach Community College*

Ranita Wyatt, *Dallas Community College*

We must thank the following instructors for their creativity and contributions to the *Microeconomics* and *Macroeconomics* card decks:

Charles Antholt, *Western Washington University*

Richard Ball, *Haverford University*

Edward Blomdahl, *Bridgewater State College*

Michael Brace, *Jamestown Community College*

Gregory Brock, *Georgia Southern University*

Joseph Cavanaugh, *Wright State University*

Tom Cooper, *Georgetown College*

James Craven, *Clark College*

Ardeshir Dalal, *Northern Illinois University*

Asif Dowla, *St. Mary's College of Maryland*

James Dulgeroff, *San Bernardino Valley Community College*

Tom Duston, *Keene State College*

Tomas Dvorak, *Union College*

Debra Dwyer, *State University of New York, Stony Brook*

Michael Ellis, *New Mexico State University*

Can Erbil, *Brandeis University*

John Erkkila, *Lake Superior State University*

Chuck Fischer, *Pittsburg State University*

Eric Fisher, *Ohio State University*

John Fitzgerald, *Bowdoin College*

Rajeev Goel, *Illinois State University*

Pat Graham, *University of Northern Colorado*

Hart Hodges, *Western Washington University*

Naphtali Hoffman, *Elmira College*

Yu Hsing, *Southeastern Louisiana University*

Miren Ivankovic, *Southern Wesleyan University*

Allan Jenkins, *University of Nebraska, Kearney*

Elia Kacapyr, *Ithaca College*

Farida Khan, *University of Wisconsin, Parkside*

Maureen Kilkenny, *Iowa State University*

Kent Klitgaard, *Wells College*

Janet Koscianski, *Shippensburg University*

Charles Kroncke, *College of Mount Saint Joseph*

Margaret Landman, *Bridgewater State College*

Bill Lee, *St. Mary's College*

Diego Mendez-Carbajo, *Illinois Wesleyan University*

Nelson Nagai, *San Joaquin Delta College*

William O'Dea, *State University of New York, Oneonta*

Douglas Orr, *Eastern Washington University*

Phil Packard, *Saint Mary's College of California*

Brian Peterson, *Central College*

Joe Pomykala, *Towson University*

Kevin Quinn, *Bowling Green State University*

Lynda Rush, *California State Polytechnic University, Pomona*

Richard Schatz, *Whitworth College*

Peter Schwartz, *University of North Carolina, Charlotte*

Kathleen Segerson, *University of Connecticut*

Esther-Mirjam Sent, *University of Nijmegen*

Millicent Sites, *Carson-Newman College*

Herrick Smith, *Nease High School*

M. N. Srinivas, *Center for Computer-Assisted Legal Instruction (CALI)*

Jean-Philippe Stijns, *Northeastern University*

Chuck Stull, *Kalamazoo College*

Michael Szenberg, *Pace University*

Ross Thomas, *Albuquerque Technical Vocational Institute*

Maurice Weinrobe, *Clark University*

James N. Wetzel, *Virginia Commonwealth University*

Gary Wolfram, *Hillsdale College*

William C. Wood, *James Madison University*

Paul Zak, *Claremont Graduate University*

Alina Zapalska, *U.S. Coast Guard Academy*

We would also like to thank the hundreds of instructors who took the time to offer their useful feedback to online marketing surveys about our project. There are nearly 800 of you out there. We only wish we had enough room in this small space to thank each of you.

The following key people critically read every page in virtually every chapter from many of our drafts and offered us so much: Andreas Bentz, Dartmouth College, oversaw accuracy checking, but his role turned into much more than that—a constant, tireless adviser who clarified our work at every step. It is extremely rare to find someone as faithful as Andreas has been to this project, and we are immensely grateful to him. Martha Olney, University of California, Berkeley, provided insightful input throughout—we had a number of moments when we realized that her advice saved us from a serious pedagogical misstep. Our deepest thanks also go to Martha. Development editor Marilyn Freedman helped us in shaping a book that instructors can really use and injected much-needed doses of common sense at crucial moments. We've even relied on her to sort out pedagogical differences between the two of us. Several other people have played an invaluable role as close readers of our chapters: Elizabeth Sawyer-Kelly, University of Wisconsin, Madison; David Findlay, Colby College; Sharon J. Ehrenburg, Eastern Michigan University; Malte Loos, Christian-Albrechts Universität Kiel; and Kristy Piccinni and Lanwei Yang, both graduate students at the University of California, Berkeley. The detailed and wise input from all of you has been enormously helpful to us! (Thanks, too, Kristy for your work on our glossary.) Special thanks go to Dave Figlio, University of Florida, for his invaluable help as a reviewer and for his contributions to the labor and inflation chapters.

Thanks to Rhona Free for her contributions, particularly for the essential role she played in the development of our graphing appendix. We must also extend special thanks to Rosemary Cunningham, Agnes Scott College, for her assistance with end-of-chapter problems.

We'd like to thank the current and former Worth people who made this project possible. Paul Shensa and Bob Worth suggested that we write this book. Craig Bleyer, publisher, kept the writing process moving, with just the right mix of patience and whip-cracking. Craig's able leadership and patience helped us realize our vision for this book and get all versions of it finished and out to the market.

Elizabeth Widdicombe, president of Freeman and Worth, and Catherine Woods, publisher at Worth, urged us on and kept faith with what must have been a very exasperating project at times.

We have had an incredible production and design team on this book. Tracey Kuehn, our associate managing editor, has worked tirelessly and with great skill to turn our rough manuscript into this beautiful textbook—and on a very tight schedule. And, thank you, Anthony Calcara, our project editor. Karen Osborne, our copyeditor, did a fine job helping us streamline and refine our writing. Babs Reingold created the spectacular cover for this book and came up with a book design that awed us each time we saw a new chapter in page proof. All we can say is "wow" and thanks. And we would not have been so awed with the look of each and every spread without the page-layout magic that Lee Mahler worked for us. Thanks, too, to Barbara Seixas for her work on the manufacturing end. We've heard about some of the miracles you've worked for us, Barbara, and we appreciate all you've done. The lovely photos you see in this book come to us courtesy of Elyse Rieder and Julie Tesser, our photo researchers. Thanks, too, to Patricia Marx and Ted Szczepanski for their assistance with photos. And for all of her help, thanks to Liz Saxon, editorial assistant.

Many thanks to Charlie Van Wagner, senior acquisitions editor, for devising and coordinating the impressive collection of media and supplements that accompany our *Microeconomics* textbook. Thanks are also extended to Marie McHale, associate editor, for doing the same on our *Macroeconomics* supplements. And many thanks to the incredible team of supplements writers and coordinators who worked with Charlie and Marie to make the supplements and media package so strong.

Thanks to Steve Rigolosi, director of market development, and Scott Guile, marketing manager, for their energetic and creative work in marketing this book. Thanks to Tom Kling, national economics consultant, for his critical role in helping to seed business for this text. And thank you, Bruce Kaplan, for all of your behind-the-scenes work supporting sales and marketing efforts. Thank you, Barbara Monteiro of Monteiro and Company as well as John Murphy and Dori Weintraub of St. Martin's Press, for your help with publicity for the book.

And most of all, special thanks to Sharon Balbos, executive development editor on this project, who must have been as stressed out as we were—but kept her cool throughout many years of tough slogging. We hope that this book lives up to the level of dedication and professionalism that she put into this project.

Paul Krugman   Robin Wells

BRIEF CONTENTS

CONTENTS

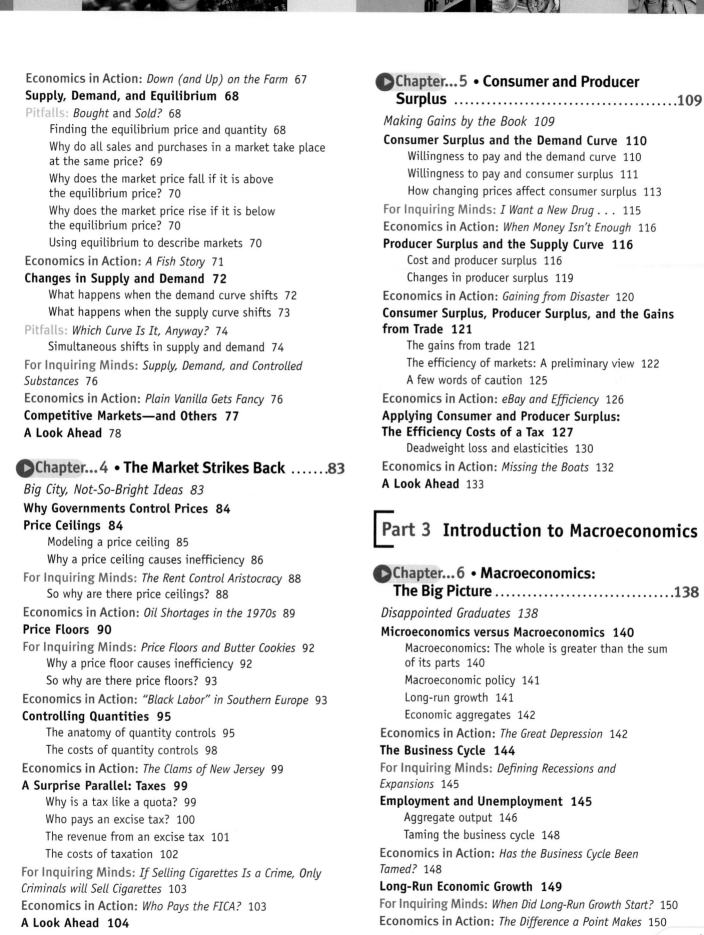

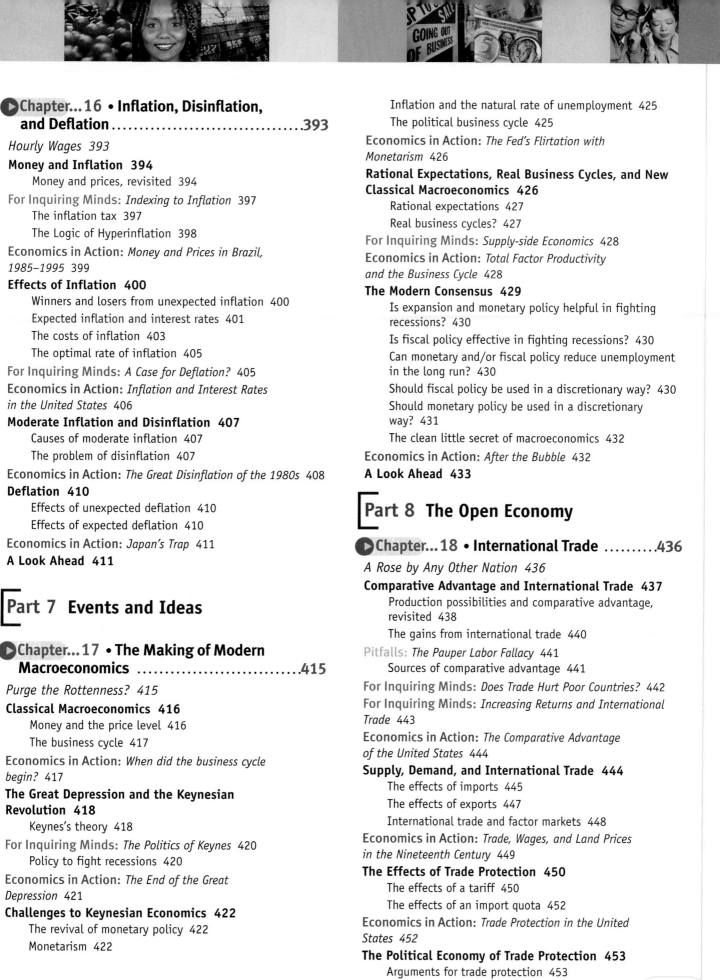

>>Introduction: The Ordinary Business of Life

ANY GIVEN SUNDAY

IT'S SUNDAY AFTERNOON IN THE SUMMER of 2003, and Route 1 in central New Jersey is a busy place. Thousands of people crowd the shopping malls that line the road for 20 miles, all the way from Trenton to New Brunswick. Most of the shoppers are cheerful—and why not? The stores in those malls offer an extraordinary range of choice; you can buy everything from sophisticated electronic equipment to fashionable clothes to organic carrots. There are probably 100,000 distinct items available

The scene along Route 1 that summer day was, of course, perfectly ordinary—very much like the scene along hundreds of other stretches of road, all across America, that same afternoon. But the discipline of economics is mainly concerned with ordinary things. As the great nineteenth-century economist Alfred Marshall put it, economics is "a study of mankind in the ordinary business of life."

What can economics say about this "ordinary business"? Quite a lot, it turns

Delivering the goods: the market economy in action

along that stretch of road. And most of these items are not luxury goods that only the rich can afford; they are products that millions of Americans can and do purchase every day.

out. What we'll see in this book is that even familiar scenes of economic life pose some very important questions—questions that economics can help answer. Among these questions are:

1

- How does our economic system work? That is, how does it manage to deliver the goods?

- When and why does our economic system go astray, leading people into counterproductive behavior?

- Why are there ups and downs in the economy? That is, why does the economy sometimes have a "bad year"?

- Finally, why is the long run mainly a story of ups rather than downs? That is, why has America, along with other advanced nations, become so much richer over time?

Let's take a look at these questions and offer a brief preview of what you will learn in this book.

The Invisible Hand

That ordinary scene in central New Jersey would not have looked at all ordinary to an American from colonial times—say, one of the patriots who helped George Washington win the battle of Trenton in 1776. (At the time, Trenton was a small village with not a shopping mall in sight, and farms lined the unpaved road that would eventually become Route 1.)

Imagine that you could transport an American from the colonial period forward in time to our own era. (Isn't that the plot of a movie? Several, actually.) What would this time-traveler find amazing?

Surely the most amazing thing would be the sheer prosperity of modern America—the range of goods and services that ordinary families can afford. Looking at all that wealth, our transplanted colonial would wonder, "How can I get some of that?" Or perhaps he would ask himself, "How can my society get some of that?"

The answer is that to get this kind of prosperity, you need a well-functioning system for coordinating productive activities—the activities that create the goods and services people want and get them to the people who want them. That kind of system is what we mean when we talk about the **economy**. And **economics** is the study of economies, at the level both of individuals and of society as a whole.

An economy succeeds to the extent that it, literally, delivers the goods. A time-traveler from the eighteenth century—or even from 1950—would be amazed at how many goods and services the modern American economy delivers and at how many people can afford them. Compared with any past economy and with all but a few other countries today, America has an incredibly high standard of living.

So our economy must be doing something right, and the time-traveler might want to compliment the person in charge. But guess what? There isn't anyone in charge. The United States has a **market economy**, in which production and consumption are the result of decentralized decisions by many firms and individuals. There is no central authority telling people what to produce or where to ship it. Each individual producer makes what he or she thinks will be most profitable; each consumer buys what he or she chooses.

The alternative to a market economy is a *command economy,* in which there *is* a central authority making decisions about production and consumption. Command economies have been tried, most notably in the Soviet Union between 1917 and 1991. But they didn't work very well. Producers in the Soviet Union routinely found themselves unable to produce because they did not have crucial raw materials, or they succeeded in producing but then found that nobody wanted their products. Consumers were often unable to find necessary items—command economies are famous for long lines at shops.

Market economies, however, are able to coordinate even highly complex activities and to reliably provide consumers with the goods and services they want. Indeed, people quite casually trust their lives to the market system: residents of any major city

---

An **economy** is a system for coordinating society's productive activities.

Economics is the study of economies, at the level both of individuals and of society as a whole.

A **market economy** is an economy in which decisions about production and consumption are made by individual producers and consumers.

would starve in days if the unplanned yet somehow orderly actions of thousands of businesses did not deliver a steady supply of food. Surprisingly, the unplanned "chaos" of a market economy turns out to be far more orderly than the "planning" of a command economy.

In 1776, in a famous passage in his book *The Wealth of Nations*, the pioneering Scottish economist Adam Smith wrote about how individuals, in pursuing their own interests, often end up serving the interests of society as a whole. Of a businessman whose pursuit of profit makes the nation wealthier, Smith wrote: "[H]e intends only his own gain, and he is in this, as in many other cases, led by an invisible hand to promote an end which was no part of his intention." Ever since, economists have used the term **invisible hand** to refer to the way a market economy manages to harness the power of self-interest for the good of society.

The study of how individuals make decisions and how these decisions interact is called **microeconomics**. One of the key themes in microeconomics is the validity of Adam Smith's insight: Individuals pursuing their own interests often do promote the interests of society as a whole.

So part of the answer to our time-traveler's question—"How can my society achieve the kind of prosperity you take for granted?"—is that his society should learn to appreciate the virtues of a market economy and the power of the invisible hand.

But the invisible hand isn't always our friend. It's also important to understand when and why the individual pursuit of self-interest can lead to counterproductive behavior.

The **invisible hand** refers to the way in which the individual pursuit of self-interest can lead to good results for society as a whole.

Microeconomics is the branch of economics that studies how people make decisions and how these decisions interact.

My Benefit, Your Cost

One thing that our time-traveler would not admire about modern Route 1 is the traffic. In fact, although most things have gotten better in America over time, traffic congestion has gotten a lot worse.

When traffic is congested, each driver is imposing a cost on all the other drivers on the road—he is literally getting in their way (and they are getting in his way). This cost can be substantial: in major metropolitan areas, each time someone drives to work, as opposed to taking public transportation or working at home, he can easily impose $15 or more in hidden costs on other drivers. Yet when deciding whether or not to drive, commuters have no incentive to take the costs they impose on others into account.

Traffic congestion is a familiar example of a much broader problem: sometimes the individual pursuit of one's own interest, instead of promoting the interests of society as a whole, can actually make society worse off. When this happens, it is known as **market failure**. Other important examples of market failure involve air and water pollution as well as the overexploitation of natural resources such as fish and forests.

The good news, as you will learn as you use this book to study microeconomics, is that economic analysis can be used to diagnose cases of market failure. And often, economic analysis can also be used to devise solutions for the problem.

When the individual pursuit of self-interest leads to bad results for society as a whole, there is **market failure**.

Good Times, Bad Times

Route 1 was bustling on that summer day in 2003—but it wasn't bustling quite as much as merchants would have liked, because in mid-2003 the U.S. economy wasn't doing all that well. The main problem was jobs: in early 2001, businesses began laying off workers in large numbers, and as of June 2003, employment had not yet started to recover.

Such troubled periods are a regular feature of modern economies. The fact is that the economy does not always run smoothly: it experiences *fluctuations,* a series of ups and downs. By middle age, a typical American will have experienced three or four downs, known as **recessions**. (The U.S. economy experienced serious recessions beginning in 1973, 1980, 1981, 1990, and 2001.) During a severe recession, millions of workers may be laid off.

Like market failure, recessions are a fact of life; but also like market failure, they are a problem to which economic analysis offers some solutions. Recessions are one of the main concerns of the branch of economics known as **macroeconomics**, which is concerned with the overall ups and downs of the economy. If you study macroeconomics, you will learn how economists explain recessions and how government policies can be used to minimize the damage from economic fluctuations.

Despite the occasional recession, however, over the long run the story of the U.S. economy contains many more ups than downs. And that long-run ascent is the subject of our final question.

> A **recession** is a downturn in the economy.

> **Macroeconomics** is the branch of economics that is concerned with overall ups and downs in the economy.

Onward and Upward

At the beginning of the twentieth century, most Americans lived under conditions that we would now think of as extreme poverty. Only 10 percent of homes had flush toilets, only 8 percent had central heating, only 2 percent had electricity, and almost nobody had a car, let alone a washing machine or air conditioning.

Such comparisons are a stark reminder of how much our lives have been changed by **economic growth**, the growing ability of the economy to produce goods and services.

Why does the economy grow over time? And why does economic growth occur faster in some times and places than in others? These are key questions for economics because economic growth is a good thing, as those shoppers on Route 1 can attest, and most of us want more of it.

> **Economic growth** is the growing ability of the economy to produce goods and services.

An Engine for Discovery

We hope we have convinced you that the "ordinary business of life" is really quite extraordinary, if you stop to think about it, and that it can lead us to ask some very interesting and important questions.

In this book, we will describe the answers economists have given to these questions. But this book, like economics as a whole, isn't a list of answers: it's an introduction to a discipline, a way to address questions like those we have just asked. Or as Alfred Marshall, who described economics as a study of the "ordinary business of life," put it: "Economics . . . is not a body of concrete truth, but an engine for the discovery of concrete truth."

So let's turn the key in the ignition.

KEY TERMS

Economy, p. 2

Economics, p. 2

Market economy, p. 2

Invisible hand, p. 3

Microeconomics, p. 3

Market failure, p. 3

Recession, p. 4

Macroeconomics, p. 4

Economic growth, p. 4

>>First Principles

COMMON GROUND

THE ANNUAL MEETING OF THE AMERICAN Economic Association draws thousands of economists, young and old, famous and obscure. There are booksellers, business meetings, and quite a few job interviews. But mainly the economists gather to talk and listen. During the busiest times, 60 or more presentations may be taking place simultaneously, on questions that range from the future of the stock market to who does the cooking in two-earner families.

What do these people have in common? An expert on the stock market probably knows very little about the economics of housework, and vice versa. Yet an economist who wanders into the wrong seminar and ends up listening to presentations on some unfamiliar topic is nonetheless likely to hear much that is familiar. The reason is that all economic analysis is based on a set of common principles that apply to many different issues.

Some of these principles involve *individual choice*—for economics is, first of all, about the choices that individuals make. Do you choose to work over the summer or take a backpacking trip? Do you buy a new CD or go to a movie? These decisions involve *making a choice* among a limited number of alternatives—limited because no one can have everything that he or she wants. Every question in economics at its most basic level involves individuals making choices.

But to understand how an economy works, you need to understand more than how individuals make choices. None of us are Robinson Crusoe, alone on an island—we must make decisions in an environment that is shaped by the decisions of others. Indeed, in a modern economy even the simplest decisions you make—say, what to have for breakfast—are shaped by the decisions of thousands of other people, from the banana grower in Costa Rica who decided to grow the fruit you eat to the farmer in Iowa who provided the corn in your cornflakes. And because each of us in a market economy depends on

One must choose.

Richard Hamilton Smith/Corbis

What you will learn in this chapter:

➤ A set of principles for understanding the economics of how individuals make choices

➤ A set of principles for understanding how individual choices interact so many others—and they, in turn, depend on us—our choices interact. So although all economics at a basic level is about individual choice, in order to understand how market economies behave we must also understand economy-wide *interaction*— how my choices affect your choices, and vice versa.

In this chapter, we will look at nine basic principles of economics—four principles involving individual choice and five involving the way individual choices interact.

Individual Choice: The Core of Economics

> **Individual choice** is the decision by an individual of what to do, which necessarily involves a decision of what not to do.

Every economic issue involves, at its most basic level, **individual choice**—decisions by an individual about what to do and what *not* to do. In fact, you might say that it isn't economics if it isn't about choice.

Step into a big store like a Wal-Mart or Home Depot. There are thousands of different products available, and it is extremely unlikely that you—or anyone else—could afford to buy everything you might want to have. And anyway, there's only so much space in your dorm room or apartment. So will you buy another bookcase or a mini-refrigerator? Given limitations on your budget and your living space, you must choose which products to buy and which to leave on the shelf.

The fact that those products are on the shelf in the first place involves choice—the store manager chose to put them there, and the manufacturers of the products chose to produce them. All economic activities involve individual choice.

Four economic principles underlie the economics of individual choice, as shown in Table 1-1. We'll now examine each of these principles in more detail.

TABLE **1-1**

Principles That Underlie the Economics of Individual Choice

1. Resources are scarce.

2. The real cost of something is what you must give up to get it.

3. "How much?" is a decision at the margin.

4. People usually exploit opportunities to make themselves better off.

Resources Are Scarce

You can't always get what you want. Everyone would like to have a beautiful house in a great location (and help with the housecleaning), two or three luxury cars, and frequent vacations in fancy hotels. But even in a rich country like the United States, not many families can afford all that. So they must make choices—whether to go to Disney World this year or buy a better car, whether to make do with a small backyard or accept a longer commute in order to live where land is cheaper.

Limited income isn't the only thing that keeps people from having everything they want. Time is also in limited supply: there are only 24 hours in a day. And because the time we have is limited, choosing to spend time on one activity also means choosing not to spend time on a different activity—spending time studying for an exam means forgoing a night at the movies. Indeed, many people are so limited by the number of hours in the day that they are willing to trade money for time. For example, convenience stores normally charge higher prices than a regular supermarket. But they fulfill a valuable role by catering to time-pressured customers who would rather pay more than travel farther to the supermarket.

> A **resource** is anything that can be used to produce something else.
>
> Resources are **scarce**—the quantity available isn't large enough to satisfy all productive uses.

Why do individuals have to make choices? The ultimate reason is that *resources are scarce*. A **resource** is anything that can be used to produce something else. Lists of the economy's resources usually begin with land, labor (the available time of workers), capital (machinery, buildings, and other man-made productive assets), and human capital (the educational achievements and skills of workers). A resource is **scarce** when the quantity of the resource available isn't large enough to satisfy all productive uses. There are many scarce resources. These include natural resources—resources that come from the physical environment, such as minerals, lumber, and petroleum. There is also a limited quantity of human resources—labor, skill, and intelligence. And in a growing world economy with a rapidly increasing human population, even clean air and water have become scarce resources.

Just as individuals must make choices, the scarcity of resources means that society as a whole must make choices. One way for a society to make choices is simply to allow them to emerge as the result of many individual choices, which is what usually happens in a market economy. For example, Americans as a group have only so many hours in a week: how many of those hours will they spend going to supermarkets to get lower prices, rather than saving time by shopping at convenience stores? The answer is the sum of individual decisions: each of the millions of individuals in the economy makes his or her own choice about where to shop, and the overall choice is simply the sum of those individual decisions.

But for various reasons, there are some decisions that a society decides are best not left to individual choice. For example, the authors live in an area that until recently was mainly farmland but is now being rapidly built up. Most local residents feel that the community would be a more pleasant place to live if some of the land were left undeveloped. But no individual has an incentive to keep his or her land as open space, rather than selling it to a developer. So a trend has emerged in many communities across the United States of local governments purchasing undeveloped land and preserving it as open space. We'll see in later chapters why decisions about how to use scarce resources are often best left to individuals but sometimes should be made at a higher, community-wide, level.

Opportunity Cost: The Real Cost of Something Is What You Must Give Up to Get It

It is the last term before you graduate, and your class schedule allows you to take only one elective. There are two, however, that you would really like to take: History of Jazz and Beginning Tennis.

Suppose you decide to take the History of Jazz course. What's the cost of that decision? It is the fact that you can't take Beginning Tennis. Economists call that kind of cost—what you must forgo in order to get something you want—the **opportunity cost** of that item. So the opportunity cost of the History of Jazz class is the enjoyment you would have derived from the Beginning Tennis class.

The concept of opportunity cost is crucial to understanding individual choice because, in the end, all costs are opportunity costs. Sometimes critics claim that economists are concerned only with costs and benefits that can be measured in dollars and cents. But that is not true. Much economic analysis involves cases like our elective course example, where it costs no extra tuition to take one elective course—that is, there is no direct monetary cost. Nonetheless, the elective you choose has an opportunity cost—the other desirable elective course that you must forgo because your limited time permits taking only one.

You might think that opportunity cost is an add-on—that is, something *additional* to the monetary cost of an item. Suppose that an elective class costs additional tuition of $750; now there is a monetary cost to taking History of Jazz. Is the opportunity cost of taking that course something separate from that monetary cost?

Well, consider two cases. First, suppose that taking Beginning Tennis also costs $750. In this case, you would have to spend that $750 no matter which class you take. So what you give up to take the History of Jazz class is still the Beginning Tennis class, period—you would have to spend that $750 either way. But suppose there isn't any fee for the tennis class. In that case, what you give up to take the jazz class is the tennis class *plus* whatever you would have bought with the $750.

Either way, the cost of taking your preferred class is what you must give up to get it. *All* costs are ultimately opportunity costs.

Sometimes the money you have to pay for something is a good indication of its opportunity cost. But many times it is not. One very important example of how poorly monetary cost can indicate opportunity cost is the cost of attending college.

The real cost of an item is its **opportunity cost**: what you must give up in order to get it.

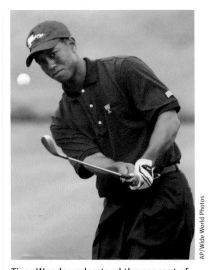

Tiger Woods understood the concept of opportunity cost. The rest is history.

Tuition and housing are major monetary expenses for most students; but even if these things were free, attending college would still be an expensive proposition because most college students, if they were not in college, would have a job. That is, by going to college, students *forgo* the income they could have made if they had worked instead. This means that the opportunity cost of attending college is what you pay for tuition and housing *plus* the forgone income you would have earned in a job.

It's easy to see that the opportunity cost of going to college is especially high for people who could be earning a lot during what would otherwise have been their college years. That is why star athletes often skip college or, like Tiger Woods, leave before graduating.

"How Much?" Is a Decision at the Margin

Some important decisions involve an "either-or" choice—for example, you decide either to go to college or to begin working; you decide either to take economics or to take something else. But other important decisions involve "how much" choices—for example, if you are taking both economics and chemistry this semester, you must decide how much time to spend studying for each. When it comes to understanding "how much" decisions, economics has an important insight to offer: "how much" is a decision made *at the margin*.

Suppose you are taking both economics and chemistry. And suppose you are a premed student, so that your grade in chemistry matters more to you than your grade in economics. Does that therefore imply that you should spend *all* your study time on chemistry and wing it on the economics exam? Probably not; even if you think your chemistry grade is more important, you should put some effort into studying for economics.

Spending more time studying for economics involves a benefit (a higher expected grade in that course) and a cost (you could have spent that time doing something else, such as studying to get a higher grade in chemistry). That is, your decision involves a **trade-off**—a comparison of costs and benefits.

How do you decide this kind of "how much" question? The typical answer is that you make the decision a bit at a time, by asking how you should spend the next hour.

You make a **trade-off** when you compare the costs with the benefits of doing something.

Say both exams are on the same day, and the night before you spend time reviewing your notes for both courses. At 6:00 P.M., you decide that it's a good idea to spend at least an hour on each course. At 8:00 P.M., you decide you'd better spend another hour on each course. At 10:00 P.M., you are getting tired and figure you have one more hour to study before bed—chemistry or economics? If you are pre-med, it's likely to be chemistry; if you are pre-MBA, it's likely to be economics.

Note how you've made the decision to allocate your time: at each point the question is whether or not to spend *one more hour* on either course. And in deciding whether to spend another hour studying for chemistry, you weigh the costs (an hour forgone of studying for economics or an hour forgone of sleeping) versus the benefits (a likely increase in your chemistry grade). As long as the benefit of studying one more hour for chemistry outweighs the cost, you should choose to study for that additional hour.

Decisions of this type—what to do with your next hour, what to do with your next dollar, and so on—are **marginal decisions**. They involve making trade-offs *at the margin*: comparing the costs and benefits of doing a little bit more of an activity versus doing a little bit less. The study of such decisions is known as **marginal analysis**.

Many of the questions that we face in economics—as well as in real life—involve marginal analysis: How many workers should I hire in my shop? At what mileage should I change the oil in my car? What is an acceptable rate of negative side effects from a new medicine? Marginal analysis plays a central role in economics because it is the key to deciding "how much" of an activity to do.

People Usually Exploit Opportunities to Make Themselves Better Off

One day, while listening to the morning financial news, the authors heard a great tip about how to park cheaply in Manhattan. Garages in the Wall Street area charge as much as $30 per day. But according to the newscaster, some people had found a better way: instead of parking in a garage, they had their oil changed at the Manhattan Jiffy Lube, where it costs $19.95 to change your oil—and they keep your car all day!

It's a great story, but unfortunately it turned out not to be true—in fact, there is no Jiffy Lube in Manhattan. But if there were, you can be sure there would be a lot of oil changes there. Why? Because when people are offered opportunities to make themselves better off, they normally take them—and if they could find a way to park their car all day for $19.95 rather than $30, they would.

When you try to predict how individuals will behave in an economic situation, it is a very good bet that they will exploit opportunities to make themselves better off. Furthermore, individuals will *continue* to exploit these opportunities until they have been fully exhausted—that is, people will exploit opportunities until those opportunities have been fully taken.

If there really were a Manhattan Jiffy Lube and an oil change really were a cheap way to park your car, we could safely predict that before long the waiting list for oil changes would be weeks, if not months.

In fact, the principle that people will exploit opportunities to make themselves better off is the basis of *all* predictions by economists about individual behavior. If the earnings of those who get MBAs soar while the earnings of those who get law degrees decline, we can expect more students to go to business school and fewer to go to law school. If the price of gasoline rises and stays high for an extended period of time, we can expect people to buy smaller cars with higher gas mileage—making themselves better off in the presence of higher gas prices by driving more fuel-efficient cars.

When changes in the available opportunities offer rewards to those who change their behavior, we say that people face new **incentives**. If the price of parking in Manhattan rises, those who can find alternative ways to get to their Wall Street jobs

Decisions about whether to do a bit more or a bit less of an activity are **marginal decisions**. The study of such decisions is known as **marginal analysis**.

An **incentive** is anything that offers rewards to people who change their behavior.

PAY FOR GRADES?

The true reward for learning is, of course, the learning itself. But teachers and schools often feel that it's worth throwing in a few extras. Elementary school students who do well get gold stars; at higher levels, students who score well on tests may receive trophies, plaques, or even gift certificates.

But what about cash?

A few years ago, some Florida schools stirred widespread debate by offering actual cash bonuses to students who scored high on the state's standardized exams. At Parrott Middle School, which offered the highest amounts, an eighth-grader with a top score on an exam received a $50 savings bond.

Many people questioned the monetary awards. In fact, the great majority of teachers feel that cash rewards for learning are a bad idea—the dollar amounts can't be made large enough to give students a real sense of how important their education is, and they make learning seem like work-for-pay. So why did the schools engage in the practice?

The answer, it turns out, is that the previous year the state government had introduced a pay-for-performance scheme for schools: schools whose students earned high marks on the state exams received extra state funds. The problem arose of how to motivate the students to take the exams as seriously as the school administrators did. Parrott's principal defended the pay-for-grades practice by pointing out that good students would often "Christmas tree" their exams—ignore the questions and fill out the bubble sheets in the shape of Christmas trees. With large sums of money for the school at stake, he decided to set aside his misgivings and pay students to do well on the exams.

Does paying students for grades lead to higher grades? Interviews with students suggest that it does spur at least some students to try harder on state exams. And some Florida schools that have introduced rewards for good grades on state exams report substantial improvements in student performance.

will save money by doing so—and so we can expect fewer people to drive to work.

One last point: economists tend to be skeptical of any attempt to change people's behavior that *doesn't* change their incentives. For example, a plan that calls on manufacturers to reduce pollution voluntarily probably won't be effective; a plan that gives them a financial incentive to reduce pollution is a lot more likely to work.

Individual Choice: Summing It Up

We have just seen that there are four basic principles of individual choice:

- *Resources are scarce.* It is always necessary to make choices.
- *The real cost of something is what you must give up to get it.* All costs are opportunity costs.
- *"How much?" is a decision at the margin.* Usually the question is not "whether," but "how much." And that is a question whose answer hinges on the costs and benefits of doing a bit more.
- *People usually exploit opportunities to make themselves better off.* As a result, people will respond to incentives.

So are we ready to do economics? Not yet—because most of the interesting things that happen in the economy are the result not merely of individual choices but of the way in which individual choices *interact*.

economics in action

A Woman's Work

One of the great social transformations of the twentieth century was the change in the nature of women's work. In 1900, only 6 percent of married women worked for pay outside the home. By the early twenty-first century, the number was about 60 percent.

What caused this transformation? Changing attitudes toward work outside the home certainly played a role: in the first half of the twentieth century, it was often considered improper for a married woman to work outside the home if she could afford not to, whereas today it is considered normal. But an important driving force was the invention and growing availability of home appliances, especially washing machines. Before these appliances became available, housework was an extremely laborious task—much more so than a full-time job. In 1945, government researchers clocked a farm wife as she did the weekly wash by hand; she spent 4 hours washing clothes and 4½ hours ironing, and she walked more than a mile. Then she was equipped with a washing machine; the same wash took 41 minutes, ironing was reduced to 1¾ hours, and the distance walked was reduced by 90 percent.

The point is that in pre-appliance days, the opportunity cost of working outside the home was very high: it was something women typically did only in the face of dire financial necessity. With modern appliances, the opportunities available to women changed—and the rest is history. ∎

> >

>> CHECK YOUR UNDERSTANDING 1-1

1. Explain how each of the following situations illustrates one of the four principles of individual choice.
   a. You are on your third trip to a restaurant's all-you-can-eat dessert buffet and are feeling very full. Although it would cost you no additional money, you forgo another slice of coconut cream pie but have a slice of chocolate cake.
   b. Even if there were more resources in the world, there would still be scarcity.
   c. Different teaching assistants teach several Economics 101 tutorials. Those taught by the teaching assistants with the best reputations fill up quickly, with spaces left unfilled in the ones taught by assistants with poor reputations.
   d. To decide how many hours per week to exercise, you compare the health benefits of one more hour of exercise to the effect on your grades of one less hour spent studying.

2. You make $45,000 per year at your current job with Whiz Kids Consultants. You are considering a job offer from Brainiacs, Inc., which will pay you $50,000 per year. Which of the following are elements of the opportunity cost of accepting the new job at Brainiacs, Inc.?
   a. The increased time spent commuting to your new job
   b. The $45,000 salary from your old job
   c. The more spacious office at your new job

Solutions appear at back of book.

Interaction: How Economies Work

As we learned in the Introduction, an economy is a system for coordinating the productive activities of many people. In a market economy, such as the one we live in, that coordination takes place without any coordinator: each individual makes his or her own choices. Yet those choices are by no means independent of each other: each individual's opportunities, and hence choices, depend to a large extent on the choices made by other people. So to understand how a market economy behaves, we have to examine this **interaction** in which my choices affect your choices, and vice versa.

When studying economic interaction, we quickly learn that the end result of individual choices may be quite different from what any one individual intends.

For example, over the past century farmers in the United States have eagerly adopted new farming techniques and crop strains that have reduced their costs and increased their yields. Clearly, it's in the interest of each farmer to keep up with the latest farming techniques. But the end result of each farmer trying to increase his or her own income has actually been to drive many farmers out of business. Because American farmers have been so successful at producing larger yields, agricultural

Interaction of choices—my choices affect your choices, and vice versa—is a feature of most economic situations. The results of this interaction are often quite different from what the individuals intend.

TABLE 1-2

Principles That Underlie the Interaction of Individual Choices

1. There are gains from trade.

2. Markets move toward equilibrium.

3. Resources should be used as efficiently as possible to achieve society's goals.

4. Markets usually lead to efficiency.

5. When markets don't achieve efficiency, government intervention can improve society's welfare.

In a market economy, individuals engage in **trade**: They provide goods and services to others and receive goods and services in return.

There are **gains from trade**: people can get more of what they want through trade than they could if they tried to be self-sufficient. This increase in output is due to **specialization**: each person specializes in the task that he or she is good at performing.

---

prices have steadily fallen. These falling prices have reduced the incomes of many farmers, and as a result fewer and fewer people find farming worth doing. That is, an individual farmer who plants a better variety of corn is better off; but when many farmers plant a better variety of corn, the result may be to make farmers as a group worse off.

A farmer who plants a new, more productive corn variety doesn't just grow more corn. Such a farmer also affects the market for corn through the increased yields attained, with consequences that will be felt by other farmers, consumers, and beyond.

Just as there are four economic principles that fall under the theme of choice, there are five principles that fall under the theme of interaction. These five principles are summarized in Table 1-2. We will now examine each of these principles more closely.

There Are Gains from Trade

Why do the choices I make interact with the choices you make? A family could try to take care of all its own needs—growing its own food, sewing its own clothing, providing itself with entertainment, writing its own economics textbooks. But trying to live that way would be very hard. The key to a much better standard of living for everyone is **trade**, in which people divide tasks among themselves and each person provides a good or service that other people want in return for different goods and services that he or she wants.

The reason we have an economy, not many self-sufficient individuals, is that there are **gains from trade**: by dividing tasks and trading, two people (or 6 billion people) can each get more of what they each want than they could get by being self-sufficient. Gains from trade arise, in particular, from this division of tasks, which economists call **specialization**—a situation in which different people each engage in a different task.

The advantages of specialization, and the resulting gains from trade, were the starting point for Adam Smith's 1776 book *The Wealth of Nations*, which many regard as the beginning of economics as a discipline. Smith's book begins with a description of an eighteenth-century pin factory where, rather than each of the 10 workers making a pin from start to finish, each worker specialized in one of the many steps in pin-making:

> One man draws out the wire, another straights it, a third cuts it, a fourth points it, a fifth grinds it at the top for receiving the head; to make the head requires two or three distinct operations; to put it on, is a particular business, to whiten the pins is another; it is even a trade by itself to put them into the paper; and the important business of making a pin is, in this manner, divided into about eighteen distinct operations . . . Those ten persons, therefore, could make among them upwards of forty-eight thousand pins in a day. But if they had all wrought separately and independently, and without any of them having been educated to this particular business, they certainly could not each of them have made twenty, perhaps not one pin a day. . . .

The same principle applies when we look at how people divide tasks among themselves and trade in an economy. *The economy, as a whole, can produce more when each person specializes in a task and trades with others.*

The benefits of specialization are the reason a person typically chooses only one career. It takes many years of study and experience to become a doctor; it also takes many years of study and experience to become a commercial airline pilot. Many doctors might well have had the potential to become excellent pilots, and vice versa;

"I hunt and she gathers—otherwise we couldn't make ends meet."

but it is very unlikely that anyone who decided to pursue both careers would be as good a pilot or as good a doctor as someone who decided at the beginning to specialize in that field. So it is to everyone's advantage that individuals specialize in their career choices.

Markets are what allow a doctor and a pilot to specialize in their own fields. Because markets for commercial flights and for doctors' services exist, a doctor is assured that she can find a flight and a pilot is assured that he can find a doctor. As long as individuals know that they can find the goods and services that they want in the market, they are willing to forgo self-sufficiency and are willing to specialize. But what assures people that markets will deliver what they want? The answer to that question leads us to our second principle of economy-wide interaction.

Markets Move Toward Equilibrium

It's a busy afternoon at the supermarket; there are long lines at the checkout counters. Then one of the previously closed cash registers opens. What happens?

The first thing that happens, of course, is a rush to that register. After a couple of minutes, however, things will have settled down; shoppers will have rearranged themselves so that the line at the newly opened register is about the same length as the lines at all the other registers.

How do we know that? We know from our fourth principle of individual choice that people will exploit opportunities to make themselves better off. This means that people will rush to the newly opened register in order to save time standing in line. And things will settle down when shoppers can no longer improve their position by switching lines—that is, when the opportunities to make themselves better off have all been exploited.

A story about supermarket checkout lines may seem to have little to do with economy-wide interactions, but in fact it illustrates an important principle. A situation in which individuals cannot make themselves better off by doing something different—the situation in which all the checkout lines are the same length—is what economists call an **equilibrium**. An economic situation is in equilibrium when no individual would be better off doing something different.

Recall the story about the mythical Jiffy Lube, where it was supposedly cheaper to leave your car for an oil change than to pay for parking. If that opportunity had

Chuck Keeler/Stone/Getty Images

Witness equilibrium in action at the checkout lines in your neighborhood supermarket.

An economic situation is in **equilibrium** when no individual would be better off doing something different.

Why do people in America drive on the right side of the road? Of course, it's the law. But long before it was the law, it was an equilibrium.

Before there were formal traffic laws, there were informal "rules of the road," practices that everyone expected everyone else to follow. These rules included an understanding that people would normally keep to one side of the road. In some places, such as England, the rule was to keep to the left; in others, such as France, it was to keep to the right.

Why would some places choose the right and others, the left? That's not completely clear, although it may have depended on the dominant form of traffic. Men riding horses and carrying swords on their left hip preferred to ride on the left (think about getting on or off the horse, and you'll see why). On the other hand, right-handed people walking but leading horses apparently preferred to walk on the right.

In any case, once a rule of the road was established, there were strong incentives for each individual to stay on the "usual" side of the road: those who didn't would keep colliding with oncoming traffic. So once established, the rule of the road would be self-enforcing—that is, it would

be an equilibrium. Nowadays, of course, which side you drive on is determined by law; some countries have even changed sides (Sweden went from left to right in 1967). But what about pedestrians? There are no laws—but there are informal rules. In the United States, urban pedestrians normally keep to the right. But if you should happen to visit Japan, watch out: the Japanese, who drive on the left, also typically walk on the left. So when in Japan, do as the Japanese do. You won't be arrested if you walk on the right, but you will be worse off than if you accept the equilibrium and walk on the left.

really existed and people were still paying $30 to park in garages, the situation would *not* have been an equilibrium.

And that should have been a giveaway that the story couldn't be true. In reality, people would have seized an opportunity to park cheaply, just as they seize opportunities to save time at the checkout line. And in so doing they would have eliminated the opportunity! Either it would have become very hard to get an appointment for an oil change or the price of a lube job would have increased to the point that it was no longer an attractive option (unless you really needed a lube job).

As we will see, markets usually reach equilibrium via changes in prices, which rise or fall until no opportunities for individuals to make themselves better off remain.

The concept of equilibrium is extremely helpful in understanding economic interactions because it provides a way of cutting through the sometimes complex details of those interactions. To understand what happens when a new line is opened at a supermarket, you don't need to worry about exactly how shoppers rearrange themselves, who moves ahead of whom, which register just opened, and so on. What you need to know is that any time there is a change, the situation will move to an equilibrium.

The fact that markets move toward equilibrium is why we can depend on them to work in a predictable way. In fact, we can trust markets to supply us with the essentials of life. For example, people who live in big cities can be sure that the supermarket shelves will always be fully stocked. Why? Because if some merchants who distribute food *didn't* make deliveries, a big profit opportunity would be created for any merchant who did—and there would be a rush to supply food, just like the rush to a newly opened cash register. So the market ensures that food will always be available for city dwellers. And, returning to our previous principle, this allows city dwellers to be city dwellers—to specialize in doing city jobs rather than living on farms and growing their own food.

A market economy also allows people to achieve gains from trade. But how do we know how well such an economy is doing? The next principle gives us a standard to use in evaluating an economy's performance.

Resources Should Be Used as Efficiently as Possible to Achieve Society's Goals

Suppose you are taking a course in which the classroom is too small for the number of students—many people are forced to stand or sit on the floor—despite the fact that large, empty classrooms are available nearby. You would say, correctly, that this is no way to run a college. Economists would call this an *inefficient* use of resources.

But if an inefficient use of resources is undesirable, just what does it mean to use resources *efficiently*? You might imagine that the efficient use of resources has something to do with money, maybe that it is measured in dollars-and-cents terms. But in economics, as in life, money is only a means to other ends. The measure that economists really care about is not money but people's happiness or welfare. Economists say that *an economy's resources are used efficiently when they are used in a way that has fully exploited all opportunities to make everyone better off*. To put it another way, an economy is **efficient** if it takes all opportunities to make some people better off without making other people worse off.

An economy is **efficient** if it takes all opportunities to make some people better off without making other people worse off.

In our classroom example, there clearly was a way to make everyone better off—moving the class to a larger room would make people in the class better off without hurting anyone else in the college. Assigning the course to the smaller classroom was an inefficient use of the college's resources, while assigning the course to the larger classroom would have been an efficient use of the college's resources.

When an economy is efficient, it is producing the maximum gains from trade possible given the resources available. Why? Because there is no way to rearrange how resources are used in a way that can make everyone better off. When an economy is efficient, one person can be made better off by rearranging how resources are used *only* by making someone else worse off. In our classroom example, if all larger classrooms were already occupied, the college would have been run in an efficient way: your class could be made better off by moving to a larger classroom only by making people in the larger classroom worse off by making them move to a smaller classroom.

Should economic policy makers always strive to achieve economic efficiency? Well, not quite, because efficiency is not the only criterion by which to evaluate an economy. People also care about issues of fairness or **equity**. And there is typically a trade-off between equity and efficiency: policies that promote equity often come at a cost of decreased efficiency in the economy, and vice versa.

> **Equity** means that everyone gets his or her fair share. Since people can disagree about what's "fair," equity isn't as well-defined a concept as efficiency.

To see this, consider the case of disabled-designated parking spaces in public parking lots. Many people have great difficulty walking due to age or disability, so it seems only fair to assign closer parking spaces specifically for their use. You may have noticed, however, that a certain amount of inefficiency is involved. To make sure that there is always an appropriate space available should a disabled person want one, there are typically quite a number of disabled-designated spaces. So at any one time there are typically more such spaces available than there are disabled people who want one. As a result, desirable parking spaces are unused. (And the temptation for non-disabled people to use them is so great that we must be dissuaded by fear of getting a ticket.) So, short of hiring parking valets to allocate spaces, there is a conflict between *equity*, making life "fairer" for disabled people, and *efficiency*, making sure that all opportunities to make people better off have been fully exploited by never letting close-in parking spaces go unused.

Exactly how far policy makers should go in promoting equity over efficiency is a very difficult question that goes to the heart of the political process. As such, it is not a question that economists can answer. What is important for economists, however, is to always seek to use the economy's resources as efficiently as possible in the pursuit of society's goals, whatever those goals may be.

Markets Usually Lead to Efficiency

No branch of the U.S. government is entrusted with ensuring the general economic efficiency of our market economy—we don't have agents who go around making sure that brain surgeons aren't plowing fields, that Minnesota farmers aren't trying to grow oranges, that prime beachfront property isn't taken up by used-car dealerships, that colleges aren't wasting valuable classroom space. The government doesn't need to enforce efficiency because in most cases the invisible hand does the job.

In other words, the incentives built into a market economy already ensure that resources are usually put to good use, that opportunities to make people better off are not wasted. If a college were known for its habit of crowding students into small classrooms while large classrooms go unused, it would soon find its enrollment dropping, putting the jobs of its administrators at risk. The "market" for college students would respond in a way that induces administrators to run the college efficiently.

A detailed explanation of why markets are usually very good at making sure that resources are used well will have to wait until we have studied how markets actually work. But the most basic reason is that in a market economy, in which individuals are free to choose what to consume and what to produce, opportunities for mutual gain are normally taken. If there is a way in which some people can be made better off, people will usually be able to take advantage of that opportunity. And that is exactly what defines efficiency: all the opportunities to make everyone better off have been exploited.

As we learned in the Introduction, however, there are exceptions to this principle that markets are generally efficient. In cases of *market failure*, the individual pursuit of self-interest found in markets makes society worse off—that is, the market outcome is inefficient. And, as we will see in examining the next principle, when markets fail, government intervention can help. But short of instances of market failure, the general rule is that markets are a remarkably good way of organizing an economy.

When Markets Don't Achieve Efficiency, Government Intervention Can Improve Society's Welfare

Let's recall from the Introduction the nature of the market failure caused by traffic congestion—a commuter driving to work has no incentive to take into account the cost that his or her action inflicts on other drivers in the form of increased traffic congestion. There are several possible remedies to this situation; examples include charging road tolls, subsidizing the cost of public transportation, or taxing sales of gasoline to individual drivers. All these remedies work by changing the incentives of would-be drivers—motivating them to drive less and use alternative transportation. But they also share another feature: each relies on government intervention in the market.

This brings us to our fifth and last principle of interaction: *When markets don't achieve efficiency, government intervention can improve society's welfare.* That is, when markets go wrong, an appropriately designed government policy can sometimes move society closer to an efficient outcome by changing how society's resources are used.

A very important branch of economics is devoted to studying why markets fail and what policies should be adopted to improve social welfare. We will study these problems and their remedies in depth in later chapters, but here we give a brief overview of why markets fail. They fail for three principal reasons:

- Individual actions have *side effects* that are not properly taken into account by the market.
- One party prevents mutually beneficial trades from occurring in the attempt to capture a greater share of resources for itself.
- Some goods, by their very nature, are unsuited for efficient management by markets.

An important part of your education in economics is learning to identify not just when markets work but also when they don't work—and to judge what government policies are appropriate in each situation.

economics in action

Restoring Equilibrium on the Freeways

In 1994 a powerful earthquake struck the Los Angeles area, causing several freeway bridges to collapse and thereby disrupting the normal commuting routes of hundreds of thousands of drivers. The events that followed offer a particularly clear example of interdependent decision making—in this case, the decisions of commuters about how to get to work.

In the immediate aftermath of the earthquake, there was great concern about the impact on traffic, since motorists would now have to crowd onto alternative routes or detour around the blockages by using city streets. Public officials and news programs warned commuters to expect massive delays and urged them to avoid unnecessary travel, reschedule their work to commute before or after the rush, or use mass transit. These warnings were unexpectedly effective. In fact, so many people heeded them that in the first few days following the quake, those who maintained their regular commuting routine actually found the drive to and from work faster than before.

Of course, this situation could not last. As word spread that traffic was actually not bad at all, people abandoned their less convenient new commuting methods and reverted to their cars—and traffic got steadily worse. Within a few weeks after the quake, serious traffic jams had appeared. After a few more weeks, however, the situation stabilized: the reality of worse-than-usual congestion discouraged enough drivers to prevent the nightmare of citywide gridlock from materializing. Los Angeles traffic, in short, had settled into a new equilibrium, in which each commuter was making the best choice he or she could, given what everyone else was doing.

This was not, by the way, the end of the story: fears that the city would strangle on traffic led local authorities to repair the roads with record speed. Within only 18 months after the quake, all the freeways were back to normal, ready for the next one. ∎

> > > > > > > > > > > > > > > > > > >

>>CHECK YOUR UNDERSTANDING 1-2

1. Explain how each of the following situations illustrates one of the five principles of interaction.
   a. Using the college website, any student who wants to sell a used textbook for at least $X is able to sell it to another who is willing to pay $X.
   b. At a college tutoring co-op, students can arrange to provide tutoring in subjects they are good in (like economics) in return for receiving tutoring in subjects they are poor in (like philosophy).
   c. The local municipality imposes a law that requires bars and nightclubs near residential areas to keep their noise levels below a certain threshold.
   d. To provide better care for low-income patients, the city of Tampa has decided to close some underutilized neighborhood clinics and shift funds to the main hospital.
   e. On the college website, books of a given title with approximately the same level of wear and tear sell for about the same price.

2. Which of the following describes an equilibrium situation? Which does not? Explain your answer.
   a. The restaurants across the street from the university dining hall serve better-tasting and cheaper meals than those served at the university dining hall. The vast majority of students continue to eat at the dining hall.
   b. You currently take the subway to work. Although taking the bus is cheaper, the ride takes longer. So you are willing to pay the higher subway fare in order to save time.

Solutions appear at back of book.

>>QUICK REVIEW

➤ A feature of most economic situations is the *interaction* of choices made by individuals, the end result of which may be quite different than what was intended. In a market economy, this takes the form of *trade* between individuals.

➤ Individuals interact because there are *gains from trade*. Gains from trade arise from *specialization*.

➤ Economic situations normally move toward *equilibrium*.

➤ As far as possible, there should be an *efficient* use of resources to achieve society's goals. But efficiency is not the only way to evaluate an economy; *equity* may also be desirable, and there is often a trade-off between equity and efficiency.

➤ Markets normally *are* efficient, except for certain well-defined exceptions.

➤ When markets fail to achieve efficiency, government intervention can improve society's welfare.

• A LOOK AHEAD •

The nine basic principles we have described lie behind almost all economic analysis. Although they can be immediately helpful in understanding many situations, they are usually not enough. Applying the principles to real economic issues takes one more step.

That step is the creation of *models*—simplified representations of economic situations. Models must be realistic enough to provide real-world guidance but simple enough that they allow us to see clearly the implications of the principles described in this chapter. So our next step is to show how models are used to actually do economic analysis.

SUMMARY

1. All economic analysis is based on a short list of basic principles. These principles apply to two levels of economic understanding. First, we must understand how individuals make choices; second, we must understand how these choices interact.

2. Everyone has to make choices about what to do and what *not* to do. **Individual choice** is the basis of economics—if it doesn't involve choice, it isn't economics.

3. The reason choices must be made is that **resources**—anything that can be used to produce something else—are **scarce.** Individuals are limited in their choices by money and time; economies are limited by their supplies of human and natural resources.

4. Because you must choose among limited alternatives, the true cost of anything is what you must give up to get it—all costs are **opportunity costs.**

5. Many economic decisions involve questions not of "whether" but of "how much"—how much to spend on some good, how much to produce, and so on. Such decisions must be taken by performing a **trade-off** at the margin—by comparing the costs and benefits of doing a bit more or a bit less. Decisions of this type are called **marginal decisions,** and the study of them, **marginal analysis,** plays a central role in economics.

6. The study of how people *should* make decisions is also a good way to understand actual behavior. Individuals usually exploit opportunities to make themselves better off. If opportunities change, so does behavior: people respond to **incentives.**

7. **Interaction**—my choices depend on your choices, and vice versa—adds another level to economic understanding.

When individuals interact, the end result may be different from what anyone intends.

8. The reason for interaction is that there are **gains from trade:** by engaging in the **trade** of goods and services with one another, the members of an economy can all be made better off. Underlying gains from trade are the advantages of **specialization,** of having individuals specialize in the tasks they are good at.

9. Economies normally move toward **equilibrium**—a situation in which no individual can make himself or herself better off by taking a different action.

10. An economy is **efficient** if all opportunities to make someone better off without making others worse off are taken. Resources should be used as efficiently as possible to achieve society's goals. But efficiency is not the sole way to evaluate an economy: **equity,** or fairness, is also desirable, and there is often a trade-off between equity and efficiency.

11. Markets usually lead to efficiency, with some well-defined exceptions.

12. When markets fail and do not achieve efficiency, government intervention can improve society's welfare.

KEY TERMS

Individual choice, p. 6
Resource, p. 6
Scarce, p. 6
Opportunity cost, p. 7
Trade-off, p. 8

Marginal decisions, p. 9
Marginal analysis, p. 9
Incentive, p. 9
Interaction, p. 11
Trade, p. 12

Gains from trade, p. 12
Specialization, p. 12
Equilibrium, p. 13
Efficient, p. 14
Equity, p. 15

PROBLEMS

1. In each of the following situations, identify which of the nine principles is at work.

   a. You choose to shop at the local discount store rather than paying a higher price for the same merchandise at the local department store.

   b. On your spring vacation trip, your budget is limited to $35 a day.

   c. The student union provides a website on which departing students can sell items such as used books, appliances, and furniture rather than giving them away to their roommates as they formerly did.

   d. You decide how many cups of coffee to have when studying the night before an exam by considering how much more work you can do by having another cup versus how jittery it will make you feel.

   e. There is limited lab space available to do the project required in Chemistry 101. The lab supervisor assigns lab time to each student based on when that student is able to come.

   f. You realize that you can graduate a semester early by forgoing a semester of study abroad.

   g. At the student union, there is a bulletin board on which people advertise used items for sale, such as bicycles. Once you have adjusted for differences in quality, all the bikes sell for about the same price.

   h. You are better at performing lab experiments, and your lab partner is better at writing lab reports. So the two of you agree that you will do all the experiments, and she will write up all the reports.

   i. State governments mandate that it is illegal to drive without passing a driving exam.

2. Describe some of the opportunity costs when you decide to do the following.

   a. Attend college instead of taking a job

   b. Watch a movie instead of studying for an exam

   c. Ride the bus instead of driving your car

3. Liza needs to buy a textbook for the next economics class. The price at the college bookstore is $65. One online site offers it for $55 and another site for $57. All prices include sales tax. The accompanying table indicates the typical shipping and handling charges for the textbook ordered online.

   a. What is the opportunity cost of buying online?

   b. Show the relevant choices for this student. What determines which of these options the student will choose?

Shipping method	Delivery time	Charge
Standard shipping	3–7 days	$3.99
Second-day air	2 business days	$8.98
Next-day air	1 business day	$13.98

4. Use the concept of opportunity cost to explain the following.

   a. More people choose to get graduate degrees when the job market is poor.

   b. More people choose to do their own home repairs when the economy is slow.

   c. There are more parks in suburban areas than in urban areas.

d. Convenience stores, which have higher prices than super-markets, cater to busy people.

e. Fewer students enroll in classes that meet before 10:00 A.M.

5. In the following examples, state how you would use the principle of marginal analysis to make a decision.

a. Deciding how many days to wait before doing your laundry

b. Deciding how much library research to do before writing your term paper

c. Deciding how many bags of chips to eat

d. Deciding how many lectures of a class to skip

6. This morning you made the following individual choices: you bought a bagel and coffee at the local café, you drove to school in your car during rush hour, and you typed your roommate's term paper because you are a fast typist—in return for which she will do your laundry for a month. In each of these actions, describe how your individual choices interacted with the individual choices made by others. Were other people left better off or worse off by your choices in each case?

7. On the east side of the Hatatoochie River lives the Hatfield family, while the McCoy family lives on the west side. Each family's diet consists of fried chicken and corn-on-the-cob, and each is self-sufficient, raising their own chickens and growing their own corn. Explain the conditions under which each of the following would be true.

a. The two families are made better off when the Hatfields specialize in raising chickens, the McCoys specialize in raising corn, and the two families trade.

b. The two families are made better off when the McCoys specialize in raising chickens, the Hatfields specialize in raising corn, and the two families trade.

8. Which of the following situations describes an equilibrium? Which does not? If the situation does not describe an equilibrium, what would an equilibrium look like?

a. Many people regularly commute from the suburbs to downtown Pleasantville. Due to traffic congestion, the trip takes 30 minutes when you travel by highway, but only 15 minutes when you go by side streets.

b. At the intersection of Main and Broadway are two gas stations. One station charges $3.00 per gallon for regular gas and the other charges $2.85 per gallon. Customers can get service immediately at the first station, but must wait in a long line at the second.

c. Every student enrolled in Economics 101 must also attend a weekly tutorial. This year there are two sections offered: section A and section B, which meet at the same time in adjoining classrooms and are taught by equally competent instructors. Section A is overcrowded, with people sitting

on the floor and often unable to see the chalkboard. Section B has many empty seats.

9. In each of the following cases, explain whether you think the situation is efficient or not. If it is not efficient, why not? What actions would make the situation efficient?

a. Electricity is included in the rent at your dorm. Some residents in your dorm leave lights, computers, and appliances on when they are not in their rooms.

b. Although they cost the same amount to prepare, the cafeteria in your dorm consistently provides too many dishes that diners don't like, such as tofu casserole, and too few dishes that diners do like, such as roast turkey with dressing.

c. The enrollment for a particular course exceeds the spaces available. Some students who need to take this course to complete their major are unable to get a space while others who are taking it as an elective do get a space.

10. Discuss the efficiency and equity implications of each of the following policies. How would you go about balancing the concerns of equity and efficiency in these areas?

a. The government pays the full tuition for every college student to study whatever subject he or she wishes.

b. When people lose their jobs, the government provides unemployment benefits until they find new ones.

11. Governments often adopt certain policies in order to promote desired behavior among their citizens. For each of the following policies, determine what the incentive is and what behavior the government wishes to promote. In each case, why do you think that the government might wish to change people's behavior, rather than allow their actions to be solely determined by individual choice?

a. A tax of $5 per pack is imposed on cigarettes.

b. The government pays parents $100 when their child is vaccinated for measles.

c. The government pays college students to tutor children from low-income families.

d. The government imposes a tax on the amount of air pollution that a company discharges.

12. In each of the following situations, explain how government intervention could improve society's welfare by changing people's incentives. In what sense is the market going wrong?

a. Pollution from auto emissions has reached unhealthy levels.

b. Everyone in Woodville would be better off if streetlights were installed in the town. But no individual resident is willing to pay for installation of a streetlight in front of his or her house because it is impossible to recoup the cost by charging other residents for the benefit they receive from it.

>web... To continue your study and review of concepts in this chapter, please visit the Krugman/Wells website for quizzes, animated graph tutorials, web links to helpful resources, and more.

www.worthpublishers.com/krugmanwells

>>Economic Models: Trade-offs and Trade

TUNNEL VISION

I N 1901 WILBUR AND ORVILLE WRIGHT built something that would change the world. No, not the airplane— their successful flight at Kitty Hawk would come two years later. What made the Wright brothers true visionaries was their wind tunnel, an apparatus that let them experiment with many different designs for wings and control surfaces. These experiments gave them the knowledge that would make heavier-than-air flight possible.

A miniature airplane sitting motionless in a wind tunnel isn't the same thing as an actual aircraft in flight. But it is a very useful model of a flying plane—a simplified representation of the real thing that can be used to answer crucial questions, such as how much lift a given wing shape will generate at a given airspeed.

Needless to say, testing an airplane design in a wind tunnel is cheaper and safer than building a full-scale version and

hoping it will fly. More generally, models play a crucial role in almost all scientific research—economics very much included.

In fact, you could say that economic theory consists mainly of a collection of models, a series of simplified representations of economic reality that allow us to understand a variety of economic issues.

Clearly, the Wright brothers believed in their model.

In this chapter, we will look at three economic models that are crucially important in their own right and also illustrate why such models are so useful. We'll conclude with a look at how economists actually use models in their work.

What you will learn in this chapter:

➤ Why **models**—simplified representations of reality—play a crucial role in economics

➤ Three simple but important models: the **production possibility frontier, comparative advantage,** and the **circular-flow diagram**

➤ The difference between **positive economics,** which tries to describe the economy and predict its behavior, and **normative economics,** which tries to prescribe economic policy

➤ When economists agree and why they sometimes disagree

Models in Economics: Some Important Examples

A **model** is any simplified representation of reality that is used to better understand real-life situations. But how do we create a simplified representation of an economic situation?

One possibility—an economist's equivalent of a wind tunnel—is to find or create a real but simplified economy. For example, economists interested in the economic role of money have studied the system of exchange that developed in World War II prison camps, in which cigarettes became a universally accepted form of payment even among prisoners who didn't smoke.

Another possibility is to simulate the workings of the economy on a computer. For example, when changes in tax law are proposed, government officials use *tax models*—large computer programs—to assess how the proposed changes would affect different types of people.

The importance of models is that they allow economists to focus on the effects of only one change at a time. That is, they allow us to hold everything else constant and study how one change affects the overall economic outcome. So the **other things equal assumption**, which means that all other relevant factors remain unchanged, is an important assumption when building economic models.

> A **model** is a simplified representation of a real situation that is used to better understand real-life situations.

> The **other things equal assumption** means that all other relevant factors remain unchanged.

FOR INQUIRING MINDS

MODELS FOR MONEY

What's an economic model worth, anyway? In some cases, quite a lot of money.

Although many economic models are developed for purely scientific purposes, others are developed to help governments make economic policies. And there is a growing business in developing economic models to help corporations make decisions.

Who models for money? There are dozens of consulting firms that use models to predict future trends, offer advice based on their models, or develop custom models for business and government clients. A notable example is Global Insight, the world's biggest economic consulting firm. It was created by a merger between Data Resources, Inc., founded by professors from Harvard and MIT, and Wharton Economic Forecasting Associates, founded by professors at the University of Pennsylvania.

One particularly lucrative branch of economics is finance theory, which helps investors figure out what assets, such as shares in a company, are worth. Finance theorists often become highly paid "rocket scientists" at big Wall Street firms because financial models demand a high level of technical expertise.

Unfortunately, the most famous business application of finance theory came spectacularly to grief. In 1994 a group of Wall Street traders teamed up with famous finance theorists—including two Nobel Prize winners—to form Long-Term Capital Management (LTCM), a fund that used sophisticated financial models to invest the money of wealthy clients. At first, the fund did very well. But in 1998 bad news from all over the world—with countries as disparate as Russia, Japan, and Brazil in trouble at the same time—inflicted huge losses on LTCM's investments. For a few anxious days, many people feared not only that the fund would collapse but also that it would bring many other companies down with it. Thanks in part to a rescue operation organized by government officials, this did not happen; but LTCM was closed a few months later, with some of its investors losing most of the money they had put in.

What went wrong? Partly it was bad luck. But experienced hands also faulted the economists at LTCM for taking too many risks. Their models said that a run of bad news like the one that actually happened was extremely unlikely—but a sensible economist knows that sometimes even the best model misses important possibilities.

But you can't always find or create a small-scale version of the whole economy, and a computer program is only as good as the data it uses. (Programmers have a saying: garbage in, garbage out.) For many purposes, the most effective form of economic modeling is the construction of "thought experiments": simplified, hypothetical versions of real-life situations.

In Chapter 1 we illustrated the concept of equilibrium with the example of how customers at a supermarket would rearrange themselves when a new cash register opens. Though we didn't say it, this was an example of a simple model—an imaginary supermarket, in which many details were ignored (what are the customers buying? never mind), that could be used to answer a "what if" question: what if another cash register were opened?

As the cash register story showed, it is often possible to describe and analyze a useful economic model in plain English. However, because much of economics involves changes in quantities—in the price of a product, the number of units produced, or the number of workers employed in its production—economists often find that using some mathematics helps clarify an issue. In particular, a numerical example, a simple equation, or—especially—a graph can be key to understanding an economic concept.

Whatever form it takes, a good economic model can be a tremendous aid to understanding. The best way to make this point is to consider some simple but important economic models and what they tell us. First, we will look at the *production possibility frontier*, a model that helps economists think about the trade-offs every economy faces. Then we will turn to *comparative advantage*, a model that clarifies the principle of gains from trade—trade both between individuals and between countries. Finally, we'll examine the *circular-flow model*, which helps economists analyze the monetary transactions taking place in the economy as a whole.

In discussing these models, we make considerable use of graphs to represent mathematical relationships. Such graphs will play an important role throughout this book. If you are already familiar with the use of graphs, the material that follows should not present any problem. If you are not, this would be a good time to turn to the appendix of this chapter, which provides a brief introduction to the use of graphs in economics.

Trade-offs: The Production Possibility Frontier

What to do? Even a castaway faces trade-offs.

The hit movie *Cast Away*, starring Tom Hanks, was an update of the classic story of Robinson Crusoe, the hero of Daniel Defoe's eighteenth-century novel. Hanks played the sole survivor of a plane crash, stranded on a remote island. As in the original story of Robinson Crusoe, the character played by Hanks had limited resources: the natural resources of the island, a few items he managed to salvage from the plane, and, of course, his own time and effort. With only these resources, he had to make a life. In effect, he became a one-man economy.

The first principle of economics we introduced in Chapter 1 was that resources are scarce and that, as a result, any economy—whether it contains one person or millions of people—faces trade-offs. For example, if a castaway devotes resources to catching fish, he cannot use those same resources to gather coconuts.

To think about the trade-offs that face any economy, economists often use the model known as the **production possibility frontier**. The idea behind this model is to improve our understanding of trade-offs by considering a simplified economy that produces only two goods. This simplification enables us to show the trade-off graphically.

Photo by 20th Century FOX Photo/ZUMA Press. © Copyright 2002 by 20th Century FOX

Figure 2-1 shows a hypothetical production possibility frontier for Tom, a castaway alone on an island, who must make a trade-off between production of fish and production of coconuts. The frontier—the curve in the diagram—shows the maximum number of fish Tom can catch during a week *given* the quantity of coconuts he gathers, and vice versa. That is, it answers questions of the form, "What is the maximum number of fish Tom can catch if he also gathers 20 (or 25, or 30) coconuts?" (We'll explain the bowed-out shape of the curve in Figure 2-1 shortly, after we've seen how to interpret the production possibility frontier.)

There is a crucial distinction between points *inside* or *on* the curve (the shaded area) and *outside* the curve. If a production point lies inside or on the frontier—like the point labeled *C*, at which Tom catches 20 fish and gathers 20 coconuts—it is feasible. After all, the frontier tells us that if Tom catches 20 fish, he could also gather a maximum of 25 coconuts, so he could certainly gather 20 coconuts. On the other hand, a production point that lies outside the frontier—such as the hypothetical production point shown in the figure as point *D*, where Tom catches 40 fish and gathers 30 coconuts—isn't feasible. (In this case, Tom could catch 40 fish and gather no coconuts *or* he could gather 30 coconuts and catch no fish, but he can't do both.)

In Figure 2-1 the production possibility frontier intersects the horizontal axis at 40 fish. This means that if Tom devoted all his resources to catching fish, he would catch 40 fish per week but would have no resources left over to gather coconuts. The production possibility frontier intersects the vertical axis at 30 coconuts; this means that if Tom devoted all his resources to gathering coconuts, he could gather 30 coconuts per week but would have no resources left over to catch fish.

The figure also shows less extreme trade-offs. For example, if Tom decides to catch 20 fish, he is able to gather 25 coconuts; this production choice is illustrated by point *A*. If Tom decides to catch 30 fish, he can gather at most only 20 coconuts, as shown by point *B*.

Thinking in terms of a production possibility frontier simplifies the complexities of reality. The real-world economy produces millions of different goods. Even a castaway on an island would produce more than two different items (for example, he would need clothing and housing as well as food). But in this model we imagine an economy that produces only two goods.

If we simplify reality, however, the production possibility frontier helps us understand some aspects of the real economy better than we could without the model.

> The **production possibility frontier** illustrates the trade-offs facing an economy that produces only two goods. It shows the maximum quantity of one good that can be produced for any given quantity produced of the other.

Figure 2-1

The Production Possibility Frontier

The production possibility frontier illustrates the trade-offs facing an economy that produces two goods. It shows the maximum quantity of one good that can be produced given the quantity of the other good produced. Here, the maximum number of coconuts that Tom can gather depends on the number of fish he catches, and vice versa. His feasible production is shown by the area *inside* or *on* the curve. Production at point *C* is feasible but not efficient. Points *A* and *B* are feasible and efficient, but point *D* is not feasible. **>web...**

>web... Throughout our book, this icon will be used to indicate which graphs are available in an interactive format on our text's website. You can work with these interactive graph tutorials and find additional learning resources if you go to www.worthpublishers.com/krugmanwells.

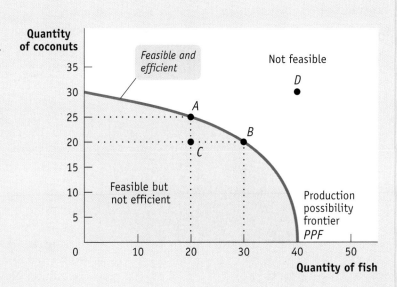

First of all, the production possibility frontier is a good way to illustrate the general economic concept of *efficiency*. Recall from Chapter 1 that an economy is efficient if there are no missed opportunities—there is no way to make some people better off without making other people worse off. A key element of efficiency is that there are no missed opportunities in production—there is no way to produce more of one good without producing less of other goods.

As long as Tom is on the production possibility frontier, his production is efficient. At point *A*, the 25 coconuts he gathers are the maximum number he can get *given* that he has chosen to catch 20 fish; at point *B*, the 20 coconuts he gathers are the maximum he can get *given* his choice to catch 30 fish; and so on.

But suppose that for some reason Tom was at point *C*, producing 20 fish and 20 coconuts. Then this one-person economy would definitely be *inefficient*: it could be producing more of both goods.

The production possibility frontier is also useful as a reminder of the fundamental point that the true cost of any good is not just the amount of money it costs to buy, but everything else in addition to money that must be given up in order to get that good—the *opportunity cost*. If Tom were to catch 30 fish instead of 20, he would be able to gather only 20 coconuts instead of 25. So the opportunity cost of those 10 extra fish is the 5 coconuts not gathered. And if 10 extra fish have an opportunity cost of 5 coconuts, each 1 fish has an opportunity cost of $5/10 = 0.5$ coconuts.

We can now explain the bowed-out shape of the production possibility frontier we saw in Figure 2-1: it reflects an assumption about how opportunity costs change as the mix of output changes. Figure 2-2 shows the same production possibility frontier as Figure 2-1. The arrows in Figure 2-2 illustrate the fact that with this bowed-out production possibility frontier, Tom faces *increasing opportunity cost*: the more fish he catches, the more coconuts he has to give up to catch an additional fish, and vice versa. For example, to go from producing zero fish to producing 20 fish, he has to give up 5 coconuts. That is, the opportunity cost of those 20 fish is 5 coconuts. But to increase his fish production to 40—that is, to produce an additional 20 fish—he must give up 25 more coconuts, a much higher opportunity cost.

Economists believe that opportunity costs are usually increasing. The reason is that when only a small amount of a good is produced, the economy can use

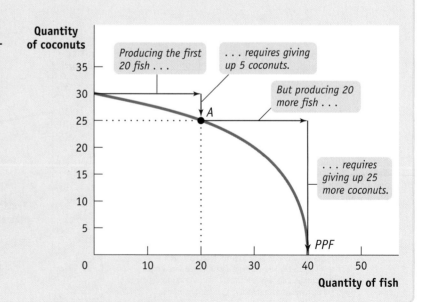

Figure 2-2

Increasing Opportunity Cost

The bowed-out shape of the production possibility frontier reflects increasing opportunity cost. In this example, to produce the first 20 fish, Tom must give up 5 coconuts. But to produce an additional 20 fish, he must give up 25 more coconuts. **>web...**

resources that are especially well suited for that production. For example, if an economy grows only a small amount of corn, that corn can be grown in places where the soil and climate are perfect for corn-growing but less suitable for growing anything else, like wheat. So growing that corn involves giving up only a small amount of potential wheat production. If the economy grows a lot of corn, however, land that isn't so great for corn and would have been well suited for wheat must be pressed into service, so the additional corn production will involve sacrificing considerably more wheat production.

Finally, the production possibility frontier helps us understand what it means to talk about *economic growth*. We introduced the concept of economic growth in the Introduction, defining it as *the growing ability of the economy to produce goods and services*. As we saw, economic growth is one of the fundamental features of the real economy. But are we really justified in saying that the economy has grown? After all, although the U.S. economy produces more of many things than it did a century ago, it produces less of other things—for example, horse-drawn carriages. Production of many goods, in other words, is actually down. So how can we say for sure that the economy as a whole has grown?

The answer, illustrated in Figure 2-3, is that economic growth means an *expansion of the economy's production possibilities*: the economy *can* produce more of everything. For example, if Tom's production is initially at point *A* (20 fish and 25 coconuts), economic growth means that he could move to point *E* (25 fish and 30 coconuts). *E* lies outside the original frontier; so in the production possibility frontier model, growth is shown as an outward shift of the frontier.

What the economy actually produces depends on the choices people make. After his production possibilities expand, Tom might not actually choose to produce both more fish and more coconuts—he might choose to increase production of only one good, or he might even choose to produce less of one good. But even if, for some reason, he chooses to produce either fewer coconuts or fewer fish than before, we would still say that his economy has grown—because he *could* have produced more of everything.

The production possibility frontier is a very simplified model of an economy. Yet it teaches us important lessons about real-life economies. It gives us our first clear sense of a key element of economic efficiency, it illustrates the concept of opportunity cost, and it makes clear what economic growth is all about.

Figure 2-3

Economic Growth

Economic growth results in an *outward shift* of the production possibility frontier because production possibilities are expanded. The economy can now produce more of everything. For example, if production is initially at point *A* (20 fish and 25 coconuts), it could move to point *E* (25 fish and 30 coconuts).

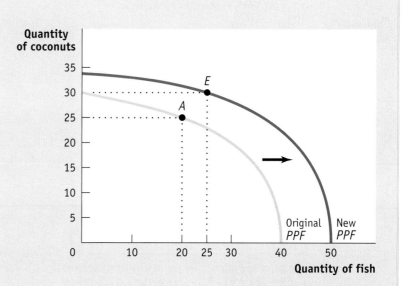

Comparative Advantage and Gains from Trade

Among the nine principles of economics described in Chapter 1 was that of *gains from trade*—the mutual gains that individuals can achieve by specializing in doing different things and trading with one another. Our second illustration of an economic model is a particularly useful model of gains from trade—trade based on *comparative advantage*.

Let's stick with Tom stranded on his island, but now let's suppose that a second castaway, who just happens to be named Hank, is washed ashore. Can they benefit from trading with each other?

It's obvious that there will be potential gains from trade if the two castaways do different things particularly well. For example, if Tom is a skilled fisherman and Hank is very good at climbing trees, clearly it makes sense for Tom to catch fish and Hank to gather coconuts—and for the two men to trade the products of their efforts.

But one of the most important insights in all of economics is that there are gains from trade even if one of the trading parties isn't especially good at anything. Suppose, for example, that Hank is less well suited to primitive life than Tom; he's not nearly as good at catching fish, and compared to Tom even his coconut-gathering leaves something to be desired. Nonetheless, what we'll see is that both Tom and Hank can live better by trading with each other than either could alone.

For the purposes of this example, let's slightly redraw Tom's production possibilities represented by the production possibility frontier in panel (a) of Figure 2-4. According to this diagram, Tom could catch at most 40 fish, but only if he gathered no coconuts, and could gather 30 coconuts, but only if he caught no fish, as before.

In Figure 2-4, we have replaced the curved production possibility frontier of Figure 2-1 with a straight line. Why do this, when we've already seen that economists regard a bowed-out production possibility frontier as normal? The answer is that it simplifies our discussion—and as we have explained, modeling is all about simplification. The principle of comparative advantage doesn't depend on the assumption of straight-line production possibility frontiers, but it is easier to explain with that assumption.

The straight-line production possibility frontier in panel (a) of Figure 2-4 has a *constant slope* of $-\frac{3}{4}$. (The appendix to this chapter explains how to calculate the slope of a line.) That is, for every 4 additional fish that Tom chooses to catch, he

Figure 2-4   Production Possibilities for Two Castaways

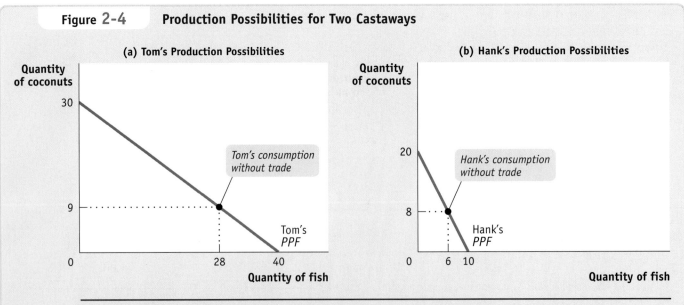

Here, each of the two castaways has a constant opportunity cost of fish and a straight-line production possibility frontier: In Tom's case, each fish always has an opportunity cost of ¾ of a coconut. In Hank's case, each fish always has an opportunity cost of 2 coconuts. **>web...**

gathers 3 fewer coconuts. So Tom's opportunity cost of a fish is ¾ of a coconut regardless of how many or how few fish he catches. In contrast, a production possibility frontier is curved when the opportunity cost of a good changes according to how much of the good has already been produced. For example, you can see from Figure 2-2 that if Tom starts at the point of having caught zero fish and gathers 30 coconuts, his opportunity cost of catching 20 fish is 5 coconuts. But once he has already caught 20 fish, the opportunity cost of an additional 20 fish increases to 25 coconuts.

Panel (b) of Figure 2-4 shows Hank's production possibilities. Like Tom's, Hank's production possibility frontier is a straight line, implying a constant opportunity cost of fish in terms of coconuts. His production possibility frontier has a constant slope of −2. Hank is less productive all around: at most he can produce 10 fish or 20 coconuts. But he is particularly bad at fishing; whereas Tom sacrifices ¾ of a coconut per fish caught, for Hank the opportunity cost of a fish is 2 whole coconuts. Table 2-1 summarizes the two castaways' opportunity costs for fish and coconuts.

Now Tom and Hank could go their separate ways, each living on his own side of the island, catching his own fish and gathering his own coconuts. Let's suppose that they start out that way and make the consumption choices shown in Figure 2-4: in the absence of trade, Tom consumes 28 fish and 9 coconuts per week, while Hank consumes 6 fish and 8 coconuts.

But is this the best they can do? No, it isn't. Given that the two castaways have different opportunity costs, they can strike a deal that makes both of them better off.

Table 2-2 shows how such a deal works: Tom specializes in the production of fish, catching 40 per week, and gives 10 to Hank. Meanwhile, Hank specializes in the production of coconuts, gathering 20 per week, and gives 10 to Tom. The result is shown in Figure 2-5 on page 28. Tom now consumes more of both goods than before: instead of 28 fish and 9 coconuts, he consumes 30 fish and 10 coconuts. And Hank also consumes more, going from 6 fish and 8 coconuts to 10 fish and 10 coconuts. As Table 2-2 also shows, both Tom and Hank experience gains from trade: Tom's consumption of fish increases by two, and his consumption of coconuts increases by one. Hank's consumption of fish increases by four, and his consumption of coconuts by two.

So both castaways are better off when they each specialize in what they are good at and trade. It's a good idea for Tom to catch the fish for both of them because his opportunity cost of a fish is only ¾ of a coconut not gathered versus 2 coconuts for Hank. Correspondingly, it's a good idea for Hank to gather coconuts for the both of them.

Or we could put it the other way around: Because Tom is so good at catching fish, his opportunity cost of gathering coconuts is high: ⁴⁄₃ fish not caught for every coconut gathered. Because Hank is a pretty poor fisherman, his opportunity cost of gathering coconuts is much less, only ½ a fish per coconut.

TABLE 2-1

Tom's and Hank's Opportunity Costs of Fish and Coconuts

	Tom's Opportunity Cost	Hank's Opportunity Cost
One fish	3/4 coconut	2 coconuts
One coconut	4/3 fish	1/2 fish

TABLE 2-2

How the Castaways Gain from Trade

		Without Trade		With Trade		Gains from Trade
		Production	Consumption	Production	Consumption	
Tom	Fish	28	28	40	30	+2
	Coconuts	9	9	0	10	+1
Hank	Fish	6	6	0	10	+4
	Coconuts	8	8	20	10	+2

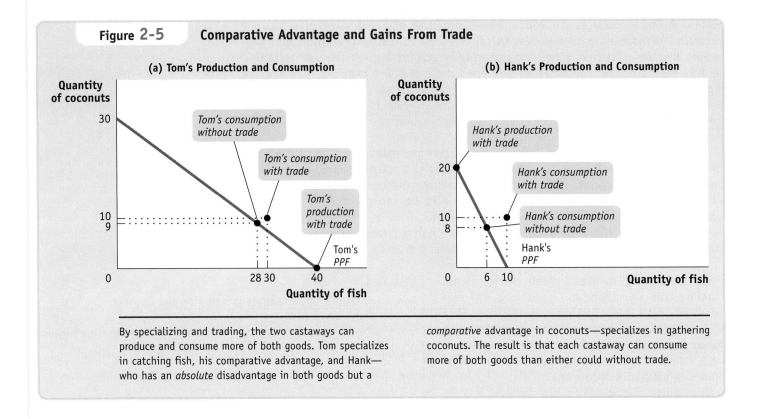

| Figure 2-5 | Comparative Advantage and Gains From Trade |

(a) Tom's Production and Consumption

Quantity of coconuts

- Tom's consumption without trade
- Tom's consumption with trade
- Tom's production with trade
- Tom's PPF

Quantity of fish

(b) Hank's Production and Consumption

Quantity of coconuts

- Hank's production with trade
- Hank's consumption with trade
- Hank's consumption without trade
- Hank's PPF

Quantity of fish

By specializing and trading, the two castaways can produce and consume more of both goods. Tom specializes in catching fish, his comparative advantage, and Hank—who has an *absolute* disadvantage in both goods but a *comparative* advantage in coconuts—specializes in gathering coconuts. The result is that each castaway can consume more of both goods than either could without trade.

An individual has a **comparative advantage** in producing a good or service if the opportunity cost of producing the good is lower for that individual than for other people.

What we would say in this case is that Tom has a **comparative advantage** in catching fish and Hank has a comparative advantage in gathering coconuts. An individual has a comparative advantage in producing something if the opportunity cost of that production is lower for that individual than for other people. In other words, Hank has a comparative advantage over Tom in producing a particular good or service if Hank's opportunity cost of producing that good or service is lower than Tom's.

The story of Tom and Hank clearly simplifies reality. Yet it teaches us some very important lessons that apply to the real economy, too.

First, the model provides a clear illustration of the gains from trade: by agreeing to specialize and provide goods to each other, Tom and Hank can produce more and therefore both be better off than if they tried to be self-sufficient.

Second, the model demonstrates a very important point that is often overlooked in real-world arguments: as long as people have different opportunity costs, *everyone has a comparative advantage in something, and everyone has a comparative disadvantage in something.*

Notice that in our example Tom is actually better than Hank at producing both goods: Tom can catch more fish in a week, and he can also gather more coconuts. That is, Tom has an **absolute advantage** in both activities: he can produce more output with a given amount of input (in this case, his time) than Hank. You might therefore be tempted to think that Tom has nothing to gain from trading with the less competent Hank.

An individual has an **absolute advantage** in an activity if he or she can do it better than other people. Having an absolute advantage is not the same thing as having a comparative advantage.

But we've just seen that Tom can indeed benefit from a deal with Hank because *comparative*, not *absolute*, advantage is the basis for mutual gain. It doesn't matter that it takes Hank more time to gather a coconut; what matters is that for him the opportunity cost of that coconut in terms of fish is lower. So Hank, despite his absolute disadvantage, even in coconuts, has a comparative advantage in coconut-gathering. Meanwhile Tom, who can use his time better by catching fish, has a comparative *disadvantage* in coconut-gathering.

If comparative advantage were relevant only to castaways, it might not be that interesting. In fact, however, the idea of comparative advantage applies to many activities in the economy. Perhaps its most important application is to trade—not between individuals, but between countries. So let's look briefly at how the model of comparative advantage helps in understanding both the causes and the effects of international trade.

Comparative Advantage and International Trade

Look at the label on a manufactured good sold in the United States, and there's a good chance you will find that it was produced in some other country—in China, or Japan, or even in Canada, eh? On the other side, many U.S. industries sell a large fraction of their output overseas (this is particularly true of agriculture, high technology, and entertainment).

Should all this international exchange of goods and services be celebrated, or is it cause for concern? Politicians and the public often question the desirability of international trade, arguing that the nation should produce goods for itself rather than buying them from foreigners. Industries around the world demand protection from foreign competition: Japanese farmers want to keep out American rice, American steelworkers want to keep out European steel. And these demands are often supported by public opinion.

Economists, however, have a very positive view of international trade. Why? Because they view it in terms of comparative advantage.

Figure 2-6 shows, with a simple example, how international trade can be interpreted in terms of comparative advantage. Although the example as constructed is hypothetical, it is based on an actual pattern of international trade: American exports of pork to Canada and Canadian exports of aircraft to the United States. Panels (a) and (b) of Figure 2-6 illustrate hypothetical production possibility frontiers for the United States and

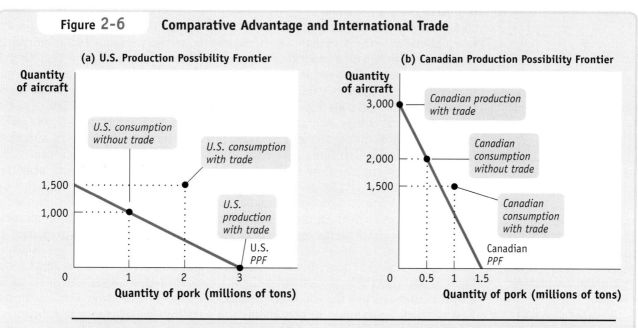

Figure 2-6   Comparative Advantage and International Trade

In this hypothetical example, Canada and the United States produce only two goods: pork and aircraft. Aircraft are measured on the vertical axis and pork on the horizontal axis. Panel (a) shows the U.S. production possibility frontier. It is relatively flat, implying that the United States has a comparative advantage in pork production. Panel (b) shows the Canadian production possibility frontier. It is relatively steep, implying that Canada has a comparative advantage in aircraft production. Just like two individuals, both countries gain from specialization and trade. **>web...**

Canada, with pork measured on the horizontal axis and aircraft measured on the vertical axis. The U.S. production possibility frontier is flatter than the Canadian frontier, implying that the United States has a comparative advantage in pork and Canada has a comparative advantage in aircraft.

Although the consumption points in Figure 2-6 are hypothetical, they illustrate a general principle: just like the example of Tom and Hank, the United States and Canada can both achieve mutual gains from trade. If the United States concentrates on producing pork and ships some of its output to Canada, while Canada concentrates on aircraft and ships some of its output to the United States, both countries can consume more than if they insisted on being self-sufficient.

Moreover, these mutual gains don't depend on each country being better at producing one kind of good. Even if one country has, say, higher output per person-hour in both industries—that is, even if one country has an absolute advantage in both industries—there are still mutual gains from trade.

But how does trade actually take place in market interactions? This brings us to our final model, the circular-flow diagram, which helps economists analyze the transactions that take place in a market economy.

Transactions: The Circular-Flow Diagram

The little economy created by Tom and Hank on their island lacks many features of the economy modern Americans live in. For one thing, though millions of Americans are self-employed, most workers are employed by someone else, usually a company with hundreds or thousands of employees. Also, Tom and Hank engage only in the simplest of economic transactions, **barter**, in which an individual directly trades a good or service he or she has for a good or service he or she wants. In the modern economy, simple barter is rare: usually people trade goods or services for money—pieces of colored paper with no inherent value—and then trade those pieces of colored paper for the goods or services they want. That is, they sell goods or services and buy other goods or services.

And they both sell and buy a lot of different things. The U.S. economy is a vastly complex entity, with more than a hundred million workers employed by hundreds of thousands of companies, producing millions of different goods and services. Yet you can learn some very important things about the economy by considering the simple model shown in Figure 2-7, the **circular-flow diagram.** This diagram represents the transactions that take place in an economy by two kinds of flows around a circle: flows of physical things such as goods, services, labor, or raw materials in one direction, and flows of money that pay for these physical things in the opposite direction. In this case the physical flows are shown in yellow, the money flows in green.

The simplest circular-flow diagram models an economy that contains only two kinds of "inhabitants": **households** and **firms.** A household consists of either an individual or a group of people (usually, but not necessarily, a family) that share their income. A firm is an organization (usually, but not necessarily, a corporation) that produces goods and services for sale—and that employs members of households.

As you can see in Figure 2-7, there are two kinds of markets in this model economy. On one side (here the left side) there are **markets for goods and services** in which households buy the goods and services they want from firms. This produces a flow of goods and services to households and a return flow of money to firms.

On the other side, there are **factor markets**. A **factor of production** is a resource used to produce goods and services. Economists usually use the term *factor of production* to refer to a resource that is not used up in production. For example, workers use sewing machines to convert cloth into shirts; the workers and the sewing machines are factors of production, but the cloth is not. Broadly speaking, the main factors of

Trade takes the form of **barter** when people directly exchange goods or services that they have for goods or services that they want.

The **circular-flow diagram** is a model that represents the transactions in an economy by flows around a circle.

A **household** is a person or a group of people that share their income.

A **firm** is an organization that produces goods and services for sale.

Firms sell goods and services that they produce to households in **markets for goods and services**.

Firms buy the resources they need to produce—**factors of production**—in **factor markets**.

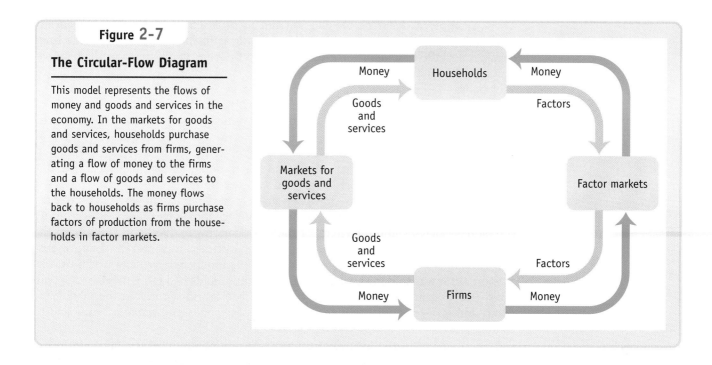

Figure 2-7

The Circular-Flow Diagram

This model represents the flows of money and goods and services in the economy. In the markets for goods and services, households purchase goods and services from firms, generating a flow of money to the firms and a flow of goods and services to the households. The money flows back to households as firms purchase factors of production from the households in factor markets.

production are labor, land, capital, and human capital. Labor is the work of human beings; land is a resource supplied by nature; capital refers to "created" resources such as machines and buildings; and human capital refers to the educational achievements and skills of the labor force, which enhance its productivity. Of course, each of these is really a category rather than a single factor: land in North Dakota is quite different from land in Florida.

The factor market most of us know best is the *labor market*, in which workers are paid for their time. Besides labor, we can think of households as owning and selling the other factors of production to firms. For example, when a corporation pays dividends to its stockholders, who are members of households, it is in effect paying them for the use of the machines and buildings that ultimately belong to those investors.

In what sense is Figure 2-7 a model? That is, in what sense is it a *simplified* representation of reality? The answer is that this picture ignores a number of real-world complications. A few examples:

- In the real world, the distinction between firms and households isn't always that clear-cut. Consider a small, family-run business—a farm, a shop, a small hotel. Is this a firm or a household? A more complete picture would include a separate box for family businesses.

- Many of the sales firms make are not to households but to other firms; for example, steel companies sell mainly to other companies such as auto manufacturers, not to households. A more complete picture would include these flows of goods and money within the business sector.

- The figure doesn't show the government, which in the real world diverts quite a lot of money out of the circular flow in the form of taxes but also injects a lot of money back into the flow in the form of spending.

Figure 2-7, in other words, is by no means a complete picture either of all the types of "inhabitants" of the real economy or of all the flows of money and physical items that take place among these inhabitants.

Despite its simplicity, the circular-flow diagram, like any good economic model, is a very useful aid to thinking about the economy.

For example, a circular-flow diagram can help us understand how the economy manages to provide jobs for a growing population. To illustrate, consider the huge expansion in the U.S. labor force—the number of people who want to work—between the early 1960s and the late 1980s. This increase was partly caused by the 15-year baby boom that followed World War II; the first baby boomers began looking for jobs in the early 1960s and the last of them went to work in the late 1980s. In addition, social changes led a much higher fraction of women to seek paid work outside the home. As a result, between 1962 and 1988 the number of Americans employed or seeking jobs increased by 71 percent.

That's a lot of new job seekers. But luckily, the number of jobs also expanded during the same period, by almost exactly the same percentage.

Or was it luck? The circular-flow diagram helps us understand why the number of jobs available grew along with the expansion of the labor force. Figure 2-8 compares the money flows around the circle for the U.S. economy in 1962 and 1988. Both the money paid to households and the money spent by households increased enormously over the period—and that was no accident. As more people went to work—that is, as more labor was sold in the factor markets—households had more income to spend. They used that increased income to buy more goods and services in the market for goods and services. And in order to produce these goods and services, firms had to hire more workers!

So, despite being an extremely simple model of the economy, the circular-flow diagram helps us to understand some important facts about the real U.S. economy. The number of jobs isn't fixed, the model tells us, because it depends on how much households spend; and the amount households spend depends on how many people are working. It is, in other words, no accident that the economy somehow creates enough jobs even when the working population grows rapidly.

Figure 2-8   Growth in the U.S. Economy from 1962 to 1988

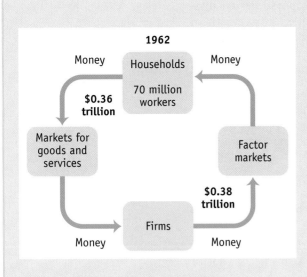
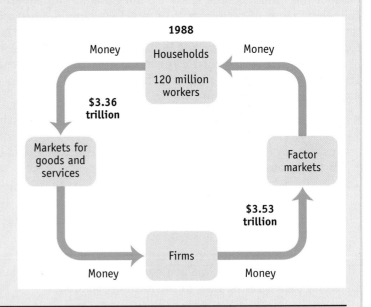

These two circular-flow diagrams—one corresponding to 1962, the other corresponding to 1988—help us understand how the U.S. economy was able to produce enough jobs for its rapidly growing labor force. A roughly twofold increase in the number of workers from 1962 to 1988 was accompanied by a ninefold increase in money flows between households and firms. As the labor force grew, money going to households increased and their spending on goods and services increased. This led firms to hire more workers to meet the increased desire for goods and services and generated more jobs for households.

economics in action

Rich Nation, Poor Nation

Try taking off your clothes—at a suitable time and in a suitable place, of course—and take a look at the labels inside that say where they were made. It's a very good bet that much, if not most, of your clothing was manufactured overseas, in a country that is much poorer than the United States—say, in El Salvador, Sri Lanka, or Bangladesh.

Why are these countries so much poorer than we are? The immediate reason is that their economies are much less *productive*—firms in these countries are just not able to produce as much from a given quantity of resources as comparable firms in the United States or other wealthy countries. Why countries differ so much in productivity is a deep question—indeed, one of the main questions that preoccupy economists. But in any case, the difference in productivity is a fact.

But if the economies of these countries are so much less productive than ours, how is it that they make so much of our clothing? Why don't we do it for ourselves?

The answer is "comparative advantage." Just about every industry in Bangladesh is much less productive than the corresponding industry in the United States. But the productivity difference between rich and poor countries varies across goods; it is very large in the production of sophisticated goods like aircraft but not that large in the production of simpler goods like clothing. So Bangladesh's position with regard to clothing production is like Hank's position with respect to coconut gathering: he's not as good at it as his fellow castaway, but it's the thing he does comparatively well.

The point is that Bangladesh, though it is at an absolute disadvantage compared with the United States in almost everything, has a comparative advantage in clothing production. This means that both the United States and Bangladesh are able to consume more because they specialize in producing different things, with Bangladesh supplying our clothing and the United States supplying Bangladesh with more sophisticated goods. ■

> > > > > > > > > > > > > > > > > > > >

Although less productive than American workers, Bengali workers have a comparative advantage in clothing production.

>>**QUICK REVIEW**

➤ Most economic *models* are "thought experiments" or simplified representations of reality, which rely on the *other things equal assumption*.

➤ An important economic model is the *production possibility frontier*, which illustrates the concepts of efficiency, opportunity cost, and economic growth.

➤ *Comparative advantage* is a model that explains the source of gains from trade but is often confused with *absolute advantage*. Every person and every country has a comparative advantage in something, giving rise to gains from trade.

➤ In the simplest economies people *barter* rather than trade with money as in a modern economy. The *circular-flow diagram* is a model representing transactions within the economy as flows of goods and services, *factors of production*, and money between *households* and *firms*. These transactions occur in *markets for goods and services* and *factor markets*.

>>**CHECK YOUR UNDERSTANDING 2-1**

1. True or false? Explain your answer.
    a. An increase in the amount of resources available to Tom for use in producing coconuts and fish does not change his production possibility frontier.
    b. A technological change that allows Tom to catch more fish for any amount of coconuts gathered results in a change in his production possibility frontier.
    c. The production possibility frontier is useful because it illustrates how much of one good an economy must give up to get more of another good regardless of whether resources are being used efficiently.

2. In Italy, an automobile can be produced by 8 workers in one day and a washing machine by 3 workers in one day. In the United States, an automobile can be produced by 6 workers in one day, and a washing machine by 2 workers in one day.
    a. Which country has an absolute advantage in the production of automobiles? In washing machines?
    b. Which country has a comparative advantage in the production of washing machines? In automobiles?
    c. What pattern of specialization results in the greatest gains from trade between the two countries?

3. Use the circular-flow diagram to explain how an increase in the amount of money spent by households results in an increase in the number of jobs in the economy. Describe in words what the circular-flow model predicts.

Solutions appear at back of book.

Using Models

Economics, we have now learned, is mainly a matter of creating models that draw on a set of basic principles but add some more specific assumptions that allow the modeler to apply those principles to a particular situation. But what do economists actually *do* with their models?

Positive versus Normative Economics

Imagine that you are an economic adviser to the governor of your state. What kinds of questions might the governor ask you to answer?

Well, here are three possible questions:

1. How much revenue will the tolls on the state turnpike yield next year?

2. How much would that revenue increase if the toll were raised from $1 to $1.50?

3. Should the toll be raised, bearing in mind that a toll increase will reduce traffic and air pollution near the road but will impose some financial hardship on frequent commuters?

There is a big difference between the first two questions and the third one. The first two are questions about facts. Your forecast of next year's toll collection will be proved right or wrong when the numbers actually come in. Your estimate of the impact of a change in the toll is a little harder to check—revenue depends on other factors besides the toll, and it may be hard to disentangle the causes of any change in revenue. Still, in principle there is only one right answer.

But the question of whether tolls should be raised may not have a "right" answer—two people who agree on the effects of a higher toll could still disagree about whether raising the toll is a good idea. For example, someone who lives near the turnpike but doesn't commute on it will care a lot about noise and air pollution but not so much about commuting costs. A regular commuter who doesn't live near the turnpike will have the opposite priorities.

This example highlights a key distinction between two roles of economic analysis. Analysis that tries to answer questions about the way the world works, which have definite right and wrong answers, is known as **positive economics**. In contrast, analysis that involves saying how the world *should* work is known as **normative economics**. To put it another way, positive economics is about description, normative economics is about prescription.

Positive economics occupies most of the time and effort of the economics profession. And models play a crucial role in almost all positive economics. As we mentioned earlier, the U.S. government uses a computer model to assess proposed changes in national tax policy, and many state governments have similar models to assess the effects of their own tax policy.

It's worth noting that there is a subtle but important difference between the first and second questions we imagined the governor asking. Question 1 asked for a simple prediction about next year's revenue—a **forecast**. Question 2 was a "what if" question, asking how revenue would change if the tax law were to change. Economists are often called upon to answer both types of questions, but models are especially useful for answering "what if" questions.

The answers to such questions often serve as a guide to policy, but they are still predictions, not prescriptions. That is, they tell you what will happen if a policy is changed; they don't tell you whether that result is good or not. Suppose that your economic model tells you that the governor's proposed increase in highway tolls will raise property values in communities near the road but will hurt those people who must use the turnpike to get to work. Does that make this proposed toll increase a good idea or a bad one? It depends on whom you ask. As we've just seen, someone who is very concerned with the communities near the road will support the increase, but someone who is very concerned with the welfare of drivers will feel differently. That's a value judgment—it's not a question of economic analysis.

Positive economics is the branch of economic analysis that describes the way the economy actually works. **Normative economics** makes prescriptions about the way the economy *should* work.

A **forecast** is a simple prediction of the future.

Still, economists often do end up giving policy advice. That is, they do engage in normative economics. How can they do this when there may be no "right" answer?

One answer is that economists are also citizens, and we all have our opinions. But economic analysis can often be used to show that some policies are clearly better than others, regardless of anyone's opinions.

Suppose that policy A makes everyone better off than policy B—or at least makes some people better off without making other people worse off. Then A is clearly more efficient than B. That's not a value judgment: we're talking about how best to achieve a goal, not about the goal itself.

For example, two different policies have been used to help low-income families obtain housing: rent control, which limits the rents landlords are allowed to charge, and rent subsidies, which provide families with additional money to pay rent. Almost all economists agree that subsidies are the more efficient policy. (In Chapter 4 we'll see why this is so.) And so the great majority of economists, whatever their personal politics, favor subsidies over rent control.

When policies can be clearly ranked in this way, then economists generally agree. But it is no secret that economists sometimes disagree. Why does this happen?

When and Why Economists Disagree

Economists have a reputation for arguing with each other. Where does this reputation come from?

One important answer is that media coverage tends to exaggerate the real differences in views among economists. If nearly all economists agree on an issue—for example, the proposition that rent controls lead to housing shortages—reporters and editors are likely to conclude that there is no story worth covering, and so the professional consensus tends to go unreported. But when there is some issue on which prominent economists take opposing sides—for example, whether cutting taxes right now would help the economy—that does make a good news story. So you hear much more about the areas of disagreement within economics than you do about the large areas of agreement.

It is also worth remembering that economics is, unavoidably, often tied up in politics. On a number of issues powerful interest groups know what opinions they want to hear; they therefore have an incentive to find and promote economists who profess those opinions, giving these economists a prominence and visibility out of proportion to their support among their colleagues.

But although the appearance of disagreement among economists exceeds the reality, it remains true that economists often *do* disagree about important things. For example, some very respected economists argue vehemently that the U.S. government should replace the income tax with a *value-added tax* (a national sales tax, which is the main source of government revenue in many European countries). Other equally respected economists disagree. Why this difference of opinion?

One important source of differences is in values: as in any diverse group of individuals, reasonable people can differ. In comparison to an income tax, a value-added tax typically falls more heavily on people of modest means. So an economist who values a society with more social and income equality for its own sake will tend to oppose a value-added tax. An economist with different values will be less likely to oppose it.

A second important source of differences arises from economic modeling. Because economists base their conclusions on models, which are simplified representations of reality, two economists can legitimately disagree about which simplifications are appropriate—and therefore arrive at different conclusions.

THE GLASS IS HALF FULL.

HALF EMPTY.

ECONOMISTS

THE CONSUMER IS HALF ALIVE.

FOR INQUIRING MINDS

WHEN ECONOMISTS AGREE

"If all the economists in the world were laid end to end, they still couldn't reach a conclusion." So goes one popular economist joke. But do economists really disagree that much?

Not according to a classic survey of members of the American Economic Association, reported in the May 1992 issue of the *American Economic Review*. The authors asked respondents to agree or disagree with a number of statements about the economy; what they found was a high level of agreement among professional economists on many of the statements. At the top, with more than 90 percent of the economists agreeing, were "Tariffs and import quotas usually reduce general economic welfare" and "A ceiling on rents reduces the quantity and quality of housing available." What's striking about these two statements is that many non-economists disagree: tariffs and import quotas to keep out foreign-produced goods are favored by many voters, and proposals to do away with rent control in cities like New York and San Francisco have met fierce political opposition.

So is the stereotype of quarreling economists a myth? Not entirely: economists do disagree quite a lot on some issues, especially in macroeconomics. But there is a large area of common ground.

Suppose that the U.S. government were considering introducing a value-added tax. Economist A may rely on a model that focuses on the administrative costs of tax systems—that is, the costs of monitoring, processing papers, collecting the tax, and so on. This economist might then point to the well-known high costs of administering a value-added tax and argue against the change. But Economist B may think that the right way to approach the question is to ignore the administrative costs and focus on how the proposed law would change savings behavior. This economist might point to studies suggesting that value-added taxes promote higher consumer saving, a desirable result.

Because the economists have used different models—that is, made different simplifying assumptions—they arrive at different conclusions. And so the two economists may find themselves on different sides of the issue.

Most such disputes are eventually resolved by the accumulation of evidence showing which of the various models proposed by economists does a better job of fitting the facts. However, in economics as in any science, it can take a long time before research settles important disputes—decades, in some cases. And since the economy is always changing, in ways that make old models invalid or raise new policy questions, there are always new issues on which economists disagree. The policy maker must then decide which economist to believe.

The important point is that economic analysis is a method, not a set of conclusions.

economics in action

Economists in Government

Many economists are mainly engaged in teaching and research. But quite a few economists have a more direct hand in events.

As described in For Inquiring Minds on page 21, economists play a significant role in the business world, especially in the financial industry. But the most striking involvement of economists in the "real" world is their extensive participation in government.

This shouldn't be surprising: One of the most important functions of government is to make economic policy, and almost every government policy decision must take economic effects into consideration. So governments around the world employ economists in a variety of roles.

In the U.S. government, a key role is played by the Council of Economic Advisers, a branch of the Executive Office (that is, the staff of the president) whose sole purpose is to advise the White House on economic matters and to prepare the annual Economic Report of the President. Unusually for a government agency, most of the economists at the Council are not long-term civil servants; instead, they are mainly professors on leave for one or two years from their universities. Many of the nation's best-known economists have served on the Council of Economic Advisers at some point during their careers.

Economists also play an important role in many other parts of the U.S. government. Indeed, as the Bureau of Labor Statistics *Occupational Outlook Handbook* says, "Some economists work in almost every area of government." Needless to say, the Bureau of Labor Statistics is itself a major employer of economists.

It's also worth noting that economists play an especially important role in two international organizations headquartered in Washington, D.C.: the International Monetary Fund, which provides advice and loans to countries experiencing economic difficulties, and the World Bank, which provides advice and loans to promote long-term economic development.

Do all these economists in government disagree with each other all the time? Are their positions largely dictated by political affiliation? The answer to both questions is no. Although there are important disputes over economic issues in government, and politics inevitably plays some role, there is broad agreement among economists on many issues, and most economists in government try very hard to assess issues as objectively as possible. ∎

> > > > > > > > > > > > > > > > > > >

>> QUICK REVIEW

➤ Economists do mostly *positive economics*, analysis of the way the world works, in which there are definite right and wrong answers and which involve making *forecasts*. But in *normative economics*, which makes prescriptions about how things ought to be, there are often no right answers and only value judgments.
➤ Economists do disagree—though not as much as legend has it—for two main reasons. One, they may disagree about which simplifications to make in a model. Two, economists may disagree—like everyone else—about values.

>> CHECK YOUR UNDERSTANDING 2-2

1. Which of the following statements is a positive statement? Which is a normative statement?
   a. Society should take measures to prevent people from engaging in dangerous personal behavior.
   b. People who engage in dangerous personal behavior impose higher costs on society through higher medical costs.

2. True or false? Explain your answer.
   a. Policy choice A and policy choice B attempt to achieve the same social goal. Policy choice A, however, results in a much less efficient use of resources than policy choice B. Therefore economists are more likely to agree on choosing policy choice B.
   b. When two economists disagree on the desirability of a policy, it's typically because one of them has made a mistake.
   c. Policy makers can always use economics to figure out which goals a society should try to achieve.

Solutions appear at back of book.

• A LOOK AHEAD •

This chapter has given you a first view of what it means to do economics, starting with the general idea of models as a way to make sense of a complicated world and then moving on to three simple introductory models.

To get a real sense of how economic analysis works, however, and to show just how useful such analysis can be, we need to move on to a more powerful model. In the next two chapters we will study the quintessential economic model, one that has an amazing ability to make sense of many policy issues, predict the effects of many forces, and change the way you look at the world. That model is known as "supply and demand."

SUMMARY

1. Almost all economics is based on **models,** "thought experiments" or simplified versions of reality, many of which use mathematical tools such as graphs. An important assumption in economic models is the **other things equal assumption,** which allows analysis of the effect of a change in one factor by holding all other relevant factors unchanged.

2. One important economic model is the **production possibility frontier.** It illustrates: opportunity cost (showing how much less of one good can be produced if more of the other good is produced); efficiency (an economy is efficient if it produces on the production possibility frontier); and economic growth (an expansion of the production possibility frontier).

3. Another important model is **comparative advantage,** which explains the source of gains from trade between individuals and countries. Everyone has a comparative advantage in something—some good or service in which that person has a lower opportunity cost than everyone else. But it is often confused with **absolute advantage,** an ability to produce a particular good or service better than anyone else. This confusion leads some to erroneously conclude that there are no gains from trade between people or countries.

4. In the simplest economies people **barter**—trade goods and services for one another—rather than trade them for money, as in a modern economy. The **circular-flow diagram** is a model representing transactions within the economy as flows of goods, services, and income between **households** and **firms**. These transactions occur in **markets for goods and services** and **factor markets,** markets for **factors of production** such as labor. It is useful in understanding how spending, production, employment, income, and growth are related in the economy.

5. Economists use economic models for both **positive economics,** which describes how the economy works, and for **normative economics,** which prescribes how the economy should work. Positive economics often involves making **forecasts.** Economists can determine correct answers for positive questions, but typically not for normative questions, which involve value judgments. The exceptions are when policies designed to achieve a certain prescription can be clearly ranked in terms of efficiency.

6. There are two main reasons economists disagree. One, they may disagree about which simplifications to make in a model. Two, economists may disagree—like everyone else—about values.

KEY TERMS

Model, p. 21
Other things equal assumption, p. 21
Production possibility frontier, p. 22
Comparative advantage, p. 28
Absolute advantage, p. 28

Barter, p. 30
Circular-flow diagram, p. 30
Household, p. 30
Firm, p. 30
Markets for goods and services, p. 30

Factor markets, p. 30
Factors of production, p. 30
Positive economics, p. 34
Normative economics, p. 34
Forecast, p. 34

PROBLEMS

1. Atlantis is a small, isolated island in the South Atlantic. The inhabitants grow potatoes and catch fresh fish. The accompanying table shows the maximum annual output combinations of potatoes and fish that can be produced. Obviously, given their limited resources and available technology, as they use more of their resources for potato production, there are fewer resources available for catching fish.

Maximum annual output options	Quantity of potatoes (pounds)	Quantity of fish (pounds)
A	1,000	0
B	800	300
C	600	500
D	400	600
E	200	650
F	0	675

a. Draw a production possibility frontier with potatoes on the horizontal axis and fish on the vertical axis illustrating these options, showing points *A–F*.

b. Can Atlantis produce 500 pounds of fish and 800 pounds of potatoes? Explain. Where would this point lie relative to the production possibility frontier?

c. What is the opportunity cost of increasing the annual output of potatoes from 600 to 800 pounds?

d. What is the opportunity cost of increasing the annual output of potatoes from 200 to 400 pounds?

e. Can you explain why the answers to parts c and d are not the same? What does this imply about the slope of the production possibility frontier?

2. In the ancient country of Roma, only two goods, spaghetti and meatballs, are produced. There are two tribes in Roma, the Tivoli and the Frivoli. By themselves, the Tivoli each month can produce either 30 pounds of spaghetti and no meatballs,

or 50 pounds of meatballs and no spaghetti, or any combination in between. The Frivoli, by themselves, each month can produce 40 pounds of spaghetti and no meatballs, or 30 pounds of meatballs and no spaghetti, or any combination in between.

a. Assume that all production possibility frontiers are straight lines. Draw one diagram showing the monthly production possibility frontier for the Tivoli and another showing the monthly production possibility frontier for the Frivoli. Show how you calculated them.

b. Which tribe has the comparative advantage in spaghetti production? In meatball production?

In A.D. 100 the Frivoli discover a new technique for making meatballs that doubles the quantity of meatballs they can produce each month.

c. Draw the new monthly production possibility frontier for the Frivoli.

d. After the innovation, which tribe now has the absolute advantage in producing meatballs? In producing spaghetti? Which has the comparative advantage in meatball production? In spaghetti production?

3. Peter Pundit, an economics reporter, states that the European Union (EU) is increasing its productivity very rapidly in all industries. He claims that this productivity advance is so rapid that output from the EU in these industries will soon exceed that of the United States and, as a result, the United States will no longer benefit from trade with the EU.

a. Do you think Peter Pundit is correct or not? If not, what do you think is the source of his mistake?

b. If the EU and the United States continue to trade, what do you think will characterize the goods that the EU exports to the United States and the goods that the United States exports to the EU?

4. You are in charge of allocating residents to your dormitory's baseball and basketball teams. You are down to the last four people, two of whom must be allocated to baseball and two to basketball. The accompanying table gives each person's batting average and free-throw average. Explain how you would use the concept of comparative advantage to allocate the players. Begin by establishing each player's opportunity cost of free throws in terms of batting average.

Name	Batting average	Free-throw average
Kelley	70%	60%
Jackie	50%	50%
Curt	10%	30%
Gerry	80%	70%

Why is it likely that the other basketball players will be unhappy about this arrangement but the other baseball players will be satisfied? Nonetheless, why would an economist say that this is an efficient way to allocate players for your dormitory's sports teams?

5. The economy of Atlantis has developed, and the inhabitants now use money in the form of cowry shells. Draw a circular-flow diagram showing households and firms. Firms produce potatoes and fish, and households buy potatoes and fish. Households also provide the land and labor to firms. Identify where in the flows of cowry shells or physical things (goods and services, or resources) each of the following impacts would occur. Describe how this impact spreads around the circle.

a. A devastating hurricane floods many of the potato fields.

b. A very productive fishing season yields a very large number of fish caught.

c. The inhabitants of Atlantis discover the Macarena and spend several days a month at dancing festivals.

6. An economist might say that colleges and universities "produce" education, using faculty members and students as inputs. According to this line of reasoning, education is then "consumed" by households. Construct a circular-flow diagram like the one found in this chapter to represent the sector of the economy devoted to college education: colleges and universities represent firms, and households both consume education and provide faculty and students to universities. What are the relevant markets in this model? What is being bought and sold in each direction? What would happen in the model if the government decided to subsidize 50 percent of all college students' tuition?

7. Your dormitory roommate plays loud music most of the time; you, however, would prefer more peace and quiet. You suggest that she buy some earphones. She responds that although she would be happy to use earphones, she has many other things that she would prefer to spend her money on right now. You discuss this situation with a friend who is an economics major. The following exchange takes place:

He: How much would it cost to buy earphones?
You: $15.
He: How much do you value having some peace and quiet for the rest of the semester?
You: $30.
He: It is efficient for you to buy the earphones and give them to your roommate. You gain more than you lose; the benefit exceeds the cost. You should do that.
You: It just isn't fair that I have to pay for the earphones when I'm not the one making the noise.

a. Which parts of this conversation contain positive statements and which parts contain normative statements?

b. Compose an argument supporting your viewpoint that your roommate should be the one to change her behavior. Similarly, compose an argument from the viewpoint of your roommate that you should be the one to buy the earphones. If your dormitory has a policy that gives residents the unlimited right to play music, whose argument is likely to win? If your dormitory has a rule that a person must stop playing music whenever a roommate complains, whose argument is likely to win?

8. A representative of the American clothing industry recently made the following statement: "Workers in Asia often work in sweatshop conditions earning only pennies an hour. American workers are more productive and as a result earn higher wages. In order to preserve the dignity of the American workplace, the government should enact legislation banning imports of low-wage Asian clothing."

   a. Which parts of this quote are positive statements? Which parts are normative statements?

   b. Is the policy that is being advocated consistent with the preceding statements about the wages and productivities of American and Asian workers?

   c. Would such a policy make some Americans better off without making any other Americans worse off? That is, would this policy be efficient from the viewpoint of all Americans?

   d. Would low-wage Asian workers benefit from or be hurt by such a policy?

9. Are the following statements true or false? Explain your answers.

   a. "When people must pay higher taxes on their wage earnings, it reduces their incentive to work" is a positive statement.

   b. "We should lower taxes to encourage more work" is a positive statement.

   c. Economics cannot always be used to completely decide what society ought to do.

   d. "The system of public education in this country generates greater benefits to society than the cost of running the system" is a normative statement.

   e. All disagreements among economists are generated by the media.

10. Evaluate the following statement: "It is easier to build an economic model that accurately reflects events that have already occurred than to build an economic model to forecast future events." Do you think that this is true or not? Why? What does this imply about the difficulties of building good economic models?

11. Economists who work for the government are often called on to make policy recommendations. Why do you think it is important for the public to be able to differentiate normative statements from positive statements in these recommendations?

12. The mayor of Gotham City, worried about a potential epidemic of deadly influenza this winter, asks an economic adviser the following series of questions. Does each question require the economic adviser to make a positive assessment or a normative assessment?

   a. How much vaccine will be in stock in the city by the end of November?

   b. If we offer to pay 10 percent more per dose to the pharmaceutical companies providing the vaccines, will they provide additional doses?

   c. If there is a shortage of vaccine in the city, whom should we vaccinate first—the elderly or the very young? (Assume that a person from one group has an equal likelihood of dying from influenza as a person from the other group.)

   d. If the city charges $25 per shot, how many people will pay?

   e. If the city charges $25 per shot, it will make a profit of $10 per shot, money that can go to pay for inoculating poor people. Should the city engage in such a scheme?

13. Assess the following statement: "If economists just had enough data, they could solve all policy questions in a way that maximizes the social good. There would be no need for divisive political debates, such as whether the government should provide free medical care for all."

>> Chapter 2 Appendix:
Graphs in Economics

Getting the Picture

Whether you're reading about economics in the *Wall Street Journal* or in your economics textbook, you will see many graphs. Visual images can make it much easier to understand verbal descriptions, numerical information, or ideas. In economics, graphs are the type of visual image used to facilitate understanding. To fully understand the ideas and information being discussed, you need to be familiar with how to interpret these visual aids. This appendix explains how graphs are constructed and interpreted and how they are used in economics.

Graphs, Variables, and Economic Models

One reason to attend college is that a bachelor's degree provides access to higher-paying jobs. Additional degrees, such as MBAs or law degrees, increase earnings even more. If you were to read an article about the relationship between educational attainment and income, you would probably see a graph showing the income levels for workers with different amounts of education. And this graph would depict the idea that, in general, more education increases income. This graph, like most of those in economics, would depict the relationship between two economic variables. A **variable** is a quantity that can take on more than one value, such as the number of years of education a person has, the price of a can of soda, or a household's income.

> A quantity that can take on more than one value is called a **variable**.

As you learned in this chapter, economic analysis relies heavily on *models*, simplified descriptions of real situations. Most economic models describe the relationship between two variables, simplified by holding constant other variables that may affect the relationship. For example, an economic model might describe the relationship between the price of a can of soda and the number of cans of soda that consumers will buy, assuming that everything else that affects consumers' purchases of soda stays constant. This type of model can be described mathematically or verbally, but illustrating the relationship in a graph makes it easier to understand. Next we show how graphs that depict economic models are constructed and interpreted.

How Graphs Work

Most graphs in economics are based on a grid built around two perpendicular lines that show the values of two variables, helping you visualize the relationship between them. So a first step in understanding the use of such graphs is to see how this system works.

Two-Variable Graphs

Figure 2A-1 on page 42 shows a typical two-variable graph. It illustrates the data in the accompanying table on outside temperature and the number of sodas a typical vendor can expect to sell at a baseball stadium during one game. The first column shows the values of outside temperature (the first variable) and the second column shows the values of the number of sodas sold (the second variable). Five combinations or pairs of the two variables are shown, each denoted by *A* through *E* in the third column.

Now let's turn to graphing the data in this table. In any two-variable graph, one variable is called the *x*-variable and the other is called the *y*-variable. Here we have made outside temperature the *x*-variable and number of sodas sold the *y*-variable. The solid

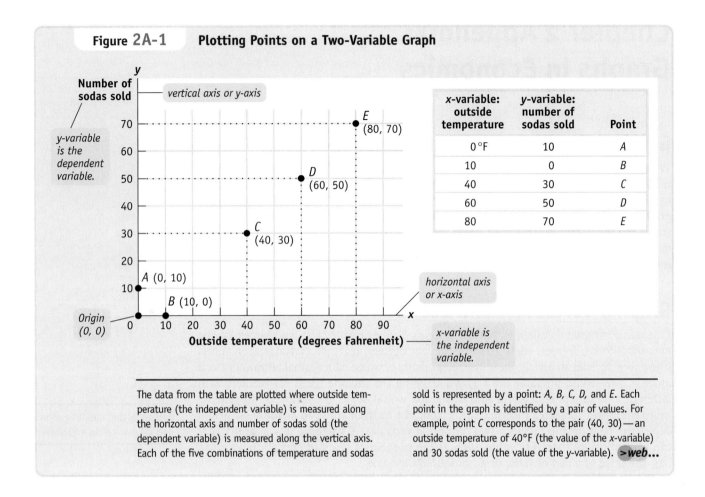

Figure 2A-1   **Plotting Points on a Two-Variable Graph**

x-variable: outside temperature	y-variable: number of sodas sold	Point
0°F	10	A
10	0	B
40	30	C
60	50	D
80	70	E

The data from the table are plotted where outside temperature (the independent variable) is measured along the horizontal axis and number of sodas sold (the dependent variable) is measured along the vertical axis. Each of the five combinations of temperature and sodas sold is represented by a point: A, B, C, D, and E. Each point in the graph is identified by a pair of values. For example, point C corresponds to the pair (40, 30)—an outside temperature of 40°F (the value of the x-variable) and 30 sodas sold (the value of the y-variable). **>web...**

The line along which values of the x-variable are measured is called the **horizontal axis** or **x-axis**. The line along which values of the y-variable are measured is called the **vertical axis** or **y-axis**. The point where the axes of a two-variable graph meet is the **origin**.

horizontal line in the graph is called the **horizontal axis** or **x-axis**, and values of the x-variable—outside temperature—are measured along it. Similarly, the solid vertical line in the graph is called the **vertical axis** or **y-axis**, and values of the y-variable—number of sodas sold—are measured along it. At the **origin**, the point where the two axes meet, each variable is equal to zero. As you move rightward from the origin along the x-axis, values of the x-variable are positive and increasing. As you move up from the origin along the y-axis, values of the y-variable are positive and increasing.

You can plot each of the five points A through E on this graph by using a pair of numbers—the values that the x-variable and the y-variable take on for a given point. In Figure 2A-1, at point C, the x-variable takes on the value 40 and the y-variable takes on the value 30. You plot point C by drawing a line straight up from 40 on the x-axis and a horizontal line across from 30 on the y-axis. We write point C as (40, 30). We write the origin as (0, 0).

Looking at point A and point B in Figure 2A-1, you can see that when one of the variables for a point has a value of zero, it will lie on one of the axes. If the value of x is zero, the point will lie on the vertical axis, like point A. If the value of y is zero, the point will lie on the horizontal axis, like point B.

A **causal relationship** exists between two variables when the value taken by one variable directly influences or determines the value taken by the other variable. In a causal relationship, the determining variable is called the **independent variable;** the variable it determines is called the **dependent variable.**

Most graphs that depict relationships between two economic variables represent a **causal relationship,** a relationship in which the value taken by one variable directly influences or determines the value taken by the other variable. In a causal relationship, the determining variable is called the **independent variable;** the variable it determines is called the **dependent variable.** In our example of soda sales, the outside temperature is the independent variable. It directly influences the number of sodas that are sold, the dependent variable in this case.

By convention, we put the independent variable on the horizontal axis and the dependent variable on the vertical axis. Figure 2A-1 is constructed consistent with this convention; the independent variable (outside temperature) is on the horizontal axis and the dependent variable (number of sodas sold) is on the vertical axis. An important exception to this convention is in graphs showing the economic relationship between the price of a product and quantity of the product: although price is generally the independent variable that determines quantity, it is always measured on the vertical axis.

Curves on a Graph

Panel (a) of Figure 2A-2 contains some of the same information as Figure 2A-1, with a line drawn through the points B, C, D, and E. Such a line on a graph is called a **curve,** regardless of whether it is a straight line or a curved line. If the curve that shows the relationship between two variables is a straight line, or linear, the variables have a **linear relationship.** When the curve is not a straight line, or nonlinear, the variables have a **nonlinear relationship.**

A point on a curve indicates the value of the *y*-variable for a specific value of the *x*-variable. For example, point *D* indicates that at a temperature of 60°F, a vendor can expect to sell 50 sodas. The shape and orientation of a curve reveal the general nature of the relationship between the two variables. The upward tilt of the curve in panel (a) of Figure 2A-2 suggests that vendors can expect to sell more sodas at higher outside temperatures.

> A **curve** is a line on a graph that depicts a relationship between two variables. It may be either a straight line or a curved line. If the curve is a straight line, the variables have a **linear relationship.** If the curve is not a straight line, the variables have a **nonlinear relationship.**

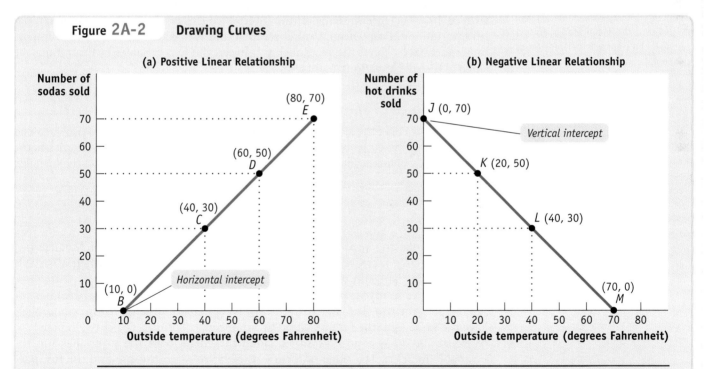

Figure 2A-2   Drawing Curves

(a) Positive Linear Relationship

(b) Negative Linear Relationship

The curve in panel (a) illustrates the relationship between the two variables, outside temperature and number of sodas sold. The two variables have a positive linear relationship: positive because the curve has an upward tilt, and linear because it is a straight line. It implies that an increase in *x* (outside temperature) leads to an increase in *y* (number of sodas sold). The curve in panel (b) is also a straight line, but it tilts downward. The two variables

here, outside temperature and number of hot drinks sold, have a negative linear relationship: an increase in *x* (outside temperature) leads to a decrease in *y* (number of hot drinks sold). The curve in panel (a) has a horizontal intercept at point *B*, where it hits the horizontal axis. The curve in panel (b) has a vertical intercept at point *J*, where it hits the vertical axis and a horizontal intercept at point *M*, where it hits the horizontal axis. **>web...**

Two variables have a **positive relationship** when an increase in the value of one variable is associated with an increase in the value of the other variable. It is illustrated by a curve that slopes upward from left to right.

Two variables have a **negative relationship** when an increase in the value of one variable is associated with a decrease in the value of the other variable. It is illustrated by a curve that slopes downward from left to right.

The **horizontal intercept** of a curve is the point at which it hits the horizontal axis; it indicates the value of the *x*-variable when the value of the *y*-variable is zero.

The **vertical intercept** of a curve is the point at which it hits the vertical axis; it shows the value of the *y*-variable when the value of the *x*-variable is zero.

The **slope** of a line or curve is a measure of how steep it is. The slope of a line is measured by "rise over run"— the change in the *y*-variable between two points on the line divided by the change in the *x*-variable between those same two points.

When variables are related this way—that is, when an increase in one variable is associated with an increase in the other variable—the variables are said to have a **positive relationship.** It is illustrated by a curve that slopes upward from left to right. Because this curve is also linear, the relationship between outside temperature and number of sodas sold illustrated by the curve in panel (a) of Figure 2A-2 is a positive linear relationship.

When an increase in one variable is associated with a decrease in the other variable, the two variables are said to have a **negative relationship.** It is illustrated by a curve that slopes downward from left to right, like the curve in panel (b) of Figure 2A-2. Because this curve is also linear, the relationship it depicts is a negative linear relationship. Two variables that might have such a relationship are the outside temperature and the number of hot drinks a vendor can expect to sell at a baseball stadium.

Return for a moment to the curve in panel (a) of Figure 2A-2 and you can see that it hits the horizontal axis at point *B*. This point, known as the **horizontal intercept,** shows the value of the *x*-variable when the value of the *y*-variable is zero. In panel (b) of Figure 2A-2 the curve hits the vertical axis at point *J*. This point, called the **vertical intercept,** indicates the value of the *y*-variable when the value of the *x*-variable is zero.

A Key Concept: The Slope of a Curve

The **slope** of a line or curve is a measure of how steep it is and indicates how sensitive the *y*-variable is to a change in the *x*-variable. In our example of outside temperature and the number of cans of soda a vendor can expect to sell, the slope of the curve would indicate how many more cans of soda the vendor could expect to sell with each 1° increase in temperature. Interpreted this way, the slope gives meaningful information. Even without numbers for *x* and *y*, it is possible to arrive at important conclusions about the relationship between the two variables by examining the slope of a curve at various points.

The Slope of a Linear Curve

Along a linear curve the slope, or steepness, is measured by dividing the "rise" between two points on the curve by the "run" between those same two points. The rise is the amount that *y* changes, and the run is the amount that *x* changes. Here is the formula:

$$\frac{\text{Change in } y}{\text{Change in } x} = \frac{\Delta y}{\Delta x} = \text{Slope}$$

In the formula, the symbol Δ (the Greek uppercase delta) stands for "change in." When a variable increases, the change in that variable is positive; when a variable decreases, the change in that variable is negative.

The slope of a curve is positive when the rise (the change in the *y*-variable) has the same sign as the run (the change in the *x*-variable). That's because when two numbers have the same sign, the ratio of those two numbers is positive. The curve in panel (a) of Figure 2A-2 has a positive slope: along the curve, both the *y*-variable and the *x*-variable increase. The slope of a curve is negative when the rise and the run have different signs. That's because when two numbers have different signs, the ratio of those two numbers is negative. The curve in panel (b) of Figure 2A-2 has a negative slope: along the curve, an increase in the *x*-variable is associated with a decrease in the *y*-variable.

Figure 2A-3 illustrates how to calculate the slope of a linear curve. Let's focus first on panel (a). From point *A* to point *B* the value of *y* changes from 25 to 20 and the value of *x* changes from 10 to 20. So the slope of the line between these two points is:

$$\frac{\text{Change in } y}{\text{Change in } x} = \frac{\Delta y}{\Delta x} = \frac{-5}{10} = -\frac{1}{2} = -0.5$$

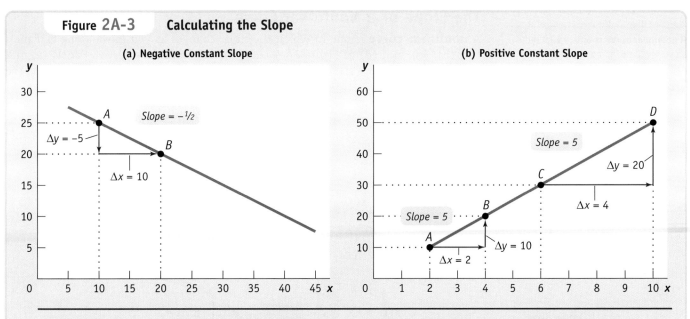

Figure 2A-3   Calculating the Slope

(a) Negative Constant Slope

Slope = $-\frac{1}{2}$

$\Delta y = -5$

$\Delta x = 10$

(b) Positive Constant Slope

Slope = 5

$\Delta y = 20$

$\Delta x = 4$

Slope = 5

$\Delta y = 10$

$\Delta x = 2$

Panels (a) and (b) show two linear curves. Between points A and B on the curve in panel (a), the change in y (the rise) is −5 and the change in x (the run) is 10. So the slope from A to B is $\Delta y/\Delta x$ $= -\frac{5}{10} = -\frac{1}{2} = -0.5$, where the negative sign indicates that the curve is downward sloping. In panel (b), the curve has a slope from A to B of $\Delta y/\Delta x = \frac{10}{2} = 5$. The slope from C to D is $\Delta y/\Delta x =$

$\frac{20}{4} = 5$. The slope is positive, indicating that the curve is upward sloping. Furthermore, the slope between A and B is the same as the slope between C and D, making this a linear curve. The slope of a linear curve is constant: it is the same regardless of where it is calculated along the curve. **>web...**

Because a straight line is equally steep at all points, the slope of a straight line is the same at all points. In other words, a straight line has a constant slope. You can check this by calculating the slope of the linear curve between points A and B and between points C and D in panel (b) of Figure 2A-3.

Between A and B:
$$\frac{\Delta y}{\Delta x} = \frac{10}{2} = 5$$

Between C and D:
$$\frac{\Delta y}{\Delta x} = \frac{20}{4} = 5$$

Horizontal and Vertical Curves and Their Slopes

When a curve is horizontal, the value of y along that curve never changes—it is constant. Everywhere along the curve, the change in y is zero. Now, zero divided by any number is zero. So, regardless of the value of the change in x, the slope of a horizontal curve is always zero.

If a curve is vertical, the value of x along the curve never changes—it is constant. Everywhere along the curve, the change in x is zero. This means that the slope of a vertical line is a ratio with zero in the denominator. A ratio with zero in the denominator is equal to infinity—that is, an infinitely large number. So the slope of a vertical line is equal to infinity.

A vertical or a horizontal curve has a special implication: it means that the x-variable and the y-variable are unrelated. Two variables are unrelated when a change in one of the variables (the independent variable) has no effect on the other variable (the dependent variable). Or to put it a slightly different way, two variables are unrelated when the dependent variable is constant regardless of the value of the independent variable. If, as is usual, the y-variable is the dependent variable, the curve is horizontal. If the dependent variable is the x-variable, the curve is vertical.

The Slope of a Nonlinear Curve

A **nonlinear curve** is one in which the slope is not the same between every pair of points.

A **nonlinear curve** is one in which the slope changes as you move along it. Panels (a), (b), (c), and (d) of Figure 2A-4 show various nonlinear curves. Panels (a) and (b) show nonlinear curves whose slopes change as you move along them, but the slopes always remain positive. Although both curves tilt upward, the curve in panel (a) gets steeper as you move from left to right in contrast to the curve in panel (b), which gets flatter. A curve that is upward sloping and gets steeper, as in panel (a), is said to have *positive increasing* slope. A curve that is upward sloping but gets flatter, as in panel (b), is said to have *positive decreasing* slope.

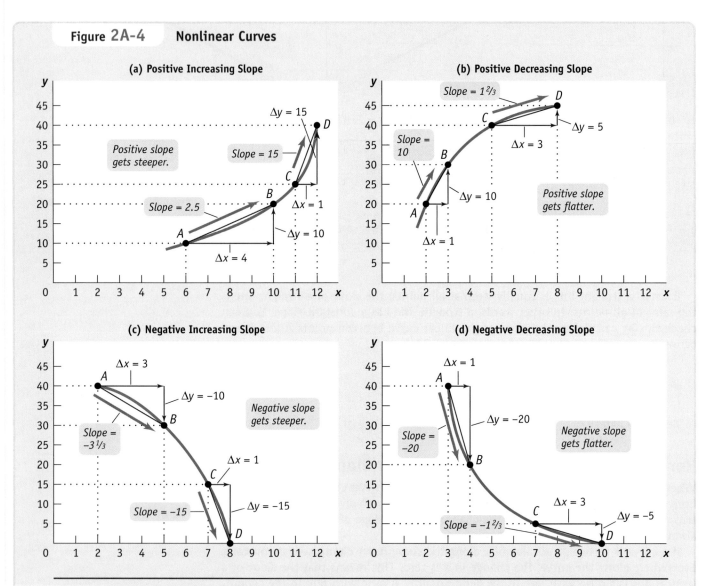

Figure 2A-4   Nonlinear Curves

In panel (a) the slope of the curve from A to B is $\Delta y/\Delta x = {}^{10}\!/_{4} = 2.5$, and from C to D it is $\Delta y/\Delta x = {}^{15}\!/_{1} = 15$. The slope is positive and increasing; it gets steeper as you move to the right. In panel (b) the slope of the curve slope from A to B is $\Delta y/\Delta x = {}^{10}\!/_{1} = 10$, and from C to D it is $\Delta y/\Delta x = {}^{5}\!/_{3} = 1{}^{2}\!/_{3}$. The slope is positive and decreasing; it gets flatter as you move to the right. In panel (c) the slope from A to B is $\Delta y/\Delta x = {}^{-10}\!/_{3} = -3{}^{1}\!/_{3}$, and from C to D it is $\Delta y/\Delta x = {}^{-15}\!/_{1} = -15$. The slope is negative and increasing; it gets steeper as you move to the

right. And in panel (d) the slope from A to B is $\Delta y/\Delta x = {}^{-20}\!/_{1} = -20$, and from C to D it is $\Delta y/\Delta x = {}^{-5}\!/_{3} = -1{}^{2}\!/_{3}$. The slope is negative and decreasing; it gets flatter as you move to the right. The slope in each case has been calculated by using the arc method—that is, by drawing a straight line connecting two points along a curve. The average slope between those two points is equal to the slope of the straight line between those two points. **>web...**

When we calculate the slope along these nonlinear curves, we obtain different values for the slope at different points. How the slope changes along the curve determines the curve's shape. For example, in panel (a) of Figure 2A-4, the slope of the curve is a positive number that steadily increases as you move from left to right, whereas in panel (b), the slope is a positive number that steadily decreases.

The slopes of the curves in panels (c) and (d) are negative numbers. Economists often prefer to express a negative number as its **absolute value,** which is the value of the negative number without the minus sign. In general, we denote the absolute value of a number by two parallel bars around the number; for example, the absolute value of –4 is written as |–4| = 4. In panel (c), the absolute value of the slope steadily increases as you move from left to right. The curve therefore has *negative increasing* slope. And in panel (d), the absolute value of the slope of the curve steadily decreases along the curve. This curve therefore has *negative decreasing* slope.

> The **absolute value** of a negative number is the value of the negative number without the minus sign.

Calculating the Slope Along a Nonlinear Curve

We've just seen that along a nonlinear curve, the value of the slope depends on where you are on that curve. So how do you calculate the slope of a nonlinear curve? We will focus on two methods: the *arc method* and the *point method*.

The Arc Method of Calculating the Slope   An arc of a curve is some piece or segment of that curve. For example, panel (a) of Figure 2A-4 shows an arc consisting of the segment of the curve between points A and B. To calculate the slope along a nonlinear curve using the arc method, you draw a straight line between the two end-points of the arc. The slope of that straight line is a measure of the average slope of the curve between those two end-points. You can see from panel (a) of Figure 2A-4 that the straight line drawn between points A and B increases along the x-axis from 6 to 10 (so that $\Delta x = 4$) as it increases along the y-axis from 10 to 20 (so that $\Delta y = 10$). Therefore the slope of the straight line connecting points A and B is:

$$\frac{\Delta y}{\Delta x} = \frac{10}{4} = 2.5$$

This means that the average slope of the curve between points A and B is 2.5.

Now consider the arc on the same curve between points C and D. A straight line drawn through these two points increases along the x-axis from 11 to 12 ($\Delta x = 1$) as it increases along the y-axis from 25 to 40 ($\Delta y = 15$). So the average slope between points C and D is:

$$\frac{\Delta y}{\Delta x} = \frac{15}{1} = 15$$

Therefore the average slope between points C and D is larger than the average slope between points A and B. These calculations verify what we have already observed— that this upward-tilted curve gets steeper as you move from left to right and therefore has positive increasing slope.

The Point Method of Calculating the Slope   The point method calculates the slope of a nonlinear curve at a specific point on that curve. Figure 2A-5 on page 48 illustrates how to calculate the slope at point B on the curve. First, we draw a straight line that just touches the curve at point B. Such a line is called a **tangent line:** the fact that it just touches the curve at point B and does not touch the curve at any other point on the curve means that the straight line is *tangent* to the curve at point B. The slope of this tangent line is equal to the slope of the nonlinear curve at point B.

> A **tangent line** is a straight line that just touches, or is tangent to, a nonlinear curve at a particular point. The slope of the tangent line is equal to the slope of the nonlinear curve at that point.

Figure 2A-5

Calculating the Slope Using the Point Method

Here a tangent line has been drawn, a line that just touches the curve at point B. The slope of this line is equal to the slope of the curve at point B. The slope of the tangent line, measuring from A to C, is $\Delta y/\Delta x = {}^{15}/_5 = 3$. **>web...**

You can see from Figure 2A-5 how the slope of the tangent line is calculated: from point A to point C, the change in y is 15 units and the change in x is 5 units, generating a slope of:

$$\frac{\Delta y}{\Delta x} = \frac{15}{5} = 3$$

By the point method, the slope of the curve at point B is equal to 3.

A natural question to ask at this point is how to determine which method to use—the arc method or the point method—in calculating the slope of a nonlinear curve. The answer depends on the curve itself and the data used to construct it. You use the arc method when you don't have enough information to be able to draw a smooth curve. For example, suppose that in panel (a) of Figure 2A-4 you have only the data represented by points A, C, and D and don't have the data represented by point B or any of the rest of the curve. Clearly, then, you can't use the point method to calculate the slope at point B; you would have to use the arc method to approximate the slope of the curve in this area by drawing a straight line between points A and C. But if you have sufficient data to draw the smooth curve shown in panel (a) of Figure 2A-4, then you could use the point method to calculate the slope at point B—and at every other point along the curve as well.

Maximum and Minimum Points

The slope of a nonlinear curve can change from positive to negative or vice versa. When the slope of a curve changes from positive to negative, it creates what is called a *maximum* point of the curve. When the slope of a curve changes from negative to positive, it creates a *minimum* point.

Panel (a) of Figure 2A-6 illustrates a curve in which the slope changes from positive to negative as you move from left to right. When x is between 0 and 50, the slope of the curve is positive. At x equal to 50, the curve attains its highest point—the largest value of y along the curve. This point is called the **maximum** of the curve. When x exceeds 50, the slope becomes negative as the curve turns downward. Many important curves in economics, such as the curve that represents how the profit of a firm changes as it produces more output, are hill-shaped like this.

In contrast, the curve shown in panel (b) of Figure 2A-6 is U-shaped: it has a slope that changes from negative to positive. At x equal to 50, the curve reaches its lowest

A nonlinear curve may have a **maximum** point, the highest point along the curve. At the maximum, the slope of the curve changes from positive to negative.

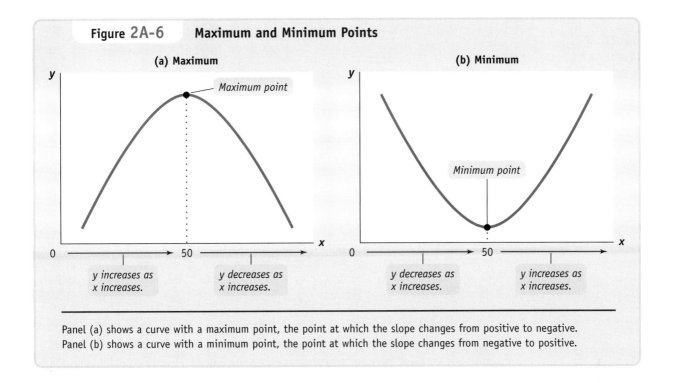

Figure 2A-6   **Maximum and Minimum Points**

(a) Maximum

Maximum point

y increases as x increases.

y decreases as x increases.

(b) Minimum

Minimum point

y decreases as x increases.

y increases as x increases.

Panel (a) shows a curve with a maximum point, the point at which the slope changes from positive to negative. Panel (b) shows a curve with a minimum point, the point at which the slope changes from negative to positive.

point—the smallest value of y along the curve. This point is called the **minimum** of the curve. Various important curves in economics, such as the curve that represents how the costs of some firms change as output increases, are U–shaped like this.

> A nonlinear curve may have a **minimum** point, the lowest point along the curve. At the minimum, the slope of the curve changes from negative to positive.

Graphs That Depict Numerical Information

Graphs can also be used as a convenient way to summarize and display data without assuming some underlying causal relationship. Graphs that simply display numerical information are called *numerical graphs*. Here we will consider four types of numerical graphs: *time-series graphs*, *scatter diagrams*, *pie charts*, and *bar graphs*. These are widely used to display real, empirical data about different economic variables because they often help economists and policy makers identify patterns or trends in the economy. But as we will also see, you must be careful not to misinterpret or draw unwarranted conclusions from numerical graphs. That is, you must be aware of both the usefulness and the limitations of numerical graphs.

Types of Numerical Graphs

You have probably seen graphs in newspapers that show what has happened over time to economic variables such as the unemployment rate or stock prices. A **time-series graph** has successive dates on the horizontal axis and the values of a variable that occurred on those dates on the vertical axis. For example, Figure 2A-7 on page 50 shows the unemployment rate in the United States from 1989 to mid-2004. A line connecting the points that correspond to the unemployment rate for each year gives a clear idea of the overall trend in unemployment over these years.

> A **time-series graph** has dates on the horizontal axis and values of a variable that occurred on those dates on the vertical axis.

Figure 2A-8 on page 50 is an example of a different kind of numerical graph. It represents information from a sample of 158 countries on average life expectancy and gross national product (GNP) per capita—a rough measure of a country's standard of living. Each point here indicates an average resident's life expectancy and the log of GNP per capita for a given country. (Economists have found that the log of GNP rather than the simple level of GNP is more closely tied to average life expectancy.) The points

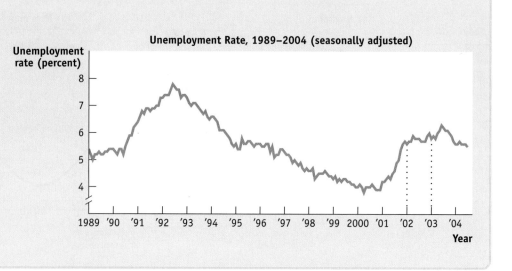

Figure 2A-7

Time-Series Graph

Time-series graphs show successive dates on the x-axis and values for a variable on the y-axis. This time-series graph shows the seasonally adjusted unemployment rate in the United States from 1989 to mid-2004.

Source: Bureau of Labor Statistics.

Unemployment Rate, 1989–2004 (seasonally adjusted)

lying in the upper right of the graph, which show combinations of high life expectancy and high log GNP per capita, represent economically advanced countries such as the United States. Points lying in the bottom left of the graph, which show combinations of low life expectancy and low log GNP per capita, represent economically less advanced countries such as Afghanistan and Sierra Leone. The pattern of points indicates that there is a positive relationship between life expectancy and log GNP per capita: on the whole, people live longer in countries with a higher standard of living. This type of graph is called a **scatter diagram,** a diagram in which each point corresponds to an actual observation of the x-variable and the y-variable. In scatter diagrams, a curve is typically fitted to the scatter of points; that is, a curve is drawn that approximates as closely as possible the general relationship between the variables. As you can see, the fitted curve in Figure 2A-8 is upward sloping, indicating the underlying positive relationship between the two variables. Scatter diagrams are often used to show how a general relationship can be inferred from a set of data.

A **scatter diagram** shows points that correspond to actual observations of the x- and y-variables. A curve is usually fitted to the scatter of points.

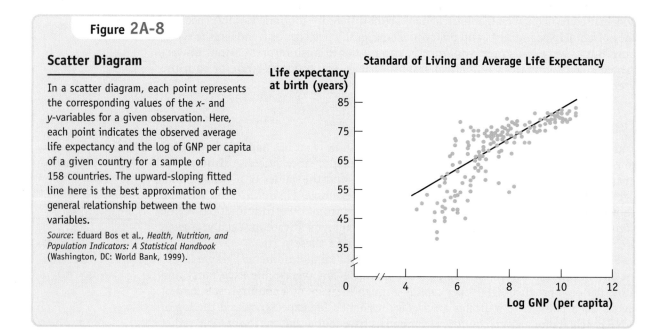

Figure 2A-8

Scatter Diagram

In a scatter diagram, each point represents the corresponding values of the x- and y-variables for a given observation. Here, each point indicates the observed average life expectancy and the log of GNP per capita of a given country for a sample of 158 countries. The upward-sloping fitted line here is the best approximation of the general relationship between the two variables.

Source: Eduard Bos et al., *Health, Nutrition, and Population Indicators: A Statistical Handbook* (Washington, DC: World Bank, 1999).

Standard of Living and Average Life Expectancy

Figure 2A-9

Pie Chart

A pie chart shows the percentages of a total amount that can be attributed to various components. This pie chart shows the percentages of total federal revenues that come from each source.

Source: Executive Office of the President, Office of Management and Budget.

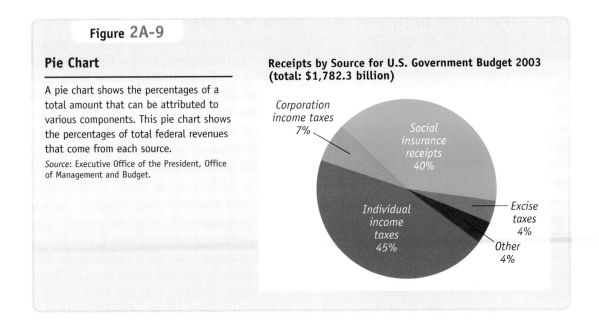

Receipts by Source for U.S. Government Budget 2003 (total: $1,782.3 billion)

A **pie chart** shows the share of a total amount that is accounted for by various components, usually expressed in percentages. For example, Figure 2A-9 is a pie chart that depicts the various sources of revenue for the U.S. government budget in 2003, expressed in percentages of the total revenue amount, $1,782.3 billion. As you can see, social insurance receipts (the revenues collected to fund Social Security, Medicare, and unemployment insurance) accounted for 40% of total government revenue and individual income tax receipts accounted for 45%.

Bar graphs use bars of various heights or lengths to indicate values of a variable. In the bar graph in Figure 2A-10, the bars show the percent change in the number of unemployed workers in the United States from 2001 to 2002, separately for White, Black or African-American, and Asian workers. Exact values of the variable that is being measured may be written at the end of the bar as in this figure. For instance, the number of unemployed Asian workers in the United States increased by 35% between 2001 and 2002. But even without the precise values, comparing the heights or lengths of the bars can give useful insight into the relative magnitudes of the different values of the variable.

> A **pie chart** shows how some total is divided among its components, usually expressed in percentages.

> A **bar graph** uses bars of varying height or length to show the comparative sizes of different observations of a variable.

Figure 2A-10

Bar Graph

A bar graph measures a variable by using bars of various heights or lengths. This bar graph shows the percent increase in the number of unemployed between 2001 and 2002, separately for White, Black or African-American, and Asian workers.

Source: Bureau of Labor Statistics.

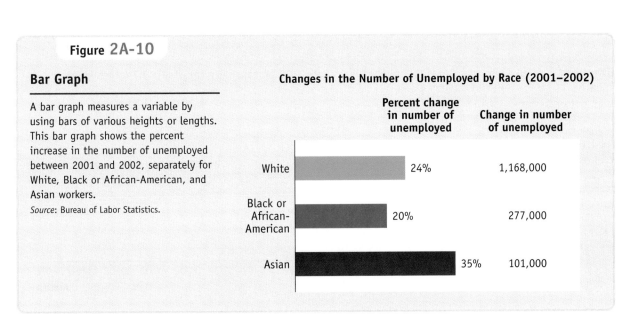

Changes in the Number of Unemployed by Race (2001–2002)

Problems in Interpreting Numerical Graphs

Although the beginning of this appendix emphasized that graphs are visual images that make ideas or information easier to understand, graphs can be constructed (intentionally or unintentionally) in ways that are misleading and can lead to inaccurate conclusions. This section raises some issues that you should be aware of when you interpret graphs.

Features of Construction Before drawing any conclusions about what a numerical graph implies, you should pay attention to the scale, or size of increments, shown on the axes. Small increments tend to visually exaggerate changes in the variables, whereas large increments tend to visually diminish them. So the scale used in construction of a graph can influence your interpretation of the significance of the changes it illustrates—perhaps in an unwarranted way.

Take, for example, Figure 2A-11, which shows the unemployment rate in the United States in 2002 using a 0.1% scale. You can see that the unemployment rate rose from 5.6% at the beginning of 2002 to 6.0% by the end of the year. Here, the rise of 0.4% in the unemployment rate looks enormous and could lead a policy maker to conclude that it was a relatively significant event. But if you go back and reexamine Figure 2A-7, which shows the unemployment rate in the United States from 1989 to 2004, you can see that this would be a misguided conclusion. Figure 2A-7 includes the same data shown in Figure 2A-11, but it is constructed with a 1% scale rather than a 0.1% scale. From it you can see that the rise of 0.4% in the unemployment rate during 2002 was, in fact, a relatively insignificant event, at least compared to the rise in unemployment during 1990 or during 2001. This comparison shows that if you are not careful to factor in the choice of scale in interpreting a graph, you can arrive at very different, and possibly misguided, conclusions.

Related to the choice of scale is the use of *truncation* in constructing a graph. An axis is **truncated** when part of the range is omitted. This is indicated by two slashes (//) in the axis near the origin. You can see that the vertical axis of Figure 2A-11 has been truncated—the range of values from 0 to 5.6 has been omitted and a // appears in the axis. Truncation saves space in the presentation of a graph and allows larger increments to be used in constructing it. As a result, changes in the variable depicted on a graph that has been truncated appear larger compared to a graph that has not been truncated and that uses smaller increments.

An axis is **truncated** when some of the values on the axis are omitted, usually to save space.

Figure 2A-11

Interpreting Graphs: The Effect of Scale

Some of the same data for 2002 used for Figure 2A-7 are represented here, except that here they are shown using 0.1% increments rather than 1% increments. As a result of this change in scale, the rise in the unemployment rate during 2002 looks much larger in this figure compared to Figure 2A-7.

Source: Bureau of Labor Statistics.

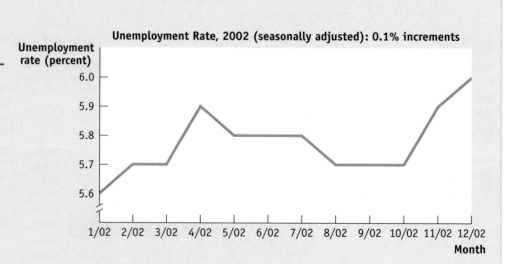

You must also pay close attention to exactly what a graph is illustrating. For example, in Figure 2A-10, you should recognize that what is being shown here are percentage changes in the number of unemployed, not numerical changes. The unemployment rate for Asian workers increased by the highest percentage, 35% in this example. If you confused numerical changes with percentage changes, you would erroneously conclude that the greatest number of newly unemployed workers were Asian. But, in fact, a correct interpretation of Figure 2A-10 shows that the greatest number of newly unemployed workers were white: the total number of unemployed white workers grew by 1,168,000 workers, which is greater than the increase in the number of unemployed Asian workers, which is 101,000 in this example. Although there was a higher percentage increase in the number of unemployed Asian workers, the number of unemployed Asian workers in the United States in 2001 was much smaller than the number of unemployed white workers, leading to a smaller number of newly unemployed Asian workers than white workers.

Omitted Variables From a scatter diagram that shows two variables moving either positively or negatively in relation to each other, it is easy to conclude that there is a causal relationship. But relationships between two variables are not always due to direct cause and effect. Quite possibly an observed relationship between two variables is due to the *unobserved* effect of a third variable on each of the other two variables. An unobserved variable that, through its influence on other variables, creates the erroneous appearance of a direct causal relationship among those variables is called an **omitted variable.** For example, in New England, a greater amount of snowfall during a given week will typically cause people to buy more snow shovels. It will also cause people to buy more de-icer fluid. But if you omitted the influence of the snowfall and simply plotted the number of snow shovels sold versus the number of bottles of de-icer fluid, you would produce a scatter diagram that showed an upward tilt in the pattern of points, indicating a positive relationship between snow shovels sold and de-icer fluid sold. To attribute a causal relationship between these two variables, however, is misguided; more snow shovels sold do not cause more de-icer fluid to be sold, or vice versa. They move together because they are both influenced by a third, determining, variable—the weekly snowfall—which is the omitted variable in this case. So before assuming that a pattern in a scatter diagram implies a cause-and-effect relationship, it is important to consider whether the pattern is instead the result of an omitted variable. Or to put it succinctly: Correlation is not causation.

> An **omitted variable** is an unobserved variable that, through its influence on other variables, creates the erroneous appearance of a direct causal relationship among those variables.

Reverse Causality Even when you are confident that there is no omitted variable and that there is a causal relationship between two variables shown in a numerical graph, you must also be careful that you don't make the mistake of **reverse causality**—coming to an erroneous conclusion about which is the dependent and which is the independent variable by reversing the true direction of causality between the two variables. For example, imagine a scatter diagram that depicts the grade point averages (GPAs) of 20 of your classmates on one axis and the number of hours that each of them spends studying on the other. A line fitted between the points will probably have a positive slope, showing a positive relationship between GPA and hours of studying. We could reasonably infer that hours spent studying is the independent variable and that GPA is the dependent variable. But you could make the error of reverse causality: you could infer that a high GPA causes a student to study more whereas a low GPA causes a student to study less.

> The error of **reverse causality** is committed when the true direction of causality between two variables is reversed.

The significance of understanding how graphs can mislead or be incorrectly interpreted is not purely academic. Policy decisions, business decisions, and political arguments are often based on interpretation of the types of numerical graphs that we've just discussed. Problems of misleading features of construction, omitted variables, and reverse causality can lead to very important and undesirable consequences.

PROBLEMS

1. Study the four accompanying diagrams. Consider the following statements and indicate which diagram matches each statement. Which variable would appear on the horizontal and which on the vertical axis? In each of these statements, is the slope positive, negative, zero, or infinity?

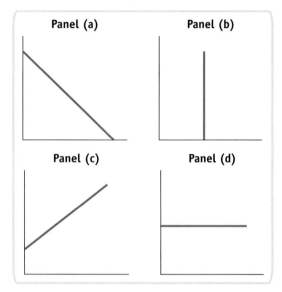

a. If the price of movies increases, fewer consumers go to see movies.

b. More experienced workers typically have higher incomes than less experienced workers.

c. Whatever the temperature outside, Americans consume the same number of hot dogs per day.

d. Consumers buy more frozen yogurt when the price of ice cream goes up.

e. Research finds no relationship between the number of diet books purchased and the number of pounds lost by the average dieter.

f. Regardless of its price, Americans buy the same quantity of salt.

2. During the Reagan administration, economist Arthur Laffer argued in favor of lowering income tax rates in order to increase tax revenues. Like most economists, he believed that at tax rates above a certain level, tax revenue would fall because high taxes would discourage some people from working and that people would refuse to work at all if they received no income after paying taxes. This relationship between tax rates and tax revenue is graphically summarized in what is widely known as the Laffer curve. Plot the Laffer curve relationship assuming that it has the shape of a nonlinear curve. The following questions will help you construct the graph.

a. Which is the independent variable? Which is the dependent variable? On which axis do you therefore measure the income tax rate? On which axis do you measure income tax revenue?

b. What would tax revenue be at a 0% income tax rate?

c. The maximum possible income tax rate is 100%. What would tax revenue be at a 100% income tax rate?

d. Estimates now show that the maximum point on the Laffer curve is (approximately) at a tax rate of 80%. For tax rates less than 80%, how would you describe the relationship between the tax rate and tax revenue, and how is this relationship reflected in the slope? For tax rates higher than 80%, how would you describe the relationship between the tax rate and tax revenue, and how is this relationship reflected in the slope?

3. In the accompanying figures, the numbers on the axes have been lost. All you know is that the units shown on the vertical axis are the same as the units on the horizontal axis.

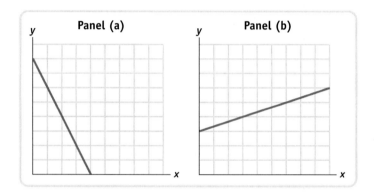

a. In panel (a), what is the slope of the line? Show that the slope is constant along the line.

b. In panel (b), what is the slope of the line? Show that the slope is constant along the line.

4. Answer each of the following questions by drawing a schematic diagram.

a. Taking measurements of the slope of a curve at three points farther and farther to the right along the horizontal axis, the slope of the curve changes from −0.3, to −0.8, to −2.5, measured by the point method. Draw a schematic diagram of this curve. How would you describe the relationship illustrated in your diagram?

b. Taking measurements of the slope of a curve at five points farther and farther to the right along the horizontal axis, the slope of the curve changes from 1.5, to 0.5, to 0, to −0.5, to −1.5, measured by the point method. Draw a schematic diagram of this curve. Does it have a maximum or a minimum?

5. The accompanying table shows the relationship between workers' hours of work per week and their hourly wage rate. Apart from the fact that they receive a different hourly wage rate and work different hours, these five workers are otherwise identical.

Name	Quantity of labor (hours per week)	Wage rate (per hour)
Athena	30	$15
Boris	35	30
Curt	37	45
Diego	36	60
Emily	32	75

a. Which variable is the independent variable? Which is the dependent variable?

b. Draw a scatter diagram illustrating this relationship. Draw a (nonlinear) curve that connects the points. Put the hourly wage rate on the vertical axis.

c. As the wage rate increases from $15 to $30, how does the number of hours worked respond according to the relationship depicted here? What is the average slope of the curve between Athena's and Boris's data points?

d. As the wage rate increases from $60 to $75, how does the number of hours worked respond according to the relationship depicted here? What is the average slope of the curve between Diego's and Emily's data points?

6. Studies have found a relationship between a country's yearly rate of economic growth and the yearly rate of increase in airborne pollutants. It is believed that a higher rate of economic growth allows a country's residents to have more cars and travel more, thereby releasing more airborne pollutants.

a. Which variable is the independent variable? Which is the dependent variable?

b. Suppose that in the country of Sudland, when the yearly rate of economic growth fell from 3.0% to 1.5%, the yearly rate of increase in airborne pollutants fell from 6% to 5%. What is the average slope of a nonlinear curve between these points using the arc method?

c. Now suppose that when the yearly rate of economic growth rose from 3.5% to 4.5%, the yearly rate of increase in airborne pollutants rose from 5.5% to 7.5%. What is the average slope of a nonlinear curve between these two points using the arc method?

d. How would you describe the relationship between the two variables here?

7. An insurance company has found that the severity of property damage in a fire is positively related to the number of firefighters arriving at the scene.

a. Draw a diagram that depicts this finding with number of firefighters on the horizontal axis and amount of property damage on the vertical axis. What is the argument made by this diagram? Suppose you reverse what is measured on the two axes. What is the argument made then?

b. In order to reduce its payouts to policyholders, should the insurance company therefore ask the city to send fewer firefighters to any fire?

8. The accompanying table illustrates annual salaries and income tax owed by five individuals. Apart from the fact that they receive different salaries and owe different amounts of income tax, these five individuals are otherwise identical.

Name	Annual salary	Annual income tax owed
Susan	$22,000	$3,304
Bill	63,000	14,317
John	3,000	454
Mary	94,000	23,927
Peter	37,000	7,020

a. If you were to plot these points on a graph, what would be the average slope of the curve between the points for Bill's and Mary's salaries and taxes using the arc method? How would you interpret this value for slope?

b. What is the average slope of the curve between the points for John's and Susan's salaries and taxes using the arc method? How would you interpret that value for slope?

c. What happens to the slope as salary increases? What does this relationship imply about how the level of income taxes affects a person's incentive to earn a higher salary?

>web... To continue your study and review of concepts in this chapter, please visit the Krugman/Wells website for quizzes, animated graph tutorials, web links to helpful resources, and more.

www.worthpublishers.com/krugmanwells

>> Supply and Demand

GRETZKY'S LAST GAME

THERE ARE SEVERAL WAYS YOU CAN GET tickets for a sporting event. You might have a season pass that gives you a seat at every home game, you could buy a ticket for a single game from the box office, or you could buy a ticket from a *scalper*. Scalpers buy tickets in advance—either from the box office or from season ticket-holders who decide to forgo the game—and then resell them shortly before the event.

Scalping is not always legal, but it is often profitable. A scalper might buy tickets at the box office and then, after the box office has sold out, resell them at a higher price to fans who have decided at the last minute to attend the event. Of course, the profits are not guaranteed. Sometimes an event is unexpectedly "hot" and scalped tickets can be sold for high prices, but sometimes an event is unexpectedly "cold" and scalpers end up selling at a loss.

Over time, however, even with some unlucky nights, scalpers can make money from eager fans.

Ticket scalpers in the Canadian city of Ottawa had a good few days in April 1999. Why? Because Wayne Gretzky, the Canadian hockey star, unexpectedly announced that he would retire from the sport and that the April 15 match between the Ottawa Senators and his team, the New York Rangers, would be his last game on Canadian soil. Many Canadian fans wanted to see the great Gretzky play one last time—and would not give up just because the box office had long since sold out.

Clearly, scalpers who had already stocked up on tickets—or who could acquire more tickets—were in for a bonanza. After the announcement, scalped tickets began selling for four or five times their face value. It was just a matter of supply and demand.

What you will learn in this chapter:

➤ What a **competitive market** is and how it is described by the **supply and demand model**

➤ What the **demand curve** is and what the **supply curve** is

➤ The difference between **movements along a curve** and **shifts of a curve**

➤ How the supply and demand curves determine a market's **equilibrium price** and **equilibrium quantity**

➤ In the case of a **shortage** or **surplus,** how price moves the market back to equilibrium

Shelly/Castellanos/Zuma

AFB/Corbis

Ronal Siemoneit/Corbis

Fans paid hundreds, even thousands, of dollars to see Wayne Gretzky and Michael Jordan play their last games. How much would you pay to see a music star, such as Jennifer Lopez, one last time? What about your favorite athlete?

But what do we mean by that? Many people use *supply and demand* as a sort of catchphrase to mean "the laws of the marketplace at work." To economists, however, the concept of supply and demand has a precise meaning: it is a *model of how a market behaves* that is extremely useful for understanding many—but not all—markets.

In this chapter, we lay out the pieces that make up the supply and demand model, put them together, and show how this model can be used to understand how many—but not all—markets behave.

Supply and Demand: A Model of a Competitive Market

Ticket scalpers and their customers constitute a market—a group of sellers and buyers. More than that, they constitute a particular type of market, known as a competitive market. Roughly, a **competitive market** is a market in which there are many buyers and sellers of the same good or service. More precisely, the key feature of a competitive market is that no individual's actions have a noticeable effect on the price at which the good or service is sold.

A **competitive market** is a market in which there are many buyers and sellers of the same good or service.

It's a little hard to explain why competitive markets are different from other markets until we've seen how a competitive market works. So let's take a rain check—we'll return to that issue at the end of this chapter. For now, let's just say that it's easier to model competitive markets than other markets. When taking an exam, it's always a good strategy to begin by answering the easier questions. In this book, we're going to do the same thing. So we will start with competitive markets.

When a market is competitive, its behavior is well described by a model known as the **supply and demand model**. And because many markets *are* competitive, the supply and demand model is a very useful one indeed.

The **supply and demand model** is a model of how a competitive market works.

There are five key elements in this model:

- The *demand curve*
- The *supply curve*
- The set of factors that cause the demand curve to shift, and the set of factors that cause the supply curve to shift
- The *equilibrium price*
- The way the equilibrium price changes when the supply or demand curves shift

To understand the supply and demand model, we will examine each of these elements.

The Demand Curve

How many people wanted to buy scalped tickets to see the New York Rangers and the Ottawa Senators play that April night? You might at first think the answer was: every hockey fan in Ontario who didn't already have a ticket. But although every hockey fan wanted to see Wayne Gretzky play one last time, most fans weren't willing to pay four or five times the normal ticket price. In general, the number of people who want to buy a hockey ticket, or any other good, depends on the price. The higher the price, the fewer people who want to buy the good; the lower the price, the more people who want to buy the good.

So the answer to the question "How many people will want to buy a ticket to Gretzky's last game?" depends on the price of a ticket. If you don't yet know what the price will be, you can start by making a table of how many tickets people would want to buy at a number of different prices. Such a table is known as a *demand schedule*. This, in turn, can be used to draw a *demand curve*, which is one of the key elements of the supply and demand model.

The Demand Schedule and the Demand Curve

A **demand schedule** is a table showing how much of a good or service consumers will want to buy at different prices. At the right of Figure 3-1, we show a hypothetical demand schedule for tickets to a hockey game.

According to the table, if scalped tickets are available at $100 each (roughly their face value), 20,000 people are willing to buy them; at $150, some fans will decide this price is too high, and only 15,000 are willing to buy. At $200, even fewer people want tickets, and so on. So the higher the price, the fewer the tickets people want to purchase. In other words, as the price rises, the quantity of tickets demanded falls.

The graph in Figure 3-1 is a visual representation of the information in the table. (You might want to review the discussion of graphs in economics in the appendix to Chapter 2.) The vertical axis shows the price of a ticket, and the horizontal axis shows the quantity of tickets. Each point on the graph corresponds to one of the entries in the table. The curve that connects these points is a **demand curve.** A demand curve is a graphical representation of the demand schedule, another way of showing how much of a good or service consumers want to buy at any given price.

Suppose scalpers are charging $250 per ticket. We can see from Figure 3-1 that 8,000 fans are willing to pay that price; that is, 8,000 is the **quantity demanded** at a price of $250.

> A **demand schedule** shows how much of a good or service consumers will want to buy at different prices.

> A **demand curve** is a graphical representation of the demand schedule. It shows how much of a good or service consumers want to buy at any given price.

> The **quantity demanded** is the actual amount consumers are willing to buy at some specific price.

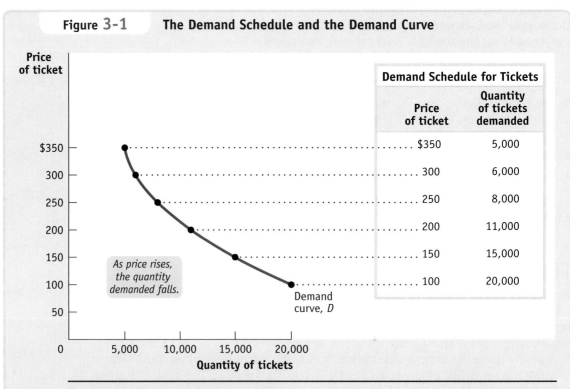

Figure 3-1   The Demand Schedule and the Demand Curve

As price rises, the quantity demanded falls.

Demand curve, *D*

Demand Schedule for Tickets	
Price of ticket	Quantity of tickets demanded
$350	5,000
300	6,000
250	8,000
200	11,000
150	15,000
100	20,000

The demand schedule for tickets is plotted to yield the corresponding demand curve, which shows how much of a good consumers want to buy at any given price. The demand curve and the demand schedule reflect the law of demand: As price rises, the quantity demanded falls. Similarly, a decrease in price raises the quantity demanded. As a result, the demand curve is downward sloping.

Note that the demand curve shown in Figure 3-1 slopes downward. This reflects the general proposition that a higher price reduces the number of people willing to buy a good. In this case, many people who would lay out $100 to see the great Gretzky aren't willing to pay $350. In the real world, demand curves almost always, with some very specific exceptions, *do* slope downward. The exceptions are goods called "Giffen goods," but economists think these are so rare that for practical purposes we can ignore them. Generally, the proposition that a higher price for a good, *other things equal*, leads people to demand a smaller quantity of that good is so reliable that economists are willing to call it a "law"—the **law of demand.**

> The **law of demand** says that a higher price for a good, other things equal, leads people to demand a smaller quantity of the good.

Shifts of the Demand Curve

When Gretzky's retirement was announced, the immediate effect was that more people were willing to buy tickets for that April 15 game at any given price. That is, at every price the quantity demanded rose as a consequence of the announcement. Figure 3-2 illustrates this phenomenon in terms of the demand schedule and the demand curve for scalped tickets.

The table in Figure 3-2 shows two demand schedules. The second one shows the demand schedule after the announcement, the same one shown in Figure 3-1. But the first demand schedule shows the demand for scalped tickets *before* Gretzky announced his retirement. As you can see, after the announcement the number of people willing to pay $350 for a ticket increased, the number willing to pay $300 increased, and so on. So at each price, the second schedule—the schedule after the announcement—shows a larger quantity demanded. For example, at $200, the quantity of tickets fans were willing to buy increased from 5,500 to 11,000.

Figure 3-2   An Increase in Demand

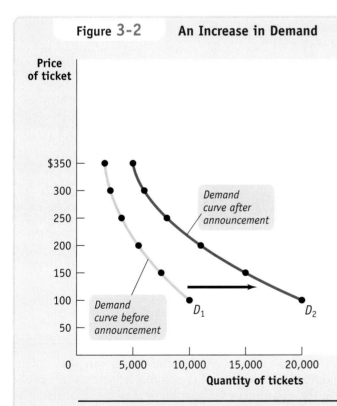

Demand Schedules for Tickets		
	Quantity of tickets demanded	
Price of ticket	Before announcement	After announcement
$350	2,500	5,000
300	3,000	6,000
250	4,000	8,000
200	5,500	11,000
150	7,500	15,000
100	10,000	20,000

Announcement of Gretzky's retirement generates an increase in demand—a rise in the quantity demanded at any given price. This event is represented by the two demand schedules—one showing demand before the announcement, the other showing demand after the announcement—and their corresponding demand curves. The increase in demand shifts the demand curve to the right. **>web...**

A **shift of the demand curve** is a change in the quantity demanded at any given price, represented by the change of the original demand curve to a new position, denoted by a new demand curve.

A **movement along the demand curve** is a change in the quantity demanded of a good that is the result of a change in that good's price.

The announcement of Gretzky's retirement generated a *new* demand schedule, one in which the quantity demanded is greater at any given price than in the original demand schedule. The two curves in Figure 3-2 show the same information graphically. As you can see, the new demand schedule after the announcement corresponds to a new demand curve, D_2, that is to the right of the demand curve before the announcement, D_1. This **shift of the demand curve** shows the change in the quantity demanded at any given price, represented by the change in position of the original demand curve D_1 to its new location at D_2.

It's crucial to make the distinction between such shifts of the demand curve and **movements along the demand curve**, changes in the quantity demanded of a good that result from a change in that good's price. Figure 3-3 illustrates the difference.

The movement from point A to point B is a movement along the demand curve: the quantity demanded rises due to a fall in price as you move down D_1. Here, a fall in price from \$350 to \$215 generates a rise in the quantity demanded from 2,500 to 5,000 tickets. But the quantity demanded can also rise when the price is unchanged if there is an increase in demand—a rightward shift of the demand curve. This is illustrated in Figure 3-3 by the shift of the demand curve from D_1 to D_2. Holding price constant at \$350, the quantity demanded rises from 2,500 tickets at point A on D_1 to 5,000 tickets at point C on D_2.

When economists say "the demand for X increased" or "the demand for Y decreased," they mean that the demand curve for X or Y shifted—*not* that the quantity demanded rose or fell because of a change in the price.

Figure 3-3

Movement Along the Demand Curve Versus Shift of the Demand Curve

The rise in quantity demanded when going from point A to point B reflects a movement along the demand curve: it is the result of a fall in the price of the good. The rise in quantity demanded when going from point A to point C reflects a shift of the demand curve: it is the result of a rise in the quantity demanded at any given price.

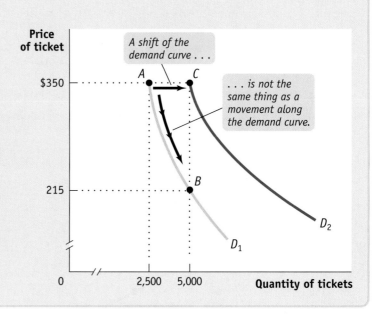

Understanding Shifts of the Demand Curve

Figure 3-4 illustrates the two basic ways in which demand curves can shift. When economists talk about an "increase in demand," they mean a *rightward* shift of the demand curve: at any given price, consumers demand a larger quantity of the good than before. This is shown in Figure 3-4 by the rightward shift of the original demand curve D_1 to D_2. And when economists talk about a "decrease in demand," they mean a *leftward* shift of the demand curve: at any given price, consumers demand a smaller quantity of the good than before. This is shown in Figure 3-4 by the leftward shift of the original demand curve D_1 to D_3.

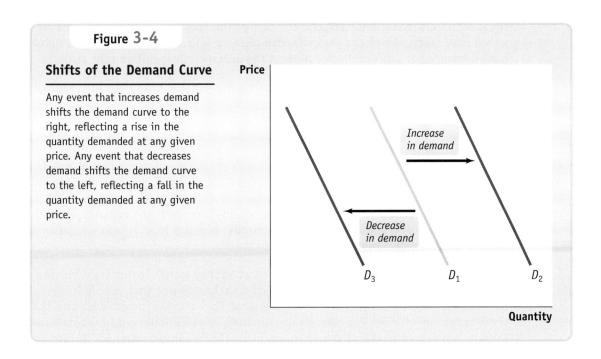

Figure 3-4

Shifts of the Demand Curve

Any event that increases demand shifts the demand curve to the right, reflecting a rise in the quantity demanded at any given price. Any event that decreases demand shifts the demand curve to the left, reflecting a fall in the quantity demanded at any given price.

But what causes a demand curve to shift? In our example, the event that shifts the demand curve for tickets is the announcement of Gretzky's imminent retirement. But if you think about it, you can come up with other things that would be likely to shift the demand curve for those tickets. For example, suppose there is a music concert the same evening as the hockey game, and the band announces that it will sell tickets at half-price. This is likely to cause a decrease in demand for hockey tickets: hockey fans who also like music will prefer to purchase half-price concert tickets rather than hockey game tickets.

Economists believe that there are four principal factors that shift the demand curve for a good:

- Changes in the prices of related goods
- Changes in income
- Changes in tastes
- Changes in expectations

Although this is not an exhaustive list, it contains the four most important factors that can shift demand curves. When we said before that the quantity of a good demanded falls as its price rises, *other things equal,* we were referring to the factors that shift demand as remaining unchanged.

Changes in the Prices of Related Goods If you want to have a good night out but aren't too particular about what you do, a music concert is an alternative to the hockey game—it is what economists call a *substitute* for the hockey game. A pair of goods are **substitutes** if a fall in the price of one good (music concerts) makes consumers less willing to buy the other good (hockey games). Substitutes are usually goods that in some way serve a similar function: concerts and hockey games, muffins and doughnuts, trains and buses. A fall in the price of the alternative good induces some consumers to purchase it *instead of* the original good, shifting the demand for the original good to the left.

But sometimes a fall in the price of one good makes consumers *more* willing to buy another good. Such pairs of goods are known as **complements**. Complements are usually goods that in some sense are consumed together: sports tickets and parking at the stadium garage, hamburgers and buns, cars and gasoline. If the garage next to the hockey arena offered free parking, more people would be willing to buy tickets to see

Two goods are **substitutes** if a fall in the price of one of the goods makes consumers less willing to buy the other good.

Two goods are **complements** if a fall in the price of one good makes people more willing to buy the other good.

the game at any given price because the cost of the "package"—game plus parking—would have fallen. When the price of a complement falls, the quantity of the original good demanded at any given price rises; so the demand curve shifts to the right.

Changes in Income When individuals have more income, they are normally more likely to purchase a good at any given price. For example, if a family's income rises, it is more likely to take that summer trip to Disney World—and therefore also more likely to buy plane tickets. So a rise in consumer incomes will cause the demand curves for most goods to shift to the right.

Why do we say "most goods," not "all goods"? Most goods are **normal goods**—the demand for them increases when consumer income rises. However, the demand for some products falls when income rises—people with high incomes are less likely to take buses than people with lower incomes. Goods for which the demand decreases when income rises are known as **inferior goods**. When a good is inferior, a rise in income shifts the demand curve to the left.

Changes in Tastes Why do people want what they want? Fortunately, we don't need to answer that question—we just need to acknowledge that people have certain preferences, or tastes, that determine what they choose to consume and that these tastes can change. Economists usually lump together changes in demand due to fads, beliefs, cultural shifts, and so on under the heading of changes in *tastes* or *preferences*.

For example, once upon a time men wore hats. Up until around World War II, a respectable man wasn't fully dressed unless he wore a dignified hat along with his suit. But the returning GIs adopted a more informal style, perhaps due to the rigors of the war. And, President Eisenhower, who had been supreme commander of Allied Forces, often went hatless. The demand curve for hats had shifted leftward, reflecting a decline in the demand for hats.

The main distinguishing feature of changes in tastes is that economists have little to say about them and usually take them as given. When tastes change in favor of a good, more people want to buy it at any given price, so the demand curve shifts to the right. When tastes change against a good, fewer people want to buy it at any given price, so the demand curve shifts to the left.

Changes in Expectations You could say that the increase in demand for tickets to the April 15 hockey game was the result of a change in expectations: fans no longer expected to have future opportunities to see Gretzky in action, so they became more eager to see him while they could.

Depending on the specifics of the case, changes in expectations can either decrease or increase the demand for a good. For example, savvy shoppers often wait for seasonal sales—say, buying holiday gifts during the post-holiday markdowns. In this case, expectations of a future drop in price lead to a decrease in demand today. Alternatively, expectations of a future rise in price are likely to cause an increase in demand today.

Expected changes in future income can also lead to changes in demand: if you expect your income to rise in the future, you will typically borrow today and increase your demand for certain goods; and if you expect your income to fall in the future, you are likely to save today and reduce your demand for some goods.

> When a rise in income increases the demand for a good—the normal case—we say that the good is a **normal good**.
>
> When a rise in income decreases the demand for a good, it is an **inferior good**.

---

economics in action

Beating the Traffic

All big cities have traffic problems, and many local authorities try to discourage driving in the crowded city center. If we think of an auto trip to the city center as a good that people consume, we can use the economics of demand to analyze anti-traffic policies.

One common strategy of local governments is to reduce the demand for auto trips by lowering the prices of substitutes. Many metropolitan areas subsidize bus and rail service, hoping to lure commuters out of their cars.

An alternative strategy is raising the price of complements: several major U.S. cities impose high taxes on commercial parking garages, both to raise revenue and to discourage people from driving into the city. (Short time limits on parking meters, combined with vigilant parking enforcement, is a related tactic.)

However, few cities have been willing to adopt the politically controversial direct approach: reducing congestion by raising the price of driving. So it was a shock when, in 2003, London imposed a "congestion charge" of £5 (about $9) on all cars entering the city center during business hours.

Compliance is monitored with automatic cameras that photograph license plates. People can either pay the charge in advance or pay it by midnight of the day they have driven. If they don't pay and are caught, a fine of £100 (about $180) is imposed for each transgression. (A full description of the rules can be found at www.cclondon.com.)

Not surprisingly, the result of the new policy confirms the law of demand: according to an August 2003 news report, traffic into central London had fallen 32 percent and cars were traveling more than a third faster as a result of the congestion charge. ■

> > > > > > > > > > > > > > > > > >

>>CHECK YOUR UNDERSTANDING 3-1

1. Explain whether each of the following events represents (i) a *shift of* the demand curve or (ii) a *movement along* the demand curve.
   a. A store owner finds that customers are willing to pay more for umbrellas on rainy days.
   b. When XYZ Telecom, a long-distance telephone service provider, offered reduced rates on weekends, the volume of weekend calling increased sharply.
   c. People buy more long-stem roses the week of Valentine's Day, even though the prices are higher than at other times during the year.
   d. The sharp rise in the price of gasoline leads many commuters to join carpools in order to reduce their gasoline purchases.

Solutions appear at back of book.

The Supply Curve

Ticket scalpers have to acquire the tickets they sell, and many of them do so from ticket-holders who decide to sell. The decision of whether to sell your own ticket to a scalper depends in part on the price offered: the higher the price offered, the more likely that you will be willing to sell.

So just as the quantity of tickets that people are willing to buy depends on the price they have to pay, the quantity that people are willing to sell—the **quantity supplied**—depends on the price they are offered. (Notice that this is the supply of tickets *to the market in scalped tickets*. The number of seats in the stadium is whatever it is, regardless of the price—but that's not the quantity we're concerned with here.)

The **quantity supplied** is the actual amount of a good or service people are willing to sell at some specific price.

The Supply Schedule and the Supply Curve

The table in Figure 3-5 on page 64 shows how the quantity of tickets made available varies with the price—that is, it shows a hypothetical **supply schedule** for tickets to Gretzky's last game.

A supply schedule works the same way as the demand schedule shown in Figure 3-1: in this case, the table shows the quantity of tickets season subscribers are willing to sell at different prices. At a price of $100, only 2,000 people are willing to part with their tickets. At $150, some more people decide that it is worth passing up the game in order to have more money for something else, increasing the quantity of tickets available to 5,000. At $200, the quantity of tickets supplied rises to 7,000, and so on.

A **supply schedule** shows how much of a good or service would be supplied at different prices.

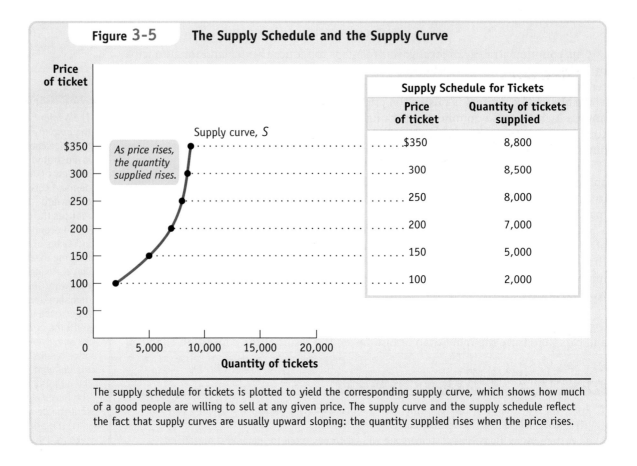

Figure 3-5   The Supply Schedule and the Supply Curve

Supply Schedule for Tickets

Price of ticket	Quantity of tickets supplied
$350	8,800
300	8,500
250	8,000
200	7,000
150	5,000
100	2,000

As price rises, the quantity supplied rises.

Supply curve, S

The supply schedule for tickets is plotted to yield the corresponding supply curve, which shows how much of a good people are willing to sell at any given price. The supply curve and the supply schedule reflect the fact that supply curves are usually upward sloping: the quantity supplied rises when the price rises.

A **supply curve** shows graphically how much of a good or service people are willing to sell at any given price.

In the same way that a demand schedule can be represented graphically by a demand curve, a supply schedule can be represented by a **supply curve,** as shown in Figure 3-5. Each point on the curve represents an entry from the table.

Suppose that the price scalpers offer rises from $200 to $250; we can see from Figure 3-5 that the quantity of tickets sold to them rises from 7,000 to 8,000. This is the normal situation for a supply curve, reflecting the general proposition that a higher price leads to a higher quantity supplied. So just as demand curves normally slope downward, supply curves normally slope upward: the higher the price being offered, the more hockey tickets people will be willing to part with—the more of any good they will be willing to sell.

Shifts of the Supply Curve

When Gretzky's retirement was announced, the immediate effect was that people who already had tickets for the April 15 game became less willing to sell those tickets to scalpers at any given price. So the quantity of tickets supplied at any given price fell: the number of tickets people were willing to sell at $350 fell, the number they were willing to sell at $300 fell, and so on. Figure 3-6 shows us how to illustrate this event in terms of the supply schedule and the supply curve for tickets.

The table in Figure 3-6 shows two supply schedules; the schedule after the announcement is the same one as in Figure 3-5. The first supply schedule shows the supply of scalped tickets *before* Gretzky announced his retirement. And just as a change in demand schedules leads to a shift of the demand curve, a change in supply schedules leads to a **shift of the supply curve**—a change in the quantity supplied at any given price. This is shown in Figure 3-6 by the shift of the supply curve before the announcement, S_1, to its new position after the announcement, S_2. Notice that S_2 lies to the left of S_1, a reflection of the fact that quantity supplied decreased at any given price in the aftermath of Gretzky's announcement.

A **shift of the supply curve** is a change in the quantity supplied of a good or service at any given price. It is represented by the change of the original supply curve to a new position, denoted by a new supply curve.

Figure 3-6   A Decrease in Supply

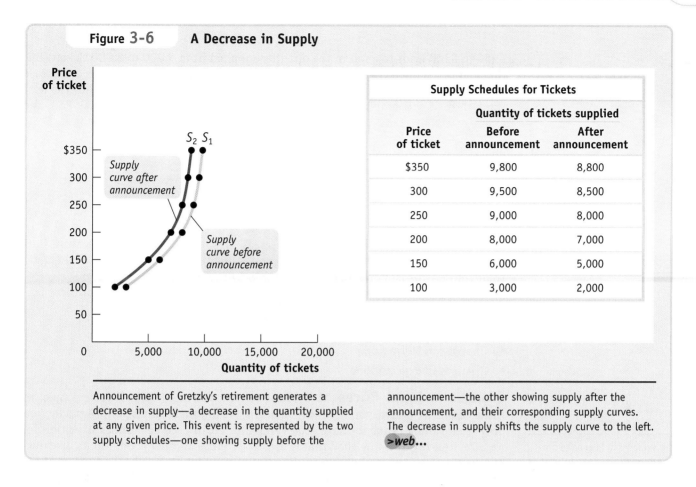

	Supply Schedules for Tickets	
	Quantity of tickets supplied	
Price of ticket	**Before announcement**	**After announcement**
$350	9,800	8,800
300	9,500	8,500
250	9,000	8,000
200	8,000	7,000
150	6,000	5,000
100	3,000	2,000

Announcement of Gretzky's retirement generates a decrease in supply—a decrease in the quantity supplied at any given price. This event is represented by the two supply schedules—one showing supply before the announcement—the other showing supply after the announcement, and their corresponding supply curves. The decrease in supply shifts the supply curve to the left. **>web...**

As in the analysis of demand, it's crucial to draw a distinction between such shifts of the supply curve and **movements along the supply curve**—changes in the quantity supplied that result from a change in price. We can see this difference in Figure 3-7. The movement from point *A* to point *B* is a movement along the supply curve: the quantity supplied falls along S_1 due to a fall in price. Here, a fall in price from

A **movement along the supply curve** is a change in the quantity supplied of a good that is the result of a change in that good's price.

Figure 3-7

Movement Along the Supply Curve Versus Shift of the Supply Curve

The fall in quantity supplied when going from point *A* to point *B* reflects a movement along the supply curve: it is the result of a fall in the price of the good. The fall in quantity supplied when going from point *A* to point *C* reflects a shift of the supply curve: it is the result of a fall in the quantity supplied at any given price.

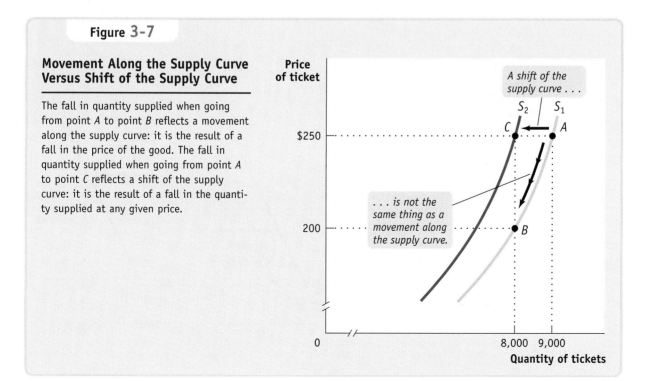

$250 to $200 leads to a fall in the quantity supplied from 9,000 to 8,000 tickets. But the quantity supplied can also fall when the price is unchanged if there is a decrease in supply—a leftward shift of the supply curve. This is shown in Figure 3-7 by the leftward shift of the supply curve from S_1 to S_2. Holding price constant at $250, the quantity supplied falls from 9,000 tickets at point A on S_1 to 8,000 at point C on S_2.

Understanding Shifts of the Supply Curve

Figure 3-8 illustrates the two basic ways in which supply curves can shift. When economists talk about an "increase in supply," they mean a *rightward* shift of the supply curve: at any given price, people will supply a larger quantity of the good than before. This is shown in Figure 3-8 by the shift to the right of the original supply curve S_1 to S_2. And when economists talk about a "decrease in supply," they mean a *leftward* shift of the supply curve: at any given price, people supply a smaller quantity of the good than before. This is represented in Figure 3-8 by the leftward shift of S_1 to S_3.

Economists believe that shifts of supply curves are mainly the result of three factors (though, as in the case of demand, there are other possible causes):

- Changes in input prices
- Changes in technology
- Changes in expectations

Changes in Input Prices To produce output, you need inputs—for example, to make vanilla ice cream, you need vanilla beans, cream, sugar, and so on. (Actually, you only need vanilla beans to make *good* vanilla ice cream; see Economics in Action on page 76.) An **input** is any good that is used to produce another good. Inputs, like output, have prices. And an increase in the price of an input makes the production of the final good more costly for those who produce and sell the good. So sellers are less willing to supply the good at any given price, and the supply curve shifts to the left. For example, newspaper publishers buy large quantities of newsprint (the paper on which newspapers are printed). When newsprint prices rose sharply in 1994–1995, the supply of newspapers fell: several newspapers went out of business and a number of new publishing ventures were canceled. Similarly, a fall in the price of an input makes the production of the final good less costly for sellers. They are more willing to supply the good at any given price, and the supply curve shifts to the right.

An **input** is a good that is used to produce another good.

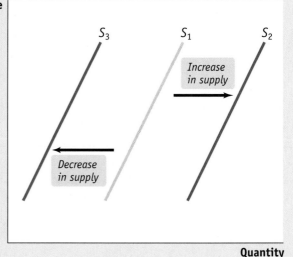

Figure 3-8

Shifts of the Supply Curve

Any event that increases supply shifts the supply curve to the right, reflecting a rise in the quantity supplied at any given price. Any event that decreases supply shifts the supply curve to the left, reflecting a fall in the quantity supplied at any given price.

Changes in Technology When economists talk about "technology," they don't necessarily mean high technology—they mean all the ways in which people can turn inputs into useful goods. The whole complex set of activities that turn corn from an Iowa farm into cornflakes on your breakfast table is technology in this sense. And when a better technology becomes available, reducing the cost of production—that is, letting a producer spend less on inputs yet produce the same output—supply increases, and the supply curve shifts to the right. For example, an improved strain of corn that is more resistant to disease makes farmers willing to supply more corn at any given price.

Changes in Expectations Imagine that you had a ticket for the April 15 game but couldn't go. You'd want to sell the ticket to a scalper. But if you heard a credible rumor about Gretzky's imminent retirement, you would know that the ticket would soon sky-rocket in value. So you'd hold off on selling the ticket until his decision to retire was made public. This illustrates how expectations can alter supply: an expectation that the price of a good will be higher in the future causes supply to decrease today, but an expectation that the price of a good will be lower in the future causes supply to increase today.

economics in action

Down (and Up) on the Farm

Many countries have designed farm policies based on the belief—or maybe the hope—that producers *won't* respond much to changes in the price of their product. But they have found out, to their dismay, that the price does indeed matter.

Advanced countries (including the United States) have historically tried to legislate farm prices *up*. (Chapter 4 describes how such price floors work in practice.) The point was to raise farmers' incomes, not to increase production—but production nonetheless did go up. Until the nations of the European Union began guaranteeing farmers high prices in the 1960s, they had limited agricultural production and imported much of their food. Once price supports were in place, production expanded rapidly, and European farmers began growing more grains and producing more dairy products than consumers wanted to buy.

In poorer countries, especially in Africa, governments have often sought to keep farm prices *down*. The typical strategy was to require farmers to sell their produce to a "marketing board," which then resold it to urban consumers or overseas buyers. A famous example is Ghana, once the world's main supplier of cocoa, the principal ingredient in chocolate. From 1965 until the 1980s, farmers were required to sell their cocoa beans to the government at prices that lagged steadily behind those chocolate manufacturers were paying elsewhere. The Ghanaian government hoped that cocoa production would be little affected by this policy and that it could profit by buying low and selling high. In fact, production fell sharply. By 1980, Ghana's share of the world market was down to 12 percent, while other cocoa-exporting countries that did not follow the same policy—including its African neighbors—were steadily increasing their sales.

Today Europe is trying to reform its agricultural policy, and most developing countries have abandoned their efforts to hold farm prices down. Governments seem finally to have learned that supply curves really do slope upward after all. ■

> > > > > > > > > > > > > > > > > > >

>>CHECK YOUR UNDERSTANDING 3-2

1. Explain whether each of the following events represents (i) a *shift of* the supply curve or (ii) a *movement along* the supply curve.
   a. More homeowners put their houses up for sale during a real estate boom that causes house prices to rise.
   b. Many strawberry farmers open temporary roadside stands during harvest season, even though prices are usually low at that time.

continued

continued

c. Immediately after the school year begins, fast-food chains must raise wages to attract workers.

d. Many construction workers temporarily move to areas that have suffered hurricane damage, lured by higher wages which represent the price of labor.

e. Since new technologies have made it possible to build larger cruise ships (which are cheaper to run per passenger), Caribbean cruise lines have offered more cabins, at lower prices, than before.

Solutions appear at back of book.

Supply, Demand, and Equilibrium

A competitive market is in equilibrium when price has moved to a level at which the quantity demanded of a good equals the quantity supplied of that good. The price at which this takes place is the **equilibrium price**, also referred to as the **market-clearing price**. The quantity of the good bought and sold at that price is the **equilibrium quantity**.

We have now covered the first three key elements in the supply and demand model: the supply curve, the demand curve, and the set of factors that shift each curve. The next step is to put these elements together to show how they can be used to predict the actual price at which a good will be bought and sold.

What determines the price at which a good is bought and sold? In Chapter 1 we learned the general principle that *markets move toward equilibrium*, a situation in which no individual would be better off taking a different action. In the case of a competitive market, we can be more specific: a competitive market is in equilibrium when the price has moved to a level at which the quantity demanded of a good equals the quantity supplied of that good. At that price, no individual seller could make herself better off by offering to sell either more or less of the good and no individual buyer could make himself better off by offering to buy more or less of the good.

The price that matches the quantity supplied and the quantity demanded is the **equilibrium price;** the quantity bought and sold at that price is the **equilibrium quantity.** The equilibrium price is also known as the **market-clearing price:** it is the price that "clears the market" by ensuring that every buyer willing to pay that price finds a seller willing to sell at that price, and vice versa.

You may notice from this point on that we will no longer focus on middlemen such as scalpers but focus directly on the market price and quantity. Why? Because the function of a middleman is to bring buyers and sellers together to trade. But what makes buyers and sellers willing to trade is in reality not the middleman, but the price they agree upon—the equilibrium price. By going deeper and examining how price functions within a market, we can safely assume that the middlemen are doing their job and leave them in the background.

So, how do we find the equilibrium price and quantity?

Finding the Equilibrium Price and Quantity

The easiest way to determine the equilibrium price and quantity in a market is by putting the supply curve and the demand curve on the same diagram. Since the supply curve shows the quantity supplied at any given price and the demand curve shows the quantity demanded at any given price, the price at which the two curves cross is the equilibrium price: the price at which quantity supplied equals quantity demanded.

Figure 3-9 combines the demand curve from Figure 3-1 and the supply curve from Figure 3-5. They *intersect* at point *E*, which is the equilibrium of this market; that is, $250 is the equilibrium price and 8,000 tickets is the equilibrium quantity.

Let's confirm that point *E* fits our definition of equilibrium. At a price of $250 per ticket, 8,000 ticket-holders are willing to resell their tickets and 8,000 people who do not have tickets are willing to buy. So at the price of $250 the quantity of tickets supplied equals the quantity demanded. Notice that at any other price the market would not clear: every willing buyer would not be able to find a willing seller, or vice versa. In other words, if the price were more than $250, the quantity supplied would exceed the quantity demanded; if the price were less than $250, the quantity demanded would exceed the quantity supplied.

PITFALLS

BOUGHT *AND* SOLD?

We have been talking about the price at which a good is bought *and* sold, as if the two were the same. But shouldn't we make a distinction between the price received by sellers and that paid by buyers? In principle, yes; but it is helpful at this point to sacrifice a bit of realism in the interests of simplicity—by assuming away the difference between the prices received by sellers and those paid by buyers. In reality, people who sell hockey tickets to scalpers, although they sometimes receive high prices, generally receive less than those who eventually buy these tickets pay. No mystery there: that difference is how a scalper or any other "middle-man"—someone who brings buyers and sellers together—makes a living. In many markets, however, the difference between the buying and selling price is quite small. It is therefore not a bad approximation to think of the price paid by buyers as being the *same* as the price received by sellers. And that is what we will assume in the remainder of this chapter.

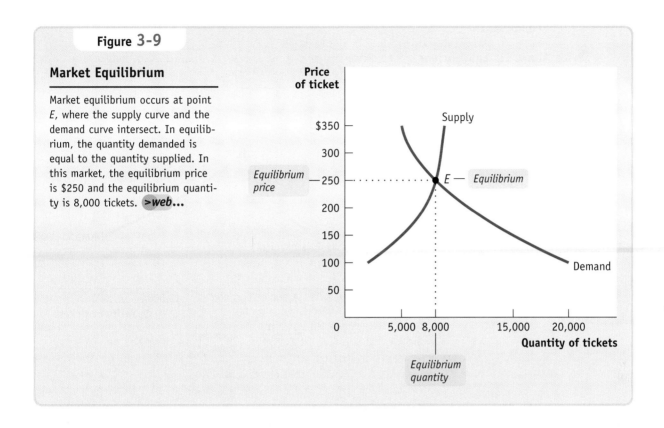

Figure 3-9

Market Equilibrium

Market equilibrium occurs at point *E*, where the supply curve and the demand curve intersect. In equilibrium, the quantity demanded is equal to the quantity supplied. In this market, the equilibrium price is $250 and the equilibrium quantity is 8,000 tickets. **>web...**

The model of supply and demand, then, predicts that given the demand and supply curves shown in Figure 3-9, 8,000 tickets would change hands at a price of $250 each.

But how can we be sure that the market will arrive at the equilibrium price? We begin by answering three simpler questions:

1. Why do all sales and purchases in a market take place at the same price?
2. Why does the market price fall if it is above the equilibrium price?
3. Why does the market price rise if it is below the equilibrium price?

Why Do All Sales and Purchases in a Market Take Place at the Same Price?

There are some markets where the same good can sell for many different prices, depending on who is selling or who is buying. For example, have you ever bought a souvenir in a "tourist trap" and then seen the same item on sale somewhere else (perhaps even in the next store) for a lower price? Because tourists don't know which shops offer the best deals and don't have time for comparison shopping, sellers in tourist areas can charge different prices for the same good.

But in any market where the buyers and sellers have both been around for some time, sales and purchases tend to converge at a generally uniform price, so that we can safely talk about *the* market price. It's easy to see why. Suppose a seller offered a potential buyer a price noticeably above what the buyer knew other people to be paying. The buyer would clearly be better off shopping elsewhere—unless the seller was prepared to offer a better deal. Conversely, a seller would not be willing to sell for significantly less than the amount he knew most buyers were paying; he would be better off waiting to get a more reasonable customer. So in any well-established, ongoing market, all sellers receive and all buyers pay approximately the same price. This is what we call the *market price*.

The market price is the same for everyone.

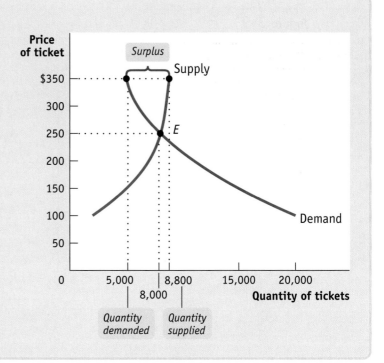

Figure 3-10

Price Above Its Equilibrium Level Creates a Surplus

The market price of $350 is above the equilibrium price of $250. This creates a surplus: at $350 per ticket, suppliers would like to sell 8,800 tickets but fans are willing to purchase only 5,000, so there is a surplus of 3,800 tickets. This surplus will push the price down until it reaches the equilibrium price of $250. **>web...**

Why Does the Market Price Fall If It Is Above the Equilibrium Price?

Suppose the supply and demand curves are as shown in Figure 3-9, but the market price is above the equilibrium level of $250—say, $350. This situation is illustrated in Figure 3-10. Why can't the price stay there?

As the figure shows, at a price of $350 there would be more tickets available than hockey fans wanted to buy: 8,800 versus 5,000. The difference of 3,800 is the **surplus**—also known as the *excess supply*—of tickets at $350.

This surplus means that some would-be sellers are being frustrated: they cannot find anyone to buy what they want to sell. So the surplus offers an incentive for those 3,800 would-be sellers to offer a lower price in order to poach business from other sellers. It also offers an incentive for would-be buyers to seek a bargain by offering a lower price. Sellers who reject the lower price will fail to find buyers, and the result of this price cutting will be to push the prevailing price down until it reaches the equilibrium price. So, the price of a good will fall whenever there is a surplus—that is, whenever the price is above its equilibrium level.

Why Does the Market Price Rise If It Is Below the Equilibrium Price?

Now suppose the price is below its equilibrium level—say, at $150 per ticket, as shown in Figure 3-11. In this case, the quantity demanded (15,000 tickets) exceeds the quantity supplied (5,000 tickets), implying that there are 10,000 would-be buyers who cannot find tickets: there is a **shortage**, also known as an *excess demand*, of 10,000 tickets.

When there is a shortage, there are frustrated would-be buyers—people who want to purchase tickets but cannot find willing sellers at the current price. In this situation, either buyers will offer more than the prevailing price or sellers will realize that they can charge higher prices. Either way, the result is to drive up the prevailing price. This bidding up of prices happens whenever there are shortages—and there will be shortages whenever the price is below its equilibrium level. So the price will always rise if it is below the equilibrium level.

There is a **surplus** of a good when the quantity supplied exceeds the quantity demanded. Surpluses occur when the price is above its equilibrium level.

There is a **shortage** of a good when the quantity demanded exceeds the quantity supplied. Shortages occur when the price is below its equilibrium level.

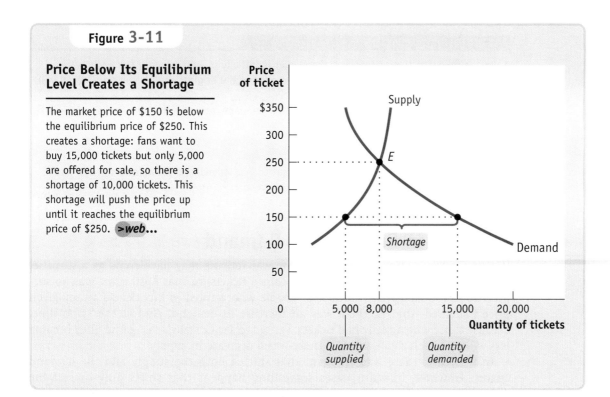

Figure 3-11

Price Below Its Equilibrium Level Creates a Shortage

The market price of $150 is below the equilibrium price of $250. This creates a shortage: fans want to buy 15,000 tickets but only 5,000 are offered for sale, so there is a shortage of 10,000 tickets. This shortage will push the price up until it reaches the equilibrium price of $250. **>web...**

Using Equilibrium to Describe Markets

We have now seen that a market tends to have a single price; that the market price falls if it is above the equilibrium level but rises if it is below that level. So the market price always *moves toward* the equilibrium price, the price at which there is neither surplus nor shortage.

economics in action

A Fish Story

In market equilibrium, something remarkable supposedly happens: everyone who wants to sell a good finds a willing buyer, and everyone who wants to buy that good finds a willing seller. It's a beautiful theory—but is it realistic?

In New York City the answer can be seen every day, just before dawn, at the famous Fulton Fish Market, which has operated since 1835 (though it has moved from its original Fulton Street location). There, every morning, fishermen bring their catch and haggle over prices with restaurant owners, shopkeepers, and a variety of middlemen and brokers.

The stakes are high. Restaurant owners who can't provide their customers with the fresh fish they expect stand to lose a lot of business, so it's important that would-be buyers find willing sellers. It's even more important for fishermen to make a sale: unsold fish loses much, if not all, of its value. But the market does reach equilibrium: just about every would-be buyer finds a willing seller, and vice versa. The reason is that every day the price of each type of fish quickly converges to a level that matches the quantity supplied and the quantity demanded.

So the tendency of markets to reach equilibrium isn't just theoretical speculation. You can see (and smell) it happening, early every morning. ∎

> —

>> QUICK REVIEW

➤ Price in a competitive market moves to the *equilibrium price*, or *market-clearing price*, where the quantity supplied is equal to the quantity demanded. This quantity is the *equilibrium quantity*.

➤ All sales and purchases in a market take place at the same price. If the price is above its equilibrium level, there is a *surplus* that drives the price down. If the price is below its equilibrium level, there is a *shortage* that drives the price up.

1. In the following three situations, the market is initially in equilibrium. After each event described below, does a surplus or shortage exist at the original equilibrium price? What will happen to the equilibrium price as a result?
   a. 1997 was a very good year for California wine-grape growers, who produced a bumper-size crop.
   b. After a hurricane, Florida hoteliers often find that many people cancel their upcoming vacations, leaving them with empty hotel rooms.
   c. After a heavy snowfall, many people want to buy secondhand snowblowers at the local tool shop.

Solutions appear at back of book.

Changes in Supply and Demand

Wayne Gretzky's announcement that he was retiring may have come as a surprise, but the subsequent rise in the price of scalped tickets for that April game was no surprise at all. Suddenly the number of people who wanted to buy tickets at any given price increased—that is, there was an increase in demand. And at the same time, because those who already had tickets wanted to see Gretzky's last game, they became less willing to sell them—that is, there was a decrease in supply.

In this case, there was an event that shifted both the supply and the demand curves. However, in many cases something happens that shifts only one of the curves. For example, a freeze in Florida reduces the supply of oranges but doesn't change the demand. A medical report that eggs are bad for your health reduces the demand for eggs but does not affect the supply. That is, events often shift either the supply curve or the demand curve, but not both; it is therefore useful to ask what happens in each case.

We have seen that when a curve shifts, the equilibrium price and quantity change. We will now concentrate on exactly how the shift of a curve alters the equilibrium price and quantity.

What Happens When the Demand Curve Shifts

Coffee and tea are substitutes: if the price of tea rises, the demand for coffee will increase, and if the price of tea falls, the demand for coffee will decrease. But how does the price of tea affect the *market* for coffee?

Figure 3-12 shows the effect of a rise in the price of tea on the market for coffee. The rise in the price of tea increases the demand for coffee. Point E_1 shows the equilibrium corresponding to the original demand curve, with P_1 the equilibrium price and Q_1 the equilibrium quantity bought and sold.

An increase in demand is indicated by a *rightward* shift of the demand curve from D_1 to D_2. At the original market price P_1, this market is no longer in equilibrium: a shortage occurs because the quantity demanded exceeds the quantity supplied. So the price of coffee rises and generates an increase in the quantity supplied, an upward *movement along the supply curve*. A new equilibrium is established at point E_2, with a higher equilibrium price P_2 and higher equilibrium quantity Q_2. This sequence of events reflects a general principle: *When demand for a good increases, the equilibrium price and the equilibrium quantity of the good both rise.*

And what would happen in the reverse case, a fall in the price of tea? A fall in the price of tea decreases the demand for coffee, shifting the demand curve to the *left*. At the original price, a surplus occurs as quantity supplied exceeds quantity demanded. The price falls and leads to a decrease in the quantity supplied, with a lower equilibrium price and a lower equilibrium quantity. This illustrates another general principle: *When demand for a good decreases, the equilibrium price of the good and the equilibrium quantity of the good both fall.*

Figure 3-12

Equilibrium and Shifts of the Demand Curve

The original equilibrium in the market for coffee is at E_1, at the intersection of the supply curve and the original demand curve D_1. A rise in the price of tea, a substitute, shifts the demand curve rightward to D_2. A shortage exists at the original price P_1, so both price and the quantity supplied rise, a movement along the supply curve. A new equilibrium is reached at E_2, with a higher equilibrium price P_2 and a higher equilibrium quantity Q_2. *When demand for a good increases, the equilibrium price and the equilibrium quantity of the good both rise.* **>web...**

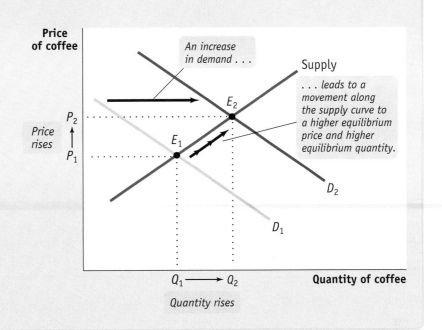

To summarize how a market responds to a change in demand: *An increase in demand leads to a rise in both the equilibrium price and the equilibrium quantity. A decrease in demand leads to a fall in both the equilibrium price and the equilibrium quantity.*

What Happens When the Supply Curve Shifts

In the real world, it is a bit easier to predict changes in supply than changes in demand. Physical factors that affect supply, like the availability of inputs, are easier to get a handle on than the fickle tastes that affect demand. Still, with supply as with demand, what we really know are the *effects* of shifts of the supply curve.

A spectacular example of a change in technology increasing supply occurred in the manufacture of semiconductors—the silicon chips that are the core of computers, video games, and many other devices. In the early 1970s, engineers learned how to use a process known as photolithography to put microscopic electronic components onto a silicon chip; subsequent progress in the technique has allowed ever more components to be put on each chip. Figure 3-13 (page 74) shows the effect of such an innovation on the market for silicon chips. The demand curve does not change. The original equilibrium is at E_1, the point of intersection of the original supply curve S_1 and the demand curve, with equilibrium price P_1 and equilibrium quantity Q_1. As a result of the technological change, supply increases and S_1 shifts *rightward* to S_2. At the original price P_1, a surplus of chips now exists and the market is no longer in equilibrium. The surplus causes a fall in price and a rise in quantity demanded, a downward movement along the demand curve. The new equilibrium is at E_2, with an equilibrium price P_2 and an equilibrium quantity Q_2. In the new equilibrium E_2, the price is lower and the equilibrium quantity higher than before. This may be stated as a general principle: *An increase in supply leads to a fall in the equilibrium price and a rise in the equilibrium quantity.*

What happens to the market when supply decreases? A decrease in supply leads to a *leftward* shift of the supply curve. At the original price, a shortage now exists; as a result, the equilibrium price rises and the quantity demanded falls. This describes the sequence of events in the newspaper market in 1994–1995, which we

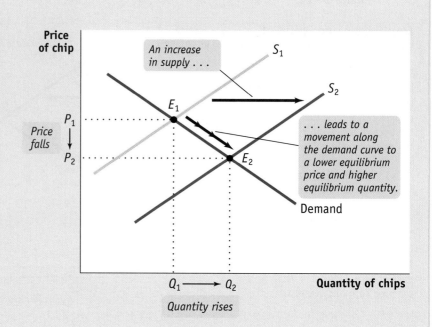

Figure 3-13

Equilibrium and Shifts of the Supply Curve

The original equilibrium in the market for silicon chips is at E_1, at the intersection of the demand curve and the original supply curve S_1. After a technological change increases the supply of silicon chips, the supply curve shifts rightward to S_2. A surplus exists at the original price P_1, so price falls and the quantity demanded rises, a movement along the demand curve. A new equilibrium is reached at E_2, with a lower equilibrium price P_2 and a higher equilibrium quantity Q_2. When supply of a good increases, the equilibrium price of the good falls and the equilibrium quantity rises. **>web...**

An increase in supply . . .

. . . leads to a movement along the demand curve to a lower equilibrium price and higher equilibrium quantity.

discussed earlier: a decrease in the supply of newsprint led to a rise in the price and the closure of many newspapers. We can formulate a general principle: *A decrease in supply leads to a rise in the equilibrium price and a fall in the equilibrium quantity.*

To summarize how a market responds to a change in supply: *An increase in supply leads to a fall in the equilibrium price and a rise in the equilibrium quantity. A decrease in supply leads to a rise in the equilibrium price and a fall in the equilibrium quantity.*

Simultaneous Shifts in Supply and Demand

Finally, it sometimes happens that events shift *both* the demand and supply curves. In fact, this chapter began with an example of such a simultaneous shift. Wayne Gretzky's announcement that he was retiring increased the demand for scalped tickets because more people wanted to see him play one last time; but it also decreased the supply because those who already had tickets became less willing to part with them.

Figure 3-14 illustrates what happened. In both panels we show an increase in demand—that is, a rightward shift of the demand curve, from D_1 to D_2. Notice that the rightward shift in panel (a) is relatively larger than the one in panel (b). Both panels also show a decrease in supply—that is, a leftward shift of the supply curve, from S_1 to S_2. Notice that the leftward shift in panel (b) is relatively larger than the one in panel (a).

In both cases, the equilibrium price rises, from P_1 to P_2, as the equilibrium moves from E_1 to E_2. But what happens to the equilibrium quantity, the quantity of scalped tickets bought and sold? In panel (a) the increase in demand is large relative to the decrease in supply, and the equilibrium quantity rises as a result. In panel (b) the decrease in supply is large relative to the increase in demand, and the equilibrium quantity falls as a result. That is, when demand increases and

PITFALLS

WHICH CURVE IS IT, ANYWAY?
When the price of some good changes, in general we can say that this reflects a change in either supply or demand. But it is easy to get confused about which one. A helpful clue is the direction of change in the quantity. If the quantity sold changes in the *same* direction as the price—for example, if both the price and the quantity rise—this suggests that the demand curve has shifted. If the price and the quantity move in *opposite* directions, the likely cause is a shift in the supply curve.

Figure 3-14 Simultaneous Shifts of the Demand and Supply Curves

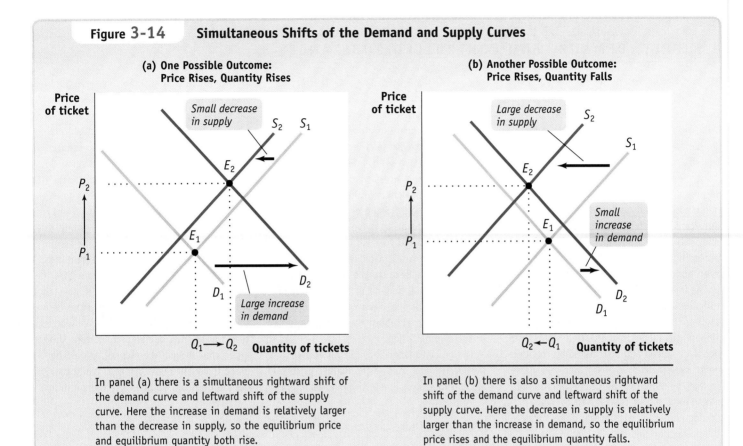

(a) One Possible Outcome:
Price Rises, Quantity Rises

(b) Another Possible Outcome:
Price Rises, Quantity Falls

In panel (a) there is a simultaneous rightward shift of the demand curve and leftward shift of the supply curve. Here the increase in demand is relatively larger than the decrease in supply, so the equilibrium price and equilibrium quantity both rise.

In panel (b) there is also a simultaneous rightward shift of the demand curve and leftward shift of the supply curve. Here the decrease in supply is relatively larger than the increase in demand, so the equilibrium price rises and the equilibrium quantity falls.

supply decreases, the actual quantity bought and sold can go either way, depending on *how much* the demand and supply curves have shifted.

In general, when supply and demand shift in opposite directions, we can't predict what the ultimate effect will be on the quantity bought and sold. What we can say is that a curve that shifts a disproportionately greater distance than the other curve will have a disproportionately greater effect on the quantity bought and sold. That said, we can make the following prediction about the outcome when the supply and demand curves shift in opposite directions:

■ When demand increases and supply decreases, the price rises but the change in the quantity is ambiguous.

■ When demand decreases and supply increases, the price falls but the change in the quantity is ambiguous.

But suppose that the demand and supply curves shift in the same direction. Can we safely make any predictions about the changes in price and quantity? In this situation, the change in quantity bought and sold can be predicted but the change in price is ambiguous. The two possible outcomes when the supply and demand curves shift in the same direction (which you should check for yourself) are as follows:

■ When both demand and supply increase, the quantity increases but the change in price is ambiguous.

■ When both demand and supply decrease, the quantity decreases but the change in price is ambiguous.

SUPPLY, DEMAND, AND CONTROLLED SUBSTANCES

The big "issue" movie of the year 2000 was *Traffic*, a panoramic treatment of the drug trade. The movie was loosely based on the 1989 British TV miniseries *Traffik*. Despite the lapse of 11 years, the basic outlines of the situation—in which the drug trade flourishes despite laws that are supposed to prevent it—had not changed. Not only has the so-called war on drugs by law enforcement officials not succeeded in eliminating the trade in illegal drugs; according to most assessments, it has not even done much to reduce consumption.

The failure of the war on drugs has a historical precedent: during Prohibition, from 1920 to 1933, the sale and consumption of alcohol was illegal in the United States. But liquor, produced and distributed by "bootleggers," nonetheless remained widely available. In fact, by 1929 per capita consumption of alcohol was higher than it had been a decade earlier. As with illegal drugs today, the production and distribution of the banned substance became a large enterprise that flourished despite its illegality.

Why is it so hard to choke off markets in alcohol and drugs? Think of the war on drugs as a policy that shifts the supply curve but has not done much to shift the demand curve.

Although it is illegal to use drugs such as cocaine, just as it was once illegal to drink alcohol, in practice the war on drugs focuses mainly on the suppliers. As a result, the cost of supplying drugs includes the risk of being caught and sent to jail, perhaps even of being executed. This undoubtedly reduces the quantity of drugs supplied *at any given price*, in effect shifting the supply curve for drugs to the left. In Figure 3-15, this is shown as a shift in the supply curve from S_1

to S_2. If the war on drugs had no effect on the price of drugs, and the price remained at P_1, this leftward shift would reflect a reduction in the quantity of drugs supplied equal in magnitude to the leftward shift of supply.

But as we have seen, when the supply curve for a good shifts to the left, the effect is to raise the market price of that good. In Figure 3-15 the effect of the war on drugs would be to move the equilibrium from E_1 to E_2, and to raise the price of drugs from P_1 to P_2, a movement along the demand curve. Because the market price rises, the actual decline in the quantity of drugs supplied is less than the decline in the quantity that would have been supplied at the original price.

The crucial reason Prohibition was so ineffective was that as the market price of alcohol rose, consumers trimmed back only

slightly on their consumption—yet the higher prices were enough to induce many potential suppliers to take the risk of jail time. So while Prohibition raised the price of alcohol, it did not do much to reduce consumption. Unfortunately, the same seems to be true of current drug policy. The policy raises the price of drugs to those who use them, but this does not do much to discourage consumption. Meanwhile, the higher prices are enough to induce suppliers to provide drugs despite the penalties.

What is the answer? Some argue that the policy should be refocused on the demand side—more antidrug education, more counseling, and so on. If these policies worked, they would shift demand to the left. Others argue that drugs, like alcohol, should be made legal but heavily taxed. While the debate goes on, so does the war on drugs.

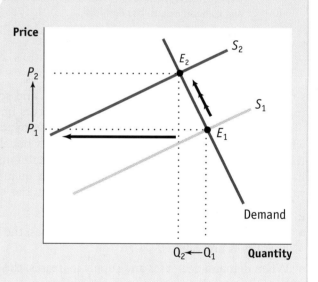

Figure 3-15

Effects of the War on Drugs

The war on drugs shifts the supply curve to the left. However, we can see by comparing the original equilibrium E_1 with the new equilibrium E_2 that the actual reduction in the quantity of drugs supplied is much smaller than the shift of the supply curve. The equilibrium price rises from P_1 to P_2—a movement along the demand curve. This leads suppliers to provide drugs despite the risks.

---

economics in action

Plain Vanilla Gets Fancy

Vanilla doesn't get any respect. It's such a common flavoring that "plain vanilla" has become a generic term for ordinary, unembellished products. But between 2000 and 2003, plain vanilla got quite fancy—at least if you looked at the price. At the supermarket, the price of a small bottle of vanilla extract rose from about $5 to about $15. The wholesale price of vanilla beans rose 400 percent.

The cause of the price spike was bad weather—not here, but in the Indian Ocean. Most of the world's vanilla comes from Madagascar, an island nation off Africa's southeast coast. A huge cyclone struck there in 2000, and a combination of colder-than-normal weather and excessive rain impeded recovery.

The higher price of vanilla led to a fall in the quantity demanded: worldwide consumption of vanilla fell about 35 percent from 2000 to 2003. Consumers didn't stop eating vanilla-flavored products; instead, they switched (often without realizing it) to ice cream and other products flavored with synthetic vanillin, which is a by-product of wood pulp and petroleum production.

Notice that there was never a shortage of vanilla: you could always find it in the store if you were willing to pay the price. That is, the vanilla market remained in equilibrium. ■

> > > > > > > > > > > > > > > > > > > >

>> **QUICK REVIEW**

➤ Changes in the equilibrium price and quantity in a market result from shifts in the supply curve, the demand curve, or both.

➤ An increase in demand—a rightward shift of the demand curve—increases both the equilibrium price and the equilibrium quantity. A decrease in demand—a leftward shift of the demand curve—pushes down both the equilibrium price and the equilibrium quantity.

➤ An increase in supply drives the equilibrium price down but increases the equilibrium quantity. A decrease in supply raises the equilibrium price but reduces the equilibrium quantity.

➤ Often the fluctuations in markets involve shifts of both the supply and demand curves. When they shift in the same direction, the change in quantity is predictable but the change in price is not. When they move in opposite directions, the change in price is predictable but the change in quantity is not. When there are simultaneous shifts of the demand and supply curves, the curve that shifts the greater distance has a greater effect on the change in price and quantity.

>> **CHECK YOUR UNDERSTANDING 3-4**

1. In each of the following examples, determine (i) the market in question; (ii) whether a shift in demand or supply occurred, the direction of the shift, and what induced the shift; and (iii) the effect of the shift on the equilibrium price and the equilibrium quantity.
   a. As the price of gasoline fell in the United States during the 1990s, more people bought large cars.
   b. As technological innovation has lowered the cost of recycling used paper, fresh paper made from recycled stock is used more frequently.
   c. As a local cable company offers cheaper pay-per-view films, local movie theaters have more unfilled seats.

2. Periodically, a computer chip maker like Intel introduces a new chip that is faster than the previous one. In response, demand for computers using the earlier chip decreases as customers put off purchases in anticipation of machines containing the new chip. Simultaneously, computer makers increase their production of computers containing the earlier chip in order to clear out their stocks of those chips.

   Draw two diagrams of the market for computers containing the earlier chip: (a) one in which the equilibrium quantity falls in response to these events and (b) one in which the equilibrium quantity rises. What happens to the equilibrium price in each diagram?

   Solutions appear at back of book.

Competitive Markets—And Others

Early in this chapter, we defined a competitive market and explained that the supply and demand framework is a model of competitive markets. But we took a rain check on the question of why it matters whether or not a market is competitive. Now that we've seen how the supply and demand model works, we can offer some explanation.

To understand why competitive markets are different from other markets, compare the problems facing two individuals: a wheat farmer who must decide whether to grow more wheat, and the president of a giant aluminum company—say, Alcoa—who must decide whether to produce more aluminum.

For the wheat farmer, the question is simply whether the extra wheat can be sold at a price high enough to justify the extra production cost. The farmer need not worry about whether producing more wheat will affect the price of the wheat he or she was already planning to grow. That's because the wheat market is competitive. There are thousands of wheat farmers, and no one farmer's decision will have much impact on the market price.

For the Alcoa executive, things are not that simple because the aluminum market is *not* competitive. There are only a few big players, including Alcoa, and each of them is well aware that its actions *do* have a noticeable impact on the market price. This adds a whole new level of complexity to the decisions producers have to make. Alcoa can't decide whether or not to produce more aluminum just by asking whether the additional product will sell for more than it costs to make. The company also has to ask whether producing more aluminum will drive down the market price and reduce its profit.

When a market is competitive, individuals can base decisions on less complicated analyses than those used in a noncompetitive market. This in turn means that it's easier for economists to build a model of a competitive market than of a noncompetitive market.

Don't take this to mean that economic analysis has nothing to say about noncompetitive markets. On the contrary, economists can offer some very important insights into how other kinds of markets work. But those insights require other models. In the next chapter, we will focus on what we can learn about competitive markets from the very useful model we have just developed: supply and demand.

• A LOOK AHEAD •

We've now developed a model that explains how markets arrive at prices and why markets "work" in the sense that buyers can almost always find sellers, and vice versa. But this model could use a little more clarification.

But, nothing demonstrates a principle quite as well as what happens when people try to defy it. And governments do, fairly often, try to defy the principles of supply and demand. In the next chapter we consider what happens when they do—the revenge of the market.

SUMMARY

1. The **supply and demand model** illustrates how a **competitive market**, one with many buyers and sellers, works.

2. The **demand schedule** shows the **quantity demanded** at each price and is represented graphically by a **demand curve**. The **law of demand** says that demand curves slope downward.

3. A **movement along the demand curve** occurs when the price changes and causes a change in the quantity demanded. When economists talk of increasing or decreasing demand, they mean **shifts of the demand curve**—a change in the quantity demanded at any given price. An increase in demand causes a rightward shift of the demand curve. A decrease in demand causes a leftward shift.

4. There are four main factors that shift the demand curve:
   - A change in the prices of related goods, such as **substitutes** or **complements**
   - A change in income: when income rises, the demand for **normal goods** increases and the demand for **inferior goods** decreases.
   - A change in tastes
   - A change in expectations

5. The **supply schedule** shows the **quantity supplied** at each price and is represented graphically by a **supply curve**. Supply curves usually slope upward.

6. A **movement along the supply curve** occurs when the price changes and causes a change in the quantity supplied. When economists talk of increasing or decreasing supply, they mean **shifts of the supply curve**—a change in the quantity supplied at any given price. An increase in supply causes a rightward shift of the supply curve. A decrease in supply causes a leftward shift.

7. There are three main factors that shift the supply curve:
   - A change in **input** prices
   - A change in technology
   - A change in expectations

8. The supply and demand model is based on the principle that the price in a market moves to its **equilibrium price**, or **market-clearing price**, the price at which the quantity demanded is equal to the quantity supplied. This quantity is the **equilibrium quantity**. When the price is above its market-clearing level, there is a **surplus** that pushes the price down. When the price is below its market-clearing level, there is a **shortage** that pushes the price up.

9. An increase in demand increases both the equilibrium price and the equilibrium quantity; a decrease in demand has the opposite effect. An increase in supply reduces the equilibrium price and increases the equilibrium quantity; a decrease in supply has the opposite effect.

10. Shifts of the demand curve and the supply curve can happen simultaneously. When they shift in opposite directions, the change in price is predictable but the change in quantity is not. When they shift in the same direction, the change in quantity is predictable but the change in price is not. In general, the curve that shifts the greater distance has a greater effect on the changes in price and quantity.

KEY TERMS

Competitive market, p. 57
Supply and demand model, p. 57
Demand schedule, p. 58
Demand curve, p. 58
Quantity demanded, p. 58
Law of demand, p. 59
Shift of the demand curve, p. 60
Movement along the demand curve, p. 60

Substitutes, p. 61
Complements, p. 61
Normal good, p. 62
Inferior good, p. 62
Quantity supplied, p. 63
Supply schedule, p. 63
Supply curve, p. 64
Shift of the supply curve, p. 64

Movement along the supply curve, p. 65
Input, p. 66
Equilibrium price, p. 68
Equilibrium quantity, p. 68
Market-clearing price, p. 68
Surplus, p. 70
Shortage, p. 70

PROBLEMS

1. A survey indicated that chocolate ice cream is America's favorite ice-cream flavor. For each of the following, indicate the possible effects on demand and/or supply and equilibrium price and quantity of chocolate ice cream.

a. A severe drought in the Midwest causes dairy farmers to reduce the number of milk-producing cattle in their herds by a third. These dairy farmers supply cream that is used to manufacture chocolate ice cream.

b. A new report by the American Medical Association reveals that chocolate does, in fact, have significant health benefits.

c. The discovery of cheaper synthetic vanilla flavoring lowers the price of vanilla ice cream.

d. New technology for mixing and freezing ice cream lowers manufacturers' costs of producing chocolate ice cream.

2. In a supply and demand diagram, draw the shift in demand for hamburgers in your hometown due to the following events. In each case show the effect on equilibrium price and quantity.

a. The price of tacos increases.

b. All hamburger sellers raise the price of their french fries.

c. Income falls in town. Assume that hamburgers are a normal good for most people.

d. Income falls in town. Assume that hamburgers are an inferior good for most people.

e. Hot dog stands cut the price of hot dogs.

3. The market for many goods changes in predictable ways according to the time of year, in response to events such as holidays, vacation times, seasonal changes in production, and so on. Using supply and demand, explain the change in price in each of the following cases. Note that supply and demand may shift simultaneously.

a. Lobster prices usually fall during the summer peak harvest season, despite the fact that people like to eat lobster during the summer months more than during any other time of year.

b. The price of a Christmas tree is lower after Christmas than before and fewer trees are sold.

c. The price of a round-trip ticket to Paris on Air France falls by more than $200 after the end of school vacation in September. This happens despite the fact that generally worsening weather increases the cost of operating flights to Paris, and Air France therefore reduces the number of flights to Paris at any given price.

4. Show in a diagram the effect on the demand curve, the supply curve, the equilibrium price, and the equilibrium quantity of each of the following events.

a. The market for newspapers in your town.

Case 1:   The salaries of journalists go up.
Case 2:   There is a big news event in your town, which is reported in the newspapers.

b. The market for St. Louis Rams cotton T-shirts.

Case 1:   The Rams win the national championship.
Case 2:   The price of cotton increases.

c. The market for bagels.

Case 1:   People realize how fattening bagels are.
Case 2:   People have less time to make themselves a cooked breakfast.

d. The market for the Krugman and Wells economics textbook.

Case 1:   Your professor makes it required reading for all of his or her students.
Case 2:   Printing costs for textbooks are lowered by the use of synthetic paper.

5. Suppose that the supply schedule of Maine lobsters is as follows:

Price of lobster (per pound)	Quantity of lobster supplied (pounds)
$25	800
20	700
15	600
10	500
5	400

Suppose that Maine lobsters can be sold only in the United States. The U.S. demand schedule for Maine lobsters is as follows:

Price of lobster (per pound)	Quantity of lobster demanded (pounds)
$25	200
20	400
15	600
10	800
5	1,000

a. Draw the demand curve and the supply curve for Maine lobsters. What is the equilibrium price and quantity of lobsters?

Now suppose that Maine lobsters can be sold in France. The French demand schedule for Maine lobsters is as follows:

Price of lobster (per pound)	Quantity of lobster demanded (pounds)
$25	100
20	300
15	500
10	700
5	900

b. What is the demand schedule for Maine lobsters now that French consumers can also buy them? Draw a supply and demand diagram that illustrates the new equilibrium price and quantity of lobsters. What will happen to the price at which fishermen can sell lobster? What will happen to the price paid by U.S. consumers? What will happen to the quantity consumed by U.S. consumers?

6. Find the flaws in reasoning in the following statements, paying particular attention to the distinction between shifts of and movements along the supply and demand curves. Draw a diagram to illustrate what actually happens in each situation.

a. "A technological innovation that lowers the cost of producing a good might seem at first to result in a reduction in the price of the good to consumers. But a fall in price will increase demand for the good, and higher demand will send the price up again. It is not certain, therefore, that an innovation will really reduce price in the end."

b. "A study shows that eating a clove of garlic a day can help prevent heart disease, causing many consumers to demand more garlic. This increase in demand results in a rise in the price of garlic. Consumers, seeing that the price of garlic has gone up, reduce their demand for garlic. This causes the demand for garlic to decrease and the price of garlic to fall. Therefore, the ultimate effect of the study on the price of garlic is uncertain."

7. Some points on a demand curve for a normal good are given here:

Price	Quantity demanded
$23	70
21	90
19	110
17	130

Do you think that the increase in quantity demanded (from 90 to 110 in the table) when price decreases (from 21 to 19) is due to a rise in consumers' income? Explain clearly (and briefly) why or why not.

8. Aaron Hank is a star hitter for the Bay City baseball team. He is close to breaking the major league record for home runs hit during one season, and it is widely anticipated that in the next game he will break that record. As a result, tickets for the team's next game have been a hot commodity. But today it is announced that, due to a knee injury, he will not in fact play in the team's next game. Assume that season ticket-holders are able to resell their tickets if they wish. Use supply and demand diagrams to explain the following.

a. Show the case in which this announcement results in a lower equilibrium price and a lower equilibrium quantity than before the announcement.

b. Show the case in which this announcement results in a lower equilibrium price and a higher equilibrium quantity than before the announcement.

c. What accounts for whether case a or case b occurs?

d. Suppose that a scalper had secretly learned before the announcement that Aaron Hank would not play in the next game. What actions do you think he would take?

9. In *Rolling Stone* magazine, several fans and rock stars, including Pearl Jam, were bemoaning the high price of concert tickets. One superstar argued, "It just isn't worth $75 to see me play. No one should have to pay that much to go to a concert." Assume this star sold out arenas around the country at an average ticket price of $75.

a. How would you evaluate the arguments that ticket prices are too high?

b. Suppose that due to this star's protests, ticket prices were lowered to $50. In what sense is this price too low? Draw a diagram using supply and demand curves to support your argument.

c. Suppose Pearl Jam really wanted to bring down ticket prices. Since the band controls the supply of its services, what do you recommend they do? Explain using a supply and demand diagram.

d. Suppose the band's next CD was a total dud. Do you think they would still have to worry about ticket prices being too high? Why or why not? Draw a supply and demand diagram to support your argument.

e. Suppose the group announced their next tour was going to be their last. What effect would this likely have on the demand for and price of tickets? Illustrate with a supply and demand diagram.

10. The accompanying table gives the annual U.S. demand and supply schedules for pickup trucks.

Price of truck	Quantity of trucks demanded (millions)	Quantity of trucks supplied (millions)
$20,000	20	14
25,000	18	15
30,000	16	16
35,000	14	17
40,000	12	18

a. Plot the demand and supply curves using these schedules. Indicate the equilibrium price and quantity on your diagram.

b. Suppose the tires used on pickup trucks are found to be defective. What would you expect to happen in the market for pickup trucks? Show this on your diagram.

c. Suppose that the U.S. Department of Transportation imposes costly regulations on manufacturers that cause them to reduce supply by one-third at any given price. Calculate and plot the new supply schedule and indicate the new equilibrium price and quantity on your diagram.

11. After several years of decline, the market for handmade acoustic guitars is making a comeback. These guitars are usually made in small workshops employing relatively few highly skilled luthiers. Assess the impact on the equilibrium price and quantity of handmade acoustic guitars as a result of each of the following events. In your answers indicate which curve(s) shift(s) and in which direction.

a. Environmentalists succeed in having the use of Brazilian rosewood banned in the United States, forcing luthiers to seek out alternative, more costly woods.

b. A foreign producer reengineers the guitar-making process and floods the market with identical guitars.

c. Music featuring handmade acoustic guitars makes a comeback as audiences tire of heavy metal and grunge music.

d. The country goes into a deep recession and the income of the average American falls sharply.

12. *Demand twisters*: Sketch and explain the demand relationship in each of the following statements.

a. I would never buy a Britney Spears CD! You couldn't even give me one for nothing.

b. I generally buy a bit more coffee as the price falls. But once the price falls to $2 per pound, I'll buy out the entire stock of the supermarket.

c. I spend more on orange juice even as the price rises. (Does this mean that I must be violating the law of demand?)

d. Due to a tuition rise, most students at a college find themselves with lower disposable income. Almost all of them eat more frequently at the school cafeteria and less often at restaurants, even though prices at the cafeteria have risen too. (This one requires that you draw both the demand and the supply curves for dormitory cafeteria meals.)

13. Will Shakespeare is a struggling playwright in sixteenth-century London. As the price he receives for writing a play increases, he is willing to write more plays. For the following situations, use a diagram to illustrate how each event affects the equilibrium price and quantity in the market for Shakespeare's plays.

a. The playwright Christopher Marlowe, Shakespeare's chief rival, is killed in a bar brawl.

b. The bubonic plague, a deadly infectious disease, breaks out in London.

c. To celebrate the defeat of the Spanish Armada, Queen Elizabeth declares several weeks of festivities, which involves commissioning new plays.

14. The small town of Middling experiences a sudden doubling of the birth rate. After three years, the birth rate returns to normal. Use a diagram to illustrate the effect of these events on the following.

a. The market for an hour of babysitting services in Middling today

b. The market for an hour of babysitting services 14 years into the future, after the birth rate has returned to normal, by which time children born today are old enough to work as babysitters

c. The market for an hour of babysitting services 30 years into the future, when children born today are likely to be having children of their own

15. Use a diagram to illustrate how each of the following events affects the equilibrium price and quantity of pizza.

a. The price of mozzarella cheese rises.

b. The health hazards of hamburgers are widely publicized.

c. The price of tomato sauce falls.

d. The incomes of consumers rise and pizza is an inferior good.

e. Consumers expect the price of pizza to fall next week.

16. Although he was a prolific artist, Pablo Picasso painted only 1,000 canvases during his "Blue Period." Picasso is now dead, and all of his Blue Period works are currently on display in museums and private galleries throughout Europe and the United States.

a. Draw a supply curve for Picasso Blue Period works. Why is this supply curve different from ones you have seen?

b. Given the supply curve from part a, the price of a Picasso Blue Period work will be entirely dependent on what factor(s)? Draw a diagram showing how the equilibrium price of such a work is determined.

c. Suppose that rich art collectors decide that it is essential to acquire Picasso Blue Period art for their collections. Show the impact of this on the market for these paintings.

17. Draw the appropriate curve in each of the following cases. Is it like or unlike the curves you have seen so far? Explain.

a. The demand for cardiac bypass surgery, given that the government pays the full cost for any patient

b. The demand for elective cosmetic plastic surgery, given that the patient pays the full cost

c. The supply of Rembrandt paintings

d. The supply of reproductions of Rembrandt paintings

>web... To continue your study and review of concepts in this chapter, please visit the Krugman/Wells website for quizzes, animated graph tutorials, web links to helpful resources, and more.

www.worthpublishers.com/krugmanwells

>> The Market Strikes Back

BIG CITY, NOT-SO-BRIGHT IDEAS

NEW YORK CITY IS A PLACE WHERE YOU can find almost anything—that is, almost anything, except a taxicab when you need one or a decent apartment at a rent you can afford. You might think that New York's notorious shortages of cabs and apartments are the inevitable price of big-city living. However, they are largely the product of government policies—specifically, of government policies that have, one way or another, tried to prevail over the market forces of supply and demand.

In the previous chapter, we learned the principle that a market moves to equilibrium—that the market price rises or falls to the level at which the quantity of a good that people are willing to supply is equal to the quantity that other people want to demand. But sometimes governments try to defy that principle. When they do, the market strikes back in predictable ways. And our ability to predict what will happen when governments try to defy supply and demand shows the power and usefulness of supply and demand analysis itself.

The shortages of apartments and taxicabs in New York are particular examples that illuminate what happens when the logic of the market is defied. New York's housing shortage is the result of *rent control,* a law that prevents landlords from raising rents except when specifically

given permission. Rent control was introduced during World War II to protect the interests of tenants, and it still remains in force. Many other American cities have had rent control at one time or another, but with the notable exceptions of New York and San Francisco, these controls have largely been done away with. Similarly, New York's limited supply of taxis is the result of a licensing system introduced in the 1930s. New York taxi licenses are known as "medallions," and only taxis with medallions are allowed to pick up passengers. And although this

New York City: An empty taxi is hard to find.

PNI Ltd./Picture Quest

system was originally intended to protect the interests of both drivers and customers, it has generated a shortage of taxis in the city. The number of medallions remained fixed from 1937 until 1995, and only a handful of additional licenses have been issued since then.

What you will learn in this chapter:

➤ The meaning of **price controls** and **quantity controls,** two kinds of government intervention in markets

➤ How price and quantity controls create problems and make a market **inefficient**

➤ Why economists are often deeply skeptical of attempts to intervene in markets

➤ Who benefits and who loses from market interventions, and why they are used despite their well-known problems

➤ What an **excise tax** is and why its effect is similar to a quantity control

➤ Why the **deadweight loss** of a tax means that its true cost is more than the amount of tax revenue collected

In this chapter, we begin by examining what happens when governments try to control prices in a competitive market, keeping the price in a market either below its equilibrium level—a *price ceiling* such as rent control—or above it—a *price floor*. We then turn to schemes such as taxi medallions that attempt to dictate the quantity of a good bought and sold. Finally, we consider the effects of taxes on sales or purchases.

Why Governments Control Prices

You learned in Chapter 3 that a market moves to equilibrium—that is, the market price moves to the level at which the quantity supplied equals the quantity demanded. But this equilibrium price does not necessarily please either buyers or sellers.

After all, buyers would always like to pay less if they could, and sometimes they can make a strong moral or political case that they should pay lower prices. For example, what if the equilibrium between supply and demand for apartments in a major city leads to rental rates that an average working person can't afford? In that case, a government might well be under pressure to impose limits on the rents landlords can charge.

Sellers, however, would always like to get more money for what they sell, and sometimes they can make a strong moral or political case that they should receive higher prices. For example, consider the labor market: the price for an hour of a worker's time is the wage rate. What if the equilibrium between supply and demand for less-skilled workers leads to wage rates that are below the poverty level? In that case, a government might well find itself pressured to require employers to pay a rate no lower than some specified minimum wage.

In other words, there is often a strong political demand for governments to intervene in markets. When a government intervenes to regulate prices, we say that it imposes **price controls**. These controls typically take the form either of an upper limit, a **price ceiling**, or a lower limit, a **price floor**.

> **Price controls** are legal restrictions on how high or low a market price may go. They can take two forms: a **price ceiling**, a maximum price sellers are allowed to charge for a good, or a **price floor**, a minimum price buyers are required to pay for a good.

Unfortunately, it's not that easy to tell a market what to do. As we will now see, when a government tries to legislate prices—whether it legislates them *down* by imposing a price ceiling or *up* by imposing a price floor—there are certain predictable and unpleasant side effects.

We should note an important caveat here: our analysis in this chapter considers only what happens when price controls are imposed on *competitive markets*, which, as you should recall from Chapter 3, are markets with many buyers and sellers in which no buyer or seller can have any influence on the price. When markets are *not* competitive—as in a monopoly, where there is only one seller—price controls don't necessarily cause the same problems. In practice, however, price controls often *are* imposed on competitive markets—like the New York apartment market. And so the analysis in this chapter applies to many important real-world situations.

Price Ceilings

Aside from rent control, there are not many price ceilings in the United States today. But at times they have been widespread. Price ceilings are typically imposed during crises—wars, harvest failures, natural disasters—because these events often lead to sudden price increases that hurt many people but produce big gains for a lucky few. The U.S. government imposed ceilings on many prices during World War II: the war sharply increased demand for raw materials, such as aluminum and steel, and price controls prevented those with access to these raw materials from earning huge profits. Price controls on oil were imposed in 1973, when an embargo by Arab oil-exporting countries seemed likely to generate huge profits for U.S. oil companies. (See

Economics in Action on page 89.) Price controls were imposed on California's whole-sale electricity market in 2001, when a shortage was creating big profits for a few power-generating companies but leading to higher bills for consumers.

Rent control in New York is, believe it or not, a legacy of World War II: it was imposed because the war produced an economic boom, which increased demand for apartments at a time when the labor and raw materials that might have been used to build them were being used to win the war instead. Although most price controls were removed soon after the war ended, New York's rent limits were retained and gradually extended to buildings not previously covered, leading to some very strange situations.

You can rent a one-bedroom apartment in Manhattan on fairly short notice—if you are able and willing to pay about $1,700 a month and live in a less-than-desirable area. Yet some people pay only a small fraction of this for comparable apartments and others pay hardly more for bigger apartments in better locations.

Aside from producing great deals for some renters, however, what are the broader consequences of New York's rent control system? To answer this question, we turn to the model we developed in Chapter 3: the supply and demand model.

Modeling a Price Ceiling

To see what can go wrong when a government imposes a price ceiling on a competitive market, consider Figure 4-1, which shows a simplified model of the market for apartments in New York. For the sake of simplicity, we imagine that all apartments are exactly the same and would therefore rent for the same price in an uncontrolled market. The table in the figure shows the demand and supply schedules; the implied demand and supply curves are shown on the left of the figure. We show the quantity of apartments on the horizontal axis and the monthly rent per apartment on the vertical axis. You can see that in an unregulated market the equilibrium would be at point E: 2 million apartments would be rented for $1,000 each per month.

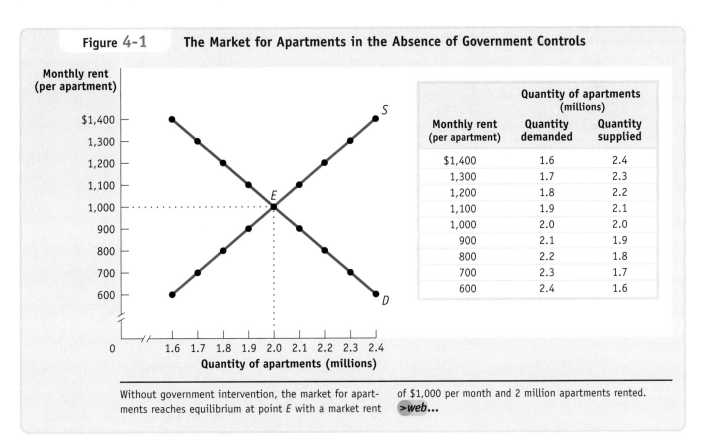

Figure 4-1   The Market for Apartments in the Absence of Government Controls

Monthly rent (per apartment)	Quantity of apartments (millions)	
	Quantity demanded	Quantity supplied
$1,400	1.6	2.4
1,300	1.7	2.3
1,200	1.8	2.2
1,100	1.9	2.1
1,000	2.0	2.0
900	2.1	1.9
800	2.2	1.8
700	2.3	1.7
600	2.4	1.6

Without government intervention, the market for apartments reaches equilibrium at point *E* with a market rent of $1,000 per month and 2 million apartments rented.

>web...

Now suppose that the government imposes a price ceiling, limiting rents to a price below the equilibrium price—say no more than $800.

Figure 4-2 shows the effect of the price ceiling, represented by the line at $800. At the enforced rental rate of $800, landlords will have less incentive to offer apartments, so they won't be willing to supply as many as they would at the equilibrium rate of $1,000. So they will choose point A on the supply curve, offering only 1.8 million apartments for rent, 200,000 fewer than in the free-market situation. At the same time, more people will want to rent apartments at a price of $800 than at the equilibrium price of $1,000; as shown at point B on the demand curve, at a monthly rent of $800 the quantity of apartments demanded rises to 2.2 million, 200,000 more than in the free-market situation and 400,000 more than are actually available at the price of $800. So there is now a persistent shortage of rental housing: at that price, 400,000 more people want to rent than are able to find apartments.

Do price ceilings always cause shortages? No. If a price ceiling is set above the equilibrium price, it won't have any effect. Suppose that the equilibrium rental rate on apartments is $1,000 per month and the city government sets a ceiling of $1,200. Who cares? In this case, the price ceiling won't be binding—it won't actually constrain market behavior—and it will have no effect.

Why a Price Ceiling Causes Inefficiency

The housing shortage shown in Figure 4-2 is not merely annoying: like any shortage induced by price controls, it can be seriously harmful because it leads to *inefficiency*. We introduced the concept of *efficiency* back in Chapter 1, where we learned that an economy is efficient if there is no way to make some people better off without making others worse off. We also learned the basic principle that a market economy, left to itself, is usually efficient.

A market or an economy becomes **inefficient** when there are missed opportunities—ways in which production or consumption could be rearranged that would make some people better off without making other people worse off.

> A market or an economy is **inefficient** if there are missed opportunities: some people could be made better off without making other people worse off.

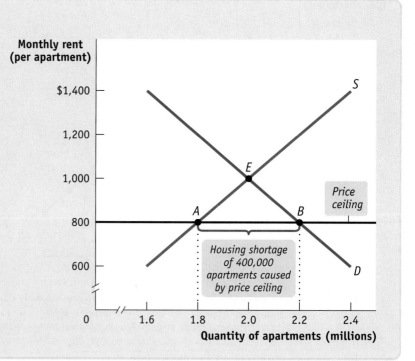

Figure 4-2

The Effects of a Price Ceiling

The dark horizontal line represents the government-imposed price ceiling on rents of $800 per month. This price ceiling reduces the quantity of apartments supplied to 1.8 million, point A, and increases the quantity demanded to 2.2 million, point B. This creates a persistent shortage of 400,000 units: 400,000 people who want apartments at the legal rent of $800 but cannot get them.

Housing shortage of 400,000 apartments caused by price ceiling

Rent control, like all price ceilings, creates inefficiency in at least three distinct ways: in the allocation of apartments to renters, in the time wasted searching for apartments, and in the inefficiently low quality or condition in which landlords maintain apartments. In addition to inefficiency, price ceilings give rise to illegal behavior as people try to circumvent them.

Inefficient Allocation to Consumers   In the case shown in Figure 4-2, 2.2 million people would like to rent an apartment at $800 per month, but only 1.8 million apartments are available. Of those 2.2 million who are seeking an apartment, some want an apartment badly and are willing to pay a high price to get one. Others have a less urgent need and are only willing to pay a low price, perhaps because they have alternative housing. An efficient allocation of apartments would reflect these differences: people who really want an apartment will get one and people who aren't all that anxious to find an apartment won't. In an inefficient distribution of apartments, the opposite will happen: some people who are not especially anxious to find an apartment will get one but others who are very anxious to find an apartment won't. And because under rent control people usually get apartments through luck or personal connections, rent control generally results in an **inefficient allocation to consumers** of the few apartments available.

To see the inefficiency involved, consider the plight of the Lees, a family with young children who have no alternative housing and would be willing to pay up to $1,500 for an apartment—but are unable to find one. Also consider George, a retiree who lives most of the year in Florida but still has a lease on the New York apartment he moved into 40 years ago. George pays $800 per month for this apartment, but if the rent were even slightly more—say, $850—he would give it up and stay with his children when he is in New York.

This allocation of apartments—George has one and the Lees do not—is a missed opportunity: there is a way to make the Lees and George both better off at no additional cost. The Lees would be happy to pay George, say, $1,200 a month to sublet his apartment, which he would happily accept since the apartment is worth no more than $850 a month to him. George would prefer the money he gets from the Lees to keeping his apartment; the Lees would prefer to have the apartment rather than the money. So both would be made better off by this transaction—and nobody else would be hurt.

Generally, if people who really want apartments could sublet them from people who are less eager to stay in them, both those who gain apartments and those who trade their leases for more money would be better off. However, subletting is illegal under rent control because it would occur at prices above the price ceiling. But just because subletting is illegal doesn't mean it never happens; in fact, it does occur in New York, although not on a scale that would undo the effects of rent control. This illegal subletting is a kind of *black market activity*, which we will discuss shortly.

Wasted Resources   A second reason a price ceiling causes inefficiency is that it leads to **wasted resources**. The Economics in Action on page 89 describes the gasoline shortages of 1979, when millions of Americans spent hours each week waiting in lines at gas stations. The *opportunity cost* of the time spent in gas lines—the wages not earned, the leisure time not enjoyed—constituted wasted resources from the point of view of consumers and of the economy as a whole. Because of rent control, the Lees will spend all their spare time for several months searching for an apartment, time they would rather have spent working or in family activities. That is, there is an opportunity cost to the Lees' prolonged search for an apartment—the leisure or income they had to forgo. If the market for apartments worked freely, the Lees would quickly find an apartment at the equilibrium rent of $1,000 and have time to earn more or to enjoy themselves—an outcome that would make them better off without making anyone else worse off. Again, rent control creates missed opportunities.

Inefficiently Low Quality   A third way a price ceiling causes inefficiency is by causing goods to be of **inefficiently low quality**.

Price ceilings often lead to inefficiency in the form of **inefficient allocation to consumers**: people who want the good badly and are willing to pay a high price don't get it, and those who care relatively little about the good and are only willing to pay a low price do get it.

Price ceilings typically lead to inefficiency in the form of **wasted resources**: people spend money and expend effort in order to deal with the shortages caused by the price ceiling.

Price ceilings often lead to inefficiency in that the goods being offered are of **inefficiently low quality**: sellers offer low-quality goods at a low price even though buyers would prefer a higher quality at a higher price.

One of the ironies of New York's rent-control system is that some of the biggest beneficiaries are not the working-class families the system was intended to help but affluent tenants whose families have lived for many decades in choice apartments that would now command very high rents.

One well-known example: the 1986 movie *Hannah and Her Sisters* took place mainly in the real-life home of actress Mia Farrow, a spectacular 11-room apartment overlooking Central Park. Ms. Farrow "inherited" this apartment from her mother, the actress Maureen O'Sullivan. A few years after the movie came out, a study found that Ms. Farrow was paying less than $2,300 a month—about what a 2-bedroom apartment in a far less desirable location would have cost on the uncontrolled market.

Again, consider rent control. Landlords have no incentive to provide better conditions because they cannot raise rents to cover their repair costs but are still able to find tenants easily. In many cases tenants would be willing to pay much more for improved conditions than it would cost for the landlord to provide them—for example, the upgrade of an antiquated electrical system that cannot safely run air conditioners or computers. But any additional payment for such improvements would be legally considered a rent increase, which is prohibited. Indeed, rent-controlled apartments are notoriously badly maintained, rarely painted, subject to frequent electrical and plumbing problems, sometimes even hazardous to inhabit. As one former manager of Manhattan buildings described his job: "At unregulated apartments we'd do most things that the tenants requested. But on the rent-regulated units, we did absolutely only what the law required. . . . We had a perverse incentive to make those tenants unhappy. With regulated apartments, the ultimate objective is to get people out of the building."

This whole situation is a missed opportunity—some tenants would be happy to pay for better conditions, and landlords would be happy to provide them for payment. But such an exchange would occur only if the market were allowed to operate freely.

Black Markets   And that leads us to a last aspect of price ceilings: the incentive they provide for *illegal activities*, specifically the emergence of **black markets**. We have already described one kind of black market activity—illegal subletting by tenants. But it does not stop there. Clearly, there is a temptation for a landlord to say to a potential tenant, "Look, you can have the place if you slip me an extra few hundred in cash each month"—and for the tenant to agree, if he or she is one of those people who would be willing to pay much more than the maximum legal rent.

> A **black market** is a market in which goods or services are bought and sold illegally—either because it is illegal to sell them at all or because the prices charged are legally prohibited by a price ceiling.

What's wrong with black markets? In general, it's a bad thing if people break *any* law, because it encourages disrespect for the law in general. Worse yet, in this case illegal activity worsens the position of those who try to be honest. If the Lees are scrupulous about not breaking the rent control law but others—who may need an apartment less than the Lees do—are willing to bribe landlords, the Lees may *never* find an apartment.

So Why Are There Price Ceilings?

We have seen three common results of price ceilings:

- A persistent shortage of the good
- Inefficiency arising from this persistent shortage in the form of inefficient allocation of the good to consumers, resources wasted in searching for the good, and the inefficiently low quality of the good offered for sale
- The emergence of illegal, black market activity

Given these unpleasant consequences, why do governments still sometimes impose price ceilings—and why does rent control, in particular, persist in New York?

One answer is that although price ceilings may have adverse effects, they do benefit some people. In practice, New York's rent control rules—which are more complex than our simple model—hurt most residents but give a small minority of renters much cheaper housing than they would get in an unregulated market. And those who benefit from the controls are typically better organized and more vocal than those who are harmed by them.

Also, when price ceilings have been in effect for a long time, buyers may not have a realistic idea of what would happen without them. In our previous example, the rental rate in an uncontrolled market (Figure 4-1) would be only 25 percent higher than in the controlled market (Figure 4-2)—$1,000 instead of $800. But how would renters know that? Indeed, they might have heard about black market transactions at much higher prices—the Lees or some other family paying George $1,200 or more—and would not realize that these black market prices are much higher than the price that would prevail in a fully free market.

A last answer is that government officials often do not understand supply and demand analysis! It is a great mistake to suppose that economic policies in the real world are always sensible or well informed.

Hurry up and wait: filling your tank circa 1979.

economics in action

Oil Shortages in the 1970s

In 1979 a revolution overthrew the government of Iran, one of the world's major petroleum-exporting countries. The political chaos in Iran disrupted oil production there, and the sudden fall in world supply caused the price of crude oil to shoot up by 300 percent.

In most of the world this price increase made gasoline more expensive at the pump but did not lead to shortages. In the United States, however, gasoline was subject to a price ceiling, imposed six years earlier during an oil crisis sparked by the Arab–Israeli war of 1973. The main purpose of those price controls was to prevent U.S. oil producers from reaping large profits as a result of temporary disruptions of supply.

As we learned in Chapter 3, a fall in supply generally raises prices. But here, because the price of gasoline at the pump couldn't rise, the reduction in supply showed up as shortages. As it turned out, these shortages became much worse because of panic: drivers who weren't sure when they would next be able to get gas rushed to fill up even if they still had plenty in their tanks. This produced a temporary surge in demand and long lines at gas stations.

For a few months the gasoline shortage dominated the national scene. Hours were wasted sitting in gasoline lines; families canceled vacations for fear of being stranded. Eventually, higher production began to work its way through the refineries, increasing supply. And the end of the summer driving season reduced demand. Both together led to a fall in price.

In 1981 price controls on gasoline, now discredited as a policy, were abolished. But the uncontrolled gasoline market faced a major test in the spring of 2000. Oil-producing nations restricted their output in order to drive up prices and achieved unexpected success, more than doubling world prices over a period of a few months. Prices at the pump rose sharply—many people altered their driving plans and some felt distinctly poorer as a result of the higher prices. But there were no shortages and life continued in the United States without nearly as much disruption as price controls had generated in the 1970s.

Interestingly, however, the oil price shock of 2000 *did* cause serious disruptions in some European countries—because truck drivers and farmers, protesting the high price of fuel, blocked deliveries. This protest was an extreme illustration of the reasons why governments sometimes try to control prices despite the known problems with price controls! ■

> >

1. Homeowners near Middletown University's stadium used to rent parking spaces in their driveways to fans at a going rate of $11. A new town ordinance now sets a maximum parking fee of $7. Use the accompanying supply and demand diagram to explain how each of the following corresponds to a price-ceiling concept.

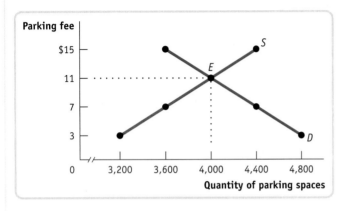

a. Some homeowners now think it's not worth the hassle to rent out spaces.

b. Some fans who used to carpool to the game now drive alone.

c. Some fans can't find parking and leave without seeing the game.

Explain how each of the following arises from the price ceiling.

d. Some fans now arrive several hours early to find parking.

e. Friends of homeowners near the stadium regularly attend games, even if they aren't big fans. But some serious fans have given up because of the parking situation.

f. Some homeowners rent spaces for more than $7 but pretend that the buyers are non-paying friends or family.

2. True or false? Explain your answer. Compared to a free market, price ceilings at a price below the equilibrium price do the following:

a. Increase quantity supplied

b. Make some people who want to consume the good worse off

c. Make all producers worse off

Solutions appear at back of book.

Price Floors

Sometimes governments intervene to push market prices up instead of down. *Price floors* have been widely legislated for agricultural products, such as wheat and milk, as a way to support the incomes of farmers. Historically, there were also price floors on such services as trucking and air travel, although these were phased out by the United States in the 1970s. If you have ever worked in a fast-food restaurant, you are likely to have encountered a price floor: the United States and many other countries maintain a lower limit on the hourly wage rate of a worker's labor—that is, a floor on the price of labor, called the **minimum wage**.

The **minimum wage** is a legal floor on the wage rate, which is the market price of labor.

Just like price ceilings, price floors are intended to help some people but generate predictable and undesirable side effects. Figure 4-3 shows hypothetical supply and demand curves for butter. Left to itself, the market would move to equilibrium at point *E*, with 10 million pounds of butter bought and sold at a price of $1 per pound.

But now suppose that the government, in order to help dairy farmers, imposes a price floor on butter of $1.20 per pound. Its effects are shown in Figure 4-4, where the line at $1.20 represents the price floor. At a price of $1.20 per pound, producers would want to supply 12 million pounds (point *B* on the supply curve) but consumers would want to buy only 9 million pounds (point *A* on the demand curve). There would therefore be a persistent surplus of 3 million pounds of butter.

Does a price floor always lead to an unwanted surplus? No. Just as in the case of a price ceiling, the floor may not be binding—that is, it may be irrelevant. If the equilibrium price of butter is $1 per pound but the floor is set at only $0.80, the floor has no effect.

But suppose that a price floor is binding: what happens to the unwanted surplus? The answer depends on government policy. In the case of agricultural price floors, governments buy up unwanted surplus. Therefore the U.S. government has at times found itself warehousing thousands of tons of butter, cheese, and other farm products. (The European Commission, which administers price floors for a number of European countries, once found itself the owner of a so-called butter mountain, equal in weight to the entire population of Austria.) The government then has to find a way to dispose of these unwanted goods.

Some countries pay exporters to sell products at a loss overseas; this is standard procedure for the European Union. (See For Inquiring Minds on page 92.) At one point the United States tried giving away surplus cheese to the poor. In some cases, governments have actually destroyed the surplus production. To avoid the problem of

Figure 4-3   The Market for Butter in the Absence of Government Controls

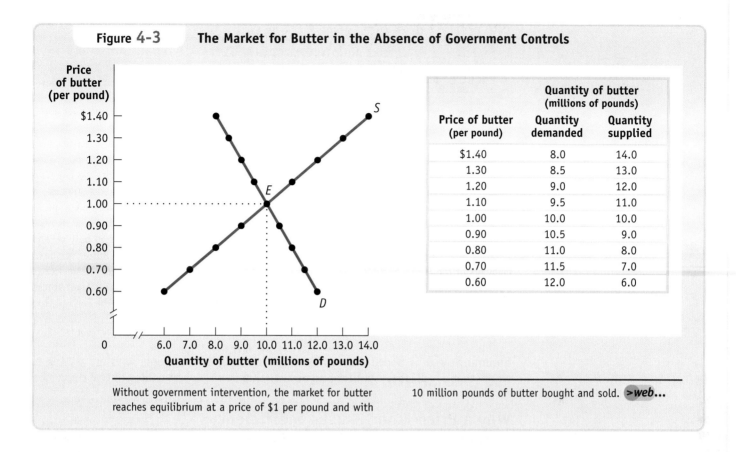

Price of butter (per pound)	Quantity of butter (millions of pounds)	
	Quantity demanded	Quantity supplied
$1.40	8.0	14.0
1.30	8.5	13.0
1.20	9.0	12.0
1.10	9.5	11.0
1.00	10.0	10.0
0.90	10.5	9.0
0.80	11.0	8.0
0.70	11.5	7.0
0.60	12.0	6.0

Without government intervention, the market for butter reaches equilibrium at a price of $1 per pound and with 10 million pounds of butter bought and sold. **>web...**

dealing with the unwanted supplies, the U.S. government typically pays farmers not to produce the products at all.

When the government is not prepared to purchase the unwanted surplus, a price floor means that would-be sellers cannot find buyers. This is what happens when there is a price floor on the wage rate paid for an hour of labor, the *minimum wage*: when the

Figure 4-4

The Effects of a Price Floor

The dark horizontal line represents the government-imposed price floor of $1.20 per pound of butter. The quantity of butter demanded falls to 9 million pounds while the quantity supplied rises to 12 million pounds, generating a persistent surplus of 3 million pounds of butter. **>web...**

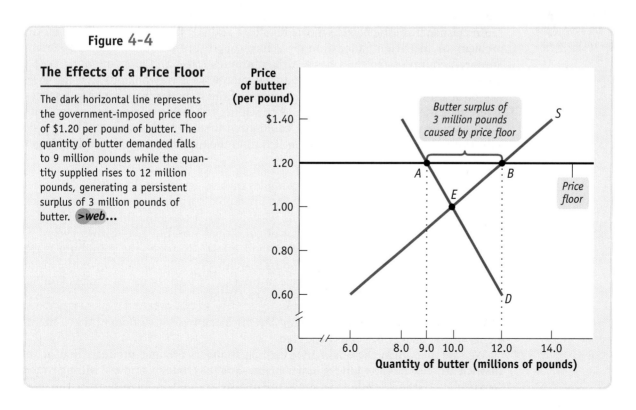

minimum wage is above the equilibrium wage rate, some people who are willing to work—that is, sell labor—cannot find buyers—that is, employers willing to give them jobs.

Why a Price Floor Causes Inefficiency

The persistent surplus that results from a price floor creates missed opportunities—inefficiencies—that resemble those created by the shortage that results from a price ceiling. These include inefficient allocation of sales among sellers, wasted resources, inefficiently high quality, and the temptation to break the law by selling below the legal price.

Inefficient Allocation of Sales Among Sellers Like a price ceiling, a price floor can lead to *inefficient allocation*—but in this case **inefficient allocation of sales among sellers** rather than inefficient allocation to consumers.

An episode from the Belgian movie *Rosetta*, a realistic fictional story, illustrates the problem of inefficient allocation of selling opportunities quite well. Like many European countries, Belgium has a high minimum wage, and jobs for young people are scarce. At one point Rosetta, a young woman who is very anxious to work, loses her job at a fast-food stand because the owner of the stand replaces her with his son—a very reluctant worker. Rosetta would be willing to work for less money, and with the money he would save, the owner could give his son an allowance and let him do something else. But to hire Rosetta for less than the minimum wage would be illegal.

> Price floors lead to **inefficient allocation of sales among sellers:** those who would be willing to sell the good at the lowest price are not always those who actually manage to sell it.

Wasted Resources Also like a price ceiling, a price floor generates inefficiency by *wasting resources*. The most graphic examples involve agricultural products with price floors when the government buys up the unwanted surplus. The surplus production is sometimes destroyed, which is a pure waste; in other cases the stored produce goes, as officials euphemistically put it, "out of condition" and must be thrown away.

Price floors also lead to wasted time and effort. Consider the minimum wage. Would-be workers who spend many hours searching for jobs, or waiting in line in the hope of getting jobs, play the same role in the case of price floors as hapless families searching for apartments in the case of price ceilings.

Inefficiently High Quality Again like price ceilings, price floors lead to inefficiency in the quality of goods produced.

We saw that when there is a price ceiling, suppliers produce products that are of inefficiently low quality: buyers prefer higher-quality products and are willing to pay for them, but sellers refuse to improve the quality of their products because the price ceiling prevents their being compensated for doing so. This same logic applies to price floors, but in reverse: suppliers offer goods of **inefficiently high quality**.

How can this be? Isn't high quality a good thing? Yes, but only if it is worth the cost. Suppose that suppliers spend a lot to make goods of very high quality but that this quality is not worth all that much to consumers, who would rather receive the money spent on that quality in the form of a lower price. This represents a missed opportunity: suppliers and buyers could make a mutually beneficial deal in which buyers got goods of somewhat lower quality for a much lower price.

A good example of the inefficiency of excessive quality comes from the days when transatlantic airfares were set artificially high by international treaty. Forbidden to compete for customers by offering lower ticket prices, airlines instead offered expensive services, like lavish in-flight meals that went largely uneaten. At one point the regulators tried to restrict this practice by defining maximum service standards—for example, that snack service should consist of no more than a sandwich. One airline then introduced what it called a "Scandinavian Sandwich," a towering affair that forced the convening of another conference to define *sandwich*. All of this was wasteful, especially considering that what passengers really wanted was less food and lower airfares.

Since the deregulation of U.S. airlines in the 1970s, American passengers have experienced a large decrease in ticket prices accompanied by a decrease in the quality of in-flight service—smaller seats, lower-quality food, and so on. Everyone complains about the service—but thanks to lower fares, the number of people flying on U.S. carriers has grown several hundred percent since airline deregulation.

Illegal Activity   Finally, like price ceilings, price floors can provide an incentive for *illegal activity*. For example, in countries where the minimum wage is far above the equilibrium wage rate, workers desperate for jobs sometimes agree to work off the books for employers who conceal their employment from the government—or bribe the government inspectors. This practice, known in Europe as "black labor," is especially common in Southern European countries such as Italy and Spain (see Economics in Action below).

> Price floors often lead to inefficiency in that goods of **inefficiently high quality** are offered: sellers offer high-quality goods at a high price, even though buyers would prefer a lower quality at a lower price.

So Why Are There Price Floors?

To sum up, a price floor creates various negative side effects:

- A persistent surplus of the good
- Inefficiency arising from the persistent surplus in the form of inefficient allocation of sales among sellers, wasted resources, and an inefficiently high level of quality offered by suppliers
- The temptation to engage in illegal activity, particularly bribery and corruption of government officials

So why do governments impose price floors when they have so many negative side effects? The reasons are similar to those for imposing price ceilings. Government officials often disregard warnings about the consequences of price floors either because they believe that the relevant market is poorly described by the supply and demand model or, more often, because they do not understand the model. Above all, just as price ceilings are often imposed because they benefit some influential buyers of a good, price floors are often imposed because they benefit some influential *sellers*.

economics in action

"Black Labor" in Southern Europe

The best-known example of a price floor is the minimum wage. Most economists believe, however, that the minimum wage has relatively little effect on the job market in the United States, mainly because the floor is set so low. (This effectively makes the U.S. minimum wage a *nonbinding* price floor—a political symbol more than a substantive policy.) In 1968, the U.S. minimum wage was 53 percent of the average wage of blue-collar workers; by 2003, it had fallen to about 34 percent.

The situation is different, however, in many European countries, where minimum wages have been set much higher than in the United States. This has happened despite the fact that European workers are somewhat less productive than their American counterparts, which means that the equilibrium wage in Europe—the wage that would clear the labor market—is probably lower in Europe than in the United States. Moreover, European countries often require employers to pay for health and retirement benefits, which are more extensive and therefore more costly than comparable American benefits. These mandated benefits make the actual cost of hiring a European worker considerably more than the worker's paycheck.

The result is that in Europe the price floor on labor is definitely binding: the minimum wage is well above the wage rate that would make the quantity of labor supplied by workers equal to the quantity of labor demanded by employers.

The persistent surplus that results from this price floor appears in the form of high unemployment—millions of workers, especially young workers, seek jobs but cannot find them. In countries where the enforcement of labor laws is lax, however, there is a second, entirely predictable result: widespread evasion of the law. In both Italy and Spain, officials believe there are hundreds of thousands, if not millions, of workers who are employed by companies that pay them less than the legal minimum, fail to provide the required health and retirement benefits, or both. In many cases the jobs are simply unreported: Spanish economists estimate that about a third of the country's reported unemployed are in the black labor market—working at unreported jobs. In fact, Spaniards waiting to collect checks from the unemployment office have been known to complain about the long lines that keep them from getting back to work!

Employers in these countries have also found legal ways to evade the wage floor. For example, Italy's labor regulations apply only to companies with 15 or more workers. This gives a big cost advantage to small Italian firms, many of which remain small in order to avoid having to pay higher wages and benefits. And sure enough, in some Italian industries there is an astonishing proliferation of tiny companies. For example, one of Italy's most successful industries is the manufacture of fine woolen cloth, centered in the Prato region. The average textile firm in that region employs only four workers! ∎

< < < < < < < < < < < < < < < < <

>> CHECK YOUR UNDERSTANDING 4-2

1. The state legislature mandates a price floor for gasoline of $4 per gallon. Assess the following statements and illustrate your answer using the figure provided:

   a. Proponents of the law claim it will increase the income of gas station owners. Opponents claim it will hurt gas station owners because they will lose customers.

   b. Proponents claim consumers will be better off because gas stations will provide better service. Opponents claim consumers will be generally worse off because they prefer to buy gas at cheaper prices.

   c. Proponents claim that they are helping gas station owners without hurting anyone else. Opponents claim that consumers are hurt and will end up doing things like buying gas in a nearby state or on the black market.

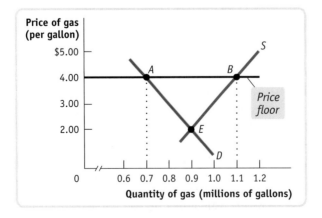

Solutions appear at back of book.

Controlling Quantities

In the 1930s, New York City instituted a system of licensing for taxicabs: only taxis with a "medallion" were allowed to pick up passengers. Because this system was intended to assure quality, medallion owners were supposed to maintain certain standards, including safety and cleanliness. A total of 11,787 medallions were issued, with taxi owners paying $10 for each medallion.

In 1995, there were still only 11,787 licensed taxicabs in New York, even though the city had meanwhile become the financial capital of the world, a place where hundreds of thousands of people in a hurry tried to hail a cab every day. (An additional 400 medallions were issued in 1995, and in 2003 plans were announced to issue 900 more over a period of three years.)

The result of this restriction on the number of taxis was that those medallions became very valuable: if you wanted to operate a New York taxi, you had to lease a medallion from someone else or buy one for a going price of about $250,000.

It turns out that the New York story is not unique; other cities introduced similar medallion systems in the 1930s and, like New York, have issued few new medallions since. In San Francisco and Boston, as in New York, taxi medallions trade for six-figure prices.

A taxi medallion system is a form of **quantity control**, or **quota**, by which the government regulates the quantity of a good that can be bought and sold rather than the price at which it is transacted. The total amount of the good that can be transacted under the quantity control is called the **quota limit**. Typically, the government limits quantity in a market by issuing **licenses;** only people with a license can legally supply the good. A taxi medallion is just such a license. The government of New York City limits the number of taxi rides that can be sold by limiting the number of taxis to only those who hold medallions. There are many other cases of quantity controls, ranging from limits on how much foreign currency (for instance, British pounds or Mexican pesos) people are allowed to buy to the quantity of clams New Jersey fishing boats are allowed to catch. Notice, by the way, that although there are price controls on both sides of the equilibrium price—price ceilings and price floors—in the real world, quantity controls always set an upper, not a lower, limit on quantities. After all, nobody can be forced to buy or sell more than they want to!

Some of these attempts to control quantities are undertaken for good economic reasons, some for bad ones. In many cases, as we will see, quantity controls introduced to address a temporary problem become politically hard to remove later because the beneficiaries don't want them abolished, even after the original reason for their existence is long gone. But whatever the reasons for such controls, they have certain predictable—and usually undesirable—economic consequences.

> A **quantity control**, or **quota**, is an upper limit on the quantity of some good that can be bought or sold. The total amount of the good that can be legally transacted is the **quota limit**.
>
> A **license** gives its owner the right to supply a good.

The Anatomy of Quantity Controls

To understand why a New York taxi medallion is worth so much money, we consider a simplified version of the market for taxi rides, shown in Figure 4-5 on page 96. Just as we assumed in the analysis of rent controls that all apartments are the same, we now suppose that all taxi rides are the same—ignoring the real-world complication that some taxi rides are longer, and thus more expensive, than others. The table in the figure shows supply and demand schedules. The equilibrium—indicated by point E in the figure and by the shaded entries in the table—is a fare of $5 per ride, with 10 million rides taken per year. (You'll see in a minute why we present the equilibrium this way.)

The New York medallion system limits the number of taxis, but each taxi driver can offer as many rides as he or she can manage. (Now you know why New York taxi drivers are so aggressive!) To simplify our analysis, however, we will assume that a medallion system limits the number of taxi rides that can legally be given to 8 million per year.

Until now, we have derived the demand curve by answering questions of the form: "How many taxi rides will passengers want to take if the price is $5 per ride?" But it is possible to reverse the question and ask instead: "At what price will consumers want to buy 10 million rides per year?" The price at which consumers want to buy a given quantity—in this case, 10 million rides at $5 per ride—is the **demand price** of that

> The **demand price** of a given quantity is the price at which consumers will demand that quantity.

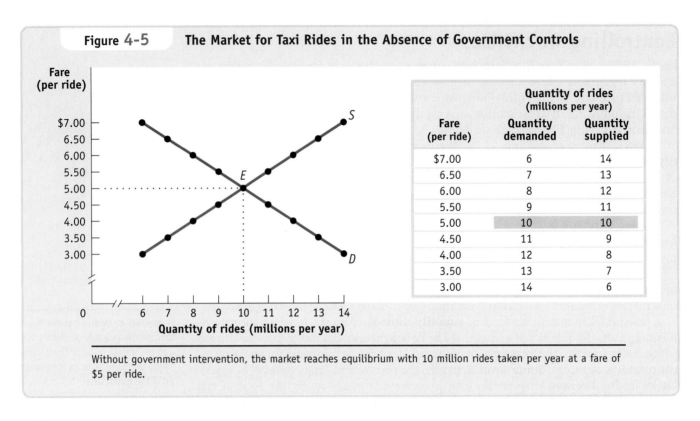

Figure 4-5 **The Market for Taxi Rides in the Absence of Government Controls**

Fare (per ride)	Quantity of rides (millions per year)	
	Quantity demanded	Quantity supplied
$7.00	6	14
6.50	7	13
6.00	8	12
5.50	9	11
5.00	10	10
4.50	11	9
4.00	12	8
3.50	13	7
3.00	14	6

Without government intervention, the market reaches equilibrium with 10 million rides taken per year at a fare of $5 per ride.

quantity. You can see from the demand schedule in Figure 4-5 that the demand price of 6 million rides is $7, the demand price of 7 million rides is $6.50, and so on.

Similarly, the supply curve represents the answer to questions of the form: "How many taxi rides would taxi drivers supply at a price of $5 each?" But we can also reverse this question to ask: "At what price will suppliers be willing to supply 10 million rides per year?" The price at which suppliers will supply a given quantity—in this case, 10 million rides at $5 per ride—is the **supply price** of that quantity. We can see from the supply schedule in Figure 4-5 that the supply price of 6 million rides is $3, the supply price of 7 million rides is $3.50, and so on.

> The **supply price** of a given quantity is the price at which producers will supply that quantity.

Now we are ready to analyze a quota. We have assumed that the city government limits the quantity of taxi rides to 8 million per year. Medallions, each of which carries the right to provide a certain number of taxi rides per year, are made available to selected people in such a way that a total of 8 million rides will be provided. Medallion holders may then either drive their own taxis or rent their medallions to others for a fee.

Figure 4-6 shows the resulting market for taxi rides, with the line at 8 million rides per year representing the quota limit. Because the quantity of rides is limited to 8 million, consumers must be at point *A* on the demand curve, corresponding to the shaded entry in the demand schedule: the demand price of 8 million rides is $6. Meanwhile, taxi drivers must be at point *B* on the supply curve, corresponding to the shaded entry in the supply schedule: the supply price of 8 million rides is $4.

But how can the price received by taxi drivers be $4 when the price paid by taxi riders is $6? The answer is that in addition to the market in taxi rides, there will also be a market in medallions. Medallion-holders may not always want to drive their taxis: they may be ill or on vacation. So those who do not want to drive their own taxis will sell the right to use the medallion to someone else. So we need to consider two sets of transactions here, and hence two prices: (1) the transactions in taxi rides and the price at which these will occur, and (2) the transactions in medallions and the price at which these will occur. It turns out that since we are looking at two markets, the $4 and $6 prices will both be right.

To see how this all works, consider two imaginary New York taxi drivers, Sunil and Harriet. Sunil has a medallion but can't use it because he's recovering from a severely sprained wrist. So he's looking to rent his medallion out to someone else. Harriet

Figure 4-6	Effect of a Quota on the Market for Taxi Rides

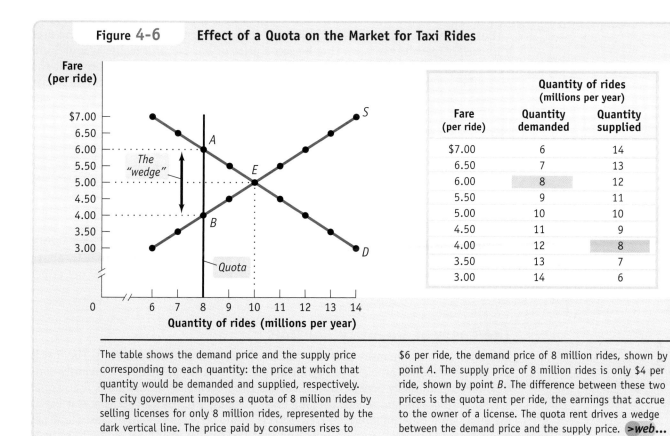

Fare (per ride)	Quantity of rides (millions per year)	
	Quantity demanded	Quantity supplied
$7.00	6	14
6.50	7	13
6.00	8	12
5.50	9	11
5.00	10	10
4.50	11	9
4.00	12	8
3.50	13	7
3.00	14	6

The table shows the demand price and the supply price corresponding to each quantity: the price at which that quantity would be demanded and supplied, respectively. The city government imposes a quota of 8 million rides by selling licenses for only 8 million rides, represented by the dark vertical line. The price paid by consumers rises to $6 per ride, the demand price of 8 million rides, shown by point A. The supply price of 8 million rides is only $4 per ride, shown by point B. The difference between these two prices is the quota rent per ride, the earnings that accrue to the owner of a license. The quota rent drives a wedge between the demand price and the supply price. **>web...**

doesn't have a medallion but would like to rent one. Furthermore, at any point in time there are many other people like Harriet who would like to rent a medallion as well as many others like Sunil who have a medallion to rent. Suppose Sunil agrees to rent his medallion to Harriet. To make things simple, assume that any driver can give only one ride per day and that Sunil is renting his medallion to Harriet for one day. What rental price will they agree on?

To answer this question, we need to look at the transactions from the viewpoints of both drivers. Once she has the medallion, Harriet knows she can make $6 per day—the demand price of a ride under the quota. And she is willing to rent the medallion only if she makes at least $4 per day—the supply price of a ride under the quota. So Sunil cannot demand a rent of more than $2—the difference between $6 and $4. And if Harriet offered Sunil less than $2—say, $1.50—there would be other eager drivers willing to offer him more, up to $2. Hence, in order to get the medallion, Harriet must offer Sunil at least $2. Therefore, since the rent can be no more than $2 and no less than $2, it must be exactly $2.

It is no coincidence that $2 is exactly the difference between $6, the demand price of 8 million rides, and $4, the supply price of 8 million rides. In every case in which the supply of a good is legally restricted, there is a **wedge** between the demand price of the quantity transacted and the supply price of the quantity transacted. This wedge, illustrated by the double-headed arrow in Figure 4-6, has a special name: the **quota rent**. It is the earnings that accrue to the license-holder from ownership of a valuable commodity, the license. In the case of Sunil and Harriet, the quota rent of $2 goes to Sunil because he owns the license, and the remaining $4 from the total fare of $6 goes to Harriet.

So Figure 4-6 also illustrates the quota rent in the market for New York taxi rides. The quota limits the quantity of rides to 8 million per year, a quantity at which the demand price of $6 exceeds the supply price of $4. The wedge between these two prices, $2, is the quota rent that results from the restrictions placed on the quantity of taxi rides in this market.

A quantity control, or quota, drives a **wedge** between the demand price and the supply price of a good; that is, the price paid by buyers ends up being higher than that received by sellers. The difference between the demand and supply price at the quota limit is the **quota rent**, the earnings that accrue to the license-holder from ownership of the right to sell the good. It is equal to the market price of the license when the licenses are traded.

But wait a second. What if Sunil doesn't rent out his medallion? What if he uses it himself? Doesn't this mean that he gets a price of $6? No, not really. Even if Sunil doesn't rent out his medallion, he could have rented it out, which means that the medallion has an *opportunity cost* of $2: if Sunil decides to drive his own taxi rather than renting it to Harriet, the $2 represents his opportunity cost of not renting out his medallion. That is, the $2 quota rent is now the rental income he forgoes by driving his own taxi. In effect, Sunil is in two businesses—the taxi-driving business and the medallion-renting business. He makes $4 per ride from driving his taxi and $2 per ride from renting out his medallion. It doesn't make any difference that in this particular case he has rented his medallion to himself! So regardless of whether the medallion owner uses the medallion himself or herself, or rents it to others, it is a valuable asset. And this is represented in the going price for a New York City taxi medallion: in 2004, it was around $250,000.

Notice, by the way, that quotas—like price ceilings and price floors—don't always have a real effect. If the quota were set at 12 million rides—that is, above the equilibrium quantity in an unregulated market—it would have no effect because it would not be binding.

The Costs of Quantity Controls

Like price controls, quantity controls can have some undesirable side effects. The first is the by-now-familiar problem of *inefficiency* due to missed opportunities: quantity controls prevent mutually beneficial transactions from occurring, transactions that would benefit both buyers and sellers. Looking back at Figure 4-6, you can see that starting at the quota limit of 8 million rides, New Yorkers would be willing to pay at least $5.50 per ride for an additional 1 million rides and that taxi drivers would be willing to provide those rides as long as they got at least $4.50 per ride. These are rides that would have taken place if there were no quota limit. The same is true for the next 1 million rides: New Yorkers would be willing to pay at least $5 per ride when the quantity of rides is increased from 9 to 10 million, and taxi drivers would be willing to provide those rides as long as they got at least $5 per ride. Again, these rides would have occurred without the quota limit. Only when the market has reached the free-market equilibrium quantity of 10 million rides are there no "missed-opportunity rides"—the quota limit of 8 million rides has caused 2 million "missed-opportunity rides." Generally, *as long as the demand price of a given quantity exceeds the supply price, there is a missed opportunity.* A buyer would be willing to buy the good at a price that the seller would be willing to accept, but such a transaction does not occur because it is forbidden by the quota.

And because there are transactions that people would like to make but are not allowed to, quantity controls generate an incentive to evade them or even to break the law. New York's taxi industry again provides clear examples. Taxi regulation applies only to those drivers who are hailed by passengers on the street. A car service that makes prearranged pickups does not need a medallion. As a result, such hired cars provide much of the service that might otherwise be provided by taxis, as in other cities. In addition, there are substantial numbers of unlicensed cabs that simply defy the law by picking up passengers without a medallion. Because these cabs are illegal, their drivers are completely unregulated, and they generate a disproportionately large share of traffic accidents in New York.

In fact, in 2004 the hardships caused by the limited number of New York taxis led city leaders to authorize an increase in the number of licensed taxis from 12,187 to a little over 13,000 by 2007—a move that certainly cheered New York riders. But those who already owned medallions were less happy with the increase; they understood that the nearly 900 new taxis would reduce or eliminate the shortage of taxis. As a result, taxi drivers might find their revenues decline as they would no longer always be assured of finding willing customers. And, in turn, the value of a medallion would fall. So to placate the medallion owners, city officials also agreed in 2004 to raise fares by 25 percent, a move that slightly diminished the newfound cheer of New York riders.

In sum, quantity controls typically create the following undesirable side effects:

- Inefficiencies, or missed opportunities, in the form of mutually beneficial transactions that don't occur
- Incentives for illegal activities

economics in action

The Clams of New Jersey

Forget the refineries along the Jersey Turnpike; one industry that New Jersey *really* dominates is clam fishing. The Garden State supplies 80 percent of the world's surf clams, whose tongues are used in fried-clam dinners, and 40 percent of the quahogs, which are used to make clam chowder.

In the 1980s, however, excessive fishing threatened to wipe out New Jersey's clam beds. To save the resource, the U.S. government introduced a clam quota, which sets an overall limit on the number of bushels of clams that may be caught and allocates licenses to owners of fishing boats based on their historical catches.

Notice, by the way, that this is an example of a quota that is probably justified by broader economic and environmental considerations—unlike the New York taxicab quota, which has long since lost any economic rationale. Still, whatever its rationale, the New Jersey clam quota works the same way as any other quota.

Once the quota system was established, many boat owners stopped fishing for clams. They realized that rather than operate a boat part time, it was more profitable to sell or rent their licenses to someone else, who could then assemble enough licenses to operate a boat full time. Today, there are about 50 boats fishing for clams; the license required to operate one is worth more than the boat itself. ■

>>CHECK YOUR UNDERSTANDING 4-3

1. Suppose that the supply and demand for taxi rides is given by Figure 4-5 but the quota is set at 6 million rides instead of 8 million. Find the following and indicate them on Figure 4-5.
   a. The price of a ride
   b. The quota rent
   c. Suppose the quota limit on taxi rides is increased to 9 million. What happens to the quota rent?
2. Assume that the quota limit is 8 million rides. Suppose demand decreases due to a decline in tourism. What is the smallest parallel leftward shift in demand that would result in the quota no longer having an effect on the market? Illustrate your answer using Figure 4-5.

Solutions appear at back of book.

A Surprise Parallel: Taxes

To provide the services we want, from national defense to public parks, governments must collect taxes. But taxes impose costs on the economy. Among the most important roles of economics is tax analysis: figuring out the economic costs of taxation, determining who bears those costs, and suggesting ways to change the tax system that will reduce the costs it imposes. It turns out that the same analysis we have just used to understand quotas can be used, with hardly any modification, to make a preliminary analysis of taxes, too.

Why Is a Tax Like a Quota?

Suppose that the supply and demand curves for New York taxis were exactly as shown in Figure 4-5. This means that in the absence of government action, the equilibrium price of a taxi ride will be $5 and 10 million rides will be bought and sold.

Figure 4-7

Effect of an Excise Tax Levied on Sales of Taxi Rides

S_1 is the supply curve before the tax. After the city requires drivers to pay a tax of $2 for every ride they give, the supply curve shifts upward by $2, to the new supply curve S_2. This means that the price drivers receive net of tax is $4, represented by point B on the old supply curve S_1. And the price paid by riders is $6, represented by point A on the new supply curve S_2. The tax drives a wedge between the demand price, $6, and the original supply price, $4.

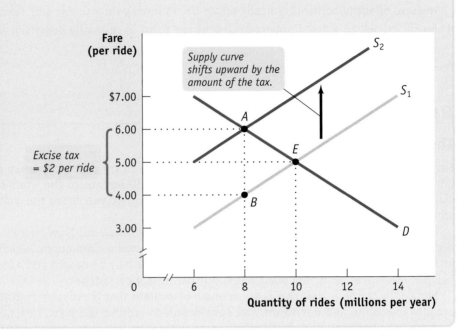

An **excise tax** is a tax on sales of a good or service.

Now suppose that instead of imposing a quota on the quantity of rides, the city imposes an **excise tax**—a tax on sales. Specifically, it charges taxi drivers $2 for each ride they provide. What is the effect of the tax?

From the point of view of a taxi driver, the tax means that he or she doesn't get to keep all of the fare: if a passenger pays $5, $2 is collected as a tax, so the driver gets only $3. For any given quantity of rides supplied, the *post-tax supply price* is higher than the pre-tax supply price. For example, drivers will now require a price of $6 to supply as many rides as they would have been willing to supply at a price of $4 in the absence of the $2 tax.

So the tax on sales shifts the supply curve upward, by the amount of the tax. This is shown in Figure 4-7, where S_1 is the supply curve before the tax is imposed and S_2 is the supply curve after the tax is imposed. The market equilibrium moves from E, where the price is $5 per ride and 10 million rides are bought and sold, to A, where the price is $6 per ride and 8 million rides are bought and sold. A is, of course, on both the demand curve D and the new supply curve S_2.

But how do we know that 8 million rides will be supplied at a price of $6? Because the price *net of the tax* is $4 and the pre-tax supply price of 8 million rides is $4, as shown by point B in Figure 4-7.

Does all this look familiar? It should. The equilibrium with a $2 tax on rides, which reduces the quantity bought and sold to 8 million rides, looks just like the equilibrium with a quota of 8 million rides, which leads to a quota rent of $2 per ride. Just like a quota, the tax *drives a wedge* between the demand price and the original, pre-tax supply price.

The only difference is that instead of paying a $2 rent to the owner of a license, drivers pay a $2 tax to the city. In fact, there is a way to make an excise tax and a quota completely equivalent. Imagine that instead of issuing a limited number of licenses, the city simply sold licenses at $2 each. This $2 license fee would, for all practical purposes, be a $2 excise tax.

Finally, imagine that instead of selling licenses at a fixed price, the city were to issue 8 million licenses and auction them off—that is, sell them for whatever price the, um, traffic will bear. What would be the price of a license? Surely it would be $2—the quota rent. And so in this case the quota rent would act just like an excise tax.

Who Pays an Excise Tax?

We have just imagined a tax that must be paid by the *sellers* of a good. But what would happen if the tax were instead paid by the *buyers*—say, if you had to pay a special $2 tax to ride in a taxicab?

Figure 4-8

Effect of an Excise Tax Levied on Purchases of Taxi Rides

D_1 is the demand curve before the tax. After the city requires riders to pay the $2 tax per ride, the demand curve shifts down by $2 to the new demand curve D_2. Drivers again receive, net of tax, $4, represented by point B, while riders again pay a total price of $6, represented by point A. The incidence of the tax is exactly the same as in Figure 4-7. This shows that who officially pays a tax is irrelevant when answering the question of who bears the burden of the tax.

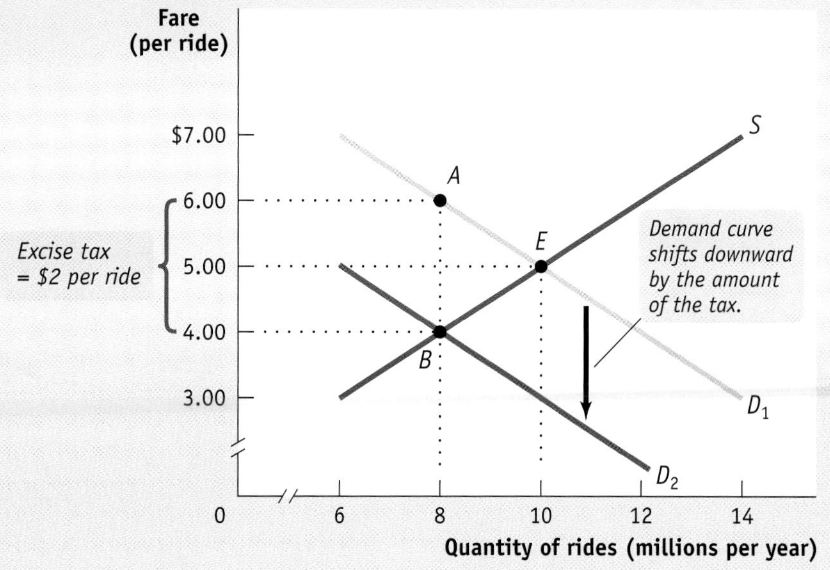

The answer is shown in Figure 4-8. If a taxi rider must pay a $2 tax on each ride, then the price riders pay must be $2 less in order for the quantity of taxi rides demanded post-tax to be the same quantity as that demanded pre-tax. So the demand curve shifts *downward*, from D_1 to D_2, by the amount of the tax. This shifts the equilibrium from E to B, where the market price is $4 per ride and 8 million rides are bought and sold. In this case, $4 is the supply price of 8 million rides and $6 is the demand price—but in effect riders do pay $6, when you include the tax. So it is just as if riders were on their original demand curve at point A.

If you compare Figures 4-7 and 4-8, you will immediately notice that they show the same price effect. In each case, buyers pay an effective price of $6, sellers receive an effective price of $4, and 8 million rides are bought and sold. *It doesn't seem to make any difference who officially pays the tax.*

This insight is a general one in analyzing taxes: the **incidence** of a tax—who really bears the burden of the tax—is often not a question you can answer by asking who actually writes the check to the government. In this particular case, a $2 tax on taxi rides is reflected in a $1 increase in the price paid by buyers and a $1 decrease in the price received by sellers; so the incidence of the tax is actually evenly split between buyers and sellers. This incidence is the same regardless of whether the check to the city government is made out by buyers or by sellers.

The incidence of an excise tax isn't always split evenly between buyers and sellers as in this example. Depending on the shapes of supply and demand curves, the incidence of an excise tax may be divided differently.

The **incidence** of a tax is a measure of who really pays it.

The Revenue from an Excise Tax

Although both buyers and sellers lose from an excise tax, the government does collect revenue—which is the whole point of the tax. How much revenue does the government collect? The revenue is equal to the area of the shaded rectangle in Figure 4-9 on the next page.

To see why this is the revenue collected by a $2 tax on taxi rides, notice that the *height* of the rectangle is $2. This is the amount of the tax per ride; it is also, as we have seen, the size of the wedge that the tax drives between the supply price and the demand price. Meanwhile, the *width* of the rectangle is 8 million rides, which is the equilibrium quantity of rides given that $2 tax.

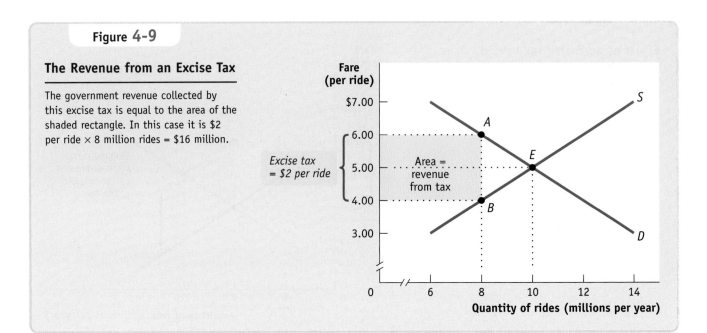

Figure 4-9

The Revenue from an Excise Tax

The government revenue collected by this excise tax is equal to the area of the shaded rectangle. In this case it is $2 per ride × 8 million rides = $16 million.

The revenue collected by the tax is

Revenue = $2 per ride × 8 million rides = $16 million

But the area of the rectangle is

Area = height × width = $2 per ride × 8 million rides = $16 million

This is a general principle: *The revenue collected by an excise tax is equal to the area of the rectangle whose height is the wedge that the tax drives between the supply and demand curves, and whose width is the quantity bought and sold under the tax.*

The Costs of Taxation

What is the cost of a tax? You might be inclined to answer that it is the money taxpayers pay to the government. But suppose the government used that money to provide services everyone wants or simply handed the money back to taxpayers. Would we then say that the tax didn't cost anything?

No—because a tax, like a quota, prevents mutually beneficial transactions from occurring. Consider Figure 4-9 once more. With a $2 tax on taxi rides, riders pay $6 per ride but drivers receive only $4. There are therefore some potential riders who would be willing to pay only, say, $5.50 per ride; and there are some drivers who would be willing to charge them, say, $4.50. If those drivers and riders could be brought together, this would be a mutually beneficial transaction. But such a deal would be illegal, because the $2 tax would not have been paid.

More broadly, we know that there are 2 million potential taxi rides that would have been taken in the absence of the tax, to the mutual benefit of riders and drivers, that do not take place because of that tax.

So an excise tax imposes additional costs, over and above the money actually paid in taxes, in the form of inefficiency, which occurs because the tax discourages mutually beneficial transactions. This is the **excess burden,** or **deadweight loss,** from a tax. And all real-world taxes do impose some excess burden, although badly designed taxes impose bigger excess burdens than well-thought-out ones.

Economists sometimes say that the real cost of a tax is not the taxes that people pay but the taxes that they *don't* pay. What they mean is that people change their

The **excess burden,** or **deadweight loss,** from a tax is the extra cost in the form of inefficiency that results because the tax discourages mutually beneficial transactions.

IF SELLING CIGARETTES IS A CRIME, ONLY CRIMINALS WILL SELL CIGARETTES

Cigarettes have long been subject to state excise taxes. As the antismoking movement has gained political power, many states and local governments have increased those taxes. Officials see high taxes on cigarettes as a way of doing well by doing good—raising more revenue while discouraging a bad habit. In 2002, increases at both the state and local levels raised the tax on a pack of cigarettes sold in New York City from $1.19 to $3.

But tobacco-growing states have not followed the trend. In Virginia, for example, the cigarette tax is only 2.5 cents per pack. And this divergence has created an opportunity for those who don't mind breaking the law: there is large-scale smuggling of cigarettes from low-tax tobacco-growing states to high-tax locations like New York.

Authorities believe that interstate cigarette smuggling, like alcohol smuggling during Prohibition, has largely been taken over by organized crime. But there is still room for smaller players: in July 2000, the FBI broke up a group, based in Charlotte, North Carolina, that had been funneling its profits to a foreign group that the U.S. government classifies as a terrorist organization.

behavior in order to avoid taxes—for example, by walking instead of taking a taxi—and in so doing miss opportunities for mutual benefit.

One final point: like all of the other government policies analyzed in this chapter, taxes create incentives for illegal activity. For Inquiring Minds above explains how excise taxes on cigarettes have given rise to a substantial smuggling business. And, of course, even seemingly respectable people have been known to be a bit creative with their income taxes.

economics in action

Who Pays the FICA?

Anyone who works for an employer receives a paycheck that itemizes not only the money received but also the money deducted for various taxes. One of the big items for most people is *FICA*, which stands for Federal Insurance Contributions Act. This is the money taken out of your paycheck for the Social Security and Medicare systems, which provide income and medical care to retired and disabled Americans.

As of the time of writing, most American workers paid 7.65 percent of their earnings in FICA. But this is literally only the half of it: employers are required to pay an equal amount.

So how should we think about FICA? Well, it's like an excise tax—a tax on the sale and purchase of labor. Half of it is a tax on the sellers—that is, workers. The other half is a tax on the buyers—that is, employers.

But we already know that the incidence of a tax does not really depend on who actually makes out the check. So the fact that employers nominally pay half the FICA tells us nothing about who really bears the burden.

In fact, most economists believe that the real effect of the FICA is, to a very good approximation, to reduce wages by the full amount of the combined employee and employer payments. That is, you not only pay your own share; your employer's share is reflected in a lower wage, so that you really pay that share, too. Your employer, though she pays the tax, is fully compensated by the lower wage rate. So workers, not employers, bear the burden of both halves of the tax.

The reason economists think that workers, not employers, really pay the FICA is that the supply of labor (the number of workers willing to take jobs) is much less responsive to the wage rate than is the demand for labor (the number of jobs employers are willing to offer). According to this reasoning, since workers are relatively unresponsive to decreases in the wage rate, employers can easily pass the burden of the tax on to them through lower wages. ∎

< < < < < < < < < < < < < < < < <

>> CHECK YOUR UNDERSTANDING 4-4

1. Use Figure 4-3 to answer the following questions.
   a. What amount of excise tax generates the same level of inefficiency as a quota of 9 million pounds of butter?
   b. What quota level generates the same level of inefficiency as an excise tax of $0.60 per pound of butter?
   c. In part a, find how the burden of an excise tax is split between buyers and sellers. That is, explain how much of the tax is paid by buyers and how much by sellers in each case.

Solutions appear at back of book.

• A LOOK AHEAD •

In the last two chapters we have gotten a first taste of how economic models help us understand the real world. As we've seen, supply and demand—a simple model of how competitive markets work—can be used to understand and predict the effects of everything from bad weather to misconceived government policies.

In the chapters to come, we'll see how models—including supply and demand, but also going beyond it—can shed light on a wide variety of economic phenomena and issues.

SUMMARY

1. Governments often intervene in markets in attempts to "defy" supply and demand. Interventions can take the form of **price controls** or **quantity controls**. But they generate predictable and undesirable side effects, consisting of various forms of inefficiency and illegal activity.

2. A **price ceiling**, a maximum market price below the equilibrium price, benefits successful buyers but creates persistent shortages: Because the price is maintained below the equilibrium price, the quantity demanded is increased and the quantity supplied is decreased compared to the equilibrium quantity. This leads to predictable problems: **inefficiencies** in the form of **inefficient allocation to consumers**, **wasted resources**, and **inefficiently low quality**. It also encourages illegal activity as people turn to **black markets** to get the good. Because of these problems, price ceilings have generally lost favor as an economic policy tool. But some governments continue to impose them either because they don't understand the effects or because the price ceilings benefit some influential group.

3. A **price floor**, a minimum market price above the equilibrium price, benefits successful sellers but creates persistent surplus: because the price is maintained above the equilibrium price, the quantity demanded is decreased and the quantity supplied is increased compared to the equilibrium quantity. This leads to predictable problems: inefficiencies in the form of **inefficient allocation of sales among sellers**, **wasted resources**, and **inefficiently high quality**. It also encourages illegal activity and black markets. The most well known kind of price floor is the **minimum wage**, but price floors are also commonly applied to agricultural products.

4. **Quantity controls**, or **quotas**, limit the quantity of a good that can be bought or sold. The amount allowed for sale is the **quota limit**. The government issues **licenses** to individuals, the right to sell a given quantity of the good. The owner of a license earns a **quota rent**, earnings that accrue from ownership of the right to sell the good. It is equal to the difference between the **demand price** at the quota limit, what consumers are willing to pay for that amount, and the **supply price** at the quota limit, what suppliers are willing to accept for that amount. Economists say that a quota drives a **wedge** between the demand price and the supply price; this wedge is equal to the quota rent. Quantity controls generate inefficiency in the form of mutually beneficial transactions that don't occur in addition to encouraging illegal activity.

5. Excise taxes—taxes on the purchase or sale of a good—have effects similar to quotas. They raise the price paid by buyers and reduce the price received by sellers, driving a wedge between the two. The **incidence** of the tax—the division of higher prices to consumers and lower prices to sellers—does not depend on who officially pays the tax. Excise taxes cause inefficiency—called **excess burden** or **deadweight loss**—because they prevent some mutually beneficial transactions. They also encourage illegal activity in attempts to avoid the tax.

KEY TERMS

Price controls, p. 84
Price ceiling, p. 84
Price floor, p. 84
Inefficient, p. 86
Inefficient allocation to consumers, p. 87
Wasted resources, p. 87
Inefficiently low quality, p. 87
Black markets, p. 88

Minimum wage, p. 90
Inefficient allocation of sales among sellers, p. 92
Inefficiently high quality, p. 93
Quantity control, p. 95
Quota, p. 95
Quota limit, p. 95
License, p. 95

Demand price, p. 95
Supply price, p. 96
Wedge, p. 97
Quota rent, p. 97
Excise tax, p. 100
Incidence, p. 101
Excess burden, p. 102
Deadweight loss, p. 102

PROBLEMS

1. Suppose it is decided that rent control in New York City will be abolished and that market rents will now prevail. Assume that all rental units are identical and are therefore offered at the same rent. To address the plight of residents who may be unable to pay the market rent, an income supplement will be paid to all low-income households equal to the difference between the old controlled rent and the new market rent.

  a. Use a diagram to show the effect on the rental market of the elimination of rent control. What will happen to the quality and quantity of rental housing supplied?

  b. Now use a second diagram to show the additional effect of the income-supplement policy on the market. What effect does it have on the market rent and quantity of rental housing supplied in comparison to your answers to part a?

  c. Are tenants better or worse off as a result of these policies? Are landlords better or worse off?

  d. From a political standpoint, why do you think cities have been more likely to resort to rent control rather than a policy of income supplements to help low-income people pay for housing?

2. In order to ingratiate himself with voters, the mayor of Gotham City decides to lower the price of taxi rides. Assume, for simplicity, that all taxi rides are the same distance and therefore cost the same. The accompanying table shows the demand and supply schedules for taxi rides.

Fare (per ride)	Quantity of rides (millions per year)	
	Quantity demanded	Quantity supplied
$7.00	10	12
6.50	11	11
6.00	12	10
5.50	13	9
5.00	14	8
4.50	15	7

  a. Assume that there are no restrictions on the number of taxi rides that can be supplied in the city (i.e., there is no medallion system). Find the equilibrium price and quantity.

  b. Suppose that the mayor sets a price ceiling at $5.50. How large is the shortage of rides? Illustrate with a diagram. Who loses and who benefits from this policy?

  c. Suppose that the stock market crashes and, as a result, people in Gotham City are poorer. This reduces the quantity of taxi rides demanded by 6 million rides per year at any given price. What effect will the mayor's new policy have now? Illustrate with a diagram.

  d. Suppose that the stock market rises and the demand for taxi rides returns to normal (that is, returns to the demand schedule given in the table). The mayor now decides to ingratiate himself with taxi drivers. He announces a policy in which operating licenses are given to existing taxi drivers; the number of licenses is restricted such that only 10 million rides per year can be given. Illustrate the effect of this policy on the market, and indicate the resulting price and quantity transacted. What is the quota rent per ride?

3. In the late eighteenth century, the price of bread in New York City was controlled, set at a predetermined price above the market price.

   a. Draw a diagram showing the effect of the policy. Did the policy act as a price ceiling or a price floor?

   b. What kinds of inefficiencies were likely to have arisen when the controlled price of bread was above the market price? Explain in detail.

   One year during this period, a poor wheat harvest caused a leftward shift in the supply of bread and therefore an increase in its market price. New York bakers found that the controlled price of bread in New York was below the market price.

   c. Draw a diagram showing the effect of the price control on the market for bread during this one-year period. Did the policy act as a price ceiling or a price floor?

   d. What kinds of inefficiencies do you think occurred during this period? Explain in detail.

4. The accompanying table shows the demand and supply schedules for milk per year. The U.S. government decides that the incomes of dairy farmers should be maintained at a level that allows the traditional family dairy farm to survive. It therefore implements a price floor of $1 per pint by buying surplus milk until the market price is $1 per pint.

Price of milk (per pint)	Quantity of milk (millions of pints per year)	
	Quantity demanded	Quantity supplied
$1.20	550	850
1.10	600	800
1.00	650	750
0.90	700	700
0.80	750	650

   a. How much surplus milk will be produced as a result of this policy?

   b. What will be the cost to the government of this policy?

   c. Since milk is an important source of protein and calcium, the government decides to provide the surplus milk it purchases to elementary schools at a price of only $0.60 per pint. Assume that schools will buy any amount of milk available at this low price. But parents now reduce their purchases of milk at any price by 50 million pints per year because they know their children are getting milk at school. How much will the dairy program now cost the government?

   d. Give two examples of inefficiencies arising from wasted resources that are likely to result from this policy. What is the missed opportunity in each case?

5. As noted in the text, European governments tend to make greater use of price controls than does the American government. For example, the French government sets minimum starting yearly wages for new hires who have completed *le bac,* certification roughly equivalent to a high school diploma. The demand schedule for new hires with *le bac* and the supply schedule for similarly credentialed new job seekers are given in the accompanying table. The price here—given in euros, the currency used in France—is the same as the yearly wage.

Wage (per year)	Quantity demanded (new job offers per year)	Quantity supplied (new job seekers per year)
€45,000	200,000	325,000
40,000	220,000	320,000
35,000	250,000	310,000
30,000	290,000	290,000
25,000	370,000	200,000

   a. In the absence of government interference, what is the equilibrium wage and number of graduates hired per year? Illustrate with a diagram. Will there be anyone seeking a job at the equilibrium wage who is unable to find one— that is, will there be anyone who is involuntarily unemployed?

   b. Suppose the French government sets a minimum yearly wage of €35,000. Is there any involuntary unemployment at this wage? If so, how much? Illustrate with a diagram. What if the minimum wage is set at €40,000? Also illustrate with a diagram.

   c. Given your answer to part b and the information in the table, what do you think is the relationship between the level of involuntary unemployment and the level of the minimum wage? Who benefits from such a policy? Who loses? What is the missed opportunity here?

6. Until recently, the standard number of hours worked per week for a full-time job in France was 39 hours, just as in the United States. But in response to social unrest over high levels of involuntary unemployment, the French government instituted a 35-hour workweek—a worker could not work more than 35 hours per week even if both the worker and employer wanted it. The motivation behind this policy was that if current employees worked fewer hours, employers would be forced to hire more new workers. Assume that it is costly for employers to train new workers. French employers were greatly opposed to this policy and threatened to move their operations to neighboring countries that did not have such employment restrictions. Can you explain their attitude? Give an example of both an inefficiency and an illegal activity that are likely to arise from this policy.

7. For the last 70 years the U.S. government has used price supports to provide income assistance to American farmers. At times the government has used price floors, which it maintains by buying up the surplus farm products. At other times, it has used target prices, a policy by which the government gives the farmer an amount equal to the difference between the market price and the target price for each unit sold. Consider the market for corn depicted in the accompanying figure.

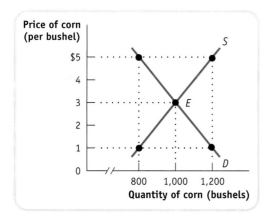

a. If the government sets a price floor of $5 per bushel, how many bushels of corn are produced? How many are purchased by consumers? By the government? How much does the program cost the government? How much revenue do corn farmers receive?

b. Suppose the government sets a target price of $5 per bushel for any quantity supplied up to 1,000 bushels. How many bushels of corn are purchased by consumers and at what price? By the government? How much does the program cost the government? How much revenue do corn farmers receive?

c. Which of these programs (in parts a and b) costs corn consumers more? Which program costs the government more? Explain.

d. What are the inefficiencies that arise in each of these cases (parts a and b)?

8. The waters off the North Atlantic coast were once teeming with fish. Now, due to overfishing by the commercial fishing industry, the stocks of fish are seriously depleted. In 1991, the National Marine Fishery Service of the U.S. government implemented a quota to allow fish stocks to recover. The quota limited the amount of swordfish caught per year by all U.S.-licensed fishing boats to 7 million pounds. As soon as the U.S. fishing fleet had met the quota limit, the swordfish catch was closed down for the rest of the year. The accompanying table gives the hypothetical demand and supply schedules for swordfish caught in the United States per year.

Price of swordfish (per pound)	Quantity of swordfish (millions of pounds per year)	
	Quantity demanded	Quantity supplied
$20	6	15
18	7	13
16	8	11
14	9	9
12	10	7

a. Use a diagram to show the effect of the quota on the market for swordfish in 1991.

b. How do you think fishermen will change how they fish in response to this policy?

c. Use your diagram from part a to show an excise tax that achieves the same reduction in the amount of pounds of swordfish caught as the quota. What is the amount of the tax per pound?

d. What kinds of activities do you think an excise tax will tempt people to engage in?

e. The excise tax is collected from the fishermen, who protest that they alone are bearing the burden of this policy. Why might this protest be misguided?

9. The U.S. government would like to help the American auto industry compete against foreign automakers that sell trucks in the United States. It can do this either by imposing a quota on the number of foreign trucks imported or by imposing an excise tax on each foreign truck sold in the United States. The hypothetical demand and supply schedules for imported trucks are given in the accompanying table.

Price of imported truck	Quantity of imported trucks (thousands)	
	Quantity demanded	Quantity supplied
$32,000	100	400
31,000	200	350
30,000	300	300
29,000	400	250
28,000	500	200
27,000	600	150

a. In the absence of government interference, what is the price of an imported truck? How many are sold in the United States? Illustrate with a diagram.

b. Suppose the government adopts a quota, allowing no more than 200,000 foreign trucks to be imported. What is the effect on the market for these trucks? Illustrate using your diagram from part a and explain.

c. Now suppose that, instead of a quota, the government imposes an excise tax of $3,000 per truck. Illustrate the effect of this excise tax in your diagram from part a. How many trucks will now be purchased and at what price? What will the foreign automaker receive per truck?

d. Calculate the government revenue raised by the excise tax in part c. Then illustrate it on your diagram from that part. Do you think the government, from a revenue standpoint, prefers an excise tax or a quota?

e. Explain how the government policy, whether it be a quota or an excise tax, benefits American automakers. Whom does it hurt? What is the missed opportunity here and how does it reflect inefficiency?

10. In Maine, you must have a license to harvest lobster commercially; these licenses are issued yearly. The state of Maine is concerned about the dwindling supplies of lobsters found off its coast. The state fishery department has decided to place a yearly quota of 80,000 pounds of lobsters harvested in all Maine waters. It has also decided to give licenses this year only to those fishermen who had licenses last year. The accompanying figure shows the demand and supply curves for Maine lobsters.

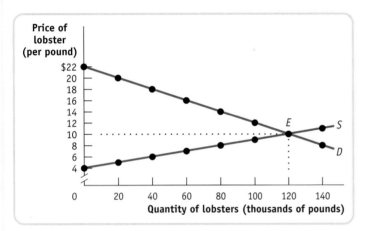

a. In the absence of government restrictions, what are the equilibrium price and quantity?

b. What is the *demand price* at which consumers wish to purchase 80,000 pounds of lobsters?

c. What is the *supply price* at which suppliers are willing to supply 80,000 pounds of lobsters?

d. What is the *quota rent* per pound of lobster when 80,000 pounds are sold?

e. Find an excise tax that achieves the same reduction in the harvest of lobsters. Show it on the figure. What is the government revenue collected from this tax?

f. Explain a transaction that benefits both buyer and seller but is prevented by the quota restriction. Explain a transaction that benefits both buyer and seller but is prevented by the excise tax.

11. In each of the following cases involving taxes, explain: (i) whether the incidence of the tax falls more heavily on consumers or producers, (ii) why government revenue raised from the tax is not a good indicator of the true cost of the tax, and (iii) what missed opportunity, or inefficiency, arises.

a. The government imposes an excise tax on the sale of all college textbooks. Before the tax was imposed, 1 million textbooks were sold every year at a price of $50. After the tax is imposed, 600,000 books are sold yearly; students pay $55 per book, $30 of which publishers receive.

b. The government imposes an excise tax on the sale of all airplane tickets. Before the tax was imposed, 3 million airline tickets were sold every year at a price of $500. After the tax is imposed, 1.5 million tickets are sold yearly; travelers pay $550 per ticket, $450 of which the airlines receive.

c. The government imposes an excise tax on the sale of all toothbrushes. Before the tax, 2 million toothbrushes were sold every year at a price of $1.50. After the tax is imposed, 800,000 toothbrushes are sold every year; consumers pay $2 per toothbrush, $1.25 of which producers receive.

>web... To continue your study and review of concepts in this chapter, please visit the Krugman/Wells website for quizzes, animated graph tutorials, web links to helpful resources, and more.

www.worthpublishers.com/krugmanwells

>> Consumer and Producer Surplus

MAKING GAINS BY THE BOOK

THERE IS A LIVELY MARKET IN SECOND-hand college textbooks. At the end of each term, some students who took a course decide that the money they can get by selling their used books is worth more to them than keeping the books. And some students who are taking the course next term prefer to buy a somewhat battered but inexpensive used textbook rather than pay the full price for a new one.

Textbook publishers and authors are not happy about these transactions, because they cut into sales of new books. But both the students who sell used books and those who buy them clearly benefit from the existence of the market. That is why many college bookstores facilitate their trade, buying used textbooks and selling them alongside the new books.

But can we put a number on what used textbook buyers and sellers gain from these transactions? Can we answer the question, "*How much* do the buyers and sellers of textbooks gain from the existence of the used-book market?"

Yes, we can. In this chapter we will see how to measure benefits, such as those to buyers of used textbooks, from being able to purchase a good—known as *consumer surplus*. And we will see that there is a corresponding measure, *producer surplus*, of the benefits sellers receive from being able to sell a good.

The concepts of consumer surplus and producer surplus are extremely useful for analyzing a wide variety of economic issues.

How much am I willing to pay for that used textbook?

They let us calculate how much benefit producers and consumers receive from the existence of a market. They also allow us to calculate how the welfare of consumers and producers is affected by changes in market

What you will learn in this chapter:

➤ The meaning of **consumer surplus** and its relationship to the demand curve

➤ The meaning of **producer surplus** and its relationship to the supply curve

➤ The meaning and importance of **total surplus** and how it can be used both to measure the gains from trade and to evaluate the efficiency of a market

➤ How to use changes in total surplus to measure the deadweight loss of taxes prices. Such calculations play a crucial role in evaluating many economic policies.

What information do we need to calculate consumer and producer surplus? The answer, surprisingly, is that all we need are the demand and supply curves for a good. That is, the supply and demand model isn't just a model of how a competitive market works—it's also a model of how much consumers and producers gain from participating in that market. So our first step will be to learn how consumer and producer surplus can be derived from the demand and supply curves. We will then see how these concepts can be applied to actual economic issues.

Consumer Surplus and the Demand Curve

The market in used textbooks is not a big business in terms of dollars and cents. But it is a convenient starting point for developing the concepts of consumer and producer surplus.

So let's look at the market for used textbooks, starting with the buyers. The key point, as we'll see in a minute, is that the demand curve is derived from their tastes or preferences—and that those same preferences also determine how much they gain from the opportunity to buy used books.

Willingness to Pay and the Demand Curve

A used book is not as good as a new book—it will be battered and coffee-stained, may include someone else's highlighting, and may not be completely up to date. How much this bothers you depends on your own preferences. Some potential buyers would prefer to buy the used book if it is only slightly cheaper than a new book, while others would buy the used book only if it is considerably cheaper. Let's define a potential buyer's **willingness to pay** as the maximum price at which he or she would buy a good, in this case a used textbook. An individual won't buy the book if it costs more than this amount but is eager to do so if it costs less. If the price is just equal to an individual's willingness to pay, he or she is indifferent between buying and not buying.

The table in Figure 5-1 shows five potential buyers of a used book that costs $100 new, listed in order of their willingness to pay. At one extreme is Aleisha, who will buy a second-hand book even if the price is as high as $59. Brad is less willing to have a used book and will buy one only if the price is $45 or less. Claudia is willing to pay only $35, Darren only $25. And Edwina, who really doesn't like the idea of a used book, will buy one only if it costs no more than $10.

How many of these five students will actually buy a used book? It depends on the price. If the price of a used book is $55, only Aleisha buys one; if the price is $40, Aleisha and Brad both buy used books, and so on. So the information in the table on willingness to pay also defines the *demand schedule* for used textbooks.

As we saw in Chapter 3, we can use this demand schedule to derive the market demand curve shown in Figure 5-1. Because we are considering only a small number of consumers, this curve doesn't look like the smooth demand curves of earlier chapters, where markets contained hundreds or thousands of consumers. This demand curve is step-shaped, with alternating horizontal and vertical segments. Each horizontal segment—each step—corresponds to one potential buyer's willingness to pay. However, we'll see shortly that for the analysis of consumer surplus it doesn't matter whether the demand curve is stepped, as in this figure, or whether there are many consumers, making the curve smooth.

A consumer's **willingness to pay** for a good is the maximum price at which he or she would buy that good.

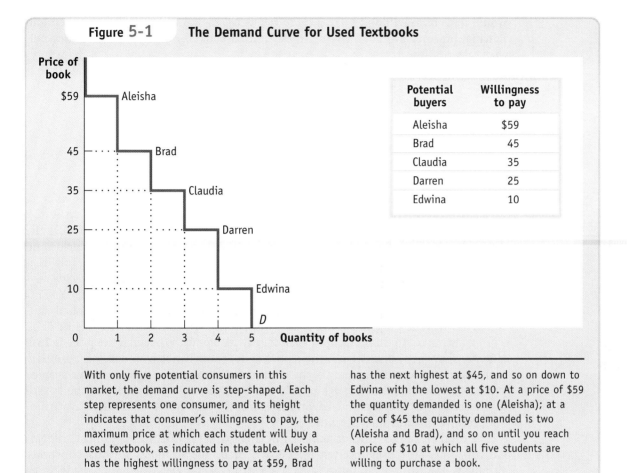

Figure 5-1   The Demand Curve for Used Textbooks

Potential buyers	Willingness to pay
Aleisha	$59
Brad	45
Claudia	35
Darren	25
Edwina	10

With only five potential consumers in this market, the demand curve is step-shaped. Each step represents one consumer, and its height indicates that consumer's willingness to pay, the maximum price at which each student will buy a used textbook, as indicated in the table. Aleisha has the highest willingness to pay at $59, Brad has the next highest at $45, and so on down to Edwina with the lowest at $10. At a price of $59 the quantity demanded is one (Aleisha); at a price of $45 the quantity demanded is two (Aleisha and Brad), and so on until you reach a price of $10 at which all five students are willing to purchase a book.

Willingness to Pay and Consumer Surplus

Suppose that the campus bookstore makes used textbooks available at a price of $30. In that case Aleisha, Brad, and Claudia will buy books. Do they gain from their purchases, and if so, how much?

The answer, shown in Table 5-1, is that each student who purchases a book does achieve a net gain but that the amount of the gain differs among students.

Aleisha would have been willing to pay $59, so her net gain is $59 − $30 = $29. Brad would have been willing to pay $45, so his net gain is $45 − $30 = $15. Claudia

TABLE 5-1

Consumer Surplus When the Price of a Used Textbook Is $30

Potential buyer	Willingness to pay	Price paid	Individual consumer surplus = willingness to pay − price paid
Aleisha	$59	$30	$29
Brad	45	30	15
Claudia	35	30	5
Darren	25	—	—
Edwina	10	—	—
		Total consumer surplus: $49	

would have been willing to pay $35, so her net gain is $35 − $30 = $5. Darren and Edwina, however, won't be willing to buy a used book at a price of $30, so they neither gain nor lose.

The net gain that a buyer achieves from the purchase of a good is called that buyer's **individual consumer surplus**. What we learn from this example is that every buyer of a good achieves some individual consumer surplus.

The sum of the individual consumer surpluses achieved by all the buyers of a good is known as the **total consumer surplus** achieved in the market. In Table 5-1, the total consumer surplus is the sum of the individual consumer surpluses achieved by Aleisha, Brad, and Claudia: $29 + $15 + $5 = $49.

Economists often use the term **consumer surplus** to refer to both individual and total consumer surplus. We will follow this practice; it will always be clear in context whether we are referring to the consumer surplus achieved by an individual or by all buyers.

Total consumer surplus can be represented graphically. Figure 5-2 reproduces the demand curve from Figure 5-1. Each step in that demand curve is one book wide and represents one consumer. For example, the height of Aleisha's step is $59, her willingness to pay. This step forms the top of a rectangle, with $30—the price she actually pays for a book—forming the bottom. The area of Aleisha's rectangle, ($59 − $30) × 1 = $29, is her consumer surplus from purchasing a book at $30. So the individual consumer surplus Aleisha gains is the *area of the dark blue rectangle* shown in Figure 5-2.

In addition to Aleisha, Brad and Claudia will also buy books when the price is $30. Like Aleisha, they benefit from their purchases, though not as much, because they each have a lower willingness to pay. Figure 5-2 also shows the consumer surplus gained by Brad and Claudia; again, this can be measured by the areas of the appropriate rectangles. Darren and Edwina, because they do not buy books at a price of $30, receive no consumer surplus.

The total consumer surplus achieved in this market is just the sum of the individual consumer surpluses received by Aleisha, Brad, and Claudia. So total consumer surplus is equal to the combined area of the three rectangles—the entire shaded area in Figure 5-2. Another way to say this is that total consumer surplus is equal to the area that is under the demand curve but above the price.

Individual consumer surplus is the net gain to an individual buyer from the purchase of a good. It is equal to the difference between the buyer's willingness to pay and the price paid.

Total consumer surplus is the sum of the individual consumer surpluses of all the buyers of a good.

The term **consumer surplus** is often used to refer to both individual and to total consumer surplus.

Figure 5-2

Consumer Surplus in the Used-Textbook Market

At a price of $30, Aleisha, Brad, and Claudia each buy a book but Darren and Edwina do not. Aleisha, Brad, and Claudia get individual consumer surpluses equal to the difference between their willingness to pay and the price, illustrated by the areas of the shaded rectangles. Both Darren and Edwina have a willingness to pay less than $30, so they are unwilling to buy a book in this market; they receive zero consumer surplus. The total consumer surplus is given by the entire shaded area—the sum of the individual consumer surpluses of Aleisha, Brad, and Claudia—equal to $29 + $15 + $5 = $49.

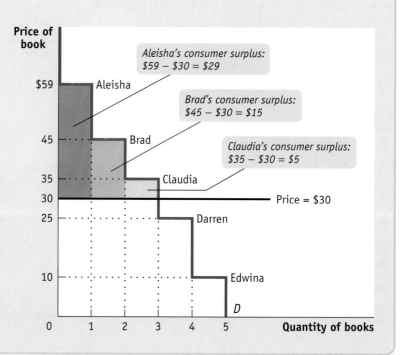

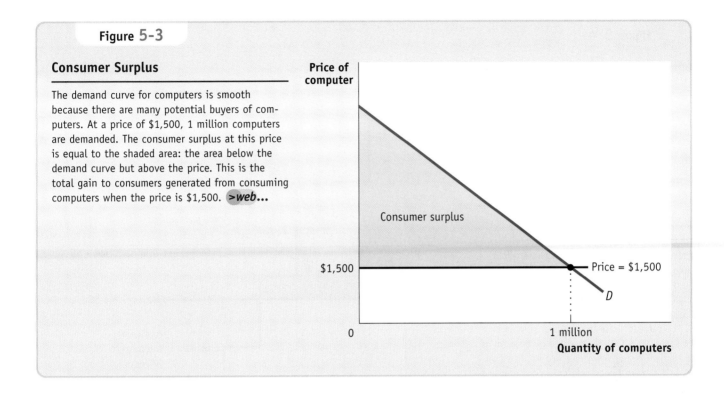

Figure 5-3

Consumer Surplus

The demand curve for computers is smooth because there are many potential buyers of computers. At a price of $1,500, 1 million computers are demanded. The consumer surplus at this price is equal to the shaded area: the area below the demand curve but above the price. This is the total gain to consumers generated from consuming computers when the price is $1,500. **>web...**

This illustrates the following general principle: *The total consumer surplus generated by purchases of a good at a given price is equal to the area below the demand curve but above that price.* The same principle applies regardless of the number of consumers.

When we consider large markets, this graphical representation becomes extremely helpful. Consider, for example, the sales of personal computers to millions of potential buyers. Each potential buyer has a maximum price that he or she is willing to pay. With so many potential buyers, the demand curve will be smooth, like the one shown in Figure 5-3.

Suppose that at a price of $1,500, a total of 1 million computers are purchased. How much do consumers gain from being able to buy those 1 million computers? We could answer that question by calculating the consumer surplus of each individual buyer and then adding these numbers up to arrive at a total. But it is much easier just to look at Figure 5-3 and use the fact that the total consumer surplus is equal to the shaded area. As in our original example, consumer surplus is equal to the area below the demand curve but above the price.

How Changing Prices Affect Consumer Surplus

It is often important to know how much consumer surplus *changes* when the price changes. For example, we may want to know how much consumers are hurt if a frost in Florida drives up orange prices or how much consumers gain if the introduction of fish farming makes salmon less expensive. The same approach we have used to derive consumer surplus can be used to answer questions about how changes in prices affect consumers.

Let's return to the example of the market for used textbooks. Suppose that the bookstore decided to sell used textbooks for $20 instead of $30. How much would this increase consumer surplus?

The answer is illustrated in Figure 5-4 on page 114. As shown in the figure, there are two parts to the increase in consumer surplus. The first part, shaded dark blue, is the gain of those who would have bought books even at the higher price. Each of the students who would have bought books at $30—Aleisha, Brad, and Claudia—pays $10 less, and therefore each gains $10 in consumer surplus from the fall in price to

Figure 5-4

Consumer Surplus and a Fall in the Price of Used Textbooks

There are two parts to the increase in consumer surplus generated by a fall in price from $30 to $20. The first is given by the dark blue rectangle: each person who would have bought at the original price of $30—Aleisha, Brad, and Claudia—receives an increase in consumer surplus equal to the total fall in price, $10. So the area of the dark blue rectangle corresponds to an amount equal to 3 × $10 = $30. The second part is given by the light blue rectangle: the increase in consumer surplus for those who would *not* have bought at the original price of $30 but who buy at the new price of $20—namely, Darren. Darren's willingness to pay is $25, so he now receives consumer surplus of $5. The total increase in consumer surplus is 3 × $10 + $5 = $35, represented by the sum of the shaded areas. Likewise, a rise in price from $20 to $30 would decrease consumer surplus by an amount equal to the sum of the shaded areas.

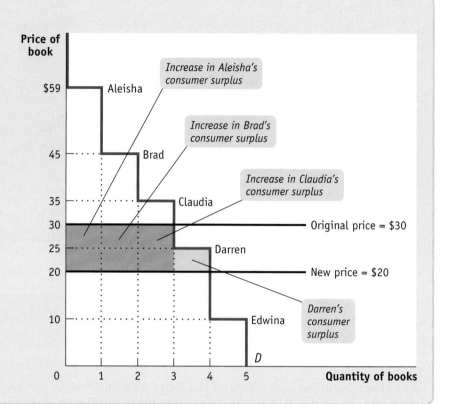

$20. So the dark blue area represents the $30 increase in consumer surplus to those three buyers. The second part, shaded light blue, is the gain to those who would not have bought a book at $30 but are willing to pay more than $20. In this case that means Darren, who would not have bought a book at $30 but does buy one at $20. He gains $5—the difference between his willingness to pay $25 and the new price of $20. So the light blue area represents a further $5 gain in consumer surplus. The total increase in consumer surplus is the sum of the shaded areas, $35. Likewise, a rise in price from $20 to $30 would decrease consumer surplus by an amount equal to the sum of the shaded areas.

Figure 5-4 illustrates that when the price of a good falls, the area under the demand curve but above the price—which we have seen is equal to the total consumer surplus—increases. Figure 5-5 shows the same result for the case of a smooth demand curve, the demand for personal computers. Here we assume that the price of computers falls from $5,000 to $1,500, leading to an increase in the quantity demanded from 200,000 to 1 million units. As in the used-textbook example, we divide the gain in consumer surplus into two parts. The dark blue rectangle in Figure 5-5 corresponds to the dark blue area in Figure 5-4: it is the gain to the 200,000 people who would have bought computers even at the higher price of $5,000. As a result of the price fall, each receives additional surplus of $3,500. The light blue triangle in Figure 5-5 corresponds to the light blue area in Figure 5-4: it is the gain to people who would not have bought the good at the higher price but are willing to do so at a price of $1,500. For example, the light blue triangle includes the gain to someone who would have been willing to pay $2,000 for a computer and therefore gains $500 in consumer surplus when he or she is able to buy a computer for only $1,500. As before, the total gain in consumer surplus is the sum of the shaded areas, the increase in the area under the demand curve but above the price.

What would happen if the price of a good were to rise instead of fall? We would do the same analysis in reverse. Suppose, for example, that for some reason the price

Figure 5-5

A Fall in the Price Increases Consumer Surplus

A fall in the price of a computer from $5,000 to $1,500 leads to an increase in the quantity demanded and an increase in consumer surplus. The change in total consumer surplus is given by the sum of the shaded areas: the total area below the demand curve but between the old and new prices. Here, the dark blue area represents the increase in consumer surplus for the 200,000 consumers who would have bought a computer at the original price of $5,000; they each receive an increase in consumer surplus of $3,500. The light blue area represents the increase in consumer surplus for those willing to buy at a price equal to or greater than $1,500 but less than $5,000. Similarly, a rise in the price of a computer from $1,500 to $5,000 generates a decrease in consumer surplus equal to the sum of the two shaded areas. **>web...**

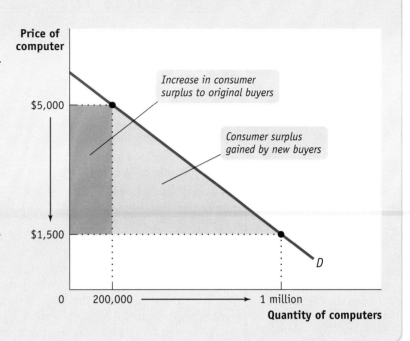

of computers rises from $1,500 to $5,000. This would lead to a fall in consumer surplus, equal to the shaded area in Figure 5-5. This loss consists of two parts. The dark blue rectangle represents the loss to consumers who would still buy a computer, even at a price of $5,000. The light blue triangle represents the loss to consumers who decide not to buy a computer at the higher price.

FOR INQUIRING MINDS

I WANT A NEW DRUG . . .

The pharmaceutical industry is constantly introducing new prescription drugs. Some of these drugs do the same thing as other, existing drugs, but a bit better—for example, pretty good allergy medicines have been around for years, but newer versions that are somewhat more effective or have fewer side effects keep emerging. Other drugs do something that was previously considered impossible—a famous example from the late 1990s was Propecia, the pill that slows and in some cases reverses hair loss.

Such innovations raise a difficult question for the people who are supposed to measure economic growth: how do you calculate the contribution of a new product to the economy?

You might at first say that it's just a matter of dollars and cents. But that could be wrong, in either direction. A new painkiller that is just slightly better than aspirin might have huge sales, because it would take over the painkiller market—but it wouldn't really add much to

consumer welfare. On the other hand, the benefits of a drug that cures the previously incurable might be much larger than the money actually spent on it—after all, people *would have been willing* to pay much more.

Consider, for example, the benefits of antibiotics. When penicillin was introduced in 1941, it transformed the treatment of infectious disease; illnesses that had previously crippled or killed millions of people were suddenly easy to treat. Presumably most people would be willing to pay a lot not to go back to the days before penicillin. Yet the average American spends only a few dollars per year on antibiotics.

The right way to measure the gains from a new drug—or any new product—is therefore to try to figure out what people would have been willing to pay for the good, and subtract what they actually pay. In other words, the gains from a new drug should be measured by calculating consumer surplus!

economics in action

When Money Isn't Enough

The key insight we get from the concept of consumer surplus is that purchases yield a net benefit to the consumer, because the consumer pays a price that is less than the amount he or she would have been willing to pay for the good. Another way to say this is that the right to buy a good at the going price is a valuable thing in itself.

Most of the time we don't think about the value associated with the right to buy a good. In a market economy, we take it for granted that we can buy whatever we want, as long as we are willing to pay the price. But that hasn't always been true. For example, during World War II many goods were rationed in order to make resources available for the war effort. To buy sugar, meat, coffee, gasoline, and many other goods, you not only had to pay cash; you also had to present stamps or coupons from special books that were issued to each family by the government. These pieces of paper, which represented nothing but the right to buy goods at the market price, quickly became valuable commodities in themselves. As a result, black markets in meat stamps and gasoline coupons sprang into existence. Moreover, criminals began stealing coupons and even counterfeiting stamps.

The funny thing was that even if you had bought a gasoline coupon on the black market, you still had to pay the regular price of gasoline to fill your tank. So what you were buying on the black market was not the good but *the right to buy the good*—that is, people who bought ration coupons on the black market were paying for the right to get some consumer surplus. ∎

< < < < < < < < < < < < < < < < <

>> CHECK YOUR UNDERSTANDING 5-1

1. Consider the market for cheese-stuffed jalapeno peppers. There are two consumers, Casey and Josie, and their willingness to pay for each pepper is given in the accompanying table. Use the table (i) to construct the demand schedule for peppers for prices of $0.00, $0.10, and so on, up to $0.90; and (ii) to calculate the total consumer surplus when the price of a pepper is $0.40.

Quantity of peppers	Casey's willingness to pay	Josie's willingness to pay
1st pepper	$0.90	$0.80
2nd pepper	0.70	0.60
3rd pepper	0.50	0.40
4th pepper	0.30	0.30

Solutions appear at back of book.

Producer Surplus and the Supply Curve

Just as buyers of a good would have been willing to pay more for their purchase than the price they actually pay, sellers of a good would have been willing to sell it for less than the price they actually receive. We can therefore carry out an analysis of producer surplus and the supply curve that is almost exactly parallel to that of consumer surplus and the demand curve.

Cost and Producer Surplus

Consider a group of students who are potential sellers of used textbooks. Because they have different preferences, the various potential sellers differ in the price at which they are willing to sell their books. The table in Figure 5-6 shows the prices at which several different students would be willing to sell. Andrew is willing to sell the book as long as he can get anything more than $5; Betty won't sell unless she can get at least $15; Carlos, unless he can get $25; Donna, unless she can get $35; Engelbert, unless he can get $45.

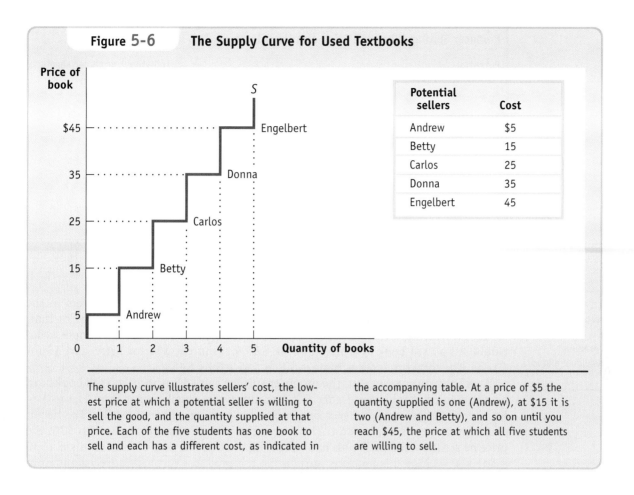

Figure 5-6   The Supply Curve for Used Textbooks

Potential sellers	Cost
Andrew	$5
Betty	15
Carlos	25
Donna	35
Engelbert	45

The supply curve illustrates sellers' cost, the lowest price at which a potential seller is willing to sell the good, and the quantity supplied at that price. Each of the five students has one book to sell and each has a different cost, as indicated in the accompanying table. At a price of $5 the quantity supplied is one (Andrew), at $15 it is two (Andrew and Betty), and so on until you reach $45, the price at which all five students are willing to sell.

The lowest price at which a potential seller is willing to sell has a special name in economics: it is called the seller's **cost**. So Andrew's cost is $5, Betty's is $15, and so on.

Using the term *cost*, which people normally associate with the monetary cost of producing a good, may sound a little strange when applied to sellers of used textbooks. The students don't have to manufacture the books, so it doesn't cost the student who sells a book anything to make that book available for sale, does it?

Yes, it does. A student who sells a book won't have it later, as part of a personal collection. So there is an *opportunity cost* to selling a textbook, even if the owner has completed the course for which it was required. And remember that one of the basic principles of economics is that the true measure of the cost of doing anything is always its opportunity cost—the real cost of something is what you must give up to get it.

So it is good economics to talk of the minimum price at which someone will sell a good as the "cost" of selling that good, even if he or she doesn't spend any money to make the good available for sale. Of course, in most real-world markets the sellers are also those who produce the good—and therefore *do* spend money to make the good available for sale. In this case the cost of making the good available for sale *includes* monetary costs—but it may also include other opportunity costs.

Getting back to the example, suppose that Andrew sells his book for $30. Clearly he has gained from the transaction: he would have been willing to sell for only $5, so he has gained $25. This gain, the difference between the price he actually gets and his cost—the minimum price at which he would have been willing to sell—is known as his **individual producer surplus.**

Just as we derived the demand curve from the willingness to pay of different consumers, we can derive the supply curve from the cost of different producers. The step-shaped curve in Figure 5-6 shows the supply curve implied by the costs shown in the

A potential seller's **cost** is the lowest price at which he or she is willing to sell a good.

Individual producer surplus is the net gain to a seller from selling a good. It is equal to the difference between the price received and the seller's cost.

TABLE 5-2

Producer Surplus When the Price of a Used Textbook Is $30

Potential seller	Cost	Price received	Individual producer surplus = price received − cost
Andrew	$5	$30	$25
Betty	15	30	15
Carlos	25	30	5
Donna	35	—	—
Engelbert	45	—	—
			Total producer surplus: $45

accompanying table. At a price less than $5, none of the students are willing to sell; at a price between $5 and $15, only Andrew is willing to sell, and so on.

As in the case of consumer surplus, we can add the individual producer surpluses of sellers to calculate the **total producer surplus**, the total gains to sellers in the market. Economists use the term **producer surplus** to refer to either total or individual producer surplus. Table 5-2 shows the net gain to each of the students who would sell a used book at a price of $30: $25 for Andrew, $15 for Betty, and $5 for Carlos. The total producer surplus is $25 + $15 + $5 = $45.

As with consumer surplus, the producer surplus gained by those who sell books can be represented graphically. Figure 5-7 reproduces the supply curve from Figure 5-6. Each step in that supply curve is one book wide and represents one seller. The height of Andrew's step is $5, his cost. This forms the bottom of a rectangle, with $30, the price he actually receives for his book, forming the top. The area of this rectangle, ($30 − $5) × 1 = $25, is his producer surplus. So the producer surplus Andrew gains from selling his book is the *area of the dark red rectangle* shown in the figure.

Let's assume that the campus bookstore is willing to buy all the used copies of this book that students are willing to sell at a price of $30. Then, in addition to Andrew, Betty and Carlos will also sell their books. They will also benefit from their sales, though not as much as Andrew, because they have higher costs. Andrew, as we have

Total producer surplus in a market is the sum of the individual producer surpluses of all the sellers of a good. Economists use the term **producer surplus** to refer both to individual and to total producer surplus.

Figure 5-7

Producer Surplus in the Used-Textbook Market

At a price of $30, Andrew, Betty, and Carlos each sell a book but Donna and Engelbert do not. Andrew, Betty, and Carlos get individual producer surpluses equal to the difference between the price and their cost, illustrated here by the shaded rectangles. Donna and Engelbert each have a cost that is greater than the price of $30, so they are unwilling to sell a book and therefore receive zero producer surplus. The total producer surplus is given by the entire shaded area, the sum of the individual producer surpluses of Andrew, Betty, and Carlos, equal to $25 + $15 + $5 = $45.

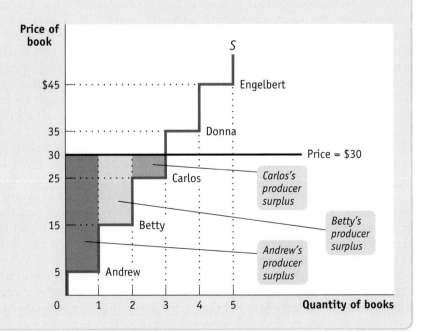

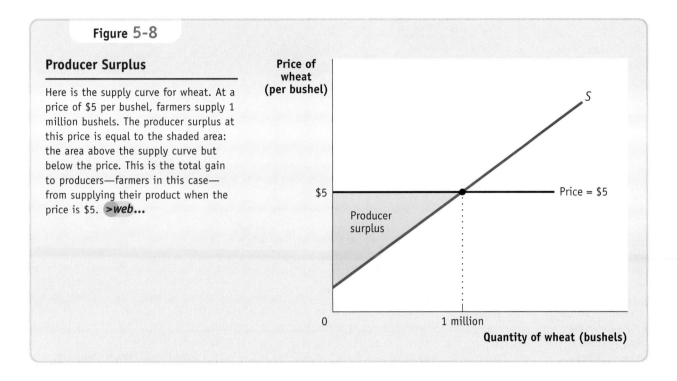

Figure 5-8

Producer Surplus

Here is the supply curve for wheat. At a price of $5 per bushel, farmers supply 1 million bushels. The producer surplus at this price is equal to the shaded area: the area above the supply curve but below the price. This is the total gain to producers—farmers in this case—from supplying their product when the price is $5. **>web...**

seen, gains $25. Betty gains a smaller amount: since her cost is $15, she gains only $15. Carlos gains even less, only $5.

Again, as with consumer surplus, we have a general rule for determining the total producer surplus from sales of a good: *The total producer surplus from sales of a good at a given price is the area above the supply curve but below that price.*

This rule applies both to examples like the one shown in Figure 5-7, where there are a small number of producers and a step-shaped supply curve, and to more realistic examples where there are many producers and the supply curve is more or less smooth.

Consider, for example, the supply of wheat. Figure 5-8 shows how producer surplus depends on the price per bushel. Suppose that, as shown in the figure, the price is $5 per bushel and farmers supply 1 million bushels. What is the benefit to the farmers from selling their wheat at a price of $5? Their producer surplus is equal to the shaded area in the figure—the area above the supply curve but below the price of $5 per bushel.

Changes in Producer Surplus

If the price of a good rises, producers of the good will experience an increase in producer surplus, though not all producers gain the same amount. Some producers would have produced the good even at the original price; they will gain the entire price increase on every unit they produce. Other producers will enter the market because of the higher price; they will gain only the difference between the new price and their cost.

Figure 5-9 on page 120 is the supply counterpart of Figure 5-5. It shows the effect on producer surplus of a rise in the price of wheat from $5 to $7 per bushel. The increase in producer surplus is the entire shaded area, which consists of two parts. First, there is a red rectangle corresponding to the gains to those farmers who would have supplied wheat even at the original $5 price. Second, there is an additional pink triangle that corresponds to the gains to those farmers who would not have supplied wheat at the original price but are drawn into the market by the higher price.

If the price were to fall from $7 to $5 per bushel, the story would run in reverse. The whole shaded area would now be the decline in producer surplus, the fall in the area above the supply curve but below the price. The loss would consist of two parts, the loss to farmers who would still grow wheat at a price of $5 (the red rectangle) and the loss to farmers who decide not to grow wheat because of the lower price (the pink triangle).

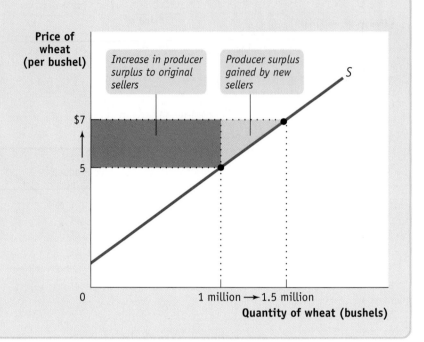

Figure 5-9

A Rise in the Price Increases Producer Surplus

A rise in the price of wheat from $5 to $7 leads to an increase in the quantity supplied and an increase in producer surplus. The change in total producer surplus is given by the sum of the shaded areas: the total area above the supply curve but between the old and new prices. The red area represents the gain to the farmers who would have supplied 1 million bushels at the original price of $5; they each receive an increase in producer surplus of $2 for each of those bushels. The triangular pink area represents the increase in producer surplus achieved by the farmers who supply the additional 500,000 bushels because of the higher price. Similarly, a fall in the price of wheat generates a decrease in producer surplus equal to the shaded areas. **>web...**

economics in action

Gaining from Disaster

In 1992 Hurricane Andrew swept through Florida, destroying thousands of homes and businesses. The state quickly began rebuilding, with the help of thousands of construction workers who moved temporarily to Florida to help out.

These construction workers were not motivated mainly by sympathy for Florida residents. They were lured by the high wages available there—and took home billions of dollars.

But how much did the temporary workers actually gain? Certainly we should not count all the money they earned in Florida as a net benefit. For one thing, most of these workers would have earned something—though not as much—if they had stayed home. In addition to this opportunity cost, the temporary move to Florida had other costs: the expense of motel rooms and of transportation, the wear and tear of being away from families and friends.

Clearly the workers viewed the benefits as being larger than the costs—otherwise they wouldn't have gone down to Florida in the first place. But the producer surplus earned by those temporary workers was much less than the money they earned. ∎

< < < < < < < < < < < < < < < < < <

▸▸CHECK YOUR UNDERSTANDING 5-2

1. Consider the market for cheese-stuffed jalapeno peppers. There are two producers, Cara and Jamie, and their costs of producing each pepper are given in the accompanying table. Use the table (i) to construct the supply schedule for peppers for prices of $0.00, $0.10, and so on, up to $0.90; and (ii) to calculate the total producer surplus when the price of a pepper is $0.70.

Quantity of peppers	Cara's cost	Jamie's cost
1st pepper	$0.10	$0.30
2nd pepper	0.10	0.50
3rd pepper	0.40	0.70
4th pepper	0.60	0.90

Solutions appear at back of book.

Consumer Surplus, Producer Surplus, and the Gains from Trade

One of the nine core principles of economics we introduced in Chapter 1 is that markets are a remarkably effective way to organize economic activity: they generally make society as well off as possible given the available resources. The concepts of consumer surplus and producer surplus can help us deepen our understanding of why this is so.

The Gains from Trade

Let's go back to the market in used textbooks but now consider a much bigger market—say, one at a large state university—where there are many potential buyers and sellers. Let's line up incoming students—who are potential buyers of the book—in order of their willingness to pay, so that the entering student with the highest willingness to pay is potential buyer number 1, the student with the next highest willingness to pay is number 2, and so on. Then we can use their willingness to pay to derive a demand curve like the one in Figure 5-10. Similarly, we can line up outgoing students, who are potential sellers of the book, in order of their cost, starting with the student with the lowest cost, then the student with the next lowest cost, and so on, to derive a supply curve like the one shown in the same figure.

As we have drawn the curves, the market reaches equilibrium at a price of $30 per book, and 1,000 books are bought and sold at that price. The two shaded triangles show the consumer surplus (blue) and the producer surplus (red) generated by this market. The sum of consumer and producer surplus is known as the **total surplus** generated in a market.

> The **total surplus** generated in a market is the total net gain to consumers and producers from trading in the market. It is the sum of the producer and the consumer surplus.

The striking thing about this picture is that both consumers and producers gain—that is, both consumers and producers are better off because there is a market in this good. But this should come as no surprise—it illustrates another core principle of economics: there are *gains from trade*. These gains from trade are the reason everyone is better off participating in a market economy than they would be if each individual tried to be self-sufficient.

But are we as well off as we could be? This brings us to the question of the efficiency of markets.

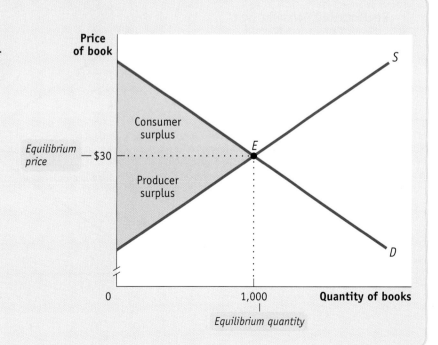

Figure 5-10

Total Surplus

In the market for used textbooks, the equilibrium price is $30 and the equilibrium quantity is 1,000 books. Consumer surplus is given by the blue area, the area below the demand curve but above the price. Producer surplus is given by the red area, the area above the supply curve but below the price. The sum of the blue and the red areas is total surplus, the total benefit to society from the production and consumption of the good. **>web...**

The Efficiency of Markets: A Preliminary View

Markets produce gains from trade, but in Chapter 1 we made a bigger claim: that markets are usually *efficient*. That is, we claimed that once the market has produced its gains from trade, there is usually no way to make some people better off without making others worse off (with some well-defined exceptions).

We're not yet ready to carry out a full discussion of the efficiency of markets—that will have to wait until we've looked in more detail at the behavior of producers and consumers. However, we can get an intuitive sense of the efficiency of markets by noticing a key feature of the market equilibrium shown in Figure 5-10: the maximum possible total surplus is achieved at market equilibrium. That is, the market equilibrium allocates the consumption of the good among potential consumers and sales of the good among potential sellers in a way that achieves the highest possible gain to society.

How do we know this? By comparing the total surplus generated by the consumption and production choices in the market equilibrium to the surplus generated by a different set of production and consumption choices. We can show that any change from the market equilibrium reduces total surplus.

Let's consider three ways in which you might try to increase the total surplus:

1. *Reallocate consumption among consumers*—take the good away from buyers who would have purchased the good in the market equilibrium, and instead give it to potential consumers who would not have bought it in equilibrium.

2. *Reallocate sales among sellers*—take sales away from sellers who would have sold the good in the market equilibrium, and instead compel potential sellers who would not have sold the good in equilibrium to sell it.

3. *Change the quantity traded*—compel consumers and producers to transact either more or less than the equilibrium quantity.

It turns out that each of these actions will not only fail to increase the total surplus; in fact, each will reduce the total surplus.

Figure 5-11 shows why reallocating consumption of the good among consumers will reduce the total surplus. Points *A* and *B* show the positions on the demand curve

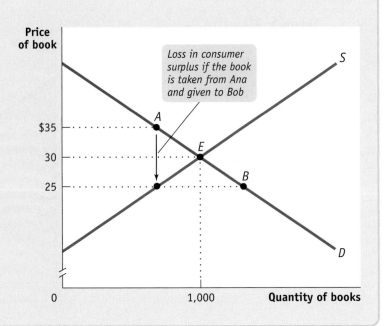

Figure 5-11

Reallocating Consumption Lowers Consumer Surplus

Ana (point *A*) has a willingness to pay of $35. Bob (point *B*) has a willingness to pay of only $25. At the market equilibrium price of $30, Ana purchases a book but Bob does not. If we rearrange consumption by taking a book from Ana and giving it to Bob, consumer surplus declines by $10 and, as a result, total surplus declines by $10. The market equilibrium generates the highest possible consumer surplus by ensuring that those who consume the good are those who value it the most. **>web...**

of two potential buyers of a used book, Ana and Bob. As we can see from the figure, Ana is willing to pay $35 for a book, but Bob is willing to pay only $25. Since the equilibrium price is $30, Ana buys a book and Bob does not.

Now suppose that we try to reallocate consumption. This would mean taking a book away from somebody who *would* have bought one at the equilibrium price of $30, like Ana, and giving that book to someone who would *not* have bought at that price, like Bob. But since the book is worth $35 to Ana, but only $25 to Bob, this would *reduce total consumer surplus* by $35 − $25 = $10.

This result doesn't depend on which two students we pick. Every student who buys a book in equilibrium has a willingness to pay that is *more* than $30, and every student who doesn't buy a book has a willingness to pay that is *less* than $30. So reallocating the good among consumers always means taking a book away from a student who values it more and giving it to a student who values it less, which necessarily reduces consumer surplus.

A similar argument, illustrated by Figure 5-12, holds for producer surplus. Here points *X* and *Y* show the positions on the supply curve of Xavier, who has a cost of $25, and Yvonne, who has a cost of $35. At the equilibrium price of $30, Xavier would sell his book but Yvonne would not. If we reallocated sales, forcing Xavier to keep his book and forcing Yvonne to give up hers, total producer surplus would be reduced by $35 − $25 = $10. Again, it doesn't matter which two students we choose. Any student who sells a book in equilibrium has a lower cost than any student who does not, so reallocating sales among sellers necessarily increases total cost and reduces producer surplus. In this way the market equilibrium generates the highest possible producer surplus: it ensures that those who sell their books are those who most value the right to sell them.

Finally, changing the quantity bought and sold reduces the sum of producer and consumer surplus. Figure 5-13 on page 124 shows all four students: potential buyers Ana and Bob, and potential sellers Xavier and Yvonne. To reduce sales, we would have to prevent someone like Xavier, who would have sold the book in equilibrium, from making the sale; and the book would then not be made available to someone like Ana who would have bought it in equilibrium. As we've seen, however, Ana would be willing to pay $35, but Xavier's cost is only $25. So preventing this sale would reduce

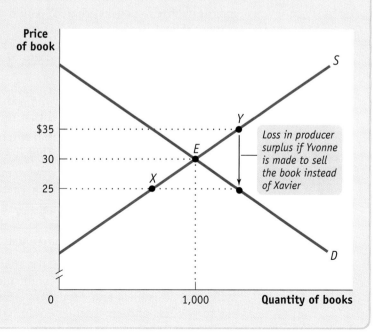

Figure 5-12

Reallocating Sales Lowers Producer Surplus

Yvonne (point *Y*) has a cost of $35, $10 more than Xavier (point *X*), who has a cost of $25. At the market equilibrium price of $30, Xavier sells a book, but Yvonne does not. If we rearrange sales by preventing Xavier from selling his book and compelling Yvonne to sell hers, producer surplus declines by $10 and, as a result, total surplus declines by $10. The market equilibrium generates the highest possible producer surplus by assuring that those who sell the good are those who value the right to sell it the most. **>web...**

Figure 5-13

Changing the Quantity Lowers Total Surplus

If Xavier (point *X*) were prevented from selling his book to someone like Ana (point *A*), total surplus would fall by $10, the difference between Ana's willingness to pay ($35) and Xavier's cost ($25). This means that total surplus falls whenever fewer than 1,000 books—the equilibrium quantity—are transacted. Likewise, if Yvonne (point *Y*) were compelled to sell her book to someone like Bob (point *B*), total surplus would also fall by $10, the difference between Yvonne's cost ($35) and Bob's willingness to pay ($25). This means that total surplus falls whenever more than 1,000 books are transacted. These two examples show that at market equilibrium, all beneficial transactions—and only beneficial transactions—occur.

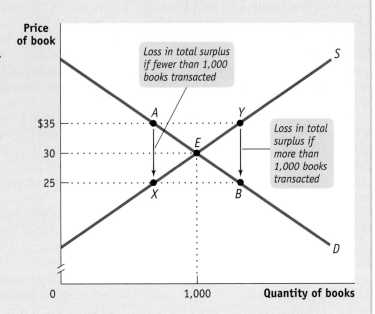

total surplus by $35 − $25 = $10. Once again, this result doesn't depend on which two students we pick: any student who would have sold the book in equilibrium has a cost of *less* than $30, and any student who would have purchased the book in equilibrium would be willing to pay *more* than $30, so preventing any sale that would have taken place in equilibrium reduces total surplus.

Finally, to increase sales would mean forcing someone like Yvonne, who would not have sold her book in equilibrium, to sell it, and giving it to someone like Bob, who would not have bought a book in equilibrium. Because Yvonne's cost is $35 but Bob is only willing to pay $25, this reduces total surplus by $10. And once again it doesn't matter which two students we pick—anyone who wouldn't have bought the book is willing to pay less than $30, and anyone who wouldn't have sold has a cost of more than $30.

What we have shown is that the market equilibrium maximizes total surplus—the sum of producer and consumer surplus. It does this because the market performs four important functions:

1. It allocates consumption of the good to the potential buyers who value it the most, as indicated by the fact that they have the highest willingness to pay.

2. It allocates sales to the potential sellers who most value the right to sell the good, as indicated by the fact that they have the lowest cost.

3. It ensures that every consumer who makes a purchase values the good more than every seller who makes a sale, so that all transactions are mutually beneficial.

4. It ensures that every potential buyer who doesn't make a purchase values the good less than every potential seller who doesn't make a sale, so that no mutually beneficial transactions are missed.

A caveat: it's important to realize that although the market equilibrium maximizes the total surplus, this does not mean that it is the best outcome for every individual consumer and producer. Other things being equal, each buyer would like to pay less and each seller would like to receive more. So some people would benefit from the price controls discussed in Chapter 4. A price ceiling that held down the market price would leave some consumers—those who managed to make a purchase—better off than they would be at equilibrium. A price floor that kept the price up would benefit some sellers—those who managed to make a sale.

But in the market equilibrium there is no way to make some people better off without making others worse off—and that's the definition of efficiency.

A Few Words of Caution

Markets are an amazingly effective way to organize economic activity; we've just demonstrated that, under certain conditions, a market is actually efficient—there is literally no way to make some people better off without making others worse off.

But how secure is this result? Are markets really that good?

The answer is "not always." As we discussed briefly in Chapter 1 in our ninth and final principle of economics (*when markets don't achieve efficiency, government intervention can improve society's welfare*), markets can fail to be efficient for a number of reasons. When a market is not efficient, we have what is known as a case of **market failure.** There are three main reasons why markets sometimes fail to deliver efficiency in reality.

Maximizing total surplus at your local hardware store.

Market failure occurs when a market fails to be efficient.

First, markets can fail when, in an attempt to capture more resources, one party prevents mutually beneficial trades from occurring. This situation arises, for instance, when a market contains only a single seller of a good, known as a *monopolist.* In this case, the assumption we have relied on in supply and demand analysis—that no individual buyer and seller can have a noticeable effect on the market price—is no longer valid. A monopolist can determine the price of its good, and it will raise the price above the competitive market equilibrium price in order to increase its profit. But the higher price discourages some consumers from buying the product who would have bought it at a lower price, and an inefficiency arises.

Second, actions of individuals sometimes have *side effects*—positive or negative—on the welfare of other individuals that markets don't take into account. These side effects are known as *externalities*. The best-known example of a negative externality is pollution. When a polluter decides how much pollution to emit, he or she doesn't take into account the cost that pollution imposes on others. Failure to take into account the cost that side effects impose on others results in an inefficiency: in this example, the polluter is likely to emit too much pollution from the point of view of society as a whole, inflicting more harm on others than gains for itself from polluting.

Third, markets for some goods can fail because the goods, by their very nature, are unsuited for efficient management by markets. Some goods fall into this category because of problems of *private information*—information about a good that some people possess but others don't. For example, imagine trying to sell your car in the used-car market. Although you know that your car is not a "lemon" (that is, it does not have any defects that are not immediately apparent), the potential buyers do not know this. Fearing that your car may be a lemon, a potential buyer may be willing only to pay less than the car is worth to you. As a result, a mutually beneficial trade goes unexploited.

Other goods are intrinsically unsuited to being traded in a market. The most important example of this type of good is a *public good*, a good that, once it has been produced, is freely accessible to everyone. An example is national defense: no individual can be excluded from consuming the protection provided by it. The problem is that no individual on his or her own has an incentive to pay for a public good: each will attempt to take a "free ride" on the provision of the good that others pay for. But if too few people pay, there is too little of the public good provided and an inefficiency arises.

But even with these caveats, it's remarkable how well markets work at maximizing the gains from trade.

economics in action

eBay and Efficiency

Garage sales are an old American tradition: they are a way for families to sell items they don't want to other families that have some use for them, to the benefit of both

"I got it from eBay"

parties. But many potentially beneficial trades were missed. For all Mr. Smith knew, there was someone 1,000 miles away who would really have loved that 1930s gramophone he had in the basement; for all Ms. Jones knew, there was someone 1,000 miles away who had that 1930s gramophone she had always wanted. But there was no way for Mr. Smith and Ms. Jones to find each other.

Enter eBay, the online auction service. eBay was founded in 1995 by Pierre Omidyar, a programmer whose fiancée was a collector of Pez candy dispensers and wanted a way to find potential sellers. The company, which says that its mission is "to help practically anyone trade practically anything on earth," provides a way for would-be buyers and would-be sellers of unique or used items to find each other, even if they don't live in the same neighborhood or even the same city.

The potential gains from trade were evidently large: in 2004, 135 million people were registered by eBay, and in the same year almost $34 billion in goods were bought and sold using the service. The Omidyars now possess a large collection of Pez dispensers. They are also billionaires. ■

>> CHECK YOUR UNDERSTANDING 5-3

1. Using the tables in Check Your Understanding 5-1 and 5-2, find the equilibrium price and quantity in the market for cheese-stuffed jalapeno peppers. What is total surplus in the equilibrium in this market, and who receives it?

2. Show how each of the following three actions reduces total surplus:
   a. Having Josie consume one less pepper, and Casey one more pepper, than in the market equilibrium
   b. Having Cara produce one less pepper, and Jamie one more pepper, than in the market equilibrium
   c. Having Josie consume one less pepper, and Cara produce one less pepper, than in the market equilibrium

Solutions appear at back of book.

>> QUICK REVIEW

- *Total surplus* measures the gains from trade in a market.
- Markets are usually efficient. We can demonstrate this by considering what happens to total surplus if we start from the equilibrium and rearrange consumption, rearrange sales, or change the quantity traded. Any outcome other than the market equilibrium reduces total surplus, which means that the market equilibrium is efficient.
- Under certain conditions, *market failure* occurs and the market produces an inefficient outcome. The three principal sources are attempts to capture more resources that produce inefficiencies, side effects from certain transactions, and problems in the nature of the goods themselves.

Applying Consumer and Producer Surplus: The Efficiency Costs of a Tax

The concepts of consumer and producer surplus are extremely useful in many economic applications. Among the most important of these is assessing the efficiency cost of taxation.

In Chapter 4 we introduced the concept of an *excise tax*, a tax on the purchase or sale of a good. We saw that such a tax drives a *wedge* between the price paid by consumers and that received by producers: the price paid by consumers rises, and the price received by producers falls, with the difference equal to the tax per unit. And as we saw in that chapter, the *incidence* of the tax—how much of the burden falls on consumers, how much on producers—does not depend on who actually writes the check to the government. Instead, the burden of the tax depends on how responsive the quantity demanded is to changes in the price and how responsive the quantity supplied is to changes in the price.

When the quantity of a good demanded is responsive to changes in that good's price, economists call the demand for that good *elastic*. When the quantity of a good demanded is not very responsive to changes in that good's price, they call the demand for that good *inelastic*. More precisely, we say that demand for a good is elastic if, for any given rise in the price of the good, the quantity demanded falls by a greater proportion than the price rises. For example, if the demand for a packet of potato chips falls by 25% when the price rises by 10%, we say that the demand for potato chips is elastic because 25% is greater than 10%. In other words, the demand for a good is elastic if the quantity demanded is relatively responsive to changes in the price. When demand is elastic, the demand curve will be relatively flat: even a small change in the price will result in a relatively large change in the quantity demanded. If the quantity of a good demanded falls by a smaller proportion than the price rises, demand for the good is said to be inelastic. For example, if the demand for gasoline falls by 5% when the price rises by 15%, we say that the demand for gasoline is inelastic because 5% is smaller than 15%. That is, the demand for a good is inelastic if the quantity demanded is relatively unresponsive to changes in price. When demand is inelastic, the demand curve will be relatively steep: even large changes in the price will result in only relatively small changes in the quantity demanded.

We use a similar concept to describe the responsiveness of the quantity of a good supplied to changes in that good's price. If the quantity of a good supplied rises by a greater proportion than the price rises, supply of the good is said to be elastic. When supply is elastic, the supply curve will be relatively flat: the quantity supplied is relatively responsive to changes in the price. But if the quantity of a good supplied rises by a smaller proportion than the price rises, supply of the good is said to be inelastic. When supply is inelastic, the supply curve will be relatively steep: large changes in the price will result in relatively small changes in the quantity supplied. In other words, when the supply of a good is inelastic, the quantity supplied is not very responsive to changes in that good's price.

How does the responsiveness of the quantity demanded and the quantity supplied to changes in a good's price account for the way in which the burden of a tax on that good is shared between consumers and producers? In other words, why is the *economic incidence* of a tax—the way that the burden of a tax actually falls on consumers and producers—different when demand is elastic from when demand is inelastic? Or why is the economic incidence different when supply is elastic from when supply is inelastic? To gain some insight into how the burden of the tax is split between consumers and producers, suppose an excise tax is imposed on producers. Producers will attempt to "pass on" some of the tax to consumers in terms of higher prices. When demand is highly elastic, the quantity of the good demanded will fall dramatically, even for a small increase in the price. If producers attempted to "pass on" much of the tax to consumers in terms of higher prices, the quantity demanded would fall disproportionately. As a result, producers will not be able to "pass on" much of the tax to consumers, and most of the burden of the tax will fall on producers. The opposite is true when supply is highly elastic: in that case, most of the burden of the tax will fall on consumers. The general rule is that the more elastic demand is, the greater the burden of a tax that falls on producers; the more elastic supply is, the greater the burden of a tax that falls on consumers.

We also learned in Chapter 4 that there is an additional cost of a tax, over and above the money actually paid to the government. A tax causes a *deadweight loss* to society, because less of the good is produced and consumed than in the absence of the tax. As a result, some mutually beneficial trades between producers and consumers do not take place.

Now we can complete the picture, because the concepts of consumer and producer surplus are what we need to pin down precisely the deadweight loss that an excise tax imposes.

Figure 5-14 shows the effects of an excise tax on consumer and producer surplus. In the absence of the tax, the equilibrium is at E, and the equilibrium price and quantity are P_E and Q_E, respectively. An excise tax drives a wedge equal to the amount of the tax between the price received by producers and the price paid by consumers, reducing the quantity bought and sold. In this case, where the tax is T dollars per unit, the quantity bought and sold falls to Q_T. The price paid by consumers rises to P_C, the demand price of the reduced quantity, Q_T, and the price received by producers falls to P_P, the supply price of that quantity. The difference between these prices, $P_C - P_P$, is equal to the excise tax, T.

What we can now do, using the concepts of producer and consumer surplus, is show exactly how much surplus producers and consumers lose as a result of the tax.

Figure 5-14

A Tax Reduces Consumer and Producer Surplus

Before the tax, the equilibrium price and quantity are P_E and Q_E, respectively. After an excise tax of T per unit is imposed, the price to consumers rises to P_C and consumer surplus falls by the sum of the dark blue rectangle, labeled A, and the light blue triangle, labeled B. The tax also causes the price to producers to fall to P_P; producer surplus falls by the sum of the red rectangle, labeled C, and the pink triangle, labeled F. The government receives revenue from the tax, $Q_T \times T$, which is given by the sum of the areas A and C. Areas B and F represent the losses to consumer and producer surplus that are not collected by the government as revenue; they are the deadweight loss to society of the tax. **>web...**

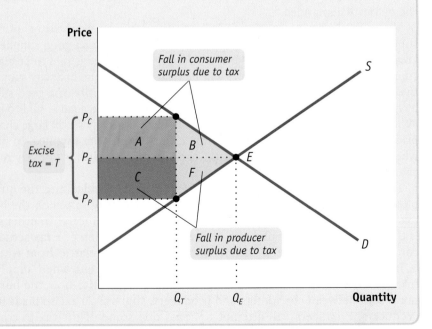

We saw earlier, in Figure 5-5, that a fall in the price of a good generates a gain in consumer surplus that is equal to the sum of the areas of a rectangle and a triangle. A price increase causes a loss to consumers that looks exactly the same. In the case of an excise tax, the rise in the price paid by consumers causes a loss equal to the sum of the area of the dark blue rectangle labeled *A* and the area of the light blue triangle labeled *B* in Figure 5-14.

Meanwhile, the fall in the price received by producers causes a fall in producer surplus. This, too, is the sum of the areas of a rectangle and a triangle. The loss in producer surplus is the sum of the areas of the red rectangle labeled *C* and the pink triangle labeled *F* in Figure 5-14.

Of course, although consumers and producers are hurt by the tax, the government gains revenue. The revenue the government collects is equal to the tax per unit sold, T, multiplied by the quantity sold, Q_T. This revenue is equal to the area of a rectangle Q_T wide and T high. And we already have that rectangle in the figure: it is the sum of rectangles *A* and *C*. So the government gains part of what consumers and producers lose from an excise tax.

But there is a part of the loss to producers and consumers from the tax that is not offset by a gain to the government—specifically, the two triangles *B* and *F*. The deadweight loss caused by the tax is equal to the combined area of these triangles. It represents the total surplus that would have been generated by transactions that do not take place because of the tax.

Figure 5-15 is a version of the same picture, leaving out the shaded rectangles—which represent money shifted from consumers and producers to the government—and showing only the deadweight loss, this time as a triangle shaded yellow. The base of that triangle is the tax wedge, T; the height of the triangle is the reduction the tax causes in the quantity sold, $Q_E - Q_T$. Notice that if the excise tax *didn't* reduce the quantity bought and sold in this market—if Q_T weren't less than Q_E—the deadweight loss represented by the yellow triangle

Figure 5-15

The Deadweight Loss of a Tax

A tax leads to a deadweight loss because it creates inefficiency: some mutually beneficial transactions never take place because of the tax, namely the transactions $Q_E - Q_T$. The yellow area here represents the value of the deadweight loss: it is the total surplus that would have been gained from the $Q_E - Q_T$ transactions. If the tax had not discouraged transactions—had the number of transactions remained at Q_E—no deadweight loss would have been incurred.

>web...

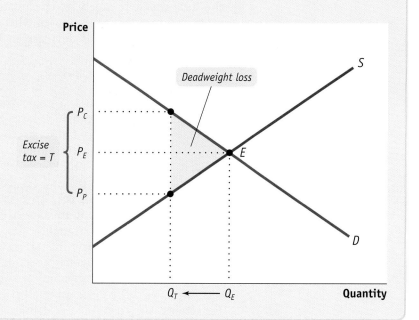

would disappear. This observation ties in with the explanation given in Chapter 4 of why an excise tax generates a deadweight loss to society: the tax causes inefficiency because it discourages mutually beneficial transactions between buyers and sellers.

The idea that deadweight loss can be measured by the area of a triangle recurs in many economic applications. Deadweight-loss triangles are produced not only by excise taxes but also by other types of taxation. They are also produced by other kinds of distortions of markets, such as monopoly. And triangles are often used to evaluate other public policies besides taxation—for example, decisions about whether to build new highways.

The general rule for economic policy is that other things equal, you want to choose the policy that produces the smallest deadweight loss. This principle gives valuable guidance on everything from the design of the tax system to environmental policy. But how can we predict the size of the deadweight loss associated with a given policy? The answer to that question depends on how elastic the demand is for the good that is being taxed and on how elastic the supply is of that good.

Deadweight Loss and Elasticities

The deadweight loss from an excise tax arises because it prevents some mutually beneficial transactions from occurring. In particular, the producer and consumer surplus that is forgone from these missing transactions is equal to the size of the deadweight loss itself. This means that the larger the number of transactions that are impeded by the tax, the larger the deadweight loss.

This gives us an important clue in understanding the relationship between how elastic or inelastic supply and demand are and the size of the deadweight loss from a tax. Recall that when demand or supply is elastic, it means that the quantity demanded or the quantity supplied is relatively responsive to price. So a tax imposed on a good for which either demand or supply, or both, is elastic will cause a relatively large decrease in the quantity bought and sold and a large deadweight loss. And when we say that demand or supply is inelastic, we mean that the quantity demanded or the quantity supplied is relatively unresponsive to price. As a result, a tax imposed when demand or supply, or both, is inelastic will cause a relatively small decrease in the quantity bought and sold and a small deadweight loss.

The four panels of Figure 5-16 illustrate how the deadweight loss of taxation increases as either supply or demand becomes more elastic. In each panel, the size of the deadweight loss is given by the area of the shaded triangle. In panel (a), the deadweight-loss triangle is large because demand is relatively elastic—a large number of transactions fail to occur because of the tax. In panel (b), the same supply curve is drawn as in panel (a), but demand is now relatively inelastic; as a result, the triangle is small because only a small number of transactions are forgone. Likewise, panels (c) and (d) contain the same demand curve but different supply curves. In panel (c), an elastic supply curve gives rise to a large deadweight-loss triangle, but in panel (d) an inelastic supply curve gives rise to a small deadweight-loss triangle.

As the following story illustrates, the implication of this result is clear: if you want to lessen the efficiency costs of taxation, you should devise taxes to fall on goods for which either demand or supply, or both, is relatively inelastic. And this lesson carries a flip-side: using a tax to purposely decrease the amount of a harmful activity, such as underage drinking, will have the most impact when that activity is elastically demanded or supplied. In the extreme case in which demand is

Figure 5-16   **Deadweight Loss and Elasticities**

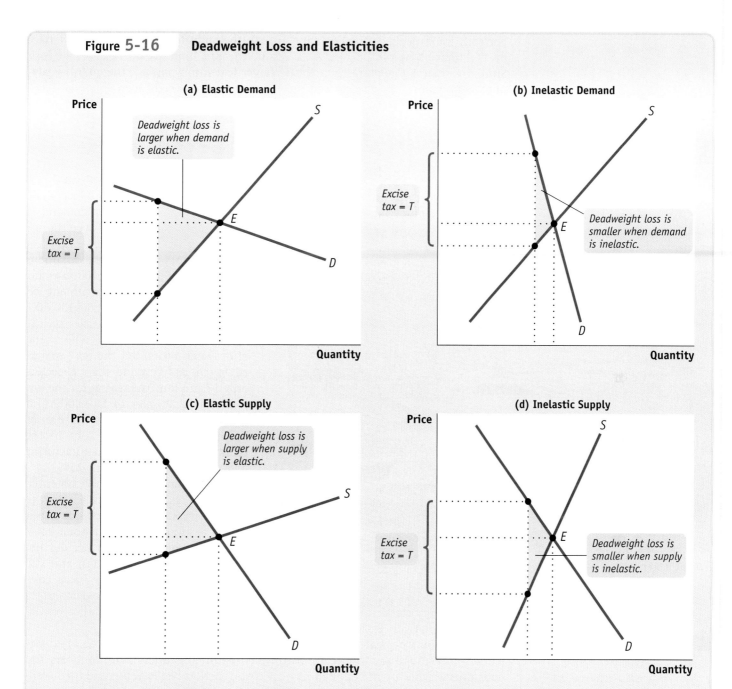

Demand is elastic in panel (a) and inelastic in panel (b), but the supply curves are the same. Supply is elastic in panel (c) and inelastic in panel (d), but the demand curves are the same. The deadweight losses are larger in panels (a) and (c) than in panels (b) and (d) because the more elastic either supply or demand is, the greater the tax-induced fall in the quantity bought and sold. In contrast, when demand or supply is inelastic, the smaller the tax-induced fall in the quantity bought and sold, and the smaller the deadweight loss.

perfectly inelastic (a vertical demand curve), the quantity demanded is unchanged by the imposition of the tax. As a result, the tax imposes no deadweight loss. Similarly, if supply is perfectly inelastic (a vertical supply curve), the quantity supplied is unchanged by the tax and there is also no deadweight loss.

economics in action

Missing the Boats

Because of deadweight losses, the costs of a tax to consumers and producers can sometimes be much larger than the actual value of taxes paid. In fact, if demand or supply, or both, is sufficiently elastic, a tax can inflict considerable losses even though it raises hardly any revenue.

The yacht tax of 1990 missed the boat and was repealed in 1993.

A case in point was the infamous "yacht tax" of 1990, a special sales tax imposed by the U.S. government on yachts whose price exceeded $100,000. The purpose was to raise taxes on the wealthy, the only people who could afford such boats. But the tax generated much less revenue than expected, only $7 million. The reason for the low yield was that sales of $100,000-plus yachts in the United States fell sharply, by 71%. The number of jobs in the yacht industry, in both manufacturing and sales, also fell, by about 25%.

What happened? Basically, potential yacht buyers changed their behavior to avoid the tax. Some decided not to buy yachts at all; others bought their boats in places where the sales tax did not apply, such as the Bahamas; and still others scaled back, buying boats costing less than $100,000 and thereby avoiding the tax. In other words, the demand for yachts was very elastic. And the size of the job losses in the industry indicates that supply was relatively elastic as well.

Despite the fact that few potential yacht buyers ended up paying the tax, you would not want to say that it imposed no costs on consumers and producers. For consumers, avoiding the tax had its own costs, such as the expense and inconvenience of buying a boat overseas or the loss in satisfaction from buying a $99,000 boat when you really wanted something fancier. Moreover, the sales force and boat builders suffered a loss in producer surplus. Policy makers eventually concluded that pain had been inflicted for little gain in tax revenue, and the tax was repealed in 1993. ∎

< < < < < < < < < < < < < < < < < <

> **QUICK REVIEW**
>
> ➤ The losses suffered by producers and consumers when an excise tax is imposed can be measured by the reduction in consumer and producer surplus.
> ➤ The government gains revenue from an excise tax, but this government revenue is less than the loss in total surplus.
> ➤ The difference between the government revenue from an excise tax and the reduction in total surplus is the deadweight loss from the tax.
> ➤ The more elastic supply or demand is, the larger the number of transactions prevented by a tax and the larger the deadweight loss.

>>**CHECK YOUR UNDERSTANDING 5-4**

1. Suppose that an excise tax of $0.40 is imposed on cheese-stuffed jalapeno peppers, raising the price paid by consumers to $0.70 and lowering the price received by producers to $0.30. Compared to the market equilibrium without the tax from Check Your Understanding 5-3, calculate the following:
   a. The loss in consumer surplus and who loses consumer surplus
   b. The loss in producer surplus and who loses producer surplus

c. The government revenue from this tax

d. The deadweight loss of the tax

2. In each of the following cases, focus on whether demand is elastic or inelastic and use a diagram to illustrate the likely size—small or large—of the deadweight loss resulting from a tax. Explain your reasoning.

a. Gasoline

b. Milk chocolate bars

Solutions appear at back of book.

• A LOOK AHEAD •

In moving from this chapter to the next, we will shift gears from the basic principles of microeconomics to the basic principles of macroeconomics. We will begin Chapter 6 by analyzing how macroeconomics is different from microeconomics. We'll see that microeconomics focuses on the behavior of individuals and individual markets; macroeconomics, however, focuses on economy-wide behavior, encompassing the actions of millions of individuals and thousands of markets. The much wider scope of macroeconomics will require the use of a largely different set of tools and concepts. However, as you move ahead it is important to remember that the basic tools and concepts of microeconomics—the nine principles and the supply and demand model—serve as an important foundation to macroeconomics. In particular, we will revisit the supply and demand models in Chapter 9, where we study the market for loanable funds, and in Chapter 18, where we study international trade.

SUMMARY

1. The **willingness to pay** of each individual consumer determines the demand curve. When price is less than or equal to the willingness to pay, the potential consumer purchases the good. The difference between price and willingness to pay is the net gain to the consumer, the **individual consumer surplus.**

2. The **total consumer surplus** in a market, the sum of all individual consumer surpluses in a market, is equal to the area below the demand curve but above the price. A rise in the price of a good reduces consumer surplus; a fall in the price increases consumer surplus. The term **consumer surplus** is often used to refer both to individual and to total consumer surplus.

3. The **cost** of each potential producer, the lowest price at which he or she is willing to supply a unit of that good, determines the supply curve. If the price of a good is above a producer's cost, a sale generates a net gain to the producer, known as the **individual producer surplus.**

4. The **total producer surplus,** the sum of the individual producer surpluses, is equal to the area above the supply curve but below the price. A rise in the price of a good increases producer surplus; a fall in the price reduces producer surplus. The term **producer surplus** is often used to refer both to the individual and to the total producer surplus.

5. **Total surplus,** the total gain to society from the production and consumption of a good, is the sum of consumer and producer surplus.

6. Usually, markets are efficient and achieve the maximum total surplus. Any possible rearrangement of consumption or sales, or change in the quantity bought and sold, reduces total surplus.

7. Under certain conditions, **market failure** occurs and markets fail to be efficient. This situation arises from three principal sources: attempts to capture more resources that create inefficiencies, side effects of some transactions, and problems in the nature of the good.

8. Economic policies can be evaluated by their effect on total surplus. For example, an excise tax generates revenue for the government but lowers total surplus. The loss in total surplus exceeds the tax revenue, resulting in a deadweight loss to society. The value of this deadweight loss is shown by the triangle that represents the value of the transactions discouraged by the tax. The more elastic supply or demand is, the larger the deadweight loss of a tax.

KEY TERMS

Willingness to pay, p. 110
Individual consumer surplus, p. 112
Total consumer surplus, p. 112
Consumer surplus, p. 112

Cost, p. 117
Individual producer surplus, p. 117
Total producer surplus, p. 118

Producer surplus, p. 118
Total surplus, p. 121
Market failure, p. 125

PROBLEMS

1. Determine the amount of consumer surplus generated in each of the following situations.

   a. Paul goes to the clothing store to buy a new T-shirt, for which he is willing to pay up to $10. He picks out one he likes with a price tag of exactly $10. At the cash register, he is told that his T-shirt is on sale for half the posted price.

   b. Robin goes to the CD store hoping to find a used copy of the *Eagles Greatest Hits* for up to $10. The store has one copy selling for $10.

   c. After soccer practice, Phil is willing to pay $2 for a bottle of mineral water. The 7-Eleven sells mineral water for $2.25 per bottle.

2. Determine the amount of producer surplus generated in each of the following situations.

   a. Bob lists his old Lionel electric trains on eBay. He sets a minimum acceptable price, known as his *reserve price*, of $75. After five days of bidding, the final high bid is exactly $75.

   b. Jenny advertises her car for sale in the used-car section of the student newspaper for $2,000, but she is willing to sell the car for any price higher than $1,500. The best offer she gets is $1,200.

   c. Sanjay likes his job so much that he would be willing to do it for free. However, his annual salary is $80,000.

3. Hollywood writers negotiate a new agreement with movie producers that they will receive 10 percent of the revenue from every video rental of a movie they worked on. They have no such agreement for movies shown on pay-per-view television.

   a. When the new writers' agreement comes into effect, what will happen in the market for video rentals—that is, will supply or demand shift, and how? As a result, how will consumer surplus in the market for video rentals change? Illustrate with a diagram. Do you think the writers' agreement will be popular with consumers who rent videos?

   b. Consumers consider video rentals and pay-per-view movies substitutable to some extent. When the new writers' agreement comes into effect, what will happen in the market for pay-per-view movies—that is, will supply or demand shift, and how? As a result, how will producer surplus in the market for pay-per-view movies change? Illustrate with a diagram. Do you think the writers' agreement will be popular with cable television companies that show pay-per-view movies?

4. There are six potential consumers of computer games, each willing to buy only one game. Consumer 1 is willing to pay $40 for a computer game, consumer 2 is willing to pay $35, consumer 3 is willing to pay $30, consumer 4 is willing pay $25, consumer 5 is willing to pay $20, and consumer 6 is willing to pay $15.

   a. Suppose the market price is $29. What is the total consumer surplus?

   b. Now the market price decreases to $19. What is the total consumer surplus now?

   c. When the price fell from $29 to $19, how much did each consumer's individual consumer surplus change?

5. In an effort to provide more affordable rental housing for low-income families, the city council of Collegetown decides to impose a rent ceiling well below the current market equilibrium rent.

   a. Illustrate the effect of this policy in a diagram. Indicate consumer and producer surplus before and after the introduction of the rent ceiling.

   b. Will this policy be popular with renters? with landlords?

   c. An economist explains to the city council that this policy is creating a deadweight loss. Illustrate the deadweight loss in your diagram.

6. On Thursday nights, a local restaurant has a pasta special. Ari likes the restaurant's pasta, and his willingness to pay for each serving is shown in the accompanying table.

Quantity of pasta (servings)	Willingness to pay for pasta (per serving)
1	$10
2	8
3	6
4	4
5	2
6	0

   a. If the price of a serving of pasta is $4, how many servings will Ari buy? How much consumer surplus does he receive?

   b. The following week, Ari is back at the restaurant again, but now the price of a serving of pasta is $6. By how much does his consumer surplus decrease compared to the previous week?

c. One week later, he goes to the restaurant again. He discovers that the restaurant is offering an "all you can eat" special for $25. How much pasta will Ari eat, and how much consumer surplus does he receive now?

d. Suppose you own the restaurant and Ari is a "typical" customer. What is the highest price you can charge for the "all you can eat" special and still attract customers?

7. The accompanying diagram shows the market for cigarettes. The current equilibrium price per pack is $4, and every day 40 million packs of cigarettes are sold. In order to recover some of the health care costs associated with smoking, the government imposes a tax of $2 per pack. This will raise the equilibrium price to $5 per pack and reduce the equilibrium quantity to 30 million packs.

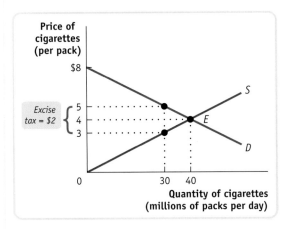

The economist working for the tobacco lobby claims that this tax will reduce consumer surplus for smokers by $40 million per day, since 40 million packs now cost $1 more per pack. The economist working for the lobby for sufferers of second-hand smoke argues that this is an enormous overestimate and that the reduction in consumer surplus will be only $30 million per day, since after the imposition of the tax only 30 million packs of cigarettes will be bought and each of these packs will now cost $1 more. They are both wrong. Why?

8. Consider the original market for pizza in Collegetown, illustrated in the accompanying table. Collegetown officials decide to impose an excise tax on pizza of $4 per pizza.

Price of pizza	Quantity of pizza demanded	Quantity of pizza supplied
$10	0	6
9	1	5
8	2	4
7	3	3
6	4	2
5	5	1
4	6	0
3	7	0
2	8	0
1	9	0

a. What is the quantity of pizza bought and sold after the imposition of the tax? What is the price paid by consumers? What is the price received by producers?

b. Calculate the consumer surplus and the producer surplus after the imposition of the tax. By how much has the imposition of the tax reduced consumer surplus? By how much has it reduced producer surplus?

c. How much tax revenue does Collegetown earn from this tax?

d. Calculate the deadweight loss from this tax.

9. Consider once more the original market for pizza in Collegetown, illustrated in the table in Problem 8. Now Collegetown officials impose a price floor on pizza of $8.

a. What is the quantity of pizza bought and sold after the imposition of the price floor?

b. Calculate the consumer surplus and the producer surplus after the imposition of the price floor.

10. You are the manager of Fun World, a small amusement park. The accompanying diagram shows the demand curve of a typical customer at Fun World.

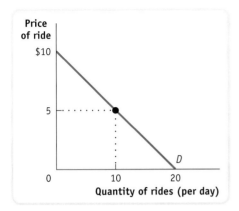

a. Suppose that the price of each ride is $5. At that price, how much consumer surplus does an individual consumer get? (Recall that the area of a triangle is ½ × the base of the triangle × the height of the triangle.)

b. Suppose that Fun World considers charging an admission fee, even though it maintains the price of each ride at $5. What is the maximum admission fee it could charge? (Assume that all potential customers have enough money to pay the fee.)

c. Suppose that Fun World lowered the price of each ride to zero. How much consumer surplus does an individual consumer get? What is the maximum admission fee Fun World could therefore charge?

11. The accompanying diagram illustrates a taxi driver's individual supply curve (assume that each taxi ride is the same distance).

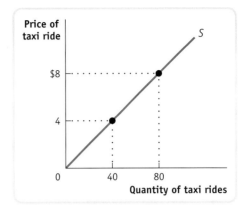

a. Suppose the city sets the price of taxi rides at $4 per ride. What is this taxi driver's producer surplus? (Recall that the area of a triangle is ½ × the base of the triangle × the height of the triangle.)

b. Suppose now that the city keeps the price of a taxi ride set at $4, but it decides to charge taxi drivers a "licensing fee." What is the maximum licensing fee the city could extract from this taxi driver?

c. Suppose that the city allowed the price of taxi rides to increase to $8 per ride. How much producer surplus does an individual taxi driver now get? What is the maximum licensing fee the city could charge this taxi driver?

12. The state needs to raise money, and the governor has a choice of imposing an excise tax of the same amount on one of two previously untaxed goods: the state can tax either sales of restaurant meals or sales of gasoline. Both the demand for and the supply of restaurant meals are more elastic than the demand for and the supply of gasoline. If the governor wants to minimize the deadweight loss caused by the tax, which good should be taxed? For each good, draw a diagram that illustrates the deadweight loss from taxation.

>web... To continue your study and review of concepts in this chapter, please visit the Krugman/Wells website for quizzes, animated graph tutorials, web links to helpful resources, and more.

www.worthpublishers.com/krugmanwells

>> Macroeconomics: The Big Picture

DISAPPOINTED GRADUATES

2000 WAS A VERY GOOD YEAR TO BE a new graduate of an American university or college. As one newspaper put it, companies were "tripping over themselves to entice graduating seniors with fat salaries and other perks." 2000 was a particularly good year for students graduating with an MBA degree. But events were not nearly as kind to those who graduated just two years later. For many members of the class of 2002 at American business schools, graduation was not the happy occasion they had expected—a golden ticket to a well-paying job and success. Even at top business schools, such as Harvard, the University of Pennsylvania, and Stanford, students and faculty watched in disbelief as recruiters reneged on job offers that had already been extended to hundreds of newly graduated MBAs. Months after commencement, many graduates still had not landed jobs. As shown in Table 6-1, graduates who did find jobs typically received lower salaries than those of graduates just two years earlier. (If you rank salaries from high to low, the median salary is the salary right at the middle.)

There was nothing wrong with the new MBAs in 2002; they were every bit as talented and motivated as the graduates two years earlier. And the phenomenon wasn't limited to business school graduates. The difference was that in the spring of 2000 the economy was booming, and employers were anxious to hire more people. In the spring of 2002 the economy was weak. Many firms were laying off employees and were in no hurry to hire more. As you can see from Table 6-1, by 2004 job prospects had improved somewhat; however, starting salaries still lagged behind the levels MBA graduates enjoyed in the spring of 2000.

The alternation between boom and bust—between years in which jobs are plentiful and years in which jobs are hard to find—is known as the *business cycle*. But why is there a business cycle, and can anything be done to smooth it out? That's one question addressed by *macroeconomics*, the area of

Even the best students had a tough time finding a job in 2002.

Jose Luis Pelaez/Corbis

What you will learn in this chapter:

➤ An overview of macroeconomics, the study of the economy as a whole, and how it differs from microeconomics

➤ The importance of the **business cycle** and why policy makers seek to diminish the severity of business cycles

➤ What **long-run growth** is and how it determines a country's standard of living

➤ The meaning of **inflation** and **deflation** and why **price stability** is preferred

➤ What is special about the macroeconomics of an **open economy**, an economy that trades goods, services, and assets with other countries

TABLE 6-1

Median Starting Salaries of New MBAs from Selected Schools in 2000, 2002, and 2004

School	2000 starting salary	2002 starting salary	2004 starting salary
Stanford	$165,500	$138,100	$150,000
Harvard	160,000	134,600	147,500
Pennsylvania	156,000	124,500	144,000
Columbia	142,500	123,600	142,500
Dartmouth	149,500	122,100	135,000

Source: *Business Week* Graduate Survey, October 18, 2004.

economics that focuses on the behavior of the economy as a whole.

In contrast, *microeconomics* is concerned with the production and consumption decisions of consumers and producers and with the allocation of scarce resources among industries. Returning to our example of business school graduates, a typical question for microeconomics would be why different industries—say, investment banking versus marketing—pay different salaries to new graduates. Macroeconomics is concerned with developments in the national economy, such as the total output level, the overall level of prices, and the total level of employment. In addition, macroeconomics analyzes how the behavior of the economy depends on and is affected by the workings of the global economy.

Another element of Table 6-1 should strike you: new MBAs get paid an awful lot of money. Most Americans don't earn as much as MBAs from elite business schools do. Still, the incomes of Americans in almost all walks of life are much higher than those typical in previous generations. The average starting salary for Stanford's MBA class of 1968 was only $12,000. A dollar doesn't go as far today as it did in the 1960s, but even after you adjust for *inflation*—a rise in the overall price level—MBA salaries in 2002 were more than twice as high as they were in 1968. This comparison touches on *long-run growth*, another fundamental area of study in macroeconomics. Long-run growth is the sustained upward trend in the economy's overall output, and is a critical factor in a country's ability to achieve higher incomes and a higher standard of living. The main reason MBAs were paid so much more in 2002 than in 1968 is that output per person in the United States had doubled over those years. As this comparison suggests, economists measure long-run growth by looking at the economy's performance over several decades—long enough to show, in retrospect, that the increase in output was a permanent trend rather than the result of a temporary boom in the economy. Historical evidence shows that over an extended period of time, long-run growth is much more important than the *business cycle*—short-run fluctuations in the economy's performance—in determining a country's living standards. The average graduate of the class of 2002, even though facing disappointing job prospects and a lower salary, would have had an enormously higher standard of living than a comparable graduate in 1968.

Earlier chapters have given you a grasp of some fundamental microeconomic concepts and principles. To understand the scope and sweep of macroeconomics, let's begin by looking more carefully at the difference between microeconomics and macroeconomics. Following that, we'll present an overview of the four main areas of macroeconomic study.

Microeconomics versus Macroeconomics

Table 6-2 lists some questions that are often asked in economics. A microeconomic version of the question appears on the left paired with a similar macroeconomic question on the right. By comparing the questions, you can begin to get a sense of the difference between microeconomics and macroeconomics.

As you can see, microeconomics focuses on how decisions are made by individuals and firms and the consequences of those decisions. For example, we use microeconomics to determine how much it would cost a university or college to offer a new course—a cost that includes the instructor's salary, the cost of class materials, and so on. The school can then decide whether or not to offer the course by weighing the costs and benefits. Macroeconomics, in contrast, examines the *aggregate* behavior of the economy—how the actions of all the individuals and firms in the economy interact to produce a particular economy-wide level of economic performance. For example, macroeconomics is concerned with the overall level of prices in the economy and how high or how low they are relative to prices last year, rather than focusing on the price of one particular good or service.

TABLE **6-2**

Microeconomic versus Macroeconomic Questions

Microeconomic Questions	Macroeconomic Questions
Should I go to business school or take a job right now?	How many people are employed in the economy as a whole this year?
What determines the salary offered by Citibank to Cherie Camajo, a new Columbia MBA?	What determines the overall salary levels paid to workers in a given year?
What determines the cost to a university or college of offering a new course?	What determines the overall level of prices in the economy as a whole?
What government policies should be adopted to make it easier for low-income students to attend college?	What government policies should be adopted to promote employment and growth in the economy as a whole?
What determines whether Citibank opens a new office in Shanghai?	What determines the overall trade in goods, services, and financial assets between the United States and the rest of the world?

You might imagine that macroeconomic questions can be answered simply by adding up microeconomic answers. For example, the model of supply and demand we introduced in Chapter 3 tells us how the equilibrium price of an individual good or service is determined in a competitive market. So you might think that applying supply and demand analysis to every good and service in the economy, then summing the results, is the way to understand the overall level of prices in the economy as a whole.

But that turns out not to be the case: although basic concepts such as supply and demand are as essential to macroeconomics as they are to microeconomics, answering macroeconomic questions requires an additional set of tools and an expanded frame of reference. We will develop the required tools in the chapters ahead. We'll start by developing the wider viewpoint that characterizes macroeconomics, and we'll consider four principal ways in which macroeconomics differs from microeconomics.

Macroeconomics: The Whole Is Greater Than the Sum of Its Parts

If you occasionally drive on a highway, you probably know what a "rubber-necking" traffic jam is and why it is so annoying. Someone pulls over to the side of the road for something minor, such as changing a flat tire, and, pretty soon, a long traffic jam occurs as drivers slow down to take a look. What makes it so annoying is that the length of the traffic jam is greatly out of proportion to the minor event that precipitated it. Because some drivers hit their brakes in order to "rubber-neck," the drivers behind them must also hit their brakes, those behind them must do the same, and so on. The accumulation of all the individual tappings of brakes eventually leads to a long, wasteful traffic jam as each driver slows down a little bit more than the driver in front of him or her.

Understanding a rubber-necking traffic jam gives us some insight into one very important way in which macroeconomics is different from microeconomics: many thousands or millions of individual actions accumulate to produce an outcome that is larger than the simple sum of those individual actions. Consider, for example, what macroeconomists call the "Paradox of Thrift": when families and businesses are worried about the possibility of economic hard times, they prepare by cutting their spending. This reduction in spending depresses the economy as consumers spend less and businesses react by laying off workers. As a result, families and businesses may end up worse off than if they hadn't tried to act responsibly by cutting their spending. This is called a paradox because seemingly virtuous behavior—cautiously preparing for hard times by saving more—ends up harming everyone. And there is a flip-side to this story: when families and businesses are feeling optimistic about the future, they spend more today. This stimulates the economy, leading businesses to hire more workers, which further expands the economy. Seemingly profligate behavior leads to good times for all.

A key insight into macroeconomics is that in the short run—a time period consisting of several years but typically less than a decade—the combined effect of individual decisions can have effects that are very different from what any one individual intended, effects that are sometimes perverse. The behavior of the macroeconomy is, indeed, greater than the sum of individual actions and market outcomes.

Macroeconomic Policy

The fact that the sum of individual decisions can sometimes lead to bad results for the macroeconomy leads us to another critical difference between microeconomics and macroeconomics: the role of government policy. Careful study of how markets work has led microeconomists to the conclusion that government should typically leave markets alone. Except in certain well-defined cases, government intervention in markets usually leaves society as a whole worse off. There are, to be sure, important tasks for microeconomic policy—ensuring that markets perform well and intervening appropriately in the well-defined cases in which markets don't work well. But the area of microeconomics, in general, suggests a limited role for government intervention.

In contrast, economists generally believe there is a much wider role for government to play in macroeconomics—most importantly, to manage short-term fluctuations and adverse events in the economy. Like the highway police who work to prevent or reduce the effects of rubber-necking traffic jams, government policy makers work to prevent or reduce the effects of adverse events on the macroeconomy.

The widely held view that the government should take an active role in the management of the macroeconomy dates back to the Great Depression of the 1930s, a pivotal event in world economic history. A global event in which output plunged, banks failed, companies went bust, and workers were laid off en masse, it was as if the world economic engine had been thrown sharply into reverse. Lasting more than a decade, from 1929 through the end of the 1930s, it caused a thorough rethinking of the principles and aims of macroeconomics. During and after the Great Depression, economists developed the modern macroeconomic toolkit—*fiscal policy,* control of government spending and taxation, and *monetary policy,* control over interest rates and the quantity of money in circulation—now used to manage the performance of the macroeconomy.

Long-Run Growth

Why, in the United States, are we able to drive at high speeds to distant destinations on well-built and (usually) well-maintained highways? For that matter, why are we able to drive at all, rather than having to rely on horses or our own two feet? The reason is long-run growth. Another fundamental area of difference between microeconomics and macroeconomics is the latter's study of long-run growth. In macroeconomics we consider questions such as: What factors lead to a higher long-run growth rate? Are there government policies capable of increasing the long-run growth rate?

Microeconomics, in contrast, focuses on problems that take the amount of ouput the economy is capable of producing as given. For example, it might consider a question like, "Given the extent of national broadband Internet access, how should access be priced so that it is used as efficiently as possible?" That is, microeconomics asks how to use a given set of resources as efficiently as possible. Macroeconomics, though, examines the longer-run problem of how a society can *increase* the total amount of productive resources so that it can achieve higher rates of growth and a higher standard of living. Moreover, what governments should or shouldn't do to promote long-run growth is also an important area of study.

You might ask why long-run growth is considered a part of macroeconomics rather than microeconomics. The reason is that the subject of long-run growth fundamentally depends on the use of *economic aggregates*. As we'll see shortly, the study of aggregates is the last of the four principal ways in which macroeconomics differs from microeconomics.

Economic Aggregates

> **Economic aggregates** are economic measures that summarize data across different markets for goods, services, workers, and assets.

A distinctive feature of modern macroeconomics is that both its theory and policy implementation focus on **economic aggregates**—economic measures that summarize data across many different markets for goods, services, workers, and *assets*. (Assets are items that serve as a store of value, like cash or real estate.) For example, macroeconomics analyzes the performance of the economy by studying *aggregate output*, the total output of the economy over a given time period, and the *aggregate price level*, a measure of the overall level of prices in the economy. Using these aggregate measures, we will study the business cycle and how fiscal policy and monetary policy can be used to manage the business cycle. As the lucky and unlucky business school grads discovered, these fluctuations affect *unemployment*, a measure of the total number of unemployed workers in the economy. We'll also see how the business cycle and long-run growth are affected by *investment spending*, additions to the economy's supply of productive *physical capital*, including machines, buildings, and inventories, as well as by *savings*, the amount that households and the government save in a given year. And we'll see how economic interactions with other countries are analyzed using the *current account*, the total net amount of goods and services exported abroad, and the *financial account*, the total net amount of assets sold to foreigners.

In the remainder of this chapter and in Chapter 7, we'll focus on how many of these economic aggregates are calculated and measured. In subsequent chapters, we'll also define these aggregates more precisely.

Now that we have an idea of how macroeconomics and microeconomics differ, we're ready to begin learning about some of the key features of modern macroeconomics, starting with the business cycle. Before we do that, however, let's take a moment to look at the episode that created macroeconomics as we know it—and almost destroyed civilization as we know it.

economics in action

The Great Depression

Historians agree that the Great Depression, which began in 1929 and lasted through the 1930s, was one of the great defining moments in American history. And its effect wasn't just limited to the United States; the catastrophe was felt in virtually all the world's market economies—in Europe, Latin America, Japan, Canada, and Australia. Germany had one of the hardest-hit economies. Historians agree that this was a major reason for the rise of Nazism, which ultimately led to World War II.

The Great Depression was also *the* defining moment for modern macroeconomics: if we had to express in a few words the central mission of modern macroeconomics, it is to prevent anything like the Great Depression from ever happening again.

The Depression began in August 1929 with a mild fall in aggregate output. This, in turn, contributed to the single event most associated with the Great Depression—the famous stock market crash of October 1929. If the economic effects had been limited to the fallout from the stock market crash, then the economy would probably have experienced a short-term downturn. But what made the Depression a long-term disaster was the catastrophic rise in unemployment and huge decline in aggregate output that occurred after the market crash. In 1929, the *unemployment rate*—loosely speaking, the percentage of the working population unable to find jobs—was only 3.2%, as shown in panel (a) of Figure 6-1. By 1933 it was 24.9%: one American worker in four was out of work, with many people forced to rely on soup kitchens and other forms of charity simply to eat. Families were evicted from their homes, and shantytowns—enclaves with dwellings made from cast-off materials—

Marion Post Wolcott/Corbis

Much of modern macroeconomics arose as a way to understand the economic devastation caused by the Great Depression. Shown here is the family of an unemployed Appalachian coal miner in 1938.

arose across the country. Labor strife was pervasive because workers felt abandoned by the market economy. (In one famous example, World War I veterans, called "Bonus Marchers," erected a shantytown on the Mall in Washington, D.C. They were driven off by the U.S. Army after they made large and vocal demands for a government-paid bonus.) Along with the collapse in employment came an extraordinary collapse in *real gross domestic product* (or *real GDP*)—a measure of aggregate output. Real GDP fell 27% from 1929 to 1933, as panel (b) of Figure 6-1 shows. It was a time of incredible, unexpected misery, all the more shocking because the previous decade, the "Roaring Twenties," had been a time of unprecedented growth and prosperity. By the 1930s, many people felt that even democracy in America was at risk.

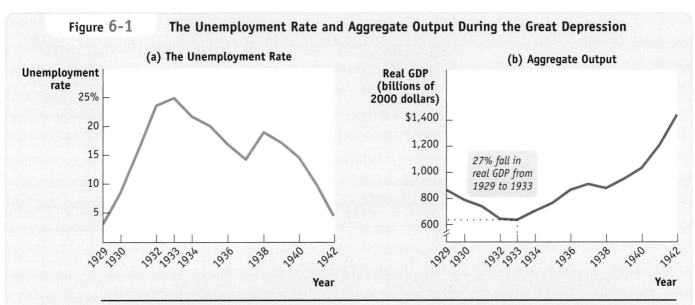

Figure 6-1   The Unemployment Rate and Aggregate Output During the Great Depression

(a) The Unemployment Rate

(b) Aggregate Output

27% fall in real GDP from 1929 to 1933

The economic slump that began in 1929 led to a drastic rise in the unemployment rate, shown in panel (a), and a drastic fall in aggregate output, shown in panel (b). Aggregate output, as measured by real GDP in 2000 dollars (we'll explain what "2000 dollars" are in Chapter 7), didn't rise above its 1929 level until 1937. The unemployment rate didn't return to single digits until 1941.

Source: U.S. Census Bureau. >*web*...

Although the economy eventually recovered, it took a very long time. In 1939, after a full decade of policy attempts to reverse the downturn, the unemployment rate was 17%—far higher than anything seen since. Real GDP did not get above its 1929 level until 1936, and it took until 1941 for the unemployment rate to drop back into single digits. Only with the coming of World War II did economic prosperity return.

The Great Depression led to a feverish effort by economists to understand what had happened and what could be done about it. This led to a breakthrough in economic measurement, and many of the statistics we now rely on to track the economy's performance first began to be collected during the 1930s. Economic theory changed dramatically with the 1936 publication of *The General Theory of Employment, Interest, and Money* by the British economist John Maynard Keynes—a book that ranks in influence with Adam Smith's *The Wealth of Nations*. Keynes's work, and the interpretations and critiques of his work by other economists, gave rise to both the field of macroeconomics and macroeconomic policy-making as we know it. ■

< < < < < < < < < < < < < < < < < <

>> **CHECK YOUR UNDERSTANDING 6-1**

1. Which of the following questions is appropriate to the study of microeconomics? Of macroeconomics? Explain your answers.
   a. How much profit is gained by installing a new piece of equipment in the Otis Furniture Factory?
   b. How does the overall level of sales of manufactured goods change as the state of the economy changes?
   c. What types of investment spending lead to a higher growth rate of the economy over time?
   d. Should Melanie buy a new car or not?

2. Explain why there is typically less scope for government intervention in microeconomics than in macroeconomics.

Solutions appear at back of book.

The Business Cycle

As we mentioned in our opening story, the poor job market of 2002 created a difficult time for all job-seekers, regardless of their skills. And it was particularly disappointing given that just two years earlier America had enjoyed a very strong job market.

The short-run alternation between economic downturns and upturns is known as the **business cycle.** A **depression** is a very deep and prolonged downturn; fortunately, the United States hasn't had one since the 1930s. But what we have had are less prolonged economic downturns known as **recessions,** periods in which output and *employment* are falling. In contrast, economic upturns, periods in which output and employment are rising, are known as **expansions** (sometimes called *recoveries*). According to the National Bureau of Economic Research there have been 10 recessions in the United States since World War II. Over that period the average recession has lasted 10 months and the average expansion has lasted 57 months. The average length of a business cycle, from the beginning of a recession to the beginning of the next recession, has been 5 years and 7 months. The shortest business cycle was 18 months and the longest was 10 years and 8 months. The recession felt by the 2002 job-seekers began in March 2001. Figure 6-2 shows the history of the U.S. unemployment rate since 1948 and the timing of post–World War II business cycles. The average unemployment rate over that period was 5.6%, and recessions are indicated in the figure by the shaded areas.

What happens during a business cycle, and what can be done about it? Let's look at three issues: the effects of recessions and expansions on unemployment; the effects on aggregate output; and the possible role of government policy.

The **business cycle** is the short-run alternation between economic downturns, known as recessions, and economic upturns, known as expansions.

A **depression** is a very deep and prolonged downturn.

Recessions are periods of economic downturns when output and employment are falling.

Expansions, or recoveries, are periods of economic upturns when output and employment are rising.

DEFINING RECESSIONS AND EXPANSIONS

Some readers may be wondering exactly how recessions and expansions are defined. The answer is that there is no exact definition!

In many countries, economists adopt the rule that a recession is a period of at least two consecutive quarters (a quarter is 3 months), during which aggregate output falls. The two-consecutive-quarter requirement is designed to avoid classifying brief hiccups in the economy's performance, with no lasting significance, as recessions. Sometimes, however, this definition seems too strict. For example, an economy that has three months of sharply declining output,

then three months of slightly positive growth, then another three months of rapid decline, should surely be considered to have endured a nine-month recession.

In the United States, we try to avoid such misclassifications by assigning the task of determining when a recession begins and ends to an independent panel of experts at the National Bureau of Economic Research (NBER). This panel looks at a variety of economic indicators, with the main focus on employment and production. But, ultimately, the panel makes a judgment call.

Sometimes this judgment is controversial. In fact, there is lingering controversy over the 2001 recession. According to the NBER, that recession began in March 2001 and ended in November 2001 when output began rising. Some critics argue, however, that the recession really began several months earlier, when industrial production began falling. Other critics argue that the recession didn't really end in 2001 because employment continued to fall and the job market remained weak for another year and a half.

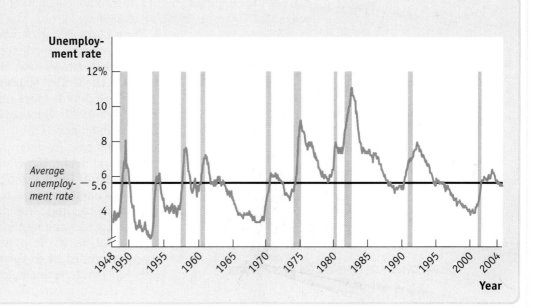

Figure 6-2

The Unemployment Rate and Recessions Since 1948

The unemployment rate normally rises during recessions and falls during expansions. As shown here, there were large fluctuations in the U.S. unemployment rate during the period after World War II. Shaded areas show periods of recession; unshaded areas are periods of expansion. Over the entire period from 1948 to 2004, the unemployment rate averaged 5.6%.

Source: Bureau of Labor Statistics; National Bureau of Economic Research.

Employment and Unemployment

Although not as severe as a depression, a recession is clearly an undesirable event. Like a depression, a recession leads to higher unemployment, reduced output, reduced incomes, and lower living standards.

To understand unemployment and how it relates to the adverse effects of recessions, we need to understand something about how the labor force is structured. **Employment** is the total number of people currently employed, and **unemployment** is the total number of people who are actively looking for work but aren't currently employed. A country's **labor force** is the sum of employment and unemployment. The official labor force doesn't include **discouraged workers,** people who are capable of working but have given up looking for jobs because they don't think they will find

Employment is the number of people currently employed in the economy.

Unemployment is the number of people who are actively looking for work but aren't currently employed.

The **labor force** is equal to the sum of employment and unemployment.

Discouraged workers are nonworking people who are capable of working but have given up looking for a job.

Underemployment is the number of people who work during a recession but receive lower wages than they would during an expansion due to fewer number of hours worked, lower-paying jobs, or both.

The **unemployment rate** is the percentage of the total number of people in the labor force who are unemployed.

them. Labor statistics don't include information on **underemployment,** the number of people who work during a recession but receive lower wages than they would during an expansion due to a smaller number of hours worked, lower-paying jobs, or both.

The **unemployment rate** is the percentage of the total number of people in the labor force who are unemployed. It is calculated as follows:

$$(6\text{-}1) \quad \frac{\text{Unemployment}}{\text{rate}} = \frac{\text{Number of unemployed workers}}{\text{Number of unemployed workers} + \text{Number of employed workers}} \times 100$$

The unemployment rate is usually a good indicator of what conditions are like in the job market: a high unemployment rate signals a poor job market in which jobs are hard to find; a low unemployment rate indicates a good job market in which jobs are relatively easy to find. (Exactly what makes for "high" or "low" has changed quite a bit over time in the United States, something we will discuss more fully in Chapter 15.) In general, during recessions the unemployment rate is rising; during expansions it is falling.

Look again at Figure 6-2, which shows the monthly unemployment rate from 1948 through 2004. The average unemployment rate for the whole period was 5.6%, but there were large fluctuations around that average. In fact, even in the most prosperous times there is some unemployment. In Chapter 15 we'll see why zero unemployment is not a realistic possibility and should not be a goal of policy makers. A booming economy, like that of the late 1960s or late 1990s, can push the unemployment rate down to 4% or even lower. But a severe recession, like that of 1981–1982, can push the unemployment rate into double digits (unemployment in that recession peaked in November 1982, at 10.8%).

"WOULD YOU LIKE A COPY OF MY MASTERS THESIS WITH THAT?"

Jim Borgman

These abstract numbers translate into enormous differences in personal experiences. For example, the 10.8% unemployment rate of late 1982 meant nearly 12 million people in the United States were actively seeking work but couldn't find jobs. More recently, as unemployment rose in the early 1990s, hundreds of thousands of workers were laid off, and many of those who did find jobs were severely underemployed. As a result, the nation was gripped by malaise and doubt. (One influential book at the time was titled *America: What Went Wrong?*) But at the end of the 1990s, as unemployment fell to 30-year lows, businesses scrambled to find workers and even students with mediocre grades and minimal experience got very good job offers. Alas, as is the nature of the business cycle, this happy era ended when the economy hit a rough patch in early 2001 and the unemployment rate rose again.

Aggregate Output

Rising unemployment is the most painful consequence of a recession, and falling unemployment the most urgently desired feature of an expansion. But the business cycle isn't just about jobs—it's also about output. Over the business cycle, the economy's level of output and its unemployment rate move in opposite directions.

Aggregate output is the economy's total production of final goods and services for a given time period.

Formally, **aggregate output** is the economy's total production of *final goods and services* for a given time period—usually a year. It excludes goods and services that are produced as inputs for the production of other goods (inputs are often called *intermediate goods*). Steel manufactured for the purpose of producing a car is not counted in aggregate output, but the car is. Real GDP is the actual numerical measure of aggregate output typically used by economists. We'll see how real GDP is calculated in Chapter 7. For now, the important point is that aggregate output normally falls in recessions but rises during expansions.

Panel (a) of Figure 6-3 shows the annual growth rate of U.S. real GDP from 1948 to 2004. That is, it plots the percent change in aggregate output from 1947 to 1948, from 1948 to 1949, and so on. On average, aggregate output grew 3.5% per year. As you can see, however, the actual growth rate fluctuated widely around that average, going as high as 8.7% in 1950 and as low as −1.9% in 1982. Comparison of panel (a) of Figure 6-3 to Figure 6-2 shows that the year in which aggregate output had its steepest post–World War II decline, 1982, was also the year in which the unemployment rate hit its post–World War II peak.

Panel (b) of Figure 6-3 shows the growth of U.S. real GDP over the same period, from 1948 to 2004. As you can see from the sustained upward trend line, declines in real GDP that occurred during recessions have been temporary events. Over the post–World War II period, real GDP has grown by more than 500% in the United States. We'll soon learn more about this long-run upward trend in aggregate output that is independent of the business cycle. For right now, however, let's learn more about the business cycle.

Figure 6-3

Growth in Aggregate Output, 1948–2004

Real GDP is a numerical measure of aggregate output, the output of the economy as a whole. Panel (a) shows the annual rate of growth of U.S. real GDP from 1948 to 2004, which averaged 3.5% over that period. Although real GDP rose in most years, the actual growth rate fluctuated with the business cycle, with real GDP actually falling in some years. Panel (b) shows the same data presented in a different form: it shows real GDP from 1948 to 2004. From it we see that when viewed from a period of time long enough to be independent of the business cycle, real GDP has grown substantially.

Source: Bureau of Economic Analysis.

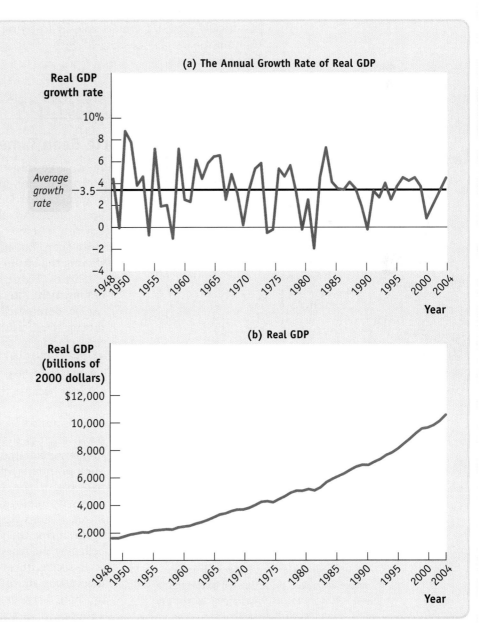

Taming the Business Cycle

As we've explained, one of the key missions of macroeconomics is to understand why recessions happen and what, if anything, can be done about them. In addition, we'll learn in Chapter 10 that another major macroeconomic concern is inflation, a rise in the overall price level that often results from an excessively strong expansion.

Policy efforts undertaken to reduce the severity of recessions or to rein in excessively strong expansions are called **stabilization policy.** Stabilization policy is based on two main tools—monetary policy and fiscal policy. **Monetary policy** attempts to stabilize the economy through changes in the quantity of money in circulation or in interest rates, or both. **Fiscal policy** attempts to stabilize the economy through changes in taxation or in government spending, or both. We'll examine these tools in Chapters 12 and 14, where we'll see how they can diminish the length and severity of recessions as well as dampen overly robust expansions. But we'll also see in those chapters why they don't work perfectly—that is, fiscal policy and monetary policy can't eliminate fluctuations in the economy altogether. So, in the end, the business cycle is still with us.

Although the business cycle is one of the main concerns of macroeconomics and historically played a crucial role in fostering the development of the field, macroeconomists are also concerned with other issues. We turn next to the question of long-run growth.

> Policy efforts undertaken to reduce the severity of recessions and to rein in excessively strong expansions are called **stabilization policy.**
>
> **Monetary policy** is a type of stabilization policy that involves changes in the quantity of money in circulation or in interest rates, or both.
>
> **Fiscal policy** is a type of stabilization policy that involves changes in taxation or in government spending, or both.

economics in action

Has the Business Cycle Been Tamed?

Macroeconomics as we know it came into existence during the Great Depression, created by economists determined to prevent anything like that from happening again. From the evidence, it appears that U.S. policy makers and economists have been successful: the United States has not suffered any downturn severe enough to be considered a depression since then. But have we succeeded in the related task of taming the business cycle?

Sort of. Figure 6-4 shows the average annual U.S. unemployment rate going all the way back to 1900. The figure is dominated by the huge rise in unemployment during the 1930s; since World War II the United States has managed to avoid anything comparably severe. Macroeconomists believe that part of the reason is that since World War II macroeconomic policies have been smarter because they are based on better macroeconomic theory.

Economists have learned, however, to be wary of pronouncements that the business cycle has been brought under control and that recessions are a thing of the past. Such pronouncements were common during the long expansion of the 1960s, but two severe recessions that drove unemployment to post–World War II highs followed. Claims that the business cycle was no more arose again during the long expansion of the 1990s, only to be belied by the recession of 2001.

In recent times other countries have suffered economic downturns almost as severe as the Great Depression. For example, between 1998 and 2002 Argentina suffered an 18% fall in its aggregate output. The unemployment rate rose to 24%, and many middle-class families were

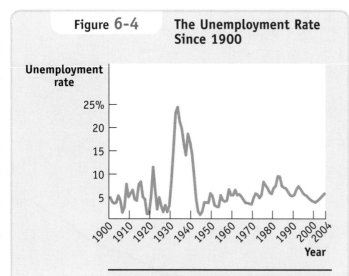

Figure 6-4   The Unemployment Rate Since 1900

Unemployment rate

Has progress in macroeconomics made the economy more stable? This figure shows average annual U.S. unemployment rates since 1900. Clearly, nothing like the Great Depression—the huge surge in unemployment that dominates the figure—has happened since. But economists who argued during the 1960s that the business cycle had been tamed were proven wrong by severe recessions in the 1970s and early 1980s.

Source: U.S. Census Bureau; Bureau of Labor Statistics.

plunged into poverty. These downturns inspired some humility in macroeconomists. Although they believe they know enough to prevent another Great Depression, the task of economic stabilization remains far from complete. ∎

> —

>>CHECK YOUR UNDERSTANDING 6-2

1. Why do the unemployment rate and aggregate output move in opposite directions over the business cycle?

2. Describe some of the costs to society of having a high unemployment rate.

3. What are likely signs that a stabilization policy has been successful over a period of time?

Solutions appear at back of book.

Long-Run Economic Growth

Although 2002 was a difficult year for all new graduates seeking jobs, the jobs actually on offer paid extremely well by historical standards. The pay package of an average U.S. worker in 2002, even after correcting for higher prices of goods and services, was worth almost three times as much as the pay of an average worker in 1948.

In fact, the purchasing power of the average American worker's wage, the average family's income, and just about any other measure of what ordinary people can afford, has been rising steadily since at least the middle of the nineteenth century. The reason is that aggregate output, despite occasional declines, has trended powerfully upward over the long run—and has grown at a much faster rate than the population.

Recall from panel (a) of Figure 6-3 that the average growth rate of aggregate output from 1948 to 2004 was 3.5%. Over that same period, the U.S. population grew at an average rate of only 1.3% each year. So the size of the economic pie per person, or per capita, grew an average of 2.2% each year, equal to the 3.5% annual growth rate of aggregate output minus the 1.3% annual growth rate of the population. That's enough to allow every American's standard of living to double every 35 years. And that, roughly speaking, is what happened.

The sustained upward trend in aggregate output is known as **secular long-run growth**, or **long-run growth** for short. The word *secular,* in this context, is used to distinguish long-run growth from the expansion phase of business cycles, which lasts less than five years on average. Secular long-run growth refers to the growth of the economy over several decades. You can get an idea of just how powerful a force long-run growth is by looking at Figure 6-5, which shows annual figures for U.S.

Secular long-run growth, or long-run growth, is the sustained upward trend in aggregate output over several decades.

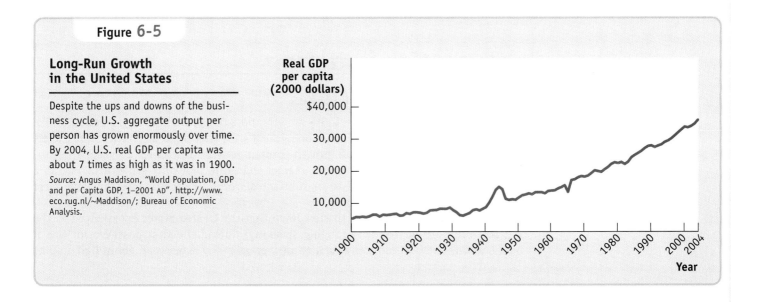

Figure 6-5

Long-Run Growth in the United States

Despite the ups and downs of the business cycle, U.S. aggregate output per person has grown enormously over time. By 2004, U.S. real GDP per capita was about 7 times as high as it was in 1900.

Source: Angus Maddison, "World Population, GDP and per Capita GDP, 1–2001 AD", http://www.eco.rug.nl/~Maddison/; Bureau of Economic Analysis.

Real GDP per capita (2000 dollars)

$40,000 —
30,000 —
20,000 —
10,000 —

1900 1910 1920 1930 1940 1950 1960 1970 1980 1990 2000 2004

Year

WHEN DID LONG-RUN GROWTH START?

We've seen that over the long run aggregate output rises steadily. In the United States it grew by more than 20-fold over the past 100 years. But did it grow that much in the previous 100 years? How far back does this process go?

The answer is that long-run growth is a relatively modern phenomenon. The U.S. economy was already growing steadily by the mid-nineteenth century—think railroads. But if you go back to the period before 1800, you find a world economy that grew extremely slowly by contemporary standards. Between the years 1000 and 1800, according to the best available estimates, the world economy grew less than 0.2% per year. Furthermore, population grew almost as fast, meaning that there was hardly any increase in aggregate output per capita. This economic stagnation was matched by unchanging living standards. For example, it's not clear that peasants in eighteenth-century Europe lived any better than Egyptian peasants in the age of the pharaohs. From examining historical records of birth and death rates, demographers know that in both periods human beings were living right on the edge of subsistence.

real GDP per capita from 1900 to 2004. As a result of this long-run growth, the U.S. economy's aggregate output per person was about 7 times as large in 2004 as it was in 1900. (Note that there was a 7-fold increase in real GDP per capita over the same period in which there was a 20-fold increase in real GDP. The difference in these two numbers is due to there being a much larger U.S. population in 2004 than in 1900.)

Long-run growth is fundamental to many of the most pressing economic questions today. In particular, *long-run growth per capita*—a sustained upward trend in aggregate output *per person*—is the key to higher wages and a rising standard of living. A major concern of macroeconomics—and the theme of Chapter 8—is trying to understand the long-run growth rate. Why was the average annual U.S. output growth rate 3.5% from 1948 to 2004? Could something have been done to make the growth rate higher?

These questions are even more urgent in poorer, less developed countries. In these countries, which would like to achieve a higher standard of living, the question of how to increase their growth rates is the central concern of economic policy.

As we'll see, macroeconomists don't use the same models to think about long-run growth that they use to think about the business cycle. It's always important to keep both sets of models in mind, because what is good in the long run can be bad in the short run, and vice versa. For example, the Paradox of Thrift shows that an attempt by households to increase their savings can be bad for the economy in the short run. But an economy's level of savings, as we'll see in Chapter 9, plays a crucial role in encouraging long-run economic growth.

economics in action

The Difference a Point Makes

What's the difference between 2.5% growth and 3.5% growth? It may not sound like much, and over the course of only one year it isn't that big a difference. But the effects of differences in long-run growth compound over time: after 25 years an economy that grows at 3.5% will be 30% larger than one that only grows at 2.5%. So a percentage point or so added to or subtracted from the growth rate can have huge economic implications over time.

A case in point is the growth slowdown that the United States experienced in the 1970s. From 1948 to 1973—roughly speaking, during the first post–World War II generation—the U.S. economy grew at an average of 3.9% per year, about half a point faster than its long-run average. For most people that meant an unprecedented rise in living standards, a general sense of miraculous prosperity.

From 1973 to 1995, however, the growth rate fell, averaging only 2.7%. The reasons for this slowdown remain disputed, but the consequences were clear: although the economic pie continued to grow, it was no longer growing fast enough to make everyone feel satisfied. Blue-collar workers believed that their wages were not keeping up with inflation, leading to a decline in their purchasing power. And investors were disappointed with company profits.

After 1995 there was a pickup in economic growth, again for reasons that remain in dispute. Many economists now believe that the U.S. economy has returned to a state in which growth may average 3.5% or so per year, that is, comparable to the miracle post–World War II generation. Let's hope that they are right! ■

> >

>> **CHECK YOUR UNDERSTANDING 6-3**

1. In the United States the 1950s and 1960s were considered times of great optimism and accomplishment on a national scale. In contrast, the 1970s and 1980s were thought of as periods of retrenchment, pessimism, and diminished expectations. Explain the economic source of the different outlooks.

2. Many poor countries have high rates of population growth. What does this imply about the long-run growth rates of aggregate output that they must achieve in order to generate a higher standard of living per person?

Solutions appear at back of book.

Inflation and Deflation

Earlier we said that the average worker in 2002 earned about three times as much as the average worker in 1948, *after correcting for higher prices of goods and services.* That's an important qualification. If we don't correct for the higher prices of goods and services, the rise in wages from 1948 to 2002 appears much larger—increasing by a factor of 20 rather than by a factor of only 3.

This example illustrates an important distinction in macroeconomics: the distinction between *nominal* versus *real.* A **nominal** measure of something, such as nominal wages, is a measure that has not been adjusted for changes in prices over time. So we say that *nominal wages* have increased by a factor of 20 from 1948 to 2002. By comparison, a **real** measure of something is a measure that has been adjusted for changes in prices over time. So we say that *real wages* have increased by a factor of 3 from 1948 to 2002. Economists typically express wages in real terms because the real wage is a better indicator of the actual change in workers' purchasing power over time: it captures how much wages have changed over and above the change in the prices of goods and services that workers buy. So although nominal wages rose by a factor of 20 in those 55 years, workers could buy only 3 times as much in goods and services rather than 20 times as much. To say this another way, an average worker's wage in 2002, expressed in *2002 dollars*—the amount of goods and services that an average worker's wage from 2002 would buy in 2002—was 3 times higher than the wage in 1948 when it is expressed in *2002 dollars*—the amount of goods and services that an average worker's wage from 1948 would buy in 2002.

We refer to the overall price level of all final goods and services in the economy—that is, the price level of aggregate output—as the **aggregate price level.** When this price level rises, we say that the economy is experiencing **inflation.** When it falls, the economy is experiencing **deflation.**

As we'll explain in Chapter 7, there are two widely used measures of the aggregate price level—the *GDP deflator* and the *consumer price index,* or *CPI.* Figure 6-6 on page 152 shows the consumer price index from 1913 to 2004.

A **nominal** measure is a measure that has not been adjusted for changes in prices over time.

A **real** measure is a measure that has been adjusted for changes in prices over time.

The **aggregate price level** is the overall price level for final goods and services in the economy.

A rising aggregate price level is **inflation.**

A falling aggregate price level is **deflation.**

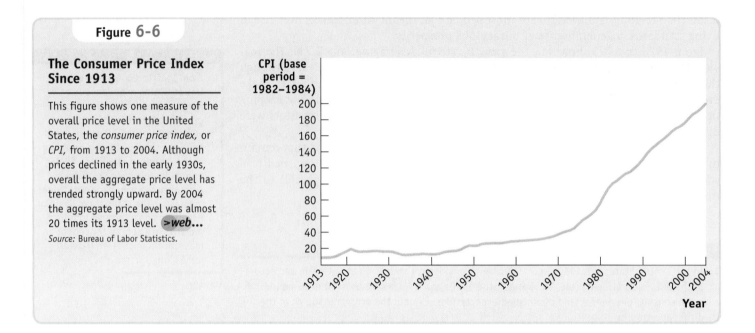

Figure 6-6

The Consumer Price Index Since 1913

This figure shows one measure of the overall price level in the United States, the *consumer price index,* or *CPI,* from 1913 to 2004. Although prices declined in the early 1930s, overall the aggregate price level has trended strongly upward. By 2004 the aggregate price level was almost 20 times its 1913 level. *>web...*

Source: Bureau of Labor Statistics.

You can see from the figure that the aggregate price level, like aggregate output (see Figure 6-3), has risen substantially over time. Overall prices were almost 20 times higher in 2004 than they were in 1913. Unlike the upward trend in aggregate output, however, the upward trend in prices is not a necessary feature of a well-performing economy. Nor is it necessarily a good thing.

Both inflation and deflation can pose problems for the economy, although these problems are subtler than those associated with recession. Here are two examples: Inflation discourages people from holding on to cash, because cash loses value over time if the aggregate price level is rising. This raises the cost of making purchases and sales for which cash is required. In extreme cases, people stop holding cash altogether and turn to barter. Deflation can cause the reverse problem. If the price level is falling, holding on to cash, which gains value over time, can become more attractive than investing in new factories and other productive assets. This can deepen a recession. We'll describe other costs of inflation and deflation in Chapter 16. For now, let's just note that in general economists regard **price stability**—in which the aggregate price level is changing, if at all, only slowly—as a desirable goal. (We say "changing slowly" instead of "not changing" because many macroeconomists believe that an inflation rate of 2 or 3% per year does little harm and may even do some good. We'll explain why in Chapter 16.) Price stability is a goal that seemed far out of reach for much of the post–World War II period but has been achieved to most macroeconomists' satisfaction in recent years.

The economy has **price stability** when the aggregate price level is changing only slowly.

The annual percent change in the aggregate price level is known as the **inflation rate** (which is negative in the case of deflation). Figure 6-7 shows the annual inflation rate in the United States from 1929 to 2004, measured as percent changes in the CPI. There were two brief bursts of inflation associated with World War II—one at the beginning, before the government imposed price controls, and one at the end, when the controls came off. Aside from those events, three main things stand out. First, there was sharp deflation in the early 1930s, associated with the onset of the Great Depression. Second, there was a prolonged period of high inflation in the 1970s and early 1980s. Finally, in the 1990s the aggregate price level returned to near-stability.

The **inflation rate** is the annual percent change in the aggregate price level.

Macroeconomists have devoted a lot of effort to understanding the causes of inflation and deflation and to providing advice to governments on how to steer a path between the two undesirable extremes.

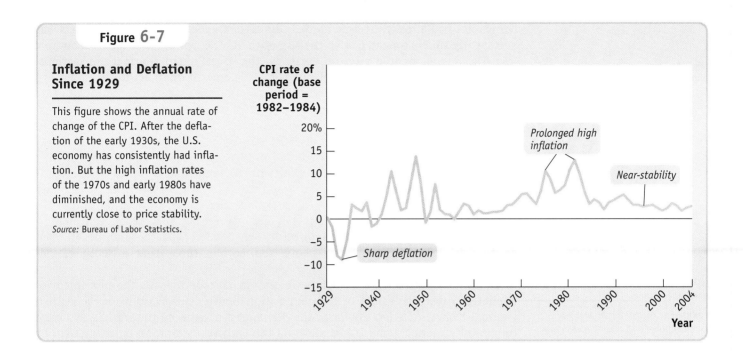

Figure 6-7

Inflation and Deflation Since 1929

This figure shows the annual rate of change of the CPI. After the deflation of the early 1930s, the U.S. economy has consistently had inflation. But the high inflation rates of the 1970s and early 1980s have diminished, and the economy is currently close to price stability.

Source: Bureau of Labor Statistics.

economics in action

A Fast (Food) Measure of Inflation

The original McDonald's opened in 1954. It offered fast service—it was, indeed, the original fast-food restaurant—and it was also very inexpensive. Hamburgers cost only $0.15; $0.25 with fries. Today a hamburger at a typical McDonald's costs five times as much—between $0.70 and $0.80. Has McDonald's lost touch with its fast-food roots? Have burgers become luxury cuisine?

No—in fact, a burger is, compared with other consumer goods, a better bargain today than it was in 1954. Burger prices have risen about 400%, from $0.15 to about $0.75, over the last half century. But the overall CPI has increased more than 600%. If McDonald's had matched the overall price-level increase, a hamburger would now cost between $0.90 and $1.00.

Inflation subsided in the 1990s—that is, the rate of increase in the aggregate price level slowed. And the same was true of burger prices—in fact, in 1997 McDonald's actually cut the price of many of its items, including the signature Big Mac. ∎

> >

>>CHECK YOUR UNDERSTANDING 6-4

1. Suppose your wages rose by 10% over the past year. In each of the following cases, determine whether you are better or worse off in comparison to the year before. Explain your answers.
   a. The yearly inflation rate was 5%.
   b. The yearly inflation rate was 15%.
   c. The economy experienced deflation, with prices falling at a rate of 2% per year.

Solutions appear at back of book.

The Open Economy

In 1954, when the original McDonald's was selling hamburgers for $0.15, the United States was very close to being a **closed economy**—an economy that does not trade goods, services, or assets with other countries. It wasn't literally closed, of course: even then the United States imported its coffee and bananas, and some U.S.

A **closed economy** is an economy that does not trade goods, services, or assets with other countries.

companies had already invested abroad. But trade in goods, services, and assets was sufficiently small compared with the size of the U.S. economy that macroeconomic analysis and policy could more or less ignore the effects of cross-border transactions.

That is no longer the case. The United States is now an **open economy**—an economy that does a lot of trade in goods, services, and assets with other countries. And the economies of most other countries are even more open than that of the United States. For example, while the U.S. sells approximately 12% of what it produces to other countries, Canada sells almost 50% of what it produces to other countries (mainly, though not entirely, to the United States).

As we discussed in Chapter 2, economies have become open over time because international trade is mutually beneficial: countries are able to specialize in activities they do comparatively well, are able to use their resources more efficiently, and so on.

By pursuing gains from trade, countries also change their macroeconomic circumstances. **Open-economy macroeconomics**—the study of macroeconomics in open economies—involves some issues above and beyond those that arise in closed-economy macroeconomics.

One important concern in open-economy macroeconomics is the movement of **exchange rates,** the values of different national currencies in terms of each other. Figure 6-8 shows the movement of the exchange rate between the world's two most important currencies, the U.S. dollar and the euro (the common currency used by many European countries), from 1999 to the beginning of 2005. As you can see, the rate swung between a minimum of $0.85 per euro and a maximum of more than $1.30 per euro. When it cost only $0.85 to buy a euro, European goods looked very cheap to Americans; when the euro rose to $1.30, the reverse was true.

One major effect of swings in exchange rates is that they have an impact on the aggregate price level. Suppose, for example, that a German car costs € 40,000. At an exchange rate of $0.85 per euro, that's $34,000. At an exchange rate of $1.30, that's $52,000. Because the prices of imported goods like foreign cars are included in some measures of the aggregate price level, changes in the exchange rate of the dollar versus other currencies affect those measures of the aggregate price level.

Another important effect of the exchange rate is its influence on the **trade balance,** the difference between the value of the goods and services a country sells to other countries and the value of the goods and services it buys from other countries. When changes in the exchange rate make American goods cheaper to foreigners, the American trade balance becomes more positive or less negative. In Chapter 19 we'll see that this

An **open economy** is an economy that trades goods, services, and assets with other countries.

Open-economy macroeconomics is the study of those aspects of macroeconomics that are affected by movements of goods, services, and assets across national boundaries.

The **exchange rate** between two national currencies is the value of one currency in terms of the other.

A country's **trade balance** is the difference between the value of the goods and services it sells to other countries and the value of the goods and services it buys from other countries.

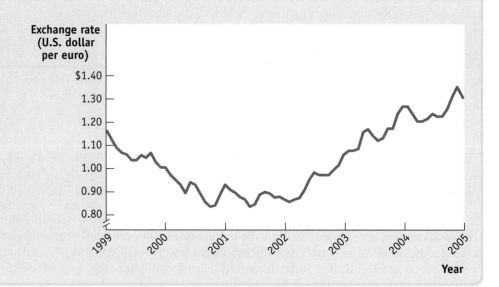

Figure 6-8

U.S. Dollars per Euro Since 1999

The U.S. dollar and Europe's euro are the world's two most important currencies. Over the course of only a few years, the exchange rate moved over a wide range, from $0.85 per euro to more than $1.30 per euro.

Source: Federal Reserve Bank of St. Louis.

increases U.S. aggregate output. When changes in the exchange rate make American goods more expensive to foreigners, the American trade balance becomes more negative or less positive.

Open economies trade goods and services as well as assets. International movements of *financial assets* are known as **capital flows.** We'll see in Chapter 9 how capital flows allow some countries to spend more on additions to their productive capacity than they would have been able to without capital flows. In the long run, this leads to a higher standard of living. We'll also see how capital flows allow international investors to get a higher return on their savings than they would have received in the absence of capital flows—also leading to a higher standard of living for investors.

Perhaps the most profound issue in open-economy macroeconomics involves the very existence of national currencies. Should the Canadian economy, which is closely intertwined with the economy of its much larger southern neighbor, even have its own currency? Or should there be a single currency for both the United States and Canada? This is not an academic question: although the Canadian dollar's independent existence seems assured for the time being, in 1999 most European countries gave up their independent national currencies in exchange for a pan-European currency, the euro. As we'll see, the question of whether other countries should follow Europe's example is the subject of intense debate, with a strong case to be made for both positions.

> **Capital flows** are international movements of financial assets.

economics in action

North of the Border

"At Windsor Crossing we welcome U.S. guests where your dollar buys you more!" So read an advertisement run in 2002 by an outlet mall that was pretty much the same as any outlet mall in the United States. But this one *wasn't* in the United States—it was in Windsor, Canada, just across the border from Detroit. (The U.S. Census considers Detroit and Windsor to be part of the same metropolitan area, even though they are in different countries.) The reason your U.S. dollar bought more was that in Windsor you could buy things with Canadian dollars—and one Canadian dollar, when this ad ran in June 2002, cost only US $0.65 (that is, $0.65 in U.S. dollars).

The Canadian dollar—known as the "loonie" because of the loon engraved on the dollar coin—isn't always that cheap. In fact, the Canadian dollar–U.S. dollar exchange rate has moved up and down significantly over the years. In 1974 a Canadian dollar was worth US $1.04. In 1986 it was down to US $0.71; in 1991 it was back up to US $0.89; in the spring of 2002 it was down to US $0.66; and by the end of 2004 it was back up to US $0.84.

These swings in the Canadian dollar–U.S. dollar exchange rate had strong effects on Canada's economy and some effect on the much larger U.S. economy. Since many of the goods Canadians buy are made in the United States, with prices set in U.S. dollars, a fall in the loonie—which means that it takes more Canadian dollars to buy a U.S. dollar—has the direct effect in Canada of raising consumer prices of goods and services imported from the United States. This sounds as if a *weak* loonie—a loonie that has fallen in value relative to other currencies like the U.S. dollar—is a bad thing for Canada, but there are compensations. Since Canadian wages and prices are largely set in Canadian dollars, a Canadian producer that sells to American customers has a cost advantage over U.S. competitors when the loonie is weak. That's because the price that it receives for its goods, in American dollars, has gone up relative to the production costs that it has to pay, which are in Canadian loonies. So it can lower its price to American customers in U.S. dollars and still make a profit—something its American competitors (whose costs are in U.S. dollars and so have not fallen) cannot match. And it's great news for Windsor's outlet malls. ∎

> >

>> QUICK REVIEW

➤ In contrast to a *closed economy*, an *open economy* is able to exploit gains from trade in goods, services, and assets.

➤ An open economy must be studied using the tools of *open-economy macroeconomics*.

➤ Changes in the *exchange rate* can affect the aggregate price level because they alter the prices of imported goods. They can also affect aggregate output through their effect on the *trade balance*.

➤ *Capital flows* of financial assets can also have important effects on aggregate output and raise a country's standard of living in the long run.

1. The euro, the currency of most countries that make up the European Union, went from approximately $1.15 in 1999 to $0.85 in 2001. Assume that over that time the price of European goods in euros, as well as the price of American goods in American dollars, did not change.

    a. Were European goods cheaper or more expensive for Americans in 1999 compared to 2001? Were American goods cheaper or more expensive for Europeans in 1999 compared to 2001?

    b. How do you think the change in the exchange rate of the euro versus the dollar from 1999 to 2001 affected the total value of European goods bought by Americans during this time? The total value of American goods bought by Europeans?

Solutions appear at back of book.

• A LOOK AHEAD •

In the chapters ahead we will examine in depth the issues described so briefly here. We'll start our discussion of macroeconomic models in Part 4 with an analysis of the long run—long-run growth, as well as the markets and institutions that channel savings in investment productive capacity. Part 5 then turns to the short run—the realm of the business cycle. There we learn how business cycles happen and how monetary policy and fiscal policy can be used to stabilize the economy. Part 6 turns to what we describe as the medium run—the period beyond the business cycle but before the long run, in which issues of inflation and deflation become central to the economic story.

Before we begin analyzing macroeconomic models, however, we need to know something about the numbers we are analyzing. How do we actually estimate aggregate output, the aggregate price level, and other key measures of macroeconomic performance?

SUMMARY

1. Macroeconomics is the study of the behavior of the economy as a whole—the total output level, the overall level of prices, total employment, and so on.

2. There are four principal ways in which macroeconomics differs from microeconomics: it focuses on how the accumulated effects of individual actions can lead to unintended macroeconomic outcomes; it allows greater scope for government intervention; it studies long-run growth; and it uses **economic aggregates,** measures that summarize data across various markets for goods, services, workers, and assets. Modern macroeconomics arose from efforts to understand the Great Depression.

3. One key concern of macroeconomics is the **business cycle,** the short-run alternation between **recessions,** periods of falling employment and output, and **expansions,** periods of rising employment and output. Modern macroeconomics arose largely in order to prevent the occurrence of another **depression,** a deep and prolonged economic downturn. The **labor force,** the sum of **employment** and **unemployment,** does not include **discouraged workers,** non-working people capable of working but who have given up looking for a job. Labor statistics also do not contain data on **underemployment,** employed workers who earn less than they would in an expansion due to lower-

paying jobs or fewer hours worked. The **unemployment rate,** which is usually a good measure of conditions in the labor market, has risen and fallen repeatedly over time. **Aggregate output,** the total level of output of final goods and services in the economy, moves in the opposite direction of unemployment over the business cycle.

4. **Stabilization policy,** the effort by governments to smooth out the business cycle, has two main tools: **monetary policy,** changes in the quantity of money in circulation or in interest rates, or both; and **fiscal policy,** changes in taxation or in government spending, or both.

5. Another key area of macroeconomic study is **secular long-run growth,** or simply **long-run growth,** the sustained upward trend in aggregate output over several decades. A sustained increase in aggregate output per capita is the key to rising living standards over time.

6. Economists distinguish between **nominal** measures, measures that haven't been adjusted for changing prices, and **real** measures, measures that have been adjusted for changing prices. Changes in real wages are a better measure of changes in workers' purchasing power. The **aggregate price level** is the overall price level for all final goods and services in the economy. The **inflation rate,** the annual percent change in the aggregate price level, is

positive when the aggregate price level is rising (**inflation**) and negative when the aggregate price level is falling (**deflation**). Because inflation and deflation can cause problems, **price stability** is generally preferred. Currently, the U.S. economy is close to price stability.

7. A **closed economy** is an economy that does not trade goods, services, or assets with other countries; an **open economy** trades goods, services, and assets with other countries. The United States has become an increasingly open economy, and **open-economy macroeconomics**

has become increasingly important. One of the main concerns introduced by open-economy macroeconomics is the **exchange rate,** the value of one currency in terms of another. Exchange rates can affect the aggregate price level. They can also affect aggregate output through their effect on the **trade balance,** the difference in value between sales to and purchases from foreigners. Another area of study is **capital flows,** movements of financial assets across borders.

KEY TERMS

Economic aggregates, p. 142
Business cycle, p. 144
Depression, p. 144
Recessions, p. 144
Expansions, p. 144
Employment, p. 145
Unemployment, p. 145
Labor force, p. 145
Discouraged workers, p. 145
Underemployment, p. 146
Unemployment rate, p. 146

Aggregate output, p. 146
Stabilization policy, p. 148
Monetary policy, p. 148
Fiscal policy, p. 148
Secular long-run growth (long-run growth), p. 149
Nominal, p. 151
Real, p. 151
Aggregate price level, p. 151
Inflation, p. 151
Deflation, p. 151

Price stability, p. 152
Inflation rate, p. 152
Closed economy, p. 153
Open economy, p. 154
Open-economy macroeconomics, p. 154
Exchange rate, p. 154
Trade balance, p. 154
Capital flows, p. 155

PROBLEMS

1. Which of the following questions are relevant for the study of macroeconomics and which for microeconomics?

   a. How will Ms. Martin's tips change when a large manufacturing plant near the restaurant where she works closes?

   b. What will happen to spending by consumers when the economy enters a downturn?

   c. How will the price of oranges change when a late frost damages Florida's orange groves?

   d. How will wages at a manufacturing plant change when its workforce is unionized?

   e. What will happen to U.S. exports as the dollar becomes less expensive in terms of other currencies?

   f. What is the relationship between a nation's unemployment rate and its inflation rate?

2. When one person saves, that person's wealth is increased, meaning that he or she can consume more in the future. But when everyone saves, everyone's income falls, meaning that everyone must consume less today. Explain this seeming contradiction.

3. What was the Great Depression? How did it affect the role of government in the economy and the macroeconomic toolkit?

4. Why do we consider a business-cycle expansion different from long-run economic growth? Why do we care about the size of the long-run growth rate of real GDP versus the size of the growth rate of the population?

5. There are 100,000 inhabitants in Macronesia. Among those 100,000 inhabitants, 25,000 are too old to work and 15,000 inhabitants are too young to work. Among the remaining 60,000 inhabitants, 10,000 are not working and have given up looking for work, 45,000 are currently employed, and the remaining 5,000 are looking for work but do not currently have a job.

   a. What is the number of people in the labor force in Macronesia?

   b. What is the unemployment rate in Macronesia?

   c. How many people in Macronesia are discouraged workers?

6. In 1798, Thomas Malthus's "Essay on the Principle of Population" was published. In it, he wrote: "Population, when unchecked, increases in a geometrical ratio. Subsistence increases only in an arithmetical ratio . . . . This implies a strong and constantly operating check on population from the difficulty of subsistence." Malthus was saying that the growth of

the population is limited by the amount of food available to eat; people will live at the subsistence level forever. Why didn't Malthus's description apply to the world after 1800?

7. At the start of 2005 in Macroland, aggregate output was $10 billion ($10,000 million) and the population was 1 million. During 2005, aggregate output increased by 3.5%, the population increased by 2.5%, and the aggregate price level remained constant.

   a. What was aggregate output per capita in Macroland at the start of 2005?

   b. What was aggregate output in Macroland at the end of 2005?

   c. What was the population of Macroland at the end of 2005?

   d. What was aggregate output per capita in Macroland at the end of 2005?

   e. What was the annual growth rate of aggregate output per capita in Macroland during 2005? *Hint:* the 2005 growth rate is equal to:

$$\frac{\text{Change in aggregate output during 2005}}{\text{Aggregate output at start of 2005}} \times 100$$

8. College tuition has risen significantly in the last few decades. From the 1971–1972 academic year to the 2001–2002 academic year, total tuition, room, and board paid by full-time undergraduate students went from $1,357 to $8,022 at public institutions and from $2,917 to $21,413 at private institutions. This is an average annual tuition increase of 6.1% at public institutions and 6.9% at private institutions. Over the same time, average personal income after taxes rose from $3,860 to $26,156 per year, which is an average annual rate of growth of personal income of 6.6%. Have these tuition increases made it more difficult for the average student to afford college tuition?

9. In May of each year, *The Economist* publishes data on the price of the Big Mac in different countries and exchange rates. The accompanying table shows some data used for the index from 2001 and 2003. Use this information to answer the questions below.

Country	2001		2003	
	Price of Big Mac (in local currency)	Exchange rate (foreign currency per U.S. dollar)	Price of Big Mac (in local currency)	Exchange rate (foreign currency per U.S. dollar)
Argentina	peso2.50	1.00 pesos per US$1	peso4.10	2.88 pesos per US$1
Canada	C$3.33	C$1.56 per US$1	C$3.20	C$1.45 per US$1
Euro area	€2.57	€1.14 per US$1	€2.71	€0.91 per US$1
Japan	¥294	¥124 per US$1	¥262	¥120 per US$1
United States	US$2.54		US$2.71	

   a. Where was it cheapest to buy a Big Mac in U.S. dollars in 2001?

   b. Where was it cheapest to buy a Big Mac in U.S. dollars in 2003?

   c. If the increase in the local currency price of the Big Mac in each country represented the average inflation rate in that country over the two-year period from 2001 to 2003, which nation experienced the most inflation? Did any of the nations experience deflation?

   d. For each currency, explain whether the dollar became more or less valuable in terms of that currency from 2001 to 2003.

>**web...** To continue your study and review of concepts in this chapter, please visit the Krugman/Wells website for quizzes, animated graph tutorials, web links to helpful resources, and more.

www.worthpublishers.com/krugmanwells

>> Tracking the Macroeconomy

AFTER THE REVOLUTION

IN DECEMBER 1975 THE GOVERNMENT of Portugal—a provisional government in the process of establishing a democracy—feared that it was facing an economic crisis. Business owners, alarmed by the rise of leftist political parties, were issuing dire warnings about plunging production. Newspapers speculated that the economy had shrunk 10 or even 15% since the 1974 revolution that had overthrown the country's long-standing dictatorship.

In the face of this supposed economic collapse, some Portuguese were pronouncing democracy itself a failure. Others declared that capitalism was the culprit and demanded that the government seize control of the nation's factories to force them to produce more. But how bad was the situation, really?

To answer this question, Portugal's top monetary official invited his old friend Richard Eckaus, an economist at the Massachusetts Institute of Technology, and two other MIT economists to look at the country's national accounts, the set of data collected on the country's economic activity. The

visiting experts had to engage in a lot of educated guesswork: Portugal's economic data collection had always been somewhat incomplete, and it had been further disrupted by political upheavals. For example, the country's statisticians normally tracked construction with data on the sales of structural steel and concrete. But in the somewhat chaotic situation of 1975, these indicators were moving in opposite directions because many builders were ignoring the construction regulations

With accurate economic data, Portugal was able to make the transition from revolution in 1975 to a prosperous democracy today.

What you will learn in this chapter:

➤ How economists use aggregate measures to track the performance of the economy

➤ What **gross domestic product,** or **GDP,** is and the three ways of calculating it

➤ The difference between **real GDP** and **nominal GDP** and why real GDP is the appropriate measure of real economic activity

➤ The significance of the **unemployment rate** and how it moves over the business cycle

➤ What a **price index** is and how it is used to calculate the **inflation rate**

and using very little steel. (Travel tip: if you find yourself visiting Portugal, try to avoid being in a 1975-vintage building during an earthquake.)

Still, they went to work with the available data, and within a week they were able to make a rough estimate: aggregate output had declined only 3% from 1974 to 1975. The economy had suffered a serious setback, but its decline was much less drastic than the calamity being portrayed in the newspapers. (Later revisions pushed the decline up to 4.5%, but that was still much less than feared.) The Portuguese government certainly had work to do, but there was no need to abandon either democracy or a market economy. In fact, the economy soon began to recover. Over the past three decades, Portugal—though

it has had its problems—has, on the whole, been a success story. A once-backward dictatorship is now a fairly prosperous, solidly democratic member of the European Union.

What's the lesson of this story? It is that economic measurement matters. If the government of Portugal had believed the scare stories some were telling at the time, it might have made major policy mistakes. Good macroeconomic policy depends on good measurement of what is happening in the economy as a whole.

In this chapter, we explain how macroeconomists measure key aspects of the economy—the level of income and aggregate output, the level of employment and unemployment, and the level and rate of change of prices.

The National Accounts

Almost all countries calculate a set of numbers known as the *national income and product accounts*. In fact, the accuracy of a country's accounts is a remarkably reliable indicator of its state of economic development—in general, the more reliable the accounts, the more economically advanced the country. When international economic agencies seek to help a less developed country, typically the first order of business is to send a team of experts to audit and improve the country's accounts.

In the United States, these numbers are calculated by the Bureau of Economic Analysis, a division of the U.S. government's Commerce Department. The **national income and product accounts,** often referred to simply as the **national accounts,** keep track of the spending of consumers, sales of producers, business investment spending, government purchases, and a variety of other flows of money between different sectors of the economy. Let's see how they work.

> The **national income and product accounts,** or **national accounts,** keep track of the flows of money between different sectors of the economy.

The Circular-Flow Diagram, Revisited and Expanded

To understand the principles behind the national accounts, it helps to look at Figure 7-1, a revised and expanded *circular-flow diagram* similar to the one we introduced in Chapter 2. Recall that in Figure 2-7 we showed the flows of money, goods and services, and factors of production through the economy. Here we restrict ourselves to flows of money but add extra elements that allow us to show the key concepts behind the national accounts. As in our original version of the circular-flow diagram, the underlying principle is that the flow of money into each market or sector is equal to the flow of money coming out of that market or sector.

Figure 2-7 showed a simplified world containing only two kinds of "inhabitants," households and firms. And it illustrated the circular flow of money between households and firms, which remains visible in Figure 7-1. In the markets for goods and services, households engage in **consumer spending,** buying goods and services from domestic firms and from firms in the rest of the world. Households also own factors of production—

> **Consumer spending** is household spending on goods and services.

Figure 7-1   An Expanded Circular-Flow Diagram: The Flows of Money Through the Economy

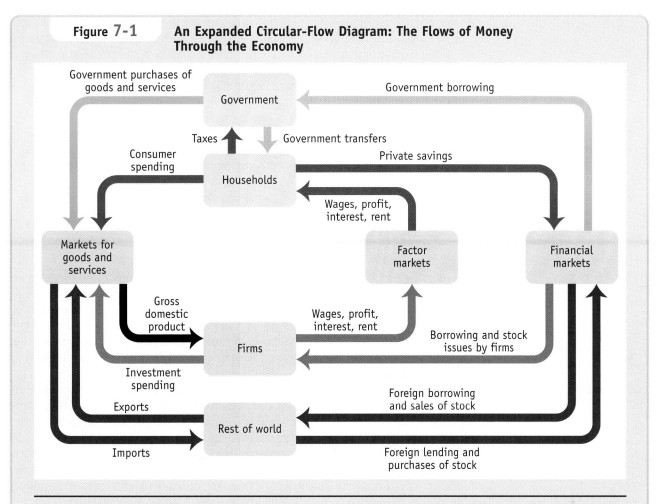

A circular flow of funds connects the four sectors of the economy—households, firms, government, and the rest of the world—via three types of markets: the factor markets, the markets for goods and services, and the financial markets. Funds flow from firms to households in the form of wages, profit, interest, and rent through the factor markets. After paying taxes to the government and receiving government transfers, households allocate the remaining income—disposable income—to private savings and consumer spending. Via the financial markets, private savings and funds from the rest of the world are channeled into investment spending by firms, government borrowing, foreign borrowing and lending, and foreign transactions of stocks. In turn, funds flow from the government and households to firms to pay for purchases of goods and services. Finally, exports to the rest of the world generate a flow of funds into the economy and imports lead to a flow of funds out of the economy. If we add up consumer spending on goods and services, investment spending by firms, government purchases of goods and services, and exports, then subtract the value of imports, the total flow of funds represented by this calculation is total spending on final goods and services produced in the United States. Equivalently, it's the value of all the final goods and services produced in the United States—that is, the gross domestic product of the economy.

labor, land, physical capital, and financial capital. They sell the use of these factors of production to firms, receiving wages, profit, interest payments, and rent in return. Firms buy and pay households for the use of those factors of production in the factor markets. Most households derive the bulk of their income from wages earned by selling labor. But households derive additional income from their indirect ownership of the physical capital used by firms, mainly in the form of **stocks,** shares in the ownership of a company, and **bonds,** borrowing in the form of an IOU that pays interest. So the income households receive from the factor markets includes profit distributed to shareholders, and the interest payments on bonds held by households. Finally, households receive rent in return for allowing firms to use land or structures that they own. So households receive income in the form of wages, profit, interest, and rent via factor markets.

A **stock** is a share in the ownership of a company held by a shareholder.

A **bond** is borrowing in the form of an IOU that pays interest.

Government transfers are payments by the government to individuals for which no good or service is provided in return.

Disposable income, equal to income plus government transfers minus taxes, is the total amount of household income available to spend on consumption and to save.

Private savings, equal to disposable income minus consumer spending, is disposable income that is not spent on consumption.

The banking, stock, and bond markets, which channel private savings and foreign lending into investment spending, government borrowing, and foreign borrowing are known as the **financial markets.**

Government borrowing is the amount of funds borrowed by the government in the financial markets.

Government purchases of goods and services are government expenditures on goods and services.

Goods and services sold to residents of other countries are **exports;** goods and services purchased from residents of other countries are **imports.**

Investment spending is spending on productive physical capital, such as machinery and construction of structures, and on changes to inventories.

In our original, simplified circular-flow diagram, households spent all the income they received via factor markets on goods and services. Figure 7-1, however, illustrates a more complicated and more realistic model. There we see two reasons why goods and services don't in fact absorb all of households' income. First, households don't get to keep all the income they receive via the factor markets. They must pay part of their income to the government in the form of taxes, such as income taxes and sales taxes. In addition, some households receive **government transfers**—payments by the government to individuals for which no good or service is provided in return, such as Social Security benefits and unemployment insurance payments. The total income households have left after paying taxes and receiving government transfers is **disposable income.**

In addition, households normally don't spend all their disposable income on goods and services. Instead, part of their income is typically set aside as **private savings,** which goes into **financial markets** where individuals, banks, and other institutions buy and sell stocks and bonds as well as make loans. As Figure 7-1 shows, the financial markets also receive funds from the rest of the world and provide funds to the government, to firms, and to the rest of the world.

Before going further, we can use the box representing households to illustrate an important general feature of the circular-flow diagram: the total sum of flows of money out of a given box is equal to the total sum of flows of money into that box. It's simply a matter of accounting: what goes in must come out. So, for example, the total flow of money out of households—the sum of taxes paid, consumer spending, and private savings—must equal the total flow of money into households—the sum of wages, profit, interest, rent, and government transfers.

Now let's look at the other types of inhabitants we've added to the circular-flow diagram, including the government and the rest of the world. The government returns part of the money it collects from taxes to households in the form of government transfers. However, it uses much of its tax revenue, plus additional funds borrowed in the financial markets through **government borrowing,** to buy goods and services. **Government purchases of goods and services,** the total purchases by federal, state, and local governments, include everything from the military spending on ammunition to your local public school's spending on chalk, erasers, and teacher salaries.

The rest of the world participates in the U.S. economy in three ways. First, some of the goods and services produced in the United States are sold to residents of other countries. For example, more than half of America's annual wheat and cotton crops are sold abroad. Goods and services sold to other countries are known as **exports.** Export sales lead to a flow of funds from the rest of the world into the United States to pay for them. Second, some of the goods and services purchased by residents of the United States are produced abroad. For example, many consumer goods are made in China. Goods and services purchased from residents of other countries are known as **imports.** Import purchases lead to a flow of funds out of the United States to pay for them. Third, foreigners can participate in U.S. financial markets by making transactions. Foreign lending—lending by foreigners to parties in the United States, and purchases by foreigners of shares of stock in American companies—generates a flow of funds into the United States from the rest of the world. Conversely, foreign borrowing—borrowing by foreigners from U.S. parties and purchases by Americans of stock in foreign companies—leads to a flow of funds out of the United States to the rest of the world.

Finally, let's go back to the markets for goods and services. In Chapter 2 we focused only on purchases of goods and services by households. We now see that there are other types of spending on goods and services, including government purchases, imports, and exports. Notice that firms also buy goods and services in our expanded economy. For example, an automobile company that is building a new factory will buy investment goods, stamping presses, welding robots, and other machines from companies that specialize in producing these items. It will also accumulate an inventory of finished cars in preparation for shipping them to dealers. The national income accounts count this **investment spending**—spending on productive physical capital, such as machinery and construction of structures, and on changes to *inventories*—as part of total spending on goods and services.

You might ask why changes to inventories are included in investment spending— finished cars aren't, after all, used to produce more cars. Additional inventories of finished goods are counted as investment spending because, like machinery, they contribute to greater future sales for a firm. So spending on additions to inventories is a form of investment spending by a firm. Conversely, a drawing-down of inventories is counted as a fall in investment spending because it leads to lower future sales. It's also important to understand that investment spending includes spending on construction of any structure, regardless of whether it is an assembly plant or a new house. Why include construction of homes? Because, like a plant, a new house produces a future stream of services—housing services for its occupants.

Suppose that we add up consumer spending on goods and services, investment spending, government purchases of goods and services, and the value of exports, then subtract the value of imports. That measure has a name: it's a country's *gross domestic product*. But before we can formally define gross domestic product, or GDP, we have to examine an important distinction between classes of goods and services: the difference between *final goods and services* versus *intermediate goods and services*.

Gross Domestic Product

A consumer's purchase of a new car from a dealer is one example of a sale of **final goods and services:** goods and services sold to the final, or end, user. But an automobile manufacturer's purchase of steel from a steel foundry or glass from a glassmaker is an example of purchasing **intermediate goods and services:** goods and services that are inputs for production of final goods and services. In the case of intermediate goods and services, the purchaser—another firm—is *not* the final user.

Gross domestic product, or **GDP,** is the total value of all *final* goods and services produced in an economy during a given period, usually a year. In 2004 the GDP of the United States was $11,734 billion, or about $40,000 per person. So if you are an economist trying to construct a country's national accounts, *one way to calculate GDP is to calculate it directly: survey firms and find out the value of their production of final goods and services.* We'll explain in detail in the next section why intermediate goods, and some other types of goods as well, are not included in the calculation of GDP.

But adding up the total value of final goods and services produced isn't the only way of calculating GDP. Since GDP is equal to the total value of final goods and services produced in the economy, it must also equal the flow of funds received by firms from sales in the goods and services market. If you look again at the circular-flow diagram in Figure 7-1, you will see that the arrow going from markets for goods and services to firms is indeed labeled "Gross domestic product." By our basic rule of accounting, which says that flows out of any box are equal to flows into the box, the flow of funds out of the markets for goods and services to firms is equal to the total flow of funds into the markets for goods and services from other sectors. And as you can see from Figure 7-1, the total flow of funds into the markets for goods and services is total or **aggregate spending** on domestically produced final goods and services—the sum of consumer spending, investment spending, government purchases of goods and services, and exports minus imports. *So a second way of calculating GDP is to add up aggregate spending on domestically produced final goods and services in the economy.*

And there is yet another way of calculating GDP. The flow from firms to the factor markets is the factor income paid out by firms to households in the form of wages, profit, interest, and rent. Again, by accounting rules, the value of the flow of factor income from firms to households must be equal to the flow of money into firms from the markets for goods and services. And this last value, we know, is the total value of production in the economy—GDP. An intuitive explanation of why

Final goods and services are goods and services sold to the final, or end, user.

Intermediate goods and services are goods and services—bought from one firm by another firm—that are inputs for production of final goods and services.

Gross domestic product, or **GDP,** is the total value of all final goods and services produced in the economy during a given year.

Aggregate spending, the sum of consumer spending, investment spending, government purchases, and exports minus imports, is the total spending on domestically produced final goods and services in the economy.

"You wouldn't think there'd be much money in potatoes, chickens, and woodchopping, but it all adds up."

GDP is equal to the total value of factor income paid by firms in the economy to households is the fact that the value of each sale in the economy must accrue to someone as income—either as wages, profit, interest, or rent. *So a third way of calculating GDP is to sum the total factor income earned by households from firms in the economy.*

Calculating GDP

We've just explained that there are in fact three methods for calculating GDP. Government statisticians use all three methods. To explain how these three methods work, we will consider a hypothetical economy, shown in Figure 7-2. This economy consists of three firms—American Motors, Inc., which produces one car per year; American Steel, Inc., which produces the steel that goes into the car; and American Ore, Inc., which mines the iron ore that goes into the steel. This economy produces one car, worth $21,500. So GDP is $21,500. Let's look at how the three different methods of calculating GDP yield the same result.

Measuring GDP as the Value of Production of Final Goods and Services
The first method for calculating GDP is to add up the value of all the final goods and services produced in the economy—a calculation that excludes the value of intermediate goods and services. Why are intermediate goods and services excluded? After all, don't they represent a very large and valuable portion of the economy?

   To understand why only final goods and services are included in GDP, look at the simplified economy described in Figure 7-2. Should we measure the GDP of this economy by adding up the total sales of the iron ore producer, the steel producer, and the auto producer? If we did, we would in effect be counting the value of the steel twice—once when it is sold by the steel plant to the auto plant, and again when the steel auto body is sold to a consumer as a finished car. And we would be counting the value of the iron ore *three* times—once when it is mined and sold to the steel company, a second time when it is made into steel and sold to the auto producer, and a third time when the steel is made into a car and sold to the consumer. So counting the full value of each producer's sales would cause us to count the same items several times and artificially inflate the

---

Figure 7-2

Calculating GDP

In this hypothetical economy consisting of three firms, GDP can be calculated in three different ways: measuring GDP as the value of production of final goods and services, by summing each firm's value added; measuring GDP as aggregate spending on domestically produced final goods and services; and measuring GDP as factor income earned from firms in the economy.

Aggregate spending on domestically produced final goods and services = $21,500

	American Ore, Inc.	American Steel, Inc.	American Motors, Inc.	Total factor income
Value of sales	$4,200 (ore)	$9,000 (steel)	$21,500 (car)	
Intermediate goods	0	4,200 (iron ore)	9,000 (steel)	
Wages	2,000	3,700	10,000	$15,700
Interest payments	1,000	600	1,000	2,600
Rent	200	300	500	1,000
Profit	1,000	200	1,000	2,200
Total expenditure by firm	4,200	9,000	21,500	
Value added per firm = **Value of sales − cost of intermediate goods**	4,200	4,800	12,500	

Total payments to factors = $21,500

Sum of value added = $21,500

calculation of GDP. For example, in Figure 7-2, the total value of all sales, intermediate and final, is $34,700: $21,500 from the sale of the car, plus $9,000 from the sale of the steel, plus $4,200 from the sale of the iron ore. Yet we know that GDP is only $21,500.

The way we avoid double-counting is to count only each producer's **value added** in the calculation of GDP: the difference between the value of its sales and the value of the inputs it purchases from other businesses. In this case, the value added of the auto producer is the dollar value of the cars it manufactures *minus* the cost of the steel it buys, or $12,500. The value added of the steel producer is the dollar value of the steel it produces *minus* the cost of the ore it buys, or $4,800. Only the ore producer, which we have assumed doesn't buy any intermediate inputs, has value added equal to its total sales, $4,200. The sum of the three producers' value added is $21,500, equal to GDP.

> The **value added** of a producer is the value of its sales minus the value of its purchases of inputs.

Measuring GDP as Spending on Domestically Produced Final Goods and Services

Another way to calculate GDP is by adding up aggregate spending on domestically produced final goods and services. That is, GDP can be measured by the flow of funds into firms. Like the method that estimates GDP as the value of production, this measurement must be carried out in a way that avoids double-counting. In terms of our steel and auto example, we don't want to count both consumer spending on a car (represented in Figure 7-2 by the sales price of the car) and the auto producer's spending on steel (represented in Figure 7-2 by the price of a car's worth of steel). If we counted both, we would be counting the steel embodied in the car twice. We solve this problem by counting only the value of sales to *final buyers,* such as consumers, firms that purchase investment goods, the government, or foreign buyers. In other words, in order to avoid double-counting of spending, we omit sales of inputs from one business to another when estimating GDP using spending data.

As we've already pointed out, however, the national accounts *do* include investment spending by firms as a part of final spending. That is, an auto company's purchase of steel to make a car isn't considered a part of final spending, but the company's purchase of new machinery for its factory *is* considered a part of final spending. What's the difference? Steel is an input that is used up in production; machinery, although it is used to make cars, will last for a number of years. Since purchases of capital goods, like machinery, that will last for a considerable time aren't closely tied to current production, the national accounts consider such purchases a form of final sales.

In later chapters, we will repeatedly make use of the proposition that GDP is equal to aggregate spending on domestically produced goods and services by final buyers. We will also develop models of how each group of final buyers decides how much to spend. So it is useful at this point to look at a breakdown of the types of spending that make up GDP.

GDP: WHAT'S IN AND WHAT'S OUT

It's easy to confuse what is included and what isn't included in GDP. So let's stop here for a moment and make sure the distinction is clear. Probably the biggest source of confusion is the difference between investment spending and spending on inputs. Investment spending—spending on investment goods, construction of structures (residential as well as commercial), and changes to inventories—is included in GDP. But spending on inputs is not. Why the difference? Recall from Chapter 2 that we made a distinction between resources that are *used up* and those that are *not used up* in production. An input, like steel, is used up in production. A metal-stamping machine, an investment good, is not; it will last for many years and will be used repeat-edly to make many cars. Since spending on investment goods and construction of structures is not directly tied to current output, economists consider such spending to be spending on final goods. And spending on changes to inventories, considered a part of investment spending, is also included in GDP. Why? Because, like a machine, additional inventory is an investment in future sales. And when a good is released for sale from inventories, its value is subtracted from the value of inventories and so from GDP. Used goods are not included in GDP because, as with inputs, to include them would be to double-count: counting them once when sold as new and again when re-sold as used. Finally, financial assets such as stocks and bonds are not included in GDP because they don't represent either the pro-duction or the sale of final goods and serv-ices. Rather, a bond represents a promise to repay with interest, and a stock represents a proof of ownership.

Here is a summary of what's included and not included in GDP.

Included
- Domestically produced final goods and services, including capital goods, new construction of structures, and changes to inventories

Not Included
- Intermediate goods and services
- Inputs
- Used goods
- Financial assets like stocks and bonds
- Foreign-produced goods and services

Look again at the markets for goods and services in Figure 7-1, and you will see that one component of sales by firms is consumer spending. Let's denote consumer spending with the symbol C. Figure 7-1 also shows three other components of sales: sales of investment spending goods to other businesses, which we will denote by *I*; government purchases of goods and services, which we will denote by *G*; and sales to foreigners—that is, exports—which we will denote by *X*.

But not all of this final spending goes toward domestically produced goods and services: spending on imports, which we will denote by *IM*, "leaks" across national borders. Putting this all together gives us the following equation that breaks GDP down by the four sources of aggregate spending:

(7-1) $GDP = C + I + G + X - IM$

We'll be seeing a lot of Equation 7-1 in later chapters.

Measuring GDP as Factor Income Earned from Firms in the Economy A final way to calculate GDP is to add up all the income earned by factors of production from firms in the economy—the wages earned by labor; the interest earned by those who lend their savings to firms and the government; the rent earned by those who lease their land or structures to firms; and the profit earned by the shareholders, the owners of the firms' physical capital. This is a valid measure because the money firms earn by selling goods and services must go somewhere; whatever isn't paid as wages, interest, or rent is profit. And part of profit is paid out to shareholders as *dividends*.

Figure 7-2 shows how this calculation works for our simplified economy. The shaded column at far right shows the total wages, interest, and rent paid by all these firms as well as their total profit. Summing up all of these yields total factor income of $21,500—again, equal to GDP.

We won't emphasize factor income as much as the other two methods of calculating GDP. It's important to keep in mind, however, that all the money spent on domestically produced goods and services generates factor income to households—that is, there really is a circular flow.

The Components of GDP Now that we know how GDP is calculated in principle, let's see what it looks like in practice.

Figure 7-3 shows the first two methods of calculating GDP side by side. The height of each bar above the horizontal axis represents the GDP of the U.S. economy in 2004: $11,734 billion. Each bar is divided to show the breakdown of that total in terms of where the value was added and how the money was spent.

FOR INQUIRING MINDS

GROSS WHAT?

Occasionally you may see references not to gross domestic product but to gross *national* product, or GNP. Is this just another name for the same thing? Not quite.

If you look at Figure 7-1 carefully, you may realize that there's a possibility that is missing from the figure. According to the figure, all factor income goes to domestic households. But what happens when profits are paid to foreigners who own stock in General Motors or Microsoft? And where do the profits earned by American companies operating overseas fit in?

The answer is that they go into GNP but not GDP. GNP is defined as the total factor income earned by residents of a country. It *excludes* factor income earned by foreigners, like profits paid to Japanese investors who own American stocks and payments to Mexican farm workers temporarily in the United States. But it *includes* factor income earned abroad by Americans, like the profits of IBM's European operations that accrue to IBM's American shareholders and the wages of American consultants who work temporarily in Asia.

In the early days of national income accounting, economists usually used GNP rather than GDP as a measure of the economy's size—although the measures were generally very close to each other. They switched to GDP mainly because it's considered a better indicator of short-run movements in production and because data on international flows of factor income are considered somewhat unreliable.

In practice, it doesn't make much difference which measure is used for large economies like that of the United States, where the flows of net factor income to other countries are small. In 2004, America's GNP was about 0.4% larger than its GDP, mainly because of the overseas profit of U.S. companies. For smaller countries, however, GDP and GNP can diverge significantly. For example, much of Ireland's industry is owned by American corporations, whose profit must be deducted from Ireland's GNP. In addition, Ireland has become a host to many temporary workers from poorer regions of Europe, whose wages must also be deducted from Ireland's GNP. As a result, in 2004 Ireland's GNP was only 84% of its GDP.

In the left bar in Figure 7-3, we see the breakdown of GDP by value added according to sector, the first method of calculating GDP. Of the $11,734 billion, $2,300 billion—less than 20%—consisted of the value added by producers of physical goods. Another $7,977 billion, or 68%, consisted of value added by private producers of services. The rest consisted of value added by government, in the form of military,

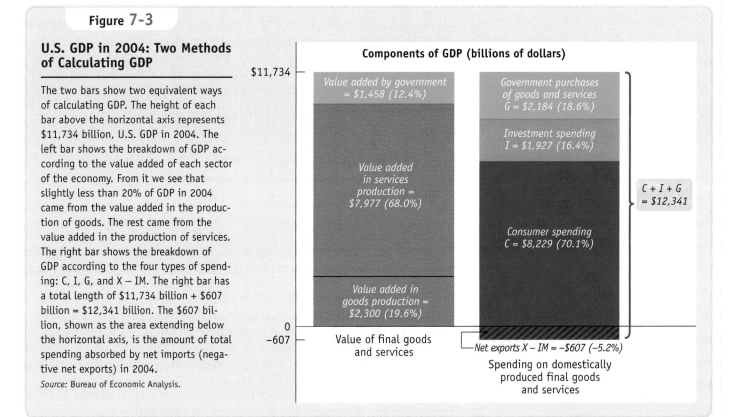

Figure 7-3

U.S. GDP in 2004: Two Methods of Calculating GDP

The two bars show two equivalent ways of calculating GDP. The height of each bar above the horizontal axis represents $11,734 billion, U.S. GDP in 2004. The left bar shows the breakdown of GDP according to the value added of each sector of the economy. From it we see that slightly less than 20% of GDP in 2004 came from the value added in the production of goods. The rest came from the value added in the production of services. The right bar shows the breakdown of GDP according to the four types of spending: C, I, G, and X − IM. The right bar has a total length of $11,734 billion + $607 billion = $12,341 billion. The $607 billion, shown as the area extending below the horizontal axis, is the amount of total spending absorbed by net imports (negative net exports) in 2004.

Source: Bureau of Economic Analysis.

Components of GDP (billions of dollars)

Value added by government = $1,458 (12.4%)

Value added in services production = $7,977 (68.0%)

Value added in goods production = $2,300 (19.6%)

Value of final goods and services

Government purchases of goods and services G = $2,184 (18.6%)

Investment spending I = $1,927 (16.4%)

Consumer spending C = $8,229 (70.1%)

C + I + G = $12,341

Net exports X − IM = −$607 (−5.2%)

Spending on domestically produced final goods and services

$11,734

0

−607

education, and other government services. As commentators often emphasize, the United States is now largely a service economy.

The right bar in Figure 7-3 corresponds to the second method of calculating GDP, showing the breakdown by the four types of aggregate spending. The total length of the right bar is longer than the total length of the left bar, a difference of $607 billion (which, as you can see, extends below the horizontal axis). That's because the total length of the right bar represents total spending in the economy, spending on both domestically produced and foreign produced final goods and services. Within the bar, consumer spending (C), which is 70.1% of GDP, dominates the picture. But some of that spending was absorbed by foreign-produced goods and services. In 2004, **net exports,** the difference between the value of exports and the value of imports (X – IM in Equation 7-1) was negative—the United States was a net importer of foreign goods and services. The 2004 value of X – IM was –$607 billion, or –5.2% of GDP. Thus a portion of the right bar extends below the horizontal axis by $607 billion to represent the amount of total spending that was absorbed by net imports and therefore did not lead to higher U.S. GDP. Investment spending (I) constituted 16.4% of GDP, while government purchases of goods and services (G) constituted 18.6% of GDP.

> **Net exports** are the difference between the value of exports and the value of imports.

What GDP Tells Us

Now we've seen the various ways that gross domestic product is calculated. But what does the measurement of GDP tell us?

The most important use of GDP is as a measure of the size of the economy, providing us a scale against which to measure the economic performance of other years, or compare the economic performance of other countries. For example, suppose you want to compare the economies of different nations. A natural approach is to compare their GDPs. In 2004, as we've seen, U.S. GDP was $11,734 billion; Japan's GDP was $4,665 billion; and the combined GDP of the 25 countries that make up the European Union was $12,758 billion. This comparison tells us that Japan, although it has the world's second-largest national economy, carries considerably less economic weight than does the United States. When taken in aggregate, Europe is America's equal.

Still, one must be careful when using GDP numbers, especially when making comparisons over time. That's because part of the increase in the value of GDP over time represents increases in the *prices* of goods and services rather than an increase in output. For example, U.S. GDP was $5,803 billion in 1990 and had roughly doubled to $11,734 billion by 2004. But the U.S. economy didn't actually double in size over that period. To measure actual changes in aggregate output, we need a modified version of GDP that is adjusted for price changes, known as *real GDP*. We'll see next how real GDP is calculated.

economics in action

Creating the National Accounts

The national accounts, like modern macroeconomics, owe their creation to the Great Depression. As the economy plunged into depression, government officials found their ability to respond crippled not only by the lack of adequate economic theories but also by the lack of adequate information. All they had were scattered statistics: railroad freight car loadings, stock prices, and incomplete indexes of industrial production. They could only guess at what was happening to the economy as a whole.

In response to this perceived lack of information, the Department of Commerce commissioned Simon Kuznets, a young Russian-born economist, to develop a set of national income accounts. (Kuznets later won the Nobel Prize in economics for his work.) The first version of these accounts was presented to Congress in 1937 and in a research report titled *National Income, 1929-35*.

There was, at first, some skepticism about the usefulness of such accounts. In 1936 the British economist John Maynard Keynes published *The General Theory of Employment,*

Interest, and Money, the book that created modern macroeconomic theory. Keynes argued against trying to use the concepts of aggregate output or the aggregate price level: "To say that net output to-day is greater, but the price-level lower, than ten years ago or one year ago, is a proposition of a similar character to the statement that Queen Victoria was a better queen but not a happier woman than Queen Elizabeth—a proposition not without meaning and not without interest, but unsuitable as material for the differential calculus." But macroeconomists soon found that the concepts of aggregate output and the aggregate price level, tied to actual measurements of these quantities, were powerful aids to understanding economic developments.

Kuznets's initial estimates fell short of the full modern set of accounts because they focused on income, not production. The push to fill out the national accounts came during World War II, when policy makers were in even more need of comprehensive measures of the economy's performance. The federal government began issuing estimates of gross domestic product and gross national product in 1942.

In January 2000, in its publication *Survey of Current Business,* the Department of Commerce ran an article titled "GDP: One of the Great Inventions of the 20th Century." This may seem a bit over the top, but national income accounting, invented in the United States, has since become a tool of economic analysis and policy making around the world. ■

$> >$

>>**CHECK YOUR UNDERSTANDING 7-1**

1. Explain why the three methods of calculating GDP produce the same estimate of GDP.

2. What are the various sectors to which firms make sales? What are the various ways in which households are linked with other sectors of the economy?

3. Consider Figure 7-2 and suppose you mistakenly believed that total value added was $30,500, the sum of the sales price of a car and a car's worth of steel. What items would you be counting twice?

Solutions appear at back of book.

Real GDP and Aggregate Output

Although the commonly cited GDP number is an interesting and useful statistic, it is not a useful measure for tracking changes in aggregate output over time. For example, GDP can rise either because the economy is producing more or simply because the prices of the goods and services it produces have increased. Likewise, GDP can fall either because the economy is producing less or because prices have fallen. In order to separate these possibilities, we must calculate how much the economy has changed in *real* terms over any given period. That is, we need to calculate how much of the change in GDP is due to a change in aggregate output separate from a change in prices. The measure that is used for this purpose is known as *real GDP.* Let's look first at how real GDP is calculated, then at what it means.

Calculating Real GDP

To understand how real GDP is calculated, imagine an economy in which only two goods, apples and oranges, are produced and in which both goods are sold only to final consumers. The outputs and prices of the two fruits for two consecutive years are shown in Table 7-1 on page 170.

The first thing we can say about these data is that the value of sales increased from year 1 to year 2. In the first year, the total value of sales was (2,000 billion × $0.25) + (1,000 billion × $0.50) = $1,000 billion; in the second it was (2,200 billion × $0.30) + (1,200 billion × $0.70) = $1,500 billion, which is 50% larger. But it is also clear from the table that this increase in the dollar value of GDP overstates the real growth in the economy. Although the quantities of both apples and oranges increased, the prices of both apples and oranges also rose. So part of the 50% increase in the dollar value of GDP simply reflects higher prices, not higher production of output.

TABLE 7-1

Calculating GDP and Real GDP in a Simple Economy

	Year 1	Year 2
Quantity of apples (billions)	2,000	2,200
Price of apple	$0.25	$0.30
Quantity of oranges (billions)	1,000	1,200
Price of orange	$0.50	$0.70
GDP (billions of dollars)	$1,000	$1,500
Real GDP (billions of year 1 dollars)	$1,000	$1,150

To estimate the true increase in aggregate output produced, we have to ask the following question: How much would GDP have gone up if prices had *not* changed? To answer this question, we need to find the value of output in year 2 expressed in year 1 prices. In year 1 the price of apples was $0.25 each and the price of oranges $0.50 each. So year 2 output *at year 1 prices* is (2,200 billion × $0.25) + (1,200 billion × $0.50) = $1,150 billion. And output in year 1 at year 1 prices was $1,000 billion. So in this example GDP measured in year 1 prices rose 15%—from $1,000 billion to $1,150 billion.

Now we can define **real GDP:** it is the total value of final goods and services produced in the economy during a year, calculated as if prices had stayed constant at the level of some given base year. A real GDP number always comes with information about what the base year is. A GDP number that has not been adjusted for changes in prices is calculated using the prices in the year in which the output is produced. Economists call this measure **nominal GDP,** GDP at current prices. If we had used nominal GDP to measure the true change in output from year 1 to year 2 in our apples and oranges example, we would have overstated the true growth in output: we would have claimed it to be 50%, when in fact it was only 15%. By comparing output in the two years using a common set of prices—the year 1 prices in this example—we are able to focus solely on changes in the quantity of output by eliminating the influence of changes in prices.

Table 7-2 shows a real-life version of our apples and oranges example. The second column shows nominal GDP in 1996, 2000, and 2004. The third column shows real GDP for each year in 2000 dollars. For 2000 the two numbers are the same. But real GDP in 1996 expressed in 2000 dollars was higher than nominal GDP in 1996, reflecting the fact that prices were in general higher in 2000 than in 1996. Real GDP in 2004 expressed in 2000 dollars, however, was less than nominal GDP in 2004 because prices in 2000 were lower than in 2004.

Real GDP is the total value of all final goods and services produced in the economy during a given year, calculated using the prices of a selected base year.

Nominal GDP is the value of all final goods and services produced in the economy during a given year, calculated using the prices current in the year in which the output is produced.

TABLE 7-2

Nominal versus Real GDP in 1996, 2000, and 2004

	Nominal GDP (billions of current dollars)	Real GDP (billions of 2000 dollars)
1996	$7,817	$8,329
2000	9,817	9,817
2004	11,734	10,842

Source: Bureau of Economic Analysis.

A Technical Detail: "Chained" Dollars

Until the 1990s, the real GDP estimates published by the Bureau of Economic Analysis were calculated in exactly the way we calculated real GDP in Table 7-1: the Bureau picked a base year and calculated each year's real GDP in the base year's prices.

But the U.S. national accounts now report real GDP in "billions of chained 2000 dollars." What does "chained" mean?

You might have noticed that there is an alternative way to calculate real GDP using the data in Table 7-1. Why not measure it using the prices of year 2 rather than year 1 as the base-year prices? This procedure seems equally valid. According to that calculation, real GDP in year 1 at year 2 prices is (2,000 billion × $0.30) + (1,000 billion × $0.70) = $1,300 billion; real GDP in year 2 in year 2 prices is $1,500 billion, the same as nominal GDP in year 2. So using year 2 prices as the base year, the growth in real GDP is equal to ($1,500 billion − $1,300 billion)/$1,300 billion = 0.154, or 15.4%. This is slightly higher than the figure we got from the previous calculation, in which year 1 prices were the base-year prices. In that calculation, we found that real GDP increased by 15%. Neither answer, 15.4% versus 15%, is more "correct" than the other.

Because 15.4% and 15% are pretty close to each other, it doesn't matter much which base year you choose in Table 7-1. But this isn't always true when calculating authentic GDP numbers. In fact, economists estimating the growth in U.S. real GDP during the 1980s and 1990s found that the results differed significantly depending on which year they used as a base. The main reason was the rapid pace of technological progress in computers, which led both to rapid growth in computer output and to falling prices of computers relative to those of other goods and services. When economists used an early base year, a year when computers were still expensive, their calculations produced a higher rate of real GDP growth than if they used a later base year, a year when computers were cheap. Because there was such a huge increase in output of computers, the two calculations produced very different estimates for real GDP.

As a result, the government economists who put together the U.S. national income accounts have adopted a method known as "chain-linking," which splits the difference between using early base years and late base years. We won't go into the details of that procedure; for the purposes of this book, we can think of calculating real GDP in the prices of a single base year.

What Real GDP Doesn't Measure

GDP is a measure of a country's aggregate output. Other things equal, a country with a larger population will have higher GDP simply because there are more people working. So if we want to compare GDP across countries but want to eliminate the effect of differences in population size, we use the measure **GDP per capita**—GDP divided by the size of the population, equivalent to the average GDP per person. Correspondingly, real GDP per capita is the average real GDP per person.

Although real GDP per capita can be a useful measure in some circumstances, it has well-known limitations as a measure of a country's living standards. Every once in a while economists are accused of believing that growth in real GDP per capita is the only thing that matters—of thinking that increasing real GDP per capita is a goal in itself. In fact, economists rarely make that mistake; the idea that economists care only about real GDP per capita is a sort of urban legend. Let's take a moment to be clear about why a country's real GDP per capita is not a sufficient measure of human welfare in that country and why growth in real GDP per capita is not an appropriate policy goal in itself.

One way to think about this issue is to say that an increase in real GDP means an expansion in the economy's production possibility frontier. Because the economy has increased its productive capacity, there are more things that society can achieve. But whether society actually makes good use of that increased potential to improve living standards is another matter. To put it in a slightly different way, your income may be higher this year than last year, but whether you use that higher income to actually improve your quality of life is your choice.

GDP per capita is GDP divided by the size of the population; it is equivalent to the average GDP per person.

The United Nations produces an annual document, the *Human Development Report,* that tries to rank countries by measures other than real GDP per capita. These measures include data on infant mortality, life expectancy, and literacy. It compiles these measures into the Human Development Index, which is an effort to determine how well societies are doing, aside from how much they produce. The index suggests that real GDP per capita is one of many important determinants of human welfare—but by no means the only one. Countries with high real GDP per capita—like the United States, European nations, and Japan—also score very well on just about every other indicator of human welfare. But there are some relatively poor countries—like Costa Rica—that have remarkably high literacy and life expectancy along with low infant mortality. And there are some relatively rich countries—especially countries with valuable natural resources—that score quite low on these criteria.

So let's say it again: real GDP per capita is a measure of an economy's average aggregate output per person—and so of what it *can* do. It is not a sufficient goal in itself because it doesn't address how a country uses that output to affect living standards. A country with a high GDP can afford to be healthy, to be well-educated, and in general to have a good quality of life. But there is not a one-to-one match between GDP and the quality of life.

economics in action

Good Decades, Bad Decades

How important is the distinction between nominal GDP and real GDP? If you are trying to interpret U.S. economic history, the answer is that it is very important indeed. Figure 7-4 tells the tale.

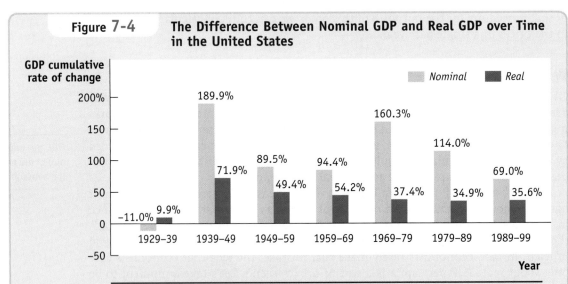

Figure 7-4   **The Difference Between Nominal GDP and Real GDP over Time in the United States**

To illustrate the difference between nominal GDP and real GDP, this figure shows the percent change in both measures over successive decades within the United States. (Real GDP was calculated using chained 2000 dollars.) The years 1929–1939 show the effect of deflation on the difference between nominal and real GDP: U.S. nominal GDP in 1939 was 11% lower than in 1929, but U.S. aggregate output as measured by real GDP was nearly 10% higher. The remaining years show the effect of inflation on the difference between the two measures: relatively high growth of U.S. nominal GDP in the years 1969–1979 and 1979–1989 contrast with relatively low growth of U.S. real GDP during those same periods. Those years experienced high levels of inflation and a simultaneous slowdown in real GDP growth. **>web...**

Source: Bureau of Economic Analysis.

Figure 7-4 shows the cumulative percent change in both U.S. nominal GDP and U.S. real GDP over successive decades since national income accounting began. That is, we show percent changes from 1929 to 1939, 1939 to 1949, and so on. In each pair, the bar on the left shows the percent change in U.S. nominal GDP over the time period, and the bar on the right shows the percent change in U.S. real GDP over the same period. (Real GDP was calculated using chained 2000 dollars.)

What we see right away is the effect of deflation during the 1930s: nominal GDP and real GDP actually moved in opposite directions during the Great Depression. Due to a falling price level, U.S. nominal GDP in 1939 was 11% lower than in 1929, but U.S. aggregate output as measured by real GDP was nearly 10% higher. After that, both nominal and real GDP rose every decade, but at different rates due to the influence of a changing price level. For example, U.S. nominal GDP grew much faster than U.S. real GDP for the years 1969–1979 and 1979–1989. The explanation is that those years saw high levels of inflation. ■

> >

>> CHECK YOUR UNDERSTANDING 7-2

1. Assume there are only two goods in the economy, french fries and onion rings. In 2004, 1,000,000 servings of french fries were sold at $0.40 each and 800,000 servings of onion rings at $0.60 each. From 2004 to 2005, the price of french fries rose by 25% and the servings sold fell by 10%; the price of onion rings fell by 15% and the servings sold rose by 5%.
   a. Calculate the nominal GDP in 2004 and 2005. Calculate real GDP in 2005 using 2004 as the base year.
   b. Why would an assessment of growth using nominal GDP be misguided?

2. From 1990 to 2000, the price of electronic equipment fell dramatically and the price of housing rose dramatically. What are the implications of this in deciding whether to use 1990 or 2000 as the base year in calculating 2005 real GDP?

Solutions appear at back of book.

The Unemployment Rate

In addition to measures of GDP, a number of other measures help us track the performance of the economy. As we learned in Chapter 6, one extremely important statistic for economic policy is the unemployment rate because unemployment leads to lost output and lower social welfare. Cases of very high unemployment, such as in a depression, often lead to political unrest. What exactly does the unemployment rate tell us about the economy?

Understanding the Unemployment Rate

Every month, the U.S. Census Bureau carries out the Current Population Survey, which involves interviewing a random sample of 60,000 American families. People are asked whether they are currently employed. If they are not employed, they are asked whether they have been looking for a job during the past four weeks. As you may recall from Chapter 6, the labor force is equal to the total of those who are either working or have recently been seeking employment; it does not include discouraged workers, those who have given up actively looking for a job. Those who are actively looking for work but have not, or at least not yet, found a job are classified as unemployed. The unemployment rate, which we showed how to calculate in Chapter 6, is the percent of the labor force that is unemployed.

What does the unemployment rate tell us? It indicates how easy or difficult it is to find a job given the current state of the economy. When the unemployment rate is low, nearly everyone who wants a job can find one. When the unemployment rate is high, jobs are hard to find. As an illustration, recall the story that we told at the beginning of Chapter 6: in the spring of 2000, when the U.S. unemployment rate was only about 4%, potential employers were anxiously wooing potential employees.

Two years later, when the unemployment rate had risen to 6%, new graduates found their job search much more difficult.

Although the unemployment rate is a good indicator of current conditions in the job market, it should not be taken literally as a measure of the percentage of people who want to work but can't find jobs. In some ways the unemployment rate exaggerates the difficulty people have in finding work. In other ways, the opposite is true: low measured unemployment can conceal deep frustration felt by discouraged workers.

Let's start with the argument that the measured unemployment rate is an overstatement of the percentage of people who want to work but can't find jobs. It's normal for someone searching for work to take at least a few weeks to find a suitable job. Yet a worker who is quite confident of getting a job, but has not yet accepted a position, is counted as unemployed. This means that even in boom times, when jobs are very easy to find, the unemployment rate does not fall to zero. As we've seen, the spring of 2000 was a very good time to be looking for a job, yet the unemployment rate was still 4%. We'll discuss in Chapter 15 why measured unemployment persists even when jobs are plentiful.

Meanwhile, an individual who has given up looking for a job for the time being—say, a laid-off steelworker in a deeply depressed steel town—isn't counted as unemployed because he or she has not been searching for work during the previous four weeks. Because it does not count discouraged workers, the measured unemployment rate may understate the percentage of people who want to work but are unable to find jobs.

Finally, it's important to realize that the unemployment rate varies greatly among demographic groups. Figure 7-5 shows unemployment rates for different groups in January 2005, when the overall unemployment rate of 5.2% was low by historical standards. As you can see, in January 2005 the unemployment rate for African-American workers was more than twice the national average, the unemployment rate for white teenagers was more than three times the national average, and the unemployment rate for African-American teenagers, at more than 30%, was almost seven times the national average. So even at a time when the overall unemployment rate was relatively low, jobs were hard to find for some groups. We'll examine the causes of persistent unemployment in Chapter 15.

So you should interpret the unemployment rate as an indicator of labor market conditions, not as a literal measure of the percentage of people unable to find jobs. Still, the

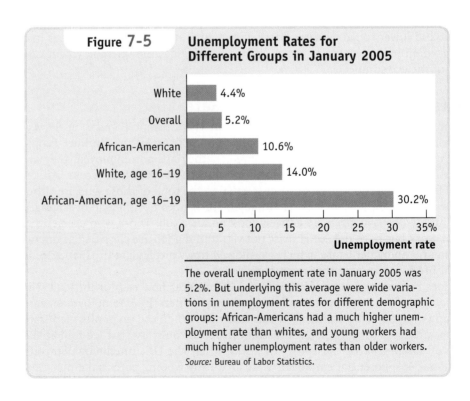

Figure 7-5 Unemployment Rates for Different Groups in January 2005

White	4.4%
Overall	5.2%
African-American	10.6%
White, age 16–19	14.0%
African-American, age 16–19	30.2%

Unemployment rate

The overall unemployment rate in January 2005 was 5.2%. But underlying this average were wide variations in unemployment rates for different demographic groups: African-Americans had a much higher unemployment rate than whites, and young workers had much higher unemployment rates than older workers.
Source: Bureau of Labor Statistics.

ups and downs of the unemployment rate have a significant impact on people's lives. What causes these fluctuations? We already saw, in Chapter 6, that the unemployment rate rises and falls with the business cycle. Now we can be more specific: there is a close relationship between the unemployment rate and the growth rate of real GDP.

Growth and Unemployment

Figure 7-6 is a scatter diagram showing observations of the growth rate of real GDP and changes in the unemployment rate over time in the United States. Each dot represents one year over the period 1949–2004. The horizontal axis measures the annual rate of growth in real GDP—the percent by which each year's real GDP changed compared to the previous year's real GDP. The vertical axis measures the *change* in the unemployment rate over the previous year in percentage points. For example, the average unemployment rate fell from 4.2% in 1999 to 4.0% in 2000; this is shown as a value of –0.2 along the vertical axis for the year 2000. Over the same period, real GDP grew by 3.7%; this is the value shown along the horizontal axis for the year 2000.

From the downward trend of the scatter points in Figure 7-6, it's clear that, in general, there is a negative relationship between growth in the economy and the rate of unemployment. Years of high growth in real GDP were years in which the unemployment rate fell, and years of low or negative growth in real GDP were years in which the unemployment rate rose. The average growth rate of real GDP over the period from 1949 to 2004 was 3.5%, and for reference we've included a dashed vertical line

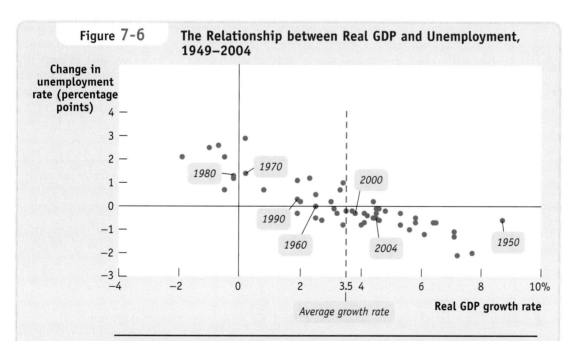

Figure 7-6   The Relationship between Real GDP and Unemployment, 1949–2004

The horizontal axis measures the annual growth rate of real GDP, the vertical axis measures the *change* in the unemployment rate over the previous year, and each dot represents one year over the period 1949–2004. The data show that there is typically a negative relationship between growth in the economy and the change in the rate of unemployment. The vertical dashed line is drawn at a value of 3.5%, the average growth rate of real GDP from 1949 to 2004. Points lying to the right of the vertical dashed line indicate that years of above-average growth were typically years of a falling unemployment rate. Points lying to the left show that years of below-average growth were typically years of a rising unemployment rate. The downward trend of the scatter points shows that there is, in general, a negative relationship between the real GDP growth rate and the change in the unemployment rate. **>web...**

Source: Bureau of Economic Analysis; Bureau of Labor Statistics.

indicating that value. You can see from examining the points lying to the right of the dashed vertical line that, with few exceptions, years when the economy grew faster than average were also years of a falling unemployment rate. For those years, the value on the vertical axis is negative. Points lying to the left of the dashed vertical line show that years when the economy grew more slowly than average were typically years with a rising unemployment rate. This relationship helps us understand why recessions, periods when real GDP falls, are so painful. As illustrated by the points to the left of the vertical axis in Figure 7-6, falling real GDP is always associated with a rising rate of unemployment, causing a great deal of hardship to families.

Our next and final subject in this chapter will be *price indexes,* which are measures of the aggregate price level.

economics in action

Jobless Recoveries

During recessions real GDP falls and the unemployment rate always rises. During expansions real GDP rises. Does the unemployment rate automatically fall?

Not necessarily. Look again at Figure 7-6. The data suggest that unemployment falls when growth is *above average* (the points lying to the right of the dashed vertical line), where the average growth rate of real GDP has been about 3.5% per year. If the economy grows at a positive rate, but below 3.5% per year, can the unemployment rate rise even as the economy grows? Put another way, can the unemployment rate rise when the economy grows at a below-average rate?

Yes, it can. The combination of slow but positive growth in real GDP with a rising unemployment rate is sometimes called a jobless recovery. It's not a usual occurrence. Normally, once an expansion gets going, growth picks up to a level that reduces unemployment. But jobless recoveries have happened. In fact, one occurred during the most recent economic expansion: the recession of 2001 officially ended in November of that year, but the unemployment rate continued to rise until the summer of 2003. ■

< < < < < < < < < < < < < < < < <

>>CHECK YOUR UNDERSTANDING 7-3

1. Suppose the advent of employment websites enables job-seekers to find a suitable job more quickly. What effect will this have on the unemployment rate over time? Also suppose that these websites encourage job-seekers who had given up their search to begin looking again. What effect will this have on the unemployment rate?

2. Which of the following are consistent with the observed relationship between growth in real GDP and changes in the unemployment rate? Which are not?
   a. A rise in the unemployment rate accompanies a fall in real GDP.
   b. A business recovery is associated with a greater percentage of the labor force being employed.
   c. Negative real GDP growth is associated with a fall in the unemployment rate.

   Solutions appear at back of book.

Price Indexes and the Aggregate Price Level

As we noted in Chapter 6, both inflation and deflation can pose problems for the economy. For that reason, we must have a way of measuring changes in the economy's overall price level over time. The aggregate price level, a single number, is supposed to be a measure of the overall price level of final goods and services. But a huge variety of goods and services are produced and consumed within the economy. How can we summarize the prices of all these goods and services with a single number? The answer lies in the concept of a *price index*—a concept best introduced with an example.

Market Baskets and Price Indexes

Suppose that a frost in Florida destroys most of the citrus harvest. As a result, the price of oranges rises from $0.20 each to $0.40 each, the price of grapefruit rises from $0.60 to $1.00, and the price of lemons rises from $0.25 to $0.45. How much has the price of citrus fruit increased?

One way to answer that question is to state three numbers, the changes in prices for oranges, grapefruit, and lemons. But this is a very cumbersome method. Rather than having to recite three numbers every time someone asks what has happened to the prices of citrus fruit, we would prefer to have some kind of overall measure of the *average* price increase.

Economists measure average price changes for consumer goods and services by asking how much more or less a typical consumer would have to spend to buy his or her previous *consumption bundle*—the typical basket of goods and services purchased before the price changes. Suppose that before the frost a typical consumer bought 200 oranges, 50 grapefruit, and 100 lemons over the course of a year. The average individual might change that pattern of consumption after the price changes caused by the frost. But we can still ask how much it would cost if he or she were to buy the same mix of fruit. A hypothetical consumption bundle, used to measure changes in the overall price level, is known as a **market basket.**

A **market basket** is a hypothetical set of consumer purchases of goods and services.

Table 7-3 shows the pre-frost and post-frost cost of the market basket. Before the frost, it cost $95. After the frost, the same bundle of goods cost $175. Since $175/$95 = 1.842, the post-frost basket costs 1.842 times the cost of the pre-frost basket, an increase in cost of 84.2%. So in this case we would say that the average price of citrus fruit increased 84.2% since the base year as a result of the frost.

TABLE 7-3

Calculating the Cost of a Market Basket

	Pre-frost	Post-frost
Price of orange	$0.20	$0.40
Price of grapefruit	$0.60	$1.00
Price of lemon	$0.25	$0.45
Cost of market basket (200 oranges, 50 grapefruit, 100 lemons)	(200 × $0.20) + (50 × $0.60) + (100 × $0.25) = $95.00	(200 × $0.40) + (50 × $1.00) + (100 × $0.45) = $175.00

Economists use the same method to measure changes in the overall price level: they track changes in the cost of buying a given market basket. In addition, economists perform another simplification in order to avoid having to keep track of the information that the market basket cost, for example, $95 in such-and-such a year. They *normalize* the measure of the aggregate price level so that it is equal to 100 in some given base year. A normalized measure of the overall price level is known as a **price index,** and it is always cited along with the year for which the aggregate price level is being measured and the base year. A price index can be calculated using the following formula:

A **price index** measures the cost of purchasing a given market basket in a given year, where that cost is normalized so that it is equal to 100 in the selected base year.

$$\text{(7-2)} \quad \text{Price index in a given year} = \frac{\text{Cost of market basket in a given year}}{\text{Cost of market basket in base year}} \times 100$$

For example, our citrus fruit market basket cost $95 before the frost; so we would define the price index for citrus fruit as (current cost of market basket/$95) × 100. This yields an index of 100 for the period before the frost and 184.2 for the period afterward. You should note that applying Equation 7-2 to calculate the price index for the base year always results in a price index equal to 100. That is, the price index in the base year is equal to: (cost of market basket in base year/cost of market basket in base year) × 100 = 100.

The price index makes it clear that the average price of citrus has risen 84.2% as a consequence of the frost. Because of its simplicity and intuitive appeal, this method is used to calculate a variety of price indexes to track the average price change among different groups of goods and services. For example, the *consumer price index* is the most widely used measure of the aggregate price level, the overall price level of final consumer goods and services across the economy. Price indexes are also the basis for measuring inflation. The **inflation rate** is the annual percent change in a price index. The inflation rate from year 1 to year 2 is calculated using the following formula:

> The **inflation rate** is the percent change per year in a price index—typically the consumer price index.

$$\textbf{(7-3)} \quad \text{Inflation rate} = \frac{\text{Price index in year 2} - \text{Price index in year 1}}{\text{Price index in year 1}} \times 100$$

Typically, a news report that cites "the inflation rate" is referring to the annual percent change in the consumer price index.

The Consumer Price Index

> The **consumer price index,** or **CPI,** measures the cost of the market basket of a typical urban American family.

The most widely used measure of prices in the United States is the **consumer price index** (often referred to simply as the **CPI**), which is intended to show how the cost of all purchases by a typical urban family has changed over time. It is calculated by surveying market prices for a market basket that is constructed to represent the consumption of a typical family of four living in a typical American city. The base period for the index is currently 1982–1984; that is, the index is calculated so that the average of consumer prices in 1982–1984 is 100.

The market basket used to calculate the CPI is far more complex than the three-fruit market basket we described above. In fact, to calculate the CPI, the Bureau of Labor Statistics sends its employees out to survey supermarkets, gas stations, hardware stores, and so on—some 21,000 retail outlets in 85 cities. Every month it tabulates about 90,000 prices, on everything from Romaine lettuce to video rentals. Figure 7-7 shows the makeup of the market basket underlying the current consumer price index by broad categories. The largest component, housing, includes all the costs of owning or renting a residence, including heating and electricity.

Figure 7-8 shows how the CPI has changed over the past 90 years. Since 1940 the CPI has risen steadily, although its annual percent increases in recent years have been much smaller than those of the 1970s and early 1980s. A proportional scale is used so that equal percent changes in the CPI appear the same.

The United States is not the only country that calculates a consumer price index. In fact, nearly every country has one. As you might expect, the market baskets that make up these indexes differ quite a lot from country to country. In poor countries, where people must spend a high proportion of their income just to feed themselves, food makes up a large share of the price index. Among high-income countries, differences in consumption patterns lead to differences in the price indexes: the Japanese price index puts a larger weight on raw fish and a smaller weight on beef than ours does, and the French price index puts a larger weight on wine.

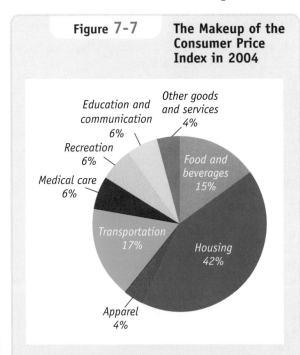

Figure 7-7   **The Makeup of the Consumer Price Index in 2004**

Education and communication 6%
Other goods and services 4%
Recreation 6%
Medical care 6%
Food and beverages 15%
Transportation 17%
Housing 42%
Apparel 4%

Housing—all the costs of owning or renting a residence—is the largest component of the market basket underlying the 2004 CPI, followed by transportation and food.
Source: Bureau of Labor Statistics.

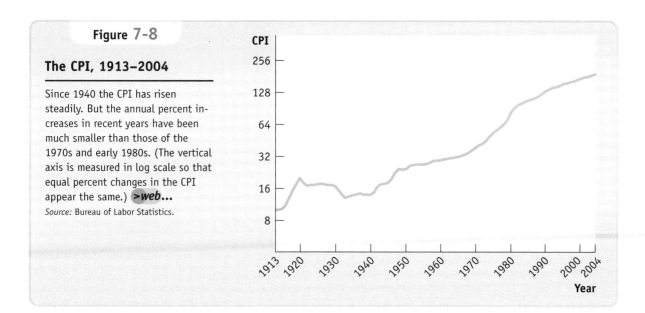

Figure 7-8

The CPI, 1913–2004

Since 1940 the CPI has risen steadily. But the annual percent increases in recent years have been much smaller than those of the 1970s and early 1980s. (The vertical axis is measured in log scale so that equal percent changes in the CPI appear the same.) **>web...**

Source: Bureau of Labor Statistics.

Other Price Measures

There are two other price measures that are also widely used to track economy-wide price changes. One is the **producer price index** (or PPI, which used to be known as the *wholesale price index*). As its name suggests, the producer price index measures the cost of a typical basket of goods and services—containing raw commodities such as steel, electricity, coal, and so on—purchased by producers. Because commodity producers are relatively quick to raise prices when they perceive a change in overall demand for their goods, the PPI often responds to inflationary or deflationary pressures more quickly than the CPI. As a result, the PPI is often regarded as an "early warning signal" of changes in the inflation rate.

> The **producer price index**, or **PPI**, measures changes in the prices of goods purchased by producers.

The other widely used price measure is the *GDP deflator;* it isn't exactly a price index, although it serves the same purpose. Recall how we distinguished between nominal GDP (GDP in current prices), and real GDP (GDP calculated using the prices of a base year). The **GDP deflator** for a given year is equal to 100 times the ratio of nominal GDP for that year to real GDP for that year expressed in prices of a selected base year. Since real GDP is currently expressed in 2000 dollars, the GDP deflator for 2000 is equal to 100. If nominal GDP doubles but real GDP does not change, the GDP deflator indicates that the aggregate price level doubled.

> The **GDP deflator** for a given year is 100 times the ratio of nominal GDP to real GDP in that year.

Perhaps the most important point about the different inflation rates generated by these three measures of prices is that they usually move closely together (although the

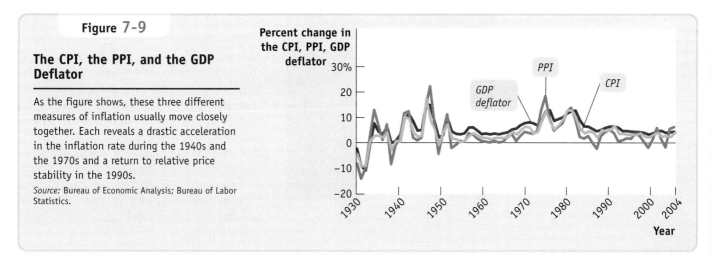

Figure 7-9

The CPI, the PPI, and the GDP Deflator

As the figure shows, these three different measures of inflation usually move closely together. Each reveals a drastic acceleration in the inflation rate during the 1940s and the 1970s and a return to relative price stability in the 1990s.

Source: Bureau of Economic Analysis; Bureau of Labor Statistics.

FOR INQUIRING MINDS

IS THE CPI BIASED?

The U.S. government takes considerable care in measuring consumer prices. Nonetheless, many—but not all—economists believe that the consumer price index systematically overstates the actual rate of inflation. Because many government payments are tied to the CPI, this is an important fact if true.

What do we mean by saying that the CPI overstates inflation? Imagine comparing two families: one in 1983, with an after-tax income of $20,000, and another in 2004, with an after-tax income of $40,000. According to the CPI, prices in 2004 were about twice as high as in 1983, so those two families should have about the same standard of living. Many economists argue, however, that the 2004 family would have a higher standard of living for two reasons.

One reason is the fact that the CPI measures the cost of buying a given market basket, when in fact consumers typically alter the mix of goods and services they buy away from products that have become relatively more expensive and toward products that have become relatively cheaper. For example, suppose that the price of hamburgers were to double suddenly. Americans currently eat a lot of burgers, but in the face of such a price rise many of them would switch to other foods—and a price index based on a market basket with a lot of hamburgers in it would overstate the true rise in the cost of living.

Actual changes in prices and in the mix of goods and services Americans consume are usually less dramatic than our hypothetical example. But the changing mix of consumption probably leads to some overstatement of inflation by the CPI.

The second reason arises from innovation. In 1983 many goods we now take for granted, especially those using information technology, didn't exist: there was no Internet and there were no iPods. By widening the range of consumer choice, innovation makes a given amount of money worth more. That is, innovation is like a fall in consumer prices.

For both these reasons, many economists believe that the CPI somewhat overstates inflation when we think of inflation as measuring the actual change in the cost of living of a typical urban American family. But there is no consensus on how large the bias is, and for the time being the official CPI remains the basis for most estimates of inflation.

---

producer price index tends to fluctuate more than either of the other two measures). Figure 7-9 on page 179 shows the annual percent changes in the three indexes since 1930. By all three measures, the U.S. economy experienced deflation during the early years of the Great Depression, wartime inflation, accelerating inflation during the 1970s, and a return to relative price stability in the 1990s.

economics in action

Indexing to the CPI

Although GDP is a very important number for shaping economic policy, official statistics on GDP don't have a direct effect on people's lives. The CPI, by contrast, has a direct and immediate impact on millions of Americans. The reason is that many payments are tied or "indexed" to the CPI—the amount paid rises or falls when the CPI rises or falls.

Donald A. Higgs Photography

A small change in the CPI has large consequences for those dependent on Social Security payments.

The practice of indexing payments to consumer prices goes back to the dawn of the United States as a nation. In 1780 the Massachusetts state legislature recognized that the pay of its soldiers fighting the British needed to be increased because of inflation that occurred during the Revolutionary War. The legislature adopted a formula that made a soldier's pay proportional to the cost of a market basket, consisting of 5 bushels of corn, $68\frac{4}{7}$ pounds of beef, 10 pounds of sheep's wool, and 16 pounds of sole leather.

Today, 48 million people, most of them old or disabled, receive checks from Social Security, a national retirement program that accounts for almost a quarter of current total federal spending—more than the defense budget. The amount of an individual's check is determined by a formula that reflects his or her previous payments into the system as well as other factors. In addition, all Social Security payments are adjusted each year to offset any increase in consumer prices over the previous year. The CPI is used to calculate the official estimate of the inflation rate used to adjust these payments yearly. So every percentage point added to the official estimate of the rate of inflation adds 1% to the checks received by tens of millions of individuals.

Other government payments are also indexed to the CPI. In addition, income tax brackets, the bands of income levels that determine a taxpayer's income tax rate, are also indexed to the CPI. (An individual in a higher income bracket pays a higher income tax rate in a progressive tax system like ours.) Indexing also extends to the private sector, where many private contracts, including some wage settlements, contain cost-of-living allowances (called COLAs) that adjust payments in proportion to changes in the CPI.

Because the CPI plays such an important and direct role in people's lives, it's a politically sensitive number. The Bureau of Labor Statistics, which calculates the CPI, takes great care in collecting and interpreting price and consumption data. They use a complex method in which households are surveyed to determine what they buy and where they shop and a carefully selected sample of stores are surveyed to get representative prices.

As explained in For Inquiring Minds on p. 180, however, there is still considerable controversy about whether the CPI accurately measures inflation. ∎

> >

>>CHECK YOUR UNDERSTANDING 7-4

1. Consider Table 7-3 but suppose that the market basket is composed of 100 oranges, 50 grapefruit, and 200 lemons. How does this change the pre-frost and post-frost price indexes? Explain. Generalize your explanation to how the construction of the market basket affects the price index.

2. Using what you have learned from Question 1, explain the effect of each of the following events on how well a CPI based on a market basket determined 10 years ago functions in measuring the change in prices today.
   a. A typical family owns more cars than it would have a decade ago. Over that time, the average price of a car has increased more than the average prices of other goods.
   b. Virtually no households had broadband Internet access a decade ago. Now, many households have it, and the price has regularly fallen each year.

3. The consumer price index in the United States (base period 1982–1984) was 184.0 in 2003 and 188.9 in 2004. Calculate the inflation rate from 2003 to 2004.

Solutions appear at back of book.

• A LOOK AHEAD •

We have now seen how economists put actual numbers to key macroeconomic variables such as aggregate output, the unemployment rate, and the aggregate price level. Now we can turn to the actual study of macroeconomics—analyzing how the values of those key macroeconomic variables are determined in the real world.

As we will learn, our analysis will depend on whether we are considering the long-run behavior of the economy or the short-run ups and downs of the business cycle. In the next two chapters we will set the short run to one side and focus on the long run. Our next topic will be the determinants of aggregate output in the long run—that is, the story behind *long-run growth*.

SUMMARY

1. Economists keep track of the flows of money between sectors with the **national income and product accounts,** or **national accounts.** Households earn income via the factor markets from wages, interest on **bonds,** profit accruing to owners of **stocks,** and rent on land. In addition, they receive **government transfers** from the government. **Disposable income,** total household income minus taxes plus government transfers, is allocated to **consumer spending** (C) and **private savings.** Via the **financial markets,** private savings and foreign lending are channeled to **investment spending** (I), government borrowing, and foreign borrowing. **Government purchases of goods and services** (G) are paid for by tax revenues and any **government borrowing. Exports** (X) generate an inflow of funds into the country from the rest of the world, but **imports** (IM) lead to an outflow of funds to the rest of the world. Foreigners can also buy stocks and bonds in the U.S. financial markets.

2. **Gross domestic product,** or **GDP,** measures the value of all **final goods and services** produced in the economy. It does not include the value of **intermediate goods and services.** It can be calculated in three ways: add up the **value added** by all producers; add up all spending on domestically produced final goods and services, leading to the equation GDP = C + I + G + X − IM; or add up all the income paid by domestic firms to factors of production. These three methods are equivalent because in the economy as a whole, total income paid by domestic firms to factors of production must equal total spending on domestically produced final goods and services. (X − IM), exports minus imports, is often called **net exports.**

3. **Real GDP** is the value of the final goods and services produced calculated using the prices of a selected base year. Except in the base year, real GDP is not the same as **nominal GDP,** aggregate output calculated using current prices. Analysis of the growth rate of aggregate output must use real GDP because doing so eliminates any change in the value of aggregate output due solely to price changes. Real **GDP per capita** is a measure of average aggregate output per person, but is not in itself an appropriate policy goal.

4. The unemployment rate is an indicator of the state of the labor market, but it should not be taken literally as a measure of the percentage of people who want to work but can't find jobs. It may overstate the true level of unemployment because a person typically spends time unemployed while searching for a job. It may also understate the true level of unemployment because it does not include discouraged workers.

5. There is a strong negative relationship between growth in real GDP and changes in the unemployment rate: when growth is above average, the unemployment rate falls; when it is below average, the unemployment rate rises.

6. To measure the aggregate price level, economists calculate the cost of purchasing a **market basket.** A **price index** is the ratio of the current cost of that market basket to the cost in a selected base year, multiplied by 100.

7. The **inflation rate** is the yearly percent change in a price index, typically based on the **consumer price index,** or **CPI,** the most common measure of the aggregate price level. A similar index for goods and services purchased by firms is the **producer price index.** Finally, economists also use the **GDP deflator,** which measures the price level by calculating the ratio of nominal to real GDP times 100.

KEY TERMS

PROBLEMS

1. At right is a simplified circular-flow diagram for the economy of Micronia.

   a. What is the value of GDP in Micronia?

   b. What is the value of net exports?

   c. What is the value of disposable income?

   d. Does the total flow of money out of households—the sum of taxes paid, consumer spending, and private savings—equal the total flow of money into households?

   e. How does the government of Micronia finance its purchases of goods and services?

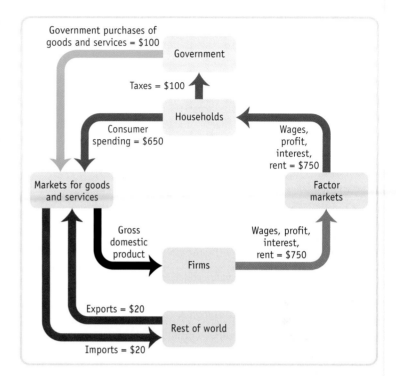

2. A more complex circular-flow diagram for the economy of Macronia is shown at right.

   a. What is the value of GDP in Macronia?

   b. What is the value of net exports?

   c. What is the value of disposable income?

   d. Does the total flow of money out of households—the sum of taxes paid, consumer spending, and private savings—equal the total flow of money into households?

   e. How does the government finance its spending?

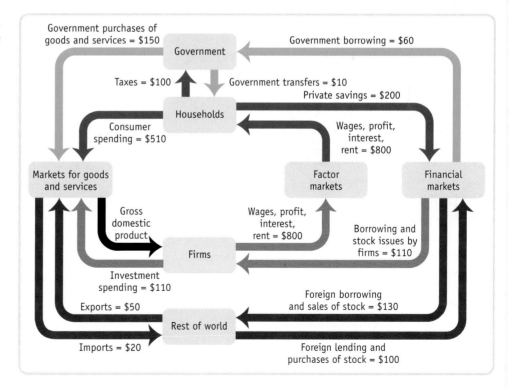

3. The small economy of Pizzania produces three goods (bread, cheese, and pizza), each produced by a separate company. The bread and cheese companies produce all the inputs they need to make bread and cheese, respectively; the pizza company uses the bread and cheese from the other companies to make its pizzas. All three companies employ labor to help produce their goods, and the difference between the value of goods sold and the sum of labor and input costs is the firm's profit. This table summarizes the activities of the three companies when all the bread and cheese produced are sold to the pizza company as inputs in the production of pizzas.

	Bread company	Cheese company	Pizza company
Cost of inputs	$0	$0	$50 Bread
			35 Cheese
Wages	15	20	75
Value of output	50	35	200

a. Calculate GDP as the value added in production.
b. Calculate GDP as spending on final goods and services.
c. Calculate GDP as factor income.

4. In the economy of Pizzania (from Problem 3), bread and cheese produced are sold both to the pizza company for inputs in the production of pizzas and to consumers as final goods. The accompanying table summarizes the activities of the three companies.

	Bread company	Cheese company	Pizza company
Cost of inputs	$0	$0	$50 Bread
			35 Cheese
Wages	25	30	75
Value of output	100	60	200

a. Calculate GDP as the value added in production.
b. Calculate GDP as spending on final goods and services.
c. Calculate GDP as factor income.

5. Which of the following transactions will be included in GDP for the United States?

a. Coca-Cola builds a new bottling plant in the United States.
b. Delta sells one of its existing airplanes to Korean Air.
c. Ms. Moneybags buys an existing share of Disney stock.
d. A California winery produces a bottle of Chardonnay and sells it to a customer in Montreal, Canada.
e. An American buys a bottle of French perfume.
f. A book publisher produces too many copies of a new book; the books don't sell this year, so the publisher adds the surplus books to inventories.

6. The economy of Britannica produces three goods: computers, DVDs, and pizza. The accompanying table shows the prices and output of the three goods for the years 2002, 2003, and 2004.

	Computers		DVDs		Pizza	
Year	Price	Quantity	Price	Quantity	Price	Quantity
2002	$900	10	$10	100	$15	2
2003	1,000	10.5	12	105	16	2
2004	1,050	12	14	110	17	3

a. What is the percent change in production of each of the goods from 2002 to 2003 and from 2003 to 2004?
b. What is the percent change in prices of each of the goods from 2002 to 2003 and from 2003 to 2004?
c. Calculate nominal GDP in Britannica for each of the three years. What is the percent change in nominal GDP from 2002 to 2003 and from 2003 to 2004?
d. Calculate real GDP in Britannica using 2002 prices for each of the three years. What is the percent change in real GDP from 2002 to 2003 and from 2003 to 2004?

7. The accompanying table shows data on nominal GDP (in billions of dollars), real GDP (in billions of dollars) using 2000 as the base year, and population (in thousands) of the U.S. in 1960, 1970, 1980, 1990, 2000, and 2004, years in which the U.S. price level consistently rose.

Year	Nominal GDP (billions of dollars)	Real GDP (billions of 2000 dollars)	Population (thousands)
1960	$526.4	$2,501.8	180,671
1970	1,038.5	3,771.9	205,052
1980	2,789.5	5,161.7	227,726
1990	5,803.1	7,112.5	250,132
2000	9,817.0	9,817.0	282,388
2004	11,734.0	10,841.9	293,907

a. Why is real GDP greater than nominal GDP for all years before 2000 and lower for 2004? Does nominal GDP have to equal real GDP in 2000?
b. Calculate the percent change in real GDP from 1960 to 1970, 1970 to 1980, 1980 to 1990, and 1990 to 2000. Which period had the highest growth rate?
c. Calculate real GDP per capita for each of the years in the table.
d. Calculate the percent change in real GDP per capita from 1960 to 1970, 1970 to 1980, 1980 to 1990, and 1990 to 2000. Which period had the highest growth rate?
e. How do the percent change in real GDP and the percent change in real GDP per capita compare? Which is larger? Do we expect them to have this relationship?

8. This table shows the Human Development Index (HDI) and real GDP per capita in U.S. dollars for six nations in 2002.

	HDI	Real GDP per capita
Brazil	0.775	$7,770
Canada	0.943	29,480
Japan	0.938	26,940
Mexico	0.802	8,970
Saudi Arabia	0.768	12,650
United States	0.939	35,750

Rank the nations according to HDI and according to real GDP per capita. Why do the two vary?

9. In general, how do changes in the unemployment rate vary with changes in real GDP? After several quarters of a severe recession, explain why we might observe a decrease in the official unemployment rate. Could we see an increase in the official unemployment rate after several quarters of a strong expansion?

10. Each month, usually on the first Friday of the month, the Bureau of Labor Statistics releases the Employment Situation Summary for the previous month. Go to www.bls.gov and find the latest report. (On the Bureau of Labor Statistics home page, click on "National unemployment rate" and then choose "Employment Situation Summary.") How does the unemployment rate compare to the rate one year earlier? What percentage of unemployed workers are long-term unemployed workers?

11. Eastland College is concerned about the rising price of textbooks that students must purchase. To better identify the increase in the price of textbooks, the dean asks you, the Economics Department's star student, to create an index of textbook prices. The average student purchases three English, two math, and four economics textbooks. The prices of these books are given in the accompanying table.

   a. Create the price index for these books for all years with a base year of 2002.

	2002	2003	2004
English textbook	$50	$55	$57
Math textbook	70	72	74
Economics textbook	80	90	100

   b. What is the percent change in the price of an English textbook from 2002 to 2004?

   c. What is the percent change in the price of a math textbook from 2002 to 2004?

   d. What is the percent change in the price of an economics textbook from 2002 to 2004?

   e. What is the percent change in the market index from 2002 to 2004?

12. The consumer price index, or CPI, measures the cost of living for the average consumer by multiplying the price for each category of expenditure (housing, food, and so on) times a measure of the importance of that expenditure in the average consumer's market basket and summing over all categories. However, using data from the consumer price index, we can see that changes in the cost of living for different types of consumers can vary a great deal. Let's compare the cost of living for a hypothetical retired person and a hypothetical college student. Let's assume that the market basket of a retired person is allocated in the following way: 10% on housing, 15% on food, 5% on transportation, 60% on medical care, 0% on education, and 10% on recreation. The college student's market basket is allocated as follows: 5% on housing, 15% on food, 20% on transportation, 0% on medical care, 40% on education, and 20% on recreation. The accompanying table shows the December 2004 CPI for each of the relevant categories.

	CPI, December 2004
Housing	190.7
Food	188.9
Transportation	164.8
Medical care	314.9
Education	112.6
Recreation	108.5

Calculate the overall CPI for the retired person and for the college student by multiplying the CPI for each of the categories by the relative importance of that category to the individual and then summing each of the categories. The CPI for all items in December 2004 was 190.3. How do your calculations for a CPI for the retired person and the college student compare to the overall CPI?

13. Each month the Bureau of Labor Statistics releases the Consumer Price Index Summary for the previous month. Go to www.bls.gov and find the latest report. (On the Bureau of Labor Statistics home page, click on "CPI" under "Latest Numbers" and then choose "Consumer Price Index Summary.") What was the CPI for the previous month? How did it change from the previous month? How does the CPI compare to the same month one year ago?

14. The accompanying table contains two price indexes for the years 2002, 2003, and 2004: the GDP deflator and the CPI. For each price index, calculate the inflation rate from 2002 to 2003 and from 2003 to 2004.

Year	GDP deflator	CPI
2002	104.1	179.9
2003	106.0	184.0
2004	108.3	188.9

>> Long-Run Economic Growth

THE BAD OLD DAYS

IN 1999 BRITAIN'S CHANNEL 4TV carried out an experiment in time travel. They filmed a documentary about a modern English family, the Bowlers, who spent three months living exactly the way an upper-middle-class family lived in the year 1900. That meant living in a house without electricity or modern appliances; doing the laundry took two days of hard, hot work, and most of their food was boiled on a coal-burning stove. There was no shampoo, toothpaste, packaged or frozen food, and frequently there was insufficient hot water for a bath. The toilet was an outdoor privy in the garden. Not surprisingly, the Bowlers found life very difficult. (At a point of desperation in the battle to stay clean, the family broke the rules and purchased a bottle of modern shampoo.) As one reviewer said, "[Viewing this] should kill any feelings of nostalgia [for the old days] once and for all."

The documentary, called *1900 House*, vividly illustrated the huge improvement in living standards that has taken place in Britain over the past century. Nowadays the vast majority of people in Britain, even those considered poor, have comforts that were not available even to well-off families in 1900. The same is true in the United States. For example, a century ago most American families didn't even have indoor plumbing.

Yet old-fashioned discomfort isn't ancient history. Today, most of the world's population still has a standard of living far worse than that of the Bowlers in their 1900 house. In fact, billions of people still lack access to clean water and don't get enough to eat.

Why do residents of countries such as the United States, Canada, Japan, Britain, and others live so much better than they did a century ago? Why is the standard of living so much lower in countries such as India or Nigeria? The answer to both questions is that some, but not all, countries have been highly successful at achieving long-run economic

The Bowlers: a late-20th-century family that found life in the year 1900 very trying indeed.

growth: their economies produce far more goods and services per capita than they did 100 years ago, which makes it possible to have a much higher average standard of living. The world's poorer countries have not yet matched this achievement.

Many economists have argued that long-run growth—why it happens and how to achieve it—is the single most important issue in macroeconomics. In this chapter, we present some facts about long-run growth, look at the factors that economists believe determine the pace at which long-run growth takes place, and examine how government policies can help or hinder growth.

Comparing Economies Across Time and Space

Before we analyze the sources of long-run economic growth, it's useful to have a sense of just how much the U.S. economy has grown over time and how large the gaps are between wealthy countries like the United States and countries that have yet to match our growth record. So let's take a look at the numbers.

Real GDP per Capita

The key statistic used to track economic growth is *real GDP per capita*—real GDP divided by the population. We focus on GDP because, as we learned in Chapter 7, GDP measures the total value of an economy's production of final goods and services as well as the income earned in that economy in a given year. We use *real* GDP because we want to separate changes in the quantity of goods and services from the effects of a rising price level. We focus on real GDP *per capita* because we want to isolate the effect of a change in the population. For example, other things equal, an increase in the population lowers the standard of living for the average person—there are now more people to share a given amount of real GDP. A rise in real GDP that only matches population growth leaves the average standard of living unchanged.

Although we learned in Chapter 7 that growth in real GDP per capita should not be a policy goal in and of itself, it does serve as a very useful summary measure of a

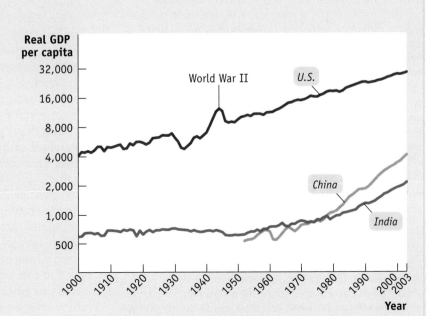

Figure 8-1

The Growth of Real GDP per Capita

Over the past century, U.S. real GDP per capita rose by nearly 600%, representing an average annual growth rate of real GDP per capita of 1.9% since 1900. Despite recent increases in growth, China and India are still poorer than the United States was in 1900.

Source: 1900–2001 data: Angus Maddison, *The World Economy: Historical Statistics* (Paris: OECD, 2003); 2002–2003 data: World Bank.

country's economic progress over time. Figure 8-1 on page 187 shows real GDP per capita for the United States, India, and China, in 2002 dollars, from 1900 to 2003. (We'll talk about India and China in a moment.) The vertical axis is drawn in a proportional scale so that equal percentage changes in real GDP per capita across countries are the same size in the graph.

To give a sense of how much the U.S. economy has grown, Table 8-1 shows real GDP per capita at 20-year intervals, expressed two ways: as a percentage of the 1900 level and as a percentage of the 2000 level. By 1920, the U.S. economy already produced 136% as much per person as it did in 1900. By 2000, it produced 688% as much per person as it did in 1900, or nearly seven times as much in output per person. Alternatively, in 1900 the U.S. economy produced only 14.5% as much per person as it did in 2000.

TABLE 8-1

U.S. Real GDP per Capita

Year	Real GDP per capita (2002 dollars)	Percentage of 1900 real GDP per capita	Percentage of 2000 real GDP per capita
1900	$5,219	100%	14.5%
1920	7,083	136	19.7
1940	8,943	171	24.9
1960	14,452	277	40.3
1980	23,700	454	66.0
2000	35,887	688	100.0

Source: Angus Maddison, *The World Economy: Historical Statistics* (Paris: OECD, 2003), adjusted using GDP deflator.

The income of the typical family normally grows in proportion to per capita income. For example, a 1% increase in real GDP per capita corresponds, roughly, to a 1% increase in the income of the median or typical family—a family in the center of the income distribution. In 2000, the median American family had an income of about $44,000. Since Table 8-1 tells us that real GDP per capita in 1900 was only 14.5% of its 2000 level, a typical family in 1900 probably had a purchasing power only 14.5% as large as the purchasing power of a typical family in 2000. That's around $6,000 in today's dollars, representing a standard of living that we would now consider severe poverty. Much like the Bowlers discovered, today's typical American family, if transported back to the United States of 1900, would feel quite a lot of deprivation.

Still many people in the world have yet to achieve the standard of living the United States had a century ago. That's the message about China and India in Figure 8-1: despite dramatic economic growth in China over the last two decades and a less dramatic acceleration of economic growth in India, as of 2003 the world's two most populous nations were still poorer than the United States was in 1900. And much of the world is poorer than China or India.

You can get a sense of how poor much of the world remains by looking at Figure 8-2, a map of the world in which countries are classified according to their 2003 levels of real gross national income per capita, a

PITFALLS

CHANGE IN LEVELS VERSUS RATE OF CHANGE

When studying economic growth, it's vitally important to understand the difference between a change in level and a rate of change. When we say that real GDP "grew," we mean that the level of real GDP increased. For example, we might say that U.S. real GDP grew during 2005 by $15 billion.

If we knew the level of U.S. real GDP in 2004, we could also represent the amount of 2005 growth in terms of a rate of change. For example, if U.S. real GDP in 2004 was $485 billion, then U.S. real GDP in 2005 was $485 billion + $15 billion = $500 billion. We could calculate the rate of change, or the growth rate, of U.S. real GDP during 2005 as: (($500 billion − $485 billion)/ $485 billion) × 100 = ($15 billion/$485 billion) × 100 = 0.0309, or 3.09%. Statements about economic growth over a period of years almost always refer to changes in the growth rate.

When talking about growth or growth rates, economists often use phrases that appear to mix the two concepts and so can be confusing. For example, when we say that "U.S. growth fell during the 1970s," we are really saying that the U.S. growth rate of real GDP was lower in the 1970s in comparison to the 1960s. When we say that "growth accelerated during the early 1990s," we are saying that the growth rate increased year after year in the early 1990s— for example, going from 3% to 3.5% to 4%.

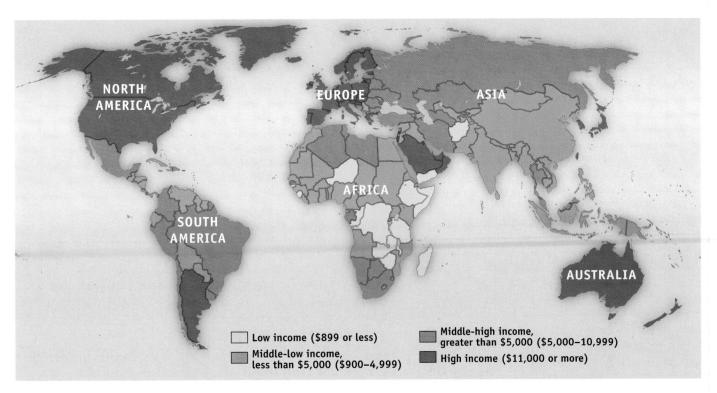

Figure 8-2 Income Around the World Income varies greatly among nations. More than half the world's population lives in countries that are poorer than the U.S. was in 1900.

Source: World Bank.

measure very close to real GDP per capita. As you can see, large parts of the world have very low incomes. Generally speaking, the countries of Europe and North America, as well as a few in the Pacific, have high incomes. The rest of the world, containing most of its population, is dominated by countries with real GDP less than $5,000 per capita—and often much less. In fact, today more than 50% of the world's people live in countries poorer than the United States was in 1900.

Growth Rates

How did the United States manage to produce nearly seven times more per person in 2000 than in 1900, a nearly 600% increase in real GDP per capita? A little bit at a time. Long-run economic growth is normally a gradual process, in which real GDP per capita grows at most a few percent per year. During the twentieth century, real GDP per capita in the United States increased an average of 1.9% each year.

To have a sense of the relationship between the annual growth rate of real GDP per capita and the long-run change in real GDP per capita, it's helpful to keep in mind the **Rule of 70,** a mathematical formula that tells us how long it takes real GDP per capita, or any other variable that grows gradually over time, to double. The approximate answer is:

The **Rule of 70** tells us that the time it takes a variable that grows gradually over time to double is approximately 70 divided by that variable's annual growth rate.

$$\text{(8-1) Number of years for variable to double} = \frac{70}{\text{Annual growth rate of variable}}$$

(Note that the rule of 70 can only be applied to a positive growth rate.) So if real GDP per capita grows at 1% per year, it will take 70 years to double. If it grows at 2% per year, it will take only 35 years to double. In fact, U.S. real GDP per capita rose on average 1.9% per year over the last century. Applying the Rule of 70 to this information implies that it should have taken 37 years for real GDP per capita to double; it would have taken 111 years—three periods of 37 years each—for U.S. real GDP per capita to double three times. That is, the Rule of 70 implies that over the course of 111 years U.S. real GDP per capita should have increased by a factor of $2 \times 2 \times 2 = 8$. And this does turn out to be a pretty good approximation to reality, once we

Figure 8-3

Average Annual Growth Rates of Real GDP per Capita, 1975–2003

Some countries, such as China and Ireland, have been very successful at achieving a rapid rise in real GDP per capita. Others, such as Argentina, have been much less successful. Still others, such as the countries of the former U.S.S.R., have slid backward. (Data for the former U.S.S.R. are for the period 1975–2001.)

Source: World Bank.

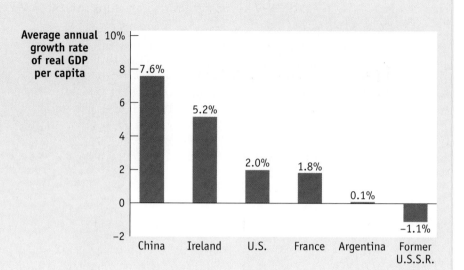

adjust for the fact that a century is a bit less than 111 years. During the twentieth century, U.S. real GDP per capita rose sevenfold, a bit less than eight-fold.

Figure 8-3 shows the average annual rate of growth of real GDP per capita for selected countries from 1975 to 2003. (Data for the former U.S.S.R. are for the period 1975–2001.) Some countries were notable success stories: for example, China, though still quite a poor country, has made spectacular progress. Ireland did very well, too, as discussed in the following Economics in Action.

Some countries, though, have had very disappointing growth. Argentina was once considered a wealthy nation—in the early years of the twentieth century, it was in the same league as the United States and Canada. But since then it has lagged far behind more dynamic economies. In 2003 it was not significantly richer than it was in 1975. The countries that made up the former U.S.S.R. suffered a severe economic decline after the Soviet Union broke up in 1991 and have not yet recovered.

What explains these differences in growth rates? To answer that question, we need to examine the sources of long-run growth.

economics in action

The Luck of the Irish

In the nineteenth century, Ireland was desperately poor, so poor that millions of its residents fled poverty and hunger by emigrating to the United States and other countries. Even as late as the 1970s, Ireland remained one of the poorest countries in Western Europe, poorer than Latin American countries such as Argentina and Venezuela.

But that was then. As Figure 8-3 shows, for the last few decades real GDP per capita has grown almost as fast in Ireland as in China, and all that growth has made Ireland *richer* than most of Europe: Irish real GDP per capita is now higher than in the United Kingdom, France, and Germany. Not surprisingly, the Irish no longer emigrate in search of a better life. In fact, these days German workers sometimes go to Ireland in search of better-paying jobs.

Why has Ireland, after centuries of poverty, done so well? That's getting a bit ahead of our story. Let's just say that economists attribute Ireland's economic performance in large part to a very good *infrastructure* and *human capital*. For example, Ireland has a very good education system, very good airports, and excellent telecommunications and shipping facilities—all of which have attracted a lot of investment by American and Japanese companies. ■

> >

>>CHECK YOUR UNDERSTANDING 8-1

1. Why do economists use real GDP per capita to measure economic progress rather than some other measure, such as nominal GDP per capita or real GDP?

2. Apply the Rule of 70 to the data in Figure 8-3 to determine how long it will take each of the countries listed there, except the former U.S.S.R., to double its real GDP per capita. Would Ireland's real GDP per capita exceed that of the United States in the future if growth rates remain the same? Why or why not?

Solutions appear at back of book.

The Sources of Long-Run Growth

Long-run economic growth depends almost entirely on one ingredient: rising *productivity*. However, a number of factors affect the growth of productivity. Let's look at why productivity is the key ingredient, and then examine what affects it.

The Crucial Importance of Productivity

Sustained economic growth occurs only when the amount of output produced by the average worker increases steadily. The term **labor productivity,** or **productivity** for short, refers to output per worker. (Where data are available, productivity is defined as output *per hour*. This is often a useful statistic for comparing countries' productivities because the number of hours worked by an average worker often differs across countries.) For the economy as a whole, productivity is simply real GDP divided by the number of people working.

You might wonder why we say that higher productivity is the only source of long-run growth. Can't an economy also increase its real GDP per capita by putting more of the population to work? The answer is "Yes, but." For short periods of time an economy can experience a burst of growth in output per capita by putting a higher percentage of the population to work. That's what happened in the United States during World War II, when millions of women entered the paid workforce. The percentage of adult civilians employed outside the home rose from 50% in 1941 to 58% in 1944, and you can see the resulting bump in real GDP per capita during those years in Figure 8-1.

But over the longer run the rate of employment growth is never very different from the rate of population growth. Over the course of the twentieth century, for example, the population of the United States rose at an average rate of 1.3% per year and employment rose 1.5% per year. Real GDP per capita rose 1.9% per year; of that, 1.7%—that is, almost 90% of the total—was the result of rising productivity. In general, overall real GDP can grow because of population growth, but any large increase in real GDP *per capita* must be the result of increased output *per worker*. That is, it must be due to higher productivity.

So increased productivity is the key to long-run economic growth. But what leads to higher productivity?

Explaining Growth in Productivity

There are three main reasons why the average U.S. worker today produces far more than his or her counterpart a century ago. First, the modern worker has far more *physical capital*, such as machinery and office space, to work with. Second, the modern worker is much better educated and so possesses much more *human capital*.

>>QUICK REVIEW

➤ Economic growth is measured using real GDP per capita.

➤ In the United States, real GDP per capita increased sevenfold during the twentieth century, resulting in a large increase in living standards.

➤ Many countries have real GDP per capita much lower than that of the United States. More than half of the world's population has living standards worse than those existing in the United States in 1900.

➤ The long-term rise in real GDP per capita is the result of gradual growth. The *Rule of 70* tells us how many years of growth at a given annual rate it takes to double real GDP per capita.

➤ Growth rates of real GDP per capita differ substantially among nations.

Labor productivity, often referred to simply as **productivity,** is output per worker.

Finally, modern firms have the advantage of a century's accumulation of technical advancements reflecting a great deal of *technological progress*.

Let's look at each of these factors in turn.

Physical Capital Economists define **physical capital** as human-made resources such as buildings and machines. Physical capital makes workers more productive. For example, a worker operating a backhoe can dig a lot more feet of trench per day than one equipped only with a shovel.

The average U.S. worker today is backed up by around $110,000 worth of physical capital—far more than a U.S. worker had 100 years ago and far more than the average worker in most other countries has today.

Human Capital It's not enough for a worker to have good equipment—he or she must also know what to do with it. **Human capital** refers to the improvement in labor created by the education and knowledge embodied in the workforce.

The human capital of the United States has increased dramatically over the past century. A century ago, although most Americans were able to read and write, very few had an extensive education. In 1910, only 13.5% of Americans over 25 had graduated from high school and only 3% had four-year college degrees. By 2003, the percentages were 85% and 27%, respectively. It would be impossible to run today's economy with a population as poorly educated as that of a century ago.

Statistical analysis comparing economic growth rates in different countries suggests that education—and its effect on productivity—is an even more important determinant of growth than increases in physical capital.

Technology Probably the most important driver of productivity growth is progress in **technology,** which is broadly defined as the technical means for the production of goods and services. We'll see shortly how economists measure the impact of technology on growth.

Workers today are able to produce more than those in the past, even with the same amount of physical and human capital, because technology has advanced over time. It's important to realize that economically important technological progress need not be flashy or rely on cutting-edge science. Historians have noted that past economic growth has been driven not only by major inventions, such as the railroad or the semiconductor chip, but also by thousands of modest innovations, such as the flat-bottomed paper bag, patented in 1870, which made packing groceries and many other goods much easier, and the Post-it® Note, introduced in 1981, which has had surprisingly large benefits for office productivity. As For Inquiring Minds on page 193 points out, experts attribute much of the productivity surge that took place in the United States late in the twentieth century to new technology adopted by retail companies like Wal-Mart rather than to high-technology companies.

> **Physical capital** consists of human-made resources such as buildings and machines.
>
> **Human capital** is the improvement in labor created by the education and knowledge embodied in the workforce.
>
> **Technology** is the technical means for the production of goods and services.

Accounting for Growth: The Aggregate Production Function

Productivity is higher, other things equal, when workers are equipped with more physical capital, more human capital, better technology, or any combination of the three. But can we put numbers to these effects? To do this, economists make use of estimates of the **aggregate production function,** which shows how productivity depends on the quantities of physical capital per worker and human capital per worker as well as the state of technology. The aggregate production function is a hypothetical relationship of the general form shown in Equation 8-2:

> The **aggregate production function** is a hypothetical function that shows how productivity (real GDP per worker) depends on the quantities of physical capital per worker and human capital per worker as well as the state of technology.

(8-2) *Aggregate production function:* $Y/L = f(K/L, H/L, T)$

where $f(\cdot)$ means a function of the variables within the parentheses. Here, Y is real GDP produced, and L is the number of workers employed, so that Y/L is real GDP produced per worker; K/L is the quantity of physical capital per worker; H/L is the quantity of human capital per worker; and T is a measure of the state of the technology used in production.

In analyzing historical economic growth, economists have discovered a crucial fact about the estimated aggregate production function: it exhibits **diminishing returns to physical capital**. That is, when the amount of human capital per worker and the state of technology are held fixed, each successive increase in the amount of physical capital per worker leads to a smaller increase in productivity. Table 8-2 gives a hypothetical example of how the level of physical capital per worker might affect the level of real GDP per worker, holding human capital per worker and the state of technology fixed. In this example, we measure the quantity of physical capital in dollars.

An aggregate production function exhibits **diminishing returns to physical capital** when, holding the amount of human capital and the state of technology fixed, each successive increase in the amount of physical capital leads to a smaller increase in productivity.

As you can see from the table, there is a big payoff for the first $15,000 of physical capital: real GDP per worker rises by $30,000. The second $15,000 of physical capital also raises productivity, but not by as much: real GDP per worker goes up only $15,000. The third $15,000 of physical capital raises real GDP per worker by only $10,000.

TABLE **8-2**

A Hypothetical Example: How Physical Capital per Worker Affects Productivity Holding Human Capital and Technology Fixed

Physical capital per worker	Real GDP per worker
$0	$0
15,000	30,000
30,000	45,000
45,000	55,000

To see why the relationship between physical capital per worker and productivity exhibits diminishing returns, think about how having farm equipment affects the productivity of farm workers. A little bit of equipment makes a big difference: a worker equipped with a tractor can do much more than a worker without one. And a worker using more expensive equipment will, other things equal, be more productive: a worker with a $30,000 tractor will normally be able to cultivate more farmland in a given amount of time than a worker with a $15,000 tractor because the more expensive machine will be more powerful, perform more tasks, or both.

IT MAY BE DIMINISHED . . . BUT IT'S STILL POSITIVE

It's important to understand what diminishing returns to physical capital means and what it doesn't mean. As we've already explained, it's an "other things equal" statement: holding the amount of human capital per worker and the technology fixed, each successive increase in the amount of physical capital per worker results in a smaller increase in real GDP per worker. But this doesn't mean that real GDP per worker eventually falls as more and more physical capital is added. It's just that the *increase* in real GDP per worker gets smaller and smaller, albeit remaining at or above zero. So an increase in physical capital per worker will never reduce productivity. But due to diminishing returns, at some point increasing the amount of physical capital per worker no longer produces an economic payoff: at some point the increase in output is so small that it is not worth the cost of the additional physical capital.

But will a worker with a $30,000 tractor, holding human capital and technology constant, be twice as productive as a worker with a $15,000 tractor? Probably not: the second $15,000 worth of equipment won't raise productivity as much as the first $15,000 worth. And we can be sure that a worker with a $150,000 tractor won't be 10 times as productive: a tractor can be improved only so much. Because the same is true of other kinds of equipment, the aggregate production function shows diminishing returns to physical capital.

Diminishing returns to physical capital imply a relationship between physical capital per worker and output per worker like the one shown in Figure 8-4. As the curve illustrates, more physical capital per worker leads to more output per worker. But each $30,000 increment in physical capital per worker adds less to productivity. By comparing points A, B, and C you can also see that as physical capital per worker rises, output per worker rises but at a diminishing rate. Starting at point A, a $30,000 increase in physical capital per worker leads to an increase of $20,000 in real GDP per worker. At point B, an additional $30,000 increase in physical capital per worker leads to an increase of only $10,000 in real GDP per worker.

It's important to realize that diminishing returns to physical capital is an "other things equal" phenomenon: additional amounts of physical capital are less productive *when the amount of human capital and the technology are held fixed*. Diminishing returns may disappear if we increase the amount of human capital, or improve the technology, or both, at the same time the amount of physical capital is increased. For example, a worker with a $30,000 tractor who has also been trained in the most advanced cultivation techniques may in fact be more than twice as productive as a worker with only a $15,000 tractor and no additional human capital. But diminishing returns to any one input—regardless of whether it is physical capital, human capital, or number of workers—is a

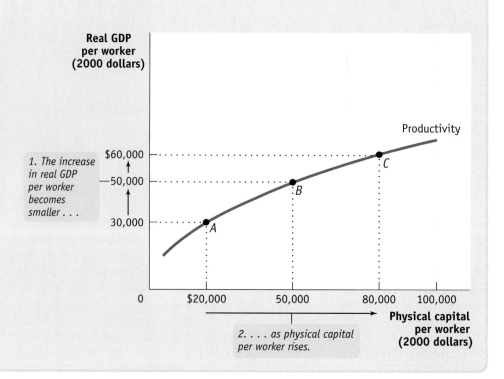

Figure 8-4

Physical Capital and Productivity

Other things equal, a greater quantity of physical capital per worker leads to higher real GDP per worker, but is subject to diminishing returns: each successive addition to physical capital per worker produces a smaller increase in productivity. Starting at point A, with $20,000 in physical capital per worker, a $30,000 increase in physical capital per worker leads to an increase of $20,000 in real GDP per worker. At point B, with $50,000 in physical capital per worker, a $30,000 increase in physical capital per worker leads to an increase of only $10,000 in real GDP per worker. **>web...**

pervasive characteristic of production. Typical estimates suggest that in practice a 1% increase in the quantity of physical capital per worker increases output per worker by only ⅓ of 1%, or 0.33%.

In practice, all the factors contributing to higher productivity rise during the course of economic growth: both physical capital and human capital per worker increase, and technology advances as well. To disentangle the effects of these factors, economists use **growth accounting,** which estimates the contribution of each major factor in the aggregate production function to economic growth. For example, suppose the following are true:

> **Growth accounting** estimates the contribution of each major factor in the aggregate production function to economic growth.

- The amount of physical capital per worker grows 3% a year.

- According to estimates of the aggregate production function, each 1% rise in physical capital per worker, holding human capital and technology constant, raises output per worker by ⅓ of 1%, or 0.33%.

In that case, we would estimate that growing physical capital per worker is responsible for 3% × 1/3 = 1 percentage point of productivity growth per year. A similar but more complex procedure is used to estimate the effects of growing human capital. The procedure is more complex because there aren't simple dollar measures of the quantity of human capital.

Growth accounting allows us to calculate the effects of greater physical and human capital on economic growth. But how can we estimate the effects of technological progress? We do so by estimating what is left over after the effects of physical and human capital have been taken into account. For example, let's imagine that there was no increase in human capital per worker so that we can focus on changes in physical capital and in technology. In Figure 8-5, the lower curve shows the same hypothetical relationship between physical capital per worker and output per worker shown in Figure 8-4.

Figure 8-5

Technological Progress and Productivity Growth

Technological progress shifts the productivity curve upward. Here we hold human capital per worker fixed. We assume that the lower curve (the same curve as in Figure 8-4) reflects technology in 1935, and the upper curve reflects technology in 2005. Holding technology and human capital fixed, quadrupling physical capital per worker from $20,000 to $80,000 leads to a doubling of real GDP per worker, from $30,000 to $60,000. This is shown by the movement from point A to point C, reflecting an approximately 1% per year rise in real GDP per worker. In reality, technological progress shifted the productivity curve upward and the actual rise in real GDP per worker is shown by the movement from point A to point D. Real GDP per worker grew 2% per year, leading to a quadrupling during the period. The extra 1% in growth of real GDP per worker is due to higher total factor productivity.

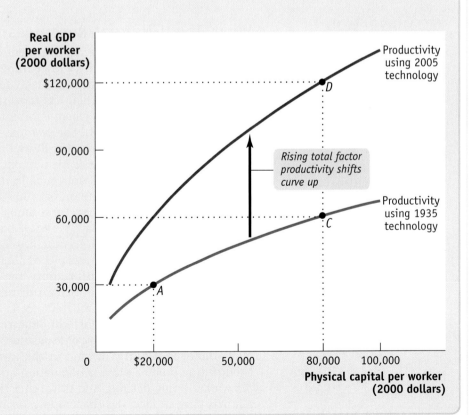

Let's assume that this was the relationship given the technology available in 1935. The upper curve also shows a relationship between physical capital per worker and productivity, but this time given the technology available in 2005. (We've chosen a 70-year stretch to make the numerical example easier to understand.) The 2005 curve is shifted up compared to the 1935 curve because technologies developed over the previous 70 years make it possible to produce more output for a given amount of physical capital per worker than was possible with the technology available in 1935.

Let's assume that between 1935 and 2005 the amount of physical capital per worker rose from $20,000 to $80,000. If this increase in physical capital per worker had taken place without any technological progress, the economy would have moved from *A* to *C*: output per worker would have risen, but only from $30,000 to $60,000, or 1% per year (remember the Rule of 70). In fact, however, the economy moved from *A* to *D*: output rose from $30,000 to $120,000, or 2% per year. There was both an increase in physical capital per worker and technological progress, which shifted the aggregate production function.

> **Total factor productivity** is the amount of output that can be achieved with a given amount of factor inputs.

In this case, 50% of the annual 2% increase in productivity—that is, 1% in productivity growth—is due to higher **total factor productivity,** the amount of output that can be produced with a given amount of factor inputs. So when total factor productivity increases, the economy can produce more output with the same quantity of physical capital, human capital, and labor.

Most estimates find that increases in total factor productivity are central to a country's economic growth. We believe that observed increases in total factor productivity do in fact measure the economic effects of technological progress. All of this implies that technological change is crucial to economic growth. The Bureau of Labor Statistics estimates the growth rate of both labor productivity and total factor productivity for nonfarm business in the United States. According to the bureau's estimates, over the period from 1948 to 2004 American labor productivity rose 2.3% per year. Only 48% of that rise is explained by increases in physical and human capital per worker; the rest is explained by rising total factor productivity—that is, by technological progress.

What About Natural Resources?

In our discussion so far, we haven't mentioned natural resources, which certainly have an effect on productivity. Other things equal, countries that are abundant in valuable natural resources, such as highly fertile land or rich mineral deposits, have higher real GDP per capita than less fortunate countries. The most obvious modern example is the Middle East, where enormous oil deposits have made a few sparsely populated countries very rich. For example, Kuwait has about the same level of real GDP per capita as South Korea, but Kuwait's wealth is based on oil, not manufacturing, the source of South Korea's high output per worker.

But other things are often not equal. In the modern world, natural resources are a much less important determinant of productivity than human or physical capital for the great majority of countries. For example, some nations with very high real GDP per capita, such as Japan, have very few natural resources. Some resource-rich nations, such as Nigeria (which has sizable oil deposits), are very poor.

Historically, natural resources played a much more prominent role in determining productivity. In the nineteenth century, the countries with the highest real GDP per capita were those abundant in rich farmland and mineral deposits: the United States, Canada, Argentina, and Australia. As a consequence, natural resources figured prominently in the development of economic thought. In a famous book published in 1798, *An Essay on the Principle of Population,* the English economist Thomas Malthus made the fixed quantity of land in the world the basis of a pessimistic prediction about future productivity. As population grew, he pointed out, the amount of land per worker would decline. And this, other things equal, would cause productivity to fall. His view, in fact, was that improvements in technology or increases in physical capital would lead to only temporary improvements in productivity because they would always be offset by the pressure of rising population and more workers on the supply of land. In the long run, he concluded, the great majority of people were condemned to living on the edge of starvation. Only then would death rates be high enough and birth rates low enough to prevent rapid population growth from outstripping productivity growth.

It hasn't turned out that way, although many historians believe that Malthus's prediction of falling or stagnant productivity was valid for much of human history. Population pressure probably did prevent large productivity increases until the eighteenth century. But in the time since Malthus wrote his book, any negative effects on productivity from population growth have been far outweighed by other, positive factors—advances in technology, increases in human and physical capital, and the opening up of enormous amounts of cultivatable land in the New World.

economics in action

The Information Technology Paradox

From the early 1970s through the mid-1990s, the United States went through a slump in productivity growth. Figure 8-6 shows the annual growth rate of U.S. labor productivity on a 10-year basis—that is, the number for 1957 is the average annual growth rate from 1947 to 1957, the number for 1958 is the average annual growth rate from 1948 to 1958, and so on. As you can see, there was a large fall in the productivity growth rate beginning in the early 1970s. Because higher output per worker is the key to long-run growth, the economy's overall growth was also disappointing, leading to a widespread sense that economic progress had ground to a halt.

Many economists were puzzled by the slowdown in the U.S. growth rate of labor productivity—a fall from an average annual growth rate of 3% in the late 1960s to slightly less than 1% in the mid-1980s. This was surprising given that there appeared to be rapid progress in technology. Modern information technology really began with the development of the first microprocessor—a computer on a chip—in 1971. In the 25 years that followed, a series of inventions that seemed revolutionary became standard equipment in the business world: fax machines, desktop computers, cell phones, and e-mail. Yet the rate of growth of productivity remained stagnant. In a famous remark, MIT economics professor and Nobel laureate Robert Solow, a pioneer in the analysis of economic growth, declared that the information technology revolution could be seen everywhere except in the economic statistics.

Why didn't information technology show large rewards? Paul David, a Stanford economic historian, offered a theory and a prediction. He pointed out that 100 years earlier another miracle technology—electric power—had spread through the economy, again with surprisingly little impact on productivity growth at first. The reason, he suggested, was that a new technology doesn't yield its full potential if you use it in old ways.

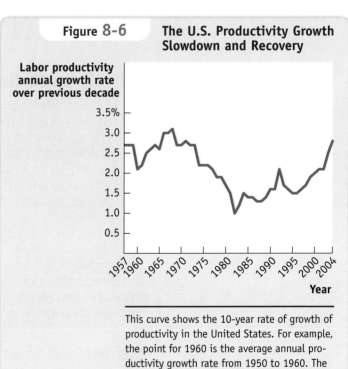

Figure 8-6 The U.S. Productivity Growth Slowdown and Recovery

Labor productivity annual growth rate over previous decade

This curve shows the 10-year rate of growth of productivity in the United States. For example, the point for 1960 is the average annual productivity growth rate from 1950 to 1960. The productivity growth rate fell in the 1970s and 1980s, despite what appeared to be rapid technological progress. However, the productivity growth rate rose again in the 1990s.

Source: Bureau of Labor Statistics.

For example, a traditional factory around 1900 was a multistory building, with the machinery tightly crowded together and designed to be powered by a steam engine in the basement. This design had problems: it was very difficult to move people and ma-terials around. Yet owners who electrified their factories initially maintained the multistory, tightly packed layout. Only with the switch to spread-out, one-story fac-tories that took advantage of the flexibility of electric power—most famously Henry Ford's auto assembly line—did productivity take off.

David suggested that the same phenomenon was happening with information technology. Productivity, he predicted, would take off when people really changed their way of doing business to take advantage of the new technology—such as, replacing letters and phone calls with electronic communications. Sure enough, productivity growth accelerated dramatically in the second half of the 1990s. And, as For Inquiring Minds on page 193 suggested, a lot of that may have been due to the discovery by companies like Wal-Mart of how to effectively use information technology. ∎

‹ ‹ ‹ ‹ ‹ ‹ ‹ ‹ ‹ ‹ ‹ ‹ ‹ ‹ ‹ ‹ ‹ ‹ ‹

>> CHECK YOUR UNDERSTANDING 8-2

1. Explain the effect of each of the following events on the growth rate of productivity.
   a. The amounts of physical and human capital per worker are unchanged, but there is signifi-cant technological progress.
   b. The amount of physical capital per worker grows, but the level of human capital per worker and technology are unchanged.

2. Multinomics, Inc., is a large company with many offices around the country. It has just adopted a new computer system that will affect virtually every function performed within the company. Why might a period of time pass before employees' productivity is improved by the new computer system? Why might there be a temporary decrease in employees' productivity?

Solutions appear at back of book.

Why Growth Rates Differ

In 1820, according to estimates by the economic historian Angus Maddison, Mexico had somewhat higher real GDP per capita than Japan. Today, Japan has higher real GDP per capita than most European nations and Mexico is a poor country, though by no means among the poorest. The difference? Over the long run, real GDP per capita grew at 1.9% per year in Japan but at only 1.2% per year in Mexico.

As this example illustrates, even small differences in growth rates have large conse-quences over the long run. But why do growth rates differ across countries and across periods of time?

The simplest answer is that economies with rapid growth tend to be economies that add physical capital, increase their human capital, experience rapid technologi-cal progress, or all three, on a sustained basis. The deeper answer lies in policies and institutions that promote economic growth—policies and institutions that ensure that those who generate additions to physical or human capital, or to technological progress, are rewarded for their efforts.

Savings and Investment Spending

To increase the physical capital available to workers, an economy must engage in in-vestment spending. There are two ways to do this. One way is for its residents to en-gage in saving—that is, for them to put aside some of their income rather than using it for consumer spending. Such domestic savings can be generated by private house-holds saving some of their disposable income, by the government spending less than its tax revenues, or both. The other source of funds for investment spending is foreign savings from residents of other countries. Let's focus first on domestic savings, those generated by a country's own residents.

Both the amount of savings and the ability of an economy to direct savings into productive investment spending depend on the economy's institutions, notably its financial system. In particular, a well-functioning banking system is very important for economic growth because in most countries it is the principal way in which savings are channeled into business investment spending. If a country's citizens trust their banks, they will place their savings in bank deposits, which the banks will then lend to their business customers. But if people don't trust their banks, they will hoard gold or foreign currency, keeping their savings in safe deposit boxes or under the mattress, where it cannot be turned into productive investment spending. As we'll discuss in Chapter 13, a well-functioning financial system requires appropriate government regulation that assures depositors that their funds are protected.

Government policy has an effect on savings and investment spending in two other important ways. As we'll see in Chapter 9, the government can engage in saving by taking in more in taxes than it spends. By doing so, the government effectively makes more funds available for investment spending. But what happens if the government spends more than it collects, requiring it to borrow money? One major concern of economists is whether government borrowing, if it is sufficiently large, "crowds out" private investment spending. In other words, does government borrowing absorb resources that would otherwise have promoted economic growth and by doing so lower investment spending compared to what it would have been without the borrowing? We'll explore the economics of savings and investment spending, the working of the financial system, and the role of government borrowing in Chapter 9.

Another way in which governments can adversely affect savings and investment spending is through irresponsible conduct of monetary policy—specifically, by generating excessive inflation. As we'll see in Chapter 16, high inflation erodes the value of many financial assets. As a result, people in countries with a history of inflation are often reluctant to save—or at least to place their savings in assets whose real value might be hurt by inflation.

Foreign Investment

A country's investment spending can be either more or less than its domestic savings because of foreign investment: residents of some countries invest part of their savings in other countries. The United States is currently a net recipient of foreign investment. In fact, foreign savings fund a large fraction of our investment spending, allowing the United States to have a quantity of investment spending higher than domestic savings. This continues a national tradition of foreign investment that goes back to the nineteenth century, when British investors financed much of the country's railroad construction.

Investors expect and normally receive a return on their investment. If a country's residents, like Americans, have borrowed from foreigners, they have to pay interest on those loans. And if foreign companies build new factories or purchase existing factories in a country, the foreign owners are entitled to receive any profits those factories earn. Still, economists argue that the increase in real GDP generated by foreign investment is usually greater than the interest and profits paid to foreigners. So, the country benefits overall from foreign investment.

In many cases there is an additional payoff to the recipient country when foreign companies invest in a country by building or purchasing factories. They often bring with them new technology that diffuses through the recipient economy, raising productivity in many sectors. In Asian nations such as Malaysia, investments in factories by U.S., European, and Japanese companies have brought modern production techniques that local Asian businesses have learned to emulate. Even U.S. businesses can learn a thing or two. In the 1980s, Japanese companies had developed production techniques, especially in the auto industry, that were superior to those used in the United States. In the 1990s, the United States closed the gap, largely by learning from Japanese-owned factories located here.

Education

An economy's physical capital is created mainly through investment spending by individuals and private companies. Much of an economy's human capital, in contrast, is the result of government spending on education. Governments pay for the great bulk of primary and secondary education, although individuals pay a significant share of the costs of higher education. The quality of education a country provides for its citizens has a large impact on its economic growth rate.

Like the Irish success story, the "East Asian economic miracle," described later in this chapter, is a case in point. Many analysts believe that the most important reason certain Asian nations did so well in the last few decades of the twentieth century is that, even when poor, they provided a very good basic education to their residents.

Infrastructure

Roads, power lines, ports, information networks, and other underpinnings for economic activity are known as **infrastructure**.

The term **infrastructure** refers to roads, power lines, ports, information networks, and other parts of an economy's physical capital that provide an underpinning, or foundation, for economic activity. Although some infrastructure is provided by private companies, much of it is either provided by the government or requires a great deal of government regulation and support. As we pointed out in Economics in Action on page 190, excellent infrastructure played a significant role in Ireland's rapid growth.

Poor infrastructure—for example, a power grid that often fails, cutting off electricity to homes and businesses—is a major obstacle to economic growth in some countries. To provide good infrastructure, an economy must be able to afford it, but it must also have the political discipline to maintain it and provide for the future.

Perhaps the most crucial infrastructure is something we rarely think about: basic public health measures in the form of a clean water supply and disease control. As we'll see in the next section, poor health infrastructure is a major problem for economic growth in poor countries, especially those in Africa.

Research and Development

The advance of technology is a key force behind economic growth. What drives technology?

Scientific advances make new technologies possible. To take the most spectacular example in today's world, the semiconductor chip—which is the basis for all modern information technology—could not have been developed without the theory of quantum mechanics in physics.

But science alone is not enough: scientific knowledge must be translated into useful products and processes. And that often requires devoting a lot of resources to **research and development,** R&D, spending to create new technologies and prepare them for practical use.

Research and development is spending to create and implement new technologies.

Much research and development is paid for by the private sector. The United States became the world's leading economy in large part because American businesses were among the first to make systematic research and development a part of their operations. For Inquiring Minds on the next page describes how Thomas Edison created the first modern industrial research laboratory.

But much important R&D is done by government agencies. In Economics in Action on page 201, we describe Brazil's recent agricultural boom. This boom was made possible by government researchers who discovered that adding crucial nutrients would allow crops to be grown on previously unusable land and also developed new varieties of soybeans and breeds of cattle that flourish in Brazil's tropical climate.

Thomas Edison is best known as the inventor of the light bulb and the phonograph. But his biggest invention may surprise you: he invented research and development.

Before Edison's time, there had, of course, been many inventors. Some of them worked in teams. But in 1875 Edison created something new: his Menlo Park, New Jersey, laboratory. It employed 25 men full-time to generate new products and processes for business. In other words, he did not set out to pursue a particular idea and then cash in. He created an organization whose purpose was to create new ideas year after year.

Edison's Menlo Park lab is now a museum. "To name a few of the products that were developed in Menlo Park," says the museum's website, "we can list the following: the carbon button mouthpiece for the telephone, the phonograph, the incandescent light bulb and the electrical distribution system, the electric train, ore separation, the Edison effect bulb, early experiments in wireless, the grasshopper telegraph, and improvements in telegraphic transmission."

You could say that before Edison's lab, technology just sort of happened: people came up with ideas, but businesses didn't plan to make continuous technological progress. Now R&D operations, often much bigger than Edison's original team, are standard practice throughout the business world.

Political Stability, Property Rights, and Excessive Government Intervention

There's not much point in investing in a business if rioting mobs are likely to destroy it or saving your money if someone with political connections can steal it. Political stability and protection of property rights are crucial ingredients in long-run economic growth.

Long-run economic growth in successful economies, like that of the United States, has been possible because there are good laws, institutions that enforce those laws, and a stable political system that maintains those institutions. The law must say that your property is really yours so that someone else can't take it away. The courts and the police must be honest so that they can't be bribed to ignore the law. And the political system must be stable so that the law doesn't change capriciously.

Americans take these preconditions for granted, but they are by no means guaranteed. Aside from the disruption caused by war or revolution, many countries find that their economic growth suffers due to corruption among the government officials who should be enforcing the law. For example, until 1991 the Indian government imposed many bureaucratic restrictions on businesses, which often had to bribe government officials to get approval for even routine activities—a tax on business, in effect. Economists have argued that a reduction in this burden of corruption is one reason Indian growth has been much faster in recent years than it was in the first 40 years after India gained independence in 1947.

Even when governments aren't corrupt, excessive government intervention can be a brake on economic growth. If large parts of the economy are supported by government subsidies, protected from imports, or otherwise insulated from competition, productivity tends to suffer because of a lack of incentives. As we'll see in the next section, excessive government intervention is one often-cited explanation for slow growth in Latin America.

economics in action

The Brazilian Breadbasket

A wry Brazilian joke says that "Brazil is the country of the future—and always will be." The world's fifth most populous country has often been seen as a possible major economic power, yet has never fulfilled that promise.

In recent years, however, Brazil's economy has made a better showing, especially in agriculture. This success depends on exploiting a natural resource, the tropical savanna land known as the *cerrado*. But until a quarter-century ago, the land was considered unsuitable for farming. A combination of three factors changed that: technological progress due to research and development, improved economic policies, and greater physical capital.

The Brazilian Enterprise for Agricultural and Livestock Research, a government-run agency, developed the crucial technologies. It showed that adding lime and phosphorus made *cerrado* land productive and developed breeds of cattle and varieties of soybeans suited for the climate. (Now they're working on wheat.) Also, until the 1980s, Brazilian international trade policies discouraged exports, as did an overvalued exchange rate that made the country's goods more expensive to foreigners. After economic reform, investing in Brazilian agriculture became much more profitable and companies began putting in place the farm machinery, buildings, and other forms of physical capital needed to exploit the land.

What limits Brazil's growth? Infrastructure. According to a report in the *New York Times,* Brazilian farmers are "concerned about the lack of reliable highways, railways and barge routes, which adds to the cost of doing business." But the Brazilian government is investing in infrastructure, and Brazilian agriculture is continuing to expand. The country has already overtaken the United States as the world's largest beef exporter and may not be far behind in soybeans.

< < < < < < < < < < < < < < < < < < <

▶▶CHECK YOUR UNDERSTANDING 8-3

1. In recent years the United States has had a very low savings rate (the percentage of GDP that is saved nationally in a given year) but has attracted much foreign investment. Some economists say this is a danger to long-run growth, but others disagree. Why might both sides be right?

2. U.S. centers of academic biotechnology research have closer connections with private biotechnology companies than their European counterparts. What effect might this have on the pace of creation and development of new drugs in the United States versus Europe?

3. During the 1990s in the former U.S.S.R., a lot of property was seized and controlled by those in power. How might this have affected the country's growth rate?

4. Many countries that once shunned foreign-owned factories now welcome them. Explain this change of attitude.

Solutions appear at back of book.

Success, Disappointment, and Failure

As we've seen, rates of long-run economic growth differ quite a lot around the world. We conclude this chapter with a look at three regions of the world that have had quite different experiences with economic growth over the last few decades.

Figure 8-7 shows trends since 1960 in real GDP per capita for three countries: Argentina, Ghana, and South Korea. (As in Figure 8-1, the vertical axis is drawn in

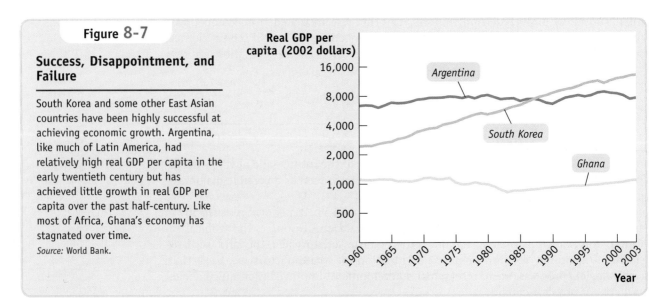

Figure 8-7

Success, Disappointment, and Failure

South Korea and some other East Asian countries have been highly successful at achieving economic growth. Argentina, like much of Latin America, had relatively high real GDP per capita in the early twentieth century but has achieved little growth in real GDP per capita over the past half-century. Like most of Africa, Ghana's economy has stagnated over time.

Source: World Bank.

proportional scale.) We have chosen these countries because each is a particularly striking example of what has happened in its region. South Korea's amazing rise is part of a broad "economic miracle" in East Asia. Argentina's stagnant real GDP per capita is more or less typical of the disappointment that has characterized Latin America. And Ghana's unhappy story—despite some recovery since the mid-1980s, real GDP per capita is still lower than it was in 1960—is, unfortunately, typical of Africa's experience.

The East Asian Miracle

In 1960 South Korea was a very poor country. In fact, in 1960 its real GDP per capita was lower than that of India today. But, as you can see from Figure 8-7, beginning in the early 1960s South Korea began an extremely rapid economic ascent: real GDP per capita grew about 7% per year for more than 30 years. Today South Korea, though still somewhat poorer than Europe or the United States, looks very much like an economically advanced country.

South Korea's economic growth is unprecedented in history: it took the country only 35 years to achieve growth that required centuries elsewhere. Yet South Korea is only part of a broader phenomenon, often referred to as the East Asian economic miracle. High growth rates first appeared in South Korea, Taiwan, Hong Kong, and Singapore but then spread across the region, most notably to China. Since 1975 the whole region has increased real GDP per capita by 6% per year, three times America's historical rate of growth.

How have the Asian countries achieved such high growth rates? The answer is that all of the sources of productivity growth have been firing on all cylinders. Very high savings rates, the percentage of GDP that is saved nationally in any given year, have allowed the countries to significantly increase the amount of physical capital per worker. Very good basic education has permitted a rapid improvement in human capital. And these countries have experienced substantial technological progress.

Why hasn't any economy achieved this kind of growth in the past? Most economic analysts think that East Asia's growth spurt was possible because of its *relative* backwardness. That is, by the time that East Asian economies began to move into the modern world, they could benefit from adopting the technological advances that had been generated in technologically advanced countries such as the United States. In 1900, the United States could not have moved quickly to a modern level of productivity because much of the technology that powers the modern economy, from jet planes to computers, hadn't been invented yet. In 1970, South Korea probably still had lower labor productivity than the United States had in 1900, but it could rapidly upgrade its productivity by adopting technology that had been developed in the United States, Europe, and Japan over the previous century.

The East Asian experience demonstrates that economic growth can be especially fast in countries that are playing catch-up to other countries with higher GDP per capita. On this basis many economists have suggested a general principle known as the **convergence hypothesis.** It says that differences in real GDP per capita among countries tend to narrow over time because countries that start with lower real GDP per capita tend to have higher growth rates. We'll look at the evidence on the convergence hypothesis in the Economics in Action on page 205.

Even before we get to that evidence, however, we can say right away that starting with a relatively low level of real GDP per capita is no guarantee of rapid growth, as the examples of Latin America and Africa both demonstrate.

China's high rate of economic growth is rapidly raising Chinese living standards.

According to the **convergence hypothesis,** international differences in real GDP per capita tend to narrow over time.

Latin America's Disappointment

In 1900, Latin America was not regarded as an economically backward region. Natural resources, including both cultivatable land and minerals, were abundant. Some countries, notably Argentina, attracted millions of immigrants from Europe, people in search of a better life. Measures of real GDP per capita in Argentina, Uruguay, and southern Brazil were comparable to that in economically advanced countries.

Since about 1920, however, growth in Latin America has been disappointing. As Figure 8-7 shows in the case of Argentina, it has remained disappointing to this day. The fact that South Korea is now much richer than Argentina would have seemed inconceivable a few generations ago.

Why has Latin America stagnated? Comparisons with East Asian success stories suggest several factors. The rates of savings and investment spending in Latin America have been much lower than in East Asia, partly as a result of irresponsible government policy that has eroded savings through high inflation, bank failures, and other disruptions. Education—especially broad basic education—has been underemphasized: even Latin American nations rich in natural resources often failed to channel that wealth into their educational systems. And political instability, leading to irresponsible economic policies, has taken a toll.

In the 1980s, many economists came to believe that Latin America was suffering from excessive government intervention in markets. They recommended opening the economies to imports, selling off government-owned companies and, in general, freeing up individual initiative. The hope was that this would produce an East Asian–type economic surge. So far, however, only one Latin American nation, Chile, has achieved really rapid growth. It now seems that pulling off an economic miracle is harder than it looks.

Africa's Troubles

Africa south of the Sahara is home to about 600 million people, more than twice the population of the United States. On average they are very poor, nowhere close to U.S. living standards 100 or even 200 years ago. Worst of all, Africa's economies have been moving backward: average real GDP per capita in 2003 was 11% lower than in 1974.

The consequence of this poor growth performance has been intense and worsening poverty. In 1970, 42% of Africans lived on less than $1 a day in today's prices. By 2001, that number was 46%.

This is a very disheartening picture. What explains it?

Several factors are probably crucial. Perhaps first and foremost is the problem of political instability. In the years since 1975, large parts of Africa have experienced savage civil wars (often with outside powers backing rival sides) that have killed millions of people and made productive investment spending impossible. The threat of war and general anarchy has also inhibited other important preconditions for growth, such as education and provision of necessary infrastructure.

Property rights are also a problem. The lack of legal safeguards means that property owners are often subject to extortion because of government corruption, making them averse to owning property or improving it. This is especially damaging in a country that is very poor.

Although many economists see political instability and government corruption as the leading causes of underdevelopment in Africa, some—most notably Jeffrey Sachs of Columbia University and the United Nations—believe the opposite. They argue that Africa is politically unstable because Africa is poor. And Africa's poverty, they go on to claim, stems from its extremely unfavorable geographic conditions—much of the continent is landlocked, hot, infested with tropical diseases, and cursed with poor soil.

Sachs, along with economists from the World Health Organization, has highlighted the importance of health problems in Africa. In poor countries, worker productivity is often severely hampered by malnutrition and disease. In particular, tropical diseases such as malaria can only be controlled with an effective public health infrastructure, something that is lacking in much of Africa. At the time of writing, within regions of Africa, economists are studying whether modest amounts of aid given directly to residents for the purposes of increasing crop yields, reducing malaria, and increasing school attendance can produce self-sustaining gains in living standards.

Although the example of African countries represents a warning that long-run economic growth cannot be taken for granted, there are some signs of hope. Mauritius has developed a successful textile industry. Several African countries that are dependent on commodities such as coffee and oil have benefited from the recent sharp rise in the prices of commodities. And Ghana has managed to maintain an increase in real GDP per capita for several years now.

economics in action

Are Economies Converging?

In the 1950s, much of Europe seemed quaint and backward to American visitors, and Japan seemed very poor. Today, a visitor to Paris or Tokyo sees a city that looks about as rich as New York. Although real GDP per capita is still somewhat higher in the United States, the differences in the standards of living among the United States, Europe, and Japan are relatively small.

Many economists have argued that this convergence in living standards is normal; the convergence hypothesis says that relatively poor countries should have higher rates of growth of real GDP per capita than relatively rich countries. And if we look at today's relatively well-off countries, the convergence hypothesis seems to be true. Panel (a) of Figure 8-8 shows data for a number of today's wealthy economies. On

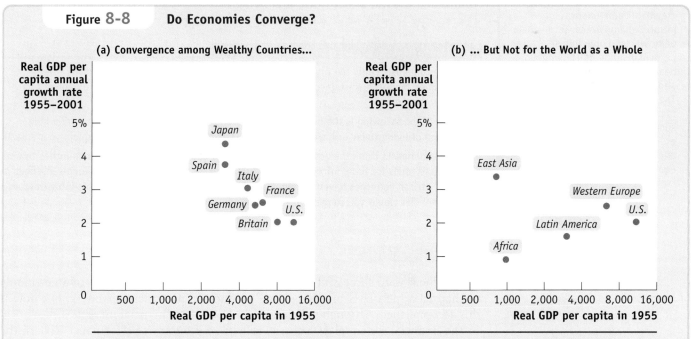

Figure 8-8   Do Economies Converge?

(a) Convergence among Wealthy Countries...

Real GDP per capita annual growth rate 1955–2001

(b) ... But Not for the World as a Whole

Real GDP per capita annual growth rate 1955–2001

Real GDP per capita in 1955

Data on today's wealthy economies seem to support the convergence hypothesis. In panel (a) we see that among wealthy countries, those that had low levels of real GDP per capita in 1955 have had high growth rates since then, and vice versa. But for the world as a whole, there has been little sign of convergence. Panel (b) shows real GDP per capita in 1955 and subsequent growth rates in major world regions. Poorer regions did not consistently have higher growth rates than richer regions: poor Africa turned in the worst performance, and relatively wealthy Europe and grew faster than Latin America. **>web...**

Source: Angus Maddison, *The World Economy: Historical Statistics,* (Paris: OECD, 2003).

the horizontal axis is real GDP per capita in 1955; on the vertical axis is the growth rate of real GDP per capita from 1955 to 2001. There is a clear negative relationship. The United States was the richest country in this group in 1955 and had the slowest rate of growth. Japan and Spain were the poorest countries in 1955 and had the fastest rate of growth. These data suggest that the convergence hypothesis is true.

But economists who looked at similar data realized that these results depend on the countries selected. If you look at successful economies that have a high standard of living today, you find that real GDP per capita has converged. But looking across the world as a whole, including countries that remain poor, there is little evidence of convergence. Panel (b) of Figure 8-8 illustrates this point using data for regions rather than individual countries (other than the United States). In 1955, East Asia and Africa were both very poor regions. Over the next 45 years, the East Asian regional economy grew quickly, as the convergence hypothesis would have predicted, but the African regional economy grew very slowly. In 1955, Western Europe had substantially higher real GDP per capita than Latin America. But, contrary to the convergence hypothesis, the Western European regional economy grew more quickly over the next 45 years, widening the gap between the regions.

So is the convergence hypothesis all wrong? No: economists still believe that countries with relatively low real GDP per capita tend to have higher rates of growth than countries with relatively high real GDP per capita, *other things equal*. But other things—education, infrastructure, rule of law, and so on—are often not equal. Statistical studies find that when you adjust for differences in these other factors, poorer countries do tend to have higher growth rates. This result is known as *conditional convergence*.

Because other factors differ, however, there is no clear tendency toward convergence in the world economy as a whole. Western Europe, North America, and parts of Asia are becoming more similar in real GDP per capita, but the gap between these regions and the rest of the world is growing.

< < < < < < < < < < < < < < < < < <

>>CHECK YOUR UNDERSTANDING 8-4

1. Some economists think the high rates of growth of productivity achieved by many Asian economies cannot be sustained. Why might they be right? What would have to happen for them to be wrong?

2. Which of the following is the better predictor of a future high long-run growth rate: a high standard of living today or high levels of savings and investment spending? Explain your answer.

3. Some economists think the best way to help African countries is for wealthier countries to provide more funds for basic infrastructure. Others think this policy will have no long-run effect unless African countries have the financial and political means to maintain this infrastructure. What policies would you suggest?

Solutions appear at back of book.

• A LOOK AHEAD •

One of the keys to successful long-run economic growth is the ability of an economy to channel a high level of savings into productive investment spending. But how is this accomplished? Through policies, institutions, and financial markets.

The financial system plays a crucial role in an economy's performance in both the long run and the short run. In the next chapter, we examine how that system works.

SUMMARY

1. Levels of real GDP per capita vary greatly around the world: more than half the world's population lives in countries that are still poorer than the United States was in 1900. Over the course of the twentieth century, real GDP per capita in the United States increased by nearly 600%.

2. Growth rates of real GDP per capita also vary widely. According to the **Rule of 70,** the number of years it takes for real GDP per capita to double is equal to 70 divided by the annual growth rate of real GDP per capita.

3. The key to long-run growth is rising **labor productivity,** or just **productivity,** which is output per worker. Increases in productivity arise from increases in **physical capital** per worker and **human capital** per worker as well as advances in **technology.** The **aggregate production function** shows how real GDP per worker depends on these three factors. Other things equal, there are **diminishing returns to physical capital:** each successive addition to physical capital yields a smaller increase in productivity than the one before. Equivalently, more physical capital per worker results in a lower, but still positive, growth rate of productivity. **Growth accounting,** which estimates the contribution of each factor to a country's economic growth, has shown that rising **total factor productivity,** the amount of output produced from a given amount of factor inputs, is key to long-run growth. It is usually interpreted as the effect of technological progress. In contrast to earlier times, natural resources are a less significant source of productivity growth in most countries today.

4. A number of factors influence differences among countries in their growth rates. These are government policies and institutions that increase savings and investment spending, foreign investment, **infrastructure, research and development,** as well as foster political stability and the protection of property rights.

5. The world economy contains examples of success and failure in the effort to achieve long-run economic growth. East Asian economies have done many things right and achieved very high growth rates. In Latin America, where some important conditions are lacking, growth has generally been disappointing. In Africa, real GDP per capita has declined for several decades, although there are some signs of progress now. The growth rates of economically advanced countries have converged, but not the growth rates of countries across the world. This has led economists to believe that the **convergence hypothesis** fits the data only when factors that affect growth, such as education, infrastructure, and favorable policies and institutions, are held equal across countries.

KEY TERMS

Rule of 70, p. 189
Labor productivity, p. 191
Productivity, p. 191
Physical capital, p. 192
Human capital, p. 192

Technology, p. 192
Aggregate production function, p. 192
Diminishing returns to physical capital, p. 193
Growth accounting, p. 195

Total factor productivity, p. 196
Infrastructure, p. 200
Research and development, p. 200
Convergence hypothesis, p. 203

PROBLEMS

1. The accompanying table shows data from the Penn World Table, Version 6.1, for real GDP per capita in 1996 U.S. dollars for Argentina, Ghana, South Korea, and the United States for 1960, 1970, 1980, 1990, and 2000.

a. Complete the table by expressing each year's real GDP per capita as a percentage of its 1960 and 2000 levels.

b. How does the growth in living standards from 1960 to 2000 compare across these four nations? What might account for these differences?

	Argentina			Ghana			South Korea			United States		
Year	Real GDP per capita (1996 dollars)	Percentage of 1960 real GDP per capita	Percentage of 2000 real GDP per capita	Real GDP per capita (1996 dollars)	Percentage of 1960 real GDP per capita	Percentage of 2000 real GDP per capita	Real GDP per capita (1996 dollars)	Percentage of 1960 real GDP per capita	Percentage of 2000 real GDP per capita	Real GDP per capita (1996 dollars)	Percentage of 1960 real GDP per capita	Percentage of 2000 real GDP per capita
1960	$7,395	?	?	$832	?	?	$1,571	?	?	$12,414	?	?
1970	9,227	?	?	1,275	?	?	2,777	?	?	16,488	?	?
1980	10,556	?	?	1,204	?	?	4,830	?	?	21,337	?	?
1990	7,237	?	?	1,183	?	?	9,959	?	?	26,470	?	?
2000	10,995	?	?	1,349	?	?	15,881	?	?	33,308	?	?

2. The accompanying table shows the average annual growth rate in real GDP per capita for Argentina, Ghana, and South Korea using data from the Penn World Table, Version 6.1, for the past few decades.

	Average annual growth rate of real GDP per capita		
Years	Argentina	Ghana	South Korea
1960–1970	2.24%	4.36%	5.86%
1970–1980	1.35	−0.57	5.69
1980–1990	−3.70	−0.18	7.51
1990–2000	4.27	1.33	4.78

a. For each decade and for each country, use the Rule of 70 where possible to calculate how long it would take for that country's real GDP per capita to double.

b. Suppose that the average annual growth rate that each country achieved over the period 1990–2000 continues indefinitely into the future. Starting from 2000, use the Rule of 70 to calculate, where possible, the year in which a country will have doubled its real GDP per capita.

3. You are hired as an economic consultant to the countries of Albernia and Brittania. Each country's current relationship between physical capital per worker (K/L) and output per worker (Y/L) is given by the curve labeled Productivity₁ in the accompanying diagram. Albernia is at point A and Brittania is at point B.

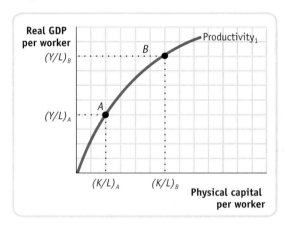

a. In the relationship depicted by the curve Productivity₁, what factors are held fixed? Do these countries experience diminishing returns to physical capital per worker?

b. Assuming that the amount of human capital per worker and the technology are held fixed in each country, can you recommend a policy to generate a doubling of real GDP per capita in each country?

c. How would your policy recommendation change if the amount of human capital per worker and the technology were not fixed? Draw a curve on the diagram that represents this policy for Albernia.

4. Why would you expect real GDP per capita in California and Pennsylvania to exhibit convergence but not in California and Baja California, a state of Mexico that borders the United States? What changes would allow California and Baja California to converge?

5. The economy of Profunctia has estimated its aggregate production function, when holding human capital per worker and technology constant, as

$$\frac{Y}{L} = 100 \times \sqrt{\frac{K}{L}}$$

Y is real GDP, L is the number of workers, and K is the quantity of physical capital. Given that Profunctia has 1,000 workers, calculate real GDP per worker and the quantity of physical capital per worker for the differing amounts of physical capital shown in the accompanying table.

K	L	K/L	Y/L
$0	1,000	?	?
10	1,000	?	?
20	1,000	?	?
30	1,000	?	?
40	1,000	?	?
50	1,000	?	?
60	1,000	?	?
70	1,000	?	?
80	1,000	?	?
90	1,000	?	?
100	1,000	?	?

a. Plot the aggregate production function for Profunctia.

b. Does the aggregate production function exhibit diminishing returns to physical capital? Explain your answer.

6. The Bureau of Labor Statistics regularly releases the "Productivity and Costs" report for the previous month. Go to www.bls.gov and find the latest report. (On the Bureau of Labor Statistics home page, click on "Productivity" under Latest Numbers and then choose the latest "Productivity and Costs" report.) What were the percent changes in business and nonfarm business productivity for the previous quarter? How does the percent change in that quarter's productivity compare to previous data?

7. What roles do physical capital, human capital, technology, and natural resources play in influencing long-run economic growth of aggregate output per capita?

8. Through its policies and institutions, how has the United States influenced U.S. long-run economic growth? Why might persistently large borrowing by the U.S. government ultimately limit long-run economic growth in the future?

9. Over the next 100 years, real GDP per capita in Groland is expected to grow at an average annual rate of 2.0%. In Sloland, however, growth is expected to be somewhat slower, at an average annual growth rate of 1.5%. If both countries have a real GDP per capita today of $20,000, how will their real GDP per capita differ in 100 years? (*Hint:* A country that has a real GDP today of x and grows at y% per year will achieve a real GDP of $\$x \times (1 + 0.0y)^z$ in z years.

10. The accompanying table shows data from the Penn World Table, Version 6.1, for real GDP per capita (1996 U.S. dollars) in France, Japan, the United Kingdom, and the United States in 1950 and 2000. Complete the table. Have these countries converged economically?

	1950		2000	
	Real GDP per capita (1996 dollars)	Percentage of U.S. real GDP per capita	Real GDP per capita (1996 dollars)	Percentage of U.S. real GDP per capita
France	$5,561	?	$22,254	?
Japan	2,445	?	24,495	?
United Kingdom	7,498	?	22,849	?
United States	10,601	?	33,308	?

11. The accompanying table shows data from the Penn World Table, Version 6.1, for real GDP per capita (1996 U.S. dollars) for Argentina, Ghana, South Korea, and the United States in 1960 and 2000. Complete the table. Have these countries converged economically?

	1960		2000	
	Real GDP per capita (1996 dollars)	Percentage of U.S. real GDP per capita	Real GDP per capita (1996 dollars)	Percentage of U.S. real GDP per capita
Argentina	$7,395	?	$10,995	?
Ghana	832	?	1,349	?
South Korea	1,571	?	15,881	?
United States	12,414	?	33,308	?

>web... To continue your study and review of concepts in this chapter, please visit the Krugman/Wells website for quizzes, animated graph tutorials, web links to helpful resources, and more.

www.worthpublishers.com/krugmanwells

chapter 9

>> Savings, Investment Spending, and the Financial System

A HOLE IN THE GROUND

ETWEEN 1987 AND 1994, A LARGE international group of private investors threw $15 billion into a hole in the ground. But this was no ordinary hole: it was the Channel Tunnel, popularly known as the Chunnel. Engineers had dreamed for centuries about linking Britain directly to France so that travelers would no longer have to cross the often-stormy seas of the English Channel. The Chunnel fulfills that dream, allowing passengers to take a comfortable fast train (and ship their cars, too) underneath the 31-mile-wide strait.

Everyone agrees that the Chunnel is a big improvement on the previously available alternatives. It's much faster than taking a ferry. Even flying from London to Paris can easily be an all-day affair, what with getting to and from the airports and air traffic delays. The *Eurostar,* the express train through the Chunnel, gets you from downtown London to downtown Paris in three hours.

How could such a massive investment be financed? The French and British governments could have built the Chunnel but chose to leave it to private initiative. Yet the size of the required investment was beyond the means of any individual. So how was the money raised?

The answer: the Eurotunnel Corporation, the company formed to build the Chunnel, was able to turn to the financial markets. It raised $4 billion by selling stock to thousands of people, who then became part-owners of the Chunnel, and an additional $12 billion through bank loans. Raising this much money was an incredible feat, in a way as incredible as the engineering required for the construction of the Chunnel.

What you will learn in this chapter:

- ➤ The relationship between savings and investment spending
- ➤ Aspects of the **loanable funds market,** which shows how savers are matched with borrowers
- ➤ The purpose of the four principal types of **financial assets:** stocks, bonds, **loans,** and **bank deposits**
- ➤ How **financial intermediaries** help investors achieve **diversification**
- ➤ Some competing views of what determines stock prices and why stock market fluctuations can be a source of macroeconomic instability

A quick and luxurious ride from London to Paris beneath the English Channel was made possible by the savings of millions of people.

Yet modern economies do this sort of thing all the time. The long-run growth we analyzed in Chapter 8 depends crucially on a set of markets and institutions, collectively known as the *financial system,* that channels the funds of savers into productive investment spending. Without this system, businesses would not be able to purchase much of the physical capital that is such an important source of productivity growth. And savers would be forced to accept a lower return on their funds. Historically, financial systems channeled funds into investment projects such as railroads, factories, electrification, and so on. Today, financial systems channel funds into sources of growth such as telecommunications, advanced technology, and investments in human capital. Without a well-functioning financial system, a country will suffer stunted economic growth.

In this chapter, we begin by focusing on the economy as a whole. We examine the relationship between savings and investment spending at the macroeconomic level. Next, we go behind this relationship and analyze the financial system, the means by which savings is transformed into investment spending. We'll see how the financial system works by creating assets, markets, and institutions that increase the welfare of both savers (those with funds to invest) and borrowers (those with investment projects to finance). Finally, we close by examining the behavior of financial markets and why that behavior often resists economists' attempts to explain it.

Matching Up Savings and Investment Spending

We learned in Chapter 8 that two of the essential ingredients in economic growth are increases in the economy's levels of *human capital* and *physical capital.* Human capital is largely provided by government through public education. (In countries with a large private education sector, like the United States, private post-secondary education is also an important source of human capital.) But physical capital, with the exception of infrastructure, is mainly created through private investment spending—that is, spending by firms rather than by the government.

Investment spending must be financed out of savings. There are two sources of savings. One source is domestic savings, created by a country's own residents. The second source is foreign savings, generated by foreigners. We'll begin with the simplest case, a *closed economy*—an economy in which there is no economic interaction with the rest of the world. There are no exports, no imports, and no capital flows. In a closed economy, the second source of acquiring savings is unavailable; so, all investment spending must come from domestic savings. However, modern economies aren't closed. So we'll follow with a discussion of an *open economy*—an economy in which there is economic interaction with the rest of the world. In an open economy, both sources of investment funds—domestic savings and foreign savings—are available.

In both a closed and an open economy, our first step in understanding the process of investment spending is to clarify the relationship between savings and investment spending. Then we can look at how savings is allocated among various investment spending projects available in the economy.

The Savings–Investment Spending Identity

The most basic point to understand about savings and investment spending is that they are always equal, regardless of whether an economy is open or closed. This is not a theory; it's a fact of accounting called the **savings–investment spending identity.**

According to the **savings–investment spending identity,** savings and investment spending are always equal for the economy as a whole.

To see why the savings–investment spending identity must be true, let's look again at the national income accounting that we examined in Chapter 7. Recall that GDP is equal to total spending on final goods and services produced in the economy and that we can write the following equation:

(9-1) $GDP = C + I + G + X - IM$

where C is spending by consumers, I is investment spending, G is government purchases of goods and services, X is the value of exports to other countries, and IM is spending on imports from other countries.

The Savings–Investment Spending Identity in a Closed Economy
In a closed economy, there are no exports or imports. So $X = 0$ and $IM = 0$, which makes Equation 9-1 simpler:

(9-2) $GDP = C + I + G$

Let's rearrange Equation 9-2, putting investment spending on one side and everything else on the other. It looks like this:

(9-3) $I = GDP - C - G$

That is, investment spending is equal to GDP minus consumer spending minus government purchases of goods and services in a closed economy.

Now let's derive savings for the total economy. We know from Chapter 7 that private savings is equal to disposable income (household income, including government transfers, net of taxes) minus consumer spending:

(9-4) $S_{Private} = GDP + TR - T - C$

where $S_{Private}$ is private savings, TR is government transfers, and T is taxes paid.

But households are not the only parties that can save in an economy. In any given year the government can save, too, if it collects more tax revenue than it spends. When this occurs, the difference is called a **budget surplus** and is equivalent to savings by government. If, alternatively, government spending exceeds tax revenue, there is a **budget deficit**—a negative surplus. In this case we often say that the government is "dissaving": by spending more than its tax revenues, the government is engaged in the opposite of saving. We'll define the term **budget balance,** $S_{Government}$, to refer to both cases, with the understanding that the budget balance can be positive (a budget surplus) or negative (a budget deficit). Then we have:

(9-5) $S_{Government} = T - TR - G$

In general, as we'll see in Chapter 12, responsible governments run deficits when faced with difficult times, such as wars or recessions, then run surpluses later to pay off the debt incurred during those deficit periods.

Putting together Equations 9-4 and 9-5 we arrive at an expression for total savings generated within the economy as a whole, called **national savings,** or NS:

(9-6) $NS = S_{Private} + S_{Government}$
$$= (GDP + TR - T - C) + (T - TR - G)$$
$$= GDP - C - G$$

At this point we can see that the right-hand sides of Equations 9-3 and 9-6 are identical. Combining these two equations brings us to our final step in showing the savings–investment spending identity in a closed economy:

(9-7) $I = NS$

or

Investment spending = National savings in a closed economy

The **budget surplus** is the difference between tax revenue and government spending when tax revenue exceeds government spending.

The **budget deficit** is the difference between tax revenue and government spending when government spending exceeds tax revenue.

The **budget balance** is the difference between tax revenue and government spending.

National savings, the sum of private savings and the budget balance, is the total amount of savings generated within the economy.

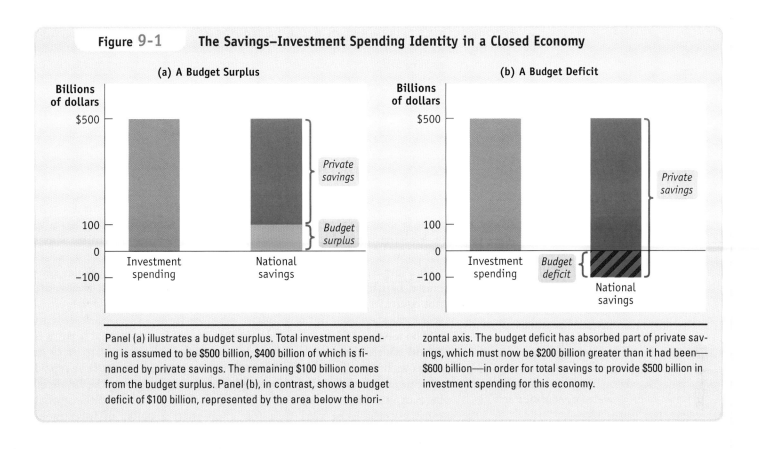

Figure 9-1   The Savings–Investment Spending Identity in a Closed Economy

Panel (a) illustrates a budget surplus. Total investment spending is assumed to be $500 billion, $400 billion of which is financed by private savings. The remaining $100 billion comes from the budget surplus. Panel (b), in contrast, shows a budget deficit of $100 billion, represented by the area below the hori-zontal axis. The budget deficit has absorbed part of private savings, which must now be $200 billion greater than it had been—$600 billion—in order for total savings to provide $500 billion in investment spending for this economy.

So the closed-economy version of the savings–investment spending identity is that investment spending is always equal to national savings.

Figure 9-1 illustrates how this works by considering a hypothetical closed economy, where we have broken national savings, NS, into its two components, $S_{Private}$, private savings, and $S_{Government}$, the budget balance (a budget surplus or deficit, as the case may be). In each panel, the height of the bar on the left represents the amount of investment spending, I, which is $500 billion. Because national savings equals investment spending in a closed economy, the bar representing investment spending must be matched by the height of the bar on the right, which represents national savings, NS. In panel (a), we show an economy in which the government runs a budget surplus of $100 billion and private savings is equal to $400 billion. The areas representing private savings and the budget surplus are stacked to create the overall pool of national savings of $500 billion, which is available for investment spending. In panel (b), we show an economy in which the government runs a budget deficit of $100 billion, represented by the area below the horizontal axis. Here part of private savings has been offset by the budget deficit. As a result, private savings must now be $200 billion greater than before—$600 billion—in order for national savings to provide $500 billion in investment spending for this economy.

We've just learned that investment spending in a closed economy is equal to national savings; that is, investment spending is equal to private savings plus the budget balance, the government's contribution to savings or dissavings, as the case may be. Now we'll examine the savings–investment spending identity when the economy is open.

The Savings–Investment Spending Identity in an Open Economy An *open economy* is an economy in which goods and money can flow into and out of the country. This changes the savings–investment spending identity because savings need not be spent on physical capital located in the same country in which the savings are generated. That's because the savings of people who live in any one country can be used to finance investment spending that takes place in other countries. So any given country can receive *inflows* of funds—foreign savings that finance investment spending in the country. Any given country can also generate *outflows* of funds—domestic savings that finance investment spending in another country.

The net effect of international inflows and outflows of funds on the total savings available for investment spending in any given country is known as the **capital inflow** into that country. It is the net inflow of funds into a country, which is equal to the total inflow of foreign funds minus the total outflow of domestic funds to other countries. We'll denote a country's capital inflow by the symbol *KI*. Like the budget balance, a capital inflow can be negative—that is, more capital can flow out of a country than flows into it. In recent years the United States has experienced a consistent net inflow of capital from foreigners, who view our economy as an attractive place to put their savings. In 2004, for example, capital inflows into the United States exceeded $600 billion.

Capital inflow is net inflow of funds into a country.

It's important to note that, from a national perspective, a dollar generated by national savings and a dollar generated by capital inflow are not equivalent. Yes, they can both finance the same dollar's worth of investment spending. But any dollar borrowed from a saver must eventually be repaid with interest. A dollar that comes from national savings is repaid with interest to someone domestically—either a private party or the government. But a dollar that comes as capital inflow must be repaid with interest to a foreigner. So a dollar of investment spending financed by a capital inflow comes at a higher *national* cost—the interest that must eventually be paid to a foreigner—than a dollar of investment spending financed by national savings.

The fact that a net capital inflow represents funds borrowed from foreigners is an important aspect of the savings–investment spending identity in an open economy. Consider an individual who spends more than his or her income; that person must borrow the difference from others. Similarly, a country that spends more on imports than it earns from exports must borrow the difference from foreigners. And that difference, the amount of funds borrowed from foreigners, is equal to the country's capital inflow. As we will explain at greater length in Chapter 19, this means that the capital inflow into a country is equal to the difference between imports and exports:

PITFALLS

THE DIFFERENT KINDS OF CAPITAL
It's important to understand clearly the three different kinds of capital: physical capital, human capital, and financial capital. As we explained in Chapter 8, physical capital consists of manufactured resources such as buildings and machines; human capital is the improvement in the labor force generated by education and knowledge. Financial capital—often referred to simply as "capital" in macroeconomics—is funds from savings that are available for investment spending. So a country that has a "capital inflow" is experiencing a flow of funds into the country from abroad for the purpose of investment spending.

(9-8) $KI = IM - X$

We can now go back to Equation 9-1 to derive the savings–investment spending identity for an open economy. By rearranging Equation 9-1, we get:

(9-9) $I = (GDP - C - G) + (IM - X)$

Using Equation 9-6, we can break $(GDP - C - G)$ into private savings and the budget balance, yielding for an open economy:

(9-10) $I = S_{Private} + S_{Government} + (IM - X)$
$$= NS + KI$$

or

Investment spending = National savings + Capital inflow in an open economy

So the savings–investment spending identity for an open economy means that investment spending is equal to savings, where savings is equal to national savings *plus* capital inflow. That is, in an open economy with a positive capital inflow, some investment spending is funded by the savings of foreigners. And in an open economy with a negative capital inflow (a net outflow), some portion of national savings is funding investment spending in other countries. In the United States in 2004, investment spending totaled $2,307 billion. Private savings were $1,927 billion, offset by a budget deficit of $358 billion and supplemented by capital inflows of $636 billion. Notice that these numbers don't quite add up; because data collection isn't perfect, there is a "statistical discrepancy" of $102 billion. But we know that this is an error in the data and not in the theory because the savings–investment spending identity must hold in reality.

Figure 9-2 shows what this identity actually looked like in 2003 for the world's two largest economies, those of the United States and Japan. To make the two economies easier to compare, we've measured savings and investment spending as percentages of GDP. As in Figure 9-1, in each panel the bars on the left show total investment spending and those on the right show the components of savings. U.S. investment spending was 18.4% of GDP, financed by a combination of private savings (18.2% of GDP) and capital inflows (4.8% of GDP) and partly offset by government dissaving (−4.6% of GDP). Japanese investment spending was higher as a percentage of GDP, at 24.2%. It was financed by a higher level of private savings as a percentage of GDP (35.3%) and was offset by both a capital outflow (−3.2% of GDP) and a relatively high budget deficit (−7.9% of GDP).

The economy's savings, then, finance its investment spending. But how are these funds available for investment spending allocated among various projects? That is, what determines which projects get financed (such as the Chunnel) and which don't (such as a new jetliner that would fly close to the speed of sound, which Boeing recently declined to fully develop and produce). We'll see shortly that funds get allocated to investment projects using a familiar method: by the market, via supply and demand.

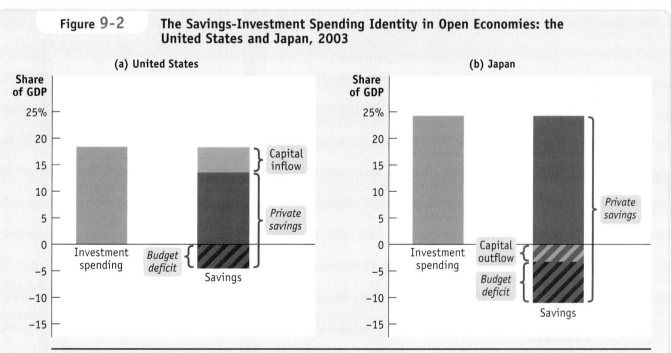

Figure 9-2   The Savings-Investment Spending Identity in Open Economies: the United States and Japan, 2003

U.S. investment spending in 2003 (equal to 18.4% of GDP) was financed by private savings (18.2% of GDP) and capital inflows (4.8% of GDP), which were partially offset by a budget deficit (−4.6% of GDP). Japanese investment spending in 2003 was higher as a percentage of GDP (24.2%). It was financed by a higher level of private savings as a percentage of GDP (35.3%), which was offset by both a capital outflow (−3.2% of GDP) and a relatively high budget deficit (−7.9% of GDP).

Source: Bureau of Economic Analysis; OECD.

WHO ENFORCES THE ACCOUNTING?

The savings–investment spending identity is a fact of accounting. By definition, savings equal investment spending for the economy as a whole. But who enforces the arithmetic? For example, what happens if the amount that businesses want to invest in capital equipment is less than the amount households want to save?

The short answer is that actual and *desired* investment spending aren't always equal. Suppose that households suddenly decide to save more by spending less. The immediate effect will be that unsold goods pile up in stores and warehouses. And this increase in inventory counts as investment spending, albeit unintended. So the savings–investment spending identity still holds, because businesses end up engaging in more investment spending than

they intended to. Similarly, if households suddenly decide to save less and spend more, inventories will drop—and this will be counted as *negative* investment spending.

A real-world example occurred in 2001. Savings and investment spending, measured at an annual rate, both fell by $126 billion between the second and the fourth quarter of 2001. But on the investment spending side, $71 billion of that fall took the form of negative inventory investment spending.

Of course, businesses respond to changes in their inventories by changing their production. The inventory reduction in late 2001 prepared the ground for a spurt in output in early 2002. We'll examine the special role of inventories in economic fluctuations in later chapters.

The Market for Loanable Funds

For the economy as a whole, savings always equals investment spending. In a closed economy, savings is equal to national savings. In an open economy, savings is equal to national savings plus capital inflow. At any given time, however, savers, the people with funds to lend, are usually not the same as borrowers, the people who want to borrow to finance their investment spending. How are savers and borrowers brought together?

Savers and borrowers are matched up with one another in much the same way producers and consumers are matched up: through markets governed by supply and demand. In Figure 7-1, the expanded circular-flow diagram, we noted that the *financial markets* channel the savings of households to businesses that want to borrow in order to purchase capital equipment. It's now time to take a look at how those financial markets work.

As we noted in Chapter 7, there are a large number of different financial markets in the financial system, such as the bond market and the stock market. However, economists often work with a simplified model in which they assume that there is just one market that brings together those who want to lend money (savers) and those who want to borrow (firms with investment spending projects). This hypothetical market is known as the **loanable funds market.** The price that is determined in the loanable funds market is the **interest rate,** denoted by r, the return a lender receives for allowing borrowers the use of a dollar for one year.

We should note at this point that there are, in reality, many different kinds of interest rates because there are many different kinds of loans—short-term loans, long-term loans, loans made to corporate borrowers, loans made to governments, and so on. In the interest of simplicity, we'll ignore those differences and assume that there is only one type of loan. But an important distinction, one that we will explore in Chapter 16, is between the *real interest rate*—the interest rate adjusted for changes in prices over the length of the loan, and the *nominal interest rate*—the interest rate unadjusted for such price changes. In the context of the hypothetical loanable funds market, we'll keep things simple by assuming that there are no price changes and that, as a result, there is no difference between the real and the nominal interest rate.

The **loanable funds market** is a hypothetical market that examines the market outcome of the demand for funds generated by borrowers and the supply of funds provided by lenders.

The **interest rate** is the price, calculated as a percentage of the amount borrowed, charged by the lender to a borrower for the use of their savings for one year.

Figure 9-3

The Demand for Loanable Funds

The demand curve for loanable funds slopes downward: the lower the interest rate, the greater the quantity of loanable funds demanded. Here, reducing the interest rate from 12% to 4% increases the quantity of loanable funds demanded from $150 billion to $450 billion. *>web*...

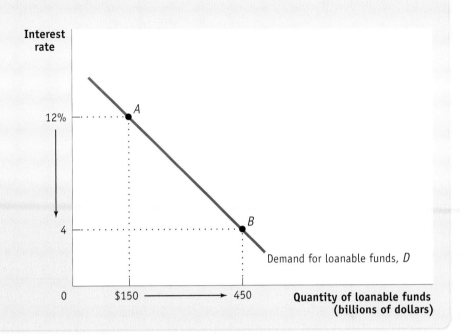

Figure 9-3 illustrates the hypothetical demand for loanable funds, represented by a downward-sloping demand curve. Imagine that there are many businesses, each of which has one potential investment project. How does a given business decide whether or not to borrow money to finance its project? The decision depends on the interest rate the business faces and the **rate of return** of its project—the profit earned on the project expressed as a percentage of its cost. This can be expressed in a formula as:

The **rate of return** of a project is the profit earned on the project expressed as a percentage of its cost.

(9-11) $Rate\ of\ return = \dfrac{(Revenue\ from\ project - Cost\ of\ project)}{Cost\ of\ project} \times 100$

A business will want a loan when the rate of return on its project is at least as great as the interest rate. So, for example, at an interest rate of 12%, only businesses with projects that yield a rate of return greater than or equal to 12% will want a loan. The demand curve in Figure 9-3 shows that if the interest rate is 12%, businesses will want to borrow $150 billion (point A); if the interest rate is only 4%, businesses will want to borrow a larger amount, $450 billion (point B). That's a consequence of our assumption that the demand curve slopes downward: the lower the interest rate, the larger the total quantity of loanable funds demanded. Why do we make that assumption? Because, in reality, the number of potential investment projects that yield at least 4% is always greater than the number that yield at least 12%.

Figure 9-4 on page 218 shows the hypothetical supply of loanable funds. Savers have an opportunity cost for the funds that they could lend to a business; they could instead be spent on consumption—say, a nice vacation. Whether a given saver becomes a lender by making funds available to borrowers depends on the interest rate received in return. By saving your money today and earning interest on it, you are rewarded with higher consumption in the future when your loan is repaid with interest. So it is a good assumption that more people are willing to forgo current consumption and make a loan when the interest rate is higher. As a result, our hypothetical supply curve of loanable funds slopes upward. In Figure 9-4, lenders will supply $150 billion to the loanable funds market at an interest rate of 4% (point X); if the interest rate rises to 12%, the quantity of loanable funds supplied will rise to $450 billion (point Y).

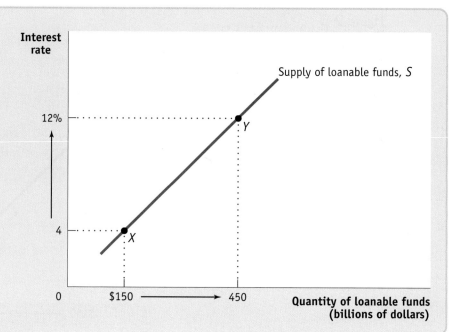

Figure 9-4

The Supply of Loanable Funds

The supply curve for loanable funds slopes upward: the higher the interest rate, the greater the quantity of loanable funds supplied. Here, increasing the interest rate from 4% to 12% increases the quantity of loanable funds supplied from $150 billion to $450 billion. **>web...**

The equilibrium interest rate is the interest rate at which the quantity of loanable funds supplied equals the quantity of loanable funds demanded. As you can see in Figure 9-5, the equilibrium interest rate, r^*, and the total quantity of lending, Q^*, are determined by the intersection of the supply and demand curves, at point E. Here, the equilibrium interest rate is 8%, at which $300 billion is lent and borrowed. Investment spending projects with a rate of return of 8% or more are funded; projects with a rate of return of less than 8% are not. Correspondingly, only lenders who are willing to accept an interest rate of 8% or less will have their offers to lend funds accepted. Potential lenders who demand an interest rate higher than 8% have a higher opportunity

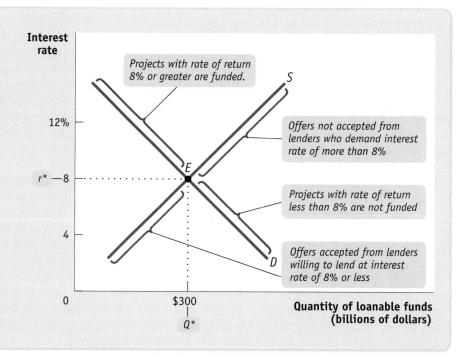

Figure 9-5

Equilibrium in the Loanable Funds Market

At the equilibrium interest rate, the quantity of loanable funds supplied equals the quantity of loanable funds demanded. Here the equilibrium interest rate is 8%, with $300 billion of funds lent and borrowed. Investment spending projects with a rate of return of 8% or higher receive financing; those with a lower rate of return do not. Lenders who demand an interest rate of 8% or lower have their offers of loans accepted; those who demand a higher interest rate do not.

cost of their funds. Their offers to lend will be turned down in the loanable funds market, and their funds will remain uninvested.

In Chapter 5 we learned that a market for an ordinary good, such as used textbooks, is usually efficient. The same is true of the hypothetical market for loanable funds. The investment spending projects that are actually financed have higher rates of return than those that do not get financed. The potential savers who actually lend funds are willing to lend for lower interest rates than those who do not. In other words, the loanable funds market maximizes the gains from trade between lenders and borrowers. Savings are allocated efficiently to investment projects throughout the economy. This result, although drawn from a highly simplified model, has important implications for real life. As we'll see shortly, it is the reason that a well-functioning financial system increases an economy's long-run economic growth rate.

Savings, Investment Spending, and Government Policy

Our model of the loanable funds market is very simple, yet it is enough to give us some preliminary insight into a source of concern about the effects of government policy on economic growth.

Consider first the impact of the government's budget. When the government runs a budget deficit, it must borrow funds to cover the gap between tax revenue and government spending—the government becomes a borrower in the loanable funds market. And we'll make an assumption, consistent with real government behavior, that the amount of government borrowing does not depend on the interest rate. At any given interest rate, private (non-government) borrowers still want to borrow as much as before the emergence of the budget deficit. But now, at any given interest rate, the government makes additional demand for funds. Figure 9-6 shows what happens. The demand curve for loanable funds shifts rightward by the amount of the government's borrowing. As a result, the equilibrium moves from E_1 to E_2. The interest rate and the total amount of borrowing rise. Because of the higher interest rate, however, the amount of private borrowing falls from Q_1 to Q_2, as shown by the movement up the demand curve D_1.

This decrease in private borrowing means that as a result of the budget deficit, businesses will engage in less investment spending than they otherwise would have.

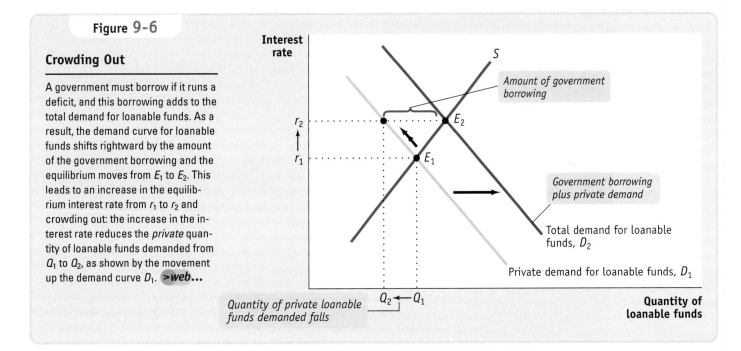

Figure 9-6

Crowding Out

A government must borrow if it runs a deficit, and this borrowing adds to the total demand for loanable funds. As a result, the demand curve for loanable funds shifts rightward by the amount of the government borrowing and the equilibrium moves from E_1 to E_2. This leads to an increase in the equilibrium interest rate from r_1 to r_2 and crowding out: the increase in the interest rate reduces the *private* quantity of loanable funds demanded from Q_1 to Q_2, as shown by the movement up the demand curve D_1. **>web**...

Crowding out is the negative effect of budget deficits on private investment.

This negative effect of budget deficits on private investment spending is called **crowding out.** When a budget deficit causes crowding out, the economy adds less private physical capital each year than it would if the budget were balanced or in surplus. And since private physical capital is one of the sources of productivity growth, budget deficits, *other things equal*, lead to lower long-run growth.

But this should not be interpreted to mean that government spending is necessarily bad for economic growth! It depends on what the government is spending its money on. In fact, as we learned in Chapter 8, much government spending is essential to growth. For example, the court system must be kept running to enforce contracts, and the public health system must be maintained to prevent the spread of disease. Governments also do quite a lot of investment spending themselves—for example, building and maintaining necessary infrastructure such as roads, schools, and airports. Our analysis of crowding out is an "other things equal" result: When government spending has *already* created the things that enhance growth (such as a court system and roads), *further* government spending that results in budget deficits reduces private investment spending and lowers growth. So we cannot say unambiguously that government spending that results in a budget deficit either decreases or increases economic growth.

Government borrowing is not the only policy that affects the loanable funds market. Many economists have argued for changes in the tax system that they believe would lead to higher private savings and lower current consumption but would generate the same amount of total tax revenue. An example would be reducing the tax on investment income (such as interest on bonds and dividends on stocks) but increasing the sales tax on consumption of goods and services. A reduction in the tax on investment income motivates people to save more because it raises the net return earned on savings after taxes are paid, while an increase in the sales taxes motivates people to consume less by making the total cost of goods and services higher. Figure 9-7 shows what would happen if their proposals were adopted and if they turned out to be right. The supply of funds to the loanable funds market would increase—that is, the supply curve would shift to the right. The equilibrium would move from E_1 to E_2, the interest rate would fall from r_1 to r_2, and private borrowing would increase from Q_1 to Q_2. So a tax reform that increases private savings would lead to higher private investment spending and, as a result, to higher long-run economic growth.

Figure 9-7

Increasing Private Savings

Some economists have urged reforms in the tax system and adoption of other policies that would, they say, increase private savings but keep tax revenue unchanged. If they are correct, the effect would be to shift the supply curve of loanable funds to the right, leading to a reduction in the equilibrium interest rate and a larger quantity of funds lent and borrowed. Private investment spending in the economy would rise and so, ultimately, would long-run economic growth.

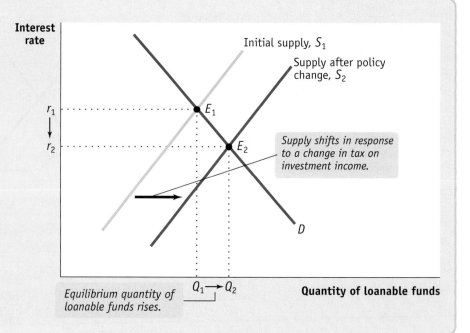

The loanable funds model is a good way to think about many issues involving savings and investment spending. Although very simple, it illustrates the trade-off involved in deciding whether to save and lend or whether to consume as well as the trade-off involved in deciding whether or not to borrow and undertake an investment spending project. It also illustrates how an interest rate moves to equalize the supply and demand for loanable funds. In reality, though, the actual markets that channel savings into investment spending are more complex than that. We turn next to an examination of those markets.

economics in action

Budgets and Investment Spending in the 1990s

Do government budget deficits really crowd out private investment spending? Does moving from deficit to surplus really encourage private investment spending? These questions aren't just academic; they have a direct bearing on political issues such as the spending priorities of the government. So what does the evidence say?

Federal, state, and local governments in the United States moved from a combined deficit of 4.2% of GDP in 1990 to a combined surplus of 1.6% of GDP in 2000. Over the same period private investment spending rose from 14.8% to 17.7% of GDP. Did the move from deficit to surplus, accompanied by a boom in private investment spending, demonstrate that deficits really do crowd out private investment spending?

The answer is that it's not clear because there was another reason for the rise in private investment spending: a sharp rise in capital inflows, which rose from 1.2% of GDP in 1990 to 4.0% of GDP in 2000. Meanwhile, private savings as a percent of GDP were falling. The increase in capital inflows, 2.8% of GDP, was almost equal to the rise in private investment spending, 2.9% of GDP. So you could say that the investment spending boom of the 1990s was basically foreign-financed.

There are two morals to this story. First, although the data don't show it unambiguously, from our model we can conclude that the move from budget deficit to budget surplus in the late 1990s made private investment spending *greater than it would have been* if there had been no increase in the budget balance. Second, we must be careful about jumping to conclusions about the impact of government policies on the basis of observed data—lots of other things tend to be happening at the same time as policy changes, and those other things may be the real story. ∎

> > > > > > > > > > > > > > > > > > > >

>> CHECK YOUR UNDERSTANDING 9-1

1. Suppose the government's deficit becomes a budget surplus. Using a diagram like Figure 9-6, show the effects on private investment spending and the equilibrium interest rate.

2. Illustrate with a diagram of the loanable funds market the effect of the following events on the equilibrium interest rate and investment spending.
   a. A closed economy becomes an open one. A capital inflow occurs.
   b. Retired people generally save less than working people at any interest rate. The proportion of retired people in the population goes up.

3. Explain what is wrong with the following statement: "Savings and investment spending may not be equal in the economy as a whole because when the interest rate rises, households will want to save more money than businesses will want to invest."

Solutions appear at back of book.

The Financial System

A well-functioning financial system that brought together the funds of British, French, and other international investors made the Chunnel possible. But to think that this is an exclusively modern phenomenon is misguided. Financial markets raised the funds that were used to develop colonial markets in India, to build canals across Europe, and to finance the Napoleonic wars in the eighteenth century. Capital inflows financed the early economic development of the United States, funding investment spending in mining, railroads, and canals. In fact, many of the principal features of financial markets and assets have been well understood in Europe and the United States since the eighteenth century. However, these features are no less relevant today. So let's begin by understanding exactly what is traded in financial markets.

Financial markets are where households invest their current savings and their accumulated savings, or **wealth,** by purchasing *financial assets*. A **financial asset** is a paper claim that entitles the buyer to future income from the seller. For example, when a saver lends funds to a company, the loan is a financial asset sold by the company that entitles the lender (the buyer) to future income from the company. A household can also invest its current savings or wealth by purchasing a **physical asset,** a claim on a tangible object, such as a preexisting house or preexisting piece of equipment. It gives the owner the right to dispose of the object as he or she wishes (for example, rent it or sell it). Recall from Pitfalls on page 211 that the purchase of a financial or physical asset is typically called investing. So if you purchase a preexisting piece of equipment—say, a used airliner—you are engaging in investing in a physical asset. But if you spend funds that *add* to the stock of physical capital in the economy—say, purchasing a newly manufactured airplane—you are engaging in investment spending.

If you were to go to your local bank and get a loan—say, to buy a new car—you and the bank would be creating a financial asset—your loan. A *loan* is one important kind of financial asset in the real world, one that is owned by the lender—in this case, your local bank. In creating that loan, you and the bank would also be creating a **liability,** a requirement to pay income in the future. So although your loan is a financial asset from the bank's point of view, it is a liability from your point of view: a requirement that you repay the loan, including any interest. In addition to loans, there are three other important kinds of financial assets: stocks, bonds, and *bank deposits*. Because a financial asset is a claim to future income that someone has to pay, it is also someone else's liability. We'll explain in detail shortly who bears the liability for each type of financial asset.

These four types of financial assets exist because the economy has developed a set of specialized markets, like the stock market and the bond market, and specialized institutions, like banks, that facilitate the flow of funds from lenders to borrowers. In Chapter 7, in the context of the circular-flow diagram, we defined the financial markets and institutions that make up the financial system. A well-functioning financial system is a critical ingredient in achieving long-run growth because it encourages greater savings and investment spending; it also ensures that savings and investment spending are undertaken efficiently. To understand how this occurs, we first need to know what tasks the financial system needs to accomplish. Then we can see how the job gets done.

Three Tasks of a Financial System

Our earlier analysis of the loanable funds market ignored three important problems facing borrowers and lenders: *transaction costs, risk,* and the desire for *liquidity*. The three tasks of a financial system are to reduce these problems in a cost-effective way. Doing so enhances the efficiency of financial markets: it makes it more likely that lenders and borrowers will make mutually beneficial trades—trades that increase society's welfare. We'll turn now to examining how financial assets are designed and how institutions are developed to cope with these problems.

Reducing Transaction Costs   **Transaction costs** are the expenses of actually putting together and executing a deal. For example, arranging a loan requires spending time and money negotiating the terms of the deal, verifying the borrower's ability to pay, drawing up and executing legal documents, and so on. Suppose a large business decided that it

---

A household's **wealth** is the value of its accumulated savings.

A **financial asset** is a paper claim that entitles the buyer to future income from the seller.

A **physical asset** is a claim on a tangible object that gives the owner the right to dispose of the object as he or she wishes.

A **liability** is a requirement to pay income in the future.

Transaction costs are the expenses of negotiating and executing a deal.

wanted to raise $100 million for investment spending. No individual would be willing to lend that much. And negotiating individual loans from thousands of different people, each willing to lend a modest amount, would impose very large total costs because each individual transaction would incur a cost. Total costs would be so large that the entire deal would probably be unprofitable for the business.

Fortunately, that's not necessary: when large businesses want to borrow money, they either go to a bank or sell bonds in the bond market. Obtaining a loan from a bank avoids large transaction costs because it involves only a single borrower and a single lender. We'll explain more about how bonds work in the next section. For now, it is enough to know that the principal reason there is a bond market is that it allows companies to borrow large sums of money without incurring large transaction costs.

Reducing Risk A second problem that real-world borrowers and lenders face is **financial risk,** uncertainty about future outcomes that involve financial losses and gains. Financial risk (which from now on we'll simply call "risk") is a problem because the future is uncertain, typically containing the potential for losses as well as gains. For example, owning and driving a car entails the financial risk of a costly accident. Most people view potential losses and gains in an *asymmetrical* way: the total loss in individual welfare from losing a given amount of money is considered larger than the total gain in welfare from gaining the same amount of money. A person who values potential losses and gains in this asymmetrical way is called *risk-averse*. This attitude toward risk is illustrated in panel (a) of Figure 9-8. Here, we show an example of a typical risk-averse person who is faced with the prospect of losing $1,000 or gaining $1,000. The bar on the left, which represents the loss in welfare from losing $1,000, is longer than the bar on the right, which represents the gain in welfare from gaining $1,000. The difference in the lengths of these two bars illustrates risk aversion: a person experiences a $1,000 loss as a significant hardship (equivalent to a $2,000 loss in welfare) and a $1,000 gain as a much less significant benefit (equivalent to a $1,000 gain in welfare). To put it a slightly different way, if you are risk-averse, you are willing to expend more

> **Financial risk** is uncertainty about future outcomes that involve financial losses and gains.

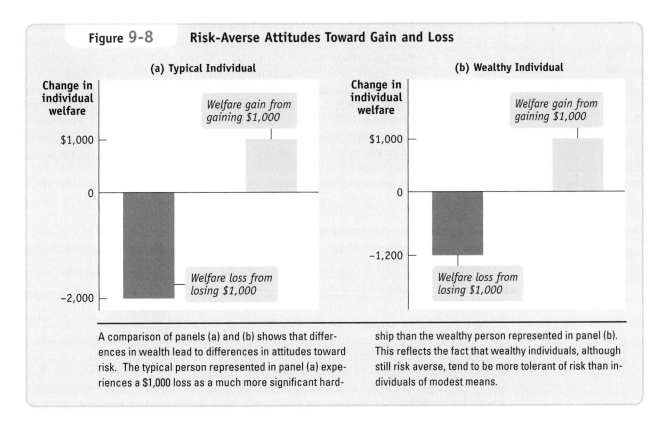

Figure 9-8   Risk-Averse Attitudes Toward Gain and Loss

A comparison of panels (a) and (b) shows that differences in wealth lead to differences in attitudes toward risk. The typical person represented in panel (a) experiences a $1,000 loss as a much more significant hardship than the wealthy person represented in panel (b). This reflects the fact that wealthy individuals, although still risk averse, tend to be more tolerant of risk than individuals of modest means.

resources to avoid losing $1,000 (say, by buying an auto insurance policy) than you are willing to expend to gain $1,000 (say, by hunting around to find the cheapest mechanic when your car needs a major repair).

Most people are risk-averse, although to differing degrees. For example, people who are wealthy are typically less risk-averse than those who are not so well-off. As panel (b) shows, a wealthy person—while still risk-averse—would consider the loss of $1,000 a lot less of a hardship than would a person of modest means. Such a loss would be experienced as only a $1,200 loss in welfare by a wealthy individual, compared to a $2,000 loss in welfare by a typical individual.

A well-functioning financial system helps people reduce their exposure to risk, which risk-averse people would like to do. Suppose the owner of a business expects to make a greater profit if she buys additional capital equipment but isn't completely sure that this will indeed happen. She could pay for the equipment by using her savings or selling her house. But if the profit is significantly less than expected, she will have lost her savings, or her house, or both. That is, she would be exposing herself to a lot of risk arising from how well or poorly the business performs. (This is why business owners, who typically have a significant portion of their own personal wealth tied up in their businesses, are usually people who are more tolerant of risk than the average person.) So, being risk-averse, this business owner wants to share the risk of purchasing new capital equipment with someone even if that requires sharing some of the profit if all goes well. How can she do this? By selling shares of her company to other people and using the money she receives from selling shares, rather than money from the sale of her other assets, to finance the equipment purchase. By selling shares in her company, she reduces her personal losses if the profit is less than expected: she won't have lost her other assets. But if things go well, the shareholders earn a share of the profit as a return on their investment.

By selling a share of her business, the owner has achieved *diversification:* she has been able to invest in several things in a way that lowers her total risk. She has maintained her investment in her bank account, a financial asset; in ownership of her house, a physical asset; and in ownership of the unsold portion of her business, also a physical asset. These investments are likely to carry some risk of their own; for example, her bank may fail or her house may burn down (though in the modern United States it is likely that she is partly protected against these risks by insurance.) But even in the absence of insurance, she is better off for having maintained investments in these different assets because their different risks are *unrelated,* or *independent, events.* This means, for example, that her house is no more likely to burn down if her business does poorly, and that her bank is no more likely to fail if her house burns down. To put it another way, if one asset performs poorly, it is very likely that her other assets will be unaffected and, as a result, her total risk of loss has been reduced. But if she had invested all her wealth in her business, she would have faced the prospect of losing everything if the business had performed poorly. By engaging in **diversification**—investing in several assets with unrelated, or independent, risks—our business owner has lowered her total risk of loss.

The desire of individuals to reduce their total risk by engaging in diversification is why we have stocks and a stock market. In the next section, we'll explain in more detail how certain features of the stock market increase the ability of individuals to manage and reduce risk.

Providing Liquidity The third and final task of the financial system is to provide investors with *liquidity,* a concern that—like risk—arises because the future is uncertain. Suppose that, once having made a loan, a lender suddenly finds himself in need of cash—say, to meet a medical emergency. Unfortunately, if that loan was made to a business that used it to buy new equipment, the business cannot repay the loan on short notice to satisfy the lender's need to recover his money. Knowing this in advance—that there is a danger of needing to get his money back before the term of the loan is up—our lender might be reluctant to lock up his money by lending it to a business.

An individual can engage in **diversification** by investing in several different things so that the possible losses are independent events.

An asset is **liquid** if it can be quickly converted into cash, without much loss of value, and it is **illiquid** if it cannot. As we'll see, stocks and bonds are a partial answer to the problem of liquidity. Banks provide a further way for individuals to hold liquid assets and still finance illiquid investments.

To help lenders and borrowers make mutually beneficial deals, then, the economy needs ways to reduce transaction costs, to reduce and manage risk through diversification, and to provide liquidity. How does it achieve these tasks?

An asset is **liquid** if it can be quickly converted into cash without much loss of value.

An asset is **illiquid** if it cannot be quickly converted into cash without much loss of value.

Types of Assets

In the modern economy there are four main types of financial assets: loans, bonds, stocks, and bank deposits. Each serves a somewhat different purpose. We'll examine loans, bonds, and stocks now, reserving our discussion of bank deposits until the following section.

Loans A **loan** is a lending agreement between a particular lender and a particular borrower. Most people encounter loans in the form of bank loans to finance the purchase of a car or a house. And small businesses usually use bank loans to buy new equipment.

A **loan** is a lending agreement between a particular lender and a particular borrower.

The good aspect of loans is that a given loan is usually tailored to the needs of the borrower. Before a small business can get a loan, it usually has to discuss its business plans, its profits, and so on with the lender. This results in a loan that meets the borrower's needs and ability to pay.

The bad aspect of loans is that making a loan to an individual person or a business typically involves a lot of transaction costs, such as the cost of negotiating the terms of the loan, investigating the borrower's credit history and ability to repay, and so on. To minimize these costs, large borrowers such as major corporations and governments often take a more streamlined approach: they sell (or issue) bonds.

Bonds As we learned in Chapter 7, a bond is a promise by the seller to pay interest each year and to repay the principal to the owner of the bond on a particular date. So a bond is a financial asset from its owner's point of view and a liability from its issuer's point of view. A bond issuer sells a number of bonds with a given interest rate and maturity date to whomever is willing to buy them, a process that avoids costly negotiation of the terms of a loan with many individual lenders.

Bond purchasers can acquire information free of charge on the quality of the bond issuer, such as the bond issuer's credit history, from *bond-rating agencies* rather than having to incur the expense of investigating it themselves. As a result, bonds can be sold on the bond market as a more or less standardized product—a product with clearly defined terms and quality.

Another important advantage of bonds is that they are easy to resell. This provides liquidity to bond purchasers. Indeed, a bond will often pass through many hands before it finally comes due. Loans, in contrast, are much more difficult to resell because, unlike bonds, they are not standardized: they differ in size, quality, terms, and so on. This makes them a lot less liquid than bonds.

"Damn it, I don't want to know about my love life. Tell me about the bond market."

Stocks As we learned in Chapter 7, a stock is a share in the ownership of a company. A share of stock is a financial asset from its owner's point of view and a liability from the the company's point of view. Not all companies sell shares of their stock; "privately held" companies are owned by an individual or a few partners, who get to keep all of the company's profit. Most large companies, however, do sell stock. For example, Microsoft has nearly 11 billion shares outstanding; if you buy one of those shares, you are entitled to one eleven-billionth of the company's profit, as well as 1 of 11 billion votes on company decisions.

Why does Microsoft, historically a very profitable company, allow you to buy a share in its ownership? Why don't Bill Gates and Paul Allen, the two founders of Microsoft, keep ownership for themselves and just sell bonds for their investment spending needs? The reason, as we have just learned, is risk: few individuals are risk-tolerant enough to face the risk involved in being the owners of a large company.

Reducing the risk that business owners face, however, is not the only way in which the existence of stocks improves society's welfare: it also improves the welfare of investors who buy stocks. Shareowners are able to enjoy the higher returns over time that stocks generally offer in comparison to bonds. Over the past century, stocks have typically yielded about 7% after adjusting for inflation; bonds have yielded only about 2%. But as investment companies warn you, "past performance is no guarantee of future performance." And there is a downside: owning the stock of a given company is riskier than owning a bond issued by the same company. Why? Loosely speaking, a bond is a promise while a stock is a hope: by law, a company must pay what it owes its lenders before it distributes any profit to its shareholders. And if the company should fail (that is, be unable to pay its interest obligations and declare bankruptcy), its physical and financial assets go to its bondholders—its lenders—while its shareholders generally receive nothing. So although a stock generally provides a higher return to an investor than a bond, it also carries higher risk.

But the financial system has devised ways to help investors as well as business owners both manage risk and enjoy somewhat higher returns. It does that through the services of institutions known as *financial intermediaries*.

Financial Intermediaries

A **financial intermediary** is an institution that transforms funds gathered from many individuals into financial assets. The most important types of financial intermediaries are *mutual funds, pension funds, life insurance companies*, and *banks*. About three-quarters of the financial assets Americans own are held through these intermediaries rather than directly.

Mutual Funds As we've explained, owning shares of a company entails risk in return for a higher potential reward. But it should come as no surprise that stock investors can lower their total risk by engaging in diversification. By owning a *diversified portfolio* of stocks—a group of stocks in which risks are unrelated to or offset one another—rather than concentrating investment in the shares of a single company or a group of related companies, investors can reduce their risk. In addition, financial advisers, aware that most people are risk-averse, almost always advise their clients to diversify not only their stock portfolio but also their entire wealth by holding other assets in addition to stocks, such as bonds, real estate, and cash. (And, for good measure, to have plenty of insurance in case of accidental losses!)

However, for individuals who don't have a large amount of money to invest—say $1 million or more—building a diversified stock portfolio can incur high transaction costs (particularly fees paid to stock brokers) because they are buying a few shares of a lot of companies. Fortunately for such investors, mutual funds solve the problem of achieving diversification without high transaction costs. A **mutual fund** is a financial intermediary that creates a stock portfolio by buying and holding shares in companies and then reselling *shares of the stock portfolio* to individual investors. By buying these shares, investors with a relatively small amount of money to invest can indirectly hold a diversified portfolio, achieving a better return for any given level of risk than they could otherwise achieve. Table 9-1 shows an example of a diversified mutual fund, the State Street Global Advisors S&P 500 Index Fund. It shows the percentage of investors' money invested in the stocks of the largest companies in the mutual fund's portfolio.

Many mutual funds also perform *market research* on the companies they invest in. This is important because there are thousands of stock-issuing U.S. companies (not to mention foreign companies), each differing in terms of its likely profitability, dividend payments, and so on. It would be extremely time-consuming and costly for an

A **financial intermediary** is an institution that transforms the funds it gathers from many individuals into financial assets.

A **mutual fund** is a financial intermediary that creates a stock portfolio and then resells shares of this portfolio to individual investors.

TABLE 9-1

State Street Global Advisors S&P 500 Index Fund, Top Holdings (as of March 31, 2005)

Company	Percent of mutual fund assets invested in company
General Electric	3.53%
Exxon Mobil	3.52
Microsoft	2.26
Citigroup	2.17
Johnson & Johnson	1.85
Pfizer	1.81
Bank of America	1.65
Wal-Mart Stores	1.57
IBM	1.38
Intel	1.34

Source: State Street Global Advisors.

individual investor to do adequate research on even a small number of companies. Mutual funds save transaction costs by doing this research for their customers.

The mutual fund industry represents a huge portion of the modern U.S. economy, not just of the U.S. financial system. The largest mutual fund at the end of 2004 was State Street Global Advisors, which managed $1.4 trillion in funds.

Pension Funds and Life Insurance Companies In addition to mutual funds, many Americans have holdings in **pension funds,** nonprofit institutions that collect the savings of their members and invest those funds in a wide variety of assets, providing their members with income when they retire. Although pension funds are subject to some special rules and receive special treatment for tax purposes, they function much like mutual funds. They invest in a diverse array of financial assets, allowing their members to achieve more cost-effective diversification and market research than they would be able to achieve individually. Pension funds in the United States hold more than $8 trillion in assets.

A **pension fund** is a type of mutual fund that holds assets in order to provide retirement income to its members.

Americans also have substantial holdings in the policies of **life insurance companies,** which guarantee a payment to the policyholder's beneficiaries (typically, the family) when the policyholder dies. By enabling policyholders to cushion their beneficiaries from financial hardship arising from their death, life insurance companies also improve welfare by reducing risk.

A **life insurance company** sells policies that guarantee a payment to a policyholder's beneficiaries when the policyholder dies.

Banks Recall the problem of liquidity: other things equal, people want assets that can be readily converted into cash. Bonds and stocks are much more liquid than physical assets or loans, yet the transaction cost of selling bonds or stocks to meet a sudden expense can be large. Furthermore, for many small and moderate-size companies, the cost of issuing bonds and stocks is too large given the modest amount of money they seek to raise. A *bank* is an institution that helps resolve the conflict between lenders' needs for liquidity and the financing needs of borrowers who don't want to use the stock or bond markets.

A bank works by first accepting funds from *depositors*: when you put your money in a bank, you are essentially becoming a lender by lending the bank your money. In return, you receive credit for a **bank deposit**—a claim on the bank, which is obliged to give you your cash if and when you demand it. So a bank deposit is a financial asset owned by the depositor and a liability of the bank that holds it.

A **bank deposit** is a claim on a bank that obliges the bank to give the depositor his or her cash when demanded.

A bank, however, keeps only a fraction of its customers' deposits in the form of ready cash. Most of its deposits are lent out to businesses, buyers of new homes, and other borrowers. These loans come with a long-term commitment by the bank to the

A **bank** is a financial intermediary that provides liquid assets in the form of bank deposits to lenders and uses those funds to finance the illiquid investments or investment spending needs of borrowers.

borrower: as long as the borrower makes his or her payments on time, the loan cannot be recalled by the bank and converted into cash. So a bank enables those who wish to borrow for long lengths of time to use the funds of those who wish to lend but simultaneously want to maintain the ability to get their cash back on demand. More formally, a **bank** is a financial intermediary that provides liquid financial assets in the form of deposits to lenders and uses their funds to finance the illiquid investments or investment spending needs of borrowers.

In essence, a bank is engaging in a kind of mismatch: lending for long periods of time but also subject to the condition that its depositors could demand their funds back at any time. How can it manage that?

The bank counts on the fact that, on average, only a small fraction of its depositors will want their cash at the same time. On any given day, some people will make withdrawals and others will make new deposits; these will roughly cancel each other out. So the bank needs to keep only a limited amount of cash on hand to satisfy its depositors. In addition, if a bank becomes financially incapable of paying its depositors, individual bank deposits are guaranteed to depositors up to $100,000 by the Federal Deposit Insurance Corporation, or FDIC, a federal agency. This reduces the risk to a depositor of holding a bank deposit, and thereby reduces the incentive to withdraw funds if concerns about the financial state of the bank should arise. So, under normal conditions, banks need hold only a fraction of their depositors' cash.

By reconciling the needs of savers for liquid assets with the needs of borrowers for long-term financing, banks play a key economic role. As the following Economics in Action explains, the creation of a well-functioning banking system was a key turning point in South Korea's economic success.

economics in action

Banks and the South Korean Miracle

As we discussed in Chapter 8, South Korea is one of the great success stories of economic growth. In the early 1960s, it was a very poor nation. Then it experienced spectacularly high rates of economic growth. South Korean banks had a lot to do with it.

In the early 1960s, South Korea's banking system was a mess. Interest rates on deposits were very low at a time when the country was experiencing a lot of inflation. So savers didn't want to save by putting money in a bank, fearing that much of their purchasing power would be eroded by rising prices. Instead, they engaged in current consumption by spending their money on goods and services or used their wealth to buy physical assets such as real estate and gold. And because savers refused to make bank deposits, businesses found it very hard to borrow money to finance investment spending.

In 1965 the South Korean government reformed the country's banks and increased interest rates to a level that was attractive to savers. Over the next five years the value of bank deposits increased 600%, and the national savings rate—the percentage of GDP going into national savings—more than doubled. The rejuvenated banking system made it possible for South Korean businesses to launch a great investment boom, a key element in the country's growth surge.

Many other factors besides banking were involved in South Korea's success, but the country's experience does show how important a good financial system is to economic growth. ∎

< < < < < < < < < < < < < < < <

> **CHECK YOUR UNDERSTANDING 9-2**

1. Rank the following assets in terms of (i) level of transaction costs, (ii) level of risk, (iii) level of liquidity.
   a. A bank deposit with a guaranteed interest rate
   b. A share of a highly diversified mutual fund, which can be quickly sold
   c. A share of the family business, which can be sold only if you find a buyer and all other family members agree to the sale

2. What relationship would you expect to find between the level of development of a country's financial system and its level of economic development? Explain in terms of the country's level of savings and level of investment spending.

Solutions appear at back of book.

Financial Fluctuations

We've learned that the financial system is an essential part of the economy; without stock markets, bond markets, and banks, long-run economic growth would be hard to achieve. Yet the news isn't entirely good: the financial system sometimes doesn't function well and instead is a source of instability. For evidence, we need look no further than the pivotal event of modern macroeconomics, the Great Depression. The worst economic slump in American history is closely identified with the U.S. stock market crash of 1929. And the 2001 U.S. recession was preceded by a sharp decline in stock prices in 2001. In Chapter 10 we'll learn about the channel by which changes in stock prices influence macroeconomic performance—how changes in households' wealth caused by asset market fluctuations alter their demand for goods and services.

We could easily write a whole book on asset market fluctuations. In fact, many people have. Here, we briefly discuss the causes of stock price fluctuations.

The Demand for Stocks

Once a company issues shares of stock to investors, those shares can then be re-sold to other investors in the stock market. And these days, thanks to cable TV and the Internet, you can easily spend all day watching stock market fluctuations—the movement up and down of the prices of individual stocks as well as the indexes. These fluctuations reflect changes in supply and demand by investors. But what causes the supply and demand for stocks to shift?

Remember that stocks are financial assets: they are shares in the ownership of a company. Unlike a good or service, whose value to its owner comes from its consumption, the value of an asset comes from its ability to generate higher *future consumption* of goods or services. A financial asset allows higher future consumption in two ways. It can generate future income through paying interest or dividends. But many companies don't pay dividends, instead retaining their earnings to finance future investment spending. Investors purchase non-dividend-paying stocks in the belief that they will earn future income from selling the stock in the future at a profit, the second way of generating higher future income. Even in the cases of a bond or a dividend-paying stock, investors will not want to purchase an asset that they believe will sell for less in the future than today because such an asset will reduce their wealth when they sell it. So the value of a financial asset today depends on investors' beliefs about the *future value* or *price* of the asset. That is, if investors believe that it will be worth more in the future, they will demand more of the asset today at any given price. As a consequence, today's equilibrium price of the asset will rise. Conversely, if investors believe the asset will be worth less in the future, they will demand less today at any given price. As a consequence, today's equilibrium price of the asset will fall. In summary, today's stock prices will change according to changes in investors' expectations about future stock prices.

Suppose an event occurs that leads to a rise in the expected future price of a company's shares—say, for example, Apple announces that it expects higher profitability due to torrential sales of its iPods. Demand for Apple shares will increase. At the same time, existing shareholders will be less willing to supply their shares to the market at any given price, leading to a decrease in the supply of Apple shares. And as we know from Chapter 3, an increase in demand or a decrease in supply (or both) leads to a rise in price. Alternatively, suppose that an event occurs that leads to a fall in the expected future price of a company's shares—say, Krispy Kreme announces that it expects lower profitability due to the popularity of low-carb diets. Demand for Krispy Kreme shares will decrease. At the same time, supply will increase because existing shareholders will

HOW NOW, DOW JONES?

Financial news reports often lead with the day's stock market action, as measured by changes in the Dow Jones Industrial Average, the S&P 500, and the NASDAQ. What are these numbers, and what do they tell us?

All three are stock market *indexes*. Like the consumer price index, they are numbers constructed as a summary of average prices—in this case, prices of stocks. The Dow, created by the financial analysis company Dow Jones (owner of the *Wall Street Journal*), is an index of the prices of stock in 30 leading companies, such as Microsoft, Wal-Mart, and General Electric. The S&P 500 is an index of 500 companies, created by Standard and Poor's, another financial company. The NASDAQ is compiled by the National Association of Securities Dealers, which trades the stocks of smaller new companies, like the satellite radio companies Sirius and XM.

It's unexpected news, not expected news, that makes for a busy day in the financial markets.

Because these indexes contain different groups of stocks, they track somewhat different things. The Dow, because it contains only 30 of the largest companies, tends to reflect the "old economy," the traditional business powerhouses. The NASDAQ is heavily influenced by technology stocks. The S&P 500, a broad measure, is in between.

Why are these indexes important? Because the movement in an index gives investors a quick, snapshot view of how stocks from certain sectors of the economy are doing. As we'll explain shortly, the price of a stock at a given point in time embodies investors' expectations about the future prospects of the underlying company. By implication, an index composed of stocks drawn from companies in a particular sector embodies investors' expectations of the future prospects of that sector of the economy. So a day on which the NASDAQ moves up but the Dow moves down implies that, on that day, prospects appear brighter for the high-tech sector than for the old economy sector. The movement in the indexes reflects the fact that investors are acting on their beliefs by selling stocks in the Dow and buying stocks in the NASDAQ.

be more willing to supply their Krispy Kreme shares to the market. Both changes lead to a fall in the stock price. So stock prices are determined by supply and demand—which, in turn, depend on investors' expectations about the future stock price.

Stock prices are also affected by changes in the attractiveness of substitute assets, like bonds. As we learned in Chapter 3, the demand for a particular good decreases when purchasing a substitute good becomes more attractive—say, due to a fall in its price. The same lesson holds true for stocks: when purchasing a bond becomes more attractive due to a rise in interest rates, stock prices will fall. And when purchasing a bond becomes less attractive due to a fall in interest rates, stock prices will rise.

But we haven't yet fully answered the question of what determines the price of a share of stock, because we haven't explained what determines investors' *expectations* about future stock prices.

Stock Market Expectations

There are two principal competing views about how stock price expectations are determined. One view, which comes from traditional economic analysis, emphasizes the rational reasons why expectations *should* change. The other, widely held by market participants and also supported by some economists, emphasizes the irrationality of market participants.

The Efficient Markets Hypothesis Suppose you were trying to assess what Krispy Kreme stock is really worth. To do this, you would look at the *fundamentals*, the underlying determinants of the company's future profits. These would include factors like the changing tastes of the American public and the price of sugar. You would also want to compare the earnings you could expect to receive from Krispy Kreme with the likely returns on other financial assets, such as bonds.

According to one view of asset prices, the value you would come up with after a careful study of this kind would, in fact, turn out to be the price at which Krispy Kreme stock is already selling in the market. Why? Because all publicly available information about Krispy Kreme's fundamentals is already embodied in its stock price. Any difference between the market price and the value suggested by a careful analysis of the underlying fundamentals would indicate a profit opportunity to smart investors, who would sell Krispy Kreme stock if it looked overpriced and buy it if it looked underpriced. The **efficient markets hypothesis** is the general form of this view; it means that asset prices always embody all publicly available information. An implication of the efficient markets hypothesis is that at any point in time stock prices are fairly valued: they reflect all currently available information about fundamentals. So they are neither overpriced nor underpriced.

> The **efficient markets hypothesis** says that asset prices embody all publicly available information.

One implication of the efficient markets hypothesis is that the prices of stocks and other assets should change only in response to new information about the underlying fundamentals. Since new information is by definition unpredictable—if it were predictable, it wouldn't be new information—movements in asset prices are also unpredictable. As a result, the movement of, say, stock prices will follow a **random walk**—the general term for the movement over time of an unpredictable variable.

> A **random walk** is the movement over time of an unpredictable variable.

The efficient markets hypothesis plays an important role in understanding how financial markets work. Most investment professionals and many economists, however, regard it as an oversimplification. Investors, they claim, aren't that rational.

Irrational Markets?   Many people who actually play the markets, such as individual investors and professional money managers, are skeptical of the efficient markets hypothesis. They believe that markets often behave irrationally and that a smart investor can engage in successful "market timing"—buying stocks when they are underpriced and selling them when they are overpriced.

Although economists are generally skeptical about claims that there are sure-fire ways to outsmart the market, many have also challenged the efficient markets hypothesis. It's important to understand, however, that finding particular examples where the market got it wrong does not disprove the efficient markets hypothesis. If the price of Krispy Kreme stock plunges from $40 to $10 because of a sudden change in eating habits, this doesn't mean that the market was inefficient in originally pricing the stock at $40. The fact that eating habits were about to change wasn't publicly available information, so it wasn't embodied in the earlier stock price.

Serious challenges to the efficient markets hypothesis focus instead either on evidence of systematic misbehavior of market prices or on evidence that individual investors don't behave in the way the theory suggests. For example, some economists believe they have found strong evidence that stock prices fluctuate more than can be explained by news about fundamentals. Others believe they have strong evidence that individual investors behave in systematically irrational ways. For example, people seem to expect that a stock that has risen in the past will keep on rising, even though the efficient markets hypothesis tells us there is no reason to expect this.

Stock Prices and Macroeconomics

How do macroeconomists and policy makers deal with the fact that stock prices fluctuate a lot and that these fluctuations can have important economic effects? The short answer is that, for the most part, they adopt an open-minded but watchful attitude.

The efficient markets hypothesis suggests that policy makers shouldn't assume that the stock market is wrong—either that stock prices are too high or too low. The best guess is always that any information that is publicly available is already accounted for in stock prices.

At the same time, policy makers shouldn't assume that stock prices will be reasonably stable and consistent with rational investor behavior. Sudden rises or falls in the market can happen for no obvious reason, and these fluctuations can have major macroeconomic effects. Policy makers have to be prepared to deal with them.

The question of how much to trust financial markets isn't academic. As the following Economics in Action explains, it was a hot issue during the 1990s.

Figure 9-9   **The S&P 500 Index from October 1982 to April 2005**

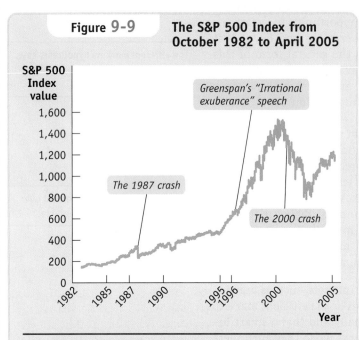

From 1982 to 1995 the stock market rose steadily with only a few setbacks, the most notable being the 1987 crash. In 1995, however, the market began growing at a much faster pace, and in 1996 Alan Greenspan cautioned that the market might be suffering from "irrational exuberance." The market, however, continued to rise for another four years—until 2000, when stock prices in general, and the prices of technology stocks in particular, suffered a large fall.

Source: Yahoo! Finance.

economics in action

"Irrational Exuberance"

Robert Shiller is an economist at Yale University and one of the best-known critics of the efficient markets hypothesis. In 1996 he gave a briefing to Alan Greenspan, the chairman of the Federal Reserve, that gave rise to a famous phrase: "irrational exuberance."

Figure 9-9 provides some background for the story. It shows the value, since October 1982, of the S&P 500, the broadest of the stock indexes we discussed in For Inquiring Minds on page 230. As you can see, from 1982 to 2000 the stock market rose steadily, with only a few setbacks.

One of those setbacks was the sudden crash in 1987, shown in the figure. There was no obvious fundamental reason for that crash. After the fact, some economists began coming up with reasons why a sudden fall in stock prices might have made sense. Shiller, however, actually surveyed investors *while* the market was crashing and found that they were selling simply because other people were selling. That is, it looked like mob psychology, not the working of an efficient market.

In 1996, when Shiller briefed Greenspan, the market was rising to unprecedented heights—and Shiller questioned whether this rise made sense. Greenspan shared his doubts and, in a famous speech, wondered whether the market was suffering from "irrational exuberance."

The big question, though, was whether Greenspan would do something about it, such as raising interest rates to discourage people from buying stocks. He didn't: he wasn't willing to second-guess the market to that extent. And, as you can see, stock prices continued to rise for another four years.

Starting in 2000, there was a large fall in stock prices, especially those of technology stocks, and many people now think that by the late 1990s, if not necessarily when Greenspan said it, there really was irrational exuberance in the market. Specifically, it's now widely accepted that there was a stock market *bubble*—a large upward movement in asset prices not based on rational factors such as fundamentals. But should Greenspan have done something about it? That's still very much a matter of debate; we'll revisit this question in Chapter 17. ∎

< < < < < < < < < < < < < < < <

▸▸ CHECK YOUR UNDERSTANDING 9-3

1. What is the likely effect of each of the following events on the stock price of a company? Explain your answers.
   a. The company announces that while profit is low this year, it has discovered a new line of business that will generate a high profit next year.
   b. The company announces that although it had a high profit this year, that profit will be less than had been previously announced.

c. Other companies in the same industry announce that sales are unexpectedly slow this year.

d. The company announces that it is on track to meet its previously forecast profit target.

2. Assess the following statement: "Although many investors may be irrational, it is unlikely that over time they will behave irrationally in exactly the same way—such as always buying stocks the day after the Dow has risen by 1%."

Solutions appear at back of book.

• A LOOK AHEAD •

At this point we've completed our study of why savings and investment spending are a critical component of long-run economic growth. We've examined how savings and investment spending are generated in the economy and how they are allocated by a well-functioning financial system. Now it's time for us to turn to the business cycle— that is, to understand the short-run fluctuations around the trend in long-run growth. Our next step, then, is to develop the Aggregate Supply–Aggregate Demand model, which we will use to analyze how the behavior of producers, consumers, and the government influences the economy's short-run performance.

SUMMARY

1. Investment in physical capital is necessary for long-run economic growth. So in order for an economy to grow, it must channel savings into investment spending.

2. According to the **savings–investment spending identity,** savings and investment spending are always equal for the economy as a whole. The government is a source of savings when it runs a positive **budget balance,** also known as a **budget surplus;** it is a source of dissavings when it runs a negative budget balance, also known as a **budget deficit.** In a closed economy, savings is equal to **national savings,** the sum of private savings plus the budget balance. In an open economy, savings is equal to national savings plus **capital inflow** of foreign savings. A capital outflow, or negative capital inflow, occurs when savings flow abroad.

3. The hypothetical **loanable funds market** shows how loans from savers are allocated among borrowers with investment spending projects. In equilibrium, only those projects with a **rate of return** greater than or equal to the equilibrium **interest rate** will be funded. By showing how gains from trade between lenders and borrowers are maximized, the loanable funds market shows why a well-functioning financial system leads to greater long-run economic growth. It also shows how government borrowing to cover a budget deficit can lead to **crowding out** of private investment spending and, other things equal, lower economic growth.

4. Households invest their current savings or **wealth**—their accumulated savings—by purchasing assets. Assets come in the form of either a **financial asset,** a paper claim that entitles the buyer to future income from the seller, or a **physical asset,** a claim on a tangible object that gives the owner the right to dispose of it as desired. A financial asset is also a **liability** from the point of view of its seller. There are four main types of financial assets: **loans,** bonds, stocks, and **bank deposits.** Each of them serves a different purpose in addressing the three fundamental tasks of a financial system: reducing **transaction costs**— the cost of making a deal; reducing **financial risk**—uncertainty about future outcomes that involves financial gains and losses; and providing **liquid** assets—assets that can be quickly converted into cash without much loss of value (in contrast to **illiquid** assets, which can't).

5. Although many small and moderate-size borrowers use bank loans to fund investment spending, larger companies typically issue bonds. Business owners reduce their risk by selling stock. Although stocks usually generate a higher return than bonds, investors typically wish to reduce their risk by engaging in **diversification,** owning a wide range of assets whose returns are based on unrelated, or independent, events. Most people are risk-averse, viewing the loss of a given amount of money as a significant hardship while viewing the gain of an equal amount of money as a much less significant benefit.

6. **Financial intermediaries**—institutions such as **mutual funds, pension funds, life insurance companies,** and **banks**—are critical components of the financial system. Mutual funds and pension funds do allow small investors to diversify; and life insurance companies reduce risk.

7. A bank allows individuals to hold liquid bank deposits that are then used to finance illiquid loans. Banks can perform this mismatch because on average only a small fraction of depositors withdraw their savings at any one time. Banks are a key ingredient of long-run economic growth.

8. Financial market fluctuations can be a source of macro-economic instability. Stock prices are determined by supply and demand as well as the desirability of competing assets, like bonds: when the interest rate rises, stock prices generally fall and vice versa. Expectations drive the supply of and demand for stocks: expectations of higher future prices push today's stock prices higher and expectations of lower future prices drive them lower. One view of how expectations are formed is the **efficient markets hypothesis,** which holds that the prices of financial assets embody all publicly available information. It implies that fluctuations are inherently unpredictable—they follow a **random walk.**

9. Many market participants and economists believe that, based on actual evidence, financial markets are not as rational as the efficient markets hypothesis claims. Such evidence includes the fact that stock price fluctuations are too great to be driven by fundamentals alone. Policy makers assume neither that markets always behave rationally nor that they can outsmart them.

KEY TERMS

Savings–investment spending identity, p. 211
Budget surplus, p. 212
Budget deficit, p. 212
Budget balance, p. 212
National savings, p. 212
Capital inflow, p. 214
Loanable funds market, p. 216
Interest rate, p. 216
Rate of return, p. 217

Crowding out, p. 220
Wealth, p. 222
Financial asset, p. 222
Physical asset, p. 222
Liability, p. 222
Transaction costs, p. 222
Financial risk, p. 223
Diversification, p. 224
Liquid, p. 225
Illiquid, p. 225

Loan, p. 225
Financial intermediary, p. 226
Mutual fund, p. 226
Pension fund, p. 227
Life insurance company, p. 227
Bank deposit, p. 227
Bank, p. 228
Efficient markets hypothesis, p. 231
Random walk, p. 231

PROBLEMS

1. Given the following information about the closed economy of Brittania, what is the level of investment spending and private savings, and what is the budget balance? What is the relationship among the three? Is national savings equal to investment spending? There are no government transfers.

   GDP = $1,000 million T = $50 million
   C = $850 million G = $100 million

2. Given the following information about the open economy of Regalia, what is the level of investment spending and private savings, and what are the budget balance and capital inflow? What is the relationship among the four? There are no government transfers.

   GDP = $1,000 million G = $100 million
   C = $850 million X = $100 million
   T = $50 million IM = $125 million

3. The accompanying table shows the percentage of GDP accounted for by private savings, investment spending, and capital inflow in the economies of Capsland and Marsalia. Capsland is currently experiencing a net capital inflow and Marsalia, a net capital outflow. What is the budget balance (as a percentage of GDP) in both countries? Are Capsland and Marsalia running a budget deficit or surplus?

	Capsland	Marsalia
Investment spending as a percentage of GDP	20%	20%
Private savings as a percentage of GDP	10	25
Capital inflow as a percentage of GDP	5	−2

4. Assume the economy is open. Answer each of the following questions.

   a. X = $125 million
      IM = $80 million
      $S_{Government}$ = − $200 million
      I = $350 million
      Calculate $S_{Private}$.

   b. X = $85 million
      IM = $135 million
      $S_{Government}$ = $100 million
      $S_{Private}$ = $250 million
      Calculate I.

   c. X = $60 million
      IM = $95 million
      $S_{Private}$ = $325 million
      I = $300 million
      Calculate $S_{Government}$.

   d. $S_{Private}$ = $325 million
      I = $400 million
      $S_{Government}$ = $10 million
      Calculate $IM − X$.

5. Use the market for loanable funds shown in the accompanying diagram to explain what happens to private savings, private investment spending, and the rate of interest if the following events occur. Assume the economy is closed.

   a. The government reduces the size of its deficit to zero.
   b. At any given interest rate, consumers decide to save more. Assume the budget balance is zero.
   c. At any given interest rate, businesses become very optimistic about the future profitability of investment spending. Assume the budget balance is zero.

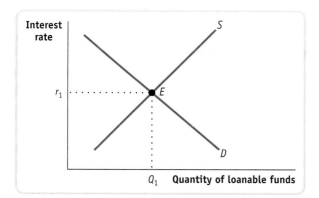

6. The government is running a budget balance of zero when it decides to increase education spending by $200 billion and finance the spending by selling bonds. The accompanying diagram shows the market for loanable funds before the government sells the bonds. Assume the economy is closed. How will the equilibrium interest rate and the equilibrium quantity of loanable funds change? Is there any crowding out in the market?

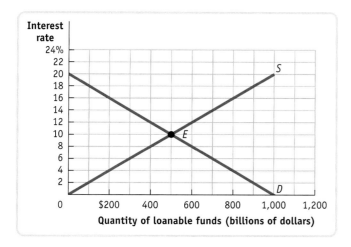

7. Explain why equilibrium in the loanable funds market maximizes efficiency.

8. How would you respond to a friend who claims that the government should eliminate all purchases that are financed by borrowing because such borrowing crowds out private investment spending?

9. Which of the following are examples of investment spending, investing in financial assets, or investing in physical assets?

   a. Rupert Moneybucks buys 100 shares of existing Coca-Cola stock.
   b. Rhonda Moviestar spends $10 million to buy a mansion built in the 1970s.
   c. Ronald Basketballstar spends $10 million to build a new mansion with a view of the Pacific Ocean.
   d. Rawlings builds a new plant to make catcher's mitts.
   e. Russia buys $100 million in U.S. government bonds.

10. Explain how a well-functioning financial system increases savings and investment spending, holding the budget balance and any capital flows fixed.

11. What are the important types of financial intermediaries in the U.S. economy? What are the primary assets of these intermediaries, and how do they facilitate investment spending and saving?

12. Explain the effect on a company's stock price today of the following events, other things held constant.

   a. The interest rate on bonds falls.
   b. Several companies in the same sector announce surprisingly slow sales.
   c. A change in the tax law passed last year reduces this year's profit.
   d. The company unexpectedly announces that due to an accounting error, it must amend last year's accounting statement and reduce last year's reported profit by $5 million. It also announces that this change has no implications for future profits.

>**web**... To continue your study and review of concepts in this chapter, please visit the Krugman/Wells website for quizzes, animated graph tutorials, web links to helpful resources, and more.

www.worthpublishers.com/krugmanwells

>>Aggregate Supply and Aggregate Demand

SHOCKS TO THE SYSTEM

ON NOVEMBER 4, 1979, MILITANT Iranian students seized the U.S. embassy in Tehran, taking 66 Americans hostage. For the next 444 days the news was dominated by the plight of the hostages, the threat of U.S. military action, and the resulting political instability. The home front was further shaken by a quadrupling of the price of oil, another repercussion of the hostage crisis in the Persian Gulf. Price controls on gasoline, which limited its price at the pump and had been imposed in response to an earlier jump in the price of oil, led to gasoline shortages and long lines. Next came a severe recession, the worst since the Great Depression. The industrial Midwest, experiencing a catastrophic loss in the number of jobs, became known as the Rust Belt. In Michigan,

ground zero of the hard-hit auto industry, the unemployment rate rose to over 16%.

But if the economic slump that followed the Persian Gulf crisis looked in many ways like a small-scale repeat of the Great Depression, it was very different in one important respect. During the Great Depression, from 1929 to 1933, the U.S. economy experienced severe *deflation*—a falling aggregate price level. During the slump from 1979 to 1982, the economy experienced severe *inflation*—a rising aggregate price level—reaching a peak rate of more than 13%. Many people were as upset by the high inflation as by the job losses because they saw the purchasing power of their incomes shrinking. And the emergence of *stagflation,* the combination of inflation and rising unemployment, also shook the confidence of economists and

What you will learn in this chapter:

➤ How the **aggregate supply curve** illustrates the relationship between the aggregate price level and the quantity of aggregate output supplied in the economy

➤ Why the aggregate supply curve is different in the short run compared to the long run

➤ How the **aggregate demand curve** illustrates the relationship between the aggregate price level and the quantity of aggregate output demanded in the economy

➤ The importance of the **multiplier,** which determines the total change in aggregate output arising from a shift of the aggregate demand curve

➤ How the **AS–AD model** is used to analyze economic fluctuations

➤ How monetary policy and fiscal policy can stabilize the economy

In the late 1970s and early 1980s, energy price increases arising from events in the Middle East led to recession and inflation here at home.

policy makers in their ability to manage the economy.

Why did the recession of 1979–1982 look different from the slump at the beginning of the Great Depression? Because it had a different cause. Indeed, the lesson of the 1970s was that recessions can have different causes and that the appropriate policy response depends on the cause. The Great Depression was caused by a crisis of confidence that led businesses and consumers to spend less, exacerbated by a banking crisis. This led to a combination of recession and deflation, which policy makers at that time didn't know how to respond to. But today we think we know what they should have done: pump cash into the economy, fighting the slump and stabilizing prices.

But the recession of 1979–1982, like the earlier recession of 1973–1975, was largely caused by events in the Middle East that led to sudden cuts in world oil production and soaring prices for oil and other fuels. These energy price increases led to a combination of recession and inflation. They also led to a dilemma: should economic policy fight the slump by pumping cash *into* the economy, or should it fight inflation by pulling cash *out* of the economy?

In this chapter, we'll develop a model that shows us how to distinguish between different types of short-run economic fluctuations—*demand shocks,* like the Great Depression, and *supply shocks,* like those of the 1970s. This model is our first step toward understanding short-run macroeconomics and macroeconomic policy.

To develop this model, we'll proceed in three steps. First, we'll develop the concept of *aggregate supply.* Then we'll turn to the parallel concept of *aggregate demand.* Finally, we'll put them together in the *AS-AD model.*

Aggregate Supply

Between 1929 and 1933, the demand curve for almost every good produced in the United States shifted to the left—the quantity demanded at any given price fell. We'll turn to the reasons for that decline in the next section, but let's focus first on the effects on producers.

One consequence of the economy-wide decline in demand was a fall in the prices of most goods and services. By 1933 the GDP deflator, one of the price indexes we defined in Chapter 7, was 26% below its 1929 level, and other indexes were down by similar amounts. A second consequence was a decline in the output of most goods and services: by 1933 real GDP was 27% below its 1929 level. A third consequence, closely tied to the fall in real GDP, was a surge in the unemployment rate from 3% to 25%.

The association between the plunge in real GDP and the plunge in prices wasn't an accident. Between 1929 and 1933, the U.S. economy was moving down its **aggregate supply curve,** which shows the relationship between the economy's aggregate price level (the overall price level of final goods and services in the economy) and the total quantity of final goods and services, or aggregate output, producers are willing to supply. (As we learned in Chapter 7, we use real GDP to measure aggregate output. So we'll often use the two terms interchangeably.) More specifically, between 1929 and 1933 the U.S. economy moved down its *short-run aggregate supply curve.*

The **aggregate supply curve** shows the relationship between the aggregate price level and the quantity of aggregate output supplied.

The Short-Run Aggregate Supply Curve

The period from 1929 to 1933 demonstrated that there is a positive relationship in the short run between the aggregate price level and the quantity of aggregate output supplied. That is, a rise in the aggregate price level leads to a rise in the quantity of aggregate output supplied, other things equal; a fall in the aggregate price level leads to a fall in the quantity of aggregate output supplied, other things equal. To understand why this positive relationship exists, let's think about the most basic question facing a producer: is producing a unit of output profitable or not? The answer depends on whether the price the producer receives for a unit of output, such as a bushel of corn, is greater or less than the cost of producing that unit of output. That is,

(10-1) Profit per unit output =
Price per unit output − Production cost per unit output

At any given point in time, many of the costs producers face are fixed and can't be changed for an extended period of time. Typically, the largest source of inflexible production cost is the wages paid to workers. *Wages* here refers to all forms of worker compensation, such as employer-paid health care and retirement benefits in addition to earnings. Wages are typically an inflexible production cost because the dollar amount of any given wage paid, called the **nominal wage,** is often determined by contracts that were signed several years earlier. And even when there are no formal contracts, there are often informal agreements between management and workers, reflecting reluctance by companies to change wages in response to economic conditions. For example, companies usually will not reduce wages during poor economic times—unless the downturn has been particularly long and severe—for fear of generating worker resentment. Correspondingly, they typically won't raise wages during better economic times—until they are at risk of losing workers to competitors—because they don't want to encourage workers to routinely demand higher wages. So as a result of both formal and informal agreements, nominal wages are "sticky": slow to fall even in the face of high unemployment, and slow to rise even in the face of labor shortages. We'll discuss the reasons for this stickiness in greater detail in Chapter 15. It's important to note, however, that nominal wages cannot be sticky forever: ultimately, formal contracts and informal agreements will be renegotiated to take into account changed economic circumstances. As the Pitfalls on page 245 explains, how long it takes for nominal wages to become flexible is an integral component of what distinguishes the short run from the long run.

Let's return to the question of the positive relationship between the aggregate price level and the quantity of aggregate output supplied in the short run. Imagine that, for some reason, the aggregate price level falls, which means that the price received by the typical producer of a final good or service falls. Because many production costs are fixed in the short run, production cost per unit of output doesn't fall by the same proportion as the fall in the price of output. So the profit per unit of output declines, leading producers to reduce the quantity supplied in the short run. In the economy as a whole, when the aggregate price level falls, aggregate output falls in the short run.

Now consider what would happen if, for some reason, the aggregate price level rises. As a result, the typical producer receives a higher price for his or her final good or service. Because many production costs are fixed in the short run, production cost per unit of output doesn't rise by the same proportion as the rise in the price of a unit. So profit per unit of output rises, the producer increases output, and aggregate output increases in the short run.

The positive relationship between the aggregate price level and the quantity of aggregate output producers are willing to supply during the time period when many production costs, particularly nominal wages, can be taken as fixed is illustrated by the **short-run aggregate supply curve.** The positive relationship between the aggregate price level and aggregate output in the short run gives the short-run aggregate supply curve its upward slope. Figure 10-1 shows a hypothetical short-run aggregate supply curve, *SRAS,* which matches actual U.S. data for 1929 and 1933.

The **nominal wage** is the dollar amount of the wage paid.

The **short-run aggregate supply curve** shows the relationship between the aggregate price level and the quantity of aggregate output supplied that exists in the short run, the time period when many production costs can be taken as fixed.

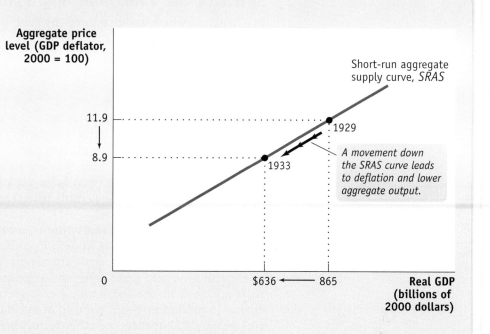

Figure 10-1

The Short-Run Aggregate Supply Curve

The short-run aggregate supply curve shows the relationship between the aggregate price level and the quantity of aggregate output supplied in the short run, the period in which many production costs such as nominal wages are fixed. It is upward-sloping because a higher aggregate price level leads to higher profit per unit of output and higher aggregate output given fixed nominal wages. Here we show numbers corresponding to the Great Depression, from 1929 to 1933: when deflation occurred and the aggregate price level fell from 11.9 (in 1929) to 8.9 (in 1933), firms responded by reducing the quantity of aggregate output supplied from $865 billion to $636 billion measured in 2000 dollars.

On the horizontal axis is aggregate output (or, equivalently, real GDP)—the total quantity of final goods and services supplied in the economy—measured in 2000 dollars. On the vertical axis is the aggregate price level as measured by the GDP deflator, with the value for year 2000 equal to 100. In 1929, the aggregate price level was 11.9 and real GDP was $865 billion. In 1933, the aggregate price level was 8.9 and real GDP was only $636 billion. The movement down the SRAS curve corresponds to the deflation and fall in aggregate output experienced over those years.

FOR INQUIRING MINDS

WHAT'S TRULY FLEXIBLE, WHAT'S TRULY STICKY

Most macroeconomists agree that the basic picture shown in Figure 10-1 is correct: there is, other things equal, a positive short-run relationship between the aggregate price level and aggregate output. But many would argue that the details are a bit more complicated.

So far we've stressed a difference in the behavior of the aggregate price level and the behavior of nominal wages. That is, we've said that the aggregate price level is flexible but nominal wages are sticky in the short run. Although this assumption is a good way to explain why the short-run aggregate supply curve is upward-sloping, empirical data on wages and prices don't wholly support a sharp distinction between flexible

prices of final goods and services and sticky nominal wages. On one side, some nominal wages are in fact flexible even in the short run because some workers are not covered by a contract or informal agreement with their employers. Since some nominal wages are sticky but others are flexible, we observe that the *average nominal wage*—the nominal wage averaged over all workers in the economy—falls when there is a steep rise in unemployment. For example, nominal wages fell substantially in the early years of the Great Depression. On the other side, some prices of final goods and services are sticky rather than flexible. For example, some firms, particularly the makers of luxury or

name-brand goods, are reluctant to cut prices even when demand falls. Instead they prefer to cut output even if their profit per unit hasn't declined.

These complications, as we've said, don't change the basic picture. When the aggregate price level falls, some producers cut output because the nominal wages they pay are sticky. And some producers don't cut their prices in the face of a falling aggregate price level, preferring instead to reduce their output. In both cases the positive relationship between the aggregate price level and aggregate output is maintained. So, in the end, the short-run aggregate supply curve is still upward-sloping.

Shifts of the Short-Run Aggregate Supply Curve

In Chapter 3, where we introduced the analysis of supply and demand in the market for an individual good, we stressed the importance of the distinction between *movements along* the supply curve and *shifts of* the supply curve. The same distinction applies to the aggregate supply curve. Figure 10-1 shows a *movement along* the short-run aggregate supply curve, as the aggregate price level and aggregate output fell from 1929 to 1933. But there can also be *shifts of* the short-run aggregate supply curve, as shown in Figure 10-2. Panel (a) shows a *decrease in short-run aggregate supply*—a leftward shift of the short-run aggregate supply curve. Aggregate supply decreases when producers reduce the quantity of aggregate output they are willing to supply at any given aggregate price level. Panel (b) shows an *increase in short-run aggregate supply*—a rightward shift of the short-run aggregate supply curve. Aggregate supply increases when producers increase the quantity of aggregate output they are willing to supply at any given aggregate price level.

To understand why the short-run aggregate supply curve can shift, it's important to recall that producers make output decisions based on their profit per unit of output. The short-run aggregate supply curve illustrates the relationship between the aggregate price level and aggregate output: because some production costs are fixed in the short run, a change in the aggregate price level leads to a change in producers' profit per unit of output and, in turn, leads to a change in aggregate output. But there are other factors besides the aggregate price level that can affect profit per unit and, in turn, aggregate output. It is changes in these other factors that will shift the short-run aggregate supply curve.

To develop some intuition, suppose that something happens that raises production costs—say an increase in the price of oil. At any given price of output, a producer now earns a smaller profit per unit of output. As a result, producers reduce the quantity supplied at any given aggregate price level, and the short-run aggregate supply curve shifts to the left. If, in contrast, something happens that lowers production costs—say a fall in the nominal wage—a producer now earns a higher profit per unit of output at any given price of output. This leads producers to increase the quantity

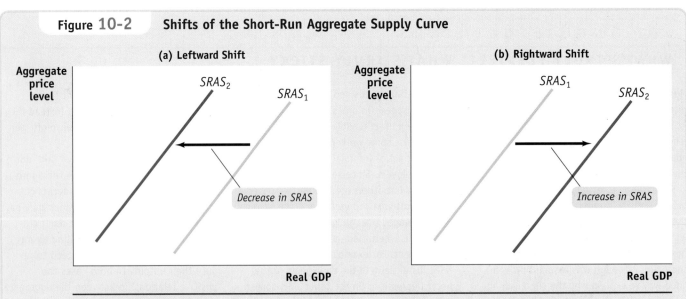

Figure 10-2 **Shifts of the Short-Run Aggregate Supply Curve**

(a) Leftward Shift

Aggregate price level

$SRAS_2$ $SRAS_1$

Decrease in SRAS

Real GDP

(b) Rightward Shift

Aggregate price level

$SRAS_1$ $SRAS_2$

Increase in SRAS

Real GDP

Panel (a) shows a decrease in short-run aggregate supply: the short-run aggregate supply curve shifts leftward from $SRAS_1$ to $SRAS_2$, and the quantity of aggregate output supplied at any given aggregate price level falls. Panel (b) shows an increase in short-run aggregate supply: the short-run aggregate supply curve shifts rightward from $SRAS_1$ to $SRAS_2$, and the quantity of aggregate output supplied at any given aggregate price level rises.

of aggregate output supplied at any given aggregate price level, and the short-run aggregate supply curve shifts to the right.

Now we'll discuss some of the other important factors that affect producers' profit per unit and so can lead to shifts of the short-run aggregate supply curve.

Changes in Commodity Prices

In this chapter's opening story, we described how a surge in the price of oil caused problems for the U.S. economy in 1979. Oil is a commodity, a standardized input bought and sold in bulk quantities. An increase in the price of a commodity—oil—raised production costs across the economy and reduced the quantity of aggregate output supplied at any given aggregate price level, shifting the short-run aggregate supply curve to the left. Conversely, a decline in commodity prices will reduce production costs, leading to an increase in the quantity supplied at any given aggregate price level and a rightward shift of the short-run aggregate supply curve.

Why isn't the influence of commodity prices already captured by the short-run aggregate supply curve? Because commodities—unlike, say, soft drinks—are not a final good, their prices are not included in the calculation of the aggregate price level. Further, commodities represent a significant cost of production to most suppliers, just like nominal wages do. So changes in commodity prices have large impacts on production costs. And in contrast to non-commodities, the prices of commodities can sometimes change drastically due to industry-specific shocks to supply—such as wars in the Middle East.

Changes in Nominal Wages

At any given point in time, the dollar wages of many workers are fixed because they are set by contracts or informal agreements made in the past. Nominal wages can change, however, once enough time has passed for contracts and informal agreements to be renegotiated. Suppose, for example, that there is an economy-wide rise in the cost of health care insurance premiums paid by employers as part of employees' wages. From the employers' perspective, this is equivalent to a rise in nominal wages because it is an increase in employer-paid compensation. So this rise in nominal wages increases production costs and shifts the short-run aggregate supply curve to the left. Conversely, suppose there is an economy-wide fall in the cost of such premiums. This is equivalent to a fall in nominal wages from the point of view of employers; it reduces production costs and shifts the short-run aggregate supply curve to the right.

An important historical fact is that during the 1970s the surge in the price of oil had the indirect effect of also raising nominal wages. This "knock-on" effect occurred because many wage contracts included *cost-of-living allowances* that automatically raised the nominal wage when consumer prices increased. Through this channel, the surge in the price of oil—which led to an increase in overall consumer prices—ultimately caused a rise in nominal wages. So the economy, in the end, experienced two leftward shifts of the aggregate supply curve: the first generated by the initial surge in the price of oil, the second generated by the induced increase in nominal wages. The negative effect on the economy of rising oil prices was greatly magnified through the cost-of-living allowances in wage contracts. Today, cost-of-living allowances in wage contracts are rare.

Changes in Productivity

An increase in productivity means that a worker can produce more units of output with the same quantity of inputs. For example, the introduction of bar-code scanners in retail stores greatly increased the ability of a single worker to stock, inventory, and resupply store shelves. As a result, the cost to a store of "producing" a dollar of sales fell and profit rose. And, correspondingly, the quantity supplied increased. (Think of Wal-Mart and the increase in the number of its stores as an increase in aggregate supply.) So a rise in productivity, whatever the source, increases producers' profits and shifts the short-run aggregate supply curve to the right. Conversely, a fall in productivity—say, due to new regulations that require workers to spend more time filling out forms—reduces the number of units of output a worker can produce with the same quantity of inputs. Consequently, the cost per unit of output rises, profit falls, and quantity supplied falls. This shifts the short-run aggregate supply curve to the left.

The Long-Run Aggregate Supply Curve

We've just seen that in the short run a fall in the aggregate price level leads to a decline in the quantity of aggregate output supplied because nominal wages are sticky in the short run. But, as we mentioned earlier, contracts and informal agreements are renegotiated in the long run. So in the long run, nominal wages—like the aggregate price level—are flexible, not sticky. This fact greatly alters the long-run relationship between the aggregate price level and aggregate supply. In fact, in the long run the aggregate price level has *no* effect on the quantity of aggregate output supplied.

To see why, let's conduct a thought experiment. Imagine that you could wave a magic wand—or maybe a magic bar-code scanner—and cut *all prices* in the economy in half at the same time. By "all prices" we mean the prices of all inputs, including nominal wages, as well as the prices of final goods and services. What would happen to aggregate output, given that the aggregate price level has been halved and all input prices, including nominal wages, have been halved?

The answer is: nothing. Consider Equation 10-1 again: each producer would receive a lower price for his or her product, but costs would fall by the same proportion. As a result, every unit of output profitable to produce before the change in prices would still be profitable to produce after the change in prices. So a halving of *all* prices in the economy has no effect on the economy's aggregate output. In other words, changes in the aggregate price level now have no effect on the quantity of aggregate output supplied.

In reality, of course, no one can change all prices by the same proportion at the same time. But in the long run, when all prices are fully flexible, inflation or deflation has the same effect as someone changing all prices by the same proportion. *As a result, changes in the aggregate price level do not change the quantity of aggregate output supplied in the long run.* That's because changes in the aggregate price level will, in the long run, be accompanied by equal proportional changes in *all* input prices, including nominal wages.

The **long-run aggregate supply curve**, illustrated in Figure 10-3 by the curve *LRAS*, shows the relationship between the aggregate price level and the quantity of aggregate output supplied that would exist if all prices, including nominal wages, were fully flexible. The long-run aggregate supply curve is vertical because changes in the aggregate price level have *no* effect on aggregate output in the long run. At an aggregate price level of 15.0, the quantity of aggregate output supplied is $800 billion in 2000 dollars. If the aggregate price level falls by 50% to 7.5, the quantity of aggregate output supplied is unchanged in the long run at $800 billion in 2000 dollars.

The **long-run aggregate supply curve** shows the relationship between the aggregate price level and the quantity of aggregate output supplied that would exist if all prices, including nominal wages, were fully flexible.

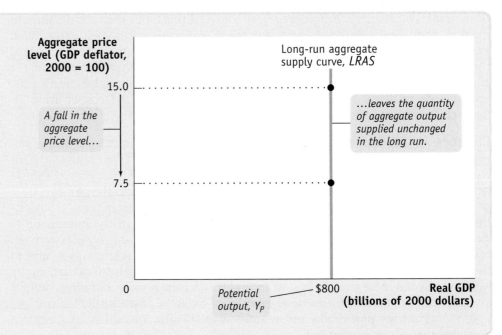

Figure 10-3

The Long-Run Aggregate Supply Curve

The long-run aggregate supply curve shows the quantity of aggregate output supplied when all prices, including nominal wages, are flexible. It is vertical at potential output, Y_P, because in the long run a change in the aggregate price level has no effect on the quantity of aggregate output supplied.

It's important to understand not only that the *LRAS* curve is vertical but also that its position along the horizontal axis represents a significant measure. The horizontal intercept in Figure 10-3, where *LRAS* touches the horizontal axis ($800 billion in 2000 dollars), is the economy's **potential output,** Y_P: the level of real GDP the economy would produce if all prices, including nominal wages, were fully flexible.

In reality, the actual level of real GDP is almost always either above or below potential output. We'll see why later in this chapter, when we discuss the *AS-AD* model. Still, an economy's potential output is an important number because it defines the trend around which actual aggregate output fluctuates from year to year.

In the United States, the Congressional Budget Office (CBO) estimates annual potential output for the purpose of federal budget analysis. Panel (a) of Figure 10-4 shows the CBO's estimates of U.S. potential output from 1989 to 2004 and the actual values of U.S. real GDP over the same period. Purple-shaded years correspond to periods in which potential output exceeded actual aggregate output; green-shaded years to periods in which actual aggregate output exceeded potential output.

As you can see in panel (a), U.S. potential output has risen steadily over time—implying a series of rightward shifts of the *LRAS* curve. What has caused these rightward shifts? The answer lies in the factors related to long-run growth that we discussed in Chapter 8, such as increases in physical capital and human capital as well as technological progress. Over the long run, as the size of the labor force and the productivity of labor both rise, the level of real GDP that the economy is capable of producing also rises. Indeed, one way to think about long-run economic growth is that it is the

Potential output is the level of real GDP the economy would produce if all prices, including nominal wages, were fully flexible.

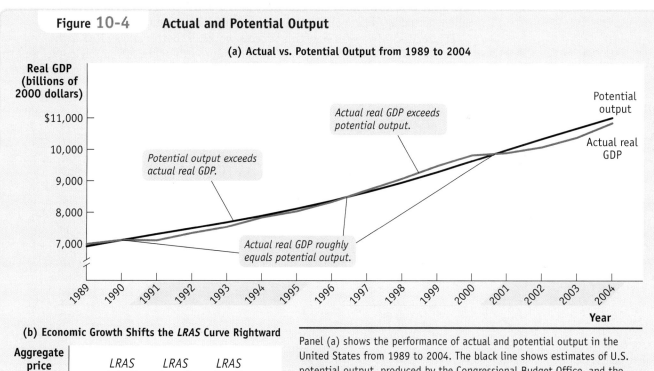

Figure 10-4   Actual and Potential Output

(a) Actual vs. Potential Output from 1989 to 2004

Panel (a) shows the performance of actual and potential output in the United States from 1989 to 2004. The black line shows estimates of U.S. potential output, produced by the Congressional Budget Office, and the blue line shows actual aggregate output. The purple-shaded years are periods in which actual aggregate output fell below potential output, and the green-shaded years are periods in which actual aggregate output exceeded potential output. As shown, significant shortfalls occurred in the recessions of the early 1990s and after 2000. Actual aggregate output was significantly above potential output in the boom of the late 1990s. Panel (b) shows how economic growth has shifted the long-run aggregate supply curve, *LRAS*, rightward over time.

growth in the economy's potential output. As illustrated in panel (b) of Figure 10-4, we generally think of the long-run aggregate supply curve as shifting to the right over time as an economy experiences long-run growth.

From the Short Run to the Long Run

As you can see in panel (a) of Figure 10-4, the economy almost always produces more or less than potential output: in only three periods during the years from 1989 to 2004 did actual aggregate output roughly equal potential output (the three years at which the two lines cross). The economy is almost always on its short-run aggregate supply curve—producing an aggregate output level more than or less than potential output—not on its long-run aggregate supply curve. So why is the long-run curve relevant? Does the economy ever move from the short run to the long run? And if so, how?

The first step to answering these questions is to understand that the economy is always in one of only two states with respect to the short-run and long-run aggregate supply curves. It can be on both curves simultaneously by being at a point where the curves cross (as in the three periods in panel (a) of Figure 10-4 in which actual aggregate output and potential output roughly coincide). Or it can be on the short-run aggregate supply curve but not the long-run aggregate supply curve (as in the years in panel (a) of Figure 10-4 in which actual aggregate output and potential output *did not* coincide). But that is not the end of the story. If the economy is on the short-run but not the long-run aggregate supply curve, the short-run aggregate supply curve will shift over time until the economy is at a point where both curves cross—a point where actual aggregate output is equal to potential output.

Figure 10-5 illustrates how this process works. In both panels *LRAS* is the long-run aggregate supply curve, *SRAS₁* is the initial short-run aggregate supply curve, and the aggregate price level is at P_1. In panel (a) the economy starts at the initial production

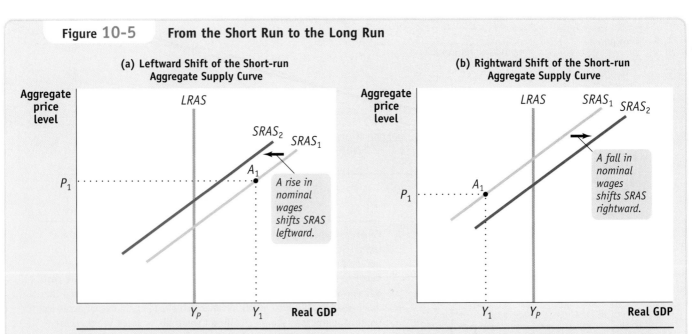

Figure 10-5   From the Short Run to the Long Run

(a) Leftward Shift of the Short-run Aggregate Supply Curve

(b) Rightward Shift of the Short-run Aggregate Supply Curve

In panel (a), the initial short-run aggregate supply curve is *SRAS₁*. At the aggregate price level, P_1, the quantity of aggregate output supplied, Y_1, exceeds potential output, Y_P. Eventually, low unemployment will cause nominal wages to rise, leading to a leftward shift of the short-run aggregate supply curve from *SRAS₁* to *SRAS₂*. In panel (b), the reverse happens: at the aggregate price level, P_1, the quantity of aggregate output supplied is less than potential output. High unemployment eventually leads to a fall in nominal wages over time and a rightward shift of the short-run aggregate supply curve.

point, A_1, which corresponds to a quantity of aggregate output supplied, Y_1, that is higher than potential output, Y_P. Producing an aggregate output level (such as Y_1) that is higher than potential output (Y_P) is possible only because nominal wages haven't yet fully adjusted upward. Until this upward adjustment in nominal wages occurs, producers are earning high profits and producing a high level of output. But a level of aggregate output higher than potential output means a low level of unemployment. Because jobs are abundant and workers are scarce, nominal wages will rise over time, gradually shifting the short-run aggregate supply curve leftward. Eventually it will be in a new position, such as $SRAS_2$. (Later in this chapter we'll show where the short-run aggregate supply curve ends up. As we'll see, that depends on the aggregate demand curve as well.)

In panel (b) of Figure 10-5, the initial production point, A_1, corresponds to the aggregate output level, Y_1, that is lower than potential output, Y_P. Producing an aggregate output level (such as Y_1) that is lower than potential output (Y_P) is possible only because nominal wages haven't yet fully adjusted downward. Until this downward adjustment occurs, producers are earning low (or negative) profits and producing a low level of output. An aggregate output level lower than potential output means high unemployment. Because workers are abundant and jobs are scarce, nominal wages will fall over time, shifting the short-run aggregate supply curve gradually to the right. Eventually it will be in a new position, such as $SRAS_2$.

We'll see shortly that these shifts of the short-run aggregate supply curve will return the economy to potential output in the long run. To explain why, however, we first need to introduce the concept of the *aggregate demand curve*.

PITFALLS

ARE WE THERE YET? WHAT THE LONG RUN REALLY MEANS

We've used the term *long run* in two different contexts. In Chapter 8 we focused on *long-run economic growth*: growth that takes place over decades. In this chapter we introduced the *long-run aggregate supply curve*, which depicts the economy's potential output: the level of aggregate output that the economy would produce if all prices, including nominal wages, were fully flexible. It might seem that we're using the same term, *long run*, for two different concepts. But we aren't: these two concepts are really the same thing.

Because the economy always tends to return to potential output in the long run, actual aggregate output *fluctuates around* potential output, rarely getting too far from it. As a result, the economy's rate of growth over long periods of time—say, decades—is very close to the rate of growth of potential output. And potential output growth is determined by the factors we analyzed in Chapter 8. So that means that the "long run" of long-run growth and the "long run" of the long-run aggregate supply curve coincide.

economics in action

Prices and Output During the Great Depression

Figure 10-6 shows the actual track of the aggregate price level, as measured by the GDP deflator, and real GDP, from 1929 to 1942. As you can see, aggregate output and the aggregate price level fell together from 1929 to 1933 and rose together during 1933 to 1937. This is what we'd expect to see if the economy were moving down the

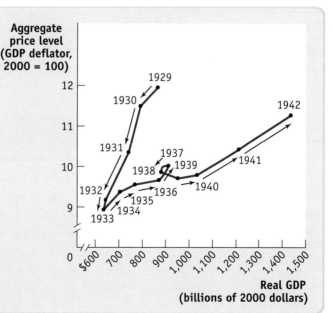

Figure 10-6

Prices and Output During the Great Depression

From 1929 to 1933, prices and aggregate output fell together. And from 1933 to 1937, prices and aggregate output rose together. That is, during the period of 1929 to 1937, the economy behaved as if it were first moving down and then up the short-run aggregate supply curve. By the late 1930s, however, aggregate output was above 1929 levels even though the aggregate price level was still lower than it was in 1929. This reflects the fact that the short-run aggregate supply curve had shifted to the right during this period, due to both the short-run adjustment process in the economy and to a rightward shift of the long-run aggregate supply curve.

short-run aggregate supply curve from 1929 to 1933 and moving up it (with a brief reversal in 1937–1938) thereafter.

But even in 1942 the aggregate price level was still lower than it was in 1929; yet real GDP was much higher. What happened?

The answer is that the short-run aggregate supply curve shifted to the right over time. This shift partly reflected rising productivity—a rightward shift of the underlying long-run aggregate supply curve. But since the U.S. economy was producing below potential output and had high unemployment during this period, the rightward shift of the short-run aggregate supply curve also reflected the adjustment process shown in panel (b) of Figure 10-5. So the movement of aggregate output from 1929 to 1942 reflected both movements along and shifts of the short-run aggregate supply curve. ∎

— < < < < < < < < < < < < < < < < < <

>>CHECK YOUR UNDERSTANDING 10-1

1. Determine the effect on short-run aggregate supply of each of the following events. Explain whether it represents a movement along the *SRAS* curve or a shift of the *SRAS* curve.
   a. A rise in the consumer price index (CPI) leads producers to increase output.
   b. A fall in the price of oil leads producers to increase output.
   c. A rise in legally mandated retirement benefits paid to workers leads producers to reduce output.

2. Suppose the economy is initially at potential output and the quantity of aggregate output supplied increases. What information would you need to determine whether this was due to a movement along the *SRAS* curve or a shift of the *LRAS* curve?

Solutions appear at back of book.

Aggregate Demand

The **aggregate demand curve** shows the relationship between the aggregate price level and the quantity of aggregate output demanded by households, businesses, the government, and the rest of the world.

Just as the aggregate supply curve shows the relationship between the aggregate price level and the quantity of aggregate output supplied by producers, the **aggregate demand curve** shows the relationship between the aggregate price level and the quantity of aggregate output demanded by households, firms, the government, and the rest of the world. Figure 10-7 shows an aggregate demand curve, *AD*. One point on

Figure 10-7

The Aggregate Demand Curve

The aggregate demand curve shows the relationship between the aggregate price level and the quantity of aggregate output demanded. The curve is downward-sloping due to the wealth effect of a change in the aggregate price level and the interest rate effect of a change in the aggregate price level. Corresponding to the actual 1933 data, here the total quantity of goods and services demanded at an aggregate price level of 8.9 is $636 billion in 2000 dollars. According to our hypothetical curve, however, if the aggregate price level had been only 5.0, the quantity of aggregate output demanded would have risen to $950 billion.

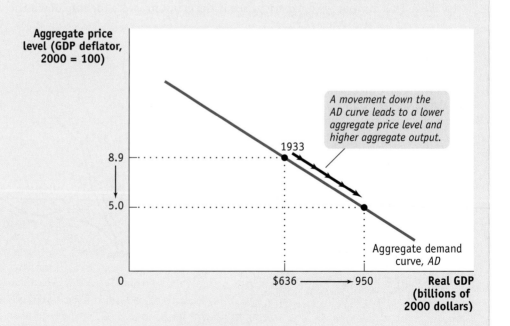

the curve corresponds to actual data for 1933, when the aggregate price level was 8.9 and the total quantity of domestic final goods and services purchased was $636 billion in 2000 dollars. *AD* is downward-sloping, indicating a negative relationship between the aggregate price level and the quantity of aggregate output demanded. A higher aggregate price level, other things equal, reduces the quantity of aggregate output demanded; a lower aggregate price level, other things equal, increases the quantity of aggregate output demanded. According to Figure 10-7, if the price level in 1933 had been 5.0 instead of 8.9, the total quantity of domestic final goods and services demanded would have been $950 billion in 2000 dollars instead of $636 billion.

Why Is the Aggregate Demand Curve Downward-Sloping?

In Figure 10-7, the curve *AD* is downward-sloping. Why? Recall the basic equation of national income accounting:

(10-2) $GDP = C + I + G + X - IM$

where *C* is consumer spending, *I* is investment spending, *G* is government purchases of goods and services, *X* is exports to other countries, and *IM* is imports. If we measure these variables in constant dollars—that is, in prices of a base year—then $C + I + G + X - IM$ is the quantity of domestically produced final goods and services demanded during a given period. *G* is decided by the government, but the other variables are private-sector decisions. To understand why the aggregate demand curve slopes downward, we need to understand why a rise in the aggregate price level reduces *C, I,* and *X – IM.*

You might think that the downward slope of the aggregate demand curve is a natural consequence of the *law of demand* we defined back in Chapter 3. That is, since the demand curve for any one good is downward-sloping, isn't it natural that the demand curve for aggregate output is downward-sloping? This turns out to be a misleading parallel. The demand curve for any individual good shows how the quantity demanded depends on the price of that good, *holding the prices of other goods and services constant.* The main reason the quantity of a good demanded falls when the price of that good rises is that people switch their consumption to other goods and services.

But when we consider movements up or down the aggregate demand curve, we're considering *a simultaneous change in the prices of all final goods and services.* Furthermore, changes in the composition of goods and services in consumer spending aren't relevant to the aggregate demand curve: if consumers decide to buy fewer clothes but more cars, this doesn't necessarily change the total quantity of final goods and services they demand.

Why, then, does a rise in the aggregate price level lead to a fall in the quantity of all domestically produced final goods and services demanded? There are two main reasons: the *wealth effect* and the *interest rate effect* of a change in the aggregate price level.

The Wealth Effect An increase in the aggregate price level, other things equal, reduces the purchasing power of many assets. Consider, for example, someone who has $5,000 in a bank account. If the aggregate price level were to rise by 25%, that $5,000 would buy only as much as $4,000 would have bought previously. With the loss in purchasing power, the owner of that bank account would probably scale back his or her consumption plans, leading to a fall in spending on final goods and services. The **wealth effect of a change in the aggregate price level** is the effect on consumer spending caused by the effect of a change in the aggregate price level on the purchasing power of consumers' assets. Because of it, consumer spending, *C,* falls when the aggregate price level rises, leading to a downward-sloping aggregate demand curve.

> The **wealth effect of a change in the aggregate price level** is the effect on consumer spending caused by the effect of a change in the aggregate price level on the purchasing power of consumers' assets.

The Interest Rate Effect Economists use the term *money* in its narrowest sense to refer to cash and bank deposits on which people can write checks. People and firms hold money because it reduces the cost and inconvenience of making transactions. An increase in the aggregate price level, other things equal, reduces the purchasing power of a given amount of money holdings. To purchase the same basket of goods and services as before, people and firms now need to hold more money. So, in response to an increase in the aggregate price level, the public tries to increase its money holdings, either by borrowing more or by selling other assets such as bonds. This reduces the funds available for lending to other borrowers and has the effect of driving interest rates up. In Chapter 9 we learned that a rise in the interest rate reduces investment spending because it makes the cost of borrowing higher. It also reduces consumer spending as households save more of their disposable income. So a rise in the aggregate price level depresses investment spending, I, and consumer spending, C, through its effect on the purchasing power of money holdings, an effect known as the **interest rate effect of a change in the aggregate price level.** This also leads to a downward-sloping aggregate demand curve.

> The **interest rate effect of a change in the aggregate price level** is the effect on consumer spending and investment spending caused by the effect of a change in the aggregate price level on the purchasing power of consumers' and firms' money holdings.

We'll have a lot more to say about money and interest rates in Chapter 14. We'll also see, in Chapter 19, that a higher interest rate indirectly tends to reduce exports (X) and increase imports (IM). For now, the important point is that the aggregate demand curve is downward-sloping due to both the wealth effect and the interest rate effect of a change in the aggregate price level.

Shifts of the Aggregate Demand Curve

When we talk about an increase in aggregate demand, we mean a shift of the aggregate demand curve to the right, as shown in panel (a) of Figure 10-8 by the shift from AD_1 to AD_2. A rightward shift occurs when the quantity of aggregate output demanded increases at any given aggregate price level. A decrease in aggregate demand means that AD shifts to the left, as in panel (b). A leftward shift implies that the quantity of aggregate output demanded falls at any given aggregate price level.

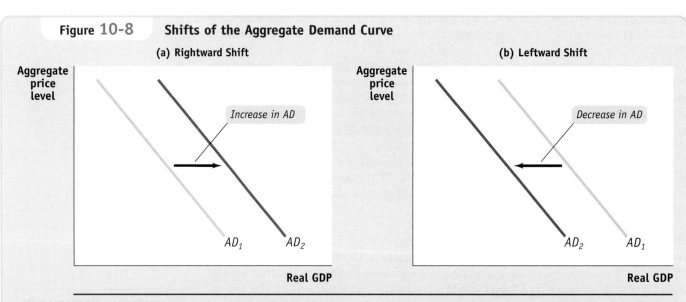

Figure 10-8 **Shifts of the Aggregate Demand Curve**

Panel (a) shows the effect of events that increase the quantity of aggregate output demanded at any given aggregate price level, such as improvements in business and consumer expectations or increased government spending. Such changes shift the aggregate demand curve to the right, from AD_1 to AD_2. Panel (b) shows the effect of events that decrease the quantity of aggregate output demanded at any given price level, such as a fall in wealth caused by a stock market decline. This shifts the aggregate demand curve leftward from AD_1 to AD_2.

A number of factors can shift the aggregate demand curve. Among the most important factors are changes in expectations, changes in wealth, and changes in the stock of physical capital. In addition, both fiscal and monetary policy can shift the aggregate demand curve.

Changes in Expectations Both consumer spending and investment spending depend in part on people's expectations about the future. Consumers base their spending not only on the income they have now but also on the income they expect to have in the future. Firms base their investment spending not only on current conditions but also on the sales they expect to make in the future. As a result, changes in expectations can push consumer spending and investment spending up or down. If consumers and firms become more optimistic, spending rises; if they become more pessimistic, spending falls. In fact, short-run economic forecasters pay careful attention to surveys of consumer and business sentiment. In particular, forecasters watch the Consumer Confidence Index, a monthly measure calculated by the Conference Board, and the Michigan Consumer Sentiment Index, a similar measure calculated by the University of Michigan.

Changes in Wealth Consumer spending depends in part on the value of household assets. When the real value of these assets rises, the purchasing power they embody also rises, leading to an increase in aggregate demand. For example, in the 1990s there was a significant rise in the stock market that shifted aggregate demand. And when the real value of household assets falls—for example, because of a stock market crash—the purchasing power they embody is reduced and aggregate demand also falls. The stock market crash of 1929 was one factor in the Great Depression. Similarly, a sharp decline in the stock market in the United States after 2000 was an important factor in the 2001 recession.

Changes in the Stock of Physical Capital Firms engage in investment spending to add to their stock of physical capital. Their incentive to spend depends in part on how much physical capital they already have: the more they have, the less they will feel a need to add more, other things equal. Investment spending fell in 2000–2001 partly because high investment spending over the previous few years had left companies with more of certain kinds of capital, such as computers and fiber-optic cable, than they needed at that time.

Government Policies and Aggregate Demand

One of the key insights of macroeconomics is that the government can have a powerful influence on aggregate demand and that, in some circumstances, this influence can be used to improve economic performance.

The two main ways the government can influence the aggregate demand curve are through fiscal policy and monetary policy. We'll briefly discuss their influence on aggregate demand, pending full-length discussions in Chapter 12 and Chapter 14.

Jim Borgman

"CONSUMER CONFIDENCE CRISIS IN AISLE THREE!"

PITFALLS

CHANGES IN WEALTH: A MOVEMENT ALONG VERSUS A SHIFT OF THE AGGREGATE DEMAND CURVE

In the last section we explained that one reason that the *AD* curve was downward-sloping was due to the wealth effect of a change in the aggregate price level: a higher aggregate price level reduces the purchasing power of households' assets and leads to a fall in consumer spending, *C*. But in this section we've just explained that changes in wealth lead to a shift of the *AD* curve. Aren't those two explanations contradictory? Which one is it—does a change in wealth move the economy along the *AD* curve or does it shift the *AD* curve? The answer is both: it depends on the *source* of the change in wealth. A movement along the *AD* curve occurs when a change in the aggregate price level changes the purchasing power of consumers' existing wealth (the real value of their assets). This is the *wealth effect of a change in the aggregate price level*—a change in the aggregate price level is the source of the change in wealth. For example, a fall in the aggregate price level increases the purchasing power of consumers' assets and leads to a movement down the *AD* curve. In contrast, a change in wealth *independent of a change in the aggregate price level* shifts the *AD* curve. For example, a rise in the stock market or a rise in real estate values leads to an increase in the real value of consumers' assets at any given aggregate price level. In this case, the source of the change in wealth is a change in the values of assets without any change in the aggregate price level—that is, a change in asset values holding the prices of all final goods and services constant.

Fiscal Policy As we learned in Chapter 6, fiscal policy is the use of either government spending—government purchases of final goods and services and government transfers—or tax policy to stabilize the economy. In practice, governments often respond to recessions by increasing spending, cutting taxes, or both. They often respond to inflation by reducing spending or increasing taxes.

The effect of government purchases of final goods and services, G, on the aggregate demand curve is *direct* because government purchases are themselves a component of aggregate demand. So an increase in government purchases shifts the aggregate demand curve to the right and a decrease shifts it to the left. History's most dramatic example of how increased government purchases affect aggregate demand was the effect of wartime government spending during World War II. Because of the war, U.S. federal purchases surged 400%. This increase in purchases is usually given the credit for ending the Great Depression. In the 1990s Japan used large public works projects—such as government-financed construction of roads, bridges, and dams—in an effort to increase aggregate demand in the face of a slumping economy. In contrast, government transfers affect aggregate demand indirectly: by changing disposable income, they change consumer spending.

In contrast, changes in tax rates (like changes in transfers) influence the economy *indirectly* through their effect on disposable income. A lower tax rate means that consumers get to keep more of what they earn, increasing their disposable income. This increases consumer spending and shifts the aggregate demand curve to the right. A higher tax rate reduces the amount of disposable income received by consumers. This reduces consumer spending and shifts the aggregate demand curve to the left.

Monetary Policy In Chapter 6 we defined monetary policy as the use of changes in the quantity of money or the interest rate to stabilize the economy. We've just discussed how a rise in the aggregate price level, by reducing the purchasing power of money holdings, causes a rise in the interest rate. That, in turn, reduces both investment spending and consumer spending.

But what happens if the quantity of money in the hands of households and firms changes? In modern economies, the quantity of money in circulation is largely determined by the decisions of a *central bank* created by the government. (As we'll learn in Chapter 13, the Federal Reserve, the U.S. central bank, is a special institution that is neither exactly part of the government nor exactly a private institution.) When the central bank increases the quantity of money in circulation, people have more money, which they are willing to lend out. The effect is to drive the interest rate down at any given aggregate price level and to increase investment spending and consumer spending. That is, increasing the quantity of money shifts the aggregate demand curve to the right. Reducing the quantity of money has the opposite effect: people have less money than before, leading them to borrow more and lend less. This raises the interest rate, reduces investment spending and consumer spending, and shifts the aggregate demand curve to the left.

economics in action

Moving Along the Aggregate Demand Curve, 1979–1980

When looking at data, it's often hard to distinguish between changes in spending that represent *movements along* the aggregate demand curve and *shifts of* the aggregate demand curve. One telling exception, however, is what happened right after the oil crisis of 1979, which we described in this chapter's opening story. Faced with a sharp increase in the aggregate price level—the rate of consumer price inflation reached 14.8% in March of 1980—the Federal Reserve stuck to a policy of increasing the quantity of money slowly. The aggregate price level was rising steeply, but the quantity of money going into the economy was growing slowly. The net result was that the purchasing power of the quantity of money in circulation in the economy fell.

This led to an increase in the demand for borrowing and a surge in interest rates. The *prime rate,* which is the interest rate banks charge their best customers, went above 20%. High interest rates, in turn, caused both consumer spending and investment spending to fall: in 1980 purchases of durable consumer goods like cars fell by 5.3% and real investment spending fell by 8.9%.

In other words, in 1979–1980 the economy responded just as we'd expect if it were moving along the aggregate demand curve: due to the wealth effect and the interest rate effect of a change in the aggregate price level, the quantity of aggregate output demanded fell as the aggregate price level rose. In the section "The *AS–AD* Model" we'll see that although this interpretation of the events in 1979–1980 is correct, the facts are a bit more complicated. There was indeed a movement along the aggregate demand curve. And the cause of this shift of the aggregate demand curve was a shift of the short-run aggregate supply curve. ∎

> >

>> **CHECK YOUR UNDERSTANDING 10-2**

1. Determine the effect on aggregate demand of each of the following events. Explain whether it represents a movement along the aggregate demand curve (up or down) or a shift of the curve (leftward or rightward).
   a. A rise in the interest rate caused by a change in monetary policy
   b. A fall in the real value of money in the economy due to a higher aggregate price level
   c. Expectations of a poor job market next year
   d. A fall in tax rates
   e. A rise in the real value of assets in the economy due to a lower aggregate price level
   f. A rise in the real value of assets in the economy due to a surge in real estate values

Solutions appear at back of book.

The Multiplier

Suppose that businesses become more optimistic about future sales and increase investment spending by $50 billion. This shifts the aggregate demand curve rightward—increasing the quantity of aggregate output demanded at any given aggregate price level. But suppose that we want to know *how much* the aggregate demand curve will shift to the right. To answer that question we use the concept of the *multiplier,* which plays an important role in the analysis of economic policy.

When we ask how far to the right a $50 billion autonomous increase in investment spending shifts the aggregate demand curve, what we really want to know is the magnitude of the shift shown in Figure 10-9 on page 252: the increase in the quantity of aggregate output demanded at a *given* aggregate price level, P^*. So we will hold the aggregate price level constant. (This means, among other things, that there is no difference between changes in *nominal* GDP and changes in *real* GDP.) We'll also make some additional simplifying assumptions: we'll hold the interest rate constant, and we'll ignore the roles of taxes and foreign trade, reserving those issues for later chapters.

Assuming a constant aggregate price level and a fixed interest rate, you might be tempted to say that a $50 billion increase in investment spending will shift the aggregate demand curve to the right by $50 billion. That, however, is an underestimate. It's true that an increase in investment spending leads firms that produce investment goods to increase output. If the process stopped there, then the rightward shift of the *AD* curve would indeed be $50 billion.

But the process doesn't stop there. The increase in output leads to an increase in disposable income that flows to households in the form of profits and wages. The increase in households' disposable income leads to a rise in consumer spending, which, in turn, induces firms to increase output yet again. This generates another rise in disposable income, which leads to another round of consumer spending increases, and so on. So there are multiple rounds of increases in aggregate output.

How large is the total effect on aggregate output if we sum the effect from all these rounds of spending increases? To answer this question, we need to introduce the concept of the **marginal propensity to consume,** or **MPC:** the increase in consumer

The **marginal propensity to consume,** or **MPC,** is the increase in consumer spending when disposable income rises by $1.

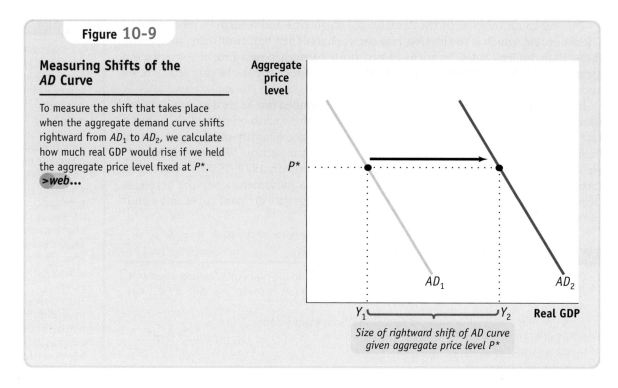

Figure 10-9

Measuring Shifts of the AD Curve

To measure the shift that takes place when the aggregate demand curve shifts rightward from AD_1 to AD_2, we calculate how much real GDP would rise if we held the aggregate price level fixed at P^*.

>web...

Size of rightward shift of AD curve given aggregate price level P^*

spending when disposable income rises by $1. When consumer spending changes because of a rise or fall in disposable income, MPC is the change in consumer spending divided by the change in disposable income:

$$(10\text{-}3) \quad MPC = \frac{\Delta \text{ Consumer spending}}{\Delta \text{ Disposable income}}$$

For example, if consumer spending goes up by $6 billion when disposable income goes up by $10 billion, MPC is $6 billion/$10 billion = 0.6.

Because consumers normally spend part but not all of an additional dollar of disposable income, MPC is a number between 0 and 1. The additional disposable income that consumers don't spend is saved; the **marginal propensity to save,** or **MPS,** is the fraction of an additional dollar of disposable income that is saved, and it is equal to $1 - MPC$.

> The **marginal propensity to save,** or **MPS,** is the increase in household savings when disposable income rises by $1.

Since we're ignoring taxes for now, we can assume that each $1 increase in real GDP raises real disposable income by $1. So the $50 billion increase in investment spending initially raises real GDP by $50 billion. This leads to a second-round increase in consumer spending, which raises real GDP by a further $MPC \times$ $50 billion. It is followed by a third-round increase in consumer spending of $MPC \times MPC \times$ $50 billion, and so on for several more rounds. The total effect on real GDP is:

Increase in investment spending	=	$50 billion
+ Second-round increase in consumer spending	= MPC	× $50 billion
+ Third-round increase in consumer spending	= MPC^2	× $50 billion
+ Fourth-round increase in consumer spending	= MPC^3	× $50 billion
⋮		⋮

Total increase in real GDP = $(1 + MPC + MPC^2 + MPC^3 + \ldots) \times$ $50 billion

So the initial $50 billion increase in investment spending arising from more optimistic expectations sets off a chain reaction in the economy. The net result of this chain reaction is that a $50 billion increase in investment spending leads to a change in real GDP that is a *multiple* of the size of that initial change in spending.

How large is this multiple? It's a mathematical fact that a series of the form $1 + x + x^2 + x^3 + \ldots$, where x is between 0 and 1, is equal to $1/(1 - x)$. So the total effect of a $50 billion increase in investment spending, taking into account all the subsequent increases in consumer spending (and assuming no taxes and no trade), is given by:

(10-4) Total increase in real GDP from $50 billion rise in I

$$= \$50 \text{ billion} \times \frac{1}{1 - MPC}$$

Let's consider a numerical example in which $MPC = 0.6$: each $1 in additional disposable income causes a $0.60 rise in consumer spending. In that case, a $50 billion increase in investment spending raises real GDP by $50 billion in the first round. The second-round increase in consumer spending raises real GDP by another $0.6 \times \$50$ billion, or $30 billion. The third-round increase in consumer spending raises real GDP by another $0.6 \times \$30$ billion, or $18 billion. Table 10-1 shows the successive stages of increases, where "..." means the process goes on an infinite number of times. In the end, real GDP rises by $125 billion as a consequence of the initial $50 billion rise in investment spending. We know that is true by Equation 10-4:

$$\$50 \text{ billion} \times \frac{1}{1 - 0.6} = \$50 \text{ billion} \times 2.5 = \$125 \text{ billion}$$

Notice that even though there are an infinite number of rounds of expansion of real GDP, the total rise in real GDP is limited to $125 billion. The reason is that at each stage some of the rise in disposable income "leaks out" because it is saved. How much of an additional dollar of disposable income is saved depends on MPS, the marginal propensity to save.

Figure 10-10 illustrates the effect of the increase in investment spending on the aggregate demand curve. Panel (a) shows the successive rounds of increasing real

TABLE 10-1

Rounds of Increases of Real GDP

	Increase in real GDP (billions of dollars)	Total increase in real GDP (billions of dollars)
First round	$50	$50
Second round	30	80
Third round	18	98
Fourth round	10.8	108.8
...	...	...
Final round	0	125

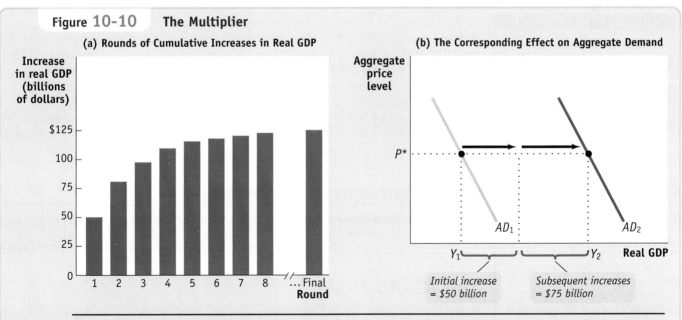

Figure 10-10   The Multiplier

(a) Rounds of Cumulative Increases in Real GDP

(b) The Corresponding Effect on Aggregate Demand

A change in expectations that leads to a rise in investment spending shifts the aggregate demand curve rightward for two reasons. Holding the aggregate price level constant, there is an initial increase in real GDP from the rise in I. Then there are subsequent increases in real GDP as rising disposable income leads to higher consumer spending. Panel (a) shows how the rise in real GDP at a given aggregate price level takes place. Panel (b) shows how this shifts the aggregate demand curve.

GDP from Table 10-1. Panel (b) shows the corresponding effect on aggregate demand: the total amount of the rightward shift of the AD curve, from AD_1 to AD_2, is $125 billion, the sum of the initial increase in investment spending, $50 billion, plus the subsequent rise in consumer spending, $75 billion.

We've described the effects of a change in investment spending arising from a change in expectations, but the same analysis can be applied to other causes of a shift in the aggregate demand curve. Since there is no foreign trade in this simple economy, we'll focus on domestic aggregate spending in the economy, the sum of consumer spending, C, investment spending, I, and government purchases of goods and services, G. Shifts in the aggregate demand curve can arise from autonomous changes in any of those three components of aggregate spending. The important thing is to distinguish between the initial change in aggregate spending, before real GDP rises, and the additional change in aggregate spending caused by the change in real GDP as the chain reaction unfolds. For example, suppose that total wealth in the economy increases for some reason. This will lead to an initial rise in consumer spending, before real GDP rises. But it will also lead to second and later rounds of higher consumer spending as real GDP rises.

An initial rise or fall in aggregate spending at a given level of real GDP is called an **autonomous change in aggregate spending.** It's autonomous—which means "self-governing"—because it's the cause, not the result, of the chain reaction we've just described. The **multiplier** is the ratio of the total change in real GDP caused by an autonomous change in aggregate spending to the size of that autonomous change. If we let ΔAAS stand for autonomous change in aggregate spending and ΔY stand for the change in real GDP, then the multiplier is equal to $\Delta Y/\Delta AAS$. And we've already seen from Equation 10-4 how to find the value of the multiplier. Assuming no taxes and no trade, it's

$$\textbf{(10-5)} \quad \text{Multiplier} = \frac{1}{1 - MPC} = \frac{\Delta Y}{\Delta AAS}$$

Accordingly, the multiplier lets us calculate the change in real GDP that arises from an autonomous change in aggregate spending. Re-arranging Equation 10-5 we get:

$$\textbf{(10-6)} \quad \Delta Y = \frac{1}{1 - MPC} \times \Delta AAS$$

Notice that the size of the multiplier—and so the size of the shift in the aggregate demand curve resulting from any given initial change in aggregate spending—depends on MPC. If the marginal propensity to consume is high, so is the multiplier. This is true because the size of MPC determines how large each round of expansion is compared with the previous round. To put it another way, the higher MPC is, the less disposable income "leaks out" into savings at each round of expansion.

In later chapters we'll use the concept of the multiplier to analyze the effects of fiscal and monetary policies. We'll also see that the formula for the multiplier changes when we introduce various complications, including taxes and foreign trade.

< < < < < < < < < < < < < < < <

An **autonomous change in aggregate spending** is an initial change in the desired level of spending by firms, households, and government at a given level of real GDP.

The **multiplier** is the ratio of the total change in real GDP caused by an autonomous change in aggregate spending to the size of that autonomous change.

>>QUICK REVIEW

> A change in investment spending arising from a change in expectations starts a chain reaction in which the initial change in real GDP leads to changes in consumer spending, leading to further changes in real GDP, and so on. The total shift in the aggregate demand curve is a multiple of the initial change in investment spending.

> Any *autonomous change in aggregate spending*, a change in *C*, *I*, or *G* that shifts the aggregate demand curve, generates the same chain reaction. The total size of the change in real GDP depends on the size of the *multiplier*. Assuming that there are no taxes and no trade, the multiplier is equal to $1/(1 - MPC)$, where *MPC* is the *marginal propensity to consume*. The total change in real GDP, ΔY, is equal to $1/(1 - MPC) \times \Delta AAS$.

>>CHECK YOUR UNDERSTANDING 10-3

1. Explain why a decline in investment spending, caused by a change in business expectations, would also lead to a fall in consumer spending.

Solution appears at back of book.

The *AS–AD* Model

From 1929 to 1933, the U.S. economy moved down the short-run aggregate supply curve as the aggregate price level fell. In contrast, from 1979 to 1980 the U.S. economy moved up the aggregate demand curve as the aggregate price level rose. In each case, the cause of the movement along the curve was a shift of the other curve. In 1929–1933, it was a leftward shift of the aggregate demand curve—a major fall in consumer spending. In 1979–1980, it was a leftward shift of the short-run aggregate supply curve—a dramatic fall in short-run aggregate supply caused by the oil price shock.

So to understand the behavior of the economy, we must put the aggregate supply curve and the aggregate demand curve together. The result is the **AS–AD model,** the basic model we use to understand economic fluctuations.

> In the **AS–AD model,** the aggregate supply curve and the aggregate demand curve are used together to analyze economic fluctuations.

Short-Run Macroeconomic Equilibrium

We'll begin our analysis by focusing on the short run. Figure 10-11 shows the aggregate demand curve and the short-run aggregate supply curve on the same diagram. The point at which the *AD* and *SRAS* curves intersect, E_{SR}, is the **short-run macroeconomic equilibrium:** the point at which the quantity of aggregate output supplied is equal to the quantity demanded by domestic households, businesses, the government, and the rest of the world. The aggregate price level at E_{SR}, P_E, is the **short-run equilibrium aggregate price level.** The level of aggregate output at E_{SR}, Y_E, is the **short-run equilibrium aggregate output.**

> The economy is in **short-run macroeconomic equilibrium** when the quantity of aggregate output supplied is equal to the quantity demanded.
>
> The **short-run equilibrium aggregate price level** is the aggregate price level in the short-run macroeconomic equilibrium.
>
> **Short-run equilibrium aggregate output** is the quantity of aggregate output produced in the short-run macroeconomic equilibrium.

In the supply and demand model of Chapter 3 we saw that a shortage of any individual good causes its market price to rise but a surplus of the good causes its market price to fall. These forces ensure that the market reaches equilibrium. The same logic applies to short-run macroeconomic equilibrium. If the aggregate price level is above its equilibrium level, the quantity of aggregate output supplied exceeds the quantity demanded. This leads to a fall in the aggregate price level and pushes it toward its equilibrium level. If the aggregate price level is below its equilibrium level, the quantity of aggregate output supplied is less than the quantity demanded. This leads to a rise in the aggregate price level, again pushing it toward its equilibrium level. In the discussion that follows, we'll assume that the economy is always in short-run macroeconomic equilibrium.

We'll also make another important simplification based on the observation that in reality there is a long-term upward trend in both aggregate output and the aggregate price level. We'll assume that a fall in either variable really means a fall compared to the long-run trend. For example, if the aggregate price level normally rises 4% per year, a year in which the aggregate price level rises only 3% would count, for

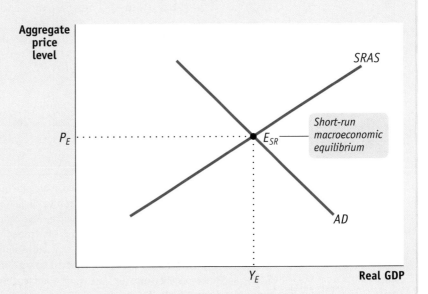

Figure 10-11

The *AS–AD* Model

The *AS–AD* model combines the short-run aggregate supply curve and the aggregate demand curve. Their point of intersection, E_{SR}, is the point of short-run macroeconomic equilibrium where the quantity of aggregate output demanded is equal to the quantity of aggregate output supplied. P_E is the short-run equilibrium aggregate price level, and Y_E is the short-run equilibrium level of aggregate output. **›web...**

our purposes, as a 1% decline. In fact, since the Great Depression there have been very few years in which the aggregate price level of any major nation actually declined—Japan's deflation after about 1995 is one of the few exceptions. We'll explain why in Chapter 16. There have, however, been many cases in which the aggregate price level fell relative to the long-run trend.

Short-run equilibrium aggregate output and the short-run equilibrium aggregate price level can change either because of shifts of the *SRAS* curve or because of shifts of the *AD* curve. Let's look at each case in turn.

Shifts of the *SRAS* Curve

An event that shifts the short-run aggregate supply curve is a **supply shock**.

An event that shifts the short-run aggregate supply curve, such as a change in commodity prices, nominal wages, or productivity, is known as a **supply shock**. A *negative* supply shock raises production costs and reduces the quantity producers are willing to supply at any given aggregate price level, leading to a leftward shift of the short-run aggregate supply curve. The U.S. economy experienced severe negative supply shocks following disruptions to world oil supplies in 1973 and 1979. In contrast, a *positive* supply shock reduces production costs and increases the quantity supplied at any given aggregate price level, leading to a rightward shift of the short-run aggregate supply curve. The United States experienced a positive supply shock between 1995 and 2000, when the increasing use of the Internet and other information technologies caused productivity growth to surge.

The effects of a negative supply shock are shown in panel (a) of Figure 10-12. The initial equilibrium is at E_1, with aggregate price level P_1 and aggregate output Y_1. The disruption in the oil supply causes the short-run aggregate supply curve to shift to the left, from $SRAS_1$ to $SRAS_2$. As a consequence, aggregate output falls and the aggregate price level rises, a movement up along the *AD* curve. At the new equilibrium,

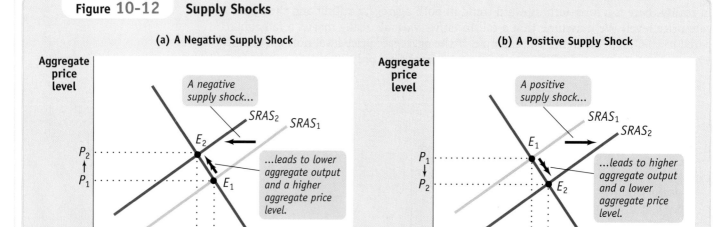

Figure 10-12 **Supply Shocks**

(a) A Negative Supply Shock

(b) A Positive Supply Shock

A supply shock shifts the short-run aggregate supply curve, moving the aggregate price level and aggregate output in opposite directions. Panel (a) shows a negative supply shock, which shifts the short-run aggregate supply curve leftward and causes stagflation—lower aggregate output and a higher aggregate price level. Here the short-run aggregate supply curve shifts from $SRAS_1$ to $SRAS_2$, and the economy moves from E_1 to E_2. The aggregate price level rises from P_1 to P_2, and aggregate output falls from Y_1 to Y_2. Panel (b) shows a positive supply shock, which shifts the short-run aggregate supply curve rightward, generating higher aggregate output and a lower aggregate price level. The short-run aggregate supply curve shifts from $SRAS_1$ to $SRAS_2$, and the economy moves from E_1 to E_2. The aggregate price level falls from P_1 to P_2, and aggregate output rises from Y_1 to Y_2.

E_2, the equilibrium aggregate price level, P_2, is higher, and the equilibrium aggregate output level, Y_2, is lower than before.

The combination of inflation and falling aggregate output shown in panel (a) has a special name: **stagflation,** for "stagnation plus inflation." When an economy experiences stagflation, it's very unpleasant: falling aggregate output leads to rising unemployment, and people feel that their purchasing power is squeezed by rising prices. Stagflation in the 1970s led to a mood of national pessimism. It also, as we'll see shortly, poses a dilemma for policy makers.

A positive supply shock, shown in panel (b), has exactly the opposite effects. A rightward shift of the $SRAS$ curve from $SRAS_1$ to $SRAS_2$ results in a rise in aggregate output and a fall in the aggregate price level, a movement down along the AD curve. The favorable supply shocks of the late 1990s led to a combination of full employment and declining inflation. That is, the aggregate price level fell compared with the long-run trend. This combination produced, for a time, a great wave of national optimism.

The distinctive feature of supply shocks, both negative and positive, is that they cause the aggregate price level and aggregate output to move in *opposite* directions.

> **Stagflation** is the combination of inflation and falling aggregate output.

Shifts of Aggregate Demand: Short-Run Effects

An event that shifts the aggregate demand curve, such as a change in expectations, wealth, the stock of physical capital, or the use of fiscal or monetary policy, is known as a **demand shock.** The Great Depression was caused by a negative demand shock, the collapse of wealth and of business and consumer confidence that followed the stock market crash of 1929 and the banking crisis of 1930–1931. The Depression was ended by a positive demand shock—the huge increase in government purchases during World War II. In 2001 the U.S. economy experienced another significant negative demand shock as the stock market boom of the 1990s turned into a bust and nervous businesses drastically scaled back their investment spending.

Figure 10-13 shows the short-run effects of negative and positive demand shocks. A negative demand shock shifts the aggregate demand curve, AD, to the left, from AD_1 to AD_2, as shown in panel (a). The economy moves down along the $SRAS$ curve from

> An event that shifts the aggregate demand curve is a **demand shock**.

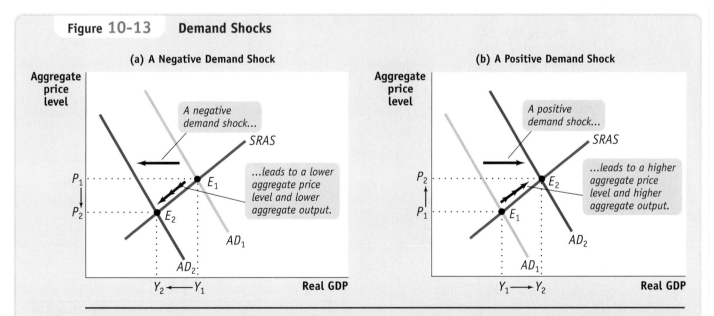

Figure 10-13   Demand Shocks

(a) A Negative Demand Shock

A negative demand shock...

...leads to a lower aggregate price level and lower aggregate output.

(b) A Positive Demand Shock

A positive demand shock...

...leads to a higher aggregate price level and higher aggregate output.

A demand shock shifts the aggregate demand curve, moving the aggregate price level and aggregate output in the same direction. In panel (a) a negative demand shock shifts the aggregate demand curve leftward from AD_1 to AD_2, reducing the aggregate price level from P_1 to P_2 and aggregate output from Y_1 to Y_2. In panel (b) a positive demand shock shifts the aggregate demand curve rightward, increasing the aggregate price level from P_1 to P_2 and aggregate output from Y_1 to Y_2.

E_1 to E_2, leading to lower equilibrium aggregate output and a lower equilibrium aggregate price level. A positive demand shock shifts the aggregate demand curve, AD, to the right, as shown in panel (b). Here, the economy moves up along the $SRAS$ curve, from E_1 to E_2. This leads to higher equilibrium aggregate output and a higher equilibrium aggregate price level. In contrast to supply shocks, demand shocks cause aggregate output and the aggregate price level to move in the *same* direction.

There's another important contrast between supply shocks and demand shocks. As we've seen, monetary policy and fiscal policy enable the government to shift the AD curve, meaning that governments are in a position to create the kinds of shocks shown in Figure 10-13. Are there good policy reasons to do this? We'll turn to that question soon. First, however, let's look at the difference between short-run macroeconomic equilibrium and long-run macroeconomic equilibrium.

Long-Run Macroeconomic Equilibrium

Figure 10-14 combines the aggregate demand curve with both the short-run and long-run aggregate supply curves. The aggregate demand curve, AD, crosses the short-run aggregate supply curve, $SRAS$, at E_{LR}. Here we assume that enough time has elapsed that the economy is also on the long-run aggregate supply curve, $LRAS$. As a result, E_{LR} is at the intersection of all three curves, $SRAS$, $LRAS$, and AD. So short-run equilibrium aggregate output is equal to potential output, Y_P. Such a situation, in which the point of short-run macroeconomic equilibrium is on the long-run aggregate supply curve, is known as **long-run macroeconomic equilibrium.**

To see the significance of long-run macroeconomic equilibrium, let's consider what happens if a demand shock moves the economy away from long-run macroeconomic equilibrium. In Figure 10-15, we assume that the initial aggregate demand curve is AD_1 and the initial short-run aggregate supply curve is $SRAS_1$. So the initial macroeconomic equilibrium is at E_1, which lies on the long-run aggregate supply curve, $LRAS$. The economy, then, starts from a point of short-run and long-run macroeconomic equilibrium, and short-run equilibrium aggregate output equals potential output at Y_1.

> The economy is in **long-run macroeconomic equilibrium** when the point of short-run macroeconomic equilibrium is on the long-run aggregate supply curve.

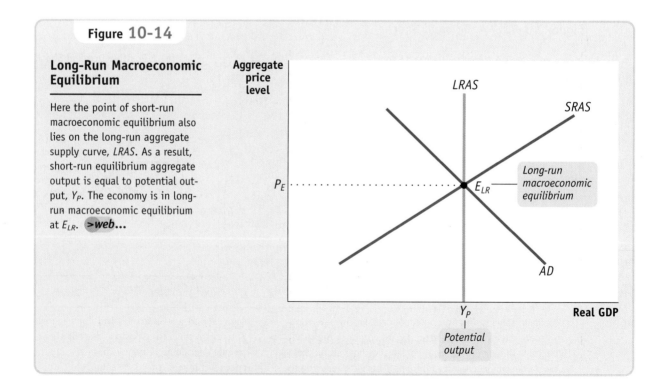

Figure 10-14

Long-Run Macroeconomic Equilibrium

Here the point of short-run macroeconomic equilibrium also lies on the long-run aggregate supply curve, *LRAS*. As a result, short-run equilibrium aggregate output is equal to potential output, Y_P. The economy is in long-run macroeconomic equilibrium at E_{LR}. **>web...**

Figure **10-15**

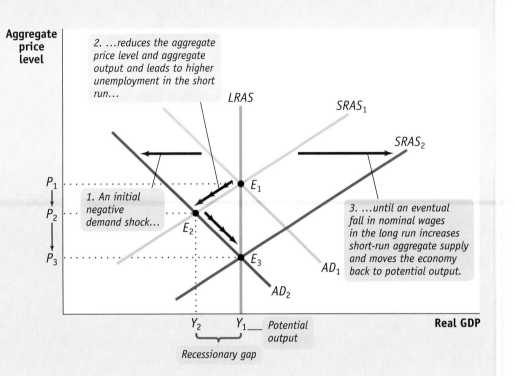

Short-Run versus Long-Run Effects of a Negative Demand Shock

In the long run the economy is self-correcting: demand shocks have only a short-run effect on aggregate output. Starting at E_1, a negative demand shock shifts AD_1 leftward to AD_2. In the short run the economy moves to E_2 and a recessionary gap arises: the aggregate price level declines from P_1 to P_2, aggregate output declines from Y_1 to Y_2, and unemployment rises. But in the long run nominal wages fall in response to high unemployment at Y_2, and $SRAS_1$ shifts rightward to $SRAS_2$. Aggregate output rises from Y_2 to Y_1, and the aggregate price level declines again, from P_2 to P_3. Long-run macroeconomic equilibrium is eventually restored at E_3.

Now suppose that for some reason—such as a sudden worsening of business and consumer expectations—aggregate demand falls and the aggregate demand curve shifts leftward to AD_2. This results in a lower equilibrium aggregate price level at P_2 and a lower equilibrium aggregate output level at Y_2 as the economy settles in the short run at E_2. The short-run effect of such a fall in aggregate demand is what the U.S. economy experienced in 1929–1933: a falling aggregate price level and falling aggregate output.

Aggregate output in this new short-run equilibrium, E_2, is below potential output. When this happens, the economy faces a **recessionary gap.** In the real world, a recessionary gap inflicts a great deal of pain because it corresponds to high unemployment. The large recessionary gap that opened up in the United States by 1933 caused intense social and political turmoil. And the devastating recessionary gap that opened up in Germany at the same time played an important role in Hitler's rise to power.

But this isn't the end of the story. In the face of high unemployment, nominal wages eventually fall, as do any other sticky prices, ultimately leading producers to increase output. As a result, a recessionary gap causes the short-run aggregate supply curve to gradually shift to the right over time. This process continues until $SRAS_1$ reaches its new position at $SRAS_2$, bringing the economy to equilibrium at E_3, where AD_2, $SRAS_2$, and $LRAS$ all intersect. At E_3, the economy is back in long-run macroeconomic equilibrium; it is back at potential output Y_1 but at a lower aggregate price level, P_3, reflecting a long-run fall in the aggregate price level. In the end, the economy is *self-correcting* in the long run.

What if, instead, there were an increase in aggregate demand? The results are shown in Figure 10-16 on page 260, where we again assume that the initial aggregate demand curve is AD_1, and the initial short-run aggregate supply curve is $SRAS_1$, so that the initial macroeconomic equilibrium, at E_1, lies on the long-run aggregate supply curve, $LRAS$. Initially, then, the economy is in long-run macroeconomic equilibrium.

Now suppose that aggregate demand rises, and the AD curve shifts rightward to AD_2. This results in a higher aggregate price level, at P_2, and a higher aggregate output

There is a **recessionary gap** when aggregate output is below potential output.

Figure 10-16

Short-Run versus Long-Run Effects of a Positive Demand Shock

Starting at E_1 a positive demand shock shifts AD_1 rightward to AD_2, and the economy moves to E_2 in the short run. This results in an inflationary gap as aggregate output rises from Y_1 to Y_2, the aggregate price level rises from P_1 to P_2, and unemployment falls to a low level. In the long run, $SRAS_1$ shifts leftward to $SRAS_2$ as nominal wages rise in response to low unemployment at Y_2. Aggregate output falls back to Y_1, the aggregate price level rises again to P_3, and the economy self-corrects as it returns to long-run macro-economic equilibrium at E_3.

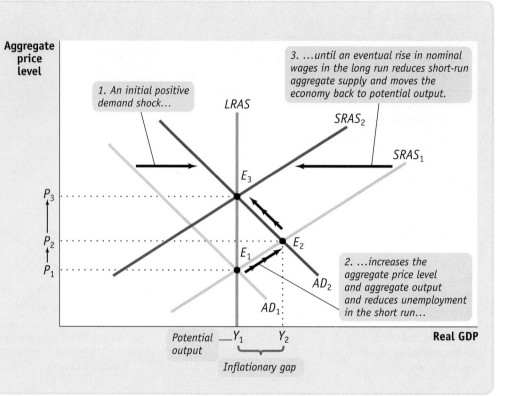

There is an **inflationary gap** when aggregate output is above potential output.

In the long run the economy is **self-correcting**: shocks to aggregate demand affect aggregate output in the short run but not the long run.

level, at Y_2, as the economy settles in the short run at E_2. Aggregate output in this new short-run equilibrium is above potential output, and unemployment is low in order to produce this higher level of aggregate output. When this happens, the economy experiences an **inflationary gap.** As in the case of a recessionary gap, this isn't the end of the story. In the face of low unemployment, nominal wages will rise, as will other sticky prices. An inflationary gap causes the short-run aggregate supply curve to shift gradually to the left as producers reduce output in the face of rising nominal wages. This process continues until $SRAS_1$ reaches its new position at $SRAS_2$, bringing the economy to equilibrium at E_3, where AD_2, $SRAS_2$, and $LRAS$ all intersect. At E_3, the economy is back in long-run macroeconomic equilibrium. It is back at potential output, but at a higher price level, P_3, reflecting a long-run rise in the aggregate price level. Again, the economy is self-correcting in the long run.

There is an important lesson about the macroeconomy to be learned from this analysis. When there is a recessionary gap, nominal wages eventually fall, moving the economy back to potential output. And when there is an inflationary gap, nominal wages eventually rise, also moving the economy back to potential output. So in the long run the economy is **self-correcting:** shocks to aggregate demand affect aggregate output in the short run but not in the long run.

economics in action

Supply Shocks versus Demand Shocks in Practice

How often do supply shocks and demand shocks, respectively, cause recessions? The verdict of most, though not all, macroeconomists is that recessions are mainly caused by demand shocks. But when a negative supply shock does happen, the resulting recession tends to be particularly nasty.

Let's get specific. Officially there have been ten recessions in the United States since World War II. However, two of these, in 1979–1980 and 1981–1982, are often treated as a single "double-dip" recession, bringing the total number down to nine. Of these nine recessions, only two—the recession of 1973–1975 and the double-dip recession of 1979–1982—showed the distinctive combination of falling aggregate output and a surge in the price level that we call stagflation. In each case, the cause of the supply shock was political turmoil in the Middle East—the Arab–Israeli war of 1973 and the Iranian revolution of 1979—that disrupted world oil supplies and sent oil prices skyrocketing. In fact, economists sometimes refer to the two slumps as "OPEC I" and "OPEC II," after the Organization of Petroleum Exporting Countries, the world oil cartel.

So seven of nine postwar recessions were the result of demand shocks, not supply shocks. The two supply-shock recessions, however, were the two worst as measured by the unemployment rate. Figure 10-17 shows the U.S. unemployment rate since 1948, with the dates of the 1973 Arab–Israeli war and the 1979 Iranian revolution marked on the graph. The two highest unemployment rates since World War II came after these two big negative supply shocks.

There's a reason the aftermath of a supply shock is particularly nasty: macroeconomic policy has a much harder time dealing with supply shocks than with demand shocks. We'll see why in a minute.

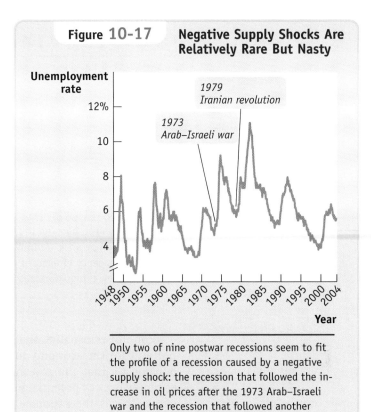

Figure 10-17   Negative Supply Shocks Are Relatively Rare But Nasty

Only two of nine postwar recessions seem to fit the profile of a recession caused by a negative supply shock: the recession that followed the increase in oil prices after the 1973 Arab–Israeli war and the recession that followed another surge in oil prices after the Iranian revolution. These two recessions were, however, the worst in terms of unemployment.

> >

1. Describe the short-run effects of each of the following shocks on the aggregate price level and on aggregate output.
   a. The government sharply increases the minimum wage, raising the wages of many workers.
   b. Solar energy firms launch a major program of investment spending.
   c. Congress raises taxes and cuts spending.
   d. Severe weather destroys crops around the world.

2. A rise in productivity increases potential output, but some worry that demand for the additional output will be insufficient even in the long run. How would you respond?

Solutions appear at back of book.

Macroeconomic Policy

We've just seen that the economy is self-correcting in the long run: it will eventually trend back to potential output. Most macroeconomists believe, however, that the process of self-correction takes several years—typically a decade or more. In particular, if aggregate output is below potential output, the economy can suffer an extended period of depressed aggregate output and high unemployment before it returns to normal.

This belief is the background to one of the most famous quotations in economics: John Maynard Keynes's declaration, "In the long run we are all dead." We explain the context in which he made this remark in For Inquiring Minds on page 262.

>>QUICK REVIEW

➤ *Short-run macroeconomic equilibrium* occurs at the intersection of the short-run aggregate supply and aggregate demand curves.
➤ A *supply shock*, a shift of the *SRAS* curve, causes the aggregate price level and aggregate output to move in opposite directions. A *demand shock*, a shift of the *AD* curve, causes them to move in the same direction. *Stagflation* is the consequence of a negative supply shock.
➤ The economy is *self-correcting* in the long run. A fall in nominal wages occurs in response to a *recessionary gap*, and a rise in nominal wages occurs in response to an *inflationary gap*. Both move the economy to *long-run macroeconomic equilibrium*, where the *AD*, *SRAS*, and *LRAS* curves intersect.

FOR INQUIRING MINDS

KEYNES AND THE LONG RUN

The British economist Sir John Maynard Keynes (1883–1946), probably more than any other single economist, created the modern field of macroeconomics. We'll look at his role, and the controversies that still swirl around some aspects of his thought, in Chapter 17. But for now let's just look at his most famous quote.

In 1923 Keynes published *A Tract on Monetary Reform,* a small book on the economic problems of Europe after World War I. In it he decried the tendency of many of his colleagues to focus on how things work out in the long run—as in the long-run macroeconomic equilibrium we have just analyzed—while ignoring the often very painful and possibly disastrous things that can happen along the way. Here's a fuller version of the quote:

> This *long run* is a misleading guide to current affairs. *In the long run* we are all dead. Economists set themselves too easy, too useless a task if in tempestuous seasons they can only tell us that when the storm is long past the sea is flat again.

Economists usually interpret Keynes as having recommended that governments not wait for the economy to correct itself. Instead, it is argued by many economists, but not all, that the government should use monetary and fiscal policy to get the economy back to potential output in the aftermath of a shift of the aggregate demand curve. This is the rationale for an active stabilization policy, which we defined in Chapter 6 as the use of government policy to reduce the severity of recessions and rein in excessively strong expansions.

Can stabilization policy improve the economy's performance? If we reexamine Figure 10-4, the answer certainly appears to be yes. Under active stabilization policy, the U.S. economy returned to potential output in 1996 after an approximately six-year recessionary gap. Likewise, in 2001 it also returned to potential output after an approximately four-year inflationary gap. These periods are much shorter than the decade or more that economists believe it would take for the economy to self-correct in the absence of active stabilization policy. However, as we'll see shortly, the ability to improve the economy's performance is not always guaranteed. It depends on the kinds of shocks the economy faces.

Policy in the Face of Demand Shocks

Imagine that the economy experiences a negative demand shock, like the one shown in Figure 10-15. As we've discussed in this chapter, monetary and fiscal policy shift the aggregate demand curve. If policy makers react quickly to the fall in aggregate demand, they can use monetary or fiscal policy to shift the aggregate demand curve back to the right. And if policy were able to perfectly anticipate shifts of the aggregate demand curve, it could short-circuit the whole process shown in Figure 10-15. Instead of going through a period of low aggregate output and falling prices, the government could manage the economy so that it would stay at E_1.

Why might a policy that short-circuits the adjustment shown in Figure 10-15, and maintains the economy at its original equilibrium, be desirable? For two reasons. First, the temporary fall in aggregate output that would happen without policy intervention is a bad thing, particularly because such a decline is associated with high unemployment. Second, as we explained briefly in Chapter 6 and will explain at greater length in Chapter 16, *price stability* is generally regarded as a desirable goal. So preventing deflation—a fall in the aggregate price level—is a good thing.

Does this mean that policy makers should always act to offset declines in aggregate demand? Not necessarily. Some policy measures to increase aggregate demand, especially those that increase budget deficits, may have long-term costs in terms of lower long-run growth, such as the crowding out of private investment spending. Furthermore, in the real world policy makers aren't perfectly informed, and the effects of their policies aren't perfectly predictable. This creates the danger that stabilization policy will do more harm than good; that is, that attempts to stabilize the economy may end up creating more instability. We'll describe the long-running debate over macroeconomic policy in Chapter 17. Despite these qualifications, most economists believe that a good case can be made for using macroeconomic policy to offset major negative shocks to the *AD* curve.

Should policy makers also try to offset positive shocks to aggregate demand? It may not seem obvious that they should. After all, even though inflation may be a bad thing, aren't more output and lower unemployment a good thing? Not necessarily. As we'll see in Chapter 16, most economists now believe that any short-run gains from an inflationary gap must be paid back later. So policy makers today usually try to offset positive as well as negative demand shocks. We can see evidence of this in panel (a) of Figure 10-4. For reasons we'll explain in Chapter 17, attempts to eliminate recessionary gaps and inflationary gaps usually rely on monetary rather than fiscal policy. During the recessionary gap of the early 1990s the Federal Reserve cut interest rates to stimulate consumer and investment spending. And it raised interest rates during the inflationary gap of the late 1990s to generate the opposite effect.

But how should macroeconomic policy respond to supply shocks?

Responding to Supply Shocks

We've now come full circle to the story that began this chapter. We can now explain why the stagflationary recessions of the 1970s posed such a policy puzzle.

Back in panel (a) of Figure 10-12 we showed the effects of a negative supply shock: in the short run such a shock leads to lower aggregate output but a higher aggregate price level. As we've noted, policy makers can respond to a negative *demand* shock by using monetary and fiscal policy to return aggregate demand to its original level. But what can or should they do about a negative *supply* shock?

In contrast to the aggregate demand curve, there are no easy policies that shift the short-run aggregate supply curve. That is, there is no government policy that can easily affect producers' profitability and so compensate for shifts of the short-run aggregate supply curve. So the policy response to a negative supply shock cannot be simply to try to push the curve that shifted back to its original position.

And if you consider using monetary or fiscal policy to shift the aggregate demand curve in response to a supply shock, the right response isn't obvious. Two bad things are happening simultaneously: a fall in aggregate output *and* a rise in the aggregate price level. Any policy that shifts the aggregate demand curve helps one problem only by making the other worse. If the government acts to increase aggregate demand, it reduces the decline in output but causes more inflation. If it acts to reduce aggregate demand, it curbs inflation but causes a further decline in output.

It's a nasty trade-off. In the end, as we'll see in Chapter 17, the United States and other economically advanced nations suffering from the supply shocks of the 1970s chose to stabilize prices. But being an economic policy maker in the 1970s meant facing even harder choices than usual.

economics in action

The End of the Great Depression

In 1939, a full decade after the 1929 stock market crash, the U.S. economy remained deeply depressed, with 17% of the labor force unemployed. But then the economy began a rapid recovery, growing an amazing 12% per year until 1944. By 1943 the unemployment rate had fallen below 2%.

Library of Congress, Washington, DC

A spectacular rise in government spending on arms during World War II spurred women to enter the workforce in droves and was the catalyst that ended the Great Depression.

What caused this turnaround? The answer, without question, was the huge increase in aggregate demand caused by World War II.

Although World War II began in September 1939, the United States didn't become a combatant until the attack on Pearl Harbor in December 1941. But the war boosted aggregate demand before the United States became involved in the fighting. A U.S. military buildup began as soon as the risk of war was apparent. In addition, Britain began buying large amounts of U.S. military equipment and other goods during 1940, boosting U.S. exports. And once the United States was directly involved, government spending on arms increased at a spectacular rate.

Did the behavior of prices match the predictions of the *AS–AD* model? Yes. At the height of the war, many goods were subject to price controls and rationing. Still, the aggregate price level as measured by the GDP deflator rose 30% during the war years and shot up further after the war as controls were removed. ∎

‹ ‹ ‹ ‹ ‹ ‹ ‹ ‹ ‹ ‹ ‹ ‹ ‹ ‹ ‹ ‹ ‹ ‹ ‹

›› CHECK YOUR UNDERSTANDING 10-5

1. Suppose someone says, "Expansionary monetary or fiscal policy does nothing but temporarily overstimulate the economy—you get a brief high, but then you have the pain of inflation."
   a. Explain what this means in terms of the *AS–AD* model.
   b. Is this a valid argument against stabilization policy? Why or why not?

Solutions appear at back of book.

• A LOOK AHEAD •

The *AS–AD* model is a powerful tool for understanding both economic fluctuations and the ways economic policy can sometimes fight adverse shocks. But in order to present the basic idea, we've been somewhat sketchy about the details.

In the next three chapters we'll put some flesh on these economic bones. We'll begin with a more detailed analysis of the factors that determine aggregate demand, then move on to how fiscal and monetary policy actually work.

›› QUICK REVIEW

➤ Stabilization policy is the use of fiscal or monetary policy to offset demand shocks. There can be drawbacks, however. Such policies may lead to a long-term rise in the budget deficit and lower long-run growth from crowding out. And, due to incorrect predictions, a misguided policy can increase economic instability.

➤ Negative supply shocks pose a policy dilemma because fighting the slump in aggregate output worsens inflation and fighting inflation worsens the slump.

➤ The role of World War II in ending the Great Depression is the classic example of how fiscal policy can increase aggregate demand and thereby increase aggregate output.

SUMMARY

1. The **aggregate supply curve** shows the relationship between the aggregate price level and the quantity of aggregate output supplied.

2. The **short-run aggregate supply curve** is upward-sloping because **nominal wages** are sticky in the short run: a higher aggregate price level leads to higher profit per unit output and increased aggregate output in the short run. Changes in commodity prices, nominal wages, and productivity lead to changes in producers' profits and shift the short-run aggregate supply curve.

3. In the long run, all prices, including nominal wages, are flexible and the economy produces at its **potential output.** If actual aggregate output exceeds potential output, nominal wages will eventually rise in response to low unemployment and aggregate output will fall. If potential output exceeds actual aggregate output, nominal wages will eventually fall in response to high unemployment and aggregate output will rise. So the **long-run aggregate supply curve** is vertical at potential output.

4. The **aggregate demand curve** shows the relationship between the aggregate price level and the quantity of aggregate output demanded. It is downward-sloping for two reasons. The first is the **wealth effect of a change in the aggregate price level**—a higher aggregate price level reduces the purchasing power of households' wealth and reduces consumer spending. The second is the **interest rate effect of a change in the aggregate price level**—a higher aggregate price level reduces the purchasing power of households' and firms' money holdings, leading to a rise in interest rates and a fall in investment spending and consumer spending. The aggregate demand curve shifts because of changes in expectations, changes in wealth not due to changes in the aggregate price level, and changes in the stock of physical capital. Policy makers can use fiscal policy and monetary policy to shift the aggregate demand curve.

5. An **autonomous change in aggregate spending** leads to a chain reaction in which the total change in real GDP is equal to the **multiplier** times the initial change in aggregate spending. The size of the multiplier, $1/(1 - MPC)$, depends on the **marginal propensity to consume,** MPC, the fraction of an additional dollar of disposable income spent on consumption. The larger the MPC, the larger the multiplier and the larger the change in real GDP for any given autonomous change in aggregate spending. The **marginal propensity to save,** MPS, is equal to $1 - MPC$.

6. In the **AS–AD model,** the intersection of the short-run aggregate supply curve and the aggregate demand curve is the point of **short-run macroeconomic equilibrium.** It determines the **short-run equilibrium aggregate price level** and the level of **short-run equilibrium aggregate output.**

7. Economic fluctuations occur because of a shift of the short-run aggregate supply curve (a *supply shock*) or the aggregate demand curve (a *demand shock*). A **supply shock** causes the aggregate price level and aggregate output to move in opposite directions as the economy moves along the aggregate demand curve . A particularly nasty occurrence is **stagflation**—inflation and falling aggregate output—which is caused by a negative supply shock. A **demand shock** causes them to move in the same direction as the economy moves along the short-run aggregate supply curve.

8. Demand shocks have only short-run effects on aggregate output because the economy is **self-correcting** in the long run. In a **recessionary gap,** an eventual fall in nominal wages moves the economy to **long-run macroeconomic equilibrium,** where aggregate output is equal to potential output. In an **inflationary gap,** an eventual rise in nominal wages moves the economy to long-run macroeconomic equilibrium.

9. The high cost—in terms of unemployment—of a recessionary gap and the future adverse consequences of an inflationary gap lead many economists to advocate active stabilization policy: using fiscal or monetary policy to offset demand shocks. Fiscal policy affects aggregate demand directly through government purchases and indirectly through changes in taxes or government transfers that affect consumer spending. Monetary policy affects aggregate demand indirectly through changes in the interest rate that affect consumer and investment spending. There can be drawbacks, however, because such policies may contribute to a long-term rise in the budget deficit and crowding out of private investment, leading to lower long-run growth. Also, erroneous predictions can increase economic instability.

10. Negative supply shocks pose a policy dilemma: a policy that counteracts the fall in aggregate output by increasing aggregate demand will lead to higher inflation, but a policy that counteracts inflation by reducing aggregate demand will deepen the output slump.

KEY TERMS

Aggregate supply curve, p. 237
Nominal wage, p. 238
Short-run aggregate supply curve, p. 238
Long-run aggregate supply curve, p. 242
Potential output, p. 243
Aggregate demand curve, p. 246
Wealth effect of a change in the aggregate price level, p. 247
Interest rate effect of a change in the aggregate price level, p. 248

Marginal propensity to consume (MPC), p. 251
Marginal propensity to save (MPS), p. 252
Autonomous change in aggregate spending, p. 254
Multiplier, p. 254
AS–AD model, p. 255
Short-run macroeconomic equilibrium, p. 255
Short-run equilibrium aggregate price level, p. 255

Short-run equilibrium aggregate output, p. 255
Supply shock, p. 256
Stagflation, p. 257
Demand shock, p. 257
Long-run macroeconomic equilibrium, p. 258
Recessionary gap, p. 259
Inflationary gap, p. 260
Self-correcting, p. 260

PROBLEMS

1. Your study partner is confused by the upward-sloping short-run aggregate supply curve and the vertical long-run aggregate supply curve. How would you explain why these slopes differ?

2. Suppose that in Wageland all workers sign annual wage contracts each year on January 1. No matter what happens to prices of final goods and services during the year, all workers earn the wage specified in their annual contract. This year, prices of final goods and services fall unexpectedly after the contracts are signed. Answer the following questions using a diagram and assume that the economy starts at potential output.

   a. In the short run, how will the quantity of aggregate output supplied respond to the fall in prices?

   b. What will happen when firms and workers renegotiate their wages?

3. In each of the following cases, in the short run, determine whether the events cause a shift of a curve or a movement along a curve. Determine which curve is involved and the direction of the change.

   a. As a result of an increase in the value of the dollar in relation to other currencies, American producers now pay less in dollar terms for foreign steel, a major commodity used in production.

   b. An increase in the quantity of money by the Federal Reserve increases the quantity of money that people and firms wish to lend, lowering interest rates.

   c. Greater union activity leads to higher nominal wages.

   d. A fall in the aggregate price level increases the purchasing power of households' money holdings. As a result, they borrow less and lend more.

4. A fall in the value of the dollar against other currencies makes U.S. final goods and services cheaper to foreigners even though the U.S. aggregate price level stays the same. As a result, foreigners demand more American aggregate output. Your study partner says that this represents a movement down the aggregate demand curve because foreigners are demanding more in response to a lower price. You, however, insist that this represents a rightward shift of the aggregate demand curve. Who is right? Explain.

5. Suppose that local, state, and federal governments were obliged to cut government purchases whenever consumer spending falls. Then suppose that consumer spending falls due to a fall in the stock market. Draw a diagram and explain the full effect of the fall in the stock market on the aggregate demand curve and on the economy. How is this similar to the experience of stagflation in the 1970s?

6. Due to an increase in consumer wealth, there is a $40 billion autonomous increase in consumer spending in the economies of Westlandia and Eastlandia. Assuming that the aggregate price level is constant, the interest rate is fixed in both countries, and there are no taxes and no foreign trade, complete the accompanying tables to show the various rounds of increased spending that will occur in both economies if the marginal propensity to consume is 0.5 in Westlandia and 0.75 in Eastlandia. What do your results indicate about the relationship between the size of the marginal propensity to consume and the multiplier?

Westlandia

Rounds	Incremental change in GDP		Total change in GDP
1	$\Delta C = \$40$ billion		?
2	$MPC \times \Delta C =$	?	?
3	$MPC \times MPC \times \Delta C =$	?	?
4	$MPC \times MPC \times MPC \times \Delta C =$	?	?
. . .		. . .	. . .
Total change in GDP	$(1/(1 - MPC)) \times \Delta C =$		?

Eastlandia

Rounds	Incremental change in GDP		Total change in GDP
1	$\Delta C = \$40$ billion		?
2	$MPC \times \Delta C =$	?	?
3	$MPC \times MPC \times \Delta C =$	?	?
4	$MPC \times MPC \times MPC \times \Delta C =$	?	?
. . .	. . . . . .		
Total change in GDP	$(1/(1 - MPC)) \times \Delta C =$		?

7. Assuming that the aggregate price level is constant, the interest rate is fixed, and there are no taxes and no foreign trade, how much will the aggregate demand curve shift and in what direction if the following events occur?

   a. An autonomous increase in consumer spending of $25 billion; the marginal propensity to consume is 2/3.

   b. Firms reduce investment spending by $40 billion; the marginal propensity to consume is 0.8.

   c. The government increases its purchases of military equipment by $60 billion; the marginal propensity to consume is 0.6.

8. The economy is at point A in the accompanying diagram. Suppose that the aggregate price level rises from P_1 to P_2. How will aggregate supply adjust in the short run and in the long run to the increase in the aggregate price level?

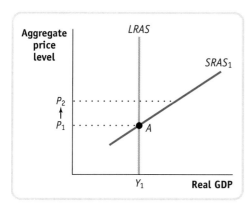

9. Suppose that all households hold all their wealth in assets that automatically rise in value when the aggregate price level rises (an example of this is what is called an "inflation-indexed bond"—a bond whose interest rate, among other things, changes one-for-one with the inflation rate). What happens to the wealth effect of a change in the aggregate price level as a result of this allocation of assets? What happens to the slope of the aggregate demand curve? Will it still slope downward? Explain.

10. Suppose that the economy is currently at potential output. Also suppose that you are an economic policy maker and that a college economics student asks you to rank, if possible, your most preferred to least preferred type of shock: positive demand shock, negative demand shock, positive supply shock, negative supply shock. How would you rank them and why?

11. Explain whether the following government policies affect the aggregate demand curve or the short-run aggregate supply curve and how.

    a. The government reduces the minimum nominal wage.

    b. The government increases Temporary Assistance to Needy Families (TANF) payments, government transfers to families with dependent children.

    c. To reduce the budget deficit, the government announces that households will pay much higher taxes beginning next year.

    d. The government reduces military spending.

12. In Wageland, all workers sign an annual wage contract each year on January 1. In late January, a new computer operating system is introduced that increases labor productivity dramatically. Explain how Wageland will move from one short-run macroeconomic equilibrium to another. Illustrate with a diagram.

13. Using aggregate demand, short-run aggregate supply, and long-run aggregate supply curves, explain the process by which each of the following economic events will move the economy from one long-run macroeconomic equilibrium to another. Illustrate with diagrams. In each case, what are the short-run and long-run effects on the aggregate price level and aggregate output?

    a. There is a decrease in households' wealth due to a decline in the stock market.

    b. The government lowers taxes, leaving households with more disposable income, with no corresponding reduction in government purchases.

14. Using aggregate demand, short-run aggregate supply, and long-run aggregate supply curves, explain the process by which each of the following government policies will move the economy from one long-run macroeconomic equilibrium to another. Illustrate with diagrams. In each case, what are the short-run and long-run effects on the aggregate price level and aggregate output?

    a. There is an increase in taxes on households.

    b. There is an increase in the quantity of money.

    c. There is an increase in government purchases.

15. The economy is in short-run macroeconomic equilibrium at point E_1 in the accompanying diagram.

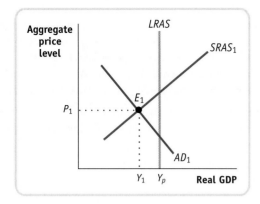

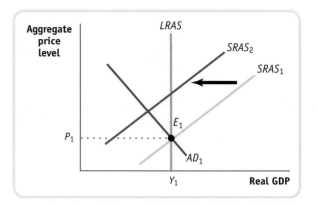

a. Is the economy facing an inflationary or a recessionary gap?

b. What policies can the government implement that might bring the economy back to long-run macroeconomic equilibrium? Illustrate with a diagram.

c. If the government did not intervene to close this gap, would the economy return to long-run macroeconomic equilibrium? Explain and illustrate with a diagram.

d. What are the advantages and disadvantages of the government's implementing policies to close the gap?

16. In the accompanying diagram, the economy is in long-run macroeconomic equilibrium at point E_1 when an oil shock shifts the short-run aggregate supply curve to $SRAS_2$.

a. How do the aggregate price level and aggregate output change in the short run as a result of the oil shock? What is this phenomenon known as?

b. What fiscal or monetary policies can the government use to address the effects of the negative supply shock? Use a diagram that shows the effect of policies chosen to address the change in real GDP. Use another diagram to show the effect of policies chosen to address the change in the aggregate price level.

c. Why do negative supply shocks present a dilemma for government policy makers?

17. The late 1990s in the United States were characterized by substantial economic growth with low inflation; that is, real GDP increased with little, if any, increase in the aggregate price level. Explain this experience using aggregate demand and aggregate supply curves. Illustrate with a diagram.

>>Income and Expenditure

BE A PATRIOT AND SPEND

AFTER THE TERRORIST ATTACKS ON September 11, 2001, many leading figures in American life made speeches urging the shocked nation to show fortitude—and keep buying consumer goods. "Do your business around the country. Fly and enjoy America's great destination spots," urged President Bush. "Go shopping," said former president Clinton.

Such words were a far cry from British prime minister Winston Churchill's famous 1940 declaration, in the face of an imminent Nazi invasion of the United Kingdom, that he had nothing to offer but "blood, toil, tears, and sweat." But there was a reason politicians of both parties called for spending, not sacrifice. The economy was already in recession, mainly because of a 14% drop in real investment spending. A plunge in consumer spending would have greatly deepened the recession. Fortunately, that didn't happen: American consumers bought less of some goods and services, such as air travel, but bought more of others.

As we explained in Chapter 10, the source of most, but not all, recessions since World War II has been negative demand shocks, leftward shifts of the aggregate demand curve. Over the course of this and the next three chapters, we'll continue to focus on the short-run behavior of the economy, looking in detail at the factors that cause such shifts of the aggregate demand curve. In this chapter, we begin by looking at the determinants of consumer

After 9/11, Americans traveled less but shopped more for goods that they could enjoy at home like barbecue grills and swimming pools.

What you will learn in this chapter:

➤ The meaning of the **aggregate consumption function,** which shows how current disposable income affects consumer spending

➤ How expected future income and aggregate wealth affect consumer spending

➤ The determinants of investment spending, and the distinction between **planned investment spending** and **unplanned inventory investment**

➤ How the inventory adjustment process moves the economy to a new equilibrium after a demand shock

➤ Why investment spending is considered a leading indicator of the future state of the economy

spending and investment spending. We'll examine in further detail the multiplier process discussed in Chapter 10, the process by which slumps or booms in aggregate spending are amplified throughout the economy over a period of time. We'll see how changes in investment spending are crucial to the multistage multiplier process that eventually moves the economy to a new equilibrium. Through this analysis we'll come to understand why investment spending and inventory levels are considered to be key indicators of the future state of the economy.

Consumer Spending

Should you splurge on a restaurant meal or save money by eating at home? Should you buy a new car and, if so, how expensive a model? Should you redo that bathroom or live with it for another year? In the real world, households are constantly confronted with such choices—not just about the consumption mix but about how much to spend in total. These choices, in turn, have a powerful effect on the economy: consumer spending normally accounts for two-thirds of total spending on final goods and services. So changes in consumer spending can produce significant shifts of the aggregate demand curve. And as we know from Chapter 10, the position of the aggregate demand curve, along with the position of the short-run aggregate supply curve, determines the economy's aggregate output and aggregate price level in the short run.

But what determines how much consumers spend? In Chapter 10, we learned that consumer spending is affected by wealth and by the interest rate. Here, we'll focus on two additional significant factors, current disposable income and expected future disposable income, in addition to exploring further the effect of wealth.

Current Disposable Income and Consumer Spending

The most important factor affecting a family's consumer spending is its current disposable income—income after taxes are paid and government transfers are received. It's obvious from daily life that people with high disposable incomes on average drive more expensive cars, live in more expensive houses, and spend more on meals and clothing than people with lower disposable incomes. And the relationship between current disposable income and spending is clear in the data.

The Bureau of Labor Statistics (BLS) collects annual data on family income and spending. Families are grouped by levels of before-tax income, and after-tax income for each group is also reported. Since the income figures include transfers from the government, what the BLS calls a household's after-tax income is equivalent to its current disposable income.

Figure 11-1 is a scatter diagram illustrating the relationship between household current disposable income and household consumer spending for American households by income group in 2003. For example, point A shows that among the group with an annual income of $40,000 to $49,999, average household current disposable income was $42,842 and average household consumer spending was $39,757 in 2003. It's clear that households with higher current disposable income had higher consumer spending.

It's very useful to represent the relationship between an individual household's current disposable income and its consumer spending with an equation. The **consumption function** is an equation showing how an individual household's consumer spending varies with the household's current disposable income. The simplest version of a consumption function is a linear equation:

(11-1) $c = a + MPC \times yd$

where lowercase letters indicate variables measured for an individual household.

The **consumption function** is an equation showing how an individual household's consumer spending varies with the household's current disposable income.

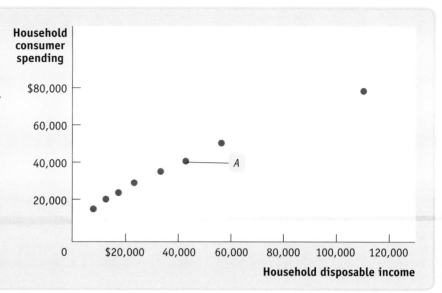

Figure 11-1

Current Disposable Income and Consumer Spending for American Households in 2003

For each income group of households, average current disposable income in 2003 is plotted versus average consumer spending in 2003. For example, point A shows that among the group with an annual income of $40,000 to $49,999, a household's average current disposable income was $42,842 and average household consumer spending was $39,757. The data clearly show a positive relationship between current disposable income and consumer spending: families with higher current disposable income have higher consumer spending.
Source: Bureau of Labor Statistics.

In this equation, c is individual household consumer spending and yd is individual household current disposable income. As we learned in Chapter 10, MPC, the marginal propensity to consume, is the amount by which consumer spending rises if current disposable income rises by $1. Finally, a is a constant term—individual household *autonomous consumer spending,* the amount of spending a household would do if it had zero disposable income. We assume that a is greater than zero because a household with zero disposable income is able to fund some consumption by borrowing or using its savings.

Recall Equation 10-3, which expressed MPC as the ratio of a change in consumer spending to the change in current disposable income. We've rewritten it for an individual household as Equation 11-2:

(11-2) $MPC = \Delta c / \Delta yd$

Multiplying both sides of Equation 11-2 by Δyd, we get:

(11-3) $MPC \times \Delta yd = \Delta c$

Equation 11-3 tells us that when yd goes up by $1, c goes up by $MPC \times \$1$. Notice, by the way, that we're using y for income. That's standard practice in macroeconomics, even though *income* isn't actually spelled "yncome." The reason is that I is reserved for investment spending.

Figure 11-2 on page 272 shows what Equation 11-1 looks like graphically, plotting yd on the horizontal axis and c on the vertical axis. Individual household autonomous consumer spending, a, is the value of c when yd is zero—it is the vertical *intercept* of the consumption function, cf. MPC is the *slope* of the line, measured by rise over run. If current disposable income rises by Δyd, household consumer spending, c, rises by Δc. Since MPC is defined as $\Delta c / \Delta yd$, the slope of the consumption function is:

(11-4) Slope of consumption function
= Rise over run
= $\Delta c / \Delta yd$
= MPC

In reality, actual data never fit Equation 11-1 perfectly, but the fit can be pretty good. Figure 11-3 on page 272 shows the data from Figure 11-1 again, together with a line drawn to fit the data as closely as possible. According to the data on households' consumer spending and current disposable income, the best estimate of a is $14,184 and of MPC is 0.597. So the consumption function fitted to the data is:

$$c = \$14,184 + 0.597 \times yd$$

Figure 11-2

The Consumption Function

The consumption function relates a household's current disposable income to its consumer spending. The vertical intercept, *a*, is individual household autonomous consumer spending: the amount of a household's consumer spending if its current disposable income is zero. The slope of the consumption function line, *cf*, is the marginal propensity to consume, or *MPC*: of every additional $1 of current disposable income, *MPC* × $1 is spent.

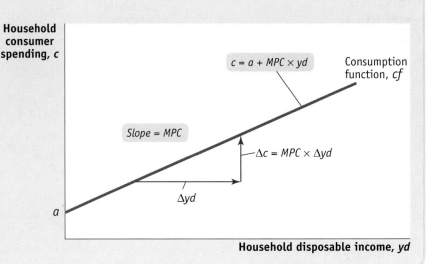

That is, the data suggest a marginal propensity to consume of approximately 0.6. This implies that the marginal propensity to save (*MPS*)—the amount of an additional $1 of disposable income that is saved—is approximately 0.4.

It's important to realize that Figure 11-3 shows a *microeconomic* relationship between the current disposable income of individual families and their spending on goods and services. However, macroeconomists assume that a similar relationship holds *for the economy as a whole*: that there is a relationship, called the **aggregate consumption function,** between aggregate current disposable income and aggregate consumer spending. So we'll assume that it has the same form as the household-level consumption function: $C = A + MPC \times YD$. Here, *C* is aggregate consumer spending (called just "consumer spending"); *YD* is aggregate current disposable income (called just "disposable income"); and *A* is aggregate autonomous consumer spending, the amount of consumer spending when *YD* equals zero. This is the relationship represented in Figure 11-4 by *CF*, analogous to *cf* in Figure 11-3.

The **aggregate consumption function** is the relationship for the economy as a whole between aggregate current disposable income and aggregate consumer spending.

Figure 11-3

A Consumption Function Fitted to Data

The data from Figure 11-1 are reproduced here, along with a line drawn to fit the data as closely as possible. For American households in 2003, the best estimate of the average household's autonomous consumer spending, *a* is $14,184 and the best estimate of *MPC* is 0.597, or approximately 0.6.

Source: Bureau of Labor Statistics.

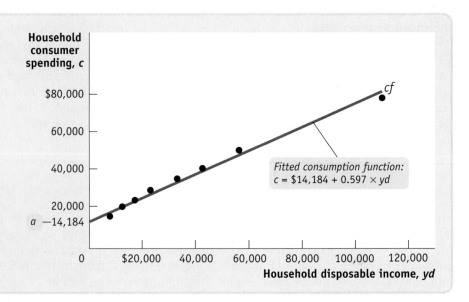

Shifts of the Aggregate Consumption Function

The aggregate consumption function shows the relationship between disposable income and consumer spending for the economy as a whole, other things equal. When things other than disposable income change, the aggregate consumption function shifts. There are two principal causes of shifts of the aggregate consumption function: changes in expected future disposable income and changes in aggregate wealth.

Changes in Expected Future Disposable Income Suppose you land a really good, well-paying job on graduating from college—but the job, and the paychecks, won't start until September. So your disposable income hasn't risen yet. Even so, it's likely that you will start spending more on final goods and services right away—maybe buying nicer work clothes than you originally planned—because you know that the income is coming.

Conversely, suppose you have a good job but learn that the company is planning to downsize your division, raising the possibility that you may lose your job and have to take a lower-paying one somewhere else. Even though your disposable income hasn't gone down yet, you might well cut back on spending even while still employed, to save for a rainy day.

Both of these examples show how expectations about future disposable income can affect consumer spending. The two panels of Figure 11-4, which plot disposable income against consumer spending, show how changes in expected future disposable income affect the aggregate consumption function. In both panels, CF_1 is the initial aggregate consumption function. Panel (a) shows the effect of good news: information that leads consumers to expect higher disposable income in the future than they

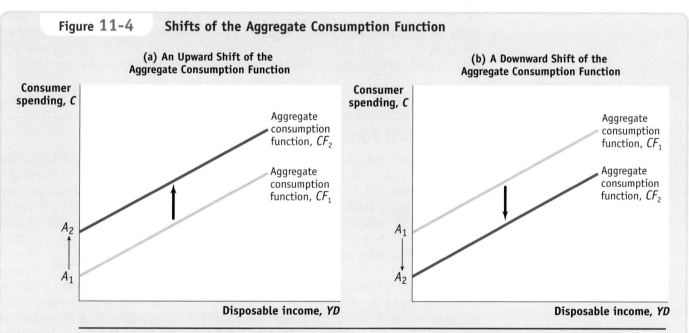

Figure 11-4   Shifts of the Aggregate Consumption Function

(a) An Upward Shift of the Aggregate Consumption Function

Consumer spending, C

Aggregate consumption function, CF_2

Aggregate consumption function, CF_1

A_2

A_1

Disposable income, YD

(b) A Downward Shift of the Aggregate Consumption Function

Consumer spending, C

Aggregate consumption function, CF_1

Aggregate consumption function, CF_2

A_1

A_2

Disposable income, YD

Panel (a) illustrates the effect of an increase in expected future disposable income. Consumers will spend more at every given level of current disposable income, YD. As a result, the initial aggregate consumption function CF_1, with aggregate autonomous consumer spending A_1, shifts up to a new position at CF_2 and aggregate autonomous consumer spending A_2. An increase in aggregate wealth will also shift the aggregate consumption function up. Panel (b), in contrast, illustrates

the effect of a reduction in expected future disposable income. Consumers will spend less at every given level of current disposable income, YD. Consequently, the initial aggregate consumption function CF_1, with aggregate autonomous consumer spending A_1, shifts down to a new position at CF_2 and aggregate autonomous consumer spending A_2. A reduction in aggregate wealth will have the same effect.

did before. Consumers will now spend more at any given level of current disposable income YD, corresponding to an increase in A, aggregate autonomous consumer spending, from A_1 to A_2. The effect is to shift the aggregate consumption function up, from CF_1 to CF_2. Panel (b) shows the effect of bad news: information that leads consumers to expect lower disposable income in the future than they did before. Consumers will now spend less at any given level of current disposable income YD, corresponding to a fall in A from A_1 to A_2. The effect is to shift the aggregate consumption function down, from CF_1 to CF_2.

Changes in Aggregate Wealth As we discussed in Chapter 10, a household's wealth influences how much of its disposable income it spends. This observation is part of an economic model of how consumers make choices about spending versus saving, called the *life-cycle hypothesis*. According to this hypothesis, consumers plan their spending over a lifetime, not just in response to their current disposable income. As a result, people try to *smooth* their consumption over their lifetimes—they save some of their current disposable income during their years of peak earnings (typically occurring during a worker's 40s and 50s) and live off the wealth they have accumulated while working during their retirement. We won't go into the details of this hypothesis but will simply point out that it implies an important role for wealth in determining consumer spending. For example, a middle-aged couple who have accumulated a lot of wealth—who have paid off the mortgage on their house and already own plenty of stocks and bonds—will, other things equal, spend more on goods and services than a couple who have the same current disposable income but still need to save for their retirement.

Because wealth affects household consumer spending, changes in wealth across the economy can shift the aggregate consumption function. A rise in aggregate wealth—say, because of rising housing values, which make homeowners wealthier—increases the vertical intercept A, aggregate autonomous consumer spending. This, in turn, shifts the aggregate consumption function up in the same way as does an expected increase in future disposable income. A decline in aggregate wealth—say, because of a stock market crash—reduces A and shifts the aggregate consumption function down.

economics in action

Famous First Forecasting Failures

The Great Depression created modern macroeconomics. It also gave birth to the modern field of econometrics—the use of statistical techniques to fit economic models to empirical data. The aggregate consumption function was one of the first things econometricians studied. And, sure enough, they quickly experienced one of the first major failures of economic forecasting: consumer spending after World War II was much higher than estimates of the aggregate consumption function based on prewar data would have predicted.

Figure 11-5 tells the story. Panel (a) shows aggregate data on disposable income and consumer spending from 1929 to 1941. A simple linear consumption function, CF_1, seems to fit the data very well. And many economists thought this relationship would continue to hold in the future. But panel (b) shows what actually happened in later years. The points in the circle at the left are the data from the Great Depression shown in panel (a). The points in the circle at the right are data from 1946 to 1960. (Data from 1942 to 1945 aren't included because rationing during World War II prevented consumers from spending normally.) The solid line in the figure, CF_1, is the consumption function fitted to 1929–1941 data. As you can see, post–World War II consumer spending was much higher than the relationship from the Depression years would have predicted. For example, in 1960 consumer spending was 13.5% higher than the level predicted by CF_1.

Why was extrapolating from the earlier relationship so misleading? The answer is that from 1946 onward both expected future disposable income and aggregate

Figure 11-5 Changes in the Aggregate Consumption Function Over Time

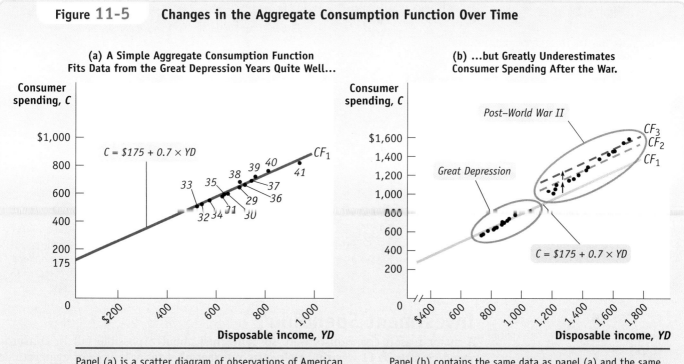

Panel (a) is a scatter diagram of observations of American households' annual disposable income measured in billions of 2000 dollars versus annual consumer spending, also in billions of 2000 dollars, during the period 1929–1941. A simple consumption function, CF_1 of the form $C = \$175 + 0.7 \times YD$, fits the data quite well and suggests that during the Great Depression the marginal propensity to consume was 0.7.

Panel (b) contains the same data as panel (a) and the same consumption function, as well as observations from the post-World War II period. CF_1 lies below the postwar observations and does not fit the data from those years well. In fact, the consumption function shifted up over time, as shown in the figure by the dashed lines, CF_2 and CF_3. **>web...**

Source: Commerce Department.

wealth were steadily rising. Consumers grew increasingly confident that the Great Depression wouldn't reemerge and that the post–World War II economic boom would continue. At the same time, wealth was steadily increasing. As indicated by the dashed lines in panel (b), CF_2 and CF_3, the increases in expected future disposable income and in aggregate wealth shifted the aggregate consumption function up a number of times.

In macroeconomics, failure—whether of economic policy or of economic prediction—often leads to intellectual progress. The embarrassing failure of early estimates of the aggregate consumption function to predict post–World War II consumer spending led to important progress in our understanding of consumer behavior. ■

> >

>>CHECK YOUR UNDERSTANDING 11-1

1. Suppose the economy consists of three people: Angelina, Felicia, and Marina. The table shows how their consumer spending varies as their current disposable income rises by $10,000.
   a. Derive each individual person's consumption function, where *MPC* is calculated for a $10,000 change in current disposable income.
   b. Derive the aggregate consumption function.

2. Suppose that problems in the capital markets make consumers unable to borrow or save.

Current disposable income	Consumer spending		
	Angelina	Felicia	Marina
$0	$8,000	$6,500	$7,250
10,000	12,000	14,500	14,250

What implication does this have for the effects of expected future disposable income on consumer spending?

Solutions appear at back of book.

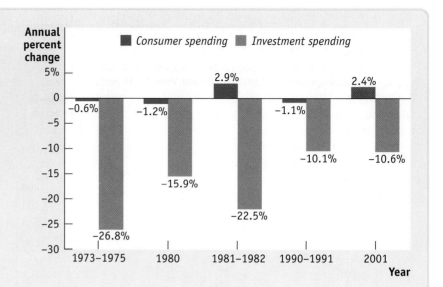

Figure 11-6

Fluctuations in Investment Spending and Consumer Spending

The bars illustrate the annual percent change in investment spending and consumer spending during the last five recessions. As the lengths of the bars show, swings in investment spending were much larger in percentage terms than those in consumer spending. This pattern has led economists to believe that recessions typically originate as a slump in investment spending.

Investment Spending

A major reason economists were so concerned about a possible fall in consumer spending after 9/11 was that there was no clear alternative source of aggregate demand that would offset a fall in consumer spending and keep the economy from plunging. At the time of the attacks, investment spending was in the midst of an 18-month slump and showed few signs of bouncing back. An increase in government spending would take too long to legislate and implement. And there was no feasible way to stimulate foreigners' demand for American goods and services.

Most economists viewed the ongoing slump in investment spending as the cause of the recession that had begun six months earlier in March 2001. As we know from the *AS–AD* model in Chapter 10, a fall in investment spending shifts the aggregate demand curve leftward, leading to a recession. In fact, most recessions originate as a fall in investment spending. Figure 11-6 illustrates this point; it shows the annual percent change of investment spending and consumer spending in the United States, both measured in 2000 dollars, during the last five recessions. As you can see, swings in investment spending are much more dramatic than those in consumer spending. In addition, due to the multiplier process introduced in Chapter 10, economists believe that declines in consumer spending are usually the result of a process that begins with a slump in investment spending. We'll examine very soon how a slump in investment spending generates a fall in consumer spending through the multiplier process. Before we do that, however, let's analyze the factors that determine investment spending, which are somewhat different from those that determine consumer spending. The most important ones are the interest rate and expected future real GDP. We'll also revisit a fact that we noted in For Inquiring Minds on page 216 in Chapter 9: the level of investment spending businesses *actually* carry out is sometimes not the same as the level they had *planned* to undertake.

The Interest Rate and Investment Spending

Planned investment spending is the investment spending that firms intend to undertake during a given period, in contrast to investment spending that occurs but is *unplanned*. Planned investment spending depends on three principal factors: the interest rate, the expected future level of real GDP, and the current level of production capacity. First, we'll analyze the effect of the interest rate.

Let's begin by recalling the loanable funds model of Chapter 9, which showed how those with funds to lend are matched with those who wish to borrow. Potential lenders are households that are deciding whether to save some of their disposable income and

Planned investment spending is the investment spending that businesses intend to undertake during a given period.

lend it out to earn interest, or to spend it on consumption. The supply curve of loanable funds is upward-sloping: as the interest rate rises, households are more willing to forgo consumption and lend their funds out. On the other side are potential borrowers, firms with investment spending projects. They will choose to borrow in order to fund a project only if the rate of return on the project equals or exceeds the interest rate charged on the loan. Otherwise, the firm would incur a loss. The demand curve for loanable funds is downward-sloping: as the interest rate rises, the number of projects with a rate of return that equals or exceeds the interest rate falls. Equilibrium in the loanable funds market is determined by the intersection of the demand and supply curves for loanable funds: at the equilibrium interest rate, the quantity of loanable funds demanded is equal to the quantity supplied. Investment projects with a rate of return equal to or exceeding the equilibrium interest rate are funded; projects with a rate of return less than the equilibrium interest rate are not.

You might think that the trade-off a firm faces is different if it can fund its investment project with its past profits rather than through borrowing. Past profits used to finance investment spending are called *retained earnings*. But even if a firm pays for investment spending out of retained earnings, the trade-off it must make in deciding whether or not to fund a project remains the same because it must take into account the opportunity cost of its funds. For example, instead of purchasing new equipment, the firm could lend out the funds and earn interest. The forgone interest earned is the opportunity cost of using retained earnings to fund an investment project. So the trade-off the firm faces when comparing a project's rate of return to the market interest rate has not changed when it uses retained earnings rather than borrowed funds.

The upshot is that regardless of whether a firm funds investment spending through borrowing or retained earnings, a rise in the market interest rate makes any given investment project less profitable. (And if it had been unprofitable before, it is even more unprofitable after a rise in the interest rate.) For example, consider a rise in the interest rate caused by a leftward shift of the supply curve of loanable funds— say, due to fear of a banking crisis that leads households to refuse to deposit their savings in banks that then lend the funds to businesses. Some projects that would have been funded under the initial, lower interest rate will not be funded now; their rates of return are now below the now-higher interest rate. Conversely, a fall in the interest rate makes some investment projects that were unprofitable before now profitable at the now lower interest rate. Some projects that had been unfunded before will be funded now.

So planned investment spending—spending on investment projects that firms voluntarily decide whether or not to undertake—is negatively related to the interest rate. Other things equal, a higher interest rate leads to a lower level of planned investment spending.

Expected Future Real GDP, Production Capacity, and Investment Spending

Suppose a firm has enough capacity to continue to produce the amount it is currently selling but doesn't expect its sales to grow in the future. Then it will engage in investment spending only to replace equipment and structures that are worn out or have been rendered obsolete by new technologies. But if, instead, the firm expects its sales to grow rapidly in the future, it will find its existing production capacity insufficient for its future production needs. So the firm will undertake investment spending to meet those needs. This implies that, other things equal, firms will undertake more investment spending when they expect their sales to grow.

Now suppose that the firm currently has considerably more capacity than necessary to meet current production needs. Even if it expects sales to grow, it won't have to undertake investment spending for a while—not until the growth in sales catches up with its excess capacity. This illustrates the fact that, other things equal, the current level of productive capacity has a negative effect on investment spending: other things equal, the higher the current capacity, the lower investment spending is.

If we put together the effects on investment spending of growth in expected future sales and the size of current production capacity, we can see one situation in which we can be reasonably sure that firms will undertake high levels of investment spending: when their sales are growing very rapidly. In that case, even excess production capacity will soon be used up, leading firms to resume investment spending.

What is an indicator of a high level of sales growth? It's the rate of growth of real GDP. A higher growth rate of real GDP results in a higher level of investment spending while a lower growth rate of real GDP leads to lower planned investment spending. This relationship is summarized in a proposition known as the **accelerator principle.** As we explain in the following Economics in Action, the effects of the accelerator principle play an important role in *investment spending slumps,* periods of low investment spending.

Inventories and Unplanned Investment Spending

Most firms maintain **inventories,** stocks of goods held to satisfy future sales. Firms hold inventories so they can quickly satisfy buyers—a consumer can purchase an item off the shelf rather than waiting for it to be manufactured. In addition, businesses often hold inventories of their inputs to be sure they have a steady supply of necessary materials and spare parts. In 2004 the overall value of inventories in the U.S. economy was estimated at $1.7 trillion, about 13% of GDP for that year.

As we explained in Chapter 7, a firm that increases its inventories is engaging in a form of investment spending. Suppose, for example, that the U.S. auto industry produces 800,000 cars per month but sells only 700,000. The remaining 100,000 cars are added to the inventory at auto company warehouses or car dealerships, ready to be sold in the future. **Inventory investment** is the value of the change in total inventories held in the economy during a given period. Unlike other forms of investment spending, inventory investment can actually be negative. If, for example, the auto industry reduces its inventory over the course of a month, we say that it has engaged in negative inventory investment.

To understand inventory investment, think about a manager stocking the canned goods section of a supermarket. The manager tries to keep the store fully stocked so that shoppers can almost always find what they're looking for. But the manager does not want the shelves too heavily stocked because shelf space is limited and products can spoil. Similar considerations apply to many firms and typically lead them to manage their inventories carefully. However, sales fluctuate. And because firms cannot always accurately predict sales, they often find themselves holding more or less inventories than they had intended. These unintended swings in inventories due to unforeseen changes in sales are called **unplanned inventory investment.** They represent investment spending, positive or negative, that occurred but was unplanned.

So in any given period, **actual investment spending** is equal to planned investment spending plus unplanned inventory investment. If we let $I_{Unplanned}$ represent unplanned inventory investment, $I_{Planned}$ represent planned investment spending, and I represent actual investment spending, then the relationship among all three can be represented as:

(11-5) $\quad I = I_{Unplanned} + I_{Planned}$

To see how unplanned inventory investment can occur, let's continue to focus on the auto industry and make the following assumptions. First, let's assume that the industry must determine each month's production volume in advance, before it knows the volume of actual sales. Second, let's assume that it anticipates selling 800,000 cars next month and that it plans neither to add to nor subtract from existing inventories. In that case, it will produce 800,000 cars to match anticipated sales.

Now imagine that next month's actual sales are less than expected, only 700,000 cars. As a result, the value of 100,000 cars will be added to investment spending as unplanned inventory investment.

According to the **accelerator principle,** a higher growth rate of GDP leads to higher planned investment spending, and a lower growth rate of real GDP leads to lower planned investment spending.

Inventories are stocks of goods held to satisfy future sales.

This lot full of cars is inventory awaiting the arrival of eager car buyers.

Inventory investment is the value of the change in total inventories held in the economy during a given period.

Unplanned inventory investment occurs when actual sales are more or less than businesses expected, leading to unplanned changes in inventories.

Actual investment spending is the sum of planned investment spending and unplanned inventory investment.

The auto industry will, of course, eventually adjust to this slowdown in sales and the resulting unplanned inventory investment. It is likely that it will cut next month's production volume in order to reduce inventories. In fact, economists who study macroeconomic variables in an attempt to determine the future path of the economy pay careful attention to changes in inventory levels. Rising inventories typically indicate positive unplanned inventory investment and a slowing economy, as sales are less than had been forecast. Falling inventories typically indicate negative unplanned inventory investment and a growing economy, as sales are greater than forecast. In the next section, we will see how production adjustments in response to fluctuations in sales and inventories ensure that the value of final goods and services actually produced is equal to desired purchases of those final goods and services.

economics in action

A Tale of Two Investment Spending Slumps

At the beginning of the 1980s there was a prolonged slump in investment spending, which played a key role in the two recessions—often treated as a single episode—of 1980 and 1981–1982. At the beginning of the twenty-first century there was another prolonged investment spending slump, which played a key role in the 2001 recession and the disappointing "jobless recovery" of the next two years.

But these investment spending slumps were very different. The 1980s slump was mainly in housing; nonresidential investment spending remained fairly strong. The slump that began in 2001 was entirely in nonresidential investment spending; by 2003 there was actually a boom in housing construction.

Figure 11-7 tells the tale. Panel (a) shows the behavior of the level of nonresidential and residential (housing) investment spending, measured in 2000 dollars, during the slump of the early 1980s. The levels of both types of investment spending are measured in real terms as an index number, with 1979 fourth-quarter real values set equal to 100. You can see that the early 1980s slump was concentrated in residential, that is, housing,

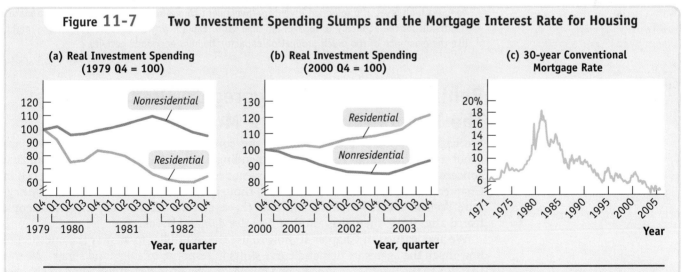

Figure 11-7 **Two Investment Spending Slumps and the Mortgage Interest Rate for Housing**

(a) Real Investment Spending (1979 Q4 = 100)

(b) Real Investment Spending (2000 Q4 = 100)

(c) 30-year Conventional Mortgage Rate

Panels (a) and (b) show the quantities of nonresidential and residential (housing) investment spending during two investment slumps. In each case, quantities are measured as index numbers, with the level just before the slump equal to 100. The slump of the early 1980s was concentrated in residential investment spending, but residential investment spending rose after 2000, and eventually turned into a boom. Panel (c) shows the source of the difference: the interest rate on 30-year mortgages, loans that many people use to buy homes, soared in the early 1980s but fell after 2000. *Source:* Commerce Department.

investment spending. Panel (b) shows the same comparison starting in the fourth quarter of 2000, measured so that 2000 fourth-quarter real values equal 100. In this case, the investment spending slump was entirely concentrated in nonresidential investment spending; housing investment spending remained high through the recession, then went up from there.

This difference in residential investment spending was due to interest rates, which shot up during the early 1980s but fell during the years after 2000. Panel (c) shows the interest rate on 30-year home mortgage loans. The rate soared to its highest level ever in the early 1980s; it fell to its lowest level in decades after 2000.

So why did nonresidential investment spending fall 15% during 2001 and 2002? It was high during the late 1990s in large part because of the accelerator principle: firms believed the economy would grow rapidly, and this encouraged investment spending. When firms became somewhat less optimistic in 2000–2001, this led to a fall in planned investment spending. Also, the high investment spending of the late 1990s left some firms with larger production capacities than they needed. This was especially true in telecommunications, where companies found themselves with lots of "dark fiber": fiber-optic cables (used to transmit phone calls and other data) that turned out not to be needed, at least for the time being. So firms cut back sharply on investment spending, waiting for demand to catch up with capacity. ∎

< < < < < < < < < < < < < < < < < < <

>>CHECK YOUR UNDERSTANDING 11-2

1. For each event, explain whether planned investment spending or unplanned inventory investment will change and in what direction.
   a. An unexpected increase in consumer spending.
   b. A sharp rise in the cost of business borrowing.
   c. A sharp increase in the economy's growth rate of real GDP.
   d. An unanticipated fall in sales.

2. Historically, investment spending has experienced more extreme upward and downward swings than consumer spending. Why do you think this is so? (*Hint:* Consider the marginal propensity to consume and the accelerator principle.)

3. Consumer demand was sluggish during 2002 and economists worried that an *inventory overhang*—a high level of unplanned inventory investment throughout the economy—would make it difficult for the economy to recover anytime soon. Explain why an inventory overhang might, like the existence of too much production capacity, depress economic activity.

Solutions appear at back of book.

Behind Shifts of the Aggregate Demand Curve: The Income-Expenditure Model

We began this chapter by describing the concern voiced by American politicians about a possible slump in consumer spending after 9/11. We can understand that concern in terms of the analysis of short-run economic fluctuations we developed in Chapter 10. There we learned that most, though not all, recessions are caused by negative *demand shocks*—leftward shifts of the aggregate demand curve. What people feared after 9/11, then, was another negative demand shock.

We also learned in Chapter 10 how to use the multiplier to answer the question of how much the aggregate demand curve shifts in response to a demand shock. We saw that due to the multistage process of a change in aggregate demand leading to changes in real GDP, disposable income, and consumer spending, the magnitude of the shift of the aggregate demand curve is several multiples of the size of the original demand shock. In this section, we will examine this multistage process more closely. We'll see that the multiple rounds of changes in real GDP are accomplished through changes in the amount of output produced by firms—changes that they make in response to changes in their inventories. And we'll come to understand why inventories play a central role in macroeconomic models of the economy in the short run, and why economists pay particular attention to the behavior of firms' inventories when trying to understand the likely future state of the economy.

Before we begin, let's quickly recap the assumptions underlying the multiplier process.

1. *The aggregate price level is fixed.* In other words, we'll analyze the determination of aggregate output as if the short-run aggregate supply curve, *SRAS,* is horizontal at a given aggregate price level. This is in contrast to the upward-sloping short-run aggregate supply curve of the *AS–AD* model. A fixed aggregate price level also implies that there is no difference between nominal GDP and real GDP. As a result, we can use the two terms interchangeably in this chapter.

2. *The interest rate is fixed.* We'll take the interest rate as predetermined and unaffected by the factors we analyze in the model. As in the case of the aggregate price level, what we're really doing here is leaving the determinants of the interest rate outside the model. As we'll see, the model can still be used to study the effects of a change in the interest rate.

3. *Taxes, government transfers, and government purchases are all zero.*

4. *There is no foreign trade.*

The Chapter 12 Appendix addresses how taxes affect the multiplier process. In all subsequent chapters we will drop the assumption that the aggregate price level is fixed. We'll explain how the interest rate is determined in Chapter 14 and bring foreign trade back into the picture in Chapter 18.

Planned Aggregate Spending and Real GDP

In an economy with no government and no foreign trade, there are only two sources of aggregate demand: consumer spending, *C,* and investment spending, *I.* And since we assume that there are no taxes or transfers, aggregate disposable income is equal to GDP (which, since the aggregate price level is fixed, is the same as real GDP): the total value of final sales of goods and services ultimately accrues to households as income. So in this highly simplified economy, there are two basic equations of national income accounting:

(11-6) $GDP = C + I$

(11-7) $YD = GDP$

As we learned earlier in this chapter, the *aggregate consumption function* shows the relationship between disposable income and consumer spending. Let's continue to assume that the aggregate consumption function is of the form:

(11-8) $C = A + MPC \times YD$

In our simplified model, we will also assume planned investment spending, $I_{Planned}$, is fixed.

We need one more concept before putting the model together: **planned aggregate spending,** the total amount of planned spending in the economy. Unlike firms, households don't take unintended actions. So planned aggregate spending is equal to the sum of consumer spending and planned investment spending. We denote planned aggregate spending by $AE_{Planned}$, so

(11-9) $AE_{Planned} = C + I_{Planned}$

The level of planned aggregate spending in a given year depends on the level of real GDP in that year. To see why, let's look at a specific example, shown in Table 11-1 on page 282. We assume that the aggregate consumption function is

(11-10) $C = 300 + 0.6 \times YD$

Planned aggregate spending is the total amount of planned spending in the economy.

TABLE 11-1

Real GDP	YD	C	$I_{Planned}$	$AE_{Planned}$
		(billions of dollars)		
$0	$0	$300	$500	$800
500	500	600	500	1,100
1,000	1,000	900	500	1,400
1,500	1,500	1,200	500	1,700
2,000	2,000	1,500	500	2,000
2,500	2,500	1,800	500	2,300
3,000	3,000	2,100	500	2,600
3,500	3,500	2,400	500	2,900

Real GDP, YD, C, $I_{Planned}$, and $AE_{Planned}$ are all measured in billions of dollars, and we assume that the level of planned investment, $I_{Planned}$, is fixed at $500 billion per year. The first column shows possible levels of real GDP. The second column shows disposable income, YD, which in our simplified model is equal to real GDP. The third column shows consumer spending, C, equal to $300 billion plus 0.6 times disposable income, YD. The fourth column shows planned investment spending, $I_{Planned}$, which we have assumed is $500 billion regardless of the level of real GDP. Finally, the last column shows planned aggregate spending, $AE_{Planned}$, the sum of aggregate consumer spending, C, and planned investment spending, $I_{Planned}$. (To economize on notation, we'll assume that it is understood from now on that all the variables in Table 11-1 are measured in billions of dollars per year.) As you can see, a higher level of real GDP leads to a higher level of disposable income: every 500 increase in real GDP raises YD by 500, which in turn raises C by 500 × 0.6 = 300 and $AE_{Planned}$ by 300.

Figure 11-8 illustrates the information in Table 11-1 graphically. Real GDP is measured on the horizontal axis. CF is the aggregate consumption function; it shows how consumer spending depends on real GDP. $AE_{Planned}$, the planned aggregate spending line, corresponds to the aggregate consumption function shifted up by 500 (the amount of $I_{Planned}$). It shows how planned aggregate spending depends on real GDP. Both lines have a slope of 0.6, equal to MPC, the marginal propensity to consume.

But this isn't the end of the story. Table 11-1 reveals that at all but one level of real GDP, when real GDP equals 2,000, planned aggregate spending, $AE_{Planned}$, doesn't equal the corresponding level of real GDP. Is that possible? Didn't we learn in Chapter 7, with the circular-flow diagram, that total spending on final goods and services in the economy is equal to the total value of output of final goods and services? The answer is that for *brief* periods of time, planned aggregate spending can differ from real GDP because of the role of *unplanned* aggregate spending—$I_{Unplanned}$, unplanned inventory investment. But as we'll see in the next section, the economy moves over time to a situation in which there is no unplanned inventory investment, called *income–expenditure equilibrium*. And when the economy is in income–expenditure equilibrium, planned aggregate spending on final goods and services equals aggregate output.

Figure 11-8

The Aggregate Consumption Function and Planned Aggregate Spending

The lower line, *CF*, is the aggregate consumption function constructed from the data in Table 11-1. The upper line, $AE_{Planned}$, is the planned aggregate spending line, also constructed from the data in Table 11-1. It is equivalent to the aggregate consumption function shifted up by $500 billion, the amount of planned investment spending, $I_{Planned}$.

>web...

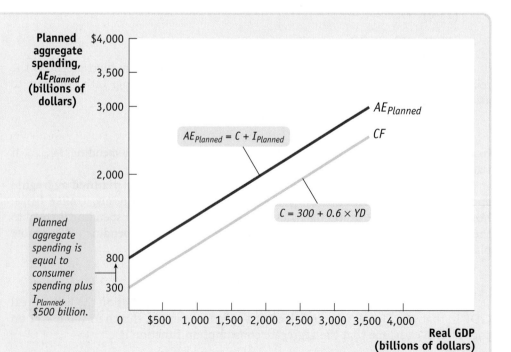

Income–Expenditure Equilibrium

For all but one value of real GDP shown in Table 11-1, real GDP is either more or less than $AE_{Planned}$, the sum of consumer spending and *planned* investment spending. For example, when real GDP is 1,000, consumer spending C is 900 and planned investment spending is 500, making planned aggregate spending 1,400. This is 400 *more* than the corresponding level of real GDP. Now consider what happens when real GDP is 2,500; consumer spending C is 1,800 and planned investment spending is 500, making planned aggregate spending only 2,300, 200 *less* than real GDP.

As we've just explained, planned aggregate spending can be different from real GDP only if there is unplanned inventory investment, $I_{Unplanned}$, in the economy. Let's examine Table 11-2, which includes the numbers for real GDP and for planned aggregate spending from Table 11-1. It also includes the levels of unplanned inventory investment, $I_{Unplanned}$, that each combination of real GDP and planned aggregate spending implies. For example, if real GDP is 2,500, planned aggregate spending is only 2,300. This 200 excess of real GDP over $AE_{Planned}$ must consist of positive unplanned inventory investment. This can happen only if firms have overestimated sales and produced too much, leading to unintended additions to inventories. More generally, any level of real GDP in excess of 2,000 corresponds to a situation in which firms are producing more than consumers and other firms want to purchase, creating an unintended increase in inventories.

Conversely, a level of real GDP below 2,000 implies that planned aggregate spending is *greater* than real GDP. For example, when real GDP is 1,000, planned aggregate spending is much larger, at 1,400. The 400 excess of $AE_{Planned}$ over real GDP corresponds to negative unplanned inventory investment of –400. More generally, any level of real GDP below 2,000 implies that firms have underestimated sales, leading to a negative level of unplanned inventory investment in the economy.

By putting together Equations 11-5, 11-6, and 11-9, we can summarize the general relationship among real GDP, planned aggregate spending, and unplanned inventory investment:

(11-11) $$\begin{aligned} GDP &= C + I \\ &= C + I_{Planned} + I_{Unplanned} \\ &= AE_{Planned} + I_{Unplanned} \end{aligned}$$

So whenever real GDP exceeds $AE_{Planned}$, $I_{Unplanned}$ is positive; whenever real GDP is less than $AE_{Planned}$, $I_{Unplanned}$ is negative.

But firms will act to correct their mistakes: they will reduce production if they have experienced an unintended rise in inventories or increase production if they have experienced an unintended fall in inventories. And these responses will eventually eliminate the unanticipated changes in inventories and move the economy to a point at which real GDP is equal to planned aggregate spending. Staying with our example, if real GDP is 1,000, negative unplanned inventory investment will lead firms to increase production, leading to a rise in real GDP. In fact, this will happen whenever real GDP is less than 2,000—that is, whenever real GDP is less than planned aggregate spending. Conversely, if real GDP is 2,500, positive unplanned inventory investment will lead firms to reduce production, leading to a fall in real GDP. This will happen whenever real GDP is greater than planned aggregate spending.

The only situation in which firms won't have an incentive to change output in the next period is when aggregate output, measured by real GDP, is equal to planned aggregate spending in the current period, an outcome known as **income–expenditure equilibrium.** In Table 11-2, income–expenditure equilibrium is achieved when real GDP is 2,000, the only level of real GDP at which unplanned inventory investment is zero. From now on, we'll denote the real GDP level at which income–expenditure equilibrium occurs as Y* and call it the **income–expenditure equilibrium GDP.**

Figure 11-9 on page 284 illustrates the concept of income–expenditure equilibrium graphically. Real GDP is on the horizontal axis and planned aggregate spending, $AE_{Planned}$, is on the vertical axis. There are two lines in the figure. The solid line is the

TABLE 11-2

Real GDP	$AE_{Planned}$	$I_{Unplanned}$
(billions of dollars)		
$0	$800	–$800
500	1,100	–600
1,000	1,400	–400
1,500	1,700	–200
2,000	2,000	0
2,500	2,300	200
3,000	2,600	400
3,500	2,900	600

The economy is in **income–expenditure equilibrium** when aggregate output, measured by real GDP, is equal to planned aggregate spending.

Income–expenditure equilibrium GDP is the level of real GDP at which real GDP equals planned aggregate spending.

Figure 11-9

Income–Expenditure Equilibrium

Income–expenditure equilibrium occurs at E, the point where the planned aggregate spending line, $AE_{Planned}$, crosses the 45-degree line. At E, the economy produces real GDP of $2,000 billion per year, the only point at which real GDP equals planned aggregate spending, $AE_{Planned}$, and unplanned inventory investment, $I_{Unplanned}$, is zero. This is the level of income–expenditure equilibrium GDP, Y^*. At any level of real GDP less than Y^*, $AE_{Planned}$ exceeds real GDP. As a result, unplanned inventory investment, $I_{Unplanned}$, is negative and firms respond by increasing production. At any level of real GDP greater than Y^*, real GDP exceeds $AE_{Planned}$. Unplanned inventory investment, $I_{Unplanned}$, is positive and firms respond by reducing production. **>web...**

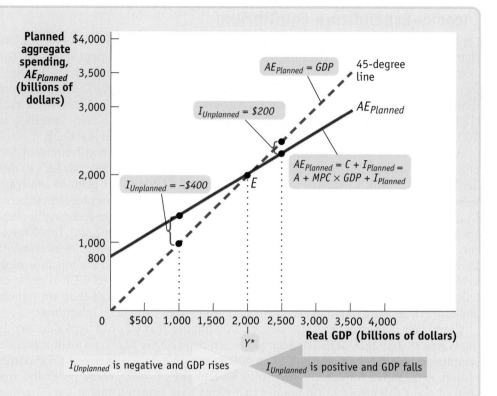

$I_{Unplanned}$ is negative and GDP rises

$I_{Unplanned}$ is positive and GDP falls

INCOME–EXPENDITURE EQUILIBRIUM VERSUS SHORT-RUN MACROECONOMIC EQUILIBRIUM

In Chapter 10 we developed the concept of short-run macroeconomic equilibrium using the *AS–AD* model. Using it, we determined the equilibrium level of real GDP as the level at which the quantity of aggregate output supplied in the short run is equal to the quantity of aggregate output demanded. Here we've introduced another concept, the income–expenditure equilibrium process. Using it, we've defined income–expenditure equilibrium GDP to be the level of real GDP at which planned aggregate spending equals real GDP. So are these concepts of equilibrium in conflict with each other? That is, do they lead to two different and therefore conflicting definitions of what real GDP is when the economy is in short-run macroeconomic equilibrium?

Definitely not. Recall that what we're doing in the income–expenditure model is analyzing how real GDP would change *holding all prices fixed*. To derive the full short-run macroeconomic equilibrium, we need to bring the flexible aggregate price level back in. So income–expenditure equilibrium is a step on the way to calculating macroeconomic equilibrium—one that allows us to closely examine the inventory adjustment process behind a shift of the aggregate demand curve—not an alternative concept.

The **Keynesian cross** diagram identifies income–expenditure equilibrium as the point where the planned aggregate spending line crosses the 45-degree line.

planned aggregate spending line. It shows how $AE_{Planned}$, equal to $C + I_{Planned}$, depends on real GDP; it has a slope of 0.6, equal to the marginal propensity to consume, *MPC*, and a vertical intercept equal to $A + I_{Planned}$ (300 + 500 = 800). The dashed line, which goes through the origin with a slope of 1 (often called a 45-degree line), shows all the possible points at which planned aggregate spending is equal to real GDP. This line allows us to easily spot the point of income-expenditure equilibrium, which must lie on both the 45-degree line and the planned aggregate spending line. So the point of income-expenditure equilibrium is at E, where the two lines cross. And the income–expenditure equilibrium GDP, Y^*, is 2,000—the same outcome we derived in Table 11-2.

Now consider what happens if the economy isn't in income-expenditure equilibrium. We can see from Figure 11-9 that whenever real GDP is less than Y^*, the planned aggregate spending line lies above the 45-degree line and $AE_{Planned}$ exceeds real GDP. In this situation, $I_{Unplanned}$ is negative: as shown in the figure, at a real GDP of 1,000, $I_{Unplanned}$ is −400. As a consequence, real GDP will rise. In contrast, whenever real GDP is greater than Y^*, the planned aggregate expenditure line lies below the 45-degree line. Here, $I_{Unplanned}$ is positive: as shown, at a real GDP of 2,500, $I_{Unplanned}$ is 200. The unanticipated accumulation of inventory leads to a fall in real GDP.

The type of diagram shown in Figure 11-9, which identifies income-expenditure equilibrium as the point at which the planned aggregate spending line crosses the 45-degree line, has a special place in the history of economic thought. Known as the **Keynesian cross,** it was developed by Paul Samuelson, one of the greatest economists of the twentieth century (as well as a Nobel Prize winner), to explain the ideas of John Maynard Keynes, the founder of macroeconomics as we know it.

The Multiplier Process and Inventory Adjustment

We've just learned about a very important feature of the macroeconomy: when planned spending by households and firms does not equal the current aggregate output by firms, there is a self-adjustment process in the economy that moves real GDP over time to the point at which real GDP and planned aggregate spending are equal. And that self-adjustment mechanism operates through inventories. That's why, as we mentioned earlier, changes in inventories are considered a leading indicator of future economic activity.

Now that we understand how real GDP moves to achieve income–expenditure equilibrium for a given level of planned aggregate spending, let's turn to understanding what happens when there is *a shift of the planned aggregate spending line.* How does the economy move from the initial point of income–expenditure equilibrium to a new point of income–expenditure equilibrium? And what are the possible sources of changes in planned aggregate spending?

In our simple model there are only two possible sources of a shift of the planned aggregate spending line: a change in planned investment spending, $I_{Planned}$, or a shift of the consumption function, C. For example, a change in $I_{Planned}$ can occur because of a change in the interest rate. (Remember, we're assuming that the interest rate is fixed by factors that are outside the model. But we can still ask what happens when the interest rate changes.) A shift of the consumption function (that is, a change in its vertical intercept, A) can occur because of a change in aggregate wealth—say, due to a rise in housing values. When the planned aggregate spending line shifts—when there is a change in the level of planned aggregate spending at any given level of real GDP—there is an autonomous change in planned aggregate spending. Recall from Chapter 10 that an autonomous change in planned aggregate spending is a change in the desired level of spending by firms, households, and government at any given level of real GDP (although we've assumed away the government for the time being). How does an autonomous change in planned aggregate spending affect real GDP in income–expenditure equilibrium?

Table 11-3 and panel (a) of Figure 11-10 on page 286 start from the same numerical example we used in Table 11-2 and Figure 11-9. They also show the effect of an autonomous increase in planned aggregate spending of 400—what happens when planned aggregate spending is 400 higher at each level of real GDP. Look first at Table 11-3. Before the autonomous increase in planned aggregate spending, the level of real GDP at which planned aggregate spending is equal to real GDP, Y*, is 2,000. After the autonomous change, Y* has risen to 3,000. The same result is visible in panel (a) of Figure 11-10. The initial income–expenditure equilibrium is at E_1, where Y_1^* is 2,000. The autonomous rise in planned aggregate spending shifts the planned aggregate spending line up, leading to a new income–expenditure equilibrium at E_2, where Y_2^* is 3,000.

The fact that the rise in income–expenditure equilibrium GDP, from 2,000 to 3,000, is much larger than the autonomous increase in aggregate spending, which is only 400, has a familiar explanation: the multiplier process. In the specific example we have just described, an autonomous increase in planned aggregate spending of 400 leads to an increase in Y* from 2,000 to 3,000, a rise of 1,000. So the multiplier in this example is $1,000/400 = 2.5$.

We can examine in detail what underlies the multistage multiplier process by continuing to use panel (a) of Figure 11-10. First, starting from E_1, the autonomous increase in planned aggregate spending leads to a gap between planned aggregate spending and real GDP. This is represented by the vertical distance between X, at 2,400, and E_1, at 2,000. This gap illustrates an unplanned fall in inventory investment: $I_{Unplanned} = -400$. Firms respond by increasing production, leading to a rise in real GDP from Y_1^*. The rise in real GDP translates into an increase in disposable income, YD. That's the first stage in the chain reaction. But it doesn't stop there—the increase in YD leads to a rise in consumer spending, C, which sets off a second-round rise in real GDP. This in turn leads to a further rise in disposable income and consumer spending, and so on. And we could play this process in reverse: an autonomous fall in

TABLE 11-3

Real GDP	$AE_{Planned}$ before autonomous change (billions of dollars)	$AE_{Planned}$ after autonomous change
$0	$800	$1,200
500	1,100	1,500
1,000	1,400	1,800
1,500	1,700	2,100
2,000	2,000	2,400
2,500	2,300	2,700
3,000	2,600	3,000
3,500	2,900	3,300
4,000	3,200	3,600

Figure 11-10

The Multiplier

Panel (a) illustrates the change in Y^* caused by an autonomous increase in planned aggregate spending. The economy is initially at equilibrium point E_1 with an income–expenditure equilibrium GDP, Y_1^*, equal to 2,000. An autonomous increase in $AE_{Planned}$ of 400 shifts the planned aggregate spending line upward by 400. The economy is no longer in income–expenditure equilibrium: real GDP is equal to 2,000 but $AE_{Planned}$ is now 2,400, represented by point X. The vertical distance between the two planned aggregate spending lines, equal to 400, represents $I_{Unplanned} = -400$—the negative inventory investment that the economy now experiences. Firms respond by increasing production, and the economy eventually reaches a new income–expenditure equilibrium at E_2 with a higher level of income–expenditure equilibrium GDP, Y_2^*, equal to 3,000. Panel (b) shows the corresponding rightward shift of the AD curve generated by the increase in $AE_{Planned}$. At the conclusion of the multiplier process, $AE_{Planned}$ will have risen by a total of 1,000, 2.5 times as much as the initial increase of 400.

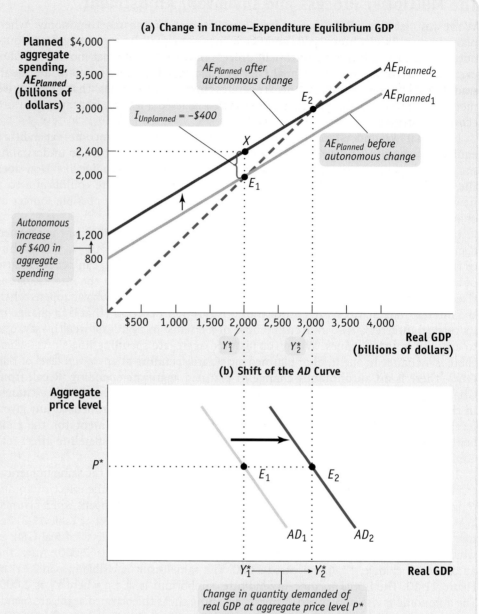

(a) Change in Income–Expenditure Equilibrium GDP

(b) Shift of the AD Curve

Change in quantity demanded of
real GDP at aggregate price level P^*

aggregate spending will lead to a chain reaction of reductions in real GDP and consumer spending.

We can summarize these results in an equation, where ΔAAE represents the autonomous change in $AE_{Planned}$:

$$(11\text{-}12) \quad \Delta Y^* = \text{Multiplier} \times \Delta AAE_{Planned}$$
$$= \frac{1}{1 - MPC} \times \Delta AAE_{Planned}$$

Like Equation 10-6, Equation 11-12 tells us that the change in income–expenditure equilibrium GDP, ΔY^*, is several times as large as the autonomous change in planned aggregate spending, $\Delta AAE_{Planned}$. Equation 11-12 also helps us recall an important point: because the marginal propensity to consume is less than 1, each increase in disposable income and each corresponding increase in consumer spending is smaller than in the previous round. That's because at each round some of the increase in disposable income leaks out into savings. As a result, although real GDP grows at each round, the increase in real GDP diminishes from each round to the next. At some point the increase in real GDP is negligible, and the economy converges to a new income–expenditure equilibrium GDP at Y_2^*.

Now we're in a position to tie the inventory adjustment that underlies the multiplier process to the question of how much the aggregate demand curve shifts in response to a slump or a boom in consumer spending or investment spending. Panel (b) of Figure 11-10 shows the corresponding shift of the aggregate demand curve generated by the events illustrated in panel (a). At a *fixed aggregate price level*, given here by P^*, the change in the quantity of aggregate output demanded is equal to the change in income–expenditure equilibrium GDP that arises from the autonomous change in $AE_{Planned}$ plus the multiplier effect. Again, we see the importance of the multiplier: the larger the multiplier, the larger the shift of the AD curve at any given aggregate price level.

The Paradox of Thrift You may recall that in Chapter 6 we mentioned the Paradox of Thrift to illustrate the fact that, in macroeconomics, the outcome of many individual actions can generate a result that is different and worse than the simple sum of those individual actions. In the Paradox of Thrift, households and firms cut their spending in anticipation of future tough economic times. These actions depress the economy, leaving households and firms worse off than if they hadn't acted virtuously to prepare for tough times. It is called a paradox because what's usually "good" (saving to provide for your family in hard times) is "bad" (because it can make everyone worse off).

Using the multiplier, we can now see exactly how this scenario unfolds. Suppose that there is a slump in consumer spending or investment spending, or both, which causes a fall in income–expenditure equilibrium GDP that is several times larger than the original fall in spending. The fall in real GDP leaves consumers and producers worse off than they would have been if they hadn't cut their spending. Conversely, prodigal behavior is rewarded: if consumers or producers increase their spending, the resulting multiplier process makes the increase in income–expenditure equilibrium GDP several times larger than the original increase in spending. So prodigal spending makes consumers and producers better off than if they had been cautious spenders.

It's important to realize that setting the multiplier equal to $1/(1 - MPC)$ depends on the simplifying assumption that there are no taxes or transfers, so that disposable income is equal to real GDP. In the Appendix to Chapter 12 we'll bring taxes into the picture, which makes the expression for the multiplier more complicated and the multiplier itself smaller. But the general principle we have just learned—an autonomous change in planned aggregate spending leads to a change in income–expenditure equilibrium GDP, both directly and through an induced change in consumer spending—remains valid.

As we noted earlier in this chapter, declines in planned investment spending are usually the major factor in recessions. So historically they have been the most common source of autonomous reductions in aggregate spending. The tendency of the consumption function to shift upward over time, which we pointed out in Economics in Action on page 274, means that autonomous changes in both planned investment spending and consumer spending play important roles in expansions. But regardless of the source, there are multiplier effects in the economy that magnify the size of the initial change in aggregate spending. Recall our opening story about how political leaders urged consumers to open their wallets and spend after 9/11. As we've now learned, the fears of those leaders were understandable: they were concerned that the shock of the terrorist attacks would lead to a reduction in consumer spending that would, through the multiplier effect, greatly worsen the existing recession. Fortunately for the economy, this didn't happen. American consumers were shocked and saddened, but they didn't stop spending. As a result, the economy began to recover only a few months later.

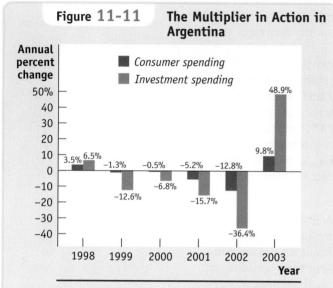

Figure 11-11 **The Multiplier in Action in Argentina**

The most severe recession in recent history was a case of the multiplier at work. The bars show annual rates of change in consumer spending and investment spending in Argentina between 1998 and 2003. A financial crisis led to a plunge in investment spending between 1998 and 2002, leading to a decline in consumer spending. Then an upturn in investment spending led to recovery in consumer spending as well.

economics in action

Bad Times in Buenos Aires

The closest thing the world has seen in recent times to a replay of the Great Depression was the severe recession that hit Argentina from 1998 to 2002. Over that period, Argentina's real GDP fell 18%, and the unemployment rate rose above 20%.

The origins of the Argentine slump lay in a financial crisis: foreign investors lost confidence in the country's ability to repay the debts owed to them, setting in motion a chain reaction that led to bank closings and widespread bankruptcy. But the channel through which the financial crisis caused a recession was the multiplier. Financial difficulties caused by the loss in confidence led to a plunge in planned investment spending. This, in turn, led to a fall in real GDP, both because of the direct effect of the reduction in investment spending and because of the induced fall in consumer spending. Figure 11-11 shows the annual rates of change of real investment spending and real consumer spending in Argentina from 1998 to 2003. As you can see, the slump in investment spending from 1998 to 2002 led to a proportionately smaller decline in consumer spending. Then, when investment spending bounced back in 2003, so did consumer spending. ∎

< < < < < < < < < < < < < < < < <

1. Although economists believe that recessions typically begin as slumps in investment spending, they also believe that consumer spending eventually slumps during a recession. Explain why.

2. a. Use a diagram like Figure 11-10 to show what happens when there is an autonomous fall in planned aggregate spending. Describe how the economy adjusts to a new income–expenditure equilibrium.

   b. Suppose Y^* is originally $500 billion, the autonomous reduction in planned aggregate spending is $300 million ($0.3 billion), and $MPC = 0.5$. Calculate Y^* after such a change.

   Solutions appear at back of book.

● **A LOOK AHEAD** ●

In this chapter we studied the inventory adjustment process that underlies the multiplier. But we used a very simplified model of the determination of aggregate output, leaving out a number of important factors in order to focus our attention on a few key relationships. Now we're ready to bring some of the complications back in—starting with the role of government and government policy.

We begin by introducing taxes, transfers, and government purchases into our model. As we'll see, putting the government in leads us immediately to one of the key insights of macroeconomics: sometimes the government can do something about the business cycle. We'll explore the potential and the difficulties of *fiscal policy*—changes in taxes, transfers, and government purchases designed to affect macroeconomic outcomes—in Chapter 12. Then in Chapters 13 and 14 we'll turn to an even more important tool in the government's hands, *monetary policy*.

SUMMARY

1. The **consumption function** shows how an individual household's consumer spending is determined by its current disposable income. The **aggregate consumption function** shows the relationship for the entire economy. According to the life-cycle hypothesis, households try to smooth their consumption over their lifetime. As a result, the aggregate consumption function shifts in response to changes in expected future disposable income and changes in aggregate wealth.

2. **Planned investment spending** depends negatively on the interest rate and on existing production capacity; it depends positively on expected future real GDP. The **accelerator principle** says that investment spending is greatly influenced by the expected growth rate of real GDP.

3. Firms hold **inventories** of goods so that they can satisfy consumer demand quickly. **Inventory investment** is positive when firms add to their inventories, negative when they reduce them. Often, however, changes in inventories are not a deliberate decision but the result of mistakes in forecasts about sales. The result is **unplanned inventory investment,** which can be either positive or negative. **Actual investment spending** is the sum of planned investment spending and unplanned inventory investment.

4. In **income–expenditure equilibrium, planned aggregate spending,** which in a simplified model with no government and no trade is the sum of consumer spending and planned investment spending, is equal to real GDP. At the **income–expenditure equilibrium GDP,** or Y^*, unplanned inventory investment is zero. When planned aggregate spending is larger than Y^*, unplanned inventory investment is negative; there is an unanticipated reduction in inventories and firms increase production. When planned aggregate spending is less than Y^*, unplanned inventory investment is positive; there is an unanticipated increase in inventories and firms reduce production. The **Keynesian cross** shows how the economy self-adjusts to income–expenditure equilibrium through inventory adjustments.

5. After an autonomous change in planned aggregate spending, the inventory adjustment process moves the economy to a new income–expenditure equilibrium. The change in income–expenditure equilibrium GDP arising from an autonomous change in spending is equal to the multiplier × $\Delta AAE_{Planned}$. Correspondingly, the amount of the shift of the AD curve at any given aggregate price level arising from an autonomous change in investment spending or consumer spending is equal to the multiplier times the autonomous change in spending.

KEY TERMS

PROBLEMS

1. Economists observed the only five residents of a very small economy and estimated each one's consumer spending at various levels of current disposable income. The accompanying table shows each resident's consumer spending at three income levels.

Individual consumer spending by	Individual current disposable income		
	$0	$20,000	$40,000
Andre	1,000	15,000	29,000
Barbara	2,500	12,500	22,500
Casey	2,000	20,000	38,000
Declan	5,000	17,000	29,000
Elena	4,000	19,000	34,000

a. What is each resident's consumption function? What is the marginal propensity to consume for each resident?

b. What is the economy's aggregate consumption function? What is the marginal propensity to consume for the economy?

2. From 2000 to 2005, Eastlandia experienced large fluctuations in both aggregate consumer spending and disposable income, but wealth, the interest rate, and expected future disposable income did not change. The accompanying table on page 290 shows the level of aggregate consumer spending and disposable income in millions of dollars for each of these years. Use this information to answer the following questions.

Year	Disposable income (millions of dollars)	Consumer spending (millions of dollars)
2000	$100	$180
2001	350	380
2002	300	340
2003	400	420
2004	375	400
2005	500	500

a. Plot the aggregate consumption function for Eastlandia.

b. What is the aggregate consumption function?

c. What is the marginal propensity to consume? What is the marginal propensity to save?

3. How will each of the following actions affect the aggregate consumption function? Explain whether the event will result in a movement along or a shift of the aggregate consumption function and in which direction.

a. The government grants an unexpected and one-time tax cut to all households.

b. The government announces permanently higher tax rates beginning next year.

c. The Social Security Administration raises the age at which workers who are currently younger than 65 can qualify for Social Security benefits from age 65 to age 75.

4. From the end of 1995 to March 2000, the Standard and Poor's 500 (S&P 500) stock index, a broad measure of stock market prices, rose almost 150%, from 615.93 to a high of 1,527.46. From that time to September 10, 2001, the index fell 28.5% to 1,092.54. How do you think the movements in the stock index influenced both the growth in real GDP in the late 1990s and the concern about maintaining consumer spending after the terrorist attacks on September 11, 2001?

5. How will the interest rate and planned investment spending change as the following events occur?

a. An increase in the quantity of money by the Federal Reserve increases the amount of money that people wish to lend at any interest rate.

b. The U.S. Environmental Protection Agency decrees that corporations must adopt new technology that reduces their emissions of sulfur dioxide.

c. Baby boomers begin to retire in large numbers and reduce their savings.

6. Explain how each of the following actions will affect the level of planned investment spending and unplanned inventory investment. Assume the economy is initially in income–expenditure equilibrium.

a. The Federal Reserve raises the interest rate.

b. There is a rise in the expected growth rate of real GDP.

c. A sizable inflow of foreign funds into the country lowers the interest rate.

7. The accompanying table shows real gross domestic product (GDP), disposable income (YD), consumer spending (C), and planned investment spending ($I_{Planned}$) in an economy. Assume there is no government or foreign sector in this economy. Complete the table by calculating planned aggregate spending ($AE_{Planned}$) and unplanned inventory investment ($I_{Unplanned}$).

GDP	YD	C	$I_{Planned}$	$AE_{Planned}$	$I_{Unplanned}$
		(billions of dollars)			
$0	$0	$100	$300	?	?
400	400	400	300	?	?
800	800	700	300	?	?
1,200	1,200	1,000	300	?	?
1,600	1,600	1,300	300	?	?
2,000	2,000	1,600	300	?	?
2,400	2,400	1,900	300	?	?
2,800	2,800	2,200	300	?	?
3,200	3,200	2,500	300	?	?

a. What is the aggregate consumption function?

b. What is Y^*, income–expenditure equilibrium GDP?

c. What is the value of the multiplier?

d. If planned investment spending falls to $200 billion, what will be the new Y^*?

e. If autonomous consumer spending rises to $200 billion, what will be the new Y^*?

8. In an economy with no government and no foreign sectors, autonomous consumer spending is $250 billion, planned investment spending is $350 billion, and the marginal propensity to consume is 2/3.

a. Plot the aggregate consumption function and planned aggregate spending.

b. What is unplanned inventory investment when real GDP equals $600 billion?

c. What is Y^*, income–expenditure equilibrium GDP?

d. What is the value of the multiplier?

e. If planned investment spending rises to $450 billion, what will be the new Y^*?

9. An economy has a marginal propensity to consume of 0.5 and Y^*, income–expenditure equilibrium GDP, equals $500 billion. Given an autonomous increase in planned investment of $10 billion, show the rounds of increased spending that take place by completing the accompanying table. The first and second rows are filled in for you. In the first row, the increase in planned investment spending of $10 billion raises real GDP and YD by $10 billion, leading to an increase in consumer spending of $5 billion ($MPC \times$ change in disposable income) in row 2.

	Change in $I_{Planned}$ or C	Change in real GDP	Change in YD
Rounds		(billions of dollars)	
1	$\Delta I_{Planned} = \$10.00$	$10.00	$10.00
2	$\Delta C = \$\ 5.00$	$ 5.00	$ 5.00
3	$\Delta C = ?$	?	?
4	$\Delta C = ?$	?	?
5	$\Delta C = ?$	?	?
6	$\Delta C = ?$	?	?
7	$\Delta C = ?$	?	?
8	$\Delta C = ?$	?	?
9	$\Delta C = ?$	?	?
10	$\Delta C = ?$	?	?

a. What is the total change in real GDP after the 10 rounds? What is the value of the multiplier? What would you expect the total change in Y^* to be based on the multiplier formula? How do your answers to the first and third qestions compare?

b. Redo the table, assuming the marginal propensity to consume is 0.75. What is the total change in real GDP after 10 rounds? What is the value of the multiplier? As the marginal propensity to consume increases, what happens to the value of the multiplier?

10. Although the U.S. is one of the richest nations in the world, it is also the world's largest debtor nation. We often hear that the problem is the nation's low savings rate. Suppose policy makers attempt to rectify this by encouraging greater savings in the economy. What effect will their successful attempts have on real GDP?

> **web...** To continue your study and review of concepts in this chapter, please visit the Krugman/Wells website for quizzes, animated graph tutorials, web links to helpful resources, and more.
> ## www.worthpublishers.com/krugmanwells

>>Chapter 11 Appendix: Deriving the Multiplier Algebraically

This appendix shows how to derive the multiplier algebraically. First recall that in this chapter planned aggregate spending, $AE_{Planned}$, is the sum of consumer spending, C, which is determined by the consumption function, and planned investment spending, $I_{Planned}$. Rewriting equation 11-9 to express all its terms fully, we have:

(11A-1) $AE_{Planned} = A + MPC \times YD + I_{Planned}$

Because there are no taxes or government transfers in this model, disposable income is equal to GDP, so equation 11A-1 becomes:

(11A-2) $AE_{Planned} = A + MPC \times GDP + I_{Planned}$

The income–expenditure equilibrium GDP, Y^*, is equal to planned aggregate spending:

(11A-3) $Y^* = AE_{Planned}$
$= A + MPC \times Y^* + I_{Planned}$
in income–expenditure equilibrium

Just two more steps. Subtract $MPC \times Y^*$ from both sides of Equation 11A-3:

(11A-4) $Y^* - MPC \times Y^* = Y^* \times (1 - MPC) = A + I_{Planned}$

Finally, divide both sides by $(1 - MPC)$:

(11A-5) $Y^* = \dfrac{A + I_{Planned}}{1 - MPC}$

Equation 11A-5 tells us that a \$1 autonomous change in planned aggregate spending— a change in either A or $I_{Planned}$—causes a \$1/(1 - MPC) change in income–expenditure equilibrium GDP, Y^*. The multiplier in our simple model is therefore:

(11A-6) $\text{Multiplier} = 1/(1 - MPC)$

PROBLEMS

1. In an economy without government purchases, transfers, or taxes, aggregate autonomous consumer spending is \$500 billion, planned investment spending is \$250 billion, and the marginal propensity to consume is 0.5.

   a. Write the expression for planned aggregate spending as in Equation 11A-1.

   b. Solve for Y^* algebraically.

   c. What is the value of the multiplier?

   d. How will Y^* change if autonomous consumer spending falls to \$450 billion?

2. Complete the following table by calculating the value of the multiplier and identifiying the change in Y^* due to the change in autonomous spending. How does the value of the multiplier change with the marginal propensity to consume?

MPC	Value of multiplier	Change in spending	Change in Y^*
0.5	?	$\Delta C = + \$50$ million	?
0.6	?	$\Delta I = - \$10$ million	?
0.75	?	$\Delta C = - \$25$ million	?
0.8	?	$\Delta I = + \$20$ million	?
0.9	?	$\Delta C = - \$2.5$ million	?

>>Fiscal Policy

A BRIDGE TO PROSPERITY?

I N 1998 THE JAPANESE GOVERNMENT completed the longest suspension bridge in the world. The 6,500-foot span linking Awaji Island to the city of Kobe cost $7.3 billion to build. Yet as skeptics had predicted, it currently carries very little traffic—about 4,000 cars a day. By comparison, America's longest suspension bridge, the Verrazano Bridge that links New York City's Staten Island to the borough of Brooklyn, carries more than 300,000 cars a day.

In Japan, stories like this are common. During the 1990s the Japanese government spent around $1.4 trillion on infrastructure that included many construction projects of questionable usefulness. But the main purpose of construction spending in Japan wasn't to provide useful infrastructure. It was to prop up aggregate demand.

During the 1990s, the Japanese government built bridges, roads, dams, breakwaters, and even parking garages in an effort to combat persistent shortfalls in aggregate demand. Japan's use of government construction spending to stimulate its economy is an example of *discretionary fiscal policy*—the deliberate use of government spending or taxation to manage aggregate demand. The U.S. government has also tried to spend its way out of economic

slumps, though on a smaller scale. Indeed, many countries attempt to manage aggregate demand by using discretionary fiscal policy. Governments also adjust taxes in an attempt to manage aggregate demand. They may reduce taxes to try to stimulate the economy or raise taxes when they believe that aggregate demand is too high.

In this chapter, we will learn how discretionary fiscal policy fits into the model of short-run fluctuations we developed in Chapter 10. We'll see how deliberate changes in government spending and tax policy affect real GDP. We'll also see how

The Akashi Kaikyo Bridge was built by the Japanese government in the 1990s to prop up aggregate demand.

changes in tax revenue caused by short-run fluctuations in GDP—an automatic response that occurs without deliberate changes in policy—help stabilize the economy. Finally, we'll examine long-run consequences of government debt and budget deficits.

What you will learn in this chapter:

➤ What fiscal policy is and why it is an important tool in managing economic fluctuations

➤ Which policies constitute an **expansionary fiscal policy** and which constitute a **contractionary fiscal policy**

➤ Why fiscal policy has a multiplier effect and how this effect is influenced by **automatic stabilizers**

➤ Why governments calculate the **cyclically adjusted budget balance**

➤ Why a large **public debt** may be a cause for concern

➤ Why **implicit liabilities** of the government are also a cause for concern

Fiscal Policy: The Basics

Let's begin with the obvious: modern governments spend a great deal of money and collect a lot in taxes. Figure 12-1 shows government spending and tax revenue as percentages of GDP for a selection of high-income countries in 2003. As you can see, the Swedish government sector is relatively large, representing nearly 60% of the Swedish

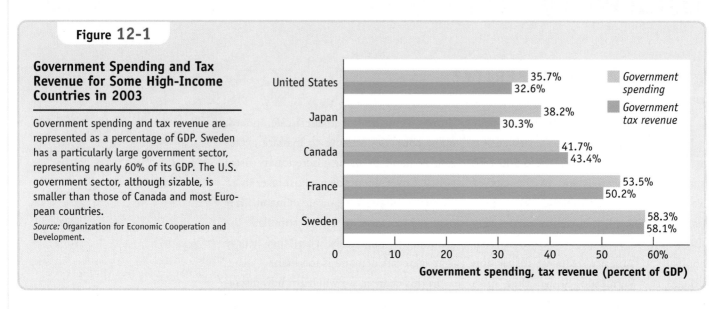

Figure 12-1

Government Spending and Tax Revenue for Some High-Income Countries in 2003

Government spending and tax revenue are represented as a percentage of GDP. Sweden has a particularly large government sector, representing nearly 60% of its GDP. The U.S. government sector, although sizable, is smaller than those of Canada and most European countries.

Source: Organization for Economic Cooperation and Development.

economy. The government of the United States plays a smaller role in the economy than those of Canada or most European countries. But that role is still sizable, meaning that the government plays a major role in the U.S. economy. Changes in the federal budget—changes in government spending or in taxation—can potentially have large effects on the American economy.

To analyze these effects, we begin by showing how taxes and government spending affect the economy's flow of income. Then we can see how changes in spending and tax policy affect aggregate demand.

Taxes, Purchases of Goods and Services, Government Transfers, and Borrowing

In Figure 7-1 we showed the circular flow of income and spending in the economy as a whole. One of the sectors represented in that figure was the government. Funds flow *into* the government in the form of taxes and government borrowing; funds flow *out* in the form of government purchases of goods and services and government transfers to households.

What kinds of taxes do Americans pay, and where does the money go? Figure 12-2 shows the composition of U.S. tax revenue in 2004. Taxes, of course, are required payments to the government. In the United States, taxes are collected at the national level by the federal government; at the state level by each state government; and at the local levels by counties, cities, and towns. At the federal level, the main taxes are income taxes on both personal income and corporate profits as well as *social insurance* taxes, which we'll explain shortly. At the state and local levels, the picture is more complex: these governments rely on a mix of sales taxes,

Figure 12-2 Sources of Tax Revenue in the United States, 2004

Other taxes, 29%

Personal income taxes, 35%

Social insurance taxes, 28%

Corporate profit taxes, 8%

Personal income taxes, taxes on corporate profits, and social insurance taxes account for most government tax revenue. The rest is a mix of property taxes, sales taxes, and other sources of revenue.

Source: Bureau of Economic Analysis.

property taxes, income taxes, and fees of various kinds. Overall, taxes on personal income and corporate profits accounted for 43% of total government revenue in 2004; social insurance taxes accounted for 28%; and a variety of other taxes, collected mainly at the state and local level, accounted for the rest.

Figure 12-3 shows the composition of total U.S. government spending in 2004, which takes two forms. One form is purchases of goods and services. This includes everything from ammunition for the army to the salaries of public schoolteachers (who are treated in the national accounts as providers of a service—education). The big items here are national defense and education. The large category labeled "other goods and services" consists mainly of state and local spending on a variety of services, from police and firefighters to highway construction and maintenance.

The other form of government spending is government transfers, which are payments by the government to households for which no good or service is provided in return. In the modern United States, as well as in Canada and Europe, government transfers represent a very large proportion of the budget. Most U.S. government spending on transfer payments is accounted for by three big programs:

- Social Security, which provides guaranteed income to older Americans, disabled Americans, and the surviving spouses and dependent children of deceased beneficiaries

- Medicare, which covers much of the cost of health care for Americans over 65

- Medicaid, which covers much of the cost of health care for Americans with low incomes

The term **social insurance** is used to describe government programs that are intended to protect families against economic hardship. These include Social Security, Medicare, and Medicaid, as well as smaller programs such as unemployment insurance and food stamps. In the United States, social insurance programs are largely paid for with special, dedicated taxes on wages—the social insurance taxes we mentioned earlier.

But how do tax policy and government spending affect the economy? The answer is that taxation and government spending have a strong effect on total aggregate spending in the economy.

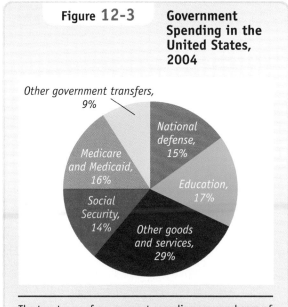

Figure 12-3   Government Spending in the United States, 2004

The two types of government spending are purchases of goods and services and government transfers. The big items in government purchases are national defense and education. The big items in government transfers are Social Security and the Medicare and Medicaid health care programs.

Source: Office of Management and Budget.

Social insurance programs are government programs intended to protect families against economic hardship.

The Government Budget and Total Spending

Let's recall the basic equation of national income accounting:

(12-1) $GDP = C + I + G + X - IM$

The left-hand side of this equation is GDP, the value of all final goods and services produced in the economy. The right-hand side is aggregate spending, total spending on final goods and services produced in the economy. It is the sum of consumer spending (C), investment spending (I), government purchases of goods and services (G), and the value of exports (X) minus the value of imports (IM). It includes all the sources of aggregate demand.

The government directly controls one of the variables on the right-hand side of Equation 12-1: government purchases of goods and services (G). But that's not the only effect fiscal policy has on aggregate spending in the economy. Through changes in taxes and transfers, it also influences consumer spending (C) and, in some cases, investment spending (I).

FOR INQUIRING MINDS

INVESTMENT TAX CREDITS

When we discuss changes in taxes in this chapter, we focus mainly on the effects of these changes on consumer spending. However, there is one tool of fiscal policy that is designed to affect investment spending—*investment tax credits*.

An investment tax credit is a tax break given to firms based on their investment spending. For example, a firm might be allowed to deduct $1 from its tax bill for every $10 it spends on investment goods. This increases the incentive for investment spending.

One more thing about investment tax credits: they're often temporary, applying only to

investment spending within a specific period. For example, Congress introduced an investment tax credit in 2002 that only applied to investment spending over the next two years. Like department store sales that encourage shoppers to spend a lot while the sale is on, temporary investment tax credits tend to generate a lot of investment spending when they're in effect. Even if a firm doesn't think it will need a new server or lathe for another year or so, it may make sense to buy it while the tax credit is available, rather than wait.

To see why the budget affects consumer spending, recall that *disposable income*, the total income households have available to spend, is equal to the total income they receive from wages, dividends, interest, and rent, *minus* taxes, *plus* government transfers. So either an increase in taxes or a decrease in government transfers *reduces* disposable income. And a fall in disposable income, other things equal, leads to a fall in consumer spending. Conversely, either a decrease in taxes or an increase in government transfers *increases* disposable income. And a rise in disposable income, other things equal, leads to a rise in consumer spending.

The government's ability to affect investment spending is a more complex story, which we won't discuss in detail (but see For Inquiring Minds above). The important point is that the government taxes profits, and changes in the rules that determine how much a business owes can increase or reduce the incentive to spend on investment goods.

Because the government itself is one source of aggregate demand in the economy, and because taxes and transfers can affect spending by consumers and firms, the government can use changes in taxes or government spending to *shift the aggregate demand curve*. And as we saw in Chapter 10, there are sometimes good reasons to shift the aggregate demand curve. For example, the Japanese government has spent trillions of dollars in an effort to increase aggregate demand. Japan's use of massive government construction spending to prop up its economy in the 1990s is a classic example of *fiscal policy*: the use of taxes, government transfers, or government purchases of goods and services to stabilize the economy by shifting the aggregate demand curve.

Expansionary and Contractionary Fiscal Policy

Why would the government want to shift the aggregate demand curve? Because it wants to close either a recessionary gap, created when aggregate output falls below potential output, or an inflationary gap, created when aggregate output exceeds potential output.

Figure 12-4 shows the case of an economy facing a recessionary gap. *SRAS* is the short-run aggregate supply curve, *LRAS* is the long-run aggregate supply curve, and AD_1 is the initial aggregate demand curve. At the initial short-run macroeconomic equilibrium, E_1, aggregate output is Y_1, below potential output, Y_P. What the government would like to do is increase aggregate demand, shifting the aggregate demand curve rightward to AD_2. This would increase aggregate output, making it equal to

Figure 12-4

Expansionary Fiscal Policy Can Close a Recessionary Gap

At E_1 the economy is in short-run macroeconomic equilibrium where the aggregate demand curve AD_1 intersects the SRAS curve. At E_1, there is a recessionary gap of $Y_P - Y_1$. An expansionary fiscal policy—an increase in government purchases, a reduction in taxes, or an increase in government transfers—shifts the aggregate demand curve rightward. It can close the recessionary gap by shifting AD_1 to AD_2, moving the economy to a new short-run macroeconomic equilibrium, E_2, which is also a long-run macroeconomic equilibrium. **>web...**

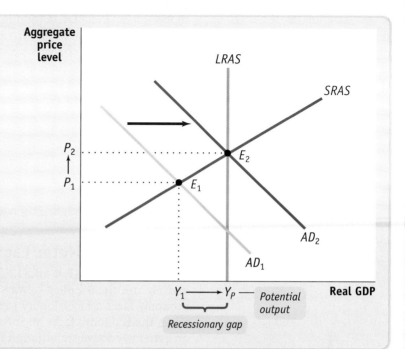

potential output. Fiscal policy that increases aggregate demand, called **expansionary fiscal policy,** normally takes one of three forms:

> **Expansionary fiscal policy** increases aggregate demand.

- An increase in government purchases of goods and services, such as the Japanese government's decision to launch a massive construction program
- A cut in taxes, such as the one the United States implemented in 2001
- An increase in government transfers, such as unemployment benefits

Figure 12-5 shows the opposite case—an economy facing an inflationary gap. Again, SRAS is the short-run aggregate supply curve, LRAS is the long-run aggregate

Figure 12-5

Contractionary Fiscal Policy Can Close an Inflationary Gap

At E_1 the economy is in short-run macroeconomic equilibrium where the aggregate demand curve AD_1 intersects the SRAS curve. At E_1, there is an inflationary gap of $Y_1 - Y_P$. A contractionary fiscal policy—reduced government purchases, an increase in taxes, or a reduction in government transfers—shifts the aggregate demand curve leftward. It can close the inflationary gap by shifting AD_1 to AD_2, moving the economy to a new short-run macroeconomic equilibrium, E_2, which is also a long-run macroeconomic equilibrium. **>web...**

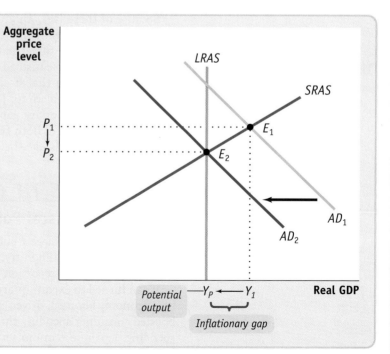

supply curve, and AD_1 is the initial aggregate demand curve. At the initial short-run macroeconomic equilibrium, E_1, aggregate output is Y_1, above potential output, Y_P. As we'll explain in later chapters, policy makers often try to head off inflation by eliminating inflationary gaps. To eliminate the inflationary gap shown in Figure 12-5, fiscal policy must reduce aggregate demand and shift the aggregate demand curve leftward to AD_2. This reduces aggregate output and makes it equal to potential output. Fiscal policy that reduces aggregate demand, called **contractionary fiscal policy,** is the opposite of expansionary fiscal policy. It is implemented by reducing government purchases of goods and services, increasing taxes, or reducing government transfers. A classic example of contractionary fiscal policy occurred in 1968, when U.S. policy makers grew worried about rising inflation. President Lyndon Johnson imposed a temporary 10% surcharge on income taxes—everyone's income taxes were increased by 10%. He also tried to scale back government purchases, which had risen dramatically because of the cost of the Vietnam War.

Contractionary fiscal policy reduces aggregate demand.

A Cautionary Note: Lags in Fiscal Policy

Looking at Figures 12-4 and 12-5, it may seem obvious that the government should actively use fiscal policy—always adopting an expansionary fiscal policy when the economy faces a recessionary gap and always adopting a contractionary fiscal policy when the economy faces an inflationary gap. But many economists caution against an extremely active stabilization policy, arguing that a government that tries too hard to stabilize the economy—through either fiscal policy or monetary policy—can end up making the economy less stable.

We'll leave discussion of the warnings associated with monetary policy to Chapter 17. In the case of fiscal policy, the reason for caution is that there are important *time lags* in its use. To understand the nature of these lags, think about what has to happen before the government increases spending to fight a recessionary gap. First, the government has to realize that the recessionary gap exists: economic data take time to collect and analyze, and recessions are often recognized only months after they have begun. Second, the government has to develop a spending plan, which can itself take months, particularly if politicians take time debating how the money should be spent and passing legislation. Finally, it takes time to spend money. For example, a road construction project begins with activities such as surveying that don't involve spending large sums. It may be quite some time before the big spending begins.

Because of these lags, an attempt to increase spending to fight a recessionary gap may take so long to get going that the recessionary gap may have turned into an inflationary gap by the time the fiscal policy takes effect. In that case, the fiscal policy will make things worse instead of better.

This doesn't mean that fiscal policy should never be actively used. After all, time lags didn't pose a problem for Japanese fiscal policy in the 1990s, which was attempting to fight a recessionary gap that lasted for many years. But the problem of lags makes the actual use of both fiscal and monetary policy harder than you might think from a simple analysis like the one we have just given.

economics in action

Expansionary Fiscal Policy in Japan

"In what may be the biggest public works bonanza since the pharaohs, Japan has spent something like $1.4 trillion trying to pave and build its way back to economic health," began one newspaper report on Japan's efforts to prop up its economy with fiscal policy.

Japan turned to expansionary fiscal policy in the early 1990s. In the 1980s the country's economy boomed, driven in part by soaring values of stocks and real estate, which boosted consumer spending through the wealth effect and also encouraged investment spending. Japanese economists now refer to this period as the "bubble economy," because the rise in stock and land values could not be justified in terms of rational calculations. At the end of the 1980s the bubble burst—stock and land values plunged, and the economy slid into recession as consumer and investment spending fell. Since the early 1990s Japan has relied on large-scale government purchases of goods and services, mainly in the form of construction spending on infrastructure, to prop up aggregate demand. This spending has been scaled back in recent years, but at its peak it was truly impressive. In 1996 Japan spent about $300 billion on infrastructure, compared with only $180 billion spent in the United States, even though Japan has less than half America's population and considerably less than half its GDP. Superb roads run through sparsely populated regions, ferries to small islands have been replaced by bridges, and many of the country's riverbeds have been paved, so that they resemble concrete aqueducts.

Has this policy been a success? Yes and no. Many economists believe that without all that government spending the Japanese economy would have slid into a 1930s-type depression after the bubble in stock and land values burst. Instead, the economy suffered a slowdown but not a severe slump: growth has been sluggish and unemployment has risen, but there has been no depression.

Furthermore, alternative policies weren't readily available. The alternative to using fiscal policy to prop up a slumping economy is using monetary policy, in which the central bank expands the money supply and drives down interest rates. Japan has done that, too; since 1998 short-term interest rates have been approximately zero! Since interest rates can't go below zero, there was no room for further interest rate cuts, yet the economy remained sluggish. So expansionary fiscal policy was the only obvious way to increase aggregate demand.

However, expansionary fiscal policy has not yet produced a full recovery in Japan. And the years of deficit spending have led to a rising government debt–GDP ratio that worries many financial experts. ■

> >

>>**CHECK YOUR UNDERSTANDING 12-1**

1. In each of the following cases, determine whether the policy is an expansionary or contractionary fiscal policy.
   a. Several military bases around the country, which together employ tens of thousands of people, are closed.
   b. The number of weeks an unemployed person is eligible for unemployment benefits is increased.
   c. The federal tax on gasoline is increased.
2. Explain why federal disaster relief, which quickly disburses funds to victims of natural disasters such as hurricanes, floods, and large-scale crop failures, will stabilize the economy more effectively than relief that must be legislated.

Solutions appear at back of book.

>>**QUICK REVIEW**

➤ Fiscal policy affects aggregate demand directly through government purchases of goods and services and indirectly through taxes and government transfers that affect consumer and investment spending. *Social insurance* programs account for most government transfers.

➤ Increased government purchases of goods and services, tax cuts, and increases in government transfers are the three principal forms of *expansionary fiscal policy*. Reduced government purchases of goods and services, tax increases, and reductions in government transfers are the three principal forms of *contractionary fiscal policy*.

➤ Because of inevitable time lags in the formulation and implementation of fiscal policy, an active fiscal policy may destabilize the economy.

Fiscal Policy and the Multiplier

An expansionary fiscal policy, like Japan's program of public works, pushes the aggregate demand curve to the right. A contractionary fiscal policy, like Lyndon Johnson's tax surcharge, pushes the aggregate demand curve to the left. For policy makers, however, knowing the direction of the shift isn't enough: they need estimates of *how much* the aggregate demand curve is shifted by a given policy. To get these estimates, they use the concept of the multiplier, which we introduced in Chapter 10.

Multiplier Effects of an Increase in Government Purchases of Goods and Services

Suppose that a government decides to spend $50 billion building bridges and roads. The government's purchases of goods and services will directly increase total spending on final goods and services by $50 billion. But as we learned in Chapter 10, there will also be an indirect effect because the government's purchases will start a chain reaction throughout the economy. The firms producing the goods and services purchased by the government will earn revenues that flow to households in the form of wages, profit, interest, and rent. This increase in disposable income will lead to a rise in consumer spending. The rise in consumer spending, in turn, will induce firms to increase output, leading to a further rise in disposable income, which will lead to another round of consumer spending increases, and so on.

In Chapter 10 we introduced the concept of the *multiplier:* the ratio of the change in real GDP caused by an autonomous change in aggregate spending to the size of that autonomous change. We saw there that in the simplest case (where there are no taxes or international trade, so that any change in real GDP accrues entirely to households, and the aggregate price level and the interest rate are fixed) the multiplier is $1/(1 - MPC)$. Recall that MPC is the *marginal propensity to consume,* the fraction of an additional dollar in disposable income that is spent. For example, if the marginal propensity to consume is 0.6, the multiplier is $1/(1 - 0.6) = 1/0.4 = 2.5$.

An increase in government purchases of goods and services is an example of an autonomous increase in aggregate spending. Its effect is illustrated in Figure 12-6. Given a multiplier of 2.5, a $50 billion increase in government purchases of goods and services will shift the AD curve rightward from AD_1 to AD_2, a distance representing an increase in real GDP of $125 billion at a given aggregate price level, P^*. Of that $125 billion, $50 billion is the initial effect from the increase in G, and the remaining $75 billion is the subsequent effect arising from the increase in consumer spending.

What happens if government purchases of goods and services are instead reduced? The math is exactly the same, except that there's a minus sign in front: if government purchases fall by $50 billion and the marginal propensity to consume is 0.6, the AD curve shifts leftward by $125 billion.

Figure 12-6

The Multiplier Effect of an Increase in Government Purchases of Goods and Services

A $50 billion increase in government purchases of goods and services has the direct effect of shifting the aggregate demand curve to the right by $50 billion. However, this is not the end of the story. The rise in real GDP causes a rise in disposable income, which leads to an increase in consumer spending, which leads to a further rise in real GDP, which leads to a further rise in consumer spending, and so on. The eventual shift, from AD_1 to AD_2, is a *multiple* of the increase in government purchases.

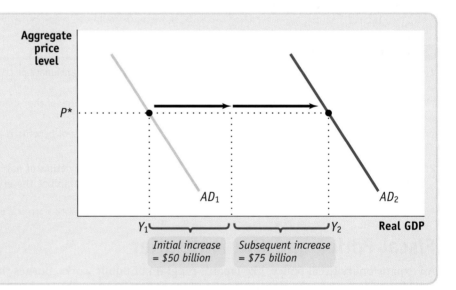

Multiplier Effects of Changes in Government Transfers and Taxes

Expansionary or contractionary fiscal policy need not take the form of changes in government purchases of goods and services. Governments can also change transfer payments or taxes. In general, however, a change in government transfers or taxes shifts the aggregate demand curve by *less* than an equal-sized change in government purchases.

To see why, imagine that instead of spending $50 billion on building bridges, the government simply hands out $50 billion in the form of government transfers. In this case, there is no direct effect on aggregate demand as there was with government purchases of goods and services. Real GDP goes up only because households spend some of that $50 billion. How much will they spend? Because the $50 billion transfer payment increases disposable income, households will engage in a first-round increase in consumer spending of $MPC \times \$50$ billion. For example, if $MPC = 0.6$, the first-round increase in consumer spending will be $30 billion ($0.6 \times \$50$ billion = $30 billion). Like an increase in government purchases, this initial rise in consumer spending will lead to a series of subsequent rounds in which real GDP, disposable income, and consumer spending rise further. In this example, although the transfer costs the government the same amount as the increase in spending on goods and services, the autonomous increase in aggregate spending from the transfer ($30 billion) is smaller than the autonomous increase in aggregate spending from government spending ($50 billion), and the overall effect on real GDP will also be smaller. In general, $1 of transfer payments will increase GDP by $MPC/(1 - MPC)$, less than the multiplier for increases in government purchases, which is $1/(1 - MPC)$. For example, if the marginal propensity to consume is 0.6, $1 of transfer payments raises real GDP by only $0.6/(1 - 0.6) = \$1.50$, while a $1 increase in government purchases of goods and services raises real GDP by $1/(1 - 0.6) = \$2.50$.

A tax cut has an effect similar to the effect of a transfer. It increases disposable income, leading to a series of increases in consumer spending. But the overall effect is smaller than that of an equal-size increase in government purchases: the autonomous increase in aggregate spending is smaller because households save part of the amount of the tax cut.

We should also note that taxes introduce a further complication: they typically change the size of the multiplier. That's because in the real world governments rarely impose "lump sum" taxes, in which the amount of tax a household owes is independent of its income. Instead, the great majority of tax revenue is raised via taxes that depend positively on the level of real GDP. (The multiplier on tax changes given above, $MPC/(1 - MPC)$, is the multiplier on lump-sum taxes.) As we'll discuss shortly, and analyze in detail in the appendix to this chapter, taxes that depend positively on real GDP reduce the size of the multiplier.

In practice, economists often argue that it also matters *who* among the population gets tax cuts or increases in government transfers. For example, compare the effects of an increase in unemployment benefits with a cut in taxes on profits distributed to shareholders as dividends. Consumer surveys indicate that the average unemployed worker will spend a higher share of any increase in his or her disposable income than would the average recipient of dividend income. That is, people who are unemployed tend to have a higher MPC than people who own a lot of stocks because the latter tend to be wealthier and to save more of any increase in disposable income. If that's true, a dollar spent on unemployment benefits increases aggregate demand more than a dollar's worth of dividend tax cuts. As the Economics in Action that follows this section explains, such arguments played an important role in recent policy debates.

How Taxes Affect the Multiplier

When we introduced the analysis of the multiplier in Chapter 10, we simplified matters by assuming that a $1 increase in real GDP raises disposable income by $1. In fact, however, government taxes capture some part of the increase in real GDP that occurs in each round of the multiplier process since most government taxes depend positively on real GDP. As a result, disposable income increases by considerably less than $1 once we include taxes in the model.

The increase in government tax revenue when real GDP rises isn't the result of a deliberate decision or action by the government. It's a consequence of the way the tax laws are written, which causes most sources of government revenue to increase *automatically* when real GDP goes up. For example, income tax receipts increase when real GDP rises because the amount each individual owes in taxes depends positively on his or her income, and households' disposable income rises when real GDP rises. Sales tax receipts increase when real GDP rises because people with more income spend more on goods and services. And corporate profit tax receipts increase when real GDP rises because profits increase when the economy expands.

The effect of these automatic increases in tax revenue is to reduce the size of the multiplier. Remember, the multiplier is the result of a chain reaction in which higher GDP leads to higher disposable income, which leads to higher consumer spending, which leads to further increases in real GDP. The fact that the government siphons off some of any increase in real GDP means that at each stage of this process the increase in consumer spending is smaller than it would be if taxes weren't part of the picture. The result is to reduce the multiplier. The appendix to this chapter shows how to derive the multiplier when taxes that depend positively on real GDP are taken into account.

Many macroeconomists believe it's a good thing that in real life taxes reduce the multiplier. In Chapter 10 we argued that most, though not all, recessions are the result of negative *demand shocks*. The same mechanism that causes tax revenue to increase when the economy expands causes it to decrease when the economy contracts. Since tax receipts decrease when real GDP falls, the effects of these negative demand shocks are smaller than they would be if there were no taxes. The decrease in tax revenue reduces the adverse effect of the initial fall in aggregate demand. By cutting the amount of taxes households pay, the automatic decrease in government tax revenue generated by a fall in real GDP acts like an automatic expansionary fiscal policy implemented in the face of a recession. Similarly, when the economy expands, the government finds itself automatically pursuing a contractionary fiscal policy—a tax increase. Government spending and taxation rules that cause fiscal policy to be expansionary when the economy contracts and contractionary when the economy expands, without requiring any deliberate action by policy makers, are called **automatic stabilizers.**

The rules that govern tax collection aren't the only automatic stabilizers, although they are the most important ones. Some types of government transfers also play a stabilizing role. For example, more people receive unemployment insurance when the economy is depressed than when it is booming. The same is true of Medicaid and food stamps. So transfer payments tend to rise when the economy is contracting and fall when the economy is expanding. Like changes in tax revenue, these changes in transfers tend to reduce the size of the multiplier because the total change in disposable income that results from a given rise or fall in real GDP is smaller.

As in the case of government tax revenue, many macroeconomists believe that it's a good thing that government transfers reduce the multiplier. More generally, expansionary and contractionary fiscal policies that are the result of automatic stabilizers are widely considered helpful to macroeconomic stabilization. But what about fiscal policy that *isn't* the result of automatic stabilizers? **Discretionary fiscal policy** is fiscal policy that is the direct result of deliberate actions by policy makers rather than automatic adjustment. For example, during a recession, the government may pass legislation that cuts taxes and purposely increases government spending in order to stimulate the economy. The use of discretionary fiscal policy to fight recessions and rein in expansions is much more controversial than the role of automatic stabilizers. We'll explain why, and describe the debates among macroeconomists on the appropriate role of fiscal policy, in Chapter 17.

Automatic stabilizers are government spending and taxation rules that cause fiscal policy to be expansionary when the economy contracts and contractionary when the economy expands.

Discretionary fiscal policy is fiscal policy that is the result of deliberate actions by policy makers rather than rules.

AP Photo

An example of a discretionary fiscal policy was the Works Progress Administration (WPA), a relief measure established during the Great Depression. The unemployed were put to work on public works projects, building bridges, roads, buildings, and parks.

economics in action

How Much Bang for the Buck?

In 2001 the U.S. economy experienced a recession, followed by a 2002–2003 "jobless recovery" in which real GDP grew but overall employment didn't. There was widespread agreement among economists that the country needed an expansionary fiscal policy to stimulate aggregate demand. And the government did, in fact, pursue an expansionary fiscal policy: tax cuts combined with increased government spending undoubtedly helped increase aggregate demand and output.

But was the expansionary fiscal policy carried out in the right way? Critics argued that a different mix of policies would have yielded more "bang for the buck"—they would have done more to increase aggregate demand, but led to a smaller rise in the budget deficit.

A particularly clear (and nonpartisan) example of this criticism was an analysis by Mark Zandi, the chief economist of economy.com, a consulting firm. Zandi estimated the multiplier effects of a number of alternative fiscal policies, shown in Table 12-1. He argued that many of the tax cuts enacted between 2001 and 2003 had smaller effects on aggregate demand compared to other types of tax cuts because they went to people who probably wouldn't spend much of the increase in their disposable income. He was particularly critical of tax cuts on dividend income and on the value of inherited estates, arguing that they did very little to raise consumer spending. According to his analysis, an alternative set of fiscal policies that put more disposable income into the hands of unemployed workers, lower-income taxpayers, and cash-strapped state and local governments would have created a larger increase in spending at the same cost. This would have led to both lower budget deficits and a larger increase in real GDP—and so to lower unemployment. This view was shared by many economists, though certainly not by all.

Despite the criticisms, there was widespread agreement that the tax cuts of 2001–2003 helped generate an economic expansion. As Richard Berner, an economist

TABLE 12-1

Differences in the Effect of Expansionary Fiscal Policies

Policy	Estimated increase in real GDP per dollar of fiscal policy	Explanation of policy
Extend emergency federal unemployment insurance benefits	$1.73	Extends the period for unemployment benefits, increasing transfers to the unemployed
10% personal income tax bracket	1.34	Reduces tax rate on some income from 15% to 10%, mainly benefiting middle-income families
State government aid	1.24	Provides financial aid to state governments during recessions so states do not have to raise taxes or cut spending
Child tax credit rebate	1.04	Increases the income tax reduction for each child, mainly benefiting middle- and lower-income families
Marriage tax penalty	0.74	Reduces the "marriage penalty," an increase in combined taxes that can occur when two working people marry
Alternative minimum tax adjustments	0.67	Revises the alternative minimum tax, designed to prevent wealthy people with many deductions from paying too little tax, to exclude those not considered sufficiently wealthy
Personal marginal tax rate reductions	0.59	Reduces tax rates for people in higher income brackets
Business investment writeoff	0.24	Temporarily allows companies to deduct some investment spending from taxable profits
Dividend–capital gain tax reduction	0.09	Reduces taxes on dividends and capital gains
Estate tax reduction	0.00	Reduces the tax paid on the value of assets passed to heirs upon a person's death

Source: economy.com

at the investment firm Morgan Stanley, put it, the tax cuts might not have generated a lot of bang per buck, but they were still effective because they involved a lot of bucks. ■

< < < < < < < < < < < < < < < < < <

>> CHECK YOUR UNDERSTANDING 12-2

1. Explain why a $500 million increase in government purchases of goods and services will generate a larger shift in the aggregate demand curve than a $500 million increase in government transfers.

2. Explain why a $500 million reduction in government purchases of goods and services will generate a larger shift in the aggregate demand curve than a $500 million reduction in government transfers.

Solutions appear at back of book.

The Budget Balance

Headlines about the government's budget tend to focus on just one point: whether the government is running a surplus or a deficit and, in either case, how big. People usually think of surpluses as good: when the federal government ran a record surplus in 2000, many people regarded it as a cause for celebration. Conversely, people usually think of deficits as bad: when the federal government ran a record deficit in 2004, many people regarded it as a cause for concern, and the White House promised to bring the deficit down over time.

How do surpluses and deficits fit into the analysis of fiscal policy? Are deficits ever a good thing and surpluses a bad thing? Let's look at the causes and consequences of surpluses and deficits.

The Budget Balance as a Measure of Fiscal Policy

What do we mean by surpluses and deficits? The budget balance, which we defined in Chapter 9, is the difference between the government's income, in the form of tax revenue, and its spending, both on goods and services and on government transfers, in a given year. That is, the budget balance is equal to government savings and is defined by Equation 12-2:

(12-2) $S_{Government} = T - G - TR$

where T is the value of tax revenues, G is government purchases and TR is the value of government transfers. As we learned in Chapter 9, a budget surplus is a positive budget balance and a budget deficit is a negative budget balance.

Other things equal, expansionary fiscal policies—increased government purchases of goods and services, higher government transfers, or lower taxes—reduce the budget balance for that year. That is, expansionary fiscal policies make a budget surplus smaller or a budget deficit bigger. Conversely, contractionary fiscal policies—reduced government purchases of goods and services, lower government transfers, or higher taxes—increase the budget balance for that year, making a budget surplus bigger or a budget deficit smaller.

You might think this means that changes in the budget balance can be used to measure fiscal policy. In fact, economists often do just that: they use changes in the budget

Patrick O' Connor

OH... SOMEONE MUST HAVE BALANCED THE BUDGET.

balance as a "quick-and-dirty" way to assess whether current fiscal policy is expansionary or contractionary. But they always keep in mind two reasons this quick-and-dirty approach is sometimes misleading:

- Two different changes in fiscal policy that have equal effects on the budget balance may have quite unequal effects on aggregate demand. As we have already seen, changes in government purchases have a larger effect on aggregate demand than equal-size changes in taxes and government transfers.

- Often, changes in the budget balance are themselves the result, not the cause, of fluctuations in the economy.

To understand the second point, we need to examine the effects of the business cycle on the budget.

The Business Cycle and the Cyclically Adjusted Budget Balance

Historically there has been a strong relationship between the federal government's budget balance and the business cycle. The budget tends to move into deficit when the economy experiences a recession, but deficits tend to get smaller or even turn into surpluses when the economy is expanding. Figure 12-7 shows the federal budget deficit as a percentage of GDP since 1970. Shaded areas indicate recessions; unshaded areas indicate expansions. As you can see, the federal budget deficit increased around the time of each recession and usually declined during expansions. In fact, in the late stages of the long expansion from 1991 to 2000 the deficit actually became negative—the budget deficit became a budget surplus.

The relationship between the business cycle and the budget balance is even clearer if we compare the budget deficit as a percentage of GDP with the unemployment rate, as we do in Figure 12-8 on page 306. The budget deficit almost always rises when the unemployment rate rises and falls when the unemployment rate falls.

Is this relationship between the business cycle and the budget balance evidence that policy makers engage in discretionary fiscal policy, using expansionary fiscal policy during recessions and contractionary fiscal policy during expansions? Not

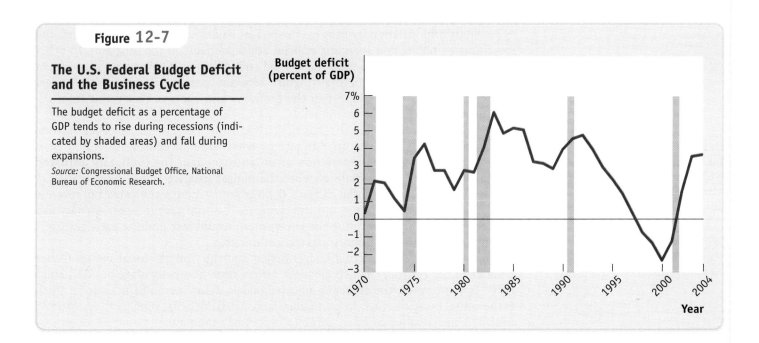

Figure 12-7

The U.S. Federal Budget Deficit and the Business Cycle

The budget deficit as a percentage of GDP tends to rise during recessions (indicated by shaded areas) and fall during expansions.

Source: Congressional Budget Office, National Bureau of Economic Research.

Budget deficit (percent of GDP)

Figure 12-8

The U.S. Federal Budget Deficit and the Unemployment Rate

There is a close relationship between the budget balance and the business cycle: a recession moves the budget balance toward deficit, but an expansion moves it toward surplus. Here, the unemployment rate serves as an indicator of the business cycle, and we should expect to see a higher unemployment rate associated with a higher budget deficit. This is confirmed by the figure: the budget deficit as a percentage of GDP moves closely in tandem with the unemployment rate. **>web**...

Source: Congressional Budget Office, Bureau of Labor Statistics.

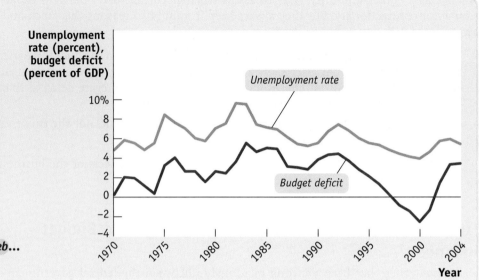

necessarily. To a large extent the relationship in Figure 12-8 reflects automatic stabilizers at work. As we learned in the discussion of automatic stabilizers, government tax revenue tends to rise and some government transfers, like unemployment benefit payments, tend to fall when the economy expands. Conversely, government tax revenue tends to fall and some government transfers tend to rise when the economy contracts. So the budget tends to move toward deficit during recessions and toward surplus during expansions even without any deliberate action on the part of policy makers.

In assessing budget policy, it's often useful to separate changes in the budget balance due to the business cycle from changes due to deliberate policy changes. The former are affected by automatic stabilizers and the latter, by deliberate changes in government purchases, government transfers, or taxes. For one thing, business-cycle effects on the budget balance are temporary: both recessionary gaps (in which real GDP is below potential output) and inflationary gaps (in which real GDP is above potential output) tend to be eliminated in the long run. So taking out the effects of recessionary and inflationary gaps on the budget balance sheds light on whether the government's taxing and spending policies are sustainable in the long run. In other words, do the government's tax policies yield enough revenue to fund its spending in the long run? Also, it's useful to distinguish between "passive" changes in the budget balance that result from changes in the economy and changes that result from actions by policy makers.

To separate the effect of the business cycle from the effects of other factors, many governments produce an estimate of what the budget balance would be if there were neither a recessionary nor an inflationary gap. The **cyclically adjusted budget balance** is an estimate of what the budget balance would be if real GDP were exactly equal to potential output. It takes into account the extra tax revenue the government would collect and the transfers it would save if a recessionary gap were eliminated—or the revenue the government would lose and the extra transfers it would make if an inflationary gap were eliminated.

Figure 12-9 shows the actual budget deficit and the Congressional Budget Office estimate of the cyclically adjusted budget deficit, both as a percentage of GDP, since 1970. As you can see, the cyclically adjusted budget deficit doesn't fluctuate as much as the actual budget deficit. In particular, large actual deficits, such as those of 1975 and 1983, are usually caused in part by a depressed economy.

The **cyclically adjusted budget balance** is an estimate of what the budget balance would be if real GDP were exactly equal to potential output.

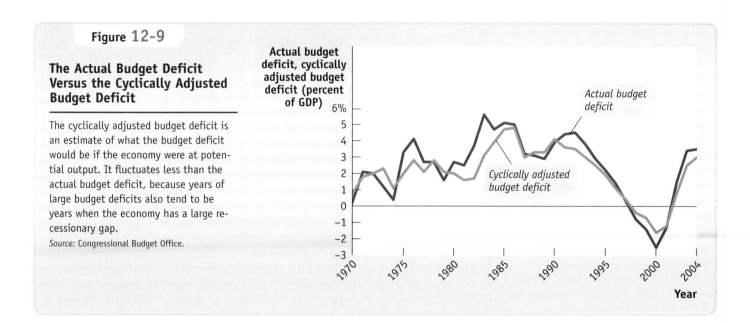

Figure 12-9

The Actual Budget Deficit Versus the Cyclically Adjusted Budget Deficit

The cyclically adjusted budget deficit is an estimate of what the budget deficit would be if the economy were at potential output. It fluctuates less than the actual budget deficit, because years of large budget deficits also tend to be years when the economy has a large recessionary gap.

Source: Congressional Budget Office.

Should the Budget Be Balanced?

As we'll see in the next section, persistent budget deficits can cause problems for both the government and the economy. Yet politicians are always tempted to run deficits because this allows them to cater to voters by cutting taxes without cutting spending or by increasing spending without increasing taxes. As a result, there are occasional attempts by policy makers to force fiscal discipline by introducing legislation—even a constitutional amendment—forbidding the government from running budget deficits. This is usually stated as a requirement that the budget be "balanced"—that revenues at least equal spending each fiscal year. Would it be a good idea to require a balanced budget annually?

Most economists don't think so. They believe that the government should only balance its budget on average—that it should be allowed to run deficits in bad years, offset by surpluses in good years. They don't believe the government should be forced to run a balanced budget *every year* because this would undermine the role of taxes and transfers as automatic stabilizers. As we learned earlier in this chapter, the tendency of tax revenue to fall and transfers to rise when the economy contracts helps to limit the size of recessions. But falling tax revenue and rising transfer payments push the budget toward deficit. If constrained by a balanced-budget rule, the government would have to respond to this deficit with contractionary fiscal policies that would tend to deepen the recession.

Yet policy makers concerned about excessive deficits sometimes feel that rigid rules prohibiting—or at least setting an upper limit on—deficits are necessary. As Economics in Action explains, Europe has had a lot of trouble reconciling rules to enforce fiscal responsibility with the problems of short-run fiscal policy.

economics in action

Stability Pact—or Stupidity Pact?

In 1999 a group of European nations took a momentous step when they adopted a common currency, the euro, to replace their national currencies, such as French francs, German marks, and Italian lira. Along with the introduction of the euro came the creation of the European Central Bank, which sets monetary policy for the whole region.

As part of the agreement creating the new currency, governments of member countries signed on to the European "stability pact." This agreement required each government to keep its budget deficit—its actual deficit, not a cyclically adjusted number—below 3% of the country's GDP or face fines. The pact was intended to prevent irresponsible deficit spending arising from political pressure that might eventually undermine the new currency. The stability pact, however, had a serious downside: it limited a country's ability to use fiscal policy.

In fact, the stability pact quickly became a problem for the two largest economies in the euro zone. In 2002 both France and Germany were experiencing rising unemployment and also running budget deficits in excess of 3% of GDP. Moreover, it seemed likely that both countries' deficits would go up in 2003, which they did. Under the rules of the stability pact, France and Germany were supposed to lower their budget deficits by raising taxes or cutting spending. Yet contractionary fiscal policy would have led to even higher unemployment.

In October 2002, reacting to these economic problems, one top European official described the stability pact as "stupid." Journalists promptly had a field day, renaming it the "stupidity pact." In fact, when push came to shove, the pact proved unenforceable. Germany and France both had enough political clout to prevent the imposition of penalties. Indeed, in March 2005 the stability pact was rewritten to allow "small and temporary" breaches of the 3% limit, with a special clause allowing Germany to describe aid to the former East Germany as a temporary expense.

Before patting themselves on the back over the superiority of their own fiscal rules, Americans should note that the United States has its own version of the stupidity pact. The federal government's budget acts as an automatic stabilizer, but 49 of the 50 states are required by their state constitutions to balance their budgets every year. When recession struck in 2001, most states were forced to—guess what?—slash spending and raise taxes in the face of a recession, exactly the wrong thing from a macroeconomic point of view. Not surprisingly, some states, like some European countries, found ways to cheat. ∎

< < < < < < < < < < < < < < < < < <

>>**QUICK REVIEW**

➤ The budget deficit tends to rise during recessions and fall during expansions. This reflects the effect of the business cycle on the budget balance.

➤ The *cyclically adjusted budget balance* is an estimate of what the budget balance would be if the economy were at potential output. It varies less than the actual budget deficit.

➤ Most economists believe that governments should run budget deficits in bad years and budget surpluses in good years. A rule requiring a balanced budget would undermine the role of automatic stabilizers.

>>**CHECK YOUR UNDERSTANDING 12-3**

1. When your work–study earnings are low, your parents help you out with expenses. When your earnings are high, they expect you to contribute toward your tuition bill. Explain how this arrangement acts like an automatic stabilizer for your economic activity.

2. Explain why states required by their constitutions to balance their budgets are likely to experience more severe economic fluctuations than states not held to that requirement.

Solutions appear at back of book.

Long-Run Implications of Fiscal Policy

The Japanese government built the bridge to Awaji Island as part of a fiscal policy aimed at increasing aggregate demand. As we've seen, that policy was partly successful: although Japan's economy was sluggish during the 1990s, it avoided a severe slump comparable to what happened to many countries in the 1930s. Yet the fact that Japan was running large deficits year after year made many observers uneasy. By 2000 there was a debate among economists about whether Japan's debt was starting to reach alarming levels.

No discussion of fiscal policy is complete if it doesn't take into account the long-run implications of government budget surpluses and deficits. We now turn to those long-run implications.

Deficits, Surpluses, and Debt

When a family spends more than it earns over the course of a year, it has to raise the extra funds either by selling assets or by borrowing. And if a family borrows year after year, it will end up with a lot of debt.

The same is true for governments. With a few exceptions, governments don't raise large sums by selling assets such as national parkland. Instead, when a government spends more than the tax revenue it receives—when it runs a budget deficit—it almost always borrows the extra funds. And governments that run persistent budget deficits end up with substantial debts.

To interpret the numbers that follow, you need to know a slightly peculiar feature of federal government accounting. For historical reasons, the U.S. government does not keep books for calendar years. Instead, budget totals are kept for **fiscal years,** which run from October 1 to September 30 and are named by the calendar year in which they end. For example, fiscal 2004 began on October 1, 2003, and ended on September 30, 2004.

At the end of fiscal 2004, the U.S. federal government had total debt equal to almost $7.4 trillion. However, part of that debt represented special accounting rules specifying that the federal government as a whole owes funds to certain government programs, especially Social Security. We'll explain those rules shortly. For now, however, let's focus on **public debt:** government debt held by individuals and institutions outside the government. At the end of fiscal 2004, the federal government's public debt was "only" $4.3 trillion, or 37% of GDP. If we include the debts of state and local governments, total government public debt was approximately 44% of GDP. Figure 12-10 compares the U.S. public debt–GDP ratio with the public debt–GDP ratios of other wealthy countries in 2003. As of 2003, the U.S. debt level was more or less typical.

U.S. federal government public debt at the end of fiscal 2004 was larger than it was at the end of fiscal 2003, because the federal government ran a budget deficit during fiscal 2004. A government that runs persistent budget deficits will experience a rising level of public debt. But why is this a problem?

Fiscal years run from October 1 to September 30 and are named by the calendar year in which they end.

Public debt is government debt held by individuals and institutions outside the government.

PITFALLS

DEFICITS VERSUS DEBT

One common mistake—it happens all the time in newspaper reports—is to confuse *deficits* with *debt.* Let's review the difference.

A *deficit* is the difference between the amount of money a government spends and the amount it receives in taxes over a given period—usually, though not always, a year. Deficit numbers always come with a statement about the time period to which they apply, as in "The U.S. budget deficit *in fiscal 2004* was $412 billion."

A *debt* is the sum of money a government owes at a particular point in time. Debt numbers usually come with a specific date, as in "U.S. public debt *at the end of fiscal 2004* was $4.3 trillion."

Deficits and debt are linked, because government debt grows when governments run deficits. But they aren't the same thing, and they can even tell different stories. At the end of fiscal 2004, U.S. *debt* as a percentage of GDP was fairly low by historical standards, but the *deficit* during fiscal 2004 was considered quite high.

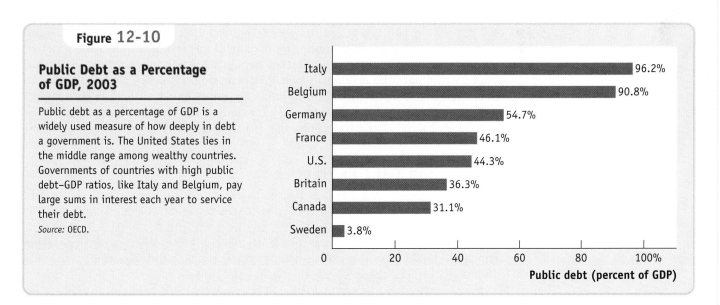

Figure 12-10

Public Debt as a Percentage of GDP, 2003

Public debt as a percentage of GDP is a widely used measure of how deeply in debt a government is. The United States lies in the middle range among wealthy countries. Governments of countries with high public debt–GDP ratios, like Italy and Belgium, pay large sums in interest each year to service their debt.
Source: OECD.

Italy 96.2%
Belgium 90.8%
Germany 54.7%
France 46.1%
U.S. 44.3%
Britain 36.3%
Canada 31.1%
Sweden 3.8%

Public debt (percent of GDP)

Problems Posed by Rising Government Debt

There are two reasons to be concerned when a government runs persistent budget deficits. We described one reason in Chapter 9: when the government borrows funds in the financial markets, it is competing with firms that plan to borrow funds for investment spending. As a result, the government's borrowing may "crowd out" private investment spending and reduce the economy's long-run rate of growth.

But there's also a second reason: today's deficits, by increasing the government's debt, place financial pressure on future budgets. The impact of current deficits on future budgets is straightforward. Like individuals, governments must pay their bills—including interest payments on their accumulated debt. When a government is deeply in debt, those interest payments can be substantial. In fiscal 2004, the U.S. federal government paid 1.4% of GDP—$160 billion—in interest on its debt. The two most heavily indebted governments shown in Figure 12-10, Italy and Belgium, each paid interest of more than 5% of GDP in 2004.

Other things equal, a government paying large sums in interest must raise more revenue from taxes or spend less than it would otherwise be able to afford—or it must borrow even more to cover the gap. But a government that borrows to pay interest on its outstanding debt pushes itself even deeper into debt. This process can eventually push a government to the point where lenders question its ability to repay. Like a consumer who has maxed out his or her credit cards, it will find that lenders are unwilling to lend any more funds. The result can be that the government defaults on its debt—it stops paying what it owes. Default is often followed by financial and economic turmoil.

The idea of a government defaulting sounds far-fetched, but it is not impossible. In the 1990s Argentina, a relatively high-income developing country, was widely praised for its economic policies—and it was able to borrow large sums from foreign lenders. By 2002, however, Argentina's interest payments were spiraling out of control, and the country stopped paying the sums that were due. We describe that default in the Economics in Action that follows this section.

Default creates havoc in a country's financial markets and badly shakes public confidence in both the government and the economy. Argentina's debt default was accompanied by a crisis in the country's banking systems and a very severe recession. And even if a highly indebted government avoids default, a heavy debt burden typically forces it to slash spending or raise taxes, politically unpopular measures that can also damage the economy.

One question some people ask is, can't a government that has trouble borrowing just print money to pay its bills? Yes, it can, but this leads to another problem: inflation. In fact, budget problems are the main cause of very severe inflation, as we'll see in Chapter 16. The point for now is that governments do not want to find themselves in a position where the choice is between defaulting on their debts and inflating those debts away.

Concerns about the long-run effects of deficits need not rule out the use of fiscal policy to stimulate the economy when it is depressed. However, these concerns do mean that governments should try to offset budget deficits in bad years with budget surpluses in good years. In other words, governments should run a budget that is approximately balanced over time. Have they actually done so?

Deficits and Debt in Practice

Figure 12-11 shows how the U.S. federal government's budget deficit and its debt have evolved since 1939. Panel (a) shows the federal deficit as a percentage of GDP. As you can see, the federal government ran huge deficits during World War II. It briefly ran surpluses after the war, but it has normally run deficits ever since, especially after 1980. This seems inconsistent with the advice that governments should offset deficits in bad times with surpluses in good times.

However, panel (b) shows that these deficits have not led to runaway debt. To assess the ability of governments to pay their debt, we often use the **debt–GDP ratio,** government debt as a percentage of GDP. We use this measure, rather than simply looking at the size of the debt, because GDP, which measures the size of the economy as a whole, is a good indicator of the potential taxes the government can collect. If the government's debt grows more slowly than GDP, the burden of paying that debt is actually falling compared with the government's potential tax revenue.

What we see from panel (b) is that although the federal debt has grown in almost every year, the debt–GDP ratio fell for 30 years after the end of World War II. This

The **debt–GDP ratio** is government debt as a percentage of GDP.

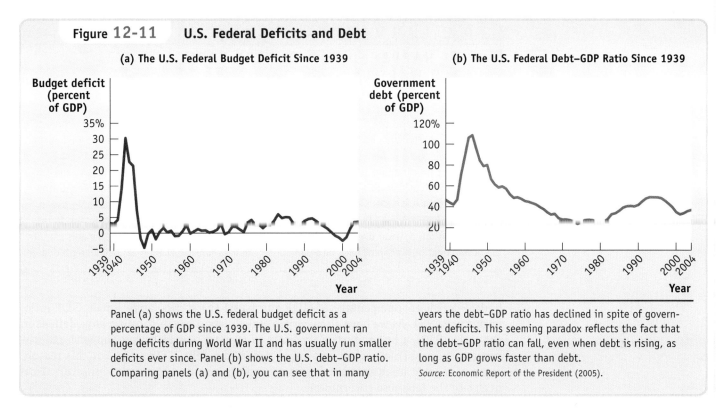

Figure 12-11 U.S. Federal Deficits and Debt

(a) The U.S. Federal Budget Deficit Since 1939

(b) The U.S. Federal Debt–GDP Ratio Since 1939

Panel (a) shows the U.S. federal budget deficit as a percentage of GDP since 1939. The U.S. government ran huge deficits during World War II and has usually run smaller deficits ever since. Panel (b) shows the U.S. debt–GDP ratio. Comparing panels (a) and (b), you can see that in many years the debt–GDP ratio has declined in spite of government deficits. This seeming paradox reflects the fact that the debt–GDP ratio can fall, even when debt is rising, as long as GDP grows faster than debt.

Source: Economic Report of the President (2005).

shows that the debt–GDP ratio can fall, even when debt is rising, as long as GDP grows faster than debt. For Inquiring Minds on page 312, which focuses on the large debt the U.S. government ran up during World War II, explains how growth and inflation sometimes allow a government that runs persistent budget deficits to nevertheless have a declining debt–GDP ratio.

Still, a government that runs persistent *large* deficits will have a rising debt–GDP ratio when debt grows faster than GDP. Panel (a) of Figure 12-12 shows Japan's

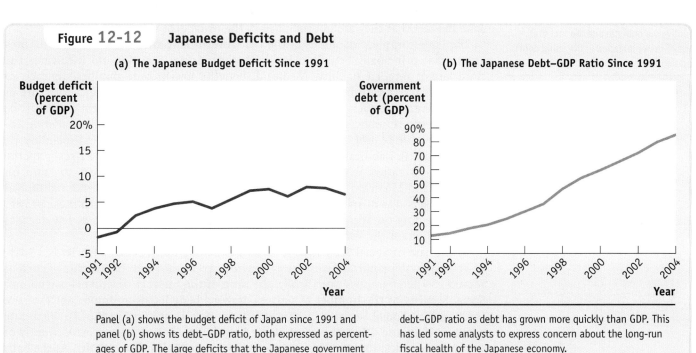

Figure 12-12 Japanese Deficits and Debt

(a) The Japanese Budget Deficit Since 1991

(b) The Japanese Debt–GDP Ratio Since 1991

Panel (a) shows the budget deficit of Japan since 1991 and panel (b) shows its debt–GDP ratio, both expressed as percentages of GDP. The large deficits that the Japanese government began running in the early 1990s have led to a rapid rise in its debt–GDP ratio as debt has grown more quickly than GDP. This has led some analysts to express concern about the long-run fiscal health of the Japanese economy.

Source: OECD.

FOR INQUIRING MINDS

WHAT HAPPENED TO THE DEBT FROM WORLD WAR II?

As you can see from Figure 12-11, the U.S. government paid for World War II by borrowing on a huge scale. By the war's end, the public debt was more than 100% of GDP, and many people worried about how it could ever be paid off.

The truth is that it never was paid off. In 1946 public debt was $270 billion; that number dipped slightly in the next few years, as the United States ran postwar budget surpluses, but the government budget went back into deficit in 1950 with the start of the Korean War. By 1956 the debt was back up to $270 billion.

But by that time nobody was worried about the fiscal health of the U.S. government because the debt–GDP ratio had fallen almost by half. The reason? Vigorous economic growth, plus mild inflation, had led to a rapid rise in GDP. The experience was a clear lesson in the peculiar fact that modern governments can run deficits forever, as long as they aren't too large.

---

budget deficit as a percentage of GDP and panel (b) shows Japan's debt–GDP ratio, both since 1991. As we have already mentioned, Japan began running large deficits in the early 1990s, a by-product of its effort to prop up aggregate demand with government spending. This has led to a rapid rise in the debt–GDP ratio. For this reason, some economic analysts have begun to express concern about the long-run fiscal health of the Japanese government.

Implicit Liabilities

Looking at Figure 12-11, you might be tempted to conclude that the U.S. federal budget is in fairly decent shape: the return to budget deficits after 2001 caused the debt–GDP ratio to rise a bit, but that ratio is still low compared with both historical experience and some other wealthy countries. In fact, however, experts on long-run budget issues view the situation of the United States (and other countries such as Japan and Italy) with alarm. The reason is the problem of *implicit liabilities*. **Implicit liabilities** are spending promises made by governments that are effectively a debt despite the fact that they are not included in the usual debt statistics.

The largest implicit liabilities of the U.S. government arise from two transfer programs that principally benefit older Americans: Social Security and Medicare. The third-largest implicit liability, Medicaid, benefits low-income families. In each of these cases the government has promised to provide transfer payments to future as well as current beneficiaries. So these programs represent a future debt that must be honored, even though the debt does not currently show up in the usual statistics. Together, these three programs currently account for about 40% of federal spending.

The implicit liabilities created by these transfer programs worry fiscal experts. Figure 12-13 shows why. It shows current spending on Social Security, and on Medicare and Medicaid as percentages of GDP, together with Congressional Budget Office projections of spending in 2010, 2030, and 2050. According to these projections, spending on Social Security will rise substantially over the next few decades and spending on the two health care programs will soar. Why?

In the case of Social Security, the answer is demography. Social Security is a "pay-as-you-go" system: current workers pay payroll taxes that fund the benefits of current retirees. So demography—specifically, the ratio of the number of workers paying into Social Security to the number of retirees drawing benefits—is an important measure for managing Social Security's finances. There was a huge surge in the U.S. birth rate between 1946 and 1964, the years of the baby boom. Baby boomers are currently of working age—which means they are paying taxes, not collecting benefits. As the baby boomers retire, they will stop earning income that is taxed and start collecting benefits. As a result, the ratio of retirees receiving benefits to workers paying into the So-

Implicit liabilities are spending promises made by governments that are effectively a debt despite the fact that they are not included in the usual debt statistics.

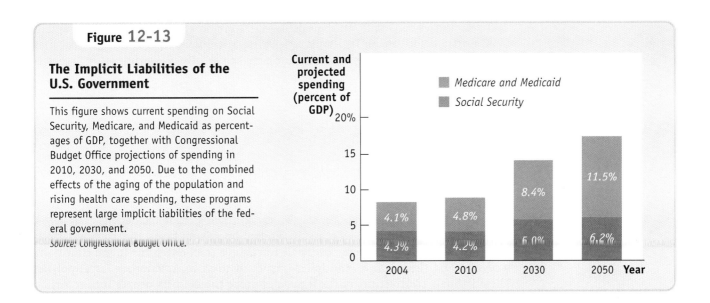

Figure 12-13

The Implicit Liabilities of the U.S. Government

This figure shows current spending on Social Security, Medicare, and Medicaid as percentages of GDP, together with Congressional Budget Office projections of spending in 2010, 2030, and 2050. Due to the combined effects of the aging of the population and rising health care spending, these programs represent large implicit liabilities of the federal government.

Source: Congressional Budget Office.

cial Security system will rise. In 2004 there were 30 retirees receiving benefits for every 100 workers paying into the system. By 2030, according to the Social Security Administration, that number will rise to 46; by 2050 it will rise to 50. This will raise benefit payments relative to the size of the economy.

The aging of the baby boomers, by itself, poses only a moderately sized long-run fiscal problem. The projected rise in Medicare and Medicaid spending is a much more serious concern. The main story behind projections of higher Medicare and Medicaid spending is the long-run tendency of health care spending to rise faster than overall spending, both for government-funded and for privately funded health care.

To some extent, the implicit liabilities of the U.S. government are already reflected in debt statistics. We mentioned earlier that the government had a total debt of $7.4 trillion at the end of 2004, but that only $4.3 trillion of that total was owed to the public. The main explanation for that discrepancy is that both Social Security and part of Medicare (the hospital insurance program) are supported by *dedicated taxes:* their expenses are paid out of special taxes on wages. At times, these dedicated taxes yield more revenue than is needed to pay current benefits. In particular, since the mid-1980s the Social Security system has been taking in more revenue than it currently needs in order to prepare for the retirement of the baby boomers. This surplus in the Social Security system has been used to accumulate a Social Security *trust fund,* which was $1.7 trillion at the end of 2004.

The $1.7 trillion in the trust fund is held in the form of U.S. government bonds, which are included in the $7.4 trillion in total debt. You could say that there's something funny about counting bonds in the Social Security trust fund as part of government debt. After all, they're owed by one part of the government (the government outside the Social Security system) to another part of the government (the Social Security system itself). But the debt corresponds to a real, if implicit, liability: promises by the government to pay future retirement benefits. So many economists argue that the gross debt of $7.4 trillion, the sum of public debt and government debt held by Social Security and other trust funds, is a more accurate indication of the government's fiscal health than the smaller amount owed to the public alone.

economics in action

Argentina's Creditors Take a Haircut

As we mentioned earlier, the idea that a government's debt can reach a level at which the government can't pay its creditors can seem far-fetched. In the United States, government debt is usually regarded as the safest asset there is.

But countries *do* default on their debts—fail to repay the money they borrowed. In 1998 Russia defaulted on its bonds, triggering a worldwide panic in financial markets. In 2001, in the biggest default of modern times, the government of Argentina stopped making payments on $81 billion in debt.

How did the Argentine default happen? During much of the 1990s, the country was experiencing an economic boom and the government was easily able to borrow money from abroad. Although deficit spending led to rising government debt, few considered this a problem. In 1998, however, the country slid into an economic slump that reduced tax revenues, leading to much larger deficits. Foreign lenders, increasingly nervous about the country's ability to repay, became unwilling to lend money except at very high interest rates. By 2001 the country was in a vicious circle: to cover its deficits and pay off old loans as they came due, it was forced to borrow at much higher interest rates, and the escalating interest rates on new borrowing made the deficits even bigger.

Argentine officials tried to reassure lenders by raising taxes and cutting government spending. But they were never able to balance the budget due to the continuing recession and the negative multiplier impact of their contractionary fiscal policies. These strongly contractionary fiscal policies drove the country deeper into recession. Late in 2001, facing popular protests, the Argentine government collapsed, and the country defaulted on its debt.

Creditors can take individuals who fail to pay debts to court. The court, in turn, can seize the debtors' assets and force them to pay part of future earnings to their creditors. But when a country defaults, it's different. Its creditors can't send in the police to seize the country's assets. They must negotiate a deal with the country for partial repayment. The only leverage creditors have in these negotiations is the defaulting government's fear that if it fails to reach a settlement, its reputation will suffer and it will be unable to borrow in the future. (A report by Reuters, the news agency, on Argentina's debt negotiations was headlined "Argentina to unhappy bondholders: so sue.")

It took three years for Argentina to reach an agreement with its creditors because the new Argentine government was determined to strike a hard bargain. And it did. Here's how Reuters described the settlement reached in March 2005: "The deal, which exchanged new paper valued at around 32 cents for every dollar in default, was the biggest 'haircut,' or loss on principal, for investors of any sovereign bond restructuring in modern times." Let's put this into English: Argentina forced its creditors to trade their "sovereign bonds"—debts of a sovereign nation, that is, Argentina—for new bonds worth only 32% as much. Such a reduction in the value of debt is known as a "haircut."

It's important to avoid two misconceptions about this "haircut." First, you might be tempted to think that because Argentina ended up paying only a fraction of the sums it owed, it paid little price for default. In fact, Argentina's default accompanied one of the worst economic slumps of modern times, a period of mass unemployment, soaring poverty, and widespread unrest. Second, it's tempting to dismiss the Argentine story as being of little relevance to countries like the United States. After all, aren't we more responsible than that? But Argentina wouldn't have been able to borrow so much in the first place if its government hadn't been well regarded by international lenders. In fact, as late as 1998 Argentina was widely admired for its economic management. What Argentina's slide into default shows is that concerns about the long-run effects of budget deficits are not at all academic. Due to its large and growing debt–GDP ratio, one recession pushed Argentina over the edge into economic collapse. ■

< < < < < < < < < < < < < < < < < < <

>> QUICK REVIEW

> - Persistent budget deficits lead to increases in *public debt*.
> - Rising public debt can lead to government default. In less extreme cases, it can crowd out investment spending, reducing long-run growth. This suggests that budget deficits in bad *fiscal years* should be offset with budget surpluses in good fiscal years.
> - A widely used indicator of fiscal health is the *debt–GDP ratio*. A country with rising GDP can have a stable debt–GDP ratio even if it runs budget deficits if GDP is growing faster than the debt.
> - In addition to their official debt, modern governments have *implicit liabilities*. The U.S. government has large implicit liabilities in the form of Social Security, Medicare, and Medicaid.

>> CHECK YOUR UNDERSTANDING 12-4

1. Explain how each of the following events would affect the public debt or implicit liabilities of the U.S. government, other things equal. Would the public debt or implicit liabilities be greater or smaller?
   a. A higher growth rate of real GDP
   b. Retirees live longer
   c. A decrease in tax revenue
   d. Government borrowing to pay interest on its current public debt

2. Suppose the economy is in a slump and the current public debt is quite large. Explain the trade-off of short-run versus long-run objectives that policy makers face when deciding whether or not to engage in deficit spending.

Solutions appear at back of book.

• A LOOK AHEAD •

Fiscal policy isn't the only way governments can stimulate aggregate demand when the economy is slumping or reduce aggregate demand when it is too high. In fact, although most economists believe that automatic stabilizers play a useful role, many are skeptical about the usefulness of discretionary fiscal policy due to the time lags in its formulation and implementation.

But there's an important alternative: monetary policy. In the next two chapters we'll learn about monetary institutions and see how monetary policy works.

SUMMARY

1. The government plays a large role in the economy, collecting a large share of GDP in taxes and spending a large share both to purchase goods and services and to make transfer payments, largely for **social insurance**. *Fiscal policy* is the use of taxes, government transfers, or government purchases of goods and services to shift the aggregate demand curve. But many economists caution that a very active fiscal policy may in fact make the economy less stable due to time lags in policy formulation and implementation.

2. Government purchases of goods and services directly affect aggregate demand, and changes in taxes and government transfers affect aggregate demand indirectly by changing households' disposable income. **Expansionary fiscal policies** shift the aggregate demand curve rightward, while **contractionary fiscal policies** shift the aggregate demand curve leftward.

3. Fiscal policy has a multiplier effect on the economy. Expansionary fiscal policy leads to an increase in real GDP larger than the initial rise in aggregate spending caused by the policy. Conversely, contractionary fiscal policy leads to a fall in real GDP larger than the initial reduction in aggregate spending caused by the policy. The size of the shift of the aggregate demand curve depends on the type of fiscal policy. The multiplier on changes in government purchases, $1/(1 - MPC)$, is larger than the multiplier on changes in (lump-sum) taxes or transfers, $MPC/(1 - MPC)$, because part of any change in taxes or transfers is absorbed by savings in the first round of spending. So changes in government purchases have a more powerful effect on the economy than equal-size changes in taxes or transfers.

4. Rules governing taxes and some transfers act as **automatic stabilizers,** reducing the size of the multiplier and automatically reducing the size of fluctuations in the business cycle. In contrast, **discretionary fiscal policy** arises from deliberate actions by policy makers rather than from the business cycle.

5. Some of the fluctuations in the budget balance are due to the effects of the business cycle. In order to separate the effects of the business cycle from the effects of discretionary fiscal policy, governments estimate the **cyclically adjusted budget balance,** an estimate of the budget balance if the economy were at potential output.

6. U.S. government budget accounting is calculated on the basis of **fiscal years.** Persistent budget deficits have long-run consequences because they lead to an increase in **public debt.** This can be a problem for two reasons. Public debt may crowd out investment spending, which reduces long-run economic growth. And in extreme cases, rising debt may lead to government default, resulting in economic and financial turmoil.

7. A widely used measure of fiscal health is the **debt–GDP ratio.** This number can remain stable or fall even in the face of moderate budget deficits if GDP rises over time. However, a stable debt–GDP ratio may give a misleading impression that all is well because modern governments often have large **implicit liabilities.** The largest implicit liabilities of the U.S. government come from Social Security, Medicare, and Medicaid, the costs of which are increasing due to the aging of the population and rising medical costs.

KEY TERMS

Social insurance, p. 295
Expansionary fiscal policy, p. 297
Contractionary fiscal policy, p. 298
Automatic stabilizers, p. 302

Discretionary fiscal policy, p. 302
Cyclically adjusted budget balance, p. 306
Fiscal years, p. 309
Public debt, p. 309

Debt–GDP ratio, p. 310
Implicit liabilities, p. 312

PROBLEMS

1. The accompanying diagram shows the current macroeconomic situation for the economy of Albernia. You have been hired as an economic consultant to help the economy move to potential output, Y_P.

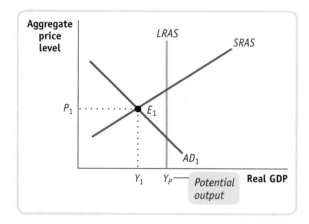

a. Is Albernia facing a recessionary or inflationary gap?

b. Which type of fiscal policy—expansionary or contractionary—would move the economy of Albernia to potential output, Y_E? What are some examples of such policies?

c. Illustrate the macroeconomic situation in Albernia with a diagram after the successful fiscal policy has been implemented.

2. The accompanying diagram shows the current macroeconomic situation for the economy of Brittania; real GDP is Y_1 and the aggregate price level is P_1. You have been hired as an economic consultant to help the economy move to potential output, Y_P.

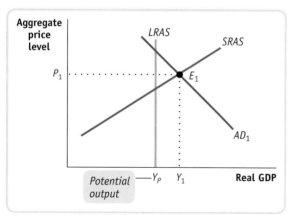

a. Is Brittania facing a recessionary or inflationary gap?

b. Which type of fiscal policy—expansionary or contractionary—would move the economy of Brittania to potential output, Y_P? What are some examples of such policies?

c. Illustrate the macroeconomic situation in Brittania with a diagram after the successful fiscal policy has been implemented.

3. An economy is in long-run macroeconomic equilibrium when each of the following aggregate demand shocks occurs. What kind of gap—inflationary or recessionary—will the economy face after the shock, and what type of fiscal policies would help move the economy back to potential output?

a. A stock market boom increases the value of stocks held by households.

b. Firms come to believe that a recession in the near future is likely.

c. Anticipating the possibility of war, the government increases its purchases of military equipment.

d. The quantity of money in the economy declines and interest rates increase.

4. Show why a $10 billion decrease in government purchases will have a larger effect on real GDP than a $10 billion reduction in government transfers by completing the table at the top of page 317 for an economy with a marginal propensity to consume (MPC) of 0.6. The first and second rows of the table are filled in for you: in the first row, the $10 billion decrease in government purchases decreases real GDP and disposable income, YD, by $10 billion, leading to a decrease in consumer spending of $6 billion (MPC × change in disposable income) in row 2. However, the $10 billion reduction in transfers has no effect on real GDP in round 1 but does lower YD by $10 billion, resulting in a decrease in consumer spending of $6 billion in round 2.

| | Decrease in G = −$10 billion | | | Decrease in TR = −$10 billion | | |
| | Billions of dollars | | | Billions of dollars | | |
Rounds	Change in G	Change in real GDP	Change in YD	Change in TR	Change in real GDP	Change in YD
1	$\Delta G = -\$10.00$	−$10.00	−$10.00	$\Delta TR = -\$10.00$	$0.00	−$10.00
2	$\Delta C =$ 6.00	−6.00	−6.00	$\Delta C =$ −6.00	−6.00	−6.00
3	$\Delta C =$?	?	?	$\Delta C =$?	?	?
4	$\Delta C =$?	?	?	$\Delta C =$?	?	?
5	$\Delta C =$?	?	?	$\Delta C =$?	?	?
6	$\Delta C =$?	?	?	$\Delta C =$?	?	?
7	$\Delta C =$?	?	?	$\Delta C =$?	?	?
8	$\Delta C =$?	?	?	$\Delta C =$?	?	?
9	$\Delta C =$?	?	?	$\Delta C =$?	?	?
10	$\Delta C =$?	?	?	$\Delta C =$?	?	?

a. When government purchases decrease by $10 billion, what is the sum of the changes in real GDP after the 10 rounds?

b. When the government reduces government transfers by $10 billion, what is the sum of the changes in real GDP after the 10 rounds?

c. Using the formula for the multiplier for changes in government purchases and for changes in transfers, calculate the total change in real GDP due to the $10 billion decrease in government purchases and the $10 billion reduction in government transfers. What explains the difference?

5. In each of the following cases, either a recessionary or inflationary gap exists. Assume that the short-run aggregate supply curve is horizontal so that the change in real GDP arising from a shift of the aggregate demand curve equals the size of the shift of the curve. Calculate both the change in government purchases of goods and services and the change in government transfers necessary to close the gap.

a. Real GDP equals $100 billion, potential output equals $160 billion, and the marginal propensity to consume is 0.75.

b. Real GDP equals $250 billion, potential output equals $200 billion, and the marginal propensity to consume is 0.5.

c. Real GDP equals $180 billion, potential output equals $100 billion, and the marginal propensity to consume is 0.8.

6. Most macroeconomists believe it is a good thing that taxes act as automatic stabilizers and lower the size of the multiplier. However, a smaller multiplier means that the change in government purchases of goods and services, government transfers, or taxes necessary to close an inflationary or recessionary gap is larger. How can you explain this apparent inconsistency?

7. The accompanying table shows how consumers' marginal propensities to consume in a particular economy are related to their level of income:

Income range	Marginal propensity to consume
$0–$20,000	0.9
$20,001–$40,000	0.8
$40,001–$60,000	0.7
$60,001–$80,000	0.6
Above $80,000	0.5

a. What is the "bang for the buck" in terms of the increase in real GDP for an additional $1 of income for consumers in each income range?

b. If the government needed to close a recessionary or inflationary gap, what types of fiscal policies would you recommend to close the gap with the smallest change in either government purchases of goods and services or taxes?

8. The government's budget surplus in Macroland has risen consistently over the past five years. Two government policy makers disagree as to why this has happened. One argues that a rising budget surplus indicates a growing economy; the other argues that it shows that the government is using contractionary fiscal policy. Can you determine which policy maker is correct? If not, why not?

9. Figure 12-9 shows the actual budget deficit and the cyclically adjusted budget deficit as a percentage of real GDP in the United States since 1970. Assuming that potential output was unchanged, use this figure to determine in which years since 1992 the government used discretionary expansionary fiscal policy and in which years it used discretionary contractionary fiscal policy.

10. You are an economic adviser to a candidate for national office. She asks you for a summary of the economic consequences of a balanced-budget rule for the federal government and for your recommendation on whether she should support such a rule. How do you respond?

11. In 2005, the policy makers of the economy of Eastlandia projected the debt–GDP ratio and the deficit–GDP ratio for the economy for the next 10 years under different scenarios for growth in the government's deficit. Real GDP is currently $1,000 billion per year and is expected to grow by 3% per year, the public debt is $300 billion at the beginning of the year, and the deficit is $30 billion in 2005.

Year	Real GDP (billions of dollars)	Debt (billions of dollars)	Budget deficit (billions of dollars)	Debt (percent of real GDP)	Budget deficit (percent of real GDP)
2005	$1,000	$300	$30	?	?
2006	1,030	?	?	?	?
2007	1,061	?	?	?	?
2008	1,093	?	?	?	?
2009	1,126	?	?	?	?
2010	1,159	?	?	?	?
2011	1,194	?	?	?	?
2012	1,230	?	?	?	?
2013	1,267	?	?	?	?
2014	1,305	?	?	?	?
2015	1,344	?	?	?	?

a. Complete the accompanying table to show the debt–GDP ratio and the deficit–GDP ratio for the economy if the government's budget deficit remains constant at $30 billion over the next 10 years. (Remember that the government's debt will grow by the previous year's deficit.)

b. Redo the table to show the debt–GDP ratio and the deficit–GDP ratio for the economy if the government's budget deficit grows by 3% per year over the next 10 years.

c. Redo the table again to show the debt–GDP ratio and the deficit–GDP ratio for the economy if the government's budget deficit grows by 20% per year over the next 10 years.

d. What happens to the debt–GDP ratio and the deficit–GDP ratio for the economy over time under the three different scenarios?

12. Your study partner argues that the distinction between the government's budget deficit and debt is similar to the distinction between consumer savings and wealth. He also argues that if you have large budget deficits, you must have a large debt. In what ways is your study partner correct and in what ways is he incorrect?

13. In which of the following cases does the size of the government's debt and the size of the budget deficit indicate potential problems for the economy?

a. The government's debt is relatively low, but the government is running a large budget deficit as it builds a high-speed rail system to connect the major cities of the nation.

b. The government's debt is relatively high due to a recently ended deficit-financed war, but the government is now running only a small budget deficit.

c. The government's debt is relatively low, but the government is running a budget deficit to finance the interest payments on the debt.

14. How did or would the following affect the current public debt and implicit liabilities of the U.S. government?

a. In 2003, Congress passed and President Bush signed the Medicare Modernization Act, which provides seniors and individuals with disabilities with a prescription drug benefit. Some of the benefits under this law took effect immediately, but others will not begin until sometime in the future.

b. The age at which retired persons can receive full Social Security benefits is raised to age 70 for future retirees.

c. For future retirees, Social Security benefits are limited to those with low incomes.

d. Because the cost of health care is increasing faster than the overall inflation rate, annual increases in Social Security benefits are increased by the annual increase in health care costs rather than the overall inflation rate.

>>Chapter 12 Appendix: Taxes and the Multiplier

In the chapter, we described how taxes that depend positively on real GDP reduce the size of the multiplier and act as an automatic stabilizer for the economy. Let's look a little more closely at the mathematics of how this works.

Specifically, let's assume that the government "captures" a fraction t of any increase in real GDP in the form of taxes, where t, the tax rate, is a fraction between 0 and 1. And let's repeat the exercise we carried out in Chapter 10, where we consider the effects of a $50 billion increase in investment spending.

The $50 billion increase in investment spending initially raises real GDP by $50 billion (the first round). In the absence of taxes, disposable income would rise by $50 billion. But because part of the rise in real GDP is collected in the form of taxes, disposable income only rises by $(1 - t) \times \$50$ billion. The second-round increase in consumer spending, which is equal to the marginal propensity to consume (MPC) multiplied by the rise in disposable income, is $MPC \times (1 - t) \times \$50$ billion. This leads to a third-round increase in consumer spending of $(MPC \times (1 - t)) \times (MPC \times (1 - t)) \times \$50$ billion, and so on. So the total effect on real GDP is

$$
\begin{aligned}
\text{Increase in investment spending} &= &&\$50 \text{ billion} \\
+ \text{ Second-round increase in consumer spending} &= (MPC \times (1 - t)) &&\times \$50 \text{ billion} \\
+ \text{ Third-round increase in consumer spending} &= (MPC \times (1 - t))^2 &&\times \$50 \text{ billion} \\
+ \text{ Fourth-round increase in consumer spending} &= (MPC \times (1 - t))^3 &&\times \$50 \text{ billion}
\end{aligned}
$$

$$
\begin{aligned}
&\bullet &&\bullet \\
&\bullet &&\bullet \\
&\bullet &&\bullet
\end{aligned}
$$

$$
\text{Total change in real GDP} = [1 + (MPC \times (1 - t)) + (MPC \times (1 - t)^2) \\
+ (MPC \times (1 - t)^3) + \ldots] \times \$50 \text{ billion}
$$

As we pointed out in Chapter 10, a series of the form $1 + x + x^2 + \ldots$, with $0 < x < 1$, is equal to $1/(1 - x)$. In this example, $x = (MPC \times (1 - t))$. So the total effect of a $50 billion increase in government purchases of goods and services, taking into account all the subsequent increases in consumer spending, is to raise real GDP by

$$
\$50 \text{ billion} \times \frac{1}{1 - (MPC \times (1 - t))}
$$

When we calculated the multiplier assuming away the effect of taxes, we found that it was $1/(1 - MPC)$. But when we assume that a fraction t of any change in real GDP is collected in the form of taxes, the multiplier is

$$
\text{Multiplier} = \frac{1}{1 - (MPC \times (1 - t))}
$$

This is always a smaller number than $1/1 - MPC$, and its size diminishes as t grows. Suppose, for example, that $MPC = 0.6$. In the absence of taxes, this implies a multiplier of $1/(1 - 0.6) = 1/0.4 = 2.5$. But now let's assume that $t = 1/3$, that is, that 1/3 of any increase in real GDP is collected by the government. Then the multiplier is

$$
\frac{1}{1 - (0.6 \times (1 - 1/3))} = \frac{1}{1 - (0.6 \times 2/3)} = \frac{1}{1 - 0.4} = \frac{1}{0.6} = 1.667
$$

PROBLEMS

1. An economy has a marginal propensity to consume of 0.6, real GDP equals $500 billion, and the government collects 20% of GDP in taxes. If government purchases increase by $10 billion, show the rounds of increased spending that take place by completing the accompanying table. The first and second rows are filled in for you. In the first row, the increase in government purchases of $10 billion raises real GDP by $10 billion, taxes increase by $2 billion, and YD increases by $8 billion; in the second row, the increase in YD of $8 billion increases consumer spending by $4.80 billion ($MPC \times$ change in disposable income).

Rounds	Change in G or C	Change in real GDP	Change in taxes	Change in YD
		(billions of dollars)		
1	$\Delta G = \$10.00$	$10.00	$2.00	$8.00
2	$\Delta C = \$4.80$	4.80	0.96	3.84
3	$\Delta C = $?	?	?	?
4	$\Delta C = $?	?	?	?
5	$\Delta C = $?	?	?	?
6	$\Delta C = $?	?	?	?
7	$\Delta C = $?	?	?	?
8	$\Delta C = $?	?	?	?
9	$\Delta C = $?	?	?	?
10	$\Delta C = $?	?	?	?

a. What is the total change in real GDP after the 10 rounds? What is the value of the multiplier? What would you expect the total change in real GDP to be, based on the multiplier formula? How do your two answers compare?

b. Redo the preceding table, assuming the marginal propensity to consume is 0.75 and the government collects 10% of the rise in real GDP in taxes. What is the total change in real GDP after 10 rounds? What is the value of the multiplier?

2. Calculate the change in government purchases of goods and services necessary to close the recessionary or inflationary gaps in the following cases. Assume that the short-run aggregate supply curve is horizontal so that the change in real GDP arising from a shift of the aggregate demand curve equals the size of the shift of the curve.

a. Real GDP equals $100 billion, potential output equals $160 billion, the government collects 20% of any change in real GDP in the form of taxes, and the marginal propensity to consume is 0.75.

b. Real GDP equals $250 billion, potential output equals $200 billion, the government collects 10% of any change in real GDP in the form of taxes, and the marginal propensity to consume is 0.5.

c. Real GDP equals $180 billion, potential output equals $100 billion, the government collects 25% of any change in real GDP in the form of taxes, and the marginal propensity to consume is 0.8.

>web... To continue your study and review of concepts in this chapter, please visit the Krugman/Wells website for quizzes, animated graph tutorials, web links to helpful resources, and more.

www.worthpublishers.com/krugmanwells

>> Money, Banking, and the Federal Reserve System

13

A WAGGON-WAY THROUGH THE AIR

THE BIRTH OF ECONOMICS AS A discipline is usually dated to 1776, when Adam Smith published *The Wealth of Nations*. His book is most famous for its early appreciation of the "invisible hand" of markets, which harnesses private interest to the public good. But there's a lot more in *The Wealth of Nations*. Among other things, it contains a passionate defense of what were, in Smith's time, new-fangled inventions: banks and paper money.

Today we take it for granted that we can trade pieces of elaborately printed paper—green paper, in the United States—for almost any good or service. We also take for granted that in many cases we don't even need the pieces of paper: we can write a check or swipe a card, both of which amount to promises that a bank will provide green paper or its equivalent at a later time.

In Adam Smith's time, however, most of the world's business was still conducted with gold or silver coins. Paper money and bank accounts—though well established in his native Scotland—were still regarded with suspicion in much of the world. That's why Smith felt it necessary to explain the virtues of a modern monetary system that would allow a nation to conduct its business

while freeing up that gold and silver for other uses. Using paper money instead of gold and silver coins, he said, was like finding a way to build a road without diverting any land from other uses—building "a sort of waggon-way through the air."

According to an old proverb, "With money in your pocket, you are wise, and you are handsome, and you sing well, too."

In this chapter, we'll look at how a modern monetary system works and at the institutions that sustain and regulate it. This topic is important in itself, and it's also essential background for the understanding of *monetary policy,* which we will examine in Chapter 14.

> ## What you will learn in this chapter:
>
> ➤ The various roles **money** plays and the many forms it takes in the economy
>
> ➤ How the actions of private banks and the Federal Reserve determine the **money supply**
>
> ➤ How the Federal Reserve uses **open-market operations** to change the **monetary base**

The Meaning of Money

In everyday conversation, people often use the word *money* to mean "wealth." If you ask, "How much money does Bill Gates have?" the answer will be something like, "Oh, $40 billion or so, but who's counting?" That is, the number will include the value of the stocks, bonds, real estate, and other assets he owns.

But the economist's definition of money doesn't include all forms of wealth. The dollar bills in your wallet are money; other forms of wealth—such as cars, houses, and stock certificates—aren't money. What, according to economists, distinguishes money from other forms of wealth?

What Is Money?

Money is any asset that can easily be used to purchase goods and services.

Money is defined in terms of what it does: **money** is any asset that can easily be used to purchase goods and services. In Chapter 9 we defined an asset as *liquid* if it can easily be converted into cash. Money consists either of cash itself, which is liquid by definition, or of other assets that are highly liquid.

You can see the distinction between money and other assets by asking yourself how you pay for groceries. The person at the cash register will accept dollar bills in return for milk and frozen pizza—but not stock certificates or a collection of vintage baseball cards. If you want to convert stock certificates into groceries, you have to sell them—trade them for money—and then use the money to buy groceries.

Currency in circulation is cash held by the public.

Checkable bank deposits are bank accounts on which people can write checks.

The **money supply** is the total value of financial assets in the economy that are considered money.

Of course, many stores allow you to write a check on your bank account in payment for goods (or to pay with a debit card that is linked to your bank account). Does that make your bank account money, even if you haven't converted it into cash? Yes. **Currency in circulation**—actual cash in the hands of the public—is considered money. So are **checkable bank deposits**—bank accounts on which people can write checks.

Are currency and checkable bank deposits the only assets that are considered money? It depends. As we'll see later, there are several widely used definitions of the **money supply,** the total value of financial assets in the economy that are considered money. The narrowest definition is the most liquid because it contains only currency in circulation, traveler's checks, and checkable bank deposits. Broader definitions include other assets that are "almost" checkable, such as savings account deposits that can be transferred into a checking account with a phone call. All definitions of the money supply, however, make a distinction between assets that can easily be used to purchase goods and services, and those that can't.

Money plays a crucial role in generating *gains from trade*, because it makes indirect exchange possible. Think of what happens when a cardiac surgeon buys a new refrigerator. The surgeon has valuable services to offer—namely, heart operations. The owner of the store has valuable goods to offer: refrigerators and other appliances. It would be extremely difficult for both parties if, instead of using money, they had to directly barter the goods and services they sell. In a barter system, a cardiac surgeon and an appliance store owner could trade only if the store owner happened to want a heart operation *and* the surgeon happened to want a new refrigerator. This is known as the problem of finding a "double coincidence of wants": in a barter system, two parties can trade only when each wants what the other has to offer. Money solves this problem: individuals can trade what they have to offer for money and trade money for what they want.

Because money makes it easier to achieve gains from trade, it increases welfare, even though it does not directly produce anything. As Adam Smith put it, money "may very properly be compared to a highway, which, while it circulates and carries to market all the grass and corn of the country, produces itself not a single pile of either."

Let's take a closer look at the roles money plays in the economy.

PITFALLS

PLASTIC AND THE MONEY SUPPLY

In twenty-first-century America, many purchases are made with neither cash nor a check, but with cards. These cards come in two varieties. *Debit cards,* like bank ATM cards that can also be used at the supermarket, automatically transfer funds from the buyer's bank account. So debit cards allow you to access your bank account balance, which is part of the money supply.

But what about credit cards? *Credit cards* in effect allow you to borrow money to buy things at the store. Shouldn't these be counted as part of the money supply? The answer is no—the money supply is the value of *financial assets,* and credit cards are not assets. Credit cards access funds you can borrow—a liability, not an asset. Your credit card balance is what you currently owe. Your available credit is the maximum amount you can borrow. Since your credit card balance and your available credit are both liabilities, not assets, neither is part of the money supply.

Both debit and credit cards make it easier for individuals to make purchases. But they don't affect measures of the money supply.

Roles of Money

Money plays three main roles in any modern economy: it is a *medium of exchange,* a *store of value,* and a *unit of account.*

Medium of Exchange Our cardiac surgeon–refrigerator example illustrates the role of money as a **medium of exchange**—an asset that individuals use to trade for goods and services rather than for consumption. People can't eat dollar bills; rather, they use dollar bills to trade for edible goods and their accompanying services.

In normal times, the official money of a given country—the dollar in the United States, the peso in Mexico, and so on—is also the medium of exchange in virtually all transactions in that country. During troubled economic times, however, other goods or assets often play that role. For example, during economic turmoil other countries' moneys frequently become the medium of exchange: U.S. dollars have played this role in Latin American countries, and euros have done so in Eastern Europe. In a famous example, cigarettes functioned as the medium of exchange in World War II prisoner-of-war camps. Even nonsmokers traded goods and services for cigarettes, because the cigarettes could in turn be easily traded for other items. During the extreme German inflation of 1923, goods such as eggs and lumps of coal became, briefly, mediums of exchange.

> **A medium of exchange** is an asset that individuals acquire for the purpose of trading rather than for their own consumption.

Store of Value In order to act as a medium of exchange, money must also be a **store of value**—a means of holding purchasing power over time. To see why this is necessary, imagine trying to operate an economy in which ice-cream cones were the medium of exchange. Such an economy would quickly suffer from, well, monetary meltdown: your medium of exchange would often turn into a sticky puddle before you could use it to buy something else. (As we'll see in Chapter 16, one of the problems caused by high inflation is that, in effect, it causes the value of money to "melt.") Of course, money is by no means the only store of value. Any asset that holds its purchasing power over time is a store of value. So the store-of-value role is necessary but not distinctive.

> **A store of value** is a means of holding purchasing power over time.

Unit of Account Finally, money normally serves as a **unit of account**—a measure individuals use to set prices and make economic calculations. A new CD costs about five times as much as a Big Mac, but Amazon.com lists the price of a CD as $14, not five Big Macs.

> **A unit of account** is a measure used to set prices and make economic calculations.

Types of Money

In some form or another, money has been in use for thousands of years. For most of that period, people used **commodity money:** the medium of exchange was a good, normally gold or silver, that had other uses. These other uses gave commodity money value independent of its role as a medium of exchange. For example, cigarettes, which served as money in World War II POW camps, were also valuable because many prisoners smoked. Gold was valuable because it was used for jewelry and ornamentation, aside from the fact that it was minted into coins.

> **Commodity money** is a good used as a medium of exchange that has other uses.

By the time Adam Smith wrote *The Wealth of Nations,* most of the money in Scotland consisted of paper notes rather than gold or silver coins. Unlike modern dollar bills, however, those notes were issued by private banks, which promised to exchange their notes for gold or silver coins on demand. That is, the paper currency of 1776 Scotland was a **commodity-backed money,** a medium of exchange with no intrinsic value whose ultimate value was guaranteed by a promise that it could always be converted into valuable goods.

> **A commodity-backed money** is a medium of exchange with no intrinsic value whose ultimate value is guaranteed by a promise that it can be converted into valuable goods.

The big advantage of commodity-backed money over gold and silver coins is that it ties up fewer valuable resources. A country in which gold and silver coins have been replaced by paper money can normally rely on the fact that on any given day holders of only a fraction of its paper notes will demand to have them converted into gold or silver coins. So the note-issuing bank needs to keep only a portion of the total value of its notes in circulation in the form of gold and silver in its vaults. It can lend out the remaining gold and silver to those who wish to use it. This allows society to use that gold and silver for other purposes, all with no loss in the ability to achieve gains from trade.

That's what Adam Smith meant by a "waggon-way through the air." Remember his analogy between money and an imaginary highway that did not absorb valuable land beneath it. An actual highway provides a useful service but at a cost: land that could be used to grow crops is instead paved over. If the highway could be built through the air, it wouldn't destroy useful land. As Smith understood, when Scottish banks replaced gold and silver money with paper, they accomplished a similar feat: they reduced the amount of real resources used by society to provide the functions of money.

At this point you may ask, why make any use at all of gold and silver as a medium of exchange in the monetary system? In fact, today's monetary system goes even further than the Scottish system Smith admired. A U.S. dollar bill isn't commodity money, and it isn't even commodity-backed. Its value arises entirely from the fact that it is generally accepted as a means of payment, a role that is ultimately decreed by the U.S. government. Money whose value derives entirely from its official status as a means of exchange is known as **fiat money** because it exists by government *fiat*, a historical term for a policy declared by a ruler.

> **Fiat money** is a medium of exchange whose value derives entirely from its official status as a means of payment.

Measuring the Money Supply

The Federal Reserve (an institution we'll talk about shortly) calculates three **monetary aggregates,** overall measures of the money supply, which differ in how strictly money is defined. The three aggregates are known, rather cryptically, as M1, M2, and M3. M1, the narrowest definition, contains only currency in circulation (also known as cash), traveler's checks, and checkable bank deposits. M2 adds several other kinds of assets, often referred to as **near-moneys**—financial assets that aren't directly usable as a medium of exchange but can be readily converted into cash or checkable bank deposits, such as savings accounts. Examples are deposits that aren't checkable but can be withdrawn at any time with little or no penalty. Most monetary analyses focus on either M1 or M2. There is, however, a third aggregate, M3, which adds yet another group of somewhat more "distant" near-moneys—assets that are somewhat harder to convert into cash or checkable bank deposits, such as deposits that come with larger penalties for early withdrawal. M1 is therefore the most liquid measure of money because currency and checkable deposits are directly usable as a medium of exchange.

> A **monetary aggregate** is an overall measure of the money supply.

> **Near-moneys** are financial assets that can't be directly used as a medium of exchange but can be readily converted into cash or checkable bank deposits.

Figure 13-1 shows the makeup of M1 and M2 in June 2005, in billions of dollars. M1, valued at $1,368.4 billion, consisted roughly of half currency in circulation and

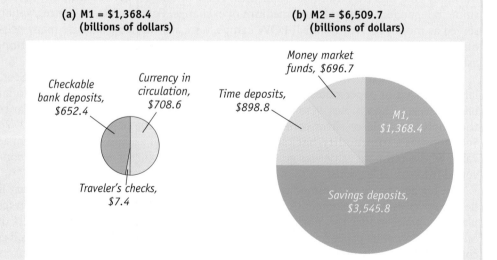

Figure 13-1

Monetary Aggregates, June 2005

The Federal Reserve uses three definitions of the money supply: M1, M2, and M3 (not shown). As panel (a) shows, M1 is almost equally split between currency in circulation and checkable bank deposits. M2, as panel (b) shows, has a much broader definition: it includes M1, plus a range of other deposits and deposit-like assets, making it almost five times as large.

Source: Federal Reserve Bank of St. Louis.

(a) M1 = $1,368.4
(billions of dollars)

Checkable bank deposits, $652.4

Currency in circulation, $708.6

Traveler's checks, $7.4

(b) M2 = $6,509.7
(billions of dollars)

Money market funds, $696.7

Time deposits, $898.8

M1, $1,368.4

Savings deposits, $3,545.8

half checkable bank deposits, with a tiny slice of traveler's checks. In turn, M1 made up slightly less than 25% of M2, valued at $6,509.7 billion. The rest of M2 consisted of two types of bank deposits, known as savings deposits and time deposits, which both are considered noncheckable, plus money market funds, which are mutual funds that invest only in liquid assets and bear a close resemblance to bank deposits.

economics in action

The History of the Dollar

U.S. dollar bills are pure fiat money: they have no intrinsic value, and they are not backed by anything that does. But money in America wasn't always like that. In the early days of European settlement, the colonies that would become the United States used commodity money, consisting in part of gold and silver coins. But such coins were scarce on this side of the Atlantic, so the colonists relied on a variety of other forms of commodity money. For example, settlers in Virginia used tobacco as money and settlers in the Northeast used "wampum," a type of clamshell.

Later in American history, commodity-backed paper money came into widespread use. But this wasn't paper money as we now know it, issued by the government and bearing the signature of the Secretary of the Treasury. Before the Civil War, the U.S. government didn't issue paper money at all. Dollar bills were issued by private banks, which promised holders that these bills could be redeemed for silver coins on demand. These promises weren't always credible because sometimes banks failed. People were reluctant to accept currency from banks suspected of being in financial trouble. In other words, some dollars were less valuable than others.

Counting money 1870s style: Iroquois chiefs from the Six Nations Reserve read wampum belts.

A curious legacy of that time was notes issued by the Citizens' Bank of Louisiana, based in New Orleans, that became among the most widely used bank notes in the southern states. These notes were printed in English on one side and French on the other. (At the time, many people in New Orleans, originally a colony of France, spoke French.) Thus, the $10 bill read *Ten* on one side and *Dix,* the French word for "ten," on the other. These $10 bills became known as "dixies," probably the source of the nickname of the U.S. South.

The U.S. government began issuing official paper money, called "greenbacks," during the Civil War. At first greenbacks had no fixed value in terms of commodities. After 1873 the U.S. government guaranteed the value of a dollar in terms of gold, effectively turning dollars into commodity-backed money.

In 1933, when President Franklin D. Roosevelt broke the link between dollars and gold, his own federal budget director declared ominously, "This will be the end of Western civilization." It wasn't. The link between the dollar and gold was restored a few years later, then dropped again—seemingly for good—in August 1971. Despite the warnings of doom, the U.S. dollar is still the world's most widely used currency. ∎

< < < < < < < < < < < < < < < < < < < <

>>CHECK YOUR UNDERSTANDING 13-1

1. Suppose you hold a gift certificate, good for certain products at participating stores. Is this gift certificate money? Why or why not?

2. Although most bank accounts pay some interest, depositors can get a higher interest rate by buying a certificate of deposit, or CD. The difference between a CD and a checking account is that the depositor pays a penalty for withdrawing the money before the CD comes due—a period of months or even years. Small CDs are counted in M2, but not in M1. Explain why they are not part of M1.

Solutions appear at back of book.

The Monetary Role of Banks

About half of M1, the narrowest definition of the money supply, consists of currency in circulation—$1 bills, $5 bills, and so on. It's obvious where currency comes from: it's printed by the U.S. Treasury. But the other half consists of bank deposits, and deposits account for the great bulk of M2 and M3, the broader definitions of the money supply. Bank deposits, then, are a major component of the money supply. And this fact brings us to our next topic: the monetary role of banks.

What Banks Do

As we learned in Chapter 9, a bank is a *financial intermediary* that uses liquid assets in the form of bank deposits to finance the illiquid investments of borrowers. Banks can create liquidity because it isn't necessary for a bank to keep all of the funds deposited with it in the form of highly liquid assets. Except in the case of a *bank run*—which we'll get to shortly—all of a bank's depositors won't want to withdraw his or her funds at the same time. So a bank can provide its depositors with liquid assets yet still invest much of the depositors' funds in illiquid assets, such as mortgages and business loans.

Banks don't, however, lend out all the funds placed in their hands by depositors because they do have to satisfy any depositor who wants to withdraw his or her funds. In order to meet these demands, banks keep substantial quantities of liquid assets on hand. In the modern U.S. banking system, these assets take the form either of currency in the banks' vaults or deposits held in the bank's own account at the Federal Reserve. The latter can be, as we'll see shortly, converted into currency more or less instantly. The currency and Federal Reserve deposits held by banks are called **bank reserves.** Because bank reserves are held by banks and the Federal Reserve, and not by the public, they are not considered part of currency in circulation.

To understand the basic role of banks in determining the money supply, let's consider a hypothetical example. Figure 13-2 shows the financial position of First Street

Bank reserves are the currency banks hold in their vaults plus their deposits at the Federal Reserve.

> **Figure 13-2**
>
> **Assets and Liabilities of First Street Bank**
>
> A T-account summarizes a bank's financial position. The bank's assets, $900,000 in outstanding loans to borrowers and reserves of $100,000, are entered on the left side. Its liabilities, $1,000,000 in bank deposits held for depositors, are entered on the right side. **>web...**
>
> | Assets | | Liabilities | |
> |---|---|---|---|
> | Loans | $900,000 | Deposits | $1,000,000 |
> | Reserves | $100,000 | | |

Bank, which is the repository of $1 million in bank deposits. The bank's financial position is described by the *T-account,* a type of financial spreadsheet, as shown in the figure. On the left side are First Street's *assets*—claims on individuals and businesses, consisting of the value of its outstanding loans—and its reserves. On the right side are the bank's *liabilities*—claims held by individuals and firms against the bank, consisting of the value of bank deposits.

In this example, First Street Bank holds reserves equal to 10% of its bank deposits. The fraction of bank deposits that a bank holds as reserves is its **reserve ratio.** In the modern American system the Federal Reserve—which, among other things, regulates banks—sets a minimum required reserve ratio that banks are required to maintain. To understand why banks are regulated, we need to look at a problem banks can face: *bank runs.*

The **reserve ratio** is the fraction of bank deposits that a bank holds as reserves.

The Problem of Bank Runs

Banks can lend out most of the funds deposited in their care because all depositors normally won't want to withdraw all their funds at the same time. But what would happen to a bank if, for some reason, all or at least a large fraction of its depositors *did* try to withdraw all their funds during a short period of time, such as a couple of days?

The answer is that the bank wouldn't have enough cash and reserves at the Federal Reserve to meet its depositors' demands for immediate cash withdrawals. The bank would have a hard time coming up with the cash, even if it had invested depositors' funds wisely, because bank loans are relatively illiquid. Bank loans can't easily be converted into cash on short notice. To see why, imagine that First Street Bank has lent $100,000 to Drive-A-Peach Used Cars, a local dealership. To raise cash, First Street can sell its loan to Drive-A-Peach to someone else—another bank or an individual investor. But if First Street tries to sell the loan quickly, potential buyers will be wary: they will suspect that First Street wants to sell the loan because there is something wrong and the loan might not be repaid. As a result, First Street Bank can sell the loan quickly only by offering it for sale at a deep discount, say a discount of 50%, or $50,000.

The upshot is that if First Street's depositors all suddenly decide to withdraw their funds, any effort to raise the necessary cash forces the bank to sell off its assets very cheaply. Inevitably, it will not be able to pay off its depositors in full.

What might start this whole process? That is, what might lead First Street's depositors to rush to pull their money out? A plausible answer is a spreading rumor that the bank is in financial trouble. Even if they aren't sure the rumor is true, depositors are likely to play it safe and get their money out while they still can. And it gets worse: a depositor who simply thinks that *other* depositors are going to panic and try to get

A **bank run** is a phenomenon in which many of a bank's depositors try to withdraw their funds due to fears of a bank failure.

their money out will realize that this could "break the bank." So he or she joins the rush. In other words, fear about a bank's financial condition can be a self-fulfilling prophecy: depositors who believe that other depositors will rush for the exit will rush for the exit themselves.

A **bank run** is a phenomenon in which many of a bank's depositors try to withdraw their funds due to fears of a bank failure. Moreover, bank runs aren't bad only for the bank in question and its depositors. Historically, they have often proved contagious, with a run on one bank leading to a loss of faith in other banks, causing additional bank runs. The Economics in Action on the following page describes just such a contagion, the wave of bank runs that swept the United States in the early 1930s. In response to that experience and similar experiences in other countries, the United States and most other modern governments have established a system of bank regulations that protect depositors and prevent bank runs.

Bank Regulation

Should you worry about losing money in the United States because of a bank run? No. After the banking crises of the 1930s, the United States and most other countries put into place a system designed to protect depositors and the economy as a whole against bank runs. This system has three main features: *deposit insurance, capital requirements,* and *reserve requirements.*

Deposit insurance guarantees that a bank's depositors will be paid even if the bank can't come up with the funds, up to a maximum amount per account.

Deposit Insurance Almost all banks in the United States advertise themselves as a "member of the FDIC"—the Federal Deposit Insurance Corporation. As we learned in Chapter 9, it provides **deposit insurance,** a guarantee by the federal government that depositors will be paid even if the bank can't come up with the funds, up to a maximum amount per account. The FDIC currently guarantees the first $100,000 of each account.

It's important to realize that deposit insurance doesn't just protect depositors if a bank actually fails. The insurance also eliminates the main reason for bank runs: since depositors know their funds are safe even if a bank fails, they have no incentive to rush to pull them out because of a rumor that the bank is in trouble.

FOR INQUIRING MINDS

IS BANKING A CON?

Banks make it possible for any individual depositor to withdraw funds whenever he or she wants. Yet the cash in a bank's vault, and its deposits at the Federal Reserve, wouldn't be enough to satisfy all or even most depositors if they all tried to withdraw funds at the same time. Does this mean that there is something fundamentally dishonest about the banking business?

Many people have thought so; every once in a while a prominent critic of the banking industry demands regulations that would stop banks from making illiquid loans. But an analogy may help explain what banks do and why it's productive.

Think about car-rental agencies. Because of

these agencies, someone who travels, say, from Atlanta to Cincinnati can normally count on having a car when he or she needs one. Yet there are many more potential travelers to Cincinnati than there are cars available to rent; the rent-a-car business depends on the fact that only a fraction of those potential visitors show up in any given week. There's no trickery involved. Travelers believe they can almost always get a car when needed, even though the number of cars actually available is limited— and they are right. Banks do the same thing. Depositors believe they can almost always get cash when they need it, even though the amount of cash actually available is limited— and they are right too.

Capital Requirements Deposit insurance, although it protects the banking system against bank runs, creates a well-known incentive problem. Because depositors are protected from loss, they have no incentive to monitor their bank's financial health. Meanwhile, the owners of banks have an incentive to engage in overly risky investment behavior, such as making risky loans at high interest. If all goes well, the owners profit; and if things go badly, the government covers the losses through federal deposit insurance.

To reduce the incentive for excessive risk taking, regulators require that the owners of banks hold substantially more assets than the value of bank deposits. That way, the bank will still have assets larger than its deposits even if some of its loans go bad, and losses will accrue against the bank owners' assets, not the government. The excess of a bank's assets over its bank deposits and other liabilities is called the bank's capital. In practice, banks' capital is equal to 7% or more of their assets.

Reserve Requirements Another way to reduce the risk of bank runs is to require banks to maintain a higher reserve ratio than they otherwise would. **Reserve requirements** are rules set by the Federal Reserve that determine a bank's minimum reserve ratio. For example, in the United States, the minimum reserve ratio for checkable bank deposits is 10%.

> **Reserve requirements** are rules set by the Federal Reserve that determine the minimum reserve ratio for a bank.

economics in action

It's a Wonderful Banking System

Next Christmas time, it's a sure thing that at least one TV station in your home town will show the 1946 film *It's a Wonderful Life,* featuring Jimmy Stewart as George Bailey, a small-town banker whose life is saved by an angel. The movie's climactic scene is a run on Bailey's bank, as fearful depositors rush to take their funds out.

When the movie was made, such scenes were still fresh in Americans' memories. There was a wave of bank runs in late 1930, a second wave in the spring of 1931, and a third wave in early 1933. By the end, more than a third of the nation's banks had failed. To bring the panic to an end, on March 6, 1933, the newly inaugurated president, Franklin Delano Roosevelt, declared a national "bank holiday," closing all banks for a week.

Since then, regulation has protected the United States and other wealthy countries against bank runs. In fact, the scene in *It's a Wonderful Life* was already out of date when the movie was made. But the last decade has seen several waves of bank runs in developing countries. For example, bank runs played a role in an economic crisis that swept Southeast Asia in 1997–1998 and in the severe economic crisis in Argentina, which began in late 2001. ∎

Argentina's economic crisis led to massive bank runs, angry public protests, and despair as many middle- and working-class families lost jobs and savings and were plunged into poverty.

> > > > > > > > > > > > > > > > > > > >

>>CHECK YOUR UNDERSTANDING 13-2

1. Suppose you are a depositor at First Street Bank. You hear a rumor that the bank has suffered serious losses on its loans. Every depositor knows that the rumor isn't true, but each thinks that most other depositors believe the rumor. Why, in the absence of deposit insurance, could this lead to a bank run? Why does deposit insurance change the situation?

> **>> QUICK REVIEW**
>
> ➤ Banks hold *bank reserves* of currency plus deposits at the Federal Reserve. The *reserve ratio* is the ratio of reserves to bank deposits.
> ➤ *Bank runs* were a serious problem in the past, but in the contemporary United States, banks and their depositors are protected by *deposit insurance*, capital requirements, and *reserve requirements*.

2. A con man has a great idea: he'll open a bank without investing any capital and lend all the deposits at high interest rates to real estate developers. If the real estate market booms, the loans will be repaid and he'll make high profits. If the real estate market goes bust, the loans won't be repaid and the bank will fail—but he will not lose any of his own wealth. How would modern bank regulation frustrate his scheme?

Solutions appear at back of book.

Determining the Money Supply

If banks didn't exist, the quantity of currency in circulation would equal the money supply. And since all U.S. currency in circulation—coins, $1 bills, $5 bills, and so on—is issued by the government, the money supply would be determined directly by whoever controls the minting and printing presses. But banks do exist, and they affect the money supply in two ways. First, they take some currency out of circulation: dollar bills that are sitting in bank vaults, as opposed to sitting in people's wallets, aren't considered part of the money supply. Second, and much more important, is that banks, by offering deposits, create money, allowing the money supply to be larger than the quantity of currency in circulation. Let's look at how banks create money and what determines the amount of money they create.

How Banks Create Money

To see how banks create money, it's useful to examine what happens when someone decides to deposit currency in a bank. So let's consider the example of Silas, a miser, who keeps shoeboxes full of currency under his mattress. Suppose he realizes that it would actually be safer, as well as more convenient, to deposit that cash in the bank and withdraw funds or write checks when necessary. And suppose he takes his money, $1,000 in cash, and deposits it into a checkable account at First Street Bank. What effect will this have on the money supply?

Panel (a) of Figure 13-3 shows the initial effect of his deposit. First Street Bank credits Silas with $1,000 in his account, so checkable bank deposits rise by $1,000. Meanwhile, Silas's cash goes into the vault, so First Street's reserves also rise by $1,000.

This initial transaction has no effect on the money supply. Currency in circulation falls by $1,000, but checkable bank deposits—which are also part of the money supply—rise by the same amount.

Figure 13-3   Effect on the Money Supply of Turning Cash into a Checkable Deposit at First Street Bank

(a) Initial Effect Before Bank Makes a New Loan

Assets		Liabilities	
Loans	No change	Checkable deposits	+$1,000
Reserves	+ $1,000		

(b) Effect After Bank Makes a New Loan

Assets		Liabilities	
Loans	+ $900	No change	
Reserves	− $900		

When Silas deposits $1,000 (which had been stashed under his mattress) into a checkable bank account, there is initially no effect on the money supply: currency in circulation falls by $1,000, but checkable bank deposits rise by $1,000. The corresponding entries on the bank's T-account (panel a) show deposits initially rising by $1,000 and the bank's reserves initially rising by $1,000. In the sec- ond stage (panel b), the bank holds 10% of Silas's deposit ($100) as reserves and lends out the rest ($900) to Mary. As a result, its reserves fall by $900 and its loans increase by $900. Its liabilities, includ- ing Silas's $1,000 deposit, are unchanged. The money supply, the sum of checkable bank deposits and cur- rency in circulation, has now increased by $900—the $900 now held by Mary.

But this is not the end of the story, because First Street Bank can now lend out part of Silas's deposit. Assume that it holds 10% of the deposit—$100—in reserves and lends the rest out in cash to Silas's neighbor, Mary. The effect of this second stage is shown in panel (b). First Street's deposits remain unchanged, and so does the value of its assets. But the composition of its assets changes. Its reserves are $900 less than if it had not made the loan (and they are $100 more than before Silas deposited his money). And in the place of that $900 it has acquired an IOU, its $900 cash loan to Mary.

By putting Silas's cash back in circulation by lending it to Mary, First Street Bank has, in fact, increased the money supply. That is, the sum of currency in circulation and checkable bank deposits has risen by $900.

And even this may not be the end of the story. Suppose that Mary uses her cash to buy a television and a DVD player from Acme Merchandise. What does Anne Acme, the store's owner, do with the cash? If she holds on to it, the money supply doesn't increase any further. But suppose she deposits the $900 into a checkable bank deposit—say, at Second Street Bank. Second Street Bank, in turn, will keep only part of that deposit in reserves, lending out the rest, creating still more money.

Assume that Second Street Bank, like First Street Bank, keeps 10% of any bank deposit in reserves and lends out the rest. Then it will keep $90 in reserves and lend out $810 of Anne's deposit, further increasing the money supply.

Table 13-1 shows the process of money creation we have described so far. At first the money supply consists only of Silas's $1,000. After he deposits the cash into a checkable bank deposit and the bank makes a loan, the money supply rises to $1,900. After the second deposit and the second loan, the money supply rises to $2,710. And the process will, of course, continue from there. (Although we have considered the case in which Silas places his cash in a checkable bank deposit, the results would be the same if he put it into any type of near-money.)

This process of money creation may sound familiar. In Chapter 10 we described the *multiplier process*: an initial increase in real GDP leads to a rise in consumer spending, which leads to a further rise in real GDP, which leads to a further rise in consumer spending, and so on. What we have here is another kind of multiplier—the *money multiplier*. Let's look at how the size of this multiplier is determined.

TABLE 13-1

How Banks Create Money

	Currency in circulation	Checkable bank deposits	Money supply
First stage (Silas keeps his cash under the mattress)	$1,000	$0	$1,000
Second stage (Silas deposits cash in First Street Bank, which lends out $900 to Mary)	900	1,000	1,900
Third stage (Mary deposits cash loan of $900 in Second Street Bank, which lends out $810 to Anne Acme.	810	1,900	2,710

Reserves, Bank Deposits, and the Money Multiplier

In tracing out the effect of Silas's deposit in Table 13-1, we assumed that the funds a bank lends out always end up being deposited either in the same bank or in another bank—so loans come back to the banking system, even if not to the lending bank itself. In reality, part of the loans may be held by borrowers in the form of currency, and so some of the loaned amount "leaks" out of the banking system because individuals add to their holdings of currency. Such leaks will reduce the size of the money multiplier, just as leaks of real income into savings reduces the size of the standard multiplier. But let's set that complication aside for a moment and consider how the money supply would be determined in a "checkable-deposits-only" monetary system.

Assume, then, that banks are subject to a rule that sets a minimum required reserve ratio. Also assume that banks lend out any of their **excess reserves,** reserves over and above required reserves. Assume, finally, that any money an individual borrows from a bank is deposited into a checkable bank account. Now suppose that for some

Excess reserves are a bank's reserves over and above its required reserves.

reason a bank suddenly finds itself with $1,000 in excess reserves. What happens? The answer is that the bank will lend out that $1,000, which will end up as a checkable bank deposit somewhere in the banking system, launching a money multiplier process very similar to the process shown in Table 13-1.

Let's examine this process more closely by assuming that the required reserve ratio is 10%. In the first stage of the process, the bank with excess reserves lends out $1,000, which becomes a checkable bank deposit somewhere. The bank that receives that deposit keeps 10%, or $100, as reserves, and lends out the remaining 90%, or $900, which again becomes a checkable bank deposit somewhere. The bank receiving this $900 deposit again keeps 10%, which is $90, as reserves, and lends out the remaining $810. The bank receiving this $810 keeps $81 in reserves, and lends out the remaining $729, and so on. As a result of this process, the total increase in checkable bank deposits is equal to a sum that looks like:

$$\$1,000 + \$900 + \$810 + \$729 + \ldots$$

We'll use the symbol rr for the reserve ratio. More generally, the total increase in checkable bank deposits that is generated when a bank lends out $1,000 in excess reserves is:

(13-1) Increase in checkable bank deposits from $1,000 in excess reserves = $$\$1,000 + \$1,000 \times (1 - rr) + \$1,000 \times (1 - rr)^2 + \$1,000 \times (1 - rr)^3 + \ldots$$

As we saw in Equation 10-4 in Chapter 10, this can be simplified to:

(13-2) Increase in checkable bank deposits from $1,000 in excess reserves = $$\$1,000/rr$$

Given a reserve ratio of 10%, or 0.1, a $1,000 increase in excess reserves will increase the total value of checkable bank deposits by $1,000/0.1 = $10,000. In fact, in a checkable-deposits-only monetary system the total value of checkable bank deposits will be equal to the value of bank reserves divided by the reserve ratio. Or to put it a different way, if the reserve ratio is 10%, each dollar of reserves held by a bank supports $1/rr = $1/0.1 = $10 of checkable bank deposits.

The Money Multiplier in Reality

In reality, the determination of the money supply is more complicated than our simple model suggests, because it depends not only on the ratio of reserves to bank deposits but also on the fraction of the money supply that individuals choose to hold in the form of currency. In fact, we already saw this in our example of Silas depositing the cash under his bed: when he chose to hold a checkable bank deposit instead of currency, he set in motion an increase in the money supply.

To define the money multiplier in practice, it's important to recognize that the monetary authorities control the *sum* of bank reserves and currency in circulation, but not the allocation of that sum between reserves and currency in circulation. Consider Silas and his deposit one more time: by taking the cash from under his bed and depositing it in a bank, he reduced the quantity of currency in circulation but increased bank reserves by an equal amount. The **monetary base,** which is the quantity the monetary authorities control, is the sum of currency in circulation and reserves held by banks.

The monetary base isn't the same thing as the money supply, for two reasons. First, bank reserves, which are part of the monetary base, aren't considered part of the money supply. A $1 bill in someone's wallet is considered money because it's available for an individual to spend, but a $1 bill held as bank reserves in a bank vault or deposited at the Federal Reserve isn't considered part of the money supply because it's not available for spending. Second, checkable bank deposits aren't part of the monetary base, but they are part of the money supply because they are available for spending.

> The **monetary base** is the sum of currency in circulation and bank reserves.

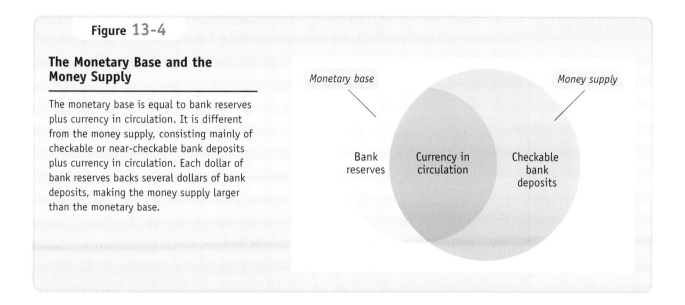

Figure 13-4

The Monetary Base and the Money Supply

The monetary base is equal to bank reserves plus currency in circulation. It is different from the money supply, consisting mainly of checkable or near-checkable bank deposits plus currency in circulation. Each dollar of bank reserves backs several dollars of bank deposits, making the money supply larger than the monetary base.

Monetary base — Money supply

Bank reserves — Currency in circulation — Checkable bank deposits

Figure 13-4 shows the two concepts schematically. The circle on the left represents the monetary base, consisting of bank reserves plus currency in circulation. The circle on the right represents the money supply, consisting mainly of currency in circulation plus checkable or near-checkable bank deposits. As the figure indicates, currency in circulation is part of both the monetary base and the money supply. But bank reserves aren't part of the money supply, and checkable or near-checkable bank deposits aren't part of the monetary base. In practice, most of the monetary base actually consists of currency in circulation, which also makes up about half of the money supply.

Now we can formally define the **money multiplier:** it's the ratio of the money supply to the monetary base. The actual money multiplier in the United States, using M1 as our measure of money, is about 1.9. That's a lot smaller than $1/0.1 = 10$, the money multiplier in a checkable-deposits-only system with a reserve ratio of 10% (the ratio for most checkable deposits in the United States). The reason the money multiplier is so small is that a dollar of currency in circulation, unlike a dollar in reserves, doesn't support multiple dollars of the money supply. And as Figure 13-4 illustrates, most of the monetary base is held as currency in circulation.

> The **money multiplier** is the ratio of the money supply to the monetary base.

economics in action

Multiplying Money Down

In our hypothetical example illustrating how banks create money, we described Silas the miser deciding to take the currency from under his mattress and turning it into a checkable bank deposit. This led to an increase in the money supply, as banks engaged in successive waves of lending backed by Silas' funds. It follows that if something happened to make Silas revert to old habits, taking his money out of the bank and putting it back under his bed, the result would be less lending and a decline in the money supply. And that's exactly what happened as a result of the bank runs of the 1930s.

Table 13-2 shows what happened between 1929 and 1933, as bank failures shook the public's confidence. The first column shows the public's holdings of currency. This increased sharply, as many Americans decided that money under the bed might be safer than money in the bank after all. The second column shows the value of checkable bank deposits. This fell sharply, through the multiplier process we have just analyzed, when individuals pulled their cash out of banks. (Loans also fell because banks that survived the waves of bank

TABLE 13-2

The Effects of Bank Runs, 1929–1933

	Currency in circulation	Checkable Bank deposits	M1
	(billions of dollars)		
1929	$3.90	$22.74	$26.64
1933	5.09	14.82	19.91
Percent change	+31%	−35%	−25%

Source: U.S Census Bureau (1975), *Historical Statistics of the United States*.

runs increased their excess reserves, just in case another wave began.) The third column shows the value of M1, the first of the monetary aggregates we described earlier. It fell sharply, because the reduction in checkable or near-checkable bank deposits was much larger than the increase in currency in circulation.

In a famous 1963 book, *A Monetary History of the United States,* Anna Schwartz and Milton Friedman drew attention to this drop in the U.S. money supply, arguing that it was the main cause of the Great Depression. They also argued that the Federal Reserve could and should have prevented it. (We should note that many economists disagree with both conclusions.) And that brings us to the nature and role of the Fed. ■

< < < < < < < < < < < < < < < < < <

▶▶ CHECK YOUR UNDERSTANDING 13-3

1. Assume that total reserves are equal to $200 and total checkable bank deposits are equal to $1,000. Also assume that the public does not hold any currency. Now suppose that the required reserve ratio falls from 20% to 10%. Trace out how this leads to an expansion in bank deposits.

2. Take the example of Silas depositing his $1,000 in cash into First Street Bank and assume that the required reserve ratio is 10%. But now assume that each time someone receives a bank loan, he or she keeps half the loan in cash. Trace out the resulting expansion in the money supply.

Solutions appear at back of book.

The Federal Reserve System

Who's in charge of ensuring that banks maintain enough reserves? Who decides how large the monetary base will be? The answer, in the United States, is an institution known as the Federal Reserve (or, informally, as the "Fed").

The Fed: America's Central Bank

A **central bank** is an institution that oversees and regulates the banking system and controls the monetary base.

The Federal Reserve is a **central bank**—an institution that oversees and regulates the banking system, and controls the monetary base. Other central banks include the Bank of England, the Bank of Japan, and the European Central Bank, or ECB. The ECB acts as a common central bank for 12 European countries: Austria, Belgium, Finland, France, Germany, Greece, Ireland, Italy, Luxembourg, the Netherlands, Portugal, and Spain. The world's oldest central bank, by the way, is Sweden's Sveriges Rijksbank, which awards the Nobel Prize in economics.

The legal status of the Fed, which was created in 1913, is unusual: it is not exactly part of the U.S. government, but it is not really a private institution either. Strictly speaking, the Federal Reserve system consists of two parts: the Board of Governors and the 12 regional Federal Reserve Banks.

The Board of Governors, which oversees the system from its offices in Washington, D.C., is set up like a government agency: its seven members are appointed by the president and must be approved by the Senate. However, they are appointed for 14-year terms, to insulate them from political pressure. The chairman is appointed on a more frequent basis, every 4 years, but it's traditional for chairmen to be reappointed and serve much longer terms. William McChesney Martin was chairman of the Fed from 1951 until 1970. Alan Greenspan, appointed in 1987, was still serving as Fed chairman in 2005.

The 12 Federal Reserve Banks each serve a region of the country, providing various banking and supervisory services. For example, they audit the books of private-sector banks, to ensure that they are financially sound. Each regional bank is run by a board of directors chosen from the local banking and business community. The Federal Reserve Bank of New York has a special role: it carries out *open-market operations*, the main tool of monetary policy. Figure 13-5 shows the Federal Reserve districts and the city in which each regional Federal Reserve Bank is located.

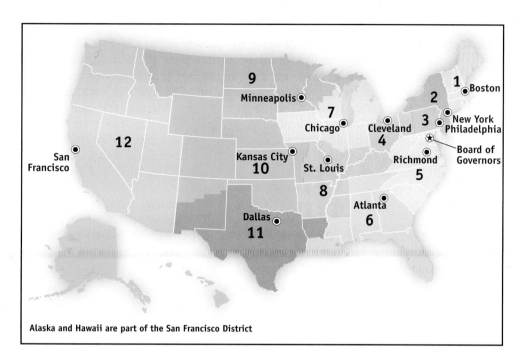

Figure 13-5 The Federal Reserve System The Federal Reserve system consists of the Board of Governors in Washington, D.C., plus regional Federal Reserve Banks, each serving its district. This map shows each of the 12 Federal Reserve districts. *Source:* Board of Governors of the Federal Reserve system.

Alaska and Hawaii are part of the San Francisco District

Decisions about monetary policy are made by the Federal Open Market Committee, which consists of the Board of Governors plus five of the regional bank presidents. The president of the Federal Reserve Bank of New York is always on the committee, and the other four seats rotate among the 11 other regional bank presidents. The chairman of the Board of Governors normally also serves as the chairman of the Open Market Committee.

The effect of this complex structure is to create an institution that is ultimately accountable to the voting public, because the Board of Governors is chosen by the president and confirmed by the Senate, all of whom are themselves elected officials. But the long terms served by board members, as well as the indirectness of the process by which they are appointed, largely insulate them from short-term political pressures.

What the Fed Does: Reserve Requirements and the Discount Rate

The Fed has three main policy tools at its disposal: *reserve requirements,* the *discount rate,* and, most importantly, *open-market operations.*

In our discussion of bank runs, we noted that the Fed sets a minimum reserve ratio requirement, currently equal to 10% for checkable bank deposits. Banks that fail to maintain at least the required reserve ratio on average over a two-week period face penalties.

What does a bank do if it looks as if it has insufficient reserves to meet the Fed's reserve requirement? Normally, it borrows additional reserves from other banks. Banks lend money to each other in the **federal funds market,** a financial market that allows banks that fall short of the reserve requirement to borrow reserves—usually just overnight—from banks that hold excess reserves. The interest rate in this market is determined by supply and demand—but the supply and demand are both strongly affected by Federal Reserve actions. As we'll see in Chapter 14, the **federal funds rate,** the interest rate determined in the federal funds market, plays a key role in modern monetary policy.

Alternatively, banks can borrow reserves from the Fed itself. The **discount rate** is the rate of interest the Fed charges on loans to banks. Currently, the discount rate is set 1 percentage point above the federal funds rate in order to discourage banks from turning to the Fed.

The **federal funds market** allows banks that fall short of the reserve requirement to borrow funds from banks with excess reserves.

The **federal funds rate** is the interest rate determined in the federal funds market.

The **discount rate** is the rate of interest the Fed charges on loans to banks.

If it chooses to do so, the Fed can change the reserve requirements or the discount rate, or both. Either change affects the money supply. If the Fed reduces reserve requirements, banks will lend a larger percentage of their deposits, leading to more loans and an increase in the money supply via the money multiplier. If the Fed increases reserve requirements, banks are forced to cut back on loans, reducing the money supply via the money multiplier. If the Fed reduces the spread between the discount rate and the federal funds rate, banks increase their lending because the cost of finding themselves short of reserves wouldn't be as high, and the money supply will increase. If the Fed increases the spread between the discount rate and the Federal funds rate, bank lending falls, and so will the money supply.

In practice, today's Fed doesn't use changes in either reserve requirements or the discount rate to actively manage the money supply. The last significant change in reserve requirements was in 1992. The discount rate, as we've noted, is set 1 percentage point above the federal funds rate. Monetary policy is, instead, conducted using the Fed's third policy tool: open-market operations.

Open-Market Operations

Like the banks it oversees, the Federal Reserve has assets and liabilities. The Fed's assets consist of government debt it holds, mainly short-term U.S. government bonds with a maturity of less than one year, known as U.S. Treasury bills. Remember, the Fed isn't exactly part of the U.S. government, so those U.S. Treasury bills are a liability of the government but an asset of the Fed. Its liabilities consist of currency in circulation and bank reserves (either in bank vaults or in deposits that private banks maintain at regional Federal Reserve Banks). In other words, the Fed's liabilities are the same as the monetary base—currency in circulation plus bank reserves. The assets and liabilities of the Fed are summarized by the T-account in Figure 13-6.

> An **open-market operation** is a purchase or sale of government debt by the Fed.

In an **open-market operation** the Federal Reserve buys or sells some of the existing stock of U.S. Treasury bills, normally through a transaction with *commercial banks*—banks that mainly make business loans, as opposed to home loans. The Fed never buys U.S. Treasury bills directly from the federal government. There's a good reason for this: when central banks lend directly to the government, they are in effect printing money to finance the budget deficit. As we'll see later in the book, this can be a route to disastrous levels of inflation.

The two panels of Figure 13-7 show the changes in the financial position of both the Fed and commercial banks that result from open-market operations. When the Fed buys U.S. Treasury bills, it pays for them by crediting the accounts of these banks with additional deposits, which increases the banks' reserves. This is illustrated in panel (a): the Fed buys $100 million of U.S. Treasury bills from commercial banks, which increases the monetary base by $100 million because it increases bank reserves by $100 million. When the Fed sells U.S. Treasury bills to commercial banks,

---

Figure 13-6

The Federal Reserve's Assets and Liabilities

The Federal Reserve holds its assets mostly in short-term government bonds called U.S. Treasury bills. Its liabilities are the monetary base—currency in circulation plus bank reserves. **>web...**

Assets	Liabilities
Government debt (Treasury bills)	Monetary base (Currency in circulation + bank reserves)

Figure 13-7 Open-Market Operations by the Federal Reserve

(a) An Open-Market Purchase of $100 Million

	Assets		Liabilities	
Federal Reserve	Treasury bills	+ $100 million	Monetary base	+ $100 million

	Assets		Liabilities
Commercial banks	Treasury bills	− $100 million	No change
	Reserves	+ $100 million	

(b) An Open-Market Sale of $100 Million

	Assets		Liabilities	
Federal Reserve	Treasury bills	− $100 million	Monetary base	− $100 million

	Assets		Liabilities
Commercial banks	Treasury bills	+ $100 million	No change
	Reserves	− $100 million	

In panel (a), the Federal Reserve increases the monetary base by purchasing U.S. Treasury bills from private commercial banks in an open-market operation. Here a $100 million purchase of U.S. Treasury bills by the Federal Reserve is paid for by a $100 million addition to private bank reserves, generating a $100 million increase in the monetary base. This will ultimately lead to an increase in the money supply via the money multiplier as banks lend out some of these new reserves. In panel (b), the Federal Reserve reduces the monetary base by selling U.S. Treasury bills to private commercial banks in an open-market operation. Here a $100 million sale of U.S. Treasury bills leads to a $100 million reduction in private bank reserves, resulting in a $100 million decrease in the monetary base. This will ultimately lead to a fall in the money supply via the money multiplier as banks reduce their loans in response to a fall in their reserves.

it debits the banks' accounts, reducing their reserves. This is shown in panel (b), where the Fed sells $100 million of U.S. Treasury bills. Here, bank reserves and the monetary base decrease.

You might wonder where the Fed gets the funds to purchase U.S. Treasury bills from banks. The answer is that it simply creates them with a stroke of the pen (or, these days, a click of the mouse). Remember, the modern dollar is fiat money, which isn't backed by anything. So the Fed can create additional monetary base at its own discretion.

The increase or decrease in reserves caused by an open-market operation doesn't directly affect the money supply. However, an open-market operation starts the money multiplier in motion. After the $100 million increase in reserves shown in panel (a), commercial banks would lend out the additional reserves, immediately increasing the money supply by $100 million. Some of those loans will be deposited back in the banking system, increasing reserves again and permitting a further round of loans, and so on. So an open-market purchase of U.S. Treasury bills sets the money multiplier in motion, leading to a rise in the money supply. An open-market sale has the reverse effect: bank reserves fall, requiring banks to reduce their loans, leading to a fall in the money supply.

The Federal Open Market Committee, as its name suggests, sets policy on open-market operations—that is, it gives instructions to the New York Fed to buy or sell U.S. Treasury bills.

Economists often say, loosely, that the Fed controls the money supply. Literally, it only controls the monetary base. But by increasing or reducing the monetary base, the Fed can exert a powerful influence on both the money supply and interest rates. This influence is the basis of monetary policy, the subject of our next chapter.

economics in action

Building Europe's Fed

Until the last year of the twentieth century, the Federal Reserve was a giant among central banks. Because the U.S. economy was far larger than any other nation's, no other nation's central bank was remotely comparable in influence. But that all changed in January 1999, when 11 European nations adopted the euro as their common currency, placing their joint monetary policy in the hands of the new European Central Bank, generally referred to as the ECB.

Like the Fed, the ECB has a special status: it's not a private institution, but it's not exactly a government agency either. In fact, it can't be a government agency, because there is no pan-European government! Luckily for puzzled Americans, there are strong analogies between European central banking and the Federal Reserve system.

First of all, the ECB, which is located in the German city of Frankfurt, isn't really the counterpart of the whole Federal Reserve system: it's the equivalent of the Board of Governors in Washington. The European counterparts of regional Federal Reserve Banks are Europe's national central banks: the Bank of France, the Bank of Italy, and so on. Until 1999, each of these national banks was the equivalent of the Fed. For example, the Bank of France controlled the French monetary base. Today these national banks, like regional Feds, provide various financial services to local banks and businesses, and actually carry out open-market operations. That doesn't mean that they are small institutions: together, the national central banks employ more than 50,000 people, while the ECB employs fewer than 1,300.

Each country gets to choose who runs its own central bank. The ECB is run by an executive board that is the counterpart of the Fed's Board of Governors; its members are chosen by unanimous consent of the governments of countries that use the euro. The counterpart of the Federal Open Market Committee is the ECB's Governing Board. Just as the Fed's Open Market Committee consists of the Board of Governors plus a rotating group of regional Fed presidents, the ECB's Governing Board consists of the executive board plus a rotating group of national central bank heads. But there's a special twist: the frequency with which any country's central bank gets a seat at the table is determined by a formula that reflects the size of the country's economy. In other words, Germany, which had a GDP of $2.7 trillion in 2004, gets a seat on the board a lot more often than Greece, which had a GDP of only $205 billion.

In the end, the details probably don't matter much. Like the Fed, the ECB is ultimately answerable to voters but is highly insulated from short-term political pressures. ∎

< < < < < < < < < < < < < < < < <

>>CHECK YOUR UNDERSTANDING 13-4

1. Assume that any money lent by a bank is deposited back in the banking system as a checkable deposit and that the reserve ratio is 10%. Trace out the effects of a $100 million open-market purchase of U.S. Treasury bills by the Fed on the value of checkable bank deposits.

Solution appears at back of book.

• A LOOK AHEAD •

We have now seen how the monetary system is organized and, in particular, the role of the Federal Reserve in determining the size of the monetary base. But why is this important? Because the actions of the Fed change the money supply and create a powerful effect on interest rates. And through changes in interest rates the Fed has a powerful effect on real GDP and the aggregate price level.

In the next chapter we'll examine how monetary policy affects the economy and how the Fed behaves in practice.

SUMMARY

1. **Money** is any asset that can easily be used to purchase goods and services. **Currency in circulation** and **checkable bank deposits** are both considered part of the **money supply.** Money plays three roles: it is a **medium of exchange** used for transactions, a **store of value** that holds purchasing power over time, and a **unit of account** in which prices are stated.

2. Over time, **commodity money,** which consists of goods possessing value aside from their role as money, such as gold and silver coins, was replaced by **commodity-backed money,** such as paper currency backed by gold. Today the dollar is pure **fiat money,** whose value derives solely from its official role.

3. The United States has several definitions of the money supply. M1 is the narrowest **monetary aggregate,** containing only currency in circulation, traveler's checks, and checkable bank deposits. M2 and M3 include a wider range of assets called **near-moneys,** mainly other forms of bank deposits, that can easily be converted into checkable bank deposits.

4. Banks allow depositors immediate access to their funds, but they also lend out most of the funds deposited in their care. To meet demands for cash, they maintain **bank reserves** composed of both currency held in vaults and deposits at the Federal Reserve. The **reserve ratio** is the ratio of bank reserves to bank deposits.

5. Historically, banks have sometimes been subject to **bank runs,** most notably in the early 1930s. To avert this danger, depositors are now protected by **deposit insurance,** bank owners face capital requirements that reduce the incentive to make overly risky loans with depositors' funds, and banks must satisfy **reserve requirements.**

6. When currency is deposited in a bank, it starts a multiplier process in which banks lend out **excess reserves,** leading to an increase in the money supply—so banks create money. If the entire money supply consisted of checkable bank deposits, the money supply would be equal to the value of reserves divided by the reserve ratio. In reality, much of the **monetary base** consists of currency in circulation, and the **money multiplier** is the ratio of the money supply to the monetary base.

7. The monetary base is controlled by the Federal Reserve, the **central bank** of the United States. The Federal Reserve system combines some aspects of a government agency with some aspects of a private institution. The Fed sets reserve requirements. To meet those requirements, banks borrow and lend reserves in the **federal funds market** at the **federal funds rate.** Banks can also borrow from the Fed at the **discount rate.**

8. **Open-market operations** by the Fed are the principal tool of monetary policy: the Fed can increase or reduce the monetary base by buying U.S. Treasury bills from banks or selling U.S. Treasury bills to banks.

KEY TERMS

Money, p. 322
Currency in circulation, p. 322
Checkable bank deposits, p. 322
Money supply, p. 322
Medium of exchange, p. 323
Store of value, p. 323
Unit of account, p. 323
Commodity money, p. 323
Commodity-backed money, p. 323

Fiat money, p. 324
Monetary aggregate, p. 324
Near-moneys, p. 324
Bank reserves, p. 326
Reserve ratio, p. 327
Bank run, p. 328
Deposit insurance, p. 328
Reserve requirements, p. 329
Excess reserves, p. 331

Monetary base, p. 332
Money multiplier, p. 333
Central bank, p. 334
Federal funds market, p. 335
Federal funds rate, p. 335
Discount rate, p. 335
Open-market operation, p. 336

PROBLEMS

1. For each of the following transactions, what is the effect (increase or decrease) on M1? On M2?

   a. You sell a few shares of stock and put the proceeds into your savings account.

   b. You sell a few shares of stock and put the proceeds into your checking account.

   c. You transfer money from your savings account to your checking account.

   d. You discover $0.25 under the floor mat in your car and deposit it in your checking account.

   e. You discover $0.25 under the floor mat in your car and deposit it in your savings account.

2. There are three types of money: commodity money, commodity-backed money, and fiat money. Which type of money is used in each of the following situations?

   a. Mother-of-pearl seashells were used to pay for goods in ancient China.

   b. Salt was used in many European countries as a medium of exchange.

   c. For a brief time, Germany used paper money (the "Rye Mark") that could be redeemed for a certain amount of grain rye.

   d. The town of Ithaca, New York, prints its own currency, the Ithaca HOURS, which can be used to purchase local goods and services.

3. The table below shows the components of M1 and M2 in billions of dollars for the month of December in the years 1995 to 2004 as published in the *2005 Economic Report of the President*. Complete the table by calculating M1, M2, currency in circulation as a percentage of M1, and currency in circulation as a percentage of M2. What trends or patterns about M1, M2, currency in circulation as a percentage of M1, and currency in circulation as a percentage of M2 do you see? What might account for these trends?

4. Indicate whether each of the following is part of M1, M2, or neither:

   a. $95 on your campus meal card

   b. $0.55 in the change cup of your car

   c. $1,663 in your savings account

   d. $459 in your checking account

   e. 100 shares of stock worth $4,000

   f. A $1,000 line of credit on your Sears credit card

5. Tracy Williams deposits $500 that was in her sock drawer into a checking account at the local bank.

   a. How does the deposit initially change the T-account of the local bank? How does it change the money supply?

   b. If the bank maintains a reserve ratio of 10%, how will it respond to the new deposit?

   c. If every time the bank makes a loan, the loan results in a new checkable bank deposit in a different bank equal to the amount of the loan, by how much could the money supply in the economy expand in total?

   d. If every time the bank makes a loan, the loan results in a new checkable bank deposit in a different bank equal to the amount of the loan and the bank maintains a reserve ratio of 5%, by how much could the money supply expand in response to an initial cash deposit of $500?

6. Ryan Cozzens withdraws $400 from his checking account at the local bank and keeps it in his wallet.

   a. How will the withdrawal change the T-account of the local bank and the money supply?

   b. If the bank maintains a reserve ratio of 10%, how will the bank respond to the withdrawal?

   c. If every time the bank decreases its loans, checkable bank deposits fall by the amount of the loan, by how much could the money supply in the economy contract in total?

   d. If every time the bank decreases its loans, checkable bank deposits fall by the amount of the loan and the bank main-

Year	Currency in circulation	Traveler's checks	Checkable bank deposits	Money market funds	Time deposits smaller than $100,000	Savings deposits	M1	M2	Currency in circulation as a percentage of M1	Currency in circulation as a percentage of M2
1995	$372.1	$9.1	$745.9	$448.8	$931.4	$1,134.0	?	?	?	?
1996	394.1	8.8	676.5	517.4	946.8	1,273.1	?	?	?	?
1997	424.6	8.5	639.5	592.2	967.9	1,399.1	?	?	?	?
1998	459.9	8.5	627.7	732.7	951.5	1,603.6	?	?	?	?
1999	517.7	8.6	597.7	832.5	954.0	1,738.2	?	?	?	?
2000	531.6	8.3	548.1	924.2	1,044.2	1,876.2	?	?	?	?
2001	582.0	8.0	589.3	987.2	972.8	2,308.9	?	?	?	?
2002	627.4	7.8	582.0	915.5	892.1	2,769.5	?	?	?	?
2003	663.9	7.7	621.8	801.1	809.4	3,158.5	?	?	?	?
2004	699.3	7.6	656.2	714.7	814.0	3,505.9	?	?	?	?

tains a reserve ratio of 20%, by how much will the money supply contract in response to a withdrawal of $400?

7. The government of Eastlandia uses measures of monetary aggregates similar to those used by the United States, and the central bank of Eastlandia imposes a required reserve ratio of 10%. Given the following information, answer the questions below.

Bank deposits at the central bank = $200 million
Currency held by public = $150 million
Currency in bank vaults = $100 million
Checkable bank deposits = $500 million
Traveler's checks = $10 million

a. What is M1?

b. What is the monetary base?

c. Are the commercial banks holding excess reserves?

d. Can the commercial banks increase checkable bank deposits? If yes, by how much can checkable bank deposits increase?

8. In Westlandia, the public holds 50% of M1 in the form of currency, and the required reserve ratio is 20%. Estimate how much the money supply will increase in response to a new cash deposit of $500 by completing the table below. (*Hint:* The first row shows that the bank must hold $100 in minimum reserves—20% of the $500 deposit—against this deposit, leaving $400 in excess reserves that can be loaned out. However, since the public wants to hold 50% of the loan in currency, only $400 × 0.5 = $200 of the loan will be deposited in round 2 from the loan granted in round 1.) How does your answer compare to an economy in which the total amount of the loan is deposited in the banking system and the public doesn't hold any of the loan in currency? What does this imply about the relationship between the public's desire for currency and the money multiplier?

Round	Deposits	Required reserves	Excess reserves	Loans	Held as currency
1	$500.00	$100.00	$400.00	$400.00	$200.00
2	200.00	?	?	?	?
3	?	?	?	?	?
4	?	?	?	?	?
5	?	?	?	?	?
6	?	?	?	?	?
7	?	?	?	?	?
8	?	?	?	?	?
9	?	?	?	?	?
10	?	?	?	?	?
Total after 10 rounds	?	?	?	?	?

9. What will happen to the money supply under the following circumstances?

a. The required reserve ratio is 25%, and a depositor withdraws $700 from his checkable bank deposit.

b. The required reserve ratio is 5%, and a depositor withdraws $700 from his checkable bank deposit.

c. The required reserve ratio is 20%, and a customer deposits $750 to her checkable bank deposit.

d. The required reserve ratio is 10%, and a customer deposits $600 to her checkable bank deposit.

10. Although the U.S. Federal Reserve doesn't use changes in reserve requirements to manage the money supply, the central bank of Albernia does. The commercial banks of Albernia have $100 million in reserves and $1,000 million in checkable deposits; the initial required reserve ratio is 10%. The commercial banks follow a policy of holding no excess reserves. The public holds a fixed amount of currency, so all loans create an equal amount of deposits in the banking system.

a. How will the money supply change if the required reserve ratio falls to 5%?

b. How will the money supply change if the minimum reserve ratio rises to 25%?

11. Using Figure 13-5, find the Federal Reserve district in which you live. Go to http://www.federalreserve.gov/bios/pres.htm and identify the president of that Federal Reserve Bank. Go to http://www.federalreserve.gov/fomc/and determine if the president of the Fed is currently a voting member of the Federal Open Market Committee (FOMC).

12. Show the changes to the T-accounts for the Federal Reserve and for commercial banks when the Federal Reserve buys $50 million in U.S. Treasury bills. If the public holds a fixed amount of currency (so that all loans create an equal amount of deposits in the banking system), the minimum reserve ratio is 10%, and banks hold no excess reserves, by how much will deposits in the commercial banks change? By how much will the money supply change? Show the final changes to the T-account for commercial banks when the money supply changes by this amount.

13. Show the changes to the T-accounts for the Federal Reserve and for commercial banks when the Federal Reserve sells $30 million in U.S. Treasury bills. If the public holds a fixed amount of currency (so that all new loans create an equal amount of checkable bank deposits in the banking system) and the minimum reserve ratio is 5%, by how much will checkable bank deposits in the commercial banks change? By how much will the money supply change? Show the final changes to the T-account for the commercial banks when the money supply changes by this amount.

14

>> Monetary Policy

EIGHT TIMES A YEAR

W HEN THE FOMC TALKS, PEOPLE listen.

Eight times a year, economists and investors around the world wait anxiously for word from the dozen men and women who make up the Federal Open Market Committee of the Federal Reserve. The FOMC controls the *federal funds rate,* the interest rate charged on reserves that banks lend each other to meet reserve requirements. What the world wants to know is the FOMC's decision—whether it has decided to increase the federal funds rate, reduce it, or leave it unchanged. Financial market analysts also carefully read the committee's accompanying statement and wait anxiously for the official minutes of the meeting, released three weeks later.

Why such a high degree of scrutiny? Because the statements of the FOMC, although usually written in jargon, offer

clues to the future stance of monetary policy. A careful reading of FOMC statements, where seemingly minor changes in wording can be highly significant, can help predict whether monetary policy will be relatively expansionary (or loose), leading to a fall in interest rates, or relatively contractionary (or tight), leading to a rise in interest rates.

For example, the FOMC statement in December 2003 said, as it had after the past several meetings, that "policy accommodation can be maintained for a considerable period." The phrase "policy accommodation" means "keeping interest rates low." But in January 2004 these words were replaced with slightly different wording: "The Committee believes that it can be patient in removing its policy accommodation." The new wording suggested that the FOMC would soon begin raising the federal funds rate, and stocks and bonds plunged at this news.

What you will learn in this chapter:

➤ What the **money demand curve** is

➤ Why the **liquidity preference model** determines the interest rate in the short run

➤ How the Federal Reserve can move interest rates

➤ How monetary policy affects aggregate output in the short run

➤ A deeper understanding of the adjustment process behind the savings–investment spending identity

➤ Why economists believe in **monetary neutrality**—that monetary policy affects only the price level, not aggregate output, in the long run

The FOMC's decision about interest rates is anxiously watched by traders like these, and by investors around the world.

Denni Brack/Bloomberg News/Landov

John Gress/Reuters/Landov

In Chapter 13 we learned about the structure of the Federal Reserve system and about how its open-market operations affect the money supply. In this chapter, we'll look at how monetary policy works—how actions by the FOMC can turn recession into expansion, and vice versa. We'll start by looking at the *demand for money* by households and firms. Then we'll see how the Fed's ability to change the money supply allows it to raise or reduce interest rates in the short run and, in doing so, shift the aggregate demand curve. Finally, we'll see why monetary policy affects the aggregate price level but doesn't affect aggregate output in the long run.

The Demand for Money

In Chapter 13 we saw that M1, the most commonly used definition of the money supply, consists of currency in circulation (cash) plus checkable bank deposits plus traveler's checks. M2, a broader definition of the money supply, consists of M1 plus deposits that can easily be transferred into checkable deposits. We also saw why people hold money—to make it easier to purchase goods and services. Now we'll go deeper, examining what determines *how much* money individuals and firms want to hold at any given time.

The Opportunity Cost of Holding Money

Individuals and firms hold some of their assets in the form of money because only money can be used to make purchases directly. But there is a price to be paid for holding money: it normally yields a lower rate of return than nonmonetary assets. For most individuals and firms, the relevant choice is between money and less liquid assets, such as short-term bonds, that can be converted fairly quickly into money but yield higher interest rates than money.

The rate-of-return disadvantage of money is obvious in the case of currency, which pays no interest. Most checkable bank deposits pay interest, but the rate is lower than that on other, less convenient assets.

Table 14-1 shows a selection of average interest rates prevailing in two months, May 2004 and March 2005. The top row shows the federal funds rate. The next row shows the rate on one-month Treasury bills, a bond issued by the U.S. government that is paid off in one month. The next row shows the interest rate on interest-bearing zero-maturity bank deposits. These are deposits, including checking account deposits, from which funds can be withdrawn at any time without penalty. The fourth row shows the interest rate on currency, which is, of course, zero.

TABLE 14-1

Selected Interest Rates

	May 2004	March 2005
Federal funds rate	1.00%	2.63%
One-month Treasury bill	0.91	2.36
Interest-bearing checkable bank deposits*	0.54	1.05
Currency	0.00	0.00
Treasury bill rate minus rate on deposits	0.37	1.31
Treasury bill rate minus rate on currency	0.91	2.36

*Average on all zero-maturity deposits (deposits that can be withdrawn at any time)
Source: Federal Reserve Bank of St. Louis.

As you can see, in both months people received a higher rate of interest on one-month U.S. Treasury bills than they did on either currency or zero-maturity deposits. There is an *opportunity cost* to holding money, which we can measure by the difference between the interest rate on assets that aren't money and the interest rate on assets that are money. The next-to-last row in Table 14-1 shows the difference between the interest rate on one-month Treasury bills and the interest rate on zero-maturity bank deposits. The last row shows the difference between the interest rate on one-month Treasury bills and the interest rate on currency. In May 2004 zero-maturity deposits yielded 0.37 percentage points less at an annual rate than Treasury bills; by March 2005 that difference had risen to 1.31 percentage points. The comparison between one-month Treasury bills and currency is even worse: in May 2004 holding currency meant forgoing 0.91 percentage points at an annual rate; by March 2005 that difference had widened to 2.36 percentage points.

As this example shows, people pay a cost for holding wealth in the form of money as opposed to nonmonetary assets such as Treasury bills. Why, then, does the public hold money? Money provides convenience and reduces the costs of transactions because it can be used immediately for spending, which other assets can't.

As an example of how convenience makes it worth incurring some opportunity costs, consider the fact that even today—with the prevalence of credit cards, debit cards, and ATMs—people continue to keep cash in their wallets rather than leave the funds in an interest-bearing account. They don't want to have to go to the bank to withdraw money every time they want to buy lunch from a place that doesn't accept credit cards at all or won't accept them for small amounts because of the processing fee. The convenience of keeping some cash in your wallet is more valuable than the interest you would earn by keeping that money in the bank.

So how much of your wealth should you hold in the form of money on any given day? Choosing the optimal quantity of money to hold requires a trade-off between the extra convenience of an additional dollar in your wallet against the higher return from keeping it in other financial assets. The terms of this trade-off change when interest rates change. Look again at Table 14-1. Between May 2004 and March 2005, the federal funds rate rose by about 1.63 percentage points. The interest rate on one-month Treasury bills rose by about the same amount. That's not an accident: all **short-term interest rates**—rates on financial assets that come due, or mature, within six months or less—tend to move together. This occurs because Treasury bills, one-month bonds, three-month bonds, and so on are in effect competing for the same business. Why? Investors will move their wealth out of any short-term financial asset that offers a lower-than-average interest rate. The selling of the asset forces the interest rate on that asset up because buyers of the asset must be rewarded with a higher rate in order to induce them to buy it. Conversely, investors will move their wealth into any short-term financial asset that offers an above-average interest rate. The purchase of the asset drives its interest rate down when sellers find they can lower the rate of return on the asset and still find willing buyers. So interest rates on short-term financial assets tend to be roughly the same because no asset will consistently offer a higher-than-average or a lower-than-average interest rate.

But the interest rates on money didn't rise by the same amount. The interest rate on currency remained at zero. The interest rate on zero-maturity bank deposits rose, but by much less than short-term interest rates. As a result, the opportunity cost of holding money increased. This reflects a general result: the higher the short-term interest rate, the higher the opportunity cost of holding money. So the quantity of money the public wants to hold—the quantity of money demanded—depends negatively on short-run interest rates.

Table 14-1 contains only short-term interest rates. At any given moment, **long-term interest rates**—rates of interest on financial assets that mature, or come due, a number of years into the future—may be different from short-term interest rates. The difference between short-term and long-term interest rates is sometimes important

Short-term interest rates are the interest rates on financial assets that mature within six months or less.

Long-term interest rates are interest rates on financial assets that mature a number of years in the future.

as a practical matter. For our current purposes, however, it's useful to ignore the distinction between short-term and long-term rates and assume that there is only one interest rate.

The Money Demand Curve

The relationship between the interest rate and the quantity of money demanded by the public is illustrated by the **money demand curve,** MD, in Figure 14-1. This curve is downward-sloping because, other things equal, a higher interest rate increases the opportunity cost of holding money, leading the public to reduce the quantity of money it demands. For example, if the interest rate is very low—say, 1%—the interest forgone by holding money is relatively small. As a result, people will tend to hold relatively large amounts of money to avoid the cost and nuisance of converting other assets into money when making purchases. By contrast, if the interest rate is relatively high—say, 15%, a level it reached in the United States in the early 1900s—the opportunity cost of holding money is high. People will respond by keeping only small amounts in cash and deposits, converting funds into money only when needed.

> The **money demand curve** shows the relationship between the quantity of money demanded and the interest rate.

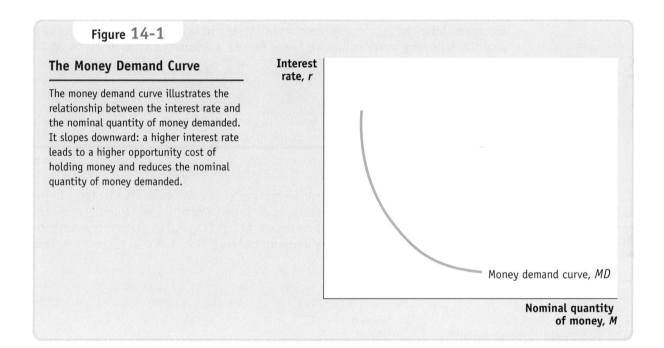

Figure 14-1

The Money Demand Curve

The money demand curve illustrates the relationship between the interest rate and the nominal quantity of money demanded. It slopes downward: a higher interest rate leads to a higher opportunity cost of holding money and reduces the nominal quantity of money demanded.

Interest rate, r

Money demand curve, MD

Nominal quantity of money, M

You might ask why we draw the money demand curve with the interest rate—as opposed to rates of return on other assets, such as stocks or real estate—on the vertical axis. As we noted earlier, for most people the relevant question in deciding how much money to hold is whether to put the funds in the form of other assets that can be turned fairly quickly into money, such as Treasury bills. And the rates of return on assets that are "close to" money—fairly liquid assets like Treasury bills that are relatively good substitutes for money—move closely with short-term interest rates.

Prices and the Demand for Money

Because the horizontal axis in Figure 14-1 measures the *nominal* quantity of money, the money demand curve shows the number of dollars demanded unadjusted for the purchasing power of a dollar. However, economists sometimes focus instead on the **real quantity of money:** the nominal quantity of money divided by the aggregate

> The **real quantity of money** is the nominal quantity of money divided by the aggregate price level.

price level. Using M for the nominal quantity of money and P for the aggregate price level, the *real* quantity of money is M/P. The real quantity of money, M/P, measures the purchasing power of the nominal quantity of money, M.

To see why economists sometimes focus on the real quantity of money, consider the effects of a doubling of the aggregate price level on the nominal quantity of money demanded, as shown in Figure 14-2. An increase in the aggregate price level means consumers must spend more money to buy a given basket of goods and services. This translates into a desire to hold more money at any given interest rate. So a rise in the aggregate price level from P_1 to P_2 shifts the money demand curve rightward from MD_1 to MD_2.

But we can be more specific about the effect of the aggregate price level on money demand: other things equal, the nominal quantity of money demanded is *proportional* to the aggregate price level. That is, a 50% rise in the aggregate price level leads to a 50% rise in the nominal quantity of money demanded at any given interest rate.

We can get a better intuitive understanding of this property with a little algebra. Suppose that the interest rate is constant at r_1 in Figure 14-2. Also suppose that the aggregate price level rises from P_1 to P_2 by a factor k, so that we can express the rise in the aggregate price level as $P_2 = k \times P_1$. Then the fact that nominal money demand is proportional to the aggregate price level means that the nominal quantity of money demanded after the aggregate price change (M_2), and before the price change (M_1) have the following relationship: $M_2 = k \times M_1$. As a result, the ratio of M_2 to M_1 is equal to the ratio of P_2 to P_1:

$$(14\text{-}1) \quad \frac{M_2}{M_1} = \frac{P_2}{P_1}$$

Equation 14-1 can be rearranged by dividing both sides by P_2 and multiplying both sides by M_1. This gives us the following result:

$$(14\text{-}2) \quad \frac{M_2}{P_2} = \frac{M_1}{P_1}$$

The **real money demand curve** shows the relationship between the real quantity of money demanded and the interest rate.

Equation 14-2 tells us that *the real quantity of money demanded after a change in the aggregate price level, M_2/P_2, other things equal, is the same as the real quantity of money demanded before the aggregate price level change, M_1/P_1.* One way to take this result into account is to draw the **real money demand curve,** *RMD*, shown in Figure 14-3. This

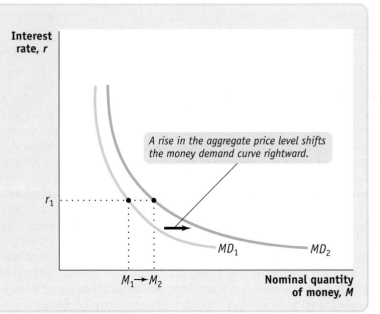

Figure 14-2

The Aggregate Price Level and Money Demand

Other things equal, an increase in the aggregate price level leads to an equal percent increase in the nominal quantity of money demanded. In this case, an increase in the aggregate price level causes a rightward shift in the money demand curve from MD_1 to MD_2. The nominal quantity of money demanded at the interest rate r_1 rises from M_1 to M_2, an increase that is proportional to the increase in the aggregate price level.

A rise in the aggregate price level shifts the money demand curve rightward.

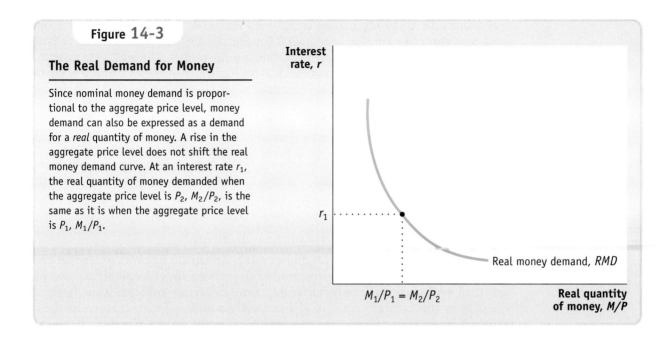

Figure 14-3

The Real Demand for Money

Since nominal money demand is proportional to the aggregate price level, money demand can also be expressed as a demand for a *real* quantity of money. A rise in the aggregate price level does not shift the real money demand curve. At an interest rate r_1, the real quantity of money demanded when the aggregate price level is P_2, M_2/P_2, is the same as it is when the aggregate price level is P_1, M_1/P_1.

Interest rate, r

r_1

Real money demand, *RMD*

$M_1/P_1 = M_2/P_2$

Real quantity of money, M/P

curve shows the relationship between the real quantity of money demanded and the interest rate. Unlike the nominal money demand curve, the real money demand curve automatically takes into account the effect of changes in the aggregate price level on the nominal quantity of money demanded. So, for example, at an interest rate r_1, the real quantity of money demanded is equal to both M_1/P_1 and M_2/P_2, shown as the same point on the real money demand curve.

Shifts of the Real Money Demand Curve

By expressing the demand for money in real terms, we take account of the effects of changes in the aggregate price level on the nominal demand for money. A number of factors can shift the real and nominal money demand curves. The most important of these are changes in the level of real aggregate spending, changes in banking technology, and changes in banking institutions.

Changes in Real Aggregate Spending   Households and firms hold money as a way to facilitate purchases of goods and services. The larger the quantity of goods and services they plan to buy, the larger the real quantity of money they will want to hold at any given interest rate. So an increase in real aggregate spending will shift the real money demand curve rightward. A fall in real aggregate spending will shift the real money demand curve leftward.

Some economists have argued that the real quantity of money demanded, other things equal, is proportional to real aggregate spending. That is, a 20% rise in real aggregate spending leads to a 20% rise in the real quantity of money demanded. This view leads to a concept known as the *velocity of money,* which we'll turn to shortly.

Changes in Technology   There was a time, not so long ago, when withdrawing cash from a bank account required a visit during the bank's hours of operation. And since most people found themselves trying to do their banking during lunch hour, this often meant standing in line. So people limited the number of times they needed to withdraw funds by keeping substantial amounts of cash on hand. Not surprisingly, this tendency diminished greatly with the advent of ATMs in the 1970s.

These events illustrate how changes in technology can affect the real demand for money. In general, advances in information technology have tended to reduce the real demand for money by making it easier for the public to make purchases without holding significant sums of money. ATM machines are only one example of how changes in technology have altered the demand for money. The ability of stores to process credit card transactions via the Internet has widened the acceptance of credit cards and similarly reduced the need for cash.

Changes in Institutions Changes in institutions can increase or decrease the demand for money. For example, until the beginning of the 1980s, U.S. banks weren't allowed to offer interest on checking accounts. As a result, the opportunity cost of holding funds in checking accounts was very high. That disincentive was greatly reduced when a change in banking regulations made interest on checking accounts legal, leading to a rise in the real demand for money.

The Velocity Approach to Money Demand

We have discussed the demand for money using the same framework we use for discussing any demand curve: first we described the reasons the curve slopes downward, and then we discussed the factors that shift the curve rightward or leftward. In some discussions about money demand and monetary policy, however, economists use a different approach, emphasizing a concept known as the *velocity of money.*

The **velocity of money** is defined as nominal GDP divided by the nominal quantity of money. That is,

$$(14\text{-}3) \quad V = \frac{P \times Y}{M}$$

where V is the velocity of money, P is the aggregate price level, Y is aggregate output measured by real GDP (so that $P \times Y$ equals nominal GDP), and M is the nominal quantity of money. This definition is often restated by multiplying both sides of the equation by the quantity of money to yield the **quantity equation:**

$$(14\text{-}4) \quad M \times V = P \times Y$$

It says that the nominal quantity of money multiplied by the velocity of money is equal to nominal GDP.

The intuition behind the concept of velocity is that each unit of money in the economy can be spent several times over the course of a year. For example, someone may use a dollar bill to pay for a cup of coffee at a cafe; the cafe may give that dollar bill as change to someone else who buys a sandwich; that person may use the dollar bill to buy a newspaper; and so on. The value of spending that takes place using a particular dollar bill in a given year depends on the number of times that dollar bill "turns over" during the year. For example, if the dollar bill is spent three times in a year, it is used for $3 worth of spending.

By analogy, aggregate spending in the economy as a whole during a year is equal to the nominal quantity of money in the economy, M, multiplied by the number of times the average unit of money is spent—the velocity of money, V. And nominal GDP, $P \times Y$, is equal to aggregate spending. So aggregate spending, measured as the number of dollars turned over, is equal to aggregate spending as measured by nominal GDP, giving us the quantity equation.

One way to think about the velocity approach is that it is a special case of the real money demand curve. To see that, let's rewrite the velocity equation, putting the real quantity of money on the left-hand side:

$$(14\text{-}5) \quad \frac{M}{P} = \frac{1}{V} \times Y$$

Equation 14-5 says that the real demand for money, M/P, is proportional to real GDP, Y, where the constant of proportionality is $1/V$. But real GDP is, in equilibrium, equal to real aggregate spending. And we already know that the real demand for

The **velocity of money** is nominal GDP divided by the nominal quantity of money.

According to the **quantity equation,** the nominal quantity of money multiplied by the velocity of money is equal to nominal GDP.

money depends positively on real aggregate spending. Equation 14-5 says that, in addition to being positive, the relationship is proportional. This is why we noted earlier that some economists believe that the real quantity of money demanded is proportional to real aggregate spending. If this is indeed true, then the effect of changes in the interest rate on real money demand is reflected in changes in the velocity of money, V. For example, a rise in the interest rate, which reduces real money demand, will lead to a fall in $1/V$—or a rise in V—other things equal. Intuitively, a smaller amount of real money holdings, M/P, will now account for the same amount of real aggregate spending, Y, because velocity, V, has increased.

We won't pursue the velocity approach to money demand any further in this chapter. As we'll see in Chapter 17, however, the concept of monetary velocity has played an important role in some debates about macroeconomic policy.

economics in action

A Yen for Cash

Japan, say financial experts, is still a "cash society." Visitors from the United States or Europe are surprised at how little use the Japanese make of credit cards and how much cash they carry around in their wallets. Yet Japan is an economically and technologically advanced country and, according to some measures, ahead of the United States in the use of telecommunications and information technology. So why do the citizens of this economic powerhouse still do business the way Americans and Europeans did a generation ago? The answer highlights the factors affecting the demand for money.

Issei Kato/Reuters/Landov

Regardless of what they are shopping for, Japanese consumers tend to pay with cash rather than plastic.

One reason the Japanese use cash so much is that their institutions never made the switch to heavy reliance on plastic. For complex reasons, Japan's retail sector is still dominated by small mom-and-pop stores, which are reluctant to invest in credit card technology. Japan's banks have also been slow about pushing transaction technology; visitors are often surprised to find that ATMs close early in the evening rather than stay open all night.

But there's another reason the Japanese hold so much cash: there's little opportunity cost to doing so. Short-term interest rates in Japan have been below 1% since the mid-1990s. It also helps that the Japanese crime rate is quite low, so you are unlikely to have your wallet full of cash stolen. So why not hold cash? ■

> >

>> QUICK REVIEW

➤ Money offers a lower rate of return than other financial assets. We usually compare the rate of return on money with *short-term*, not *long-term, interest rates*.

➤ Holding money provides liquidity but has an opportunity cost that rises with the interest rate, leading to the downward slope of the *money demand curve*.

➤ Because the nominal demand for money is proportional to the aggregate price level, the money demand curve can also be represented by the *real money demand curve*.

➤ Changes in aggregate spending, institutions, and technology shift the real and nominal money demand curves.

➤ A widely used approach to money demand focuses on the *velocity of money*. The *quantity equation* implies that the real demand for money is proportional to real aggregate spending.

>>CHECK YOUR UNDERSTANDING 14-1

1. Explain how each of the following would affect the real and nominal quantity of money demanded:
   a. Short-term interest rates rise from 5% to 30%.
   b. All prices fall by 10%.
   c. New wireless technology automatically charges supermarket purchases to credit cards, eliminating the need to stop at the cash register.
   d. For some reason, firms return to the old practice of paying employees in cash rather than with checks.

Solutions appear at back of book.

Money and Interest Rates

"The Federal Open Market Committee decided today to raise its target for the federal funds rate by 25 basis points to 2¾%." So reads the first sentence of the press release from the FOMC after its meeting of March 22, 2005. (A basis point is equal to 0.01 percentage point. So the statement says that the Fed raised the target from 2.50% to 2.75%.) We learned about the federal funds rate in Chapter 13: it's the rate at which banks lend reserves to each other to meet the required reserve ratio. As the statement implies, at each of its eight-times-a-year meetings, the Federal Open Market Committee sets a target value for the federal funds rate. It's then up to Fed officials to achieve that target. This is done by the Open Market Desk at the Federal Reserve Bank of New York, which buys and sells Treasury bills to achieve that target.

Other short-term interest rates, such as the rates on bank loans to businesses, move with the federal funds rate. So when the Fed raised its target for the federal funds rate from 2.50% to 2.75% in March 2005, all short-term interest rates rose as well by about a quarter of a percentage point.

How does the Fed go about achieving a *target federal funds rate*? And more to the point, how is the Fed able to affect interest rates at all?

The Equilibrium Interest Rate

According to the **liquidity preference model of the interest rate**, the interest rate is determined by the supply and demand for money.

The **money supply curve** shows how the nominal quantity of money supplied varies with the interest rate.

Recall that, for simplicity, we've assumed that there is only one interest rate paid on nonmonetary financial assets, both in the short run and in the long run. To understand how the interest rate is determined, consider Figure 14-4, which illustrates the **liquidity preference model of the interest rate;** this model says that the interest rate is determined by the supply and demand for money in the market for money. Figure 14-4 combines the nominal money demand curve, *MD*, with the **money supply curve,** *MS*, which shows how the nominal quantity of money supplied by the Federal Reserve varies with the interest rate. (From now on we will drop the word *nominal* with the understanding that *MD* and *MS* represent nominal quantities.) In Chapter 13 we learned how the Federal Reserve can increase or decrease the money supply by buying or selling Treasury bills. Let's assume for simplicity that the Fed simply chooses the level of the money

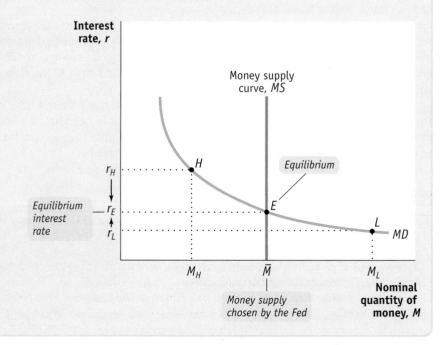

Figure 14-4

Equilibrium in the Money Market

The money supply curve, *MS*, is vertical at the money supply chosen by the Federal Reserve, $\bar{M}$. The money market is in equilibrium at the interest rate r_E: the quantity of money demanded by the public is equal to $\bar{M}$, the quantity of money supplied. At a point such as *L*, the interest rate, r_L, is below r_E and the corresponding quantity of money demanded, M_L, exceeds the money supply, $\bar{M}$. In an attempt to shift their wealth out of nonmonetary interest-bearing financial assets and raise their money holdings, investors drive the interest rate up to r_E. At a point such as *H*, the interest rate r_H is above r_E and the corresponding quantity of money demanded, M_H, is less than the money supply $\bar{M}$. In an attempt to shift out of money holdings into nonmonetary interest-bearing financial assets, investors drive the interest rate down to r_E.

supply that it believes will achieve its interest rate target. Then the money supply curve is a vertical line, MS, in Figure 14-4, with a horizontal intercept corresponding to the money supply chosen by the Fed, $\overline{M}$. The money market equilibrium is at E, where MS and MD cross. At this point the quantity of money demanded equals the money supply, $\overline{M}$, leading to an equilibrium interest rate of r_E.

To understand why r_E is the equilibrium interest rate, consider what happens if the money market is at a point like L, where the interest rate, r_L, is below r_E. At r_L the public wants to hold the quantity of money M_L, an amount larger than the actual money supply, $\overline{M}$. This means that at point L, the public wants to shift some of its wealth out of nonmonetary interest-bearing financial assets such as Treasury bills and into money. This has two implications. One is that the quantity of money demanded is *more* than the quantity of money supplied. The other is that the quantity of nonmonetary interest-bearing financial assets demanded is *less* than the quantity supplied. So those trying to sell interest-bearing assets will find that they have to offer a higher interest rate to attract buyers. As a result, the interest rate will be driven up from r_L until the public wants to hold the quantity of money that is actually available, $\overline{M}$. That is, the interest rate will rise until it is equal to r_E.

Now consider what happens if the money market is at a point such as H in Figure 14-4, where the interest rate r_H is above r_E. In that case the quantity of money demanded, M_H, is less than the quantity of money supplied, $\overline{M}$. Correspondingly, the quantity of nonmonetary interest-bearing financial assets demanded is greater than the quantity supplied. Those trying to sell interest-bearing financial assets will find that they can offer a lower interest rate and still find willing buyers. This leads to a fall in the interest rate from r_H. It falls until the public wants to hold the quantity of money that is actually available, $\overline{M}$. Again, the interest rate will end up at r_E.

Two Models of Interest Rates?

At this point you may be a bit puzzled. This is the second time we have discussed the determination of the interest rate. In Chapter 9 we studied the *loanable funds model* of the interest rate; according to that model, the interest rate is determined by the equalization of the supply of funds from lenders and the demand for funds by borrowers in the market for loanable funds. But here we have described a seemingly different model in which the interest rate is determined by the equalization of the supply and demand for money in the money market. Which of these models is correct?

The answer is both. But that will take a little time to explain, something we will do later in this chapter. For now, let's put the loanable funds model to one side and concentrate on the liquidity preference model of the interest rate. The most important insight from this model is that it shows us how monetary policy—actions by the Federal Reserve and other central banks—works.

Monetary Policy and the Interest Rate

Let's examine how the Federal Reserve can use changes in the money supply to change the interest rate. Figure 14-5 on page 352 shows what happens when the Fed increases the money supply from $\overline{M}_1$ to $\overline{M}_2$. The economy is originally in equilibrium at E_1, with an equilibrium interest rate of r_1 and money supply $\overline{M}_1$. An increase in the money supply by the Fed to $\overline{M}_2$ shifts the money supply curve to the right, from MS_1 to MS_2, and leads to a fall in the equilibrium interest rate to r_2. Why? Because r_2 is the only interest rate at which the public is willing to hold the quantity of money actually supplied, $\overline{M}_2$. So an increase in the money supply drives the interest rate down. Similarly, a reduction in the money supply drives the interest rate up. By adjusting the money supply up or down, the Fed can set the interest rate.

PITFALLS

THE TARGET VERSUS THE MARKET

Over the years, the Federal Reserve has changed the details of how it makes monetary policy. At one point, in the late 1970s and early 1980s, it set a target level for the money supply and altered the monetary base to achieve that target. Under this policy, the federal funds rate fluctuated freely. Today the Fed does the reverse, setting a target for the federal funds rate and allowing the money supply to fluctuate as it pursues that target.

A common mistake is to imagine that these changes in the way the Federal Reserve operates alter the way the money market works. That is, you'll sometimes hear people say that the interest rate no longer reflects the supply and demand for money because the Fed sets the interest rate.

In fact, the money market works the same way as always: the interest rate is determined by the supply and demand for money. The only difference is that now the Fed adjusts the supply of money to achieve its target interest rate. It's important not to confuse a change in the Fed's operating procedure with a change in the way the economy works.

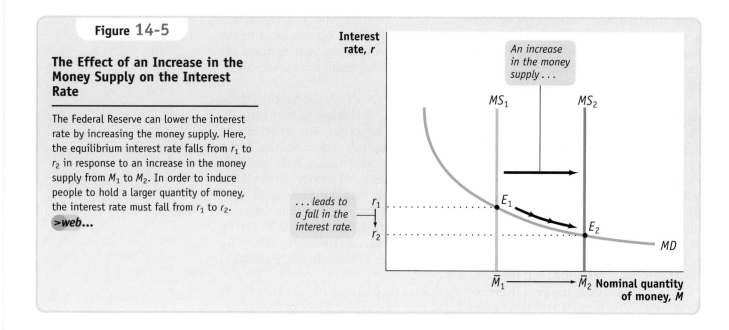

Figure 14-5

The Effect of an Increase in the Money Supply on the Interest Rate

The Federal Reserve can lower the interest rate by increasing the money supply. Here, the equilibrium interest rate falls from r_1 to r_2 in response to an increase in the money supply from M_1 to M_2. In order to induce people to hold a larger quantity of money, the interest rate must fall from r_1 to r_2.

>web...

An increase in the money supply . . .

. . . leads to a fall in the interest rate.

The **target federal funds rate** is the Federal Reserve's desired federal funds rate.

In practice, at each meeting the FOMC decides on the interest rate to prevail for the next six weeks, until its next meeting. The Fed sets a **target federal funds rate,** a desired level for the federal funds rate. The Open Market Desk of the Federal Reserve Bank of New York adjusts the money supply through the purchase and sale of Treasury bills until the actual federal funds rate equals the target rate.

Figure 14-6 shows how this works. In both panels, r_T is the target federal funds rate. In panel (a), the initial money supply curve is MS_1 with money supply $\overline{M}_1$, and

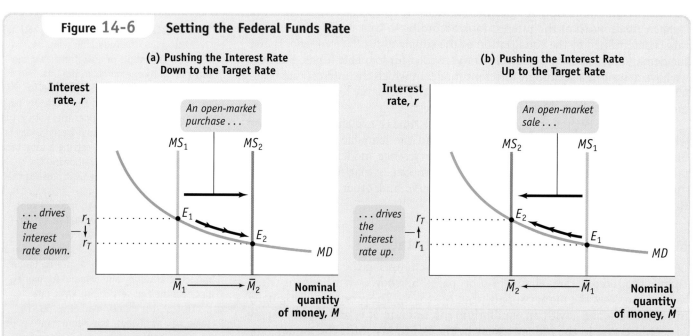

Figure 14-6   **Setting the Federal Funds Rate**

(a) Pushing the Interest Rate Down to the Target Rate

An open-market purchase . . .

. . . drives the interest rate down.

(b) Pushing the Interest Rate Up to the Target Rate

An open-market sale . . .

. . . drives the interest rate up.

The Federal Reserve sets a target for the federal funds rate and uses open-market operations to achieve that target. In both panels the target rate is r_T. In panel (a) the initial equilibrium interest rate, r_1, is above the target rate. The Fed increases the money supply by making an open-market purchase of Treasury bills, pushing the money supply curve rightward from MS_1 to MS_2, and driving the interest rate down to r_T. In panel (b) the initial equilibrium interest rate, r_1, is below the target rate. The Fed reduces the money supply by making an open-market sale of Treasury bills, pushing the money supply curve leftward from MS_1 to MS_2, and driving the interest rate up to r_T.

LONG-TERM INTEREST RATES

Earlier in this chapter we mentioned that *long-term interest rates*—rates on bonds or loans that mature in several years—don't necessarily move with short-term interest rates. How is that possible?

Consider the case of Millie, who has already decided to place $1,000 in certificates of deposit (CDs) for the next two years. However, she hasn't decided whether to put the money in a one-year CD, at a 4% rate of interest, or a two-year CD, at a 5% rate of interest.

You might think that the two-year CD is a clearly better deal—but it may not be. Suppose that Millie expects the rate of interest on one-year CDs to rise sharply next year. If she puts her funds in a one-year CD this year, she will be able to reinvest the money at a much higher rate next year. And this could give her a two-year rate of return that is higher than if she put her funds into the two-year CD. For exam-

ple, if the rate of interest on one-year CDs rises from 4% this year to 8% next year, putting her funds in a one-year CD will give her a rate of return over the next two years of about 6%, better than the rate on two-year CDs.

The same considerations apply to investors deciding between short-term and long-term bonds. If they expect short-term interest rates to rise, investors may buy short-term bonds even if long-term bonds offer a higher interest rate. If they expect short-term interest rates to fall, investors may buy long-term bonds even if short-term bonds offer a higher interest rate.

In practice, long-term interest rates reflect the average expectation in the market about what's going to happen to short-term rates in the future. When long-term rates are much higher than short-term rates, as they were in 2003, the market is signaling that it expects short-term rates to rise in the future.

the equilibrium interest rate, r_1, is above the target rate. To lower the interest rate to r_T, the Fed makes an open-market purchase of Treasury bills. As we learned in Chapter 13, an open-market purchase of Treasury bills leads to an increase in the money supply via the money multiplier. This is illustrated in panel (a) by the rightward shift of the money supply curve from MS_1 to MS_2 and an increase in the money supply to $\overline{M}_2$. This drives the equilibrium interest rate down to the target rate, r_T.

Panel (b) shows the opposite case. Again, the initial money supply curve is MS_1 with money supply $\overline{M}_1$. But this time the equilibrium interest rate, r_1, is below the target federal funds rate, r_T. In this case, the Fed will make an open-market sale of Treasury bills, leading to a fall in the money supply to $\overline{M}_2$ via the money multiplier. The money supply curve shifts leftward from MS_1 to MS_2, driving the equilibrium interest rate *up* to the target federal funds rate, r_T.

economics in action

The Fed Takes Action

In January 2001 the Federal Reserve, alarmed by signs of a looming recession, began cutting the target federal funds rate. We'll explain in the next section why the Fed believed this would be the correct response to a recession. But for now, let's focus on the Fed's ability to move interest rates.

Figure 14-7 on page 354 shows the movements of three interest rates between 1999 and 2005: the actual federal funds rate, the *prime rate*, and the 30-year mortgage rate. As you can see, the January 2001 cut in the federal funds rate was followed by several more. In fact, by the end of 2001 the Fed had cut the target federal funds rate 10 times, bringing it down from 6% at the beginning of 2001 to 1.75% at the end of 2001. (This was achieved by making cuts between regular meetings of the FOMC.) In 2002 the Fed cut the target again, to 1.25%; in 2003 it cut the target even further, to just 1%. In 2004, in response to signs of a growing economy, the Fed began gradually raising its target again, by 0.25 percentage points at each meeting.

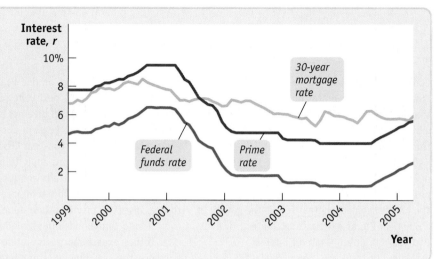

Figure 14-7

The Fed Moves Interest Rates

In early 2001, in response to a weakening economy, the Fed began cutting the federal funds rate. The prime rate—the interest rate on short-term bank loans to their best customers—fell in parallel. The 30-year mortgage rate, which is used by many consumers buying homes, fell, too, though not as much. By 2004, in the face of a growing economy, the Fed began raising the federal funds rate.

Source: Federal Reserve Bank of St. Louis.

The second interest rate shown in Figure 14-7, the prime rate, is the short-term rate that banks charge on loans to their best customers. This is a measure of how much it costs businesses to borrow. It's always above the federal funds rate because lending to a business customer always involves some risk of nonpayment. But the prime rate moves almost perfectly in parallel with the federal funds rate.

The last interest rate in Figure 14-7 is the rate on 30-year mortgages—loans that many people use to buy homes. As you can see, this rate didn't move nearly as much in synch with the federal funds rate as did the prime rate. This illustrates a point we mentioned earlier in this chapter: long-term interest rates don't always move closely together with short-term rates.

Still, mortgage rates did fall significantly as the Fed cut the federal funds rate repeatedly in 2001. And the fall in mortgage rates helped start a housing boom, which had an expansionary effect on the economy. Housing starts—the number of new homes on which construction has begun—rose by one-third, from 1.2 million in 2000 to 1.6 million in 2004. ■

< < < < < < < < < < < < < < < < < <

>>CHECK YOUR UNDERSTANDING **14-2**

1. Assume that there is an increase in the demand for money at every interest rate. Using a diagram, show what effect this will have on the equilibrium interest rate for a given money supply.

2. Now assume that the Fed is following a policy of targeting the federal funds rate. What will the Fed do in the situation described in Question 1 to keep the federal funds rate unchanged? Illustrate with a diagram.

Solutions appear at back of book.

Monetary Policy and Aggregate Demand

In Chapter 12 we saw how fiscal policy can be used to stabilize the economy. Now we will see how monetary policy—changes in the money supply or the interest rate, or both—can play the same role.

Expansionary and Contractionary Monetary Policy

As we have just seen, the Fed moves the interest rate down or up by increasing or decreasing the money supply. Changes in the interest rate, in turn, change aggregate demand. Other things equal, a fall in the interest rate leads to a rise in investment and consumer spending and therefore a rise in aggregate demand. And, other things equal, a rise in the interest rate leads to a fall in investment and consumer spending and therefore a fall in aggregate demand. As a result, monetary policy, like fiscal pol-icy, can be used to close either a recessionary gap or an inflationary gap.

Figure 14-8 shows the case of an economy facing a recessionary gap, where aggre-gate output is below potential output. *SRAS* is the short-run aggregate supply curve, *LRAS* is the long-run aggregate supply curve, and AD_1 is the initial aggregate demand curve. At the initial short-run macroeconomic equilibrium, E_1, aggregate output is Y_1, below potential output, Y_P. Suppose the Fed would like to increase aggregate de-mand, shifting the aggregate demand curve rightward to AD_2. This would increase ag-gregate output to potential output. The Fed can accomplish that goal by increasing the money supply, which drives the interest rate down. A lower interest rate leads to higher investment and consumer spending leading to a rise in aggregate demand. Monetary policy that increases aggregate demand is called **expansionary monetary policy.** Commentators often call an expansionary monetary policy a "loose" mone-tary policy because it is associated with a loosening of the money supply.

Expansionary monetary policy is mone-tary policy that increases aggregate demand.

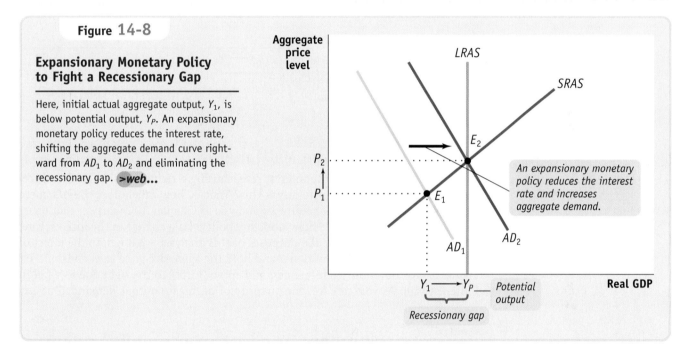

Figure 14-8

Expansionary Monetary Policy to Fight a Recessionary Gap

Here, initial actual aggregate output, Y_1, is below potential output, Y_P. An expansionary monetary policy reduces the interest rate, shifting the aggregate demand curve right-ward from AD_1 to AD_2 and eliminating the recessionary gap. **>web...**

An expansionary monetary policy reduces the interest rate and increases aggregate demand.

Figure 14-9 on page 356 shows the opposite case—an econ-omy facing an inflationary gap, where actual output is above potential output. *SRAS* is the short-run aggregate supply curve, *LRAS* is the long-run aggregate supply curve, and AD_1 is the ini-tial aggregate demand curve. At the initial short-run macroeco-nomic equilibrium, aggregate output, Y_1, is above potential output, Y_P. As we've previously mentioned, policy makers often try to head off inflation by eliminating inflationary gaps. To eliminate the inflationary gap illustrated in Figure 14-9, aggre-gate demand must be reduced. By raising the interest rate, the Fed can cause a leftward shift of the aggregate demand curve, from AD_1 to AD_2, which reduces aggregate output to potential output. Monetary policy that reduces aggregate demand is called **contractionary monetary policy.** Commentators often refer to this as a "tight" monetary policy because it is associated with a restriction of the money supply.

"I told you the Fed should have tightened."

Does monetary policy, like fiscal policy, have a multiplier effect on aggregate de-mand? Yes, although it's important to have a clear understanding of what is being multiplied.

Contractionary monetary policy is monetary policy that reduces aggregate demand.

Figure 14-9

Contractionary Monetary Policy to Fight an Inflationary Gap

Here, initial actual aggregate output, Y_1, is above potential output, Y_P. A contractionary monetary policy raises the interest rate, shifting the aggregate demand curve leftward from AD_1 to AD_2 and eliminating the inflationary gap.

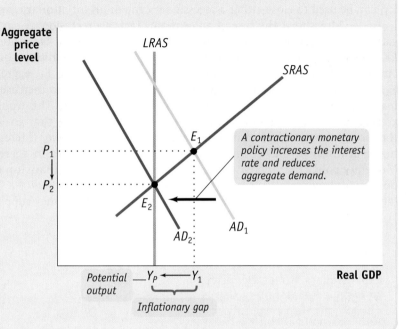

A contractionary monetary policy increases the interest rate and reduces aggregate demand.

Monetary Policy and the Multiplier

Suppose the Fed drives down the interest rate, causing a rightward shift of the aggregate demand curve. How expansionary is this? That is, how much does the AD curve shift to the right? We'll use the multiplier analysis of Chapter 10 to answer that question. In particular, we'll analyze how monetary policy, via a change in the interest rate, affects aggregate demand. (For the purposes of this analysis, we'll ignore the effect of taxes or foreign trade on the multiplier and hold the aggregate price level constant.)

Figure 14-10 shows the aggregate demand curve shifted to the right due to a fall in the interest rate. As you can see, the quantity of aggregate output demanded at any

Figure 14-10

Monetary Policy and the Multiplier

An expansionary monetary policy drives down the interest rate, leading to an initial rise in investment spending, ΔI. This raises disposable income, which causes a rise in consumer spending, which further raises disposable income, and so on. In the end, the AD curve shifts rightward by a *multiple* of the initial rise in I.

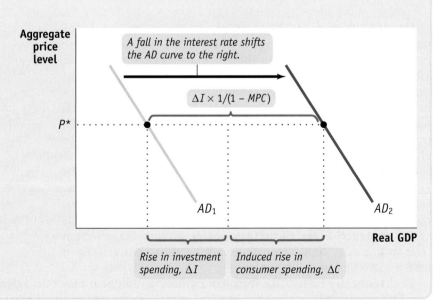

A fall in the interest rate shifts the AD curve to the right.

$\Delta I \times 1/(1 - MPC)$

given aggregate price level increases. To calculate how much the quantity of aggregate output demanded increases, we need to know how much a fall in the interest rate increases real GDP at a given aggregate price level, such as P^*. To keep things simple, we'll focus exclusively on the change in investment spending caused by a change in the interest rate, ignoring the direct effect of a change in the interest rate on consumer spending. Although they are present in reality, they are also likely to be much smaller than the effects on investment spending.

Assume that the initial aggregate demand curve is AD_1, and that the decline in the interest rate increases investment spending at the aggregate price level P^* by an amount ΔI. This is an example of an autonomous rise in aggregate spending, a phenomenon we studied in Chapter 10. From this point on, the analysis is exactly the same as that of any autonomous change in aggregate spending. The initial increase in real GDP translates into an increase in disposable income. This causes a rise in consumer spending, C, and a second-round rise in real GDP. This second-round increase in real GDP leads to yet another rise in consumer spending, and so on. At each round, however, the increase in real GDP is smaller than in the previous round, because some of the increase in disposable income "leaks out" into savings due to the fact that the marginal propensity to save, MPS, is positive. In the end, the AD curve shifts to a new position such as AD_2.

So a fall in the interest rate, r, leads to a rise in investment spending, ΔI. This rise in investment spending leads, in turn, to a rightward shift of the AD curve that reflects both the increase in investment spending, ΔI, and an induced rise in consumer spending, ΔC. As we saw in Chapter 12, the total rise in real GDP, assuming a fixed aggregate price level and no taxes or foreign trade, is a multiple of the initial rise in investment spending:

(14-6) $\Delta Y = \Delta I \times \dfrac{1}{1 - MPC}$

where MPC is the marginal propensity to consume—the increase in consumer spending if disposable income rises by $1.

Two Models of Interest Rates, Revisited

Earlier in this chapter we developed the liquidity preference model of the interest rate. In this model, the equilibrium interest rate is the rate at which the quantity of money demanded equals the quantity of money supplied. We promised to explain how this is consistent with the loanable funds model of the interest rate we developed in Chapter 9. In this model, the equilibrium interest rate matches the quantity of loanable funds supplied by savers with the quantity of loanable funds demanded for investment spending. We will now take the first of two steps toward providing that explanation, focusing on what happens in the short run.

As we have just discussed, a fall in the interest rate leads to a rise in investment spending, I, which then leads to a rise in both real GDP and consumer spending, C. The rise in real GDP doesn't lead only to a rise in consumer spending, however. As we noted, it also leads to a rise in savings: at each stage of the multiplier process, part of the increase in disposable income is saved. How much do savings rise? In Chapter 9 we introduced the *savings–investment spending identity:* total savings in the economy is always equal to investment spending. This tells us that when a fall in the interest rate leads to higher investment spending, the resulting increase in real GDP generates exactly enough additional savings to match the rise in investment spending. To put it another way, after a fall in the interest rate, the quantity of savings supplied rises exactly enough to match the quantity of savings demanded.

Figure 14-11 on page 358 shows how our two models of the interest rate are reconciled in the short run by the links among changes in the interest rate, changes in real GDP, and changes in savings. Panel (a) represents the liquidity preference model

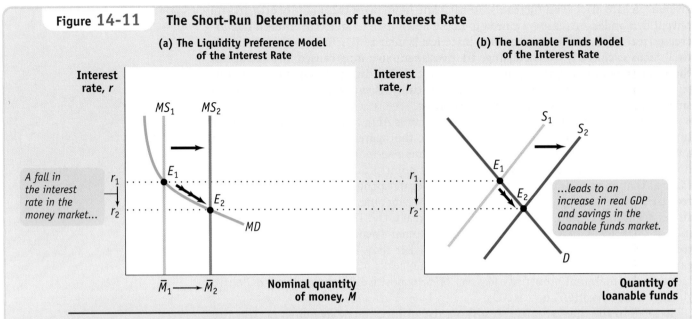

Figure 14-11   The Short-Run Determination of the Interest Rate

(a) The Liquidity Preference Model of the Interest Rate

(b) The Loanable Funds Model of the Interest Rate

Panel (a) shows the liquidity preference model of the interest rate: the equilibrium interest rate matches the money supply to the quantity of money demanded. In the short run, the interest rate is determined in the money market, where an increase in the money supply from $\bar{M}_1$ to $\bar{M}_2$ pushes the equilibrium interest rate down from r_1 to r_2. Panel (b) shows the loanable funds model of the interest rate. The fall in the interest rate in the

money market leads, through the multiplier effect, to an increase in real GDP and savings, to a rightward shift of the supply curve of loanable funds, from S_1 to S_2, and to a fall in the interest rate, from r_1 to r_2. As a result, the new equilibrium interest rate in the loanable funds market matches the new equilibrium interest rate in the money market at r_2.

of the interest rate. MS_1 and MD are the initial supply and demand curves for money. According to the liquidity preference model, the equilibrium interest rate in the economy is the rate at which the quantity of money supplied is equal to the quantity of money demanded in the money market. Panel (b) represents the loanable funds model of the interest rate. S_1 is the initial supply curve and D is the demand curve for loanable funds. According to the loanable funds model, the equilibrium interest rate in the economy is the rate at which the quantity of loanable funds supplied is equal to the quantity of loanable funds demanded in the market for loanable funds.

In Figure 14-11 both the money market and the market for loanable funds are initially in equilibrium at the same interest rate, r_1. You might think that this would only happen by accident, but in fact it will always be true. To see why, let's look at what happens when the Fed increases the money supply. This action pushes the money supply curve rightward to MS_2, and the equilibrium interest rate in the market for money falls to r_2. What happens in panel (b), in the market for loanable funds? In the short run, the fall in the interest rate leads to a rise in real GDP, which generates a rise in savings through the multiplier process. This rise in savings shifts the supply curve for loanable funds rightward from S_1 to S_2, reducing the equilibrium interest rate in the loanable funds market, too. And we know that savings rise by exactly enough to match the rise in investment spending. This tells us that the equilibrium rate in the loanable funds market falls to r_2, the same as the new equilibrium interest rate in the money market.

In the short run, then, the supply and demand for money determine the interest rate, and the loanable funds market follows the lead of the money market. When a change in the money supply leads to a change in the interest rate, the resulting change in real GDP causes the supply of loanable funds to change as well. As a result, the equilibrium interest rate in the loanable funds market is the same as the equilibrium interest rate in the money market.

Notice our use of the phrase "in the short run." Recall from Chapter 10 that changes in aggregate demand affect aggregate output only in the short run. In the long run, aggregate output is equal to potential output. So our story about how a fall in the interest rate leads to a rise in aggregate output, which leads to a rise in savings, applies only to the short run. In the long run, as we'll see in the next section, the determination of the interest rate is quite different, because the roles of the two markets are reversed. In the long run, the loanable funds market determines the equilibrium interest rate, and it is the market for money that follows the lead of the loanable funds market.

economics in action

The Fed and the Output Gap, 1985–2004

In Figures 14-8 and 14-9 we showed how monetary policy can play a useful role: expansionary monetary policy can close recessionary gaps, and contractionary monetary policy can close inflationary gaps. A look back at U.S. monetary policy between 1985 and 2004 shows that the Federal Reserve did indeed tend to cut interest rates when the economy had a recessionary gap and raise interest rates when the economy had an inflationary gap.

The vertical axis on the left of Figure 14-12 shows the federal funds rate; the line labeled "federal funds rate" shows the average yearly value of that rate between 1985 and 2004. The vertical axis on the right shows the Congressional Budget Office estimate of the output gap, measured as a percentage of potential output. This number is positive when there is an inflationary gap, as in 1999 and 2000, and negative when there is a recessionary gap, as in 2001 through 2004.

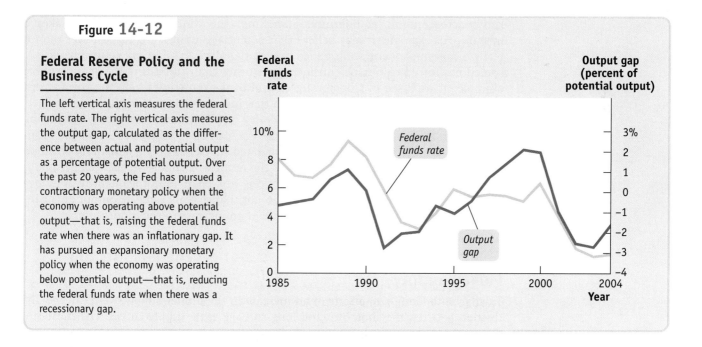

Figure 14-12

Federal Reserve Policy and the Business Cycle

The left vertical axis measures the federal funds rate. The right vertical axis measures the output gap, calculated as the difference between actual and potential output as a percentage of potential output. Over the past 20 years, the Fed has pursued a contractionary monetary policy when the economy was operating above potential output—that is, raising the federal funds rate when there was an inflationary gap. It has pursued an expansionary monetary policy when the economy was operating below potential output—that is, reducing the federal funds rate when there was a recessionary gap.

As you can see, there's a positive association between the federal funds rate and the output gap: the Fed tended to raise interest rates when aggregate output was moving above potential output and to reduce them when aggregate output was moving below potential output. In other words, the Fed was following pretty much the policy illustrated in Figures 14-8 and 14-9.

The two lines aren't perfectly synchronized. As you can see, the Fed did not raise interest rates in 1998 and 1999, even though the economy had developed a substantial inflationary gap. The main reason was that the Federal Reserve wasn't sure at the time that there was an output gap. As we'll see in Chapter 17, some economists believe that the Fed *should* have raised rates during that period. Also, data from years earlier than 1985 look very different. Prior to 1985 the Fed was grappling with the problem of *inflationary expectations,* which we will discuss in Chapter 16.

The important lesson, however, is that over the past two decades the Fed's actual policy has largely followed our basic analysis of how monetary policy should work. ■

< < < < < < < < < < < < < < < < < < <

>>CHECK YOUR UNDERSTANDING 14-3

1. Suppose the economy is currently suffering from a recessionary gap and the Federal Reserve uses an expansionary monetary policy to close that gap. Describe the short-run effect of this policy on the following:
   a. The money supply curve
   b. The equilibrium interest rate
   c. Investment spending
   d. Consumer spending
   e. Aggregate output
   f. The aggregate price level
   g. Savings
   h. The supply curve of loanable funds in the loanable funds market

Solutions appear at back of book.

Money, Output, and Prices in the Long Run

Through its expansionary and contractionary effects, monetary policy can be used to move the economy more quickly to long-run macroeconomic equilibrium. Sometimes, however, there are monetary events that move the economy *away* from long-run macroeconomic equilibrium. Sometimes the central bank simply makes a mistake. For example, it may believe that potential output is higher or lower than it really is and implement a misguided monetary policy. In addition, central banks are sometimes forced to pursue considerations other than stabilizing the economy. For example, as we'll see in Chapter 16, central banks sometimes help the government pay its bills by printing money, an action that increases the money supply.

What happens when a change in the money supply pushes the economy away from, rather than toward, long-run equilibrium? We learned in Chapter 10 that the economy is self-correcting in the long run: a demand shock has only a temporary effect on aggregate output. If the demand shock is the result of a change in the money supply, we can make a stronger statement: in the long run, changes in the quantity of money affect the aggregate price level, but they do not change real aggregate output or the interest rate. To see why, let's look at the case of an increase in the money supply.

Short-Run and Long-Run Effects of an Increase in the Money Supply

To analyze the long-run effects of an increase in the money supply, we recall the distinction between the short-run and long-run aggregate supply curves. The short-run aggregate supply curve slopes upward: in the short run, a higher aggregate price level leads to higher production. The long-run aggregate supply curve, however, is vertical at potential output: in the long run, a rise in prices of final goods and services leads to an equal rise in nominal wages, and real GDP remains equal to potential output.

Figure 14-13 shows the short-run and long-run effects of an increase in the money supply when the economy begins at potential output, Y_1. The initial short-run aggregate supply curve is $SRAS_1$, the long-run aggregate supply curve is *LRAS,* and the initial aggregate demand curve is AD_1. The economy's initial equilibrium is at E_1, a point of both short-run and long-run macroeconomic equilibrium because it is on

Figure 14-13

The Short-Run and Long-Run Effects of an Increase in the Money Supply

An increase in the money supply generates a positive short-run effect, but no long-run effect, on real GDP. Here, the economy begins at E_1, a point of short-run and long-run equilibrium. An increase in the money supply shifts the AD curve rightward, and the economy moves to a new short-run equilibrium at E_2 and a new real GDP of Y_2. But E_2 is not a long-run equilibrium: Y_2 exceeds potential output, Y_1, leading over time to an increase in nominal wages. In the long run, the increase in nominal wages shifts the short-run aggregate supply curve leftward, to a new position at $SRAS_2$. The economy reaches a new short-run and long-run equilibrium at E_3 on the $LRAS$ curve, and output falls back to potential output, Y_1. The only long-run effect of an increase in the money supply is an increase in the aggregate price level to P_3. **>web...**

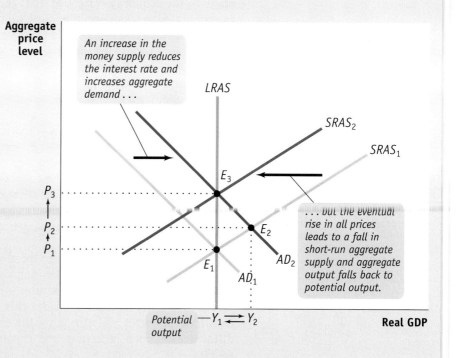

An increase in the money supply reduces the interest rate and increases aggregate demand . . .

. . . but the eventual rise in all prices leads to a fall in short-run aggregate supply and aggregate output falls back to potential output.

both the short-run and the long-run aggregate supply curves. Real GDP is at potential output, Y_1.

Now suppose there is an increase in the money supply. This shifts the AD curve to the right, to AD_2. In the short run, the economy moves to a new short-run macroeconomic equilibrium at E_2. The price level rises from P_1 to P_2, and real GDP rises from Y_1 to Y_2. That is, both the aggregate price level and aggregate output increase in the short run.

But the aggregate output level Y_2 is above potential output. As a result, nominal wages will rise over time, causing the short-run aggregate supply curve to shift leftward. This process stops only when the $SRAS$ curve ends up at $SRAS_2$ and the economy ends up at point E_3, a point of both short-run and long-run macroeconomic equilibrium. The long-run effect of an increase in the money supply, then, is that the aggregate price level has increased from P_1 to P_3, but aggregate output is back at potential output, Y_1. In the long run, a monetary expansion raises the aggregate price level but has no effect on real GDP.

We won't describe the effects of a monetary contraction in detail, but the same logic applies. In the short run, a fall in the money supply leads to a fall in aggregate output as the economy moves down the short-run aggregate supply curve. In the long run, however, the monetary contraction reduces only the aggregate price level, and real GDP returns to potential output.

Monetary Neutrality

How much does a change in the money supply change the aggregate price level in the long run? A change in the money supply leads to a proportional change in the aggregate price level in the long run. For example, if the money supply falls 25%, the aggregate price level falls 25% in the long run; if the money supply rises 50%, the aggregate price level rises 50% in the long run.

How do we know this? Consider the following thought experiment: suppose all prices in the economy—prices of final goods and services and also factor prices, such as nominal wage rates—double. And suppose the money supply doubles at the same time. What difference does this make to the economy in real terms? The answer is none. All real variables in the economy—including the real value of the money supply—are unchanged, so there is no reason for anyone to behave any differently.

We can state this argument in reverse: if the economy starts out in long-run macroeconomic equilibrium and the nominal money supply changes, restoring long-run macroeconomic equilibrium requires restoring all real values to their original values. This includes restoring the real money supply to its original level. So if the money supply falls 25%, the aggregate price level must fall 25%; if the money supply rises 50%, the price level must rise 50%; and so on.

> There is **monetary neutrality** when changes in the money supply have no real effects on the economy.

This analysis demonstrates the concept known as **monetary neutrality,** in which changes in the money supply have no real effects on the economy—no effects on real GDP or its components. The only effect of an increase in the money supply is to raise the aggregate price level by an equal percentage. Economists argue that *money is neutral in the long run.*

This is, however, a good time to recall the dictum of John Maynard Keynes: "In the long run we are all dead." In the long run, changes in the money supply don't have any effect on real GDP, interest rates, or anything else except the price level. But it would be foolish to conclude from this that the Fed is irrelevant. Monetary policy does have powerful real effects on the economy in the short run, often making the difference between recession and expansion. And that matters a lot for society's welfare.

The Interest Rate in the Long Run

In the short run an increase in the money supply leads to a fall in the interest rate, and a decrease in the money supply leads to a rise in the interest rate. In the long run, however, changes in the money supply don't affect the interest rate.

Figure 14-14 shows why. It is similar to Figure 14-11, but in this case panel (a) shows the *real* money demand curve, RMD. Panel (b), as in Figure 14-11, shows the supply and demand for loanable funds. We assume that in both panels the economy is initially at E, in long-run macroeconomic equilibrium at potential output with the nominal money supply equal to $\overline{M}_1$ and the price level equal to P_1. The demand curve for loanable funds is D, and the initial supply curve for loanable funds is S_1. The initial equilibrium interest rate is r_1.

Now suppose the nominal money supply rises from $\overline{M}_1$ to $\overline{M}_2$. We already know from the neutrality of money that in the long run the aggregate price level rises by the same proportion as the increase in the money supply but that in the short run the price level rises by a smaller amount. So the initial effect of an increase in the nominal money supply is a rise in the *real* money supply, from $\overline{M}_1/P_1$ to $\overline{M}_2/P_2$. Given the real money demand curve, RMD, this reduces the equilibrium interest rate from r_1 to r_2, and the money market moves to X in panel (a). And as we saw earlier, the supply of loanable funds shifts rightward by just enough that the quantity of loanable funds supplied and the quantity of loanable funds demanded are equalized at r_2. Correspondingly, the loanable funds market moves to X in panel (b). X corresponds to an aggregate output greater than potential output because the interest rate at X, r_2, is lower than the interest rate that holds at potential output, r_1.

In the long run, however, the aggregate price level rises further, from P_2 to P_3. As we've already seen, this reduces the real money supply back to its original level: $\overline{M}_2/P_3$ is equal to $\overline{M}_1/P_1$. As a result, the equilibrium interest rate goes back to r_1 and each market moves back to E. Meanwhile, aggregate output also falls back to potential output—which means that savings return to their original level, too. In panel (b), the supply of loanable funds, which initially shifted from S_1 to S_2, shifts back to S_1.

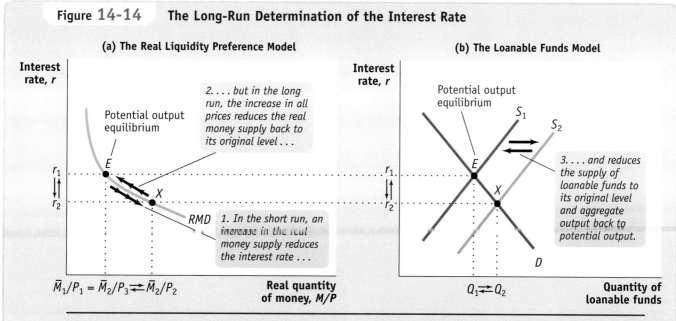

Figure 14-14 **The Long-Run Determination of the Interest Rate**

Panel (a) shows the money market expressed in real terms and panel (b) shows the loanable funds market. Each market starts at point E, where the economy is at potential output. In the short run, an increase in the money supply increases the real money supply from $\bar{M}_1/P_1$ to $\bar{M}_2/P_2$ and reduces the equilibrium interest rate from r_1 to r_2 as the money market moves from point E to point X. The fall in the interest rate leads to higher real GDP and higher savings through the multiplier effect. This shifts the supply curve of loanable funds rightward, from S_1 to S_2, also moving the market for loanable funds from point E to point X. In the long run, however, the increase in the money supply raises prices: the real money supply returns to its original level, $\bar{M}_2/P_3 = \bar{M}_1/P_1$, and the supply curve of loanable funds shifts back to its initial position, S_1. So in the long run the equilibrium interest rate is determined by the supply and demand for loanable funds that arise at potential output.

In the long run, then, changes in the money supply do not affect the interest rate. So what determines the interest rate in the long run—that is, what determines r_1 in Figure 14-14? The answer is the supply and demand for loanable funds. More specifically, in the long run the equilibrium interest rate matches the supply and demand for loanable funds that arise at potential output.

economics in action

International Evidence of Monetary Neutrality

These days monetary policy is quite similar among wealthy countries. Each major nation (or, in the case of the euro, group of nations) has a central bank that is insulated from political pressure; all of these central banks try to keep the aggregate price level roughly stable, which usually means inflation of at most 2% to 3% per year.

But if we look at a longer period and a wider group of countries, we see large differences in the growth of the money supply. Between 1970 and the present the money supply rose only a few percent per year in some countries, such as Switzerland and the United States, but rose much more rapidly in some poorer countries, such as Bolivia. These differences allow us to see whether it is really true that increases in the money supply lead, in the long run, to equal percentage rises in the aggregate price level.

Figure 14-15 on page 364 shows the annual percentage increases in the money supply and in the aggregate price level for a sample of countries during the period

Figure 14-15

The Long-Run Relationship Between Money and Inflation

The horizontal axis measures the annual percent increase in a country's money supply between 1970 and 2000. The vertical axis measures the annual percent increase in a country's aggregate price level over the same period. Each point represents a specific country. The scatter of points lies close to a 45-degree line, demonstrating that in the long run increases in the money supply lead to roughly equal percent increases in the aggregate price level.

Source: United Nations Statistical Database.

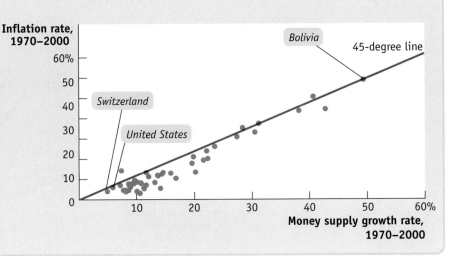

1970–2000, with each point representing a country. If the relationship between increases in the money supply and changes in the aggregate price level were exact, the points would lie precisely on a 45-degree line. In fact, the relationship isn't exact, because other factors besides money affect the aggregate price level. But the scatter of points clearly lies close to a 45-degree line, showing a more or less proportional relationship between money and the aggregate price level. That is, the data support the idea that money is neutral in the long run. ■

< < < < < < < < < < < < < < < < <

▶▶CHECK YOUR UNDERSTANDING 14-4

1. Assume the central bank increases the quantity of money by 25%, even though the economy is initially in both short-run and long-run macroeconomic equilibrium. Describe the effects, in the short run and in the long run (giving numbers where possible), on the following:
   a. Aggregate output
   b. Aggregate price level
   c. Real quantity of money
   d. Interest rate

Solutions appear at back of book.

• A LOOK AHEAD •

Monetary and fiscal policy can be used to help close gaps: a recessionary gap, in which the economy is producing less than potential output, or an inflationary gap, in which it is producing more than potential output. We have not yet explained, however, why closing such gaps is so important.

In the case of a recessionary gap, the answer is that recessionary gaps are associated with high unemployment. To deepen our understanding of that concern, however, we need to look more deeply into the causes and meaning of unemployment. That's the subject of Chapter 15.

The causes and costs of inflation are a more subtle issue, which we deal with in Chapter 16.

SUMMARY

1. The **money demand curve** arises from a trade-off between the opportunity cost of holding money and the liquidity that money provides. The opportunity cost of holding money depends on **short-term interest rates,** not **long-term interest rates.**

2. Other things equal, the nominal quantity of money demanded is proportional to the aggregate price level. So money demand can also be represented using the **real money demand curve.** Changes in real aggregate spending, technology, and institutions shift the real and nominal money demand curves. According to the **quantity equation,** the real quantity of money demanded is proportional to real aggregate spending, where the constant of proportionality is one over the **velocity of money.**

3. The **liquidity preference model of the interest rate** says that the interest rate is determined in the money market by the money demand curve and the **money supply curve.** The Federal Reserve can change the interest rate in the short run by shifting the money supply curve. In practice, the Fed uses open-market operations to achieve a **target federal funds rate,** which other interest rates generally track.

4. **Expansionary monetary policy,** which reduces the interest rate and increases aggregate demand by increasing the money supply, is used to close recessionary gaps. **Contractionary monetary policy,** which increases the interest rate and reduces aggregate demand by decreasing the money supply, is used to close inflationary gaps.

5. Like fiscal policy, monetary policy has a multiplier effect, because changes in the interest rate lead to changes in consumer spending and savings as well as investment spending. In the short run, a change in the equilibrium interest rate determined in the money market results in a change in real GDP and in savings through the multiplier effect. The change in savings shifts the supply of loanable funds in the market for loanable funds until it reaches equilibrium at the new equilibrium interest rate.

6. In the long run, changes in the money supply affect the aggregate price level but not real GDP or the interest rate. In fact, there is **monetary neutrality:** changes in the money supply have no real effect on the economy in the long run. So monetary policy is ineffectual in the long run.

7. In the long run, the equilibrium interest rate matches the supply and demand for loanable funds that arise at potential output in the market for loanable funds.

KEY TERMS

Short-term interest rates, p. 344
Long-term interest rates, p. 344
Money demand curve, p. 345
Real quantity of money, p. 345
Real money demand curve, p. 346

Velocity of money, p. 348
Quantity equation, p. 348
Liquidity preference model of the interest rate, p. 350
Money supply curve, p. 350

Target federal funds rate, p. 353
Expansionary monetary policy, p. 355
Contractionary monetary policy, p. 355
Monetary neutrality, p. 362

PROBLEMS

1. Go to the FOMC page of the Federal Reserve Board's website (http://www.federalreserve.gov/FOMC/) to find the statement issued after the most recent FOMC meeting. (Go to the bottom of the web page and click on the most recent statement listed in the calendar.)

   a. What is the target federal funds rate?

   b. Is the target federal funds rate different from the target federal funds rate from the previous FOMC statement? If yes, by how much does it differ?

   c. Does the statement comment on macroeconomic conditions in the United States? How does it describe the U.S. economy?

2. How will the following events affect the nominal demand for money as defined by M1? In each case, specify whether there

   is a shift of the money demand curve or a movement along the money demand curve and its direction.

   a. There is a fall in the interest rate from 12% to 10%.

   b. Thanksgiving arrives and, with it, the beginning of the holiday shopping season.

   c. McDonald's and other fast-food restaurants begin to accept credit cards.

   d. The Fed engages in an open-market purchase of U.S. Treasury bills.

3. The table on page 366 shows nominal GDP, M1, and M2 in billions of dollars in five-year increments from 1960 to 2000 as published in the *2005 Economic Report of the President.* Complete the table by calculating the velocity of money using both M1 and M2. What trends or patterns in the velocity of money do you see? What might account for these trends?

Year	Nominal GDP (billions of dollars)	M1 (billions of dollars)	M2 (billions of dollars)	Velocity using M1	Velocity using M2
1960	$526.4	$140.7	$312.4	?	?
1965	719.1	167.8	459.2	?	?
1970	1,038.5	214.4	626.5	?	?
1975	1,638.3	287.1	1,016.2	?	?
1980	2,789.5	408.5	1,599.8	?	?
1985	4,220.3	619.8	2,495.7	?	?
1990	5,803.1	824.8	3,279.2	?	?
1995	7,397.7	1,127.0	3,641.2	?	?
2000	9,817.0	1,087.9	4,932.5	?	?

4. The accompanying table shows the annual growth of M1 and nominal GDP in Japan during the early 2000s. What must have been happening to velocity during this time?

Year	M1 growth	Nominal GDP growth
2000	8.2%	2.9%
2001	8.5%	0.4%
2002	27.6%	−0.5%
2003	8.2%	2.5%

5. An economy is facing the recessionary gap shown in the accompanying diagram. To eliminate the gap, should the central bank use expansionary or contractionary monetary policy? How will the interest rate, investment spending, consumer spending, real GDP, and the aggregate price level change as the monetary policy closes the recessionary gap?

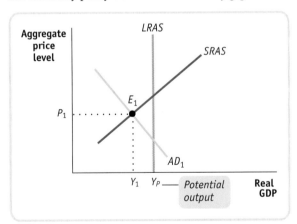

6. An economy is facing the inflationary gap shown in the accompanying diagram. To eliminate the gap, should the central bank use expansionary or contractionary monetary policy? How will the interest rate, investment spending, consumer spending, real GDP, and the aggregate price level change as the monetary policy closes the inflationary gap?

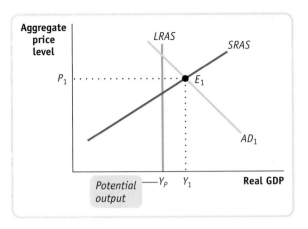

7. In the economy of Eastlandia, the money market is initially in equilibrium when the economy begins to slide into a recession.

   a. Using the accompanying diagram, explain what will happen to the interest rate if the central bank of Eastlandia keeps the money supply constant at $\overline{M}_1$.

   b. If the central bank is instead committed to maintaining an interest rate target of r_1, how should the central bank react as the economy slides into recession?

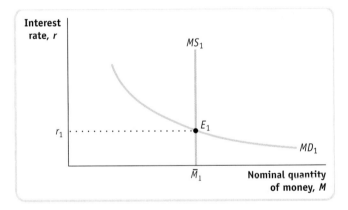

8. An economy is in long-run macroeconomic equilibrium with an unemployment rate of 5% when the government passes a law requiring the central bank to use monetary policy to lower the unemployment rate to 3% and keep it there. How could the central bank achieve this goal in the short run? What would happen in the long run? Illustrate with a diagram.

9. According to the European Central Bank website, the treaty establishing the European Community "makes clear that ensuring price stability is the most important contribution that monetary policy can make to achieve a favourable economic environment and a high level of employment." If price stability is the only goal of monetary policy, explain how monetary policy would be conducted during recessions. Analyze both the case of a recession that is the result of a demand shock and the case of a recession that is the result of a supply shock.

10. The effectiveness of monetary policy depends on how easy it is for changes in the money supply to change interest rates. By

changing interest rates, monetary policy affects investment spending and the aggregate demand curve. The economies of Albernia and Brittania have very different money demand curves, as shown in the accompanying diagram. In which economy will changes in the money supply be a more effective policy tool? Why?

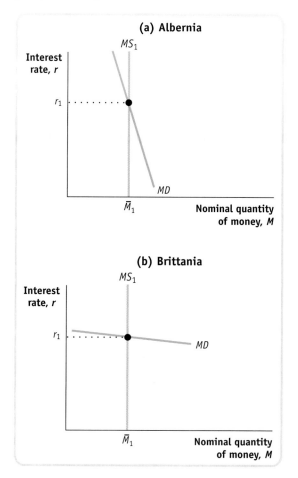

(a) Albernia

(b) Brittania

11. During the Great Depression, businesspeople in the United States were very pessimistic about the future of economic growth and reluctant to increase investment spending even when interest rates fell. How did this limit the potential for monetary policy to help alleviate the Depression?

12. Using a figure similar to Figure 14-11, explain how the money market and the loanable funds market react to a reduction in the money supply in the short run.

13. Contrast the short-run effects of an increase in the money supply on the interest rate to the long-run effects of an increase in the money supply on the interest rate. Which market determines the interest rate in the short run? Which market does so in the long run? What are the implications of your answers for the effectiveness of monetary policy in the short run and the long run in influencing real GDP?

>>Labor Markets, Unemployment, and Inflation

TWO PATHS TO UNEMPLOYMENT

MICHAEL WATSON, A SOFTWARE developer in Colorado Springs, has been moving in and out of unemployment for three years. Ever since his high-tech employer closed its doors in July 2002, Watson has been without a permanent job and traveling to places as far-flung as Virginia and Djibouti to do temporary contract work. He isn't alone: Colorado Springs, home to many high-tech workers, lost nearly 20% of its high-tech jobs between 2000 and 2004. Some workers who lost their jobs have since found new ones in Colorado Springs, others have left the area, and others—like Watson—are still looking for permanent work.

The economy in North Carolina, where textile engineer Tommy Patterson lives, is booming relative to that in the rest of the country. But Patterson, who lost his job at a Charlotte textile mill in November 2004, is still looking for work as a process engineer in the chemical industry. Still, despite

sending out between 50 and 75 résumés, he has had few bites to date. In North Carolina there are more jobs than there were a few years ago, but manufacturing and engineering jobs are still hard to come by.

Because both Watson and Patterson are currently jobless and actively seeking employment, they are considered to be unemployed. Both are in professions on the decline or stagnating in their given locations, but each is hesitant to move his family to a new city in search of work. So both men continue to search actively for permanent employment that's a good match for their skills and ambitions.

At any given point in time, millions of Americans are actively pursuing employment but have not found the right match. Others have recently been laid off, and still others have just entered the workforce but haven't yet found jobs. This "natural" churning of the labor force means that at any given point in time some fraction of the population is

Job loss strikes many kinds of workers, from computer programmers like Michael Watson to process engineers like Tommy Patterson. These two, like the millions of other workers who lose jobs in any given year, would like to see themselves as pictured above: employed again.

unemployed. But the size of that fraction depends on the state of the economy: there are more people in Watson's and Patterson's situation when the economy is depressed than when the economy is booming.

In this chapter, we look more closely at the nature of unemployment, why the unemployment rate goes up and down over time, and what economic policy can and cannot do about it.

The Nature of Unemployment

U.S. government statistics count as unemployed a worker who is actively looking for a job but hasn't found one. Recall from Chapter 6 that the unemployment rate is the ratio of the number of people unemployed to the total number of people in the labor force, where the labor force consists of people who are either currently working or looking for jobs. If everyone who wanted a job had one, the unemployment rate would be 0%. But American public policy considers the unemployment rate at "full employment," which you might think means that everyone who wants to work has a job, to be a number well above 0%. Indeed, as explained in For Inquiring Minds, a famous piece of legislation known as the Humphrey–Hawkins bill was passed by Congress in 1978. It called on the government to seek full employment—but defined full employment to be an unemployment rate of 4%.

Although a 4% unemployment rate may seem like a large number—after all, this implies that even with "full employment" millions of Americans looking for work would be jobless—at the time Humphrey–Hawkins was passed the vast majority of economists considered this target to be unrealistic. In fact, the Congressional Budget Office currently calculates the cyclically adjusted budget balance, the budget balance if the economy were at potential output and, hence, at full employment, under the assumption that full employment means a 5.2% unemployment rate.

To understand why there are so many unemployed workers even when the economy is considered to be at full employment, we need to look at the realities of the labor market.

FOR INQUIRING MINDS

FULL EMPLOYMENT: IT'S THE LAW!

Is there a law requiring the U.S. government to ensure full employment? No, and there never was. But the Full Employment and Balanced Growth Act of 1978, usually referred to as the Humphrey–Hawkins bill, did call on the U.S. government to achieve an unemployment rate of 4% or less through macroeconomic policy.

Nothing in the bill specified penalties for government officials who failed to achieve these goals, and policy makers began ignoring the unemployment target from the start. The only provision that really had teeth was the requirement that the chairman of the Federal Reserve Board of Governors testify about monetary policy before Congress twice a year, a tradition that continues to this day. That testimony is still often referred to as the "Humphrey–Hawkins testimony," even though the 1978 bill was allowed to lapse in 2000.

Despite the fact that Humphrey–Hawkins never had much direct effect on policy, it came to have symbolic importance. A 4% unemployment rate became the seemingly unattainable goal of economic policy. In late 1998, when the unemployment rate finally (and briefly) dropped toward the elusive goal, columnist Walter Shapiro asked in the online magazine *Slate*, "Where are the ticker-tape parades, the patriotic speeches, the red-white-and-blue fireworks, and the photographs of beautiful women embracing exuberant economists in Times Square?"

Job Creation and Job Destruction

At any given time, most Americans know someone who has lost his or her job recently. On average, about one worker in seven loses his or her job each year (in some cases because of leaving voluntarily) even in good years.

"They just like to remind you about the job market."

Dave Carpenter

There are many reasons for such job loss. One is that industries rise and fall as new technologies emerge and consumers' tastes change. For example, employment in high-tech industries such as telecommunications surged in the late 1990s but slumped severely after 2000. That's a major reason why Michael Watson, the software developer, lost his job in 2002 and has had difficulty finding another. Another reason is that individual companies do well or badly depending on the quality of their management or simply depending on luck: for example, in 2005 General Motors announced plans to close a number of auto plants even as Japanese companies such as Toyota announced plans to open new plants in North America. In addition, individual workers are constantly leaving jobs for personal reasons—family moves, dissatisfaction, better job prospects elsewhere.

This constant churning of the workforce is an inevitable feature of the modern economy. It is also one main reason that there is a considerable amount of unemployment even when the economy is at full employment.

Frictional Unemployment

Workers who spend time looking for employment are engaged in **job search.**

Frictional unemployment is unemployment due to the time workers spend in job search.

When a worker loses a job—or a young worker enters the job market for the first time—he or she often doesn't take the first new job offered. For example, suppose a skilled programmer, laid off because her company's product line was unsuccessful, sees a help-wanted sign in the window of a shop. She might well be able to walk in and get the job—but that would usually be foolish. Instead, she should take the time to look for a job that takes advantage of her skills and pays accordingly.

Economists say that workers who spend time looking for employment are engaged in **job search.** If all workers and all jobs were alike, job search wouldn't be necessary; if information about jobs and workers were perfect, job search would be very quick. In practice, however, it's normal for a worker who loses a job (or a young worker seeking a first job) to spend at least a few weeks searching.

Frictional unemployment is unemployment due to the time workers spend in job search. A certain amount of frictional unemployment is inevitable, for two reasons. One is the constant process of job creation and job destruction, which we have just described. The other is the fact that new workers are always entering the job market. For example, in July 2005, out of 7.8 million workers counted as unemployed, 882,000 were new entrants to the workforce.

A limited amount of frictional unemployment is relatively harmless and may even be a good thing. The economy is more productive if workers take the time to find jobs that are well matched to their skills, and workers who are unemployed for a brief period while searching for the right job don't experience great hardship. In fact, when there is a low unemployment rate, periods of unemployment tend to be quite short, suggesting that much of the unemployment is frictional. Figure 15-1 shows the composition of unemployment in 2000, when the unemployment rate was only 4%. Forty-five percent of the unemployed had been unemployed for less than 5 weeks and only 23% had been unemployed for 15 or more weeks. Just 11% were considered to be "long-term unemployed"—unemployed for 27 or more weeks.

Figure 15-1

Distribution of the Unemployed by Duration of Unemployment, 2000

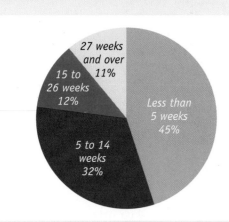

27 weeks and over 11%

15 to 26 weeks 12%

Less than 5 weeks 45%

5 to 14 weeks 32%

In years when the unemployment rate is low, most unemployed workers are unemployed for only a short period. In 2000, a year of low unemployment, 45% of the unemployed had been unemployed for less than 5 weeks and 77% for less than 15 weeks. The short duration of unemployment for most workers suggests that most unemployment in 2000 was frictional.

Source: Bureau of Labor Statistics.

In periods of higher unemployment, however, workers tend to be jobless for longer periods of time, suggesting that a smaller share of unemployment is frictional. By 2003, for instance, the fraction of workers considered "long-term unemployed" had jumped to 22%.

Structural Unemployment

Frictional unemployment exists even when the number of people seeking jobs is equal to the number of jobs being offered—that is, frictional unemployment doesn't signal a surplus of labor. Sometimes, however, there is a *persistent surplus* of job-seekers in a particular labor market. For example, there may be more workers with a particular skill than there are jobs available using that skill, or there may be more workers in a particular geographic region than there are jobs available in that region. **Structural unemployment** is unemployment that results when there are more people seeking jobs in a labor market than there are jobs available at the current wage rate.

> **Structural unemployment** is unemployment that results when there are more people seeking jobs in a labor market than there are jobs available at the current wage rate.

The supply and demand model tells us that the price of a good, service, or factor of production tends to move toward an equilibrium level that matches the quantity supplied with the quantity demanded. This is equally true, in general, of labor markets. Figure 15-2 shows a typical market for labor. The labor demand curve indicates that when the price of labor—the wage rate—increases, employers demand less labor. The labor supply curve indicates that when the price of labor increases, more workers will be willing to supply labor at the prevailing wage rate. These two forces coincide to lead to an equilibrium wage rate for any given type of labor in a particular location. That equilibrium wage rate is shown as W_E.

Figure 15-2

The Effect of a Minimum Wage on the Labor Market

When the government sets a minimum wage, W_F, that exceeds the market equilibrium wage rate, W_E, the number of workers, Q_S, who would like to work at that minimum wage, is greater than the number of workers, Q_D, demanded at that wage rate. This surplus of labor is considered structural unemployment.
>web...

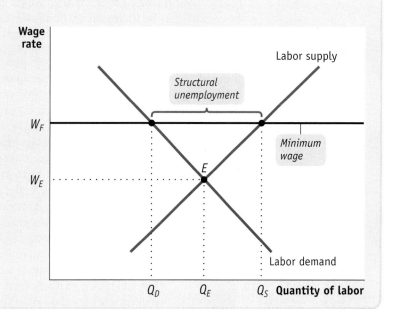

Even at the equilibrium wage rate W_E, there will still be some frictional unemployment. That's because there will always be some workers engaged in job search even when the number of jobs available is equal to the number of workers seeking jobs. But there wouldn't be any structural unemployment in this labor market. *Structural unemployment occurs when the wage rate is, for some reason, persistently above W_E.* There are several factors that can lead to a wage rate in excess of W_E, the most important being minimum wages, labor unions, *efficiency wages*, and the side effects of government policies.

Minimum Wages As we learned in Chapter 4, a minimum wage is a government-mandated floor on the price of labor. In the United States, the national minimum wage in 2005 was $5.15 an hour. For many types of labor, the minimum wage is irrelevant; the market equilibrium wage is well above this price floor. But for some types of labor, the minimum wage may be binding—it affects the wages that people are actually paid.

Figure 15-2 on page 371 shows just such a situation. In this market, there is a legal floor on wages, W_F, which is above the equilibrium wage rate, W_E. This leads to a persistent surplus in the labor market: the quantity of labor supplied, Q_S, is larger than the quantity demanded, Q_D. In other words, more people want to work than can find jobs at the minimum wage, leading to structural unemployment.

Given that minimum wages—that is, binding minimum wages—generally lead to structural unemployment, you might be wondering why governments impose them. The rationale is to help ensure that people who work can earn enough income to afford at least a minimally comfortable lifestyle. However, this comes at a cost, because it forecloses the opportunity to work for some workers who would have willingly worked for lower wages. As illustrated in Figure 15-2, not only are there more sellers of labor than there are buyers, but there are also fewer people working at a minimum wage (Q_D) than there would have been with no minimum wage at all (Q_E).

We should note, however, that although economists broadly agree that a high minimum wage has the employment-reducing effects shown in Figure 15-2, there is some question about whether this is a good description of how the minimum wage works in the United States. As a percentage of average wages, the minimum wage in the United States is quite low by international standards. (See the Economics in Action that follows this section.) Some researchers have produced evidence that increases in the minimum wage actually lead to higher employment when the minimum wage is low compared with average wages. They argue that firms that employ low-skilled workers sometimes restrict their hiring in order to keep wages low and that, as a result, the minimum wage can sometimes be increased without any loss of jobs. Most economists, however, agree that a sufficiently high minimum wage *does* lead to structural unemployment.

Labor Unions The actions of *labor unions* can have effects similar to those of minimum wages, leading to structural unemployment. By bargaining for all a firm's workers collectively, unions can often win higher wages from employers than the market would have otherwise provided when workers bargained individually. This process, known as *collective bargaining,* is intended to tip the scales of bargaining power more to workers and away from employers. Labor unions exercise bargaining power by threatening firms with a *labor strike,* a collective refusal to work. The threat of a strike can be very serious for firms that would have difficulty replacing striking workers. In such cases, workers acting collectively can exercise more power than they could if they acted independently.

When workers have greater bargaining power, they tend to demand and receive higher wages. Unions also bargain over benefits, such as health care and retirement benefits, which we can think of as additional wages. Indeed, economists who study the effects of unions on wages find that unionized workers earn higher wages and benefits than non-union workers with similar skills. The result of these increased wages is the same as the result of a minimum wage: labor unions push the wage that workers receive above the equilibrium wage. Consequently, there are more people willing to work at the wage being paid than there are jobs available. Like a binding minimum wage, this leads to structural unemployment.

Another way in which labor unions lead to unemployment involves the ways in which the labor contracts that result from collective bargaining are structured. Union members tend to have long-term contracts of two or three years duration. Independent of the increased wages associated with unions, these long-term contracts could also lead to structural unemployment. If the demand for labor is falling but employers and

Unions are one reason why wages are sometimes higher than the level that matches the supply and demand for labor.

employees have previously agreed to a higher wage rate, this has the same effect as a floor on wages—leading to more workers being willing to work for the negotiated wage rate than there are jobs available at that wage rate.

If non-unionized firms also commit to a given advertised wage for a period of time, the same effects could occur even without labor unions. The fact that some firms are on a different timetable for negotiating their labor contracts than other firms—a phenomenon known as *wage staggering*—leads the labor market to move slowly from one equilibrium to another when the demand for labor changes. In the meantime, while the labor market is out of equilibrium, structural unemployment can occur. We will turn to this topic again later in this chapter when we explore in more detail why the labor market moves slowly from one equilibrium to another.

Efficiency Wages Actions by firms may also contribute to structural unemployment in the absence of labor unions and wage staggering. Firms may choose to pay *efficiency wages*—wages that employers set above the equilibrium wage rate as an incentive for better performance.

> **Efficiency wages** are wages that employers set above the equilibrium wage rate as an incentive for better performance.

Employers may do this for several reasons. One is that workers know more about their other work opportunities than do their employers. An employer that pays as little as possible risks losing its better workers and retaining more of its lower-quality workers—the ones who wouldn't be able to find better work elsewhere. This is less likely to happen if the firm pays a wage above the equilibrium wage rate. In such a situation, high-quality workers will be less likely to move to a different employer.

Employers may also pay above-market wages in order to ensure a higher degree of worker effort when they can't directly observe how hard an employee works. Employees receiving these higher wages are more likely to maintain a higher level of effort to ensure that they do not suffer a wage reduction by being fired.

If many firms pay wages that are above the market equilibrium wage rate, this will result in a pool of workers who want higher-paying jobs but can't find them. So the use of efficiency wages by firms leads to structural unemployment.

Side Effects of Public Policy In addition, public policy designed to help workers who lose their jobs can lead to structural unemployment as an unintended side effect. Most economically advanced countries provide benefits to laid-off workers as a way to tide them over until they find a new job. In the United States, these benefits typically replace only a small fraction of a worker's income and expire after 26 weeks. In other countries, particularly in Europe, benefits are more generous and last longer. The drawback to this generosity is that it reduces a worker's incentive to seek a new job. Generous unemployment benefits are widely believed to be one of the main causes of "Eurosclerosis," described in Economics in Action on page 376.

The Natural Rate of Unemployment

We can now return to the question of why national goals for unemployment are so modest. Why settle for an unemployment rate of 4% or more?

Because some frictional unemployment is inevitable and many economies also suffer from structural unemployment, a certain amount of unemployment is normal, or "natural," although actual unemployment fluctuates around this normal level. The **natural rate of unemployment** is the normal unemployment rate around which the actual unemployment rate fluctuates. It is the rate of unemployment that arises from the effects of frictional plus structural unemployment. Deviations in the actual rate of unemployment from the natural rate are called **cyclical unemployment.** As the name suggests, cyclical unemployment is unemployment that arises from the business cycle. We'll see later in this chapter that public policy cannot keep the unemployment rate persistently below the natural rate without leading to accelerating inflation. We can summarize the relationships between the various types of unemployment as follows:

> The **natural rate of unemployment** is the normal unemployment rate around which the actual unemployment rate fluctuates.
>
> **Cyclical unemployment** is the deviation in the actual rate of unemployment from the natural rate.

(15-1) Natural unemployment = Frictional unemployment +
Structural unemployment

(15-2)   Actual unemployment = Natural unemployment +
                                      Cyclical unemployment

Perhaps because of its name, people often imagine that the natural rate of unemployment is a constant that doesn't change over time and can't be affected by policy. Neither proposition is true. Let's take a moment to stress two facts: the natural rate of unemployment changes over time, and it can be affected by economic policies.

Changes in the Natural Rate of Unemployment

Both private-sector economists and government agencies need estimates of the natural rate of unemployment for forecasts and policy analyses. Almost all these estimates show the U.S. natural rate rising and falling over time. For example, the Congressional Budget Office believes that the natural rate was 5.3% in 1950, rose to 6.3% by the end of the 1970s, then fell to 5.2% by the end of the 1990s. The United States is not alone in its changes in the natural rate of unemployment over time. In fact, Europe has experienced even larger swings in the natural rate of unemployment.

What causes the natural rate of unemployment to change? The most important factors are changes in the characteristics of the labor force, changes in labor market institutions, changes in government policies, and changes in productivity. Let's look briefly at each factor.

Changes in Labor Force Characteristics   In 2000, as we've seen, the overall rate of unemployment in the United States was 4%. Young workers, however, had much higher unemployment rates: 13% for teenagers and 7% for workers aged 20 to 24. Workers over 25 had an unemployment rate of only 3%.

In general, unemployment rates tend to be lower for experienced workers than for inexperienced workers. Because experienced workers tend to stay in a given job longer than do inexperienced workers, they have lower frictional unemployment. Also, because older workers are more likely than young workers to be family breadwinners, they have a stronger incentive to find and keep jobs.

One reason the natural rate of unemployment rose during the 1970s was a large rise in the number of new workers—children of the post World War II baby boom entered the labor force, as did a rising percentage of married women. As Figure 15-3 shows, both the percentage of the labor force less than 25 years old and the percentage of women in the labor force surged in the 1970s. By the end of the 1990s, however, the share of women in the labor force had leveled off, and the percentage of

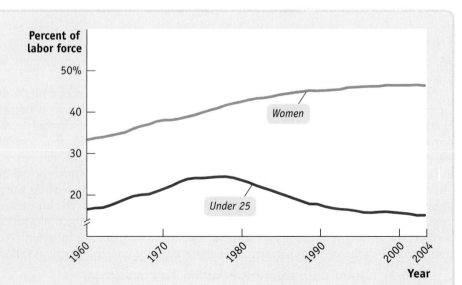

Figure 15-3

The Changing Makeup of the U.S. Labor Force

In the 1970s the percentage of the labor force consisting of women rose rapidly, as did the percentage under age 25. These changes reflected the entry of large numbers of women into the paid labor force for the first time and the fact that baby boomers were reaching working age. The natural rate of unemployment may have risen because many of these workers were relatively inexperienced. Today, the labor force is much more experienced, which is one possible reason the natural rate has fallen since the 1970s.

Source: Bureau of Labor Statistics.

workers under 25 had fallen sharply. This means that the labor force as a whole is more experienced today than it had been in the 1970s, one likely reason that the natural rate of unemployment is lower today than in the 1970s.

Changes in Labor Market Institutions

As we pointed out earlier, unions that negotiate wages above the equilibrium level can be a source of structural unemployment. Some economists believe that strong labor unions are one reason for the high natural rate of unemployment in Europe, discussed below. In the United States, the sharp fall in union membership after 1980 may have been one reason the natural rate of unemployment fell between the 1970s and the 1990s.

Other institutional changes may also be at work. For example, some labor economists believe that temporary employment agencies, which have proliferated in recent years, have reduced frictional unemployment by helping match workers to jobs.

Technological change, coupled with labor market institutions, can also play a role in affecting the natural rate of unemployment. Technological change probably leads to an increase in the demand for skilled workers who are familiar with the technology and a reduction in the demand for unskilled workers. Economic theory predicts that wages should increase for skilled workers and decrease for unskilled workers. But if wages for unskilled workers cannot go down, say due to a binding minimum wage, increased structural unemployment, and hence a higher natural rate of unemployment, will result.

Changes in Government Policies

A high minimum wage can cause structural unemployment. Generous unemployment benefits can increase both structural and frictional unemployment. So government policies intended to help workers can have the undesirable side effect of raising the natural rate of unemployment.

Some government policies, however, may reduce the natural rate. Two examples are job training and employment subsidies. Job-training programs are supposed to provide unemployed workers with skills that widen the range of jobs they can perform. Employment subsidies are payments either to workers or to employers that provide a financial incentive to offer or accept jobs.

Changes in Productivity

Another explanation for changes over time in the natural rate of unemployment involves changes in *labor force productivity*. Productivity changes are an attractive explanation for the changes in the natural rate of unemployment because it's an explanation consistent with the timing of actual events. The rise in the natural rate of unemployment in the 1970s came at the same time as a slowdown in productivity growth, and a fall in the natural rate of unemployment in the 1990s came at the same time as an acceleration in productivity growth.

That said, it is now easy to explain why higher productivity growth should reduce the natural rate of unemployment, as opposed to simply raising real wages. Suppose, for example, there is an acceleration in productivity growth. If workers do not immediately recognize that productivity is rising faster than before, they will be slow to demand wage increases that reflect their productivity gains. Until wages catch up with productivity gains, hiring an additional worker will be profitable for employers. For a while, then, increases in productivity growth can translate into lower unemployment rates.

Alternatively, suppose there is a slowdown in productivity growth. If workers do not immediately recognize that productivity is growing more slowly, they may continue to demand higher wage increases that were consistent with an earlier, higher rate of productivity growth. Until wage demands diminish, an employer will be better off not hiring, and sometimes firing, workers. As a result, a persistent surplus of labor may develop. For a while, then, a productivity slowdown can translate into higher unemployment rates.

In the end, a number of factors can be proposed to explain the patterns in the natural rate of unemployment experienced over the past 30 years. Although each of these explanations seems reasonable, none can be considered solely responsible for the changes over time in the natural rate of unemployment. Different elements have been at work at different times, and there are surely other determinants of the natural rate of unemployment that we have yet to fully understand.

economics in action

Eurosclerosis

Unemployment rates in Western Europe are normally higher than in the United States. Most estimates suggest that the natural rate of unemployment in France and Germany is currently above 8%, compared with somewhere between 5% and 5.5% in the U.S. today.

It wasn't always that way. In fact, in the early 1970s the natural rate of unemployment seemed to be lower in France and Germany than in the United States. As you can see from Figure 15-4, the actual unemployment rate was lower in France than in the United States, but the situation reversed in the 1980s. Why is the natural rate in Europe so high today?

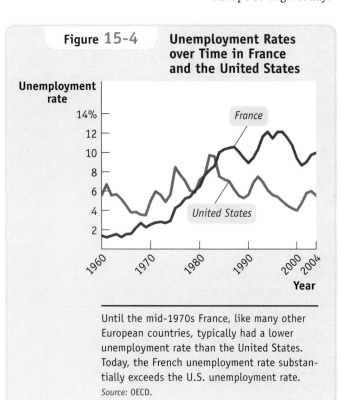

Figure 15-4 Unemployment Rates over Time in France and the United States

Until the mid-1970s France, like many other European countries, typically had a lower unemployment rate than the United States. Today, the French unemployment rate substantially exceeds the U.S. unemployment rate.
Source: OECD.

The answer of many (but not all) economists is that high European natural rates of unemployment are an unintended side-effect of government policies. This is often referred to as *Eurosclerosis.*

The Eurosclerosis hypothesis says that persistently high European unemployment is the result of policies intended to help workers. One such set of policies involves the generous benefits to unemployed workers. In many European countries, there is no limit to the amount of time that the unemployed can collect benefits, and the benefits that the unemployed collect at any given point in time tend to be considerably greater than in the United States. For example, benefits replace 48% of the earnings of a typical French worker, compared with only 14% for the typical U.S. worker.

The importance of the European "welfare state" in explaining unemployment differences between Europe and the United States has further increased as the demand for unskilled workers has fallen. If unskilled wages continue to fall, the benefit to these workers of taking a job—as compared to collecting benefits—also falls. Therefore, unskilled workers are increasingly likely to choose unemployment as a long-term option.

In addition, many European countries have high minimum-wage rates. For example, as of 1999 the minimum wage in France was 47% of the average wage rate, compared with only 34% in the United States. Union membership is greater in many European countries than in the United States as well, and unions seem to have strong bargaining power even in European countries such as France that have relatively low union membership. Both of these factors could also contribute to higher unemployment rates in Europe than in the United States.

If the Eurosclerosis explanation of high European unemployment is correct, a European country that moved its policies in an "American" direction—such as by reducing unemployment benefits and limiting the power of unions—should reduce its natural rate of unemployment. In fact, this seems to have happened in the United Kingdom, which had one of the highest unemployment rates in Europe in the early 1980s. Britain undertook a number of economic reforms under Prime Minister Margaret Thatcher and today typically has an unemployment rate of around 5%.

It should be noted, however, that an "Americanization" of European policies would come at a cost: reducing welfare benefits would probably reduce unemployment by encouraging individuals to take low-wage jobs. But at the same time it would make many workers worse off, increasing the inequities that were the motivation for the creation of the European social welfare systems. ■

> >

1. Explain the following:
   a. Why frictional unemployment is inevitable in a modern economy.
   b. Why frictional unemployment accounts for a larger share of total unemployment when the unemployment rate is low.

2. Why does collective bargaining have the same general effect on unemployment as a minimum wage? Illustrate with a diagram.

3. Suppose the United States dramatically increases benefits for unemployed workers. Explain what will happen to the natural rate of unemployment.

Solutions appear at back of book.

Unemployment and the Business Cycle

Although the natural rate of unemployment can change over time, it changes only gradually. The actual rate of unemployment, however, fluctuates around the natural rate, reflecting changes in cyclical unemployment. Panel (a) of Figure 15-5 on page 378 illustrates these fluctuations, showing both the actual unemployment rate and Congressional Budget Office (CBO) estimates of the natural rate of unemployment in the United States from 1959 to 2004. (We'll explain later in the chapter how the CBO arrives at these estimates.)

Fluctuations of the actual unemployment rate around the natural rate reflect fluctuations in aggregate output over the course of the business cycle: the unemployment rate normally rises during recessions and falls during expansions. To understand why, and to understand the exceptions to this rule, we need to look at the links between changes in aggregate output and the unemployment rate.

The Output Gap and the Unemployment Rate

In Chapter 10 we introduced the concept of *potential output,* the level of real GDP that the economy would produce once all prices had adjusted. Potential output typically grows steadily over time, reflecting long-run growth. However, as we learned in the aggregate supply–aggregate demand model, actual aggregate output fluctuates around potential output in the short run: a recessionary gap arises when actual aggregate output falls short of potential output; an inflationary gap arises when actual aggregate output exceeds potential output. In either case, the percentage difference between the actual level of real GDP and potential output is called the **output gap.** A positive or negative output gap occurs when an economy is producing more than or less than what would be "expected" because all prices have not yet adjusted. And wages, as we've learned, are the prices in the labor market.

This realization implies a straightforward relationship between the unemployment rate and the output gap. This relationship consists of two rules:

■ When actual aggregate output is equal to potential output, the actual unemployment rate is equal to the natural rate of unemployment.

■ When the output gap is positive (an inflationary gap), the unemployment rate is *below* the natural rate. When the output gap is negative (a recessionary gap), the unemployment rate is *above* the natural rate.

In other words, fluctuations of aggregate output around the long-run trend of potential output correspond to fluctuations of the unemployment rate around the natural rate.

The percentage difference between the actual level of real GDP and potential output is the **output gap.**

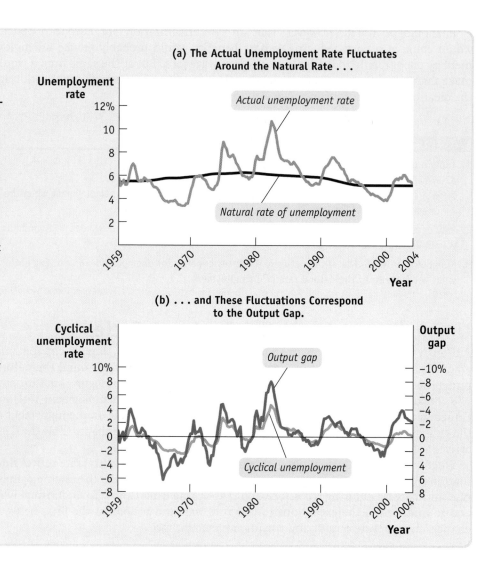

Figure 15-5

Cyclical Unemployment and the Output Gap

Panel (a) shows the actual U.S. unemployment rate from 1959 to 2004, together with the Congressional Budget Office estimate of the natural rate of unemployment. The actual rate fluctuates around the natural rate, often for extended periods. Panel (b) shows cyclical unemployment—the difference between the actual unemployment rate and the natural rate—and the output gap, also estimated by the CBO. The output gap is shown with an inverted scale, so that it moves in the same direction as the unemployment rate: when the output gap is positive, the actual unemployment rate is below the natural rate; when the output gap is negative, the actual unemployment rate is above the natural rate. **>web...**

Source: Congressional Budget Office; Bureau of Labor Statistics.

(a) The Actual Unemployment Rate Fluctuates Around the Natural Rate . . .

Actual unemployment rate

Natural rate of unemployment

(b) . . . and These Fluctuations Correspond to the Output Gap.

Output gap

Cyclical unemployment

This makes sense. When the economy is producing less than potential output—when the output gap is negative—it is not making full use of its productive resources. Among the resources that are not fully utilized is labor, the economy's most important resource. So we would expect a negative output gap to be associated with unusually high unemployment. Conversely, when the economy is producing more than potential output, it is temporarily using resources at more than normal rates. With this positive output gap, we would expect to see lower-than-normal unemployment.

Figure 15-5 confirms this rule. Panel (a) shows the actual and natural rates of unemployment. Panel (b) shows two series. One is cyclical unemployment: the difference between the actual unemployment rate and the CBO estimate of the natural rate of unemployment, measured on the left. The other is the CBO estimate of the output gap, measured on the right. To make the relationship clearer, the output gap series is "inverted"—shown upside down—so that the line goes down if actual output rises above potential output and up if actual output falls below potential output. As you can see, the two series move together: years of high cyclical unemployment, like 1982 or 1992, were also years of a strongly negative output gap. Years of low cyclical unemployment, like the late 1960s or 2000, were also years of a strongly positive output gap.

You may notice something else, however: although cyclical unemployment and the output gap move together, cyclical unemployment seems to move *less* than the output gap. For example, the output gap reached −8% in 1982, but the cyclical unemployment rate reached only 4%. This observation is the basis of an important relationship known as *Okun's law.*

Okun's Law

In the early 1960s Arthur Okun, who was John F. Kennedy's chief economic adviser, pointed out an important fact about the relationship between aggregate output and the unemployment rate. Although the ups and downs of the unemployment rate correspond closely to fluctuations in real GDP around its long-run trend, fluctuations in the unemployment rate are normally much smaller than the corresponding changes in the output gap. Okun originally estimated that a rise in real GDP of 1 percentage point above potential output would lead to a fall in the unemployment rate of only ⅓ of a percentage point. Today, estimates of **Okun's law**—the negative relationship between the output gap and the unemployment rate—typically find that a rise in the output gap of 1 percentage point reduces the unemployment rate by about ½ of a percentage point. That is, a modern version of Okun's law reads

> According to **Okun's law**, each additional percentage point of output gap reduces the unemployment rate by less than 1 percentage point.

(15-3) Unemployment rate = Natural rate of unemployment − (0.5 × Output gap)

For example, suppose that the natural rate of unemployment is 5.2% and that the economy is currently producing only 98% of potential output. In that case, the output gap is −2%, and Okun's law predicts an unemployment rate of 5.2% − (0.5 × (−2%)) = 6.2%.

You should be aware that the "0.5" coefficient in Okun's law is an *estimate*, rather than a physical property, and this relationship can change over time. Indeed, there have been numerous estimates of this coefficient, which vary according to the time period considered and the context in which it is estimated.

Importantly, however, the estimates of the Okun's law coefficient all tend to be considerably less than 1. You might have expected this coefficient to be 1—that is, you might have expected to see a one-to-one relationship between the output gap and unemployment. Doesn't a 1% rise in aggregate output require a 1% increase in employment? And shouldn't that take 1% off the unemployment rate? No.

There are two well-understood reasons for the relationship between changes in the output gap and changes in the unemployment rate to be less than one-to-one. The first is that companies often meet changes in demand in part by changing the number of hours their existing employees work. For example, a company that experiences a sudden increase in demand for its products may cope by asking (or requiring) its workers to put in longer hours, rather than by hiring more workers. Conversely, a company that sees sales drop will often reduce workers' hours rather than lay off employees. This behavior dampens the effect of output fluctuations on the number of workers employed.

The second reason is that the number of workers looking for jobs is affected by the availability of jobs. Suppose that the number of jobs falls by 1 million. Often, measured unemployment will rise by less than 1 million because some unemployed workers become discouraged and give up actively looking for work. (Recall from Chapter 7 that workers aren't counted as unemployed unless they are actively seeking work.) Conversely, if the economy adds 1 million jobs, some people who haven't been actively looking for work will begin doing so; as a result, measured unemployment will fall by less than 1 million. This behavior dampens the effect of output fluctuations on the measured unemployment rate.

In addition to these well-understood factors, the rate of growth of labor productivity generally accelerates during booms (when actual aggregate output is growing faster than potential output) and slows down or even turns negative during busts (when actual aggregate output is growing more slowly than potential output). The reasons for this phenomenon are the subject of some dispute among economists. The consequence, however, is that the effects of booms and busts on the unemployment rate are dampened.

PITFALLS

WHEN IS A "LAW" NOT A LAW?
Economists occasionally refer to a generally observed and accepted pattern of behavior as a "law." The term *law* brings to mind unalterable physical properties or formulaic explanations of the ways in which the world operates. In some cases in economics, such as the law of demand, the economic theory has been so consistent with experience that it approaches the certainty that you may associate with chemical or physical laws.

Economics, however, is a study of human beings, and human behavior is difficult to predict. We may know that the quantity demanded of a given product falls when its price rises, but the law of demand does not tell us *by how much* the quantity demanded will fall.

The same holds true for Okun's law. Okun's law is based on *estimates* that can and do change over time and in different settings. The constant feature of these estimates is not precisely how much the unemployment rate falls when the output gap increases, but that the unemployment rate falls at a ratio of less than 1:1 with increases in the output gap. Okun's law says not that this relationship is, for example, 1:3 or 1:2, but that this relationship is less than 1:1.

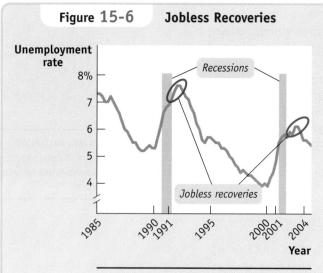

Figure 15-6 **Jobless Recoveries**

The graph shows the unemployment rate in the United States from 1985 to 2004. The shaded areas show official periods of recession. In the recessions of 1990–1991 and 2001, unemployment rose sharply. In both cases, however, unemployment continued to rise for a time after, even though the economy was officially expanding.

Sources: Bureau of Labor Statistics; National Bureau of Economic Research.

economics in action

Jobless Recoveries

Our explanation of the relationship between the output gap and the unemployment rate is slightly more complex than a statement that the unemployment rate falls when the economy is expanding and rises when the economy is contracting. A good way to see the subtlety is to look at those occasions when the economy expands but unemployment nonetheless rises.

Figure 15-6 shows the U.S. unemployment rate from 1985 to 2004. It also shows, as shaded areas, the periods of recession according to the National Bureau of Economic Research. Officially, the U.S. economy went into recession in July 1990 and began an expansion in March 1991. But tell that to workers: the unemployment rate continued rising and didn't turn downward until July 1992. The same thing happened after the next recession, 11 years later. The recession that began in March 2001 officially ended in November 2001, but the unemployment rate didn't turn downward until July 2003. Both recessions, in other words, were followed by periods of jobless recovery.

Why do jobless recoveries happen? The unemployment rate reflects the output gap: the unemployment rate falls only when the output gap is rising, which happens when real GDP is growing faster than potential output. If real GDP is growing more slowly than potential output—as it did in both 1991–1992 and 2001–2003—the output gap continues to fall even though the economy is officially considered to be expanding. And this falling output gap leads to rising, not falling, unemployment. ∎

< < < < < < < < < < < < < < < < < < <

>>CHECK YOUR UNDERSTANDING 15-2

1. Examine panel (a) of Figure 15-5. In which years would you expect a large positive output gap? How does your expectation compare with the reality of panel (b)?

2. Suppose the United States imposes strict limits on the number of hours that employees can work in a week. How would this policy affect the relationship between the output gap and the unemployment rate?

Solutions appear at back of book.

Why Doesn't the Labor Market Move Quickly to Equilibrium?

We've now seen that the unemployment rate fluctuates around the natural rate of unemployment. A look back at Figure 15-5 shows that these fluctuations can last for long periods. For example, the actual unemployment rate was above the natural rate from 1980 to 1987.

One way to think about the natural rate of unemployment is that it is an *equilibrium* rate, the rate of unemployment that the labor market achieves when employers and workers have had time to adjust. Deviations from the natural rate, then, are situations in which the labor market is out of equilibrium. Figure 15-5 shows that the labor market often remains out of equilibrium for long stretches of time.

Yet in most economic analyses we assume that markets move quickly to equilibrium. Why is the labor market different?

One compelling answer is that wages behave differently from the prices of many goods and services. Wages do not fall quickly in the face of labor surpluses or rise quickly in the face of shortages. Almost all macroeconomists agree that wages adjust slowly to surpluses or shortages of labor.

There is, however, some dispute about why wages adjust slowly. Broadly speaking, there are two main theories: *misperceptions* and *sticky wages*.

Misperceptions Some macroeconomists believe that an important source of slow wage adjustment is that workers are slow to realize that the equilibrium wage rate has changed. For example, a worker searching for a new job may have expectations based on last year's wage rate. If wage rates have dropped, that worker may spend a long time looking for a job with an unrealistically high wage rate. When workers take longer to find jobs because they are holding out for a wage that may no longer be appropriate, this contributes not only to slow wage adjustment but also to an increased unemployment rate.

Misperceptions by firms can also contribute to slow wage adjustment. Firms, especially those that hire infrequently, may base their wage decisions on old information; this, in turn, causes wages to change slowly. If a firm sets its wages below the market-clearing wage rate, it will have difficulty hiring workers but may be slow to realize this fact and respond to it. If a firm sets its wages above the market-clearing wage rate, it will turn away excess job applicants—and perhaps also contribute to worker misperceptions about the market-clearing wage rate.

You might wonder why firms and workers would not quickly realize when their perceptions about wages are out of line with the reality of market-clearing wages. One reason labor markets may clear more slowly than other markets is that they are so complex. Market-clearing wages are constantly changing as demand conditions change, and firms and workers are collectively responding to ever-changing perceptions about these wages. As a result, when conditions change in the labor market, it may take quite some time before the labor market returns to equilibrium.

Sticky Wages Economists say that **sticky wages** occur when employers are slow to change wages in the face of a surplus or shortage of labor, even when everyone understands that the wage rate isn't at its equilibrium level. Wages may be sticky for several reasons. Some wages are governed by long-term contracts, which set the wage rate a year or more in advance and don't reflect changes in the labor market after the contract has been signed. In other cases there is no formal contract, but there is an implicit agreement between workers and their employers not to change wage rates too often.

Workers and employers are often concerned about *relative wages*—how the wages of one group of workers compare with those of other workers. Companies believe that the productivity or morale of workers will suffer—or even that they will go on strike—if wages are cut compared with those paid by other companies. As a result, each company is reluctant to reduce wages until other companies do the same, making wages as a whole slow to adjust.

Concerns about relative wages can interact with explicit or implicit contracts to slow down wage adjustment. Even if a worker's contract has just expired, the employer will be cautious about reducing his or her wage rate compared with that of other workers who are still covered by contracts signed in the past. Economists have shown that if employers are concerned about relative wages and contracts are staggered over time, even short contracts—such as contracts that set wages one year ahead—can cause the adjustment of the average wage rate to its equilibrium level to take a number of years.

Wages tend to be stickier when equilibrium wages are falling than when they are rising. When wages are rising, workers may put pressure on firms to renegotiate

> **Sticky wages** occur when employers are slow to change wage rates in the face of a surplus or shortage of labor.

wages to reflect the new wage reality. This pressure could occur either through negotiation or through worker departure, as competing firms bid up wages. But when wages are falling, firms may be contractually unable to lower wages in response to prevailing market conditions—and even if they are able to lower wages, it may not be in their best interest to do so. Recall the discussion of efficiency wages earlier in this chapter: firms may pay above-market wages to give workers an incentive for better performance.

Although this discussion has focused only on the slow adjustment of wages, prices of some goods and services also seem to adjust slowly. Because it is time-consuming and costly to constantly devise new sets of prices, firms may change prices infrequently even if the market-clearing prices change frequently. An influential economic theory says that these small costs associated with the act of changing prices—known as **menu costs**—can have a surprisingly large effect in postponing price adjustment to surpluses and shortages. (This term derives from the fact that it costs time and money for restaurants to print new menus and that, as a result, restaurants rarely change their prices.) Sticky prices can interact with sticky wages to slow the adjustment of prices and wages in the economy as a whole.

For our purposes, the distinctions between different theories of slow wage and price adjustment don't matter very much. The important point is that wages move toward their equilibrium level, but only slowly.

> **Menu costs** are small costs associated with the act of changing prices.

economics in action

Sticky Wages During the Great Depression

History's most extreme example of disequilibrium in the labor market is the Great Depression, the era of high unemployment between 1929 and World War II. At its peak in 1933, the U.S. unemployment rate exceeded 25%. The Depression also provides the clearest illustration of the sluggish adjustment of wages, which plays a crucial role in our understanding of aggregate supply.

Recent analyses suggest that during the 1930s manufacturing wages in particular were sticky. Nominal hourly wages in manufacturing—wages in dollar amounts—remained almost unchanged during the first two years of the Great Depression. Since prices of almost all goods and services fell during the early years of the Depression, the *real* wages of manufacturing workers—their nominal wages divided by the price level—actually *rose* even though there was a massive surplus of labor. ∎

‹ ‹ ‹ ‹ ‹ ‹ ‹ ‹ ‹ ‹ ‹ ‹ ‹ ‹ ‹ ‹ ‹ ‹ ‹

> **›› QUICK REVIEW**
>
> ➤ Prolonged deviations from the natural rate of unemployment show that the labor market, unlike the markets for many goods and services, does not move quickly to equilibrium.
>
> ➤ The majority of economists agree that wages adjust slowly to surpluses or shortages of labor, due to either misperceptions or *sticky wages*.
>
> ➤ Several factors, including concern for relative wages, *menu costs,* and staggered contracts, may explain why wages and other prices are sticky.

››CHECK YOUR UNDERSTANDING 15-3

1. The country of Willovia has a tradition of three-year labor contracts, but Malavia has a tradition of one-year labor contracts. In which country would you expect the labor market to move more quickly to equilibrium when demand conditions change? Explain your answer.

2. Why might workers misperceive changes in the market-clearing wage rate? Suppose the market-clearing wage rate is rising but workers are slow to recognize this growth. What does this misperception imply about unemployment in the short run?

Solutions appear at back of book.

Unemployment and Inflation: The Phillips Curve

Earlier in this chapter we saw that in 1978, when the Humphrey–Hawkins bill set a target unemployment rate of 4%, many economists were concerned: they feared an attempt to achieve that target would lead to high and accelerating inflation. What was the basis for these concerns?

We've seen part of the answer: 4% was well below estimates of the natural rate of unemployment. But what's wrong with trying to keep unemployment below the natural rate? To answer that question we need to look at the relationship between unemployment and inflation.

The Short-Run Phillips Curve

In a famous 1958 paper the New Zealand–born economist A. W. H. Phillips found that historical data for the United Kingdom showed that when the unemployment rate is high, the wage rate tends to fall, and when the unemployment rate is low, the wage rate tends to rise. Using data from Britain, the United States, and elsewhere, other economists soon found similar patterns between the unemployment rate and the rate of inflation—that is, the rate of change in the aggregate price level. The negative short-run relationship between the unemployment rate and the inflation rate is called the **short-run Phillips curve,** or *SRPC*. (We'll explain the difference between the short run and the long run in a little while.) Figure 15-7 shows a hypothetical short-run Phillips curve.

Why is there a negative short-run relationship between the unemployment rate and the inflation rate? Recall the short-run aggregate supply curve from earlier chapters. The *SRAS* curve shows that when a rightward shift of the aggregate demand curve leads to an increase in the aggregate price level, real GDP increases as well. In other words, there is a positive relationship between the aggregate price level and real GDP.

But how does this relate to unemployment? Remember that there is a negative relationship between real GDP and the unemployment rate: Okun's law tells us that when real GDP is higher than potential output, the unemployment rate will be lower than when real GDP is below potential output. So increases in the aggregate price level are associated with increases in real GDP, which in turn tend to lead to lower unemployment rates.

The relationship between the short-run Phillips curve and the short-run aggregate supply curve is a bit trickier than presented here. Specifically, the preceding discussion of the short-run aggregate supply curve describes a relationship between *changes* in the unemployment rate and inflation; the short-run Phillips curve, however, describes a relationship between the *level* of the unemployment rate and inflation. For Inquiring Minds on page 384 explains the relationship between the two concepts in more detail.

> The **short-run Phillips curve** is the negative short-run relationship between the unemployment rate and the inflation rate.

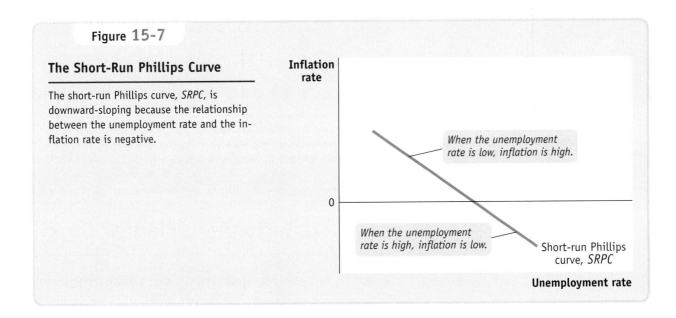

Figure 15-7

The Short-Run Phillips Curve

The short-run Phillips curve, *SRPC*, is downward-sloping because the relationship between the unemployment rate and the inflation rate is negative.

When the unemployment rate is low, inflation is high.

When the unemployment rate is high, inflation is low.

Short-run Phillips curve, *SRPC*

Inflation rate

Unemployment rate

0

THE AGGREGATE SUPPLY CURVE AND THE SHORT-RUN PHILLIPS CURVE

In earlier chapters we made extensive use of the *AS–AD* model, in which the short-run aggregate supply curve—a relationship between real GDP and the aggregate price level—plays a central role. Now we've introduced the concept of the short-run Phillips curve, a relationship between the unemployment rate and the rate of inflation. How do these two concepts fit together?

We can get a partial answer to this question by looking at panel (a) of Figure 15-8, which shows how changes in the aggregate price level and the output gap depend on changes in aggregate demand. Assume that in year 1 the aggregate demand curve is AD_1, the long-run aggregate supply curve is *LRAS,* and the short-run aggregate supply curve is *SRAS*. The initial macroeconomic equilibrium is at E_1, where the price level is 100 and real GDP is $10 trillion. Notice that at E_1 real GDP is equal to potential output, so the output gap is zero.

Now consider two possible paths for the economy over the next year. One is that aggregate demand remains unchanged and the economy stays at E_1. The other is that aggregate demand shifts out to AD_2 and the economy moves to E_2.

At E_2, real GDP is $10.4 trillion, $0.4 trillion more than potential output—a 4% output gap. Meanwhile, at E_2 the aggregate price level is 102—a 2% increase. So panel (a) tells us that in this example a zero output gap is associated with zero inflation and a 4% output gap is associated with 2% inflation.

Panel (b) shows what this implies for the relationship between unemployment and inflation. Assume that the natural rate of unemployment is 6%, and that a rise of 1 percentage point in the output gap causes a fall of ½ percentage point in the unemployment rate by Okun's law. In that case, the two cases shown in panel (a)—aggregate demand either staying put or rising—

correspond to the two points in panel (b). At E_1, the unemployment rate is 6% and the inflation rate is 0%. At E_2, the unemployment rate is 4%, because an output gap of 4% reduces the unemployment rate by 4% × 0.5 = 2%—and the inflation rate is 2%. So there is a negative relationship between unemployment and inflation.

So does the short-run aggregate supply curve say exactly the same thing as the short-run Phillips curve? Not quite. The short-run aggregate supply curve seems to imply a relationship between the *change* in the unemployment rate and the inflation rate, but the short-run Phillips curve shows a relationship between the *level* of the unemployment rate and the inflation rate. Reconciling these views completely would go beyond the scope of this book. The important point is that the short-run Phillips curve is a concept that is closely related, though not identical, to the short-run aggregate supply curve.

Figure 15-8   The *AS–AD* Model and the Short-Run Phillips Curve

(a) An Increase in Aggregate Demand . . .

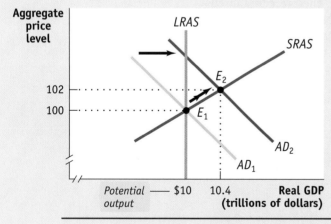

(b) . . . Leads to Both Inflation and a Fall in the Unemployment Rate.

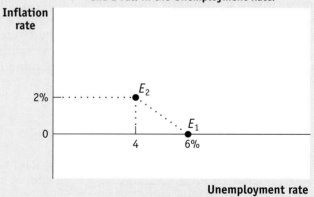

The short-run Phillips curve is closely related to the short-run aggregate supply curve. In panel (a), the economy is initially in equilibrium at E_1, with the aggregate price level at 100 and aggregate output at $10 trillion, which we assume is potential output. Now consider two possibilities. If the aggregate demand curve remains at AD_1, there is an output gap of zero and 0% inflation. If the aggregate demand curve shifts out to AD_2, there is an output gap of 4% and 2% inflation, as shown in panel (b). Assuming that the natural rate of unemployment is 6%, the implications for unemployment and inflation are as follows: if aggregate demand does not increase, 6% unemployment and 0% inflation will result; if aggregate demand does increase, 4% unemployment and 2% inflation will result.

The short-run Phillips curve relationship itself, however, is very intuitive. In general, a low rate of unemployment corresponds to an economy in which there are shortages of labor and other resources, leading to rising prices. But when unemployment is high,

the economy is far from capacity. When there are surpluses of labor and other resources, prices will fall.

Early estimates of the short-run Phillips curve for the United States were very simple: they showed a relationship between the unemployment rate and the inflation
rate, without taking account of any other variables. During the 1960s this simple
approach seemed, for a while, to be adequate. Figure 15-9 plots average annual rates
of unemployment and inflation from 1961 to 1969. The data look a lot like a simple
short-run Phillips curve.

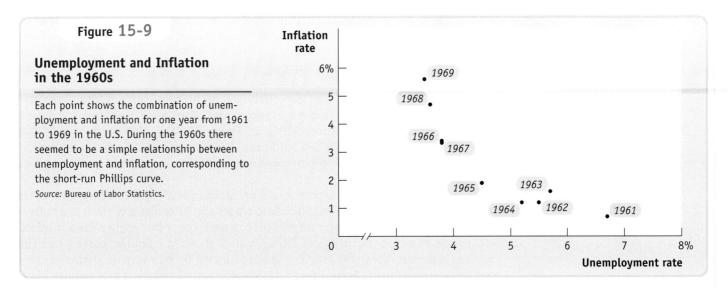

Figure 15-9

Unemployment and Inflation in the 1960s

Each point shows the combination of unemployment and inflation for one year from 1961
to 1969 in the U.S. During the 1960s there
seemed to be a simple relationship between
unemployment and inflation, corresponding to
the short-run Phillips curve.

Source: Bureau of Labor Statistics.

Even at the time, however, some economists argued that a more accurate short-
run Phillips curve would include other factors. In Chapter 10 we discussed the effect
of *supply shocks,* such as sudden changes in the price of oil, which shift the short-run
aggregate supply curve. Such shocks also shift the short-run Phillips curve: surging oil
prices were an important factor in the inflation of the 1970s and also played an important role in the acceleration of inflation in early 2004. In general, a negative supply shock shifts *SRPC* up, while a positive supply shock shifts it down.

But supply shocks are not the only factors that could change the inflation rate. In
the early 1960s, Americans had little experience with inflation: inflation rates had
been low for decades. But by the late 1960s, after inflation had been steadily increasing for a while, they had probably started to expect future inflation. In 1968 two
economists—Milton Friedman of the University of Chicago and Edmund Phelps of
Columbia University—independently set forth a crucial hypothesis that expectations
about future inflation directly affect the present inflation rate. Today most economists accept that the *expected inflation rate*—the rate of inflation that employers and
workers expect in the near future—is the most important factor affecting inflation
other than the unemployment rate.

Inflation Expectations and the Short-Run Phillips Curve

The **expected rate of inflation** is the rate of inflation that employers and workers
expect in the near future. One of the crucial discoveries of modern macroeconomics
is that the expected rate of inflation affects the short-run trade-off between unemployment and inflation.

Why does expected inflation affect the short-run Phillips curve? The answer lies in
part with the fact that wages are sticky, as discussed earlier in this chapter. Put yourself in the position of a worker or employer about to sign a contract setting the
worker's wages over the next year. For a number of reasons, the wage rate they agree
to will be higher if everyone expects high inflation (including rising wages) than if

The **expected rate of inflation** is the rate
of inflation that employers and workers
expect in the near future.

everyone expects prices to be stable. The worker will want a wage rate that takes into account future declines in the purchasing power of earnings. He or she will also want a wage rate that won't fall behind the wages of other workers. And the employer will be more willing to agree to a wage increase now if hiring workers later will be even more expensive. Also, rising prices will make paying a higher wage rate more afford-able for the employer because the employer's output will sell for more.

For these reasons, an increase in expected inflation shifts the short-run Phillips curve upward: the actual rate of inflation at any given unemployment rate is higher when the expected inflation rate is higher. In fact, macroeconomists believe that the relationship between expected inflation and actual inflation is one-to-one. That is, when the expected inflation rate increases, the actual inflation rate at any given un-employment rate will increase by the same amount. When the expected inflation rate falls, the actual inflation rate at any given level of unemployment will fall by the same amount.

Figure 15-10 shows how the expected rate of inflation affects the short-run Phillips curve. First, suppose that the expected rate of inflation is 0%: people expect 0% inflation in the near future. $SRPC_0$ in Figure 15-10 is the short-run Phillips curve when the public expects 0% inflation. According to $SRPC_0$, the actual infla-tion rate will be 0% if the unemployment rate is 6%; it will be 2% if the unemploy-ment rate is 4%.

Alternatively, suppose the expected rate of inflation is 2%. In that case, employers and workers will build this expectation into wages and prices: at any given unemploy-ment rate, the actual inflation rate will be 2 percentage points higher than it would be if people expected 0% inflation. $SRPC_2$, which shows the Phillips curve when the expected inflation rate is 2%, is $SRPC_0$ shifted upward by 2 percentage points at every level of unemployment. According to $SRPC_2$, the actual inflation rate will be 2% if the unemployment rate is 6%; it will be 4% if the unemployment rate is 4%.

What determines the expected rate of inflation? In general, people base their ex-pectations about inflation on experience. If the inflation rate has hovered around 0% in the last few years, people will expect it to be around 0% in the near future. But if the inflation rate has averaged around 5% lately, people will expect inflation to be around 5% in the near future.

Since expected inflation is an important part of the modern short-run Phillips curve discussion, you might wonder why it was not in the original formulation of the Phillips curve. But think back to what we said about the early 1960s: at that point,

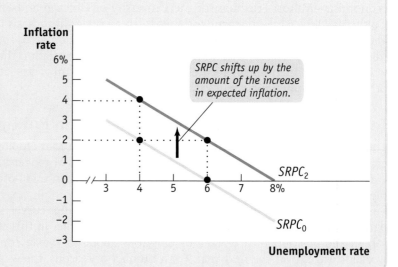

Figure 15-10

Expected Inflation and the Short-Run Phillips Curve

Expected inflation shifts the short-run Phillips curve up. $SRPC_0$ is the short-run Phillips curve with an expected inflation rate of 0%; $SRPC_2$ is the short-run Phillips curve with an expected inflation rate of 2%. Each additional percentage point of ex-pected inflation raises the actual inflation rate at any given unemployment rate by 1 percentage point.   **>web...**

people were accustomed to low inflation rates and reasonably expected that future inflation rates would also be modest. It was only after 1965 that persistent inflation became a fact of life as a consequence of the government's attempts to pay for the Vietnam War. So it was only at that point that it became clear that expected inflation would play an important role in price-setting.

The Long-Run Phillips Curve

We can now explain why economists were skeptical of the 4% target for unemployment contained in the Humphrey–Hawkins bill, and believed that an attempt to achieve that target would lead to high and accelerating inflation.

Figure 15-11 reproduces the two short-run Phillips curves from Figure 15-10, $SRPC_0$ and $SRPC_2$. It also adds an additional short-run Phillips curve, $SRPC_4$, representing a 4% expected rate of inflation. We'll explain why these are short-run curves in a moment, and we'll also explain the significance of the vertical long-run Phillips curve, $LRPC$.

Suppose that the economy has, in the past, had a 0% inflation rate. In that case the current short-run Phillips curve will reflect a 0% expected inflation rate, so it will be $SRPC_0$. If the unemployment rate is 6%, the actual inflation rate will be 0%.

Also suppose that policy makers decide to take Humphrey–Hawkins seriously and try to trade off lower unemployment for a higher rate of inflation. They use monetary policy, fiscal policy, or both to drive the unemployment rate down to 4%. This puts the economy at point A on $SRPC_0$, leading to an actual inflation rate of 2%.

Over time, the public will come to expect a 2% inflation rate. *This will shift the short-run Phillips curve upward to $SRPC_2$.* Now, when the unemployment rate is 6%, the actual inflation rate will be 2%. Given this new short-run Phillips curve, keeping the unemployment rate at 4% will lead to a 4% actual inflation rate—point B on $SRPC_2$—rather than 2%.

Eventually, this 4% inflation rate gets built into expectations, and the short-run Phillips curve shifts upward again, to $SRPC_4$. To keep the unemployment rate at 4% would now require accepting a 6% actual inflation rate (point C on $SRPC_4$), and so on. In short, a persistent attempt to trade off lower unemployment for higher inflation leads to *accelerating* inflation over time.

Figure 15-11

The NAIRU and the Long-Run Phillips Curve

$SRPC_0$ is the short-run Phillips curve when the expected inflation rate is 0%. At a 4% unemployment rate, the economy is at point A with an inflation rate of 2%. The higher inflation rate will get built into expectations, and the $SRPC$ will shift upward to $SRPC_2$. If the unemployment rate remains at 4%, the economy will be at B and the inflation rate will rise to 4%. Inflationary expectations will be revised again, and $SRPC$ will shift upward to $SRPC_4$. At a 4% unemployment rate, the economy will be at C, and the inflation rate will rise to 6%.

Here, 6% is the NAIRU, or nonaccelerating inflation rate of unemployment. As long as unemployment is at the NAIRU, the inflation rate will match expectations and remain constant. An unemployment rate below 6% requires ever-accelerating inflation. The long-run Phillips curve, $LRPC$, which passes through E_0, E_2, and E_4, is vertical: no long-run trade-off between unemployment and inflation exists.

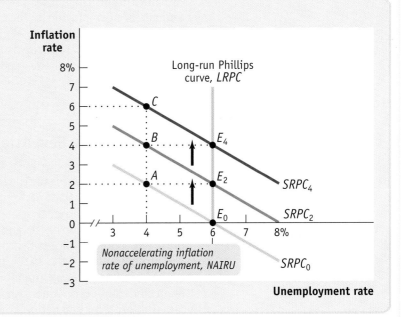

To avoid accelerating inflation over time, the unemployment rate must be high enough so that the actual rate of inflation matches the expected rate of inflation. This is the situation at E_0 on $SRPC_0$: when the expected inflation rate is 0% and the unemployment rate is 6%, the actual inflation rate is 0%. It is also the situation at E_2 on $SRPC_2$: when the expected inflation rate is 2% and the unemployment rate is 6%, the actual inflation rate is 2%. And it is the situation at E_4 on $SRPC_4$: when the expected inflation rate is 4% and the unemployment rate is 6%, the actual inflation rate is 4%.

The unemployment rate at which inflation does not change over time—6% in Figure 15-11—is known as the **nonaccelerating inflation rate of unemployment, or NAIRU** for short. Unemployment rates below the NAIRU lead to ever-accelerating inflation and cannot be maintained. Most macroeconomists believe that there is a NAIRU and that there is no long-run trade-off between unemployment and inflation.

We can now explain the significance of the vertical line *LRPC*. It is the **long-run Phillips curve,** the relationship between unemployment and inflation in the long run, after expectations of inflation have had time to adjust to experience. It is vertical because any unemployment rate below the NAIRU leads to ever-accelerating inflation (and, a point we have not yet emphasized, any unemployment rate above the NAIRU leads to decelerating inflation). In other words, it shows that an unemployment rate below the NAIRU cannot be maintained in the long run.

> The **nonaccelerating inflation rate of unemployment,** or **NAIRU,** is the unemployment rate at which inflation does not change over time.
>
> The **long-run Phillips curve** shows the relationship between unemployment and inflation after expectations of inflation have had time to adjust to experience.

The Natural Rate, Revisited

Earlier in this chapter, we introduced the concept of the *natural rate of unemployment,* the normal rate of unemployment around which the actual unemployment rate fluctuates. Now we have introduced the concept of the *NAIRU.* How do these two concepts relate to each other?

The answer is that the NAIRU is another name for the natural rate. The level of unemployment the economy "needs" in order to avoid accelerating inflation is equal to the sum of frictional unemployment plus structural unemployment.

In fact, economists estimate the natural rate of unemployment by looking for evidence about the NAIRU. For example, the way European countries learned, to their dismay, that their natural rates of unemployment were 9% or more was through unpleasant experience: in the late 1980s, and again in the late 1990s, European inflation began to accelerate as the unemployment rates in major economies, which had been above 9%, began to fall, approaching 8%.

Earlier in this chapter we used Congressional Budget Office estimates of the U.S. natural rate of unemployment. The CBO has a model that predicts changes in the inflation rate based on the deviation of the actual unemployment rate from the natural rate. Given data on actual unemployment and inflation, this model can be used to deduce estimates of the natural rate—and that's where the CBO numbers come from.

economics in action

From the Scary Seventies to the Nifty Nineties

Earlier we saw that experience during the 1960s seemed to show the existence of a short-run Phillips curve for the U.S. economy, with a short-run trade-off between unemployment and inflation.

After 1969, however, that apparent relationship fell apart. Figure 15-12 plots the track of the unemployment and inflation rates from 1961 to 1990. The track looks more like a tangled piece of yarn than like a smooth curve.

Through much of the 1970s and early 1980s, the economy suffered from a combination of above-average unemployment rates coupled with inflation rates unprecedented in modern American history. This condition came to be known as "stagflation"—for stagnation combined with inflation. In the late 1990s, by contrast,

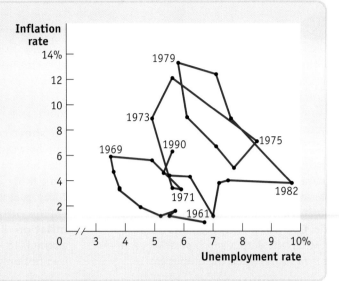

Figure 15-12

Unemployment and Inflation, 1961–1990

During the 1970s, the short-run Phillips curve relationship that seemed to work in the 1960s broke down as the economy experienced a combination of high unemployment and high inflation. Economists believe this was the result both of adverse supply shocks and a buildup of expected inflation. Inflation came down during the 1980s, and the 1990s were a time of both low unemployment and low inflation.

Source: Bureau of Labor Statistics.

the economy was experiencing a blissful combination of low unemployment and low inflation. What explains these developments?

Part of the answer lies in the role of supply shocks. During the 1970s the economy suffered a series of adverse supply shocks. The price of oil, in particular, soared as wars and revolutions in the Middle East led to a reduction in oil supplies and as oil-exporting countries deliberately curbed production to drive up prices. There was also a slowdown in labor productivity growth, which may have contributed to the poor economic performance.

During the 1990s, by contrast, supply shocks were positive. Prices of oil and other raw materials were generally falling, and productivity growth accelerated.

Equally important, however, was the role of expected inflation. As mentioned earlier in the chapter, inflation accelerated during the 1960s as the result of an economic boom. During the 1970s the public came to expect high inflation, and this got built into the short-run Phillips curve. It took a sustained and costly effort during the 1980s to get inflation back down. We'll describe that effort in Chapter 16. The result, however, was that expected inflation was very low by the late 1990s, allowing actual inflation to be low even with low rates of unemployment. ■

> —

>>**CHECK YOUR UNDERSTANDING 15-4**

1. Explain how the short-run Phillips curve can be thought of as the relationship between cyclical unemployment and the actual inflation rate above and beyond the expected inflation rate.

2. Why is there no long-run trade-off between unemployment and inflation?

Solutions appear at back of book.

• A LOOK AHEAD •

Few economists now believe that government policy can trade off higher inflation for lower unemployment except in the short run. Nonetheless, the United States and other economies have had periods of substantial inflation; in some times and places, the inflation rate has gone into the thousands of percent. In contrast, in some other countries *deflation*—falling prices—has become a concern.

In Chapter 16 we'll look at why inflation occurs and the harm that it can do if not managed well. We'll also look at why inflation can be hard to eliminate once the public comes to expect it. And we'll explore the flip-side of the coin—the perils of deflation.

SUMMARY

1. There is always a positive amount of unemployment in the economy: **job search** leads to **frictional unemployment.** There may also be **structural unemployment,** which is the result of factors that include minimum wages, unions, **efficiency wages,** and side effects of government policies.

2. Frictional plus structural unemployment make up the **natural rate of unemployment.** It's a rate that can and does shift over time. At any given time, the actual unemployment rate fluctuates around the natural rate because of the business cycle. **Cyclical unemployment** is linked to the **output gap:** when the output gap is positive, cyclical unemployment is negative; when the output gap is negative, cyclical unemployment is positive. Swings in cyclical unemployment are, however, smaller than swings in the output gap, a fact captured by **Okun's law.**

3. Unlike many markets, the labor market doesn't move quickly to equilibrium. This may, in part, reflect misperceptions on the part of workers and employers about the state of the market. **Sticky wages** also appear to play a

role, slowing the adjustment of wages even in the absence of misperceptions. Prices (including the wage rate) are also slow to adjust in some cases, in part reflecting the **menu costs** of changing prices.

4. The **short-run Phillips curve** shows a negative relationship between the unemployment rate and inflation rate. The short-run Phillips curve is related to, but not the same thing as, the short-run aggregate supply curve. Today, macroeconomists believe that the short-run Phillips curve shifts with changes in the **expected rate of inflation.** Because expectations change with experience, attempts to keep the unemployment rate persistently low lead not only to high inflation but also to constantly accelerating inflation. The **nonaccelerating inflation rate of unemployment,** or **NAIRU,** is the rate of unemployment at which inflation is stable. It is equal to the natural rate of unemployment. The **long-run Phillips curve** is vertical because there is no trade-off between the unemployment rate and the inflation rate in the long run.

KEY TERMS

Job search, p. 370
Frictional unemployment, p. 370
Structural unemployment, p. 371
Efficiency wages, p. 373
Natural rate of unemployment, p. 373

Cyclical unemployment, p. 373
Output gap, p. 377
Okun's law, p. 379
Sticky wages, p. 381
Menu costs, p. 382

Short-run Phillips curve, p. 383
Expected rate of inflation, p. 385
Nonaccelerating inflation rate of unemployment, or NAIRU, p. 388
Long-run Phillips curve, p. 388

PROBLEMS

1. In each of the following situations, what type of unemployment is Melanie facing?

   a. After completing a complex programming project, Melanie is laid off. Her prospects for a new job requiring similar skills are good, and she has signed up with a programmer placement service. She has passed up low-paying job offers.

   b. When Melanie and her co-workers refused to accept pay cuts, her employer outsourced their programming tasks to workers in another country. This phenomenon is occurring throughout the programming industry.

   c. Due to the current slump in investment spending, Melanie has been laid off from her programming job. Her employer promises to re-hire her when business picks up.

2. Each month, usually on the first Friday of the month, the Bureau of Labor Statistics releases the Employment Situation Summary for the previous month. Part of the information released concerns how long individuals have been unemployed. Go to www.bls.gov to find the latest report. On the Bureau of

Labor Statistics home page, click on the unemployment rate in the middle of the page, choose the Employment Situation Summary, and then click on the table titled "Unemployed persons by duration of unemployment." Use the seasonally adjusted numbers to answer the following questions.

   a. How many workers were unemployed less than 5 weeks? What percentage of all unemployed workers do these workers represent? How do these numbers compare to the previous month's data?

   b. How many workers were unemployed 27 or more weeks? What percentage of all unemployed workers do these workers represent? How do these numbers compare to the previous month's data?

   c. How long has the average worker been unemployed (average duration, in weeks)? How does this compare to the average for the previous month's data?

   d. Comparing the latest month for which there is data with the previous month, has the problem of long-term unemployment improved or deteriorated?

3. There is only one labor market in Profunctia. All workers have the same skills and all firms hire workers with these skills. Use the accompanying diagram, which shows the supply of and demand for labor, to answer the following questions.

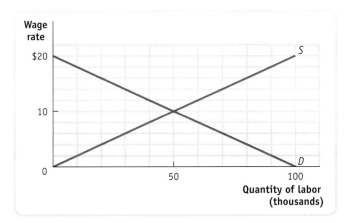

a. What is the equilibrium wage rate in Profunctia? At this wage rate, what is the level of employment, the size of the labor force, and the unemployment rate?

b. If the government of Profunctia sets a minimum wage equal to $12, what will be the level of employment, the size of the labor force, and the unemployment rate?

c. If unions bargain with the firms in Profunctia and set a wage rate equal to $14, what will be the level of employment, the size of the labor force, and the unemployment rate?

d. If the concern for retaining workers and encouraging high quality work leads firms to set a wage rate equal to $16, what will be the level of employment, the size of the labor force, and the unemployment rate?

4. In Northlandia, there are no labor contracts; that is, wage rates can be renegotiated at any time. But in Southlandia, wage rates are set at the beginning of each odd year and last for two years. Why would equal-sized falls in aggregate output due to a fall in aggregate demand have different effects on the magnitude and duration of unemployment in these two economies?

5. In which of the following cases is it more likely for efficiency wages to exist? Why?

a. Jane and her boss work as a team selling ice cream.

b. Jane sells ice cream without any direct supervision by her boss.

c. Jane speaks Korean and sells ice cream in a neighborhood in which Korean is the primary language. It is difficult to find another worker who speaks Korean.

6. How will the following changes affect the natural rate of unemployment?

a. The government reduces the time during which an unemployed worker can receive benefits.

b. More teenagers focus on their studies and do not look for jobs until after college.

c. Greater access to the Internet leads both potential employers and potential employees to use the Internet to list and find jobs.

d. Union membership declines.

7. With its tradition of a job for life for most citizens, Japan once had a much lower unemployment rate than that of the United States; from 1960 to 1995, the unemployment rate in Japan exceeded 3% only once. However, since the crash of its stock market in 1989 and slow economic growth in the 1990s, the job-for-life system has broken down and unemployment has risen to more than 5% in 2003. Explain the likely effect of these recent changes in Japan on the Japanese natural rate of unemployment.

8. The accompanying scatter diagram shows the relationship between the unemployment rate and the output gap in the United States from 1990 to 2004. Draw a straight line through the scatter of dots in the figure. Assume that this line represents Okun's law:

$$\text{Unemployment rate} = b - (m \times \text{Output gap})$$

where b is the vertical intercept and m is the slope

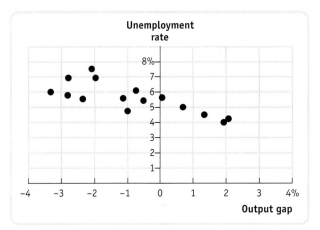

What is the unemployment rate when aggregate output equals potential output? What would the unemployment rate be if the output gap were 2%? What if the output gap were −3%? What do these results tell us about the coefficient m in Okun's law?

9. After experiencing a recession for the past two years, the residents of Albernia were looking forward to a decrease in the unemployment rate. Yet after six months of positive economic growth, the unemployment rate remains the same as it was at the end of the recession. How can you explain why the unemployment rate did not fall although the economy was experiencing economic growth?

10. Due to historical differences, countries often differ in how quickly a change in actual inflation is incorporated into a change in expected inflation. In a country such as Japan that has had very little inflation in recent memory, it will take longer for a change in the actual inflation rate to be reflected in a corresponding change in the expected inflation rate. In contrast, in a country such as Argentina, one that has recently had very high inflation, a change in the actual inflation rate will immediately be reflected in a corresponding change in the expected inflation rate. What does this imply about the short-run and long-run Phillips curves in these two types of countries? What does this imply about the effectiveness of monetary and fiscal policy to reduce the unemployment rate?

11. The accompanying table shows data for the average annual rates of unemployment and inflation for the economy of Britannia from 1995 to 2004. Use it to construct a scatterplot similar to Figure 15-9.

Are the data consistent with a short-run Phillips curve? If the government pursues expansionary monetary policies in the future to keep the unemployment rate below the natural rate of unemployment, how effective will such a policy be?

Year	Unemployment rate	Inflation rate
1995	4.0%	2.5%
1996	2.0%	5.0%
1997	10.0%	1.0%
1998	8.0%	1.3%
1999	5.0%	2.0%
2000	2.5%	4.0%
2001	6.0%	1.7%
2002	1.0%	10.0%
2003	3.0%	3.0%
2004	7.0%	1.5%

>*web*... To continue your study and review of concepts in this chapter, please visit the Krugman/Wells website for quizzes, animated graph tutorials, web links to helpful resources, and more.

www.worthpublishers.com/krugmanwells

>>Inflation, Disinflation, and Deflation

HOURLY WAGES

IN MODERN AMERICA, WE COMPLAIN about inflation when the overall level of prices rises a few percent over the course of a year. But those who lived through the late 1970s scoff—they remember when prices rose as much as 13% in a year. And in other times and places, inflation has gone much, much higher. For example, the accompanying figure shows the inflation rate in Brazil from 1980 to 2004. As you can see, there were many years when the Brazilian inflation rate was in triple digits—and even years when it went into four digits. For a sense of what it felt like to be a Brazilian consumer during this period, consider what happens to the price of a gallon of gas over the course of a year at an inflation rate of 3,000%, equal to Brazil's inflation rate in 1990. At that rate, a gallon of gas that cost $3 at the beginning of the year would cost $90 by the end of the year.

In some months, inflation in Brazil briefly reached the 50%-per-month level

that economists use as a rough dividing line between merely high inflation and *hyperinflation*. Yet Brazil's experience was actually quite mild compared with history's most famous example of hyperinflation, which took place

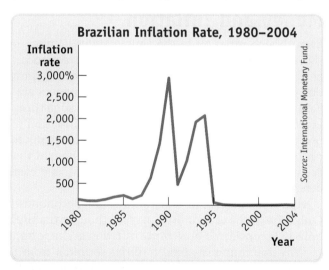

Brazilian Inflation Rate, 1980–2004

Source: International Monetary Fund.

You call what we've seen in the United States inflation? As shown in the graph above, between 1985 and 1995 Brazil demonstrated what really serious inflation—up to almost 3,000% per year—looks like. In 1992, hoping for relief, Brazilians were out on the street demanding new leadership.

What you will learn in this chapter:

➤ Why efforts to collect an **inflation tax** by printing money can lead to high rates of inflation

➤ How high inflation can spiral into hyperinflation as the public tries to avoid paying the inflation tax

➤ The economy-wide costs of inflation and **disinflation**, and the debate over the optimal rate of inflation

➤ Why even moderate levels of inflation can be hard to end

➤ Why deflation is a problem for economic policy and leads policy makers to prefer a low but positive inflation rate

in Germany in 1922–1923. Toward the end of the German hyperinflation, prices were rising 16% a *day,* which—through compounding—meant an increase of approximately 500 billion percent over the course of five months. People became so reluctant to hold paper money, which lost value by the hour, that eggs and lumps of coal began to circulate as currency. German firms would pay their workers several times a day so that they could spend their earnings before they lost value (lending new meaning to the term *hourly wage*). Legend has it that men sitting down at a bar would order two beers at a time, out of fear that the price of a beer would rise before they could order a second round!

What causes episodes of high inflation? How do they come to an end? In this chapter, we'll look at the underlying reasons for inflation. We'll also examine the costs of inflation, which aren't as obvious as you might imagine. We'll see that a falling price level, or deflation, has its own special problems. And we'll look at the issues associated with *disinflation,* a reduction in the inflation rate.

Money and Inflation

Even though inflation in the United States is much lower today than it was during the 1970s—and a far cry from the recent experience of Brazil—the American public and media still pay close attention to inflation. Ask any American to name some serious problems that an economy faces and chances are you'll hear the word *inflation.* Yale University economist Robert Shiller did something similar in the mid-1990s, and indeed, he found that Americans consider inflation to be a problem. Three-quarters of those surveyed thought that "inflation hurts my real buying power; it makes me poorer." And over half of the respondents thought that "preventing high inflation is an important national priority, as important as preventing drug abuse or preventing deterioration in the quality of our schools."

However, Shiller found that professional economists rarely shared these concerns. Only 12% of the economists surveyed thought that inflation makes them poorer, and only 18% considered preventing inflation an important national priority.

Why do economists tend to differ so much from the general public in their impressions about inflation, at least at the moderate levels encountered in countries such as the United States? The answer lies in people's perception of how inflation affects them. People often view inflation as reducing the value of their pay raises; however, economists argue that inflation leads to higher nominal pay increases and therefore doesn't automatically reduce households' purchasing power. But even economists who do not consider a moderate level of inflation to be a serious problem still believe there can be costs associated with it.

To understand the true costs of inflation, we first need to analyze its causes. As we'll see later in this chapter, moderate levels of inflation such as those experienced in the United States—even the double-digit inflation of the late 1970s—can have complex causes. But very high inflation is always associated with rapid increases in the money supply.

To understand why, we need to revisit the effect of changes in the money supply on the overall price level. Then we'll turn to the reasons governments sometimes increase the money supply very rapidly.

Money and Prices, Revisited

In Chapter 14 we learned that in the short run an increase in the money supply increases real GDP by lowering the interest rate and stimulating investment spending and consumer spending. However, in the long run, as nominal wages and other sticky prices rise, real GDP falls back to its original level. So in the long run, any given percent increase in the money supply does not change real GDP. Instead, other things equal, it leads to an equal percent rise in the overall price level; that is, the prices of all goods and services in the economy, including nominal wages and the prices of intermediate goods, rise. And when the overall price level rises, the aggregate price level—the prices of all final goods and services—rises as well. As a result, an increase in the *nominal* money supply, M, leads in the long run to an increase in the aggregate price level that leaves the *real* quantity of money, M/P, at its original level. For example, when Turkey dropped six zeros from its currency, the Turkish lira, in January 2005, Turkish real GDP did not change. The only thing that changed was the number of zeros in prices: instead of something costing 2,000,000 lira, it cost 2 lira.

When analyzing large changes in the aggregate price level, macroeconomists often find it useful to ignore the distinction between the short run and the long run. Instead, they work with a simplified model in which the effect of a change in the money supply on the aggregate price level takes place instantaneously rather than over a long period of time. You might be concerned about this assumption given that in previous chapters we've emphasized the difference between the short run and the long run. However, for reasons we'll explain shortly, this is a reasonable assumption to make in the case of high inflation.

A simplified model in which the real quantity of money, M/P, is always at its long-run equilibrium level is known as the **classical model of the price level,** because it was commonly used by "classical" economists who wrote before the work of John Maynard Keynes. To understand the classical model and why it is useful in this context, let's revisit the *AS–AD* model and what it says about the effects of an increase in the money supply. (Unless otherwise noted, we will always be referring to changes in the *nominal* supply of money.)

According to the **classical model of the price level,** the real quantity of money is always at its long-run equilibrium level.

Figure 16-1 reviews the effects of an increase in the money supply according to the *AS–AD* model. The economy starts at E_1, a point of short-run and long-run macroeconomic equilibrium. It lies at the intersection of the aggregate demand curve AD_1 and the short-run aggregate supply curve $SRAS_1$. It also lies on the long-run aggregate supply curve, *LRAS*. At E_1, the equilibrium aggregate price level is P_1.

Now suppose there is an increase in the money supply. This is an expansionary monetary policy, which shifts the aggregate demand curve to the right, to AD_2, and moves the economy to a new short-run equilibrium at E_2. Over time, however, nominal wages adjust upward in response to the rise in the aggregate price level, and the

Figure 16-1

The Classical Model of the Price Level

Starting at E_1, an increase in the money supply shifts the aggregate demand curve rightward, as shown by the movement from AD_1 to AD_2. There is a new short-run equilibrium at E_2 and a higher price level at P_2. In the long run, nominal wages adjust upward and push the *SRAS* curve leftward to $SRAS_2$. The total percent increase in the price level from P_1 to P_3 is equal to the percent increase in the money supply. In the *classical model of the price level,* we ignore the transition period and think of the price level as rising to P_3 immediately. This is a good approximation under conditions of high inflation. **>web...**

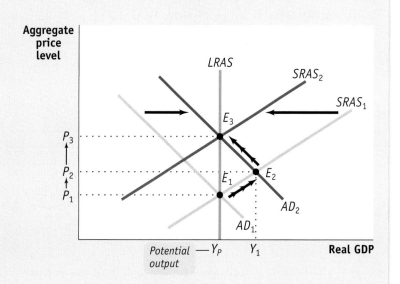

SRAS curve shifts to the left, to *SRAS*$_2$. The new long-run equilibrium is at E_3, and real GDP returns to its initial level. As we learned in Chapter 14, the long-run increase in the aggregate price level from P_1 to P_3 is proportional to the increase in the money supply. As a result, in the long run changes in the money supply have no effect on the real quantity of money, *M/P,* or on real GDP. In the long run, money—as we learned—is *neutral.*

The classical model of the price level ignores the short-run movement from E_1 to E_2, assuming that the economy moves directly from one long-run equilibrium to another long-run equilibrium. In other words, it assumes that the economy moves directly from E_1 to E_3 and that real GDP never changes in response to a change in the money supply. In effect, in the classical model the effects of money supply changes are analyzed as if the short-run as well as the long-run aggregate supply curves were vertical.

In reality, this is a poor assumption during periods of low inflation. With a low inflation rate, it may take a while for workers and firms to react to a monetary expansion by raising wages and prices. In this scenario, some nominal wages and the prices of some goods are sticky in the short run. As a result, there is an upward-sloping *SRAS* curve and changes in the money supply can indeed change real GDP in the short run.

But what about periods of high inflation? In the face of high inflation, economists have observed that the short-run stickiness of nominal wages and prices tends to vanish. Workers and businesses, sensitized to inflation, are quick to raise their wages and prices in response to changes in the money supply. This implies that under high inflation there is a quicker adjustment of wages and prices of intermediate goods than occurs in the case of low inflation. So the short-run aggregate supply curve shifts leftward more quickly and there is a more rapid return to long-run equilibrium under high inflation. As a result, the classical model of the price level is much more likely to be a good approximation of reality for economies experiencing persistently high inflation. The following For Inquiring Minds explains this point further.

The consequence of this rapid adjustment of all prices in the economy is that in countries with persistently high inflation, changes in the money supply are quickly translated into changes in the inflation rate. Let's look again at Brazil. Figure 16-2 shows the annual rate of growth in the money supply (as measured by M1) and the annual rate of change of consumer prices from 1980 to 2004. As you can see, surges

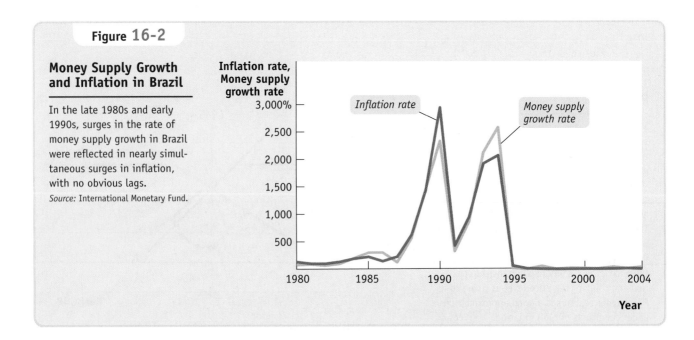

Figure 16-2

Money Supply Growth and Inflation in Brazil

In the late 1980s and early 1990s, surges in the rate of money supply growth in Brazil were reflected in nearly simultaneous surges in inflation, with no obvious lags.

Source: International Monetary Fund.

INDEXING TO INFLATION

When an economy experiences high inflation year after year, people take steps to protect themselves from future inflation—and these steps typically have the effect of making prices highly sensitive to changes in the money supply, even in the short run.

The usual response to inflation is *indexation*—contracts of all kinds are written in ways that adjust for inflation. For example, wage contracts typically include a cost-of-living adjustment, or COLA: payments to workers rise automatically with the consumer price index. The best-known COLA in the United States today involves Social Security benefits, which are automatically adjusted upward each year by the previous year's inflation rate: if the consumer price index rose 3% last year, every retiree's benefits are increased by 3%.

Most wage contracts in the United States no longer have COLAs. In the late 1970s, however, when inflation was much higher than it is today, COLAs were widespread. Economist Steven Holland reports that the rate of wage indexation in the American economy increased through the 1970s and then fell during the early 1980s, once inflation began to fall. In high-inflation economies, similar adjustments are regularly written into labor contracts, rental agreements, loan contracts, and so on. For example, during the late 1980s and early 1990s in Brazil, almost every contract that involved delaying payment into the future was indexed for inflation.

Indexation has the effect of speeding up the response of the overall price level to changes in the money supply. Even in an economy without indexation, an increase in the money supply quickly pushes up the prices of some types of goods, such as raw materials. In a highly indexed economy, these higher prices feed into changes in the consumer price index. That, in turn, quickly leads to increases in wages, further leading to increases in other prices, which feed back into wages, and so on. The result is that the long run, the period in which an increase in the money supply raises the overall price level by the same percentage, arrives very quickly—typically in a matter of months.

---

in the money supply in the late 1980s and early 1990s coincide with roughly equal surges in the inflation rate.

What leads a country to increase its money supply so much that the result is an inflation rate in the hundreds or thousands of percent?

The Inflation Tax

Modern economies use fiat money—pieces of paper that have no intrinsic value but are accepted as a medium of exchange. In the United States and most other wealthy countries, the decision about how many pieces of paper to issue is placed in the hands of a central bank that is somewhat independent of the political process. However, political leaders make the ultimate decision of whether or not to print more money.

So what is to prevent a government from paying for some of its expenses, not by raising taxes or borrowing, but simply by printing money? Nothing. In fact, governments, including the U.S. government, do it all the time. How can the U.S. government do this, given that the Federal Reserve issues money and not the Treasury? The answer is that the Treasury and the Federal Reserve work in concert. The Treasury issues debt to finance the government's purchases of goods and services, and the Fed *monetizes* the debt by creating money and buying the debt back from the public through open-market purchases of Treasury bills. In effect, the U.S. government can and does raise revenue by printing money.

For example, in July 2005 the U.S. monetary base—bank reserves plus currency in circulation—was $26 billion larger than it had been a year earlier. This occurred because, over the course of that year, the Federal Reserve had issued $26 billion in money or its electronic equivalent and put it into circulation through open-market operations. To put it another way, the Fed created money out of thin air and used it to buy valuable government securities from the private sector. Despite the fact that the Fed is officially independent of the U.S. government, its actions enabled the government to pay off $26 billion in outstanding government debt not by raising revenue through taxes but simply by printing money.

An alternative way to look at this is to say that the right to print money is itself a source of revenue. Governments have the exclusive right to print money, and they frequently do so in order to finance government spending. Economists refer to the revenue generated by the government's right to print money as *seigniorage,* an archaic term that goes back to the Middle Ages. It refers to the right to stamp gold and silver into coins, and charge a fee for doing so, that medieval lords—seigneurs, in France—reserved for themselves.

Seigniorage accounts for only a tiny fraction (about 1.5%) of the U.S. government's budget. So the government doesn't rely on the printing press to pay its bills. But there have been many occasions in history when governments turned to their printing presses as a crucial source of revenue. According to the usual scenario, a government finds itself running a large budget deficit—and lacks either the competence or the political will to eliminate this deficit by raising taxes or cutting spending. And the government can't borrow to cover the gap because potential lenders won't extend loans given the fear that the government's weakness will continue and leave it unable to repay its debts.

In such a situation, governments end up printing money to cover the budget deficit. But by printing money to pay its bills, a government increases the quantity of money in circulation. And as we've just seen, increases in the money supply translate into equally large increases in the aggregate price level. So printing money to cover a budget deficit leads to inflation.

Who ends up paying for the goods and services the government purchases with newly printed money? The people who currently hold money pay. They pay because inflation erodes the purchasing power of their money holdings. In other words, a government imposes an **inflation tax,** the reduction in the value of the money held by the public, by printing money to cover its budget deficit and creating inflation.

It's helpful to think about what this tax represents. If the inflation rate is 5%, then a year from now $1 will buy goods and services only worth $0.95 today. This is equivalent to a tax rate of 5% on the value of all money held by the public. So the size of the inflation tax over a given period is equal to the inflation rate over that period multiplied by the money supply:

> The **inflation tax** is the reduction in the value of money held by the public caused by inflation.

(16-1)   Inflation tax = Inflation rate × (Nominal) money supply

However, the inflation tax as we've just calculated it may not be a good indicator of the real amount of resources captured by the government from the public because it is a *nominal* measure. If we want to know the *real* burden of the inflation tax on the public, we have to calculate the *real* inflation tax, which is equal to the inflation rate multiplied by the real money supply:

(16-2)   Real inflation tax = Inflation rate × Real money supply

Because it adjusts for changes in the price level, the real inflation tax measures the real value of the goods and services lost by the public through the inflation tax.

As we'll now see, the real inflation tax plays a key role in the process by which high inflation turns into explosive hyperinflation.

The Logic of Hyperinflation

In 1923, Germany's money was worth so little that children used stacks of banknotes as building blocks.

Inflation imposes a tax on individuals who hold money. And, like any tax, it will lead people to change their behavior. In particular, when inflation is high, people will try to avoid holding money and will instead substitute real goods as well as interest-bearing assets for money. In the introduction to this chapter, we described how, during the German hyperinflation, people began using eggs or lumps of coal as a medium of exchange. They did this because lumps of coal maintained their real value over time but money didn't. Indeed, during the peak of German hyperinflation, people often burned paper money, which was less valuable than wood. Moreover, people don't just reduce their nominal money holdings—they reduce their *real* money holdings. Why? Because the more real money holdings they have, the greater the real amount of resources the government captures from them through the inflation tax.

We are now prepared to understand how countries can get themselves into situations of extreme inflation. High inflation arises when the government must collect a large inflation tax to cover a large budget deficit. According to Equation 16-2, the real inflation tax is equal to the inflation rate multiplied by the real money supply.

But as we've just explained, in the face of high inflation the public reduces the real amount of money it holds. In turn, the government must generate a higher rate of inflation to collect the same amount of real inflation tax that it collected before people reduced their money holdings—an amount it needs to raise in order to cover a large budget deficit. And people respond to this new higher rate of inflation by reducing their real money holdings yet again. As the process becomes self-reinforcing, it can easily spiral out of control. Although the amount of real inflation tax that the government must ultimately collect to pay off its deficit does not change, the inflation rate the government needs to impose to collect that amount rises. So the government is forced to increase the money supply more rapidly, leading to an even higher rate of inflation, and so on.

Here's an analogy: Imagine a city government that tries to raise a lot of money with a special fee on taxi rides. The fee will raise the cost of taxi rides, and this will cause people to turn to easily available substitutes such as walking or taking the bus. As taxi use declines, the government finds its tax revenue declines and must impose a higher fee to raise the same amount of revenue as before. You can imagine the ensuing vicious circle: the government imposes fees on taxi rides, which leads to less taxi use, which causes the government to raise the fee on taxis, which leads to even less taxi use, and so on.

Substitute the real money supply for taxi rides and the inflation rate for the fee on taxis, and you have the story of hyperinflation. A race develops between the government printing presses and the public: the presses churn out money at a faster and faster rate, to try to compensate for the fact that the public is reducing its real money holdings. At some point the inflation rate explodes into hyperinflation, and people are unwilling to hold any money at all (and resort to trading in eggs and lumps of coal). The government is then forced to abandon its use of the inflation tax and shut down the printing presses.

economics in action

Money and Prices in Brazil, 1985–1995

As we noted in the introduction to this chapter, Brazil offers a relatively recent example of a country experiencing very high inflation. Figure 16-2 showed that surges in Brazil's money supply were matched by almost simultaneous surges in Brazil's inflation rate. But looking at rates of change doesn't give a true feel for just how much prices went up in Brazil.

Figure 16-3 shows Brazil's money supply and aggregate price level from 1985 to 1995. We measure both the money supply and the aggregate price level as index numbers, with their 1985 levels set equal to 1. We also use a logarithmic scale, because equal-size percent changes are drawn as the same size. Over the course of a decade, both the money supply and the aggregate price level increased by approximately 100 billion percent. As you can see, the aggregate price level and the money supply rose in close tandem.

Why did the Brazilian government increase its money supply so excessively over the course of a decade? The reason boils down to political conflict, which made

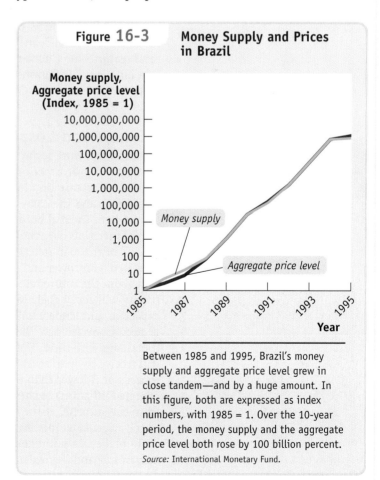

Figure 16-3   Money Supply and Prices in Brazil

Between 1985 and 1995, Brazil's money supply and aggregate price level grew in close tandem—and by a huge amount. In this figure, both are expressed as index numbers, with 1985 = 1. Over the 10-year period, the money supply and the aggregate price level both rose by 100 billion percent.
Source: International Monetary Fund.

it impossible for the country's government to balance its budget by either raising taxes or by cutting spending. Financial difficulties during the 1980s left Brazil unable to borrow money in world markets. Like many others before it, Brazil's government turned to the printing press to cover the gap—leading to massive inflation. ■

< < < < < < < < < < < < < < < < < <

>>CHECK YOUR UNDERSTANDING 16-1

1. Suppose there is a large increase in the money supply in an economy that previously had low inflation. As a consequence, aggregate output expands in the short run. What does this say about situations in which the classical model of the price level applies?

2. Suppose that all wages and prices in an economy are indexed to inflation. Can there still be an inflation tax?

Solutions appear at back of book.

Effects of Inflation

We've seen how the use of the printing press to cover a government deficit leads to inflation. And we've also learned how a government's attempt to collect a large real inflation tax can lead to fiscal disaster. But even in the absence of such a disaster, inflation can have important consequences.

Recall the widespread belief that inflation makes everyone worse off by raising the cost of living. As we discussed earlier, this is a fallacy. It misses the point that inflation raises the prices received by firms—which in turn determine incomes paid in the economy—as well as the prices paid by consumers. In fact, recall from the *AS–AD* model that when an increase in the money supply leads to a rise in the aggregate price level, in the long run real GDP and aggregate real income are unchanged.

Although it is incorrect that inflation makes everyone worse off, inflation does have important effects on the economy that are not fully captured by the *AS–AD* model. We'll soon learn that *unexpected* inflation, although leaving real GDP and total real income unchanged, hurts some people while helping others. Then we'll see that *anticipated* inflation can indeed impose real costs on the economy; if sufficiently high, it can reduce real GDP and real incomes.

Winners and Losers from Unexpected Inflation

Inflation can hurt some people while helping others for one main reason: contracts that extend over a period of time, such as loans, are normally specified in nominal terms. In the case of a loan, the borrower receives a certain amount of funds at the beginning, and the loan contract specifies how much he or she must repay at some future date. The real burden of that repayment to the borrower depends greatly on the rate of inflation over the intervening years of the loan because the inflation rate over the life of the loan determines how large the repayment is in real terms.

When a borrower and a lender enter into a loan contract, each party has an expectation about the future rate of inflation. If the inflation rate is *higher* than expected, borrowers will repay their loans with funds that have a lower real value than they had expected, and lenders will receive payment with a lower real value than they had expected. Conversely, if the inflation rate is *lower* than expected, borrowers will repay their loans with funds that have a higher real value than they had expected, and lenders will receive payment with a higher real value than they had expected. So when inflation exceeds or is lower than expectations, either the borrower (in the case of higher-than-expected inflation) or the lender (in the case of lower-than-expected inflation) benefits from the surprise, at the other party's expense. But if the actual inflation rate is equal to the anticipated rate, inflation does not create winners or losers in loan contracts.

To make this point concrete, we need to recall the distinction between the *nominal interest rate* and the *real interest rate*. The best way to understand the difference between them is with an example. Suppose the owner of a firm borrows $10,000 for one year at a 10% interest rate. At the end of the year, he or she must repay $11,000—the amount borrowed plus interest. But suppose that over the course of the year the average level of prices increases by 10%. Then the $11,000 repayment has the same purchasing power as the original $10,000 loan. In real terms, the borrower has in effect received a zero-interest loan.

In this example, economists would say that the **nominal interest rate** (the interest rate in money terms) is 10%, but the **real interest rate** (the interest rate adjusted for inflation) is 0%. As the example shows, the real interest rate is equal to the nominal interest rate minus the rate of inflation:

(16-3)   Real interest rate = Nominal interest rate − Inflation rate

> The **nominal interest rate** is the interest rate in money terms.
>
> The **real interest rate** is the interest rate adjusted for inflation, equal to the nominal rate minus the inflation rate.

You might be tempted to say that inflation necessarily helps borrowers and hurts lenders; but what really matters is how actual inflation compares with the inflation that borrowers and lenders *expected when they entered into the loan contract*. Suppose a borrower and a lender agreed on a one-year loan at a nominal interest rate of 7%, and both expected the inflation rate to be 5% over the next year. Then the expected inflation rate was taken into account when they entered into the contract: the 7% nominal interest rate represented a 2% real interest rate plus 5% for inflation. But suppose people expected a 5% inflation rate and actually experienced a 10% rate. In this case, lenders thought they were lending at a 2% real interest rate, but they actually received a negative real interest rate of *minus* 3%. That is, by lending at a 7% nominal interest rate (2% real interest rate plus 5% expected inflation rate) but experiencing a 10% *actual* inflation rate, lenders received a real interest rate equal to 7% − 10% = −3%. Borrowers won, and lenders lost. Conversely, suppose the actual inflation rate turned out to be 0% rather than 5%. In that case, borrowers who thought they were paying a 2% real interest rate actually ended up paying a real interest rate equal to 7% (7% nominal interest rate minus 0% actual inflation rate). Lenders won, and borrowers lost.

In modern America, home mortgages provide the most important example of how inflation can create winners and losers. A standard mortgage specifies a monthly dollar payment over a period of 15 to 40 years. If the overall price level is rising, the borrower's real payment per month falls over time. How fast the payment falls depends on the rate of inflation. For example, Americans who took out mortgages in the early 1970s quickly found their real payments reduced by higher-than-expected inflation: by 1983 the purchasing power of a dollar was only 45% of what it had been in 1973. Those who took out mortgages in the early 1990s were not so lucky because the inflation rate fell to lower-than-expected levels in the following years: in 2003 the purchasing power of a dollar was 78% of what it had been in 1993.

So borrowers who took out mortgages in the early 1970s gained at the expense of lenders, who found the real value of their loans rapidly eroded by inflation. In fact, one side effect of inflation during the 1970s was to push many savings and loan institutions—a type of bank that traditionally specialized in home loans—into bankruptcy. They failed because the value of the long-term loans they had made were greatly reduced by inflation, but the interest rates they paid on short-term deposits had to keep up with inflation in order to attract depositors.

Expected Inflation and Interest Rates

As the preceding discussion makes clear, people should base the decision of whether or not to borrow on their expectation of the real interest rate, not the nominal rate. It is the real interest rate that measures the quantity of real purchasing power the borrower will have to give up to repay the loan. A loan at 10% interest is very expensive at a time of 0% inflation; it's very cheap if inflation is near 10%; and it's better than free in real terms if the inflation rate is above 10%.

And like borrowers, lenders should be concerned with the real rather than the nominal interest rate. A loan at 10% interest is a very good investment if inflation is at 0% but a poor investment if inflation is running at 15%.

Because inflation affects the real interest rate actually paid by borrowers and received by lenders, *expected* inflation has strong effects on the nominal interest rate. Recall the loanable funds model of the interest rate we developed in Chapter 9, where we described how the equilibrium nominal interest rate equalizes the quantity of loanable funds supplied and the quantity of loanable funds demanded. As with all supply and demand models, this result depends on the "other things equal" assumption. And in this market, one very important thing that must be held equal (that is, unchanged) is the expected inflation rate. So how are the results of the loanable funds model affected by changes in the expected inflation rate?

In Figure 16-4, the curves S_0 and D_0 show the supply and demand for loanable funds given that the expected rate of inflation is 0%. In that case, equilibrium is at E_0 and the equilibrium nominal interest rate is 4%. Because expected inflation is 0%, the equilibrium expected real interest rate, the real interest rate expected by borrowers and lenders when the loan is contracted, is also 4%.

Now suppose that the expected inflation rate rises to 10%. The demand curve for funds shifts upward to D_{10}: borrowers are now willing to borrow as much at a nominal interest rate of 14% as they were previously willing to borrow at 4%. That's because with a 10% inflation rate, a 14% nominal interest rate corresponds to a 4% real interest rate. Similarly, the supply curve of funds shifts upward to S_{10}: lenders require a nominal interest rate of 14% to persuade them to lend as much as they would previously have lent at 4%. The new equilibrium is at E_{10}: the result of an expected inflation rate of 10% is that the equilibrium nominal interest rate rises from 4% to 14%.

This situation can be summarized as a general principle, known as the **Fisher effect** (after the American economist Irving Fisher, who proposed it in 1930): *the expected real interest rate is unaffected by the change in expected inflation.* According to the Fisher effect, expected inflation drives up nominal interest rates, and each additional percentage point of expected inflation drives up the nominal interest rate by 1 percentage point. The central point is that both lenders and borrowers base their decisions on the expected real rate of interest. As long as inflation is expected, it does not affect the equilibrium quantity of loanable funds or the expected real interest rate; all it affects is the equilibrium nominal interest rate.

According to the **Fisher effect**, an increase in expected inflation drives up the nominal interest rate, leaving the expected real interest rate unchanged.

Figure 16-4

The Fisher Effect

D_0 and S_0 are the demand and supply curves for loanable funds when the expected inflation rate is 0%. At an expected inflation rate of 0%, the equilibrium nominal interest rate is 4%. Expected inflation pushes both the demand and supply curves upward by 1 percentage point for every percentage point increase of expected inflation. D_{10} and S_{10} are the demand and supply curves for loanable funds when the expected inflation rate is 10%. Expected inflation raises the equilibrium nominal interest rate to 14%. The expected real interest rate remains at 4%, and the equilibrium quantity of loanable funds also remains unchanged. **>web...**

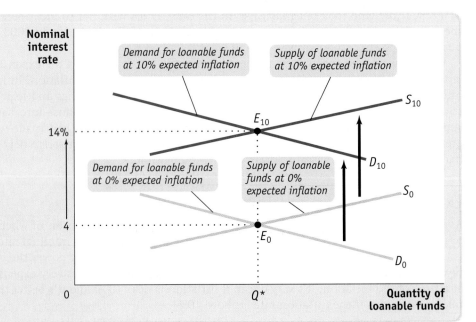

The Costs of Inflation

We've now seen how unexpected inflation produces winners and losers. The question we want to ask now is whether *anticipated* inflation imposes costs on the economy as a whole and whether, as a result, it changes the overall level of income in the economy. (We are considering the costs that even low or moderate inflation can cause, excluding the costs of a fiscal crisis that high inflation or hyperinflation can impose on an economy.)

The answer to our question is yes; anticipated inflation can impose real costs on the economy. Economists have identified several of these, the most important being *shoe-leather costs*, *menu costs*, and *unit-of-account costs*. We'll discuss each in turn.

Shoe-Leather Costs People hold money for convenience in making transactions. Inflation, as we've seen, discourages people from holding money. The result is that making transactions becomes more difficult.

One typical response to inflation is that people make more transactions in order to purchase the same amount of goods and services. In 1984–1985, when Israel experienced an episode of very high inflation, Israelis tried to hold as little money as possible, which required visiting a bank or ATM several times a week to move money into or out of interest-bearing accounts. During the German hyperinflation, merchants employed runners to take their cash to the bank many times a day to deposit it into interest-bearing assets or to convert it into a more stable foreign currency. In each case, in an effort to avoid the inflation tax, people devoted valuable resources—the time of Israeli citizens, the labor of those German runners—that could have been used productively elsewhere. During the German hyperinflation, so many banking transactions were taking place that the number of employees at German banks nearly quadrupled—from around 100,000 in 1913 to 375,000 in 1923. Similarly, during the Brazilian hyperinflation, the financial sector of the economy accounted for 15% of GDP, more than twice the size of the financial sector in the United States measured as a share of GDP. The large increase in the banking sector needed to cope with the consequences of inflation represented a loss of real resources to society.

Ricki Rosen / Corbis Saba

Such are the shoe-leather costs of inflation: when the inflation rate in Israel hit 500% in 1985, people spent a lot of time in line at ATMs.

The increased costs of transactions caused by inflation are known as **shoe-leather costs,** an allusion to the wear and tear of the extra running around that takes place when people are trying to avoid holding money. Shoe-leather costs are substantial in very high-inflation economies, as anyone who has lived through a hyperinflation—or even inflation of, say, 100% per year—can attest. Most estimates suggest, however, that the shoe-leather costs of inflation at the rates seen in the United States—which in peacetime has never had inflation above 13%—are quite small.

> The **shoe-leather costs** of inflation are the increased costs of making transactions that arise from the public's efforts to avoid the inflation tax.

PITFALLS

WHAT INTEREST RATE FOR MONEY DEMAND?

We learned in Chapter 14 that the demand for money depends on the interest rate. But now we've made a distinction between the *nominal* interest rate and the *real* interest rate. Which one affects money demand?

You might be tempted to answer that it's the real interest rate. After all, we know that the demand for money can be viewed as a demand for a *real* quantity of money. So shouldn't it be real values, all the way?

No. Think about the opportunity cost of holding cash: a dollar bill or a *real* (Brazil's currency) offers a 0% interest rate—a 0%

nominal interest rate. The alternative is to hold a bond that yields positive interest—positive *nominal* interest. So the interest rate that matters for money demand is the nominal rate of interest because that is what you forgo by holding money.

In fact, that's why expected inflation leads to reduced holding of money as people substitute money for interest-bearing assets. The real rate of interest doesn't rise, but the nominal rate does. And the nominal rate is the opportunity cost of holding money because it is the rate paid on interest-bearing assets.

Menu Costs   We introduced the concept of menu costs—the literal cost of changing listed prices—in Chapter 15 as one reason firms are reluctant to change prices in the face of changes in aggregate demand. In the face of inflation, of course, firms are forced to change prices more often than they would if the aggregate price level was more or less stable. This means higher costs for the economy as a whole.

In times of hyperinflation, menu costs can be very substantial. During the Brazilian hyperinflation, for instance, supermarket workers reportedly spent half of their time replacing old price stickers with new ones. When inflation is high, merchants may decide to stop listing prices in terms of the local currency and use either an artificial unit—in effect, measuring prices relative to one another—or a more stable currency, such as the U.S. dollar. This is exactly what the Israeli real estate market began doing in the mid-1980s: prices were quoted in U.S. dollars, even though payment was made in Israeli shekels.

Menu costs are present in low-inflation economies, but they are not severe. In low-inflation economies, businesses might update their prices only sporadically—not daily or even more frequently, as is the case in high-inflation or hyperinflation economies. Also, with technological advances, menu costs are becoming less and less important, since prices can be changed electronically and fewer merchants attach price stickers to merchandise.

Unit-of-Account Costs   Article I, Section 8 of the U.S. Constitution gives Congress the power to "fix the standard of weights and measures" for the nation. The Founding Fathers realized that trade among the states would be greatly facilitated if there were no confusion about units of measurement—a pound in Massachusetts should weigh the same amount as a pound in Virginia; a foot in New York should be the same length as a foot in South Carolina.

As we explained in Chapter 13, one of the roles of money is as a unit of account—a measure individuals use to set prices and make economic calculations. Just as trade among states is facilitated when everyone knows how much a pound weighs, exchange in the economy as a whole is facilitated when everyone knows how much a dollar is worth. Yet inflation causes the real value of a dollar to change over time—a dollar next year is worth less than a dollar this year. The effect, many economists argue, is to reduce the quality of economic decisions: the economy as a whole makes less efficient use of its resources. The **unit-of-account costs** of inflation are the costs arising from the way inflation makes money a less reliable unit of measurement.

> The **unit-of-account costs** of inflation are the costs arising from the way inflation makes money a less reliable unit of measurement.

Unit-of-account costs may be particularly important in the tax system. The United States has a progressive income tax, meaning that people with higher incomes pay a higher income tax rate on their incomes. In addition, the schedule of income tax rates in the United States is indexed to inflation. That is, the threshold level of income above which a taxpayer must pay a higher tax rate goes up every year with inflation to prevent people from having to pay a higher tax rate on their income if their income is just keeping up with inflation. But in the United States and most other countries, taxable income *itself* is still calculated in nominal terms. For example, taxable profits are calculated as the difference between a company's nominal costs and its nominal revenues. If costs are paid before revenues are received, inflation can distort the calculation of profit in nominal terms, making a case of no profit or loss in real terms appear like a positive profit in nominal terms.

In times of high inflation, this is a serious risk. Imagine a clothing store that buys a coat at a wholesale price of $600 during the summer and sells it at a retail price of $1,000 three months later. By law, the difference between the price at which the store buys the coat and the price at which it sells it is considered a profit—$400 in this case—and is subject to taxes. But under high inflation the store cannot replace coats at the same cost it paid for the coats it just sold. It must pay the prevailing wholesale price of a coat to replace its inventory. If the wholesale price had risen to $800 at the time of the sale, then from the viewpoint of the store's owner, his or her profit on the sale is only $1,000 − $800 = $200, not $400. But the Internal Revenue Service does not see it this way; it assesses taxes based on the difference between what the firm actually paid in nominal terms and what the firm received in nominal terms.

During the 1970s, when the United States had relatively high inflation, the distorting effects of inflation on the tax system were a serious problem. Some businesses were discouraged from productive investment spending because inflation caused the IRS to exaggerate their true profits. Conversely, inflation encouraged excessive spending on homeownership. The U.S. income tax system allows taxpayers to deduct interest payments on home mortgages, so at a time when nominal—but not real—interest rates were high, owning a home became a very good deal. When inflation (and tax rates) were reduced in the 1980s, these problems became much less important.

The Optimal Rate of Inflation

What is the optimal rate of inflation for an economy? You might be tempted to say 0%—aren't stable prices a good thing? And haven't we just listed several real costs to the economy from inflation? However, some economists argue that there should be a small positive inflation rate, while others suggest that even 0% inflation may be too high!

In a famous analysis, University of Chicago economist Milton Friedman argued that economic policy should aim for steady *deflation* as a way to minimize shoe-leather costs. As explained in For Inquiring Minds, Friedman suggested that the only way to truly eliminate the shoe-leather costs of inflation would be to make people indifferent between holding money and not holding money. This would mean that the nominal interest rate would need to be near 0%. But if the real interest rate is positive, a 0% nominal interest rate requires a negative rate of inflation.

In practice, no central bank has tried to put Friedman's rule into effect. Most central banks aim for **price stability,** usually defined as a low but positive rate of inflation. For example, it is clear from the Federal Reserve's actions that it prefers an inflation rate of 2% to 3%, but it has never made a formal statement to that effect. Other central banks are less cagey. For example, the Bank of England has an explicit inflation rate target of 2.5%.

Most central banks target **price stability,** a low but positive rate of inflation.

The main reason most central banks aim for slightly positive inflation is their belief that monetary policy is better able to respond to adverse events when the public expects modest inflation than when the public expects 0% inflation. We'll explain why later in this chapter, when we discuss deflation.

FOR INQUIRING MINDS

A CASE FOR DEFLATION?

In 1960, Milton Friedman used the analysis of shoe-leather costs of inflation to arrive at a radical conclusion: the optimal rate of inflation is negative. That is, there should be persistent deflation.

His argument ran as follows. Even at 0% inflation, people incur shoe-leather costs when they economize on the use of money in order to avoid the opportunity cost of interest forgone. Yet it does not cost the economy anything to provide people with fiat money. So Friedman argued that even at 0% inflation, people's efforts to limit their money holdings in favor of holding interest-bearing assets lead to inefficiency.

To eliminate this inefficiency, Friedman concluded that the government should try to push the nominal interest rate close to 0%. But the only way to do this on a sustained basis would be to have a policy dictating a negative inflation rate. A negative expected inflation rate reduces the nominal interest rate through the Fisher effect, leading people to hold a larger real quantity of money.

Although an ingenious analysis, it has never been used as a basis for policy. Negative inflation—deflation—poses risks to economic policy, which most economists believe outweigh any gains from reduced shoe-leather costs.

economics in action

Inflation and Interest Rates in the United States

Does expected inflation really push up interest rates? A quick look at nominal interest rates and inflation in the United States over the past 50 years is strong evidence that it does.

Figure 16-5 shows the nominal interest rate on U.S. Treasury bills and the inflation rate in the United States since 1955. Both peaked around 1980, when inflation rose into double digits—and so did interest rates.

Figure 16-5

Inflation and Nominal Interest Rates

The Fisher effect tells us that each percentage point of expected inflation raises the nominal interest rate by 1 percentage point. These data show the short-term nominal interest rate and the inflation rate in the United States over the past half-century. They moved roughly together, both reaching a double-digit peak around 1980. To the extent that actual inflation eventually represents previously held expectations of inflation, the data are strong evidence for the Fisher effect. **>web...**

Sources: Bureau of Labor Statistics; Federal Reserve Bank of St. Louis.

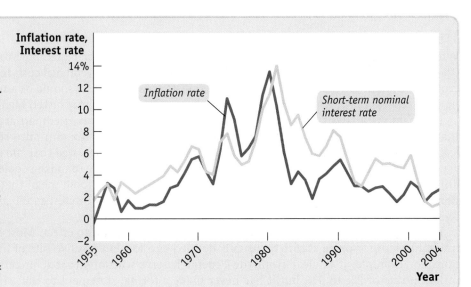

Movements in inflation and nominal interest rates do not, of course, match exactly. For one thing, other factors besides inflation affect the nominal interest rate. For another, the nominal interest rate reflects *expected* inflation, not actual inflation. To the extent that actual inflation is either higher or lower than expected inflation, the nominal interest rate will not move in tandem with the actual inflation rate. Through much of the 1970s, inflation ran faster than people expected, leading to negative real interest rates. During the 1980s inflation ran below most people's expectations, leading to very high real interest rates.

But, to the extent that the actual inflation rate eventually represents what people had expected the inflation rate to be, the key message from Figure 16-5 is that inflation does push up nominal interest rates. And it does this roughly one-for-one, as the Fisher effect predicts. ■

‹ ‹ ‹ ‹ ‹ ‹ ‹ ‹ ‹ ‹ ‹ ‹ ‹ ‹ ‹ ‹ ‹ ‹ ‹

►►QUICK REVIEW

- ➤ An unexpectedly high inflation rate benefits borrowers and hurts lenders by reducing the *real interest rate* paid on loans.
- ➤ Higher expected inflation raises *nominal interest rates* through the *Fisher effect*.
- ➤ Even anticipated inflation imposes *shoe-leather costs*, *menu costs*, and *unit-of-account costs*.
- ➤ Most central banks target *price stability*.

►►CHECK YOUR UNDERSTANDING 16-2

1. For each of the following cases, calculate the real interest rate paid on the loans as well as who gained and who lost from unexpected inflation.
   a. The nominal interest rate is 8%, and both borrowers and lenders expect an inflation rate of 5% over the life of their loans. The actual inflation rate is 3%.
   b. The nominal interest rate is 6%, and both borrowers and lenders expect an inflation rate of 4% over the life of their loans. The actual inflation rate is 7%.

2. The widespread use of technology has revolutionized the banking industry, making it much easier for customers to access and manage their assets. Does this mean that the shoe-leather costs of inflation are higher or lower than they used to be?

Solutions appear at back of book.

Moderate Inflation and Disinflation

The governments of wealthy, politically stable countries like the United States and Britain don't find themselves forced to print money to pay their bills. Yet over the past 40 years both countries, along with a number of other nations, have experienced uncomfortable episodes of inflation. In the United States, the inflation rate peaked at 13% at the beginning of the 1980s. In Britain, the inflation rate reached 26% in 1975. Why did policy makers allow this to happen?

To understand inflation rates in such cases, it is helpful to shift our focus away from the link between money and prices and look at the policy trade-offs that governments face.

Causes of Moderate Inflation

In Chapter 15 we learned that most economists believe that in the short run there is a trade-off between unemployment and inflation. If the government makes an effort to keep unemployment below the natural rate of unemployment, the short-run Phillips curve implies that this will lead to a higher inflation rate than people expect. Over time, however, people will come to expect this higher level of inflation, and the short-run Phillips curve will shift upward. If the government insists on keeping unemployment below its natural rate, this will lead to further increases in expected inflation, and so on. So keeping unemployment below its natural rate requires an ever-higher rate of inflation.

This analysis suggests that policy makers should not try to achieve an unemployment rate below the natural rate. However, imagine yourself as a politician facing an election in a year or two, and suppose that inflation is fairly low at the moment. You might well be tempted to create an inflationary gap, pushing the unemployment rate down right now, as a way to please voters. These gains will eventually have to be paid back: low unemployment will lead to gradually rising inflation, and future governments will face an unpleasant choice between raising unemployment or living with inflation. But that's a problem for the future—right now you have an election to win.

This scenario explains why governments might follow expansionary monetary and fiscal policies that lead the economy into inflation. Does this happen in the real world? The evidence is mixed: it's hard to find a systematic pattern of opportunistic behavior, but there are some specific cases in which governments appear to have attempted to stimulate the economy for short-term electoral gain but at long-term economic cost.

A less cynical but similar scenario emphasizes the role of wishful thinking. The natural rate of unemployment changes over time, and estimates of the natural rate are often controversial. A government can easily convince itself that it's safe to target an unemployment rate that is, in fact, well below the natural rate. (It's especially easy to reach that conclusion when it's politically advantageous to do so.) By the time it becomes clear that the target was too ambitious, substantial inflation may be embedded in people's expectations.

Situations like these explain how countries with no need to impose an inflation tax nonetheless developed double-digit inflation rates in the 1970s. And once they found themselves experiencing moderately high inflation, it was difficult to bring inflation back down.

The Problem of Disinflation

Suppose that, for whatever reason, an economy gets into a situation of moderate inflation. Why doesn't it just reverse policy and end the inflation? The answer is that once the public has come to expect continuing inflation, bringing inflation down is painful.

Recall our description in Chapter 15 of how a persistent attempt to keep unemployment below the natural rate leads to accelerating inflation. To reduce inflation that is built into expectations, policy makers need to run the process in reverse, adopting contractionary policies that keep the unemployment rate above the natural rate for an extended period of time. The process of bringing down inflation that has become embedded in expectations is known as **disinflation.**

Disinflation is the process of bringing down inflation that has become embedded in expectations.

Disinflation can be very expensive. As the following Economics in Action documents, the U.S. retreat from high inflation at the beginning of the 1980s appears to have cost the equivalent of about 18% of a year's real GDP. The justification for paying these costs is that they lead to a permanent gain. Although the economy does not recover the short-term productivity losses caused by disinflation, it no longer suffers from the other costs associated with the persistently high inflation. In fact, the United States, Britain, and other wealthy countries that experienced inflation in the 1970s eventually decided that the pain of bringing inflation down—the large reduction in real GDP in the short term—was worth the required suffering.

Some economists argue that the costs of disinflation can be reduced if policy makers explicitly state their determination to reduce inflation. A clearly announced, credible policy of disinflation, they contend, can reduce expectations of future inflation and so shift the short-run Phillips curve downward. Some economists believe that the clear determination of the Federal Reserve to combat the inflation of the 1970s was credible enough that the costs of disinflation, huge though they were, were lower than they might otherwise have been.

Supply Shocks

Another factor that contributed to the rise of U.S. inflation in the 1970s and its decline in the 1980s was a series of *supply shocks,* first negative and then positive.

In Chapter 10 we showed how negative supply shocks can lead both to a fall in aggregate output and to a rise in the aggregate price level. During the 1970s there were major negative supply shocks, driven by political events in the Middle East that drove up the price of oil. These supply shocks led directly to inflation. They also made it hard for the government to pursue an anti-inflationary policy, because high inflation was coupled with relatively high unemployment rates. When it is already high, risking further increases in unemployment is a particularly bitter pill to swallow in order to achieve lower inflation rates.

In the 1980s the same process operated in reverse. A fall in oil prices, especially after 1985, allowed policy makers to preside over declining inflation without the need to impose high unemployment.

economics in action

The Great Disinflation of the 1980s

As we've mentioned several times in this chapter, the United States ended the 1970s with a high rate of inflation, at least by its own peacetime historical standards—13% in 1980. Part of this inflation was the result of one-time events, especially a world oil crisis. But expectations of future inflation at 10% or more per year appeared to be firmly embedded in the economy.

By the mid-1980s, however, inflation was running at about 4% per year. Panel (a) of Figure 16-6 shows the annual rate of change in the "core" consumer price index (CPI)—also called the *core inflation rate.* This index, which excludes energy and food prices, is widely regarded as a better indicator of underlying inflation trends than the

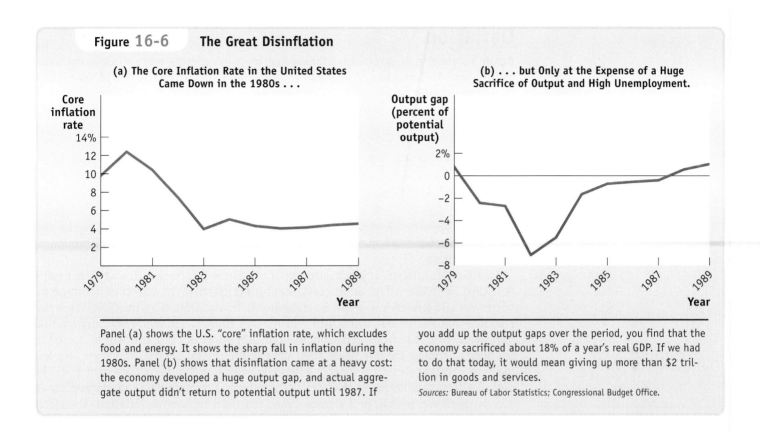

Figure 16-6   **The Great Disinflation**

(a) The Core Inflation Rate in the United States Came Down in the 1980s . . .

(b) . . . but Only at the Expense of a Huge Sacrifice of Output and High Unemployment.

Panel (a) shows the U.S. "core" inflation rate, which excludes food and energy. It shows the sharp fall in inflation during the 1980s. Panel (b) shows that disinflation came at a heavy cost: the economy developed a huge output gap, and actual aggregate output didn't return to potential output until 1987. If you add up the output gaps over the period, you find that the economy sacrificed about 18% of a year's real GDP. If we had to do that today, it would mean giving up more than $2 trillion in goods and services.

Sources: Bureau of Labor Statistics; Congressional Budget Office.

overall CPI. By this measure, inflation fell from about 12% at the end of the 1970s to about 4%.

How was this disinflation achieved? At great cost. Beginning in late 1979, the Federal Reserve imposed strongly contractionary monetary policies, which pushed the economy into its worst recession since the Great Depression. Panel (b) shows the Congressional Budget Office estimate of the U.S. output gap from 1979 to 1989: by 1982, actual output was 7% below potential output, corresponding to an unemployment rate of more than 9%. Aggregate output didn't get back to potential output until 1987.

Our analysis of the Phillips curve in Chapter 15 tells us that a temporary rise in unemployment, like that of the 1980s, is needed to break the cycle of inflationary expectations. Once expectations of inflation are reduced, the economy can return to the natural rate of unemployment at a lower inflation rate. And that's just what happened.

But the cost was huge. If you add up the output gap over 1980–1987, you find that the economy sacrificed approximately 18% of an average year's output over the period. If we had to do the same thing today, that would mean giving up more than $2 trillion worth of goods and services. ∎

> >

>>QUICK REVIEW

➤ Countries can get into situations of moderate inflation because governments are tempted to seek an unemployment rate below the natural rate for political reasons.

➤ *Disinflation*—bringing down inflation that has become embedded in expectations—can impose high costs in unemployment and lost output.

>>CHECK YOUR UNDERSTANDING 16-3

1. British economists believe that the natural rate of unemployment in that country rose sharply during the 1970s, from around 3% to as much as 10%. During that period Britain experienced a sharp acceleration of inflation, which for a time went above 20%. How might these facts be related?

2. Why is disinflation so costly for an economy? Are there ways to reduce these costs?

Solutions appear at back of book.

Deflation

Before World War II, *deflation*—a falling aggregate price level—was almost as common as inflation. In fact, the U.S. consumer price index on the eve of World War II was 30% lower than it had been in 1920. After World War II, inflation became the norm in all countries. But in the 1990s deflation reappeared in Japan and proved difficult to reverse. Other countries, including the United States, became concerned that they might face similar problems.

Why is deflation a problem? And why is it hard to end?

Effects of Unexpected Deflation

Unexpected deflation, like unexpected inflation, produces both winners and losers—but in the opposite direction. Lenders, who are owed money, gain because the real value of borrowers' payments increases. Borrowers lose because the real burden of their debt rises.

In a famous analysis at the beginning of the Great Depression, Irving Fisher (who described the Fisher effect on interest rates) suggested that the effects of deflation on borrowers and lenders can worsen an economic slump. Deflation, in effect, takes real resources away from borrowers and redistributes them to lenders. Fisher argued that borrowers, who lose from deflation, are typically short of cash and will be forced to cut their spending sharply when their debt burden rises. Lenders, however, are less likely to increase spending sharply when the values of the loans they own rise. The overall effect, said Fisher, is that deflation reduces aggregate demand, deepening an economic slump, which, in a vicious circle, may lead to further deflation. The effect of deflation in reducing aggregate demand, known as **debt deflation,** probably played a role in the Great Depression.

Debt deflation is the reduction in aggregate demand arising from the increase in the real burden of outstanding debt caused by deflation.

Effects of Expected Deflation

The effects of expected deflation are, as you might expect, the reverse of the effects of expected inflation: deflation leads to lower nominal interest rates and to increased demand for money. There is, however, a limit to the effect of expected deflation on nominal interest rates. Look back at the example in Figure 16-4, where the equilibrium nominal interest rate is 4% if the expected inflation rate is 0%. Clearly, if the expected inflation rate is −3%—if the public expects deflation at 3% per year—the equilibrium nominal interest rate will be 1%.

But what would happen if the expected rate of inflation is −5%? Would the nominal interest rate fall to −1%? No. Nobody would lend money at a negative nominal rate of interest because they could do better by simply holding cash. Economists say that there is a **zero bound** on the nominal interest rate: it cannot go below zero.

There is a **zero bound** on the nominal interest rate: it cannot go below zero.

This zero bound can limit the effectiveness of monetary policy. Suppose the economy is depressed, with output below potential output and the unemployment rate above the natural rate. Normally the central bank can respond by cutting interest rates so as to increase aggregate demand. If the nominal interest rate is already zero, however, the central bank cannot push it down any further. Any further increases in the monetary base will either be held in bank vaults or held as cash by individuals and firms, without being spent. (With a negative inflation rate and a 0% nominal interest rate, holding cash yields a positive real interest rate.)

A situation in which monetary policy can't be used because nominal interest rates cannot fall below the zero bound is known as a **liquidity trap.** A liquidity trap can occur whenever there is a sharp reduction in demand for loanable funds. The U.S. economy was up against the zero bound for much of the 1930s. Such situations are, however, more likely to arise when the public expects deflation than when it expects inflation. After World War II, when inflation became the norm around the world, the zero bound largely vanished as a problem—until the 1990s.

A **liquidity trap** is a situation in which monetary policy can't be used because nominal interest rates cannot fall below zero.

In the 1990s, however, Japan found itself up against the zero bound, and it also experienced persistent deflation. The Japanese experience alarmed other countries, which feared that they might experience similar problems. In 2001 and 2002, deflation concerns increased in the United States as the inflation rate dipped below 2%.

As we first mentioned in Chapter 6, these fears are the main reason most central banks prefer price stability, a low but positive inflation rate—say 2 or 3%—rather than 0% inflation. Studies by economists at the Federal Reserve and elsewhere indicate that inflation at such low rates imposes very small costs on the economy and makes a liquidity trap unlikely.

economics in action

Japan's Trap

After a boom in the late 1980s, Japan experienced a recession in the early 1990s. The recession was not particularly severe, but it proved very persistent. And in the face of a sustained recessionary gap, the inflation rate in Japan steadily declined. By the middle of the 1990s Japan had become the first major economy to experience deflation since the 1930s.

Figure 16-7 shows Japan's inflation rate and the call money rate—the short-term nominal interest rate that corresponds to the Federal funds rate in the United States—from 1990 to 2004. With a brief exception in 1996 and 1997, the inflation rate fell steadily, becoming negative in the late 1990s. The Bank of Japan, the counterpart of the Federal Reserve, steadily reduced interest rates in an effort to fight deflation. By 1998, however, it had reduced the call money rate all the way to 0%—and the economy was still depressed. This experience demonstrated that the liquidity trap is a real problem in the modern world.

Japan's inability to stimulate the economy by reducing interest rates was one reason for its extensive use of expansionary fiscal policy during the 1990s. In Chapter 12 we described the "bridge to nowhere" linking Awaji Island to the Japanese mainland. Such construction projects were, in part, a substitute for monetary expansion. ∎

> —

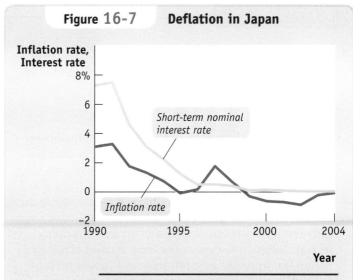

Figure 16-7   Deflation in Japan

During the 1990s, Japan slipped into deflation. The Bank of Japan tried to fight this by reducing the call money rate, the short-term nominal interest rate that corresponds to the Federal funds rate in the U.S. By 1996, however, the call money rate was close to 0%—and by 2004 it actually was 0%, its lower limit. Japan found itself in a liquidity trap, with no room for monetary expansion.

Source: International Monetary Fund.

>>CHECK YOUR UNDERSTANDING 16-4

1. Why won't anyone lend money at a negative nominal rate of interest? How can this pose problems for monetary policy?

Solution appears at back of book.

>> QUICK REVIEW

➤ Unexpected deflation helps lenders and hurts borrowers. This can lead to *debt deflation*, which has a contractionary effect on aggregate demand.
➤ Deflation makes it more likely that interest rates will end up against the *zero bound*. When this happens, the economy is in a *liquidity trap*, and monetary policy is ineffective.

• A LOOK AHEAD •

In the course of our presentation of macroeconomics, we've referred a number of times to history—both the history of events, such as the Great Depression, and the history of ideas, like those of John Maynard Keynes. Both types of history help us understand why macroeconomics is the way it is.

In the next chapter we'll step back from the details of specific models, and look at the making of modern macroeconomics—at how events and ideas interacted to produce the analysis we now rely on.

SUMMARY

1. In analyzing high inflation, economists use the **classical model of the price level,** which says that changes in the money supply lead to proportional changes in the aggregate price level even in the short run.

2. Governments sometimes print money in order to finance budget deficits. When they do, they impose an **inflation tax,** equal to the inflation rate times the money supply, on those who hold money. The real value of resources captured by the government is reflected by the real inflation tax, the inflation rate times the real money supply. In order to avoid paying the inflation tax, people reduce their real money holdings and force the government to increase inflation to capture the same amount of real inflation tax. In some cases, this leads to a vicious circle of a shrinking real money supply and a rising rate of inflation, leading to hyperinflation and a fiscal crisis.

3. The **real interest rate** is equal to the **nominal interest rate** minus the inflation rate. The expected inflation rate is accounted for in the nominal interest rate on a loan. Inflation that is higher than expected benefits borrowers and hurts lenders; inflation that is lower than expected benefits lenders and hurts borrowers. According to the **Fisher effect,** expected inflation raises the nominal interest rate one-to-one so that the expected real interest rate remains unchanged.

4. Inflation imposes **shoe-leather costs,** costs of making transactions incurred as people try to avoid holding money; menu costs, the costs of changing prices; and **unit-of-account costs,** costs that arise because money ceases to be a reliable measure of value. Although there are arguments for a negative rate of inflation (deflation), in practice policy makers tend to aim for price stability—low but positive rates of inflation.

5. Countries that don't need to print money to cover government deficits can still stumble into moderate inflation, either because of political opportunism or because of wishful thinking. When this happens, getting inflation back down can be difficult because **disinflation** can be very costly, requiring the sacrifice of large amounts of aggregate output and imposing high levels of unemployment. However, policy makers in the United States and other wealthy countries were willing to pay the price of bringing down the high inflation of the 1970s.

6. Deflation poses several problems. It can lead to **debt deflation,** in which a rising real burden of outstanding debt intensifies an economic downturn. Also, interest rates are more likely to run up against the **zero bound** in an economy experiencing deflation. When this happens, the economy enters a **liquidity trap,** rendering monetary policy ineffective. Fears of a liquidity trap are the primary reason policy makers prefer price stability, a low but positive inflation rate.

KEY TERMS

Classical model of the price level, p. 395
Inflation tax, p. 398
Nominal interest rate, p. 401
Real interest rate, p. 401

Fisher effect, p. 402
Shoe-leather costs, p. 403
Unit-of-account costs, p. 404
Price stability, p. 405

Disinflation, p. 408
Debt deflation, p. 410
Zero bound, p. 410
Liquidity trap, p. 410

PROBLEMS

1. In the economy of Scottopia, policy makers want to lower the unemployment rate and raise real GDP by using monetary policy. Using the accompanying diagram, show why this policy will ultimately result in a higher aggregate price level but no change in real GDP.

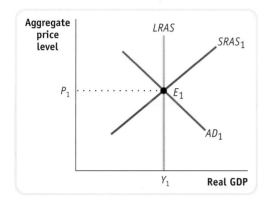

2. In the following examples, would the classical model of the price level be relevant?

   a. There is a great deal of unemployment in the economy and no history of inflation.

   b. The economy has just experienced five years of hyperinflation.

   c. Although the economy experienced inflation in the 10% to 20% range 3 years ago, prices have recently been stable and the unemployment rate has approximated the natural rate of unemployment.

3. The Federal Reserve regularly releases data on the U.S. monetary base. You can access that data at various websites, including the website for the Federal Reserve Bank of St. Louis. Go to http://research.stlouisfed.org/fred2/ and click on "Reserves and Monetary Base" and then on "Board of Governors Monetary Base, Adjusted for Changes in Reserve Requirements, Seasonally Adjusted (SA)" for the latest report.

   a. How much did the monetary base grow in the last month?

   b. How did this help in the government's efforts to finance its deficit?

   c. Why is it important for the central bank to be independent from the part of the government responsible for spending?

4. Answer the following questions about the (real) inflation tax, assuming that the price level starts at 1.

   a. Maria Moneybags keeps $1,000 in her sock drawer for a year. Over the year, the inflation rate is 10%. What is the real inflation tax for this year?

   b. Maria continues to keep the $1,000 in her drawer for a second year. What is the real value of this $1,000 at the beginning of the second year? Over the year, the inflation rate is again 10%. What is the real inflation tax for the second year?

   c. For a third year, Maria keeps the $1,000 in the drawer. What is the real value of this $1,000 at the beginning of

the third year. Over the year, the inflation rate is again 10%. What is the real inflation tax for the third year?

   d. After three years, what is the cumulative real inflation tax?

   e. Redo parts a through d with an inflation rate of 25%. Why is hyperinflation such a problem?

5. Concerned about the crowding-out effects of government borrowing on private investment spending, a candidate for president argues that the United States should just print money to cover the government's budget deficit. What are the advantages and disadvantages of such a plan?

6. Boris Borrower and Lynn Lender agree that Lynn will lend Boris $10,000 and that Boris will repay the $10,000 with interest in one year. They agree to a nominal interest rate of 8%, reflecting a real interest rate of 3% on the loan and a commonly shared expected inflation rate of 5% over the next year.

   a. If the inflation rate is actually 4% over the next year, how does that lower-than-expected inflation rate affect Boris and Lynn? Who is better off?

   b. If the actual inflation rate is 7% over the next year, how does that affect Boris and Lynn? Who is better off?

7. Using the accompanying diagram, explain what will happen to the market for loanable funds when there is a fall of 2 percentage points in the expected future inflation rate. How will the change in the expected future inflation rate affect the equilibrium quantity of loanable funds?

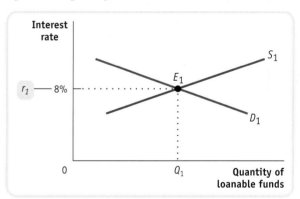

8. In the following examples, is inflation creating winners and losers at no net cost to the economy or is inflation imposing a net cost on the economy? If a net cost is being imposed, which type of cost is involved?

   a. When inflation is expected to be high, workers get paid more frequently and make more trips to the bank.

   b. Lanwei is reimbursed by her company for her work-related travel expenses. Sometimes, however, the company takes a long time to reimburse her. So when inflation is high, she is less willing to travel for her job.

   c. Hector Homeowner has a mortgage with a fixed nominal 6% interest rate that he took out five years ago. Over the years, the inflation rate has crept up unexpectedly to its present level of 7%.

d. In response to unexpectedly high inflation, the manager of Cozy Cottages of Cape Cod must reprint and resend expensive color brochures correcting the price of rentals this season.

9. The accompanying diagram shows mortgage interest rates and inflation during 1990–2005 in the economy of Albernia. When would home mortgages have been especially attractive and why?

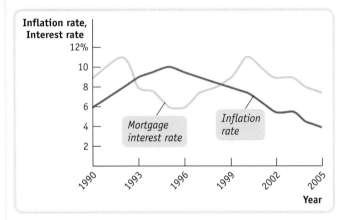

10. The accompanying diagram shows data for the short-term (three-month) nominal interest rate as reported by the European Central Bank and inflation for the euro area for 1996 through mid-2005. How would you describe the relationship between the two? How does the pattern compare to that of the United States in Figure 16-5?

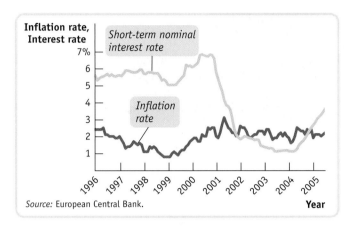

Source: European Central Bank.

11. The economy of Brittania has been suffering from high inflation with an unemployment rate equal to its natural rate. Policy makers would like to disinflate the economy with the lowest economic cost possible. Assume that the state of the economy is not the result of a negative supply shock. How can they try to minimize the unemployment cost of disinflation? Is it possible for there to be no cost of disinflation?

12. Who are the winners and losers when a mortgage company lends $100,000 to the Miller family to buy a house worth $105,000 and during the first year prices unexpectedly fall by 10%? What would you expect to happen if the deflation continued over the next few years? How would continuing deflation affect the economy as a whole?

›web... To continue your study and review of concepts in this chapter, please visit the Krugman/Wells website for quizzes, animated graph tutorials, web links to helpful resources, and more.

www.worthpublishers.com/krugmanwells

>>The Making of Modern Macroeconomics

PURGE THE ROTTENNESS?

"AGGRESSIVE MONETARY POLicy," declared the *2004 Economic Report of the President*, "can reduce the depth of a recession." Few modern macroeconomists would disagree. There are many public arguments about macroeconomic policy—arguments that can play a central role in political campaigns. But there is a broad consensus among macroeconomists about how the economy works. The view that expansionary monetary policy can be effective in fighting recessions is part of that consensus. And that consensus is reflected in actual policy: as the two panels of the accompanying figure show, monetary policy responded very aggressively to the 2001 recession.

Yet today's consensus about monetary policy didn't always exist. There was a time when many economists opposed any effort to fight recessions. At the beginning of the Great Depression, Herbert Hoover's secretary of the treasury, Andrew Mellon, was firmly opposed to any monetary expansion. Hoover would later claim that Mellon's advice was to let the slump take its course: "It will purge the rottenness out of the system." This advice reflected the views of many eminent economists of the day, who regarded aggressive monetary policy as dangerous and ineffective.

When Franklin Roosevelt, Hoover's successor, took office, there was an intense debate among his advisers about whether to

What you will learn in this chapter:

➤ Why classical macroeconomics wasn't adequate for the problems posed by the Great Depression

➤ The core ideas of **Keynesian economics**

➤ How challenges led to a revision of Keynesian ideas

➤ The ideas behind **new classical macroeconomics**

➤ The elements of the modern consensus, and the main remaining disputes

---

An Example of Aggressive Monetary Policy

(a) The Money Supply Rose Sharply in Response to the 2001 Recession...

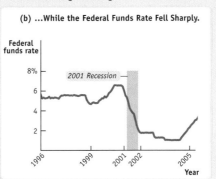

(b) ...While the Federal Funds Rate Fell Sharply.

The Fed responded to the 2001 recession, indicated by the shaded area in both panels, with a rapid expansion of the money supply (panel (a)) and sharp cuts in the federal funds rate (panel (b)).

Source: Federal Reserve Bank of St. Louis; National Bureau of Economic Research.

In 1930, as the U.S. economy plunged into the Great Depression, Herbert Hoover's economic advisers told him to let the economy suffer—it would "purge the rottenness." By contrast, in 2001, George W. Bush's economic advisers supported "aggressive" measures to fight a recession.

pursue expansionary monetary and fiscal policies or to do the opposite. When the expansionists won the debate and the United States went off the gold standard in order to permit monetary expansion, Roosevelt's budget director declared, "This is the end of Western civilization." As far as we can tell, Western civilization is still standing.

How did we get from there to here? How did modern macroeconomics evolve? In preceding chapters we've developed a framework for understanding growth, the business cycle, and inflation. In this chapter, we'll look at how this framework was created—how events and ideas interacted in the making of modern macroeconomics.

Classical Macroeconomics

The term *macroeconomics* appears to have been coined in 1933 by the Norwegian economist Ragnar Frisch; the date, during the worst year of the Great Depression, is no accident. Still, there were economists analyzing what we now consider macroeconomic issues—the behavior of the aggregate price level and aggregate output—before then.

Money and the Price Level

In Chapter 16 we described the *classical model of the price level.* According to the classical model, prices are flexible, making the aggregate supply curve vertical even in the short run. In this model, an increase in the money supply leads, other things equal, to an equal proportional rise in the aggregate price level, with no effect on aggregate output. As a result, increases in the money supply lead to inflation, and that's all. Before the 1930s, the classical model of the price level dominated economic thinking about the effects of monetary policy.

Did classical economists really believe that changes in the money supply affected only aggregate prices, without any effect on aggregate output? Probably not. Historians of economic thought argue that before 1930 most economists were aware that changes in the money supply affect aggregate output as well as aggregate prices in the short run—or, to use modern terms, they were aware that the short-run aggregate supply curve slopes upward. But they regarded such short-run effects as unimportant, stressing the long run instead. It was this attitude that led John Maynard Keynes to scoff at the focus on the long run, in which "we are all dead."

The Business Cycle

Classical economists were, of course, aware that the economy did not grow smoothly. The American economist Wesley Mitchell pioneered the quantitative study of business cycles. In 1920 he founded the National Bureau of Economic Research, an independent, nonprofit organization that to this day has the official role of declaring the beginnings of recessions and expansions. Thanks to Mitchell's work, the *measurement* of business cycles was well advanced by 1930. But there was no widely accepted *theory* of business cycles.

In the absence of any clear theory, views about how policy makers should respond to a recession were conflicting. Some economists favored expansionary monetary and fiscal policies to fight a recession. Others believed that such policies would worsen the slump or merely postpone the inevitable. For example, in 1934 Harvard's Joseph Schumpeter, now famous for his early recognition of the importance of technological change, warned that any attempt to alleviate the Great Depression with expansionary monetary policy "would, in the end, lead to a collapse worse than the one it was called in to remedy." When the Great Depression hit, policy was paralyzed by this lack of consensus. In many cases, economists now believe, policy moved in the wrong direction.

Necessity was, however, the mother of invention. As we'll explain next, the Great Depression provided a strong incentive for economists to develop theories that could serve as a guide to policy—and economists responded.

economics in action

When Did the Business Cycle Begin?

The official chronology of past U.S. business cycles maintained by the National Bureau of Economic Research goes back only to 1854. There are two reasons for this. One is that the farther back in time you go, the less economic data are available. The other is that business cycles, in the modern sense, may have not occurred often in the United States before 1854.

In the first half of the nineteenth century the United States was overwhelmingly a rural, agricultural economy. Figure 17-1 shows estimates of the changing percentages of GDP coming from agriculture and from manufacturing and mining over the period from 1840 to 1900. The figure shows that agriculture dwarfed manufacturing in

---

Figure 17-1

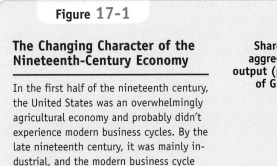

The Changing Character of the Nineteenth-Century Economy

In the first half of the nineteenth century, the United States was an overwhelmingly agricultural economy and probably didn't experience modern business cycles. By the late nineteenth century, it was mainly industrial, and the modern business cycle had emerged.

Source: Robert E. Gallman, "Economic Growth and Structural Change in the Long Nineteenth Century," in Stanley L. Engerman and Robert E. Gallman, editors. *The Cambridge Economic History of the United States, vol. II: The Long Nineteenth Century* (Cambridge, UK: Cambridge University Press, 2000), pp. 1–55.

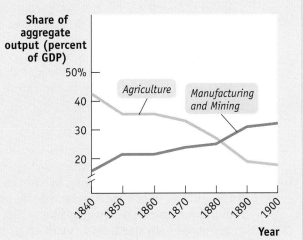

1840 and that manufacturing didn't overtake agriculture in economic importance until the 1880s.

Why does this matter? Fluctuations in aggregate output in agricultural economies are very different from the business cycles we know today. That's because prices of agricultural goods tend to be highly flexible. As a result, the short-run aggregate supply curve of a mainly agricultural economy is probably close to vertical, so demand shocks don't cause output fluctuations. Instead, fluctuations on the farm are driven mainly by weather, making shifts of the short-run aggregate supply curve the primary source of fluctuations. In contrast, modern business cycles are largely the result of shifts in the aggregate demand curve.

The modern business cycle probably originated in Britain—home of the Industrial Revolution—which was already a largely industrial and urban society by 1820. The British recession of 1846–1847 had a particularly modern feel: it followed a bout of "irrational exuberance" in which firms spent heavily on an exciting new technology—railroads—and then realized they had overdone it. ■

< < < < < < < < < < < < < < < < < <

>> CHECK YOUR UNDERSTANDING 17-1

1. Panel (a) of the figure that opened this chapter, on page 415, shows the behavior of M1 before, during, and after the 2001 recession.
   a. How do these data tie in with the quotation from the *Economic Report of the President* that opens this chapter?
   b. What would a classical economist have said about the Fed's policy?

Solutions appear at back of book.

The Great Depression and the Keynesian Revolution

The Great Depression demonstrated, once and for all, that economists cannot safely ignore the short run. Not only was the economic pain severe; it threatened to destabilize societies and political systems. In particular, the economic plunge helped Adolf Hitler rise to power in Germany.

The whole world wanted to know how this economic disaster could be happening and what should be done about it. But because there was no widely accepted theory of the business cycle, economists gave conflicting and, we now believe, often harmful advice. Some believed that only a huge change in the economic system—such as having the government take over much of private industry and replace markets with a command economy—could end the slump. Others argued that slumps were natural—even beneficial—and that nothing should be done.

Some economists, however, argued that the slump both could and should be cured—without giving up on the basic idea of a market economy. In 1930 the British economist John Maynard Keynes compared the problems of the U.S. and British economies to those of a car with a defective alternator. Getting the economy running, he argued, would require only a modest repair, not a complete overhaul.

Nice metaphor. But what was the nature of the trouble?

Keynes's Theory

In 1936 Keynes presented his analysis of the Great Depression—his explanation of what was wrong with the economy's alternator—in a book titled *The General Theory of Employment, Interest, and Money*. In 1946 the great American economist Paul Samuelson wrote that "it is a badly written book, poorly organized. . . . Flashes of insight and intuition intersperse tedious algebra . . . We find its analysis to be obvious and at the same time new. In short, it is a work of genius." *The General Theory* isn't easy reading, but it stands with Adam Smith's *The Wealth of Nations* as one of the most influential books on economics ever written.

As Samuelson's description suggests, Keynes's book is a vast stew of ideas. The school of thought that came to be known as **Keynesian economics** mainly reflected two innovations.

First, Keynes emphasized the short-run effects of shifts in aggregate demand on aggregate output, rather than the long-run determination of the aggregate price level. As Keynes's famous remark about being dead in the long run suggests, until his book appeared most economists had treated short-run macroeconomics as a minor issue. Keynes focused the attention of economists on situations in which the short-run aggregate supply curve slopes upward and shifts in the aggregate demand curve affect aggregate output and employment as well as aggregate prices.

Figure 17-2 illustrates the difference between Keynesian and classical macroeconomics. Both panels of the figure show the short-run aggregate supply curve, *SRAS*; in both it is assumed that for some reason the aggregate demand curve shifts leftward from AD_1 to AD_2—let's say in response to a fall in stock market values that leads households to reduce consumer spending.

Panel (a) shows the classical view: the short-run aggregate supply curve is vertical. The decline in aggregate demand leads to a fall in the price level, from P_1 to P_2, but no change in real GDP. Panel (b) shows the Keynesian view: the short-run aggregate supply curve slopes upward, so the decline in aggregate demand leads to both a fall in the price level, from P_1 to P_2, and a fall in real GDP, from Y_1 to Y_2. As we've already explained, many classical macroeconomists would have agreed that panel (b) was an accurate story in the short run—but they regarded the short run as unimportant. Keynes disagreed. (Just to be clear, there isn't any diagram that looks like panel (b) of Figure 17-2 in Keynes's *General Theory*. But Keynes's discussion of aggregate supply, translated into modern terminology, clearly implies an upward-sloping *SRAS* curve.)

Second, classical economists emphasized the role of changes in the money supply in shifting the aggregate demand curve, paying little attention to other factors. Keynes, however, argued that other factors, especially changes in "animal spirits"— these days usually referred to with the bland term *business confidence*—are mainly responsible for business cycles. Before Keynes, economists often argued that a decline in business confidence would have no effect on either the aggregate price level or aggregate output, as long as the money supply stayed constant. Keynes offered a very different picture.

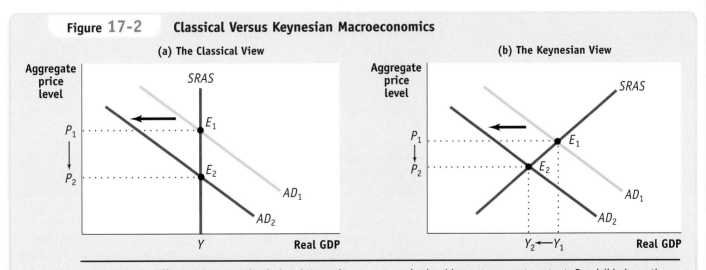

Figure 17-2 **Classical Versus Keynesian Macroeconomics**

(a) The Classical View

(b) The Keynesian View

One important difference between classical and Keynesian economics involves the short-run aggregate supply curve. Panel (a) shows the classical view: the *SRAS* curve is vertical, so shifts in aggregate demand affect the aggregate price level but not aggregate output. Panel (b) shows the Keynesian view: in the short run the *SRAS* curve slopes upward, so shifts in aggregate demand affect aggregate output as well as aggregate prices. **>web...**

FOR INQUIRING MINDS

THE POLITICS OF KEYNES

The term *Keynesian economics* is sometimes used as a synonym for *left-wing economics:* authors seem to believe that because Keynes offered a rationale for some kinds of government activism, he was a leftist of some kind, maybe even a socialist. But the truth is more complicated.

As we explain in the text, Keynesian ideas have actually been accepted across a broad part of the political spectrum. In 2004 the president was a conservative, as was his top economist, N. Gregory Mankiw; but Mankiw is also the editor of a collection of readings titled *New Keynesian Economics.*

And Keynes himself was no socialist—and not much of a leftist. At the time the *General Theory* was published, many intellectuals in Britain believed that the Great Depression was the final crisis of the capitalist economic system and that only a

Some people use *Keynesian economics* as a synonym for *left-wing economics*—but the truth is that the ideas of John Maynard Keynes have been accepted across a broad part of the political spectrum.

government takeover of industry could save the economy. Keynes, in contrast, argued that all the system needed was a narrow technical fix. In that sense, his ideas were pro-capitalist and politically conservative.

What is true is that the rise of Keynesian economics in the 1940s, 1950s, and 1960s went along with a general rise in the role of government in the economy and that those who favored a larger role for government tended to be enthusiastic Keynesians. Conversely, a swing of the pendulum back toward free-market policies in the 1970s and 1980s was accompanied by a series of challenges to Keynesian ideas, which we describe later in this chapter. But it's perfectly possible to have conservative political preferences while respecting Keynes's contribution and equally possible to be very liberal while questioning Keynes's ideas.

Keynes's ideas have penetrated deeply into the public consciousness, to the extent that many people who have never heard of Keynes, or have heard of him but think they disagree with his theory, use Keynesian ideas all the time. For example, suppose that a business commentator says something like this: "Because of a decline in business confidence, investment spending slumped, causing a recession." Whether the commentator knows it or not, that statement is pure Keynesian economics.

Keynes himself more or less predicted that his ideas would become part of what "everyone knows." In another famous passage, this from the end of *The General Theory*, he wrote: "Practical men, who believe themselves to be quite exempt from any intellectual influences, are usually the slaves of some defunct economist."

Policy to Fight Recessions

Macroeconomic policy activism is the use of monetary and fiscal policy to smooth out the business cycle.

The main practical consequence of Keynes's work was that it legitimized **macroeconomic policy activism**—the use of monetary and fiscal policy to smooth out the business cycle.

Macroeconomic policy activism wasn't something completely new. Before Keynes, many economists had argued for using monetary expansion to fight economic downturns—though others were fiercely opposed. Some economists had even argued that temporary budget deficits were a good thing in times of recession—though others disagreed strongly. In practice, during the 1930s many governments followed policies that we would now call Keynesian. In the United States, the administration of Franklin Roosevelt engaged in modest deficit spending in an effort to create jobs.

But these efforts were half-hearted. As we saw in the introduction, Roosevelt's advisers were deeply divided over the appropriate policies to take. In fact, in 1937 Roosevelt gave in to advice from non-Keynesian economists who urged him to balance the budget and raise interest rates, even though the economy was still depressed. The result was a renewed slump.

Today, by contrast, there is broad consensus about the useful role monetary and fiscal policy can play in fighting recessions. The *2004 Economic Report of the President*, quoted at the beginning of this chapter, was issued by a conservative Republican administration that was generally opposed to government intervention in the economy. Yet its view on economic policy in the face of recession was far more like that of Keynes than like that of most economists before 1936.

It would be wrong, however, to suggest that Keynes's ideas have been fully accepted by modern macroeconomists. In the decades that followed the publication of *The General Theory*, Keynesian economics faced a series of challenges, some of which succeeded in modifying the macroeconomic consensus in important ways.

economics in action

The End of the Great Depression

It would make a good story if Keynes's ideas had led to a change in economic policy that brought the Great Depression to an end. Unfortunately, that's not what happened. Still, the way the Depression ended did a lot to convince economists that Keynes was right.

The basic message many of the young economists who adopted Keynes's ideas in the 1930s took from his work was that economic recovery requires aggressive fiscal expansion—deficit spending on a large scale to create jobs. And that is what they eventually got, but it wasn't because politicians were persuaded. Instead, what happened was a very large war.

Figure 17-3 shows the U.S. unemployment rate and the federal budget deficit as a share of GDP from 1930 to 1947. As you can see, deficit spending during the 1930s was on a modest scale. As the risk of war grew larger, the United States began a large military buildup, and the budget moved deep into deficit. After the attack on Pearl Harbor on December 7, 1941, the country began deficit spending on an enormous scale: in fiscal 1943, which began in July 1942, the deficit was 30% of GDP. Today that would be a deficit of $3.5 trillion.

And the economy recovered. World War II wasn't intended as a Keynesian fiscal policy, but it demonstrated that expansionary fiscal policy can, in fact, create jobs in the short run. ■

> >

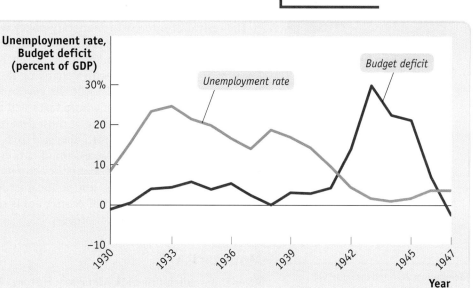

Figure 17-3

Fiscal Policy and the End of the Great Depression

During the 1930s, in an effort to prop up the economy, the U.S. government began deficit spending. The deficits were, however, fairly small as a percentage of GDP. In 1937 the government even tried to balance the budget, only to face a renewed rise in unemployment. The onset of World War II brought on deficit spending on a massive scale and ended the Great Depression.

Source: U.S. Census Bureau.

1. In addition to praising aggressive monetary policy, the *2004 Economic Report of the President* says that "tax cuts can boost economic activity by raising after-tax income and enhancing incentives to work, save, and invest." Is this a Keynesian statement? Why or why not?

Solution appears at back of book.

Challenges to Keynesian Economics

Keynes's ideas fundamentally changed the way economists think about business cycles. They did not, however, go unquestioned. In the decades that followed the publication of *The General Theory*, Keynesian economics faced a series of challenges. As a result, the consensus of macroeconomists retreated somewhat from the strong version of Keynesianism that prevailed in the 1950s. In particular, economists became much more aware of the limits to macroeconomic policy activism.

The Revival of Monetary Policy

Keynes's *General Theory* suggested that monetary policy wouldn't be very effective in depression conditions. Many modern macroeconomists agree: in Chapter 16 we introduced the concept of a *liquidity trap,* a situation in which monetary policy is ineffective because the nominal interest rate is down against the zero bound. In the 1930s, when Keynes wrote, interest rates were, in fact, very close to 0%. (The term *liquidity trap* was first introduced by the British economist John Hicks in a 1937 paper, "Mr. Keynes and The Classics: A Suggested Interpretation," that summarized Keynes's ideas.)

But even when the era of near-0% interest rates came to an end after World War II, many economists continued to emphasize fiscal policy and downplay the usefulness of monetary policy. Eventually, however, macroeconomists reassessed the importance of monetary policy. A key milestone in this reassessment was the 1963 publication of *A Monetary History of the United States, 1867–1960* by Milton Friedman, of the University of Chicago, and Anna Schwartz of the National Bureau of Economic Research. Friedman and Schwartz showed that business cycles had historically been associated with fluctuations in the money supply. In particular, the money supply fell sharply during the onset of the Great Depression. Friedman and Schwartz persuaded many, though not all, economists that the Great Depression could have been avoided if the Federal Reserve had acted to prevent that monetary contraction. They persuaded most economists that monetary policy should play a key role in economic management.

The revival of interest in monetary policy was significant because it suggested that the burden of managing the economy could be shifted away from fiscal policy—meaning that economic management could largely be taken out of the hands of politicians. Fiscal policy, which must involve changing tax rates or government spending, necessarily involves political choices. If the government tries to stimulate the economy by cutting taxes, it must decide whose taxes will be cut. If it tries to stimulate the economy with government spending, it must decide what to spend the money on.

Monetary policy, in contrast, does not involve such choices: when the central bank cuts interest rates to fight a recession, it cuts everyone's interest rate at the same time. So a shift from relying on fiscal policy to relying on monetary policy makes macroeconomics a more technical, less political issue. In fact, as we learned in Chapter 14, monetary policy in most major economies is set by an independent central bank that is insulated from the political process.

Milton Friedman and his co-author Anna Schwartz played a key role in convincing macroeconomists of the importance of monetary policy.

Monetarism asserted that GDP will grow steadily if the money supply grows steadily.

Monetarism

After the publication of *A Monetary History,* Milton Friedman led a movement that sought to eliminate macroeconomic policy activism while maintaining the importance of monetary policy. **Monetarism** asserted that GDP will grow steadily if the money supply grows steadily. The monetarist policy prescription was to have the central bank target a constant rate of growth of the money supply, such as 3% per year, and maintain that target regardless of any fluctuations in the economy.

It's important to realize that monetarism retained many Keynesian ideas. Like Keynes, Friedman asserted that the short run is important and that short-run changes in aggregate demand affect aggregate output as well as aggregate prices. Like Keynes, he argued that policy should have been much more expansionary during the Great Depression.

Monetarists argued, however, that most of the efforts of policy makers to smooth out the economy's ups and downs actually make things worse. In Chapter 12 we discussed the reasons macroeconomists are skeptical about the usefulness of *discretionary fiscal policy*—changes in taxes or spending, or both, in response to the perceived state of the economy. As we explained there, government perceptions about the economy often lag behind reality, and there are further lags both in changing fiscal policy and in the effects of fiscal policy on the economy. As a result, discretionary fiscal policies intended to fight a recession often end up feeding a boom, and vice versa.

Friedman also argued that if the central bank followed his advice and refused to change the money supply in response to fluctuations in the economy, fiscal policy would be much less effective than Keynesians believed. In Chapter 9 we analyzed the phenomenon of *crowding out*, in which government deficits drive up interest rates and lead to reduced investment spending. Friedman and others pointed out that if the money supply is held fixed while the government pursues an expansionary fiscal policy, crowding out will limit the effect of the fiscal expansion on aggregate demand.

Figure 17-4 illustrates this argument. Panel (a) shows aggregate output and the aggregate price level. AD_1 is the initial aggregate demand curve and $SRAS$ is the short-run aggregate supply curve. At the initial equilibrium E_1, the level of aggregate output is Y_1 and the aggregate price level is P_1. Panel (b) shows the money market. MS is the money supply curve and MD_1 is the initial money demand curve, so the initial interest rate is r_1.

Now suppose the government increases purchases of goods and services. We know that this will shift the AD curve rightward, as illustrated by the shift from AD_1 to

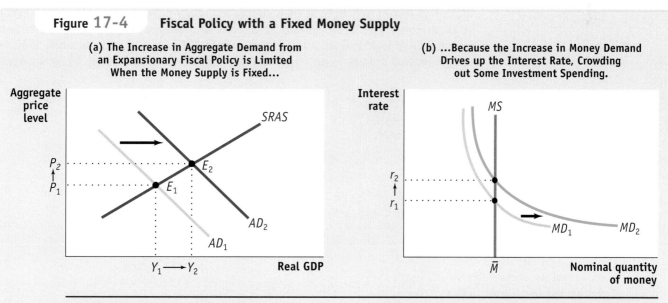

Figure 17-4 Fiscal Policy with a Fixed Money Supply

(a) The Increase in Aggregate Demand from an Expansionary Fiscal Policy is Limited When the Money Supply is Fixed...

(b) ...Because the Increase in Money Demand Drives up the Interest Rate, Crowding out Some Investment Spending.

In panel (a) an expansionary fiscal policy shifts the AD curve rightward, driving up both the aggregate price level and aggregate output. However, this leads to an increase in the demand for money. If the money supply is held fixed, as in panel (b), the increase in money demand drives up the interest rate, reducing investment spending and offsetting part of the fiscal expansion. So the shift of the AD curve is less than it would otherwise be: fiscal policy becomes less effective when the money supply is held fixed.

AD_2, and that aggregate output will rise, from Y_1 to Y_2, and the aggregate price level will rise, from P_1 to P_2. Both the rise in aggregate output and the rise in the aggregate price level will, however, increase the demand for money, shifting the money demand curve rightward from MD_1 to MD_2. This drives up the equilibrium interest rate, to r_2. Friedman's point was that this rise in the interest rate reduces investment spending, partially offsetting the initial rise in government spending. As a result, the rightward shift of the AD curve is smaller than the multiplier analysis in Chapter 12 indicated. And Friedman argued that with a constant money supply, the multiplier is so small that there's not much point in using fiscal policy.

But Friedman didn't favor activist monetary policy either. He argued that the same problems that limit the ability of the government to stabilize the economy using discretionary fiscal policy also apply to **discretionary monetary policy,** in which the central bank changes interest rates or the money supply based on its assessment of the state of the economy.

Friedman's solution was to put monetary policy on "autopilot." The central bank, he argued, should follow a **monetary policy rule,** a formula that determines its actions. During the 1960s and 1970s, most monetarists believed that the best monetary policy rule was to target slow, steady growth in the money supply. They thought this would work because they believed that the *velocity of money,* which we defined in Chapter 14 as the ratio of nominal GDP to the quantity of money, was stable in the short run and changes only gradually. Recall the velocity equation:

$$M \times V = P \times Y$$

In this equation, M is the money supply, V is the velocity of money, P is the aggregate price level, and Y is real GDP (so that $P \times Y$ is nominal GDP.) Monetarists believed that V was stable, so they believed that if the Federal Reserve kept M on a steady growth path, nominal GDP would also grow steadily.

Monetarism strongly influenced actual monetary policy in the late 1970s and early 1980s, as described in the Economics in Action that follows this section. It quickly became clear, however, that steady growth in the money supply didn't ensure steady growth in the economy: the velocity of money wasn't stable enough for such a simple policy rule to work. Figure 17-5 shows both why monetarists of the 1960s and 1970s had reason to believe in their simple monetary policy rule and how later events let them down. The figure shows the velocity of money, as measured by the ratio of nominal GDP to M1, from 1960 to the start of 2005. As you can see, until 1980 velocity followed a fairly smooth, seemingly predictable trend. After 1980, however,

> When the central bank changes interest rates or the money supply based on its assessment of the state of the economy, it is engaging in **discretionary monetary policy.**
>
> A **monetary policy rule** is a formula that determines the central bank's actions.

Figure 17-5

The Velocity of Money

From 1960 to 1980, the velocity of money was stable, leading monetarists to believe that steady growth in the money supply would lead to a stable economy. After 1980, however, velocity began moving erratically, undermining the case for traditional monetarism. 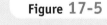**web...**

Source: Federal Reserve Bank of St. Louis.

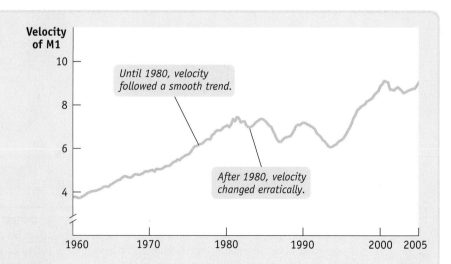

after the Fed began to adopt monetarist ideas, the velocity of money began shifting around erratically—probably due to financial market innovations.

Traditional monetarists are hard to find among today's macroeconomists. As we'll see later in the chapter, however, the monetarist idea that too much discretion in monetary policy is counterproductive has been widely accepted by macroeconomists.

Inflation and the Natural Rate of Unemployment

At the same time that monetarists were challenging Keynesian views about how macroeconomic policy should be conducted, other economists—some but not all of them monetarists—were emphasizing the limits to what activist macroeconomic policy could achieve.

In the 1940s and 1950s, many Keynesian economists believed that expansionary fiscal policy could be used to achieve full employment on a permanent basis. In the 1960s, however, many economists realized that expansionary policies could cause problems with inflation, but they still believed policy makers could choose to trade off low unemployment for higher inflation even in the long run.

In 1968, however, Milton Friedman and Edmund Phelps of Columbia University, working independently, proposed the concept of the natural rate of unemployment, which we discussed in Chapter 15. We showed there that the natural rate of unemployment is also the nonaccelerating inflation rate of unemployment, or NAIRU. According to the hypothesis of the NAIRU, inflation eventually gets built into expectations, so any attempt to keep the unemployment rate below the natural rate will lead to an ever-rising inflation rate.

The natural rate hypothesis gives a more limited role to activist macroeconomic policy than did earlier ideas. Because the government can't keep unemployment below the natural rate, its task is not to keep unemployment low but to keep it *stable*—to prevent large fluctuations in unemployment in either direction.

The important point to notice about the Friedman–Phelps hypothesis is that it made a strong prediction. Friedman and Phelps claimed that the apparent trade-off between unemployment and inflation would not survive an extended period of rising prices: once inflation was embedded in the public's expectations, inflation would continue even in the face of high unemployment. Sure enough, that's exactly what happened in the 1970s. This successful prediction was one of the triumphs of macroeconomic analysis, and it convinced the great majority of economists that the natural rate hypothesis was correct. In contrast to traditional monetarism, which declined in influence as more evidence accumulated, the natural rate hypothesis has become almost universally accepted among macroeconomists, with a few qualifications. (Some macroeconomists believe that at very low or negative rates of inflation the hypothesis doesn't work.)

The Political Business Cycle

One final challenge to Keynesian economics focused not on the validity of the economic analysis but on its political consequences. A number of economists and political scientists pointed out that activist macroeconomic policy lends itself to political manipulation.

Statistical evidence suggests that election results tend to be determined by the state of the economy in the months just before the election. In the United States, if the economy is growing rapidly and the unemployment rate is falling in the six months or so before Election Day, the incumbent party tends to be re-elected even if the economy performed poorly in the preceding three years.

This creates an obvious temptation to abuse activist macroeconomic policy: pump up the economy in an election year, and pay the price in higher inflation and/or higher unemployment later. The result can be unnecessary instability in the economy, a **political business cycle** caused by the use of macroeconomic policy to serve political ends.

An often-cited example is the combination of expansionary fiscal and monetary policy that led to rapid growth in the U.S. economy just before the 1972 election and a sharp acceleration in inflation after the election. Kenneth Rogoff, a respected macroeconomist

A **political business cycle** results when politicians use macroeconomic policy to serve political ends.

who served as chief economist at the International Monetary Fund, has proclaimed Richard Nixon, the president at the time, "the all-time hero of political business cycles."

As we saw in Chapter 14, one way to avoid a political business cycle is to place monetary policy in the hands of an independent central bank, insulated from political pressure. The political business cycle is also a reason to rule out the use of discretionary fiscal policy except in extreme circumstances.

economics in action

The Fed's Flirtation with Monetarism

In the late 1970s and early 1980s the Federal Reserve flirted with monetarism. For most of its prior existence, the Fed had targeted interest rates, adjusting its target based on the state of the economy. In the late 1970s, however, the Fed began announcing target ranges for several measures of the money supply. It also stopped setting targets for interest rates. Most people saw these changes as a strong move toward monetarism.

In 1982, however, the Fed turned its back on monetarism. Since 1982 the Fed has pursued a discretionary monetary policy, which has led to large swings in the money supply. And at the end of the 1980s, the Fed went back to setting target levels for the interest rate.

Why did the Fed flirt with monetarism, then give it up? The turn to monetarism largely reflected the events of the 1970s, when a sharp rise in inflation had the effect of discrediting traditional economic policies. Also, the fact that the natural rate hypothesis had successfully predicted a worsening of the trade-off between unemployment and inflation increased the prestige of Milton Friedman and his intellectual followers. So policy makers were willing to try Friedman's policy proposals.

The turn away from monetarism also reflected events: as we saw in Figure 17-5, the velocity of money, which had followed a smooth trend before 1980, became erratic after 1980. This made monetarism seem like a much less good idea. ■

< < < < < < < < < < < < < < < < < < <

>>CHECK YOUR UNDERSTANDING 17-3

1. Panel (a) of the figure on page 415 shows recent movements in M1. What would that diagram have looked like if the Fed had been following a monetarist policy since 1996?

2. Now look at Figure 17-5 on page 424. What problems do you think the United States would have had since 1996 if the Fed had followed a monetarist policy?

Solutions appear at back of book.

Rational Expectations, Real Business Cycles, and New Classical Macroeconomics

As we have seen, one key difference between classical economics and Keynesian economics is that classical economists believed that the short-run aggregate supply curve is vertical, but Keynes emphasized the idea that the aggregate supply curve slopes upward in the short run. As a result, Keynes argued that demand shocks—shifts in the aggregate demand curve—can cause fluctuations in aggregate output.

The challenges to Keynesian economics that arose in the 1950s and 1960s—the renewed emphasis on monetary policy and the natural rate hypothesis—didn't question the view that an increase in aggregate demand leads to a rise in aggregate output in the short run and that a decrease in aggregate demand leads to a fall in aggregate output in the short run. In the 1970s and 1980s, however, some economists developed an approach to the business cycle known as **new classical macroeconomics,** which returned to the classical view that shifts in the aggregate demand curve affect only the aggregate price level, not aggregate output. The new approach evolved in two steps. First, some economists challenged traditional arguments about the slope of the short-run aggregate supply curve based on the concept

New classical macroeconomics is an approach to the business cycle that returns to the classical view that shifts in the aggregate demand curve affect only the aggregate price level, not aggregate output.

of *rational expectations.* Second, some economists suggested that changes in productivity cause economic fluctuations, a view known as *real business cycle theory.*

Rational Expectations

In the 1970s a concept known as *rational expectations* had a powerful impact on macroeconomics. **Rational expectations,** a theory originally introduced by John Muth in 1961, is the view that individuals and firms make decisions optimally, using all available information.

> **Rational expectations** is the view that individuals and firms make decisions optimally, using all available information.

For example, workers and employers bargaining over long-term wage contracts need to estimate the inflation rate they expect over the life of that contract. Rational expectations says that in making estimates of future inflation, they won't just look at past rates of inflation; they will also take into account available information about monetary and fiscal policy. Suppose that prices didn't rise last year but that the monetary and fiscal policies announced by policy makers make it clear to economic analysts that there will be substantial inflation over the next few years. According to rational expectations, long-term wage contracts will reflect this future inflation, even though prices didn't rise in the past.

Rational expectations can make a major difference in the effects of government policy. According to the original version of the natural rate hypothesis, a government attempt to trade off higher inflation for lower unemployment would work in the short run but would eventually fail because higher inflation would get built into expectations. According to rational expectations, we should remove the word *eventually:* if it's clear that the government intends to trade off higher inflation for lower unemployment, the public will understand this, and inflation expectations will immediately rise.

In the 1970s Robert Lucas of the University of Chicago, in a series of very influential papers, used this logic to argue that monetary policy can change the level of unemployment only if it comes as a surprise to the public. If his analysis was right, monetary policy isn't useful in stabilizing the economy after all. In 1995, Lucas won the Nobel Prize in economics for this work, which remains widely admired. However, many—perhaps most—macroeconomists, especially those advising policy makers, now believe that his conclusions were overstated. The Federal Reserve certainly thinks that it can play a useful role in economic stabilization, a view seconded by the quote from the *2004 Economic Report of the President* that opened this chapter. Nonetheless, the idea of rational expectations did serve as a useful caution for macroeconomists who had become excessively optimistic about their ability to manage the economy.

Real Business Cycles

In Chapter 8 we introduced the concept of *total factor productivity,* the amount of output that can be generated with a given level of factor inputs. Total factor productivity grows over time, but that growth isn't smooth. In the 1980s a number of economists argued that slowdowns in productivity growth, which they attributed to pauses in technological progress, are the main cause of recessions. **Real business cycle theory** says that fluctuations in the rate of growth of total factor productivity cause the business cycle. In the early days of real business cycle theory, the theory's proponents denied that changes in aggregate demand have any effect on aggregate output.

> According to **real business cycle theory,** fluctuations in the rate of growth of total factor productivity cause the business cycle.

This theory was strongly influential, as shown by the fact that two of the founders of real business cycle theory, Finn Kydland of Carnegie-Mellon University and Edward Prescott of the Federal Reserve Bank of Minneapolis, won the 2004 Nobel Prize in economics. The current status of real business cycle theory, however, is somewhat similar to that of rational expectations. The theory is widely recognized as having made valuable contributions to our understanding of the economy, and it serves as a useful caution against too much emphasis on aggregate demand. But many of the real business cycle theorists themselves now acknowledge that their models need an upward-sloping aggregate supply curve to fit the data—and that this gives aggregate demand a potential role in determining aggregate output. And as we have seen, policy makers believe strongly that aggregate demand policy has an important role to play in fighting recessions.

SUPPLY-SIDE ECONOMICS

During the 1970s a group of economic writers began propounding a view of economic policy that came to be known as "supply-side economics." The core of this view was the belief that reducing tax rates, and so increasing the incentives to work and invest, would have a powerful positive effect on the growth rate of potential output. The supply-siders urged the government to cut taxes without worrying about matching spending cuts: economic growth, they argued, would offset any negative effects from budget deficits. Some supply-siders even argued that a cut in tax *rates* would have such a miraculous effect on economic growth that tax *revenues*—the total

amount taxpayers pay to the government—would actually rise.

In the 1970s supply-side economics was enthusiastically supported by the editors of the *Wall Street Journal* and other figures in the media, and it became popular with politicians. In 1980 Ronald Reagan made supply-side economics the basis of his presidential campaign.

Because supply-side economics emphasizes supply rather than demand, and because the supply-siders themselves are harshly critical of Keynesian economics, it might seem as if supply-side theory belongs in our discussion of new classical macroeconomics. But unlike rational expectations and real business cycle

theory, supply-side economics is generally dismissed by economic researchers.

The main reason for this dismissal is lack of evidence. Almost all economists agree that tax cuts increase incentives to work and invest, but attempts to estimate these incentive effects indicate that at current U.S. levels they aren't nearly strong enough to back the strong claims made by supply-siders. In particular, the supply-side doctrine implies that large tax cuts, such as those implemented by Ronald Reagan in the early 1980s, should sharply raise potential output. Yet estimates of potential output by the Congressional Budget Office and others show no sign of an acceleration in growth after the Reagan tax cuts.

economics in action

Total Factor Productivity and the Business Cycle

Real business cycle theory argues that fluctuations in the rate of growth of total factor productivity are the principal cause of business cycles. Although many macroeconomists dispute that claim, the theory did draw attention to the fact that there is a strong correlation between the rate of total factor productivity growth and the business cycle. Figure 17-6 shows the annual rate of total factor productivity growth estimated by the Bureau of Labor Statistics. The shaded areas represent recessions. Clearly, recessions tend also to be periods in which the growth of total factor productivity slows sharply or even turns negative. And real business cycle theorists deserve a lot of credit for drawing economists' attention to this fact.

There are, however, disputes about how to interpret this correlation. In the early days of real business cycle theory, new classical macroeconomists argued that

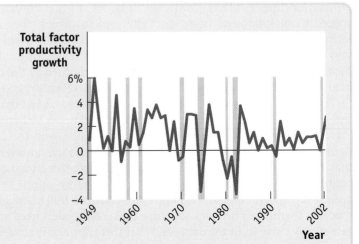

Figure 17-6

Total Factor Productivity and the Business Cycle

There is a clear correlation between declines in the rate of total factor productivity growth and recessions (indicated by the shaded areas). Real business cycle theory says that fluctuations in productivity growth are the main cause of business cycles. Other economists argue, however, that business cycles cause productivity fluctuations, not the other way around.

Source: Bureau of Labor Statistics; National Bureau of Economic Research.

productivity fluctuations are entirely the result of uneven technological progress. Critics pointed out, however, that in really severe recessions, like those of 1974–1975 or the early 1980s, total factor productivity actually declines. And it's hard to believe that technology actually moved backward during those periods.

So what is going on during these periods of declining total factor productivity? Some economists argue that declining productivity during recessions is a result, not a cause, of economic downturns. An example may be helpful. Suppose we measure productivity at the local post office by the number of pieces of mail handled, divided by the number of postal workers. Since the post office doesn't lay off workers whenever there's a slow mail day, days on which not much mail comes in will seem to be days on which the workers are especially unproductive. But the slump in business is causing the apparent decline in productivity, not the other way around.

It's now widely accepted that some of the correlation between total factor productivity and the business cycle is the result of the effect of the business cycle on productivity, rather than the reverse. But the extent to which this is true is a subject of continuing research. ■   >

>> CHECK YOUR UNDERSTANDING 17-4

1. In early 2001, as it became clear that the United States was experiencing a recession, the Fed stated that it would fight the recession with an aggressive monetary policy. By 2004, most observers concluded that this aggressive monetary expansion should be given credit for ending the recession.

   a. What would rational expectations theorists say about this conclusion?
   b. What would real business cycle theorists say?

   Solutions appear at back of book.

The Modern Consensus

As we've seen, there were intense debates about macroeconomics in the 1960s, 1970s, and 1980s. More recently, however, things have settled down. The age of macroeconomic controversy is by no means over, but there is now a broad consensus about several crucial macroeconomic issues.

To understand the modern consensus, where it came from, and what still remains in dispute, we'll look at how macroeconomists have changed their answers to five key questions about macroeconomic policy. The five questions, and the answers given by macroeconomists over the past 70 years, are summarized in Table 17-1. Notice that classical macroeconomics said no to each question; basically, classical macroeconomists didn't think macroeconomic policy could accomplish very much. But let's go through the questions one by one.

TABLE 17-1

Five Key Questions About Macroeconomic Policy

	Classical macroeconomics	Keynesian macroeconomics	Monetarism	Modern consensus
Is expansionary monetary policy helpful in fighting recessions?	No	Not very	Yes	Yes, except in special circumstances
Is fiscal policy effective in fighting recessions?	No	Yes	No	Yes
Can monetary and/or fiscal policy reduce unemployment in the long run?	No	Yes	No	No
Should fiscal policy be used in a discretionary way?	No	Yes	No	No, except in special circumstances
Should monetary policy be used in a discretionary way?	No	Yes	No	Still in dispute

Is Expansionary Monetary Policy Helpful in Fighting Recessions?

As we've seen, classical macroeconomists generally believed that expansionary monetary policy was ineffective or even harmful in fighting recessions. In the early years of Keynesian economics, macroeconomists weren't against monetary expansion during recessions, but they tended to believe that it was of doubtful effectiveness. Milton Friedman and his followers convinced economists that monetary policy is effective after all.

Nearly all macroeconomists now agree that monetary policy can be used to shift the aggregate demand curve and to reduce economic instability. The classical view that changes in the money supply affect only aggregate prices, not aggregate output, has few supporters today. The view once held by some Keynesian economists—that changes in the money supply have little effect—has equally few supporters. The exception to this view is the case of a liquidity trap, in which monetary policy is ineffective.

Is Fiscal Policy Effective in Fighting Recessions?

Classical macroeconomists were, if anything, even more opposed to fiscal expansion than monetary expansion. Keynesian economists, on the other hand, gave fiscal policy a central role in fighting recessions. Monetarists argued that fiscal policy was ineffective as long as the money supply was held constant. But that strong view has become relatively rare.

Most macroeconomists now agree that fiscal policy, like monetary policy, can shift the aggregate demand curve. Most macroeconomists also agree that the government should not seek to balance the budget regardless of the state of the economy: they agree that the role of the budget as an automatic stabilizer, as discussed in Chapter 12, helps keep the economy on an even keel.

Can Monetary and/or Fiscal Policy Reduce Unemployment in the Long Run?

Classical macroeconomists didn't believe the government could do anything about unemployment. Some Keynesian economists moved to the opposite extreme, arguing that expansionary policies could be used to achieve a permanently low unemployment rate, perhaps at the cost of some inflation. Monetarists believed that unemployment could not be kept below the natural rate.

Almost all macroeconomists now accept the natural rate hypothesis. This hypothesis leads them to accept sharp limits to what monetary and fiscal policy can accomplish. Effective monetary and fiscal policy, most macroeconomists believe, can limit the size of fluctuations of the actual unemployment rate around the natural rate, but they can't be used to keep unemployment below the natural rate.

Should Fiscal Policy Be Used in a Discretionary Way?

As we've already seen, views about the effectiveness of fiscal policy have gone back and forth, from rejection by classical macroeconomists, to a positive view by Keynesian economists, to a negative view once again by monetarists. Today most macroeconomists believe that tax cuts and spending increases are at least somewhat effective in increasing aggregate demand.

Many, but not all, macroeconomists, however, believe that *discretionary fiscal policy* is usually counterproductive, for the reasons discussed in Chapter 12: the lags in adjusting fiscal policy mean that all too often, policies intended to fight a slump end up intensifying a boom.

As a result, the macroeconomic consensus gives monetary policy the lead role in economic stabilization. Discretionary fiscal policy plays the leading role only in special circumstances when monetary policy may not be able to do the job, such as those facing Japan in the 1990s.

Should Monetary Policy Be Used in a Discretionary Way?

Classical macroeconomists didn't think that monetary policy should be used to fight recessions; Keynesian economists didn't oppose discretionary policy, but they were skeptical about its effectiveness. Monetarists argued that discretionary monetary policy was doing more harm than good. Where are we today? This remains an area of dispute.

Today there is a broad consensus among macroeconomists on these points:

- Monetary policy should play the main role in stabilization policy.
- The central bank should be independent, insulated from political pressures, in order to avoid a political business cycle.
- Discretionary fiscal policy should be used sparingly, both because of policy lags and because of the risks of a political business cycle.

There are, however, debates over how the central bank should set its policy. Should the central bank be given a simple, clearly defined target for its policies, or should it be given discretion to manage the economy as it sees fit? If the central bank has a target, what should it be? And—a particular concern in recent years—should the central bank consider the management of asset prices, such as stock prices, part of its responsibility?

Central Bank Targets It may sound funny to say this, but it's not clear exactly what the Federal Reserve, the central bank of the United States, is trying to achieve. Clearly it wants a stable economy with price stability, but there isn't any document setting out the Fed's official view about exactly how stable the economy should be or what the inflation rate should be.

This is not necessarily a bad thing. Experienced staff at the Fed generally believe that the absence of specific guidelines gives the central bank flexibility in coping with economic events, and that history proves the Fed uses that flexibility well. In practice, chairmen of the Fed tend to stay in office for a long time—William McChesney Martin was chairman from 1951 to 1970, and Alan Greenspan, appointed in 1987, was still serving as chairman in 2005. These long-serving chairmen acquire personal credibility that reassures the public that the central bank's power will be used well.

But other countries believe that their central banks need formal guidelines, and some American economists—including some members of the Federal Reserve Board of Governors—believe that the United States should follow suit. The best-known example of a central bank using formal guidelines is the Bank of England. Until 1997, the Bank of England was simply an arm of the British Treasury Department, with no independence. When it became an independent organization like the Federal Reserve, it was also given a guideline: it is supposed to keep the inflation rate at 2.1%.

Inflation targeting—requiring the central bank to seek to keep the inflation rate near a predetermined target rate—is now advocated by many macroeconomists. Others, however, believe that such a rule can limit the ability of the central bank to respond to events, such as a stock market crash or a world financial crisis.

In practice, the Fed acts as if it seeks to keep the inflation rate somewhere between 2% and 3%. That is, the Fed's informal policy doesn't look very different from the Bank of England's formal policy. But there is likely to be intense debate over the next few years about whether to give the Fed an explicit inflation target.

Setting a Target Inflation Rate If a central bank has an inflation target, formal or informal, what should that target be? The Bank of England has a 2.1% target; the

Alan Greenspan was appointed chairman of the Federal Reserve Board of Governors in 1987. His long tenure helped give the Fed credibility. In 2006, Ben Bernanke succeeded him.

Inflation targeting requires that the central bank try to keep the inflation rate near a predetermined target rate.

European Central Bank's rules say that it should seek "price stability," which it has defined as 0%–2% inflation. Does it matter, and which target is better?

Some macroeconomists believe that *strict price stability*—an inflation rate close to 0%—helps stabilize the economy because it leads the public to consider money a truly stable measure of value. As we explained in Chapter 16, however, other macroeconomists worry that too low an inflation rate creates a risk that the interest rate will fall to 0% during a recession, making monetary policy ineffective. The rule for the Bank of England reflects that concern. If the Fed ever moves to an explicit inflation target, there will be an intense debate over the issue in the United States.

Asset Prices During the 1990s many economists warned that the stock market was losing touch with reality—that people buying shares in American corporations were paying prices much higher than made sense given realistic forecasts of those companies' future profits. Among these economists was Alan Greenspan, the chairman of the Federal Reserve, who warned about "irrational exuberance" in a famous speech. In 2000 the stock market headed downward. Americans who had invested in the stock market suddenly felt poorer and so cut back on spending, helping push the economy into a recession.

These events brought new emphasis to a long-standing debate over monetary policy. Should the central bank restrict its concerns to inflation and possibly unemployment, or should it also try to prevent extreme movements in asset prices, such as the average value of stocks or the average price of houses?

One view is that the central bank shouldn't try to second-guess the value investors place on assets like stocks or houses, even if it suspects that those prices are getting out of line. That is, the central bank shouldn't raise interest rates to curb stock prices or housing prices if overall consumer price inflation remains low. If an overvalued stock market eventually falls and depresses aggregate demand, the central bank can deal with that by cutting interest rates.

The alternative view warns that after a bubble bursts—after over-valued asset prices fall to earth—it may be difficult to offset the effects on aggregate demand. After having seen the Japanese economy struggle for years with deflation in the aftermath of the collapse of its bubble economy, proponents of this view argue that the central bank should act to rein in irrational exuberance when it is happening, even if consumer price inflation isn't a problem.

As we explain in the Economics in Action that follows, the 2001 recession and its aftermath gave ammunition to both sides in this debate, which shows no sign of ending.

The Clean Little Secret of Macroeconomics

It's important to keep the debates we have just described in perspective. Macroeconomics has always been a contentious field, much more so than microeconomics. There will always be debates about appropriate policies. But the striking thing about current debates is how modest the differences among macroeconomists really are. The clean little secret of modern macroeconomics is how much consensus economists have reached over the past 70 years.

economics in action

After the Bubble

During the 1990s, many economists worried that stock prices were irrationally high, and these worries proved justified. By late 2002 the NASDAQ, an index made up largely of technology stocks, had lost two-thirds of its peak value. And in 2001 the plunge in stock prices helped push the United States into recession.

The Fed responded with large, rapid interest rate cuts. But should it have tried to burst the stock bubble when it was happening?

Many economists expected the aftermath of the 1990s stock market bubble to settle, once and for all, the question of whether central banks should concern themselves about asset prices. But the test results came out ambiguous, failing to settle the issue.

If the Fed had been unable to engineer a recovery—if the U.S. economy had slid into a liquidity trap like that of Japan—critics of the Fed's previous inaction would have had a very strong case. But the recession was, in fact, short: the National Bureau of Economic Research says that the recession began in March 2001 and ended in November 2001.

But if the Fed had been able to produce a quick, strong recovery, its inaction during the 1990s would have been strongly vindicated. Unfortunately, that didn't happen either. Although the economy began recovering in late 2001, the recovery was initially weak—so weak that employment continued to drop until the summer of 2003. Also, the fact that the Fed had to cut the federal funds rate to only 1%—not much above 0%—suggested that the U.S. economy had come dangerously close to a liquidity trap.

In other words, the events of 2001–2003 probably intensified the debate over monetary policy and asset prices, rather than resolving it. ∎

> >—

>> QUICK REVIEW

➤ There is a broad consensus that monetary policy is effective but that it can only stabilize the economy, not reduce unemployment below the natural rate.

➤ There is also a broad consensus that discretionary fiscal policy should be avoided except in exceptional cases.

➤ There is a broad consensus that central banks should be independent, but there are disagreements about whether they should have formal *inflation targets*, what these targets should be, and how to deal with asset prices.

>>CHECK YOUR UNDERSTANDING 17-5

1. The United States entered the 2001 recession with an inflation rate of about 3%. Suppose that the inflation rate in early 2001 had been much lower, maybe even 0%. How would this have created problems for monetary policy?

2. Why would the Fed's job after 2001 have been easier if it had somehow managed to prevent stock prices from escalating at the end of the 1990s?

Solutions appear at back of book.

• A LOOK AHEAD •

We have now given a comprehensive overview of the state of modern macroeconomics, with one major exception: we haven't looked at the implications of international trade and international movements of capital. These have become increasingly important in the modern world economy. In the next two chapters we will turn to *open-economy macroeconomics*, the issues raised by the fact that modern economies are "open" to the world.

SUMMARY

1. Classical macroeconomics asserted that monetary policy affected only the aggregate price level, not aggregate output, and that the short run was unimportant. By the 1930s, measurement of business cycles was a well-established subject, but there was no widely accepted theory of business cycles.

2. **Keynesian economics** attributed the business cycle to shifts of the aggregate demand curve, often the result of changes in business confidence. Keynesian economics also offered a rationale for **macroeconomic policy activism.**

3. In the decades that followed Keynes's work, economists came to agree that monetary policy as well as fiscal policy is effective under certain conditions. **Monetarism,** a doctrine that called for a **monetary policy rule** as opposed to **discretionary monetary policy,** and which argued that GDP would grow steadily if the money supply grew steadily, was influential for a time but was eventually rejected by many macroeconomists.

4. The natural rate hypothesis became almost universally accepted, limiting the role of macroeconomic policy to stabilizing the economy rather than seeking a permanently lower unemployment rate. Fears of a **political business cycle** led to a consensus that monetary policy should be insulated from politics.

5. **Rational expectations** suggested that even in the short run there might not be a trade-off between inflation and unemployment because expected inflation would change immediately in the face of expected changes in policy.

Real business cycle theory argued that changes in the rate of growth of total factor productivity are the main cause of business cycles. Both of these versions of **new classical macroeconomics** received wide attention and respect, but policy makers and many economists haven't accepted the conclusion that monetary and fiscal policy are ineffective in changing aggregate output.

6. The modern consensus is that monetary and fiscal policy are both effective in the short run but that neither can re-

duce the unemployment rate in the long run. Discretionary fiscal policy is considered generally unadvisable, except in special circumstances.

7. There are continuing debates about the appropriate role of monetary policy. Some economists advocate the explicit use of an **inflation target,** but others oppose it. There's also a debate about whether monetary policy should take steps to manage asset prices.

KEY TERMS

Keynesian economics, p. 419
Macroeconomic policy activism, p. 420
Monetarism, p. 422
Discretionary monetary policy, p. 424

Monetary policy rule, p. 424
Political business cycle, p. 425
New classical macroeconomics, p.426

Rational expectations, p. 427
Real business cycle theory, p. 427
Inflation targeting, p. 431

PROBLEMS

1. Since the crash of its stock market in 1989, the Japanese economy has seen little economic growth and some deflation. The accompanying table from the Organization for Economic Cooperation and Development (OECD) shows some key macroeconomic data for Japan for 1991 (a "normal" year) and 1995–2003. How did Japan's policy makers try to promote growth in the economy during this time? How does this fit in with the Keynesian and classical models of the macroeconomy?

Year	Real GDP annual growth rate	Short-term interest rate	Government debt (percent of GDP)	Government budget deficit (percent of GDP)
1991	3.4%	7.38%	64.8%	−1.81%
1995	1.9	1.23	87.1	4.71
1996	3.4	0.59	93.9	5.07
1997	1.9	0.6	100.3	3.79
1998	−1.1	0.72	112.2	5.51
1999	0.1	0.25	125.7	7.23
2000	2.8	0.25	134.1	7.48
2001	0.4	0.12	142.3	6.13
2002	−0.3	0.06	149.3	7.88
2003	2.5	0.04	157.5	7.67

2. The National Bureau of Economic Research (NBER) maintains the official chronology of past U.S. business cycles. Go to its website at http://www.nber.org/cycles/cyclesmain.html to answer the following questions.

a. How many business cycles have occurred since the end of World War II in1945?

b. What was the average duration of a business cycle when measured from the end of one expansion (its peak) to the end of the next? That is, what was the average duration of a business cycle in the period from1945 to the present?

c. When and what was the last announcement by the NBER's Business Cycle Dating Committee?

3. The fall of the Soviet Union in 1989 and the subsequent reduction in U.S. defense spending helped ease some of the inflationary pressure in the United States that could have occurred during the strong economic growth of the late 1990s. Using the data in the accompanying table from the *Economic Report of the President,* replicate Figure 17-3 for the 1990–2000 period. Why would a Keynesian see the decrease in defense spending as fortunate?

Year	Budget deficit (percent of GDP)	Unemployment rate
1990	3.9%	5.6%
1991	4.5	6.8
1992	4.7	7.5
1993	3.9	6.9
1994	2.9	6.1
1995	2.2	5.6
1996	1.4	5.4
1997	0.3	4.9
1998	−0.8	4.5
1999	−1.4	4.2
2000	−2.4	4.0

4. In the modern world, central banks are free to increase or reduce the money supply as they see fit. However, some people harken back to the "good old days" of the gold standard. Under the gold standard, the money supply could only expand when the amount of available gold increased.

   a. Under the gold standard, if the velocity of money was stable when the economy was expanding, what would have had to happen to keep prices stable?

   b. John Maynard Keynes once dismissed the gold standard as a "barbarous relic." Why would he have considered it a bad idea?

5. The chapter explains that Kenneth Rogoff proclaimed Richard Nixon "the all-time hero of political business cycles." Using the accompanying table of data from the *Economic Report of the President,* explain why Nixon may have earned that title. (*Note:* Nixon entered office in January 1969 and was re-elected in November 1972. He resigned in August 1974.)

6. The economy of Albernia is facing a recessionary gap, and the leader of that nation calls together four of its best economists representing the classical, Keynesian, monetarist, and modern consensus views of the macroeconomy. Explain what policies each economist would recommend and why.

7. Which of the following policy recommendations are consistent with the classical, Keynesian, monetarist, and/or modern consensus views of the macroeconomy?

   a. Since the long-run growth of real GDP is 2%, the money supply should grow at 2%.

   b. Decrease government spending in order to decrease inflationary pressure.

   c. Increase the money supply in order to alleviate a recessionary gap.

   d. Always maintain a balanced budget.

   e. Decrease the budget deficit as a percent of GDP when facing a recessionary gap.

Year	Government receipts (billions of dollars)	Government spending (billions of dollars)	Government budget balance (billions of dollars)	M1 growth	M2 growth	3-month Treasury bill rate
1969	$186.9	$183.6	$3.2	3.3%	3.7%	6.68%
1970	192.8	195.6	−2.8	5.1	6.6	6.46
1971	187.1	210.2	−23.0	6.5	13.4	4.35
1972	207.3	230.7	−23.4	9.2	13.0	4.07
1973	230.8	245.7	−14.9	5.5	6.6	7.04

>**web...** To continue your study and review of concepts in this chapter, please visit the Krugman/Wells website for quizzes, animated graph tutorials, web links to helpful resources, and more.

www.worthpublishers.com/krugmanwells

18

>> International Trade

A ROSE BY ANY OTHER NATION

GIVING YOUR BELOVED ROSES ON Valentine's Day is a well-established tradition in the United States. But in the past it was a very expensive gesture: in the northern hemisphere, Valentine's Day falls not in summer, when roses are in bloom, but in the depths of winter. Until recently, that meant that the roses in the florist's shop were grown at great cost in heated greenhouses. Nowadays, however, most of the Valentine's Day roses sold in this country are flown in from South America, mainly from Colombia, where growing a rose in February is no trouble at all.

Is it a good thing that we now buy our winter roses from abroad? The vast majority of economists say yes: international trade, in which countries specialize in producing different goods and trade those goods with each other, is a source of mutual benefit to the countries involved. In Chapter 2 we laid out the basic principle that there are *gains from trade*; it's a principle that applies to countries as well as individuals.

But politicians and the public are often not convinced. In fact, during the 1996 presidential campaign one contender used the occasion of Valentine's Day to visit a flower-growing greenhouse in New Hampshire, where he denounced imports of South American roses as a threat to U.S. jobs.

Up to now this book has analyzed the economy as if it were self-sufficient, as if the economy produced all the goods and services it consumes, and vice versa. This is, of course, true of the world economy as a whole. But it is not true of any individual country. It's true that 40 years ago the United States exported only a small fraction of what it produced and imported only a

What do these sweethearts and this rose farmer have in common? They are enjoying the mutual benefits of international trade.

small fraction of what it consumed. Since then, however, both U.S. imports and U.S. exports have grown much faster than the U.S. economy as a whole. And other countries engage in far more foreign trade, relative to the size of their economies, than does the United States. To have a full picture of how national economies work, we must understand international trade.

This chapter examines the economics of international trade. We start from the model of comparative advantage, which, as we saw in Chapter 2, explains why there are gains from international trade. It's also important, however, to understand how some individuals can be hurt by international trade and the effects of trade policies that countries use to limit imports or promote exports.

Comparative Advantage and International Trade

The United States buys roses—and many other goods and services—from other countries. At the same time, it sells many goods and services to other countries. Goods and services purchased from abroad are **imports;** goods and services sold abroad are **exports.**

As illustrated by the opening story, imports and exports have taken on an increasingly important role in the U.S. economy. Over the last 40 years, both imports into the United States and exports from the United States have grown faster than the U.S. economy; panel (a) of Figure 18-1 shows how the values of imports and exports have grown as a percentage of gross domestic product. As panel (b) demonstrates, foreign trade is even more important for many other countries than for the United States.

To understand why international trade occurs and why economists believe it is beneficial to the economy, we will first review the concept of comparative advantage.

> Goods and services purchased from other countries are **imports;** goods and services sold to other countries are **exports.**

Figure 18-1   The Growing Importance of International Trade

Panel (a) illustrates the fact that over the past 40 years, the United States has exported a steadily growing share of its output (that is, its gross domestic product) to other countries and imported a growing share of what it consumes from abroad. Panel (b) demonstrates that international trade is even more important to many other countries than it is to the United States.

Source: U.S. Department of Commerce, National Income and Product Accounts [for panel (a)] and United Nations Human Development Report 2004 [for panel (b)].

Production Possibilities and Comparative Advantage, Revisited

To grow Valentine's Day roses, any country must use resources—labor, energy, capital, and so on—that could have been used to produce other things. The potential production of other goods a country must forgo to produce a rose is the opportunity cost of that rose.

It's a lot easier to grow Valentine's Day roses in Colombia, where the weather in January and February is nearly ideal, than it is in the United States. Conversely, other goods are not produced as easily in Colombia as in the United States. For example, Colombia doesn't have the base of skilled workers and technological know-how that makes the United States so good at producing high-technology goods. So the opportunity cost of a Valentine's Day rose, in terms of other goods such as computers, is much less in Colombia than it is in the United States.

And so we say that Colombia has a comparative advantage in producing roses. Let's repeat the definition of comparative advantage from Chapter 2: *a country has a comparative advantage in producing a good if the opportunity cost of producing the good is lower for that country than for other countries.*

Figure 18-2 provides a hypothetical numerical example of comparative advantage in international trade. We assume that only two goods are produced and consumed, roses and computers, and there are only two countries in the world, the United States and Colombia. We also assume that roses are shipped in standard refrigerated boxes, each containing 100 roses. The figure shows hypothetical production possibility frontiers for the United States and Colombia. As in Chapter 2, we simplify the model by assuming that the production possibility frontiers are straight lines, rather than the more realistic bowed-out shape shown in Figure 2-1. The straight-line shape implies that the opportunity cost of a box of roses in terms of computers in each country is constant—it does not depend on how many units of each good the country produces. The analysis of international trade under the assumption that opportunity costs are constant and therefore production possibility frontiers are

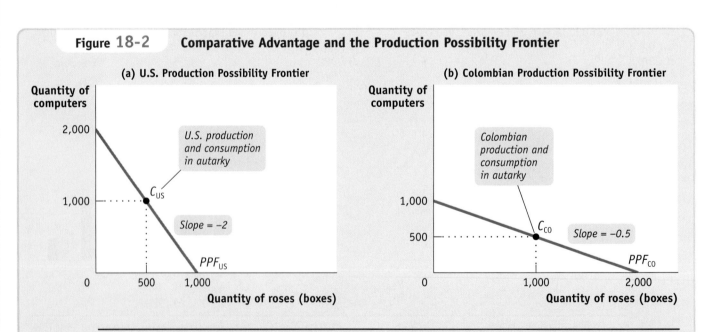

Figure 18-2   **Comparative Advantage and the Production Possibility Frontier**

(a) U.S. Production Possibility Frontier

(b) Colombian Production Possibility Frontier

The U.S. opportunity cost of a box of roses in terms of a computer is 2: 2 computers must be forgone for every additional box of roses produced. The Colombian opportunity cost of a box of roses in terms of a computer is 0.5: only 0.5 computer must be forgone for every additional box of roses produced. Therefore, Colombia has a comparative advantage in roses and the United States has a comparative advantage in computers. In autarky, C_{US} is the U.S. production and consumption bundle and C_{CO} is the Colombian production and consumption bundle. **>web...**

TABLE 18-1

Production Possibilities

(a) United States

	Production	
	One possibility	Another possibility
Quantity of roses (boxes)	1,000	0
Quantity of computers	0	2,000

(b) Colombia

	Production	
	One possibility	Another possibility
Quantity of roses (boxes)	2,000	0
Quantity of computers	0	1,000

straight lines is known as the **Ricardian model of international trade,** named after the English economist David Ricardo, who introduced this analysis in the early nineteenth century.

Table 18-1 presents the same information that is shown in Figure 18-2. We assume that the United States can produce 1,000 boxes of roses if it produces no computers or 2,000 computers if it produces no roses. The slope of the production possibility frontier in panel (a) is −2,000/1,000, or −2: to produce an additional box of roses, the United States must forgo the production of 2 computers.

Similarly, we assume that Colombia can produce 2,000 boxes of roses if it produces no computers or 1,000 computers if it produces no roses. The slope of the production possibility frontier in panel (b) is −1,000/2,000, or −0.5: to produce an additional box of roses, Colombia must forgo the production of 0.5 computer.

Economists use the term **autarky** to describe a situation in which a country cannot trade with other countries. We assume that in autarky the United States would choose to produce and consume 500 boxes of roses and 1,000 computers. This autarky production and consumption bundle is shown by point C_{US} in panel (a) of Figure 18-2. We also assume that in autarky Colombia would choose to produce and consume 1,000 boxes of roses and 500 computers, shown by point C_{CO} in panel (b). The outcome in autarky is summarized in Table 18-2, where world production and consumption is the sum of U.S. and Colombian production and consumption.

If the countries trade with each other, they can do better than they can in autarky. In this example, Colombia has a comparative advantage in the production of roses. That

> The **Ricardian model of international trade** analyzes international trade under the assumption that opportunity costs are constant.

> **Autarky** is a situation in which a country cannot trade with other countries.

TABLE 18-2

Production and Consumption Under Autarky

(a) United States

	Production	Consumption
Quantity of roses (boxes)	500	500
Quantity of computers	1,000	1,000

(b) Colombia

	Production	Consumption
Quantity of roses (boxes)	1,000	1,000
Quantity of computers	500	500

(c) World (United States and Colombia)

	Production	Consumption
Quantity of roses (boxes)	1,500	1,500
Quantity of computers	1,500	1,500

is, the opportunity cost of roses is lower in Colombia than in the United States: 0.5 computer per box of roses in Columbia versus 2 computers per box of roses in the United States. Conversely, the United States has a comparative advantage in the production of computers: to produce an additional computer, the United States must forgo the production of 0.5 box of roses, but producing an additional computer in Colombia requires forgoing the production of 2 boxes of roses. International trade allows each country to specialize in producing the good in which it has a comparative advantage: computers in the United States, roses in Colombia. And that leads to gains for both when they trade.

The Gains from International Trade

Figure 18-3 illustrates how both countries gain from specialization and trade. Again, panel (a) represents the United States and panel (b) represents Colombia. As a result of international trade, the United States produces at point Q_{US}: 2,000 computers but no roses. Colombia produces at Q_{CO}: 2,000 boxes of roses but no computers. The new production choices are given in the second column of Table 18-3.

By comparing Table 18-3 with Table 18-2, you can see that specialization increases total world production of *both* goods. In the absence of specialization, total world production consists of 1,500 computers and 1,500 boxes of roses. After specialization, total world production rises to 2,000 computers and 2,000 boxes of roses. These goods can now be traded, with the United States consuming roses produced in Colombia and Colombia consuming computers produced in the United States. The result is that each country can consume more of *both* goods than it did in autarky.

In addition to showing production under trade, Figure 18-3 shows one of many possible pairs of consumption bundles for the United States and Colombia, which is also given in Table 18-3. In this example, the United States moves from its autarky consumption of 1,000 computers and 500 boxes of roses, shown by C_{US}, to consumption after trade of 1,250 computers and 750 boxes of roses, represented by C'_{US}. Colombia moves from its autarky consumption of 500 computers and 1,000 boxes of

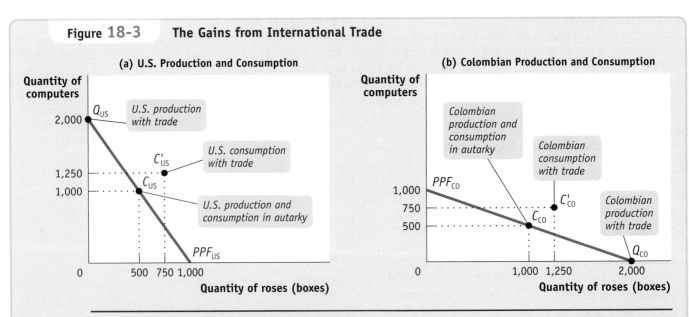

Figure 18-3   The Gains from International Trade

Trade increases world production of both goods, allowing both countries to consume more. Here, each country specializes its production as a result of trade: the United States produces at Q_{US} and Colombia produces at Q_{CO}. Total world production of computers has risen from 1,500 to 2,000

and of roses from 1,500 boxes to 2,000 boxes. The United States can now consume bundle C'_{US}, and Colombia can now consume bundle C'_{CO}—consumption bundles that were unattainable without trade.

TABLE 18-3

Production and Consumption After International Trade

(a) United States

	Production	Consumption
Quantity of roses (boxes)	0	750
Quantity of computers	2,000	1,250

(b) Colombia

	Production	Consumption
Quantity of roses (boxes)	2,000	1,250
Quantity of computers	0	750

(c) World (United States and Colombia)

	Production	Consumption
Quantity of roses (boxes)	2,000	2,000
Quantity of computers	2,000	2,000

roses, shown by C_{CO}, to consumption after trade of 750 computers and 1,250 boxes of roses, shown by C'_{CO}.

What makes this possible is the fact that with international trade countries are no longer required to consume the same bundle of goods that they produce. Each country produces at one point (Q_{US} for the United States, Q_{CO} for Colombia) but consumes at a different point (C'_{US} for the United States, C'_{CO} for Colombia). The difference reflects imports and exports: the 750 boxes of roses the United States consumes are imported from Colombia; the 750 computers Colombia consumes are imported from the United States.

In this example we have simply assumed the post-trade consumption bundles of the two countries. In fact, just as in the case of individual consumption choices, the consumption choices of countries reflect both the preferences of its residents and the *relative prices* in international markets—the prices of one good in terms of another. Although we have not explicitly given the price of computers in terms of roses, that price is implicit in our example: Colombia exports 750 boxes of roses and receives 750 computers in return, so that each box of roses is traded for 1 computer. This tells us that the price of a computer on world markets must be equal to the price of a box of roses in our example.

What determines the actual relative prices in international trade? The answer is supply and demand—and we'll turn to supply and demand in international trade in the next section. However, first let's look behind the production possibility frontiers and ask what determines a country's comparative advantage.

Sources of Comparative Advantage

International trade is driven by comparative advantage, but where does comparative advantage come from? Economists who study international trade have found three main sources of comparative advantage: international differences in *climate*, international differences in *factor endowments*, and international differences in *technology*.

Differences in Climate A key reason the opportunity cost of producing a Valentine's Day rose in Colombia is less than in the United States is that nurseries in Colombia can grow roses outdoors all year

PITFALLS

THE PAUPER LABOR FALLACY

One common argument about international trade goes as follows: it's true that Bangladesh (to pick an example) can produce some goods, such as clothing, more cheaply than we can—but that cost advantage is based only on lower wages. In fact, it takes *fewer* hours of labor to produce a shirt in the United States than in Bangladesh. So importing goods produced by "pauper labor" (workers who are paid very low wages), goes the argument, reduces the American standard of living.

Why is this a misconception? Because it confuses *comparative advantage* with *absolute advantage*. Yes, it takes less labor to produce a shirt in the United States than it does in Bangladesh. But what determines comparative advantage is not the amount of resources used to produce a good but the opportunity cost of that good—the quantity of other goods forgone in order to produce a shirt.

Low wages in countries such as Bangladesh reflect low productivity of labor across the board. Because labor productivity in other Bangladeshi industries is very low, using a lot of labor to produce a shirt does not require forgoing the production of large quantities of other goods. But in the United States, the opposite is true: very high productivity in other industries (such as high-technology goods) means that producing a shirt in the United States requires sacrificing lots of other goods. So the opportunity cost of producing a shirt is less in Bangladesh than in the United States. Despite its lower labor productivity, Bangladesh has a comparative advantage in clothing production, although the United States has an absolute advantage. As a result, importing clothing from Bangladesh actually raises the standard of living in the United States.

round but nurseries in the United States can't. In general, differences in climate are a significant source of international trade. Tropical countries export tropical products like coffee, sugar, and bananas. Countries in the temperate zones export crops like wheat and corn. Some trade is even driven by the difference in seasons between the northern and southern hemispheres: winter deliveries of Chilean grapes and New Zealand apples have become commonplace in U.S. and European supermarkets.

Differences in Factor Endowments   Canada is a major exporter of forest products—lumber and products derived from lumber, like pulp and paper—to the United States. These exports don't reflect the special skill of Canadian lumberjacks. Instead, Canada has a comparative advantage in forest products because its forested area is much greater compared to the size of its labor force than the ratio of forestland to the labor force in the United States.

Forestland, like labor and capital, is a factor of production. Due to history and geography, the mix of available factors of production differs among countries, providing an important source of comparative advantage. The relationship between comparative advantage and factor availability is found in an influential model of international trade, the *Heckscher-Ohlin model* (developed by two Swedish economists in the first half of the twentieth century).

A key concept in the model is *factor intensity*. Producers use different ratios of factors of production in the production of different goods. For example, at any given wage rate and rental rate of capital, oil refineries will use much more capital per worker than clothing factories. Economists use the term **factor intensity** to describe this difference among goods: oil refining is capital-intensive, because it tends to use a high ratio of capital to labor, but clothing manufacture is labor-intensive, because it tends to use a high ratio of labor to capital.

According to the **Heckscher–Ohlin model,** a country will have a comparative advantage in a good whose production is intensive in the factors that are abundantly available in that country. So a country that has an abundance of capital will have a comparative advantage in capital-intensive industries such as oil refining, but a country that has an abundance of labor will have a comparative advantage in labor-intensive industries such as clothing production. The basic intuition behind this result is simple and based on opportunity cost. The opportunity cost of a given factor—the value that the factor would generate in alternative uses—is low for a country when it possesses an abundance of that factor. (For example, in rainy parts of the United States, the opportunity cost of water for residences is low because there is a plentiful supply for other uses, such as agriculture.) So the opportunity cost of producing goods that are intensive in the use of an abundantly available factor is also low.

The **factor intensity** of production of a good is a measure of which factor is used in relatively greater quantities than other factors in production.

According to the **Heckscher–Ohlin model,** a country has a comparative advantage in a good whose production is intensive in the factors that are abundantly available in that country.

FOR INQUIRING MINDS

DOES TRADE HURT POOR COUNTRIES?

It's a good bet that the clothes you are wearing right now were produced in a labor-abundant country such as Bangladesh or Sri Lanka. If so, the workers who produced those clothes were paid very low wages by Western standards: in 2002 (the most recent data available) workers in Sri Lankan factories were paid an average of $0.33 an hour. Doesn't this mean that Sri Lankan workers are getting a bad deal?

The answer of most economists is that it doesn't. The wages paid to export workers in poor countries should be compared not to what workers get in rich countries but to what they would get if those export jobs weren't available. The reason Sri Lankans are willing to work for so little is that in an underdeveloped economy, with lots of labor but very little of other factors of production like capital, the opportunities available to workers are very limited. It's almost certain that international trade makes Sri Lanka and other low-wage countries *less* poor than they would be otherwise and raises workers' wages relative to what they would be without international trade.

Nonetheless, many people in advanced countries—students in particular—are disturbed by the thought that their consumer goods are produced by such poorly paid workers and want to see those workers receive higher pay and better working conditions. The dilemma is whether it is possible to insist on higher wages and better working conditions without eliminating the job altogether, thereby choking off the benefits of international trade.

The most dramatic example of the validity of the Heckscher–Ohlin model is world trade in clothing. Clothing production is a labor-intensive activity: it doesn't take much physical capital, nor does it require a lot of human capital in the form of highly educated workers. So you would expect labor-abundant countries such as China and Bangladesh to have a comparative advantage in clothing production. And they do.

That much international trade is the result of differences in factor endowments helps explain another fact: international specialization of production is often *incomplete*. That is, a country often maintains some domestic production of a good that it imports. A good example of this is the United States and oil. Saudi Arabia exports oil to the United States because Saudi Arabia has an abundant supply of oil relative to its other factors of production; the United States exports medical devices to Saudi Arabia because it has an abundant supply of medical technical expertise relative to its other factors of production. But the United States also produces some oil domestically because the size of its domestic oil reserves make it economical to do so. In our demand and supply analysis in the next section, we'll consider incomplete specialization by a country to be the norm. We should emphasize, however, that the fact that countries often incompletely specialize does not in any way change the conclusion that there are gains from trade.

Differences in Technology In the 1970s and 1980s, Japan became by far the world's largest exporter of automobiles, selling large numbers to the United States and the rest of the world. Japan's comparative advantage in automobiles wasn't the result of climate. Nor can it easily be attributed to differences in factor endowments: aside from a scarcity of land, Japan's mix of available factors is quite similar to that in other advanced countries. Instead, Japan's comparative advantage in automobiles was based on the superior production techniques developed by that country's manufacturers, which allowed them to produce more cars with a given amount of labor and capital than their American or European counterparts.

Japan's comparative advantage in automobiles was a case of comparative advantage caused by differences in technology—the techniques used in production.

The causes of differences in technology are somewhat mysterious. Sometimes they seem to be based on knowledge accumulated through experience—for example, Switzerland's comparative advantage in watches reflects a long tradition of watchmaking. Sometimes they are the result of a set of innovations that for some reason occur in one country but not in others. Technological advantage is also often transitory. American auto manufacturers have now closed much of the gap in productivity with their Japanese competitors; Europe's aircraft industry has closed a similar gap with the U.S. aircraft industry. At any given point in time, however, differences in technology are a major source of comparative advantage.

FOR INQUIRING MINDS

INCREASING RETURNS AND INTERNATIONAL TRADE

Most analysis of international trade focuses on how differences between countries—differences in climate, factor endowments, and technology—create national comparative advantage. However, economists have also pointed out another reason for international trade: the role of *increasing returns*.

Production of a good is characterized by increasing returns if the productivity of labor and other resources rises with the quantity of output. For example, in an industry characterized by increasing returns, increasing output by 10% might require only 8% more labor and 9% more raw materials. Increasing returns (sometimes also called economies of scale) can give rise to monopoly, because they give large firms an advantage over small firms.

But increasing returns can also give rise to international trade. The logic runs as follows: if production of a good is characterized by increasing returns, it makes sense to concentrate production in only a few locations, so as to achieve a high level of production in each location. But that also means that the good is produced in only a few countries, which export that good to other countries. A commonly cited example is the North American auto industry: although both the United States and Canada produce automobiles and their components, each particular model or component tends to be produced in only one of the two countries and exported to the other. Increasing returns probably play a large role in the trade in manufactured goods between advanced countries, which is about 25% of the total value of world trade.

In the United States, an abundance of engineering know-how has led to a comparative advantage in aircraft.

economics in action

The Comparative Advantage of the United States

The United States is a country of superlatives: a nation richly endowed with many resources, human and natural, it has an *absolute* advantage in almost everything—that is, it is better at producing almost everything than anyone else. But what is its *comparative* advantage?

In 1953 the economist Wassily Leontief made a surprising discovery. Until his work, many economists had assumed that because U.S. workers were clearly better-equipped with machinery than their counterparts in other countries, the production of U.S. exports was more capital-intensive than the production of U.S. imports. That is, they expected that U.S. exports were more capital-intensive than U.S. imports. But Leontief's work showed that this wasn't true: in fact, goods that the United States exported were slightly less capital-intensive than goods the country imported. The "Leontief paradox" led to a sustained effort to make sense of U.S. trade patterns.

The main resolution of this paradox, it turns out, depends on the definition of capital. U.S. exports aren't intensive in *physical* capital—machines and buildings. Instead, they are intensive in *human* capital. U.S. exporting industries use a substantially higher ratio of highly educated workers to other workers than is found in U.S. industries that compete against imports. For example, one of America's biggest export sectors is aircraft; the aircraft industry employs large numbers of engineers and other people with graduate degrees relative to the number of manual laborers. Conversely, we import a lot of clothing, which is often produced by workers with little formal education. ∎

< < < < < < < < < < < < < < < < < <

>>CHECK YOUR UNDERSTANDING 18-1

1. In the United States, the opportunity cost of 1 ton of corn is 50 bicycles. In China, the opportunity cost of 1 bicycle is 0.01 ton of corn.
   a. Determine the pattern of comparative advantage.
   b. In autarky, the United States can produce 200,000 bicycles if no corn is produced, and China can produce 3,000 tons of corn if no bicycles are produced. Draw each country's production possibility frontier assuming constant opportunity cost, with tons of corn on the vertical axis and bicycles on the horizontal axis.
   c. With trade, each country specializes its production. The United States consumes 1,000 tons of corn and 200,000 bicycles; China consumes 3,000 tons of corn and 100,000 bicycles. Indicate the production and consumption points on your diagrams, and use them to explain the gains from trade.
2. Explain the following patterns of trade using the Heckscher–Ohlin model:
   a. France exports wine to the United States, and the United States exports movies to France.
   b. Brazil exports shoes to the United States, and the United States exports shoe-making machinery to Brazil.

Solutions appear at back of book.

>>QUICK REVIEW

> *Imports* and *exports* account for a growing share of the U.S. economy and of the economies of many other countries.
> International trade is driven by comparative advantage. The *Ricardian model of international trade* shows that trade between two countries makes both countries better off than they would be in *autarky*—that is, there are gains from trade.
> The main sources of comparative advantage are international differences in climate, factor endowments, and technology.
> The *Heckscher–Ohlin model* shows how comparative advantage can arise from differences in factor endowments: goods differ in their *factor intensity*, and countries tend to export goods that are intensive in the factors they have in abundance.
> Trade in manufactured goods amongst developed countries is best explained by increasing returns in production.

Supply, Demand, and International Trade

Simple models of comparative advantage are helpful for understanding the fundamental causes of international trade. However, to analyze the effects of international trade at a more detailed level and to understand trade policy, it helps to return to the supply and demand model. We'll start by looking at the effects of imports on domestic producers and consumers, then turn to the effect of exports.

The Effects of Imports

Figure 18-4 shows the U.S. market for roses, ignoring international trade for a moment. It introduces a few new concepts: the *domestic demand curve,* the *domestic supply curve,* and the domestic or autarky price.

The **domestic demand curve** shows how the quantity of a good demanded by residents of a country depends on the price of that good. Why "domestic"? Because people living in other countries may demand the good, too. Once we introduce international trade, we need to distinguish between purchases of a good by domestic consumers and purchases by foreign consumers. So the domestic demand curve reflects only the demand of residents of our own country. Similarly, the **domestic supply curve** shows how the quantity of a good supplied by producers inside a country depends on the price of that good. Once we introduce international trade, we need to distinguish between the supply of domestic producers and foreign supply—supply brought in from abroad.

In autarky, with no international trade in roses, the equilibrium in this market would be determined by the intersection of the domestic demand and domestic supply curves, point A. The equilibrium price of roses would be P_A, and the equilibrium quantity of roses produced and consumed would be Q_A. As always, both consumers and producers would gain from the existence of the domestic market. Consumer surplus would be equal to the area of the upper shaded triangle in Figure 18-4. Producer surplus would be equal to the area of the lower shaded triangle. And total surplus would be equal to the sum of these two shaded triangles.

Now let's imagine opening up this market to imports. To do this, we must make some assumption about the supply of imports. The simplest assumption, which we will adopt here, is that unlimited quantities of roses can be purchased from abroad at a fixed price, known as the **world price** of roses. Figure 18-5 on page 446 shows a situation in which the world price of roses, P_W, is lower than the price of roses that would prevail in the domestic market in autarky, P_A.

Given the world price of roses is below the domestic price of roses, it is profitable for importers to buy roses abroad and resell them domestically. The imported roses increase the supply of roses to the domestic market, driving down the domestic market price. Roses will continue to be imported until the domestic price falls to a level equal to the world price.

The result is shown in Figure 18-5. Because of imports, the domestic price of roses falls from P_A to P_W. The quantity of roses demanded by domestic consumers rises from Q_A to C_T, and the quantity supplied by domestic producers falls from Q_A to Q_T.

The **domestic demand curve** shows how the quantity of a good demanded by domestic consumers depends on the price of that good.

The **domestic supply curve** shows how the quantity of a good supplied by domestic producers depends on the price of that good.

The **world price** of a good is the price at which that good can be bought or sold abroad.

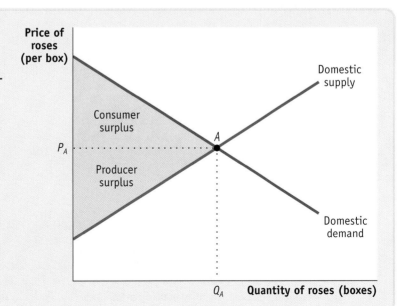

Figure 18-4

Consumer and Producer Surplus in Autarky

In the absence of trade, domestic price is P_A, the autarky price at which the domestic supply curve and the domestic demand curve intersect. The quantity produced and consumed domestically is Q_A. Consumer surplus is represented by the blue-shaded area, and producer surplus is represented by the red-shaded area.

> *web...*

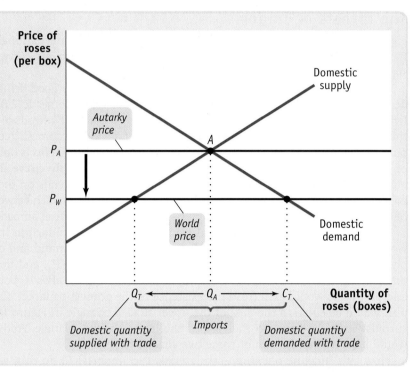

Figure 18-5

The Domestic Market with Imports

Here the world price of roses, P_W, is below the autarky price, P_A. When the economy is opened to international trade, imports enter the domestic market, and the domestic price falls from the autarky price, P_A, to the world price, P_W. As the price falls, the domestic quantity demanded rises from Q_A to C_T and domestic production falls from Q_A to Q_T. The difference between domestic quantity demanded and domestic quantity supplied at P_W, the quantity $C_T - Q_T$, is filled by imports.

>web...

The difference between the domestic quantity demanded and the domestic quantity supplied, $C_T - Q_T$, is filled by imports.

Now let's turn to the effects of imports on consumer surplus and producer surplus. Because imports of roses lead to a fall in their domestic price, consumer surplus rises and producer surplus falls. Figure 18-6 shows how this works. We label four areas: W,

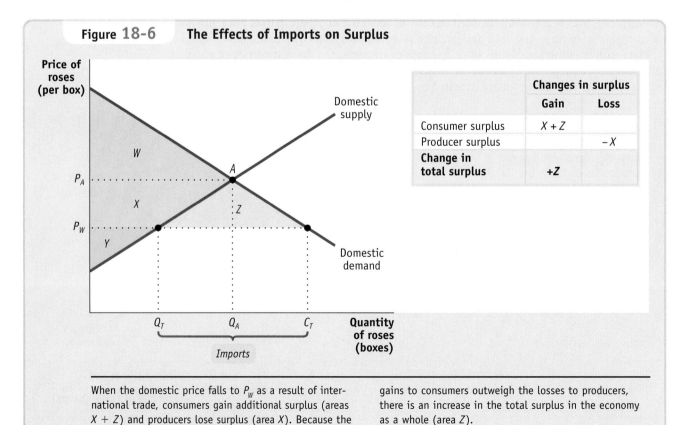

Figure 18-6   The Effects of Imports on Surplus

	Changes in surplus	
	Gain	**Loss**
Consumer surplus	$X + Z$	
Producer surplus		$-X$
Change in total surplus	**$+Z$**	

When the domestic price falls to P_W as a result of international trade, consumers gain additional surplus (areas $X + Z$) and producers lose surplus (area X). Because the gains to consumers outweigh the losses to producers, there is an increase in the total surplus in the economy as a whole (area Z).

X, *Y*, and *Z*. The autarky consumer surplus we identified in Figure 18-4 corresponds to *W*, and the autarky producer surplus corresponds to the sum of *X* and *Y*. The fall in the domestic price to the world price leads to an increase in consumer surplus; it increases by the areas *X* and *Z*, so that it now equals the sum of *W*, *X*, and *Z*. At the same time, producers lose the area *X* in surplus, so that producer surplus now equals only *Y*.

The table in Figure 18-6 summarizes the changes in consumer and producer surplus when the rose market is opened to imports. Consumers gain surplus equal to the area *X* + *Z*. Producers lose surplus equal to the area *X*. So the sum of producer and consumer surplus—the total surplus generated in the rose market—increases by the area *Z*. As a result of trade, consumers gain and producers lose, but the gain to consumers exceeds the loss to producers.

This is an important result. We have just shown that opening up a market to imports leads to a net gain in total surplus, which is what we should have expected given the proposition that there are gains from international trade. However, we have also learned that although the country as a whole gains, some groups—in this case, domestic producers of roses—lose as a result of international trade. As we'll see shortly, the fact that international trade typically creates losers as well as winners is crucial for understanding the politics of trade policy.

We turn next to the case in which a country exports a good.

The Effects of Exports

Figure 18-7 shows the effects on a country when it exports a good, in this case computers. For this example, we assume that unlimited quantities of computers can be sold abroad at a given world price, P_W, which is higher than the price that would prevail in the domestic market in autarky, P_A.

The higher world price makes it profitable for exporters to buy computers domestically and sell them overseas. The purchases of domestic computers drives the domestic price up until the domestic price is equal to the world price. As a result, the quantity demanded by domestic consumers falls from Q_A to C_T, and the quantity supplied by domestic producers rises from Q_A to Q_T. This difference between domestic production and domestic consumption, $Q_T - C_T$, is exported.

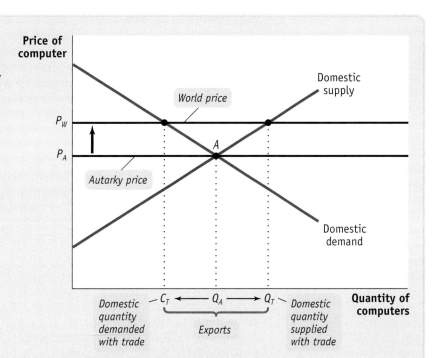

Figure 18-7

The Domestic Market with Exports

Here the world price, P_W, is greater than the autarky price, P_A. When the economy is opened to international trade, some of the domestic supply is now exported. The domestic price rises from the autarky price, P_A, to the world price, P_W. As the price rises, the domestic quantity demanded falls from Q_A to C_T and domestic production rises from Q_A to Q_T. The remainder of the domestic quantity supplied, $Q_T - C_T$, is exported.

> *web...*

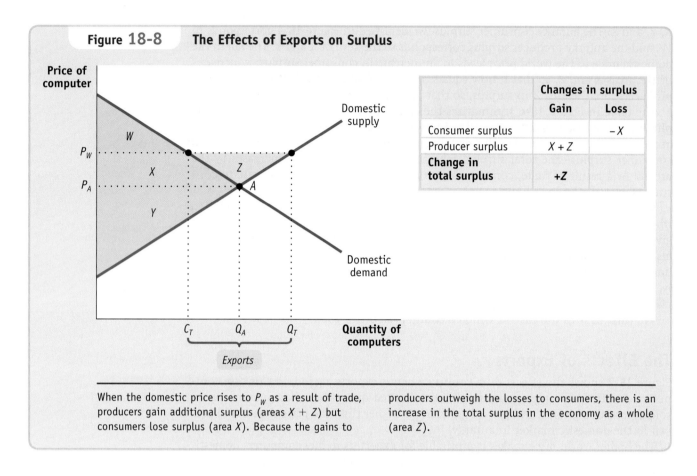

Figure 18-8   **The Effects of Exports on Surplus**

	Changes in surplus	
	Gain	**Loss**
Consumer surplus		– X
Producer surplus	X + Z	
Change in total surplus	**+Z**	

When the domestic price rises to P_W as a result of trade, producers gain additional surplus (areas $X + Z$) but consumers lose surplus (area X). Because the gains to producers outweigh the losses to consumers, there is an increase in the total surplus in the economy as a whole (area Z).

Like imports, exports lead to an overall gain in total surplus for the exporting country, but also create losers as well as winners. Figure 18-8 shows the effects of computer exports on producer and consumer surplus. In the absence of trade, the price of computers would be P_A. Consumer surplus in the absence of trade is the sum of the areas W and X, and producer surplus would be the area Y. As a result of trade, price rises from P_A to P_W, consumer surplus falls to W, and producer surplus rises to $Y + X + Z$. So producers gain $X + Z$, consumers lose X, and, as shown in the table accompanying the figure, the economy as a whole gains total surplus in the amount of Z.

We have learned, then, that imports of a particular good hurt domestic producers of that good but help domestic consumers, whereas exports of a particular good hurt domestic consumers but help domestic producers of that good. In each case, the gains are larger than the losses.

International Trade and Factor Markets

So far we have focused on the effects of international trade on producers and consumers in a particular industry. For many purposes this is a very helpful approach. But to understand the long-run effects of international trade on income distribution, this approach can be inadequate, because factors of production move between industries.

To see the problem, consider the position of Maria, a trained accountant who currently works for a U.S. company that grows flowers. If the economy is opened up to imports of roses from South America, the domestic rose-growing industry will contract, and it will hire fewer accountants. But accounting is a profession with employment opportunities in many industries, and Maria might well find a better job in the computer industry, which expands as a result of international trade. So it may not be appropriate to think of her as a producer of flowers who is hurt by competition from imported roses. Rather, what matters to her is the effect of international trade on the salaries of accountants, wherever they are employed. In other words, sometimes it is important to analyze the effect of trade on *factor prices*.

Earlier in this chapter we described the Heckscher–Ohlin model of trade, which states that comparative advantage is determined by a country's factor endowment. This model also suggests how international trade affects factor prices in a country: compared to autarky, international trade tends to raise the prices of factors that are abundantly available and reduce the prices of factors that are scarce.

We won't work this out in detail, but the idea is intuitively simple. Think of a country's industries as consisting of two kinds: **exporting industries,** which produce goods and services that are sold abroad, and **import-competing industries,** which produce goods and services that are also imported. Compared with autarky, international trade leads to higher production in exporting industries and lower production in import-competing industries. This indirectly increases the demand for the factors used by exporting industries and decreases the demand for factors used by import-competing industries. In addition, the Heckscher–Ohlin model says that a country tends to export goods that are intensive in its abundant factors and to import goods that are intensive in its scarce factors. *So international trade tends to increase the demand for factors that are abundant in our country compared with other countries, and to decrease the demand for factors that are scarce in our country compared with other countries. As a result, the prices of abundant factors tend to rise, and the prices of scarce factors tend to fall.*

The Economics in Action on page 444 pointed out that U.S. exports tend to be human-capital-intensive and U.S. imports tend to be unskilled-labor-intensive. This suggests that the effect of international trade on U.S. factor markets is to raise the wage rate of highly educated workers and to reduce the wage rate of unskilled workers.

This effect has been a source of some concern in recent years. Wage inequality—the gap between the wages of highly paid and low-paid workers—has increased substantially over the last 25 years. Some economists believe that growing international trade is an important factor in that trend. If international trade has the effects predicted by the Heckscher–Ohlin model, it raises the wages of highly educated workers, who already have relatively high wages, and lowers the wages of less educated workers, who already have relatively low wages.

How important are these effects? In some historical episodes, the impacts of international trade on factor prices have been very large. As we explain in the Economics in Action that follows, the opening of transatlantic trade in the late nineteenth century had a large negative impact on land rents in Europe, hurting landowners but helping workers and owners of capital. The effects of trade on wages in the United States have generated considerable controversy in recent years. Most economists who have studied the issue agree that growing imports of labor-intensive products from newly industrializing economies, and the export of high-technology goods in return, have helped cause a widening wage differential between highly educated and less educated workers in this country. However, other forces, especially technological change, are probably more important in explaining growing wage inequality.

Exporting industries produce goods and services that are sold abroad.

Import-competing industries produce goods and services that are also imported.

economics in action

Trade, Wages, and Land Prices in the Nineteenth Century

Beginning around 1870, there was an explosive growth of world trade in agricultural products, based largely on the steam engine. Steam-powered ships could cross the ocean much more quickly and reliably than sailing ships. Until about 1860, steamships had higher costs than sailing ships, but after that rates dropped sharply. At the same time, steam-powered rail transport made it possible to bring grain and other bulk goods cheaply from the interior to ports. The result was that land-abundant countries—the United States, Canada, Argentina, Australia—began shipping large quantities of agricultural goods to the densely populated, land-scarce countries of Europe.

An economy has **free trade** when the government does not attempt either to reduce or to increase the levels of exports and imports that occur naturally as a result of supply and demand.

Policies that limit imports are known as **trade protection** or simply as **protection.**

A **tariff** is a tax levied on imports.

This opening up of international trade led to higher prices of agricultural products, such as wheat, in exporting countries and a decline in their prices in importing countries. Notably, the difference between wheat prices in the midwestern United States and England plunged.

The change in agricultural prices created both winners and losers on both sides of the Atlantic as factor prices adjusted. In England, land prices fell by half compared with average wages; landowners found their purchasing power sharply reduced, but workers benefited from cheaper food. In the United States, the reverse happened: land prices doubled compared with wages. Landowners did very well, but workers found the purchasing power of their wages dented by rising food prices. ∎

< < < < < < < < < < < < < < < < < <

The Effects of Trade Protection

Ever since David Ricardo laid out the principle of comparative advantage in the early nineteenth century, most economists have advocated **free trade.** That is, they have argued that government policy should not attempt either to reduce or to increase the levels of exports and imports that occur naturally as a result of supply and demand. Despite the free-trade arguments of economists, however, many governments use taxes and other restrictions to limit imports. Much less frequently, governments offer subsidies to encourage exports. Policies that limit imports, usually with the goal of protecting domestic producers in import-competing industries from foreign competition, are known as **trade protection** or simply as **protection.**

Let's look at the two most common protectionist policies, tariffs and import quotas, then turn to the reasons governments follow these policies.

The Effects of a Tariff

A **tariff** is a form of excise tax, one that is levied only on sales of imported goods. For example, the U.S. government could declare that anyone bringing in roses from Colombia must pay a tariff of $2 per rose, or $200 per box of 100 roses. In the distant past, tariffs were an important source of government revenue because they were relatively easy to collect. But in the modern world, tariffs are usually intended to discourage imports and protect import-competing domestic producers rather than as a source of government revenue.

The effect of a tariff is to raise both the price received by domestic producers and the price paid by domestic consumers. Suppose, for example, that our country imports roses, and a box of 100 roses is available on the world market at $400. As we saw earlier, under free trade the domestic price would also be $400. But if a tariff of $200 per box is imposed, the domestic price will rise to $600, and it won't be profitable to import roses unless the price in the domestic market is high enough to compensate importers for the cost of paying the tariff.

Figure 18-9 illustrates the effects of a tariff on rose imports. As before, we assume that P_W is the world price of roses. Before the tariff is imposed, imports have driven the domestic price down to P_W, so that pre-tariff domestic production is Q_1, pre-tariff domestic consumption is C_1, and pre-tariff imports are $C_1 - Q_1$.

Now suppose that the government imposes a tariff on each box of roses imported. As a consequence, it is no longer profitable to import roses unless the domestic price

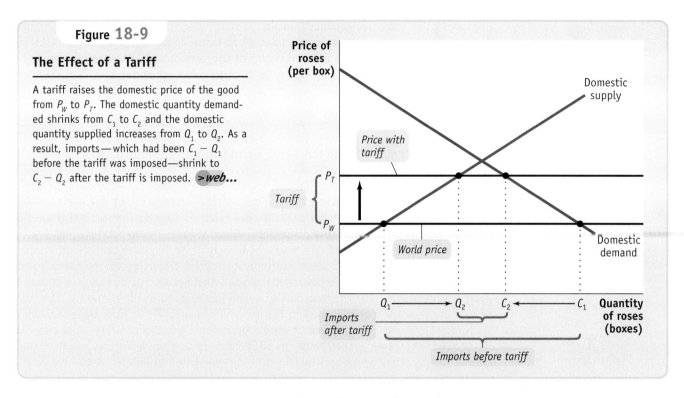

Figure 18-9

The Effect of a Tariff

A tariff raises the domestic price of the good from P_W to P_T. The domestic quantity demanded shrinks from C_1 to C_2 and the domestic quantity supplied increases from Q_1 to Q_2. As a result, imports—which had been $C_1 - Q_1$ before the tariff was imposed—shrink to $C_2 - Q_2$ after the tariff is imposed. **>web...**

received by the importer is greater than or equal to the world price *plus* the tariff. So the domestic price rises to P_T, which is equal to the world price, P_W, plus the tariff. Domestic production rises to Q_2, domestic consumption falls to C_2, and imports fall to $C_2 - Q_2$.

A tariff, then, raises domestic prices, and leads to increased domestic production and reduced domestic consumption compared to the situation under free trade. Figure 18-10 shows the effects on surplus. There are three effects. First, the higher

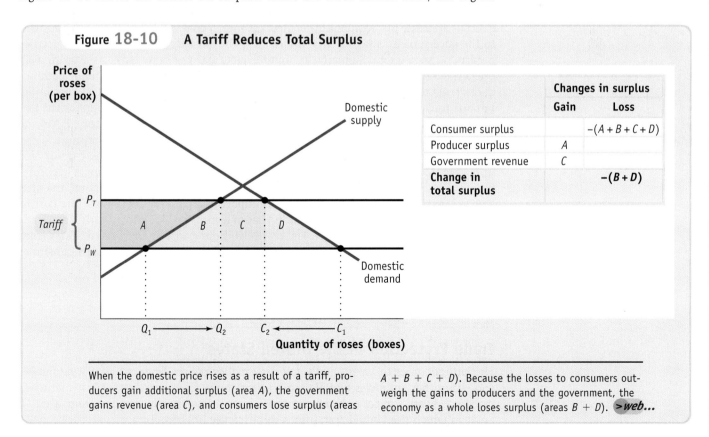

Figure 18-10   A Tariff Reduces Total Surplus

	Changes in surplus	
	Gain	**Loss**
Consumer surplus		$-(A + B + C + D)$
Producer surplus	A	
Government revenue	C	
Change in total surplus		$-(B + D)$

When the domestic price rises as a result of a tariff, producers gain additional surplus (area A), the government gains revenue (area C), and consumers lose surplus (areas $A + B + C + D$). Because the losses to consumers outweigh the gains to producers and the government, the economy as a whole loses surplus (areas $B + D$). **>web...**

domestic price increases producer surplus, a gain equal to area *A*. Second, the higher domestic price reduces consumer surplus, a reduction equal to the sum of areas *A*, *B*, *C*, and *D*. Finally, the tariff yields revenue to the government. How much revenue? The government collects the tariff—which, remember, is equal to the difference between P_T and P_W on each of the $C_2 - Q_2$ roses imported. So total revenue is $(P_T - P_W) \times (C_2 - Q_2)$. This is equal to area *C*.

The welfare effects of a tariff are summarized in the table in Figure 18-10. Producers gain, consumers lose, the government gains. But consumer losses are greater than the sum of producer and government gains, leading to a net reduction in total surplus equal to areas *B* + *D*.

Recall that in Chapter 4 we analyzed the effect of an excise tax—a tax on buyers or sellers of a good. We saw that an excise tax creates inefficiency, or deadweight loss, because it prevents mutually beneficial trades from occurring. The same is true of a tariff, where its deadweight loss on society is equal to the loss in total surplus represented by areas *B* + *D*. Tariffs generate deadweight losses because they create inefficiencies in two ways. First, some mutually beneficial trades go unexploited: some consumers who are willing to pay more than the world price, P_W, do not purchase the good, even though P_W is the true cost of a unit of the good to the economy. The cost of this inefficiency is represented in Figure 18-10 by area *D*. Second, the economy's resources are wasted on inefficient production: some producers whose cost exceeds P_W produce the good, even though an additional unit of the good can be purchased abroad for P_W. The cost of this inefficiency is represented in Figure 18-10 by area *B*.

The Effects of an Import Quota

An **import quota** is a legal limit on the quantity of a good that can be imported.

An **import quota,** another form of trade protection, is a legal limit on the quantity of a good that can be imported. For example, a U.S. import quota on Colombian roses might limit the number imported each year to 50 million. Import quotas are usually administered through licenses: a number of licenses are issued, each giving the license-holder the right to import a limited quantity of the good each year.

We discussed quotas in Chapter 4, where we saw that a quota on sales has the same effect as an excise tax, with one difference: the money that would otherwise have accrued to the government as tax revenue under an excise tax becomes quota rents to license-holders under a quota. Similarly, an import quota has the same effect as a tariff, with one difference: the money that would otherwise have been government revenue becomes quota rents to license-holders. Look again at Figure 18-10. An import quota that limits imports to $C_2 - Q_2$ will raise the domestic price of roses by the same amount as the tariff we considered previously. That is, it will raise the domestic price from P_W to P_T. However, area *C* will now represent quota rents rather than government revenue.

Who receives import licenses and so collects the quota rents? In the case of U.S. import protection, the answer may surprise you: the most important import licenses—mainly for clothing, to a lesser extent for sugar—are granted to foreign governments.

Because the quota rents for most U.S. import quotas go to foreigners, the cost to the nation of such quotas is larger than that of a comparable tariff (a tariff that leads to the same level of imports). In Figure 18-10 the net loss to the United States from such an import quota would be equal to *B* + *C* + *D*, the difference between consumer losses and producer gains.

economics in action

Trade Protection in the United States

The United States today generally follows a policy of free trade, at least in comparison with other countries and also in comparison with its own past. Most manufactured goods are subject either to no tariff or to a low tariff. However, there are two areas in which the United States does significantly limit imports.

One is agriculture. The typical U.S. policy here is something called a "tariff quota." A certain amount of the imports are subject to a low tariff rate; this acts like an import quota because an importer is allowed to pay the low rate only if she has a license. Any additional imports are subject to a much higher tariff rate. We have tariff quotas on beef, dairy products, sugar, peanuts, and other things. For Inquiring Minds on page 454 discusses the sugar quota in the context of worldwide sugar policy.

The other area in which the United States significantly limits imports is clothing and textiles, where the government applies an elaborate system of import quotas.

The peculiar thing about U.S. trade protection is that in most cases quota licenses are assigned to foreigners, often foreign governments. For example, rights to sell clothing in the United States are allotted to various exporting countries, which can then hand those rights out as they see fit. This means that the quota rents go overseas, greatly increasing the cost to the United States of the import limitations. In fact, according to some estimates, about 70% of the total cost of U.S. import restrictions comes not from deadweight loss but from the transfer of quota rents to foreigners. ■

KAL, Cartoonists & Writers Syndicate http://CartoonWeb.com

> >

The Political Economy of Trade Protection

We have seen that international trade produces mutual benefits to the countries that engage in it. We have also seen that tariffs and import quotas, although they produce winners as well as losers, reduce total surplus. Yet many countries continue to impose tariffs and import quotas, and to enact other protectionist measures.

To understand why trade protection takes place, we will first look at some common justifications for protection. Then we will look at the politics of trade protection. Finally, we will look at an important feature of trade protection in today's world: tariffs and import quotas are the subject of international negotiation and are policed by international organizations.

Arguments for Trade Protection

Advocates of tariffs and import quotas offer a variety of arguments. Three common arguments are *national security*, *job creation*, and the *infant industry argument*.

The national security argument is based on the proposition that overseas sources of goods are vulnerable to disruption in times of international conflict; therefore a country should protect domestic suppliers of crucial goods with the aim to be self-sufficient in those goods. In the 1960s, the United States—which had begun to import oil as domestic oil reserves ran low—had an import quota on oil, justified on national

If there's one good in which we can be absolutely sure that neither the European Union nor the United States has a comparative advantage, it's sugar. The cheapest way to produce sugar is by growing sugar cane, a crop that requires a tropical climate. A few places in the United States can grow cane sugar (basically along the Gulf of Mexico and in Hawaii), but they are no match for the sugar-growing capacity of genuinely tropical countries. And it's almost impossible to grow sugar cane in Western Europe.

Yet Europe is a net *exporter* of sugar, and the United States imports only a fraction of its consumption. How is this possible, and why does it happen?

It's possible because there is another less efficient way to produce sugar: sugar beets can survive even in cold climates. On both sides of the Atlantic, sugar producers receive huge amounts of government support. In the United States, an import quota keeps prices on average at twice world levels. In Europe, import restrictions are supplemented by huge government subsidies to farmers.

What's the rationale for this trade protection? Governments hardly even bother to make excuses: on both sides of the Atlantic, there's a powerful farm lobby. In fact, agriculture in industrial countries is heavily subsidized, at the expense of both consumers and taxpayers.

The really sad thing is that some of the protected goods—sugar in particular—would be major exports of poor countries (and major sources of income for their poor farmers) if it weren't for the import quotas and subsidies in advanced countries.

security grounds. Some people have argued that we should again have policies to discourage imports of oil, especially from the Middle East.

The job creation argument points to the additional jobs created in import-competing industries as a result of trade protection. Economists argue that these jobs are offset by the jobs lost elsewhere, such as industries that use imported inputs and now face higher input costs. But noneconomists don't always find this argument persuasive.

Finally, the infant industry argument, often raised in newly industrializing countries, holds that new industries require a temporary period of trade protection to get established. For example, in the 1950s many countries in Latin America imposed tariffs and import quotas on manufactured goods, in an effort to switch from their traditional role as exporters of raw materials to a new status as industrial countries.

The Politics of Trade Protection

In reality, much trade protection has little to do with the arguments just described. Instead, it reflects the political influence of import-competing producers.

We've seen that a tariff or import quota leads to gains for import-competing producers and losses for consumers. Producers, however, usually have much more influence over trade policy decisions. The producers who compete with imports of a particular good are usually a smaller, more cohesive group than the consumers of that good.

An example is trade protection for sugar, discussed in For Inquiring Minds above. The United States has an import quota on sugar, which on average leads to a domestic price about twice the world price. This quota is difficult to rationalize in terms of any economic argument. However, consumers rarely complain about the quota because they are unaware that it exists: Because no individual consumer buys large amounts of sugar, the cost of the quota is only a few dollars per family each year, not enough to attract notice. But there are only a few thousand sugar growers in the United States. They are very aware of the benefits they receive from the quota and make sure that their representatives in Congress are aware of their interest in the matter.

Given these political realities, it may seem surprising that trade is as free as it is. As explained in Economics in Action on page 455, the United States has low tariffs, and its import quotas are mainly confined to clothing and a few agricultural products. It would be nice to say that the main reason trade protection is so limited is that economists have convinced governments of the virtues of free trade. A more important reason, however, is the role of *international trade agreements*.

International Trade Agreements and the World Trade Organization

When a country engages in trade protection, it hurts two groups. We've already emphasized the adverse effect on domestic consumers, but protection also hurts foreign export industries. This means that countries care about each others' trade policies: the Canadian lumber industry has a strong interest in keeping U.S. tariffs on forest products low.

Because countries care about each others' trade policies, they engage in **international trade agreements:** treaties in which a country promises to engage in less trade protection against the exports of another country in return for a promise by the other country to do the same for its exports. Most world trade is now governed by such agreements.

Some international trade agreements involve just two countries or a small group of countries. In 1993, the U.S. Congress approved the North American Free Trade Agreement (NAFTA) between the United States, Canada, and Mexico. Once fully implemented, this agreement will remove all barriers to trade among the three nations. Free trade has already been implemented among the 25 nations of the European Union.

There are also global trade agreements, covering most of the world. Such global agreements are overseen by the **World Trade Organization,** or WTO, which plays two roles. First, it provides the framework for the massively complex negotiations involved in a major international trade agreement (the full text of the last major agreement, approved in 1994, was 24,000 pages long). Second, the WTO resolves disputes between members. These disputes typically arise when one country claims that another country's policies violate its previous agreements.

Here are two examples that illustrate the WTO's role. First, in 1999 the WTO ruled that the European Union's import restrictions on bananas, which discriminate in favor of producers in former European colonies and against Central American producers, are in violation of international trade rules. The banana dispute had threatened to become a major source of conflict between the European Union and the United States because the United States has taken the side of the Central American countries. Europe is currently in the process of revising its system. In 2002 the United States was on the losing side of a WTO decision: the European Union complained that a provision in U.S. tax law, intended to help exporting companies, is in effect an export subsidy—which is not allowed according to international agreements. The WTO ruled in Europe's favor and the United States is now obliged to revise its tax law.

The WTO is sometimes, with great exaggeration, described as a world government. In fact, it has no army, no police, and no direct enforcement power. The grain of truth in that description is that when a country joins the WTO, it agrees to accept the organization's judgments—and these judgments apply not only to tariffs and import quotas but also to domestic policies that, according to the organization, are in effect trade protection under another name. So in joining the WTO a country does give up a bit of its sovereignty.

> **International trade agreements** are treaties in which a country promises to engage in less trade protection against the exports of other countries in return for a promise by other countries to do the same for its own exports.

> The **World Trade Organization** oversees international trade agreements and rules on disputes between countries over those agreements.

economics in action

Declining Tariffs

The United States began basing its trade policy on international agreements in the 1930s, and global trade negotiations began soon after World War II. The success of these agreements in reducing trade protection is illustrated by Figure 18-11 on page 456 which shows the average U.S. tariff rate on imports subject to tariffs since the 1920s.

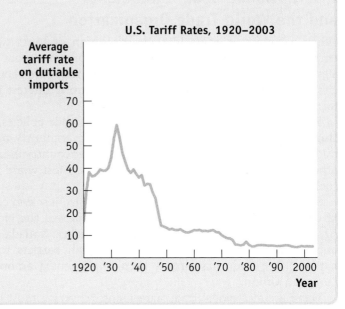

Figure 18-11

Declining Tariff Rates

U.S. tariff rates were very high in the early 1930s but have steadily fallen since then. This move toward relatively free trade has been achieved in large part through international trade agreements.

Source: U.S. International Trade Commission.

Tariffs reached a peak in the early 1930s after the passage of a very protectionist bill, known as the Smoot-Hawley tariff, in 1930. (Some people blame Smoot-Hawley for causing the Great Depression of the 1930s, though few economists think it was *that* bad.) From then on, tariff rates have steadily ratcheted down, with U.S. moves matched in other advanced countries, and later in many poorer countries as well.

At this point world trade in manufactured goods is subject to low tariffs and relatively few import quotas, with clothing the main exception. Agricultural products are subject to many more restrictions, reflecting the political power of farmers in advanced countries. ∎

< < < < < < < < < < < < < < < < < <

>> CHECK YOUR UNDERSTANDING 18-4

1. In 2002 the U.S. imposed tariffs on steel imports, which are an input in a large number and variety of U.S. industries. Explain why political lobbying to eliminate these tariffs is more likely to be effective than political lobbying to eliminate tariffs on consumer goods such as sugar or clothing.

2. Over the years, the WTO has increasingly found itself adjudicating trade disputes that involve not just tariffs or quota restrictions but also restrictions based on quality, health, and environmental considerations. Why do you think this has occurred? What method would you, as a WTO official, use to decide whether a quality, health, or environmental restriction is in violation of a free-trade agreement?

Solutions appear at back of book.

• A LOOK AHEAD •

As we move ahead to new topics, it is important that we carry with us the insights learned here about the logic of comparative advantage and the gains from international trade. They will provide us with a deeper understanding of what drives the world economy and of the reasons countries differ economically. In addition, the study of international trade teaches us how economic policies can create both winners and losers despite the fact that society as a whole gains, an important consideration in any study of how policies are actually made.

SUMMARY

1. International trade is of growing importance to the United States and of even greater importance to most other countries. International trade, like trade among individuals, arises from comparative advantage: the opportunity cost of producing an additional unit of a good is lower in some countries than in others. Goods and services purchased abroad are **imports;** those sold abroad are **exports.**

2. The **Ricardian model of international trade** assumes that opportunity costs are constant. It shows that there are gains from trade: two countries are better off with trade than in **autarky.**

3. In practice, comparative advantage reflects differences between countries in climate, factor endowments, and technology. The **Heckscher–Ohlin model** shows how differences in factor endowments determine comparative advantage: goods differ in **factor intensity,** and countries tend to export goods that are intensive in the factors they have in abundance.

4. The **domestic demand curve** and the **domestic supply curve** determine the price of a good in autarky. When international trade occurs, the domestic price is driven to equality with the **world price,** the price at which the good may be bought or sold abroad.

5. If the world price is below the autarky price, a good is imported. This leads to an increase in consumer surplus, a fall in producer surplus, and a gain in total surplus. If the world price is above the autarky price, a good is exported. This leads to an increase in producer surplus, a fall in consumer surplus, and a gain in total surplus.

6. International trade leads to expansion in **exporting industries** and contraction in **import-competing industries.** This raises the domestic demand for abundant factors of production, reduces the demand for scarce factors, and so affects factor prices.

7. Most economists advocate **free trade,** but in practice many governments engage in **trade protection.** The two most common forms of **protection** are tariffs and quotas; in rare occasions, export industries are subsidized.

8. A **tariff** is a tax levied on imports. It raises the domestic price above the world price, hurting consumers, benefiting domestic producers, and generating government revenue. As a result, total surplus falls. An **import quota** is a legal limit on the quantity of a good that can be imported. It has the same effects as a tariff, except that the revenue goes not to the government but to those who receive import licenses.

9. Although several popular arguments have been made in favor of trade protection, in practice the main reason for protection is probably political: import-competing industries are well organized and well informed about how they gain from trade protection, while consumers are unaware of the costs they pay. Still, U.S. trade is fairly free, mainly because of the role of **international trade agreements,** in which countries agree to reduce trade protection against each others' exports. Trade negotiations are overseen, and the resulting agreements are enforced, by the **World Trade Organization.**

KEY TERMS

Imports, p. 437
Exports, p. 437
Ricardian model of international trade, p. 439
Autarky, p. 439
Factor intensity, p. 442
Heckscher–Ohlin model, p. 442

Domestic demand curve, p. 445
Domestic supply curve, p. 445
World price, p. 445
Exporting industries, p. 449
Import-competing industries, p. 449
Free trade, p. 450
Trade protection, p. 450

Protection, p. 450
Tariff, p. 450
Import quota, p. 452
International trade agreements, p. 455
World Trade Organization, p. 455

PROBLEMS

1. Assume Saudi Arabia and the United States face the production possibilities for oil and cars shown in the accompanying table.

Saudi Arabia		United States	
Quantity of oil (millions of barrels)	Quantity of cars (millions)	Quantity of oil (millions of barrels)	Quantity of cars (millions)
0	4	0	10.0
200	3	100	7.5
400	2	200	5.0
600	1	300	2.5
800	0	400	0

a. What is the opportunity cost of producing a car in Saudi Arabia? In the United States? What is the opportunity cost of producing a barrel of oil in Saudi Arabia? In the United States?

b. Which country has the comparative advantage in producing oil? In producing cars?

c. Suppose that in autarky, Saudi Arabia produces 200 million barrels of oil and 3 million cars; and that the United States produces 300 million barrels of oil and 2.5 million cars. Without trade, can Saudi Arabia produce more oil *and* more cars? Without trade, can the United States produce more oil *and* more cars?

2. The production possibilities for the United States and Saudi Arabia are given in Problem 1. Suppose now that each country specializes in the good in which it has the comparative advantage, and the two countries trade. Also assume that for each country the value of imports must equal the value of exports.

a. What is the total quantity of oil produced? What is the total quantity of cars produced?

b. Is it possible for Saudi Arabia to consume 400 million barrels of oil and 5 million cars, and for the United States to consume 400 million barrels of oil and 5 million cars?

c. Suppose that, in fact, Saudi Arabia consumes 300 million barrels of oil and 4 million cars and the United States consumes 500 million barrels of oil and 6 million cars. How many barrels of oil does the United States import? How many cars does the United States export? Suppose a car costs $10,000 on the world market. How much, then, does a barrel of oil cost on the world market?

3. Both Canada and the United States produce lumber and music CDs with constant opportunity costs. The United States can produce either 10 tons of lumber and no CDs, or 1,000 CDs and no lumber, or any combination in between. Canada can produce either 8 tons of lumber and no CDs, or 400 CDs and no lumber, or any combination in between.

a. Draw the U.S. and Canadian production possibility frontiers in two separate diagrams, with CDs on the horizontal axis and lumber on the vertical axis.

b. In autarky, if the United States wants to consume 500 CDs, how much lumber can it consume at most? Label this point A in your diagram. Similarly, if Canada wants

to consume 1 ton of lumber, how many CDs can it consume in autarky? Label this point C in your diagram.

c. Which country has the absolute advantage in lumber production?

d. Which country has the comparative advantage in lumber production?

Suppose each country specializes in the good in which it has the comparative advantage, and there is trade.

e. How many CDs does the United States produce? How much lumber does Canada produce?

f. Is it possible for the United States to consume 500 CDs and 7 tons of lumber? Label this point B in your diagram. Is it possible for Canada at the same time to consume 500 CDs and 1 ton of lumber? Label this point D in your diagram.

4. For each of the following trade relationships, explain the likely source of the comparative advantage of each of the exporting countries.

a. The United States exports software to Venezuela, and Venezuela exports oil to the United States.

b. The United States exports airplanes to China, and China exports clothing to the United States.

c. The United States exports wheat to Colombia, and Colombia exports coffee to the United States.

5. Shoes are labor-intensive and satellites are capital-intensive to produce. The United States has abundant capital. China has abundant labor. According to the Heckscher–Ohlin model, which good will China export? Which good will the United States export? In the United States, what will happen to the price of labor (the wage) and to the price of capital?

6. Before the North American Free Trade Agreement (NAFTA) gradually eliminated import tariffs on goods, the autarky price of tomatoes in Mexico was below the world price and in the United States was above the world price. Similarly, the autarky price of poultry in Mexico was above the world price and in the United States was below the world price. Draw diagrams with domestic supply and demand curves for each country and each of the two goods. As a result of NAFTA, the United States now imports tomatoes from Mexico and the United States now exports poultry to Mexico. How would you expect the following groups to be affected?

a. Mexican and U.S. consumers of tomatoes. Illustrate the effect on consumer surplus in your diagram.

b. Mexican and U.S. producers of tomatoes. Illustrate the effect on producer surplus in your diagram.

c. Mexican and U.S. tomato workers.

d. Mexican and U.S. consumers of poultry. Illustrate the effect on consumer surplus in your diagram.

e. Mexican and U.S. producers of poultry. Illustrate the effect on producer surplus in your diagram.

f. Mexican and U.S. poultry workers.

7. The accompanying table indicates the U.S. domestic demand schedule and domestic supply schedule for commercial jet

airplanes. Suppose that the world price of a commercial jet airplane is $100 million.

Price of jet (millions)	Quantity of jets demanded	Quantity of jets supplied
$120	100	1,000
110	150	900
100	200	800
90	250	700
80	300	600
70	350	500
60	400	400
50	450	300
40	500	200

a. In autarky, how many commercial jet airplanes does the United States produce, and at what price are they bought and sold?

b. With trade, what will the price for commercial jet airplanes be? Will the United States import or export airplanes? How many?

8. The accompanying table shows the U.S. domestic demand schedule and domestic supply schedule for oranges. Suppose that the world price of oranges is $0.30 per orange.

Price of orange	Quantity of oranges demanded (thousands)	Quantity of oranges supplied (thousands)
$1.00	2	11
0.90	4	10
0.80	6	9
0.70	8	8
0.60	10	7
0.50	12	6
0.40	14	5
0.30	16	4
0.20	18	3

a. Draw the U.S. domestic supply curve and domestic demand curve.

b. With free trade, how many oranges will the United States import or export?

Suppose that the U.S. government imposes a tariff on oranges of $0.20 per orange.

c. How many oranges will the United States import or export after introduction of the tariff?

d. In your diagram, shade the gain or loss to the economy as a whole from the introduction of this tariff.

9. The U.S. domestic demand schedule and domestic supply schedule for oranges was given in Problem 8. Suppose that the world price of oranges is $0.30. The United States introduces an import quota of 3,000 oranges. Draw the domestic demand and supply curves and answer the following questions.

a. What will the domestic price of oranges be after introduction of the quota?

b. What is the value of the quota rents that importers of oranges receive?

10. The accompanying diagram illustrates the U.S. domestic demand curve and domestic supply curve for beef.

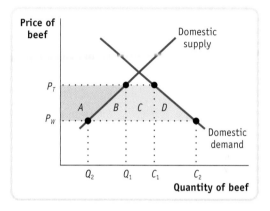

The world price of beef is P_W. The United States currently imposes an import tariff on beef, so the price of beef is P_T. Congress decides to eliminate the tariff. In terms of the areas marked in the diagram, answer the following questions.

a. What is the gain/loss in consumer surplus?

b. What is the gain/loss in producer surplus?

c. What is the gain/loss to the government?

d. What is the gain/loss to the economy as a whole?

11. As the United States has opened up to trade, it has lost many of its low-skill manufacturing jobs, but it has gained jobs in high-skill industries, such as the software industry. Explain whether the United States as a whole has been made better off by trade.

12. The United States is highly protective of its agricultural industry, imposing import tariffs, and sometimes quotas, on imports of agricultural goods. The chapter has presented three arguments for trade protection. For each argument, discuss whether it is a valid justification for trade protection of U.S. agricultural products.

13. In World Trade Organization (WTO) negotiations, if a country agrees to reduce trade barriers (tariffs or quotas), it usually refers to this as a *concession* to other countries. Do you think that this terminology is appropriate?

14. Producers in import-competing industries often make the following argument: "Other countries have an advantage in production of certain goods purely because workers abroad are paid lower wages. In fact, American workers are much more productive than foreign workers. So import-competing industries need to be protected." Is this a valid argument? Explain your answer.

>>Open-Economy Macroeconomics

EURO DILEMMAS

To join or not to join, that is the question.

Not long ago, the menu in a French bistro listed prices in francs, the menu in a German Gasthouse listed prices in marks, and the menu in an Italian trattoria listed prices in lire. Today, however, menus in all three countries list prices with a "€" in front—the symbol of the euro.

The euro came into existence on January 1, 1999. France, Germany, and Italy all gave up their national currencies in favor of the euro. So did most, but not all, of their neighbors. The new "eurozone"—the group of countries using the euro—has a combined GDP almost as large as that of the dollar zone, otherwise known as the United States.

But not all of Europe is part of the euro-zone. The most conspicuous holdout is Britain, which has decided to keep its national currency, the pound, for the time being. Why hasn't Britain adopted the euro?

Part of the answer is national pride: if Britain gave up the pound, it would also have to give up currency that bears the portrait of the queen. But there are also serious economic concerns about giving up the pound in favor of the euro. British economists who favor adoption of the euro argue that if Britain used the same currency as its neighbors, Britain's international trade would expand and its economy would become more productive. But other economists point out that adopting the euro would take away Britain's ability to have an independent monetary policy and might lead to macroeconomic problems.

For the time being, those who want to keep the pound seem to have the upper hand: Britain doesn't seem likely to adopt the euro anytime soon. But the argument will probably go on for a long time, because both sides have a point. To see why, we need to look at the special issues raised by macroeconomics in the open economy.

What you will learn in this chapter:

➤ The meaning and measurement of the **balance of payments**

➤ The determinants of international capital flows

➤ The role of the **foreign exchange market** and the **exchange rate**

➤ The importance of **real exchange rates** and their role in the **current account**

➤ The considerations that lead countries to choose different **exchange rate regimes,** such as **fixed exchange rates** and **floating exchange rates**

➤ Why open-economy considerations affect macroeconomic policy under floating exchange rates

Most of Europe has given up national currencies in favor of the euro, but for now, at least, the British are sticking with the pound.

Capital Flows and the Balance of Payments

In 2004 people living in the United States sold about $3 trillion worth of stuff to people living in other countries and bought about $3 trillion worth of stuff in return. What kind of stuff? All kinds. Residents of the United States (including firms operating in the United States) sold airplanes, bonds, wheat, and many other items to residents of other countries. Residents of the United States bought cars, stocks, oil, and many other items from residents of other countries.

How can we keep track of these transactions? In Chapter 7 we learned that economists keep track of the domestic economy using the national income and product accounts. Economists keep track of international transactions using a different but related set of numbers, the *balance of payments accounts*.

Balance of Payments Accounts

A country's **balance of payments accounts** are a summary of the country's transactions with other countries. The most important feature of that summary is the distinction between the *balance on current account* and the *balance on financial account*.

Look back at the examples we just gave of U.S. sales to foreigners: airplanes, bonds, wheat. When a U.S. resident sells a good such as wheat to a foreigner, that's the end of the transaction. But a financial asset, such as a bond, is different. Remember, a bond is a promise to pay interest and principal in the future. So when a U.S. resident sells a bond to a foreigner, that sale creates a liability: the U.S. resident will have to pay interest and repay principal in the future. The balance of payments accounts distinguish between transactions that don't create liabilities and those that do.

Most of the transactions that enter the current account consist of international sales and purchases of goods, such as wheat and oil, and services, such as computer consulting and hotel rooms. The **balance of payments on goods and services** is the difference between the value of exports (sales of goods and services to foreigners) and the value of imports (purchases of goods and services from foreigners) during a given period. The difference between a country's exports and imports of goods alone—not including services—is the **merchandise trade balance**, sometimes referred to as the **trade balance** for short. Economists sometimes focus on the merchandise trade balance, even though it's an incomplete measure, because data on international trade in services aren't as accurate as data on trade in physical goods.

The **balance of payments on current account,** often referred to simply as the **current account,** is a slightly broader measure than the balance of payments on goods and services. It consists of the balance of payments on goods and services plus net international transfer payments and net international factor income. Transfer payments are funds sent by residents of one country to residents of another—for example, money that Mexican immigrants to the United States send to their families back home. Factor income consists mainly of the income on assets held abroad—for example, the interest paid on U.S. bonds owned by Japanese pension funds. But it also includes labor payments, such as the fees paid to American oil experts hired as consultants in African nations.

Table 19-1 on page 462 shows the composition of the U.S. balance of payments on current account in 2004. The most important feature of that balance was a huge deficit in the balance of payments on goods and services: $618 billion, or 5.3% of GDP. One way to understand this is to say that in 2004, for every dollar's worth of goods and services the United States sold abroad, Americans spent $1.54 on imports. The United States ran a small surplus on factor income and a larger deficit on transfer payments, for an overall current account deficit of $668 billion.

How did the United States pay for all those imports? By selling a lot of assets to the rest of the world, causing it to run a surplus on its *financial account*. A country's **balance of payments on financial account,** or simply **financial account,** is the difference between the country's sales of assets to foreigners and its purchases of assets from

A country's **balance of payments accounts** are a summary of the country's transactions with other countries.

A country's **balance of payments on goods and services** is the difference between its exports and its imports during a given period.

The **merchandise trade balance**, or **trade balance**, is the difference between a country's exports and imports of goods.

A country's **balance of payments on current account**, or **current account**, is its balance of payments on goods and services plus net international transfer payments and factor income.

A country's **balance of payments on financial account**, or simply its **financial account**, is the difference between its sales of assets to foreigners and its purchases of assets from foreigners during a given period.

TABLE 19-1

The U.S. Balance of Payments on Current Account, 2004

	Payments from foreigners (billions of dollars)	Payments to foreigners (billions of dollars)	Balance (billions of dollars)
Goods and services	Exports of goods and services: $1,151	Imports of goods and services: $1,769	−$618
Factor income	Income receipts: 379	Income payments: 349	30
Transfers	*	*	−81
Total (balance of payments on current account)	*	*	−668

*The U.S. government provides only an estimate of net transfers, without the amounts going in and out.

Note: Numbers do not add due to rounding.

Source: Bureau of Economic Analysis.

foreigners during a given period. (Until a few years ago, economists often referred to the financial account as the *capital account*. We'll use the modern term, but you may run across the older term.) The financial account measures *capital flows,* flows of savings from one country to another.

Like the current account, the financial account can be broken into several subaccounts. The most important distinction, as we'll see later in the chapter, is between private and official sales and purchases—between, for example, purchases of U.S. government bonds by private investors in Europe and purchases of these bonds by the central banks of Japan and China. Table 19-2 shows this breakdown of the U.S. financial account for 2004. As you can see, official purchases of U.S. assets were $395 billion in 2004. We'll turn to the reasons for these purchases later in the chapter, when we discuss exchange rate policy. As Table 19-2 shows, there was also a net capital flow into the United States from private investors.

The negative balance of payments on current account and the positive balance of payments on financial account for the United States in 2004 were not an accident. They reflect a basic rule of balance of payments accounting for any country:

(19-1)   Balance of payments on current account (*CA*) + Balance of payments on financial account (*FA*) = 0

or,

$$CA = -FA$$

To understand why Equation 19-1 must be true, it helps to look at Figure 19-1, a variant on the circular-flow diagram we have found useful in discussing domestic

TABLE 19-2

The U.S. Balance of Payments on Financial Account, 2004

	Sales of assets to foreigners (billions of dollars)	Purchases of assets from foreigners (billions of dollars)	Balance (billions of dollars)
Official sales and purchases	$395	−$4	$399
Private sales and purchases	1,045	860	185
Total (balance of payments on financial account)	1,440	856	584

Source: Bureau of Economic Analysis.

Figure 19-1

The Balance of Payments

The green arrows represent payments that are counted in the balance of payments on current account. The red arrows represent payments that are counted in the balance of payments on financial account. Because the total flow into the United States must equal the total flow out of the United States, the sum of the balance of payments on current account plus the balance of payments on financial account is zero.

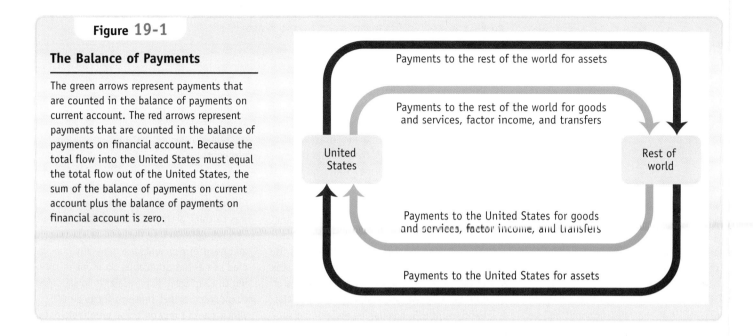

macroeconomics. Instead of showing the flow of money *within* a national economy, Figure 19-1 shows the flow of money *between* national economies. Money flows into the United States from the rest of the world as payment for U.S. exports of goods and services, as payment for the use of U.S.-owned factors of production, and as transfer payments. These flows (indicated by the green arrow) are the positive components of the U.S. balance of payments on current account. Money also flows into the United States from foreigners who purchase U.S. assets (as shown by the red arrow)—the positive component of the U.S. balance of payments on financial account.

At the same time, money flows from the United States to the rest of the world as payment for U.S. imports of goods and services, as payment for the use of foreign-owned factors of production, and as transfer payments. These flows, indicated by another green arrow, are the negative components of the U.S. balance of payments on current account. Money also flows from the United States to purchase foreign assets, as shown by the red arrow—the negative component of the U.S. balance of payments on financial account. As in all circular-flow diagrams, the flow into a box and the flow out of a box are equal. This means that the sum of the red and green arrows going into the United States is equal to the sum of the red and green arrows going out of the United States. That is,

(19-2) Positive entries on current account + Positive entries on financial account = Negative entries on current account + Negative entries on financial account

Equation 19-2 can be rearranged as follows:

(19-3) Positive entries on current account − Negative entries on current account + Positive entries on financial account − Negative entries on financial account = 0

Equation 19-3 is equivalent to Equation 19-1: the balance of payments on current account plus the balance of payments on financial account—both equal to positive entries minus negative entries—is equal to zero.

Even though the balance of payments on current account and the balance of payments on financial account sum to zero by the rules of accounting, you can see by

FOR INQUIRING MINDS

GDP, GNP, AND THE CURRENT ACCOUNT

When we discussed national income accounting in Chapter 7, we derived the basic equation relating GDP to the components of spending:

$$Y = C + I + G + X - IM$$

where X and IM are exports and imports, respectively, of goods and services. But as we've learned, the balance of payments on goods and services is only one component of the current account balance. Why doesn't the national income equation use the current account as a whole?

The answer is that gross domestic product, which is the value of goods and services produced in a country, doesn't include two sources of income that are included in calculating the current account balance: international factor income and international transfers. The profits of Ford Motors U.K. aren't included in America's GDP, and the funds Latin American immigrants send home to their families aren't subtracted from GDP.

Shouldn't we have a broader measure that does include these sources of income? Actually, gross *national* product—GNP—does include international factor income. Estimates of U.S. GNP differ slightly from estimates of GDP because GNP adds in items such as the earnings of U.S. companies abroad and subtracts items such as the interest payments on bonds owned by residents of China and Japan. There isn't, however, any regularly calculated measure that includes transfer payments.

Why do economists use GDP rather than a broader measure? Two reasons. First, the original purpose of the national accounts was to track production rather than income. Second, data on international factor income and transfer payments are generally considered somewhat unreliable. So if you're trying to keep track of movements in the economy, it makes sense to focus on GDP, which doesn't rely on these unreliable data.

comparing Table 19-1 with Table 19-2 that the *measured* balance of payments on current account and the *measured* balance of payments on financial account didn't add up to zero in 2004. The U.S. deficit on current account was offset by a surplus of $584 billion on financial account, but this was $84 billion less than the $668 billion deficit on current account. That difference is known as the *statistical discrepancy*. It tells us that there was an error in the numbers. The reason for such errors is that economic data collection isn't perfect. Economists generally consider current account data more reliable than financial account data, so they often assume that any discrepancy represents unmeasured financial account transactions.

Modeling Private International Capital Flows

In Chapter 18 we described how comparative advantage gives rise to international trade, an exchange of goods and services between countries. Our discussion of the balance of payments already tells us that the picture we gave in Chapter 18 was somewhat simplified, because countries don't exchange just goods and services. They also trade assets—not just for other assets, but for goods and services. In fact, in 2004 inflows of capital paid for about a third of U.S. imports. That is, the United States paid for a large fraction of its imports not by exporting other goods and services but by selling assets to foreigners, creating liabilities that will have to be repaid at some future date. So it's important to understand the determinants of international capital flows.

Part of our explanation will have to wait for a little while, because some international capital flows are carried out by governments and central banks, who sometimes act very differently from private investors. For example, in 2004 non-Chinese individuals and firms were buying Chinese assets, but the Chinese government

more than offset this capital inflow by buying assets overseas, especially in the United States. We'll turn later in the chapter to the reasons governments and central banks buy and sell foreign assets. But we can gain insight into the motivations for capital flows that are the result of private decisions by using the *loanable funds model* we developed in Chapter 9. In using this model, we make two important simplifications:

- We simplify the reality of international capital flows by assuming that all flows are in the form of loans. In reality, capital flows take many forms, including purchases of shares of stock in foreign companies and foreign real estate, as well as *direct foreign investment,* in which companies build factories or acquire other productive assets abroad.

- We also ignore the effects of expected changes in *exchange rates,* the relative values of different national currencies. We will analyze the determination of exchange rates later in the chapter.

Figure 19-2 recaps the loanable funds model for a closed economy. Equilibrium corresponds to point *E,* at an interest rate of 4%, where the supply of loanable funds, curve *S,* intersects the demand for loanable funds, curve *D.* But if international capital flows are possible, this diagram changes and *E* may no longer be the equilibrium. We can analyze the causes and effects of international capital flows using Figure 19-3 on page 466, which places the loanable funds market diagrams for two countries side by side.

Figure 19-3 on page 466 illustrates a world consisting of only two countries, the United States and Britain. Panel (a) shows the loanable funds market in the U.S., where the equilibrium in the absence of international capital flows is at point E_{US} with an interest rate of 6%. Panel (b) shows the loanable funds market in Britain, where the equilibrium in the absence of international capital flows is at point E_B with an interest rate of 2%.

Will the actual interest rate in the United States remain at 6% and that in Britain at 2%? Not if it is easy for British residents to make loans to Americans. In that case, British lenders, attracted by high American interest rates, will send some of their loanable funds to the United States. This capital inflow will increase the quantity of loanable funds supplied to American borrowers, pushing the U.S. interest rate down. At the same time, it will reduce the quantity of loanable funds supplied to British borrowers, pushing the British interest rate up. So, international capital flows will narrow the gap between U.S. and British interest rates.

Let's further suppose that British lenders regard a loan to an American as being just as good as a loan to one of their own compatriots, and American borrowers regard a debt to a British lender as no more costly than a debt to an American lender.

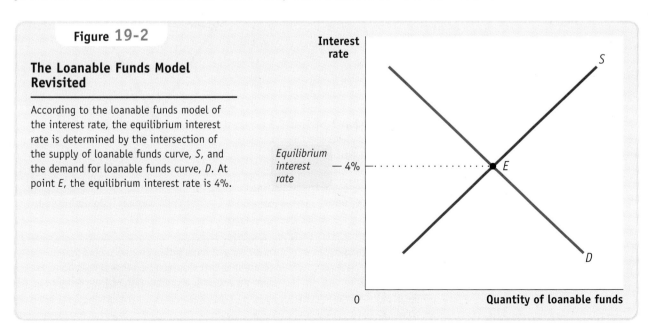

Figure 19-2

The Loanable Funds Model Revisited

According to the loanable funds model of the interest rate, the equilibrium interest rate is determined by the intersection of the supply of loanable funds curve, *S,* and the demand for loanable funds curve, *D.* At point *E,* the equilibrium interest rate is 4%.

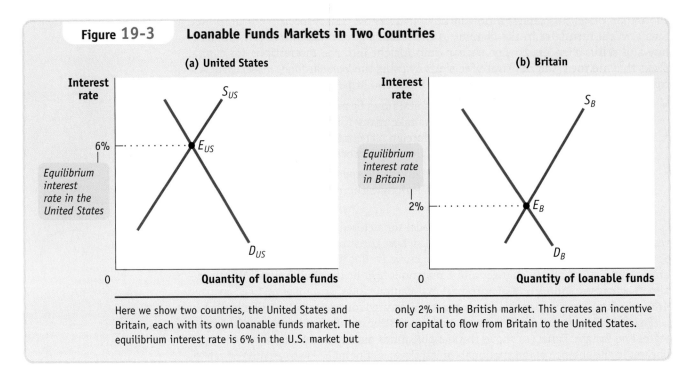

Figure 19-3 **Loanable Funds Markets in Two Countries**

(a) United States

Equilibrium interest rate in the United States

(b) Britain

Equilibrium interest rate in Britain

Here we show two countries, the United States and Britain, each with its own loanable funds market. The equilibrium interest rate is 6% in the U.S. market but only 2% in the British market. This creates an incentive for capital to flow from Britain to the United States.

In that case, the flow of funds from Britain to the United States will continue until the gap between their interest rates is eliminated. In other words, when residents of the two countries believe that a foreign asset is as good as a domestic one and that a foreign liability is as good as a domestic one, then international capital flows will equalize the interest rates in the two countries. Figure 19-4 shows an international

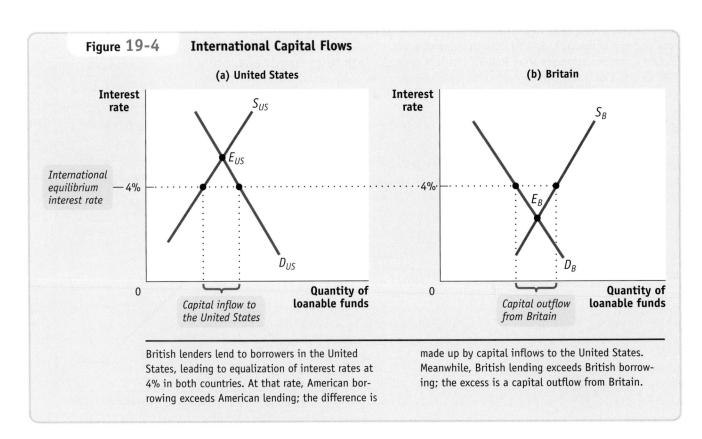

Figure 19-4 **International Capital Flows**

(a) United States

International equilibrium interest rate

Capital inflow to the United States

(b) Britain

Capital outflow from Britain

British lenders lend to borrowers in the United States, leading to equalization of interest rates at 4% in both countries. At that rate, American borrowing exceeds American lending; the difference is made up by capital inflows to the United States. Meanwhile, British lending exceeds British borrowing; the excess is a capital outflow from Britain.

equilibrium in the loanable funds markets where the equilibrium interest rate is 4% in both the United States and Britain. At this interest rate, the quantity of loanable funds demanded by American borrowers exceeds the quantity of loanable funds supplied by American lenders. This gap is filled by "imported" funds—a capital inflow from Britain. At the same time, the quantity of loanable funds supplied by British lenders is greater than the quantity of loanable funds demanded by British borrowers. This excess is "exported" in the form of a capital outflow to the United States. And the two markets are in equilibrium at a common interest rate of 4%—at that interest rate, the total quantity of loans demanded by borrowers across the two markets is equal to the total quantity of loans supplied by lenders across the two markets.

In short, international flows of capital are like international flows of goods and services. Capital moves from places where it would be cheap in the absence of international capital flows to places where it would be expensive in the absence of such flows.

Underlying Determinants of International Capital Flows

The open-economy version of the loanable funds model helps us understand international capital flows in terms of the supply and demand for funds. But what underlies differences across countries in the supply and demand for funds? Why, in the absence of international capital flows, would interest rates differ internationally, creating an incentive for international capital flows?

International differences in the demand for funds reflect underlying differences in investment opportunities. In particular, a country with a rapidly growing economy, other things equal, tends to offer more investment opportunities than a country with a slowly growing economy. So rapidly growing economies typically—though not always—offer higher returns to investors than slowly growing economies in the absence of capital flows. As a result, capital tends to flow from slowly growing to rapidly growing economies.

The classic example, described in the Economics in Action that follows on page 468, is the flow of capital from Britain to the United States, among other countries, between 1870 and 1914. During that era, the U.S. economy was growing rapidly as the population increased and spread westward and as the nation industrialized. This

---

FOR INQUIRING MINDS

TWIN DEFICITS?

In the 1980s the United States began to run both large budget deficits and large deficits in its balance of payments on current account; for a time these deficits were roughly the same size. And they soon came to be known as the "twin deficits." But were they linked?

The argument for linkage ran as follows: Budget deficits reduce overall national savings. Capital tends to flow into countries with low savings, other things equal. And capital inflows are always matched by equal-sized deficits in the balance of payments on current account. So there was a chain of economic links from the budget deficit to the current account deficit.

Even at the time, however, economists cautioned that the fact that the budget deficit and the current account deficit were about the same size was largely an accident, because there are many other factors besides budget deficits that affect international capital flows. As a result, there isn't a close relationship between the size of a country's budget deficit and its balance of payments on current account. In fact, sometimes the two numbers have the opposite sign. Japan has large budget deficits but runs large surpluses on its current account. In the late 1990s the United States had a budget surplus but ran a large deficit on its current account.

Still, the concept of the twin deficits did highlight the relationship between savings and international capital flows. And twin deficits reemerged in the United States after 2000.

created a demand for investment spending on railroads, factories, and so on. Meanwhile, Britain had a much more slowly growing population, was already industrialized, and already had a railroad network covering the country. This left Britain with savings to spare, much of which were lent out to the United States and other New World economies.

International differences in the supply of funds reflect differences in savings across countries. These may be the result of differences in private savings rates, which vary widely among countries. For example, in 2002 private savings were 33.6% of Japan's GDP but only 17.6% of U.S. GDP. They may also reflect differences in savings by governments. In particular, as discussed in For Inquiring Minds on page 467, government budget deficits, which reduce overall national savings, can lead to capital inflows.

economics in action

The Golden Age of Capital Flows

Technology, it's often said, shrinks the world. Jet planes have put most of the world's cities within a few hours of one another; modern telecommunications transmit information instantly around the globe. So you might think that international capital flows must now be larger than ever.

But if capital flows are measured as a share of world savings and investment, that belief turns out not to be true. The golden age of capital flows actually preceded World War I—from 1870 to 1914.

These capital flows went mainly from European countries, especially Britain, to what were then known as "zones of recent settlement," countries that were attracting large numbers of European immigrants. Among the big recipients of capital inflows were Australia, Argentina, Canada, and the United States.

The large capital flows reflected differences in investment opportunities. Britain, a mature industrial economy with limited natural resources and a slowly growing population, offered relatively limited opportunities for new investment. The regions of recent settlement, with rapidly growing populations and abundant natural resources, offered investors a higher return and attracted capital inflows. Estimates suggest that over this period Britain sent about 40% of its savings abroad, largely to finance railroads and other large projects. No country has matched that record in modern times.

Why can't we match the capital flows of our great-great-grandfathers? Economists aren't completely sure, but they have pointed to two causes: migration restrictions and political risks.

During the golden age of capital flows, capital movements were complementary to population movements: the big recipients of capital from Europe were also places to which large numbers of Europeans were moving. These large-scale population movements were possible before World War I because there were few legal restrictions on immigration. In today's world, by contrast, migration is limited by extensive legal barriers, as anyone considering a move to the United States or Europe can tell you.

The other factor that has changed is political risk. Modern governments often limit foreign investment because they fear it will diminish their national autonomy. And due to political or security concerns, governments sometimes seize foreign property, a risk that deters investors from sending more than a relatively modest share of their wealth abroad. In the nineteenth century such actions were rare, partly because some major destinations of investment were still European colonies, partly because in those days governments had a habit of sending troops and gunboats to enforce the claims of their investors. ■

< < < < < < < < < < < < < < < < < < <

1. Which of the balance of payments accounts do the following events affect?
   a. Boeing, a U.S.-based company, sells a newly built airplane to China.
   b. Chinese investors buy stock in Boeing from Americans.
   c. A Chinese company buys a used airplane from American Airlines and ships it to China.
   d. A Chinese investor who owns property in the United States buys a corporate jet, which he will keep in the United States so he can travel around America.

2. In a widely reported speech, a Federal Reserve official declared that there is a "global savings glut": savings are high, and investment returns are low, in the rest of the world. Explain how such a glut would affect the U.S. financial account and interest rates.

Solutions appear at back of book.

The Role of the Exchange Rate

We've just seen how differences in the supply of loanable funds from savings and the demand for loanable funds for investment spending lead to international capital flows. We've also learned that a country's balance of payments on current account plus its balance of payments on financial account add to zero: a country that receives net capital inflows must run a matching current account deficit, and a country that generates net capital outflows must run a matching current account surplus.

The behavior of the financial account—reflecting inflows or outflows of capital—is best described by equilibrium in the international loanable funds market. At the same time, the balance of payments on goods and services, the main component of the current account, is determined by decisions in the international markets for goods and services. So given that the financial account reflects the movement of capital and the current account reflects the movement of goods and services, what ensures that the balance of payments really does balance? That is, what ensures that the two accounts actually offset one another?

The answer lies in the role of the *exchange rate,* which is determined in the *foreign exchange market.*

Understanding Exchange Rates

In general, goods, services, and assets produced in a country must be paid for in that country's currency. American products must be paid for in dollars; European products must be paid for in euros; Japanese products must be paid for in yen. Occasionally, sellers will accept payment in foreign currency, but they will then exchange that currency for domestic money.

International transactions, then, require a market—the **foreign exchange market**—in which currencies can be exchanged for each other. This market determines **exchange rates,** the prices at which currencies trade. (The foreign exchange market is, in fact, not located in any one geographic location. Rather, it is a global electronic market that traders around the world use to buy and sell currencies.)

Table 19-3 shows exchange rates among the world's three most important currencies as of 4:25 P.M., EST, on August 22, 2005. Each entry shows the price of the "row" currency in terms of the "column" currency. For example, at that time US\$1 exchanged for €0.8178, so it took €0.8178 to buy US\$1. Similarly, it took US\$1.2228 to buy one €1. These two numbers reflect the same rate of exchange between the euro and the U.S. dollar: 1/1.2228 = 0.8178.

There are two ways to write any given exchange rate. In this case, there were €0.8178 to US\$1 and US\$1.2228 to €1. Which is the correct way to write it? The answer is that there is no fixed rule. In most countries people tend to express the exchange rate as the price of a dollar in domestic currency. However, this rule isn't universal, and the U.S. dollar–euro rate is commonly quoted both ways. The important thing is to be sure you know which one you are using! See Pitfalls on page 470.

Currencies are traded in the **foreign exchange market**.

The prices at which currencies trade are known as **exchange rates**.

TABLE 19-3

Exchange Rates, August 22, 2005, 4:25 P.M.

	U.S. dollars	Yen	Euros
One U.S. dollar exchanged for	1	109.7050	0.8178
One yen exchanged for	0.009115	1	0.007454
One euro exchanged for	1.2228	134.1473	1

When a currency becomes more valuable in terms of other currencies, it **appreciates.**

When a currency becomes less valuable in terms of other currencies, it **depreciates.**

When discussing movements in exchange rates, economists use specialized terms to avoid confusion. When a currency becomes more valuable in terms of other currencies, economists say that the currency **appreciates.** When a currency becomes less valuable in terms of other currencies, it **depreciates.** Suppose, for example, that the value of €1 went from $1 to $1.25, which means that the value of US$1 went from €1 to €0.8 (because 1/1.25 = 0.8). In this case we would say that the euro appreciated and the U.S. dollar depreciated.

Movements in exchange rates, other things equal, affect the relative prices of goods, services, and assets in different countries. Suppose, for example, that the price of an American hotel room is US$100 and the price of a French hotel room is €100. If the exchange rate is €1 = US$1, these hotel rooms have the same price. If the exchange rate is €1.25 = US$1, the French hotel room is 20% cheaper than the American hotel room. If the exchange rate is €0.80 = US$1, the French hotel room is 25% more expensive than the American hotel room.

But what determines exchange rates? Supply and demand in the foreign exchange market.

PITFALLS

WHICH WAY IS UP?

Suppose someone says, "The U.S. exchange rate is up." What does that person mean?

It isn't clear. Sometimes the exchange rate is measured as the price of a dollar in terms of foreign currency, sometimes as the price of foreign currency in terms of dollars. So the statement could mean that the dollar either appreciated or that it depreciated!

You have to be particularly careful when using published statistics. Most countries other than the United States state their exchange rates in terms of the price of a dollar in their domestic currency—for example, Mexican officials will say that the exchange rate is 10, meaning 10 pesos per dollar. But Britain, for historical reasons, usually states its exchange rate the other way. At 4:25 P.M. on August 22, 2005, US$1 was worth £0.5553, and £1 was worth US$1.8009. More often than not, this number is reported as an exchange rate of 1.8009. In fact, on occasion, professional economists and consultants embarrass themselves by getting the direction in which the pound is moving wrong!

By the way, Americans generally follow other countries' lead: we usually say that the exchange rate against Mexico is 10 pesos per dollar but the exchange rate against Britain is 1.8 dollars per pound. But this rule isn't reliable; exchange rates against the euro are often stated both ways.

So it's always important to check before using exchange rate data: which way is the exchange rate being measured?

The Equilibrium Exchange Rate

Imagine, for the sake of simplicity, that there are only two currencies in the world: U.S. dollars and euros. Europeans wanting to purchase American goods, services, and assets come to the foreign exchange market, wanting to exchange euros for U.S. dollars. That is, Europeans demand U.S. dollars from the foreign exchange market and, correspondingly, supply euros to that market. Americans wanting to buy European goods, services, and assets come to the foreign exchange market to exchange U.S. dollars for euros. That is, Americans supply U.S. dollars to the foreign exchange market and, correspondingly, demand euros from that market. (International transfers and payments of factor income also enter into the foreign exchange market, but to make things simple we'll ignore these.)

Figure 19-5 shows how the foreign exchange market works. The quantity of dollars demanded and supplied at any given euro–U.S. dollar exchange rate is shown on the horizontal axis, and the euro–U.S. dollar exchange rate is shown on the vertical axis. The exchange rate plays the same role as the price of a good or service in an ordinary supply and demand diagram.

The figure shows two curves, the demand curve for U.S. dollars and the supply curve for U.S. dollars. The demand curve slopes downward: the more euros it takes to buy a dollar, the fewer dollars Europeans will demand. The key to understanding the slopes of these curves is that the level of the exchange rate affects exports and imports. When a country's currency appreciates (becomes more valuable), exports fall and imports rise. When a country's currency depreciates (becomes less valuable), exports rise and imports fall.

To understand why the demand curve for U.S. dollars slopes downward, recall that the exchange rate, other things equal, determines the prices of American goods, services, and assets relative to those of European goods, services, and assets. If the U.S. dollar rises against the euro (the dollar appreciates), American products will become more expensive to Europeans relative to European goods. So Europeans will buy less from the United States and will acquire fewer dollars in the foreign exchange market: the quantity of U.S. dollars demanded falls as the number of euros needed to buy a U.S. dollar rises. If the U.S. dollar falls against the euro (the dollar depreciates), American products will become cheaper for Europeans. Europeans will respond by buying more from the United States and acquiring more dollars in the foreign exchange market: the quantity of U.S. dollars demanded rises as the number of euros needed to buy a U.S. dollar falls.

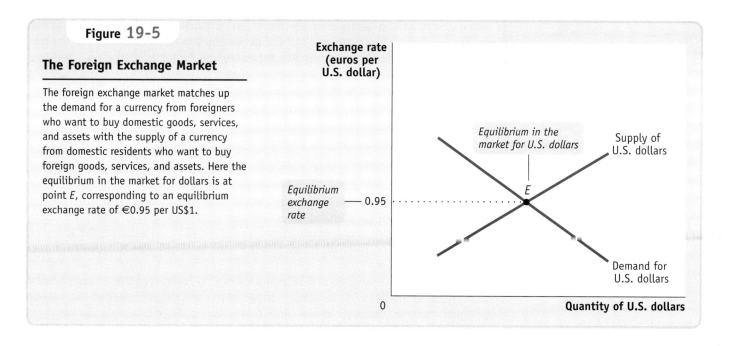

Figure 19-5

The Foreign Exchange Market

The foreign exchange market matches up the demand for a currency from foreigners who want to buy domestic goods, services, and assets with the supply of a currency from domestic residents who want to buy foreign goods, services, and assets. Here the equilibrium in the market for dollars is at point *E*, corresponding to an equilibrium exchange rate of €0.95 per US$1.

A similar argument explains why the supply curve of U.S. dollars in Figure 19-5 slopes upward: the more euros required to buy a U.S. dollar, the more dollars Americans will supply. Again, the reason is the effect of the exchange rate on relative prices. If the U.S. dollar rises against the euro, European products look cheaper to Americans—who will demand more of them. This will require Americans to convert more dollars into euros.

The **equilibrium exchange rate** is the exchange rate at which the quantity of U.S. dollars demanded in the foreign exchange market is equal to the quantity of U.S. dollars supplied. In Figure 19-5, the equilibrium is at point *E*, and the equilibrium exchange rate is 0.95. That is, at an exchange rate of €0.95 per US$1, the quantity of U.S. dollars supplied to the foreign exchange market is equal to the quantity of U.S. dollars demanded.

To understand the significance of the equilibrium exchange rate, it's helpful to consider a numerical example of what equilibrium in the foreign exchange market looks like. Such an example is shown in Table 19-4. (This is a hypothetical table that isn't intended to match real numbers.) The first row shows European purchases of U.S. dollars, either to buy U.S. goods and services or to buy U.S. assets. The second row shows U.S. sales of U.S. dollars, either to buy European goods and services or to buy European assets. At the equilibrium exchange rate, the total quantity of U.S. dollars Europeans want to buy is equal to the total quantity of U.S. dollars Americans want to sell.

The **equilibrium exchange rate** is the exchange rate at which the quantity of a currency demanded in the foreign exchange market is equal to the quantity supplied.

TABLE 19-4

Equilibrium in the Foreign Exchange Market: A Hypothetical Example

European purchases of U.S. dollars (trillions of U.S. dollars)	To buy U.S. goods and services: 1.0	To buy U.S. assets: 1.0	Total purchases of dollars: 2.0
U.S. sales of U.S. dollars (trillions of U.S. dollars)	To buy European goods and services: 1.5	To buy European assets: 0.5	Total sales of dollars: 2.0
	U.S. balance of payments on current account: −0.5	U.S. balance of payments on financial account: +0.5	

Remember that the balance of payments accounts divide international transactions into two types. Purchases and sales of goods and services are counted in the current account. (Again, we're leaving out transfers and factor income to keep things simple.) Purchases and sales of assets are counted in the financial account. At the equilibrium exchange rate, then, we have the situation shown in Table 19-4: the sum of the balance of payments on current account plus the balance of payments on financial account is zero.

Now let's briefly consider how a shift in the demand for U.S. dollars affects equilibrium in the foreign exchange market. Suppose that for some reason capital flows from Europe to the United States increase—say, due to a change in the preferences of European investors. The effects are shown in Figure 19-6. The demand for U.S. dollars in the foreign exchange market increases as European investors convert euros into dollars to fund their new investments in the United States. This is shown by the shift in the demand curve from D_1 to D_2. As a result, the U.S. dollar appreciates: the number of euros per U.S. dollar at the equilibrium exchange rate rises from X_1 to X_2.

What are the consequences of this increased capital inflow for the balance of payments? The total quantity of U.S. dollars supplied to the foreign exchange market still must equal the total quantity of U.S. dollars demanded. So the increased capital inflow to the United States—an increase in the balance of payments on financial account—must be matched by a decline in the balance of payments on current account. What causes the balance of payments on current account to decline? The appreciation of the U.S. dollar. A rise in the number of euros per U.S. dollar leads Americans to buy more European goods and services and Europeans to buy fewer American goods and services.

Table 19-5 shows how this might work. Europeans are buying more U.S. assets, increasing the balance on financial account from 0.5 to 1.0. This is offset by a reduction in European purchases of U.S. goods and services and a rise in U.S. purchases of European goods and services, both the result of the dollar's appreciation. *So any change in the U.S. balance of payments on financial account generates an equal and opposite reaction in the balance of payments on current account. Movements in the exchange*

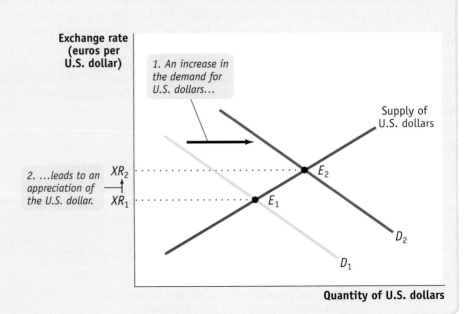

Figure 19-6

An Increase in the Demand for U.S. Dollars

An increase in the demand for U.S. dollars might result from a change in the preferences of European investors. The demand curve for U.S. dollars shifts from D_1 to D_2. So the equilibrium number of euros per U.S. dollar rises—the dollar *appreciates*. As a result, the balance of payments on current account falls as the balance of payments on financial account rises.

>web...

TABLE 19-5

Effects of Increased Capital Inflows

European purchases of U.S. dollars (trillions of U.S. dollars)	To buy U.S. goods and services: 0.75 (down 0.25)	To buy U.S. assets: 1.5 (up 0.5)	Total purchases of U.S. dollars: 2.25
U.S. sales of U.S. dollars (trillions of U.S. dollars)	To buy European goods and services: 1.75 (up 0.25)	To buy European assets: 0.5 (no change)	Total sales of U.S. dollars: 2.25
	U.S. balance of payments on current account: −1.0 (down 0.5)	U.S. balance of payments on financial account: +1.0 (up 0.5)	

rate ensure that changes in the financial account and in the current account offset each other.

Let's briefly run this process in reverse. Suppose there is a reduction in capital flows from Europe to the United States—again due to a change in the preferences of European investors. The demand for U.S. dollars in the foreign exchange market falls, and the dollar depreciates: the number of euros per U.S. dollar at the equilibrium exchange rate falls. This leads Americans to buy fewer European products and Europeans to buy more American products. Ultimately, this generates an increase in the U.S. balance of payments on current account. So a fall in capital flows into the United States leads to a weaker dollar, which in turn generates an increase in U.S. net exports.

Inflation and Real Exchange Rates

In 1992 one U.S. dollar exchanged, on average, for 3.1 Mexican pesos. By 2003, the peso had fallen against the dollar by more than two-thirds, with an average exchange rate in 2003 of 10.8 pesos per dollar. Did Mexican products also become much cheaper relative to U.S. products over that 11-year period? Did the price of Mexican products expressed in terms of U.S. dollars also fall by two-thirds? The answer is no, because Mexico had much higher inflation than the United States over that period. In fact, the relative price of U.S. and Mexican products changed little between 1992 and 2003, although the exchange rate changed a lot.

To take account of the effects of differences in inflation rates, economists calculate **real exchange rates,** exchange rates adjusted for international differences in aggregate price levels. Suppose that the exchange rate we are looking at is the number of Mexican pesos per U.S. dollar. Let P_{US} and P_{Mex} be indexes of the aggregate price levels in the United States and Mexico, respectively. Then the real exchange rate between the Mexican peso and the U.S. dollar is defined as

(19-4) Real exchange rate = Mexican pesos per U.S. dollar $\times \dfrac{P_{US}}{P_{Mex}}$

To distinguish it from the real exchange rate, the exchange rate unadjusted for aggregate price levels is sometimes called the *nominal* exchange rate.

To understand the significance of the difference between the real and nominal exchange rates, let's consider the following example. Suppose that the Mexican peso depreciates against the U.S. dollar, with the exchange rate going from 10 pesos per U.S. dollar to 15 pesos per U.S. dollar, a 50% change. But suppose that at the same time the price of everything in Mexico, measured in pesos, increases by 50%, so that the Mexican price index rises from 100 to 150. At the same time, suppose that there is no

Real exchange rates are exchange rates adjusted for international differences in aggregate price levels.

change in U.S. prices, so that the U.S. price index remains at 100. Then the initial real exchange rate is

$$\text{Pesos per dollar} \times \frac{P_{US}}{P_{Mex}} = 10 \times \frac{100}{100} = 10$$

After the peso depreciates and the Mexican price level increases, the real exchange rate is

$$\text{Pesos per dollar} \times \frac{P_{US}}{P_{Mex}} = 15 \times \frac{100}{150} = 10$$

In this example, the peso has depreciated substantially in terms of the U.S. dollar, but the *real* exchange rate between the peso and the U.S. dollar hasn't changed at all. And because the real peso–U.S. dollar exchange rate hasn't changed, the nominal depreciation of the peso against the U.S. dollar will have no effect either on the quantity of goods and services exported by Mexico to the United States or on the quantity of goods and services imported by Mexico from the United States. To see why, consider again the example of a hotel room. Suppose that this room initially costs 1,000 pesos per night, which is $100 at an exchange rate of 10 pesos per dollar. After both Mexican prices and the number of pesos per dollar rise by 50%, the hotel room costs 1,500 pesos per night—but 1,500 pesos divided by 15 pesos per dollar is $100, so the Mexican hotel room still costs $100. As a result, a U.S. tourist considering a trip to Mexico will have no reason to change plans.

The same is true for all goods and services that enter into trade: *the current account responds only to changes in the real exchange rate, not the nominal exchange rate.* A country's products become cheaper to foreigners only when that country's currency depreciates in real terms, and those products become more expensive to foreigners only when the currency appreciates in real terms. As a consequence, economists who analyze movements in exports and imports of goods and services focus on the real exchange rate, not the nominal exchange rate.

Figure 19-7 illustrates just how important it can be to distinguish between nominal and real exchange rates. The line labeled "nominal exchange rate" shows the number of pesos it took to buy a U.S. dollar from 1992 to 2003. As you can see, the peso depreciated massively over that period. But the line labeled "real exchange rate"

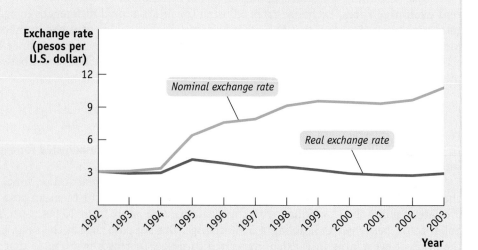

Figure 19-7

Real versus Nominal Exchange Rates, 1992–2003

Between 1992 and 2003, the price of a dollar in Mexican pesos tripled. But because Mexico had higher inflation than the United States, the real exchange rate, which measures the relative price of Mexican goods and services, ended up roughly where it started.

Source: OECD Factbook 2005.

shows the real exchange rate: it was calculated using Equation 19-4, with price indexes for both Mexico and the United States set so that 1992 = 100. In real terms, the peso depreciated between 1992 and 1995, but not by nearly as much as the nominal depreciation. By the end of the period, the real peso–U.S. dollar exchange rate was just about back where it started.

Purchasing Power Parity

A useful tool for analyzing exchange rates, closely connected to the concept of the real exchange rate, is known as *purchasing power parity.* The **purchasing power parity** between two countries' currencies is the nominal exchange rate at which a given basket of goods and services would cost the same amount in each country. Suppose, for example, that a basket of goods and services that costs $100 in the United States costs 1,000 pesos in Mexico. Then the purchasing power parity is 10 pesos per U.S. dollar: at that exchange rate, 1,000 pesos = $100, so the market basket costs the same amount in both countries.

> The **purchasing power parity** between two countries' currencies is the nominal exchange rate at which a given basket of goods and services would cost the same amount in each country.

Calculations of purchasing power parities are usually made by estimating the cost of buying broad market baskets containing many goods and services—everything from automobiles and groceries to housing and telephone calls. But as For Inquiring Minds on page 476 explains, once a year the magazine *The Economist* publishes a list of purchasing power parities based on the cost of buying a market basket that contains only one item—a McDonald's Big Mac.

Nominal exchange rates almost always differ from purchasing power parities. Some of these differences are systematic: in general, prices are lower in poor countries than in rich countries because services tend to be cheaper in poor countries. But even among countries at roughly the same level of economic development, nominal exchange rates vary quite a lot from purchasing power parity. Figure 19-8 shows the nominal exchange rate between the Canadian dollar and the U.S. dollar, measured as the number of Canadian dollars per U.S. dollar, from 1990 to 2003, together with an estimate of the purchasing power parity exchange rate between the United States and Canada over the same period. The purchasing power parity didn't change much over the whole period because the United States and Canada had about the same rate of inflation. But at the beginning of the period the nominal exchange rate was below purchasing power parity, so a given market basket was more expensive in Canada than in the United States. By 2002 the nominal exchange rate

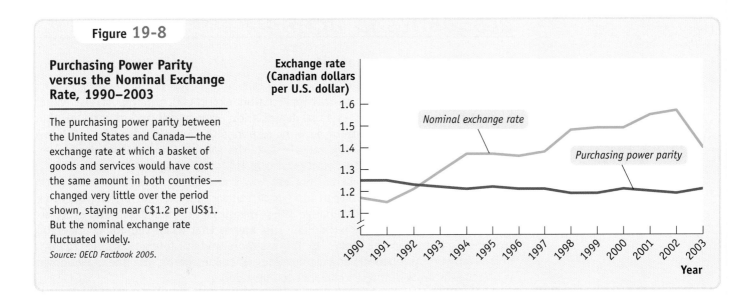

Figure 19-8

Purchasing Power Parity versus the Nominal Exchange Rate, 1990–2003

The purchasing power parity between the United States and Canada—the exchange rate at which a basket of goods and services would have cost the same amount in both countries— changed very little over the period shown, staying near C$1.2 per US$1. But the nominal exchange rate fluctuated widely.

Source: OECD Factbook 2005.

For a number of years the British magazine *The Economist* has produced an annual comparison of the cost in different countries of one particular consumption item that is found around the world—a McDonald's Big Mac. The magazine finds the price of a Big Mac in local currency, then computes two numbers: the price of a Big Mac in U.S. dollars using the prevailing exchange rate, and the exchange rate at which the price of a Big Mac would equal the U.S. price. If purchasing power parity held for Big Macs, the dollar price of a Big Mac would be the same everywhere. If purchasing power parity is a good theory for the long run, the exchange rate at which a Big Mac's price matches the U.S. price should offer some guidance about where the exchange rate will eventually end up.

In the May 2004 version of the Big Mac index, there were some wide variations in the dollar price of a Big Mac. In the U.S.,

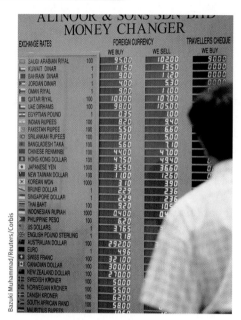

But how much money do I need to exchange if I want to buy lunch?

the price was $2.90. In China, converting at the official exchange rate, a Big Mac cost only $1.26. In Denmark, though, the price was $4.46.

The Big Mac index suggested that the euro would eventually fall against the dollar: the purchasing power parity exchange rate was $1.06 per €1 versus an actual market exchange rate of $1.24. The yen, on the other hand, looked undervalued: at burger purchasing power parity, the yen price of a dollar would be ¥90.3 versus the actual market exchange rate of ¥108.

Serious economic studies of purchasing power parity require data on the prices of many goods and services. It turns out, however, that estimates of purchasing power parity based on the Big Mac index usually aren't that different from more elaborate measures. Fast food seems to make for pretty good fast research.

was far above the purchasing power parity, so a market basket was much cheaper in Canada than in the United States.

Over the long run, however, purchasing power parities are pretty good at predicting actual changes in nominal exchange rates. In particular, nominal exchange rates between countries at similar levels of economic development tend to fluctuate around levels that lead to similar costs for a given market basket. In fact, by July 2005 the nominal exchange rate between the United States and Canada was C$1.22 per US$1—just about the purchasing power parity.

economics in action

The Dollar and the Deficit

As we've seen, the level of the *real* exchange rate affects exports and imports. When a country's currency undergoes a real appreciation, exports fall and imports rise. When a country's currency undergoes a real depreciation, exports rise and imports fall. And as we've just stated, the current account responds to changes in the real exchange rate, not the nominal exchange rate. In fact, the relationship between the real exchange rate and the current account is clear in U.S. data, as shown in Figure 19-9.

In Figure 19-9, the line labeled "real exchange rate" is an index of the value of the U.S. dollar in terms of a basket of foreign currencies, adjusted for differences in aggregate price levels. The real exchange rate is measured on the left axis and expressed in units of foreign currency per dollar. This means that when the dollar undergoes real appreciation, the line moves up: it takes more units of foreign currency to buy a dollar. Conversely, when the dollar undergoes real depreciation, the line moves down: it takes fewer units of foreign currency to buy a dollar.

Figure 19-9

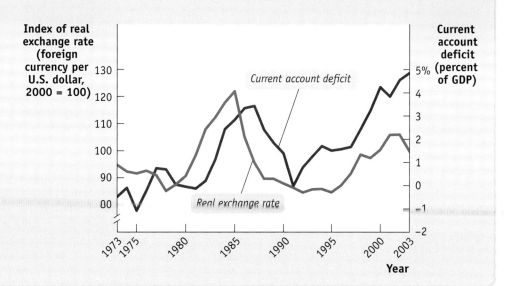

The Dollar and the Current Account Deficit, 1973–2003

The U.S. balance of payments on current account has generally followed movements in the real exchange rate. Here we compare the real exchange rate of the U.S. dollar against a basket of foreign currencies with the current account deficit, measured as a percentage of GDP. Notice how the large appreciation and depreciation of the U.S. dollar in the 1980s were followed, with a lag, by a large rise and fall in the current account deficit.

Source: OECD Economic Outlook.

The line labeled "current account deficit" is the U.S. current account deficit as a percentage of GDP, measured on the right axis. Because it shows the *deficit,* it goes up when exports fall or imports rise, and it falls when exports rise or imports fall.

In the 1980s there was a completely clear relationship between the real exchange rate and the current account. On a real basis, the dollar appreciated dramatically in the first half of the 1980s; with a bit of a lag, this caused exports to slump and imports to soar, which in turn caused the current account to move deep into deficit. (We haven't stressed lags in the effect of the exchange rate, but experience shows that it takes time for exporters and importers to respond to exchange rate changes.) When the dollar came down again, so did the current account deficit.

The dollar and the current account deficit both rose again in the late 1990s. The real increase in the dollar wasn't as large as the episode in the 1980s, but the current account deficit grew even larger. This probably reflected other factors, such as the rapid growth of export industries in China. Still, the overall picture strongly confirms the idea that changes in the real exchange rate have a strong effect on the current account balance. ∎

> >

>> CHECK YOUR UNDERSTANDING 19-2

1. Mexico discovers huge reserves of oil and starts exporting oil to the United States. Describe how this would affect the following:
   a. The nominal peso–U.S. dollar exchange rate
   b. Mexican exports of other goods and services
   c. Mexican imports of goods and services

2. A basket of goods and services that costs $100 in the United States costs 800 pesos in Mexico, and the current nominal exchange rate is 10 pesos per U.S. dollar. Over the next five years, the cost of that market basket rises to $120 in the United States and to 1,200 pesos in Mexico, although the nominal exchange rate remains at 10 pesos per U.S. dollar. Calculate the following:
   a. The real exchange rate now and five years from now, if today's price index in both countries is 100
   b. Purchasing power parity today and five years from now

Solutions appear at back of book.

>> QUICK REVIEW

- Currencies are traded in the *foreign exchange market,* which determines *exchange rates.*
- Exchange rates can be measured two ways. To avoid confusion, economists say that a currency *appreciates* or *depreciates.* The *equilibrium exchange rate* matches the supply and demand for currencies on the foreign exchange market.
- To take account of differences in national price levels, economists calculate *real exchange rates.*
- *Purchasing power parities* indicate the nominal exchange rates that would equalize the price of a market basket.

Exchange Rate Policy

The nominal exchange rate, like other prices, is determined by supply and demand. Unlike the price of wheat or oil, however, the exchange rate is the price of a country's money (in terms of another country's money). Money isn't a good or service produced by the private sector; it's an asset whose quantity is determined by government policy. As a result, governments have much more power to influence nominal exchange rates than they have to influence ordinary prices.

The nominal exchange rate is a very important price for many countries: the exchange rate determines the price of imports; it determines the price of exports; in economies where exports and imports are large percentages of GDP, movements in the exchange rate can have major effects on aggregate output and the aggregate price level. What do governments do with their power to influence this important price?

The answer is, it depends. At different times and in different places, governments have adopted a variety of *exchange rate regimes*. Let's talk about these regimes, how they are enforced, and how governments choose a regime. (From now on we'll adopt the convention that we mean the nominal exchange rate when we refer to the exchange rate.)

Exchange Rate Regimes

An **exchange rate regime** is a rule governing policy toward the exchange rate.

A country has a **fixed exchange rate** when the government keeps the exchange rate against some other currency at or near a particular target.

A country has a **floating exchange rate** when the government lets the exchange rate go wherever the market takes it.

An **exchange rate regime** is a rule governing policy toward the exchange rate. There are two main kinds of exchange rate regime. A country has a **fixed exchange rate** when the government keeps the exchange rate against some other currency at or near a particular target. For example, Hong Kong has an official policy of setting an exchange rate of HK$7.4 per US$1. A country has a **floating exchange rate** when the government lets the exchange rate go wherever the market takes it. This is the policy followed by Britain, Canada, and the United States.

Fixed exchange rates and floating exchange rates aren't the only possibilities. At various times countries have adopted compromise policies that lie somewhere between fixed and floating exchange rates. These include exchange rates that are fixed at any given time but are adjusted frequently, exchange rates that aren't fixed but are "managed" by the government to avoid wide swings, and exchange rates that float within a "target zone" but are prevented from leaving that zone. In this book, however, we'll focus on the two main exchange rate regimes.

The immediate question about a fixed exchange rate is how it is possible for governments to fix the exchange rate when the exchange rate is determined by supply and demand.

How Can an Exchange Rate Be Held Fixed?

To understand how it is possible for a country to fix its exchange rate, let's consider a hypothetical country, Genovia, which for some reason has decided to fix the value of its currency, the geno, at 1.50 U.S. dollars.

The obvious problem is that $1.50 may not be the equilibrium exchange rate in the foreign exchange market: the equilibrium rate may be either higher or lower than the target exchange rate. Figure 19-10 shows the foreign exchange market for genos, with the quantities of genos supplied and demanded on the horizontal axis and the exchange rate of the geno, measured in U.S. dollars per geno, on the vertical axis. Panel (a) shows the case in which the equilibrium value of the geno is *below* the target exchange rate. Panel (b) shows the case in which the equilibrium value of the geno is *above* the target exchange rate.

Consider first the case in which the equilibrium value of the geno is below the target exchange rate. As panel (a) of Figure 19-10 shows, at the target exchange rate there is a surplus of genos in the foreign exchange market, which would normally push the value of the geno down. How can the Genovian government support the

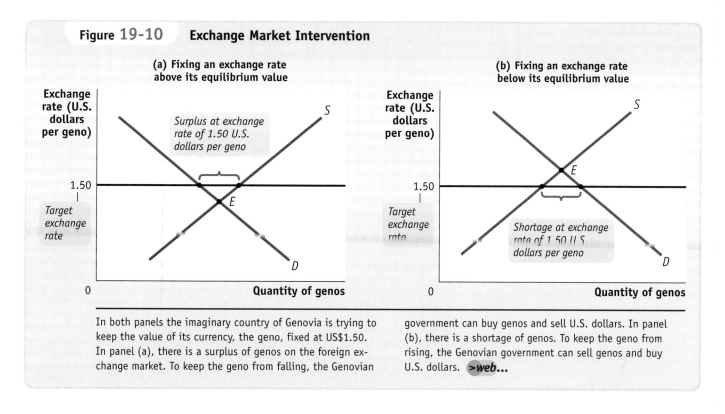

Figure 19-10   Exchange Market Intervention

In both panels the imaginary country of Genovia is trying to keep the value of its currency, the geno, fixed at US$1.50. In panel (a), there is a surplus of genos on the foreign exchange market. To keep the geno from falling, the Genovian government can buy genos and sell U.S. dollars. In panel (b), there is a shortage of genos. To keep the geno from rising, the Genovian government can sell genos and buy U.S. dollars. **>web...**

value of the geno to keep the rate where it wants? There are three possible answers, all of which have been used by governments at some point.

One way the Genovian government can support the geno is to "soak up" the surplus of genos by buying its own currency in the foreign exchange market. Government purchases or sales of currency in the foreign exchange market are called **exchange market intervention.** To buy genos in the foreign exchange market, of course, the Genovian government must have U.S. dollars to exchange for genos. In fact, most countries maintain **foreign exchange reserves,** stocks of foreign currency (usually U.S. dollars or euros) that they can use to buy their own currency to support its price.

We mentioned earlier in the chapter that an important part of international capital flows is the result of purchases and sales of foreign assets by governments and central banks. Now we can see why governments sell foreign assets: they are supporting their currency through exchange market intervention. As we'll see in a moment, governments that keep the value of their currency *down* through exchange market intervention must *buy* foreign assets. First, however, let's talk about the other ways governments fix exchange rates.

As an alternative to exchange market intervention, the Genovian government can try to shift the supply and demand curves for the geno in the foreign exchange market. Governments usually do this by changing monetary policy. For example, to support the geno the Genovian central bank can raise the Genovian interest rate. This will increase capital flows into Genovia, increasing the demand for genos, at the same time that it reduces capital flows out of Genovia, reducing the supply of genos. So, other things equal, an increase in a country's interest rate will increase the value of its currency.

Finally, the Genovian government can support the geno by reducing the supply of genos to the foreign exchange market. It can do this by requiring domestic residents who want to buy foreign currency to get a license and giving these licenses only to people engaging in approved transactions (such as the purchase of imported goods the Genovian government thinks are essential). Licensing systems that limit the right

Government purchases or sales of currency in the foreign exchange market are **exchange market intervention.**

Foreign exchange reserves are stocks of foreign currency that governments maintain to buy their own currency on the foreign exchange market.

Foreign exchange controls are licensing systems that limit the right of individuals to buy foreign currency.

of individuals to buy foreign currency are called **foreign exchange controls.** Other things equal, foreign exchange controls increase the value of a country's currency.

So far we've been discussing a situation in which the government is trying to prevent a depreciation of the geno. Suppose, instead, that the situation is as shown in panel (b) of Figure 19-10, where the equilibrium value of the geno is *above* the target exchange rate and there is a shortage of genos. To maintain the target exchange rate, the Genovian government can apply the same three basic options in the reverse direction. It can intervene in the foreign exchange market, in this case *selling* genos and acquiring U.S. dollars, which it can add to its foreign exchange reserves. It can *reduce* interest rates to increase the supply of genos and reduce the demand. Or it can impose foreign exchange controls that limit the ability of foreigners to buy genos. All of these actions, other things equal, will reduce the value of the geno.

As we said, all three techniques have been used to manage fixed exchange rates. But we haven't said whether fixing the exchange rate is a good idea. In fact, the choice of exchange rate regime poses a dilemma for policy makers, because fixed and floating exchange rates each have both advantages and disadvantages.

The Exchange Rate Regime Dilemma

Few questions in macroeconomics produce as many arguments as that of whether a country should adopt a fixed or a floating exchange rate. The reason there are so many arguments is that both sides have a case.

To understand the case for a fixed exchange rate, consider for a moment how easy it is to conduct business across state lines in the United States. There are a number of things that make interstate commerce trouble-free, but one of them is the absence of any uncertainty about the value of money: a dollar is a dollar, in both New York and Los Angeles.

By contrast, a dollar isn't a dollar in transactions between New York and Toronto. The exchange rate between the Canadian dollar and the U.S. dollar fluctuates, sometimes widely. If a U.S. firm promises to pay a Canadian firm a given number of U.S. dollars a year from now, the value of that promise in Canadian currency can vary by 10% or more. This uncertainty has the effect of deterring trade between the two countries. So one benefit of a fixed exchange rate is certainty about the future value of a currency.

There is also, in some cases, an additional benefit to adopting a fixed exchange rate: by committing itself to a fixed rate, a country is also committing itself not to engage in inflationary policies. For example, in 1991 Argentina, which has a long history of irresponsible policies leading to severe inflation, adopted a fixed exchange rate of US$1 per Argentine peso in an attempt to commit itself to noninflationary policies in the future. (Argentina's fixed exchange rate regime collapsed disastrously in late 2001. But that's another story.)

The point is that there is some economic value in having a stable exchange rate. Indeed, as the upcoming For Inquiring Minds explains, the presumed benefits of stable exchange rates motivated the international system of fixed exchange rates created after World War II and was one major reason for creating the euro.

Unfortunately, there are also costs to fixing the exchange rate. To stabilize an exchange rate through intervention, a country must keep large quantities of foreign currency on hand—usually a low-return investment. Furthermore, even large reserves can be quickly exhausted when there are large capital flows out of a country. If a country chooses to stabilize an exchange rate by adjusting monetary policy rather than through intervention, it must divert monetary policy from other goals, notably stabilizing output and the inflation rate. Finally, exchange controls, like import quotas and tariffs, distort incentives for importing and exporting. They can also create substantial costs in terms of red tape and corruption.

So there's a dilemma. Should a country let its currency float, which leaves monetary policy available for macroeconomic stabilization but creates uncertainty for busi-

FROM BRETTON WOODS TO THE EURO

In 1944, while World War II was still raging, representatives of Allied nations met in Bretton Woods, New Hampshire, to establish a postwar international monetary system of fixed exchange rates among major currencies. The system was highly successful at first, but it broke down in 1971. After a confusing interval during which policy makers tried unsuccessfully to establish a new fixed exchange rate system, by 1973 most economically advanced countries had moved to floating exchange rates.

In Europe, however, many policy makers were unhappy with floating exchange rates, which they believed created too much uncertainty for business. From the late 1970s onward they tried several times to create a system of more or less fixed exchange rates in Europe, culminating in an arrangement known as the Exchange Rate Mechanism. (The Exchange Rate Mechanism was, strictly speaking, a "target zone" system—exchange rates were free to move within a narrow band, but not outside it.) And in 1991 they agreed to move to the ultimate in fixed exchange rates: a common European currency, the euro. To the surprise of many analysts, they pulled it off: today most of Europe has abandoned national currencies for euros.

Figure 19-11 illustrates the history of European exchange rate arrangements. It shows the exchange rate between the French franc and the German mark, measured as francs per mark, since 1971. The

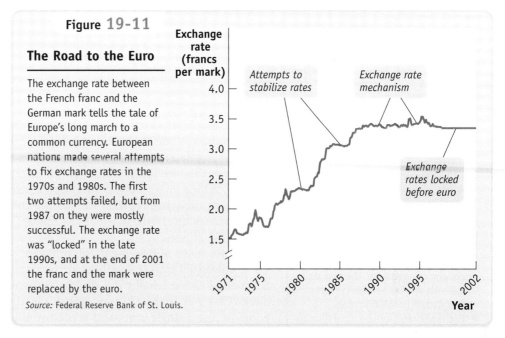

Figure 19-11

The Road to the Euro

The exchange rate between the French franc and the German mark tells the tale of Europe's long march to a common currency. European nations made several attempts to fix exchange rates in the 1970s and 1980s. The first two attempts failed, but from 1987 on they were mostly successful. The exchange rate was "locked" in the late 1990s, and at the end of 2001 the franc and the mark were replaced by the euro.

Source: Federal Reserve Bank of St. Louis.

exchange rate fluctuated widely at first. The "plateaus" you can see in the data—eras when the exchange rate fluctuated only modestly—are periods when attempts to restore fixed exchange rates were in process. The Exchange Rate Mechanism, after a couple of false starts, became effective in 1987, stabilizing the exchange rate at about 3.4 francs per mark. (The wobbles in 1992–1993 reflect two *currency crises*—episodes in which widespread expectations of imminent devaluations led to large but temporary capital flows.)

In 1999 the exchange rate was "locked"—no further fluctuations were allowed as the countries prepared to switch

from francs and marks to euros. At the end of 2001, the franc and the mark ceased to exist.

The transition to the euro has not been without costs. With most of Europe sharing the same currency, it must also share the same monetary policy. Yet economic conditions in the different countries aren't always the same—there may be a boom in Spain while there's a slump in Germany. In such cases Spain wants to raise interest rates, but Germany wants to cut them. Europeans now complain about a "one size fits all" monetary policy. In fact, a May 2005 poll found that 56% of Germans would prefer a return to their old currency, the mark.

ness? Or should it fix the exchange rate, which eliminates the uncertainty but means giving up monetary policy, adopting exchange controls, or both? Different countries reach different conclusions at different times. Most European countries, except for Britain, have long believed that exchange rates among major European economies, which do most of their international trade with each other, should be fixed. But Canada seems happy with a floating exchange rate with the United States, even though the United States accounts for most of Canada's trade.

Luckily, we don't have to resolve this dilemma. For the rest of the chapter, we'll take exchange rate regimes as given and ask how they affect macroeconomic policy.

economics in action

China Pegs the Yuan

In the early years of the twenty-first century, China provided a striking example of the lengths to which countries sometimes go to maintain a fixed exchange rate. Here's the background: China's spectacular success as an exporter led to a rising surplus on current account. At the same time, private investors became increasingly eager to shift funds into China, to take advantage of its growing domestic economy. These capital flows were somewhat limited by foreign exchange controls—but kept coming in anyway. As a result of the current account surplus and private capital inflows, China found itself in the position described by panel (b) of Figure 19-10: at the target exchange rate the demand for yuan exceeded the supply. Yet the Chinese government was determined to keep the exchange rate fixed at 8.28 yuan per U.S. dollar.

To keep the rate fixed, China had to engage in large-scale exchange market intervention, selling yuan, buying up other countries' currencies (mainly U.S. dollars) on the foreign exchange market, and adding them to its reserves. In 2004, China's foreign currency intervention was $194 billion, bringing total foreign exchange reserves up to $655 billion.

To get a sense of how big these totals are, you have to know that China's nominal GDP, converted into U.S. dollars at the prevailing exchange rate, was $1.65 trillion. So in 2004 China bought U.S. dollars and other currencies equal to almost 12% of its GDP. That's as if the U.S. government had bought $1.3 trillion worth of yen and euros in just a single year—and was continuing to buy yen and euros even though it was already sitting on a $4 trillion pile of foreign currencies. Economists expected China to buy even more foreign currency in 2005.

Will China continue accumulating foreign exchange reserves at this pace? On July 21, 2005, China announced a new scheme under which it would fix the value of the yuan in terms of a basket of currencies, rather than in terms of the U.S. dollar alone. It also suggested that it might gradually increase the value of the yuan in terms of this basket over time. Initially, however, this new scheme led to an appreciation of the yuan by only 2%. ■

< < < < < < < < < < < < < < < < < < <

>> **CHECK YOUR UNDERSTANDING 19-3**

1. Draw a diagram, similar to Figure 19-10, representing the foreign exchange situation of China in early 2005, before the change in exchange rate policy. (*Hint:* Express the exchange rate as U.S. dollars per yuan.) Then show with a diagram how each of the following policy changes might eliminate the disequilibrium in the market:
   a. An appreciation of the yuan
   b. Placing restrictions on foreigners who want to invest in China
   c. Removing restrictions on Chinese who want to invest abroad
   d. Imposing taxes on Chinese exports, such as shipments of clothing, that are causing a political backlash in the importing countries

Solutions appear at back of book.

Exchange Rates and Macroeconomic Policy

A look at the history of British macroeconomic policy over the past 50 years touches on all the themes we've covered in our study of macroeconomics so far: British policy makers have wrestled with inflation and unemployment and wondered how to get faster long-run growth. But British macroeconomic history also reveals other concerns—notably, whether to fix the exchange rate of the pound, and if so at what level. As we learned in the opening story, the possibility of future changes in the exchange rate regime looms large even when the exchange rate is floating. And the analysis of monetary policy focuses to a large degree on how it affects the exchange rate and the balance of payments. In other words, the fact that modern economies are open to international trade and capital flows adds a new level of complication to our analysis of macroeconomic policy. Let's look at three policy issues raised by open-economy macroeconomics.

Devaluation and Revaluation of Fixed Exchange Rates

Historically, fixed exchange rates haven't been permanent commitments. Sometimes countries with a fixed exchange rate switch to a floating rate, as Argentina did in 2001. In other cases they retain a fixed rate but change the target exchange rate. Such adjustments in the target were common during the Bretton Woods era described in For Inquiring Minds on page 481. For example, in 1967 Britain changed the exchange rate of the pound against the U.S. dollar from US$2.80 per £1 to US$2.40 per £1. A modern example is China: as we explained in Economics in Action on page 402, China maintained a fixed exchange rate against the U.S. dollar from 1994 to 2005 but changed its exchange rate regime in July 2005.

A reduction in the value of a currency that is set under a fixed exchange rate regime is called a **devaluation.** As we've already learned, a *depreciation* is a downward move in a currency. A devaluation is a depreciation that is due to a revision in a fixed exchange rate target. An increase in the value of a currency that is set under a fixed exchange rate regime is called a **revaluation.**

A devaluation, like any depreciation, makes domestic goods cheaper in terms of foreign currency, which leads to higher exports. At the same time, it makes foreign goods more expensive in terms of domestic currency, which reduces imports. The effect is to increase the balance of payments on current account. Similarly, a revaluation makes domestic goods more expensive in terms of foreign currency, which reduces exports, and makes foreign goods cheaper in domestic currency, which increases imports. So a revaluation reduces the balance of payments on current account.

Devaluations and revaluations serve two purposes under fixed exchange rates. First, they can be used to eliminate shortages or surpluses in the foreign exchange market. For example, in early 2005, some economists were urging China to revalue the yuan so that it would not have to buy up so many U.S. dollars on the foreign exchange market.

Second, devaluation and revaluation can be used as tools of macroeconomic policy. A devaluation, by increasing exports and reducing imports, increases aggregate demand. So a devaluation can be used to reduce or eliminate a recessionary gap. A revaluation has the opposite effect, reducing aggregate demand. So a revaluation can be used to reduce or eliminate an inflationary gap.

> A **devaluation** is a reduction in the value of a currency that is set under a fixed exchange rate regime.
>
> A **revaluation** is an increase in the value of a currency that is set under a fixed exchange rate regime.

Monetary Policy Under Floating Exchange Rates

Under a floating exchange rate regime, a country's central bank retains its ability to pursue independent monetary policy: it can increase aggregate demand by cutting the interest rate or decrease aggregate demand by raising the interest rate. But the exchange rate adds another dimension to the effects of monetary policy. To see why, let's return to the hypothetical country of Genovia and ask what happens if the central bank cuts the interest rate.

Just as in a closed economy, a lower interest rate leads to higher investment spending and higher consumer spending. But the decline in the interest rate also affects the foreign exchange market. Foreigners have less incentive to move funds into Genovia, because they will receive a lower rate of return on their loans. As a result, they have less need to exchange U.S. dollars for genos, so the demand for genos falls. At the same time, Genovians have *more* incentive to move funds abroad because the rate of return on loans at home has fallen, making investments outside the country more attractive. As a result, they need to exchange more genos for U.S. dollars, so the supply of genos rises.

Figure 19-12

Monetary Policy and the Exchange Rate

Here we show what happens in the foreign exchange market if Genovia cuts its interest rate. Residents of Genovia have a reduced incentive to keep their funds at home, so they invest more abroad. As a result, the supply of genos shifts rightward from S_1 to S_2. Meanwhile, foreigners have less incentive to put funds into Genovia, so the demand for genos shifts leftward from D_1 to D_2. The geno depreciates: the equilibrium exchange rate falls from XR_1 to XR_2. **>web...**

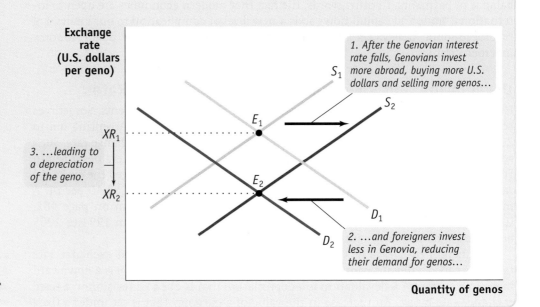

Figure 19-12 shows the effect of an interest rate reduction on the foreign exchange market. The demand curve for genos shifts leftward, from D_1 to D_2, and the supply curve shifts rightward, from S_1 to S_2. The equilibrium exchange rate, as measured in U.S. dollars per geno, falls from XR_1 to XR_2. That is, a reduction in the Genovian interest rate causes the geno to *depreciate*.

The depreciation of the geno, in turn, affects aggregate demand. We've already seen how a devaluation—a depreciation that is the result of a change in a fixed exchange rate—raises exports and reduces imports, thereby increasing aggregate demand. A depreciation that results from an interest rate cut has the same effect: it increases exports and reduces imports, increasing aggregate demand.

In other words, monetary policy under floating rates has effects beyond those we've described in looking at closed economies. In a closed economy, a reduction in the interest rate leads to a rise in aggregate demand because it leads to more investment spending and consumer spending. In an open economy with a floating exchange rate, the interest rate reduction leads to increased investment spending and consumer spending, but it also increases aggregate demand in another way: it leads to a currency depreciation, which increases exports and reduces imports, increasing aggregate demand.

International Business Cycles

Up to this point we have discussed macroeconomics, even in an open economy, as if all demand shocks originate from the domestic economy. In reality, however, economies sometimes face shocks coming from abroad. For example, recessions in the United States have historically led to recessions in Mexico.

The key point is that changes in aggregate demand affect the demand for goods and services produced abroad as well as at home: other things equal, a recession leads to a fall in imports and an expansion leads to a rise in imports. And one country's imports are another country's exports. This link between aggregate demand in different national economies is one reason business cycles in different countries sometimes—but not always—seem to be synchronized. The prime example is the Great Depression, which affected countries around the world.

The extent of this link depends, however, on the exchange rate regime. To see why, think about what happens if a recession abroad reduces the demand for Genovia's exports. A reduction in foreign demand for Genovian goods and services is also a reduction in demand for genos on the foreign exchange market. If Genovia has a fixed exchange rate, it responds to this decline with exchange market intervention. But if Genovia has a floating exchange rate, the geno depreciates. Because Genovian goods and services become cheaper to foreigners when the demand for exports falls, the quantity of goods and services exported doesn't fall by as much as it would under a fixed rate. At the same time, the fall in the geno makes imports more expensive to Genovians, leading to a fall in imports. Both effects limit the decline in Genovia's aggregate demand.

One of the virtues of a floating exchange rate, according to advocates of such exchange rates, is that they help insulate countries from recessions originating abroad. This theory looked pretty good in the early 2000s: Britain, with a floating exchange rate, managed to stay out of a recession that affected the rest of Europe, and Canada, which also has a floating rate, suffered a less severe recession than the United States.

economics in action

The Joy of a Devalued Pound

In For Inquiring Minds on page 481 we mentioned the Exchange Rate Mechanism, the system of European fixed exchange rates that paved the way for the creation of the euro in 1999. Britain joined that system in 1990 but dropped out in 1992. The story of Britain's exit from the Exchange Rate Mechanism is a classic example of open-economy macroeconomic policy.

Britain originally fixed its exchange rate for both the reasons we described earlier in the chapter: British leaders believed that a fixed exchange rate would help promote international trade, and they also hoped that it would help fight inflation. But by 1992 Britain was suffering from high unemployment: the unemployment rate in September 1992 was over 10%. And as long as the country had a fixed exchange rate, there wasn't much the government could do. In particular, the government wasn't able to cut interest rates because it was using high interest rates to help support the value of the pound.

In the summer of 1992, investors began speculating against the pound—selling pounds in the expectation that the currency would drop in value. This speculation helped force the British government's hand. On September 16, 1992, Britain abandoned its fixed exchange rate. The pound promptly dropped 20% against the German mark, the most important European currency at the time.

At the time, the devaluation of the pound greatly damaged the prestige of the British government. But the chancellor of the exchequer—the equivalent of the U.S. treasury secretary—claimed to be happy about it. "My wife has never before heard me singing in the bath," he told reporters. There were several reasons for his joy. One was that the British government would no longer have to engage in large-scale exchange market intervention to support the pound's value. Another was that devaluation increases aggregate demand, so the pound's fall would help reduce unemployment. Finally, because Britain no longer had a fixed exchange rate, it was free to pursue an expansionary monetary policy.

Indeed, events made it clear that the chancellor's joy was well founded. British unemployment fell over the next two years, even as the unemployment rate rose in France and Germany. One person who did not share in the improving employment picture, however, was the chancellor himself. Soon after his remark about singing in the bath, he was fired. ∎

> >

> **QUICK REVIEW**
>
> ➤ Countries can change fixed exchange rates. *Devaluation* or *revaluation* can help reduce surpluses or shortages in the foreign exchange market and can increase or reduce aggregate demand.
>
> ➤ In an open economy with a floating exchange rate, interest rates also affect the exchange rate, and so monetary policy affects aggregate demand through the effects of the exchange rate on imports and exports.
>
> ➤ Because one country's imports are another country's exports, business cycles are sometimes synchronized across countries. However, floating exchange rates may reduce this link.

1. Look at the data in Figure 19-11. Where do you see devaluations and revaluations of the franc against the mark?

2. In the late 1980s Canadian economists argued that the high interest rate policies of the Bank of Canada weren't just causing high unemployment—they were also making it hard for Canadian manufacturers to compete with the United States. Explain this complaint, using our analysis of how monetary policy works under floating exchange rates.

Solutions appear at back of book.

● If your interest was sparked by references in this chapter to speculation and currency crises, you can find a supplemental chapter online that explains how expectations can move exchange rates and the balance of payments—sometimes violently. To see the chapter, go to www.worthpublishers.com/krugmanwells.

SUMMARY

1. A country's **balance of payments accounts** summarize its transactions with the rest of the world. The **balance of payments on current account** includes the **balance of payments on goods and services** together with balances on factor income and transfers. The **merchandise trade balance** is a frequently cited component of the balance of payments on goods and services. The **balance of payments on financial account** measures capital flows. By definition, the balance of payments on current account plus the balance of payments on financial account is zero.

2. Capital flows respond to international differences in interest rates and other rates of return; they can be usefully analyzed using an international version of the loanable funds model, which shows how a country where the interest rate would be low in the absence of capital flows sends funds to a country where the interest rate would be high in the absence of capital flows. The underlying determinants of capital flows are international differences in savings and opportunities for investment spending.

3. Currencies are traded in the **foreign exchange market;** the prices at which they are traded are **exchange rates.** When a currency rises against another currency, it **appreciates;** when it falls, it **depreciates.** The **equilibrium exchange rate** matches the quantity of that currency supplied to the foreign exchange market to the quantity demanded.

4. To correct for international differences in inflation rates, economists calculate **real exchange rates,** which multiply the exchange rate between two countries' currencies by the ratio of the countries' price levels. A related concept, **purchasing power parity,** is the exchange rate that makes the cost of a basket of goods and services equal in two countries.

5. Countries adopt different **exchange rate regimes,** rules governing exchange rate policy. The main types are **fixed exchange rates,** where the government takes action to keep the exchange rate at a target level, and **floating exchange rates,** where the exchange rate is free to fluctuate. Countries can fix exchange rates using **exchange market intervention,** which requires them to hold **foreign exchange reserves** that they use to buy any surplus of their currency. Alternatively, they can use **foreign exchange controls.** Finally, they can change domestic policies, especially monetary policy, to shift the demand and supply curves in the foreign exchange market.

6. Exchange rate policy poses a dilemma: there are economic payoffs to stable exchange rates, but the policies used to fix the exchange rate have costs. Exchange market intervention requires large reserves, and exchange controls distort incentives. If monetary policy is used to help fix the exchange rate, it isn't available to use for domestic policy.

7. Fixed exchange rates aren't always permanent commitments: countries with a fixed exchange rate sometimes engage in **devaluations** or **revaluations.** In addition to helping eliminate a surplus of domestic currency on the foreign exchange market, a devaluation increases aggregate demand. Similarly, a revaluation reduces shortages of domestic currency and reduces aggregate demand.

8. Under floating exchange rates, expansionary monetary policy works in part through the exchange rate: cutting domestic interest rates leads to a depreciation, and through that to higher exports and lower imports, which increases aggregate demand. Contractionary monetary policy has the reverse effect.

9. The fact that one country's imports are another country's exports creates a link between the business cycle in different countries. Floating exchange rates, however, may reduce the strength of that link.

PROBLEMS

1. How would the following transactions be categorized in the U.S. balance of payments accounts? Would they be entered in the current account (as a payment to or from a foreigner) or the financial account (as a sale to or purchase of assets from a foreigner)? How will the balance of payments on the current and financial accounts change?

a. A French importer buys a case of California wine for $500.

b. An American who works for a French company deposits her paycheck, drawn on a Paris bank, into her San Francisco bank.

c. An American buys a bond from a Japanese company for $10,000.

d. An American charity sends $100,000 to Africa to help local residents buy food after a harvest shortfall.

2. In the economy of Scottopia in 2005, exports equaled $400 billion of goods and $300 billion of services, imports equaled $500 billion of goods and $350 billion of services, and the rest of the world purchased $250 billion of Scottopia's assets. What was the merchandise trade balance for Scottopia? What was the balance of payments on current account in Scottopia? What was the balance of payments on financial account? What was the value of Scottopia's purchases of assets from the rest of the world?

3. In the economy of Popania in 2005, total Popanian purchases of assets in the rest of the world equaled $300 billion, purchases of Popanian assets by the rest of the world equaled $400 billion, and Popania exported goods and services equal to $350 billion. What was Popania's balance of payments on financial account in 2005? What was its balance of payments on current account? What was the value of its imports?

4. Suppose that Northlandia and Southlandia are the only two trading countries in the world, that each nation runs a balance of payments on both current and financial accounts equal to zero, and that each nation sees the other's assets as identical to its own. Using the accompanying diagrams, explain how the demand and supply of loanable funds, the interest rate, and the balance of payments on current and financial accounts will change in each country if international capital flows are possible.

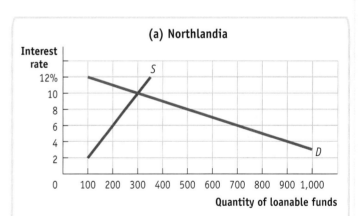

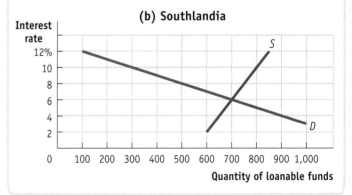

5. Based on the exchange rates for the first trading days of 2004 and 2005 shown in the accompanying table, did the U.S. dollar appreciate or depreciate during 2004? Did the movement in the value of the U.S. dollar make American goods and services more or less attractive to foreigners?

January 2, 2004	January 3, 2005
US$1.79 to buy 1 British pound sterling	US$1.91 to buy 1 British pound sterling
33.98 Taiwan dollars to buy US$1	31.71 Taiwan dollars to buy US$1
US$0.78 to buy 1 Canadian dollar	US$0.83 to buy 1 Canadian dollar
104.27 Japanese yen to buy US$1	106.95 Japanese yen to buy US$1
US$1.26 to buy 1 euro	US$1.38 to buy 1 euro
1.24 Swiss francs to buy US$1	1.15 Swiss francs to buy US$1

6. Suppose the United States and Japan are the only two trading countries in the world. What will happen to the value of the U.S. dollar if the following occur, other things equal?

   a. Japan relaxes some of its import restrictions.

   b. The United States imposes some import tariffs on Japanese goods.

   c. Interest rates in the United States rise dramatically.

   d. A report indicates that Japanese cars last much longer than previously thought, especially compared with American cars.

7. In each of the following scenarios, suppose that the two nations are the only trading nations in the world. Given inflation and the change in the nominal exchange rate, which nation's goods become more attractive?

   a. Inflation is 10% in the United States and 5% in Japan; the U.S. dollar–Japanese yen exchange rate remains the same.

   b. Inflation is 3% in the United States and 8% in Mexico; the price of the U.S. dollar falls from 12.50 to 10.25 Mexican pesos.

   c. Inflation is 5% in the United States and 3% in the Euro-area; the price of the euro falls from $1.30 to $1.20.

   d. Inflation is 8% in the United States and 4% in Canada; the price of the Canadian dollar rises from US$0.60 to US$0.75.

8. Starting from a position of equilibrium in the foreign exchange market under a fixed exchange rate system, how must a government react to an increase in the demand for the nation's goods and services by the rest of the world to keep the exchange rate at its fixed value?

9. Suppose that Albernia's central bank has fixed the value of its currency, the bern, to the U.S. dollar (at a rate of US$1.50 to 1 bern) and is committed to that exchange rate. Initially, the foreign exchange market for the bern is also in equilibrium, as shown in the accompanying diagram. However, both Albernians and Americans begin to believe that there are big risks in holding Albernian assets, and as a result, they become unwilling to hold Albernian assets unless they receive a higher rate of return on them than they do on U.S. assets. How would this affect the diagram? If the Albernian central bank tries to keep the exchange rate fixed using monetary policy, how will this affect the Albernian economy?

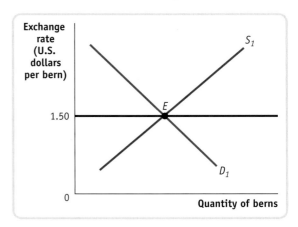

10. Your study partner asks you, "If central banks lose the ability to use discretionary monetary policy under fixed exchange rates, why would nations agree to a fixed exchange rate system?" How do you respond?

>> **Solutions to
"Check Your Understanding" Questions**

This section offers suggested answers to the "Check Your Understanding" questions found within chapters.

Chapter One

1. a. This illustrates the concept of opportunity cost. Given that a person can only eat so much at one sitting, having an additional slice of chocolate cake requires that you forgo eating something else, such as a slice of the coconut cream pie.
   b. This illustrates the concept that resources are scarce. Even if there were more resources in the world, the total amount of those resources would be limited. As a result, scarcity would still arise. For there to be no scarcity, there would have to be unlimited amounts of everything (including unlimited time in a human life), which is clearly impossible.
   c. This illustrates the concept that people usually exploit opportunities to make themselves better off. Students will seek to make themselves better off by signing up for the tutorials of teaching assistants with good reputations and avoiding those teaching assistants with poor reputations. It also illustrates the concept that resources are scarce. If there were unlimited spaces in tutorials with good teaching assistants, they would not fill up.
   d. This illustrates the concept of marginal analysis. Your decision about allocating your time is a "how much" decision: how much time spent exercising versus how much time spent studying. You make your decision by comparing the benefit of an additional hour of exercising to its cost, the effect on your grades of one less hour spent studying.

2. a. Yes. The increased time spent commuting is a cost you will incur if you accept the new job. That additional time spent commuting—or equivalently, the benefit you would get from spending that time doing something else—is an opportunity cost of the new job.
   b. Yes. One of the benefits of the new job is that you will be making $50,000. But if you take the new job, you will have to give up your current job; that is, you have to give up your current salary of $45,000. So $45,000 is one of the opportunity costs of taking the new job.
   c. No. A more spacious office is an additional benefit of your new job and does not involve forgoing something else. So, it is not an opportunity cost.

1. a. This illustrates the concept that markets usually lead to efficiency. Any seller who wants to sell a book for at least $X does indeed sell to someone who is willing to buy a book for $X. As a result, there is no way to change how used textbooks are distributed among buyers and sellers in a way that would make one person better off without making someone else worse off.
   b. This illustrates the concept that there are gains from trade. Students trade tutoring services based on their different abilities in academic subjects.
   c. This illustrates the concept that when markets don't achieve efficiency, government intervention can improve society's welfare. In this case the market, left alone, will permit bars and nightclubs to impose costs on their neighbors in the form of loud music, costs that the bars and nightclubs have no incentive to take into account. This is an inefficient outcome because society as a whole can be made better off if bars and nightclubs are induced to reduce their noise.
   d. This illustrates the concept that resources should be used as efficiently as possible to achieve society's goals. By closing neighborhood clinics and shifting funds to the main hospital, better health care can be provided at a lower cost.
   e. This illustrates the concept that markets move toward equilibrium. Here, because books with the same amount of wear and tear sell for about the same price, no buyer or seller can be made better off by engaging in a different trade than he or she undertook. This means that the market for used textbooks has moved to an equilibrium.

2. a. This does not describe an equilibrium situation. Many students should want to change their behavior and switch to eating at the restaurants. Therefore, the situation described is not an equilibrium. An equilibrium will be established when students are equally as well off eating at the restaurants as eating at the dining hall—which would happen if, say, prices at the restaurants were higher than at the dining hall.
   b. This does describe an equilibrium situation. By changing your behavior and riding the bus, you would not be made better off. Therefore, you have no incentive to change your behavior.

Chapter Two

Check Your Understanding
2-1

1. **a.** False. An increase in the resources available to Tom for use in producing coconuts and fish changes his production possibility frontier by shifting it outward. This is because he can now produce more fish and coconuts than before. In the accompanying figure, the line labeled Tom's original *PPF* represents Tom's original production possibility frontier, and the line labeled Tom's new *PPF* represents the new production possibility frontier that results from an increase in resources available to Tom.

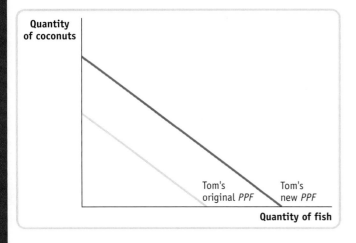

b. True. A technological change that allows Tom to catch more fish for any amount of coconuts gathered results in a change in his production possibility frontier. This is illustrated in the accompanying figure: the new production possibility frontier is represented by the line labeled Tom's new *PPF*, and the original production frontier is represented by the line labeled Tom's original *PPF*. Since the maximum quantity of coconuts that Tom can gather is the same as before, the new production possibility frontier intersects the vertical axis at the same point as the old frontier. But since the maximum possible quantity of fish is now greater than before, the new frontier intersects the horizontal axis to the right of the old frontier.

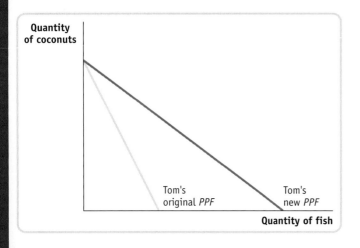

c. False. The production possibility frontier illustrates how much of one good an economy must give up to get more of another good only when resources are used efficiently. If an economy is producing inefficiently—that is, inside the frontier—then it does not have to give up a unit of one good in order to get another unit of the other good. Instead, by becoming more efficient, this economy can have more of both goods.

2. **a.** The United States has an absolute advantage in automobile production because it takes fewer Americans (6) to produce a car in one day than Italians (8). The United States also has an absolute advantage in washing machine production because it takes fewer Americans (2) to produce a washing machine in one day than Italians (3).

b. In Italy the opportunity cost of a washing machine in terms of an automobile is $3/8$: $3/8$ of a car can be produced with the same number of workers and in the same time it takes to produce 1 washing machine. In the United States the opportunity cost of a washing machine in terms of an automobile is $2/6 = 1/3$: $1/3$ of a car can be produced with the same number of workers and in the same time it takes to produce 1 washing machine. Since $1/3 < 3/8$, the United States has a comparative advantage in the production of washing machines: to produce a washing machine, only $1/3$ of a car must be given up in the United States but $3/8$ of a car must be given up in Italy. This means that Italy has a comparative advantage in automobiles. This can be checked as follows. The opportunity cost of an automobile in terms of a washing machine in Italy is $8/3$, equal to $2 2/3$: $2 2/3$ washing machines can be produced in the time it takes to produce 1 car in Italy. And the opportunity cost of an automobile in terms of a washing machine in the United States is $6/2$, equal to 3: 3 washing machines can be produced in the time it takes to produce 1 car in the United States.

c. The greatest gains are realized when each country specializes in producing the good for which it has a comparative advantage. Therefore the United States should specialize in washing machines and Italy should specialize in automobiles.

3. An increase in the amount of money spent by households results in an increase in the flow of goods to households. This, in turn, generates an increase in demand for factors of production by firms. Therefore there is an increase in the number of jobs in the economy.

Check Your Understanding
2-2

1. **a.** This is a normative statement because it stipulates what should be done. In addition, it may have no "right" answer. That is, should people be prevented from all dangerous personal behavior if they enjoy that behavior—like skydiving? Your answer will depend on your point of view.

b. This is a positive statement because it is a description of fact.

2. **a.** True. Economists often have different value judgments about the desirability of a particular social goal. But despite those differences in value judgments, they will tend to agree that society, once it has decided to pursue a given social goal, should adopt the most efficient policy to achieve that goal. Therefore economists are likely to agree on adopting policy choice B.

b. False. Disagreements between economists are more likely to arise because they base their conclusions on different models or because they have different value judgments about the desirability of the policy.

c. False. Deciding which goals a society should try to achieve is a matter of value judgments, not a question of economic analysis.

Chapter Three

3-1

1. a. The quantity of umbrellas demanded is higher at any given price on a rainy day than on a dry day. This is a rightward *shift of* the demand curve, since at any given price the quantity demanded rises. This implies that any specific quantity can now be sold at a higher price.

b. The quantity of weekend calls demanded rises in response to a price reduction. This is a *movement along* the demand curve for weekend calls.

c. The demand for roses increases the week of Valentine's Day. This is a rightward *shift of* the demand curve.

d. The quantity of gasoline demanded falls in response to a rise in price. This is a *movement along* the demand curve.

3-2

1. a. The quantity of houses supplied rises as a result of an increase in prices. This is a *movement along* the supply curve.

b. The quantity of strawberries supplied is higher at any given price. This is a rightward *shift of* the supply curve.

c. The quantity of labor supplied is lower at any given wage. This is a leftward *shift of* the supply curve compared to the supply curve during the school vacation. So, in order to attract workers, fast-food chains have to offer higher wages.

d. The quantity of labor supplied rises in response to a rise in wages. This is a *movement along* the supply curve.

e. The quantity of cabins supplied is higher at any given price. This is a rightward *shift of* the supply curve.

3-3

1. a. The supply curve shifts rightward. At the original equilibrium price of the year before, the quantity of grapes supplied exceeds the quantity demanded. This is a case of surplus. The price of grapes will fall.

b. The demand curve shifts leftward. At the original equilibrium price, the quantity of hotel rooms supplied exceeds the quantity demanded. This is a case of surplus. The rates for hotel rooms will fall.

c. The demand curve for secondhand snowblowers shifts rightward. At the original equilibrium price, the quantity of secondhand snowblowers demanded exceeds the quantity supplied. This is a case of shortage. The equilibrium price of secondhand snowblowers will rise.

3-4

1. a. The market for large cars: this is a rightward shift in demand caused by a decrease in the price of a complement, gasoline. As a result of the shift, the equilibrium price of large cars will rise and the equilibrium quantity of large cars bought and sold will also rise.

b. The market for fresh paper made from recycled stock: this is a rightward shift in supply due to a technological innovation. As a result of this shift, the equilibrium price of fresh paper made from recycled stock will fall and the equilibrium quantity bought and sold will rise.

c. The market for movies at a local movie theater: this is a leftward shift in demand caused by a fall in the price of a substitute, pay-per-view movies. As a result of this shift, the equilibrium price of movie tickets will fall and the equilibrium number of people who go to the movies will also fall.

2. Upon the announcement of the new chip, the demand curve for computers using the earlier chip shifts leftward, as demand decreases, and the supply curve for these computers shifts rightward, as supply increases.

a. If demand decreases relatively more than supply increases, then the equilibrium quantity falls, as shown here:

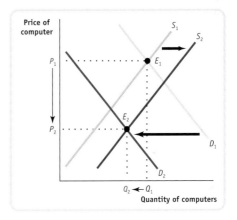

b. If supply increases relatively more than demand decreases, then the equilibrium quantity rises, as shown here:

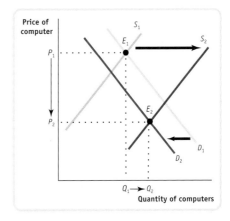

In both cases, the equilibrium price falls.

Chapter Four

Check Your Understanding 4-1

1. **a.** Fewer homeowners are willing to rent out their driveways because the price ceiling has caused a decrease in the payment they receive. This reflects the concept that the quantity supplied decreases as the price decreases. It is shown in the following diagram by the movement from point *E* to point *A* along the supply curve, a reduction in quantity of 400 parking spaces.

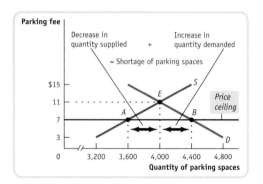

b. The quantity demanded increases by 400 spaces as the price decreases. At a lower price, more fans are willing to drive and rent a parking space. It is shown in the diagram by the movement from point *E* to point *B* along the demand curve.

c. Under a price ceiling, the quantity demanded exceeds the quantity supplied; as a result, shortages arise. In this case, there will be a shortage of 800 parking spaces. It is shown by the horizontal distance between points *A* and *B*.

d. Price ceilings result in wasted resources. The additional time fans spend to guarantee a parking space is wasted time.

e. Price ceilings lead to inefficient allocation of a good—here, the parking spaces—to consumers.

f. Price ceilings lead to black markets.

2. **a.** False. By lowering the price that producers receive, price ceilings lead to a decrease in the quantity supplied.

b. True. Price ceilings lead to a lower quantity supplied than in a free market. As a result, some people who would have been willing to pay the market price, and therefore would have gotten the good in a free market, are unable to obtain it when a price ceiling is imposed.

c. True. Those producers who still sell the product now receive less for it and are therefore worse off. Other producers will no longer find it worthwhile to sell the product at all and therefore will also be made worse off.

Check Your Understanding 4-2

1. **a.** Some gas station owners will benefit from getting a higher price. Point *A* indicates the sales (0.7 million gallons) made by these owners. But some will lose; there are those who made sales at the market price of $2 but do not make sales at the regulated price of $4. These missed sales are indicated on the graph by the fall in the quantity demanded along the demand curve, from point *E* to point *A*. Overall, the effect on station owners is ambiguous.

b. Those who buy gas at the higher price of $4 probably will receive better service; this is an example of *inefficiently high quality* caused by a price floor as gas station owners compete on quality rather than price. But opponents are correct to claim that consumers are generally worse off—those who buy at $4 would have been happy to buy at $2, and many who were willing to buy at a price between $2 and $4 are now unwilling to buy. This is indicated on the graph by the fall in the quantity demanded along the demand curve, from point *E* to point *A*.

c. Proponents are wrong because consumers and some gas station owners are hurt by the price floor, which creates "missed opportunities"—desirable transactions between consumers and station owners that never take place. Moreover, the inefficiency of wasted resources arises as consumers spend time and money driving to other states. The price floor tempts people to engage in black market activity. With the price floor of $4, only 0.7 million gallons are sold. But at prices between $2 and $4, there are drivers who cumulatively want to buy more than 0.7 million gallons and owners who are willing to sell to them, a situation likely to lead to illegal activity.

Check Your Understanding 4-3

1. **a.** The price of a ride is $7 since the quantity demanded at this price is 6 million: $7 is the *demand price* of 6 million rides. This is represented by point *A* in the following figure.

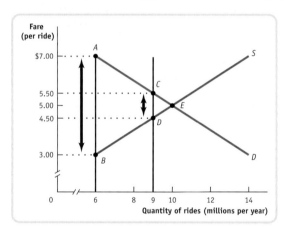

b. At 6 million rides, the supply price is $3, represented by point *B* in the figure. The wedge between the demand price of $7 and the supply price of $3 is the quota rent per ride, $4. This is represented in the figure above by the vertical distance between points *A* and *B*.

c. At 9 million rides, the demand price is $5.50, indicated by point *C* on the figure, and the supply price is $4.50, indicated by point *D*. The quota rent is the difference between the demand price and the supply price: $1.

2. The figure shows how a decrease in demand by 4 million rides, represented by a leftward shift of the demand curve from D_1 to D_2: at any given price, the quantity demanded falls by 4 million rides. This eliminates the effect of a quota limit of 8 million rides. At point E_2, the new market equilibrium, the equilibrium quantity is equal to the quota limit; as a result, the quota has no effect on the market.

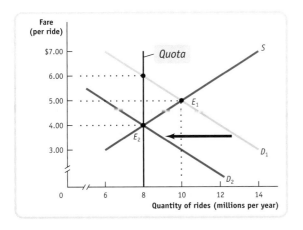

Check Your Understanding

4-4

1. a. Under the quota, only 9 million pounds of butter are bought and sold. We can limit the amount of butter that dairies want to sell to 9 million pounds by setting the supply price to $0.90, as indicated by point D in the following figure, which is a replication of Figure 4-3. Similarly, we can limit the amount of butter consumers want to buy to 9 million pounds by setting the demand price to $1.20, as indicated by point C. The difference between these two prices, $0.30, is therefore equal to the tax that reduces sales to only 9 million pounds, indicated by the vertical distance between points C and D. Thus a tax of $0.30 per pound generates the same inefficiency as a quota of 9 million pounds.

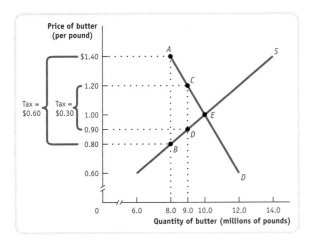

b. To answer this question, we must find a supply price and a demand price that generate the same quantity of butter but differ by $0.60. Examination of the supply and demand schedules shows that the supply price of $0.80 (indicated by point B) and the demand price of $1.40 (indicated by point A) satisfy these conditions: They give rise to the same quantity transacted, 8 million pounds, and they differ by $0.60. Therefore, a quota of 8 million pounds will generate the same level of inefficiency as a tax of $0.60. (Note that a supply price of $1.20 and a demand price of $0.60 also differ by $0.60 and give rise to the same quantity, 12 million pounds. Why is this choice not the right answer here? Because 12 million pounds is more than people want to buy in the free market, so it can't be a valid quota level.)

c. In part a, the unrestricted equilibrium price is $1 per pound. So consumers pay $0.20 ($1.20 – $1.00) of the $0.30 tax and producers pay $0.10 ($1.00 – $0.90).

Chapter Five

Check Your Understanding

5-1

1. A consumer buys each pepper if the price is less than (or just equal to) the consumer's willingness to pay for that pepper. The demand schedule is constructed by asking how many peppers will be demanded at any price. The accompanying table illustrates the demand schedule.

Price of pepper	Quantity of peppers demanded	Quantity of peppers demanded by Casey	Quantity of peppers demanded by Josie
$0.90	1	1	0
0.80	2	1	1
0.70	3	2	1
0.60	4	2	2
0.50	5	3	2
0.40	6	3	3
0.30	8	4	4
0.20	8	4	4
0.10	8	4	4
0.00	8	4	4

When the price is $0.40, Casey's consumer surplus from the first pepper is $0.50, from his second pepper $0.30, from his third pepper $0.10, and he does not buy any more peppers. Casey's individual consumer surplus is therefore $0.90. Josie's consumer surplus from her first pepper is $0.40, from her second pepper $0.20, from her third pepper $0.00 (she is just indifferent between buying it and not buying it, so let's assume she does buy it), and she does not buy any more peppers. Josie's individual consumer surplus is therefore $0.60. Total consumer surplus at a price of $0.40 is therefore $0.90 + $0.60 = $1.50.

Check Your Understanding 5-2

1. A producer supplies each pepper if the price is greater than (or just equal to) the producer's cost of producing that pepper. The supply schedule is constructed by asking how many peppers will be supplied at any price. The accom-panying table illustrates the supply schedule.

Price of pepper	Quantity of peppers supplied	Quantity of peppers supplied by Cara	Quantity of peppers supplied by Jamie
$0.90	8	4	4
0.80	7	4	3
0.70	7	4	3
0.60	6	4	2
0.50	5	3	2
0.40	4	3	1
0.30	3	2	1
0.20	2	2	0
0.10	2	2	0
0.00	0	0	0

When the price is $0.70, Cara's producer surplus from the first pepper is $0.60, from her second pepper $0.60, from her third pepper $0.30, from her fourth pepper $0.10, and she does not supply any more peppers. Cara's individual producer surplus is therefore $1.60. Jamie's producer surplus from his first pepper is $0.40, from his second pepper $0.20, from his third pepper $0.00 (he is just indifferent between supplying it and not supplying it, so let's assume he does supply it), and he does not supply any more peppers. Jamie's individual producer surplus is therefore $0.60. Total producer surplus at a price of $0.70 is therefore $1.60 + $0.60 = $2.20.

Check Your Understanding 5-3

1. The quantity demanded equals the quantity supplied at a price of $0.50, the equilibrium price. At that price, a total quantity of five peppers will be bought and sold. Casey will buy three peppers and receive consumer surplus of $0.40 on his first, $0.20 on his second, and $0.00 on his third pepper. Josie will buy two peppers and receive consumer surplus of $0.30 on her first and $0.10 on her second pepper. Total consumer surplus is therefore $1.00. Cara will supply three peppers and receive producer surplus of $0.40 on her first, $0.40 on her second, and $0.10 on her third pepper. Jamie will supply two peppers and receive producer surplus of $0.20 on his first and $0.00 on his second pepper. Total producer surplus is therefore $1.10. Total surplus in this market is therefore $1.00 + $1.10 = $2.10.

2. a. If Josie consumes one less pepper, she loses $0.60 (her willingness to pay for her second pepper); if Casey consumes one more pepper, he gains $0.30 (his willingness to pay for his fourth pepper). This results in an overall loss of consumer surplus of $0.60 − $0.30 = $0.30.

b. Cara's cost of the last pepper she supplied (the third pepper) is $0.40, and Jamie's cost of producing one more (his third pepper) is $0.70. Total producer surplus therefore falls by $0.70 − $0.40 = $0.30.

c. Josie's willingness to pay for her second pepper is $0.60; this is what she would lose if she were to consume one less pepper. And Cara's cost of producing her third pepper is $0.40; this is what she would save if she were to produce one less pepper. If we therefore reduced quantity by one pepper, we would lose $0.60 − $0.40 = $0.20 of total surplus.

Check Your Understanding 5-4

1. a. At a price paid by consumers of $0.70, Casey's consumer surplus is $0.20 from his first pepper (he loses $0.20 compared to the market equilibrium), $0.00 from his second pepper (he loses $0.20), and he no longer buys the third pepper. Josie's consumer surplus is $0.10 from her first pepper (she loses $0.20), and she no longer buys the second pepper (she loses $0.10 of consumer surplus that she previously got from that second pepper). So the loss in consumer surplus is $0.70.

b. At a price received by producers of $0.30, Cara's producer surplus is $0.20 from her first pepper (she loses $0.20), $0.20 from her second pepper (she loses $0.20), and she no longer produces the third pepper (she loses $0.10 that she previously got from that third pepper). Jamie's producer surplus is $0.00 from his first pepper (he loses $0.20), and he no longer produces his second pepper. So the loss in producer surplus is $0.70.

c. Since three peppers are now sold and the tax on each is $0.40, the government tax revenue is 3 × $0.40 = $1.20.

d. Introduction of the tax resulted in a loss of total surplus of $0.70 + $0.70 = $1.40. Of that amount, $1.20 went to the government in the form of tax revenue. But $0.20 is lost: that is the amount of deadweight loss from this tax.

2. a. The demand for gasoline is inelastic because there is no close substitute for gasoline itself, and it is difficult for drivers to arrange substitutes for driving, such as taking public transportation. As a result, the deadweight loss from a tax on gasoline would be relatively small, as shown in the accompanying diagram.

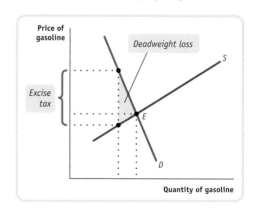

b. The demand for milk chocolate bars is elastic because there are close substitutes: dark chocolate bars, milk chocolate kisses, and so on. As a result, the deadweight loss from a tax on milk chocolate bars would be relatively large, as shown in the accompanying diagram.

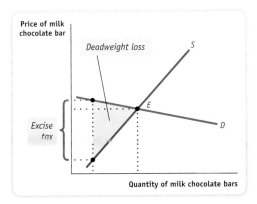

Chapter Six

Check Your Understanding

6-1

1. a. This is a microeconomic question because it considers the economic circumstances facing an individual firm.

b. This is a macroeconomic question because it considers how the overall level of an activity changes as the whole economy changes.

c. This is a macroeconomic question because it addresses the causes of long-run growth.

d. This is a microeconomic question because it addresses the economic decision-making of a single individual.

2. There is typically less scope for government intervention in microeconomics because government intervention in markets reduces society's welfare except in certain well-defined cases. There is more scope for government intervention in macroeconomics because society's welfare is enhanced when the government can reduce the severity of economic fluctuations or promote factors that increase a country's long-run growth.

Check Your Understanding

6-2

1. When fewer people are employed, the unemployment rate rises. Because fewer people are employed in production, the amount of aggregate output produced falls. As a result, the unemployment rate rises when aggregate output falls. When more people are employed, the unemployment rate falls. The amount of aggregate output produced rises because more people are employed in production. So the unemployment rate falls when aggregate output rises. Putting all these facts together means that the unemployment rate and aggregate output move in opposite directions over the business cycle.

2. A high unemployment rate results in lost wages for people who would like to be employed but aren't. It results in lost output for firms, output of goods and services that

consumers could have enjoyed. It can also result in political instability.

3. An economy with a successful stabilization policy experiences relatively few and shallow recessions. Equivalently, the economy experiences a low unemployment rate over time. It also experiences few overly robust expansions and therefore fewer inflationary pressures.

Check Your Understanding

6-3

1. The 1950s and 1960s were characterized by a high growth rate of real GDP, which significantly improved Americans' living standards over that period. In contrast, the 1970s and 1980s were characterized by a much lower growth rate of real GDP, which made Americans feel poorer, particularly when viewed in comparison to the gains that had been achieved in the 1950 and 1960s.

2. Countries with high rates of population growth will have to maintain higher growth rates of aggregate output than countries with low rates of population growth in order to achieve an increased standard of living per person because aggregate output will have to be divided among a larger number of people.

Check Your Understanding

6-4

1. a. You are better off because your wages have risen 5 percentage points more than prices (10% increase in wages – 5% increase in prices = 5%).

b. You are worse off because your wages have risen 5 percentage points less than prices (10% increase in wages – 15% increase in prices = – 5%).

c. You are better off because your wages have risen 12 percentage points more than prices (10% increase in wages + 2% fall in prices = 12%).

Check Your Understanding

6-5

1. a. The fall in the euro from $1.15 in 1999 to $0.85 in 2001 made European goods less expensive for Americans because a euro cost less to buy with a dollar. Conversely, American goods became more expensive for Europeans because a dollar cost more to buy with a euro.

b. The total value of European goods bought by Americans would have risen, and the total value of American goods bought by European, would have fallen.

Chapter Seven

Check Your Understanding

7-1

1. Let's start by considering the relationship between the total value added of all domestically produced final goods and services and aggregate spending on domestically produced final goods and services. These two quantities are equal because every final good and service produced in the economy is either purchased by someone or added to inventories. And additions to inventories are counted as spending by firms. Next, consider the relationship between aggregate spending on domestically produced final goods and services and total factor income. These two quantities are equal because all spending that is channeled to firms to pay for purchases of domestically produced final goods and services is revenue for firms. Those revenues must be paid out by firms to their factors of production in the form of wages, profit, interest, and rent. Taken together, this means that all three methods of calculating GDP are equivalent.

2. Firms make sales to other firms, households, the government, and the rest of the world. Households are linked to firms through the sale of factors of production to firms, through purchases from firms of final goods and services, and through lending funds to firms in the financial markets. Households are linked to the government through their payment of taxes, their receipt of transfers, and their lending of funds to the government to finance government borrowing via the financial markets. Finally, households are linked to the rest of the world through their purchases of imports and transactions with foreigners in financial markets.

3. You would be counting the value of the steel twice—once as it was sold by American Steel to American Motors and once as part of the car sold by American Motors.

Check Your Understanding

7-2

1. **a.** In 2004 nominal GDP was (1,000,000 × $0.40) + (800,000 × $0.60) = $400,000 + $480,000 = $880,000. A 25% rise in the price of french fries from 2004 to 2005 means that the 2005 price of french fries was 1.25 × $0.40 = $0.50. A 10% fall in servings means that 1,000,000 × 0.9 = 900,000 servings were sold in 2005. As a result, the total value of sales of french fries in 2005 was 900,000 × $0.50 = $450,000. A 15% fall in the price of onion rings from 2004 to 2005 means that the 2005 price of onion rings was 0.85 × $0.60 = $0.51. A 5% rise in servings sold means that 800,000 × 1.05 = 840,000 servings were sold in 2005. As a result, the total value of sales of onion rings in 2005 was 840,000 × $0.51 = $428,400. Nominal GDP in 2005 was $450,000 + $428,400 = $878,400. To find real GDP in 2005, we must calculate the value of sales in 2005 using 2004 prices: (900,000 french fries × $0.40) + (840,000 onion rings × $0.60) = $360,000 + $504,000 = $864,000.

   b. A comparison of nominal GDP in 2004 to nominal GDP in 2005 shows a decline of (($880,000 – $878,400) / $880,000) × 100 = 0.18%. But a comparison using real GDP shows a decline of (($880,000 – $864,000) / $880,000) × 100 = 1.8%. That is, a calculation based on real GDP shows a drop 10 times larger (1.8%) than a calculation based on nominal GDP (0.18%): in this case, the calculation based on nominal GDP underestimates the true magnitude of the change.

2. A price index based on 1990 prices will contain a relatively high price of electronics and a relatively low price of housing compared to a price index based on 2000 prices. This means that a 1990 price index used to calculate real GDP in 2005 will magnify the value of electronics production in the economy, but a 2000 price index will magnify the value of housing production in the economy.

Check Your Understanding

7-3

1. The advent of websites that enable job-seekers to find jobs more quickly will reduce the unemployment rate over time. However, websites that induce discouraged workers to begin actively looking for work again will lead to an increase in the unemployment rate over time.

2. Both parts a and b are consistent with the relationship between growth in real GDP and changes in the unemployment rate that is illustrated in Figure 7-6: during years of above-average growth, the unemployment rate fell, and vice versa. They are consistent with this relationship because they both entail either a fall in the unemployment rate during a recovery or a rise in the unemployment rate during a recession. However, part c is not consistent: it implies that a recession is associated with a fall in the unemployment rate.

Check Your Understanding

7-4

1. This market basket costs, pre-frost, (100 × $0.20) + (50 × $0.60) + (200 × $0.25) = $20 + $30 + $50 = $100. The same market basket, post-frost, costs (100 × $0.40) + (50 × $1.00) + (200 × $0.45) = $40 + $50 + $90 = $180. So the price index is ($100/$100) × 100 = 100 before the frost and ($180/$100) × 100 = 180 after the frost, implying a rise in the price index of 80%. This increase in the price index is less than the 84.2% increase calculated in the text. The reason for this difference is that the new market basket of 100 oranges, 50 grapefruit, and 200 lemons contains proportionately more of the items that have experienced relatively lower price increases (the lemons, whose price has increased by 80%) and proportionately fewer of the items that have experienced relatively large price increases (the oranges, whose price has increased by 100%). This shows that the price index can be very sensitive to the composition of the market basket. If the market basket contains a large proportion of goods whose prices have risen faster than the prices of other goods, it will lead to a higher estimate of the increase in the price level. If it contains a large proportion of goods whose prices have risen more slowly than the prices of other goods, it will lead to a lower estimate of the increase in the price level.

2. **a.** A market basket determined 10 years ago will contain fewer cars than at present. Given that the average price of a car has grown faster than the average prices of other goods, this basket will underestimate the true increase in the price level because it contains relatively too few cars.

   b. A market basket determined 10 years ago will not contain broadband Internet access. So, it cannot track the fall in prices of Internet access over the past few years. As a result, it will overestimate the true increase in the price level.

3. Using Equation 7-3, the inflation rate from 2003 to 2004 is (188.9 – 184.0)/184.0 × 100 = 2.7%.

Chapter Eight

Check Your Understanding

8-1

1. Economic progress raises the living standards of the average resident of a country. An increase in overall real GDP

does not accurately reflect an increase in an average resident's living standard because it does not account for growth in the number of residents. If, for example, real GDP rises by 10% but population grows by 20%, the living standard of the average resident falls: after the change, the average resident has only (110/120) × 100 = 91.6% as much real income as before the change. Similarly, an increase in nominal GDP does not accurately reflect an increase in living standards because it does not account for any change in prices. For example, a 5% increase in nominal GDP generated by a 5% increase in prices implies that there has been no change in living standards. Real GDP per capita is the only measure that accounts for both changes in the population and changes in prices.

2. Using the rule of 70, the amount of time it will take for China to double its real GDP per capita is (70/7.6) = 9.2 years; Ireland, (70/5.2) = 13.5 years; the United States, (70/2.0) = 35 years; France, (70/1.8) = 38.9 years; and Argentina (70/0.1) = 700 years. If Ireland continues to have a higher growth rate of real GDP per capita than the United States, then Irish real GDP per capita will eventually surpass that of the United States.

Check Your Understanding
8-2

1. **a.** Significant technological progress will result in an increase in the growth rate of productivity even though physical capital per worker and human capital per worker are unchanged.

   b. The growth rate of productivity will fall but remain positive due to diminishing returns to physical capital.

2. It will take a period of time for workers to learn how to use the new computer system and to adjust their routines. And because there are often setbacks in learning a new system, such as accidentally erasing your computer files, productivity at Multinomics may decrease for a period of time.

Check Your Understanding
8-3

1. Funds borrowed from abroad must eventually be paid back to foreigners, meaning that in the future there will be fewer funds available to the country for investment spending. In contrast, funds that are paid back to domestic savers stay in the country and are available for future investment spending. This is why some economists believe that foreign investment may result in a lower growth rate than if the same amount of funds were generated by domestic savings. Other economists disagree because they believe that foreign investment brings with it new technology, which leads to an increase in a country's growth rate that more than offsets the reduction in funds that occurs when funds from abroad must be paid back to foreigners.

2. It is likely that the United States will experience a greater pace of creation and development of new drugs because closer links between private companies and academic research centers will lead to work more directly focused on producing new drugs than on pure research.

3. It is likely that these events resulted in a fall in the country's growth rate because the lack of property rights would have dissuaded people from making investments in productive capacity.

4. Countries have found that foreign investment usually brings new technology that increases the country's growth rate and living standards.

Check Your Understanding
8-4

1. The conditional version of the convergence hypothesis says that countries grow faster, other things equal, when they start from relatively low GDP per capita and grow more slowly, other things equal, when their GDP per capita is relatively higher; this points to lower future Asian growth. However, other things might not be equal: if Asian economies continue investing in human capital, if savings rates continue to be high, if governments invest in infrastructure, and so on, growth might continue at an accelerated pace.

2. As you can see from panel (b) of Figure 8-8, although it is important in determining the growth rate for some countries (such as those of Western Europe), the initial level of GDP per capita isn't the only factor. High rates of savings and investment appear to be better predictors of future growth than today's standard of living.

3. The evidence suggests that both sets of factors matter: better infrastructure is important for growth, but so is political stability. Policies should try to address both areas.

Chapter Nine

Check Your Understanding
9-1

1. As the budget deficit becomes a budget surplus, the government needs to borrow less money; as a result, the demand for loanable funds decreases. In the accompanying diagram, the demand curve, D_1, represents the demand for government borrowing plus private demand. The elimination of government borrowing shifts D_1 leftward to D_2, where D_2 represents only the private demand for loanable funds. The equilibrium interest rate falls from r_1 to r_2. As a result—although the *total* quantity of lending falls—the *private* quantity of loanable funds demanded rises from Q_1 to Q_2.

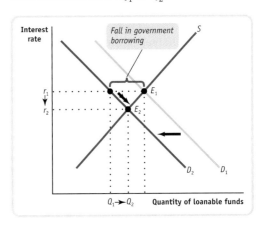

2. a. As capital flows into the economy, the supply of loanable funds increases. This is illustrated by the shift of the supply curve from S_1 to S_2 in the accompanying diagram. As the equilibrium moves from E_1 to E_2, the equilibrium interest rate falls from r_1 to r_2, and the equilibrium quantity of loanable funds increases from Q_1 to Q_2.

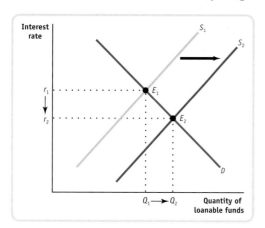

b. Savings fall due to the higher proportion of retired people and the supply of loanable funds decreases. This is illustrated by the leftward shift of the supply curve from S_1 to S_2 in the accompanying diagram. The equilibrium moves from E_1 to E_2, the equilibrium interest rate rises from r_1 to r_2, and the equilibrium quantity of loanable funds falls from Q_1 to Q_2.

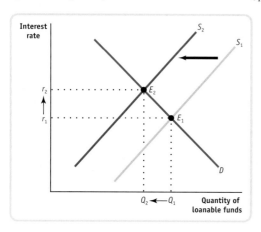

3. We know from the loanable funds market that as the interest rate rises, households want to save more and consume less. But at the same time, an increase in the interest rate lowers the number of investment spending projects with returns at least as high as the interest rate. The statement "households will want to save more money than businesses will want to invest" cannot represent an equilibrium in the loanable funds market because it says that the quantity of loanable funds offered exceeds the quantity of loanable funds demanded. If that were to occur, the interest rate must fall to make the quantity of loanable funds offered equal to the quantity of loanable funds demanded.

1. The transaction costs for (a) a bank deposit and (b) a share of a mutual fund are approximately equivalent because each can typically be accomplished by making a phone call, going online, or visiting a branch office. Transaction costs are highest for (c) a share of the family business, since finding a buyer for the share consumes time and resources. The level of risk is probably lowest for (a) a bank deposit, since these deposits are insured by the Federal Deposit Insurance Corporation (FDIC) up to $100,000; somewhat higher for (b) a share of a mutual fund, since despite diversification, there is still risk associated with holding stocks; and highest for (c) a share of the family business, since this investment is not diversified. The level of liquidity is highest for (a) a bank deposit, since withdrawals can usually be made immediately; somewhat lower for (b) a share of a mutual fund, since it may take a few days between selling your shares and the payment being processed; and lowest for (c) a share of the family business, since it can only be sold with the unanimous agreement of other members and it will take some time to find a buyer.

2. Economic development and growth are the result of, among other factors, investment spending on physical capital. Since investment spending is equal to savings, the greater the amount saved, the higher investment spending will be, and so the higher growth and economic development will be. So the existence of institutions that facilitate savings will help a country's growth and economic development. As a result, a country with a financial system that provides low transaction costs, simple opportunities for diversification of risk, and high liquidity to its savers will experience faster growth and economic development than a country that doesn't.

1. a. Today's stock prices reflect the market's expectation of future stock prices, and according to the efficient markets hypothesis, stock prices always take account of all available information. The fact that this year's profits are low is not new information, so it is already built into the share price. However, when it becomes known that the company's profit will be high next year, the price of a share of its stock will rise today, reflecting this new information.

b. The expectations of investors about high profits were already built into the stock price. Since profits are lower than expected, the market's expectations about the company's future stock price will be revised downward. This new information will lower the stock price.

c. These announcements will lower investors' expectations about the company's future stock price. This new information will lower the stock price.

d. This announcement will either have no effect on the company's stock price or will increase it only slightly. It does not add any new information, beyond removing some uncertainty about whether the profit forecast was correct. It should therefore result in either no increase, or only a small increase in the stock price.

2. The efficient markets hypothesis states that all available information is immediately taken account in stock prices. So if investors consistently bought stocks the day after the Dow rose by 1%, a smart investor would *sell* on that day because demand—and therefore stock prices—would be high. If a profit can be made that way, eventually many investors would be selling, and it would no longer be true that investors always bought stocks the day after the Dow rose by 1%.

Chapter Ten

Check Your Understanding
10-1

1. a. This represents a movement along the SRAS curve because the CPI—like the GDP deflator—is a measure of the aggregate price level, the overall price level of final goods and services in the economy.

b. This represents a shift of the SRAS curve because oil is a commodity. The SRAS will shift to the right because production costs are now lower, leading to a higher quantity of aggregate output supplied at any given aggregate price level.

c. This represents a shift of the SRAS curve because it involves a change in nominal wages. An increase in legally mandated benefits to workers is equivalent to an increase in nominal wages. As a result, the SRAS curve will shift leftward because production costs are now higher, leading to a lower quantity of aggregate output supplied at any given aggregate price level.

2. You would need to know what happened to the aggregate price level. If the increase in the quantity of aggregate output supplied was due to a movement along the SRAS curve, the aggregate price level would increase at the same time as the quantity of aggregate output supplied increases. If the increase in the quantity of aggregate output supplied was due to a rightward shift of the LRAS curve, the aggregate price level might not rise. Alternatively, you could make the determination by observing what happened to aggregate output in the long run. If it falls back to its initial level in the long run, then the temporary increase in aggregate output was due to a movement along the SRAS curve. If it stays at the higher level in the long run, the increase in aggregate output was due to a rightward shift of the LRAS curve.

Check Your Understanding
10-2

1. a. This is a shift of the aggregate demand curve. A decrease in the quantity of money raises the interest rate, since people now want to borrow more and lend less. A higher interest rate reduces investment and consumer spending at any given aggregate price level, so the aggregate demand curve shifts to the left.

b. This is a movement up along the aggregate demand curve. As the aggregate price level rises, the real value of money holdings falls. This is the interest rate effect of a change in the aggregate price level: as the value of money falls, people want to hold more money. They do so by borrowing more and lending less. This leads to a rise in the interest rate and a reduction in consumer and investment spending. So it is a movement along the aggregate demand curve.

c. This is a shift of the aggregate demand curve. Expectations of a poor job market, and so lower average disposable incomes, will reduce people's consumer spending today at any given aggregate price level. So the aggregate demand curve shifts to the left.

d. This is a shift of the aggregate demand curve. A fall in tax rates raises people's disposable income. At any given aggregate price level, consumer spending is now higher, so the aggregate demand curve shifts to the right.

e. This is a movement down along the aggregate demand curve. As the aggregate price level falls, the real value of assets rises. This is the wealth effect of a change in the aggregate price level: as the value of assets rises, people will increase their consumption plans. This leads to higher consumer spending, so it is a movement along the aggregate demand curve.

f. This is a shift of the aggregate demand curve. A rise in the real value of assets in the economy due to a surge in real estate values raises consumer spending at any given aggregate price level. So the aggregate demand curve shifts to the right.

Check Your Understanding
10-3

1. A decline in investment spending, like a rise in investment spending, has a multiplier effect on real GDP—the only difference in this case is that real GDP falls instead of rises. The fall in I leads to an initial fall in real GDP, which leads to a fall in disposable income, which leads to lower consumer spending, which leads to another fall in real GDP, and so on. So consumer spending falls as an indirect result of the fall in investment spending.

Check Your Understanding
10-4

1. a. An increase in the minimum wage raises the nominal wage and, as a result, shifts the short-run aggregate supply curve to the left. As a result of this negative supply shock, the aggregate price level rises, and aggregate output falls.

b. Increased investment spending shifts the aggregate demand curve to the right. As a result of this positive demand shock, both the aggregate price level and aggregate output rise.

c. An increase in taxes and a reduction in government spending both result in negative demand shocks, shifting the aggregate demand curve to the left. As a result, both the aggregate price level and aggregate output fall.

d. This is a negative supply shock, shifting the short-run aggregate supply curve to the left. As a result, the aggregate price level rises and aggregate output falls.

2. As long-run growth increases potential output, the long-run aggregate supply curve shifts to the right. If, in the short run, there is now a recessionary gap (aggregate output is less than potential output), nominal wages will fall, shifting the short-run aggregate supply curve to the right. This results in a falling aggregate price level and a rise in aggregate output. As prices fall, we move along the aggregate demand curve due to the wealth and interest rate effects of a change in the aggregate price level. Eventually, as long-run macroeconomic equilibrium is reestablished, aggregate output will rise to be equal to potential output.

Check Your Understanding 10-5

1. a. An economy is overstimulated when an inflationary gap is present. This will arise if an expansionary monetary or fiscal policy is implemented when the economy is currently in long-run macroeconomic equilibrium. This shifts the aggregate demand curve to the right, in the short run raising the aggregate price level and aggregate output and creating an inflationary gap. Eventually nominal wages will rise and shift the short-run aggregate supply curve to the left, and aggregate output will fall back to potential output. This is the scenario envisaged by the speaker.

b. No, this is not a valid argument. When the economy is not currently in long-run macroeconomic equilibrium, an expansionary monetary or fiscal policy does not lead to the outcome described above. Suppose a negative demand shock has shifted the aggregate demand curve to the left, resulting in a recessionary gap. An expansionary monetary or fiscal policy can shift the aggregate demand curve back to its original position in long-run macroeconomic equilibrium. In this way, the short-run fall in aggregate output and deflation caused by the original negative demand shock can be avoided. So, if used in response to demand shocks, fiscal or monetary policy is a an effective policy tool.

Chapter Eleven

Check Your Understanding 11-1

1. a. Angelina's autonomous consumer spending is $8,000. When her current disposable income rises by $10,000, her consumer spending rises by $4,000 ($12,000 – $8,000). So her *MPC* is $4,000/$10,000 = 0.4 and her consumption function is $c = \$8,000 + 0.4 \times yd$.

Felicia's autonomous consumer spending is $6,500. When her current disposable income rises by $10,000, her consumer spending rises by $8,000 ($14,500 – $6,500). So her *MPC* is $8,000/$10,000 = 0.8 and her consumption function is $c = \$6,500 + 0.8 \times yd$.

Marina's autonomous consumer spending is $7,250. When her current disposable income rises by $10,000, her consumer spending rises by $7,000 ($14,250 – $7,250). So her *MPC* is $7,000/$10,000 = 0.7 and her consumption function is $c = \$7,250 + 0.7 \times yd$.

b. The aggregate autonomous consumer spending in this economy is $8,000 + $6,500 + $7,250 = $21,750. A $30,000 increase in disposable income (3 × $10,000) leads to a $4,000 + $8,000 + $7,000 = $19,000 increase in consumer spending. So the economy-wide *MPC* is $19,000/$30,000 = 0.63 and the aggregate consumption function is $C = \$21,750 + 0.63 \times YD$.

2. If you expect your future disposable income to fall, you would like to save some of today's disposable income to tide you over in the future. But you cannot do this if you cannot save. If you expect your future disposable income to rise, you would like to spend some of tomorrow's higher income today. But you cannot do this if you cannot borrow. If you cannot save or borrow, your expected future disposable income will have no effect on your consumer spending today. In fact, your *MPC* must always equal 1: you must consume all your current disposable income today, and you will be unable to smooth your consumption over time.

Check Your Understanding 11-2

1. a. This unexpected increase in consumer spending will result in a reduction in inventories as producers sell items from their inventories to satisfy this short-term increase in demand. This is negative unplanned inventory investment: it reduces the value of producers' inventories.

b. A rise in the cost of borrowing is equivalent to a rise in the interest rate: fewer investment spending projects are now profitable to producers, whether they are financed through borrowing or retained earnings. As a result, producers will reduce the amount of planned investment spending.

c. A sharp increase in the rate of real GDP growth leads to a higher level of planned investment spending by producers, according to the accelerator principle, as they increase production capacity to meet higher demand.

d. As sales fall, producers sell less, and their inventories grow. This leads to positive unplanned inventory investment.

2. Since the marginal propensity to consume is less than 1, consumer spending does not fully respond to fluctuations in current disposable income. This behavior is explained by the life-cycle hypothesis: households engage in "consumption smoothing" by borrowing against future income if current disposable income falls or by saving if current disposable income rises. This behavior diminishes the effect of fluctuations in the economy on consumer spending. In contrast, by the accelerator principle, fluctuations in the economy have magnified effects on investment spending.

3. When consumer demand is sluggish, firms with excess production capacity will cut back on planned investment spending because they think their existing capacities are sufficient for expected future sales. Similarly, when consumer demand is sluggish and firms have a large amount of unplanned inventory investment, they are likely to cut back their production of output because they think their existing inventories are sufficient for expected future sales. So an inventory overhang is likely to depress economic activity as firms cut back their output.

Check Your Understanding 11-3

1. A slump in planned investment spending will lead to a fall in real GDP in response to an unanticipated increase in inventories. The fall in real GDP will translate into a fall in households' disposable income, and households will respond by reducing consumer spending. The decrease in consumer spending leads producers to further decrease output, further lowering disposable income and leading to further reductions in consumer spending. So although the slump originated in investment spending, it will cause a reduction in consumer spending.

2. a. After an autonomous fall in planned aggregate spending, the economy is no longer in equilibrium: real GDP is greater than planned aggregate spending. Panel (a) of the accompanying figure shows this autonomous fall in planned aggregate spending by the shift of the aggregate spending curve from AE_1 to AE_2. The difference between the two results in positive unplanned inventory investment: there is an unanticipated increase in inventories. Firms will respond by reducing production. This will eventually move the economy to a new equilibrium. In the accompanying figure, this is illustrated by the movement from the initial income-expenditure equilibrium at E_1 to the new income-expenditure equilibrium at E_2. As the economy moves to its new equilibrium, real GDP falls from its initial income-expenditure equilibrium level at Y_1^* to its new lower level, Y_2^*. As panel (b) shows, at the fixed aggregate price level P^*, aggregate output falls from Y_1^* to Y_2^*, and therefore the aggregate demand curve shifts leftward from AD_1 to AD_2.

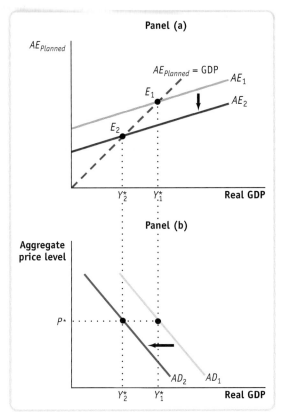

b. We know from Equation 11-12 that the change in income-expenditure equilibrium GDP is given by: $\Delta Y^* =$ Multiplier $\times \Delta AAE_{Planned}$. Here, the multiplier $= 1/(1 - 0.5) = 1/0.5 = 2$. So a $300 million autonomous fall in planned aggregate spending will lead to a $2 \times \$300$ million $= \$600$ million ($0.6 billion) fall in income-expenditure equilibrium GDP. The new Y^* will be $500 billion − $0.6 billion = $499.4 billion.

Chapter Twelve

Check Your Understanding

12-1

1. a. This is a contractionary fiscal policy because it is a reduction in government purchases of goods and services.
   b. This is an expansionary fiscal policy because it is an increase in government transfers that will increase disposable income.

c. This is a contractionary fiscal policy because it is an increase in taxes that will reduce disposable income.

2. Federal disaster relief that is quickly disbursed is more effective than legislated aid because there is very little time lag between the time of the disaster and the time it is received by victims. Hence, it will stabilize the economy after a disaster. In contrast, legislated aid is likely to entail a time lag in its disbursment, leading to potential destabilization of the economy.

Check Your Understanding

12-2

1. A $500 million increase in government purchases of goods and services directly increases aggregate spending by $500 million, which then starts the multiplier in motion. It will increase real GDP by $500 million $\times 1/(1 - MPC)$. A $500 million increase in government transfers increases aggregate spending only to the extent that it leads to an increase in consumer spending. Consumer spending rises by $$MPC$ for every $1 increase in disposable income, where MPC is less than 1. Thus, a $500 million increase in government transfers shifts the aggregate demand curve only MPC times as much as a $500 million increase in government purchases of goods and services. It will increase real GDP by $500 million $\times MPC/(1 - MPC)$.

2. This is the same issue as in problem 1, but in reverse. If government purchases of goods and services fall by $500 million, the initial fall in aggregate spending is $500 million. If there is a $500 million reduction in government transfers, the initial fall in aggregate spending is $MPC \times$ $500 million, which is less than $500 million.

Check Your Understanding

12-3

1. When your work-study earnings are low, your parents help softens the impact on your disposable income: your disposable income (and so your consumer spending) does not fall by as much as it otherwise would. But when your earnings are high, the requirement that you contribute to your tuition bill dampens the increase in your disposable income: your disposable income (and so your consumer spending) does not rise by as much as it otherwise would. As a result, the arrangement reduces the size of the fluctuations of your disposable income: it acts like the automatic stabilizing effect of the government's budget.

2. In recessions, real GDP falls. This implies that consumers' incomes, consumer spending, and producers' profits also fall. So in recessions, states' tax revenue (which depends in large part on consumers' incomes, consumer spending, and producers' profits) falls. In order to balance the state budget, states have to cut spending or raise taxes. But that implies deepening the recession. Without a balanced-budget requirement, states could use expansionary fiscal policy during a recession to lessen the fall in real GDP. The same is true during an expansion but with contractionary fiscal policy instead of expansionary fiscal policy. As real GDP rises, government revenue also rises. To balance the budget, states have to increase spending or cut taxes, further boosting real GDP and leading to an even greater expansion. Without a

balanced-budget requirement, states could use contractionary fiscal policy during expansions to dampen the rise in real GDP.

Check Your Understanding 12-4

1. **a.** A higher growth rate of real GDP implies that tax revenue will increase. If government spending remains constant and the government runs a budget surplus, the size of the public debt will be less than it would otherwise have been.

b. If retirees live longer, the average age of the population increases. As a result, the implicit liabilities of the government increase because spending on programs for older Americans, such as Social Security and Medicare, will rise.

c. A decrease in tax revenue without offsetting reductions in government spending will cause the public debt to increase.

d. Public debt will increase as a result of government borrowing to pay interest on its current public debt.

2. In order to stimulate the economy in the short run, the government can use fiscal policy to increase real GDP. This entails borrowing, increasing the size of the public debt further and leading to undesirable consequences: in extreme cases, governments can be forced to default on their debts. Even in less extreme cases, a large public debt is undesirable because government borrowing "crowds out" borrowing for private investment spending. This reduces the amount of investment spending, reducing the long-run potential of the economy to grow.

Chapter Thirteen

Check Your Understanding 13-1

1. The defining characteristic of money is its liquidity: how easily it can be used to purchase goods and services. Although a gift certificate can easily be used to purchase a very defined set of goods or services (the goods or services available at the store issuing the gift certificate), it cannot be used to purchase any other goods and services. A gift certificate is therefore not money, since it cannot easily be used to purchase all goods or services.

2. Again, the important characteristic of money is its liquidity: how easily it can be used to purchase goods and services. M1, the narrowest definition of the money supply, contains only currency in circulation, traveler's checks, and checkable bank deposits. CDs aren't checkable—and they can't be made checkable without incurring a cost because there's a penalty for early withdrawal. This makes them less liquid than the assets counted in M1.

Check Your Understanding 13-2

1. Even though you know that the rumor about the bank is not true, you are concerned about other depositors pulling their money out of the bank. And you know that if enough other depositors pull their money out, the bank will fail. In that case, it is rational for you to pull your money out before the bank fails. All depositors will think like this, so even if they all know that the rumor is false, they may still rationally pull their money out, leading to a bank run. Deposit insurance leads depositors to worry less about the possibility of a bank run. Even if a bank fails, the FDIC will pay each depositor up to $100,000 per account. This will make you much less likely to pull your money out in response to a rumor. Since other depositors will think the same, there will be no bank run.

2. The aspects of modern bank regulation that would frustrate this scheme are *capital requirements* and *reserve requirements*. Capital requirements mean that a bank has to have a certain amount of capital—the difference between its assets (loans plus reserves) and its liabilities (deposits). So the con man could not open a bank without putting any of his own wealth in because the bank needs a certain amount of capital—that is, it needs to hold more assets (loans plus reserves) than deposits. So the con man would be at risk of losing his own wealth if his loans turn out badly.

Check Your Understanding 13-3

1. Since they only have to hold $100 in reserves, instead of $200, banks now lend out $100 of their reserves. Whoever borrows the $100 will deposit it in a bank, which will lend out $100 × (1 − rr) = $100 × 0.9 = $90. Whoever borrows the $90 will put it into a bank, which will lend out $90 × 0.9 = $81, and so on. Overall, deposits will increase by $100/0.1 = $1,000.

2. Silas puts $1,000 in the bank, of which the bank lends out $1,000 × (1 − rr) = $1,000 × 0.9 = $900. Whoever borrows the $900 will keep $450 in cash and deposit $450 in a bank. The bank will lend out $450 × 0.9 = $405. Whoever borrows the $405 will keep $202.50 in cash and deposit $202.50 in a bank. The bank will lend out $202.50 × 0.9 = $182.25, and so on. Overall, this leads to an increase in deposits of $1,000 + $450 + $202.50 + . . . But it decreases the amount of currency in circulation: the amount of cash is reduced by the $1,000 Silas puts into the bank. This is offset, but not fully, by the amount of cash held by each borrower. The amount of currency in circulation therefore changes by −$1,000 + $450 + $202.50 + . . . The money supply therefore increases by the sum of the increase in deposits and the change in currency in circulation, which is $1,000 − $1,000 + $450 + $450 + $202.50 + $202.50 + . . . and so on.

Check Your Understanding 13-4

1. An open-market purchase of $100 million by the Fed increases banks' reserves by $100 million as the Fed credits their accounts with additional reserves. In other words, this open-market purchase increases the monetary base (currency in circulation plus bank reserves) by $100 million. Banks lend out the additional $100 million. Whoever borrows the money puts it back into the banking system in the form of deposits. Of these deposits, banks lend out $100 million × (1 − rr) = $100 million × 0.9 = $90 million. Whoever borrows the money deposits it back into the banking system. And banks lend out $90 million × 0.9 = $81 million, and so on. As a result, bank deposits increase by $100 million + $90 million + $81 million + . . . = $100 million/rr = $100 million/0.1 = $1,000 million = $1 billion. Since in this simplified example all money lent out is deposited back in the banking system, there is no increase of currency in circulation, so the increase in bank deposits is equal to the increase in the money supply. In other words, the money supply increases by $1 billion. This is greater than the increase in the monetary base by a factor of 10: in this simplified model in which deposits are the only component of the money supply and in which banks hold no excess reserves, the money multiplier is $1/rr = 10$.

Chapter Fourteen

14-1

1. a. By increasing the opportunity cost of holding money, a high interest rate reduces the nominal and the real quantity of money demanded. This is a movement along the (nominal and real) money demand curve.
   b. A 10% fall in prices, other things equal, reduces the nominal quantity of money demanded by exactly 10% at any given interest rate, shifting the nominal money demand curve leftward. Because the real quantity of money demanded is unchanged, the real money demand curve does not shift.
   c. This technological change, which is widely expected in the fairly near future, would make currency unnecessary for many purchases, reducing the nominal and real quantity of money demanded at any given interest rate. That is, it would shift the nominal and real money demand curves leftward.
   d. Payment in cash would require firms to hold more money, increasing the nominal and real quantity of money demanded at any given interest rate. That is, it would shift the nominal and real money demand curves rightward.

14-2

1. In the accompanying diagram, the increase in the demand for money is shown as a rightward shift of the money demand curve, from MD_1 to MD_2. This raises the equilibrium interest rate from r_1 to r_2.

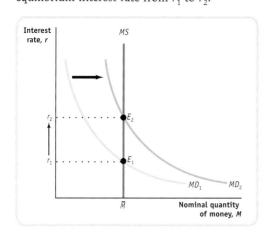

2. In order to prevent the interest rate from rising, the Federal Reserve must make an open-market purchase of Treasury bills, shifting the money supply curve rightward. This is shown in the accompanying diagram as the move from MS_1 to MS_2.

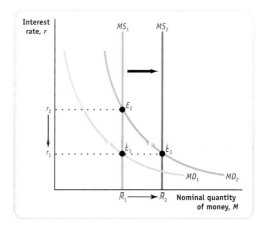

14-3

1. a. The money supply curve shifts to the right.
   b. The equilibrium interest rate falls.
   c. Investment spending rises, due to the fall in the interest rate.
   d. Consumer spending rises, due to the multiplier process.
   e. Aggregate output rises because of the rightward shift in the aggregate demand curve.
   f. The aggregate price level rises because the economy moves up the short-run aggregate supply curve.
   g. Savings rise because disposable income rises; part of the increase in disposable income is saved.
   h. The supply curve of loanable funds shifts rightward because savings rise.

14-4

1. a. Aggregate output rises in the short run, then falls back to equal potential output in the long run.
   b. The aggregate price level rises in the short run, but by less than 25%. It rises further in the long run, for a total increase of 25%.
   c. The real quantity of money rises in the short run, but by less than 25% because the aggregate price level also rises. In the long run, the real quantity of money returns to its original level.
   d. The interest rate falls in the short run, then rises back to its original level in the long run.

Chapter Fifteen

15-1

1. a. Frictional unemployment is unemployment due to the time workers spend searching for jobs. It is inevitable because workers may leave one job in search of another for a variety of reasons. Furthermore, there will always be

new entrants in the labor force who are seeking a first job. During the search process, these individuals will be counted as part of the frictionally unemployed.

b. When the unemployment rate is low, frictional unemployment will account for a larger share of total unemployment because other sources of unemployment—in particular, cyclical unemployment—will be diminished. So the share of total unemployment composed of the frictionally unemployed will rise.

2. A binding minimum wage represents a price floor below which wages cannot fall. As a result, actual wages cannot move toward equilibrium. So a minimum wage causes the quantity of labor supplied to exceed the quantity of labor demanded. Because this surplus of labor reflects unemployed workers, it affects the unemployment rate. Collective bargaining has a similar effect—unions are able to raise the wage above the equilibrium level. This will act like a minimum wage by causing the number of job seekers to be larger than the number of workers firms are willing to hire. Collective bargaining causes the unemployment rate to be higher than it otherwise would be, as shown in in the accompanying figure.

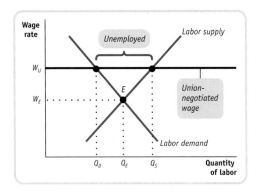

3. An increase in unemployment benefits reduces the cost to individuals of being unemployed, causing them to spend more time searching for a new job. So the natural rate of unemployment would increase.

Check Your Understanding
15-2

1. a. A positive output gap implies that actual output is above potential output. Given the relationship between output and unemployment, we would expect the output gap to be most positive when the difference between the natural unemployment rate and actual unemployment rate is greatest. Specifically, the output gap will be positive when the actual unemployment rate is below the natural rate of unemployment. This occurs from 1964 to 1972 and again from 1996 to 2001. There were several other brief periods when actual unemployment was below the natural rate of unemployment (the mid-1970s and again in the mid- to late 1980s). Although the relationship is not perfect, these periods are similar to those predicted by an examination of the actual and natural rates of unemployment.

2. Such a policy would increase the magnitude of the relationship between the output gap and the unemployment rate. An increase in output generally causes firms to

increase first the number of hours they employ their workforce. This is one of the reasons there is not a one-for-one relationship between the percent change in output and the unemployment rate. However, if there is a limit on the number of hours a worker can be employed, firms will not have the same flexibility to change output without changing the number of workers employed. With such a policy, firms will be more likely to respond to an increase in output by increasing employment. This would result in a greater reduction in the unemployment rate for a given increase in output.

Check Your Understanding
15-3

1. The more rapidly labor contracts can adjust to changing macroeconomic conditions, the more rapidly the economy will return to potential output. Since contracts of shorter duration often will be renegotiated more than those of longer duration, the country that has contracts of shorter duration (Malavia) will move more quickly to equilibrium when demand changes.

2. Workers may misperceive changes in the market-clearing wage rate because they are using old information to assess current equilibrium wage rates. More generally, workers may not be aware of rapidly changing supply and demand conditions in particular segments of the labor market. Until information about changes in labor supply or labor demand becomes more widespread, workers may misperceive the market-clearing wage. If the market-clearing wage is rising but workers are slow to recognize this, the extent to which the wage will rise in the short run will be diminished. With less upward pressure on the actual wage paid to workers, employment will be higher than it otherwise would be. This implies that the unemployment rate will be lower than it otherwise would be.

Check Your Understanding
15-4

1. The short-run Phillips curve illustrates the negative relationship between the unemployment rate and the inflation rate for a given expected inflation rate (and natural rate of unemployment). The economy will operate at the NAIRU only if the actual inflation rate and the expected inflation rate are equal. Now suppose that demand increases, causing an increase in employment, a reduction in the unemployment rate, and an increase in economic activity. As output rises above the potential output, the actual inflation rate will rise above the expected inflation rate. The subsequent reduction in the unemployment rate reflects a reduction in cyclical unemployment. So we will observe an increase in the inflation rate above the expected rate and a reduction in cyclical unemployment.

2. There is no long-run trade-off between inflation and unemployment because once expectations of inflation adjust, wages will also adjust, returning employment and the unemployment rate to their equilibrium (natural) levels. This implies that once expectations of inflation fully adjust to any change in actual inflation, the unemployment rate will return to the natural rate of unemployment, or NAIRU. This also implies that the long-run Phillips curve is vertical.

Chapter Sixteen

Check Your Understanding

16-1

1. The inflation rate is more likely to quickly reflect changes in the money supply when the economy has had an extended period of high inflation. That's because an extended period of high inflation sensitizes workers and firms to raise nominal wages and prices of intermediate goods when the aggregate price level rises. As a result, there will be little or no increase in real output in the short run after an increase in the money supply, and the increase in the money supply will simply be reflected in an equal-size percent increase in prices. In an economy where people are not sensitized to high inflation because of low inflation in the past, an increase in the money supply will lead to an increase in real output in the short run. This illustrates the fact that the classical model of the price level best applies to economies with *persistently* high inflation and not those with little or no history of high inflation while currently having high inflation.

2. Yes, there can still be an inflation tax because the tax is levied on people who hold money. As long as people hold money, regardless of whether prices are indexed or not, the government is able to use seigniorage to capture real resources from the public.

Check Your Understanding

16-2

1. a. With a nominal interest rate of 8% and an actual inflation rate of 3%, the real interest rate paid on the loan is 8% − 3% = 5%. Borrowers and lenders, however, expected the loan to have a real interest rate of 8% − 5% = 3%. Since this is lower than the actual real interest rate of 5%, lenders benefited and borrowers lost from the unexpected change in inflation.

   b. With a nominal interest rate of 6% and an actual inflation rate of 7%, the real interest rate paid on the loan is 6% − 7% = −1%. Borrowers and lenders, however, expected the loan to have a real interest rate of 6% − 4% = 2%. Since this is higher than the actual real interest rate of −1%, borrowers benefited and lenders lost from the unexpected change in inflation.

2. Shoe-leather costs as a result of inflation will be lower because it is now less costly for individuals to manage their assets in order to economize on their money holdings. This reduction in the costs associated with converting non-money assets into money translates into the lower shoe-leather costs.

Check Your Understanding

16-3

1. There are two possible explanations for this. First, negative supply shocks (for example, increases in the price of oil) will cause an increase in unemployment and an increase in inflation. Second, it is possible that British policy makers attempted to peg the unemployment rate below the natural rate of unemployment. Any attempt to peg unemployment below the natural rate will result in an increase in inflation.

2. Disinflation is costly because to reduce the inflation rate, aggregate output in the short run must typically fall below potential output. This, in turn, results in an increase in the unemployment rate above the natural rate. In general, we would observe a reduction in real GDP. The costs of disinflation can be reduced by not allowing inflation to increase in the first place. Second, the costs of any disinflation will be lower if the central bank is credible and it announces in advance its policy to reduce inflation. In this situation, the adjustment to the disinflationary policy will be more rapid, resulting in a smaller loss of aggregate output.

Check Your Understanding

16-4

1. If the nominal interest rate is negative, an individual is better off simply holding cash, which has a 0% nominal rate of return. If the options facing an individual are to lend and receive a negative nominal interest rate or to hold cash and receive a 0% nominal interest rate, the individual will hold cash. Such a scenario creates the possibility of a liquidity trap, in which monetary policy is ineffective because the nominal interest rate cannot fall below zero. Once the nominal interest rate falls to zero, further increases in the monetary base will lead banks, firms, and individuals to simply hold the additional cash.

Chapter Seventeen

Check Your Understanding

17-1

1. a. The figure on page 415 shows that the Fed pursued a policy that led to a rapid rise in the money supply during and after the 2001 recession. So the data support the first part of the quotation—that there was an "aggressive monetary policy." Whether this did in fact "reduce the depth" of that particular recession is a different question, one that cannot be answered just by looking at the data in the figure. To address the latter part of the quotation, we would have to ask what the size and depth of the 2001 recession would have been had the Fed not aggressively pursued an expansionary monetary policy.

   b. A classical economist would have said that the aggressive monetary expansion would have had no short-run effect on aggregate output and would simply have resulted in a proportionate increase in the aggregate price level.

Check Your Understanding

17-2

1. This is partly a Keynesian statement. Tax cuts will increase after-tax income and, from a Keynesian perspective, increase economic activity. A Keynesian would typically argue that a tax cut will increase disposable income, causing households to increase consumer spending. This increase in consumer spending will cause an increase in aggregate demand and, given an upward-sloping aggregate supply curve, will cause an increase in aggregate output. The Keynesian explanation of the way in which tax cuts affect economic activity, however, is not based on the latter part of the quotation. The latter part of the quotation suggests that the tax cuts will increase economic activity by increasing "incentives to work, save, and invest." That part doesn't seem to have much to do with Keynesian ideas.

Check Your Understanding 17-3

1. Monetarists argue that central banks should implement policy so that the money supply grows at some constant rate. Had the Fed pursued a monetarist policy during this period, we would have observed movements in M1 that would have shown a fixed rate of growth during this period. We would not, therefore, have observed any of the reductions in M1 that are observed in the figure nor would we have observed the acceleration in the rate of growth of M1 that occured in 2001.

2. As in Question 1, a monetarist policy would have resulted in a constant rate of growth in M1. Between 1960 and approximately 1981, the velocity of M1 rose smoothly. After 1981, the velocity of money experienced a number of shocks, where we observe increases and reductions in velocity. Given a constant rate of money growth, these changes in the velocity of M1 would have caused changes in aggregate demand and in economic activity, other things equal. In this situation, a monetarist policy would have allowed these shocks to the velocity of money to cause fluctuations in economic activity.

Check Your Understanding 17-4

1. **a.** Rational expectations theorists would argue that only unexpected changes in the money supply would have any short-run effect on economic activity. They would also argue that expected changes in the money supply would affect only the aggregate price level, with no short-run effect on aggregate output. So such theorists would give credit to the Fed for limiting the severity of the 2001 recession only if the Fed's monetary policy had been more aggressive than individuals expected during this period.
   b. Real business cycle theorists would argue that the Fed's policy had no effect on ending the 2001 recession because they believe that fluctuations in aggregate output are caused largely by changes in total factor productivity.

Check Your Understanding 17-5

1. Had inflation been much lower in early 2001, we would also expect that nominal interest rates would have been lower. In a situation like this, where inflation is near 0% and nominal interest rates are already low as well, a liquidity trap could occur. In a liquidity trap, the nominal interest rate is already low and close to 0%. In such a situation, it would be difficult for the Fed to further reduce the interest rate. This would have limited the Fed's ability to increase aggregate demand and, by doing so, attempt to limit the severity of any recession.

2. The large drop in stock prices is believed to have had at least two negative effects on the macroeconomy. First, the drop in stock prices reduced individuals' wealth, causing them to reduce consumer spending and so causing aggregate demand to fall. Second, the drop in stock prices may also have caused a reduction in consumer confi-

dence that would also have resulted in a reduction in consumer spending and a fall in aggregate demand. Any reduction in aggregate demand caused by lower stock prices would have meant that the Fed had to be even more aggressive in implementing expansionary monetary policy in order to reduce the length and severity of the recession.

Chapter Eighteen

Check Your Understanding 18-1

1. **a.** To determine comparative advantage, we must compare the two countries' opportunity costs for a given good. Take the opportunity cost of 1 ton of corn in terms of bicycles. In China, the opportunity cost of 1 bicycle is 0.01 ton of corn; so the opportunity cost of 1 ton of corn is 1/0.01 bicycles = 100 bicycles. The United States has the comparative advantage in corn since its opportunity cost in terms of bicycles is 50, a smaller number. Similarly, the opportunity cost in the United States of 1 bicycle in terms of corn is 1/50 ton of corn = 0.02 ton of corn. This is greater than 0.01, the Chinese opportunity cost of 1 bicycle in terms of corn, implying that China has a comparative advantage in bicycles.
   b. Given that the United States can produce 200,000 bicycles if no corn is produced, it can produce 200,000 bicycles × 0.02 ton of corn/bicycle = 4,000 tons of corn when no bicycles are produced. Likewise, if China can produce 3,000 tons of corn if no bicycles are produced, it can produce 3,000 tons of corn × 100 bicycles/ton of corn = 300,000 bicycles if no corn is produced. These points determine the vertical and horizontal intercepts of the U.S. and Chinese production possibility frontiers as shown in the accompanying diagram.

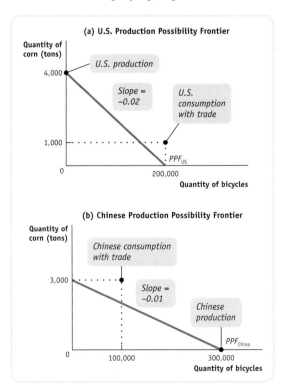

(a) U.S. Production Possibility Frontier

Quantity of corn (tons)

U.S. production

4,000

Slope = −0.02

U.S. consumption with trade

1,000

0   200,000

PPF_{US}

Quantity of bicycles

(b) Chinese Production Possibility Frontier

Quantity of corn (tons)

Chinese consumption with trade

3,000

Slope = −0.01

Chinese production

0   100,000   300,000

PPF_{China}

Quantity of bicycles

c. The figure shows the production and consumption points of the two countries. Each country is clearly better off with international trade because each now consumes a bundle of the two goods that lies outside its own production possibility frontier, indicating that these bundles were unattainable when each country was in autarky.

2. a. According to the Heckscher–Ohlin model, this pattern of trade occurs because the United States has a relatively larger endowment of factors of production, such as human capital and physical capital, that are suited to the production of movies, but France has a relatively larger endowment of factors of production suited to wine-making, such as vineyards and the human capital of vintners.

b. According to the Heckscher–Ohlin model, this pattern of trade occurs because the United States has a relatively larger endowment of factors of production, such as human and physical capital, that are suited to making machinery, but Brazil has a relatively larger endowment of factors of production suited to shoe-making, such as labor and leather.

Check Your Understanding

18-2

1. In the accompanying diagram, P_A is the price of U.S. grapes in autarky and P_W is the world price of grapes under international trade. With trade, U.S. consumers pay a price of P_W for grapes and consume quantity C_T, U.S. grape producers produce quantity Q_T, and the difference, $C_T - Q_T$, represents imports of Mexican grapes. As a consequence of the strike by truckers, imports are halted, the price paid by American consumers rises to the autarky price, P_A, and U.S. consumption falls to the autarky quantity Q_A.

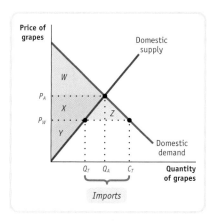

a. Before the strike, U.S. consumers enjoy consumer surplus equal to the area $W + X + Z$. After the strike, their consumer surplus shrinks to the area W. So consumers are worse off, losing consumer surplus represented by the area $X + Z$.

b. Before the strike, U.S. producers have producer surplus equal to the area Y. After the strike, their producer surplus increases to the area $Y + X$. So U.S. producers are better off, gaining producer surplus represented by the area X.

c. U.S. total surplus falls as a result of the strike by an amount represented by the area Z, the loss in consumer surplus that does not accrue to producers.

2. Mexican grape producers are worse off because they lose sales in the amount of $C_T - Q_T$, and Mexican grape pickers are worse off because they lose the wages that were associated with the lost sales. The lower demand for Mexican grapes caused by the strike implies that the price that Mexican consumers pay for grapes falls, making them better off. American grape pickers are better off because their wages increase as a result of the increase of $Q_A - Q_T$ in U.S. sales.

Check Your Understanding

18-3

1. a. If the tariff is $0.50, the price paid by domestic consumers for a pound of imported butter is $0.50 + $0.50 = $1.00, the same price as a pound of domestic butter. Imported butter will no longer have a price advantage over domestic butter, imports will cease, and domestic producers will capture all the feasible sales to domestic consumers, selling amount Q_A in the accompanying figure. But if the tariff is less than $0.50—say only $0.25—the price paid by domestic consumers for a pound of imported butter is $0.50 + $0.25 = $0.75, $0.25 cheaper than a pound of domestic butter. American butter producers will gain sales in the amount of $Q_2 - Q_1$ as a result of the $0.25 tariff. But this is smaller than the amount they would have gained under the $0.50 tariff, the amount $Q_A - Q_1$.

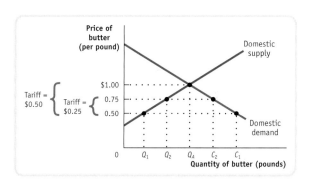

b. As long as the tariff is at least $0.50, increasing it more has no effect. At a tariff of $0.50, all imports are effectively blocked.

2. All imports are effectively blocked at a tariff of $0.50. So such a tariff corresponds to an import quota of 0.

Check Your Understanding

18-4

1. There are many fewer businesses that use steel as an input than there are consumers who buy sugar or clothing. So it will be easier for such businesses to communicate and coordinate among themselves to lobby against tariffs than it will be for consumers. In addition, each business will perceive that the cost of a steel tariff is quite costly to its profits, but an individual consumer is either unaware of or perceives little loss from tariffs on sugar or clothing.

2. Countries are often tempted to protect domestic industries by claiming that an import poses a quality, health, or environmental danger to domestic consumers. A WTO official should examine whether domestic producers are subject to the same stringency in the application of quality, health, or environmental regulations as foreign producers. If they are, then it is more likely that the regulations are for legitimate, non–trade protection purposes; if they are not, then it is more likely that the regulations are intended as trade protection measures.

Chapter Nineteen

Check Your Understanding
19-1

1. a. The sale of the new airplane to China represents an export of a good to China, and so affects the current account.
   b. The sale of Boeing stock to Chinese investors is a sale of a U.S. asset and so enters into the financial account.
   c. Even though the plane already exists, when it is shipped to China it is an export of a good from the United States. So the sale of the plane enters the current account.
   d. Because the plane stays in the United States, the Chinese investor is buying a U.S. asset. So this is identical to the answer to part b: the sale of the jet enters the financial account.

2. The high savings combined with the low returns in the rest of the world will cause an increase in the capital inflow into the United States—an increase in the U.S. balance of payments on financial account. This will cause an increase in the quantity of loanable funds supplied in the United States, which will cause the U.S. interest rate to fall.

Check Your Understanding
19-2

1. a. The increased purchase of Mexican oil will cause U.S. individuals (and firms) to increase their demand for the peso. To purchase pesos, individuals will increase their supply of U.S. dollars to the foreign exchange market, causing a rightward shift in the supply curve of U.S. dollars. This will cause the peso price of the dollar to fall (the amount of pesos per dollar will fall). The peso has appreciated and the U.S. dollar has depreciated as a result.
   b. This appreciation of the peso means it will take more U.S. dollars to obtain the same quantity of Mexican pesos. If we assume that the price level (measured in Mexican pesos) of other Mexican goods and services does not change, other Mexican goods and services become more expensive to U.S. households and firms. The dollar cost of other Mexican goods and services will rise as the peso appreciates. So Mexican exports of goods and services other than oil will fall.
   c. U.S. goods and services become cheaper in terms of pesos, so Mexican imports of goods and services will rise.

2. a. The real exchange rate equals

$$\text{Pesos per U.S. dollar} \times \frac{\text{Aggregate price level in the U.S.}}{\text{Aggregate price level in Mexico}}$$

Today, the aggregate price levels in both countries are both equal to 100. The real exchange rate today is: 10 × (100/100) = 10. The aggregate price level in five years in the U.S. is 100 × (120/100) = 120 and in Mexico it will be 100 × (1,200/800) = 150. The real exchange rate in five years, assuming the nominal exchange rate does not change, will be 10 × (120/150) = 8.
   b. Today, a basket of goods and services that costs $100 costs 800 pesos; so the purchasing power parity is 8 pesos per U.S. dollar. In five years, a basket that costs $120 will cost 1,200 pesos, so the purchasing power parity will be 10 pesos per U.S. dollar.

Check Your Understanding
19-3

1. The accompanying diagram shows the supply of and demand for the yuan with the U.S. dollar price of the yuan on the vertical axis. In 2005, prior to the revaluation, the exchange rate was pegged at 8.28 yuan per U.S. dollar or, equivalently, 0.121 U.S. dollars per yuan ($0.121). At the target exchange rate of $0.121, the quantity of yuan demanded exceeded the quantity of yuan supplied, creating the shortage depicted in the diagram. Without any intervention by the Chinese government, the U.S. dollar price of the yuan would be bid up, causing an appreciation of the yuan. The Chinese government, however, intervened to prevent this appreciation.

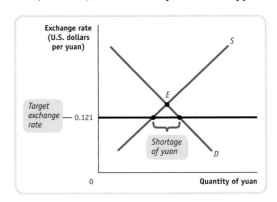

a. If the exchange rate were allowed to move freely, the U.S. dollar price of the exchange rate would move toward the equilibrium exchange rate (labeled XR* in the accompanying diagram). This would occur as a result of the shortage, when buyers of the yuan would bid up its U.S. dollar price. As the exchange rate increases, the quantity of yuan demanded would fall and the quantity of yuan supplied would increase. If the exchange rate were to increase to XR*, the disequilibrium would be entirely eliminated.

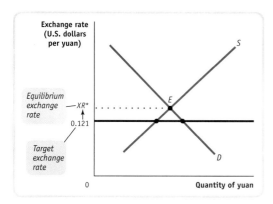

b. Placing restrictions on foreigners who want to invest in China would reduce the demand for the yuan, causing the demand curve to shift in the accompanying diagram from D_1 to something like D_2. This would cause a reduction in the shortage of the yuan. If demand fell to D_3, the disequilibrium would be completely eliminated.

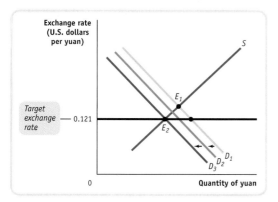

c. Removing restrictions on Chinese who wish to invest abroad would cause an increase in the supply of the yuan and a rightward shift in the supply curve. This increase in supply would also cause a reduction in the size of the shortage. If, for example, supply increased from S_1 to S_2, the disequilibrium would be eliminated completely in the accompanying diagram.

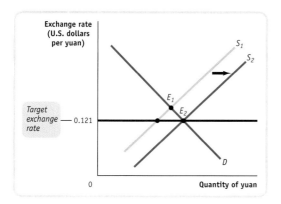

d. Imposing a tax on exports (Chinese goods sold to foreigners) would raise the price of these goods and decrease the amount of Chinese goods purchased. This would also decrease the demand for the yuan. The graphical analysis here is virtually identical to that found in the figure accompanying part b.

19-4

1. The devaluations and revaluations most likely occurred in those periods when there was a sudden change in the franc–mark exchange rate: 1974, 1976, the early 1980s, 1986, and 1993–1994.

2. The high Canadian interest rates would likely have caused an increase in capital inflows to Canada. To obtain these assets (which yielded a relatively higher interest rate) in Canada, investors would first have had to obtain Canadian dollars. The increase in the demand for the Canadian dollar would have caused the Canadian dollar to appreciate. This appreciation of the Canadian currency would have raised the price of Canadian goods to foreigners (measured in terms of the foreign currency). This would have made it more difficult for Canadian firms to compete in other markets.

MACROECONOMIC DATA 1929–2004

The following section presents macroeconomic data for the United States. The data include selected early years that illustrate the behavior of the economy during the Great Depression and the postwar boom. The series also include data for each from 1970 to 2004 for full coverage of recent years.

MACROECONOMIC DATA 1929–2004[1]

	1929	1933	1939	1945	1950	1955	1960	1965	1966
Nominal GDP and Its Components									
1. + Consumer spending (C)	77.4	45.9	67.2	120.0	192.2	258.8	331.7	443.8	480.9
2. + Investment spending (I)	16.5	1.7	9.3	10.8	54.1	69.0	78.9	118.2	131.3
3. + Government purchases of goods and services (G)	9.4	8.7	14.8	93.0	46.8	86.5	111.6	151.5	171.8
4. + Exports (X)	5.9	2.0	4.0	6.8	12.4	17.7	27.0	37.1	40.9
5. − Imports (IM)	5.6	1.9	3.1	7.5	11.6	17.2	22.8	31.5	37.1
6. = Gross domestic product (GDP)	**103.6**	**56.4**	**92.2**	**223.1**	**293.8**	**414.8**	**526.4**	**719.1**	**787.8**
7. + Income from abroad earned by Americans	1.1	0.4	0.7	0.8	2.2	3.5	4.9	7.9	8.1
8. − Income paid to foreigners	0.4	0.1	0.3	0.5	0.7	1.1	1.8	2.6	3.0
9. = Gross national product	**104.4**	**56.7**	**92.5**	**223.4**	**295.2**	**417.2**	**529.5**	**724.4**	**792.9**
10. National income	94.2	48.9	82.2	198.4	264.4	372.7	474.9	653.4	711.0
11. Government transfers	1.2	1.7	2.5	5.6	14.0	15.7	25.7	36.2	39.6
12. Taxes	1.7	0.8	1.5	19.4	18.9	32.9	46.1	57.7	66.4
13. Disposable income (YD)	83.4	46.1	71.4	152.2	210.1	283.3	365.4	498.1	537.5
14. Private savings ($S_{private}$)	3.8	−0.7	3.2	31.1	15.1	19.7	26.7	43.0	44.4
Real GDP and Growth Measures									
15. Real GDP (billions of 2000 dollars)	865.2	635.5	950.7	1,786.3	1,777.3	2,212.8	2,501.8	3,191.1	3,399.1
16. Real GDP growth (percent change from previous year)	-	−1.3%	8.1%	−1.1%	8.7%	7.1%	2.5%	6.4%	6.5%
17. Real GDP per capita (2000 dollars)	7,099	5,056	7,256	12,766	11,717	13,389	13,840	16,420	17,290
18. Real GDP per capita growth (percent change from previous year)	-	−1.9%	7.2%	−2.2%	6.9%	5.3%	0.4%	5.1%	5.3%
Prices and Inflation									
19. Consumer Price Index (1982 − 1984 = 100)	17.1	13.0	13.9	18.0	24.1	26.8	29.6	31.5	32.4
20. CPI Inflation rate	-	−5.1%	−1.4%	2.3%	1.3%	−0.4%	1.7%	1.6%	2.9%
21. Producer Price Index (all commodities, 1982 = 100)	16.4	11.4	13.3	18.2	27.3	29.3	31.7	32.3	33.3
22. PPI Inflation rate	-	1.8%	−1.5%	1.7%	3.8%	0.0%	0.0%	2.2%	3.1%
23. GDP deflator (2000 = 100)	11.9	8.9	9.7	12.5	16.5	18.7	21.0	22.5	23.2
24. GDP deflator inflation rate	-	−2.6%	−1.2%	2.6%	0.8%	1.5%	1.4%	1.8%	2.8%
Population and Employment									
25. Population (thousands)	121,878	125,690	131,028	139,928	151,684	165,275	180,760	194,347	196,599
26. Labor force (thousands)[2]	49,180	51,590	55,230	53,860	62,208	65,023	69,628	74,455	75,770
27. Unemployed (thousands)[2]	1,550	12,830	9,480	1,040	3,288	2,852	3,852	3,366	2,875
28. Unemployment rate	3.2%	24.9%	17.2%	1.9%	5.3%	4.4%	5.5%	4.5%	3.8%
Government Finance and Money									
29. Government (federal, state and local) budget balance	2.6	−0.5	−0.1	−27.4	6.8	9.2	11.5	9.9	10
30. Budget balance (percent of GDP)	2.5%	−0.9%	−0.1%	−12.3%	2.3%	2.2%	2.2%	1.4%	1.3%
31. M1	-	-	-	-	-	-	140	163	171
32. M2	-	-	-	-	-	-	304	443	471
33. Federal funds rate (yearly average)	-	-	-	-	-	1.8%	3.2%	4.1%	5.1%
International Trade									
34. Current account balance	-	-	-	-	-	-	2.8	5.4	3.0

Sources: Bureau of Economic Analysis, Bureau of Labor Statistics, Federal Reserve Bank of St. Louis.

1. Data in billions of current dollars unless otherwise stated.
2. Until 1947, includes workers 14 years and older; 1948 and after, includes workers 16 years and older.

1967	1968	1969	1970	1971	1972	1973	1974	1975	1976	1977	1978	1979	1980
507.8	558.0	605.2	648.5	701.9	770.6	852.4	933.4	1,034.4	1,151.9	1,278.6	1,428.5	1,592.2	1,757.1
128.6	141.2	156.4	152.4	178.2	207.6	244.5	249.4	230.2	292.0	361.3	438.0	492.9	479.3
192.7	209.4	221.5	233.8	246.5	263.5	281.7	317.9	357.7	383.0	414.1	453.6	500.8	566.2
43.5	47.9	51.9	59.7	63.0	70.8	95.3	126.7	138.7	149.5	159.4	186.9	230.1	280.8
39.9	46.6	50.5	55.8	62.3	74.2	91.2	127.5	122.7	151.1	182.4	212.3	252.7	293.8
832.6	**910.0**	**984.6**	**1,038.5**	**1,127.1**	**1,238.3**	**1,382.7**	**1,500.0**	**1,638.3**	**1,825.3**	**2,030.9**	**2,294.7**	**2,563.3**	**2,789.5**
8.7	10.1	11.8	12.8	14.0	16.3	23.5	29.8	28.0	32.4	37.2	46.3	68.3	79.1
3.3	4.0	5.7	6.4	6.4	7.7	10.9	14.3	15.0	15.5	16.9	24.7	36.4	44.9
838.0	**916.1**	**990.7**	**1,044.9**	**1,134.7**	**1,246.8**	**1,395.3**	**1,515.5**	**1,651.3**	**1,842.1**	**2,051.2**	**2,316.3**	**2,595.3**	**283.7**
751.9	823.2	889.7	930.9	1,008.1	1,111.2	1,247.4	1,342.1	1,445.9	1,611.8	1,798.9	2,027.4	2,249.1	2,439.3
48.0	56.1	62.3	74.7	88.1	97.9	112.6	133.3	170.0	184.0	194.2	209.6	235.3	279.5
73.0	87.0	104.5	103.1	101.7	123.6	132.4	151.0	147.6	172.3	197.5	229.4	268.7	298.8
575.3	625.0	674.0	735.7	801.8	869.1	978.3	1,071.6	1,187.4	1,302.5	1,435.7	1,608.3	1,793.5	2,009.0
54.4	52.8	52.5	69.5	80.6	77.2	102.7	113.6	125.6	122.3	125.3	142.5	159.1	201.4
3,484.6	3,652.7	3,765.4	3,771.9	3,898.6	4,105.0	4,341.5	4,319.6	4,311.2	4,540.9	4,750.5	5,015.0	5,173.4	5,161.7
2.5%	4.8%	3.1%	0.2%	3.4%	5.3%	5.8%	−0.5%	−0.2%	5.3%	4.6%	5.6%	3.2%	−0.2%
17,533	18,196	18,573	18,391	18,771	19,555	20,484	20,195	19,961	20,822	21,565	22,526	22,982	22,666
1.4%	3.8%	2.1%	−1.0%	2.1%	4.2%	4.8%	−1.4%	−1.2%	4.3%	3.6%	4.5%	2.0%	−1.4%
33.4	34.8	36.7	38.8	40.5	41.8	44.4	49.3	53.8	56.9	60.6	65.2	72.6	82.4
3.1%	4.2%	5.5%	5.7%	4.4%	3.2%	6.2%	11.0%	9.1%	5.8%	6.5%	7.6%	11.3%	13.5%
33.4	34.2	35.6	36.9	38.1	39.8	45	53.5	58.4	61.1	64.9	69.9	78.7	89.8
0.3%	2.4%	4.1%	3.7%	3.3%	4.5%	13.1%	18.9%	9.2%	4.6%	6.2%	7.7%	12.6%	14.1%
23.9	24.9	26.2	27.5	28.9	30.2	31.9	34.7	38.0	40.2	42.8	45.8	49.6	54.1
3.1%	4.3%	5.0%	5.3%	5.0%	4.3%	5.6%	9.0%	9.5%	5.8%	6.4%	7.0%	8.3%	9.1%
198,752	200,745	202,736	205,089	207,692	209,924	211,939	213,898	215,981	218,086	220,289	222,629	225,106	227,726
77,347	78,737	80,734	82,771	84,382	87,034	89,429	91,949	93,775	96,158	99,009	102,251	104,962	106,940
2,975	2,817	2,832	4,093	5,016	4,882	4,365	5,156	7,929	7,406	6,991	6,202	6,137	7,637
3.8%	3.6%	3.5%	4.9%	5.9%	5.6%	4.9%	5.6%	8.5%	7.7%	7.1%	6.1%	5.8%	7.1%
−2.4	5.2	16.7	−8.1	−21.9	−8.8	4.4	−4.4	−66.6	−44.4	−31	−7.8	1.7	−44.8
−0.3%	0.6%	1.7%	−0.8%	−1.9%	−0.7%	0.3%	−0.3%	−4.1%	−2.4%	−1.5%	−0.3%	0.1%	−1.6%
178	190	201	209	223	239	256	269	281	297	320	346	373	396
504	545	579	601	674	758	832	881	964	1,087	1,221	1,322	1,426	1,540
4.2%	5.7%	8.2%	7.2%	4.7%	4.4%	8.7%	10.5%	5.8%	5.0%	5.5%	7.9%	11.2%	13.4%
2.6	0.6	0.4	2.3	−1.4	−5.8	7.1	2.0	18.1	4.3	−14.3	−15.1	−0.3	2.3

MACROECONOMIC DATA 1929–2004[1]

	1981	1982	1983	1984	1985	1986	1987	1988	1989	1990
Nominal GDP and Its Components										
1. + Consumer spending (C)	1,941.1	2,077.3	2,290.6	2,503.3	2,720.3	2,899.7	3,100.2	3,353.6	3,598.5	3,839.9
2. + Investment spending (I)	572.4	517.2	564.3	735.6	736.2	746.5	785.0	821.6	874.9	861.0
3. + Government purchases of goods and services (G)	627.5	680.5	733.5	797.0	879.0	949.3	999.5	1,039.0	1,099.1	1,180.2
4. + Exports (X)	305.2	283.2	277.0	302.4	302.0	320.5	363.9	444.1	503.3	552.4
5. − Imports (IM)	317.8	303.2	328.6	405.1	417.2	453.3	509.1	554.5	591.5	630.3
6. = Gross domestic product (GDP)	3,128.4	3,255.0	3,536.7	3,933.2	4,220.3	4,462.8	4,739.5	5,103.8	5,484.4	5,803.1
7. + Income from abroad earned by Americans	92.0	101.0	101.9	121.9	112.4	111.4	123.2	152.1	177.7	189.1
8. − Income paid to foreigners	59.1	64.5	64.8	85.6	85.9	93.6	105.3	128.5	151.5	154.3
9. = Gross national product	3,161.4	3,291.5	3,573.8	3,969.5	4,246.8	4,480.6	4,757.4	5,127.4	5,510.6	5,837.9
10. National income	2,742.4	2,864.3	3,084.2	3,482.3	3,723.4	3,902.3	4,173.7	4,549.4	4,826.6	5,089.1
11. Government transfers	318.4	354.8	383.7	400.1	424.9	451.0	467.6	496.6	543.4	595.2
12. Taxes	345.2	354.1	352.3	377.4	417.4	437.3	489.1	505.0	566.1	592.8
13. Disposable income (YD)	2,246.1	2,421.2	2,608.4	2,912.0	3,109.3	3,285.1	3,458.3	3,748.7	4,021.7	4,285.8
14. Private savings ($S_{private}$)	244.3	270.8	233.6	314.8	280.0	268.4	241.4	272.9	287.1	299.4
Real GDP and Growth Measures										
15. Real GDP (billions of 2000 dollars)	5,291.7	5,189.3	5,423.8	5,813.6	6,053.7	6,263.6	6,475.1	6,742.7	6,981.4	7,112.5
16. Real GDP growth (percent change from previous year)	2.5%	−1.9%	4.5%	7.2%	4.1%	3.5%	3.4%	4.1%	3.5%	1.9%
17. Real GDP per capita (2000 dollars)	23,007	22,346	23,146	24,593	25,382	26,024	26,664	27,514	28,221	28,429
18. Real GDP per capita growth (percent change from previous year)	1.5%	−2.9%	3.6%	6.3%	3.2%	2.5%	2.5%	3.2%	2.6%	0.7%
Prices and Inflation										
19. Consumer Price Index (1982 − 1984 = 100)	90.9	96.5	99.6	103.9	107.6	109.6	113.6	118.3	124.0	130.7
20. CPI Inflation rate	10.3%	6.2%	3.2%	4.3%	3.6%	1.9%	3.6%	4.1%	4.8%	5.4%
21. Producer Price Index (all commodities, 1982 = 100)	98	100	101.3	103.7	103.2	100.2	102.8	106.9	112.2	116.3
22. PPI Inflation rate	9.1%	2.0%	1.3%	2.4%	−0.5%	−2.9%	2.6%	4.0%	5.0%	3.7%
23. GDP deflator (2000 = 100)	59.1	62.7	65.2	67.7	69.7	71.3	73.2	75.7	78.6	81.6
24. GDP deflator inflation rate	9.4%	6.1%	3.9%	3.8%	3.0%	2.2%	2.7%	3.4%	3.8%	3.9%
Population and Employment										
25. Population (thousands)	230,008	232,218	234,333	236,394	238,506	240,683	242,843	245,061	247,387	250,181
26. Labor force (thousands)[2]	108,670	110,204	111,550	113,544	115,461	117,834	119,865	121,669	123,869	125,840
27. Unemployed (thousands)[2]	8,273	10,678	10,717	8,539	8,312	8,237	7,425	6,701	6,528	7,047
28. Unemployment rate	7.6%	9.7%	9.6%	7.5%	7.2%	7.0%	6.2%	5.5%	5.3%	5.6%
Government Finance and Money										
29. Government (federal, state and local) budget balance	−45.7	−134.1	−168.1	−144.1	−152.6	−169.9	−132.6	−116.6	−109.3	−164.8
30. Budget balance (percent of GDP)	−1.5%	−4.1%	−4.8%	−3.7%	−3.6%	−3.8%	−2.8%	−2.3%	−2.0%	−2.8%
31. M1	425	453	503	539	587	666	743	775	782	811
32. M2	1,680	1,833	2,058	2,222	2,420	2,616	2,787	2,937	3,060	3,228
33. Federal funds rate (yearly average)	16.4%	12.3%	9.1%	10.2%	8.1%	6.8%	6.7%	7.6%	9.2%	8.1%
International Trade										
34. Current account balance	5.0	−5.5	−38.7	−94.3	−118.2	−147.2	−160.7	−121.2	−99.5	−79.0

Sources: Bureau of Economic Analysis, Bureau of Labor Statistics, Federal Reserve Bank of St. Louis.

1. Data in billions of current dollars unless otherwise stated.
2. Until 1947, includes workers 14 years and older; 1948 and after, includes workers 16 years and older.

1991	1992	1993	1994	1995	1996	1997	1998	1999	2000	2001	2002	2003	2004
3,986.1	4,235.3	4,477.9	4,743.3	4,975.8	5,256.8	5,547.4	5,879.5	6,282.5	6,739.4	7,055.0	7,376.1	7,760.9	8,229.9
802.9	864.8	953.4	1,097.1	1,144.0	1,240.3	1,389.8	1,509.1	1,625.7	1,735.5	1,614.3	1,579.2	1,665.8	1,927.3
1,234.4	1,271.0	1,291.2	1,325.5	1,369.2	1,416.0	1,468.7	1,518.3	1,620.8	1,721.6	1,825.6	1,956.6	2,075.5	2,183.9
596.8	635.3	655.8	720.9	812.2	868.6	955.3	955.9	991.2	1,096.3	1,032.8	1,005.0	1,046.2	1,175.5
624.3	668.6	720.9	814.5	903.6	964.8	1,056.9	1,115.9	1,251.7	1,475.8	1,399.8	1,429.9	1,544.3	1,781.6
5,995.9	**6,337.7**	**6,657.4**	**7,072.2**	**7,397.7**	**7,816.9**	**8,304.3**	**8,747.0**	**9,268.4**	**9,817.0**	**10,128.0**	**10,487.0**	**11,004.0**	**11,735.0**
168.9	152.7	156.2	186.4	233.9	248.7	286.7	287.1	320.8	382.7	322.4	301.8	329.0	405.8
138.5	123.0	124.3	160.2	198.1	213.7	253.7	265.8	287.0	343.7	278.8	274.7	273.9	361.9
6,026.3	**6,367.4**	**6,689.3**	**7,098.4**	**7,433.4**	**7,851.9**	**8,337.3**	**8,768.3**	**9,302.2**	**9,855.9**	**10,171.6**	**10,514.1**	**11,059.2**	**11,778.9**
5,227.9	5,512.8	5,773.4	6,122.3	6,453.9	6,840.1	7,292.2	7,752.8	8,236.7	8,795.2	8,979.8	9,225.4	9,679.6	10,339.6
666.4	749.4	790.1	827.3	877.4	925.0	951.2	978.6	1,022.1	1,084.0	1,193.9	1,282.7	1,335.4	1,405.9
586.7	610.6	646.6	690.7	744.1	832.1	926.3	1,027.0	1,107.5	1,235.7	1,237.3	1,051.2	1,001.9	1,042.6
4,464.3	4,751.4	4,911.9	5,151.8	5,408.2	5,688.5	5,988.8	6,395.9	6,695.0	7,194.0	7,486.8	7,827.7	8,159.9	8,646.9
324.2	366.0	284.0	249.5	250.9	228.4	218.3	276.8	158.6	168.5	132.3	159.2	110.6	115.0
7,100.5	7,336.6	7,532.7	7,835.5	8,031.7	8,328.9	8,703.5	9,066.9	9,470.3	9,817.0	9,890.7	10,074.8	10,381.3	10,841.9
−0.2%	3.3%	2.7%	4.0%	2.5%	3.7%	4.5%	4.2%	4.5%	3.7%	0.8%	1.9%	3.0%	4.4%
28,007	28,556	28,940	29,741	30,128	30,881	31,886	32,833	33,904	34,759	34,660	34,955	35,666	36,883
−1.5%	2.0%	1.3%	2.8%	1.3%	2.5%	3.3%	3.0%	3.3%	2.5%	−0.3%	0.9%	2.0%	3.4%
136.2	140.3	144.5	148.2	152.4	156.9	160.5	163.0	166.6	172.2	177.1	179.9	184.0	188.9
4.2%	3.0%	3.0%	2.6%	2.8%	3.0%	2.3%	1.6%	2.2%	3.4%	2.8%	1.6%	2.3%	2.7%
116.5	117.2	118.9	120.4	124.7	127.7	127.6	124.4	125.5	132.7	134.2	131.1	138.1	146.7
0.2%	0.6%	1.5%	1.3%	3.6%	2.4%	−0.1%	−2.5%	0.9%	5.7%	1.1%	−2.3%	5.3%	6.2%
84.5	86.4	88.4	90.3	92.1	93.9	95.4	96.5	97.9	100.0	102.4	104.1	106.0	108.3
3.5%	2.3%	2.3%	2.1%	2.0%	1.9%	1.7%	1.1%	1.4%	2.2%	2.4%	1.7%	1.8%	2.2%
253,530	256,922	260,282	263,455	266,588	269,714	272,958	276,154	279,328	282,429	285,366	288,217	291,073	293,951
126,346	128,105	129,200	131,056	132,304	133,943	136,297	137,673	139,368	142,583	143,734	144,863	146,510	147,401
8,628	9,613	8,940	7,996	7,404	7,236	6,739	6,210	5,880	5,692	6,801	8,378	8,774	8,149
6.8%	7.5%	6.9%	6.1%	5.6%	5.4%	4.9%	4.5%	4.2%	4.0%	4.7%	5.8%	6.0%	5.5%
−217.9	−296.7	−272.6	−201.9	−184.9	−116	−16.7	90.8	154	239.4	51.5	−279.5	−367.8	−351.9
−3.6%	−4.7%	−4.1%	−2.9%	−2.5%	−1.5%	−0.2%	1.0%	1.7%	2.4%	0.5%	−2.7%	−3.3%	−3.0%
859	966	1,079	1,145	1,143	1,106	1,069	1,080	1,101	1,104	1,136	1,191	1,267	1,337
3,349	3,412	3,449	3,495	3,566	3,737	3,920	4,206	4,523	4,799	5,216	5,610	5,998	6,270
5.7%	3.5%	3.0%	4.2%	5.8%	5.3%	5.5%	5.4%	5.0%	6.2%	3.9%	1.7%	1.1%	1.3%
2.9	−50.1	−84.8	−121.6	−113.7	−124.9	−140.9	−214.1	−300.1	−416.0	−389.5	−475.2	−519.7	−668.1

Glossary

Italicized terms within definitions are key terms that are defined elsewhere in this glossary.

absolute advantage: the advantage conferred by the ability to produce a good more efficiently—at lower cost of *resources*—than other producers.

absolute value: the value of a number without regard to a plus or minus sign.

accelerator principle: the proposition that a higher rate of growth in real GDP leads to higher planned investment spending, because high growth in real GDP is indicative of high growth in sales, which encourages firms to invest.

actual investment spending: the sum of *planned investment spending* and *unplanned inventory investment*.

aggregate consumption function: an equation relating aggregate current disposable income and aggregate consumer spending for the economy as a whole. A common form for the aggregate consumption function is $C = A + MPC \times YD$.

aggregate demand curve: a graphical representation of the relationship between the aggregate price level and the quantity of aggregate output demanded by households, businesses, the government, and the rest of the world. The aggregate demand curve has a negative slope due to the *wealth effect of a change in the aggregate price level* and the *interest rate effect of a change in the aggregate price level*.

aggregate output: the economy's total production of final goods and services for a given time period, usually a year. Real GDP is the numerical measure of aggregate output typically used by economists.

aggregate price level: the overall price level for final goods and services in the economy.

aggregate production function: a hypothetical function that describes how productivity (real GDP per worker) depends on the quantities of physical capital per worker and human capital per worker as well as the state of technology. It has the general form $Y/L = f(K/L, H/L, T)$.

aggregate spending: the sum of consumer spending, investment spending, government purchases, and exports minus imports. It is the total spending on domestically produced final goods and services in the economy.

aggregate supply curve: a graphical representation of the relationship between the aggregate price level and the quantity of aggregate output supplied.

appreciation: a rise in the value of one currency in terms of other currencies.

AS–AD model: the basic model used to understand fluctuations in aggregate output and the aggregate price level. It uses the *aggregate supply curve* and the *aggregate demand curve* together to analyze the behavior of the economy in response to shocks or government policy.

autarky: occurs when a country cannot trade with other countries.

automatic stabilizers: government spending and taxation rules that cause fiscal policy to be expansionary when the economy contracts and contractionary when the economy expands. Taxes that depend on disposable income are the most important example of automatic stabilizers.

autonomous change in aggregate spending: a change in the desired level of spending by firms, households, or government at a constant level of GDP.

balance of payments accounts: a summary of a country's transactions with other countries, including two main elements: the *balance of payments on current account* and the *balance of payments on financial account*.

balance of payments on current account (current account): a country's *balance of payments on goods and services* plus net international transfer payments and factor income.

balance of payments on financial account (financial account): the difference between a country's sales of assets to foreigners and its purchases of assets from foreigners during a given period.

balance of payments on goods and services: the difference between a country's exports of goods and services and its imports of goods and services during a given period.

bank: a *financial intermediary* that provides *liquid* assets in the form of *bank deposits* to lenders and uses those funds to finance the *illiquid* investments or investment spending needs of borrowers.

bank deposit: a claim on a *bank* that obliges the bank to give the depositor his or her cash when demanded.

bank reserves: currency held by banks in their vaults plus their deposits at the Federal Reserve.

bank run: a phenomenon in which many of a bank's depositors try to withdraw their funds due to fears of a bank failure.

bar graph: a graph that uses bars of varying height or length to show the comparative sizes of different observations of a variable.

barter: the direct exchange of goods or services without the use of money.

black market: a market in which goods or services are bought and sold illegally, either because it is illegal to sell them at all or because the prices charged are legally prohibited by a *price ceiling*.

bond: a legal document issued by a corporation or government promising the repayment of a loan, usually with interest.

budget balance: the difference between net tax revenue and government spending. A positive budget balance is referred to as a *budget surplus*; a negative budget balance is referred to as a *budget deficit*.

budget deficit: the difference between net tax revenue and government spending when government spending exceeds tax revenue; dissaving by the government in the form of a budget deficit is a negative contribution to national savings.

budget surplus: the difference between net tax revenue and government spending when tax revenue exceeds government spending; saving by the government in the form of a budget surplus is a positive contribution to national savings.

business cycle: the short-run alternation between economic downturns, known as *recessions*, and economic upturns, known as *expansions*.

capital flows: international movements of *financial assets*.

capital inflow: the net inflow of funds into a country; the difference between the total inflow of foreign funds to the home country and the total outflow of domestic funds to other countries. A positive net capital inflow represents funds borrowed from foreigners to finance domestic investment; a negative net capital inflow represents funds lent to foreigners to finance foreign investment.

causal relationship: the relationship between two variables in which the value taken by one variable directly influences or determines the value taken by the other variable.

central bank: an institution that oversees and regulates the banking system and controls the *monetary base*.

checkable bank deposits: bank accounts on which people can write checks.

circular-flow diagram: a model that represents the transactions in an *economy* by two kinds of flows around a circle: a flow of physical things such as goods or labor and the flow of money to pay for these physical things.

classical model of the price level: a model of the price level in which the real quantity of money is always at its long-run equilibrium level. This model ignores the distinction between the short run and the long run but is useful for analyzing the case of high inflation.

closed economy: an economy that does not trade goods, services, or assets with other countries.

commodity money: a good that is used as a medium of exchange but also has intrinsic worth because it has other uses. Gold or silver coins are commodity money.

commodity-backed money: a medium of exchange that has no intrinsic value but is guaranteed by a promise that it can be converted into valuable goods. Paper money that can be exchanged freely for gold or silver coins is commodity-backed money.

comparative advantage: the advantage conferred on an individual or nation if it can produce a good at a lower *opportunity cost* than another producer.

competitive market: a market in which all market participants are price-takers.

complements: pairs of goods for which a fall in the price of one good results in greater demand for the other.

consumer price index (CPI): a measure of the cost of a market basket intended to represent the consumption of a typical urban American family of four. It is the most commonly used measure of prices in the United States.

consumer spending: household spending on goods and services produced by domestic and foreign firms.

consumer surplus: a term often used to refer both to *individual consumer surplus* and to *total consumer surplus*.

consumption function: an equation showing how an individual household's consumer spending varies with current disposable income. Generally, consumption is positively related to disposable income. A common and simple version of a consumption function that captures this relationship is linear: $c = a + MPC \times yd$.

contractionary fiscal policy: *fiscal policy* that reduces aggregate demand by increasing taxes, decreasing transfers, or decreasing government purchases.

contractionary monetary policy: monetary policy that, through the raising of the interest rate, reduces aggregate demand and therefore output.

convergence hypothesis: a theory of economic growth that holds that international differences in real GDP per capita tend to narrow over time because countries with low GDP per capita generally have higher growth rates.

cost (of potential seller): the lowest price at which a seller is willing to sell a good.

crowding out: the negative effect of budget deficits on private investment, which occurs because government borrowing drives up interest rates.

currency in circulation: cash, in either paper or coin form, held by the public.

curve: a line on a graph, which may be curved or straight, that depicts a relationship between two variables.

cyclical unemployment: unemployment resulting from the business cycle; equivalently, the difference between the actual rate of unemployment and the *natural rate of unemployment*.

cyclically adjusted budget balance: an estimate of what the *budget balance* would be if real GDP were exactly equal to potential output.

deadweight loss (from a tax): the extra cost in the form of inefficiency that results because a tax discourages mutually beneficial transactions; also referred to as *excess burden*.

debt deflation: the reduction in aggregate demand arising from the increase in the real burden of outstanding debt caused by deflation; occurs because borrowers, whose real debt rises as a result of deflation, are likely to cut spending sharply, and lenders, whose real assets are now more valuable, are less likely to increase spending.

debt–GDP ratio: government debt as a percentage of GDP, frequently used as a measure of a government's ability to pay its debts.

deflation: a falling *aggregate price level*.

demand curve: a graphical representation of the *demand schedule*, showing how much of a good or service consumers would buy at a given price.

demand price: the price of a given quantity at which consumers will demand that quantity.

demand schedule: a list or table showing the relationship between price and the quantity of a good consumers would buy.

demand shock: any event that shifts the *aggregate demand curve*. A positive demand shock is associated with higher demand for aggregate output at any price level and shifts the curve to the right. A negative demand shock is associated with lower demand for aggregate output at any price level and shifts the curve to the left.

dependent variable: the determined variable in a causal relationship.

deposit insurance: a guarantee that a bank's depositors will be paid even if the bank can't come up with the funds, up to a maximum amount per account.

depreciation: a fall in the value of one currency in terms of other currencies.

depression: a very deep and prolonged downturn.

devaluation: a reduction in the value of a currency that is set under a fixed *exchange rate* regime.

diminishing returns to physical capital: property of an *aggregate production function* whereby each successive increase in the amount of physical capital, holding the amount of human capital and the state of technology fixed, leads to a smaller increase in productivity.

discount rate: the rate of interest the Federal Reserve charges on loans to banks that fall short of *reserve requirements*.

discouraged workers: nonworking people who are capable of working but have given up looking for a job because they believe no jobs are available.

discretionary fiscal policy: *fiscal policy* that is the result of deliberate actions by policy makers rather than rules.

discretionary monetary policy: policy actions, either changes in interest rates or changes in the money supply, undertaken by the central bank based on its assessment of the state of the economy.

disinflation: the process of lowering inflation that has become embedded in expectations by keeping the unemployment rate above the natural rate for an extended period of time.

disposable income: income plus *government transfers* minus taxes; the total amount of household income available to use for consumption and saving.

diversification: investment in several different assets with unrelated risks, so that the possible losses are independent events.

domestic demand curve: a *demand curve* for domestic consumers.

domestic supply curve: a *supply curve* for domestic producers.

economic aggregate: an economic measure that summarizes data across different markets for goods, services, workers, and assets.

economic growth: a *long-run* trend toward the production of more goods and services.

economics: the study of *economies,* at the level of individuals and of society as a whole.

economy: a system for coordinating a society's productive activities.

efficiency wages: wages that employers set above the equilibrium wage rate as an incentive for better performance.

efficient markets hypothesis: a theory of asset price determination that holds that asset prices embody all publicly available information. The theory implies that stock prices should be unpredictable, or follow a *random walk*, since changes should occur only in response to new information about fundamentals.

efficient: description of a market or *economy* that uses its resources in such a way as to exploit all opportunities to make some individuals better off without making others worse off.

employment: the number of people currently employed for pay in the economy.

equilibrium: an economic balance in which no individual would be better off doing something different; an equality of supply and demand.

equilibrium exchange rate: the *exchange rate* at which the quantity of a currency demanded in the *foreign exchange market* is equal to the quantity supplied.

equilibrium price: the price at which the market is in *equilibrium,* that is, the quantity of a good demanded equals the quantity supplied; also referred to as the *market-clearing price.*

equilibrium quantity: the quantity of a good bought and sold at the *equilibrium* (or *market-clearing*) price.

equity: fairness; because individuals can disagree about what is "fair," equity is not as well defined a concept as efficiency.

excess burden (from a tax): the extra cost in the form of inefficiency that results because a tax discourages mutually beneficial transactions; also referred to as *deadweight loss.*

excess reserves: a *bank's reserves* over and above the reserves required by law or regulation.

exchange market intervention: government purchases or sales of currency in the *foreign exchange market.*

exchange rate: the price of one currency in terms of another, determined by the *foreign exchange market.* The nominal exchange rate is unadjusted for international differences in price levels; the *real exchange rate* is adjusted for those differences.

exchange rate regime: a rule governing a country's policy toward the *exchange rate.*

excise tax: a tax on the consumption of a given good or service.

expansion: a period when output and employment are rising; also referred to as a *recovery.*

expansionary fiscal policy: *fiscal policy* that increases aggregate demand by decreasing taxes, increasing transfers, or increasing government purchases.

expansionary monetary policy: monetary policy that, through the lowering of the interest rate, increases aggregate demand and therefore output.

expected rate of inflation: the rate of inflation that employers and workers expect in the near future.

exporting industries: industries that produce goods or services for sale abroad.

exports: goods and services sold to residents of other countries.

factor intensity: the difference in the ratio of *factors* used to produce a good in various industries. For example, oil refining is capital-intensive compared to clothing manufacture because oil refiners use a higher ratio of capital to labor than do clothing producers.

factor markets: markets in which firms buy *factors of production.*

factors of production: the *resources* needed to produce goods or services. Labor and capital are examples of factors.

federal funds market: the market in which banks that fall short of *reserve requirements* can borrow funds from banks with *excess reserves.*

federal funds rate: the interest rate at which banks short of reserves can borrow from other banks with *excess reserves.* It is determined in the *federal funds market.*

fiat money: a medium of exchange that derives its value entirely from its

official status as a means of payment. The U.S. dollar is fiat money.

final goods and services: goods and services sold to the final, or end, user.

financial asset: a paper claim that entitles the buyer to future income from the seller. Loans, stocks, bonds, and bank deposits are types of financial assets.

financial intermediary: an institution, such as a *mutual fund, pension fund, life insurance company,* or *bank,* that transforms the funds it gathers from many individuals into financial assets.

financial markets: the banking, stock, and bond markets, which channel private savings and foreign lending into investment spending, government borrowing, and foreign borrowing.

financial risk: uncertainty about future outcomes that involve financial losses and gains.

firm: an organization that produces goods or services for sale.

fiscal policy: a type of stabilization policy that involves the use of changes in taxation, government transfers, or government purchases of goods and services.

fiscal year: the time period used for much of government accounting, running from October 1 to September 30. Fiscal years are named by the calendar year in which they end.

Fisher effect: the principle by which an increase in expected inflation drives up the nominal interest rate, leaving the expected real interest rate unchanged.

fixed exchange rate: an *exchange rate regime* in which the government keeps the exchange rate against some other currency at or near a particular target.

floating exchange rate: an *exchange rate regime* in which the government lets the exchange rate go wherever the market takes it.

forecast: a simple prediction of the future under current assumptions.

foreign exchange controls: licensing systems that limit the right of individuals to buy foreign currency.

foreign exchange market: the market in which currencies are traded.

foreign exchange reserves: stocks of foreign currency that governments maintain in order to buy their own currency on the *foreign exchange market.*

free trade: *trade* that is unregulated by government *tariffs* or other artificial barriers; the levels of *exports* and *imports* occur naturally, as a result of supply and demand.

frictional unemployment: unemployment due to time spent searching for a job. Because this type of unemployment can occur even when jobs exist for all of the unemployed, it does not necessarily signal a labor surplus.

gains from trade: the benefit that each party receives from a trade, which, because of *specialization,* is greater than if each attempted to be self-sufficient.

GDP deflator: for a given year, 100 times the ratio of *nominal GDP* to *real GDP* in that year.

GDP per capita: GDP divided by the size of the population; equivalent to the average GDP per person.

government borrowing: funds borrowed by the government in financial markets.

government purchases of goods and services: government expenditures on goods and services.

government transfers: payments by the government to individuals for which no good or service is provided in return.

gross domestic product (GDP): the total value of all final goods and services produced in the economy during a given year.

growth accounting: an estimation of the contribution to economic growth of each of the major factors (physical and human capital, labor, and technology) in the aggregate production function. Most growth accounting finds that increases in *total factor productivity* are central to a country's economic growth.

Hecksher–Olin model: a *model* of international trade that shows how a country's *comparative advantage* can be determined by its supply of *factors of production.*

horizontal axis: the horizontal number line of a graph along which values

of the *x*-variable are measured; also referred to as the *x-axis.*

horizontal intercept: the point at which a curve intersects the horizontal axis, showing the value of the *x*variable when the value of the *y*-variable is zero.

household: a group of people that share a dwelling and their income (a household may also consist of one person).

human capital: the improvement in labor created by the education and knowledge embodied in the workforce.

illiquid: refers to an asset that cannot be quickly converted into cash without much loss of value.

implicit liabilities: spending promises made by governments that are like a debt although they are not included in the usual debt statistics. In the United States, the largest implicit liabilities arise from Social Security and Medicare, which promise transfer payments to current and future retirees (Social Security) and to the elderly (Medicare).

import quota: a legal limit on the quantity of a good that can be imported.

import-competing industries: industries that produce goods or services that are also imported.

imports: goods and services purchased from residents of other countries.

incentive: a reward offered to people who change their behavior.

incidence (of a tax): a measure of who actually bears the burden of a tax.

income–expenditure equilibrium GDP: the level of real GDP at which real GDP equals *planned aggregate spending.*

income–expenditure equilibrium: a situation in which aggregate output, measured by real GDP, is equal to planned aggregate spending and firms have no incentive to change output.

independent variable: the determining variable in a causal relationship.

individual choice: the decision by an individual of what to do, which necessarily involves a decision of what not to do.

individual consumer surplus: the net gain to an individual buyer from the purchase of a good; equal to the

difference between the buyer's *willingness to pay* and the price paid.

individual producer surplus: the net gain to an individual seller from selling a good; equal to the difference between the price received and the seller's *cost*.

inefficient allocation of sales among sellers: a form of inefficiency in which sellers who are willing to sell a good at a lower price are not always those who actually manage to sell it; often the result of a *price floor*.

inefficient allocation to consumers: a form of inefficiency in which consumers who are willing to pay a high price for a good do not get it, and those willing to pay only a low price do; often a result of a *price ceiling*.

inefficient: describes a market or *economy* in which there are missed opportunities for making some individuals better off without making others worse off.

inefficiently high quality: a form of inefficiency in which sellers offer high-quality goods at a high price even though buyers would prefer a lower quality at a lower price; often the result of a *price floor*.

inefficiently low quality: a form of inefficiency in which sellers offer lowquality goods at a low price even though buyers would prefer a higher quality at a higher price; often a result of a *price ceiling*.

inferior good: a good for which a rise in income decreases the demand for the good.

inflation: a rising *aggregate price level*.

inflation rate: the percent change per year in a price index—typically the *consumer price index*. The inflation rate is positive when the aggregate price level is rising (*inflation*) and negative when the aggregate price level is falling (*deflation*).

inflation targeting: an approach to *monetary policy* that requires that the central bank try to keep the inflation rate near a predetermined target rate.

inflation tax: the reduction in the value of money held by the public caused by inflation.

inflationary gap: occurs when aggregate output is above *potential output*.

infrastructure: physical capital, such as roads, power lines, ports, and information networks, that provides the foundation for economic activity.

input: a good used to produce another good.

interaction (of choices): the mutual influence of the choices of various parties (the results are often quite different from what was intended).

interest rate: the price, calculated as a percentage of the amount borrowed, charged by lenders to borrowers for the use of their savings for one year.

interest rate effect of a change in the aggregate price level: the effect on consumer and investment spending caused by a change in the purchasing power of consumers' money holdings when the aggregate price level changes. A rise (fall) in the aggregate price level decreases (increases) the purchasing power of consumers' money holdings. In response, consumers try to increase (decrease) their money holdings, which drives up (down) interest rates, thereby decreasing (increasing) consumption and investment.

intermediate goods and services: goods and services, bought from one firm by another firm, that are inputs for production of final goods and services.

international trade agreements: treaties by which countries agree to lower *trade protections* against one another.

inventories: stocks of goods held to satisfy future sales.

inventory investment: the value of the change in total inventories held in the economy during a given period. Unlike other types of investment spending, inventory investment can be negative, if inventories fall.

investment spending: spending on productive physical capital, such as machinery and construction of structures, and on changes to inventories.

invisible hand: a phrase used by Adam Smith to describe the way in which an individual's pursuit of self-interest can lead, without the individual intending it, to good results for society as a whole.

job search: the act of looking for employment.

Keynesian cross: a diagram that identifies income–expenditure equilibrium as the point where the planned aggregate spending line crosses the 45-degree line.

Keynesian economics: the school of thought emerging out of the works of John Maynard Keynes and emphasizing two important concepts: the short run effects of shifts in *aggregate demand* on output and the ability of factors other than the money supply to create *business cycles*.

labor force: the number of people who are either actively employed for pay or unemployed and actively looking for work; the sum of *employment* and *unemployment*.

labor productivity: output per worker; also referred to as simply *productivity*. Increases in labor productivity are the only source of long-run economic growth.

law of demand: a higher price charged for a good, other things equal, leads to a smaller quantity of the good demanded.

liability: a requirement to pay income in the future.

license: the right, conferred by the government or an owner, to supply some good or perform some activity, often in exchange for a fee.

life insurance company: a *financial intermediary* that sells policies guaranteeing a payment to a policyholder's beneficiaries when the policyholder dies.

linear relationship: the relationship between two variables in which the *slope* is constant and therefore is depicted on a graph by a *curve* that is a straight line.

liquid: refers to an asset that can be quickly converted into cash without much loss of value.

liquidity preference model of the interest rate: a model of the market for money, in which the interest rate is determined by the supply and demand for money.

liquidity trap: a situation in which the nominal interest rate has hit its lower bound of zero; as a result, expansionary monetary policy can no longer be used.

loan: a lending agreement between a particular lender and a particular

borrower. Loans are usually tailored to the individual borrower's needs and ability to pay but carry relatively high transaction costs.

loanable funds market: a hypothetical market in which the demand for funds is generated by borrowers and the supply of funds is provided by lenders. The market equilibrium determines the quantity and price, or *interest rate*, of loanable funds.

long-run aggregate supply curve: a graphical representation of the relationship between the aggregate price level and the quantity of aggregate output supplied if all prices, including nominal wages, were fully flexible. The long-run aggregate supply curve is vertical because the aggregate price level has no effect on aggregate output in the long run; in the long run, aggregate output is determined by the economy's *potential output.*

long-run growth: See *secular long-run growth.*

long-run macroeconomic equilibrium: a situation in which *short-run macroeconomic equilibrium* is also on the *long-run aggregate supply curve;* so *short-run equilibrium aggregate output* is equal to *potential output.*

long-run Phillips curve: a graphical representation of the relationship between unemployment and inflation after expectations of inflation have had time to adjust to experience. It is vertical at the *natural rate of unemployment.*

long-term interest rate: the interest rate on financial assets that mature a number of years in the future.

macroeconomic policy activism: the use of monetary and fiscal policy to smooth out the *business cycle.*

macroeconomics: the branch of *economics* concerned with the overall ups and downs in the *economy.*

marginal analysis: the study of *marginal decisions,* those resulting from small changes in an activity.

marginal decision: a decision made at the "margin" of an activity to do a little more or a little less.

marginal propensity to consume, or MPC: the increase in consumer spending when income rises by $1. Because consumers normally spend part but not all of an additional dollar

of disposable income, *MPC* is between zero and one.

marginal propensity to save, or MPS: the increase in household savings when disposable income rises by $1.

market basket: a hypothetical set of consumer purchases of goods and services, used to measure changes in the overall price level.

market economy: an *economy* in which decisions about production and consumption are made by individual producers and consumers.

market failure: occurs when a market fails to be efficient.

market-clearing price: the price at which the market is in *equilibrium,* that is, the quantity of a good demanded equals the quantity supplied; also referred to as the *equilibrium price.*

markets for goods and services: markets in which households buy goods and services from *firms.*

medium of exchange: an asset that individuals acquire for the purpose of trading rather than for their own consumption. One of *money*'s main roles in the economy is to serve as the primary medium of exchange.

menu costs: small costs associated with the act of changing prices.

merchandise trade balance: the difference between a country's exports of goods and its imports of goods.

microeconomics: the branch of *economics* that studies how individuals make decisions and how those decisions interact.

minimum: the lowest point on a *nonlinear curve,* where the *slope* changes from negative to positive.

minimum wage: a legal floor on the wage rate. The wage rate is the market price of labor.

model: a simplified representation of a real-life situation that uses data and assumptions to make predictions about that situation and understand it better.

monetarism: a theory of *business cycles,* associated primarily with Milton Friedman, that asserts that GDP will grow steadily if the money supply grows steadily; implies that policy makers' attempts to smooth business cycles are often counterproductive.

monetary aggregate: an overall measure of the money supply. The most common monetary aggregates in the United States are M1, which includes *currency in circulation,* traveler's checks, and *checkable bank deposits,* and M2, which includes M1 as well as *near-moneys.*

monetary base: the sum of currency in circulation and *bank reserves;* controlled by the monetary authority.

monetary neutrality: the principle by which changes in the money supply have no real effects on the economy in the long run and only result in a proportional change in the price level.

monetary policy: a type of *stabilization policy* that involves changes in the quantity of money in circulation or in the interest rate, or both.

monetary policy rule: a formula that determines the central bank's actions.

money: any asset that can easily be used to purchase goods and services.

money demand curve: a graphical representation of the negative relationship between the quantity of money demanded and the interest rate. The money demand curve slopes downward because, other things equal, a higher interest rate increases the opportunity cost of holding money.

money multiplier: the ratio of the *money supply* to the *monetary base.*

money supply: the total value of financial assets in the economy that are considered money. There are several different measures of the money supply, called *monetary aggregates.*

money supply curve: a graphical representation of the relationship between the nominal quantity of money supplied by the Federal Reserve and the interest rate. The money supply curve is vertical at the money supply chosen by the Fed.

movement along the demand curve: a change in the *quantity demanded* of a good that results from a change in the price of that good.

movement along the supply curve: a change in the *quantity supplied* of a good that results from a change in the price of that good.

multiplier: the ratio of the eventual change in GDP caused by an

autonomous change in aggregate spending to the size of that autonomous change.

mutual fund: a *financial intermediary* that creates a stock portfolio and then resells shares of this portfolio to individual investors.

national income and product accounts: an accounting of *consumer spending*, sales of producers, business *investment spending*, and other flows of money between different sectors of the economy; also referred to as *national accounts*. Calculated by the Bureau of Economic Analysis.

national savings: the total amount of savings generated within the economy, which equals the sum of private savings and the government's *budget balance*.

natural rate of unemployment: the normal unemployment rate arising from *frictional* and *structural unemployment*. The actual unemployment rate fluctuates around the natural rate.

near-money: a financial asset that can't be directly used as a medium of exchange but can be readily converted into cash or checkable bank deposits.

negative relationship: a relationship between two variables in which an increase in the value of one variable is associated with a decrease in the value of the other variable. It is described by a *curve* that slopes downward from left to right.

net exports: the difference between the value of *exports* and the value of *imports*. A positive value for net exports indicates that a country is a net exporter of goods and services; a negative value indicates that a country is a net importer of goods and services.

new classical macroeconomics: an approach to the *business cycle* that returns to the classical view that, even in the short run, shifts in the *aggregate demand curve* affect only the aggregate price level, not aggregate output.

nominal: refers to a measure or quantity that has not been adjusted for changes in prices over time.

nominal GDP: the value of all final goods and services produced in the economy during the year, calculated using the prices current in the year in which the output is produced.

nominal interest rate: the interest rate unadjusted for inflation.

nominal wage: the dollar amount of the wage paid.

nonaccelerating inflation rate of unemployment (NAIRU): the unemployment rate at which, other things equal, inflation does not change over time.

nonlinear curve: a curve whose *slope* is not constant.

nonlinear relationship: the relationship between two variables in which the *slope* is not constant and therefore is depicted on a graph by a *curve* that is not a straight line.

normal good: a good for which a rise in income increases the demand for that good—the "normal" case.

normative economics: the branch of economic analysis that makes prescriptive statements about how the *economy* should work.

Okun's law: the generally observed relationship between the output gap and the unemployment rate, whereby each additional percentage point of output gap reduces the unemployment rate by less than 1 percentage point.

omitted variable: an unobserved *variable* that, through its influence on other variables, creates the erroneous appearance of a direct *causal relationship* among those variables.

open economy: an economy that trades goods, services, and assets with other countries.

open-economy macroeconomics: the study of those aspects of macroeconomics that are affected by movements of goods, services, and assets across national boundaries.

open-market operation: a purchase or sale of U.S. Treasury bills by the Federal Reserve, undertaken to change the *monetary base*, which in turn changes the *money supply*.

opportunity cost: the real cost of an item, including what must be given up to obtain it.

origin: the point where the axes of a two-variable graph meet.

other things equal assumption: in the development of a model, the assumption that all relevant factors

except the one under study remain unchanged.

output gap: the percentage difference between the actual level of real GDP and potential output.

pension fund: a type of *mutual fund* that holds assets in order to provide retirement income to its members.

physical asset: a claim on a tangible object that gives the owner the right to dispose of the object as he or she wishes.

physical capital: human-made physical resources, such as buildings and machines, that are used in production.

pie chart: a circular graph that shows how some total is divided among its components; the proportions are indicated by the sizes of the "wedges."

planned aggregate spending: the total amount of planned spending in the economy, which includes consumer spending, planned investment spending, government spending, and net export spending.

planned investment spending: the investment spending that businesses intend to undertake during a given period. Planned investment spending may differ from actual investment spending due to *unplanned inventory investment*.

political business cycle: a *business cycle* that results from politicians using macroeconomic policy to serve political ends.

positive economics: the branch of economic analysis that describes the way the *economy* actually works.

positive relationship: a relationship between two variables in which an increase in the value of one variable is associated with an increase in the value of the other variable. It is described by a *curve* that slopes upward from left to right.

potential output: the level of real GDP the economy would produce if all prices, including nominal wages, were fully flexible. Although an economy's actual output is rarely exactly at potential output, potential output defines the trend around which actual output fluctuates from year to year.

price ceiling: a government-set maximum price that sellers are

allowed to charge for a good; a form of *price control*.

price controls: legal restrictions on how high or low a market price may go.

price floor: a government-set minimum price that buyers are required to pay for a good; a form of price control.

price index: a measure of the overall price level; it measures the cost of purchasing a given market basket in a given year, where that cost is normalized so that it is equal to 100 in the selected base year.

price stability: a low but positive rate of inflation targeted by most central banks.

private savings: *disposable income* minus *consumer spending*; disposable income that is not spent on consumption.

producer price index (PPI): a measure of the cost of a typical basket of goods and services purchased by producers. Because these commodity prices respond quickly to changes in demand, the PPI is often regarded as a leading indicator of changes in the inflation rate.

producer surplus: a term often used to refer both to *individual producer surplus* and to *total producer surplus*.

production possibility frontier: illustrates the trade-offs facing an economy that produces only two goods. It shows the maximum quantity of one good that can be produced for any given production of the other.

protection: an alternative term for *trade protection;* policies that limit *imports*.

public debt: government debt held by individuals and institutions outside the government.

purchasing power parity (between two countries' currencies): the nominal *exchange rate* at which a given basket of goods and services would cost the same amount in each country.

quantity control: an upper limit, set by the government, on the quantity of some good that can be bought or sold; also referred to as a *quota*.

quantity demanded: the actual amount of a good or service consumers are willing to buy at some specific price.

quantity equation: an equation that states that the nominal quantity of

money multiplied by the velocity of money is equal to nominal GDP.

quantity supplied: the actual amount of a good or service sellers are willing to sell at some specific price.

quota: an upper limit, set by the government, on the quantity of some good that can be bought or sold; also referred to as a *quantity control*.

quota limit: the total amount of a good under a *quota* or *quantity control* that can be legally transacted.

quota rent: the difference between the *demand price* and the *supply price* at the *quota limit;* this difference, the earnings that accrue to the license-holder, is equal to the market price of the *license* when the license is traded.

random walk: the movement over time of an unpredictable variable.

rate of return (of an investment project): the profit earned on an investment project expressed as a percentage of its cost.

rational expectations: a theory of expectation formation that holds that individuals and firms make decisions optimally, using all available information.

real: refers to a measure or quantity that has been adjusted for changes in prices over time.

real business cycle theory: a theory of *business cycles* that asserts that fluctuations in the growth rate of *total factor productivity* cause the business cycle.

real exchange rate: the *exchange rate* adjusted for international differences in aggregate price levels.

real GDP: the total value of all final goods and services produced in the economy during a given year, calculated using the prices of a selected base year.

real interest rate: the interest rate adjusted for inflation, equal to the nominal interest rate minus the inflation rate.

real money demand curve: a graphical representation of the negative relationship between the real quantity of money demanded and the interest rate. The real money demand curve slopes downward because, other things equal, a higher interest rate increases the opportunity cost of holding money.

real quantity of money: the nominal quantity of money divided by the aggregate price level; equivalently, the quantity of money adjusted for the purchasing power of a dollar.

recession: a period when output and employment are falling.

recessionary gap: occurs when aggregate output is below *potential output*.

research and development: spending to create and implement new technologies.

reserve ratio: the fraction of deposits that a bank holds as reserves. In the United States, the minimum required reserve ratio is set by the Federal Reserve.

reserve requirements: rules set by the Federal Reserve that determine the minimum reserve ratio for a bank. For checkable bank deposits in the United States, the minimum reserve ratio is set at 10%.

resource: anything, such as land, labor, and capital, that can be used to produce something else; includes natural resources (from the physical environment) and human resources (labor, skill, intelligence).

revaluation: an increase in the value of a currency that is set under a fixed *exchange rate* regime.

reverse causality: the error committed when the true direction between *variables* is reversed, and the *independent variable* and the *dependent variable* are incorrectly identified.

Ricardian model of international trade: a model that analyzes international *trade* under the assumption that *production possibility frontiers* are straight lines.

Rule of 70: a formula that states that the time it takes a variable growing at some annual rate to double is approximately 70 divided by that variable's annual growth rate.

savings–investment spending identity: an accounting fact that states that savings and investment spending are always equal for the economy as a whole. For a closed economy, savings are composed of *national savings*, so that national savings is equal to investment. For an open economy, savings are composed of national savings plus foreign savings (also called *capital*

inflow), so that investment is equal to national savings plus capital inflow.

scarce: in short supply; a *resource* is scarce when the quantity available is insufficient to satisfy all productive uses.

scatter diagram: a graph that displays points that correspond to actual observations of the *x*- and *y*-variables; a curve is usually fitted to the scatter of points to indicate the trend in the data.

secular long-run growth: the sustained upward trend in aggregate output over several decades; also referred to as *long-run growth*.

self-correcting: refers to the fact that in the long run, shocks to aggregate demand affect aggregate output in the short run, but not the long run.

shift of the demand curve: a change in the *quantity demanded* at any given price, represented graphically by the movement of the original *demand curve* to a new position.

shift of the supply curve: a change in the *quantity supplied* at any given price, represented graphically by the movement of the original *supply curve* to a new position.

shoe-leather costs (of inflation): the increased costs associated with making transactions that arise from the public's efforts to avoid the inflation tax.

shortage: the insufficiency of a good when the quantity supplied is less than the quantity demanded; shortages occur when the price is below the *equilibrium price.*

short-run aggregate supply curve: a graphical representation of the relationship between the aggregate price level and the quantity of aggregate output supplied that exists in the short run, the time period when many production costs can be taken as fixed. The short-run aggregate supply curve has a positive slope because a rise in the aggregate price level leads to a rise in profits, and therefore output, when production costs are fixed

short-run equilibrium aggregate output: the quantity of aggregate output produced in *short-run macroeconomic equilibrium.*

short-run equilibrium aggregate price level: the aggregate price level

in *short-run macroeconomic equilibrium.*

short-run macroeconomic equilibrium: a situation in which the quantity of aggregate output supplied is equal to the quantity demanded.

short-run Phillips curve: a graphical representation of the negative short-run relationship between the unemployment rate and the inflation rate.

short-term interest rate: the interest rate on financial assets that mature within six months or less.

slope: the ratio of the "rise" (the change between two points on the *y*-axis) to the "run" (the difference between the same two points on the *x*-axis); a measure of the steepness of a curve.

social insurance: government programs—like Social Security, Medicare, unemployment insurance, and food stamps—intended to protect families against economic hardship.

specialization: occurs when each person concentrates on the task that he or she is good at performing; generally leads to improved quality or to increase in output.

stabilization policy: policy efforts undertaken to reduce the severity of recessions and to rein in excessively strong expansions. There are two main tools of stabilization policy: *monetary policy* and *fiscal policy.*

stagflation: the combination of rising inflation and falling aggregate output.

sticky wages: refers to a situation in which employers are slow to change wage rates in the face of a surplus or shortage of labor.

stock: a share in the ownership of a company held by a shareholder.

store of value: an asset that is a means of holding purchasing power over time. In a well-functioning economy, *money* is one of the assets that plays this role.

structural unemployment: unemployment that results when there are more people seeking jobs in a labor market than there are jobs available at the current wage rate.

substitutes: pairs of goods for which a fall in the price of one results in less demand for the other.

supply and demand model: a model that describes how a *competitive market* works.

supply curve: a graphical representation of the *supply schedule,* showing how much of a good or service would be supplied at a given price.

supply price: the price of a given quantity at which producers will supply that quantity.

supply schedule: a list or table showing the relationship between price and the quantity of a good or service that would be supplied to consumers.

supply shock: any event that shifts the *short-run aggregate supply curve.* A negative supply shock raises production costs and reduces the quantity supplied at any aggregate price level, shifting the curve leftward. A positive supply shock decreases production costs and increases the quantity supplied at any aggregate price level, shifting the curve rightward.

surplus: the excess of a good that occurs when the quantity supplied is greater than the quantity demanded; surpluses occur when the price is above the *equilibrium price.*

tangent line: a straight line that touches a *nonlinear curve* at a given point; the *slope* of the tangent line equals the slope of the nonlinear curve at that point.

target federal funds rate: the Federal Reserve's desired *federal funds rate.* The Federal Reserve adjusts the money supply through the purchase and sale of Treasury bills until the actual rate equals the desired rate.

tariff: a tax levied on *imports.*

technology: the technical means for the production of goods and services.

time-series graph: a two-variable graph in which the values on the *horizontal axis* are dates and those on the *vertical axis* are values of a variable that occurred on those dates.

total consumer surplus: the sum of the *individual consumer surpluses* of all the buyers of a good.

total factor productivity: the total amount of output that can be achieved with a given amount of the factor inputs physical capital, human capital, and labor. Increases in total

factor productivity are central to economic growth.

total producer surplus: the sum of the *individual producer surpluses* of all the sellers of a good.

total surplus: the total net gain to consumers and producers from trading in a market; the sum of the *consumer surplus* and the *producer surplus*.

trade: the exchange of goods or services for other goods or services.

trade balance: the difference between the value of the goods and services a country sells to other countries and the value of the goods and services it buys from other countries.

trade protection: policies that limit *imports*.

trade-off: a comparison of costs and benefits; the amount of a good that must be sacrificed to obtain another good.

transaction costs: the expenses of negotiating and executing a deal.

truncated: cut; in a truncated axis, some of the range of values are omitted, usually to save space.

underemployment: the number of people who work during a *recession* but receive lower wages than they would during an *expansion* due to fewer number of hours worked, lower-paying jobs, or both.

unemployment: the number of people who are actively looking for work but aren't currently employed.

unemployment rate: the percentage of the total number of people in the

labor force who are unemployed. It is calculated as: unemployment rate = *unemployment* / (*unemployment* + *employment*).

unit of account: a measure used to set prices and make economic calculations.

unit-of-account costs (of inflation): the costs arising from the way inflation makes money a less reliable unit of measurement.

unplanned inventory investment: unplanned changes in inventories, which occur when actual sales are more or less than businesses expected.

value added (of a producer): the value of sales minus the value of input purchases.

variable: a quantity that can take on more than one value.

velocity of money: nominal GDP divided by the nominal quantity of money; a measure of how many times a unit of money is spent over the course of a year.

vertical axis: the vertical number line of a graph along which values of the *y*-variable are measured; also referred to as the *y-axis*.

vertical intercept: the point at which a curve intersects the vertical axis, showing the value of the *y*-variable when the value of the *x*-variable is zero.

wasted resources: a form of inefficiency; consumers waste resources when they must spend money and expend effort to deal with shortages caused by a *price ceiling*.

wealth (of a household): the value of accumulated savings.

wealth effect of a change in the aggregate price level: the effect on consumer spending caused by the change in the purchasing power of consumers' assets when the aggregate price level changes. A rise in the aggregate price level decreases the purchasing power of consumers' assets, so they decrease their consumption; a fall in the aggregate price level increases the purchasing power of consumers' assets, so they increase their consumption.

wedge: the difference between the *demand price* of the quantity transacted and the *supply price* of the quantity transacted for a good when the supply of the good is legally restricted. Often created by a quota or a tax.

willingness to pay: the maximum price a consumer is prepared to pay for a good.

world price: the price at which a good can be bought or sold abroad.

World Trade Organization: an international organization of member countries that oversees *international trade agreements* and rules on *trade* disputes.

***x*-axis:** the horizontal number line of a graph along which values of the *x*variable are measured; also referred to as the *horizontal axis*.

***y*-axis:** the vertical number line of a graph along which values of the *y*variable are measured; also referred to as the *vertical axis*.

zero bound: the lower bound of zero on the nominal interest rate.

Key terms and the pages on which they are defined appear in **boldface** in this index.